AAA
Vacations®

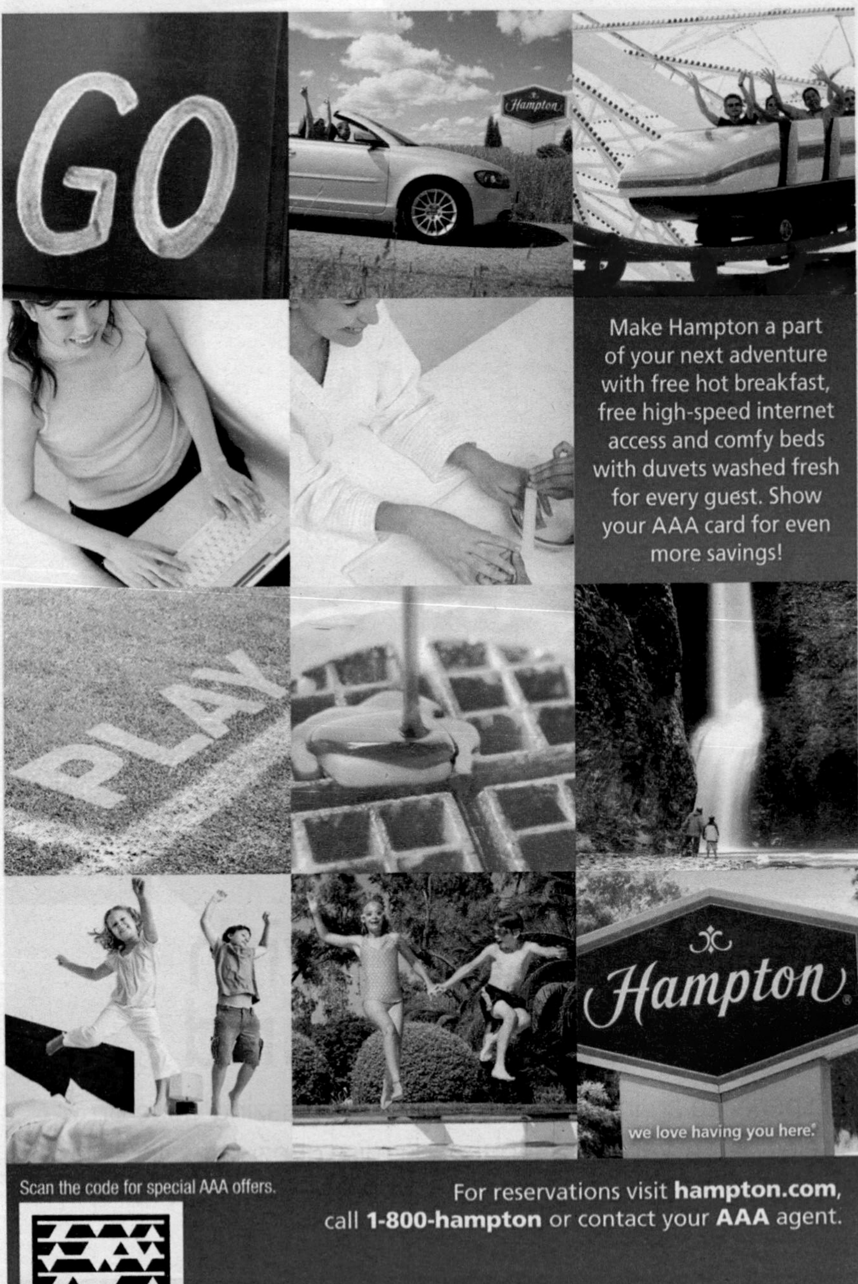
GO
Hampton
Make Hampton a part of your next adventure with free hot breakfast, free high-speed internet access and comfy beds with duvets washed fresh for every guest. Show your AAA card for even more savings!
PLAY
Hampton®
we love having you here.®
Scan the code for special AAA offers.
For reservations visit hampton.com, call 1-800-hampton or contact your AAA agent.
Get the free mobile app at http://gettag.mobi
HHONORS
HILTON WORLDWIDE
Show Your Card & Save

Colorado & Utah

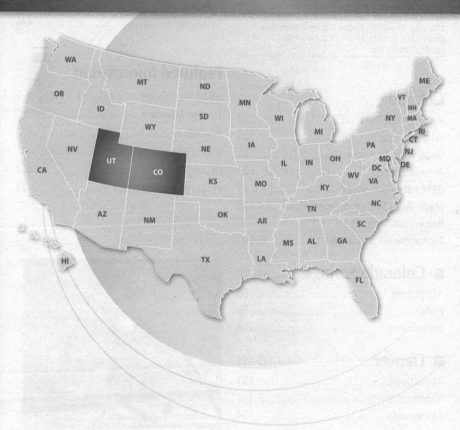

Published by AAA Publishing
1000 AAA Drive, Heathrow, FL 32746-5063

Advertising Rate and Circulation Information: (407) 444-8280

Printed in the USA by Quad/Graphics

This book is printed on paper certified by third-party standards for sustainably managed forestry and production.

Printed on recyclable paper.
Please recycle whenever possible.

Stock #4606

CONTENTS

Attractions, hotels, restaurants and other travel experience information are all grouped under the alphabetical listing of the city in which those experiences are physically located—or the nearest recognized city.

Our New Look!

We've taken the travel series members use more than any other trip planning resource and made it even better, from the inside out.

Discover a colorful twist on your favorite features plus new additions that make the 2012 series our richest, most robust TourBook® edition yet.

Central Florida

Historic Timeline	20
What To Pack	20
Good Facts To Know	21
Annual Events	22
GEM Attraction Index	24
Maps: Atlas Section & Orientation	25
Recreation Areas Chart	34
Alphabetical City Listings	37
MAJOR DESTINATIONS:	
Jacksonville	130
Orlando	278
Tampa	493

24 CENTRAL FLORIDA

Great Experience for Members

AAA editor's picks of exceptional note

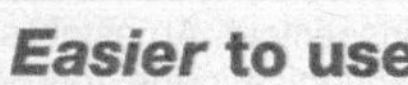

Easier to use
- Lighter to carry
- Improved readability
- Reorganized A to Z by city

Easier to navigate
- Mini tables of contents
- Page cross-referencing
- Quick-reference indexes

Easier to travel
- Navigable Atlas maps
- More destination photos
- Recommendations from AAA travel experts

Turn inside. It's a better guide — just for members.

A to Z City Listings

Cities and places are listed alphabetically within each state or province. Attractions, hotels and restaurants are listed once — under the city in which they are physically located.

Cities that are considered part of a larger destination city or area have an expanded city header. The header identifies the larger region and cross-references pages that contain shared trip planning resources:

- Destination map – outline map of the cities that comprise a destination city or area
- Attraction spotting map – regional street map marked with attraction locations
- Hotel/restaurant spotting map and index – regional street map numbered with hotel and restaurant locations identified in an accompanying index

Cities that are not considered part of a larger destination city or area but have a significant number of listings may have these resources within the individual city section:

- Attraction spotting map
- Hotel/restaurant spotting map and index

About Listed Establishments

AAA/CAA Approved attractions, hotels and restaurants are listed on the basis of merit alone after careful evaluation and approval by full-time, professionally trained AAA/CAA inspectors. An establishment's decision to advertise in the TourBook guide has no bearing on its evaluation or rating; nor does inclusion of advertising imply AAA endorsement of products and services.

Information in this guide was believed accurate at the time of publication. However, since changes inevitably occur between annual editions, please contact your AAA travel professional or visit AAA.com to confirm prices and schedules.

Location Abbreviations

Directions are from the center of town unless otherwise specified, using these highway abbreviations:

Bus. Rte.=business route

CR=county road

FM=farm to market

FR=forest road

Hwy.=Canadian highway

I=interstate highway

LR=legislative route

R.R.=rural route

SR/PR=state or provincial route

US=federal highway

Atlas Section

The Atlas Section provides navigable road maps from the AAA Road Atlas series. The overview map displays the entire coverage area. Corresponding, numbered detail maps offer a closer view for route planning and navigation.

Mobile Tags

Look for codes like this Microsoft Tag in the ads and restaurant listings to access special online offers, menus, videos and more.

To use Microsoft Tags:

- Download the free Tag Reader app to your smartphone at http://gettag.mobi.
- Start scanning Tags.
- Link to featured content.

Some advertisers use codes other than Microsoft Tags. In those cases, please note any accompanying text that indicates where to download the required reader.

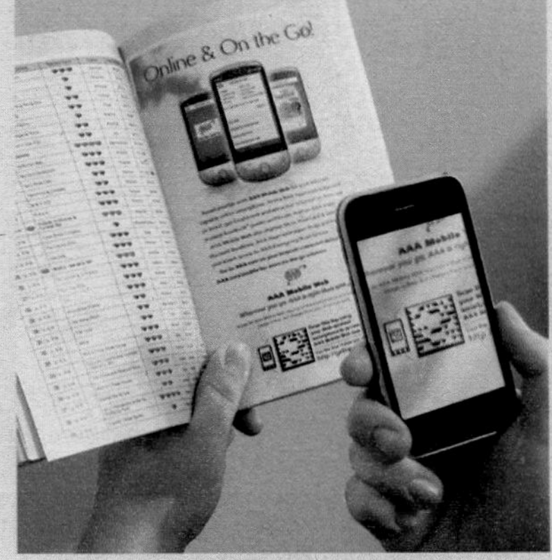

Attraction Listings

ATTRACTION NAME, 3 mi. n. off SR 20A (Main Ave.), consists of 250 acres with Olmsted-designed gardens, a 205-foot marble and coquina bell tower and a Mediterranean-style mansion. One of the state's oldest attractions, the tower and gardens were dedicated to the American people in 1929 by President Calvin Coolidge on behalf of their founder, a Dutch immigrant.

Other features include daily concerts from the 60-bell carillon, a nature observatory and Nature Preserve Trail. The visitor center presents art exhibits, an orientation film and exhibits about the family legacy, the carillon and endangered plants and animals found on the property.

Hours: Gardens daily 8-6. Last admission 1 hour before closing. Visitor center daily 9-5. Estate tours are given at noon and 2. Carillon concerts are given at 1 and 3. Phone ahead to confirm schedule. **Cost:** $10; $3 (ages 5-12). Gardens and estate $16; $8 (ages 5-12). **Phone:** (555) 555-5555.

AAA/CAA inspectors may designate an attraction of exceptional interest and quality as a GEM — a *Great Experience for Members*®. See GEM Attraction Index (listed on CONTENTS page) for complete list of locations.

Adventure Travel

Activities such as air tours, hiking, skiing and white-water rafting are listed to provide member information and do not imply AAA/CAA endorsement. For your safety, be aware of inherent risks and adhere to all safety instructions.

Cost

Prices are quoted without sales tax in the local currency (U.S. or Canadian dollars). Children under the lowest age specified are admitted free when accompanied by an adult. Most establishments accept credit cards, but a small number require cash, so please call ahead to verify.

Icons

- SAVE Show Your Card & Save member discount
- Camping facilities
- Food on premises
- Recreational activities
- Pets on leash allowed
- Picnicking allowed

District of Columbia only:

- Metro station within 1 mile
  Icon is followed by station name and AAA/CAA designated station number

Information-Only Attraction Listings

Bulleted listings, which include the following categories, are listed for informational purposes as a service to members:

- **Gambling establishments** (even if located in a AAA/CAA Approved hotel)
- **Participatory recreational activities** (those requiring physical exertion or special skills)
- **Wineries** that offer tours and tastings

Hotel and Restaurant Listings

1 Diamond Rating – AAA/CAA Approved hotels and restaurants are assigned a rating of one to five Diamonds. Red Diamonds distinguish establishments that participate in the AAA/CAA logo licensing program. For details, see p. 11 or AAA.com/Diamonds.

[fyi] indicates hotels and restaurants that are not AAA/CAA Approved and Diamond Rated but are listed to provide additional choices for members:

- **Hotels** may be unrated if they are: too new to rate, under construction, under major renovation, not evaluated, do not meet all AAA requirements. Hotels that do not meet all AAA requirements may be included if they offer member value or are the only option; details are noted in the listing.
- **Restaurants** may be unrated if they have not yet been evaluated by AAA.

2 Classification or Cuisine Type – noted immediately below the Diamond Rating

- **Hotel Classifications** indicate the style of operation, overall concept and service level. Subclassifications may also be added. (See p. 12 list.)
- **Restaurant Cuisine Types** identify the food concept from more than 100 categories. If applicable, a classification may also be added. (See p. 13 list.)

3 Dollar Amounts – Quoted without sales tax in the local currency (U.S. or Canadian dollars), rounded up to the nearest dollar. Most establishments accept credit cards, but a small number require cash, so please call ahead to verify.

- **Hotel Rates** indicate the publicly available two-person rate or rate range for a standard room, applicable all year unless effective dates are indicated.
- **Restaurant Prices** represent the minimum and maximum entree cost per person. Exceptions may include one-of-a-kind or special market priced items.

4 Spotting Symbol – Ovals containing numbers correspond with numbered location markings on hotel and restaurant spotting maps.

5 Parking – Unless otherwise noted, parking is free, on-site self parking.

6 Hotel Value Nationwide – Blue boxes highlight everyday member benefits available at all AAA/CAA Approved locations across a hotel chain. (See Just For Members section for details.)

7 Hotel Unit Limited Availability – Unit types, amenities and room features preceded by "some" are available on a limited basis, potentially as few as one.

8 Hotel Terms – Cancellation and minimum stay policies are listed. Unless otherwise noted, most properties offer a full deposit refund with cancellations received at least 48 hours before standard check-in. Properties that require advance payment may not refund the difference for early departures.

9 Hotel Check-in/Check-out – Unless otherwise noted, check-in is after 3 p.m. and check-out is before 10 a.m.

10 Restaurant Dress Code – Unless otherwise noted, dress is casual or dressy casual.

11 Restaurant Menu – Where indicated, menus may be viewed in a secure online environment at AAA.com or, if a mobile tag is provided, via the restaurant's website.

12 Hotel Icons – May be preceded by CALL, FEE and/or SOME UNITS.

Member Information:

- SAVE Rate guarantee: discounted standard room rate or lowest public rate available at time of booking for dates of stay.
- ECO Eco-certified by government or private organization. Visit AAA.com/eco for details.
- Smoke-free premises

Services:

- Wireless Internet service on premises
- Airport transportation
- Pets allowed (call property for restrictions and fees)
- Restaurant on premises
- Restaurant off premises (walking distance)
- Room service for 2 or more meals

HOTEL LISTING

RESTAURANT LISTING

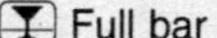

Full bar

Child care

BIZ Business services

Accessible features (Call property for available services and amenities.)

Activities:

Full-service casino

Pool

Health club on premises

Health club off premises

In-Room Amenities:

Pay movies

Refrigerator

Microwave

Coffee maker

No air conditioning

No TV

No cable TV

No telephones

13 Restaurant Icons

SAVE Show Your Card & Save member discount

No air conditioning

Accessible features (Call property for available services and amenities.)

Designated smoking section

B Breakfast

L Lunch

D Dinner

24 Open 24 hours

LATE Open after 11 p.m.

Just For Members

Understanding the Diamond Ratings

Hotel and restaurant evaluations are unscheduled to ensure our professionally trained inspectors encounter the same experience members do.

- When an establishment is Diamond Rated, it means members can expect a good fit with their needs. The inspector assigns a rating that indicates the type of experience to expect.
- While establishments at high levels must offer increasingly complex personalized services, establishments at every level are subject to the same basic requirements for cleanliness, comfort and hospitality. Learn more at AAA.com/Diamonds.

Hotels

Budget-oriented, offering basic comfort and hospitality.

Affordable, with modestly enhanced facilities, decor and amenities.

Distinguished, multi-faceted with enhanced physical attributes, amenities and guest comforts.

Refined, stylish with upscale physical attributes, extensive amenities and high degree of hospitality, service and attention to detail.

Ultimate luxury, sophistication and comfort with extraordinary physical attributes, meticulous personalized service, extensive amenities and impeccable standards of excellence.

What's the difference?

Red Diamonds mark establishments that participate in the AAA/CAA logo licensing program for increased visibility to members.

Black Diamonds identify all other AAA/CAA Approved and Diamond Rated establishments.

Restaurants

Simple, familiar specialty food at an economical price. Often self-service, basic surroundings.

Familiar, family-oriented experience. Home-style foods and family favorites, often cooked to order, modestly enhanced and reasonably priced. Relaxed service, casual surroundings.

Fine dining, often adult-oriented. Latest cooking trends and/or traditional cuisine, expanded beverage offerings. Professional service staff and comfortable, well-coordinated ambience.

Distinctive fine-dining, typically expensive. Highly creative chefs, imaginative presentations and fresh, top-quality ingredients. Proficient service staff, upscale surroundings. Wine steward may offer menu-specific knowledge.

Luxurious and consistently world-class. Highly acclaimed chefs, artistic and imaginative menu selections using the finest ingredients. Maitre d' and unobtrusive, expert service staff.

Hotel Classifications

Quality and comfort are usually consistent across each Diamond Rating level, but decor, facilities and service levels vary by classification.

1884 Paxton House Inn
Thomasville, GA

Bed & Breakfast – Typically small-scale, emphasizing personal touches. Individually decorated units may not include televisions, telephones or private bathrooms. Usually a common room and continental or full, hot breakfast.

Greenbrier Valley Resorts at Cobbly Nob, Gatlinburg, TN

Cabin – Vacation-oriented, typically small-scale, freestanding units with simple construction and basic decor. Often in wooded, rural or waterfront location. Cleaning supplies, utensils and bath linens provided. Check-in may be off site.

Camelot by the Sea
Myrtle Beach, SC

Condominium – Vacation-oriented, commonly for extended stays. Routinely rented through a management company. Generally one or more bedrooms, living room, full kitchen and eating area. Studio units combine sleeping and living areas. Cleaning supplies, utensils and linens provided. Check-in may be off site.

The Dunes on the Waterfront
Ogunquit, ME

Cottage – Vacation-oriented, typically small-scale, freestanding units with homey design and decor. Often in wooded, rural or waterfront location. Cleaning supplies, utensils and linens provided. Check-in may be off site.

The Lodge at Moosehead Lake, Greenville, ME

Country Inn – Similar to bed and breakfasts but larger scale with spacious public areas and dining facility that serves, at a minimum, breakfast and dinner.

The Grand America Hotel
Salt Lake City, UT

Hotel – Commonly multistory with interior room entrances. Unit styles vary. Public areas determined by overall theme, location and service level, but may include restaurant, shops, fitness center, spa, business center and meeting rooms.

Best Western Plus Sea Island Inn, Beaufort, SC

Motel – Commonly one- or two-story with exterior room entrances and drive-up parking. Typically one bedroom with bathroom. Limited public areas and facilities.

Lost Valley Ranch
Deckers, CO

Ranch – Typically a working ranch with rustic, Western theme, equestrian activities and various unit styles.

Indian Creek-Alexander Holiday Homes
Kissimmee, FL

Vacation Rental House – Commonly for extended stays. Typically large scale, freestanding and of varying design. Routinely rented through a management company. Often two or more bedrooms, living room, full kitchen, dining room and multiple bathrooms. Cleaning supplies, utensils and linens supplied. Check-in may be off site.

Hotel Subclassifications

These additional descriptives may be added to the classification for more information:

- **Boutique** – Often thematic and informal, highly personalized experience. May have fashionable, luxurious or quirky style.
- **Casino** – (Identified by listing icon) Extensive gambling facilities such as blackjack, craps, keno and slot machines.
- **Classic** – Landmark property, older than 50 years, renowned style and ambience.
- **Contemporary** – Design and theme reflective of current mainstream tastes and style.
- **Extended Stay** – Predominantly long-term units with full-service kitchens.
- **Historic** – Typically 75 years or older with historic architecture, design, furnishings, public record or acclaim and at least one of the following: maintains integrity of the historical nature, listed on the National Register of Historic Places, designated a National Historic Landmark or located in a National Register Historic District.
- **Resort** – Recreation-oriented, geared to a specific destination experience. Typically offer travel packages, meal plans, themed entertainment and social and recreational programs. Extensive recreational facilities may include spa treatments, golf, tennis, skiing, fishing or water sports. Larger resorts may offer a variety of unit types.
- **Retro** – Contemporary design and theme that reinterpret styles of a bygone era.
- **Vacation Rental** – Typically a house, condo, cottage or cabin offering space, value and conveniences such as full kitchens and washers/dryers. Located in a resort or popular destination area near major points of interest. May require reservations and off-site check-in. Limited housekeeping services.
- **Vintage** – Design and theme reflective of a bygone era.

Service Animals

Under the Americans with Disabilities Act (ADA), U.S. businesses that serve the public must allow people with disabilities to bring their service animals into all areas of the facility where customers are normally allowed to go.

Businesses may ask if an animal is a service animal and what tasks the animal has been trained to perform. Businesses may not ask about the person's disability, require special identification for the animal or request removal of the animal from the premises except in limited cases that require alternate assistance. Businesses may not charge extra fees for service animals, including standard pet fees, but may charge for damage caused by service animals if guests are normally charged for damage they cause.

Call the U.S. Department of Justice ADA Information Line: (800) 514-0301 or TTY (800) 514-0383, or visit ada.gov. Regulations may differ in Canada.

Restaurant Classifications

If applicable, in addition to the cuisine type noted under the Diamond Rating, restaurant listings may also include one or both classifications:

- **Classic** – Renowned and landmark operation in business for 25 plus years; unique style and ambience.
- **Historic** – Meets one of the following: Listed on National Register of Historic Places, designated a National Historic Landmark or located in a National Register Historic District.

AAA/CAA Approved Hotels

For members, AAA/CAA Approved means quality assured.

- Only properties that meet basic requirements for cleanliness, comfort and hospitality pass inspection.
- Approved hotels receive a Diamond Rating that tells members the type of experience to expect.

Guest Safety

Inspectors view a sampling of rooms during evaluations and, therefore, AAA/CAA cannot guarantee the presence of working locks and operational fire safety equipment in every guest unit.

Member Rates

AAA/CAA members can generally expect to pay no more than the maximum TourBook listed rate for a standard room. Member discounts apply to rates quoted within the rate range and are applicable at the time of booking. Listed rates are usually based on last standard room availability. Within the range, rates may vary by season and room type. Obtain current AAA/CAA member rates and make reservations at AAA.com.

Exceptions

- Rates for properties operating as concessionaires for the U.S. National Park Service are not guaranteed due to governing regulations.
- Special advertised rates and short-term promotional rates below the rate range are not subject to additional member discounts.
- During special events, hotels may temporarily increase room rates, not recognize discounts or modify pricing policies. Special events may include Mardi Gras, the Kentucky Derby (including pre-Derby events), college football games, holidays, holiday periods and state fairs. Although some special events are listed in the TourBook guides and on AAA.com, it's always wise to check in advance with AAA travel professionals for specific dates.

If you are charged more than the maximum TourBook listed rate, question the additional charge. If an exception is not in effect and management refuses to adhere to the published rate, pay for the room and contact AAA/CAA. The amount paid above the stated maximum will be refunded if our investigation indicates an unjustified charge.

Reservations and Cancellations

When making your reservation, identify yourself as a AAA/CAA member and request written confirmation of your room type, rate, dates of stay, and cancellation and refund policies. At registration, show your membership card.

To cancel, contact the hotel or your AAA/CAA club office, depending on how you booked your reservation. Request a cancellation number or proof of cancellation.

If your room is not as specified and you have written confirmation of your reservation for a specific room type, you should be given the option of choosing a different room or receiving a refund. If management refuses to issue a refund, contact AAA/CAA.

Contacting AAA/CAA About Approved Properties

If your visit to a AAA/CAA Approved attraction, hotel or restaurant doesn't meet your expectations, please tell us about it — ***during your visit or within 30 days***.

Use the easy online form at AAA.com/TourBookComments to send us the details, and save your receipts and other documentation for reference.

Or, send your written comments to us at: AAA Member Comments, 1000 AAA Dr., Heathrow, FL 32746.

AAA/CAA Preferred Hotels

All AAA/CAA Approved hotels are committed to providing quality, value and member service. In addition, those designated as AAA/CAA Preferred Hotels also offer these extra values at Approved locations nationwide. Valid AAA/CAA membership required.

- **Best AAA/CAA member rates for your dates of stay.**
- **Seasonal promotions and special member offers.** Visit AAA.com to view current offers.
- **Everyday member benefit.** Look for the blue boxes in the TourBook listings to find everyday values offered at all AAA/CAA Approved locations nationwide. Chains and offers valid at time of publication may change without notice.
- **Total satisfaction guarantee.** If you book your stay with AAA/CAA Travel and your stay fails to meet your expectations, you can apply for a full refund. Bring the complaint to the hotel's attention during the stay and request resolution; if the complaint is not resolved by the hotel, ask your AAA/CAA travel agent to request resolution through the AAA/CAA Assured Stay program.

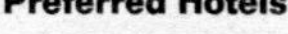

Best Western, Best Western Plus and Best Western Premier

Conrad Hotels & Resorts, DoubleTree by Hilton, Embassy Suites, Hampton Inns & Suites, Hilton Hotels & Resorts, Hilton Garden Inns, Hilton Grand Vacations, Home2 Suites, Homewood Suites and Waldorf Astoria Collection

ANdAZ, Grand Hyatt, Hyatt Place, Hyatt Regency, Hyatt Summerfield Suites and Park Hyatt

Autograph Collection by Marriott, Courtyard, EDITION Hotels by Marriott, Fairfield Inn, JW Marriott, Marriott Hotels & Resorts, Renaissance Hotels, Residence Inn, Ritz-Carlton Hotels & Resorts, SpringHill Suites and TownePlace Suites

Aloft, Element, Four Points, Le Meridien, Sheraton, St. Regis Hotels & Resorts, The Luxury Collection, Westin and W Hotels

Show Your Card & Save® Member Discounts

Visit AAA.com/Discounts to find local Show Your Card & Save discounts. Your AAA/CAA club may offer even greater discounts on theme park tickets. Amtrak, Gray Line and theme park discounts may be used for up to six tickets; restaurant savings may be used for up to six patrons. Other restrictions may apply.

ATTRACTIONS

SeaWorld, Busch Gardens, Sesame Place

SEAWORLD PARKS & ENTERTAINMENT

- Save on admission at the gate, participating AAA/CAA offices or AAA.com/SeaWorld.
- Save 10% on up-close dining; visit Guest Relations for details.

Six Flags

- Save on admission at the gate, participating AAA/CAA offices or AAA.com/SixFlags.
- Save 10% on merchandise of $15 or more at in-park stores.

Universal Orlando Resort and Universal Studios Hollywood

- Save on admission at the gate, participating AAA/CAA offices or AAA.com/Universal.
- Save 10% at select food and merchandise venues in-park and at Universal CityWalk®.

DINING & SHOPPING

Hard Rock Cafe

- Save 10% on food, nonalcoholic beverages and merchandise at all U.S., Canadian and select international locations.

Hard Rock CAFE

Landry's Seafood House, The Crab House, Chart House, Oceanaire, Saltgrass Steak House, Muer Seafood Restaurants and Aquarium Restaurants

CHART HOUSE

- Save 10% on food and nonalcoholic beverages at all of the above restaurants.
- Save 10% on merchandise at Aquarium and Downtown Aquarium restaurants.

Tanger Outlet Centers

Tanger Outlets

- Save up to 20% on total purchase at select merchants with FREE coupon booklet available with registration at AAA customer service desk.
- After first visit, get $5 gift card for each additional location visited in same calendar year.
- Location information: tangeroutlet.com.

TravelCenters of America/Petro Stopping Centers

TA   PETRO Stopping Centers

- Save 10% at the more than 350 full-service and fast-food restaurants inside participating locations nationwide.

TRANSPORTATION & TOURS

Amtrak

AMTRAK

- Save 10% on rail fare booked at least 3 days in advance of travel date at AAA.com/Amtrak.

Gray Line

- Save 10% on sightseeing tours of 1 day or less worldwide at AAA.com/GrayLine.

Hertz

- Save on daily, weekend, weekly and monthly rentals at AAA.com/hertz or 1-800-654-3080.

Sprague Lake, Rocky Mountain National Park

Colorado

If you find yourself fed up with the congestion, stress and fast pace of everyday life, change your altitude. In Colorado, people tend to breathe a little easier, focus better and take themselves less seriously.

Geography is a good reason why. Colorado is awe-inspiring: The Continental Divide saws a jagged line through the state, leaving the eastern portion to resemble Kansas with rolling hills and golden plains that expand for miles. But central Colorado gets vertical—its sharp outline reaches for the sky.

The Rocky Mountains resemble a calico quilt in soothing shades of greens. Cathedral-shaped mountains wrap around you under a blanket of blue, and crisp air goes right to your head to sweep out any cobwebs.

Surrounded by a circle of peaks, you'll feel small yet invigorated. John Denver could only describe the oxymoronic feeling as a "Rocky Mountain High"—a humbling yet empowering drive to find a place for yourself in the midst of such bold surroundings. The sheer majesty of 58 pinnacles surpassing the 14,000-foot mark crowns everyday hassles runners-up.

Downtown Leadville

Purple Peaks and Red Rocks

Pack your suitcase full of bad karma and head for Pikes Peak National Forest, where a cog railway ascends to the tiptop of the magnificent summit. En route, you'll pass bighorn sheep who are just as eager to check you out as you are to snap a photo. It was this peak, named for Col. Zebulon Pike (who never actually made it to the top but admired it during his survey of the Louisiana Purchase), which inspired poet Katherine Lee Bates to write "America the Beautiful."

You'll see firsthand at the Garden of the Gods Park in Colorado Springs why early Spanish *conquistadores* called the state *colorado*—meaning "the color red." Giant sandstone rock formations take the shapes of Kissing Camels, a Cathedral and a Sleeping Giant.

Nearby, a mountain of a different sort—fashioned from glass and silver spires—will lift your spirits as well. The Cadet Chapel at the U.S. Air Force Academy, with its pointed aluminum steeples and brightly colored stained glass, contains Catholic, Protestant and Jewish chapels and two All Faiths Rooms, each individually breathtaking.

Golden Days of Ore

Denver, dubbed the "Mile High City" due to its elevation of exactly 5,280 feet, is the gateway to the Rocky Mountains. Early residents came in search of clean air, believed to cure tuberculosis. Others, such as the legendary Buffalo Bill, rode in on the coattails of the Pikes Peak gold rush.

Leadville, the highest city in America—positioned at a whopping 10,152 feet above sea level—is another escape to the past. If the thin air alone doesn't make your head spin, frontier tales of mining, gunfights and love triangles surely will. Wander through the historic district and hear about the "get-rich-quick" story of H.A.W. Tabor and his mine.

Many visitors to this state fall under the spell of its dry air, snowcapped summits, dark canyons, icy mountain streams and dusty ghost towns. A trip here instills a deep appreciation for the power of environmental surroundings. Colorado just might change you, bringing vigor, creativity, solace and emotional riches—and diminishing anxieties.

Recreation

If you're looking for adventure, Colorado is the place. On what might be a lazy Saturday anywhere else, choose from vigorous options like climbing a bluff, tackling river rapids, storming a mountain on a bike or skis, hiking through backwoods to sleep under the stars or observing wildlife.

Aspen, Beaver Creek, Breckenridge, Copper Mountain, Crested Butte, Keystone, Purgatory, Snowmass Village, Steamboat Springs, Telluride, Vail, Winter Park and Wolf Creek are just *some* of the places where you can maneuver the moguls. If skis bore you, try snowboarding down a black diamond or snowmobiling along a mountain trail for an added kick.

Where there are mountains, there are trails. Horseback riding through Devils Canyon provides views of red rocks, while paths at Colorado National Monument snake along 600-foot canyons. Trails suitable for two wheels are nearly everywhere. Hit the ski resorts in summer for mountain biking; you can load your bike onto a ski lift and ride down. Cycle the Rio Grande Trail near Aspen, which skirts the Roaring Fork River and follows the path of the old Denver & Rio Grande Railroad system, or choose from some 600 miles of connecting mountain bike trails at Winter Park in the Fraser River Valley.

Hiking is just as enticing, with thousands of miles of trails winding through nearly every park and national forest. Near Golden, try the Lookout Mountain Trail—it connects Beaver Brook Trail to the top of Lookout Mountain—or the Red Rocks/Dakota Ridge Trail, which meanders through red rock formations and across streams.

The section of Los Pinos River (called "the Pine" by locals) from the wilderness boundary to the Continental Divide offers excellent back country fly fishing. Various streams in the state are stocked with eastern brook, brown and rainbow trout. Walleyed pike, white bass, catfish and perch are hooked from larger lakes and reservoirs.

The Arkansas River is a favored rafting spot. Its upper portion provides for a crazy jaunt, but lower waters are more novice-friendly. The wild at heart will want to tackle the class III and IV waters that charge through Brown Canyon; you'll catch glimpses of some of Colorado's tallest peaks. The Colorado, Dolores, Gunnison and North Platte rivers also cater to rafters. And those who find themselves wandering around downtown Durango are sure to be tempted to slide into a wetsuit and brave the waters of the Animas River.

Garden of the Gods Park, Colorado Springs

Historic Timeline

1540 Francisco de Coronado's expedition begins the journey through what is now southeastern Colorado.

1803 The United States acquires the area as part of the Louisiana Purchase.

1850 Gold is discovered at what is now Arvada; other strikes in 1858 begin Colorado's first gold rush.

1876 Colorado becomes the 38th state in the Union.

1881 Ute tribes are forced onto reservations.

1906 The U.S. Mint at Denver issues its first coins.

1947 Colorado's first commercial ski resort opens for business in Aspen.

1954 The U.S. Air Force Academy is established at Colorado Springs.

1999 Lynxes are reintroduced to Colorado after not being seen in the wild for more than 25 years.

2000 Denver celebrates the news that its public library is named the nation's best.

2010 A wildfire west of Boulder becomes one of the most destructive in Colorado history.

What To Pack

Temperature Averages Maximum/Minimum	JANUARY	FEBRUARY	MARCH	APRIL	MAY	JUNE	JULY	AUGUST	SEPTEMBER	OCTOBER	NOVEMBER	DECEMBER
Colorado Springs	43/14	45/17	50/22	59/31	68/41	80/49	85/55	84/54	77/45	66/35	52/23	46/18
Denver	43/17	46/19	51/25	61/34	70/44	81/53	87/59	86/58	78/49	67/38	53/27	46/20
Durango	38/12	43/17	51/24	60/30	69/36	80/43	83/51	82/49	75/42	64/32	53/23	39/13
Grand Junction	35/17	42/23	53/30	65/40	75/49	86/57	93/64	89/62	81/54	67/43	50/28	38/20
Steamboat Springs	28/1	33/4	42/15	53/24	64/32	75/36	82/42	81/41	72/33	59/24	41/13	29/2
Sterling	38/10	44/15	54/21	62/32	70/43	81/52	87/57	86/55	78/45	67/32	53/20	36/11

From the records of The Weather Channel Interactive, Inc.

Good Facts To Know

ABOUT THE STATE

POPULATION: 5,029,196.

AREA: 104,247 square miles; ranks 8th.

CAPITAL: Denver.

HIGHEST POINT: 14,433 ft., Mount Elbert.

LOWEST POINT: 3,315 ft., Arickaree River.

TIME ZONE(S): Mountain. DST.

GAMBLING

MINIMUM AGE FOR GAMBLING: 21.

REGULATIONS

TEEN DRIVING LAWS: No unrelated passengers under age 21 for the first six months; no more than one unrelated passenger under age 21 for the following six months. Driving is not permitted midnight-5 a.m. Minimum age for an unrestricted driver's license is 17. For more information about Colorado driver's license regulations, phone (303) 205-5600.

SEAT BELT/CHILD RESTRAINT LAWS: Seat belts are required for driver and front-seat passengers ages 16 and older. Children ages 8 until 16 are required to be in a seat belt; booster seat required for children ages 4 until 8; child restraints required for under age 4 and under 40 pounds.

CELL PHONE RESTRICTIONS: Drivers under 18 are not permitted to use cell phones. Texting is prohibited for all drivers.

HELMETS FOR MOTORCYCLISTS: Required for all riders under 18.

RADAR DETECTORS: Permitted.

MOVE OVER LAW: Driver is required to slow down and vacate a lane nearest police, fire and rescue vehicles stopped on the side of the road using audible or flashing signals. Law includes tow trucks.

FIREARMS LAWS: Vary by state and/or county. Contact Colorado Bureau of Investigation, 690 Kipling St., Denver, CO 80215; phone (303) 239-4300.

HOLIDAYS

HOLIDAYS: Jan. 1 ■ Martin Luther King Jr. Day, Jan. (3rd Mon.) ■ Presidents Day, Feb. (3rd Mon.) ■ Memorial Day, May (last Mon.) ■ July 4 ■ Labor Day, Sept. (first Mon.) ■ Veterans Day, Nov. 11 ■ Thanksgiving, Nov. (4th Thurs.) ■ and Christmas, Dec. 25.

MONEY

TAXES: Colorado's statewide sales tax is 2.9 percent, with local options for additional increments. Cities and counties also may levy a lodging tax. Additional taxes, such as a tribal tax, can be levied.

VISITOR INFORMATION

INFORMATION CENTERS: State welcome centers that provide details about state attractions, accommodations, historic sites, parks and events are at Alamosa, 601 State St. ■ Burlington, on I-70 between exits 437 and 438 ■ Cortez, US 160 at 928 E. Main St. ■ Dinosaur, US 40 at 101 E. Stegosaurus St. ■ Fort Collins, I-25 at exit 268 ■ Fruita, I-70 at exit 19 ■ Julesburg, I-76 exit 180 at 20934 CR 28 ■ Lamar, US 50 at 109 E. Beech St. ■ Red Rocks, 18300 W. Alameda Pkwy. at Red Rocks Park and Amphitheatre ■ and Trinidad, I-25 exit 14 at 309 Nevada Ave.

FURTHER INFORMATION FOR VISITORS:
Colorado Tourism Office
1625 Broadway, Suite 1700
Denver, CO 80202-4729
(800) 265-6723

NATIONAL FOREST INFORMATION:
U.S. Forest Service
Rocky Mountain Region
740 Simms St.
Golden, CO 80401
(303) 275-5350
(877) 444-6777 (reservations)

FISHING AND HUNTING REGULATIONS:
Colorado Division of Wildlife
6060 Broadway
Denver, CO 80216
(303) 297-1192

RECREATION INFORMATION:
Colorado Parks and Outdoor Recreation
1313 Sherman St., Room 618
Denver, CO 80203
(303) 866-3437

SKIING INFORMATION:
Colorado Ski Country USA
1444 Wazee St., Unit 320
Denver, CO 80202
(303) 837-0793

Colorado Annual Events

Please call ahead to confirm event details.

JANUARY	FEBRUARY	MARCH
■ National Western Stock Show, Rodeo and Horse Show / Denver 888-551-5004 ■ Budweiser International Snow Sculpture Championships Breckenridge 800-936-5573 ■ Winterskol / Aspen 970-925-1940	■ Frisco Gold Rush Weekend Frisco 970-668-5276 ■ Winter Carnival Steamboat Springs 970-879-0695 ■ Snowdown / Durango 970-247-0312	■ Nature Valley Championships Winter Park 970-726-1573 ■ Denver March Powwow Denver 303-934-8045 ■ Ski Joring and Crystal Carnival / Leadville 719-486-3900
APRIL	**MAY**	**JUNE**
■ University of Northern Colorado/Greeley Jazz Festival / Greeley 970-351-2394 ■ Coca-Cola Classic Spring Splash at Winter Park Winter Park 970-726-1564 ■ Breckenridge Spring Fever Festival / Breckenridge 800-936-5573	■ Downtown Grand Junction Art and Jazz Festival Grand Junction 970-245-9697 ■ Tesoro Foundation Indian Market and Powwow Morrison 303-839-1671 ■ Music and Blossom Festival Cañon City / 719-275-7234	■ Palisade Bluegrass and Roots Music Festival Palisade 970-464-5602 ■ Manitou Springs Colorado Wine Festival Manitou Springs 719-685-5089 ■ Frisco Colorado Barbecue Challenge / Frisco 970-668-5276
JULY	**AUGUST**	**SEPTEMBER**
■ Pikes Peak or Bust Rodeo Colorado Springs 719-635-1101, ext. 2 ■ Colorado Dragon Boat Festival / Denver 303-722-6852 ■ Crested Butte Wildflower Festival / Crested Butte 970-349-2571	■ Leadville Boom Days and International Pack Burro Race / Leadville 719-486-3900 ■ Gold Rush Days Buena Vista 719-395-6612 ■ Durango and Silverton Narrow Gauge Railfest Durango / 970-247-2733	■ Colorado Balloon Classic Colorado Springs 719-471-4833 ■ Telluride Blues and Brews Festival / Telluride 970-728-8037 ■ Longs Peak Scottish-Irish Highland Festival Estes Park 970-586-6308
OCTOBER	**NOVEMBER**	**DECEMBER**
■ Glenwood's Historic Ghost Walk / Glenwood Springs 970-945-4448 ■ Emma Crawford Festival, Memorial Coffin Race and Parade / Manitou Springs 719-685-5089 ■ Cider Days / Lakewood 303-987-7850	■ Victorian Christmas at Miramont Castle Manitou Springs 719-685-1011 ■ Hometown Holidays Trinidad 719-846-9285 ■ Denver Holiday Food and Gift Festival / Denver 888-412-5015	■ Winter Festival and Parade of Lights / Grand Junction 970-245-9697 ■ New Year's Eve Fireworks Downtown / Denver 303-534-6161 ■ Georgetown Christmas Market / Georgetown 303-569-2840

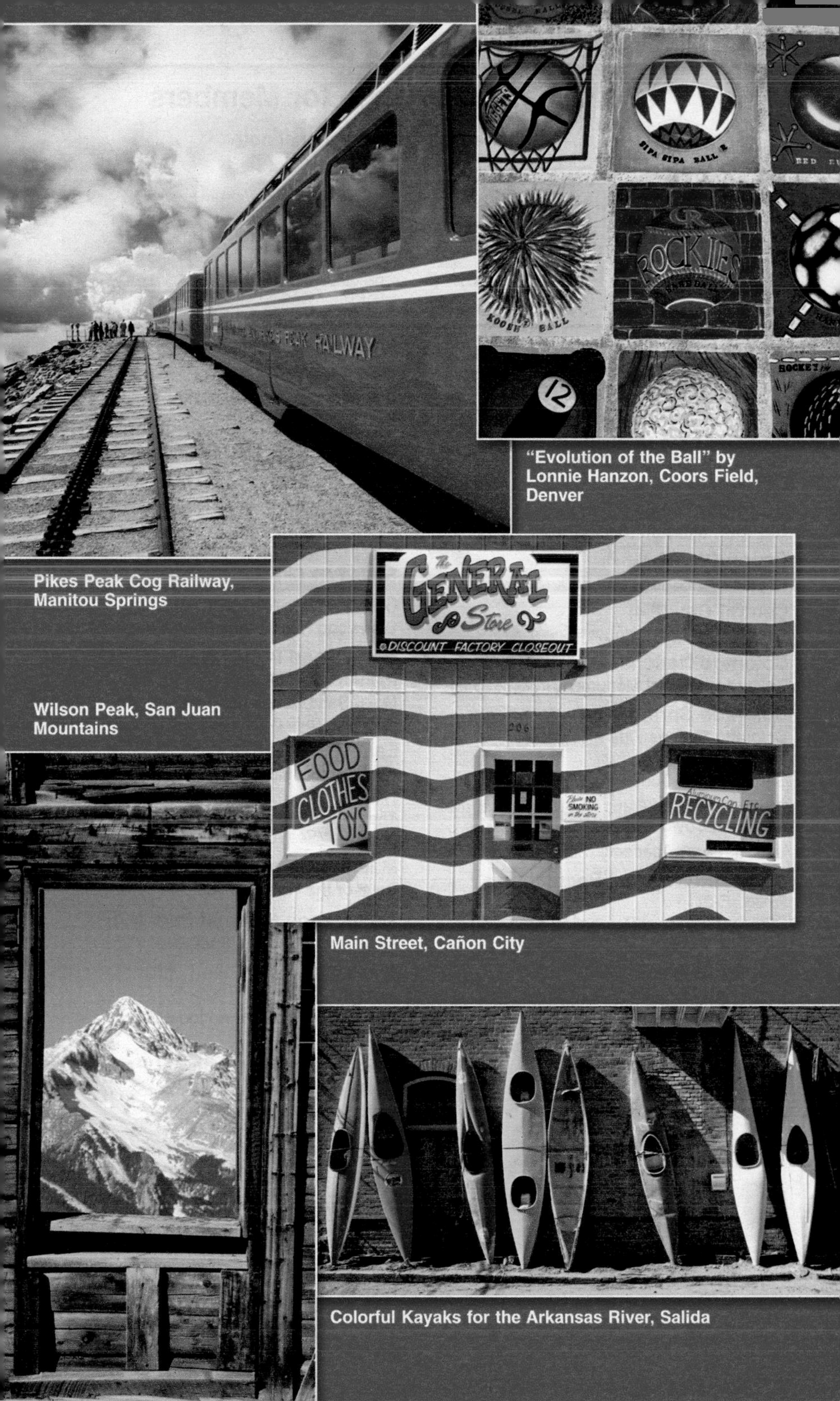

"Evolution of the Ball" by Lonnie Hanzon, Coors Field, Denver

Pikes Peak Cog Railway, Manitou Springs

Wilson Peak, San Juan Mountains

Main Street, Cañon City

Colorful Kayaks for the Arkansas River, Salida

Great Experience for Members

AAA editor's picks of exceptional note

Denver Art Museum

Royal Gorge Bridge and Park

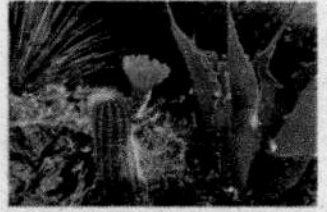
Denver Botanic Gardens

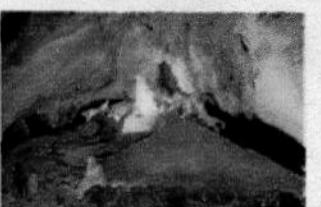
Cave of the Winds

Antonito (F-3)
Cumbres & Toltec Scenic Railroad *(See p. 39.)*

Black Canyon of the Gunnison National Park (D-2)
Black Canyon Of The Gunnison National Park *(See p. 55.)*

Burlington (D-6)
Old Town Museum *(See p. 75.)*

Cañon City (E-4)
Royal Gorge Bridge and Park *(See p. 76.)*

Central City (B-4)
Central City Opera House *(See p. 81.)*

Colorado National Monument (D-1)
Colorado National Monument *(See p. 83.)*

Colorado Springs (D-4)
Colorado Springs Fine Arts Center *(See p. 90.)*

Garden of the Gods Park *(See p. 90.)*

ProRodeo Hall of Fame and Museum of the American Cowboy *(See p. 92.)*

U.S. Air Force Academy *(See p. 92.)*

Curecanti National Recreation Area (E-2)
Curecanti National Recreation Area *(See p. 120.)*

Denver (B-4)
Denver Art Museum *(See p. 133.)*

Denver Botanic Gardens *(See p. 134.)*

Denver Museum of Nature & Science *(See p. 131.)*

Denver Zoo *(See p. 133.)*

Downtown Aquarium *(See p. 134.)*

State Capitol *(See p. 135.)*

U.S. Mint *(See p. 135.)*

Dinosaur National Monument (B-1)
Dinosaur National Monument *(See p. 342.)*

Durango (F-2)
The Durango and Silverton Narrow Gauge Railroad & Museum *(See p. 173.)*

Fairplay (D-3)
South Park City Museum *(See p. 196.)*

Glenwood Springs (D-2)
Glenwood Hot Springs Pool *(See p. 207.)*

Great Sand Dunes National Park and Preserve (E-3)
Great Sand Dunes National Park And Preserve *(See p. 220.)*

Leadville (D-3)
Healy House Museum and Dexter Cabin *(See p. 238.)*

The National Mining Hall of Fame and Museum *(See p. 239.)*

Manitou Springs (D-4)
Cave of the Winds *(See p. 249.)*

Mesa Verde National Park (F-1)
Mesa Verde National Park *(See p. 252.)*

Pikes Peak and Pike National Forest (D-4)
Pikes Peak And Pike National Forest *(See p. 269.)*

Rocky Mountain National Park (A-3)
Rocky Mountain National Park *(See p. 276.)*

Colorado Atlas Section

ROADS/HIGHWAYS

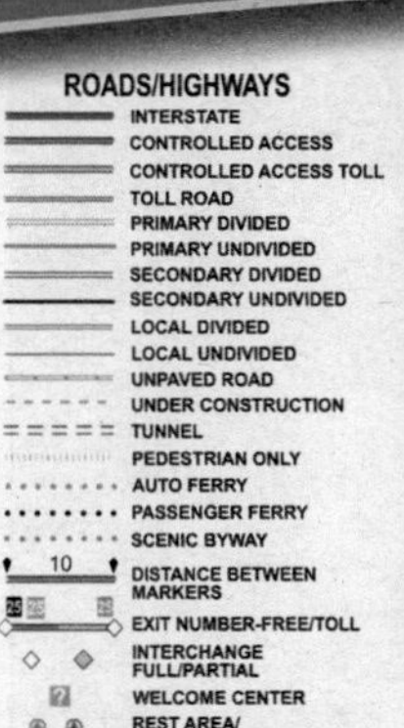

INTERSTATE
CONTROLLED ACCESS
CONTROLLED ACCESS TOLL
TOLL ROAD
PRIMARY DIVIDED
PRIMARY UNDIVIDED
SECONDARY DIVIDED
SECONDARY UNDIVIDED
LOCAL DIVIDED
LOCAL UNDIVIDED
UNPAVED ROAD
UNDER CONSTRUCTION
TUNNEL
PEDESTRIAN ONLY
AUTO FERRY
PASSENGER FERRY
SCENIC BYWAY
DISTANCE BETWEEN MARKERS
EXIT NUMBER-FREE/TOLL
INTERCHANGE FULL/PARTIAL
WELCOME CENTER
REST AREA/ SERVICE CENTER

BOUNDARIES

INTERNATIONAL
STATE
COUNTY
TIME ZONE
CONTINENTAL DIVIDE

ROAD SHIELDS

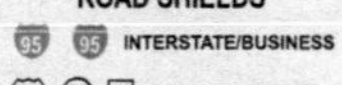

INTERSTATE/BUSINESS

U.S./STATE/COUNTY

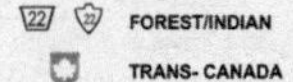

FOREST/INDIAN
TRANS- CANADA
PROVINCIAL AUTOROUTE
MEXICO
HISTORIC ROUTE 66
VT 41 REFERENCE PAGE INDICATOR

AREAS OF INTEREST

INDIAN
MILITARY
PARK
FOREST
GRASSLANDS
HISTORIC
INT'L/REGIONAL AIRPORT
INCORPORATED CITY

POINTS OF INTEREST

TOWN
NATIONAL CAPITAL
STATE/PROVINCIAL CAPITAL
AAA/CAA CLUB LOCATION
FEATURE OF INTEREST
COLLEGE/UNIVERSITY
CAMPGROUND
CUSTOMS STATION
HISTORIC
LIGHTHOUSE
MONUMENT/MEMORIAL
STATE/PROVINCIAL PARK
NATIONAL WILDLIFE REFUGE
SKI AREA
SPORTS COMPLEX

CITIES/TOWNS are color-coded by size, showing where to find AAA Approved and Diamond rated lodgings or restaurants listed in the AAA TourBook guides and on AAA.com:

- RED - major destinations and capitals; many listings
- Black - destinations; some listings
- Grey - no listings

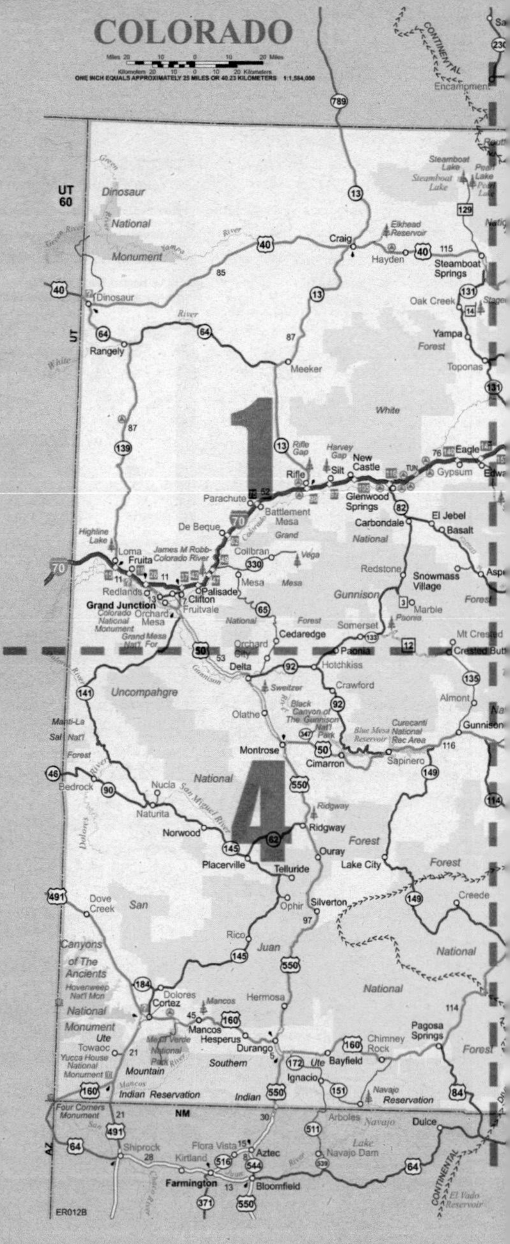

COLORADO

Miles 20 10 0 10 20 Miles
Kilometers 20 10 0 10 20 Kilometers
ONE INCH EQUALS APPROXIMATELY 25 MILES OR 40.23 KILOMETERS 1:1,584,000

ER012B

Use driving maps from the AAA Road Atlas to plan your itinerary and route. Purchase the complete 2012 AAA Road Atlas at participating AAA/CAA offices, retail stores and online booksellers.

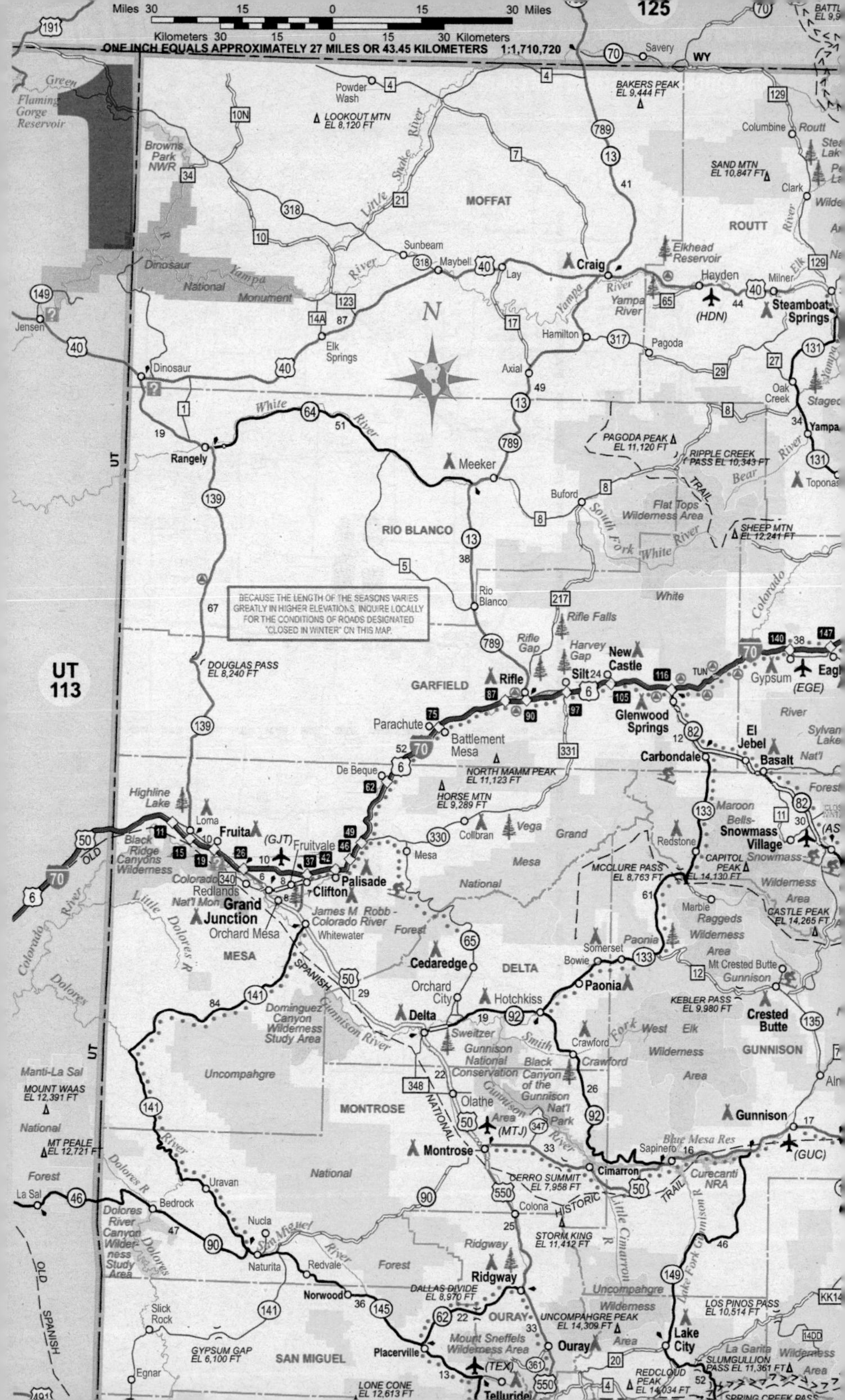
Miles 30 15 0 15 30 Miles
Kilometers 30 15 0 15 30 Kilometers
ONE INCH EQUALS APPROXIMATELY 27 MILES OR 43.45 KILOMETERS 1:1,710,720
WY
UT
UT 113
BECAUSE THE LENGTH OF THE SEASONS VARIES GREATLY IN HIGHER ELEVATIONS, INQUIRE LOCALLY FOR THE CONDITIONS OF ROADS DESIGNATED "CLOSED IN WINTER" ON THIS MAP.
N
MOFFAT
ROUTT
RIO BLANCO
GARFIELD
MESA
DELTA
MONTROSE
GUNNISON
OURAY
SAN MIGUEL
Flaming Gorge Reservoir
Browns Park NWR
Dinosaur National Monument
Powder Wash
LOOKOUT MTN EL 8,120 FT
BAKERS PEAK EL 9,444 FT
SAND MTN EL 10,847 FT
Savery
Columbine
Clark
Sunbeam
Maybell
Lay
Craig
Elkhead Reservoir
Hayden
(HDN)
Milner
Steamboat Springs
Jensen
Dinosaur
Elk Springs
Hamilton
Pagoda
Axial
Oak Creek
Yampa
Rangely
Meeker
PAGODA PEAK EL 11,120 FT
RIPPLE CREEK PASS EL 10,343 FT
Buford
Flat Tops Wilderness Area
SHEEP MTN EL 12,241 FT
Rio Blanco
Rifle Falls
Rifle Gap
Harvey Gap
New Castle
Silt
Rifle
Glenwood Springs
Gypsum
(EGE)
DOUGLAS PASS EL 8,240 FT
Parachute
Battlement Mesa
De Beque
NORTH MAMM PEAK EL 11,123 FT
HORSE MTN EL 9,289 FT
Carbondale
El Jebel
Basalt
Highline Lake
Loma
Fruita
(GJT)
Fruitvale
Palisade
Clifton
Grand Junction
Redlands
Colorado Nat'l Mon
Orchard Mesa
James M Robb - Colorado River
Whitewater
Collbran
Vega
Mesa
Grand Mesa National Forest
Redstone
Maroon Bells-Snowmass Wilderness
Snowmass Village
MCCLURE PASS EL 8,763 FT
CAPITOL PEAK EL 14,130 FT
CASTLE PEAK EL 14,265 FT
Marble
Raggeds Wilderness Area
Black Ridge Canyons Wilderness
Cedaredge
Orchard City
Somerset
Bowie
Paonia
Mt Crested Butte
Crested Butte
KEBLER PASS EL 9,980 FT
Delta
Hotchkiss
Dominguez Canyon Wilderness Study Area
Sweitzer
Crawford
West Elk Wilderness Area
Gunnison National Conservation Area
Black Canyon of the Gunnison Nat'l Park
Olathe
Uncompahgre National Forest
Manti-La Sal National Forest
MOUNT WAAS EL 12,391 FT
MT PEALE EL 12,721 FT
Montrose
(MTJ)
Gunnison
(GUC)
Blue Mesa Res
Sapinero
Cimarron
CERRO SUMMIT EL 7,958 FT
Curecanti NRA
OLD SPANISH TRAIL
Uravan
La Sal
Bedrock
Dolores River Canyon Wilderness Study Area
Nucla
Naturita
Redvale
Colona
STORM KING EL 11,412 FT
Ridgway
DALLAS DIVIDE EL 8,970 FT
Norwood
Uncompahgre Wilderness
UNCOMPAHGRE PEAK EL 14,309 FT
LOS PINOS PASS EL 10,514 FT
Lake City
Slick Rock
Placerville
Mount Sneffels Wilderness Area
Ouray
GYPSUM GAP EL 6,100 FT
(TEX)
Telluride
Egnar
LONE CONE EL 12,613 FT
REDCLOUD PEAK EL 14,034 FT
SLUMGULLION PASS EL 11,361 FT
La Garita Wilderness Area

2
WY
Foxpark
Laramie
Platte River
Cowdrey
North Fork
Zirkel
MT ZIRKEL EL 12,180 FT
State Canadian
Rawah
Walden
Arapaho
JACKSON
MOUNT ETHEL EL 11,924 FT
NWR
Michigan R
Illinois River
State Park
Hebron
Gould
Rand
Roosevelt
N Fk Cache La Poudre R
HALLIGAN DAM
Red Feather Lakes
SOUTH BALD MTN EL 11,003 FT
Rustic
Comanche Peak Wilderness
Cache La Poudre Wilderness Area
LOOKOUT MTN EL 10,626 FT
CAMERON PASS EL 10,276 FT
HAGUES PEAK EL 13,560 FT
Never Summer Wildnrs Area
WILLOW CREEK PASS EL 9,621 FT
PARKVIEW MTN EL 12,296 FT
CASCADE MTN EL 12,303 FT
LARIMER
Livermore
Wellington
Fort Collins
Laporte
Masonville
Carr
Nunn
Ault
Eaton
Windsor
Greeley
Gill
Kersey
(FNL)
Loveland
Pawnee
Hereford
Grover
Briggsdale
WELD
South Platte
Big Thompson R
Rocky Mountain National Park
CONTINENTAL DIVIDE
Forest
BOULDER
Lake Granby
Arapaho NRA
GRAND
Kremmling
Granby
Hot Sulphur Springs
Parshall
Williams Fork Res
SHEEP MTN EL 10,671 FT
ELK MTN EL 11,419 FT
GORE PASS EL 9,527 FT
McCoy
Bond
Green Mountain Res
Vasquez Peak Wilderness Area
BYERS PEAK EL 12,804 FT
BERTHOUD PASS EL 11,315 FT
Fraser R
GILPIN
Central City
Ptarmigan Peak Wilderness Area
Eagles Nest Wilderness Area
Georgetown
LOVELAND PASS EL 11,990 FT
SQUAW PASS EL 9,790 FT
CLEAR CREEK
Silverthorne
Dillon
Keystone
Frisco
SUMMIT
Breckenridge
Wolcott
Vail
Edwards
Avon
Minturn
EAGLE
VAIL PASS EL 10,603 FT
MT JACKSON EL 13,670 FT
Red Cliff
Holy Cross Wilderness
Copper Mountain
TENNESSEE PASS EL 10,424 FT
FREMONT PASS EL 11,320 FT
HOOSIER PASS EL 11,532 FT
Alma
Leadville
LAKE
Mount Massive Wilderness Area
INDEPENDENCE PASS EL 12,093 FT
Twin Lakes
LA PLATA PEAK EL 14,361 FT
MT HARVARD EL 14,420 FT
MOUNT SHERMAN EL 14,036 FT
BLACK MOUNTAIN EL 10,568 FT
Granite
Buffalo Peaks Wilderness Area
Fairplay
RED HILL PASS EL 9,986 FT
Como
Jefferson
KENOSHA PASS EL 10,000 FT
Grant
Mount Evans Wilderness Area
Lost Creek Wilderness Area
Bailey
BISON MOUNTAIN EL 12,431 FT
PARK
Tarryall
WILKERSON PASS EL 9,502 FT
Hartsel
Spinney Mountain Res
Eleven Mile
Antero Res
Antero Junction
Buena Vista
TROUT CREEK PASS EL 9,487 FT
Taylor Park Res
San
Arkansas R
COTTONWOOD PASS EL 12,126 FT
CHAFFEE
Nathrop
Fossil Ridge Wilderness Area
Arkansas Headwaters Recreation Area
Isabel
Pitkin
MT SHAVANO EL 14,229 FT
BLACK SAGE PASS EL 9,745 FT
Parlin
Monarch
Salida
MONARCH PASS EL 11,312 FT
Poncha Springs
PONCHA PASS EL 9,010 FT
Doyleville
Sargents
Howard
Cotopaxi
Coaldale
Villa Grove
Mineral Hot Springs
NORTH PASS EL 10,149 FT
SAGUACHE
Saguache
Moffat
Crestone
CRESTONE PEAK
Sangre de Cristo Wilderness Area
Westcliffe
Silver Cliff
CUSTER
National
Boulder
Broomfield
Golden
Lakewood
DENVER
Aurora
(DEN)
Brighton
Hudson
Keenesburg
Roggen
Bennett
Strasburg
ARAPAHOE
Littleton
Conifer
JEFFERSON
Buffalo Creek
Sedalia
Parker
Ponderosa Park
Elizabeth
Kiowa
Castle Rock
Castlewood Canyon
DOUGLAS
Larkspur
Elbert
DEVILS HEAD EL 9,748 FT
Deckers
Palmer Lake
Monument
SIGNAL BUTTE EL 9,459 FT
Woodland Park
USAF Academy
Black Forest
Lake George
TELLER
Divide
Florissant Fossil Beds Nat'l Mon
Mueller
Cascade
COLORADO SPRINGS
Peyton
Calhan
PIKES PEAK EL 14,110 FT
(COS)
Fort Carson
EL PASO
Yoder
SADDLE MTN EL 10,801 FT
Guffey
Cripple Creek
Victor
VICTOR PASS EL 10,202 FT
Cheyenne Mountain
Fountain
FREMONT
WAUGH MTN EL 11,718 FT
Canon City
TUNNEL
Penrose
Lincoln Park
Florence
Williamsburg
CURLEY PEAK EL 9,622 FT
Pueblo West
(PUB)
Pueblo Ordnance Depot
Lake Pueblo
Boone
Avondale
Pueblo
PUEBLO
Wetmore
RUDOLPH MTN EL 10,334 FT
Beulah
Rye
Saint Charles River
INSET

3
Sidney
Kimball
Chappell
Julesburg
Ovid
Sedgwick
Peetz
PANORAMA POINT
(HIGHEST POINT)
EL 5,424 FT
WY
NE
LOGAN
SEDGWICK
PHILLIPS
Crook
Iliff
North
Sterling
Fleming
Haxtun
Amherst
Holyoke
NE
70
National
Grassland
Stoneham
Sterling
Willard
Atwood
Merino
Jackson
Lake
Log
Lane
Village
Weldona
Orchard
Snyder
Hillrose
Wiggins
MORGAN
Ft
Morgan
Brush
Akron
Otis
Yuma
Eckley
Wray
Laird
YUMA
North
Fk
Republican
KS
TIME
CENTRAL
MOUNTAIN T
Hoyt
Woodrow
WASHINGTON
ADAMS
Last
Chance
Lindon
Anton
Cope
Joes
Kirk
Idalia
River
Bonny
Lake
Deer
Trail
Agate
ELBERT
KIT CARSON
Arikaree
Fork
Stratton
Bethune
Burlington
Genoa
Arriba
Flagler
Seibert
Limon
Simla
Matheson
Hugo
South
Smoky
Hill
River
MT SUNFLOWER
EL 4,039 FT
LINCOLN
CHEYENNE
Cheyenne
Wells
Smokey
Hill
River
Arapahoe
Wild
Horse
Aroya
Kit Carson
Yoder
Rush
Punkin
Center
Karval
Sand Creek
Massacre NHS
Galatea
Eads
Haswell
Brandon
Chivington
Sheridan
Lake
Towner
KS
42
CROWLEY
KIOWA
Arlington
Sugar
City
Crowley
Ordway
Olney
Springs
Boone
Arkansas
Fowler
Rocky
Ford
Cheraw
Bent's Old
Fort NHS
Swink
Hawley
La Junta
River
McClave
Hasty
Wiley
Bristol
Hartman
SANTA FE
TRAIL
Las
Animas
John
Martin
Res
John Martin
Reservoir
Lamar
Granada
Holly
HISTORIC
NAT'L
Platte
R
Republican

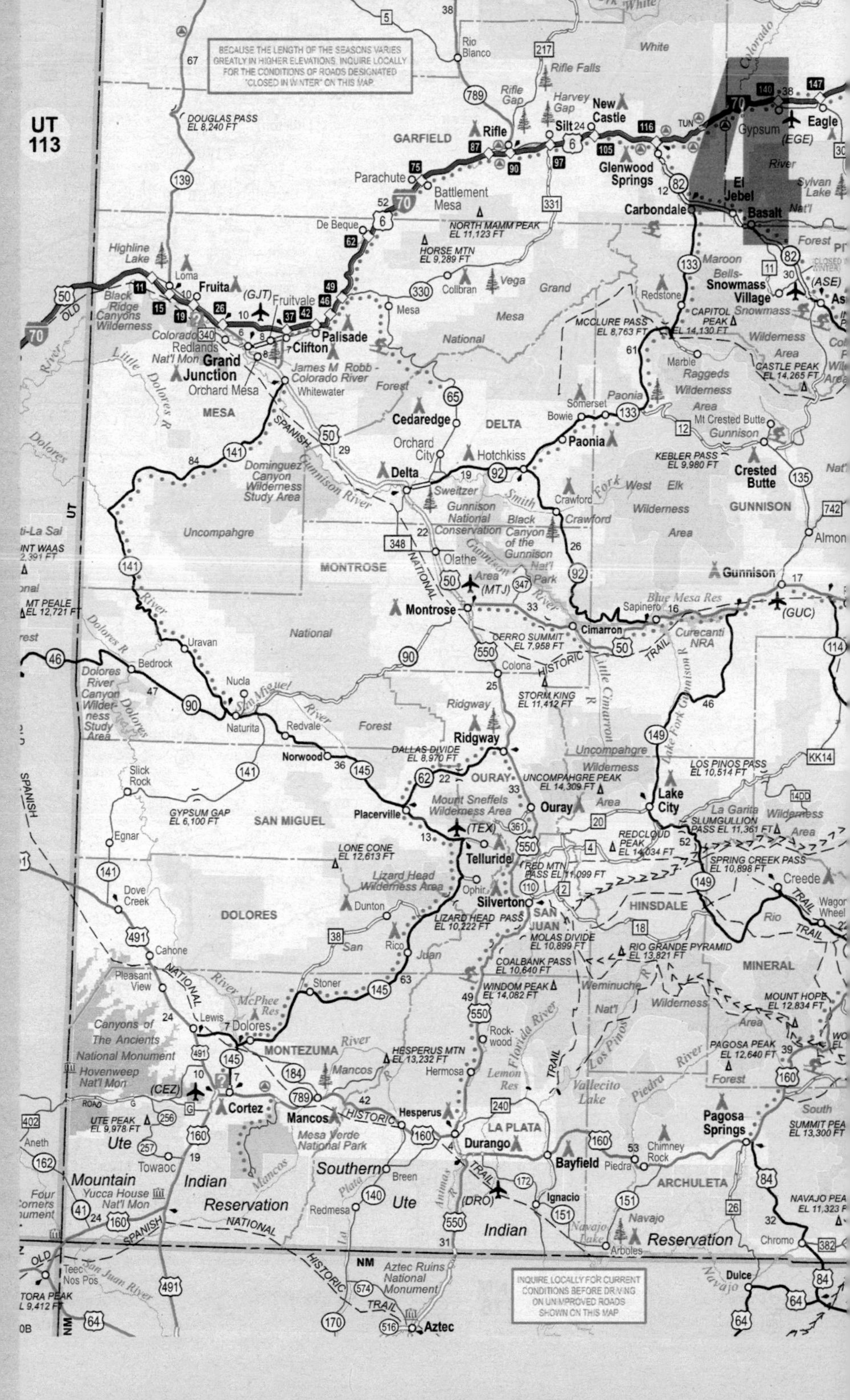
UT
113
BECAUSE THE LENGTH OF THE SEASONS VARIES GREATLY IN HIGHER ELEVATIONS, INQUIRE LOCALLY FOR THE CONDITIONS OF ROADS DESIGNATED "CLOSED IN WINTER" ON THIS MAP.
DOUGLAS PASS
EL 8,240 FT
Rio Blanco
Rifle Falls
Rifle Gap
Harvey Gap
New Castle
Rifle
Silt
GARFIELD
Glenwood Springs
Gypsum
(EGE)
Eagle
El Jebel
Carbondale
Basalt
Sylvan Lake
Parachute
Battlement Mesa
NORTH MAMM PEAK
EL 11,123 FT
HORSE MTN
EL 9,289 FT
De Beque
Highline Lake
Loma
Fruita
(GJT)
Fruitvale
Collbran
Vega
Grand
Mesa
National
Forest
Black Ridge Canyons Wilderness
Colorado
Redlands
Nat'l Mon
Grand Junction
Orchard Mesa
Clifton
Palisade
Mesa
James M Robb - Colorado River
Whitewater
MESA
Little Dolores R
Dolores
Redstone
MCCLURE PASS
EL 8,763 FT
CAPITOL PEAK
EL 14,130 FT
Maroon Bells-Snowmass Wilderness Area
Snowmass Village
(ASE)
Snowmass
CASTLE PEAK
EL 14,265 FT
Marble
Raggeds Wilderness Area
Paonia
Somerset
Bowie
Mt Crested Butte
Gunnison
KEBLER PASS
EL 9,980 FT
Crested Butte
Cedaredge
DELTA
Orchard City
Hotchkiss
Delta
Sweitzer
Gunnison National Conservation Area
Black Canyon of the Gunnison Nat'l Park
Crawford
West Elk Wilderness Area
GUNNISON
Almont
SPANISH
Gunnison River
Dominguez Canyon Wilderness Study Area
Uncompahgre
MONTROSE
Olathe
(MTJ)
Montrose
NATIONAL
Gunnison
Blue Mesa Res
Sapinero
Cimarron
(GUC)
CERRO SUMMIT
EL 7,958 FT
Curecanti NRA
HISTORIC
TRAIL
Colona
Uravan
Bedrock
Dolores River Canyon Wilderness Study Area
Nucla
San Miguel River
Naturita
Redvale
Forest
STORM KING
EL 11,412 FT
Little Cimarron
Lake Fork Gunnison R
Ridgway
Norwood
DALLAS DIVIDE
EL 8,970 FT
OURAY
UNCOMPAHGRE PEAK
EL 14,309 FT
Uncompahgre Wilderness Area
LOS PINOS PASS
EL 10,514 FT
Lake City
Slick Rock
GYPSUM GAP
EL 6,100 FT
SAN MIGUEL
Placerville
Mount Sneffels Wilderness Area
Ouray
(TEX)
Telluride
La Garita Wilderness Area
SLUMGULLION PASS EL 11,361 FT
REDCLOUD PEAK
EL 14,034 FT
SPRING CREEK PASS
EL 10,898 FT
Creede
Egnar
LONE CONE
EL 12,613 FT
RED MTN PASS EL 11,099 FT
Lizard Head Wilderness Area
Ophir
Dove Creek
Dunton
DOLORES
Silverton
SAN JUAN
HINSDALE
Wagon Wheel
LIZARD HEAD PASS
EL 10,222 FT
MOLAS DIVIDE
EL 10,899 FT
RIO GRANDE PYRAMID
EL 13,821 FT
Rio
MINERAL
Cahone
San Juan
Rico
COALBANK PASS
EL 10,640 FT
Pleasant View
Stoner
WINDOM PEAK
EL 14,082 FT
Weminuche Wilderness Area
MOUNT HOPE
EL 12,834 FT
River
McPhee Res
Canyons of The Ancients National Monument
Lewis
Dolores
Rockwood
Florida River
Nat'l
Los Pinos
MONTEZUMA
HESPERUS MTN
EL 13,232 FT
PAGOSA PEAK
EL 12,640 FT
Hovenweep Nat'l Mon
Mancos
Hermosa
Lemon Res
Vallecito Lake
Piedra River
(CEZ)
Cortez
Mancos
HISTORIC
Hesperus
LA PLATA
South
UTE PEAK
EL 9,978 FT
Mesa Verde National Park
Durango
Pagosa Springs
SUMMIT PEAK
EL 13,300 FT
Ute
Aneth
Towaoc
Bayfield
Piedra
Chimney Rock
Southern
Breen
Mountain
Indian
ARCHULETA
Four Corners Monument
Yucca House Nat'l Mon
(DRO)
Ignacio
Reservation
Redmesa
Ute
Navajo
NAVAJO PEAK
EL 11,323 FT
Indian
Navajo Lake
Reservation
Chromo
Arboles
NATIONAL
SPANISH
OLD
Teec Nos Pos
San Juan River
HISTORIC
NM
Aztec Ruins National Monument
TRAIL
Aztec
Dulce
Navajo
INQUIRE LOCALLY FOR CURRENT CONDITIONS BEFORE DRIVING ON UNIMPROVED ROADS SHOWN ON THIS MAP
UT
NM

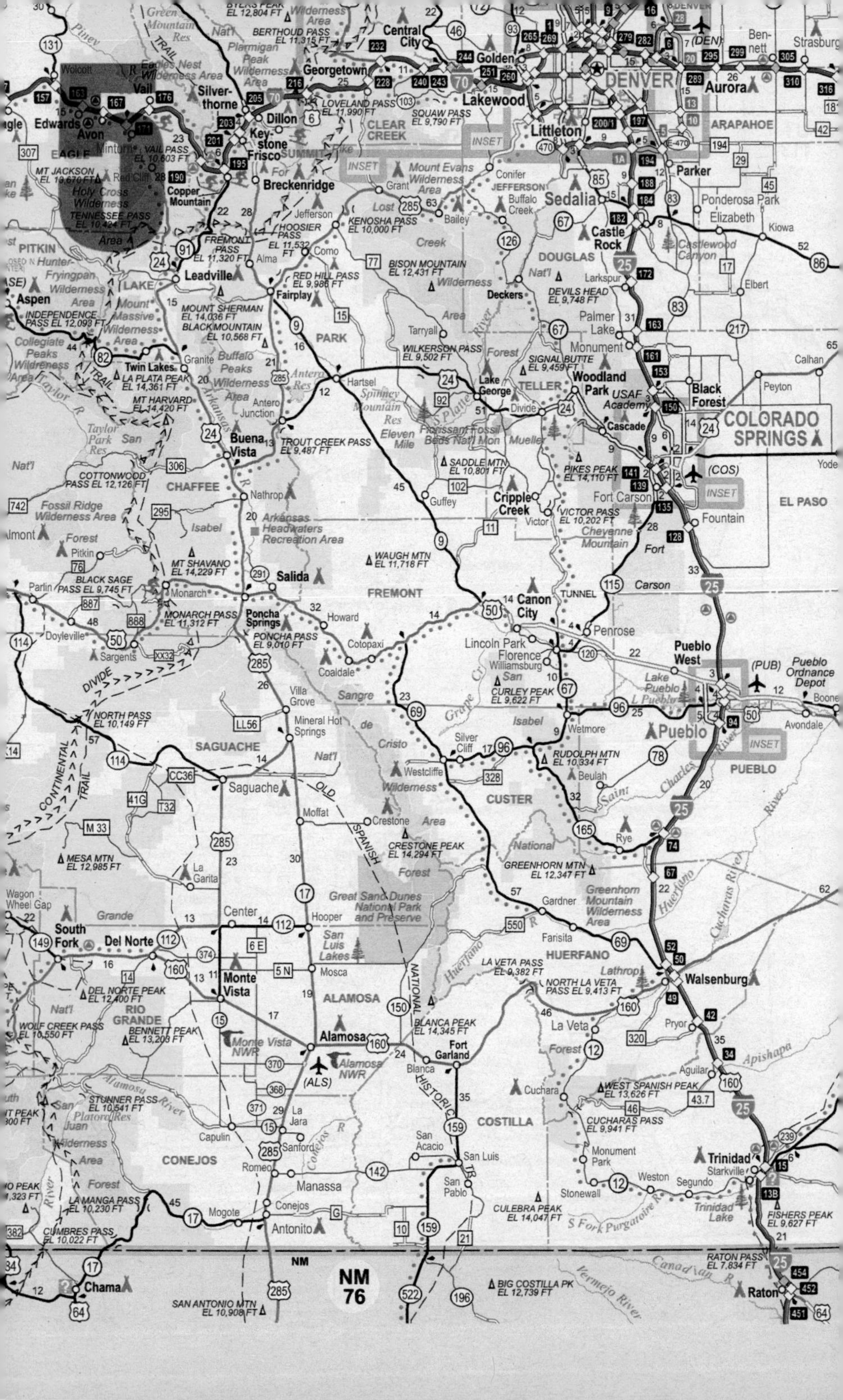

5
Denver
Aurora
Lakewood
Golden
Littleton
Central City
Georgetown
Silverthorne
Dillon
Keystone
Frisco
Vail
Avon
Edwards
Wolcott
Minturn
Red Cliff
Copper Mountain
Breckenridge
Leadville
Aspen
Twin Lakes
Granite
Alma
Fairplay
Como
Jefferson
Grant
Bailey
Conifer
Buffalo Creek
Deckers
Sedalia
Castle Rock
Parker
Ponderosa Park
Elizabeth
Kiowa
Elbert
Larkspur
Palmer Lake
Monument
Woodland Park
Black Forest
Calhan
Peyton
Colorado Springs
Cascade
Fort Carson
Fountain
Yoder
El Paso
Lake George
Divide
Tarryall
Hartsel
Antero Junction
Buena Vista
Nathrop
Salida
Poncha Springs
Monarch
Parlin
Doyleville
Sargents
Pitkin
Almont
Howard
Cotopaxi
Coaldale
Canon City
Penrose
Lincoln Park
Florence
Williamsburg
Guffey
Cripple Creek
Victor
Pueblo West
Pueblo
Pueblo Ordnance Depot
Boone
Avondale
Lake Pueblo
Wetmore
Beulah
Rye
Silver Cliff
Westcliffe
Villa Grove
Mineral Hot Springs
Saguache
Moffat
Crestone
La Garita
Center
Hooper
Mosca
Alamosa
Monte Vista
South Fork
Del Norte
Wagon Wheel Gap
Fort Garland
Blanca
San Luis
San Acacio
San Pablo
La Jara
Sanford
Capulin
Romeo
Manassa
Conejos
Mogote
Antonito
Chama
Gardner
Farisita
Walsenburg
Lathrop
La Veta
Pryor
Aguilar
Cuchara
Monument Park
Stonewall
Weston
Segundo
Trinidad
Starkville
Trinidad Lake
Raton
EAGLE
PITKIN
LAKE
SUMMIT
CLEAR CREEK
JEFFERSON
DOUGLAS
ARAPAHOE
PARK
TELLER
CHAFFEE
FREMONT
CUSTER
SAGUACHE
PUEBLO
HUERFANO
ALAMOSA
RIO GRANDE
COSTILLA
CONEJOS
NM
NM 76
INSET
(DEN)
(COS)
(PUB)
(ALS)
BERTHOUD PASS EL 11,315 FT
LOVELAND PASS EL 11,990 FT
SQUAW PASS EL 9,790 FT
VAIL PASS EL 10,603 FT
MT JACKSON EL 10,670 FT
TENNESSEE PASS EL 10,424 FT
FREMONT PASS EL 11,320 FT
HOOSIER PASS EL 11,532 FT
KENOSHA PASS EL 10,000 FT
RED HILL PASS EL 9,986 FT
BISON MOUNTAIN EL 12,431 FT
DEVILS HEAD EL 9,748 FT
INDEPENDENCE PASS EL 12,093 FT
MOUNT SHERMAN EL 14,036 FT
BLACK MOUNTAIN EL 10,568 FT
LA PLATA PEAK EL 14,361 FT
MT HARVARD EL 14,420 FT
WILKERSON PASS EL 9,502 FT
SIGNAL BUTTE EL 9,459 FT
TROUT CREEK PASS EL 9,487 FT
SADDLE MTN EL 10,801 FT
PIKES PEAK EL 14,110 FT
COTTONWOOD PASS EL 12,126 FT
VICTOR PASS EL 10,202 FT
MT SHAVANO EL 14,229 FT
WAUGH MTN EL 11,718 FT
BLACK SAGE PASS EL 9,745 FT
MONARCH PASS EL 11,312 FT
PONCHA PASS EL 9,010 FT
CURLEY PEAK EL 9,622 FT
NORTH PASS EL 10,149 FT
RUDOLPH MTN EL 10,334 FT
MESA MTN EL 12,985 FT
CRESTONE PEAK EL 14,294 FT
GREENHORN MTN EL 12,347 FT
LA VETA PASS EL 9,382 FT
NORTH LA VETA PASS EL 9,413 FT
DEL NORTE PEAK EL 12,400 FT
WOLF CREEK PASS EL 10,550 FT
BENNETT PEAK EL 13,203 FT
BLANCA PEAK EL 14,345 FT
WEST SPANISH PEAK EL 13,626 FT
CUCHARAS PASS EL 9,941 FT
STUNNER PASS EL 10,541 FT
LA MANGA PASS EL 10,230 FT
CUMBRES PASS EL 10,022 FT
CULEBRA PEAK EL 14,047 FT
FISHERS PEAK EL 9,627 FT
RATON PASS EL 7,834 FT
BIG COSTILLA PK EL 12,739 FT
SAN ANTONIO MTN EL 10,908 FT
Eagles Nest Wilderness Area
Ptarmigan Peak Wilderness Area
Mount Evans Wilderness Area
Holy Cross Wilderness Area
Hunter-Fryingpan Wilderness Area
Mount Massive Wilderness Area
Collegiate Peaks Wilderness Area
Buffalo Peaks Wilderness Area
Lost Creek Wilderness Area
Fossil Ridge Wilderness Area
Sangre de Cristo Wilderness Area
Greenhorn Mountain Wilderness Area
South San Juan Wilderness Area
Florissant Fossil Beds Nat'l Mon
Arkansas Headwaters Recreation Area
Great Sand Dunes National Park and Preserve
Monte Vista NWR
Alamosa NWR
San Luis Lakes
Castlewood Canyon
Antero Res
Spinney Mountain Res
Eleven Mile Res
Taylor Park Res
Platoro Res
USAF Academy
Cheyenne Mountain
TUNNEL
CONTINENTAL DIVIDE TRAIL
OLD SPANISH NATIONAL HISTORIC TR
Arkansas R
Taylor R
Huerfano R
Cucharas River
Apishapa R
Saint Charles River
Purgatoire R
Vermejo River
Canadian R
Alamosa River
Conejos R
Grande

6
KS 42
OK 92
ADAMS
ELBERT
KIT CARSON
LINCOLN
CHEYENNE
CROWLEY
KIOWA
OTERO
BENT
PROWERS
BACA
LAS ANIMAS
Last Chance
Lindon
Anton
Cope
Joes
Kirk
Idalia
St Francis
Bonny Lake
MOUNTAIN TIME
CENTRAL
Goodland
Deer Trail
Agate
Limon
Genoa
Arriba
Flagler
Seibert
Stratton
Bethune
Burlington
Simla
Matheson
Hugo
MT SUNFLOWER EL 4,039 FT
Sharon Springs
Wild Horse
Cheyenne Wells
Arapahoe
Rush
Punkin Center
Aroya
Kit Carson
Karval
Sand Creek Massacre NHS
Galatea
Eads
Haswell
Sheridan Lake
Towner
Tribune
Brandon
Chivington
Arlington
Sugar City
Crowley
Olney Springs
Ordway
Fowler
Rocky Ford
Cheraw
Bent's Old Fort NHS
Las Animas
John Martin Res
John Martin Reservoir
McClave
Hasty
Wiley
Lamar
Bristol
Hartman
Granada
Holly
Syracuse
SANTA FE TRAIL
Swink
La Junta
Hawley
Timpas
Toonerville
Yarber Reservoir
Comanche
Delhi
Pinon
Thatcher
Canyon
Tyrone
Maneuver
Site
Model
Johnson City
Two Buttes
Springfield
Bartlett
Vilas
Walsh
Pritchett
Stonington
National
Grasslands
Kim
Campo
Branson
Elkhart
CIMARRON CUTOFF
BLACK MESA (HIGHEST POINT) EL 4,973 FT
Kenton
Arkansas River
Purgatoire
Cimarron River
Dry
Arikaree
South Fork
N Fork Smoky Hill River
Smokey Hill River
Republican River
North Fork Cimarron
NM
OK
KS

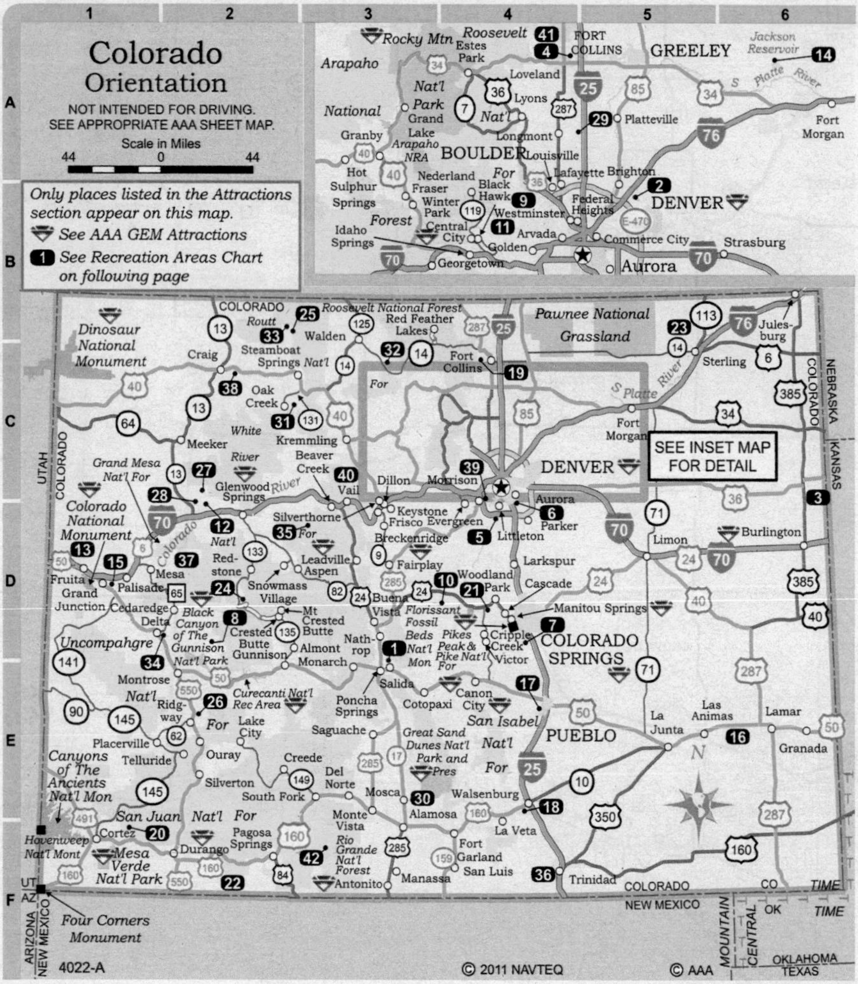

Colorado
Orientation
NOT INTENDED FOR DRIVING.
SEE APPROPRIATE AAA SHEET MAP.
Scale in Miles
44 0 44
Only places listed in the Attractions section appear on this map.
See AAA GEM Attractions
1 See Recreation Areas Chart on following page
SEE INSET MAP FOR DETAIL
Rocky Mtn Nat'l Park
Roosevelt Nat'l For
Estes Park
FORT COLLINS
GREELEY
Jackson Reservoir
Arapaho National Forest
Loveland
Lyons
Granby
Grand Lake
Arapaho NRA
Longmont
Platteville
Fort Morgan
BOULDER
Louisville
Lafayette
Brighton
Hot Sulphur Springs
Nederland
Fraser
Winter Park
Black Hawk
Westminster
Federal Heights
DENVER
Idaho Springs
Central City
Arvada
Golden
Commerce City
Strasburg
Georgetown
Aurora
Dinosaur National Monument
Craig
Routt
Steamboat Springs
Walden
Red Feather Lakes
Roosevelt National Forest
Pawnee National Grassland
Julesburg
Sterling
Oak Creek
Meeker
White River
Kremmling
Beaver Creek
Grand Mesa Nat'l For
Glenwood Springs
Colorado National Monument
Vail
Dillon
Morrison
Keystone
Frisco
Evergreen
Silverthorne
Breckenridge
Littleton
Parker
Limon
Burlington
Fruita
Grand Junction
Palisade
Mesa
Redstone
Snowmass Village
Leadville
Aspen
Fairplay
Larkspur
Woodland Park
Cascade
Manitou Springs
Cedaredge
Delta
Black Canyon of The Gunnison Nat'l Park
Crested Butte
Mt Crested Butte
Gunnison
Almont
Monarch
Buena Vista
Nathrop
Florissant Fossil Beds Nat'l Mon
Pikes Peak & Pike Nat'l For
Cripple Creek
Victor
COLORADO SPRINGS
Uncompahgre
Montrose
Curecanti Nat'l Rec Area
Salida
Poncha Springs
Cotopaxi
Canon City
San Isabel Nat'l For
PUEBLO
La Junta
Las Animas
Lamar
Granada
Ridgway
Placerville
Telluride
Ouray
Lake City
Saguache
Great Sand Dunes Nat'l Park and Pres
Canyons of The Ancients Nat'l Mon
Creede
Silverton
Del Norte
South Fork
Mosca
Walsenburg
Alamosa
San Juan Nat'l For
Monte Vista
La Veta
Hovenweep Nat'l Mont
Cortez
Pagosa Springs
Rio Grande Nat'l Forest
Fort Garland
San Luis
Mesa Verde Nat'l Park
Durango
Antonito
Manassa
Trinidad
COLORADO
NEW MEXICO
Four Corners Monument
UTAH
NEBRASKA
KANSAS
OKLAHOMA
TEXAS
ARIZONA
MOUNTAIN
CENTRAL
TIME
4022-A
© 2011 NAVTEQ
© AAA

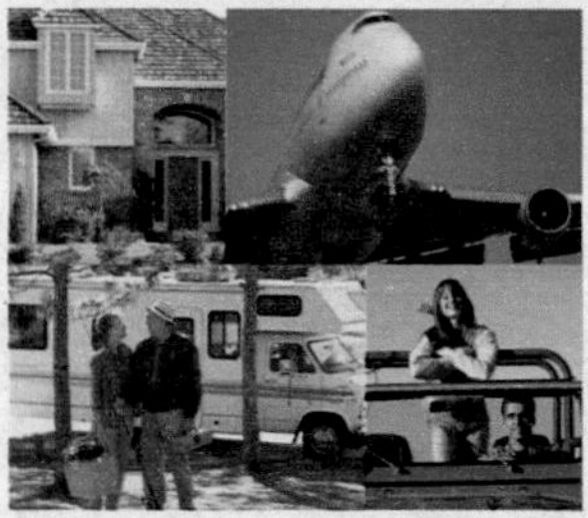

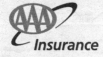

Recreation Areas Chart

The map location numerals in column 2 show an area's location on the preceding map.

	MAP LOCATION	CAMPING	PICNICKING	HIKING TRAILS	BOATING	BOAT RAMP	BOAT RENTAL	FISHING	SWIMMING	PETS ON LEASH	BICYCLE TRAILS	WINTER SPORTS	VISITOR CENTER	LODGE/CABINS	FOOD SERVICE
NATIONAL PARKS *(See place listings.)*															
Black Canyon of the Gunnison (D-2) 30,750 acres.		●	●	●				●		●		●	●		
Great Sand Dunes National Park and Preserve (E-3) 149,137 acres. Nature programs. Nature trails.		●	●	●						●		●	●		
Mesa Verde (F-1) 52,000 acres.		●	●	●						●		●	●	●	
Rocky Mountain (A-3) 265,800 acres. Cross-country skiing, rock climbing, snowshoeing; equestrian camping, horse rental.		●	●	●				●		●		●	●		
NATIONAL FORESTS *(See place listings.)*															
Arapaho and Roosevelt/Pawnee National Grassland (A-3, A-4, B-4) 1,280,000 acres. North-central Colorado.		●	●	●	●	●	●	●	●	●	●	●	●		
Grand Mesa-Uncompahgre-Gunnison (D-1) 2,952,549 acres. West-central Colorado.		●	●	●	●	●		●		●	●	●	●		●
Pike (D-4) 1,105,704 acres. Central Colorado. Horse rental.		●	●	●	●	●		●		●	●	●	●	●	●
Rio Grande (F-3) 1,851,792 acres. South-central Colorado. Horse rental.		●	●	●	●	●		●	●	●	●	●	●	●	
Routt (B-2) 1.26 million acres. Northwest Colorado. Cross-country skiing, hunting, snowshoeing; horseback trails, motorized vehicle trails.		●	●	●	●	●		●	●	●	●	●	●	●	
San Isabel (E-4) 1,109,782 acres. South-central Colorado. Horse rental.		●	●	●	●	●		●		●	●	●	●	●	●
San Juan (E-1) 1,881,586 acres. Southwestern Colorado.		●	●	●	●	●	●	●	●	●	●	●	●	●	●
White River (C-2) 2.3 million acres. Northwestern and north-central Colorado.		●	●	●	●	●	●	●	●	●	●	●	●	●	●
NATIONAL RECREATION AREAS *(See place listings.)*															
Arapaho (A-3) 36,000 acres. North-central Colorado.		●	●	●	●	●	●	●	●	●	●	●	●		
Curecanti (E-2) 41,971 acres. West-central Colorado.		●	●	●	●	●	●	●	●	●		●	●		●
STATE															
Arkansas Headwaters Recreation Area (D-3) 6,190 acres 150 mi. along the Arkansas River from Leadville to Lake Pueblo State Park. Main access roads: US 24, 285 and 50. Cross-country skiing, gold panning, ice fishing, rock climbing, snowmobiling, snowshoeing, white-water rafting and boating; nature programs, off-road vehicle trails.	1	●	●	●	●	●		●		●	●	●	●		
Barr Lake (B-5) 2,609 acres n.e. of Denver off I-76 and Bromley Ln. Bird-watching, cross-country skiing, hunting, ice fishing, snowshoeing; horse rental, nature programs.	2		●	●	●	●		●		●	●	●	●		
Bonny Lake (C-6) 6,940 acres 4 mi. s. of Idalia on US 385. Cross-country skiing, hunting, ice fishing, ice skating, jet skiing; equestrian camping, horseback trails, nature trail, off-road vehicle trials.	3	●	●		●	●		●		●	●	●	●		
Boyd Lake (A-4) 2,186 acres 1 mi. e. of Loveland on US 34. Jet skiing, water skiing; marina.	4	●	●	●	●	●	●	●	●	●	●				●
Chatfield (D-4) 6,750 acres 8 mi. s.w. of Denver at SR 470 and Wadsworth. Cross-country skiing, hot-air ballooning, jet skiing, snowshoeing, water skiing; horse rental, marina, nature programs.	5	●	●	●	●	●	●	●	●	●	●	●			●
Cherry Creek (D-4) 4,795 acres 10 mi. s.e. of Denver near I-225 and Parker Rd. Bird-watching, cross-country skiing, ice skating, jet skiing, water skiing; horse rental, marina, nature programs.	6	●	●	●	●	●	●	●	●	●	●	●			
Cheyenne Mountain (D-4) 1,680 acres on the s.e. side of Colorado Springs off SR 115 across from Fort Carson Gate 1. Geocaching; nature programs.	7	●	●	●							●		●		●
Crawford (D-2) 1,218 acres 1 mi. s. of Crawford on SR 92. Cross-country skiing, hunting, ice fishing, jet skiing, scuba diving, snowshoeing, water skiing; nature programs.	8	●	●	●	●	●		●	●	●	●	●	●		
Eldorado Canyon (B-4) 845 acres 7 mi. s.w. of Boulder on SR 93. Cross-country skiing, hunting, snowshoeing, technical rock climbing; horseback trails, nature programs, nature trails.	9		●	●				●		●	●	●	●		

Recreation Areas Chart

The map location numerals in column 2 show an area's location on the preceding map.

Recreation Area	MAP LOCATION	CAMPING	PICNICKING	HIKING TRAILS	BOATING	BOAT RAMP	BOAT RENTAL	FISHING	SWIMMING	PETS ON LEASH	BICYCLE TRAILS	WINTER SPORTS	VISITOR CENTER	LODGE/CABINS	FOOD SERVICE
Eleven Mile (D-4) 7,662 acres about 11 mi. s.w. of Lake George off US 24 on CR 92. Bird-watching, cross-country skiing, hunting, ice fishing, ice skating, sailboarding; nature programs, nature trails, marina.	10	•	•	•	•	•	•	•		•	•	•	•		
Golden Gate Canyon (B-4) 12,000 acres 12 mi. w. of Golden off SR 93. Cross-country skiing, hunting, ice fishing, ice skating, rock climbing, snowshoeing; horseback trails, nature programs, nature trails.	11	•	•	•				•		•	•	•	•	•	
Harvey Gap (D-2) 320 acres 5 mi. n. of Silt off US 6. Cross-country skiing, hunting, ice fishing, snowshoeing, windsurfing.	12		•		•	•		•	•			•			
Highline Lake (D-1) 824 acres 14 mi. n.w. of Grand Junction off I-70 and SR 139. Bird-watching, hunting, ice fishing, ice skating, jet skiing, water skiing; jet ski rental, nature programs.	13	•	•	•	•	•		•	•	•	•	•	•		
Jackson Lake (A-6) 3,350 acres 20 mi. n.w. of Fort Morgan off SR 144. Bird-watching, hunting, ice fishing, jet skiing, sailboarding, water skiing, wildlife viewing; marina, nature programs, nature trail, off-road vehicle track.	14	•	•	•	•	•	•	•	•	•	•	•	•		•
James M. Robb-Colorado River (D-1) 475 acres in five sections along the Colorado River through the Grand Junction area from Island Acres to Fruita. Ice fishing, ice skating, snowmobiling; nature programs, nature trails.	15	•	•	•	•	•		•	•	•	•	•	•		
John Martin Reservoir (E-6) 5,700 acres 15 mi. e. of Las Animas off US 50. Bird-watching, hunting, jet skiing, water skiing; horseback trails, nature programs. *(See Las Animas p. 237.)*	16	•	•	•	•	•		•	•	•	•		•		
Lake Pueblo (E-4) 17,155 acres 6 mi. w. of Pueblo on SR 96. Hunting, jet skiing, sailboarding, water skiing; marina, nature programs.	17	•	•	•	•	•	•	•	•	•	•		•		•
Lathrop (E-4) 1,596 acres 3 mi. w. of Walsenburg on US 160. Bird-watching, golf, hunting, jet skiing, water skiing; nature trails.	18	•	•	•	•	•		•	•	•	•		•		
Lory (C-4) 2,419 acres 15 mi. n.w. of Fort Collins off US 287. Back-country camping, cross-country skiing, geocaching, hunting, rock climbing, snowshoeing, water skiing; horseback trails.	19		•	•	•			•		•	•	•	•		
Mancos (F-1) 577 acres .25 mi. n. of Mancos on SR 184, 4 mi. e. on CR 42, then .5 mi. w. on CR N. Bird-watching, cross-country skiing, hunting, ice fishing, snowshoeing; horseback trails, nature programs.	20	•	•	•	•	•	•	•		•	•	•		•	
Mueller (D-4) 5,121 acres 3.5 mi. s. of Divide off SR 67. Cross-country skiing, hunting, sledding, snowshoeing; horseback trails, nature programs.	21	•	•	•							•	•	•	•	
Navajo (F-2) 17,600 acres 2 mi. s. of Arboles on CR 982. Cross-country skiing, hunting, jet skiing, water skiing; horseback trails, marina, nature trails.	22	•	•	•	•	•	•	•	•	•	•	•	•	•	
North Sterling (B-5) 3,000 acres 12 mi. n. of Sterling via N. 7th Ave. Hunting, ice fishing, jet skiing, sailboarding, star gazing, water skiing; horseback trails, nature programs. *(See Sterling p. 291.)*	23	•	•	•	•	•		•	•	•	•		•		•
Paonia (D-2) 1,816 acres 14 mi. n. of Paonia on SR 133. Cross-country skiing, horseback riding, hunting, jet skiing, water skiing.	24	•	•		•	•		•		•		•			
Pearl Lake (B-3) 274 acres 25 mi. n. of Steamboat Springs off CR 129. Cross-country skiing, ice fishing, snowmobiling, snowshoeing.	25	•	•	•	•	•		•		•		•		•	
Ridgway (E-2) 3,201 acres 4 mi. n. of Ridgway on US 550. Bird-watching, cross-country skiing, geocaching, hot-air ballooning, hunting, rock climbing, sledding, snowmobiling, snowshoeing, water skiing, windsurfing.	26	•	•	•	•	•		•	•	•	•	•	•	•	
Rifle Falls (C-2) 93 acres 14 mi. n. of Rifle on SR 325. Hunting; nature programs, triple waterfall.	27	•	•	•				•		•		•			
Rifle Gap (C-1) 2,535 acres 10 mi. n. of Rifle on SR 325. Ice fishing, jet skiing, snowshoeing, water skiing; nature programs, nature trails.	28	•	•		•	•		•	•	•		•	•		
St. Vrain (A-5) 130 acres 7 mi. e. of Longmont off I-25. Bird-watching, ice fishing; nature trails.	29	•	•	•	•			•		•	•	•			

Recreation Areas Chart

The map location numerals in column 2 show an area's location on the preceding map.

	MAP LOCATION	CAMPING	PICNICKING	HIKING TRAILS	BOATING	BOAT RAMP	BOAT RENTAL	FISHING	SWIMMING	PETS ON LEASH	BICYCLE TRAILS	WINTER SPORTS	VISITOR CENTER	LODGE/CABINS	FOOD SERVICE
San Luis (E-3) 586 acres e. of Mosca on Six Mile Ln. Hunting; wildlife area.	30	•	•	•	•	•		•		•	•	•			
Stagecoach (C-2) 1,641 acres 6 mi. w. of Oak Creek off CR 14. Cross-country skiing, hunting, ice fishing, jet skiing, snowshoeing, water skiing, wildlife viewing; horseback trails.	31	•	•	•	•	•	•	•	•	•	•	•			
State Forest (C-3) 72,130 acres 21 mi. s.e. of Walden off SR 14. Bird-watching, cross-country skiing, geocaching, hunting, ice fishing, sledding, snowmobiling, snowshoeing; equestrian camping, horseback trails, motorized vehicles trail, nature programs, nature trails.	32	•	•	•	•	•		•		•	•	•	•	•	
Steamboat Lake (B-2) 2,773 acres 25 mi. n. of Steamboat Springs on CR 129. Cross-country skiing, hunting, ice fishing, jet skiing, sailboarding, snowmobiling, snowshoeing, water skiing; horseback trails, nature programs.	33	•	•	•	•	•	•	•	•	•	•	•	•	•	•
Sweitzer Lake (E-1) 210 acres 1.5 mi. s.e. of Delta off US 50. Bird-watching, canoeing, cross-country skiing, hunting, jet skiing, scuba diving, waterfowl hunting, water skiing; horseback trails.	34		•	•	•	•		•	•	•	•	•			
Sylvan Lake (D-2) 1,272 acres 10 mi. s. of Eagle on Brush Creek Rd. Cross-country skiing, ice fishing, ice skating, sledding, snowshoeing; motorized vehicles trail, nature programs.	35	•	•	•	•	•	•	•		•	•	•	•	•	
Trinidad Lake (F-4) 2,800 acres 3 mi. w. of Trinidad on SR 12. Cross-country skiing, ice fishing, jet skiing, snowshoeing, water skiing; horseback trails, nature programs.	36	•	•	•	•	•		•		•	•	•	•		
Vega (D-2) 2,730 acres 8 mi. e. of Collbran on CR 330. Historic. Bird-watching, cross-country skiing, hunting, ice fishing, ice skating, jet skiing, sledding, snowmobiling, snowshoeing, water skiing; motorized vehicles trail, nature trails.	37	•	•	•	•	•		•		•	•	•	•	•	
Yampa River (C-2) 70 acres 2 mi. w. of Hayden on US 40, managing 125 mi. of the Yampa River with 13 public access sites. Bird-watching, hunting, white-water rafting; nature programs, nature trail.	38	•	•	•	•	•		•		•			•		
OTHER															
Bear Creek Lake (C-4) 2,600 acres 14 mi. s.w. of Denver on US 285. Horse rental.	39	•	•	•	•	•		•		•	•	•	•	•	•
Green Mountain (C-3) 3,563 acres 17 mi. s. of Kremmling on SR 9. Ice fishing.	40	•	•		•	•	•	•	•	•		•			•
Horsetooth Reservoir (A-4) 3,900 acres 3 mi. w. of Fort Collins on CR 52. Waterskiing; nature trails.	41	•	•		•	•	•	•	•	•				•	
Platoro Reservoir (F-3) 22 mi. w. of Antonito on SR 17, then 23 mi. n.w. on access road. Hunting, ice fishing; horseback trails, nature trails.	42	•	•	•	•	•		•	•	•	•	•			

ALAMOSA (F-3) pop. 8,780, elev. 7,544'

When the Denver & Rio Grande Western Railroad reached the stagecoach stop on the cottonwood *(alamosa)*-blanketed bend of the Rio Grande, it brought with it the houses, stores and churches from its former terminus, Garland City. In a matter of days, Alamosa was in business. As the rails extended beyond the town, Alamosa became the transportation and trading center for the San Luis Valley.

The valley—a high, flat, semiarid plain about 50 miles wide and 125 miles long—once was the bed of an ancient lake. Irrigated by the Rio Grande and artesian wells, it is one of the most productive farming areas in the state. Red McClure potatoes, lettuce and barley are among crops shipped from Alamosa. Many wetlands and lakes make this a popular stopping place for migratory birds, including the 20,000 cranes that grace the valley each spring.

Great Sand Dunes National Park and Preserve *(see place listing p. 220)* lies 38 miles northeast of Alamosa; recreational opportunities such as camping, hiking and birding are available in the park. Fishing, boating and soaking in hot springs are available in the valley and nearby mountain ranges.

Colorado Welcome Center at Alamosa: 610 State Ave., Alamosa, CO 81101. **Phone:** (719) 589-4840 or (800) 258-7597.

ALAMOSA NATIONAL WILDLIFE REFUGE, 3 mi. e. on US 160, then 2 mi. s. on El Rancho Ln., is a 12,000-acre refuge. Ducks, geese and shorebirds nest on the marshes. Bald eagles are common November through March. A 2-mile nature trail along the Rio Grande, a 3.5-mile driving tour and the Bluff Overlook provide wildlife viewing opportunities. A visitor center offers interpretive displays. **Hours:** Refuge daily dawn-dusk. Visitor center hours vary; phone ahead. Closed major holidays. **Cost:** Free. **Phone:** (719) 589-4021.

RIO GRANDE SCENIC RAILROAD departs from the station at 601 State Ave. at jct. 6th St. The San Luis Express carries passengers through the Sangre de Cristo mountains, surrounded by dramatic 14,000-foot peaks along the edge of the San Isabel National Forest, past serene high mountain meadows and spectacular canyons to eventually arrive in the historic small town of La Veta *(see place listing p. 238)* for a 2-hour lunch and shopping stop. Travel takes place in either the 1950s passenger cars or panoramic dome cars. Steam engines run daily. Both one-way and round trips are available.

The Toltec Gorge Limited travels to Antonito daily, providing passengers a connection with the Cumbres & Toltec Scenic Railroad *(see attraction listing in Antonito)*. The Monte Vista Mixed runs daily between Alamosa and Monte Vista *(see place listing p. 258)* with a mixed passenger and freight train reminiscent of small town train travel generations ago.

Hours: San Luis Express departs daily at 9, late May through Oct. 31. The train returns to Alamosa between 6 and 6:30. **Cost:** One-way fare $48; $38 (ages 60+); $28 (ages 2-11). Round-trip fare $58; $48 (ages 60+); $38 (ages 2-11). Toltec Gorge Limited and Monte Vista fares start at $15. **Phone:** (719) 587-0520 or (877) 726-7245.

BEST WESTERN ALAMOSA INN **Phone:** (719)589-2567

Motel

$93-$140

AAA Benefit: Members save up to 20%, plus 10% bonus points with Best Western Rewards®.

Address: 2005 W Main St 81101 **Location:** On US 160, 1 mi w. **Facility:** 53 units. 2 stories (no elevator), exterior corridors. **Amenities:** *Some:* high-speed Internet. **Pool(s):** heated indoor. **Activities:** whirlpool, exercise room. **Guest Services:** coin laundry. **Free Special Amenities: local telephone calls and high-speed Internet.**

 / SOME UNITS FEE

COMFORT INN OF ALAMOSA **Phone:** (719)587-9000

Hotel

$71-$159

Address: 6301 Rd 107 S 81101 **Location:** On US 160, 2.3 mi w. **Facility:** 52 units. 2 stories, interior corridors. **Terms:** cancellation fee imposed. **Amenities:** high-speed Internet. **Pool(s):** heated indoor. **Activities:** whirlpool, exercise room. **Guest Services:** coin laundry. **Free Special Amenities: full breakfast and high-speed Internet.**

SAVE / SOME UNITS FEE

HOLIDAY INN EXPRESS **Phone:** (719)589-4026

Hotel

$139-$148 5/1-9/30
$108-$126 10/1-4/30

Address: 3418 Mariposa St 81101 **Location:** On US 160, 1.8 mi w. **Facility:** 74 units. 3 stories, interior corridors. **Terms:** 3 day cancellation notice. **Amenities:** high-speed Internet. **Pool(s):** heated indoor. **Activities:** sauna, whirlpool, exercise room. **Guest Services:** valet and coin laundry.

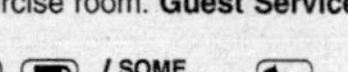

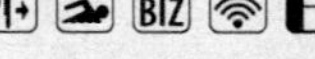 BIZ / SOME UNITS FEE

HAMPTON INN ALAMOSA **Phone:** 719/480-6023

fyi

AAA Benefit: Members save up to 10% everyday!

Not evaluated. **Address:** 710 Mariposa St 81101 **Location:** 2 mi w of center via Main St, then just n. Facilities, services, and decor characterize a mid-scale property.

WHERE TO EAT

CALVILLO'S MEXICAN RESTAURANT & BAR
Phone: 719/587-5500

Mexican

$6-$14

AAA Inspector Notes: You can explore the buffet all day long at this friendly and spacious eatery. **Bar:** full bar. **Address:** 400 Main St 81101 **Location:** 0.5 mi e on US 160.

B L D

MRS. RIVERA'S KITCHEN
Menu on AAA.com **Phone:** 719/589-0277

Mexican

$5-$11

AAA Inspector Notes: The family-owned restaurant, with an enclosed patio, features a wide variety of traditional Mexican dishes such as nachos, tamales, flautas, chalupas and combo plates. They also offer burgers, sandwiches, shrimp, steak, margaritas and Mexican beer. **Bar:** beer & wine. **Address:** 1019 6th St 81101 **Location:** Jct US 160 and 285, just s, just e. L D

ALMONT (D-2)

Originally christened Fishers after the man who first settled the area, in 1881 the town was named Almont after a famous stallion of the time. Near the headwaters of the Gunnison River, where the Taylor and East rivers meet, Almont is an outdoor playground with a plethora of activities including fishing, hiking, white-water rafting, kayaking, horseback riding, mountain biking and cross-country skiing.

RECREATIONAL ACTIVITIES

Fishing

- **Almont Anglers Fly Shop and Guide Service** departs from jct. SR 135 and CR 742 at the Almont Resort. **Hours:** Daily dawn-dusk, Mar.-Nov. **Phone:** (970) 641-7404.
- **Willowfly Anglers** is n. on SR 135, then .25 mi. e. on CR 742 to Three Rivers Resort. **Hours:** Daily dawn-dusk, Mar.-Nov. **Phone:** (970) 641-1303 or (888) 761-3474.

White-water Rafting

- **Three Rivers Outfitting** is n. on SR 135, then .25 mi. e. on CR 742 to Three Rivers Resort. **Hours:** Daily dawn-dusk, May-Oct. **Phone:** (970) 641-1303 or (888) 761-3474.

ANTONITO (F-3) pop. 781, elev. 7,882'

Originating with the arrival of the railroads, as did many Colorado settlements, Antonito is still a shipping point for perlite and lava rock of the southern San Luis Valley. It also is the Colorado terminal for the Cumbres & Toltec Scenic Railroad and offers many opportunities for recreation including mountain biking, wildlife viewing, sightseeing, hunting and fishing.

Conejos County Tourism: P.O. Box 829, Antonito, CO 81120. **Phone:** (719) 376-2049 or (800) 835-1098.

CUMBRES & TOLTEC SCENIC RAILROAD (GEM) trips depart from the depot at jct. US 285 and SR 17. Built in the 1880s, the line connected commercial outposts and mining camps in the Rocky Mountain region and was part of the original Denver & Rio Grande railway system. The 64-mile line, jointly owned by the states of Colorado and New Mexico, has departures from both Antonito and Chama, N.M.

All-day trips on vintage, narrow-gauge, coal-burning steam trains afford spectacular views of the scenic San Juan and Sangre de Cristo mountain ranges. Passengers may choose from three types of class: coach, tourist or parlor. The parlor car offers refreshments and the services of an attendant.

Osier, an old stagecoach stop, is the transfer and lunch point. From there, guests can choose to continue on by train to Chama or return to Antonito. Various combinations of train and motorcoach transportation are offered; all trips include lunch. One-way trips also are available.

AAA offices in Colorado and New Mexico can make reservations. **Hours:** Round-trip train excursions depart from Antonito and Chama daily at 10, Memorial Day weekend to mid-Oct. Train/bus combination trip schedules vary; phone ahead. **Cost:** Round-trip coach fare $74; $37 (ages 2-11). Round-trip parlor car fare $139. Through coach fare with bus return $88 (coach class); $120 (tourist class); $153 (parlor car). All fares include lunch. Children are permitted in coach and tourist class only. Reservations are recommended. **Phone:** (719) 376-5483 in Colo., (505) 756-2151 in N.M. or (888) 286-2737. ***(See ad this page.)***

▼ *See AAA listing this page* ▼

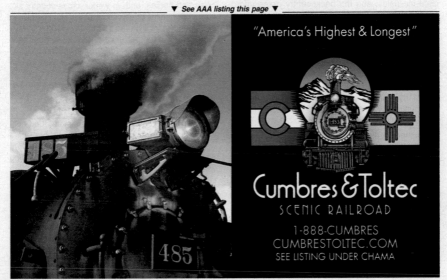

ARAPAHO AND ROOSEVELT NATIONAL FORESTS AND PAWNEE NATIONAL GRASSLAND (A-3, A-4, B-4)

Elevations in the forests range from 4,300 ft. at Pawnee National Grassland to 14,270 ft. at Grays Peak in Arapaho National Forest. Refer to AAA maps for additional elevation information.

In north-central Colorado past and present co-exist within the 1,280,000 mountainous acres of the Arapaho and Roosevelt National Forests, which embrace some of the higher and more visited areas of the region. Creaking ghost towns in the Arapaho region set off lively ski resorts, and the rotted roadbeds of abandoned narrow-gauge railways contrast with the well-maintained highways that provide access to this rooftop of the continent.

One of these modern routes, the road to the 14,260-foot summit of Mount Evans, is part of a popular day trip from Denver. The highway, SR 5, is commonly known as Mount Evans Highway or Mount Evans Road. **Note:** There is a fee of $10 per private vehicle to drive to the top of Mount Evans. The Indian Peaks and Mount Evans wilderness areas can be explored on foot or horseback; camping permits are required at Indian Peaks. Trout fishing is available in the many lakes and streams as well as in Granby and Green Mountain reservoirs. Hunting is available in season with a valid license.

Major winter sports developments within the forests are Eldora, Loveland Basin and Winter Park. Scenic gondola rides, an alpine slide and chairlift rides also are available.

In a region dotted with alpine lakes and divided by high mountains and deep canyons, Roosevelt National Forest sits along the eastern slope of the Rockies. Numerous small glaciers, remnants of ancient ice fields, and the backcountry areas afford magnificent scenery and varied recreational facilities.

Scenic SR 14, the mountainous route over Cameron Pass and along the Cache La Poudre River, provides access to the adjoining Routt National Forest *(see place listing p. 279)*. A second scenic route, the Peak to Peak National Scenic Byway (SR 7/72/119), connects Estes Park with the mining communities of Black Hawk *(see place listing p. 56)* and Central City *(see place listing p. 81)*.

Another scenic route, the Colorado River Headwaters, follows the Colorado River 75 miles westward from SR 34 in Grand Lake, SR 40 in Kremmling and along CR 1 in State Bridge.

The fragile uplands of the Rawah Wilderness are accessible only by foot or horseback. Permits are required for camping in the Indian Peaks Wilderness. Hunting for deer, elk, mountain sheep and bears is permitted. Other wilderness areas include Byers Peak, Cache La Poudre, Comanche Peak, James Peak, Neota, Never Summer, Ptarmigan Peak and Vasquez Peak. Motorized vehicles are not permitted in wilderness areas.

The almost 200,000 acres of the Pawnee National Grassland are widely scattered in two units east of Fort Collins. Restored from the devastation of the 1930s dust bowl, the short-grass prairie is inhabited by more than 200 species of wildlife, including falcons, hawks, badgers, prairie dogs and coyotes. Hiking, camping, horseback riding and bird-watching are popular activities.

The Pawnee Pioneer Trails is a scenic route that winds 125 miles east from Ault, Colo., along SR 14 and various county roads. Contact Pawnee National Grassland, 660 O St., Greeley, CO 80631-3033, for additional information, or phone (970) 346-5000.

The U.S. Forest Service has a visitor information office at 2150 Centre Ave., Building E, Fort Collins, CO 80526. Phone (970) 295-6600 for information or (877) 444-6777 for campground reservations. *See Recreation Chart.*

ARAPAHO NATIONAL RECREATION AREA (A-3)

In north-central Colorado, next to Rocky Mountain National Park *(see place listing p. 276)*, Arapaho National Recreation Area comprises more than 36,000 acres. Willow Creek Reservoir, Monarch Lake, Lake Granby, Shadow Mountain Lake and Meadow Creek Reservoir are open for fishing year-round; ice fishing is available December through April. Fishing licenses are required. Boat ramps are located at Arapaho Bay, Green Ridge, Hilltop, Stillwater, Sunset Point and Willow Reservoir locations. (Note: These lakes have tested positive for zebra/quagga mussel larvae. To slow the spread of the mussels to other state lakes and reservoirs, the Colorado Division of Wildlife is conducting boat inspections in the area. Some waters may be closed to trailered and motorized boats.)

Other recreational activities include camping, hiking and picnicking. Visitors may ride mountain bikes and horses, and, in winter, cross-country ski, ride snowmobiles or use snowshoes. Hunting also is permitted. Recreation fee $5 per day, $10 for 3 days or $15 for 7 days per private vehicle. Annual pass $30. Phone (970) 887-4100 for information or (877) 444-6777 for campground reservations. *See Recreation Chart.*

ARVADA (B-4) pop. 106,433, elev. 5,340'

• Part of Denver area — see map p. 123

It was June 1850 when Lewis Ralston found gold in what is now known as Ralston Creek. His strike was just the beginning, however, as other miners would soon come to Colorado with hopes of finding wealth and fortune. Founded in 1870, 6 years before Colorado achieved statehood, Arvada was initially a trading hub for the surrounding agricultural region.

The town recalls its early days in its Historic Olde Town section, where some of the commercial and residential buildings date to the 19th century, and at Gold Strike Park, the site of the 1850 gold discovery, at the confluence of Ralston and Clear creeks.

Arvada Chamber of Commerce: 7305 Grandview Ave., Arvada, CO 80002. **Phone:** (303) 424-0313.

Self-guiding tours: Brochures describing buildings in Historic Olde Town Arvada are available from many local merchants.

ARVADA CENTER FOR THE ARTS AND HUMANITIES, 6901 Wadsworth Blvd., is the cultural center of the community. Summer concerts are presented under the stars at the 1,500-seat outdoor amphitheater. Two indoor theater hosts professional theater productions, concerts and dance events throughout the year. Three galleries feature rotating exhibits of contemporary art by regional, national and international artists. A museum devoted to local history is part of the center.

Time: Allow 1 hour minimum. **Hours:** Tues.-Sat. 9-9, Sun. 1-5, Mon. 9-6. Closed major holidays. **Cost:** Galleries and museum free. Performances $8-$57. **Phone:** (720) 898-7200.

CUSSLER MUSEUM is at 14959 W. 69th Ave. The museum is owned by Clive Cussler, a best-selling novelist who also is a collector of classic automobiles. Among the more than 75 restored cars on display are a 1913 Marmon, a 1929 Model J Duesenberg, a 1932 Stutz Town Car, a 1952 Allard J2X roadster and a 1932 Auburn Speedster. **Time:** Allow 30 minutes minimum. **Hours:** Mon.-Tues. 10-7, May-Sept. **Cost:** $7; $5 (ages 65+); $3 (ages 0-11). **Phone:** (303) 420-2795.

ASPEN (D-2) pop. 6,658, elev. 7,907'

• **Hotels p. 45** • **Restaurants p. 46**
• **Hotels & Restaurants map & index p. 43**

Mines and mills have given way to beautiful homes on the hillsides above Aspen, a town whose transformation from riches to rags to riches is part of the fabric of Colorado. A 2,350-pound, 93-percent-pure silver nugget taken in three pieces from Aspen's Smuggler Mine was to be displayed at the Chicago Columbian Exposition in 1893 along with the Silver Queen, a sculpture made of silver, gold and minerals from the Aspen area. Yet the nugget never made it, symbolizing both the apex and the beginning of the end of the silver era.

With the repeal of the Sherman Silver Act in 1893, supply exceeded demand and prices fell. As the nation succumbed to the Panic of 1893, Colorado's economy collapsed. Aspen's revival was due to another natural resource, this time a recurrent one—snow. In the late 1930s a simple ski area was built and in 1946 Aspen Ski Corporation launched the ski runs on Aspen Mountain. Seeing the potential, private enterprises quickly turned the little city in the Roaring Fork Valley into a year-round resort and cultural center.

The Ute Indians called the area Shining Mountains, and early pioneers referred to the settlement as Ute City. It wasn't until 1880 that the city officially became known as Aspen, chosen because of the bountiful number of trees of the same name. The city's historic Victorian buildings, its eclectic personality, cultural amenities, nightlife and, of course, the blessing of its natural surroundings have made it an increasingly popular choice for vacationers.

Local events include Winterskól, Aspen's toast to winter, held in mid-January. In June the Food and Wine Magazine Classic in Aspen is offered. Mid-June through August the Aspen Music Festival and School presents classical music concerts and recitals by guest artists. Seminars, lectures and classes also are part of a summer-long festival of the mind at the Aspen Institute. The restored 1889 Wheeler Opera House presents operas, dramas, concerts, films and dances throughout the year.

Concessionaires in Aspen offer hiking, paragliding, bicycle tours, white-water rafting, horseback riding, river expeditions, back-country jeep excursions, balloon rides, guided rock and mountain climbing, trail rides and overnight pack trips, not to mention the wintry offerings of cross-country and downhill skiing, snowmobiling, sleigh rides and ice-skating.

Guided tours of Victorian buildings in the West End are offered by the Aspen Historical Society. The tours are available June through August and depart from the Wheeler-Stallard Museum *(see attraction listing)*. For additional information, phone (970) 925-3721.

Aspen Chamber Resort Association: 425 Rio Grande Pl., Aspen, CO 81611. **Phone:** (970) 925-1940 or (800) 670-0792.

Self-guiding tours: Self-guiding walking tours of the downtown area are available. Maps may be purchased for $2 at the Aspen Historical Society, 620 W. Bleeker St., and at the Wheeler Opera House Visitor's Center, 320 E. Hyman St.

ASPEN ART MUSEUM is at 590 N. Mill St. The focus at this museum is on contemporary art; all exhibitions are temporary. Art workshops and lectures are available. **Time:** Allow 30 minutes minimum. **Hours:** Tues.-Sat. 10-6, Sun. noon-6. Closed major holidays. **Cost:** Free. **Phone:** (970) 925-8050.

GHOST TOWN OF ASHCROFT, 11 mi. s. on Castle Creek Rd., is a weather-beaten vestige of its mining camp heyday. Lack of rail service to the mines caused the town's demise by 1890, although residents had hoped their town would someday rival Aspen in importance. The Aspen Historical Society in partnership with the Aspen Center for Environmental Studies conducts 30-minute tours of the town; self-guiding tours also are available. Interpretive signage and brochures are available on site.

Note: Do not enter obviously sagging structures that could collapse. **Hours:** Tours are offered daily at 11, 1 and 3, Memorial Day-Labor Day. **Cost:** $3; free (ages 0-10). **Phone:** (970) 925-3721.

GHOST TOWN OF INDEPENDENCE, 16 mi. e. on SR 82, is the faded relic of the Roaring Fork Valley's original gold mining community. After the first gold strike in 1879 the town boomed; decline set in by the end of the 1880s when the nearby mines stopped

(See map & index p. 43.)

producing. The Aspen Historical Society in the Wheeler-Stallard Museum *(see attraction listing)* offers information about self-guiding tours. Interpretive signage and brochures are available at the site.

Note: Do not enter obviously sagging structures that could collapse. **Hours:** Self-guiding tours are available Memorial Day-Oct. 31 (weather permitting; Independence Pass is closed in winter). **Cost:** $3. **Phone:** (970) 925-3721.

HOLDEN/MAROLT MINING AND RANCHING MUSEUM is at 40180 SR 82. Located in an 1890s barn, this living-history museum tells the story of the silver mining boom in Aspen 1879-93. It also depicts the "quiet years" of ranching between the silver bust and the skiing/cultural boom that began in the 1940s. **Time:** Allow 1 hour minimum. **Hours:** Tues.-Sat. 1-5. **Cost:** (includes Wheeler-Stallard Museum) $6; $5 (ages 65+); free (ages 0-11). **Phone:** (970) 925-3721.

MAROON BELLS is 9 mi. s.w. off SR 82. The jagged peaks of the Maroon Bells are some of the country's most photographed mountains. Many souvenir snapshots feature their reflection in the waters of Maroon Lake. The loftiest of the peaks towers at 14,156 feet. Hiking trails, picnicking and fishing are available in front of the mountain at the lake. Aspen Center for Environmental Studies offers free naturalist-led 45-minute guided walks along the lake from early June through Labor Day.

Note: From mid-June through Labor Day access to the road to the base of the mountain is open daily 9-5 only to private vehicles carrying those staying at the campgrounds, those with children in car seats or physically impaired passengers. Round-trip bus service is provided from the Aspen Highlands ski area. The road reopens to all traffic 5 p.m.-8:30 a.m. **Hours:** Buses depart daily every 20 minutes 9:05-2:05 and every 30 minutes 2:05-4:30, early June-early Sept.; Sat.-Sun. every 20 minutes 9-1 and every 30 minutes 1-4:30, early Sept.-late Sept. **Cost:** Fare $6; $4 (ages 6-16 and 65+); $3 (Wed. for all passengers). **Phone:** (970) 925-8484, or (800) 854-5588 for bus information.

WHEELER-STALLARD MUSEUM, 620 W. Bleeker St., in an 1888 Queen Anne Revival style house, is dedicated to preserving Aspen Valley history. As home to the Aspen Historical Society, it features rotating exhibits, weekly summer and winter events on Tuesday evenings, and a variety of historic tours, such as walking tours of the historic West End. Activities for all ages are presented June through August. **Hours:** Tues.-Sat. 1-5. Phone for tour and event schedules. **Cost:** (includes Holden/Marolt Mining and Ranching Museum) $6; $5 (ages 65+); free (ages 0-11). Walking tour $12; $10 (ages 65+); phone for admission costs of other tours. **Phone:** (970) 925-3721.

RECREATIONAL ACTIVITIES

Skiing

- **Aspen Highlands** is 2 mi. w. on SR 82. **Hours:** Daily 9-3:30, late Nov.-late Apr. (weather permitting). **Phone:** (970) 925-1220 or (800) 525-6200.
- **Aspen Mountain** is at 601 Dean St. **Hours:** Daily 9-3:30, late Nov. to mid-Apr. (weather permitting). **Phone:** (970) 925-1220 or (800) 525-6200.
- **Buttermilk** is 3 mi. w. on SR 82. **Hours:** Daily 9-3:30, mid-Dec. to early Apr. (weather permitting). **Phone:** (970) 925-1220 or (800) 525-6200.

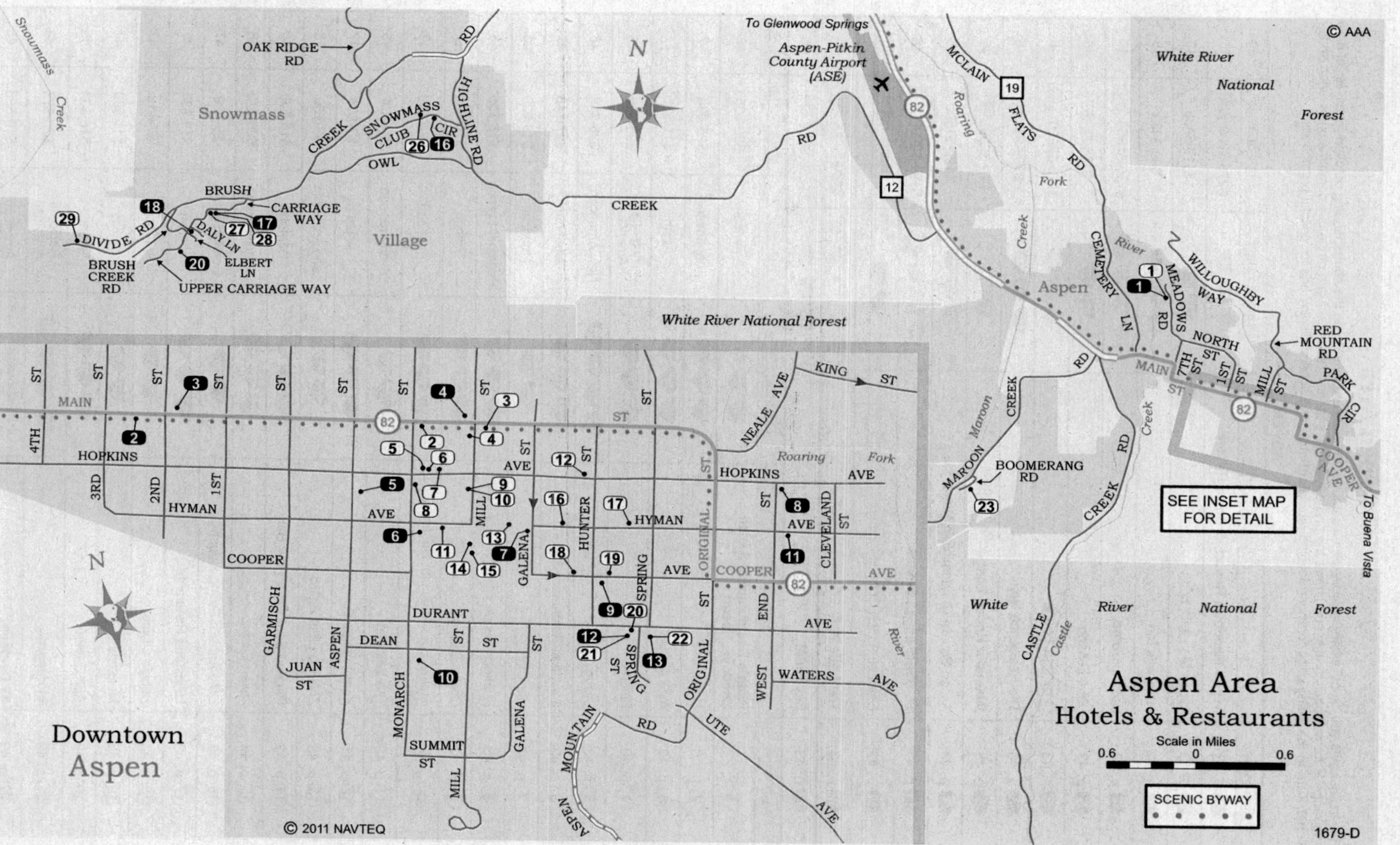
Aspen Area
Hotels & Restaurants
Scale in Miles
0.6
0
0.6
SCENIC BYWAY
1679-D
© AAA
SEE INSET MAP FOR DETAIL
To Buena Vista
To Glenwood Springs
Aspen-Pitkin County Airport (ASE)
White River National Forest
White River National Forest
Snowmass Village
Aspen
Roaring Fork River
Maroon Creek
Castle Creek
Snowmass Creek
MCLAIN FLATS RD
CEMETERY LN
MEADOWS RD
WILLOUGHBY WAY
RED MOUNTAIN RD
PARK CIR
COOPER AVE
MILL ST
NORTH ST
1ST ST
7TH ST
MAIN ST
MAROON CREEK RD
BOOMERANG RD
CASTLE CREEK RD
OWL CREEK RD
HIGHLINE RD
SNOWMASS CLUB CIR
BRUSH CREEK RD
CARRIAGE WAY
UPPER CARRIAGE WAY
DALY LN
ELBERT LN
DIVIDE RD
OAK RIDGE RD
82
19
12
Downtown Aspen
© 2011 NAVTEQ
KING ST
NEALE AVE
HOPKINS AVE
CLEVELAND ST
WEST END ST
ORIGINAL ST
HYMAN AVE
SPRING ST
HUNTER ST
GALENA ST
MILL ST
DURANT AVE
MONARCH ST
DEAN ST
ASPEN ST
JUAN ST
GARMISCH ST
SUMMIT ST
UTE AVE
WATERS AVE
ASPEN MOUNTAIN RD
COOPER AVE
1ST ST
2ND ST
3RD ST
4TH ST
N

Aspen Area

This index helps you "spot" where approved hotels and restaurants are located on the corresponding detailed maps. Hotel daily rate range is for comparison only and shows the property's high season. Restaurant rate range is a combination of lunch and/or dinner. Turn to the listing page for more detailed rate information and consult display ads for special promotions.

ASPEN

Map Page	Hotels	Diamond Rated	High Season	Page
1 p. 43	**Aspen Meadows Resort, A Dolce Resort**	◆◆◆	$275-$800 SAVE	45
2 p. 43	Aspen Mountain Lodge	◆◆	$119-$435	45
3 p. 43	Annabelle Inn	◆◆◆	$89-$489	45
4 p. 43	**Hotel Jerome**	◆◆◆◆	$180-$1850 SAVE	45
5 p. 43	Hotel Lenado	◆◆	$175-$645	46
6 p. 43	**Limelight Lodge**	◆◆◆	$115-$2520 SAVE	46
7 p. 43	The Residence Hotel	◆◆◆	$199-$1195	46
8 p. 43	**Mountain House Lodge**	◆◆	$79-$299 SAVE	46
9 p. 43	Aspen Square Condominium Hotel	◆◆◆	$129-$1500	45
10 p. 43	**St. Regis Aspen Resort**	◆◆◆◆	$199-$2099 SAVE	46
11 p. 43	Chateau Aspen Condominiums	◆◆	Rates not provided	45
12 p. 43	**The Little Nell**	◆◆◆◆◆	$420-$3300 SAVE	46
13 p. 43	**Sky Hotel**	◆◆◆	$259-$869 SAVE	46

Map Page	Restaurants	Diamond Rated	Cuisine	Meal Range	Page
1 p. 43	**Plato's Restaurant at Aspen Meadows Resort**	◆◆◆	American	$20-$35	48
2 p. 43	Matsuhisa	◆◆◆	Japanese	$25-$38	47
3 p. 43	Asie	◆◆◆	Asian	$11-$35	47
4 p. 43	Pinons	◆◆◆	Regional American	$25-$50	48
5 p. 43	Syzygy	◆◆◆◆	New American	$25-$49	48
6 p. 43	Elevation Restaurant & Bar	◆◆◆	American	$27-$48	47
7 p. 43	Ute City	◆◆	American	$18-$29	48
8 p. 43	Rustique Bistro	◆◆◆	Regional French	$18-$35	48
9 p. 43	Cache Cache	◆◆◆	French	$16-$62	47
10 p. 43	Jimmy's, An American Restaurant & Bar	◆◆◆	American	$24-$48	47
11 p. 43	The Wild Fig	◆◆	Mediterranean	$9-$34	48
12 p. 43	Kenichi Aspen	◆◆◆	Asian	$7-$38	47
13 p. 43	Zocalito Latin Bistro	◆◆	Latin American	$8-$30	48
14 p. 43	Pacifica Seafood & Raw Bar	◆◆◆	Seafood	$15-$39	48
15 p. 43	Takah Sushi	◆◆◆	Pacific Rim	$26-$70	48
16 p. 43	Little Annie's Eating House	◆◆	Comfort Food	$9-$29	47
17 p. 43	L'Hostaria Ristorante	◆◆◆	Italian	$18-$34	47
18 p. 43	Boogie's Diner	◆◆	American	$7-$16	47
19 p. 43	Mezzaluna	◆◆	Italian	$11-$30	47
20 p. 43	Ajax Tavern	◆◆◆	American	$16-$34	46
21 p. 43	**Montagna**	◆◆◆◆	Regional American	$20-$75	47
22 p. 43	**39 Degrees**	◆◆	American	$10-$28	46

Map Page	Restaurants (cont'd)	Diamond Rated	Cuisine	Meal Range	Page
23 p. 43	Willow Creek Bistro	♦♦♦	American	$6-$19	48

SNOWMASS VILLAGE

Map Page	Hotels	Diamond Rated	High Season	Page
16 p. 43	Villas at Snowmass Club	♦♦♦	$200-$1100	286
17 p. 43	Stonebridge Inn	♦♦♦	Rates not provided	285
18 p. 43	Snowmass Mountain Chalet	♦♦	$150-$364	285
20 p. 43	Timberline Condominiums	♦♦♦	$150-$1220	285

Map Page	Restaurants	Diamond Rated	Cuisine	Meal Range	Page
26 p. 43	Sage Restaurant & Patio	♦♦♦	American	$10-$36	286
27 p. 43	Garnish Cafe	♦♦♦	American	$19-$32	286
28 p. 43	Artisan Restaurant & Bar	♦♦♦	American	$12-$29	286
29 p. 43	Krabloonik Restaurant	♦♦♦	Regional American	$8-$62	286

ANNABELLE INN

Phone: (970)925-3822 3

♦♦♦ Hotel

$89-$489

Address: 232 W Main St 81611 **Location:** 0.4 mi w on SR 82; jct Main and 2nd sts. **Facility:** 35 units. 3 stories, exterior corridors. **Terms:** office hours 7:30 am-8 pm, check-in 4 pm, 2-7 night minimum stay - seasonal, 14 day cancellation notice-fee imposed. **Amenities:** high-speed Internet. **Activities:** whirlpools. *Fee:* massage. **Guest Services:** coin laundry.

ASPEN MEADOWS RESORT, A DOLCE RESORT

Phone: (970)925-4240 1

♦♦♦ Classic Hotel

$275-$800 12/16-4/30
$125-$800 5/1-12/15

Address: 845 Meadows Rd 81611 **Location:** 0.3 mi n of SR 82 via 7th Ave, just w. Located in a quiet area. **Facility:** Designed by Bauhaus architect Hebert Bayer, the buildings for this resort and the incorporated Aspen Institute reflect the era's best design elements. 98 units, some two bedrooms. 2 stories (no elevator), interior/exterior corridors. **Terms:** check-in 4 pm, 30 day cancellation notice-fee imposed. **Amenities:** high-speed Internet, safes. **Dining:** 2 restaurants, also, Plato's Restaurant at Aspen Meadows Resort, see separate listing. **Pool(s):** heated outdoor. **Activities:** whirlpool, steamrooms, 6 tennis courts, rental bicycles, hiking trails, jogging, basketball. *Fee:* massage. **Guest Services:** valet and coin laundry, area transportation-ski areas & town. **Free Special Amenities: local transportation and airport transportation.**

/ SOME UNITS FEE

ASPEN MOUNTAIN LODGE

Phone: (970)925-7650 2

♦♦ Hotel

$119-$435 11/22-4/24
$116-$274 5/22-10/21

Address: 311 W Main St 81611 **Location:** 0.3 mi w on SR 82; between 2nd and 3rd sts. **Facility:** 38 units. 3 stories (no elevator), interior corridors. **Terms:** open 5/22-10/21 & 11/22-4/24, office hours 7:30 am-10 pm, check-in 4 pm, 7 day cancellation notice, 14 day in winter-fee imposed. **Amenities:** safes, honor bars. **Pool(s):** heated outdoor. **Activities:** whirlpool, hiking trails, jogging.

/ SOME UNITS FEE

ASPEN SQUARE CONDOMINIUM HOTEL

Phone: (970)925-1000 9

♦♦♦ Condominium

$129-$1500 11/21-4/30
$129-$850 5/1-11/20

Address: 617 E Cooper Ave 81611 **Location:** Between Cooper and Durant aves. **Facility:** Just steps from the gondola, these well-appointed condominium units have fans, a humidifier, a wood-burning fireplace and a lovely patio. 101 condominiums. 3-4 stories, interior/exterior corridors. **Terms:** office hours 7 am-midnight, check-in 4 pm, 1-5 night minimum stay - seasonal, 14 day cancellation notice, 30 day in winter-fee imposed. **Amenities:** high-speed Internet, safes. **Pool(s):** heated outdoor. **Activities:** whirlpools, hiking trails, exercise room. *Fee:* massage. **Guest Services:** valet and coin laundry.

CHATEAU ASPEN CONDOMINIUMS

Phone: 970/925-8717 11

♦♦ Condominium

Rates not provided

Address: 630 E Cooper Ave 81611 **Location:** Jct E Cooper Ave and S Hunter St; downtown. **Facility:** 10 condominiums. 3 stories (no elevator), exterior corridors. **Terms:** office hours 9 am-5 pm, off-site registration, check-in 4 pm. **Activities:** bicycle trails, hiking trails, jogging. **Guest Services:** complimentary laundry.

FEE

HOTEL JEROME

Phone: (970)920-1000 4

♦♦♦♦ Classic Boutique Hotel

$180-$1850

Address: 330 E Main St 81611 **Location:** Jct Main and Mill sts. **Facility:** The restored 1889 hotel has elegant public areas and guest rooms furnished with Victorian antiques and reproductions. 94 units. 3-4 stories, interior corridors. **Parking:** valet only. **Terms:** check-in 4 pm, 30 day cancellation notice, 10 day in summer-fee imposed. **Amenities:** high-speed Internet, safes, honor bars. **Dining:** 2 restaurants. **Pool(s):** heated outdoor. **Activities:** whirlpool, rental bicycles, hiking trails, jogging, exercise room. *Fee:* massage. **Guest Services:** valet laundry, area transportation (fee)-Aspen ski areas.

/ SOME UNITS FEE

(See map & index p. 43.)

HOTEL LENADO **Phone:** (970)925-6246 5

Hotel

$175-$645 11/28-4/16
$145-$425 5/30-10/31

Address: 200 S Aspen St 81611 **Location:** 0.3 mi w on SR 82, just s via Aspen St to Hopkins St. Located in a residential area. **Facility:** 19 units. 2 stories (no elevator), interior/exterior corridors. **Terms:** open 5/30-10/31 & 11/28-4/16, office hours 7 am-10 pm, check-in 4 pm, 1-4 night minimum stay - seasonal and/or weekends, 30 day cancellation notice-fee imposed. **Activities:** whirlpool. *Fee:* massage. **Guest Services:** valet laundry.

BIZ / SOME UNITS

LIMELIGHT LODGE **Phone:** (970)925-3025 6

Hotel

$115-$2520

Address: 355 S Monarch St 81611 **Location:** Just s of SR 82; at Monarch and Cooper sts. Opposite Wagner Park. **Facility:** 126 units, some two bedrooms and kitchens. 4 stories, interior corridors. **Parking:** on-site (fee). **Terms:** check-in 4 pm, 14 day cancellation notice-fee imposed. **Amenities:** safes. **Pool(s):** heated outdoor. **Activities:** whirlpools, exercise room. **Guest Services:** valet and coin laundry, area transportation-within 3 mi. **Free Special Amenities: continental breakfast and airport transportation.**

SAVE BIZ / SOME UNITS FEE

THE LITTLE NELL **Phone:** (970)920-4600 12

Contemporary Hotel

$420-$3300 11/24-4/12
$255-$2190 5/18-11/23

Address: 675 E Durant Ave 81611 **Location:** 0.3 mi e on SR 82, 0.3 mi s on Spring St; jct Durant Ave and Spring St; beside gondola at base of Aspen Mountain. **Facility:** Centered in town at the base of the mountain, the ski-in/ski-out hotel has fireplaces and humidifiers in all of its newly renovated rooms. 92 units, some two bedrooms. 4 stories, interior corridors. **Parking:** valet only. **Terms:** open 5/18-4/12, check-in 4 pm, 3-4 night minimum stay - seasonal and/or weekends, 30 day cancellation notice-fee imposed. **Amenities:** high-speed Internet, safes, honor bars. **Dining:** Ajax Tavern, Montagna, see separate listings. **Pool(s):** heated outdoor. **Activities:** whirlpool, steamroom, bicycles, hiking trails, jogging, exercise room. *Fee:* downhill & cross country skiing, massage. **Guest Services:** valet laundry, area transportation-within 5 mi. **Free Special Amenities: high-speed Internet and airport transportation.**

SAVE BIZ / SOME UNITS FEE

MOUNTAIN HOUSE LODGE **Phone:** (970)920-2550 8

Motel

$79-$299 9/17-4/30
$79-$209 5/1-9/16

Address: 905 E Hopkins St 81611 **Location:** 0.3 mi e on SR 82, just e. Located in a quiet residential area. **Facility:** 26 units, some two bedrooms and kitchens. 2 stories (no elevator), interior corridors. **Terms:** office hours 7:30 am-8:30 pm, 30 day cancellation notice-fee imposed. **Activities:** whirlpool, hiking trails, jogging. **Guest Services:** coin laundry. **Free Special Amenities: expanded continental breakfast and high-speed Internet.**

SAVE BIZ / SOME UNITS FEE

THE RESIDENCE HOTEL **Phone:** (970)920-6532 7

Boutique Contemporary Hotel

$199-$1195

Address: 305 S Galena St 81611 **Location:** Jct S Galena St and E Hyman Ave; downtown. **Facility:** This wonderful boutique hotel offers guests a perfect location and large, well-appointed rooms that are comfortable for any length of stay. 7 units, some two bedrooms and kitchens. 1 story, interior corridors. **Parking:** street only. **Terms:** office hours 8:30 am-9 pm, 2 night minimum stay - seasonal and/or weekends, cancellation fee imposed. **Amenities:** safes. **Guest Services:** coin laundry.

FEE BIZ / SOME UNITS

ST. REGIS ASPEN RESORT

Phone: (970)920-3300 10

Hotel

$199-$2099

AAA Benefit: Legendary stays at a preferred rate.

Address: 315 E Dean St 81611 **Location:** Just w on SR 82; jct Monarch and Dean sts. **Facility:** At the foot of the mountain, the elegant resort allows easy access to skiing and shopping. Many rooms have views and fireplaces; all have humidifiers. 179 units. 3-5 stories, interior corridors. **Parking:** valet only. **Terms:** check-in 4 pm, 60 day cancellation notice-fee imposed. **Amenities:** high-speed Internet, safes, honor bars. **Pool(s):** heated outdoor. **Activities:** whirlpools, rental bicycles, hiking trails, jogging, spa. *Fee:* downhill & cross country skiing, ice skating. **Guest Services:** valet and coin laundry, area transportation-within city limits.

SAVE BIZ / SOME UNITS FEE

SKY HOTEL **Phone:** (970)925-6760 13

Boutique Contemporary Hotel

$259-$869 11/24-4/30
$200-$665 5/1-11/23

Address: 709 E Durant Ave 81611 **Location:** At base of Aspen Mountain. **Facility:** This trendy boutique hotel has custom furniture, bold design features and one of the area's most popular outdoor pool lounges. 90 units. 2-3 stories, interior/exterior corridors. **Parking:** valet and street only. **Terms:** check-in 4 pm, 2-4 night minimum stay - seasonal and/or weekends, 30 day cancellation notice-fee imposed. **Amenities:** safes, honor bars. **Dining:** 39 Degrees, see separate listing. **Pool(s):** heated outdoor. **Activities:** whirlpool, bicycles, hiking trails, jogging, exercise room. *Fee:* downhill skiing, massage. **Guest Services:** valet laundry, area transportation-within town. **Free Special Amenities: high-speed Internet and manager's reception.**

SAVE ECO BIZ / SOME UNITS

THE GANT ASPEN **Phone:** 970/925-5000

fyi Not evaluated. **Address:** 610 S West End St 81611 **Location:** Through town to 4-way stop (Cooper St), 1 blk e, then n. Facilities, services, and decor characterize a mid-scale property.

MOLLY GIBSON LODGE **Phone:** 970/925-3434

fyi Not evaluated. **Address:** 101 W Main St 81611 **Location:** 0.3 mi w of jct Main and Garmisch sts. Facilities, services, and decor characterize an economy property.

WHERE TO EAT

39 DEGREES **Phone:** 970/925-6760 22

American

$10-$28

AAA Inspector Notes: The stylish lounge and restaurant offers an eclectic selection of appetizers and light fare with an Asian accent, as well as a great selection of wines and spirits. **Bar:** full bar. **Address:** 709 E Durant Ave 81611 **Location:** Corner of Spring St and Durant Ave; at the base of Aspen Mountain; in Sky Hotel. **Parking:** on-site (fee) and valet. L D LATE

AJAX TAVERN **Phone:** 970/920-6334 20

American

$16-$34

AAA Inspector Notes: The French-American bistro offers innovative dishes prepared with sustainably raised meats and locally grown, seasonal produce. The Raw Bar features littleneck clams, crab, oysters and shrimp. Skiers can come down the run and stop off for lunch on a gorgeous slopeside outdoor patio. It's also a great option for apres-ski or apres-bike relaxation. **Bar:** full bar. **Address:** 685 E Durant Ave 81611 **Location:** 0.3 mi e on SR 82, 0.3 mi s on Spring St; corner of Durant Ave and Spring St, beside gondola at base of Aspen Mountain; in The Little Nell. **Parking:** valet and street only. L D

(See map & index p. 43.)

ASIE Phone: 970/920-9988 (3)

Asian
$11-$35

AAA Inspector Notes: This popular spot offers artfully presented, varied Asian cuisine. Sushi and tempura dishes sit comfortably next to chicken satay, Thai curry and roasted Peking duck. Friendly, attentive servers and modern décor enhance the dining experience. **Bar:** full bar. **Address:** 413 E Main St 81611 **Location:** Just e of Main and Mill sts. **Parking:** street only. L D AC

BOOGIE'S DINER Phone: 970/925-6610 (18)

American
$7-$16

AAA Inspector Notes: This 1950s diner offers a wide variety of hearty fare, including blue-plate specials, meatloaf, mashed potatoes, burgers, soda-fountain delights and homemade desserts, all of which is served by a friendly staff. **Bar:** full bar. **Address:** 534 E Cooper Ave 81611 **Location:** Corner of Cooper Ave and Hunter St. **Parking:** on-site (fee). B L D

CACHE CACHE Phone: 970/925-3835 (9)

French
$16-$62

AAA Inspector Notes: Signature dishes include seared lemon sole, Colorado rack of lamb, osso buco and rotisserie game fowl. The ambience is intimate, with attractive drop-lamp lighting and a feel of Provence. **Bar:** full bar. **Reservations:** suggested. **Address:** 205 S Mill St 81611 **Location:** At Hyman and Mill sts; downtown; in square. **Parking:** on-site (fee). D

ELEVATION RESTAURANT & BAR
Phone: 970/544-5166 (6)

American
$27-$48

AAA Inspector Notes: Flavorful, distinctive preparations such as wasabi Caesar salad, Thai green curry bowl, caramelized black cod and grilled pesto-rubbed Colorado lamb are fitting lead-ins to the restaurant's decadent desserts. The menu lists a good choice of seafood, beef, pork and lamb dishes. Diners can relax amid the warm, intimate décor inside or watch Aspen life from a seat on the patio. **Bar:** full bar. **Reservations:** suggested. **Address:** 304 E Hopkins Ave 81611 **Location:** Corner of Hopkins Ave and Monarch St. **Parking:** street only. D

JIMMY'S, AN AMERICAN RESTAURANT & BAR
Phone: 970/925-6020 (10)

American
$24-$48

AAA Inspector Notes: This restaurant and bar offers a great dining room and a large outdoor patio where patrons can feast on tender steaks, wild-caught seafood, Alaskan king crab legs, Chesapeake Bay jumbo lump blue crab and classic comfort dishes such as the popular barbecue meatloaf. Delicious and attractively presented desserts are paired with wines and spirits. **Bar:** full bar. **Address:** 205 S Mill St 81611 **Location:** Just n of Mill St and Hopkins Ave. **Parking:** street only. D CALL AC

KENICHI ASPEN Phone: 970/920-2212 (12)

Asian
$7-$38

AAA Inspector Notes: Asian cuisine, including top-rate sushi, is served in an atmosphere that is both hip and elegant. **Bar:** full bar. **Address:** 533 E Hopkins Ave 81611 **Location:** Just s on Galena St, then just e. **Parking:** street only. D AC

L'HOSTARIA RISTORANTE Phone: 970/925-9022 (17)

Italian
$18-$34

AAA Inspector Notes: The warm and gracious staff delivers a variety of courses such as braised pork shank served in a terra cotta dish with roasted shallots, osso buco, baked organic chicken, goat cheese-crusted Colorado lamb chops served with truffle mashed potatoes and halibut with milk-braised leeks. Tempting desserts may include tiramisu, crème brûle and a selection of Italian cheeses served with walnuts and toast. **Bar:** full bar. **Reservations:** suggested. **Address:** 620 E Hyman Ave 81611 **Location:** Just s of Galena St, then just e. **Parking:** street only. D

LITTLE ANNIE'S EATING HOUSE
Phone: 970/925-1098 (16)

Comfort Food
$9-$29

AAA Inspector Notes: This cozy eatery offers a wide variety of delicious items such as daily soups, chili, their famous beef stew, a thick and juicy grilled prime rib sandwich, the spinach pie vegetable plate, curry chicken salad and jumbo shrimp cocktail. Dinner platters include Colorado lamb chops, Caribbean marinated pork rib-eye, fresh Rocky Mountain trout, Annie's rotisserie chicken and tempting homemade desserts. **Bar:** full bar. **Address:** 517 E Hyman Ave 81611 **Location:** Just s on Galena St, then just e. **Parking:** street only. L D AC

MATSUHISA Phone: 970/544-6628 (2)

Japanese
$25-$38

AAA Inspector Notes: Created by noted celebrity chef Nobu Matsuhisa and his partner Nobuko Kang, this popular eatery draws locals and tourists alike. The basement of this blue Victorian house transports guests to a warm enclave featuring modern décor. Attractively presented delicious dishes and flavors from around the world are sure to please and surprise. The extensive beverage menu offers various wines and cocktails and even a variety of cocktails with shochu, a Japanese distilled alcohol. **Bar:** full bar. **Reservations:** suggested. **Address:** 303 E Main St 81611 **Location:** Corner of Main and Monarch sts. **Parking:** street only. D

MEZZALUNA Phone: 970/925-5882 (19)

Italian
$11-$30

AAA Inspector Notes: This trendy, high-energy dining room offers internationally flavored cuisine that includes creative appetizers, entrées and pastas. The menu lists crab cakes, oven-fired brie, veal chop Milanese, penne with rock shrimp and wood-fired pizzas. It's a great place for people-watching. **Bar:** full bar. **Address:** 624 E Cooper Ave 81611 **Location:** Opposite Aspen Square; downtown. **Parking:** street only. L D

MONTAGNA
Menu on AAA.com Phone: 970/920-6313 (21)

Regional American
$20-$75

AAA Inspector Notes: Regional ingredients flavor such preparations of Montagna's Alpine mountain cuisine as elk loin, wild mushroom crepes, foie gras and seafood pot au feu. An excellent cheese course is offered. Creme brulee, sorbets, flourless chocolate cake and golden watermelon soup are just a few of the tempting desserts. The elegant mountain setting serves as a backdrop for fine dining, and service is professional and attentive. Patio tables are available off the dining room and bar. **Bar:** full bar. **Reservations:** suggested. **Address:** 675 E Durant Ave 81611 **Location:** 0.3 mi e on SR 82, 0.3 mi s on Spring St; jct Durant Ave and Spring St; beside gondola at base of Aspen Mountain; in The Little Nell. **Parking:** valet only. B L D

(See map & index p. 43.)

PACIFICA SEAFOOD & RAW BAR

Phone: 970/920-9775 (14)

Seafood
$15-$39

AAA Inspector Notes: Good service, high energy and a creative and artistic menu are hallmarks of this restaurant and raw bar. Choices can range from cocktails and crab at the bar to a five-course dinner. **Bar:** full bar. **Address:** 307 S Mill St 81611 **Location:** Just e to S Hunter St, 0.3 mi s to E Durant Ave, just w to S Mill St, then just n. **Parking:** street only. D CALL &M

PINE CREEK COOKHOUSE **Phone:** 970/925-1044

American
$13-$45

AAA Inspector Notes: Have lunch or dinner while enjoying the flowers and mountain scenery. The menu includes a signature smoked trout melt sandwich, wild game, artisan cheeses, dry-cured meats, fresh-baked breads and homemade desserts. Enjoy cocktails and appetizers beside the outdoor wood-burning stove before enjoying dishes featuring buffalo, elk, venison and line-caught fresh fish. In winter, a horse-drawn sleigh will take you here. The more adventurous can arrive on skis or snowshoes. **Bar:** full bar. **Reservations:** suggested. **Address:** 11399 Castle Creek Rd 81611 **Location:** At roundabout, exit Castle Creek Rd (CR 15), then 12.5 mi s. L D

PINONS **Phone:** 970/920-2021 (4)

Regional American
$25-$50

AAA Inspector Notes: This restaurant's contemporary Western-ranch setting features Colorado-themed cuisine with a Southwestern flair and includes roasted and pan-seared fish, wild game, lobster strudel and crispy Malpeque oysters. The spacious outdoor patio offers the best views of Aspen Mountain. **Bar:** full bar. **Reservations:** suggested. **Address:** 105 S Mill St 81611 **Location:** Just s of Main and Mill sts. **Parking:** street only.

D

PLATO'S RESTAURANT AT ASPEN MEADOWS RESORT **Phone:** 970/925-4240 (1)

American
$20-$35

AAA Inspector Notes: A must for any visitor, this restaurant is a favorite for its flavorful dishes that are artistically presented and perfectly prepared. The talented team of chefs creates food for an innovative menu more typically seen at a fine-dining restaurant. The menu changes seasonally, but if it's available, peach and Champagne soup with jumbo lump crab is divine. Gorgeous mountain views enhance the dining experience. **Bar:** full bar. **Reservations:** suggested. **Address:** 845 Meadows Rd 81611 **Location:** 0.3 mi n of SR 82 via 7th Ave, just w; in Aspen Meadows Resort, A Dolce Resort. D

RUSTIQUE BISTRO **Phone:** 970/920-2555 (8)

Regional French
$18-$35

AAA Inspector Notes: Hearty fare evokes the feel of country French kitchens, where thick soups, freshly prepared vegetables and great bread are served daily. A casual atmosphere and kind service make for a fine evening. **Bar:** full bar. **Address:** 216 S Monarch St 81611 **Location:** Corner of Hopkins Ave and Monarch St; downtown. **Parking:** street only. D

SYZYGY **Phone:** 970/925-3700 (5)

New American
$25-$49

AAA Inspector Notes: Syzygy means "being in alignment," and elegant presentations hold true to the definition in their appeal to both the palate and eye. Appetizers such as silky water chestnut soup and pan-seared foie gras and main courses such as maple-glazed wild king salmon contribute to a dining experience that synchronizes delectable taste and vision. **Bar:** full bar. **Reservations:** required. **Address:** 308 E Hopkins Ave 81611 **Location:** Jct E Hopkins Ave and Monarch St; Lower Level. **Parking:** street only. D

TAKAH SUSHI **Phone:** 970/925-8588 (15)

Pacific Rim
$26-$70

AAA Inspector Notes: Those who walk down the stairs enter an intimate space with a fresh sushi bar where guests can watch the preparation as well as an inviting dining room. In the summer, many patrons choose to enjoy their meals al fresco on the outdoor patio. The friendly, helpful waitstaff provides guidance through the eclectic Asian-fusion menu, which ranges from sushi and sashimi to such classics as pad thai and crispy Chinese duck. **Bar:** full bar. **Reservations:** suggested. **Address:** 320 S Mill St 81611 **Location:** At Cooper and Mill sts; in Hyman Ave Mall.

D

UTE CITY **Phone:** 970/925-2900 (7)

American
$18-$29

AAA Inspector Notes: This American-style bistro offers a nice selection of appetizers, salads, pasta, meat, fowl and fish. Dishes include braised lamb shank, stuffed veal breast, duck confit with pine nuts and sable fish with pomegranate reduction. Decadent desserts are sure to please. **Bar:** full bar. **Reservations:** suggested. **Address:** 308 E Hopkins Ave 81611 **Location:** Corner of Hopkins Ave and Monarch St. **Parking:** street only.

L D

THE WILD FIG **Phone:** 970/925-5160 (11)

Mediterranean
$9-$34

AAA Inspector Notes: This casual eatery features an open patio, quite popular in the warm summer months. The menu offers a diverse selection of Mediterranean fare such as falafel, hummus with pita bread, panini, and a variety of pasta dishes. Lunch is served June through August only. **Bar:** full bar. **Address:** 315 E Hyman Ave 81611 **Location:** Between Monarch and Mill sts. **Parking:** street only. D

WILLOW CREEK BISTRO **Phone:** 970/429-2327 (23)

American
$6-$19

AAA Inspector Notes: Creative and artistically presented soups, appetizers, salads, sandwiches and entrees are served in secluded surroundings. **Bar:** full bar. **Address:** 75 Prospector Rd 81611 **Location:** Exit Maroon Creek Rd at roundabout, 1.5 mi sw to Thunderbowl Ln, then just e on Boomerang Rd; at The Ritz-Carlton Club. **Parking:** no self-parking.

B L D

ZOCALITO LATIN BISTRO **Phone:** 970/920-1991 (13)

Latin American
$8-$30

AAA Inspector Notes: Latin specialties and cold cocktails from the rum bar are offered at this colorful eatery. **Bar:** full bar. **Address:** 420 E Hyman Ave 81611 **Location:** Corner of S Galena St and E Hyman Ave. **Parking:** no self-parking. D

AURORA (B-5) pop. 325,078, elev. 5,435'

- **Restaurants p. 51**
- **Hotels & Restaurants map & index p. 140**
- **Part of Denver area — see map p. 123**

Aurora is home to the Aurora Reservoir. This municipal park offers recreational activities year-round, including swimming and boating. The city also offers hiking and bicycling trails as well as 16 golf courses. Saturdays from May through October vendors offer fruit, vegetables, specialty items and baked goods for sale at the Southlands Farmer's Market, at the Southlands Outdoor Retail Center at Smoky Hill Road and E470.

Special events proliferate in Aurora and include Kidspree, a two-day event in mid-July. It takes place in Bicentennial Park with live entertainment and

(See map & index p. 140.)

hands-on activities for children. Early October brings PumpkinFest, held at the historic Delaney Farm; festivities include hay rides, music, scarecrow building, a pumpkin patch and a pumpkin launch.

Aurora Chamber of Commerce: 14305 E. Alameda Ave., Suite 300, Aurora, CO 80012. **Phone:** (303) 344-1500.

AURORA HISTORY MUSEUM is at 15051 E. Alameda Pkwy. The museum's permanent exhibit, Living Aurora, contains a collection of artifacts from the late 1800s to the 1990s. Changing exhibits are featured in the second and third galleries. The Children's Hands-on Room includes touchable artifacts, clothes and games. **Time:** Allow 30 minutes minimum. **Hours:** Tues.-Fri. 9-4, Sat.-Sun. 11-4. Closed major holidays. **Cost:** Free. Parking is available in the library lot. **Phone:** (303) 739-6666 or (303) 739-6660.

ALOFT DENVER INTERNATIONAL AIRPORT
Phone: (303)371-9500 91

Contemporary Hotel
$79-$199

aloft
AAA Benefit: Enjoy the new twist, get up to 15% off + Starwood Preferred Guest® bonuses.

Address: 16470 E 40th Cir 80011 **Location:** I-70 exit 283 (Chambers Rd), just n, 0.7 mi e, then just s. **Facility:** 144 units. 5 stories, interior corridors. *Bath:* shower only. **Amenities:** high-speed Internet, safes. **Pool(s):** heated indoor. **Activities:** exercise room. **Guest Services:** valet and coin laundry. **Free Special Amenities: high-speed Internet and airport transportation.**

SAVE FEE / SOME UNITS

BEST WESTERN PLUS GATEWAY INN & SUITES
Phone: (720)748-4800 92

Hotel
$79-$150

AAA Benefit: Members save up to 20%, plus 10% bonus points with Best Western Rewards®.

Address: 800 S Abilene St 80012 **Location:** I-225 exit 7 (Mississippi Ave), just e, then 0.3 mi n. **Facility:** 67 units. 4 stories, interior corridors. **Amenities:** high-speed Internet, safes (fee). **Pool(s):** heated indoor. **Activities:** whirlpool, exercise room. **Guest Services:** valet and coin laundry. **Free Special Amenities: full breakfast and high-speed Internet.**

SAVE CALL FEE / SOME UNITS FEE

CAMBRIA SUITES DENVER AIRPORT
Phone: (303)576-9600 85

Contemporary Hotel
$89-$229

Address: 16001 E 40th Cir 80011 **Location:** I-70 exit 283 (Chambers Rd), just n, then 0.4 mi e. **Facility:** 151 units. 6 stories, interior corridors. **Terms:** cancellation fee imposed. **Amenities:** high-speed Internet. **Pool(s):** heated indoor. **Activities:** whirlpool, exercise room. **Guest Services:** valet and coin laundry, area transportation-within 5 mi. *(See ad p. 103.)*

DENVER AIRPORT MARRIOTT AT GATEWAY PARK
Phone: (303)371-4333 90

Hotel
$79-$239

AAA Benefit: AAA hotel discounts of 5% or more.

Address: 16455 E 40th Cir 80011 **Location:** I-70 exit 283 (Chambers Rd), just n, 0.5 mi e, then just s. **Facility:** 238 units. 6 stories, interior corridors. **Pool(s):** heated indoor. **Activities:** whirlpool, exercise room. **Guest Services:** valet laundry. **Free Special Amenities: high-speed Internet and airport transportation.**

SAVE CALL FEE / SOME UNITS

DOUBLETREE BY HILTON HOTEL DENVER - AURORA
Phone: (303)337-2800 94

Hotel
$89-$169

DOUBLETREE BY HILTON
AAA Benefit: Members save 5% or more everyday!

Address: 13696 E Iliff Pl 80014 **Location:** I-225 exit 5 (E Iliff Ave), just w. **Facility:** 248 units. 6 stories, interior corridors. **Terms:** 1-7 night minimum stay, cancellation fee imposed. **Amenities:** *Fee:* video games, high-speed Internet. **Pool(s):** heated indoor. **Activities:** whirlpool, exercise room. **Guest Services:** valet laundry, area transportation-within 5 mi. **Free Special Amenities: newspaper.** *(See ad p. 50.)*

SAVE CALL FEE / SOME UNITS

FAIRFIELD INN-DENVER/AURORA
Phone: (303)745-6700 95

Hotel
$80-$98

AAA Benefit: AAA hotel discounts of 5% or more.

Address: 13851 E Harvard Ave 80014 **Location:** I-225 exit 5 (E Iliff Ave), just e to Blackhawk St, then s. **Facility:** 82 units. 3 stories, interior corridors. **Pool(s):** heated indoor. **Activities:** whirlpool, exercise room. **Guest Services:** valet and coin laundry.

CALL / SOME UNITS

HILTON GARDEN INN-DENVER INTERNATIONAL AIRPORT
Phone: (303)371-9393 89

Hotel
$99-$199

Hilton Garden Inn
AAA Benefit: Unparalleled hospitality at a special Member rate.

Address: 16475 E 40th Cir 80011 **Location:** I-70 exit 283 (Chambers Rd), just n to 40th Ave E, then 0.5 mi e. **Facility:** 157 units. 6 stories, interior corridors. **Terms:** 1-7 night minimum stay, cancellation fee imposed. **Amenities:** video games (fee), high-speed Internet. **Pool(s):** heated indoor. **Activities:** whirlpool, exercise room. *Fee:* massage. **Guest Services:** valet and coin laundry, area transportation-University of Colorado Hospital at Fitzsimmons. **Free Special Amenities: high-speed Internet and airport transportation.** *(See ad p. 50.)*

SAVE CALL FEE

(See map & index p. 140.)

▼ See AAA listing p. 49 ▼

▼ See AAA listing p. 49 ▼

(See map & index p. 140.)

HOLIDAY INN EXPRESS & SUITES DENVER-AURORA

Phone: 303/369-8400 93

Hotel

Rates not provided

Address: 1500 S Abilene St 80012 **Location:** I-225 exit 7 (Mississippi Ave), just e, then 0.5 mi s. **Facility:** 129 units. 4 stories, interior corridors. **Amenities:** video games (fee). **Pool(s):** heated outdoor. **Activities:** exercise room. **Guest Services:** valet and coin laundry, area transportation-within 5 mi.

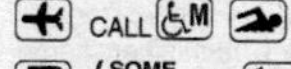

CALL BIZ FEE / SOME UNITS FEE

WHERE TO EAT

AURORA SUMMIT **Phone:** 303/751-2112 100

Steak

$10-$46

AAA Inspector Notes: There's a loyal local following for this restaurant's wonderful offerings of USDA Prime aged beef, seafood, chicken and lamb. Meals are served by an attentive, capable serving staff in a décor of subdued lighting and bas-relief walls. **Bar:** full bar. **Reservations:** suggested. **Address:** 2700 S Havana St 80014 **Location:** I-25 exit E Hampden Ave (which becomes S Havana St), 3.5 mi e; I-225 exit 5 (E Iliff Ave), w to S Havana St, then 0.3 mi s on east side. L D

HYATT PLACE DENVER AIRPORT

Phone: (303)371-0700 87

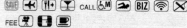

Hotel

$79-$229

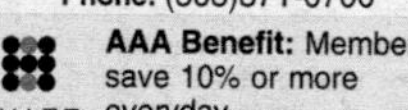

HYATT PLACE

AAA Benefit: Members save 10% or more everyday.

Address: 16250 E 40th Ave 80011 **Location:** I-70 exit 283 (Chambers Rd), just n, then 0.5 mi e. **Facility:** 126 units. 6 stories, interior corridors. **Terms:** cancellation fee imposed. **Amenities:** safes. *Some:* high-speed Internet. **Pool(s):** heated indoor. **Activities:** exercise room. **Guest Services:** valet laundry, area transportation-within 5 mi. **Free Special Amenities: expanded continental breakfast and high-speed Internet.**

SAVE CALL BIZ

FEE

BENT FORK AMERICAN GRILL

Phone: 303/337-6600 99

American

$9-$26

AAA Inspector Notes: Lamb, buffalo, beef, pork and seafood dishes share menu space with burgers and sandwiches. Among the choices that reflect a modern twist on classic favorites are salmon fish and chips, lobster shell pasta and cheese and buffalo pot roast. Specialty martinis merit a look. **Bar:** full bar. **Address:** 12191 E Iliff Ave 80014 **Location:** I-225 exit 5 (E Iliff Ave), 0.8 mi w. L D

CAFÉ PAPRIKA **Phone:** 303/755-4150 97

Moroccan

$7-$18

AAA Inspector Notes: Tucked away in an unassuming strip mall, this little place has been a local favorite for more than a decade. Desert-themed murals on the wall, complete with camels and their nomadic masters, add to the ambience. The mouthwatering North African and Middle Eastern dishes include kebabs, hummus, tagine stews and gyros. Among the choices of must-try desserts are flaky baklava and the m'hencha, a pastry filled with almond paste and cinnamon. **Address:** 13160 E Mississippi Ave 80012 **Location:** I-225 exit 7 (Mississippi Ave), 0.4 mi w; in Uvalda Shoppette strip mall. L D

RESIDENCE INN BY MARRIOTT

Phone: (303)459-8000 88

Extended Stay Hotel

$98-$152

AAA Benefit: AAA hotel discounts of 5% or more.

Address: 16490 E 40th Cir 80011 **Location:** I-70 exit 283 (Chambers Rd), just n, 0.5 mi e, then just s. **Facility:** 124 units, some two bedrooms. 4 stories, interior corridors. **Amenities:** *Some:* high-speed Internet. **Pool(s):** heated indoor. **Activities:** whirlpool, exercise room. **Guest Services:** valet and coin laundry.

CALL BIZ FEE / SOME UNITS FEE

CALDONIA'S BARBECUE **Phone:** 303/752-3829 98

Barbecue

$8-$17

AAA Inspector Notes: The menu lists a variety of barbecue dishes with the usual suspects: beef, pork, chicken, ribs and combination plates. The emphasis for a good plate of barbecue is on key ingredients: the smoker, the wood, the meat and the sauce. For those in the mood for something else, the menu also features comfort foods such as chicken-fried steak, mac 'n' cheese and Philly cheesesteak. The mostly female waitstaff wears short shorts and low-cut tops. **Bar:** full bar. **Address:** 2252 S Parker Rd 80231 **Location:** Jct E Iliff Ave and Parker Rd, just nw.

L D LATE

SLEEP INN DENVER INTERNATIONAL AIRPORT

Phone: (303)373-1616 86

Hotel

$69-$130

Address: 15900 E 40th Ave 80011 **Location:** I-70 exit 283 (Chambers Rd); from airport, Pena Blvd S to 40th Ave W. **Facility:** 119 units. 3 stories, interior corridors. *Bath:* shower only. **Terms:** cancellation fee imposed. **Amenities:** video games (fee). **Pool(s):** heated indoor. **Guest Services:** valet laundry. **Free Special Amenities: continental breakfast and high-speed Internet.**

SAVE CALL BIZ FEE / SOME UNITS FEE FEE FEE

LA CUEVA RESTAURANTE

Phone: 303/367-1422 96

Mexican

$8-$16

AAA Inspector Notes: Serving guests since 1974, the family-owned restaurant features friendly service, a festive atmosphere and a good variety of tasty, made-from-scratch dishes. Colorful and tastefully appointed, the eatery is popular with local residents. **Bar:** full bar. **Address:** 9742 E Colfax Ave 80010 **Location:** I-225 exit 10, 2.5 mi w.

L D

SPRINGHILL SUITES BY MARRIOTT

Phone: 720/859-1100 95

Hotel

Rates not provided

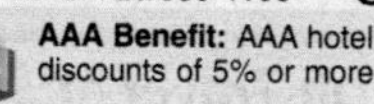

AAA Benefit: AAA hotel discounts of 5% or more.

Address: 13400 E Colfax Ave 80011 **Location:** I-225 exit 10, 0.5 mi w. **Facility:** 153 units. 4 stories, interior corridors. **Amenities:** high-speed Internet. **Pool(s):** heated indoor. **Activities:** whirlpool, exercise room. **Guest Services:** valet and coin laundry, area transportation-within 5 mi.

SAVE CALL BIZ

Safety tip: Keep a current AAA/CAA Road Atlas in every vehicle

AVON pop. 6,447

COMFORT INN VAIL/BEAVER CREEK

Phone: (970)949-5511

Hotel

$100-$225

Address: 161 W Beaver Creek Blvd 81620 **Location:** I-70 exit 167, just s on Avon Rd, then just w. **Facility:** 146 units. 4 stories, interior corridors. **Terms:** cancellation fee imposed. **Pool(s):** heated outdoor. **Activities:** whirlpool, exercise room. **Guest Services:** valet and coin laundry. **Free Special Amenities: expanded continental breakfast and high-speed Internet.**

/ SOME UNITS FEE FEE

FALCON POINT RESORT

Phone: (970)949-4416

Condominium

$110-$528

Address: 175 Lake St 81620 **Location:** I-70 exit 167, just s on Avon Rd, just w on W Beaver Creek Blvd, just s on Benchmark Rd, then just w. **Facility:** Across from Nottingham Park, these studio to three-bedroom condos feature contemporary décor with ceiling fans and humidifiers in each unit. Ski, snowboard and bicycle storage is available. 58 condominiums. 5 stories, interior corridors. **Terms:** office hours 8 am-10 pm, check-in 4 pm, 2 night minimum stay - seasonal and/or weekends, 60 day cancellation notice. **Pool(s):** heated indoor/outdoor. **Activities:** sauna, whirlpools, recreation programs in season, exercise room. **Guest Services:** coin laundry.

SHERATON MOUNTAIN VISTA

Phone: (970)748-6000

Condominium

$95-$409

Sheraton HOTELS & RESORTS **AAA Benefit:** Members get up to 15% off, plus Starwood Preferred Guest® bonuses.

Address: 160 W Beaver Creek Blvd 81620 **Location:** I-70 exit 167, just s on Avon Rd, then just w. **Facility:** Located in the center of town convenient to shops and restaurants, the modern, well-appointed condos feature the latest in decor and amenities. 158 condominiums. 8 stories, interior corridors. **Terms:** check-in 4 pm, 3 day cancellation notice-fee imposed. **Amenities:** safes. **Pool(s):** heated outdoor. **Activities:** sauna, whirlpools, steamroom, rental bicycles, exercise room. *Fee:* massage. **Guest Services:** complimentary and valet laundry.

CALL

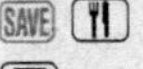

WEST BEAVER CREEK LODGE

Phone: (970)949-9073

Bed & Breakfast

$269-$289 12/15-4/30
$149 5/1-12/14

Address: 220 W Beaver Creek Blvd, Suite B 81620 **Location:** I-70 exit 167, just s on Avon Rd, then just w. **Facility:** Two blocks from the gondola, this B&B has spaces for guests to relax, play pool or cook (a full breakfast is included). Shuttles stop outside, but restaurants and shops are within walking distance. 9 units, some two bedrooms and kitchens. 2 stories (no elevator), interior corridors. **Terms:** check-in 4 pm, 45 day cancellation notice-fee imposed. **Activities:** whirlpool, game room. **Guest Services:** complimentary laundry.

/ SOME UNITS

WESTIN RIVERFRONT RESORT & SPA, AVON

Phone: (970)790-6000

Contemporary Hotel

$179-$889

WESTIN HOTELS & RESORTS **AAA Benefit:** Enjoy up to 15% off your next stay, plus Starwood Preferred Guest® bonuses.

Address: 126 Riverfront Ln 81620 **Location:** I-70 exit 167, 0.6 mi s on Avon Rd, then just w. **Facility:** This upscale riverside condominium hotel offers easy access to the mountain via a gondola. The modern décor features subtle mountain-themed accents. All units have a humidifier; some have a fireplace. 346 units, some two bedrooms, three bedrooms, efficiencies, kitchens and condominiums. 9 stories, interior corridors. **Parking:** valet only. **Terms:** check-in 4 pm, 30 day cancellation notice-fee imposed. **Amenities:** high-speed Internet, safes. **Dining:** Restaurant Avondale, see separate listing. **Pool(s):** heated outdoor. **Activities:** whirlpools, recreation programs in season, rental bicycles, hiking trails, jogging, exercise room, spa. *Fee:* downhill & cross country skiing, game room. **Guest Services:** valet and coin laundry.

FEE / SOME UNITS

WHERE TO EAT

AVON BAKERY & DELI

Phone: 970/949-3354

Deli

$7-$9

AAA Inspector Notes: The small and busy bakery serves freshly made soups, salads, cold and hot sandwiches and a nice selection of combination lunches featuring delicious daily lunch specials. The artisan bread is baked fresh daily on the premises using 100 percent organic flour. **Address:** 0025 Hurd Ln, Suite 4 81620 **Location:** I-70 exit 167, 0.4 mi s on Avon Rd, then just e.

B L

BLUE PLATE BISTRO

Phone: 970/845-2252

American

$4-$22

AAA Inspector Notes: This casual eatery provides comfort food at reasonable prices. The lunch menu features a variety of soups, salads, sandwiches and hamburgers, while the expanded dinner menu lists meatloaf, Rocky Mountain trout, New England pot roast, barbecue pork ribs, shrimp scampi and other American classics. **Bar:** full bar. **Address:** 48 E Beaver Creek Blvd 81620 **Location:** I-70 exit 167, 0.4 mi s, take 3rd exit at second roundabout, then just e; in Boat Bldg.

L D

PAZZO'S PIZZERIA

Phone: 970/949-9900

Italian

$8-$14

AAA Inspector Notes: The menu at this lively eatery includes delicious hand-tossed pizza, strombolis and calzones with a variety of toppings, lasagna, ravioli, rigatoni, spinach manicotti, and chicken and eggplant Parmigiana. The soft sub roll, sauteed green peppers, onions and mushrooms steamed with provolone cheese made this one of the best Philly cheesesteaks I have tasted, and the fresh pasta salad was delicious. Enjoy outdoor dining on the patio when the weather is fair. **Bar:** full bar. **Address:** 82 E Beaver Creek Blvd 81620 **Location:** I-70 exit 167, 0.3 mi s to 2nd roundabout, take 3rd exit, then just e; in Benchmark Shopping Center. L D

RESTAURANT AVONDALE **Phone:** 970/790-5500

American
$12-$40

AAA Inspector Notes: Chef/owner Thomas Salamunovich receives high praise for his various eateries, including this casual spot for fine-dining cuisine. Although the menu changes seasonally, the quality and variety of ingredients is consistent. Entrees range from the simple gourmet pizza to the complex lamb osso buco. Other choices include preparations of beef, chicken, pork, lamb, local trout or fresh seafood, which is flown in daily. Handmade pasta enhances some dishes. Mountain views are gorgeous. **Bar:** full bar. **Reservations:** suggested. **Address:** 126 Riverfront Ln 81620 **Location:** I-70 exit 167, 0.5 mi s on Avon Rd, then just w; in The Westin Riverfront Resort & Spa, Avon. **Parking:** valet only. L D

VIN 48 RESTAURANT & WINE BAR **Phone:** 970/748-9463

Northern American
$16-$29

AAA Inspector Notes: The Italian-influenced contemporary American cuisine features a seasonal menu of small and large plates such as sauteed sea scallops with a caramelized red onion puree, duck confit sliders, Waygu beef carpaccio and braised pork cheeks. Seasonal creative desserts such as the banana chocolate tart or the lemon mascarpone parfait are a must. The wine bar features 40 wines by the glass and distinctive flights. **Bar:** full bar. **Reservations:** suggested. **Address:** 48 E Beaver Creek Blvd 81620 **Location:** I-70 exit 167, 0.4 mi s, take 3rd exit at second roundabout, then just e; in Boat Bldg. D

BASALT pop. 3,857

ASPENALT LODGE **Phone:** (970)927-3191

Motel
$99-$150

Address: 157 Basalt Center Cir 81621 **Location:** Off SR 82; center. **Facility:** 35 units. 2 stories (no elevator), exterior corridors. **Terms:** office hours 6:30 am-9 pm. **Amenities:** *Some:* high-speed Internet. **Activities:** whirlpool, fishing. BIZ

WHERE TO EAT

CAFE BERNARD **Phone:** 970/927-4292

American
$7-$27

AAA Inspector Notes: The charming and casual bistro features freshly baked croissants every morning, truffle mousse pâté, organic field greens, filet mignon, Rocky Mountain smoked trout pasta and a variety of delicious dessert selections. The high-quality ingredients mix well with the cozy ambience. **Bar:** beer & wine. **Reservations:** suggested, for dinner. **Address:** 200 Midland Ave 81621 **Location:** Off SR 82, just n at Basalt Ave traffic light, then just w at roundabout toward downtown. **Parking:** street only. B L D

CUVEE WORLD BISTRO **Phone:** 970/927-4000

New American
$15-$25

AAA Inspector Notes: Seasonally changing menus are paired with a well-crafted wine list. The wild mushroom cakes over avocado pesto, tamarind marinated pork tenderloin, and mascarpone cheesecake with pine nut crust and coffee blueberry syrup make this bistro the perfect spot to enjoy a fantastic meal. **Bar:** full bar. **Reservations:** suggested. **Address:** 305 Gold Rivers Ct, Suite 140-B 81621 **Location:** Off SR 82, just n at Basalt Ave traffic light, w at roundabout toward downtown, then just n on Midland Ave. **Parking:** street only. L D

TEMPRANILLO **Phone:** 970/927-3342

Spanish
$11-$35

AAA Inspector Notes: Rich colors, high ceilings and warm fireplaces enhance the atmosphere at this charming Old World-style home, where food from Spain and Italy pairs with more than 100 wine choices. Guests can sit in the softly lit dining room or lively bar to feast on delicious Spanish tapas, grilled calamari with arugula and aioli, classic Caesar or Greek salad, fettuccine mambo with jamón serrano, chicken, mushrooms and cream, or grilled salmon with Mediterranean olives and citrus and basil pesto. **Bar:** full bar. **Address:** 165 Midland Ave 81621 **Location:** Off SR 82, just n at Basalt Ave traffic light, w at roundabout toward downtown. L D CALL

BAYFIELD pop. 2,333

WILDERNESS TRAILS RANCH **Phone:** (970)247-0722

Resort Ranch
$199-$2495

Address: 23486 CR 501 81122 **Location:** 35 mi e of Durango to CR 501 via US 160, continue 8 mi nw and 11 mi ne on CR 501, then 4.5 mi se on dirt road via CR 501. Located in San Juan National Forest. **Facility:** The secluded valley along the Pine River affords plenty of active pursuits via all-inclusive and a la carte packages that generate great memories. The family-owned ranch offers well-appointed cabins. 9 cabins. 1 story, exterior corridors. **Terms:** open 6/5-10/1, 2-6 night minimum stay - seasonal, 120 day cancellation notice-fee imposed. **Activities:** whirlpool, waterskiing, fishing, recreation programs, hiking trails, horseback riding, playground, horseshoes. *Fee:* massage. **Guest Services:** coin laundry.

FEE

/ SOME UNITS FEE

BEAVER CREEK (D-3) elev. 8,100'

• **Restaurants p. 54**

RECREATIONAL ACTIVITIES

Skiing

- **Beaver Creek Resort** is 3 mi. s. of I-70 exit 167. Other activities are offered. **Hours:** Daily 9-4, mid.-Nov. to mid-Apr. (weather permitting). **Phone:** (970) 754-4636.

BEAVER CREEK LODGE **Phone:** (970)845-9800

Boutique Hotel
$119-$1099

Address: 26 Avondale Ln 81620 **Location:** I-70 exit 167, 3 mi s on Avon and Village rds, then just e. Located in Beaver Creek Village. **Facility:** This ski-in/ski-out hotel attracts visitors with its well-appointed guest rooms, each with a gas fireplace, original artwork, a living room and air-conditioning with humidification. 72 units. 6 stories, interior corridors. **Parking:** valet only. **Terms:** 3 day cancellation notice-fee imposed. **Amenities:** video games (fee), safes. **Dining:** Rocks Modern Grill, see separate listing. **Pool(s):** heated indoor/outdoor. **Activities:** sauna, whirlpool, steamroom, hiking trails, jogging, exercise room. *Fee:* downhill & cross country skiing, ice skating, massage. **Guest Services:** valet and coin laundry, area transportation-within 5 mi. **Free Special Amenities: newspaper and high-speed Internet.** Affiliated with A Preferred Hotel.

BIZ FEE

PARK HYATT BEAVER CREEK RESORT & SPA
Phone: (970)949-1234

Resort Hotel
$119-$949

AAA Benefit: Members save 10% or more everyday.

Address: 136 E Thomas Pl 81620 **Location:** I-70 exit 167, 3 mi s on Avon and Village rds to Offerson Rd, then 0.4 mi e. Located in Beaver Creek Village. **Facility:** Enticing views of the surrounding valley and mountains at this ski-in/ski-out hotel are available from most of the stylish guest rooms. 190 units. 4 stories, interior corridors. **Parking:** valet only. **Terms:** check-in 4 pm, 3 day cancellation notice-fee imposed. **Amenities:** high-speed Internet, safes. **Dining:** 2 restaurants. **Pool(s):** heated outdoor. **Activities:** saunas, whirlpools, steamrooms, recreation programs, rental bicycles, hiking trails, jogging, playground, horseshoes, volleyball, spa. *Fee:* downhill & cross country skiing, ice skating, horseback riding. **Guest Services:** valet and coin laundry.

POSTE MONTANE LODGE **Phone:** (970)845-7500

Boutique Hotel
$200-$775 11/15-4/30
$130-$330 5/1-11/14

Address: 76 Avondale Ln 81620 **Location:** I-70 exit 167, 3 mi s on Avon and Village rds, then just e. **Facility:** The traditional European inn features wood-burning fireplaces in lodge rooms. Some amenities include terry robes, down comforters, grocery and sundry delivery, ski lockers and overnight ski tuning. 24 units, some two bedrooms. 4 stories, interior corridors. **Terms:** office hours 7 am-8 pm, check-in 4 pm, 2-5 night minimum stay - seasonal, 30 day cancellation notice-fee imposed. **Amenities:** safes. **Activities:** sauna, whirlpool, steamroom, hiking trails, jogging. *Fee:* fishing, downhill & cross country skiing, ice skating. **Guest Services:** complimentary laundry.

THE RITZ-CARLTON, BACHELOR GULCH
Phone: 970/748-6200

Resort Hotel
Rates not provided

AAA Benefit: Unequaled service at Special Member Savings.

Address: 130 Daybreak Ridge 81620 **Location:** I-70 exit 167, just s past the Beaver Creek Village gatehouse to Prater Rd, then just w; follow signs to Bachelor Gulch Village. **Facility:** This upscale, ski-in/ski-out resort has a secluded location and a spa. Many suites have kitchens, and all rooms have extra clothing storage and humidifiers. Happy hour for dogs is held on Fido Friday. 180 units, some two bedrooms, efficiencies and kitchens. 8 stories, interior corridors. **Parking:** valet only. **Amenities:** video games (fee), high-speed Internet, safes, honor bars. **Dining:** 3 restaurants, also, Spago, see separate listing. **Pool(s):** heated outdoor. **Activities:** saunas, whirlpools, steamrooms, hiking trails, jogging, game room, horseshoes, volleyball, spa. *Fee:* 4 tennis courts, downhill & cross country skiing. **Guest Services:** valet laundry, area transportation-within 5 mi.

WHERE TO EAT

FOXNUT SLOPESIDE SUSHI **Phone:** 970/845-0700

Japanese
$9-$25

AAA Inspector Notes: Although the menu offers standard sushi rolls, the more innovative fare is where this restaurant excels. The waiter recommended the crab in avocado, in which thick slices of avocado are topped with a spicy Dungeness crab mixture prepared with Kewpie mayo. The macadamia nut-crusted goat cheese salad featured mango slices and a mango-yuzu vinaigrette. The new location has a toned-down, sophisticated décor, yet it still has a modern '50s aesthetic. **Bar:** full bar. **Address:** 15 W Thomas Pl 81620 **Location:** I-70 exit 167, 3 mi s on Avon and Village rds, then 0.4 mi e on Offerson Rd; in Beaver Creek Village; at base of Centennial Lift.

L D AC

GOLDEN EAGLE INN **Phone:** 970/949-1940

American
$8-$40

AAA Inspector Notes: Fresh fish and wild game entrees, such as elk fillet and caribou medallions, are menu highlights at this family-friendly restaurant, which sits at the base of the Beaver Creek ski area. The atmosphere is casual, and the décor is country elegant. **Bar:** full bar. **Address:** 118 Beaver Creek Plaza 81620 **Location:** In Beaver Creek Plaza. L D AC

GROUSE MOUNTAIN GRILL **Phone:** 970/949-0600

Regional American
$11-$44

AAA Inspector Notes: This mountain grill features an elegant alpine atmosphere and offers outstanding seasonally focused preparations of fine meats and fish. Panoramic views and capable service enhance your dining experience. A hand-picked selection of limited-production wines is available. Terrace dining is available, weather permitting. **Bar:** full bar. **Reservations:** suggested. **Address:** 141 Scott Hill Rd 81620 **Location:** I-70 exit 167, 3 mi s via Avon and Village rds; in The Pines Lodge. **Parking:** valet only. B L D AC

MIRABELLE AT BEAVER CREEK **Phone:** 970/949-7728

Continental
$29-$45

AAA Inspector Notes: At the gatehouse entry to Beaver Creek, this restored 1898 farmhouse has charming decor and a lounge area with a fireplace. Belgian master chef Daniel Joly prepares creative European cuisine, including Dover sole, warm sweetbread salad, hot foie gras, Colorado lamb chops and roasted elk medallions. **Bar:** full bar. **Reservations:** suggested. **Address:** 55 Village Rd 81620 **Location:** I-70 exit 167, s to gatehouse; entrance to Beaver Creek Resort. **Historic**

D AC

ROCKS MODERN GRILL **Phone:** 970/845-9800

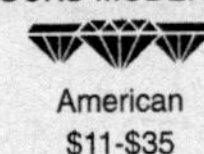
American
$11-$35

AAA Inspector Notes: The restaurant puts international twists on traditional American favorites such as fresh seafood, steaks and salads. Seating is available indoors in an informal yet comfortable upscale setting with stunning views and on an outside terrace with two inviting fire pits. **Bar:** full bar. **Address:** 26 Avondale Ln 81620 **Location:** I-70 exit 167, 3 mi s on Avon and Village rds, then just e; in Beaver Creek Lodge. B L D

SPAGO **Phone:** 970/343-1555

American

$14-$70

AAA Inspector Notes: Famed celebrity chef Wolfgang Puck decided to expand his restaurant brand by opening this restaurant. Artful presentations and fresh, high-quality ingredients make every mouthwatering bite enjoyable. The menu changes seasonally but includes local meats such as Colorado lamb as well as fresh seafood flown in daily. Discussing wine options with the knowledgeable sommelier is a delight. **Bar:** full bar. **Reservations:** suggested. **Address:** 130 Daybreak Ridge 81620 **Location:** I-70 exit 167, just s past the Beaver Creek Village gatehouse to Prater Rd, then just w; follow signs to Bachelor Gulch Village; in The Ritz-Carlton, Bachelor Gulch. **Parking:** valet only. B L D

SPLENDIDO AT THE CHATEAU **Phone:** 970/845-8808

American

$36-$52

AAA Inspector Notes: Chef David Walford delights patrons with his creative, innovative and contemporary cuisine that exhibit global influences. The menu changes seasonally, but if elk or any dish with hand-made pasta is available, that's a highly recommended choice. Other options include seafood, lamb, rabbit, steak and chicken. The extensive wine list features wines from 17 countries. Live piano music enhances the warm, opulent setting, which is reminiscent of a luxurious European country estate. **Bar:** full bar. **Reservations:** suggested. **Address:** 17 Chateau Ln 81620 **Location:** I-70 exit 167, s on Avon and Village rds (beyond gatehouse), 2.4 mi s on Village Rd, then just nw on Scott Hill Rd; in Chateau at Beaver Creek. **Parking:** valet only. D

BLACK CANYON OF THE GUNNISON NATIONAL PARK (D-2)

Elevations in the park range from 6,547 ft. at East Portal to 9,040 ft. at Poison Spring Hill. Refer to AAA maps for additional elevation information.

Black Canyon of the Gunnison National Park has several observation points on the South Rim, reached via SR 347, leading off US 50, 8 miles east of Montrose; the North Rim is reached by an 11-mile road (the last half is gravel) from SR 92 east of Crawford.

Embracing approximately 30,000 acres, the park contains 14 miles of the deepest portion of the Black Canyon of the Gunnison. Some of Earth's oldest base rocks have been cut by the river to a depth of 2,722 feet. At the narrowest point along the top of the canyon, the distance between the canyon walls measures about 1,100 feet across, but narrows to only 40 feet near the riverbed below.

The name Black Canyon comes from the many shadows cast on the cliff walls due to the narrowness of the canyon and from the dark-colored schists, granites and other Precambrian rocks. Descent into the canyon is arduous and hazardous; do not attempt it without consulting a ranger.

Summer recreational options include camping, hiking along the canyon rim, picnicking, fishing, rock climbing and extreme kayaking. Winter recreation offers cross-country skiing and snowshoeing.

The South Rim Visitor Center at Gunnison Point provides information about current interpretive programs and houses exhibits and a video describing the park's history, geology, flora and fauna. Recreational activities taking place in the inner gorge require a permit, which can be obtained from the visitor center. Programs are held daily, mid-June through Labor Day. Camping and rangers are available year-round at the South Rim, and in summer at the North Rim.

The park provides several options for scenic drives. South Rim Drive is a 7-mile paved road; 12 overlooks provide grand views of the canyon and the river. East Portal Road is a very steep paved drive; vehicles longer than 22 feet are prohibited. The road ends at the Gunnison River, a popular spot for camping, fishing and sightseeing.

The South Rim Visitor Center is open daily 8-6, Memorial Day weekend-Labor Day; 8:30-4, rest of year. South Rim Drive and East Portal Road are open early April to mid-Nov. (weather permitting). North Rim Road is open May-Oct. (weather permitting). Admission $15 per private vehicle or $7 per person arriving by other means (valid for 7 days); free (ages 0-16). Camping $12-$18. Phone (970) 249-1914 , ext. 423. *See Recreation Chart.*

BLACK FOREST pop. 13,116

• Part of Colorado Springs area — see map p. 85

BLACK FOREST BED & BREAKFAST LODGE

Phone: (719)495-4208

Bed & Breakfast

$75-$350

Address: 11170 Black Forest Rd 80908 **Location:** Jct Shoup and Black Forest rds, 1.3 mi s, then w at stone columns. Located in a quiet area. **Facility:** On 20 acres of pines, aspens and open meadow, the B&B is convenient to jogging and hiking areas. Rooms are individually decorated. 5 units, some efficiencies and kitchens. 1-2 stories (no elevator), interior/exterior corridors. **Terms:** check-in 4 pm, 2 night minimum stay - seasonal, 15 day cancellation notice-fee imposed. **Activities:** playground, volleyball. **Guest Services:** complimentary laundry.

SAVE

BLACK HAWK (B-4) pop. 118, elev. 8,056'

GAMBLING ESTABLISHMENTS

- **Ameristar Casino** is at 11 Richman St. **Hours:** Daily 24 hours. **Phone:** (720) 946-4000 or (866) 667-3386.
- **Bullwhackers Casinos** is at 101 Gregory St. **Hours:** Daily 24 hours. **Phone:** (303) 271-2500 or (800) 426-2855.
- **Canyon Casino** is at 131 Main St. **Hours:** Fri.-Sat. 24 hours; Sun.-Thurs. 9 a.m.-3 a.m. **Phone:** (303) 777-1111.
- **Fitzgeralds** is at 101 Main St. **Hours:** Daily 8 a.m.-2 a.m. **Phone:** (303) 582-6100 or (800) 538-5825.
- **The Gilpin Casino** is at 111 Main St. **Hours:** Daily 24 hours. **Phone:** (303) 582-1133.
- **Golden Gates Casino** is at 261 Main St. **Hours:** Daily 24 hours. Phone ahead to confirm schedule. **Phone:** (303) 582-5600.
- **Golden Mardi Gras Casino** is at 300 Main St. **Hours:** Daily 24 hours. Phone ahead to confirm schedule. **Phone:** (303) 582-5600.
- **Isle Casino Hotel Black Hawk** is at 401 Main St. **Hours:** Daily 24 hours. **Phone:** (303) 998-7777.
- **Lady Luck Casino** is at 340 Main St. **Hours:** Daily 24 hours. **Phone:** (303) 582-3000.
- **The Lodge Casino** is at 240 Main St. **Hours:** Daily 24 hours. **Phone:** (303) 582-1771.
- **Riviera** is at 444 Main St. **Hours:** Daily 24 hours. **Phone:** (303) 582-1000.

AMERISTAR CASINO RESORT SPA BLACK HAWK, COLORADO **Phone:** 720/946-4000

Resort Hotel
Rates not provided

Address: 111 Richman St 80422 **Location:** Just w of jct SR 119. **Facility:** The resort's spa features dry saunas, steam rooms, whirlpools and a quiet lounging area. Rooms feature flat-screen TVs and separate tubs and showers. 536 units. 33 stories, interior corridors. **Parking:** on-site and valet. **Terms:** check-in 4 pm. **Amenities:** safes. **Dining:** 5 restaurants. **Pool(s):** heated indoor. **Activities:** whirlpools, exercise room, spa. **Guest Services:** valet laundry.

(See ad p. 160, p. 57.)

SAVE BIZ   

WHERE TO EAT

TIMBERLINE GRILL **Phone:** 720/946-4000

American
$14-$36

AAA Inspector Notes: Escape the hustle and bustle of the casino by walking into this inviting mountain lodge restaurant, complete with Western-themed oil paintings, wood accents and a fireplace. Menu items include a variety of steaks, pasta dishes, chicken, ribs, and fish. Try to save room for the decadent desserts-the sampler includes a shot of lemon berry trifle, a small hot cocoa with homemade marshmallows and an amazing chocolate hazelnut torte. **Bar:** full bar. **Address:** 111 Richman St 80422 **Location:** Just w of jct SR 119; in Ameristar Casino Resort Spa Black Hawk, Colorado. **Parking:** on-site and valet.

D

▼ See AAA listing p. 56 ▼

BOULDER (B-4) pop. 97,385, elev. 5,344'

• Hotels p. 62 • Restaurants p. 64
• Hotels & Restaurants map & index p. 60

Boulder was settled on the outwash plain of Boulder Creek in 1858 because, according to Capt. Thomas A. Aikens, "the mountains look right for gold, and the valleys ... rich for grazing." It has since grown from a cluster of crude log houses into one of the leading educational and scientific research and development centers in the Rocky Mountain states.

The combination of climate, scenery and the 25,000-student University of Colorado attracted such agencies as the National Center for Atmospheric Research, the laboratories of the National Institute of Standards and Technology and the Joint Institute for Laboratory Astrophysics as well as other large corporate installations.

The University of Colorado's establishment in 1876 spurred the struggling gold and agricultural community, then called Boulder City, to a new vigor. The 1,590-acre campus has a computer center, the Fiske Planetarium/Sommers-Bausch Observatory and the Mary Rippon Outdoor Theatre. The theater hosts the Colorado Shakespeare Festival from early July to mid-August. Campus tours can be arranged; phone (303) 492-6301, ext. 2.

The Dushanbe Teahouse, presented as a gift from its sister city of Dushanbe, Tajikistan, is a traditionally decorated Tajik teahouse that sits at 13th Street in Boulder. The hand-carved, hand-painted structure, which arrived in 200 crates, was assembled by Tajik artisans.

An 8,555-acre system of mountain parks includes Boulder Creek Path, Boulder Falls, Colorado Chautauqua *(see attraction listing)*, Flagstaff Mountain and the Flatirons. Boulder Creek, which flows through the city, offers a multitude of recreational activities. In combination with Boulder Creek Path, which winds for 16 miles alongside the creek, opportunities exist for casual strolling, picnicking, tubing and fishing.

Boulder obtains its water supply from a municipally owned glacier. Twenty-eight miles of pipe channel the clear, soft water from Arapaho Glacier to the town's taps.

You'll find both residents and visitors gathering at the Boulder County Farmers' Market to shop for fresh produce from local growers as well as baked goods, flowers and crafts. The market, on 13th Street adjacent to Central Park, is open Wednesday evenings, early May to early October and Saturday mornings, early April to early November.

Boulder Convention and Visitors Bureau: 2440 Pearl St., Boulder, CO 80302. **Phone:** (303) 442-2911 or (800) 444-0447.

Shopping areas: In Boulder's downtown historic area, not far from the University of Colorado campus, is Pearl Street, a four-block, pedestrian-only outdoor mall lined with bookstores, art galleries, coffeehouses, boutiques and restaurants. Street performers and seasonal arts and crafts shows help contribute to a fun atmosphere.

Just east of 28th Street (US 36) between Arapahoe Avenue and Walnut Street is Twenty Ninth Street, an open-air lifestyle center combining retail establishments with dining and outdoor gathering spots. Joining Macy's are shops such as Ann Taylor Loft, Anthropologie and an Apple Store.

BOULDER BEER COMPANY TOUR is at 2880 Wilderness Place. The facility offers interactive tours of Colorado's first microbrewery. Visitors learn about the company's history as well as the science behind making beer and the production process. Free samples are offered to those 21+. **Hours:** Guided tours Mon.-Fri. at 2. Closed Jan. 1, Thanksgiving and Christmas. **Cost:** Free. **Phone:** (303) 444-8448.

BOULDER HISTORY MUSEUM is at 1206 Euclid Ave. on University Hill. This museum, in the 1899 Harbeck-Bergheim House, documents the history of the Boulder Valley with artifacts from pioneer days to the present. The house features a Tiffany window, Italian tile fireplaces and many period details. **Hours:** Tues.-Fri. 10-5, Sat.-Sun. noon-4. Closed major holidays. **Cost:** $6; $4 (ages 62+); $3 (ages 5-18 and college students with ID). **Phone:** (303) 449-3464.

BOULDER MUSEUM OF CONTEMPORARY ART, 1750 13th St., presents a rotating collection of local, national and international exhibits of contemporary art in its three galleries. **Time:** Allow 45 minutes minimum. **Hours:** Tues.-Fri. 11-5, Sat. 9-4, Sun. noon-3. **Cost:** $5; $4 (ages 65+ and students and teachers with ID); free (ages 0-11 and Wed. 4-8, Sat. 9-4, Apr.-Oct.). **Phone:** (303) 443-2122.

CELESTIAL SEASONINGS FREE TOUR OF TEA, 4600 Sleepytime Dr., offers tours of the company's manufacturing facility. Highlights of the facility, which produces more than 90 varieties of tea, include a gallery of original Celestial Seasonings artwork, marketing displays, a tea tasting, a guided tour of the production and packaging facilities, plus the aromatic mint room.

Food is available Mon.-Fri. **Time:** Allow 1 hour minimum. **Hours:** Guided 45-minute tours are given Mon.-Sat. on the hour 10-4, Sun. 11-3. Closed major holidays. **Cost:** Free. Ages 0-4 are not permitted in the production area. **Phone:** (303) 581-1202 or (800) 525-0347.

COLORADO CHAUTAUQUA, 1 mi. w. of US 36 at 900 Baseline Rd., occupies 26 acres at the base of Boulder's iconic mountain. Founded in 1898, the park was part of the Chautauqua movement, which sought to bring culture to rural areas of the country. Music, dance, silent films and lectures are presented during summer in the historic auditorium. Cultural and educational programs are given year-round. Most of the original buildings remain intact and are still being used for their original intent.

(See map & index p. 60.)

Hiking, bicycling, rock climbing and a playground can be enjoyed. Overnight accommodations are available year-round in cottages and lodges. **Hours:** Daily 24 hours. **Cost:** Free. **Phone:** (303) 442-3282.

FLAGSTAFF SCENIC HIGHWAY leaves Baseline Rd. and winds to the summit of Flagstaff Mountain, 1,600 feet above Boulder. It affords splendid views of the Continental Divide, city, valley and plains. Picnic tables are provided at Panorama Point; hiking trails wind around the summit. **Note:** Drivers should use caution due to the numerous rock-climbers and bicyclists.

LEANIN' TREE MUSEUM AND SCULPTURE GARDEN OF WESTERN ART, n.e. on SR 119, e. on Jay Rd., n. on 63rd St., then w. to 6055 Longbow Dr., is housed in the corporate headquarters of the Leanin' Tree greeting card company. Some 250 paintings and 150 bronze sculptures illustrate the landscape, cowboys, American Indians and wildlife of the American West. An outdoor sculpture garden contains more than 20 large bronze creations.

Time: Allow 1 hour minimum. **Hours:** Mon.-Fri. 8-5, Sat.-Sun. 10-5. Closed Jan. 1, Easter, July 4, Thanksgiving and Christmas. **Cost:** Free. **Phone:** (303) 729-3440.

NATIONAL CENTER FOR ATMOSPHERIC RESEARCH (NCAR), 1850 Table Mesa Dr., is a National Science Foundation-sponsored scientific research laboratory offering interactive exhibits and informational displays on such topics as weather; past, present and future climate; Earth's atmosphere and Sun; and NCAR supercomputing capabilities including weather and climate modeling. The building, designed by renowned architect I.M. Pei, is nestled against Boulder's Flatiron Mountains, overlooking the city in a picturesque setting. An interpretive .25-mile outdoor weather trail and art galleries with changing exhibits are offered.

Guided 1-hour tours are available Mon.-Fri. at noon or by appointment. Self-guiding "Guide-by-Cell" audio tours, in both adult and child versions, are offered in English and Spanish daily. **Hours:** Visitor center Mon.-Fri. 8-5, Sat.-Sun. and some holidays 9-4. Guided tours depart daily at noon. **Cost:** Free. Audio tours $2; $5 (family rate). **Phone:** (303) 497-1000.

UNIVERSITY OF COLORADO MUSEUM OF NATURAL HISTORY is in the Henderson Building at 15th St. and Broadway. The museum offers exhibits and activities that focus on the natural and cultural history of the Rocky Mountain west. Subjects include dinosaurs and other fossils, southwestern archeology and Colorado's plants and wildlife. A children's Discovery Corner also is available. **Time:** Allow 1 hour minimum. **Hours:** Mon.-Fri. 9-5, Sat. 9-4, Sun. 10-4. Closed major holidays. **Cost:** Donations. **Phone:** (303) 492-6892.

WINERIES

- **Boulder Creek Winery** is off SR 119 (63rd St. exit), s. to Lookout Rd., e. to Spine Rd., then n. to 6440 Odell Place. **Hours:** Self-guiding tour and tastings Thurs.-Sun. 1-5:30. **Phone:** (303) 516-9031.
- **Redstone Meadery** is e. on Pearl St. past Foothills Pkwy. (SR 157), then n. on 47th St. to 4700 Pearl St. **Hours:** Tasting room open Mon.-Fri. noon-6:30, Sat. noon-5. Tours are offered Mon.-Fri. at 1 and 3, Sat. at 12:30. **Phone:** (720) 406-1215.

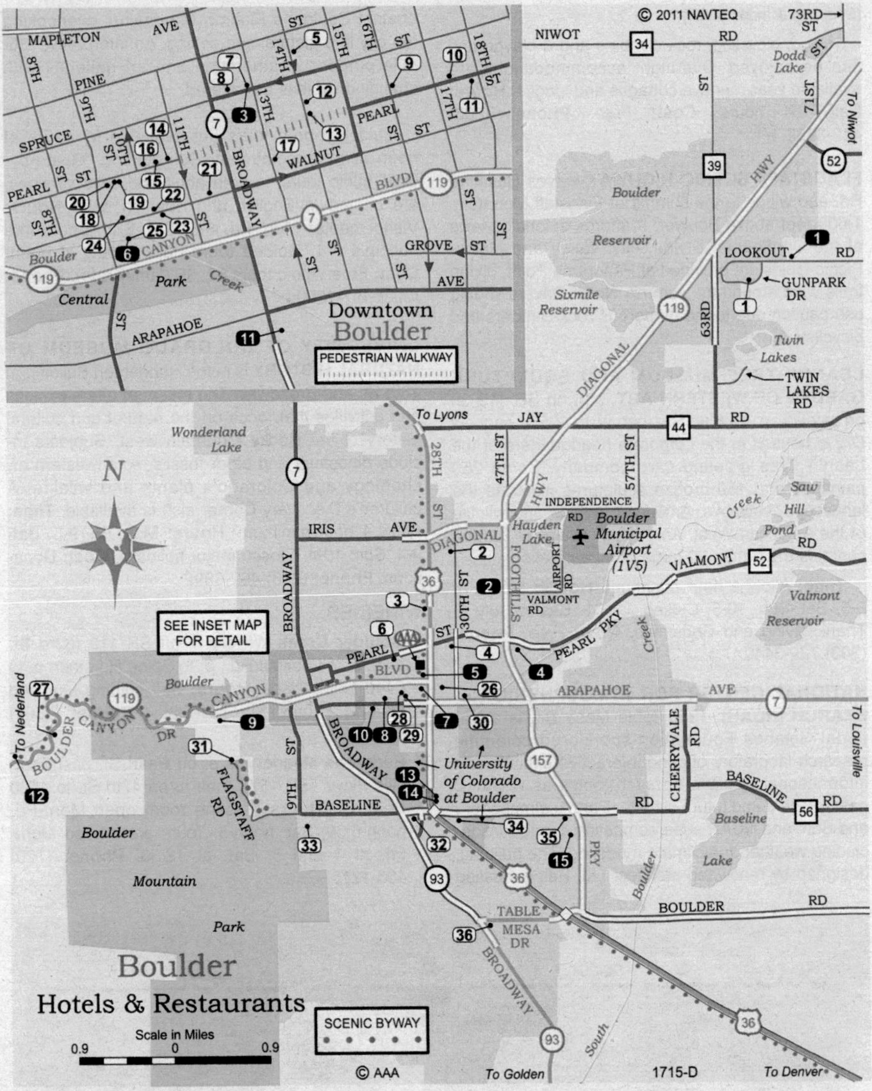

Downtown Boulder

PEDESTRIAN WALKWAY

SEE INSET MAP FOR DETAIL

MAPLETON AVE · PINE · SPRUCE · PEARL ST · WALNUT · CANYON · BLVD · GROVE ST · AVE · ARAPAHOE · BROADWAY · 8TH · 9TH · 10TH ST · 11TH · 13TH · 14TH · 15TH · 16TH · 17TH · 18TH · Central Park · Boulder Creek

NIWOT RD · 73RD ST · Dodd Lake · 71ST ST · To Niwot · Boulder Reservoir · LOOKOUT RD · GUNPARK DR · Sixmile Reservoir · 63RD · Twin Lakes · TWIN LAKES RD · DIAGONAL HWY · To Lyons · JAY RD · Wonderland Lake · 28TH ST · 47TH ST · 57TH ST · INDEPENDENCE RD · Boulder Municipal Airport (1V5) · Hayden Lake · FOOTHILLS · AIRPORT RD · Saw Hill Pond · Creek · VALMONT RD · Valmont Reservoir · IRIS AVE · DIAGONAL · 30TH ST · PEARL PKY · PEARL ST · ARAPAHOE AVE · CHERRYVALE RD · To Louisville · To Nederland · BOULDER CANYON DR · FLAGSTAFF RD · 9TH ST · BASELINE RD · University of Colorado at Boulder · Baseline Lake · Boulder Mountain Park · TABLE MESA DR · BROADWAY · South Boulder Creek · BOULDER RD · To Golden · To Denver

Boulder

Hotels & Restaurants

Scale in Miles

0.9 0 0.9

SCENIC BYWAY

© 2011 NAVTEQ

© AAA

1715-D

Boulder

This index helps you "spot" where approved hotels and restaurants are located on the corresponding detailed maps. Hotel daily rate range is for comparison only and shows the property's high season. Restaurant rate range is a combination of lunch and/or dinner. Turn to the listing page for more detailed rate information and consult display ads for special promotions.

BOULDER

Map Page	Hotels	Diamond Rated	High Season	Page
1 p. 60	Lookout Inn Guesthouse & Suites	♦♦	$104-$134	63
2 p. 60	Residence Inn by Marriott	♦♦♦	$119-$309	64
3 p. 60	**Hotel Boulderado**	♦♦♦	$194-$414 SAVE	63
4 p. 60	**Courtyard by Marriott-Boulder**	♦♦♦	$109-$260 SAVE	63
5 p. 60	**Best Western Golden Buff Lodge**	♦♦	$84-$134 SAVE	62
6 p. 60	**St Julien Hotel & Spa**	♦♦♦♦	$249-$479 SAVE	64
7 p. 60	Boulder Marriott	♦♦♦	$175-$370	62
8 p. 60	The Briar Rose Bed & Breakfast	♦♦♦	Rates not provided	63
9 p. 60	**Foot of The Mountain Motel**	♦	$90 SAVE	63
10 p. 60	**Quality Inn & Suites Boulder Creek**	♦♦♦	$120-$170 SAVE	63
11 p. 60	**Boulder University Inn**	♦♦	$89-$179 SAVE	63
12 p. 60	Alps Boulder Canyon Inn	♦♦♦	$169-$279	62
13 p. 60	**Boulder Outlook Hotel & Suites**	♦♦	$79-$159 SAVE	62
14 p. 60	**Best Western Plus Boulder Inn**	♦♦♦	$110-$190 SAVE	62
15 p. 60	Homewood Suites by Hilton	♦♦♦	$189-$229	63

Map Page	Restaurants	Diamond Rated	Cuisine	Meal Range	Page
1 p. 60	Gunbarrel Deli	♦	Deli	$5-$9	65
2 p. 60	Boulder Cork	♦♦♦	American	$9-$35	64
3 p. 60	Chez Thuy	♦♦	Vietnamese	$8-$24	65
4 p. 60	Ras Kassa's Ethiopian Restaurant	♦♦	Ethiopian	$10-$16	66
5 p. 60	Lucile's Creole Cafe	♦♦	Creole	$6-$12	66
6 p. 60	John's	♦♦♦	Continental	$21-$42	65
7 p. 60	Q's	♦♦♦	American	$8-$27	66
8 p. 60	Sushi Zanmai	♦♦	Sushi	$15-$25	67
9 p. 60	Leaf Vegetarian Restaurant	♦♦♦	Vegetarian	$8-$16	66
10 p. 60	L'Atelier	♦♦♦	French	$10-$29	66
11 p. 60	Frasca	♦♦♦♦	Regional Italian	$28-$38	65
12 p. 60	Himalayas Restaurant	♦♦	Indian	$10-$17	65
13 p. 60	The Cheesecake Factory	♦♦♦	American	$9-$30	65
14 p. 60	The Kitchen	♦♦♦	Natural/Organic	$11-$28	65
15 p. 60	Salt	♦♦♦	Natural/Organic	$12-$26	66
16 p. 60	Pasta Jay's	♦♦	Italian	$8-$17	66
17 p. 60	Black Cat	♦♦♦	Natural/Organic	$22-$29	64
18 p. 60	West End Tavern	♦♦	American	$9-$24	67
19 p. 60	Centro Latin Kitchen & Refreshment Palace	♦♦♦	Latin American	$9-$20	64
20 p. 60	Jax Fish House	♦♦♦	Seafood	$12-$29	65

Map Page	Restaurants (cont'd)	Diamond Rated	Cuisine	Meal Range	Page
21 p. 60	Walnut Brewery	2 diamonds	American	$9-$22	67
22 p. 60	Brasserie Ten Ten	3 diamonds	French	$9-$29	64
23 p. 60	The Mediterranean	3 diamonds	American	$9-$27	66
24 p. 60	Boulder Chophouse & Tavern	3 diamonds	Steak	$10-$36	64
25 p. 60	Jill's	3 diamonds	American	$10-$25	65
26 p. 60	**Cantina Laredo**	2 diamonds	Mexican	$8-$20	64
27 p. 60	Red Lion Restaurant	3 diamonds	Regional American	$14-$36	66
28 p. 60	Naraya Thai & Sushi	2 diamonds	Thai	$8-$13	66
29 p. 60	Zolo Grill	3 diamonds	American	$8-$26	67
30 p. 60	Moe's Broadway Bagel	1 diamond	Deli	$3-$8	66
31 p. 60	**The Flagstaff House Restaurant**	4 diamonds	New American	$32-$68	65
32 p. 60	Taj Indian Cuisine	2 diamonds	Indian	$8-$17	67
33 p. 60	Chautauqua Dining Hall	2 diamonds	American	$12-$26	64
34 p. 60	Carelli's of Boulder	3 diamonds	Italian	$8-$32	64
35 p. 60	Namaste Nepal Restaurant	2 diamonds	Nepali	$10-$16	66
36 p. 60	Tandoori Grill	2 diamonds	Eastern Indian	$10-$20	67

ALPS BOULDER CANYON INN

Phone: (303)444-5445 12

Historic Bed & Breakfast

$169-$279 5/1-10/31
$159-$269 11/1-4/30

Address: 38619 Boulder Canyon Dr 80302 **Location:** Jct SR 93 (Broadway) and 119, 3.3 mi w on SR 119. **Facility:** All rooms in this restored 1870s log cabin inn have ceiling fans and fireplaces, and several rooms have a patio or porch. 12 units. 2 stories (no elevator), interior corridors. **Terms:** office hours 8 am-10 pm, check-in 4 pm, age restrictions may apply, 7 day cancellation notice-fee imposed. **Amenities:** high-speed Internet. **Activities:** fishing, hiking trails, jogging. *Fee:* bicycles, massage.

FEE / SOME UNITS

BEST WESTERN PLUS BOULDER INN

Phone: (303)449-3800 14

Hotel

$110-$190

AAA Benefit: Members save up to 20%, plus 10% bonus points with Best Western Rewards®.

Address: 770 28th St 80303 **Location:** US 36 (28th St) at Baseline Rd. Opposite University of Colorado. **Facility:** 98 units. 2 stories (no elevator), interior corridors. **Pool(s):** heated outdoor. **Activities:** sauna, whirlpool, bicycles. **Guest Services:** valet and coin laundry. **Free Special Amenities: full breakfast and high-speed Internet.**

SAVE BIZ / SOME UNITS FEE FEE

BEST WESTERN GOLDEN BUFF LODGE

Phone: (303)442-7450 5

Hotel

$84-$134

AAA Benefit: Members save up to 20%, plus 10% bonus points with Best Western Rewards®.

Address: 1725 28th St 80301 **Location:** US 36 (28th St) and SR 119; just s of AAA club. **Facility:** 112 units, some kitchens. 2 stories (no elevator), exterior corridors. **Amenities:** high-speed Internet. **Pool(s):** heated outdoor. **Activities:** saunas, whirlpool, putting green, exercise room. **Guest Services:** valet and coin laundry. **Free Special Amenities: local telephone calls and high-speed Internet.**

SAVE / SOME UNITS

BOULDER MARRIOTT **Phone:** (303)440-8877 7

Hotel

$175-$370

AAA Benefit: AAA hotel discounts of 5% or more.

Address: 2660 Canyon Blvd 80302 **Location:** US 36 (28th St), just w on Canyon Blvd, then s on 26th St. **Facility:** 157 units. 5 stories, interior corridors. **Terms:** check-in 4 pm. **Amenities:** high-speed Internet (fee), safes. **Pool(s):** heated indoor. **Activities:** whirlpool, exercise room. **Guest Services:** valet and coin laundry.

CALL BIZ / SOME UNITS

BOULDER OUTLOOK HOTEL & SUITES

Phone: (303)443-3322 13

Hotel

$79-$159 5/1-8/31
$79-$129 9/1-4/30

Address: 800 28th St 80303 **Location:** US 36 (28th St), exit Baseline Rd via Frontage Rd. Opposite University of Colorado. **Facility:** 162 units. 2 stories (no elevator), interior/exterior corridors. **Amenities:** safes (fee). **Pool(s):** heated indoor. **Activities:** saunas, whirlpool, bicycles, exercise room. *Fee:* game room, massage. **Guest Services:** valet and coin laundry. **Free Special Amenities: continental breakfast and high-speed Internet.**

SAVE 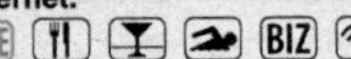 BIZ / SOME UNITS  

(See map & index p. 60.)

BOULDER UNIVERSITY INN

Phone: (303)417-1700 11

Motel

$89-$179 5/1-9/30
$79-$139 10/1-4/30

Address: 1632 Broadway 80302 **Location:** US 36 (28th St) exit Baseline Rd, 0.3 mi s, then 3 mi nw. **Facility:** 40 units. 2 stories (no elevator), exterior corridors. **Pool(s):** heated outdoor. **Guest Services:** valet and coin laundry. **Free Special Amenities: continental breakfast and high-speed Internet.**

SAVE ECO FEE BIZ / SOME UNITS FEE FEE FEE

THE BRIAR ROSE BED & BREAKFAST

Phone: 303/442-3007 8

Bed & Breakfast

Rates not provided

Address: 2151 Arapahoe Ave 80302 **Location:** 0.5 mi w of US 36 (28th St). Located in a residential area. **Facility:** Guest rooms feature original artwork and queen beds with fine linens and a Federbett comforter, a German-style down cover. 10 units. 2 stories (no elevator), interior/exterior corridors. **Terms:** office hours 7 am-9 pm. BIZ / SOME UNITS

COURTYARD BY MARRIOTT-BOULDER

Phone: (303)440-4700 4

Hotel

$109-$260

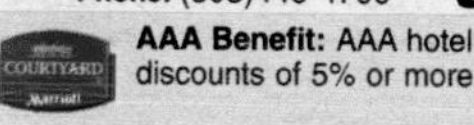

AAA Benefit: AAA hotel discounts of 5% or more.

Address: 4710 Pearl East Cir 80301 **Location:** Just e of SR 157 (Foothills Pkwy) exit Pearl St, just e to Pearl East Cir, just s, then just w. **Facility:** 149 units. 3 stories, interior corridors. **Amenities:** high-speed Internet. **Pool(s):** heated indoor. **Activities:** whirlpool, jogging, exercise room. **Guest Services:** valet and coin laundry. **Free Special Amenities: local telephone calls and high-speed Internet.**

SAVE ECO CALL BIZ

FOOT OF THE MOUNTAIN MOTEL

Phone: (303)442-5688 9

Motel

$90 5/1-10/31
$80 11/1-4/30

Address: 200 Arapahoe Ave 80302 **Location:** 1.8 mi w of US 36 (28th St). **Facility:** 20 units, some two bedrooms and kitchens. 1 story, exterior corridors. **Activities:** hiking trails, jogging. **Free Special Amenities: continental breakfast and high-speed Internet.**

SAVE / SOME UNITS FEE

HOLIDAY INN EXPRESS

Phone: (303)442-6600

Hotel

$99-$199

Address: 4777 N Broadway 80304 **Location:** 3 mi n of Pearl Street Pedestrian Mall; jct US 36 (28th St), 0.3 mi s. **Facility:** 106 units. 3 stories, interior corridors. **Terms:** cancellation fee imposed. **Amenities:** video games (fee). **Pool(s):** heated outdoor. **Activities:** whirlpool, exercise room. **Guest Services:** valet and coin laundry. **Free Special Amenities: expanded continental breakfast and high-speed Internet.**

SAVE BIZ FEE / SOME UNITS FEE

HOMEWOOD SUITES BY HILTON

Phone: (303)499-9922 15

Extended Stay Hotel

$189-$229 5/1-10/31
$159-$189 11/1-4/30

AAA Benefit:
Contemporary luxury at a special Member rate.

Address: 4950 Baseline Rd 80303 **Location:** 1.2 mi e of US 36 (28th St); jct SR 157 (Foothills Pkwy), just w; entry off Baseline Rd. Located behind Meadows Shopping Center. **Facility:** 112 efficiencies, some two bedrooms. 2 stories, interior/exterior corridors. **Terms:** 1-7 night minimum stay, cancellation fee imposed. **Amenities:** video games (fee), high-speed Internet. **Pool(s):** heated outdoor. **Activities:** whirlpool, basketball, exercise room. **Guest Services:** valet and coin laundry, area transportation-within 10 mi.

BIZ FEE / SOME UNITS FEE

HOTEL BOULDERADO **Phone:** (303)442-4344 3

Classic Historic Hotel

$194-$414 1/1-4/30
$189-$399 5/1-12/31

Address: 2115 13th St 80302 **Location:** At 13th and Spruce sts, just n of Pearl Street Pedestrian Mall. **Facility:** In a historic downtown building furnished with antiques, the hotel has a Victorian feel. Some modern amenities, like flat-screen TVs, are offered. 160 units. 4-5 stories, interior corridors. **Parking:** valet only. **Terms:** check-in 4 pm, cancellation fee imposed. **Amenities:** video games (fee). *Some:* safes. **Dining:** 2 restaurants, also, Q's, see separate listing. **Activities:** *Fee:* massage. **Guest Services:** valet laundry. **Free Special Amenities: local telephone calls and high-speed Internet.**

SAVE BIZ FEE / SOME UNITS

LOOKOUT INN GUESTHOUSE & SUITES

Phone: (303)530-1513 1

Hotel

$104-$134

Address: 6901 Lookout Rd 80301 **Location:** SR 119 exit 63rd St, just s, 0.7 mi e on Lookout Rd, then just n on Idylwild Tr. **Facility:** 13 units. 1-2 stories, exterior corridors. **Terms:** office hours 8 am-9 pm, 2 night minimum stay, 3 day cancellation notice-fee imposed. **Amenities:** high-speed Internet. **Activities:** hiking trails. **Guest Services:** coin laundry. BIZ

QUALITY INN & SUITES BOULDER CREEK

Phone: (303)449-7550 10

Hotel

$120-$170

Address: 2020 Arapahoe Ave 80302 **Location:** US 36 (28th St), 0.5 mi w. **Facility:** 49 units. 1-2 stories (no elevator), interior/exterior corridors. **Terms:** cancellation fee imposed. **Amenities:** high-speed Internet. **Pool(s):** heated indoor. **Activities:** sauna, whirlpool, exercise room. **Guest Services:** valet and coin laundry. **Free Special Amenities: full breakfast and high-speed Internet.**

SAVE BIZ / SOME UNITS FEE

(See map & index p. 60.)

RESIDENCE INN BY MARRIOTT
Phone: (303)449-5545 2

Extended Stay Hotel
$119-$309

AAA Benefit:
AAA hotel discounts of 5% or more.

Address: 3030 Center Green Dr 80301 **Location:** 0.5 mi e of US 36 (28th St), e on Valmont Rd; from Foothills Pkwy, just w on Valmont Rd. **Facility:** 128 units, some efficiencies and kitchens. 2 stories (no elevator), exterior corridors. **Amenities:** high-speed Internet. **Pool(s):** heated outdoor. **Activities:** whirlpool, sports court, exercise room. **Guest Services:** valet and coin laundry.

ECO BIZ / SOME UNITS FEE

ST JULIEN HOTEL & SPA **Phone:** (720)406-9696 6

Address: 900 Walnut St 80302 **Location:** Jct 9th and Walnut sts; downtown. **Facility:** Although space is a little tight, the guest rooms offer luxurious appointments and many amenities. The bathrooms are more spacious. 201 units. 4 stories, interior corridors. **Parking:** on-site (fee) and valet. **Terms:** cancellation fee imposed. **Amenities:** high-speed Internet, safes, honor bars. **Dining:** Jill's, see separate listing, entertainment. **Pool(s):** heated indoor. **Activities:** saunas, whirlpool, steamrooms, bicycle trails, hiking trails, jogging, exercise room, spa. **Guest Services:** valet laundry, area transportation-within 5 mi. Affiliated with A Preferred Hotel.

BIZ FEE

WHERE TO EAT

BLACK CAT **Phone:** 303/444-5500 17

Natural/Organic
$22-$29

AAA Inspector Notes: The highlight of this cozy restaurant is the innovative cuisine of chef/owner Eric Skokan. The menu changes based on what is available from the restaurant's organic farm, located just northwest of town. Fresh ingredients, Skokan's inspired dishes and an enthusiastic, knowledgeable staff make for an unforgettable meal. Sample dishes include roasted beet salad, duck confit and tagine of lamb. **Bar:** full bar. **Reservations:** suggested. **Address:** 1964 13th St 80302 **Location:** Just s of Pearl Street Pedestrian Mall. **Parking:** street only. D

BOULDER CHOPHOUSE & TAVERN
Phone: 303/443-1188 24

Steak
$10-$36

AAA Inspector Notes: This popular eatery offers various steaks, seafood and other meats, as well as sides and appetizers; tavern fare is served until midnight. The main dining room offers subdued lighting and interesting historic photos of Boulder. Patio seating also is available. **Bar:** full bar. **Reservations:** suggested. **Address:** 921 Walnut St 80302 **Location:** Just s of Pearl Street Pedestrian Mall; adjacent to Merrill Lynch; near downtown area. **Parking:** street only. D LATE CALL

BOULDER CORK **Phone:** 303/443-9505 2

American
$9-$35

AAA Inspector Notes: A favorite spot for delicious steaks since 1969, the restaurant presents a Southwestern menu that also features prime rib, seafood, salad, sandwiches, artichokes and lighter fare. Patio dining is a nice seasonal option. **Bar:** full bar. **Reservations:** suggested. **Address:** 3295 30th St 80301 **Location:** US 36 (28th St) exit SR 157 (Foothills Pkwy) to Valmont Rd, 0.4 mi w, then 0.3 mi n. L D

BRASSERIE TEN TEN **Phone:** 303/998-1010 22

French
$9-$29

AAA Inspector Notes: Offering French-based cuisine, this restaurant has a casual bistro feel. I loved the brique poulet served in beurre blanc sauce with Kennebec frites. The sauce was buttery but not overwhelmingly rich. The frites were thin and savory. Portions are large. For dessert, I had the mocha pot de crème. The macaroons were dense and chewy. The happy hour menu has reasonably priced small plates, allowing patrons to sample a variety of items in one sitting. **Bar:** full bar. **Address:** 1011 Walnut St 80302 **Location:** Between 9th and 11th sts. **Parking:** street only. L D

CANTINA LAREDO **Phone:** 303/444-2260 26

Mexican
$8-$20

AAA Inspector Notes: Modern yet relaxed, this restaurant features creative Mexican fare. A great starter of top-shelf guacamole, which is prepared tableside, primes the palate for an entree of enchiladas, tacos, fajitas and chiles rellenos. **Bar:** full bar. **Address:** 1680 29th St 80301 **Location:** Just n of Arapahoe Ave. L D

Gourmet Mexican food, fresh-squeezed lime margaritas

CARELLI'S OF BOULDER **Phone:** 303/938-9300 34

Italian
$8-$32

AAA Inspector Notes: The centerpiece of this inviting dining room is a large fireplace that makes you feel at home and comfortable. The salmon carpaccio is a delicious appetizer. For the main course, try the carelli bianco penne pasta with fresh vegetables and chicken breast. **Bar:** full bar. **Reservations:** suggested. **Address:** 645 30th St 80303 **Location:** Jct Baseline Rd (SR 93); in Williams Village Shopping Center. L D

CENTRO LATIN KITCHEN & REFRESHMENT PALACE
Phone: 303/442-7771 19

Latin American
$9-$20

AAA Inspector Notes: The lively atmosphere and friendly staff draw locals and visitors in droves, so making reservations at dinner would be wise. The menu features a variety of Mexican-style dishes including tacos, carne asada and chicken enchiladas as well as dishes from other Latin American countries, such as white sea bass ceviche verde, lobster arepas and baked clams chimichurri. The menu changes seasonally, but if it's available, the dulce de leche flan with grapefruit is delicious. **Bar:** full bar. **Address:** 950 Pearl St 80302 **Location:** West end of Pearl Street Pedestrian Mall. **Parking:** street only.

L D CALL

CHAUTAUQUA DINING HALL
Phone: 303/440-3776 33

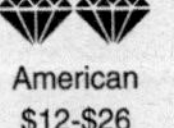

American
$12-$26

AAA Inspector Notes: Built in 1898, the historic restaurant is part of one of the few surviving Chautauqua meeting places, which were first instituted in the late 19th century as a way to educate communities through seasonal lectures, plays and other forms of entertainment. Although the restaurant recalls a time in the past, the menu reflects modern tastes by offering hamburgers, sandwiches, pasta and comfort food. **Bar:** full bar. **Address:** 900 Baseline Rd 80302 **Location:** US 36 (28th St) exit Baseline Rd, 1.2 mi w. B L D

(See map & index p. 60.)

THE CHEESECAKE FACTORY

Phone: 303/546-0222 (13)

American

$9-$30

AAA Inspector Notes: A display case of mouthwatering cheesecakes is the first thing visitors see as they walk through the door. The extensive menu incorporates many types of cuisine, including Asian, Italian, Greek and Spanish. **Bar:** full bar. **Address:** 1401 Pearl St 80302 **Location:** Corner of 14th St and Pearl Street Pedestrian Mall. **Parking:** on-site (fee). L D CALL M

CHEZ THUY

Phone: 303/442-1700 (3)

Vietnamese

$8-$24

AAA Inspector Notes: Examples of this popular restaurant's traditional cuisine include grilled appetizers, a nice noodle lamb dish, combination rice-noodle bowls and vegetarian dishes. Couples and professionals like this place. **Bar:** full bar. **Address:** 2655 28th St 80301 **Location:** US 36 (28th St), 0.4 mi n of Walnut St.

L D

THE FLAGSTAFF HOUSE RESTAURANT

Phone: 303/442-4640 (31)

New American

$32-$68

AAA Inspector Notes: You'll enjoy fine dining and marvelous views at this mountainside restaurant offering an extraordinary wine list, ever-changing New American cuisine, wild game, fresh fish and vegetarian selections, a tasting menu and a terrace. Family-owned and operated since 1971, this reputable establishment has hosted the royal family of Japan, Paul Bocuse and other prominent chefs. **Bar:** full bar. **Reservations:** suggested. **Address:** 1138 Flagstaff Rd 80302 **Location:** US 36 (28th St), 2.5 mi w on Baseline Rd. **Parking:** valet only. D

FRASCA

Phone: 303/442-6966 (11)

Regional Italian

$28-$38

AAA Inspector Notes: On Monday, a prix fixe wine-tasting menu (with optional wines) is the only option, but during the rest of the week, a seasonal menu is set up to enable patrons to sample four small-portioned courses at a discounted price (although they may order as few or as many as they choose). The food is influenced by Italy's Friuli-Venezia Giulia region, where a neighborhood gathering place for people to eat and socialize is traditionally called a "frasca" and the entrance is marked with a branch. **Bar:** full bar. **Reservations:** suggested. **Address:** 1738 Pearl St 80302 **Location:** Just w of jct 18th St; just e of Pearl Street Pedestrian Mall; downtown. **Parking:** on-site and street. D

THE GREENBRIAR INN

Phone: 303/440-7979

American

$18-$39

AAA Inspector Notes: Nestled in the foothills, the well-established restaurant lures patrons for fine dining in an antique Colorado setting. Dark woodwork, ceramic and copper chandeliers, a huge moose head over the fireplace and candle lamps on the tables contribute to an intimate atmosphere. Friendly, capable servers prepare Caesar salad tableside. Other favorites include Colorado lamb, beef, fowl and seafood. **Bar:** full bar. **Reservations:** suggested. **Address:** 8735 N Foothills Hwy 80302 **Location:** N of town on US 36 (28th St), west side of highway. **Historic** D

GUNBARREL DELI

Phone: 303/530-5595 (1)

Deli

$5-$9

AAA Inspector Notes: This quick-serve eatery provides a fast food fix while using fresh ingredients, not processed food. This is a great place for soup, sandwiches, salads, coffee and cookies. **Address:** 6545 Gun Park Dr, #280 80301 **Location:** Jct Diagonal Hwy and 63rd St, just s to Lookout Rd, then w; jct Spine and Lookout rds; in Gunbarrel Square. B L D

HIMALAYAS RESTAURANT

Phone: 303/442-3230 (12)

Indian

$10-$17

AAA Inspector Notes: The varied cuisine at this restaurant features Himalayan, Tibetan, and Nepalese dishes, with several vegetarian, lamb, tandoori chicken and seafood entrees, and baked breads offered. Service is friendly and casual the decor is tasteful and pleasing. Daily luncheon buffet. **Bar:** beer & wine. **Address:** 2010 14th St 80302 **Location:** Just off Pearl Street Pedestrian Mall; opposite courthouse; adjacent to Boulder Theater. **Parking:** street only. L D

JAX FISH HOUSE

Phone: 303/444-1811 (20)

Seafood

$12-$29

AAA Inspector Notes: This snug and very popular people-watching spot features delicious fresh seafood, an oyster bar, great microbrews and excellent martinis. The restaurant looks like a New England fish house with touches of New Orleans. The serving staff is very friendly. **Bar:** full bar. **Address:** 928 Pearl St 80302 **Location:** West end of Pearl Street Pedestrian Mall. **Parking:** street only. D

JILL'S

Phone: 720/406-7399 (25)

American

$10-$25

AAA Inspector Notes: Especially popular on the weekends, this casual eatery offers a combination of standard comfort food and more creative options. Burgers, pasta dishes and steaks share space with lamb kebabs, potato manicotti with wild mushrooms, and crispy duck breast and leg confit. Artful décor and friendly service add to the dining experience. **Bar:** full bar. **Reservations:** suggested. **Address:** 900 Walnut St 80302 **Location:** Jct 9th and Walnut sts; downtown; in St Julien Hotel & Spa. **Parking:** on-site (fee) and valet.

B L D

JOHN'S

Phone: 303/444-5232 (6)

Continental

$21-$42

AAA Inspector Notes: After taking over this local favorite from the original owner in 2004, the brother-and-sister team of chef Corey Buck and manager Ashley Maxwell continues to earn accolades. Their approach focuses on innovative cuisine mixed with relaxed, knowledgeable and friendly service. Chef Buck creates seasonal menus, purchases ingredients from local farms and purveyors, and presents a dining experience comparable to that of higher rated restaurants. **Bar:** full bar. **Address:** 2328 Pearl St 80301 **Location:** Jct US 36 (28th St), just w. **Parking:** street only. D

THE KITCHEN

Phone: 303/544-5973 (14)

Natural/Organic

$11-$28

AAA Inspector Notes: Well-suited to the vast list of wines, beers and cocktails, the frequently changing menu of pasta, salmon, pork, lamb, beef, vegetarian and other dishes reflects the seasonal availability of ingredients. Local purveyors provide many organic ingredients. Among the decadent desserts are a lemon tart and sticky toffee pudding. Original flooring and exposed brick walls define the dining room, where the distinctive décor blends simplicity with elegance. **Bar:** full bar. **Address:** 1039 Pearl St 80302 **Location:** Between 10th and 11th sts; downtown. **Parking:** street only. L D LATE

(See map & index p. 60.)

L'ATELIER Phone: 303/442-7233 (10)

French
$10-$29

AAA Inspector Notes: The cozy French brasserie, decorated with custom displays of French figurines, prepares excellent, gorgeously presented food. Service is spotty when the dining room is busy, which is often at this extremely popular spot. At lunchtime, the tuna carpaccio with house-made crackers is a delicious treat. The sophisticated dinner menu includes duck, rack of lamb, filet mignon and lobster. It's difficult to choose from the extensive list of decadent desserts. **Bar:** full bar. **Reservations:** suggested. **Address:** 1739 Pearl St 80302 **Location:** Between 17th and 18th sts. **Parking:** street only. L D

LEAF VEGETARIAN RESTAURANT Phone: 303/442-1485 (9)

Vegetarian
$8-$16

AAA Inspector Notes: This eatery does more than serve vegetables, it honors them. The complex flavors and visual appeal of the sweet onion tart, which also includes sun-dried tomatoes, chevre, red peppers and a basil-walnut pesto, made my day. I also had the opportunity to sample the refreshing chilled apple and fennel soup. If it sounds strange, it will probably taste great. Entrées include huevos rancheros, Jamaican jerk tempeh, vegan Alfredo and flatbread pizza. Martinis and teas are on the beverage menu. **Bar:** full bar. **Address:** 2010 16th St 80302 **Location:** Just n of jct Pearl St. **Parking:** street only. L D

LUCILE'S CREOLE CAFE Phone: 303/442-4743 (5)

Creole
$6-$12

AAA Inspector Notes: Friendly folks serve up large portions of Cajun-influenced home-style fare at this eatery. The beignets come hot and fresh and covered in powdered sugar. **Address:** 2124 14th St 80302 **Location:** 1 blk n of Pearl Street Pedestrian Mall. **Parking:** street only. B L

THE MEDITERRANEAN Phone: 303/444-5335 (23)

American
$9-$27

AAA Inspector Notes: This place is fun and noisy, so diners may experience a wait. College students mix with yuppies while the chefs and cooks work in the open kitchen. Hot and cold tapas, pizza and pasta are among the many offerings. I enjoyed the tender calamari, which had a light, crispy batter and came with a flavorful tomato sauce. The watermelon gazpacho had a light, refreshing flavor with just a slight sweetness and a little kick of onion. The mussels are wood-fire roasted, adding a smoky flavor. **Bar:** full bar. **Address:** 1002 Walnut St 80302 **Location:** Between 9th and 10th sts. **Parking:** street only. L D

MOE'S BROADWAY BAGEL Phone: 303/442-4427 (30)

Deli
$3-$8

AAA Inspector Notes: Like their outlet on North Broadway, this location is popular with the locals but closer to nearby lodgings. It offers a wide variety of bagels and juices, as well as other breakfast items, coffee, soup and sandwiches. **Address:** 3075 Arapahoe Ave 80303 **Location:** Just e of jct 30th St and Arapahoe Ave; in Sunrise Center. B L

NAMASTE NEPAL RESTAURANT Phone: 303/499-2234 (35)

Nepali
$10-$16

AAA Inspector Notes: The menu features interesting herb combinations and sauces, including Tibetan combination soup and curry chicken with basmati rice. **Bar:** full bar. **Address:** 4800 Baseline Rd 80303 **Location:** 0.3 mi e of US 36 (28th St); SR 157 (Foothills Pkwy) exit Baseline Rd (SR 93), just w; in Meadows Shopping Center. L D

NARAYA THAI & SUSHI Phone: 303/447-9718 (28)

Thai
$8-$13

AAA Inspector Notes: Popular with locals, this cozy restaurant with casual décor features a full Japanese and Thai menu. Offerings include chicken satay, pad thai, curry dishes, sushi, teriyaki and much more. Staff could be more attentive. **Bar:** full bar. **Reservations:** suggested, weekends. **Address:** 1575 Folsom St 80302 **Location:** Jct Arapahoe Ave and Folsom St. L D

PASTA JAY'S Phone: 303/444-5800 (16)

Italian
$8-$17

AAA Inspector Notes: Enjoying pizza and pasta here is a Boulder tradition. The dining rooms may be small, but the food flavors are big. Service is friendly, and people-watching is an event on the patio. Takeout is available. **Bar:** full bar. **Address:** 1001 Pearl St 80302 **Location:** On Pearl Street Pedestrian Mall. **Parking:** street only. L D

Q'S Phone: 303/442-4880 (7)

American
$8-$27

AAA Inspector Notes: Located on the main level of the hotel, this stylish Art Deco restaurant allows diners to watch the chef/proprietor as he creates his renowned, seasonal and artfully presented cuisine in an exhibition kitchen. Fresh fish, beef, fowl and vegetarian selections are available. **Bar:** full bar. **Reservations:** suggested. **Address:** 2115 13th St 80302 **Location:** At 13th and Spruce sts, just n of Pearl Street Pedestrian Mall; in Hotel Boulderado. **Parking:** valet and street only. **Historic** B L D

RAS KASSA'S ETHIOPIAN RESTAURANT Phone: 303/447-2919 (4)

Ethiopian
$10-$16

AAA Inspector Notes: Operating in the area for more than 20 years, the ethnic establishment remains a favorite for locals looking for something different. Diners sit at low tables and eat a variety of stews, vegetarian dishes, meats, chicken and salads with a spongy bread. Brunch is offered on Saturday and Sunday. **Bar:** full bar. **Address:** 2111 30th St, Unit E 80301 **Location:** SR 157 (Foothills Pkwy) exit Pearl St, w to 30th St, then just s. L D

RED LION RESTAURANT Phone: 303/442-9368 (27)

Regional American
$14-$36

AAA Inspector Notes: A country dining experience is the specialty of the house at this restaurant, which has been serving guests since 1915. Housed in a converted 1890 stone-and-frame home, the restaurant boasts a beautiful mountain setting. The menu features seafood, wild game specialties and German dishes. **Bar:** full bar. **Reservations:** suggested. **Address:** 38470 Boulder Canyon Hwy 119 80302 **Location:** 6.5 mi w of US 36 (28th St) via Canyon Blvd and SR 119. **Historic** D

SALT Phone: 303/444-7258 (15)

Natural/Organic
$12-$26

AAA Inspector Notes: I have to admit, the food, although fabulous, is not my favorite thing at this upscale eatery. I love the look and taste of the pre-Prohibition spirituals (i.e. cocktails). The option of having a "shorty" size allows me to sample a couple. There also are plenty of local craft beers and wines. The food menu changes seasonally and focuses on local, organic ingredients. The flavorful, innovative dishes have brought chef/owner Bradford Heap well-deserved local and national attention. **Bar:** full bar. **Address:** 1049 Pearl St 80302 **Location:** Between 10th and 11th sts; downtown. **Parking:** street only. L D

(See map & index p. 60.)

SUSHI ZANMAI **Phone:** 303/440-0733 (8)

Sushi
$15-$25

AAA Inspector Notes: A longtime Boulder favorite, this restaurant offers super sushi at a great downtown location; it can get a bit crowded and loud at times. **Bar:** full bar. **Reservations:** suggested, weekends. **Address:** 1221 Spruce St 80302 **Location:** Just n of Pearl Street Pedestrian Mall; 1 blk e of Broadway. **Parking:** street only. (L) (D)

TAJ INDIAN CUISINE **Phone:** 303/494-5216 (32)

Indian
$8-$17

AAA Inspector Notes: In a shopping plaza, the dining spot has a popular buffet and offers the usual favorites, such as mulligatawny soup, tandoori breads and chicken, lamb and taj thali. **Bar:** full bar. **Address:** 2630 Baseline Rd 80303 **Location:** Baseline Rd (SR 93) exit US 36 (28th St), just w; in Basemar Shopping Plaza, 2nd Floor. (L) (D)

TANDOORI GRILL **Phone:** 303/543-7339 (36)

Eastern Indian
$10-$20

AAA Inspector Notes: In a shopping center near the corner of Broadway and Table Mesa, this restaurant offers Indian cuisine on its full menu and on the popular daily buffet. **Bar:** full bar. **Address:** 619 S Broadway St 80305 **Location:** US 36 (28th St) exit Table Mesa Dr, 1 mi w; in Table Mesa Shopping Center. (L) (D)

WALNUT BREWERY **Phone:** 303/447-1345 (21)

American
$9-$22

AAA Inspector Notes: This upscale, trendy and very popular pub features tasty dishes and several homemade brews, some of which are part of the food recipes. Brunch is offered on Saturday and Sunday. Service is friendly and attentive. **Bar:** full bar. **Address:** 1123 Walnut St 80302 **Location:** Between 11th St and Broadway. (L) (D)

WEST END TAVERN **Phone:** 303/444-3535 (18)

American
$9-$24

AAA Inspector Notes: This popular local eatery offers rooftop dining and a great view of the Flatirons. Burgers, sandwiches, salads and Mexican fare are served in a casual atmosphere. **Bar:** full bar. **Address:** 926 Pearl St 80302 **Location:** On west end of Pearl Street Pedestrian Mall. **Parking:** street only. (L) (D)

ZOLO GRILL **Phone:** 303/449-0444 (29)

American
$8-$26

AAA Inspector Notes: Rob Rosser, this restaurant's popular chef, prepares imaginative and flavorful Southwestern cuisine that combines with a fun atmosphere to create a great place to dine. The restaurant also offers what may be the best guacamole in town, a variety of tequila drinks and patio dining. **Bar:** full bar. **Address:** 2525 Arapahoe Ave 80302 **Location:** Between 28th and Folsom sts; in Village Shopping Center. (L) (D)

BRECKENRIDGE (D-3) pop. 4,540, elev. 9,602'

• Hotels p. 68 • Restaurants p. 70

Breckenridge offers all the perks of a high-altitude environment and then some. With the winter months comes the thrill of snowboarding, downhill skiing, snowmobiling and dog-sledding. There also are more laid-back snow-related activities to indulge in, like snowshoeing and cross-country skiing; those ready to explore these pursuits on scenic trails can visit the Breckenridge Nordic Center, where the varied terrain satisfies beginners and experts alike. If gliding across the ice is more your style, hit Maggie Pond at the Village at Breckenridge for some quality outdoor skating.

When the summer months arrive, locals stash their cold-weather gear to bike the area's trail system or hike through meadows dotted with wildflowers. The Breckenridge Welcome Center provides visitors with information on trails suitable for hiking and mountain biking. For less-strenuous bicycle touring, a popular choice is the Blue River Bikeway, a 10-mile paved stretch between Breckenridge and Frisco—if you get tired, you can ride the bus back to "Breck." Fly-fishers cast their lines in the meandering Blue River year-round to hopefully snare some trout, and duffers hit the links at the Breckenridge Golf Club, a 27-hole course designed by Jack Nicklaus that's nestled in a valley.

This recreational paradise traces its roots to the gold rush, when prospectors panned gold from the Blue River in 1859. Some 250 historic structures reminiscent of the mining era are preserved in one of Colorado's largest National Historic Districts, and Breckenridge's charming Main Street houses galleries, shops, eateries and nightspots within these colorfully restored Victorians. Weary shoppers can hop on the free Breckenridge Trolley, which travels down the main drag and provides access to the ski slopes and other points throughout town.

For those inclined to learn more about the town's storied past, the Breckenridge Heritage Alliance, (800) 980-1859, conducts historic walking and mine tours; athletically oriented individuals also can take advantage of their guided ski and snowshoe excursions. If you prefer to do your sightseeing behind the wheel, catch Boreas Pass Road (FR 223) south of town, a route traveling along an old narrow-gauge railroad bed and cresting at 11,482 feet; you'll see stunning views of the Blue River Valley and an old railroad camp perched at the summit.

Breckenridge presents a medley of enticing events throughout the year. One of the most unique is the Budweiser International Snow Sculpture Championships in late January, when teams from throughout the globe create frosty works of art from massive 20-ton snow blocks. Plenty of activities are packed into 3 weeks during April at the Spring Massive Festival; outdoor concerts, competitions, family events, comedy shows and a beer festival are all part of the agenda. Late June to mid-August brings the sounds of classical music at the internationally acclaimed Breckenridge Music Festival, offering a variety of styles including chamber music, country and jazz.

Breckenridge Welcome Center: 203 S. Main St., P.O. Box 1909, Breckenridge, CO 80424. **Phone:** (877) 864-0868.

Self-guiding tours: Information about a walking tour through Breckenridge's historic district is available at the Breckenridge Welcome Center.

INSIDER INFO:
High Altitude Health

Temples throbbing, gasping for breath and nauseated, you barely notice the scudding clouds or the spectacular view.

You might be suffering from Acute Mountain Sickness (AMS). Usually striking at around 8,000 feet (2,450 m) in altitude, AMS is your body's way of coping with the reduced oxygen and humidity of high altitudes. Among the symptoms are headaches, shortness of breath, loss of appetite, insomnia and lethargy. Some people complain of temporary weight gain or swelling in the face, hands and feet.

You can reduce the effect of high altitude by being in top condition. If you smoke or suffer from heart or lung ailments, consult your physician before your trip. Certain drugs will intensify the symptoms. To avoid Acute Mountain Sickness, adjust to elevations slowly; a gradual ascent with a couple days of acclimatization is best if you have time. For example, if you are planning a trip to the Rocky Mountains of Colorado, you might want to spend the first night in a lower altitude city such as Denver as opposed to heading directly to an environment with extreme elevations.

On the way up, eat light, nutritious meals and stay hydrated by drinking a large amount of water, taking care to avoid caffeine, alcohol and salt. In addition, your doctor may be able to prescribe medication that can offset the effects of high-altitude.

If you develop AMS, you should stop ascending; you will recover in a few days. If the AMS is mild, a quick descent will end the suffering immediately.

Other high-altitude health problems include sunburn and hypothermia. Dress in layers to protect yourself from the intense sun and wide fluctuations in temperature.

Finally, after you lounge in the sauna or whirlpool bath at your lodgings, remember to stand up carefully, for the heat has relaxed your blood vessels and lowered your blood pressure.

BARNEY FORD HOUSE MUSEUM is at 111 E. Washington Ave. The museum depicts the life of Ford, a former slave that escaped via the Underground Railroad. His travels eventually led him to Colorado, where he became a civil rights pioneer and a successful restaurant and hotel owner. Exhibits focus on Ford and other African-Americans of the era; articles from the 1800s also are displayed. **Time:** Allow 30 minutes minimum. **Hours:** Tues.-Sun. 11-3, summer and winter seasons. Phone ahead to confirm schedule. **Cost:** $5. **Phone:** (970) 453-9767.

COUNTRY BOY MINE, off Wellington Rd. at 0542 French Gulch Rd., offers 45-minute guided underground tours of a late 1800s gold mine deeper than 1,000 feet, as well as mining exhibits and old buildings. Gold panning activities also are offered. Roaming miniature donkeys add to the mining camp environment.

Hard hats are provided. **Time:** Allow 1 hour minimum. **Hours:** Tours depart daily on the hour 10-4, mid-May through Labor Day; Mon.-Fri. 11, noon and 1, day after Labor Day-Oct. 31; Wed.-Sun. 11, noon and 1, day before Thanksgiving-Apr. 30. **Cost:** Fee $18.95; $12.95 (ages 4-12). Gold panning only $9.95. **Phone:** (970) 453-4405.

RECREATIONAL ACTIVITIES

Skiing

- **Breckenridge Resort** is at 1599C Summit County Rd. within the Arapaho and Roosevelt National Forests. Other activities are offered. **Hours:** Daily mid-Nov. to late Apr. (weather permitting). **Phone:** (970) 453-5000 or (800) 789-7669.

Snowmobiling

- **Good Times Adventure Tours and Dog Sledding** is 2.5 mi. n. on SR 9, e. at Breckenridge Golf Course, then 6.5 mi. to 6061 Tiger Rd. **Hours:** Daily 9-5, mid-Nov. to mid-Apr. **Phone:** (970) 453-7604 or (800) 477-0144.

White-water Rafting

- **Good Times Rafting** provides pick-up service at area hotels for transfer to rafting sites. **Hours:** Daily mid-May to mid-Sept. **Phone:** (970) 453-5559 or (800) 997-3448.

ALLAIRE TIMBERS INN **Phone:** 970/453-7530

Bed & Breakfast
$129-$290

Address: 9511 Hwy 9 80424 **Location:** 0.7 mi s of center to River Parks Rd; on west side of SR 9. **Facility:** The beautiful inn has wonderful common areas, including a sunroom and loft. Named for historic Colorado mountain passes, rooms are individually decorated and have log furnishings and handmade duvets. 10 units. 2 stories (no elevator), interior corridors. *Bath:* shower only. **Terms:** open 5/25-10/21 & 11/23-4/21, office hours 9 am-6 pm, check-in 4 pm, 3 night minimum stay, age restrictions may apply, 30 day cancellation notice-fee imposed. **Activities:** whirlpool. **Free Special Amenities: full breakfast and local telephone calls.**

BARN ON THE RIVER **Phone:** 970/453-2975

Bed & Breakfast
$169-$249 12/5-4/15
$139-$169 5/25-10/19

Address: 303B N Main St 80424 **Location:** On SR 9; between French and Watson sts. **Facility:** A timber-frame barn, this B&B has balconies overlooking the river. Known for its hospitality, the property has a small riverbank garden filled with wildflowers and a cozy sitting area with a library. 4 units. 2 stories (no elevator), interior corridors. *Bath:* shower only. **Terms:** open 5/25-10/19 & 12/5-4/15, office hours 8 am-8 pm, check-in 4 pm, 4 night minimum stay - seasonal, age restrictions may apply, 45 day cancellation notice-fee imposed. **Activities:** whirlpool. **Guest Services:** area transportation.

BEAVER RUN RESORT & CONFERENCE CENTER
Phone: (970)453-6000

Resort Hotel
$105-$585

Address: 620 Village Rd 80424 **Location:** 0.3 mi w of SR 9, on S Park Ave and Village Rd; at base of peak 9. **Facility:** The ski-in/ski-out resort next to the Peak 9 gondola has underground parking and condominium-style units, including a deluxe studio. All have a fan and humidifier, and most have a fireplace. 500 units, some two bedrooms, efficiencies and kitchens. 5-8 stories, interior corridors. **Terms:** check-in 4 pm, 1-7 night minimum stay - seasonal, 3 day cancellation notice-fee imposed. **Amenities:** video games (fee). **Dining:** 4 restaurants. **Pool(s):** heated outdoor, heated indoor/outdoor. **Activities:** sauna, whirlpools, steamroom, tennis court, basketball, exercise room. *Fee:* miniature golf, downhill skiing, game room, massage. **Guest Services:** valet and coin laundry, area transportation-within 5 mi. **Free Special Amenities: newspaper.**

SAVE FEE BIZ
FEE / SOME UNITS FEE

BRECK INN **Phone:** 970/547-9861

Motel
$89-$239

Address: 11078 Hwy 9 80424 **Location:** 0.8 mi n of center. **Facility:** 35 units, some kitchens. 2 stories (no elevator), interior corridors. **Terms:** office hours 7 am-7 pm, check-in 4 pm, 14 day cancellation notice-fee imposed. **Activities:** whirlpool. / SOME UNITS

DOUBLETREE BY HILTON BRECKENRIDGE
Phone: (970)547-5550

Hotel
$149-$299 11/9-4/30
$129-$219 5/1-11/8

AAA Benefit: Members save 5% or more everyday!

Address: 550 Village Rd 80424 **Location:** Jct Main St, just w on S Park Ave, then just sw. **Facility:** 208 units. 8 stories, interior corridors. **Parking:** on-site and valet. **Terms:** check-in 4 pm, 1-7 night minimum stay, cancellation fee imposed. **Pool(s):** heated indoor. **Activities:** saunas, whirlpools, hiking trails, exercise room. *Fee:* downhill skiing, game room, massage. **Guest Services:** valet laundry, area transportation-within 4 mi.

ECO BIZ FEE
/ SOME UNITS FEE

THE LODGE & SPA AT BRECKENRIDGE
Phone: (970)453-9300

Hotel
$129-$340 11/11-4/30
$79-$195 5/1-11/10

Address: 112 Overlook Dr 80424 **Location:** Jct Main St and Park Ave, just s to Boreas Pass Rd, 2.1 mi w. **Facility:** 47 units, some houses. 2 stories, interior/exterior corridors. **Terms:** check-in 4 pm, cancellation fee imposed. **Activities:** whirlpools. *Fee:* massage.

SAVE
/ SOME UNITS FEE

Nestled cliff side overlooking Breckenridge Ski Resort and the Rocky Mountains!

MOUNTAIN THUNDER LODGE **Phone:** 970/547-5650

Condominium
Rates not provided

Address: 50 Mountain Thunder Dr 80424 **Location:** Jct Main St, 0.5 mi w on Park Ave. **Facility:** This property offers upscale accommodations near the newest gondola. Guests walk to the gondola but ski down directly to their townhome or condominium building. 100 condominiums. 2-4 stories, interior/exterior corridors. **Terms:** check-in 4 pm. **Amenities:** high-speed Internet (fee), safes. **Pool(s):** heated outdoor. **Activities:** whirlpools, hiking trails, exercise room. **Guest Services:** complimentary and valet laundry, area transportation-within 3 mi.

FEE

RESORTQUEST MAIN STREET STATION
Phone: 970/453-4000

Condominium
Rates not provided

Address: 505 S Main St 80424 **Location:** 0.4 mi s of center. **Facility:** The new property has large units with scenic views and fireplaces. Shops, restaurants and ski lifts are within walking distance. Heated underground parking, and ski and bicycle storage are available. 50 condominiums. 4-5 stories, interior corridors. **Terms:** check-in 4 pm. **Amenities:** high-speed Internet. **Dining:** Quandary Grille, see separate listing. **Pool(s):** heated outdoor. **Activities:** whirlpools, steamrooms, exercise room, spa. *Fee:* downhill skiing. **Guest Services:** complimentary and valet laundry, area transportation-within 4 mi.

RESORTQUEST RIVER MOUNTAIN LODGE
Phone: 970/453-4711

Condominium
Rates not provided

Address: 100 S Park Ave 80424 **Location:** Jct Main St and Ski Hill Rd, just w, then just s. Located near downtown area. **Facility:** 100 condominiums. 3-4 stories, interior corridors. **Terms:** check-in 4 pm. **Amenities:** *Some:* high-speed Internet. **Pool(s):** heated outdoor. **Activities:** sauna, whirlpools, steamroom, hiking trails, jogging, exercise room. **Guest Services:** area transportation-within 3 mi.

BIZ
/ SOME UNITS

GOLD POINT RESORT **Phone:** 970/453-1910

fyi Not evaluated. **Address:** 53 View Ln 80424 **Location:** Jct SR 9 and Boreas Pass Rd, 1.9 mi se, then 1:1 mi e on Baldy Rd. Facilities, services, and decor characterize a mid-scale property.

HIGHLAND GREENS TOWNHOMES
Phone: 970/468-7851

fyi Not evaluated. **Address:** 34 Highfield Tr 80424. Facilities, services, and decor characterize a mid-scale property.

THE LODGE AT HIGHLAND GREENS
Phone: 970/468-7851

fyi Not evaluated. **Address:** 34 Highfield Tr 80424. Facilities, services, and decor characterize a mid-scale property.

MARRIOTT'S MOUNTAIN VALLEY LODGE
Phone: 970/453-8500

fyi

AAA Benefit: AAA hotel discounts of 5% or more.

Not evaluated. **Address:** 655 Columbine Rd 80424 **Location:** 0.5 mi s on SR 9, just w on Broken Lance Dr, then just n. Facilities, services, and decor characterize a mid-scale property.

TANNHAUSER AT BRECKENRIDGE
Phone: 970/453-2136

fyi Not evaluated. **Address:** 420 S Main St 80424 **Location:** Just s of Jefferson Ave and S Main St. Facilities, services, and decor characterize an economy property.

VILLAGE AT BRECKENRIDGE **Phone:** 970/453-2000

fyi Not evaluated. **Address:** 535 S Park Ave 80424 **Location:** 0.3 mi w of Main St. Facilities, services, and decor characterize a mid-scale property.

VILLAGE HOTEL **Phone:** 970/453-2000

fyi Not evaluated. **Address:** 535 S Park Ave 80424 **Location:** 0.3 mi w of Main St. Facilities, services, and decor characterize a mid-scale property.

WHERE TO EAT

AMAZING GRACE NATURAL EATERY
Phone: 970/453-1445

Natural/Organic
$9-$10

AAA Inspector Notes: Heated by an antique woodstove, this adorable historic cabin is an old-fashioned gathering place to enjoy a hearty breakfast, spicy tofu salad, hummus and natural turkey, hearty winter soups, blue chip nachos, turkey veggie and turkey berry sandwiches. Scones, biscuits, muffins and oversize vegan chocolate chip cookies are made fresh daily. Gluten and dairy-free options are available. Look for the yellow cabin on the corner. **Bar:** beer & wine. **Address:** 213 Lincoln Ave 80424 **Location:** Just e of Main St; corner of Lincoln Ave and French St; downtown. **Parking:** street only.

B L AC

BLUE RIVER BISTRO **Phone:** 970/453-6974

American
$9-$29

AAA Inspector Notes: This bistro sustains a lively, energetic atmosphere in part due to the live entertainment. On this creekside eatery's menu is a wide selection of appetizers, salads, pasta and seafood dishes, including Kobe beef and roasted pulled pork sliders, classic escargot, grilled New York strip steak finished with tarragon and shallot compound butter, shellfish cioppino, seafood primavera and tortellini carbonara. Servers are friendly, casual and well informed. Happy hour happens twice a day. **Bar:** full bar. **Address:** 305 N Main St 80424 **Location:** Just n of center. **Parking:** street only. L D AC

BRECKENRIDGE BREWERY & PUB
Phone: 970/453-1550

American
$9-$23

AAA Inspector Notes: This place has an airy, inviting and fun atmosphere where guests can watch the brewing process then sample a handcrafted ale. The menu includes soups and salads, fish and chips, pork spare ribs and country-fried steak. Sandwiches include barbecued pulled pork, hot turkey and Swiss, and steak and cheese. Burgers, grilled chicken sandwiches and Boca burgers can be ordered in such styles as Las Vegas, alpine or Tijuana. Patio dining is offered in summer, and entertainment is occasionally provided. **Bar:** full bar. **Address:** 600 S Main St 80424 **Location:** On SR 9, south end of town; corner of S Main and Ridge sts. L D AC

BRIAR ROSE CHOPHOUSE & SALOON
Phone: 970/453-9948

Steak
$19-$44

AAA Inspector Notes: Visiting this elegant downtown landmark is a must. Menu items include a creatively presented shrimp cocktail with horseradish panna cotta, escargot with parsley-garlic butter, a popular roasted beet and arugula salad with goat cheese crisps, Australian Wagyu beef, Kurobuta heirloom double-cut pork chops, and roasted duck with cranberry orange demi-glace. Desserts include berries topped with Grand Marnier cream, Key lime pie and a chocolate terrine with pistachio crème anglaise. **Bar:** full bar. **Reservations:** suggested. **Address:** 109 E Lincoln Ave 80424 **Location:** Just e of Main St and Lincoln Ave; downtown. D

THE DREDGE RESTAURANT & BAR
Phone: 970/453-4877

American
$14-$40

AAA Inspector Notes: Patrons must walk across a small bridge to reach the floating "dredge," which is right in the heart of town. Menu items include interesting salads, hearty steaks, and specialties such as pork loin, pan-seared ahi tuna and ruby red trout. **Bar:** full bar. **Address:** 180 W Jefferson Ave 80424 **Location:** Jct S Main St and W Jefferson Ave, just w; on Blue River. **Parking:** street only.

D AC

EMBER **Phone:** 970/547-9595

International
$16-$29

AAA Inspector Notes: Globally inspired cuisine is served in a Victorian home with a contemporary style. Seasonal menu items may include pulled Wagyu beef resting on noodle cakes with watermelon radish; veal roulade with lemon risotto and apricot chutney resting in a chocolate chai coulis; and lentil-crusted scallops. Delicious desserts may include a pecan tamale with strawberry mango salsa, Kahlua and banana cream or a walnut brie cheesecake with cherry caramel surrounded by grapefruit pearls and maple foam. **Bar:** full bar. **Reservations:** suggested. **Address:** 106 E Adams Ave 80424 **Location:** Just s of Main St. **Parking:** street only. D AC

HEARTHSTONE RESTAURANT **Phone:** 970/453-1148

Regional American
$18-$36

AAA Inspector Notes: Contemporary and regional dishes are served in a century-old Victorian home with barn-wood walls and a seasonal patio. Menu items such as the smoked trout platter, tilapia pepita and granola-crusted elk chop are complemented by an excellent wine list. The waitstaff is capable and personable. **Bar:** full bar. **Reservations:** suggested. **Address:** 130 S Ridge St 80424 **Location:** Just e of Main St; at Washington and Ridge sts; in historic town center. **Parking:** street only. **Historic**

D CALL M AC

KENOSHA STEAKHOUSE **Phone:** 970/453-7313

Steak
$8-$32

AAA Inspector Notes: The casual, unpretentious eatery prepares some great steaks, a great variety of tasty smoked meats, sandwiches and side dishes. A big-screen TV and pool table are upstairs. **Bar:** full bar. **Address:** 301 S Main St 80424 **Location:** Corner of Main St and Adams Ave. **Parking:** street only. L D AC

LA FRANCAISE FRENCH BAKERY **Phone:** 970/547-7173

Deli
$8-$13

AAA Inspector Notes: Those who appreciate the simplicity of a crunchy baguette with a soft center, the tangy flavor of Brie and the decadence of French pastries must stop in this tiny, quick-serve restaurant. The menu features savory and sweet crepes, quiches, sandwiches, omelets, specialty coffees and a variety of tarts and pastries. When picking out a tart or baked good, it's a good idea to peek around the deli case to view all the options. **Address:** 411 S Main St 80424 **Location:** 0.3 mi s; in Four Seasons Plaza; Lower Level. **Parking:** street only.

B L D AC

LE PETIT PARIS **Phone:** 970/547-5335

French
$19-$35

AAA Inspector Notes: Spend a night in Paris in this charming bistro, which serves traditional French cuisine in an elegant setting. The dining room is cozy with French decorations and music, pink tablecloths, wine-colored cloth napkins and fresh-cut flowers throughout. The seasonal menu changes often and may feature elk- and bleu cheese-stuffed mushrooms, a wild-boar duo, hazelnut- and pancetta-encrusted Idaho trout and house-made ricotta gnocchi. With advance notice, vegetarian options are available. **Bar:** full bar. **Reservations:** suggested. **Address:** 161 Adams Ave 80424 **Location:** Just e of Main St and Adams Ave; downtown. **Parking:** street only. D AC

MI CASA MEXICAN RESTAURANT & CANTINA **Phone:** 970/453-2071

Mexican
$7-$16

AAA Inspector Notes: Through a courtyard entrance and perched over the creek, the festive cantina prepares dishes with Southwestern flavor. Two favorites are duck quesadillas with mango sauce and buffalo fajitas. **Bar:** full bar. **Address:** 600 S Park Ave 80424 **Location:** Just w of Main St; center. L D AC

MICHAEL'S ITALIAN RESTAURANT **Phone:** 970/453-5800

Italian
$10-$18

AAA Inspector Notes: This relaxed, family-friendly and casual eatery with an extensive menu serves up pizza as well as favorites such as chicken Parmigiana, lasagna and fettuccine Alfredo. Nightly dinner specials and an extensive wine and beer list also are featured. **Bar:** full bar. **Address:** 326 S Main St 80424 **Location:** Jct S Main St and Jefferson Ave, just e; in Centennial Square. **Parking:** street only. D AC

MODIS **Phone:** 970/453-4330

American
$9-$40

AAA Inspector Notes: One of the more upscale restaurants in this casual ski town, Modis focuses on elegant, flavorful cuisine. Heartier dishes feature pork, steak, lamb and duck, while less rich options include the vegetable tower, yellowfin tuna or grilled salmon. Among decadent items are butternut squash with brown butter cream and port wine reduction, as well as the chocolate-glazed chocolate tart for dessert. The decor blends modern colors and historic Victorian accents. **Bar:** full bar. **Reservations:** suggested. **Address:** 113 S Main St 80424 **Location:** Downtown. **Parking:** street only. D AC

MOUNTAIN FLYING FISH **Phone:** 970/453-1502

Japanese
$8-$20

AAA Inspector Notes: Chef/owner Tetsuo Shimoda, who trained in Japan, has worked in sushi restaurants in both Japan and New York City. Fresh fish is flown in from Japan and all over the world. The extensive sake menu will please both beginners and connoisseurs. The parking lot is in the back of the mall on South Ridge Road, not on Main Street. **Bar:** full bar. **Address:** 500 S Main St 80424 **Location:** At Town Center; in La Cima Mall, 3rd Floor. D

QUANDARY GRILLE **Phone:** 970/547-5969

American
$8-$25

AAA Inspector Notes: This eatery, with its excellent views of Peak Nine, is a favorite in winter and summer alike. Burgers, sandwiches, Mexican fare and full dinner plates such as hand-cut steaks and a barbecue platter make this a crowd-pleaser. Travelers will appreciate the free heated underground parking. **Bar:** full bar. **Address:** 505 S Main St 80424 **Location:** 0.3 mi s of downtown on SR 9; in ResortQuest Main Street Station. L D

RELISH **Phone:** 970/453-0989

American
$17-$29

AAA Inspector Notes: Climbing upstairs is the last strenuous thing patrons must do before dinner. Then, friendly servers assist them through a meal with innovative elements and satisfying flavors. Hearty and warming made-in-house soups prime the palate for entrees such as Colorado lamb, ruby red trout, elk, sea scallops and beef. **Bar:** full bar. **Reservations:** suggested. **Address:** 137 S Main St 80424 **Location:** Just off Main St via Washington St toward big white tent; center. **Parking:** street only. D AC

SALT CREEK STEAK HOUSE **Phone:** 970/453-4949

Steak
$8-$29

AAA Inspector Notes: Steaks, seafood, pasta and Texas-style barbecue are on the menu at this casual eatery with a mountain-lodge theme. It also offers an extensive, award-winning wine list; live music can be heard in the upstairs nightclub. **Bar:** fuil bar. **Address:** 110 E Lincoln Ave 80424 **Location:** Just e of corner of Main St and Lincoln Ave; downtown. L D

SOUTH RIDGE SEAFOOD GRILL **Phone:** 970/547-0063

Seafood
$15-$25

AAA Inspector Notes: Although the casual and familiar vibe of this intimate eatery makes it feel like an ordinary neighborhood grill, the artistry and sophistication of the menu makes it a special place to dine. Items such as tandoori spiced gulf shrimp, Jamaican jerk pork chop and Colorado red trout are illustrative of the broad and innovative menu offerings. **Bar:** full bar. **Reservations:** suggested. **Address:** 215 S Ridge St 80424 **Location:** Jct Main St and Washington Ave, just e, then just s. **Parking:** street only. D AC

THE SWISS HAVEN **Phone:** 970/453-6969

Swiss
$16-$35

AAA Inspector Notes: This restaurant offers authentic Swiss cuisine that includes tasty fondues with combinations of Appenzeller, Gruyère and Emmentaler cheeses. Popular starters are kaseschnitte, provincial mushrooms, baked brie and beef carpaccio. Patrons follow up with meat, seafood or cheese fondue or select from a variety of other Swiss staples. The menu also includes pasta and wild game. An outdoor patio is available. **Bar:** full bar. **Reservations:** suggested. **Address:** 325 S Main St 80424 **Location:** On SR 9; downtown; in Columbine Square Building. **Parking:** street only. L D

WHALE'S TAIL **Phone:** 970/453-2221

Seafood
$6-$37

AAA Inspector Notes: With its cozy fireplace, this Cape Cod-style, nautically decorated restaurant offers a variety of menu items such as charbroiled filet mignon, jumbo shrimp cocktail, honey-smoked salmon and coconut curry sea scallops. **Bar:** full bar. **Address:** 323 S Main St 80424 **Location:** Just s of center. **Parking:** street only. L D AC

BRIGHTON (B-5) pop. 33,352, elev. 4,983'

• Hotels p. 72 • Restaurants p. 72
• Part of Denver area — see map p. 123

ADAMS COUNTY MUSEUM COMPLEX is at 9601 Henderson Rd. Adams County and Colorado history, from prehistoric times to the early 20th century, is presented in three galleries. Buildings include a restored 1887 Victorian house; a working blacksmith's shop; and replicas of a one-room schoolhouse, a 1930s-era Conoco service station and a fire station with a restored antique fire truck inside. A restored early 1940s-era red caboose also can be seen.

Hoffman Hall includes antique and military equipment. The Heritage Center features displays on earth sciences and fluorescents. The Carlson Cultural Center displays quilts, art and vintage cameras. **Time:** Allow 1 hour minimum. **Hours:** Tues.-Sat. 10-4; closed Jan. 1, July 4, Thanksgiving and Dec. 21-31. **Cost:** Museum building free. Guided tour of other buildings $2. **Phone:** (303) 659-7103.

BEST WESTERN BRIGHTON INN Phone: (303)637-7710

Hotel
$99-$119

AAA Benefit: Members save up to 20%, plus 10% bonus points with Best Western Rewards®.

Address: 15151 Brighton Rd 80601 **Location:** US 85, 1 mi s of jct SR 7, just w. **Facility:** 58 units. 3 stories, interior corridors. **Amenities:** *Some:* high-speed Internet. **Pool(s):** heated indoor. **Activities:** whirlpool, limited exercise equipment. **Guest Services:** valet and coin laundry. **Free Special Amenities: local telephone calls and high-speed Internet.**

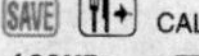
CALL

/ SOME UNITS FEE

COMFORT INN OF BRIGHTON Phone: (303)654-1400

Hotel
$89-$99

Address: 15150 Brighton Rd 80601 **Location:** I-76 exit 12, 7.3 mi n on US 85. **Facility:** 52 units. 3 stories, interior corridors. **Terms:** cancellation fee imposed. **Pool(s):** heated indoor. **Activities:** whirlpool. **Guest Services:** valet and coin laundry.

CALL

HAMPTON INN Phone: (303)654-8055

Hotel
$89-$107

AAA Benefit: Members save up to 10% everyday!

Address: 992 Platte River Blvd 80601 **Location:** I-76 exit 12, 7.3 mi n on US 85, just w, then just s. **Facility:** 76 units. 4 stories, interior corridors. **Terms:** 1-7 night minimum stay, cancellation fee imposed. **Amenities:** high-speed Internet. **Pool(s):** heated indoor. **Activities:** whirlpool, exercise room. **Guest Services:** valet and coin laundry.

HOLIDAY INN EXPRESS HOTEL & SUITES
Phone: 720/685-1500

Hotel
Rates not provided

Address: 2180 S Medical Center Dr 80601 **Location:** I-76 exit 21, just nw, just n, then just e. **Facility:** 88 units. 3 stories, interior corridors. **Amenities:** high-speed Internet. **Pool(s):** heated indoor. **Activities:** whirlpool, exercise room. **Guest Services:** valet and coin laundry.

WHERE TO EAT

LA ESTRELLITA Phone: 303/654-9900

Mexican
$7-$13

AAA Inspector Notes: Although the location inside a small shopping center is a little odd, it's worth wandering down to this family-owned eatery to taste recipes from the owners' grandparents, who also owned a restaurant. Diners have come to expect large portions of stuffed sopaipillas, Mayan enchiladas, carnitas and fajitas. The homemade flan is delicious. Due to high demand from customers, the owners began bottling their salsas, so it's possible to take a little taste of Colorado home. **Bar:** full bar. **Address:** 45 N Main St, Suite 9 80601 **Location:** I-76 exit 12, 8 mi ne on US 85 exit SR 7/Brighton, 0.3 mi e, then just n; in Old Town Shops building. **Parking:** on-site and street.

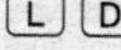

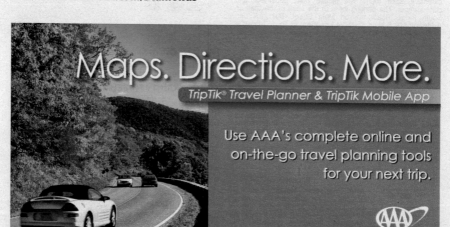

BROOMFIELD pop. 55,889

• Restaurants p. 74

ALOFT BROOMFIELD DENVER

Phone: (303)635-2000

Contemporary Hotel $89-$169

AAA Benefit: Enjoy the new twist, get up to 15% off + Starwood Preferred Guest® bonuses.

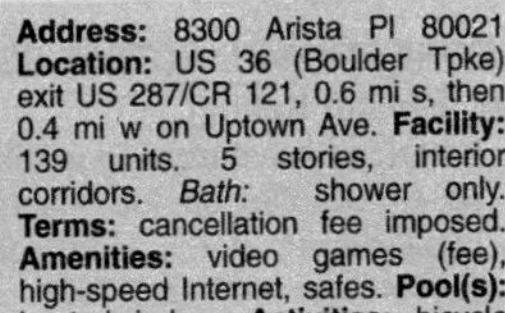

Address: 8300 Arista Pl 80021 **Location:** US 36 (Boulder Tpke) exit US 287/CR 121, 0.6 mi s, then 0.4 mi w on Uptown Ave. **Facility:** 139 units. 5 stories, interior corridors. *Bath:* shower only. **Terms:** cancellation fee imposed. **Amenities:** video games (fee), high-speed Internet, safes. **Pool(s):** heated indoor. **Activities:** bicycle trails, jogging, exercise room. **Guest Services:** valet and coin laundry, area transportation-within 5 mi. **Free Special Amenities: newspaper.** *(See ad this page.)*

SAVE BIZ FEE / SOME UNITS 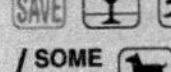

HYATT SUMMERFIELD SUITES BOULDER/BROOMFIELD

Phone: (720)890-4811

Extended Stay Hotel $89-$239

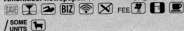

AAA Benefit: Members save 10% or more everyday.

Address: 13351 W Midway Blvd 80020 **Location:** US 36 (Boulder Tpke) exit Storagetek Dr/Interlocken Loop, 0.3 mi n, then just e on Via Varra Rd. **Facility:** 123 units, some two bedrooms, efficiencies and kitchens. 4 stories, interior corridors. **Terms:** cancellation fee imposed. **Amenities:** high-speed Internet. **Pool(s):** heated outdoor. **Activities:** exercise room. **Guest Services:** valet and coin laundry, area transportation-within 5 mi. **Free Special Amenities: full breakfast and high-speed Internet.**

   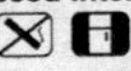  SAVE BIZ / SOME UNITS FEE

OMNI INTERLOCKEN RESORT

Phone: (303)438-6600

Resort Hotel $119-$389

Address: 500 Interlocken Blvd 80021 **Location:** US 36 (Boulder Tpke) exit Interlocken Loop, 0.4 mi s, then 0.4 mi e. **Facility:** Public areas display artwork by Colorado artists, and spacious units offer golf course or mountain views; a pool and sunbathing area has waterfalls. 390 units. 11 stories, interior corridors. **Parking:** on-site and valet. **Terms:** cancellation fee imposed. **Amenities:** high-speed Internet (fee), safes, honor bars. **Dining:** 2 restaurants, also, Meritage, see separate listing. **Pool(s):** 2 heated outdoor. **Activities:** whirlpool, steamroom, bicycle trails, jogging, spa. *Fee:* golf-27 holes. **Guest Services:** valet laundry, area transportation-within 2 mi.

SAVE CALL BIZ  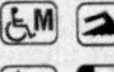 FEE  / SOME UNITS FEE

RENAISSANCE BOULDER FLATIRON HOTEL

Phone: (303)464-8400

Hotel $110-$280

R RENAISSANCE HOTELS & RESORTS

AAA Benefit: AAA hotel discounts of 5% or more.

Address: 500 Flatiron Blvd 80021 **Location:** US 36 (Boulder Tpke) exit Interlocken Loop, 0.4 mi s, just w on Interlocken Blvd, then just s. **Facility:** The mountain resort-style hotel, with an upscale lodge ambience, offers spacious guest rooms with mountain views and numerous amenities. 232 units. 10 stories, interior corridors. **Parking:** on-site and valet. **Terms:** check-in 4 pm. **Amenities:** high-speed Internet (fee). **Pool(s):** heated indoor. **Activities:** whirlpool, exercise room. *Fee:* massage. **Guest Services:** valet and coin laundry, area transportation-within 3 mi. **Free Special Amenities: newspaper and local transportation.**

SAVE CALL BIZ FEE 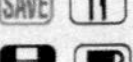

▼ See AAA listing this page ▼

TOWNEPLACE SUITES BY MARRIOTT BOULDER/ BROOMFIELD
Phone: (303)466-2200

Extended Stay Hotel
$179-$196

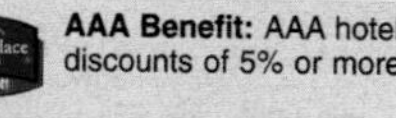

AAA Benefit: AAA hotel discounts of 5% or more.

Address: 480 Flatiron Blvd 80021 **Location:** US 36 (Boulder Tpke) exit Interlocken Loop, 0.4 mi s, just w on Interlocken Blvd, then just s. Located above a shopping center. **Facility:** 151 kitchen units, some two bedrooms. 4 stories, interior corridors. **Amenities:** high-speed Internet. **Pool(s):** heated outdoor. **Activities:** exercise room. **Guest Services:** valet and coin laundry. **Free Special Amenities: continental breakfast and high-speed Internet.**

 CALL BIZ

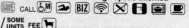

/ SOME UNITS FEE

WHERE TO EAT

MERITAGE
Phone: 303/464-3330

American
$10-$35

AAA Inspector Notes: Accomplished service matched with innovative food combinations makes dinner at the sophisticated restaurant more than just a special occasion. Creative flavorings mingled with a wide variety of seafood and meats will satisfy any palate. **Bar:** full bar. **Reservations:** suggested. **Address:** 500 Interlocken Blvd 80021 **Location:** US 36 (Boulder Tpke) exit Interlocken Loop, 0.4 mi s, then 0.4 mi e; in Omni Interlocken Resort. **Parking:** on-site and valet. B L D

P.F. CHANG'S CHINA BISTRO
Phone: 720/887-6200

Chinese
$10-$23

AAA Inspector Notes: Trendy, upscale decor provides a pleasant backdrop for New Age Chinese dining. Appetizers, soups and salads are a meal by themselves. Vegetarian plates and sides, noodles, meins, chicken and meat dishes are created from exotic, fresh ingredients. **Bar:** full bar. **Address:** 1 W Flatiron Cir 80021 **Location:** US 36 (Boulder Tpke) exit Flatiron Cir, 0.9 mi e, then just n on Interlocken Blvd. L D CALL

VILLAGE TAVERN
Phone: 720/887-6900

Steak
$9-$30

AAA Inspector Notes: Attentive, personable servers bring out fresh entrees of steak, seafood, chicken, wood-oven pizzas, sandwiches, soups, salads and some downright tasty made-in-house potato chips. The comprehensive offerings, including a children's menu, ensure there is something for everyone. **Bar:** full bar. **Address:** 100 W Flatiron Crossing Dr 80021 **Location:** US 36 (Boulder Tpke) exit Interlocken Loop/Storagetek Dr; in Flatiron Shopping District. L D

BUENA VISTA (D-3) pop. 2,617, elev. 7,955'

Buena Vista means "beautiful view." The Sawatch Range, which includes the Collegiate Peaks—mounts Yale, Harvard and Princeton, all more than 14,000 feet in elevation—forms a backdrop for this pastoral community. An overlook 1.5 miles east of the junction of US 24 and US 285 provides a view of the range.

Though rooted in ranching and mining, Buena Vista's economic base also includes tourism and recreation. The area is popular for hot springs, scenic drives, hiking, skiing, off-road driving, backpacking, hunting, fishing and gold panning. Horseback, snowmobile and mountain bicycle tours are available from local tour providers.

Often referred to as the "Whitewater Capital of Colorado," the town is one of the main gateways to the 148-mile Arkansas Headwaters Recreation Area *(see Recreation Chart)* which is favored by rafters and kayakers.

Buena Vista Chamber of Commerce: 343 US 24S, P.O. Box 2021, Buena Vista, CO 81211. **Phone:** (719) 395-6612.

RECREATIONAL ACTIVITIES

White-water Rafting

- **American Adventure Expeditions** is off US 24 to 12844 US 285 on the Arkansas River. **Hours:** Trips depart daily, May-Sept. **Phone:** (719) 395-2409 or (800) 288-0675.
- **Buffalo Joe Whitewater Rafting** is at 113 N. Railroad St. **Hours:** Daily 7-7, May 1-Labor Day. **Phone:** (719) 395-8757 or (866) 283-3563.
- **Good Times Rafting** is 1 mi. n. of jct. US 285 and US 24. **Hours:** Daily mid-May to mid-Sept. **Phone:** (970) 453-5559 or (800) 997-3448.
- **Performance Tours** is 1 mi. s. at 115 Gregg Dr. **Hours:** Daily May 1-Labor Day. **Phone:** (800) 328-7238.
- **River Runners Riverside Resort** is at jct. US 285 and CR 301. **Hours:** Daily 7 a.m.-9 p.m., late Apr. to mid-Sept. **Phone:** (719) 395-2466 or (800) 525-2081.
- **Wilderness Aware Rafting** is at 12600 US 285. **Hours:** Daily 7:30 a.m.-8 p.m., May 1-Labor Day. **Phone:** (719) 395-2112 or (800) 462-7238.

BEST WESTERN PLUS VISTA INN
Phone: (719)395-8009

Hotel
$100-$165

AAA Benefit: Members save up to 20%, plus 10% bonus points with Best Western Rewards®.

Address: 733 US Hwy 24 N 81211 **Location:** 0.5 mi n of center. **Facility:** 52 units. 2 stories (no elevator), interior corridors. **Parking:** winter plug-ins. **Amenities:** *Some:* high-speed Internet. **Pool(s):** heated indoor. **Activities:** whirlpool, exercise room. **Guest Services:** coin laundry. **Free Special Amenities: local telephone calls and high-speed Internet.**

WHERE TO EAT

BONGO BILLY'S CAFE
Phone: 719/395-2634

Coffee/Tea
$5-$8

AAA Inspector Notes: This eatery is a great place to stop while biking or traveling for a delicious bite to eat. The daily quiche selection is a treat. Chicken, tuna, turkey and veggie sandwiches go well with the daily made-in-house soup and bow-tie, green leaf, multi-bean or tortellini salad. Espressos, cappuccinos, lattes, teas and hot chocolate warm patrons in the winter, and their iced counterparts satisfy during the summer. **Address:** 713 S US 24 81211 **Location:** 0.6 mi s of center. B L D

CASA DEL SOL Phone: 719/395-8810

Mexican
$7-$16

AAA Inspector Notes: This popular eatery has several colorful and nicely appointed dining nooks and a lovely garden patio. **Bar:** full bar. **Reservations:** suggested, in summer. **Address:** 333 US 24 N 81211 **Location:** Corner of E Arkansas St and US 24. **Historic**

L D

COYOTE CANTINA Phone: 719/395-3755

Mexican
$5-$10

AAA Inspector Notes: Popular for its unpretentious décor, rustic theme and straightforward menu, dishes include salad in tortilla bowls, hand-made tamales, burritos, fajitas, fresh salsa and veggie plates. Rounding out the menu are green chili soup, country breakfasts and such traditional desserts as flan, sopaipillas and chocolate chimi. The patio affords a spectacular view of the Collegiate Peaks. **Bar:** full bar. **Address:** 12985 Hwy 24 & 285 81211 **Location:** 2.3 mi s on US 24, 0.4 mi e on US 24/285; in Johnson Village. B L D

BURLINGTON (D-6) pop. 4,254, elev. 4,163'

KIT CARSON COUNTY CAROUSEL is off I-70 exit 437, following signs to Kit Carson County Fairgrounds. Forty-six carved animals adorn the restored 1905 carousel. Visitors may choose from a lion, giraffe, camel or other whimsical creatures for a nostalgic ride, accompanied by music from a Wurlitzer band organ. A museum offers a historical perspective, from the early years of the Philadelphia Toboggan Co. to how carousel animals are crafted. **Time:** Allow 30 minutes minimum. **Hours:** Daily 11-6, Memorial Day weekend-Labor Day. **Cost:** Museum $1; free (ages 0-9); rides 25¢. **Phone:** (800) 825-0208.

GEM **OLD TOWN MUSEUM,** 420 S. 14th St., is a 6.5-acre site with a collection of original and re-created buildings furnished with early 1900s artifacts. The 21 buildings include a schoolhouse, church, sod house, windmill, grocery store, jail, saloon, drugstore, soda fountain, Texaco station and blacksmith shop as well as a museum. Belgian horses pull the Old Town Express to the Kit Carson County Carousel, and cancan dancers perform in the saloon during the summer.

Time: Allow 1 hour minimum. **Hours:** Mon.-Sat. 9-5, Sun. noon-5. **Cost:** $6; $5 (ages 60+); $4 (ages 12-17); $2 (ages 3-11). **Phone:** (719) 346-7382 or (800) 288-1334.

BEST WESTERN PLUS CAROUSEL INN & SUITES Phone: 719/346-7777

fyi
Hotel
Rates not provided

AAA Benefit: Members save up to 20%, plus 10% bonus points with Best Western Rewards®.

Too new to rate, opening scheduled for November 2011. **Address:** 605 S Lincoln St 80807 **Location:** I-70 exit 437, just s. **Amenities:** 66 units, pets, restaurant, coffeemakers, microwaves, refrigerators, pool, exercise facility.

CHAPARRAL MOTOR INN Phone: (719)346-5361

Motel
$50-$65 5/1-9/15
$49-$59 9/16-4/30

Address: 405 S Lincoln St 80807 **Location:** I-70 exit 437, just n on US 385. **Facility:** 39 units. 1 story, exterior corridors. **Amenities:** high-speed Internet. **Pool(s):** heated outdoor. **Free Special Amenities: continental breakfast and high-speed Internet.**

SAVE / SOME UNITS FEE

COMFORT INN BURLINGTON Phone: (719)346-7676

Hotel
$70-$149

Address: 282 S Lincoln St 80807 **Location:** I-70 exit 437, just n on US 385. **Facility:** 57 units. 2 stories (no elevator), interior corridors. **Terms:** cancellation fee imposed. **Pool(s):** heated indoor. **Activities:** whirlpool, exercise room. **Guest Services:** coin laundry.

BIZ / SOME UNITS FEE

WHERE TO EAT

THE ROUTE STEAKHOUSE Phone: 719/346-8790

Steak
$7-$33

AAA Inspector Notes: The restaurant is a good stopping spot for interstate travelers or those staying in Burlington. Among offerings are traditional American food, steaks and seafood. **Bar:** full bar. **Address:** 218 S Lincoln St 80807 **Location:** I-70 exit 437, just n on US 385.

L D CALL M

CAÑON CITY (E-4) pop. 16,400, elev. 5,332'

• Hotels p. 77 • Restaurants p. 77

Cañon City's history can be traced back to prehistoric times. Dinosaur Depot, on Royal Gorge Boulevard, displays replicas of dinosaur remains found in the area. A life-size allosaurus welcomes visitors.

Shadowed and sheltered by a close ring of mountains, Cañon City is at the head of the Arkansas Valley, where the Arkansas River bursts from its canyon confines to begin a 1,900-mile open-country run to the Mississippi. The canyon scenery attracted filmmakers to Cañon City in the early 20th century. Tom Mix, hero of silent Westerns, launched his career in Cañon City in 1910. Such films as "Cat Ballou" and "True Grit" as well as "Conagher," a made-for-television movie, were made in the vicinity.

Stock raising, agriculture, mining, 13 correctional facilities and tourism provide a broad economic base. The Blossom and Music Festival and the Royal Gorge Rodeo are held the first weekend in May.

Greater Cañon City Chamber of Commerce: 403 Royal Gorge Blvd., Cañon City, CO 81212. **Phone:** (719) 275-2331 or (800) 876-7922.

MUSEUM OF COLORADO PRISONS, off US 50 at 201 N. 1st St., is located in the original women's prison built in 1935. Displays feature a gas chamber, confiscated inmate weapons, disciplinary paraphernalia and inmates' original photographs and art work. Other displays feature Roy Best, one of the prison's most famous wardens, and other inmates such as cannibal Alfred Packer and 11-year-old murderer Anton Woode. The Historic Ghost Walk tour of Cañon City departs from the museum.

▼ See AAA listing this page ▼

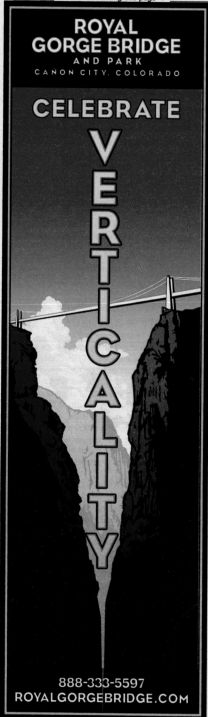

Audiotapes are available for self-guiding tours. **Time:** Allow 1 hour minimum. **Hours:** Daily 8:30-6, Memorial Day-Labor Day; daily 10-5, day after Labor Day to mid-Oct.; Wed.-Sun. 10-5, rest of year. Ghost Walk tour departs Fri.-Mon. at 6:30, Memorial Day-Labor Day. Closed Easter, Thanksgiving and Christmas. **Cost:** $7; $6 (ages 65+); $5 (ages 6-12, military with ID and department of corrections employees with ID). Historic Ghost Walk $8; $5 (ages 6-12). **Phone:** (719) 269-3015.

PHANTOM CANYON ROAD (SR 67), 6 mi. e. on US 50 to SR 67, twists and turns for 35 miles through a canyon leading to Cripple Creek *(see place listing p. 118)*. Several old train tunnels cut through red rock formations. Phantom Canyon Road is part of the "Gold Belt Tour," a national historical route. Another one of the legs of the tour is Shelf Road, also departing from the north side of Cañon City. **Note:** This gravel road is narrow and winding and should not be attempted in an RV or by those unaccustomed to mountain driving. The posted speed limit is 20 mph; the drive takes 1.5 to 2 hours. Check road conditions before starting. **Phone:** (719) 275-2331 or (800) 876-7922.

GEM **ROYAL GORGE BRIDGE AND PARK** is 8 mi. w. on US 50, then 4.3 mi. s. on CR 3A. The bridge is the highest suspension bridge in the United States. Built in 1929, the bridge spans the scenic Royal Gorge nearly 1,000 feet above the Arkansas River.

The park offers more than 360 acres of scenery, history and rides, including an incline railway to the bottom of the gorge, the Royal Rush Skycoaster, an aerial tram across the canyon, many children's attractions, a theater, a trolley, a miniature train, a carousel, a petting zoo, a wildlife park and scenic trails for walking and bicycling. Only the bridge, incline railway, aerial tram, theater and wildlife park are open early October through April.

Note: Park admission is charged before crossing the bridge. Due to the narrowness of the bridge, RVs and large vehicles are not permitted to cross; parking is free, and transportation across the bridge is provided May through September. Allow 3 hours, 30 minutes minimum during peak season. **Hours:** Bridge open daily 7-dusk (weather permitting). Park opens daily at 10. Closing times vary; phone ahead.

Cost: $25 (includes park and all attractions except the Skycoaster, mule team rides and Jeep tours); $21 (ages 60+); $19 (ages 4-11). Half-price second admission applies mid-Oct. to late Apr. Skycoaster $25. **Phone:** (719) 275-7507 or (888) 333-5597. ***(See ad this page.)***

ROYAL GORGE REGIONAL MUSEUM & HISTORY CENTER, 612 Royal Gorge Blvd., depicts the history of the Royal Gorge region. Exhibits encompass ranching, firearms, military veterans, community leader Dall DeWeese, artist Robert Wesley Amick and a display of phonographs that includes Victor, Edison and Columbia models.

Also featured are a natural history bison diorama and an 1860s log cabin. The History Center contains genealogical and research material related to the area. **Hours:** Mon.-Sat. 10-4. **Cost:** Free. **Phone:** (719) 269-9036.

ROYAL GORGE ROUTE RAILROAD departs from the historic Santa Fe Depot at 401 Water St. The 24-mile journey follows the Arkansas River through the scenic Royal Gorge and crosses a hanging bridge where the gorge narrows to 30 feet wide. Passengers select from six classes of service. Coach, Vista Dome, Ride in the Cab, lunch, dinner and wine excursions are offered. The bar car features a copper bar and large plate glass windows for viewing the gorge. Special events include Murder Mystery and Wine Excursion dinner trains, and the Santa Express, an evening departure Nov.-Dec. featuring Santa, gifts for kids, cookies and hot cocoa.

Time: Allow 2 hours minimum. **Hours:** Scenic train excursion departs Mon.-Fri. at 9:30 and 12:30, Sat.-Sun. at 9:30, 12:30 and 3:30, mid-May to mid-Oct.; Sat.-Sun. at 12:30, early Mar. to mid-May and mid-Oct. through Dec. 31. Call for schedules of other theme train rides. **Cost:** Coach fare $33; $22 (ages 3-12). Additional fees apply for Vista Dome, Murder Mystery, Santa Express, wine tasting, Ride in the Cab, lunch and dinner trains. Reservations are recommended. **Phone:** (888) 724-5748.

SKYLINE DRIVE, starting 3 mi. w. off US 50, is a 3-mile, paved, one-way road that traverses the crest of a "hogback" ridge 800 feet above town. The view from Skyline Drive is spectacular and includes actual dinosaur tracks in the rocks. **Note:** Motor homes, vans, campers and vehicles towing trailers are not permitted on the narrow, steep and winding road. **Hours:** The road is closed in inclement weather.

WHITEWATER ADVENTURE OUTFITTERS is 1 mi. w. of Cañon City at 50905 US 50W. Quarter-day, half-day, full-day and overnight trips are available on the Arkansas River. Experienced, professional guides provide narrated highlights along the route.

Time: Allow 3 hours minimum. **Hours:** Daily 8-8, mid-Apr. to mid-Sept. **Cost:** Fare $42-$105; $28-$69 (ages 6-12). Reservations are recommended. **Phone:** (719) 275-5344 or (800) 530-8212.

RECREATIONAL ACTIVITIES

White-water Rafting

- **American Adventure Expeditions** is at 41746 US 50W on the Arkansas River. **Hours:** Trips depart daily, May-Sept. **Phone:** (719) 395-2409 or (800) 288-0675.
- **Bill Dvorak Rafting & Kayak Expeditions** meets at Parkdale State River Site, 12 mi. w. of Cañon City off US 50W. **Hours:** Daily 7 a.m.-9 p.m., May-Sept. **Phone:** (719) 539-6851 or (800) 824-3795.
- **Buffalo Joe Whitewater Rafting** is at 45000 US 50. **Hours:** Daily 7-7, May 1-early Sept. **Phone:** (719) 395-8757 or (866) 283-3563.
- **Clear Creek Rafting Co.** is 8 mi. w. at 44650 US 50W. **Hours:** Daily 7 a.m.-9 p.m., May-Sept. **Phone:** (719) 275-4500 or (800) 353-9901.
- **Echo Canyon River Expeditions** is 8 mi. w. at 45000 US 50W. **Hours:** Daily 7-7, May 1-Sept. 15. Times may vary. **Phone:** (719) 275-3154 or (800) 748-2953.
- **Performance Tours** is 8 mi. w. on US 50 at 35 CR 3A. **Hours:** Daily, May 1-Labor Day. **Phone:** (800) 328-7238.
- **Raft Masters** is at 2315 E. Main St. **Hours:** Daily 8-6, mid-Mar. to mid-Oct. **Phone:** (719) 275-6645 or (800) 568-7238.
- **River Runners Royal Gorge Rafting Center** is 8 mi. w. at the turnoff for the Royal Gorge Bridge and Park at 44641 US 50W. **Hours:** Daily 7 a.m.-9 p.m., May 1 to mid-Sept. **Phone:** (719) 395-2466.
- **Wilderness Aware Rafting** departs from Pinnacle Rock Recreation Area, 11.6 mi. w. of jct. US 50 and SR 9. **Hours:** Trips depart daily at 9, May 1-Labor Day. **Phone:** (719) 395-2112 or (800) 462-7238.

ARKANSAS RIVER INN & SUITES **Phone:** (719)275-3377

Motel

$74-$143 5/1-9/15
$59-$101 9/16-4/30

Address: 1925 Fremont Dr 81212 **Location:** From 9th St, 0.8 mi e on US 50. **Facility:** 67 units. 2 stories (no elevator), interior/exterior corridors. **Terms:** office hours 7 am-11 pm, cancellation fee imposed. **Pool(s):** heated outdoor. **Activities:** whirlpool, putting green, playground, horseshoes. **Guest Services:** coin laundry.

BARRYMORE HOTEL **Phone:** (719)275-2400

Hotel

$80-$149

Address: 110 Latigo Ln 81212 **Location:** From 9th St, 3 mi e on US 50, then just n. **Facility:** 82 units. 2 stories, interior corridors. **Terms:** cancellation fee imposed. **Amenities:** high-speed Internet. **Pool(s):** heated indoor. **Activities:** whirlpool, exercise room.

SOME UNITS FEE

HAMPTON INN **Phone:** (719)269-1112

Hotel

$105-$155

AAA Benefit:
Members save up to 10% everyday!

Address: 102 McCormick Pkwy 81212 **Location:** From 9th St, 2.7 mi e on US 50, then just n. **Facility:** 64 units. 3 stories, interior corridors. **Terms:** 1-7 night minimum stay, cancellation fee imposed. **Amenities:** high-speed Internet. **Pool(s):** heated indoor. **Activities:** whirlpool, exercise room. **Guest Services:** valet and coin laundry.

SOME UNITS FEE

WHERE TO EAT

DIRITO'S ITALIAN RESTAURANT **Phone:** 719/276-7240

Italian

$5-$18

AAA Inspector Notes: Family-owned and -operated, the eatery serves traditional Italian favorites in a casual atmosphere. **Bar:** full bar. **Address:** 231 Main St 81212 **Location:** Corner of 3rd and Main sts. **Parking:** street only.

EL CAPORAL

Phone: 719/276-2001

Mexican
$6-$16

AAA Inspector Notes: Colorful décor sets the stage for this dining experience. The local favorite features daily lunch and dinner specials and offers many authentic dishes to choose from, including meat, seafood and vegetarian options. You also may create your own combination. **Bar:** beer & wine. **Address:** 1028 Main St 81212 **Location:** Just e of Main and 10th sts; downtown.

L D

LE PETIT CHABLIS

Phone: 719/269-3333

French
$9-$29

AAA Inspector Notes: A touch of elegance in the heart of the West, this cozy French restaurant is the hidden jewel of Cañon City. The menu consists mainly of seafood, lamb, duck and a variety of decadent desserts. **Bar:** full bar. **Reservations:** suggested, for dinner. **Address:** 512 Royal Gorge Blvd 81212 **Location:** On US 50, between 5th and 6th sts. L D

MERLINOS' BELVEDERE

Menu on AAA.com

Phone: 719/275-5558

Italian
$6-$29

AAA Inspector Notes: An establishment for savory family dining since 1946, the restaurant prepares fresh pasta dishes, aged cut beef, seafood and chicken. **Bar:** full bar. **Address:** 1330 Elm Ave 81212 **Location:** 1.2 mi s of jct US 50 and 9th St to Elm Ave, then 0.6 mi e. L D

CANYONS OF THE ANCIENTS NATIONAL MONUMENT (E-1)

In the Four Corners region 20 miles northwest of Cortez and west of US 491, Canyons of the Ancients National Monument preserves one of the richest archeological areas in the United States, covering 166,000 acres of remote and difficult terrain. More than 6,000 archeological sites, including dwellings, shrines, hunting camps and petroglyphs, provide information about cultures and traditions spanning thousands of years.

The 12th-century Lowry Pueblo, a National Historic Landmark containing 40 rooms and ceremonial kivas, is among the largest and most easily accessible of the ruins. Visitors are advised to stop at the Anasazi Heritage Center in Dolores prior to visiting the national monument for maps, advice and current road conditions.

Note: The monument is a primitive backcountry area with gravel and dirt roads, minimal facilities and no permanent source of water. Visitors are advised to bring sufficient water, fuel and maps, and to stay on existing roads and trails. Daily 24 hours. Free. Phone (303) 239-3600.

ANASAZI HERITAGE CENTER, 3.5 mi. w. of Dolores on SR 184, interprets the history and culture of the Four Corners region, including Canyons of the Ancients National Monument. Ancient pottery displays, interactive exhibits, two 12th-century pueblos and special exhibits and events are presented. Visitors can try their hand at weaving on a Pueblo-style loom or grinding corn.

As the visitor center for Canyons of the Ancients National Monument, it offers maps, brochures and orientation, as well as two short video programs about the ancient culture: "Visit With Respect" is an appeal from American Indians to protect their ancestral homesites; "The Cultural History of the Great Sage Plain" focuses on archaeologists' work of the 19th and 20th centuries. A paved, half-mile nature trail leads to the hilltop Escalante Pueblo.

Time: Allow 1 hour minimum. **Hours:** Daily 9-5, Mar.-Oct.; 10-4, rest of year. Closed Jan. 1, Thanksgiving and Christmas. **Cost:** Mar.-Oct. $3; free (ages 0-17). Rest of year, free. **Phone:** (970) 882-5600.

CARBONDALE pop. 6,427

COMFORT INN & SUITES

Phone: (970)963-8880

Hotel
$79-$169

Address: 920 Cowen Dr 81623 **Location:** Jct SR 82 and 133, just s. **Facility:** 76 units. 2 stories (no elevator), interior corridors. **Terms:** check-in 4 pm, cancellation fee imposed. **Pool(s):** heated indoor. **Activities:** whirlpool, fishing. **Guest Services:** valet and coin laundry.

FEE BIZ

/ SOME UNITS FEE

WHERE TO EAT

ECO-GODDESS ALL ORGANIC CUISINE

Phone: 970/963-7316

Natural/Organic
$8-$16

AAA Inspector Notes: Patrons will appreciate the gluten-free and vegan options at this downtown eatery, which also features an-all organic juice, wine and drink bar and menu items such as wild Alaskan salmon pâté, linguine noodles topped with sauteed spinach and served with tempeh or tofu, and a savory house-made black bean burger. Tempting desserts are displayed in a glass case. **Bar:** full bar. **Address:** 335 Main St 81623 **Location:** Just e of center. **Parking:** street only. L D

PHAT THAI

Phone: 970/963-7001

Thai
$9-$19

AAA Inspector Notes: This eatery is the sister property to Chef Mark Fischer's Carbondale Restaurant Six89 and offers a delicious selection of salads, soups, small and large plates, curries, noodles, rice and stir-fries such as a northern Thai herb salad, beef satay, spring rolls with tofu, coconut pumpkin soup, asparagus fried rice with pineapple, chicken basil and more. **Bar:** full bar. **Address:** 343 Main St 81623 **Location:** East end of downtown. **Parking:** street only. D

RUSSETS RESTAURANT

Phone: 970/963-3036

New American
$9-$25

AAA Inspector Notes: Friendly service enhances the charming and comfortable atmosphere in this welcoming neighborhood setting. Among menu items are fresh seafood dishes such as oysters Rockefeller, hormone-free chicken, hand-cut steaks and made-in-house desserts, including a tasty mocha torte. **Bar:** full bar. **Address:** 225 Main St 81623 **Location:** Jct Main and 2nd sts; east end of downtown. **Parking:** street only.

L D

SIX89 Phone: 970/963-6890

American
$16-$26

AAA Inspector Notes: Creative cuisine, a seasonal, irreverent menu and rational prices are what chef Mark Fischer and his staff serve at this popular down valley, farm-to-table restaurant. Diners can enjoy Colorado wine in the warm and comfortable, turn-of-the-century house or out on the patio. **Bar:** full bar. **Reservations:** suggested. **Address:** 689 Main St 81623 **Location:** West end of Main St. D

VILLAGE SMITHY RESTAURANT Phone: 970/963-9990

American
$5-$18

AAA Inspector Notes: This family-owned restaurant must be doing something right as it's been in business since 1975. The menu includes daily specials, Mexican dishes, salads, pasta, a popular Asian chicken salad, sandwiches, espresso, cappuccino, lattes and limited cocktails. Vegetarian items also are available. **Bar:** full bar. **Address:** 26 S 3rd St 81623 **Location:** At 3rd and Main sts; downtown. **Parking:** street only. **Historic**

B L D

WHITE HOUSE PIZZA & PASTA Phone: 970/704-9400

Italian
$7-$24

AAA Inspector Notes: Patrons can enjoy dining upstairs, outside on the patio, in a cozy booth in the bar or in the sunroom. Menu offerings include a variety of tasty appetizers, salads, two types of delicious lasagna, oven-baked sandwiches, pulled pork, noodles galore and last but not least, pizza pies. **Bar:** full bar. **Address:** 801 Main Ct 81623 **Location:** West end of Main St; downtown.

L D

CASCADE (D-4) elev. 7,375'

• Part of Colorado Springs area — see map p. 85

SANTA'S WORKSHOP—NORTH POLE, 10 mi. w. on US 24, is a 27-acre theme park. Highlights include a 60-foot Ferris wheel, children's rides and Santa's house. Inquire about weather policies. **Time:** Allow 2 hours minimum. **Hours:** Daily 10-5, mid-May to mid-Aug.; Fri.-Tues. 10-5, mid-Aug. to late Dec. Phone ahead to confirm schedule. **Cost:** $17.95; free (ages 0-1 and 60+). **Phone:** (719) 684-9432.

AMERICA'S ROCKY MOUNTAIN LODGE & CABINS
Phone: 719/684-2521

Bed & Breakfast
$95-$250

Address: 4680 Hagerman Ave 80809 **Location:** US 24 exit Severy Ave, just n on Ute Pass, e on Topeka Ave, then n. **Facility:** 6 units. 2 stories (no elevator), interior corridors. **Terms:** check-in 4 pm, 2-7 night minimum stay - seasonal and/or weekends, 30 day cancellation notice-fee imposed. **Activities:** whirlpool.

/ SOME UNITS

CASTLE ROCK pop. 48,231

BEST WESTERN INN & SUITES OF CASTLE ROCK
Phone: (303)814-8800

Hotel
$85-$130

AAA Benefit: Members save up to 20%, plus 10% bonus points with Best Western Rewards®.

Address: 595 Genoa Way 80109 **Location:** I-25 exit 184 (Meadows Pkwy), just w to Castleton Way, just s, then e. Opposite an outlet mall. **Facility:** 69 units. 4 stories, interior corridors. **Terms:** check-in 4 pm. **Amenities:** high-speed Internet. *Some:* safes. **Pool(s):** heated indoor. **Activities:** whirlpool, exercise room. **Guest Services:** valet and coin laundry. **Free Special Amenities: local telephone calls and high-speed Internet.**

/ SOME UNITS FEE

HAMPTON INN Phone: (303)660-9800

Hotel
$89-$149

AAA Benefit: Members save up to 10% everyday!

Address: 4830 Castleton Way 80104 **Location:** I-25 exit 184 (Meadows Pkwy), sw to N Castleton Rd, just s, then e. **Facility:** 72 units. 4 stories, interior corridors. **Terms:** 1-7 night minimum stay, cancellation fee imposed. **Amenities:** video games (fee), high-speed Internet. **Pool(s):** heated indoor. **Activities:** whirlpool, exercise room. **Guest Services:** valet and coin laundry. ***(See ad p. 103.)***

CALL   FEE  

/ SOME UNITS

WHERE TO EAT

AUGUSTINE GRILL Phone: 303/814-3663

American
$8-$28

AAA Inspector Notes: Converted from a historic Victorian house into a cheerful restaurant, the grill prepares a mix of seafood, pasta and meat dishes. The grilled beef tenderloin is highly recommended. **Bar:** full bar. **Reservations:** suggested. **Address:** 519 Wilcox St 80104 **Location:** I-25 exit 182, just w to Park St, 0.6 mi se, then just n. **Parking:** street only. L D

CASTLE CAFE Phone: 303/814-2233

American
$9-$27

AAA Inspector Notes: This Western-style café is located in a tastefully renovated 1910 hotel. Delicious fried chicken, Yankee pot roast, mashed potatoes with homemade gravy, burgers and sandwiches are among the menu choices. **Bar:** full bar. **Address:** 403 Wilcox St 80104 **Location:** I-25 exit 182, just e to Wilcox St, then 0.4 mi s; corner of 4th and Wilcox sts. **Parking:** street only. **Historic** L D

EL PARRAL MEXICAN RESTAURANT
Phone: 303/660-9905

Mexican
$5-$13

AAA Inspector Notes: This place prepares varied dishes, including tamales, burritos and taquitos, to name a few options. Margaritas, smoothies and specialty drinks are good accompaniments. The sopaipillas alone are worth a detour off I-25 to the restaurant's location near the center of town. Patio seating is available. **Bar:** full bar. **Address:** 215 Wilcox St 80104 **Location:** I-25 exit 181 northbound, just e to Wilcox St, then 0.5 mi n; southbound, just e to Wilcox St, then 0.5 mi s.

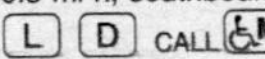

ROCKYARD AMERICAN GRILL & BREWING COMPANY
Phone: 303/814-9273

American
$9-$21

AAA Inspector Notes: Just off the interstate, the popular brewpub has a high, beamed ceiling, patio seating and a fireplace that separates the lounge from the main dining room. Four hand-crafted beers complement the typical pub grub. **Bar:** full bar. **Address:** 880 W Castleton Rd 80109 **Location:** I-25 exit 184 (Meadows Pkwy), w to Castleton Rd. L D CALL

CEDAREDGE (D-2) pop. 2,253, elev. 6,264'

PIONEER TOWN is 2 blks. s. of Main St. on SR 65. This 5-acre site includes more than 20 buildings depicting turn-of-the-20th-century life. Wooden sidewalks line Main Street, which features barn silos, a 1906 jail, a schoolhouse, a general store, a depot, a fruit-packing shed and a log cabin.

The Sutherland Indian Museum, Doris Doll and Toy House, blacksmith shop, railroad depot and Chapel of the Cross also are offered. **Time:** Allow 1 hour minimum. **Hours:** Mon.-Sat. 10-4, Sun. 1-4, Memorial Day-late Sept. **Cost:** $3; $2 (ages 62+); free (ages 0-7). **Phone:** (970) 856-7554.

HOWARD JOHNSON EXPRESS INN
Phone: (970)856-7824

Motel
$59-$90

Address: 530 S Grand Mesa Dr 81413 **Location:** 0.3 mi s of Main St on SR 65. **Facility:** 30 units. 2 stories (no elevator), interior corridors. **Amenities:** safes (fee). **Pool(s):** heated indoor. **Activities:** whirlpool. **Guest Services:** coin laundry.

SOME UNITS FEE

WHERE TO EAT

APPLE SHED
Phone: 970/856-7007

Deli
$7-$9

AAA Inspector Notes: Diners can choose the soup of the day or any of a variety of delicious salads and sandwich favorites including the roasted raspberry chipotle turkey or cranberry chicken. Cream and fruit pies are featured daily. The large patio is the desired seating spot in the summer. **Bar:** wine only. **Address:** 250 S Grand Mesa Dr 81413 **Location:** Just s on SR 65.
B L D

RJ'S STEAKHOUSE
Phone: 970/856-3841

American
$8-$22

AAA Inspector Notes: Although the seasonal menu changes frequently, patrons usually find Angus beef, delicious St. Louis pork ribs and chicken, along with creative, made-from-scratch appetizers, soups, sandwiches, specials and made-in-house desserts. **Bar:** full bar. **Address:** 2323 Grand Mesa Dr 81413 **Location:** 1 mi s on SR 65. L D

CENTENNIAL pop. 100,377

- **Hotels & Restaurants map & index p. 140**
- **Part of Denver area — see map p. 123**

CANDLEWOOD SUITES
Phone: (303)792-5393 115

Extended Stay Hotel
$49-$99

Address: 6780 S Galena St 80112 **Location:** I-25 exit 197 (Arapahoe Rd), 0.7 mi e, then just s. **Facility:** 131 efficiencies. 3 stories, interior corridors. **Amenities:** high-speed Internet. **Activities:** exercise room. **Guest Services:** complimentary and valet laundry. **Free Special Amenities: newspaper and high-speed Internet.**
SAVE SOME UNITS FEE

COMFORT SUITES DENVER TECH CENTER
Phone: (303)858-0700 119

Hotel
$85-$140

Address: 7374 S Clinton St 80112 **Location:** I-25 exit 196 (Dry Creek Rd), just e, then n. **Facility:** 78 units. 3 stories, interior corridors. **Terms:** cancellation fee imposed. **Amenities:** safes (fee). *Some:* high-speed Internet. **Pool(s):** heated indoor. **Activities:** whirlpool, exercise room. **Guest Services:** valet and coin laundry. **Free Special Amenities: full breakfast and high-speed Internet.**
SAVE CALL BIZ

DRURY INN & SUITES-DENVER NEAR THE TECH CENTER
Phone: (303)694-3400 121

Hotel
$85-$139

Address: 9445 E Dry Creek Rd 80112 **Location:** I-25 exit 196 (Dry Creek Rd), just w; on northwest corner. **Facility:** 161 units. 6 stories, interior corridors. **Terms:** cancellation fee imposed. **Amenities:** high-speed Internet. **Pool(s):** heated indoor/outdoor. **Activities:** whirlpool, exercise room. **Guest Services:** valet and coin laundry, area transportation-within 5 mi. BIZ SOME UNITS

EMBASSY SUITES DENVER TECH CENTER
Phone: (303)792-0433 116

Hotel
$129-$199

EMBASSY SUITES HOTELS

AAA Benefit: Members save 5% or more everyday!

Address: 10250 E Costilla Ave 80112 **Location:** I-25 exit 197 (Arapahoe Rd), 1 mi e, 0.3 mi s on Havana St, then w. **Facility:** 236 units, some two bedrooms. 9 stories, interior corridors. **Terms:** 1-7 night minimum stay, cancellation fee imposed. **Amenities:** video games (fee). **Pool(s):** heated indoor. **Activities:** whirlpool, exercise room. **Guest Services:** valet and coin laundry, area transportation-within 6 mi. **Free Special Amenities: full breakfast and manager's reception.**
SAVE CALL BIZ FEE SOME UNITS FEE

EXTENDED STAY DELUXE-DENVER TECH CENTER SOUTH
Phone: (303)858-0292 118

Extended Stay Hotel
$80-$90

Address: 9604 E Easter Ave 80112 **Location:** I-25 exit 197 (Arapahoe Rd), just e to Clinton St, 0.5 mi s, then just e. **Facility:** 72 kitchen units. 3 stories, interior corridors. **Terms:** cancellation fee imposed. **Pool(s):** heated outdoor. **Activities:** exercise room. **Guest Services:** coin laundry.
SOME UNITS FEE

(See map & index p. 140.)

HOLIDAY INN EXPRESS HOTEL & SUITES

Phone: (303)662-0777 120

Hotel

$80-$139 5/1-9/30
$70-$129 10/1-4/30

Address: 7380 S Clinton St 80112 **Location:** I-25 exit 196 (Dry Creek Rd), e to S Clinton St, then just n. **Facility:** 92 units. 4 stories, interior corridors. **Amenities:** high-speed Internet. **Pool(s):** heated indoor. **Activities:** whirlpool, exercise room. **Guest Services:** valet and coin laundry, area transportation-within 10 mi.

BIZ FEE

/ SOME UNITS

STAYBRIDGE SUITES DENVER TECH CENTER

Phone: (303)858-9990 117

Extended Stay Hotel

$85-$105

Address: 7150 S Clinton St 80112 **Location:** I-25 exit 197 (Arapahoe Rd), just e to Clinton St, 0.5 mi s, then just e. **Facility:** 128 efficiencies. 3 stories, interior corridors. **Amenities:** high-speed Internet. **Pool(s):** heated outdoor. **Activities:** whirlpool, exercise room. **Guest Services:** complimentary and valet laundry, area transportation-within 5 mi.

CALL BIZ

/ SOME UNITS FEE

TOWNEPLACE SUITES DENVER TECH CENTER

Phone: (720)875-1113 122

Extended Stay Hotel

$69-$149

AAA Benefit: AAA hotel discounts of 5% or more.

Address: 7877 S Chester St 80112 **Location:** I-25 exit 196 (Dry Creek Rd), just w to Chester St, then 0.3 mi s. **Facility:** 95 kitchen units, some two bedrooms. 3 stories, interior corridors. **Amenities:** high-speed Internet. **Pool(s):** heated outdoor. **Activities:** exercise room. **Guest Services:** valet and coin laundry. **Free Special Amenities: continental breakfast and high-speed Internet.**

SAVE CALL BIZ

/ SOME UNITS FEE

WHERE TO EAT

CANTINA LAREDO **Phone:** 303/795-0339

Mexican

$8-$20

AAA Inspector Notes: Modern yet relaxed, this restaurant features creative Mexican fare. A great starter of top-shelf guacamole, which is prepared tableside, primes the palate for an entree of enchiladas, tacos, fajitas and chiles rellenos. **Bar:** full bar. **Address:** 6851 S Gaylord St 80122 **Location:** SR 470 exit University Blvd, 2 mi n, then just w. L D

Gourmet Mexican food, fresh-squeezed lime margaritas

THE EGG & I **Phone:** 303/804-0902 128

Breakfast

$6-$9

AAA Inspector Notes: Near the Denver Tech Center, this location of a small chain prepares a wide variety of popular breakfast items, including eggs Benedict, frittatas, crepes, waffles and pancakes. The lunch menu includes creative sandwiches, soups and salads. **Address:** 6818 S Yosemite St 80112 **Location:** I-25 exit 197 (Arapahoe Rd), just w to S Yosemite St, then just w; in Southgate Center. B L

MAGGIANO'S LITTLE ITALY

Phone: 303/858-1405 129

Italian

$11-$38

AAA Inspector Notes: Diners savor scrumptious, traditional favorites served in a bustling atmosphere reminiscent of Little Italy. The dining area projects an early-20th-century feel; loud conversations bouncing off high ceilings evoke a sense of the Roaring '20s. **Bar:** full bar. **Reservations:** suggested. **Address:** 7401 S Clinton St 80112 **Location:** I-25 exit 196 (Dry Creek Rd), just e, then just n. L D

PESCE FRESCO **Phone:** 303/290-9705 127

Italian

$8-$26

AAA Inspector Notes: Though Pesce Fresco means fresh fish, the menu is extensive and includes lamb, beef and nightly fresh seafood specials. This romantic eatery's attentive staff is quick to assist with meal selections and a choice of excellent wine that will complement your meal; their desire is for you to have a wonderful experience. The flavorful risotto and tiramisu are attractively presented and satisfying. **Bar:** full bar. **Reservations:** suggested, weekends. **Address:** 6600 S Quebec St 80111 **Location:** I-25 exit 197 (Arapahoe Rd), 0.9 mi w, then just n.

L D

CENTRAL CITY (B-4) pop. 663, elev. 8,496'

• Hotels p. 82

Within weeks of John Gregory's discovery of gold in 1859, hordes of prospectors were swarming over the steep sides of Gregory Gulch, which soon earned the title "the richest square mile on Earth." Although later eclipsed by the lodes at Cripple Creek, the gold dug from Gregory Gulch amounted to more than $67 million.

Central City, the middle camp among several that sprang up along the precipitous gulch, soon absorbed its immediate neighbors. Train loads of theatergoers came from Denver to enjoy Central City's cultural advantages. In 1932 the Opera Festival featured Lillian Gish in "Camille." The festival still attracts crowds every July and August.

With its preserved 1870s main street, Central City is part of a national historic district that is surrounded by hills and dotted with Victorian houses. Outdoor enthusiasts enjoy camping, hiking, hunting, mountain biking and cross-country skiing. The city offers a variety of museums, casinos and summer festivals.

City of Central Visitors Center: 125 Main St., P.O. Box 249, Central City, CO 80427. **Phone:** (303) 582-3345, (303) 582-5251 or (800) 542-2999.

GEM **CENTRAL CITY OPERA HOUSE,** w. of jct. Lawrence and Main sts. on Eureka St., was built in 1878 by the Welsh and Cornish as a reminder of the musical heritage of their homeland. The elaborate 550-seat opera house fell into disrepair when area mines closed shortly thereafter. Volunteers fortunately came to the rescue, and in 1932 the opera house was restored to its original Victorian splendor. Traditional operas have been presented in the grand theater each summer since its reopening. Tours feature the opera house and the adjoining 1872 Teller House hotel.

Hours: Guided tours are offered Tues.-Sun. 10:30-4, Memorial Day-Labor Day. Tour times may vary; phone ahead. Opera season runs late June-early Aug. **Cost:** Tour $5 for opera house, $5 for Teller House hotel. Opera performance prices vary; phone box office for information. **Phone:** (303) 582-5283 for tour information, or (303) 292-6700 for ticket information.

THE GILPIN HISTORY MUSEUM, 1 blk. from Lawrence at 228 E. High St., is in a restored 1870 schoolhouse. Displays include a miniature mining town, mining memorabilia, Main Street, Victorian rooms and changing exhibits. **Time:** Allow 1 hour minimum. **Hours:** Tues.-Sun. 11-4. **Cost:** $6; free (ages 0-11). Combination ticket with Thomas House Museum $10. **Phone:** (303) 582-5283.

Thomas House Museum is at 209 Eureka St. Virtually unchanged since 1897 when Ben Thomas bought it for his bride, the Colorado Greek Revival house contains family memorabilia, including quilts, clothes, calendars, clocks, kitchen items and family photographs.

Tours: Guided tours are available. **Time:** Allow 30 minutes minimum. **Hours:** Tours are offered Tues.-Sun. 11-4, Memorial Day-Labor Day. Last tour departs at closing. **Cost:** $6; free (ages 0-11). Combination ticket with The Gilpin History Museum $10. **Phone:** (303) 582-5283.

"OH MY GAWD" ROAD (CR 279), s. on Spring St. out of town to the dirt road entering Virginia Canyon, is a half-hour drive to Idaho Springs that offers spectacular views of Mount Evans and the Continental Divide. The bumpy gravel road, with intermittent paved areas, passes through old mining towns, including Russell Gulch, Old Glory Hole and Central City. **Note:** This road is narrow and winding and should not be attempted by camping vehicles or drivers unaccustomed to mountain driving. Check road conditions with the visitor center before starting. **Phone:** (303) 567-4382.

GAMBLING ESTABLISHMENTS

- **Doc Holliday Casino** is at 131 Main St. **Hours:** Sun.-Thurs. 9 a.m.-midnight, Fri.-Sat. 9 a.m.-3 a.m. **Phone:** (303) 582-1400.
- **Easy Street Casino** is at 120 Main St. **Hours:** Daily 8 a.m.-2 a.m. **Phone:** (303) 582-5914, ext. 235.
- **Fortune Valley Hotel and Casino** is at 321 Gregory St. **Hours:** Daily 24 hours. **Phone:** (303) 582-0800 or (800) 924-6646.

FORTUNE VALLEY HOTEL AND CASINO **Phone:** 303/582-0800

Hotel
Rates not provided

Address: 321 Gregory St 80427 **Location:** US 6 to SR 119, to Gregory St, 1 mi to town; I-70 exit 243 (Hidden Valley/Central City), 8 mi nw on Central City Pkwy, then just e. **Facility:** A popular hotel and casino in the heart of the historic city, Fortune Valley has a nightclub where visitors enjoy live music, dancing and video poker. 118 units. 4 stories, interior corridors. **Parking:** on-site and valet. **Terms:** check-in 4 pm, age restrictions may apply. **Amenities:** video games (fee). **Dining:** 2 restaurants.

CALL FEE

CHIPITA PARK

• Part of Colorado Springs area — see map p. 85

CHIPITA LODGE B & B **Phone:** (719)684-8454

Bed & Breakfast
$125-$190

Address: 9090 Chipita Park Rd 80809 **Location:** Jct US 24, just s on Fountain Blvd (Pine Peak Hwy), then 1.5 mi w; right at fork. **Facility:** The pine-shrouded 1927 log lodge has a great room with a stone fireplace and cozy, inviting rooms with wood floors and Western/outdoor motifs. 5 units, some cabins. 1 story, interior/exterior corridors. **Terms:** open 5/1-10/31, office hours 9 am-7 pm, check-in 4 pm, 2 night minimum stay - seasonal and/or weekends, age restrictions may apply, 7 day cancellation notice-fee imposed. **Activities:** whirlpool.

/ SOME UNITS FEE

CIMARRON

THE INN AT ARROWHEAD **Phone:** 970/862-8206

Country Inn
$135-$175

Address: 21401 Alpine Plateau Rd 81220 **Location:** 11 mi e of Montrose on US 50, 5.1 mi s, follow signs. **Facility:** 12 units. 2 stories (no elevator), interior corridors. **Terms:** open 5/17-11/18 & 12/28-3/31, check-in 4 pm, 2 night minimum stay - weekends, 14 day cancellation notice-fee imposed. **Activities:** whirlpool, hiking trails, jogging.

/ SOME UNITS FEE

CLARK

VISTA VERDE GUEST RANCH **Phone:** (970)879-3858

Resort Ranch
$830-$1100 6/5-9/30
$700-$900 12/16-3/16

Address: 58000 Cowboy Way 80428 **Location:** 0.8 mi n to jct SR 129 and 64, 4.7 mi ne to Slavonia, then 1 mi on dirt road, follow signs. **Facility:** This all-inclusive luxury dude ranch has modern but small lodge rooms and luxury cabins, each with a deck and outdoor hot tub. Endless summer and winter activities cater to the entire family. 12 units, some two bedrooms, three bedrooms and cabins. 1-2 stories (no elevator), interior/exterior corridors. **Terms:** open 6/5-9/30 & 12/16-3/16, check-in 4 pm, check-out 9 am, 3-7 night minimum stay - seasonal, 90 day cancellation notice-fee imposed. **Pool(s):** heated outdoor. **Activities:** whirlpool, fishing, cross country skiing, snowmobiling, recreation programs, bicycles, hiking trails, jogging, horseback riding, horseshoes, volleyball, exercise room. *Fee:* massage. **Guest Services:** complimentary and valet laundry, area transportation-Steamboat Springs. **Free Special Amenities: full breakfast and airport transportation.**

SAVE

CLIFTON pop. 19,889

BEST WESTERN GRANDE RIVER INN & SUITES **Phone:** (970)434-3400

Hotel
$80-$150

AAA Benefit: Members save up to 20%, plus 10% bonus points with Best Western Rewards®.

Address: 3228 I-70 Business Loop 81520 **Location:** I-70 exit 37, 0.8 mi s. **Facility:** 49 units. 2 stories (no elevator), exterior corridors. **Amenities:** *Some:* high-speed Internet. **Pool(s):** heated indoor. **Activities:** whirlpool, exercise room. **Guest Services:** coin laundry. **Free Special Amenities: full breakfast and high-speed Internet.**

SAVE / SOME UNITS FEE

WHERE TO EAT

DOS HOMBRES Phone: 970/434-5078

Mexican
$8-$14

AAA Inspector Notes: There are several comfortable dining rooms in which diners sample many appetizers, salads and build-your-own combinations. Favorites include white bean chili, Navajo tacos, seafood enchiladas and Southwest pasta with grilled chicken and jalapeno cream sauce. A daily lunch special is made seven days a week, along with a poquito and New Mexican combination. **Bar:** full bar. **Address:** 3245 I-70 Business Loop 81520 **Location:** I-70 exit 37, 0.8 mi s, east corner of US 6. (L) (D)

COLORADO NATIONAL MONUMENT (D-1)

Colorado National Monument is reached from Fruita via I-70 exit 19 or Grand Junction via SR 340 (Broadway). This bold, big and brilliantly colored canyon country, with its towering and fascinating rock sculptures, covers 32 square miles of rugged terrain. Rim Rock Drive is one of the grandest scenic drives in the American West and offers both motorists and bicyclists access to 23 miles of breathtaking scenery. The drive also provides access to the visitor center and campground, 19 interpretive viewpoints and 14 hiking trails varying in length from 1 to 14 miles.

It is a semi-desert landscape of pinyon pines and Utah juniper; low-growing plants and wildflowers grace the area in spring. Camping and picnicking areas, self-guiding nature trails and longer hiking paths are available. Back-country camping requires a permit, available free at the visitor center.

Allow 2 hours, 30 minutes minimum. Daily 24 hours. Entrance fee $7 per private vehicle or $4 per person arriving by other means (valid for 7 days). Annual permits $20. Camping $10. Phone (970) 858-3617.

VISITOR CENTER, near the Fruita entrance, presents cultural and natural history exhibits as well as two 12-minute video programs. **Hours:** Daily 8-6, Memorial Day-Sept. 30; 9-5, Oct.-Nov. and Mar. 1-day before Memorial Day; 9-4, rest of year. Closed Christmas. **Cost:** Free. **Phone:** (970) 858-3617.

Colorado Springs

Then & Now

Gen. William J. Palmer, forging westward with his Denver & Rio Grande Railroad in 1871, saw the area's potential early on and formulated a plan of creating a playground for the wealthy on what was essentially a sagebrush flat. The village already at the site, a miners' and millers' town called Colorado City, hardly met his stringent requirements. Palmer and his associates moved a few miles away and drove the first stake at what is now Pikes Peak and Cascade avenues.

Within the year there were more than 150 temporary and two permanent structures, irrigation ditches, countless seedling cottonwoods and land donated for a college. All were placed according to an orderly plan with broad boulevards, school lots and parks.

A road linked the new town with the mineral springs at Manitou Springs, 6 miles west. Colorado Springs, its name derived from the spa and from Colorado City, was on the way to becoming everything Palmer wanted, and more.

Many of the younger sons of the English gentry arrived. Polo, riding to hounds, gentlemen's clubs and Tudor architecture became so much a part of the Springs that it was soon known as Little London.

When not playing cricket or attending social functions, these Britons and their American counterparts speculated in mining. They made millions, especially after the bonanza in Cripple Creek. The city benefited in the form of parks, office buildings, mansions and hotels. By the first decade of the 20th century, Colorado Springs ranked among the wealthiest cities per capita in the country.

Meanwhile, Colorado City flourished, partly because of liquor trafficking and other temptations prohibited by its neighbor. Allegedly, tunnels ran between the two communities to protect the anonymity of those citizens who liked to visit the other side of the tracks. Colorado City was ultimately absorbed by the Springs and its respectability.

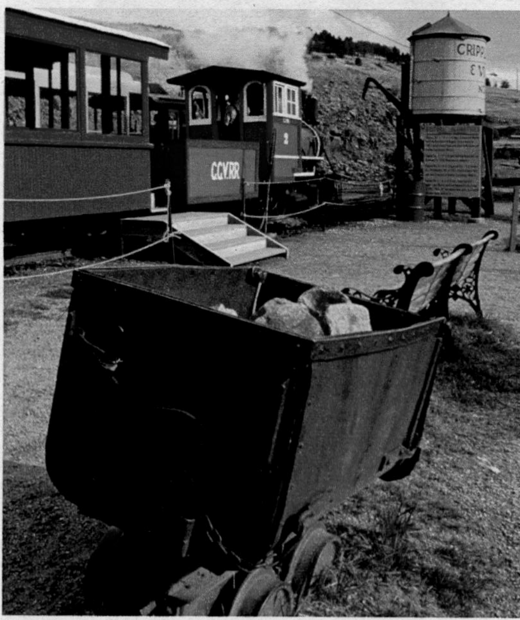

Cripple Creek and Victor Narrow Gauge Railroad

Some of the old buildings still exist, particularly in the Old Colorado City Historic District between 24th and 28th streets. They house specialty shops, restaurants, galleries and municipal offices.

Today, Colorado Springs continues to enjoy the reputation it received upon its creation—a destination for recreation, relaxation and bountiful sightseeing opportunities. A few miles west, scenic US 24 climbs to the 14,100-foot summit of Pikes Peak; the journey to the top offers stunning panoramas, ranging from lush alpine forest to the stark beauty above the timberline. And, if the prospect of driving the twisting route makes you a bit nervous, you can hop on a train at the Manitou Springs depot and travel upward via the cog railway.

(Continued on p. 86.)

Destination Colorado Springs

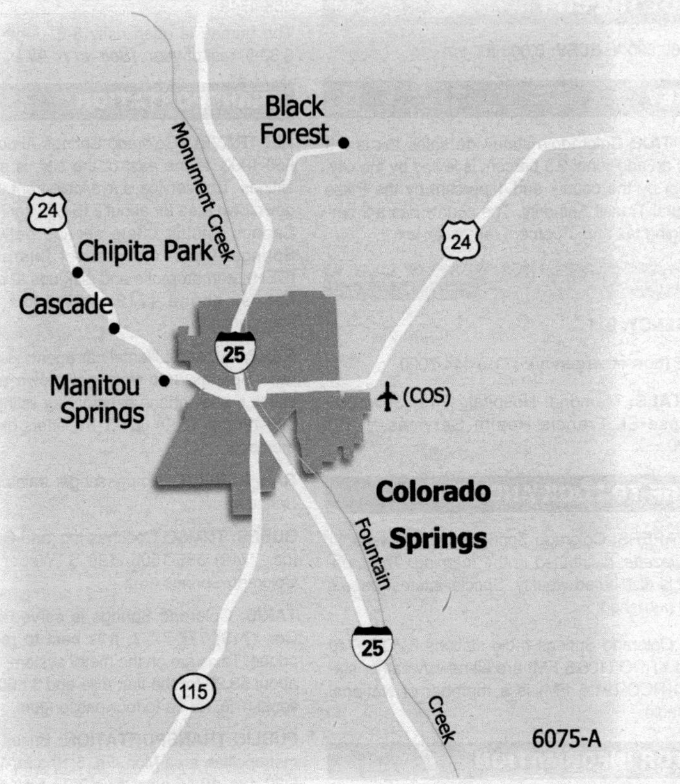

This map shows cities in the Colorado Springs vicinity where you will find attractions, hotels and restaurants. Cities are listed alphabetically in this book on the following pages.

Fast Facts

ABOUT THE CITY

POP: 360,890 ▪ **ELEV:** 6,008 ft.

MONEY

SALES TAX: Colorado's statewide sales tax is 2.9 percent; an additional 2.5 percent is levied by the city, 1 percent by the county and 1 percent by the Pikes Peak Rural Transit Authority. The county has a 2 percent lodging tax and 1 percent rental car tax.

WHOM TO CALL

EMERGENCY: 911

POLICE (non-emergency): (719) 444-7000

HOSPITALS: Memorial Hospital, (719) 365-5000 ▪ Penrose-St. Francis Health Services, (719) 776-5000.

WHERE TO LOOK AND LISTEN

NEWSPAPERS: Colorado Springs' major newspaper is *The Gazette,* distributed in the morning. *The Independent* is distributed weekly. Special-interest papers also are published.

RADIO: Colorado Springs radio stations KVOR (740 AM) and KRDO (105.5 FM) are all-news/weather stations ▪ KRCC (91.5 FM) is a member of National Public Radio.

VISITOR INFORMATION

Colorado Springs Convention & Visitors Bureau: 515 S. Cascade Ave., Colorado Springs, CO 80903. **Phone:** (719) 635-7506, (800) 888-4748 or (800) 368-4748.

The bureau is open daily 8-6, June-Aug.; Mon.-Fri. 8:30-5, rest of year. ***(See ad p. 93.)***

TRANSPORTATION

AIR TRAVEL: Colorado Springs Airport (COS), (719) 550-1900, to the east of the city, is served by major airlines. Taxi service is available from the airport to the downtown area for about $15-$20 each way. Colorado Springs Shuttle offers service between Colorado Springs Airport and Denver International Airport (DEN), with drop-offs and pick-ups at designated area hotels; phone (719) 687-3456 for schedule information.

RENTAL CARS: Rental car agencies serve the Colorado Springs area from downtown and the airport; check the telephone directory for listings. Hertz, (719) 596-1863 or (800) 654-3131, offers discounts to AAA members.

RAIL SERVICE: No passenger trains serve Colorado Springs.

BUSES: TNM&O Coaches Inc. and Greyhound Lines Inc., (719) 635-1505, 120 S. Weber St., serve the Colorado Springs area.

TAXIS: Colorado Springs is served by Yellow Cab Co., (719) 777-7777. It is best to request cabs by phone. Taxis are on the meter system, with the charge about $3.20 for the first mile and $1.60 for each additional mile, for up to four passengers.

PUBLIC TRANSPORTATION: Buses operate in the metropolitan area Mon.-Fri. 5:10 a.m.-10:45 p.m., Sat. 5:30 a.m.-10:45 p.m., Sun 7:30 a.m.-5:35 p.m.; night service is limited. The fare for in-town routes is $1.75, zone routes $1. Phone (719) 385-7433.

(Continued from p. 84.)

Garden of the Gods Park, another must-see, offers dramatic views of towering sandstone rock formations with Pikes Peak looming in the background. The erosion-sculpted, red-hued marvels have morphed into such shapes as Kissing Camels, Siamese Twins and a Sleeping Giant, and depending on the time of day you visit, the light produces a vast array of mesmerizing effects. The park is a natural playground for hikers, rock climbers and those just happy to snap photos of the impressive birdlife and geologic wonders. Given the environment, mountain bikers, golfers and horseback riders find the community a perfect setting in which to indulge their passions.

The city has become an important military center. The North American Air Defense Command (NORAD), sequestered in the granite heart of Cheyenne Mountain, was command-central for American defensive troops during the Desert Storm conflict. More visible are the U.S. Air Force Academy, Fort Carson Army Base, Peterson Air Force Base and U.S. Space Command.

Especially prominent is the Air Force Academy's Cadet Chapel: Majestic glass and silver spires jutting skyward resemble 17 swept-wing, vertical-takeoff planes poised to break Earth's bonds. The academy's visitor center welcomes guests, who are typically free to explore the chapel and such sites as Arnold Hall, the Field House and the Honor Court, but they should inquire first due to fluctuating security levels.

Southwest of the city via SRs 115 and 122 is The Broadmoor resort. Since its opening in 1918 as a grand hotel, it has grown into a recreational retreat and includes two spas, three 18-hole golf courses, 16 tennis courts, squash courts, hiking trails and horseback riding.

Arriving

By Car

North-south access is via I-25, which skirts the eastern face of the Rocky Mountains and is concurrent with US 85/87 through much of Colorado. I-25 is the fast route into or through Colorado Springs, with interchanges at major streets; US 85/87 leaves the interstate briefly in favor of downtown streets. Another major north-south thoroughfare is Powers Boulevard (SR 21), which runs near the airport in the eastern section of the city.

Yet another north-south route leading into town is Nevada Avenue (SR 115 in the southern part of the city), which offers a shortcut from US 50 between Cañon City and Pueblo. East-west travel is via US 24, which comes into the city from the eastern plains as Platte Avenue and from the western mountains through Ute Pass.

Getting Around

Street System

I-25 is the major north-south artery and fastest means of travel through Colorado Springs. Nevada Avenue (SR 115 in the southern section of the city) runs parallel to I-25 and provides access to many downtown streets.

US 24 (Martin Luther King, Jr. Bypass) travels east to west, becoming Platte Avenue when it crosses I-25 into the eastern section of the city; it leads to Manitou Springs and Pikes Peak in the west. East-west roads that interchange with I-25 are Garden of the Gods Road, Fillmore Street, Woodmen Road and Uintah Street.

Parking

Downtown on-street parking is metered, 75c-$1 per hour. Commercial garages and lots are available for 75c-$1 per hour, with a daily maximum of $6.75-$7.50. Prepaid "Easy Park" cards are accepted at most meters and can be purchased at the City Administration Building at Nevada and Colorado avenues.

Shopping

Malls and shopping centers provide most of the shopping opportunities in Colorado Springs. Some of the popular centers include Chapel Hills Mall, with anchor stores Dillard's, JCPenney, Macy's and Sears, at Academy and Briargate boulevards; The Citadel, with anchors Dillard's and JCPenney, N. Academy Boulevard and US 24; The Promenade Shops at Briargate, Briargate Parkway and SR 83; and downtown Colorado Springs, Pikes Peak and Tejon. Other centers include Rustic Hills, Palmer Park and Academy Boulevard, and Broadmoor Towne Center, S. Nevada Avenue and Southgate Road.

A 19th-century haven of fur trappers, cowboys, gamblers and a few outlaws and gunfighters, Old Colorado City Historic District, between 24th and 28th streets, now houses specialty shops. The Garden of the Gods Trading Post, built in the late 1920s to resemble Pueblo Indian houses, offers Indian arts, crafts, jewelry, rugs and pottery as well as signed prints by well-known artists.

Big Events

Two street festivals featuring local vendors and entertainment herald the arrival of spring to Colorado Springs. Territory Days in Old Colorado City takes place in May, and June brings Spring Spree to Memorial Park.

Colorado Springs' sports facilities play host to athletic events throughout the year, but the major events take place in summer. The Ride for the Brand Championship Ranch Rodeo and the GEM Pikes Peak or Bust Rodeo at the Norris-Penrose Events Center, both held in early July, attract top rodeo cowboys from around the country. A Rodeo Parade takes place the Tuesday evening prior to Rodeo Week in downtown Colorado Springs. Sports fans also will enjoy the Pikes Peak International Hill Climb in July on Pikes Peak Highway and the Pikes Peak Ascent and Marathon at Pikes Peak in August.

Over the Labor Day weekend, watch more than 100 colorful balloons ascend in Memorial Park during the GEM Colorado Balloon Classic. The Festival of Lights Parade downtown ushers in the holiday season in early December.

Sports & Rec

The surrounding lands of the Pike National Forest *(see Pikes Peak and Pike National Forest p. 269)* provide opportunities for outdoor recreation. Green Mountain Falls and Woodland Park are northwest of the city. **Hiking** and **horseback riding** on the Barr

Colorado Balloon Classic

Colorado Springs Philharmonic

National Recreation Trail are enjoyable ways to travel to the summit of Pikes Peak. **Camping** also is popular in this area.

Horseback riding through Garden of the Gods Park, North Cheyenne Cañon Park or at area dude ranches can be arranged at a variety of locations in the area. A list is available at the convention and visitors bureau; phone (719) 635-7506, (800) 888-4748 or (800) 368-4748.

Golf enthusiasts have their choice of three 18-hole championship golf courses at The Broadmoor resort, (719) 577-5775, or the 18-hole championship Pete Dye course at the Cheyenne Mountain Resort, (719) 538-4000. Golfers also can tee off at the Patty Jewett Municipal Golf Course (27 holes), E. Española and N. Prospect streets, (719) 385-6938, or the Pine Creek Golf Course (18 holes), 9850 Divot Tr., (719) 594-9999. The Valley Hi Municipal Course (18 holes), 610 Chelton Rd., (719) 385-6919, also has a swimming pool and driving range. Vineyard Golf Club (nine holes) is at 3819 Janitell Rd., (719) 226-2466.

Most city parks have **tennis** courts and **bicycling** trails. The Broadmoor resort also has tennis courts. Guided 20-mile **mountain biking** trips from the 14,110-summit of Pikes Peak are offered daily late April through early October by Challenge Unlimited; phone (719) 633-6399 or (800) 798-5954. **Swimming** is available at several indoor and outdoor aquatic facilities operated by the City of Colorado Springs; phone (719) 385-5984. Memorial Park, at the corner of Pikes Peak and Union, is home to a 40,000-square-foot Skate Park that welcomes skate boarders, inline skaters and BMX riders.

Hometown fans come out to cheer the Air Force Academy **football** team, phone (719) 472-1895, the Colorado Sky Sox **baseball** team, phone (719) 591-7699, and the Colorado College **hockey** team, phone (719) 389-6324.

Performing Arts

The Colorado Springs Fine Arts Center *(see attraction listing p. 90)*, 30 W. Dale St., is the scene of permanent and traveling art exhibits, theatrical performances, concerts, dance productions and film showings. The Civic Music Theater also holds performances at the fine arts center throughout the year.

Pikes Peak Center, 190 S. Cascade Ave., plays host to more than 200 performances a year, running the gamut from ballet, opera, theater and the symphony to country and rock music. The Colorado Springs Philharmonic plays its September through May season here; phone (719) 884-2110 for ticket information. The center is also the home of Broadway in Colorado Springs; phone (719) 799-4139. Festival of World Theater, at various locations, stages more than 30 productions from late summer through early fall that appeal to a variety of ages.

Colorado Springs World Arena features top-name performers in both theatrical productions and concerts, ice hockey and skating shows. The Iron Springs Chateau and Playhouse dinner theater is at 444 Ruxton Ave. Plays also are staged at Colorado College and the University of Colorado-Colorado Springs. Check the local newspapers for complete listings of current events.

ATTRACTIONS

AMERICAN NUMISMATIC ASSOCIATION MONEY MUSEUM, 818 N. Cascade Ave., claims to be the country's largest museum dedicated to coins, paper money, medals and related items. The museum presents changing and permanent exhibits featuring coins from ancient civilizations to the present. Of special interest is a collection of American gold coins. A library features more than 40,000 volumes related to numismatics.

Time: Allow 1 hour minimum. **Hours:** Museum Tues.-Sat. 10:30-5. Closed major holidays. **Cost:** $5; $4 (ages 55+, active military and students with ID); free (third Sat. of the month). **Phone:** (719) 632-2646, Ext. 134 or (800) 367-9723.

BEAR CREEK NATURE CENTER, off 26th St. at 245 Bear Creek Rd. in Bear Creek Regional Park, features hands-on, interactive Colorado wildlife exhibits and multimedia nature videotapes. Self-guiding nature trails begin at the center. **Time:** Allow 1 hour minimum. **Hours:** Wed.-Fri. 9-2, Sat. 9-4. Park and nature trails daily dawn-dusk. Closed major holidays. **Cost:** Free. **Phone:** (719) 520-6387.

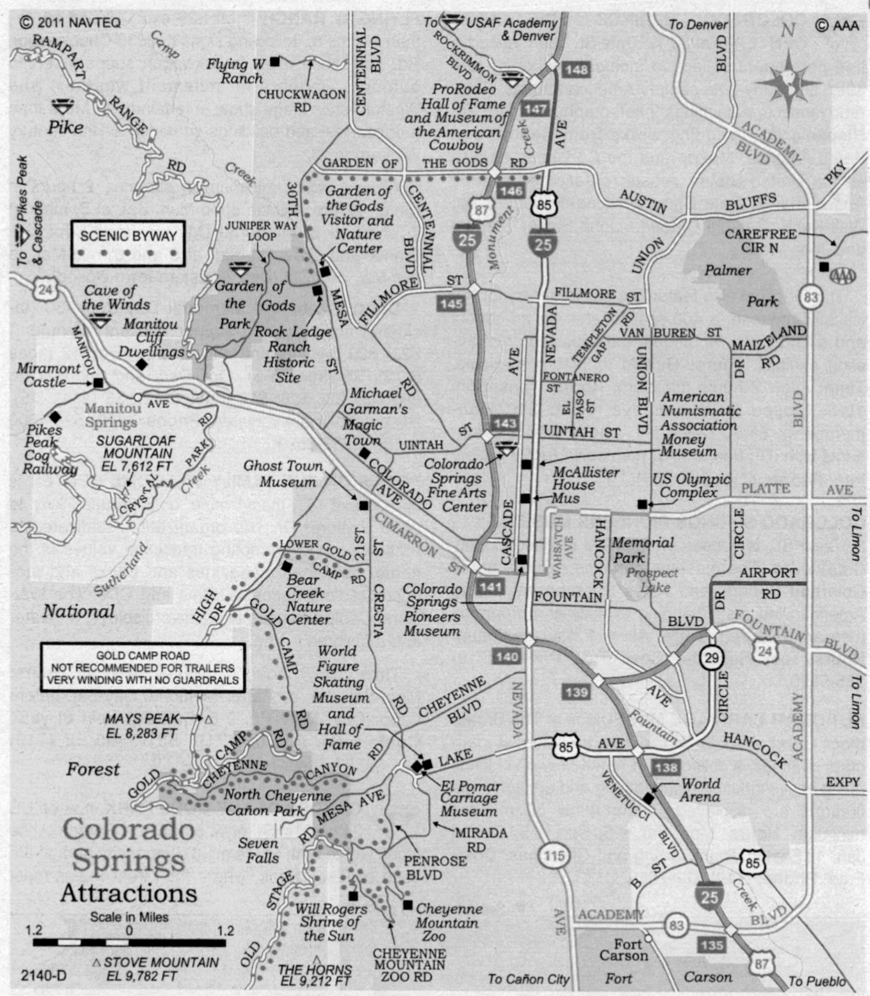

CAVE OF THE WINDS—see Manitou Springs p. 249.

CHEYENNE MOUNTAIN ZOO, 2.75 mi. w. of I-25 exit 138, then 2 mi. s.w. following signs to 4250 Cheyenne Mountain Zoo Rd., claims the distinction of being America's only mountain zoo. The Rocky Mountain Wild exhibit features grizzly bears, river otters, mountain lions and moose among many other animals. The African Rift Valley exhibit highlights the zoo's noted giraffe herd. More than 750 animals, including many endangered species, are featured. The landscaped grounds also contain an antique carousel and a tot train as well as the Mountaineer Sky Ride, an open-air chairlift providing spectacular views of the Pikes Peak region.

Time: Allow 3 hours minimum. **Hours:** Daily 9-6, Memorial Day-Labor Day; 9-5, rest of year. Last admission is at 4 year-round. Mountaineer Sky Ride Mon.-Thurs. 9-6 (last ride at 5:30), Memorial Day weekend-Labor Day. Sat.-Sun. 10-4 (last ride at 3:30), rest of year (weather permitting). **Cost:** Memorial Day-Labor Day (includes Will Rogers Shrine of the Sun) $17.25; $15.25 (ages 65+); $14.25 (military with ID); $12.25 (ages 3-11); $9.25 (military children). Rest of year $14.25; $12.25 (ages 65+); $11.25 (military with ID); $10.25 (ages 3-11); $7.25 (military children). Mountaineer Sky Ride $5; $4 (ages 3-11). **Phone:** (719) 633-9925.

Will Rogers Shrine of the Sun, reached via Cheyenne Mountain Zoo Rd., which runs through the zoo, is a stone tower memorial to the 20th-century humorist. Built at an elevation of 8,136 feet, the shrine provides spectacular views of Colorado Springs and the surrounding area. **Time:** Allow 1 hour minimum. **Hours:** Daily 9-4, Memorial Day weekend-Labor Day; 9-3, rest of year (weather permitting). Closed Jan. 1, Thanksgiving and Christmas. **Cost:** Included with Cheyenne Mountain Zoo. **Phone:** (719) 578-5367.

GEM **COLORADO SPRINGS FINE ARTS CENTER** is at 30 W. Dale St. The museum's fine permanent collection includes works by late 19th- and early 20th-century American artists; Colorado landscape paintings; photography; modern art; Hispanic art, including works from Central and South America, Mexico and the Caribbean as well as the United States. Artists represented include Ansel Adams, Dale Chihuly, Richard Diebenkorn, Walt Kuhn, Georgia O'Keeffe, John Singer Sargent and John Waters.

The museum also features a tactile gallery for the visually impaired, a 400-seat theater, an art school and a courtyard. Additional galleries feature traveling exhibits. **Tours:** Guided tours are available. **Time:** Allow 2 hours minimum. **Hours:** Tues.-Sun. 10-5. Closed major holidays. **Cost:** $10 (nonmembers); $8.50 (ages 5-17, ages 62+ and students with ID); free to FAC members. Tactile gallery free. **Phone:** (719) 634-5581.

COLORADO SPRINGS PIONEERS MUSEUM, 215 S. Tejon St., is housed in the 1903 El Paso County Courthouse. The museum contains exhibits about Colorado Springs and Pikes Peak heritage, and American Indians. Changing exhibits and programs also are featured. **Time:** Allow 1 hour minimum. **Hours:** Tues.-Sat. 10-4. **Cost:** Free. **Phone:** (719) 385-5990.

EL POMAR CARRIAGE MUSEUM is at The Broadmoor resort at 11 Lake Cir. Two presidential inaugural coaches, a collection of horse-drawn vehicles, riding accessories, Indian clothing and artifacts, and firearms are displayed. **Time:** Allow 30 minutes minimum. **Hours:** Mon.-Sat. 9-5, Sun. 1-5. Closed Jan. 1, Easter, Thanksgiving and Christmas. **Cost:** Free. **Phone:** (719) 577-7065.

FLYING W RANCH is off I-25 exit 146, 2.4 mi. w., then 1.6 mi. n., following signs to 3330 Chuckwagon Rd. The ranch offers chuckwagon suppers served outdoors (indoors in inclement weather) and Western-style stage show entertainment. More than a dozen restored buildings comprise a 19th-century Western town.

Allow 4 hours minimum in summer, 2 hours in winter. **Hours:** Village open Mon.-Sat. at 5, meal at 7, show at 8, Memorial Day weekend-Sept. 30. Dinner and show Fri.-Sat. at 5 and 8, mid-Mar. to mid-May and Oct.-Dec. (Western town closed).

Cost: Fri. before Memorial Day-Sept. 30 (including chuck wagon supper and entertainment) $22; $20 (seniors and military with ID); $12 (ages 6-12); $5 (ages 3-5). Oct.-Dec. and mid-Mar. to mid-May $25-$28; $12 (ages 6-12); $5 (ages 3-5). Reservations are required. **Phone:** (719) 598-4000 or (800) 232-3599.

FOCUS ON THE FAMILY WELCOME CENTER is off I-25 exit 151, then 1 mi. e. on Briargate Pkwy. to 8685 Explorer Dr. The organization, dedicated to preserving and promoting traditional values in the home, publishes magazines and books and produces radio broadcasts, films and CDs. The Welcome Center includes interactive displays, a theater and a children's area.

Time: Allow 1 hour, 30 minutes minimum. **Hours:** Mon.-Sat. 9-5, day after Memorial Day-Sat. before Labor Day; Mon.-Fri. 9-5, Sat. 9-4, rest of year. **Cost:** Free. **Phone:** (719) 531-3400, or (719) 531-3328 for tour reservations.

GEM **GARDEN OF THE GODS PARK,** n.w. off US 24 on 31st St. or w. off I-25 on Garden of the Gods Rd. to 30th St., is a 1,319-acre city park at the base of Pikes Peak, where the Great Plains meet

▼ See AAA listing p. 92 ▼

the Rockies. Flora and fauna within the park reflect the rich diversity of this crossroad. In 1909, railroad magnate Charles Elliot Perkins bequeathed to the city the parkland he purchased in 1879 with the stipulation that it remain open and free to the public.

The park is known for its towering red sandstone formations, which include Kissing Camels and Balanced Rock. The soft sunlight of early morning and late afternoon enhances the beauty of the formations. Beautifully framed snapshots of Pikes Peak are available from many viewpoints.

In addition, the park offers a diverse list of recreational options. Visitors can explore miles of both paved and unpaved trails and try mountain biking, horseback riding and guided nature walks. The park's many footpaths have easy slopes. Visitors safe on the ground can watch climbers scale the cliffs. **Time:** Allow 1 hour minimum. **Hours:** Visitor center open daily 8-8, May-Oct.; 9-5, rest of year. Park hours 5 a.m.-11 p.m., May-Oct; 5 a.m.-9 p.m., rest of year. **Cost:** Free. **Phone:** (719) 634-6666.

Garden of the Gods Visitor and Nature Center, 1805 N. 30th St., offers maps, exhibits, a museum, a 14-minute multimedia show featuring park history, a 20-minute bus tour of the park, guided nature walks, Segway tours, interactive natural history exhibits and brochures and information about the area.

Time: Allow 1 hour minimum. **Hours:** Daily 8-8, Memorial Day-Labor Day; 9-5, rest of year. Guided nature walks are given daily at 10 and 2. Bus tour daily 9:30-4:30, Memorial Day-Labor Day. Closed Jan. 1, Thanksgiving and Christmas. **Cost:** Museum and nature walks free. Multimedia show $5; $2 (ages 5-12). Bus tour $5; $3 (ages 5-12). **Phone:** (719) 634-6666.

GHOST TOWN MUSEUM is off I-25 exit 141, then 1.5 mi. w. to 400 S. 21st St., next to Van Briggle Pottery and Tile. This 1800s Old West town, relocated and preserved within the former Colorado Midland Railroad depot, is comprised of buildings abandoned after the gold rush era. Included are a general store, saloon, Victorian house, blacksmith shop, jail, livery stable, rooming house and other buildings, each containing artifacts of the period. Gold panning and other hands-on activities are offered.

Hours: Mon.-Sat. 9-6, Sun. 10-6, June-Aug.; daily 10-5, rest of year. **Cost:** $6.50; $5 (ages 6-16). **Phone:** (719) 634-0696.

GOLD CAMP ROAD is 1 mi. e. off US 115 on Cheyenne Blvd., then 2 mi. n. on 21st St. The road is a narrow, twisting, 36-mile gravel trail that follows the Cripple Creek Short Line Railroad roadbed through North Cheyenne Canyon. President Theodore Roosevelt described it as the "trip that bankrupts the English language." It is a favorite scenic route for cyclists.

Note: The road has no guardrails and is unsuitable for trailers and some RVs. Only experienced mountain drivers should attempt it. Phone ahead for road conditions. An 8-mile section of the road is closed due to a tunnel collapse; Old Stage Road provides a detour. **Time:** Allow 2 hours, 30 minutes minimum. **Phone:** (719) 636-1602 for the U.S. Forest Service.

THE JOHN MAY MUSEUM CENTER, 8 mi. s.w. on SR 115 (Nevada Ave.) to 710 Rock Creek Canyon Rd., exhibits more than 7,000 giant and exotic insects from the jungles of the world. Also featured are exhibits chronicling space exploration. **Time:** Allow 1 hour, 30 minutes minimum. **Hours:** Daily 9-6, May-Sept. **Cost:** $6; $5 (ages 60+); $3 (ages 6-12). **Phone:** (719) 576-0450 or (800) 666-3841.

MANITOU CLIFF DWELLINGS—see Manitou Springs p. 249.

McALLISTER HOUSE MUSEUM, 423 N. Cascade Ave., was built for Maj. Henry McAllister, who assisted Gen. William Palmer in developing Colorado Springs. The restored 1873 house contains original and period furnishings. **Time:** Allow 30 minutes minimum. **Hours:** Wed.-Sat. 10-4, Sun. noon-4, May-Aug.; Thurs.-Sat. 10-4, rest of year. Last tour begins 30 minutes before closing. **Cost:** $5; $4 (ages 62+); $3 (ages 6-12). **Phone:** (719) 635-7925.

MICHAEL GARMAN'S MAGIC TOWN, 2418 W. Colorado Ave., is a 3-D cityscape sculpted by artist Michael Garman. Through the use of mirrors, holographs, videotape projection and illusion, Garman has designed a miniature city of yesterday, complete with mom-and-pop cafés, pool halls, flophouses and saloons. **Time:** Allow 30 minutes minimum. **Hours:** Mon.-Sat. 10-5:30, Sun. 11-4. **Cost:** $7; $5 (ages 65+); $3 (ages 7-12). **Phone:** (719) 471-9391 or (800) 731-3908.

MIRAMONT CASTLE—see Manitou Springs p. 249.

NORTH CHEYENNE CAÑON PARK is reached via Cheyenne Blvd. Striking rock formations and waterfalls, notably Helen Hunt Falls and Silver Cascade Falls, characterize the canyon. Hiking and biking trails, some challenging, are available. A permit is required for technical rock climbing.

Starsmore Discovery Center, at the east entrance of the park, is a visitor center with exhibits about area wildlife, the history of the park and nature programs. Another visitor center is at Helen Hunt Falls, 3 miles up the canyon. Both centers offer special programs and hummingbird watching in summer. **Hours:** Starsmore Discovery Center daily 9-5, June-Aug.; Tues.-Sat. 9-3, rest of year. Helen Hunt Falls Visitor Center 11-5, June-Aug. Phone ahead to confirm schedule. **Cost:** Free. **Phone:** (719) 385-6086.

High Drive begins at the end of N. Cheyenne Cañon Rd. The one-way dirt route ascends a steep mountain for 1 mile, then descends 2.4 miles, eventually intersecting with Gold Camp Road. Maps and information about the drive are available at the Starsmore Discovery Center at the base of N. Cheyenne Canon Road.

Note: The route has no guardrails, and drivers should expect hairpin turns and loose gravel; only experienced mountain drivers should attempt the drive. **Time:** Allow 1 hour minimum. **Hours:** Daily 5 a.m.-dusk, May-Sept. **Cost:** Free. **Phone:** (719) 385-6086.

PALMER PARK, about 3 mi. n.e., has entrances off Maizeland and Paseo rds. Comprising 737 acres on Austin Bluffs, the park affords a view of the mountains and offers scenic drives and hiking trails. **Time:** Allow 30 minutes minimum. **Hours:** Daily 5 a.m.-11 p.m., May-Oct.; 5 a.m.-9 p.m., rest of year. **Cost:** Free. **Phone:** (719) 385-5940.

PETERSON AIR AND SPACE MUSEUM, 7 mi. e. on US 24 (use the west gate into Peterson AFB) to 150 E. Ent Ave., has exhibits about North American air defense, Colorado Springs' aviation heritage, the Air Force Space Command and the North American Aerospace Defense Command (NORAD). Displays include 21 historic aircraft and missiles, military uniforms, model airplanes and a World War II-era Peterson Army Air Base exhibit. The museum is in the original 1941 Colorado Springs airport terminal at Peterson Air Force Base.

Note: Visitor passes are required for those without a military or Department of Defense ID. Visitors must provide full names of visitors ages 18+, driver's license number, car license plate number and state, and dates of birth. This information is required at least 24 hours prior to arrival; for Saturday visits, information is required 72 hours prior to visit. Those driving on the base must have a valid driver's license, current vehicle registration and proof of insurance to enter. Security levels may fluctuate; phone ahead for updates. Photo ID is required for all adults. **Hours:** Tues.-Sat. 9-4. **Cost:** Free. **Phone:** (719) 556-4915.

PIKES PEAK—see Pikes Peak and Pike National Forest p. 269.

PRORODEO HALL OF FAME AND MUSEUM OF THE AMERICAN COWBOY, w. of I-25 exit 148 at 101 ProRodeo Dr., depicts the history of rodeo and honors the sport's champions through multimedia presentations, art, audiovisual programs and artifacts. Setting the tone, a statue of legendary world champion bronc rider Casey Tibbs resides at the entrance to the hall.

The attraction, appropriately enough, is adjacent to the national headquarters of the Professional Rodeo Cowboys Association. Exhibits in Heritage Hall trace the evolution of the modern rodeo. The Hall of Champions honors rodeo greats, both human and equine, and displays statues, trophies and tack belonging to the sport's heroes. A garden, bronzes, an arena and a corral can be found outdoors.

Time: Allow 1 hour, 30 minutes minimum. **Hours:** Daily 9-5, Apr. 1-Sept. 1; Wed.-Sun. 9-5, rest of year. Closed Jan. 1, Easter, Labor Day, Thanksgiving, Christmas Eve, Christmas and Dec. 31. **Cost:** $6; $5 (ages 55+); $3 (ages 6-12). **Phone:** (719) 528-4764.

ROCK LEDGE RANCH HISTORIC SITE, at the e. entrance to Garden of the Gods Park off 30th St., is a living-history museum and working farm where interpreters in period clothing depict American Indian and pioneer life in the Pikes Peak region. Displays include an 1860s homestead, an 1880s farm, a 1907 estate house, a 19th-century blacksmith shop and an American Indian camp and general store.

Time: Allow 1 hour minimum. **Hours:** Wed.-Sat. 10-5, early June to mid-Aug. **Cost:** $8; $4 (ages 6-17); $5 (ages 55+). **Phone:** (719) 578-6777.

SEVEN FALLS, 7 mi. w. on Cheyenne Blvd., cascade down a steep canyon in seven distinct falls. The most spectacular view of the falls is seen from the Eagle's Nest platform, reached by an in-mountain elevator or by walking up a 185-step stairway alongside the falls. Self-guiding audio tours highlight features found along two nature trails, one leading to Midnight Falls. Native wildlife abounds with deer and hummingbirds. On summer nights and during the Christmas season, the falls are illuminated in the evening.

Time: Allow 1 hour, 30 minutes minimum. **Hours:** Daily 8:30 a.m.-10:30 p.m., June 1 to mid-Aug.; Sun.-Thurs. 9-5:15, Fri.-Sat. 9 a.m.-9:30 p.m. in May and Sept.; daily 9-4:15, rest of year. Closed Jan. 1, Thanksgiving and Christmas Eve. **Cost:** $9.25-$10.75; $5.75-$6.75 (ages 6-15). **Phone:** (719) 632-0765. ***(See ad p. 90.)***

U.S. AIR FORCE ACADEMY, 14 mi. n. on I-25 to exit 156B, prepares cadets for careers in the Air Force. Guests may visit the Cadet Chapel, Field House, Arnold Hall, the Honor Court and the Visitor Center. The newest of the nation's service academies, the U.S. Air Force Academy graduated its first class in 1959.

The strikingly modern aluminum, glass and steel Cadet Chapel and its 17 spires are a campus landmark. The chapel provides worship facilities for cadets of all faiths. The Field House is the site of cadet athletic events and Arnold Hall is a concert and entertainment venue. The academy's Honor Court, between the chapel and Arnold Hall, displays statues and Air Force memorials. Throughout the academy grounds are static displays of aircraft.

Note: Fluctuating security levels may affect public access; phone ahead to verify status. **Time:** Allow 2 hours minimum. **Hours:** Academy daily 8-6. Visitor center daily 9-5. Chapel Mon.-Sat. 9-5, Sun. 1-5. Chapel hours may vary due to services and events. **Cost:** Free. **Phone:** (719) 333-3818, (719) 333-2025 to check public access status, or (719) 333-2636 for chapel information.

The Barry Goldwater Air Force Academy Visitor Center is off I-25 exit 156B, 4 mi. from the north entrance. The center presents a 14-minute film about cadet life at the academy. There also are displays and an information desk. A .3-mile nature walk connects the visitor center with the chapel. **Hours:** Daily 9-5; closed Jan. 1, Thanksgiving, Christmas Eve, Christmas and Dec. 31. **Cost:** Free. **Phone:** (719) 333-2025.

U.S. OLYMPIC COMPLEX, 1750 E. Boulder St., is a 37-acre sports training center for the U.S. Olympic Committee. Nearly 130 athletes representing nine sports live and train at the complex on a full-time basis; thousands train here part-time. Guided tours feature an Olympic highlights film and a walking tour that includes the multisport gymnasium, the Olympic-size swimming pool and the indoor shooting center. **Time:** Allow 1 hour, 15 minutes minimum. **Hours:** Tours are offered Mon.-Sat. 9-4. **Cost:** Free. **Phone:** (719) 866-4618 or (888) 659-8687.

WESTERN MUSEUM OF MINING AND INDUSTRY, e. of I-25 exit 156A (Gleneagle Dr.) at 225 North Gate Blvd., displays restored, operating steam engines and mining equipment used in early Western mines on its 27 acres. The museum offers a 20-minute film, a rock and mineral display, gold panning demonstrations, exhibits about mining life and a re-created mine drift as well as hands-on exhibits. Guests may pan for gold and mine for gems, visit with the museum's mascot burros and see machinery, a stamp mill and a reclamation project. A research library is available with advance notice.

Hours: Mon.-Sat. 9-4. Guided tours are offered at 10 and 1. Closed major holidays. **Cost:** $8; $7 (military with ID); $6 (ages 60+); $4 (ages 3-12). Gold panning $5. **Phone:** (719) 488-0880 or (800) 752-6558.

WORLD FIGURE SKATING MUSEUM AND HALL OF FAME, .5 mi. n.e. of The Broadmoor resort at 20 First St., honors the history of figure skating with changing displays and the Hall of Fame. Exhibits feature such international and American Olympic champions as Dick Button, Scott Hamilton, Sonja Henie and Michelle Kwan. Displays include films, costumes, medals, trophies and thematic artwork by world renowned artists.

Time: Allow 1 hour minimum. **Hours:** Tues.-Fri. 10-4. Closed major holidays. **Cost:** $5; $3 (ages 6-12 and 60+). **Phone:** (719) 635-5200.

Sightseeing

Sightseeing tours of the Pikes Peak region with stops at attractions in and around Colorado Springs are offered by SAVE Gray Line, (719) 633-1181 or (800) 345-8197. Some excursions include a trek to the summit of Pikes Peak.

Tours of Peterson Air Force Base can be arranged in advance for groups of 15 or more people; phone (719) 556-4696.

▼ See AAA listing p. 86 ▼

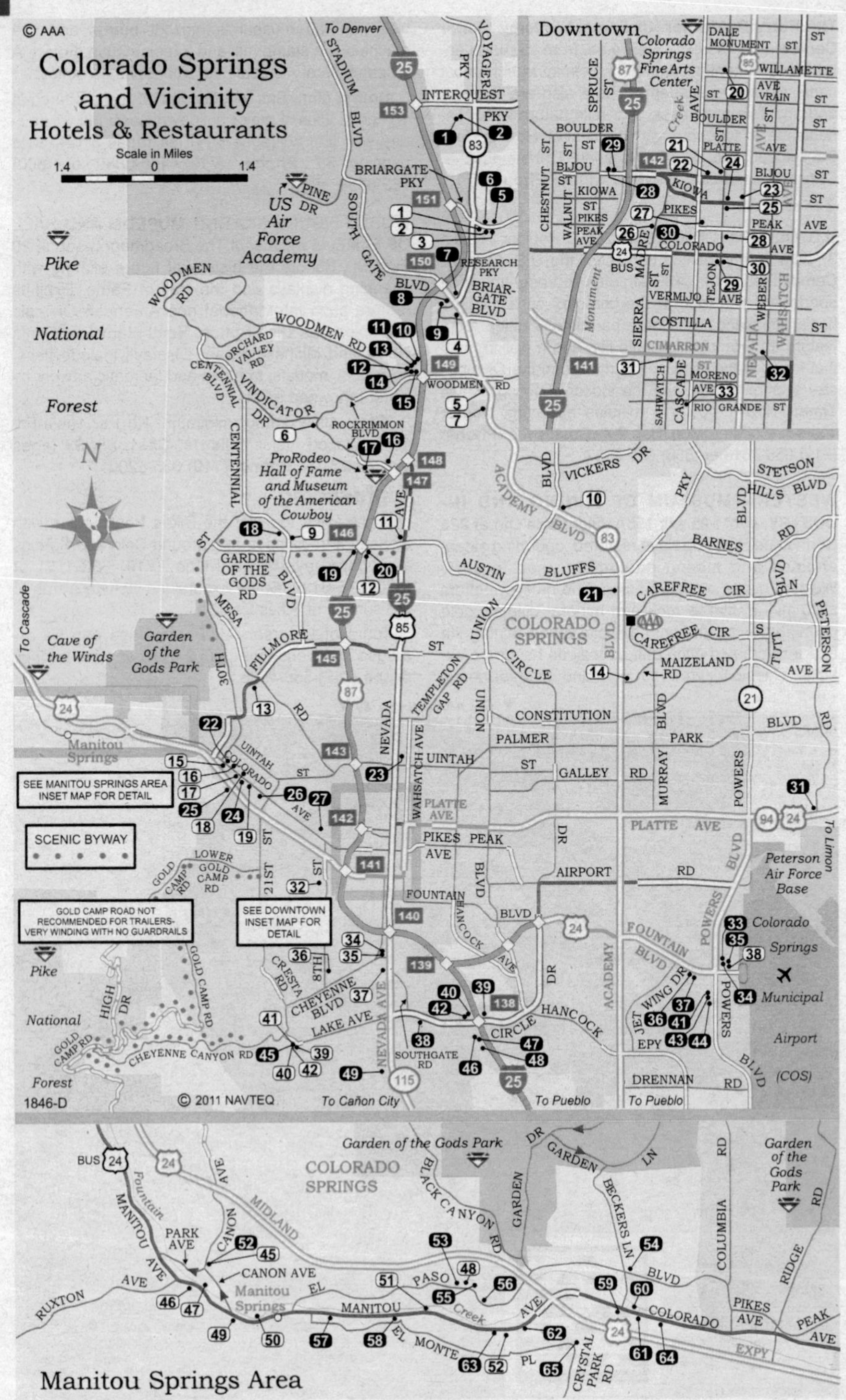
© AAA
Colorado Springs and Vicinity
Hotels & Restaurants
Scale in Miles
1.4 0 1.4
Downtown
Colorado Springs Fine Arts Center
US Air Force Academy
Pike National Forest
ProRodeo Hall of Fame and Museum of the American Cowboy
Garden of the Gods Park
Cave of the Winds
COLORADO SPRINGS
SEE MANITOU SPRINGS AREA INSET MAP FOR DETAIL
SCENIC BYWAY
GOLD CAMP ROAD NOT RECOMMENDED FOR TRAILERS-VERY WINDING WITH NO GUARDRAILS
SEE DOWNTOWN INSET MAP FOR DETAIL
Peterson Air Force Base
Colorado Springs Municipal Airport (COS)
To Denver
To Cascade
To Limon
To Cañon City
To Pueblo
1846-D
© 2011 NAVTEQ
Manitou Springs Area
Garden of the Gods Park

Airport Accommodations

Map Page	**COLORADO SPRINGS AIRPORT**	Diamond Rated	High Season	Page
44 p. 94	**Comfort Inn, 2 mi w of terminal**	◆◆	$90-$160 SAVE	101
43 p. 94	Hampton Inn Airport, 2 mi w of terminal	◆◆◆	$89-$149	103
37 p. 94	Holiday Inn Airport, 2.5 mi nw of terminal	◆◆◆	$119-$179	105
36 p. 94	Holiday Inn Express-Airport, 2.5 mi nw of terminal	◆◆	$109-$169	105
35 p. 94	**Radisson Hotel Colorado Springs Airport, 2.5 mi nw of terminal**	◆◆◆	$119-$185 SAVE	107
34 p. 94	SpringHill Suites Colorado Springs South, 3 mi w of terminal	◆◆◆	$119-$149	108
33 p. 94	TownePlace Suites Colorado Springs South, 3 mi w of terminal	◆◆◆	$119-$139	108

Colorado Springs and Vicinity

This index helps you "spot" where approved hotels and restaurants are located on the corresponding detailed maps. Hotel daily rate range is for comparison only and shows the property's high season. Restaurant rate range is a combination of lunch and/or dinner. Turn to the listing page for more detailed rate information and consult display ads for special promotions.

COLORADO SPRINGS

Map Page	Hotels	Diamond Rated	High Season	Page
1 p. 94	Residence Inn by Marriott Colorado Springs North at Interquest Pkwy	◆◆◆	$89-$349	107
2 p. 94	**Hampton Inn & Suites Colorado Springs Air Force Academy/I-25 North @ Interquest** *(See ad p. 104.)*	◆◆◆	$79-$189 SAVE	104
5 p. 94	Homewood Suites by Hilton Colorado Springs-North	◆◆◆	$114-$134	105
6 p. 94	Hilton Garden Inn	◆◆◆	$109-$119	104
7 p. 94	Drury Inn-Pikes Peak	◆◆	$70-$154	102
8 p. 94	**The Academy Hotel Colorado Springs** *(See ad p. 99.)*	◆◆	Rates not provided SAVE	99
9 p. 94	**Sleep Inn**	◆◆	$45-$129 SAVE	107
10 p. 94	Embassy Suites Hotel Colorado Springs	◆◆◆	$139-$159	102
11 p. 94	**Microtel Inn & Suites** *(See ad p. 106.)*	◆◆	$53-$71 SAVE	106
12 p. 94	**Staybridge Suites-Air Force Academy** *(See ad p. 103.)*	◆◆◆	$99-$159 SAVE	108
13 p. 94	**Hampton Inn Colorado Springs Central Air Force Academy**	◆◆◆	$79-$189 SAVE	104
14 p. 94	**Holiday Inn Express Air Force Academy** *(See ad p. 103.)*	◆◆◆	$79-$209 SAVE	105
15 p. 94	Colorado Springs Fairfield Inn Air Force Academy	◆◆	$90-$110	101
16 p. 94	**Hyatt Summerfield Suites Colorado Springs**	◆◆◆	$79-$209 SAVE	105
17 p. 94	Colorado Springs Marriott	◆◆◆	$143-$185	101
18 p. 94	TownePlace Suites by Marriott-Colorado Springs	◆◆	$129-$159	108
19 p. 94	**Hyatt Place Colorado Springs/Garden of the Gods**	◆◆◆	$79-$209 SAVE	105
20 p. 94	La Quinta Inn Colorado Springs Garden of the Gods	◆◆	$58-$165	105
21 p. 94	**Residence Inn by Marriott Colorado Springs Central**	◆◆◆	$149-$229 SAVE	107
22 p. 94	**Garden of the Gods Motel**	◆◆	$48-$125 SAVE	103
23 p. 94	Lennox House Bed and Breakfast	◆◆◆	Rates not provided	105
24 p. 94	**Old Town GuestHouse**	◆◆◆	$99-$235 SAVE	106

COLORADO SPRINGS (cont'd)

Map Page	Hotels (cont'd)	Diamond Rated	High Season	Page
25 p. 94	**Travelodge**	◆◆	$45-$94 SAVE	108
26 p. 94	Our Hearts Inn Old Colorado City	◆◆◆	$100-$165	106
27 p. 94	**Holden House 1902 Bed & Breakfast Inn**	◆◆◆	$145-$160 SAVE	105
28 p. 94	**Clarion Hotel & Conference Center**	◆◆◆	$70-$150 SAVE	100
29 p. 94	**Quality Suites Downtown**	◆◆◆	$80-$150 SAVE	106
30 p. 94	**Antlers Hilton Colorado Springs**	◆◆◆◆	Rates not provided SAVE	99
31 p. 94	Econo Lodge-Airport	◆◆	$44-$75	102
32 p. 94	Travelers Uptown Motel	◆◆	Rates not provided	108
33 p. 94	TownePlace Suites Colorado Springs South	◆◆◆	$119-$139	108
34 p. 94	SpringHill Suites Colorado Springs South	◆◆◆	$119-$149	108
35 p. 94	**Radisson Hotel Colorado Springs Airport** *(See ad p. 107.)*	◆◆◆	$119-$185 SAVE	107
36 p. 94	Holiday Inn Express-Airport	◆◆	$109-$169	105
37 p. 94	Holiday Inn Airport	◆◆◆	$119-$179	105
38 p. 94	Courtyard by Marriott	◆◆◆	$115-$149	101
39 p. 94	**Crowne Plaza Colorado Springs**	◆◆◆	$75-$169 SAVE	102
40 p. 94	**Best Western Executive Inn & Suites** *(See ad p. 100.)*	◆◆	$80-$140 SAVE	99
41 p. 94	Hilton Garden Inn Colorado Springs Airport *(See ad p. 103.)*	◆◆◆	$99-$179	105
42 p. 94	**Comfort Inn South**	◆◆	$79-$139 SAVE	101
43 p. 94	Hampton Inn Airport *(See ad p. 103.)*	◆◆◆	$89-$149	103
44 p. 94	**Comfort Inn** *(See ad p. 103.)*	◆◆	$90-$160 SAVE	101
45 p. 94	**The Broadmoor**	◆◆◆◆◆	$420-$7500 SAVE	100
46 p. 94	Fairfield Inn & Suites Colorado Springs/South	◆◆◆	$79-$189	103
47 p. 94	Residence Inn by Marriott-Colorado Springs South	◆◆◆	$109-$259	107
48 p. 94	Hampton Inn & Suites I-25 South-Colorado Springs	◆◆◆	$119-$159	104
49 p. 94	**Cheyenne Mountain Resort** *(See ad p. 101.)*	◆◆◆◆	$99-$349 SAVE	100

Map Page	Restaurants	Diamond Rated	Cuisine	Meal Range	Page
1 p. 94	Bird Dog BBQ	◆	Barbecue	$5-$13	108
2 p. 94	P.F. Chang's China Bistro	◆◆◆	Chinese	$10-$23	111
3 p. 94	Biaggi's Ristorante Italiano	◆◆◆	Italian	$9-$22	108
4 p. 94	La Baguette French Bakery and Espresso Cafe	◆	Breads/Pastries	$6-$9	110
5 p. 94	Lemongrass Bistro	◆◆	Vietnamese	$7-$13	110
6 p. 94	Salsa Brava Fresh Mexican Grill	◆◆	Mexican	$9-$18	111
7 p. 94	Jun Japanese Restaurant	◆◆	Japanese	$7-$13	110
9 p. 94	**Marigold Cafe & Bakery**	◆◆◆	French	$7-$28	110
10 p. 94	Mirch Masala-Kabab & Curry Dining	◆◆	Indian	$9-$16	110
11 p. 94	Senor Manuel Mexican Cuisine	◆◆	Mexican	$8-$18	111
12 p. 94	Caspian Cafe Mediterranean Restaurant	◆◆	Mediterranean	$9-$27	109
13 p. 94	Pizzeria Rustica	◆◆	Pizza	$11-$14	111

Map Page	Restaurants (cont'd)	Diamond Rated	Cuisine	Meal Range	Page
14 p. 94	Steaksmith	◆◆	Steak	$16-$34	112
15 p. 94	**The Mason Jar**	◆◆	American	$8-$16	110
16 p. 94	Paravicini's Italian Bistro	◆◆	Italian	$8-$20	111
17 p. 94	Gertrude's Restaurant	◆◆◆	American	$9-$32	109
18 p. 94	Jake and Telly's Greek Taverna	◆◆	Greek	$9-$24	109
19 p. 94	La Baguette French Bakery and Espresso Cafe	◆	Breads/Pastries	$6-$9	110
20 p. 94	Panino's Restaurant Downtown	◆◆	Italian	$8-$16	110
21 p. 94	Jose Muldoon's	◆◆	Mexican	$7-$17	109
22 p. 94	Everest Nepal Restaurant	◆◆	Nepali	$10-$17	109
23 p. 94	**Fratelli Ristorante Italiano**	◆◆◆	Italian	$6-$21	109
24 p. 94	Mediterranean Cafe	◆◆	Mediterranean	$6-$14	110
25 p. 94	The Famous "A Steak House"	◆◆	Steak	$9-$50	109
26 p. 94	Giuseppe's Old Depot Restaurant	◆◆	Italian	$8-$33	109
27 p. 94	Phantom Canyon Brewing Co	◆◆	American	$8-$24	111
28 p. 94	The Ritz Grill	◆◆	American	$8-$22	111
29 p. 94	MacKenzie's Chop House	◆◆	Steak	$9-$35	110
30 p. 94	Nosh	◆◆◆	American	$9-$23	110
31 p. 94	**The Warehouse**	◆◆◆	American	$11-$36	112
32 p. 94	The Pepper Tree Restaurant	◆◆◆	Continental	$19-$50	111
33 p. 94	Shuga's Restaurant & Bar	◆◆	Deli	$8-$9	112
34 p. 94	The Blue Star	◆◆◆	American	$11-$30	108
35 p. 94	**Edelweiss Restaurant**	◆◆	German	$7-$27	109
36 p. 94	Little Nepal	◆◆	Indian	$11-$17	110
37 p. 94	Walter's Bistro	◆◆◆	American	$10-$46	112
38 p. 94	The Airplane Restaurant	◆◆	American	$9-$16	108
39 p. 94	The Tavern	◆◆◆	American	$10-$55	112
40 p. 94	**The Penrose Room**	◆◆◆◆◆	Continental	$72-$102	111
41 p. 94	**Summit**	◆◆◆◆	American	$16-$28	112
42 p. 94	**Charles Court**	◆◆◆◆	Regional American	$22-$42	109

MANITOU SPRINGS

Map Page	Hotels	Diamond Rated	High Season	Page
52 p. 94	**The Cliff House at Pikes Peak**	◆◆◆◆	$117-$370 SAVE	250
53 p. 94	Bed and Breakfast at Historic Onaledge	◆◆◆	$100-$200	250
54 p. 94	Red Wing Motel	◆	Rates not provided	250
55 p. 94	Rockledge Country Inn	◆◆◆	$185-$355	250
56 p. 94	Red Crags Bed & Breakfast Inn	◆◆◆	$100-$200	250
57 p. 94	**Americas Best Value Inn Villa Motel**	◆◆	$77-$129 SAVE	249
58 p. 94	Eagle Motel	◆◆	$64-$89	250
59 p. 94	**Rodeway Inn at the Castaways**	◆◆	$60-$190 SAVE	251

MANITOU SPRINGS (cont'd)

Map Page	Hotels (cont'd)	Diamond Rated	High Season	Page
60 p. 94	**Park Row Lodge**	♦♦	$59-$89 SAVE	250
61 p. 94	Comfort Inn	♦♦♦	$89-$149	250
62 p. 94	**Silver Saddle Motel**	♦♦	$59-$129 SAVE	251
63 p. 94	**Best Western Sky Way Inn & Suites**	♦♦	$89-$139 SAVE	250
64 p. 94	**El Colorado Lodge**	♦♦	$90-$175 SAVE	250
65 p. 94	Town-N-Country Cottages	♦♦	$85-$145	251

Map Page	Restaurants	Diamond Rated	Cuisine	Meal Range	Page
45 p. 94	**The Cliff House Dining Room**	♦♦♦♦	New Continental	$16-$26	251
46 p. 94	The Loop	♦♦	Mexican	$8-$15	251
47 p. 94	Adam's Mountain Cafe	♦♦	Vegetarian	$8-$17	251
48 p. 94	**Craftwood Inn**	♦♦♦	Regional American	$20-$35	251
49 p. 94	The Mona Lisa Fondue Restaurant	♦♦♦	Fondue	$17-$30	251
50 p. 94	**Stagecoach Inn**	♦♦	Regional American	$8-$25	252
51 p. 94	**Briarhurst Manor**	♦♦♦	Regional American	$20-$45	251
52 p. 94	Savelli's	♦♦	Italian	$7-$13	251

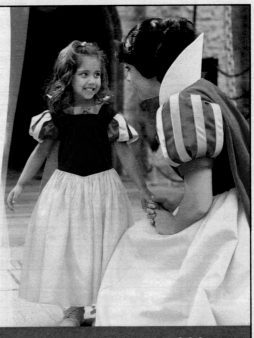

COLORADO SPRINGS

• Restaurants p. 108
• Hotels & Restaurants map & index p. 94

THE ACADEMY HOTEL COLORADO SPRINGS

Phone: 719/598-5770 8

Hotel
Rates not provided

Address: 8110 N Academy Blvd 80920 **Location:** I-25 exit 150, just s. **Facility:** 196 units. 2-4 stories, interior corridors. **Terms:** check-in 4 pm. **Amenities:** video games (fee), high-speed Internet. **Pool(s):** heated indoor. **Activities:** whirlpool, exercise room. *Fee:* game room. **Guest Services:** valet and coin laundry. **Free Special Amenities: full breakfast and newspaper.**

(See ad this page.)

SAVE CALL FEE / SOME UNITS

BEST WESTERN EXECUTIVE INN & SUITES

Phone: (719)576-2371 40

Hotel
$80-$140

AAA Benefit: Members save up to 20%, plus 10% bonus points with Best Western Rewards®.

Address: 1440 Harrison Rd 80905 **Location:** I-25 exit 138, just w; on northwest corner of interchange; entrance through restaurant. **Facility:** 84 units. 2 stories (no elevator), interior corridors. **Amenities:** *Some:* high-speed Internet. **Pool(s):** heated indoor. **Activities:** whirlpool, exercise room. **Guest Services:** valet and coin laundry. **Free Special Amenities: expanded continental breakfast and room upgrade (subject to availability with advance reservations).**

(See ad p. 100.)

SAVE CALL BIZ / SOME UNITS FEE

ANTLERS HILTON COLORADO SPRINGS

Phone: 719/473-5600 30

Hotel
Rates not provided

Hilton **AAA Benefit:** Members save 5% or more everyday!

Address: 4 S Cascade Ave 80903 **Location:** I-25 exit 142 (Bijou St), just e, then just s; downtown. **Facility:** Mountain views are offered from many rooms at this hotel; a brew pub is on site. 292 units. 13 stories, interior corridors. **Parking:** on-site (fee) and valet. **Amenities:** high-speed Internet. **Dining:** 2 restaurants. **Pool(s):** heated indoor. **Activities:** whirlpool, exercise room. *Fee:* massage. **Guest Services:** valet laundry, area transportation-within 5 mi. **Free Special Amenities: high-speed Internet.**

SAVE CALL BIZ / SOME UNITS FEE

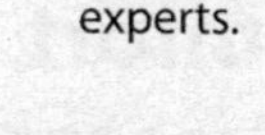

▼ See AAA listing this page ▼

(See map & index p. 94.)

THE BROADMOOR Phone: (719)634-7711 45

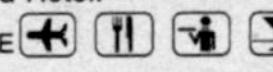

Classic Historic Resort Hotel

$420-$7500 5/1-10/31
$300-$6000 11/1-4/30

Address: 1 Lake Ave 80906 **Location:** I-25 exit 138, 3 mi w on Circle Dr (which becomes Lake Ave). **Facility:** This grand 1918 hotel incorporates modern tastes while maintaining its historic character. Hand-painted ceilings and custom furnishings give public areas a look reminiscent of the Old World. 744 units, some two bedrooms, three bedrooms and cottages. 1-8 stories, interior/exterior corridors. **Parking:** valet only. **Terms:** check-in 4 pm, 7 day cancellation notice-fee imposed. **Amenities:** video games (fee), high-speed Internet, safes, honor bars. **Dining:** 9 restaurants, also, Charles Court, The Penrose Room, The Tavern, see separate listings, nightclub, entertainment. **Pool(s):** heated outdoor, heated indoor. **Activities:** saunas, whirlpools, steamrooms, waterslide, rental paddleboats, 6 tennis courts, recreation programs, rental bicycles, jogging, playground, spa. *Fee:* golf-54 holes, horseback riding. **Guest Services:** valet laundry, area transportation (fee)-within state. Affiliated with A Preferred Hotel.

SAVE FEE CALL BIZ FEE

/ SOME UNITS FEE FEE FEE

Learn about
AAA/CAA Diamond Ratings
at AAA.com/Diamonds

CHEYENNE MOUNTAIN RESORT
Phone: (719)538-4000 49

Resort Hotel
$99-$349

Address: 3225 Broadmoor Valley Rd 80906 **Location:** I-25 exit 138, 1.4 mi w to SR 115, 0.5 mi s, just w on Cheyenne Mountain Blvd, then just s. **Facility:** The balconies in the well-appointed guest rooms at this expansive resort provide breathtaking views of the Colorado Rockies. 316 units. 3 stories (no elevator), interior/exterior corridors. **Parking:** on-site and valet. **Terms:** check-in 4 pm, cancellation fee imposed. **Amenities:** video games (fee), safes. **Dining:** 2 restaurants. **Pool(s):** 3 heated outdoor, heated indoor. **Activities:** sauna, whirlpools, steamroom, fishing, 4 lighted indoor tennis courts, jogging, playground, sports court, basketball, volleyball. *Fee:* golf-18 holes, massage. **Guest Services:** valet laundry, area transportation (fee)-within 10 mi.

(See ad p. 101.)

SAVE FEE CALL BIZ

FEE / SOME UNITS FEE
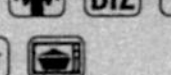

CLARION HOTEL & CONFERENCE CENTER
Phone: (719)471-8680 28

Hotel
$70-$150

Address: 314 W Bijou St 80905 **Location:** I-25 exit 142 (Bijou St), just w. **Facility:** 98 units. 3 stories, interior corridors. **Terms:** cancellation fee imposed. **Pool(s):** heated indoor. **Activities:** whirlpool, exercise room. **Guest Services:** valet and coin laundry, area transportation-within 3 mi. **Free Special Amenities: full breakfast and manager's reception.**

SAVE BIZ

▼ See AAA listing p. 99 ▼

(See map & index p. 94.)

COLORADO SPRINGS FAIRFIELD INN AIR FORCE ACADEMY
Phone: (719)533-1903 15

Hotel
$90-$110

AAA Benefit:
AAA hotel discounts of 5% or more.

Address: 7085 Commerce Center Dr 80919 **Location:** I-25 exit 149 (Woodmen Rd), just w, then just n. **Facility:** 67 units. 4 stories, interior corridors. **Pool(s):** heated indoor. **Activities:** whirlpool. **Guest Services:** valet laundry.

BIZ / SOME UNITS

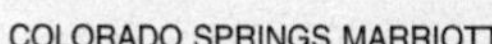

COLORADO SPRINGS MARRIOTT
Phone: (719)260-1800 17

Hotel
$143-$185

AAA Benefit:
AAA hotel discounts of 5% or more.

Address: 5580 Tech Center Dr 80919 **Location:** I-25 exit 148 (Rockrimmon Blvd), 0.5 mi w, then just s. **Facility:** 309 units. 9 stories, interior corridors. **Amenities:** safes. *Fee:* video games, high-speed Internet. **Pool(s):** heated outdoor, heated indoor. **Activities:** sauna, whirlpools, hiking trails, volleyball, exercise room. **Guest Services:** valet and coin laundry, area transportation-within 7 mi.

BIZ FEE

COMFORT INN
Phone: (719)380-9000 44

Hotel
$90-$160

Address: 2115 Aerotech Dr 80916 **Location:** I-25 exit 139, 4.2 mi e on US 24 Bypass, 0.4 mi s on Powers Blvd, just w on Astrozon Blvd, then just n. **Facility:** 88 units, some kitchens. 2 stories (no elevator), interior corridors. **Terms:** cancellation fee imposed. **Amenities:** high-speed Internet. **Pool(s):** heated indoor. **Activities:** whirlpool, exercise room. **Guest Services:** valet and coin laundry. *(See ad p. 103.)*

SAVE BIZ / SOME UNITS FEE

COMFORT INN SOUTH
Phone: (719)579-6900 42

Hotel
$79-$139

Address: 1410 Harrison Rd 80905 **Location:** I-25 exit 138, just w to Rand Rd, then ne. **Facility:** 111 units. 3 stories, interior corridors. **Terms:** cancellation fee imposed. **Pool(s):** heated indoor. **Activities:** whirlpool, exercise room. **Guest Services:** valet and coin laundry. **Free Special Amenities: expanded continental breakfast and high-speed Internet.**

SAVE BIZ / SOME UNITS FEE

COURTYARD BY MARRIOTT
Phone: (719)226-5006 38

Hotel
$115-$149

AAA Benefit:
AAA hotel discounts of 5% or more.

Address: 2570 Tenderfoot Hill St 80906 **Location:** I-25 exit 138, 0.6 mi w on Lake Ave, then s. **Facility:** 90 units. 3 stories, interior corridors. **Amenities:** video games (fee), high-speed Internet. **Pool(s):** heated indoor. **Activities:** whirlpool, exercise room. **Guest Services:** valet and coin laundry.

CALL BIZ FEE / SOME UNITS

▼ See AAA listing p. 100 ▼

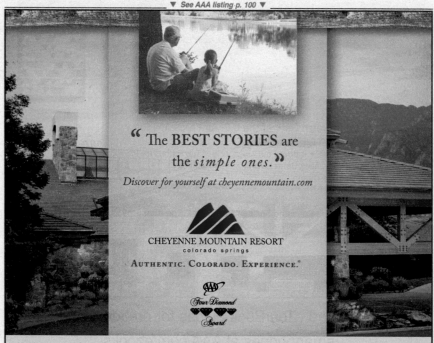

(See map & index p. 94.)

CROWNE PLAZA COLORADO SPRINGS
Phone: (719)576-5900 39

Hotel
$75-$169

Address: 2886 S Circle Dr 80906 **Location:** I-25 exit 138, just e. **Facility:** 500 units. 2-3 stories, interior corridors. **Terms:** cancellation fee imposed. **Amenities:** video games (fee). **Dining:** 2 restaurants. **Pool(s):** heated outdoor, heated indoor. **Activities:** whirlpool. *Fee:* massage. **Guest Services:** valet and coin laundry.

SAVE FEE / SOME UNITS FEE

DRURY INN-PIKES PEAK Phone: (719)598-2500 7

Hotel
$70-$154

Address: 8155 N Academy Blvd 80920 **Location:** I-25 exit 150, just s, then e. **Facility:** 117 units. 4 stories, interior corridors. **Terms:** cancellation fee imposed. **Amenities:** high-speed Internet. **Pool(s):** heated indoor/outdoor. **Activities:** whirlpool, exercise room. **Guest Services:** valet and coin laundry.

BIZ / SOME UNITS

ECONO LODGE-AIRPORT
Phone: (719)638-5800 31

Motel
$44-$75

Address: 6715 Panamint Ct 80915 **Location:** I-25 exit 141, 1 mi e on Cimarron Ave, 0.7 mi n on Wahsatch Ave, 6.3 mi e on Platte Ave, exit Space Village Ave, just e, then just n on Peterson Rd. Located next to golf course and near Peterson AFB. **Facility:** 37 units. 2 stories (no elevator), interior corridors. **Terms:** cancellation fee imposed. **Pool(s):** heated indoor. **Activities:** whirlpool. **Guest Services:** coin laundry.

EMBASSY SUITES HOTEL COLORADO SPRINGS
Phone: (719)599-9100 10

Hotel
$139-$159

AAA Benefit: Members save 5% or more everyday!

Address: 7290 Commerce Center Dr 80919 **Location:** I-25 exit 149 (Woodmen Rd), just w, then n. **Facility:** 206 units. 4 stories, interior corridors. **Terms:** 1-7 night minimum stay, cancellation fee imposed. **Amenities:** video games (fee). **Pool(s):** heated indoor. **Activities:** whirlpool, exercise room. *Fee:* game room. **Guest Services:** valet and coin laundry.

BIZ FEE / SOME UNITS FEE

FAIRFIELD INN & SUITES COLORADO SPRINGS AIR FORCE ACADEMY
Phone: (719)488-4644

Hotel
$98-$120

AAA Benefit: AAA hotel discounts of 5% or more.

Address: 15275 W Struthers Rd 80921 **Location:** I-25 exit 158, just e on Baptist Rd, then just s. **Facility:** 85 units. 3 stories, interior corridors. **Amenities:** high-speed Internet. **Pool(s):** heated indoor. **Activities:** whirlpool, jogging, exercise room. **Guest Services:** valet and coin laundry. **Free Special Amenities: expanded continental breakfast and high-speed Internet.**

(See ad this page.)

SAVE CALL BIZ / SOME UNITS FEE

(See map & index p. 94.)

FAIRFIELD INN & SUITES COLORADO SPRINGS/SOUTH
Phone: (719)576-1717 46

Hotel
$79-$189

AAA Benefit:
AAA hotel discounts of 5% or more.

Address: 2725 Geyser Dr 80906 **Location:** I-25 exit 138, just w to E Cheyenne Mountain Blvd, then just s. **Facility:** 84 units. 3 stories, interior corridors. **Amenities:** video games (fee). **Pool(s):** heated indoor. **Activities:** whirlpool, exercise room. **Guest Services:** valet and coin laundry.

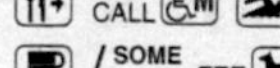

CALL FEE / SOME UNITS FEE

GARDEN OF THE GODS MOTEL
Phone: (719)636-5271 22

Motel
$48-$125

Address: 2922 W Colorado Ave 80904 **Location:** I-25 exit 141, 2.5 mi nw on US 24, just n on 31st St, then e. **Facility:** 33 units, some two bedrooms. 2 stories (no elevator), interior/exterior corridors. **Terms:** office hours 8 am-11:30 pm, cancellation fee imposed. **Pool(s):** heated indoor. **Activities:** sauna. **Free Special Amenities: continental breakfast and local telephone calls.**

   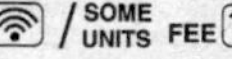  

SAVE / SOME UNITS FEE

HAMPTON INN AIRPORT **Phone:** (719)591-1100 43

Hotel
$89-$149

AAA Benefit:
Members save up to 10% everyday!

Address: 2077 Aerotech Dr 80916 **Location:** I-25 exit 139, 4.2 mi e on US 24 Bypass, 0.4 mi s on Powers Blvd, just w on Astrozon Blvd, then just n. **Facility:** 80 units. 3 stories, interior corridors. **Terms:** 1-7 night minimum stay, cancellation fee imposed. **Amenities:** video games (fee), high-speed Internet. **Pool(s):** heated indoor. **Activities:** whirlpool, exercise room. **Guest Services:** valet and coin laundry, area transportation-within 4 mi. ***(See ad this page.)***

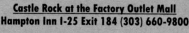

   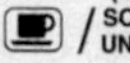 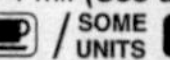 

FEE / SOME UNITS

(See map & index p. 94.)

HAMPTON INN & SUITES COLORADO SPRINGS AIR FORCE ACADEMY/I-25 NORTH @ INTERQUEST **Phone:** (719)598-6911 2

Hotel $79-$189

AAA Benefit: Members save up to 10% everyday!

Address: 1307 Republic Dr 80921 **Location:** I-25 exit 153, 0.5 mi e, then just s. **Facility:** 75 units. 3 stories, interior corridors. **Terms:** 1-7 night minimum stay, cancellation fee imposed. **Amenities:** high-speed Internet. **Pool(s):** heated indoor. **Activities:** whirlpool, exercise room. **Guest Services:** valet and coin laundry. **Free Special Amenities: full breakfast and high-speed Internet.** *(See ad this page.)*

SAVE BIZ / SOME UNITS FEE

HAMPTON INN & SUITES I-25 SOUTH-COLORADO SPRINGS **Phone:** (719)884-0330 48

Hotel $119-$159

AAA Benefit: Members save up to 10% everyday!

Address: 2910 Geyser Dr 80906 **Location:** I-25 exit 138, just w, just s on Cheyenne Mountain Blvd, then just e. **Facility:** 101 units. 4 stories, interior corridors. **Terms:** 1-7 night minimum stay, cancellation fee imposed. **Amenities:** video games (fee), high-speed Internet. **Pool(s):** heated indoor. **Activities:** whirlpool, exercise room. **Guest Services:** valet and coin laundry.

BIZ FEE / SOME UNITS

HAMPTON INN COLORADO SPRINGS CENTRAL AIR FORCE ACADEMY **Phone:** (719)593-9700 13

Hotel $79-$189

AAA Benefit: Members save up to 10% everyday!

Address: 7245 Commerce Center Dr 80919 **Location:** I-25 exit 149 (Woodmen Rd), just w, then n. **Facility:** 125 units. 4 stories, interior corridors. **Terms:** 1-7 night minimum stay, cancellation fee imposed. **Amenities:** *Some:* high-speed Internet. **Pool(s):** heated indoor. **Activities:** exercise room. **Guest Services:** valet and coin laundry. **Free Special Amenities: expanded continental breakfast and high-speed Internet.**

SAVE BIZ / SOME UNITS 

HILTON GARDEN INN **Phone:** (719)598-6866 6

Hotel $109-$119

AAA Benefit: Unparalleled hospitality at a special Member rate.

Address: 1810 Briargate Pkwy 80920 **Location:** I-25 exit 151 (Briargate Pkwy), 0.7 mi e. **Facility:** 154 units. 3 stories, interior corridors. **Terms:** check-in 4 pm, 1-7 night minimum stay, cancellation fee imposed. **Pool(s):** heated indoor. **Activities:** whirlpool, exercise room. **Guest Services:** valet and coin laundry.

 BIZ

▼ *See AAA listing this page* ▼

(See map & index p. 94.)

HILTON GARDEN INN COLORADO SPRINGS AIRPORT
Phone: (719)622-0300 41

Hotel
$99-$179

AAA Benefit:
Unparalleled hospitality at a special Member rate.

Address: 2035 Aerotech Dr 80916 **Location:** I-25 exit 139, 4.2 mi e on US 24 Bypass, 0.4 mi s on Powers Blvd, just w on Astrozon Blvd, then just n. **Facility:** 119 units. 3 stories, interior corridors. **Parking:** winter plug-ins. **Terms:** 1-7 night minimum stay, cancellation fee imposed. **Amenities:** video games (fee), high-speed Internet. **Pool(s):** heated indoor. **Activities:** whirlpool, exercise room. **Guest Services:** valet and coin laundry, area transportation-within 3 mi.
(See ad p. 103.)

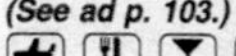
FEE
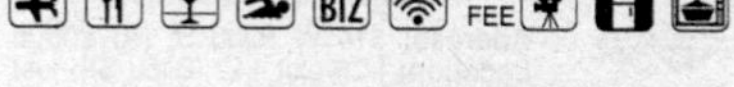

HOLDEN HOUSE 1902 BED & BREAKFAST INN
Phone: (719)471-3980 27

Historic Bed & Breakfast
$145-$160

Address: 1102 W Pikes Peak Ave 80904 **Location:** I-25 exit 141, 0.3 mi w on US 24, just n on 8th St, just w on Colorado Ave, then just n on 11th St. **Facility:** Victorian furnishings, in-room fireplaces and lace curtains impart traditional charm to this restored 1902 home and carriage house. The lovely garden adds a touch of class to the front yard. 5 units. 2 stories (no elevator), interior/exterior corridors. **Terms:** office hours 8 am-10 pm, check-in 4 pm, 2-3 night minimum stay - seasonal and/or weekends, age restrictions may apply, 14 day cancellation notice-fee imposed. **Free Special Amenities: full breakfast and manager's reception.**

HOLIDAY INN AIRPORT **Phone:** (719)380-8516 37

Hotel
$119-$179 5/1-9/30
$109-$169 10/1-4/30

Address: 1855 Aeroplaza Dr 80916 **Location:** I-25 exit 139, 4.5 mi e on US 24 Bypass, then just w. **Facility:** 115 units. 4 stories, interior corridors. **Amenities:** high-speed Internet, safes. **Pool(s):** heated indoor. **Activities:** whirlpool, exercise room. **Guest Services:** valet and coin laundry.

CALL
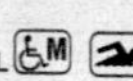

HOLIDAY INN EXPRESS AIR FORCE ACADEMY
Phone: (719)592-9800 14

Hotel
$79-$209

Address: 7110 Commerce Center Dr 80919 **Location:** I-25 exit 149 (Woodmen Rd), just w, then just n. **Facility:** 78 units. 4 stories, interior corridors. **Amenities:** video games (fee), high-speed Internet. **Pool(s):** heated indoor. **Activities:** whirlpool, exercise room. **Guest Services:** valet and coin laundry. **Free Special Amenities: expanded continental breakfast and high-speed Internet.** *(See ad p. 103.)*

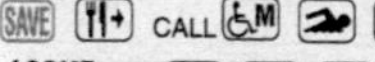
CALL FEE / SOME UNITS FEE

HOLIDAY INN EXPRESS-AIRPORT
Phone: (719)591-6000 36

Hotel
$109-$169 5/1-9/30
$99-$159 10/1-4/30

Address: 1815 Aeroplaza Dr 80916 **Location:** I-25 exit 139, 4.5 mi e on US 24 Bypass, then just w. **Facility:** 94 units. 4 stories, interior corridors. **Amenities:** high-speed Internet. **Activities:** exercise room. **Guest Services:** valet and coin laundry, area transportation-within 2 mi.

CALL

HOMEWOOD SUITES BY HILTON COLORADO SPRINGS-NORTH
Phone: (719)265-6600 5

Extended Stay Hotel
$114-$134

AAA Benefit:
Contemporary luxury at a special Member rate.

Address: 9130 Explorer Dr 80920 **Location:** I-25 exit 151 (Briargate Pkwy), 0.8 mi e; across from Focus on the Family. **Facility:** 127 efficiencies. 3 stories, interior corridors. **Terms:** 1-7 night minimum stay, cancellation fee imposed. **Pool(s):** heated outdoor. **Activities:** putting green, exercise room. **Guest Services:** valet and coin laundry.

CALL / SOME UNITS FEE

HYATT PLACE COLORADO SPRINGS/GARDEN OF THE GODS
Phone: (719)265-9385 19

Hotel
$79-$209

HYATT PLACE

AAA Benefit: Members save 10% or more everyday.

Address: 503 W Garden of the Gods Rd 80907 **Location:** I-25 exit 146 (Garden of the Gods Rd), just w. **Facility:** 124 units. 4 stories, interior corridors. **Terms:** cancellation fee imposed. **Amenities:** video games (fee). *Some:* high-speed Internet. **Pool(s):** heated outdoor. **Activities:** exercise room. **Guest Services:** valet laundry. **Free Special Amenities: expanded continental breakfast and high-speed Internet.**

FEE

HYATT SUMMERFIELD SUITES COLORADO SPRINGS
Phone: (719)268-9990 16

Extended Stay Hotel
$79-$209

HYATT SUMMERFIELD SUITES

AAA Benefit: Members save 10% or more everyday.

Address: 5805 Delmonico Dr 80919 **Location:** I-25 exit 148 (Rockrimmon Blvd), just nw, then ne; entry around the bank. Located near railroad tracks. **Facility:** 125 efficiencies, some two bedrooms. 3 stories, interior corridors. **Terms:** cancellation fee imposed. **Amenities:** high-speed Internet. **Pool(s):** heated outdoor. **Activities:** whirlpool, exercise room. **Guest Services:** valet and coin laundry. **Free Special Amenities: full breakfast and high-speed Internet.**

/ SOME UNITS FEE

LA QUINTA INN COLORADO SPRINGS GARDEN OF THE GODS
Phone: (719)528-5060 20

Hotel
$58-$165

Address: 4385 Sinton Rd 80907 **Location:** I-25 exit 146 (Garden of the Gods Rd), just e. **Facility:** 105 units. 3 stories, interior/exterior corridors. **Amenities:** *Some:* high-speed Internet. **Pool(s):** heated outdoor. **Guest Services:** coin laundry.

/ SOME UNITS

LENNOX HOUSE BED AND BREAKFAST
Phone: 719/471-9265 23

Historic Bed & Breakfast
Rates not provided

Address: 1339 N Nevada Ave 80903 **Location:** I-25 exit 143 (Uintah St), 0.5 mi e, then just n. **Facility:** This 1891 inn has tastefully decorated rooms with Victorian touches, and most rooms have ceiling fans. A sun deck allows for outdoor lounging. 5 units, some two bedrooms and kitchens. 3 stories (no elevator), interior corridors. **Terms:** check-in 4 pm. **Activities:** whirlpool, basketball. **Guest Services:** valet and coin laundry.

/ SOME UNITS

(See map & index p. 94.)

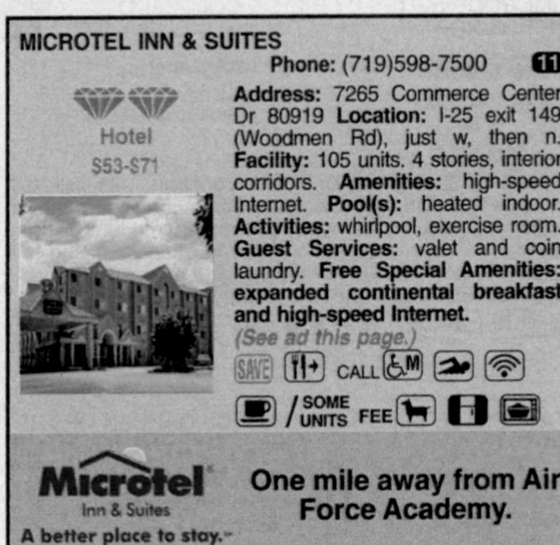

MICROTEL INN & SUITES Phone: (719)598-7500 11

Hotel $53-$71

Address: 7265 Commerce Center Dr 80919 **Location:** I-25 exit 149 (Woodmen Rd), just w, then n. **Facility:** 105 units. 4 stories, interior corridors. **Amenities:** high-speed Internet. **Pool(s):** heated indoor. **Activities:** whirlpool, exercise room. **Guest Services:** valet and coin laundry. **Free Special Amenities: expanded continental breakfast and high-speed Internet.**

(See ad this page.)

SAVE CALL / SOME UNITS FEE

OLD TOWN GUESTHOUSE Phone: (719)632-9194 24

Bed & Breakfast $99-$235

Address: 115 S 26th St 80904 **Location:** I-25 exit 141, w on US 24, then just n. **Facility:** Rooms in this guest house near Old Colorado City are individually decorated, and many feature a balcony. 8 units. 3 stories, interior corridors. *Bath:* shower only. **Terms:** office hours 9 am-9 pm, check-in 4 pm, age restrictions may apply, 30 day cancellation notice-fee imposed. **Amenities:** high-speed Internet. **Activities:** game room, limited exercise equipment. *Fee:* massage. **Guest Services:** valet laundry. **Free Special Amenities: full breakfast and high-speed Internet.**

SAVE CALL BIZ

OUR HEARTS INN OLD COLORADO CITY Phone: (719)473-8684 26

Historic Bed & Breakfast $100-$165

Address: 2215 W Colorado Ave 80904 **Location:** I-25 exit 141, 1.4 mi w on US 24, just n on 21st St, then just w. **Facility:** This 1895 Victorian country home has elaborate hand-stenciling throughout. Rooms are individually decorated and offer a variety of amenities. Dogs are allowed in the cottage with a deposit. 4 units, some cottages. 2 stories (no elevator), interior/exterior corridors. **Terms:** office hours 9 am-9 pm, check-in 4 pm, 2-4 night minimum stay - seasonal and/or weekends, 7 day cancellation notice-fee imposed. **Guest Services:** valet laundry. / SOME UNITS

QUALITY SUITES DOWNTOWN Phone: (719)471-8681 29

Hotel $80-$150

Address: 314 W Bijou St (A) 80905 **Location:** I-25 exit 142 (Bijou St), just w. **Facility:** 50 units. 3 stories, interior corridors. **Terms:** cancellation fee imposed. **Pool(s):** heated indoor. **Activities:** whirlpool, exercise room. **Guest Services:** valet and coin laundry, area transportation-within 3 mi. **Free Special Amenities: full breakfast and manager's reception.**

SAVE BIZ 

Safety tip: Keep a current AAA/CAA Road Atlas in every vehicle

▼ *See AAA listing this page* ▼

(See map & index p. 94.)

RADISSON HOTEL COLORADO SPRINGS AIRPORT
Phone: (719)597-7000 35

Hotel
$119-$185

Address: 1645 N Newport Rd 80916 **Location:** I-25 exit 139, 4.5 mi e on US 24 Bypass. **Facility:** 200 units. 2 stories, interior corridors. **Terms:** cancellation fee imposed. **Amenities:** video games (fee). *Some:* safes. **Pool(s):** heated indoor. **Activities:** whirlpool, exercise room. *Fee:* game room. **Guest Services:** valet and coin laundry. **Free Special Amenities: full breakfast and high-speed Internet.** *(See ad this page.)*

SAVE CALL FEE / SOME UNITS FEE

RESIDENCE INN BY MARRIOTT COLORADO SPRINGS CENTRAL
Phone: (719)574-0370 21

Extended Stay Hotel
$149-$229

AAA Benefit: AAA hotel discounts of 5% or more.

Address: 3880 N Academy Blvd 80917 **Location:** I-25 exit 146 (Garden of the Gods Rd), 4.5 mi e, then 0.3 mi s. **Facility:** 96 kitchen units. 2 stories (no elevator), exterior corridors. **Amenities:** *Some:* high-speed Internet. **Pool(s):** heated outdoor. **Activities:** whirlpool, playground, sports court, volleyball, exercise room. **Guest Services:** valet and coin laundry. **Free Special Amenities: full breakfast and high-speed Internet.**

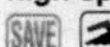     

/ SOME UNITS FEE

Visit AAA.com or CAA.ca
for one-stop travel
planning and reservations

RESIDENCE INN BY MARRIOTT COLORADO SPRINGS NORTH AT INTERQUEST PKWY
Phone: (719)388-9300 1

Extended Stay Hotel
$89-$349

AAA Benefit:
AAA hotel discounts of 5% or more.

Address: 9805 Federal Dr 80921 **Location:** I-25 exit 153, just e, then s. **Facility:** 113 units, some two bedrooms, efficiencies and kitchens. 4 stories, interior corridors. **Amenities:** video games (fee), high-speed Internet. **Pool(s):** heated indoor. **Activities:** whirlpool, putting green, sports court, exercise room. **Guest Services:** valet and coin laundry.

CALL FEE  

/ SOME UNITS FEE

RESIDENCE INN BY MARRIOTT-COLORADO SPRINGS SOUTH
Phone: (719)576-0101 47

Extended Stay Hotel
$109-$259

AAA Benefit:
AAA hotel discounts of 5% or more.

Address: 2765 Geyser Dr 80906 **Location:** I-25 exit 138, just w to E Cheyenne Mountain Blvd, then just s. **Facility:** 72 units, some two bedrooms, efficiencies and kitchens. 3 stories, interior corridors. **Amenities:** video games (fee), high-speed Internet. **Pool(s):** heated indoor. **Activities:** whirlpool, sports court, exercise room. **Guest Services:** valet and coin laundry.

CALL FEE / SOME UNITS FEE

SLEEP INN
Phone: (719)260-6969 9

Hotel
$45-$129

Address: 1075 Kelly Johnson Blvd 80920 **Location:** I-25 exit 150, just s on Academy Blvd to Kelly Johnson Blvd, then w. **Facility:** 83 units. 3 stories, interior corridors. *Bath:* shower only. **Terms:** cancellation fee imposed. **Guest Services:** valet laundry. **Free Special Amenities: continental breakfast and high-speed Internet.**

SAVE CALL / SOME UNITS FEE

▼ *See AAA listing this page* ▼

(See map & index p. 94.)

SPRINGHILL SUITES COLORADO SPRINGS SOUTH
Phone: (719)637-0800 34

Hotel
$119-$149

AAA Benefit:
AAA hotel discounts of 5% or more.

Address: 1570 N Newport Rd 80916 **Location:** I-25 exit 139, 5 mi e on US 24 Bypass, then just n. **Facility:** 101 units. 4 stories, interior corridors. **Amenities:** high-speed Internet. **Pool(s):** heated indoor. **Activities:** whirlpool, exercise room. **Guest Services:** valet and coin laundry.

 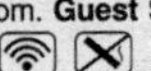  FEE

STAYBRIDGE SUITES-AIR FORCE ACADEMY
Phone: (719)590-7829 12

Extended Stay Hotel
$99-$159 5/1-8/31
$89-$149 9/1-4/30

Address: 7130 Commerce Center Dr 80919 **Location:** I-25 exit 149 (Woodmen Rd), just w, then n. **Facility:** 79 efficiencies, some two bedrooms. 4 stories, interior corridors. **Terms:** 3 day cancellation notice. **Amenities:** video games (fee), high-speed Internet. **Pool(s):** heated outdoor. **Activities:** whirlpool, sports court, exercise room. **Guest Services:** complimentary and valet laundry. **Free Special Amenities: expanded continental breakfast and manager's reception.** *(See ad p. 103.)*

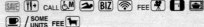

CALL FEE
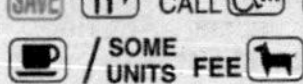 / SOME UNITS FEE

TOWNEPLACE SUITES BY MARRIOTT-COLORADO SPRINGS
Phone: (719)594-4447 18

Extended Stay Hotel
$129-$159

AAA Benefit:
AAA hotel discounts of 5% or more.

Address: 4760 Centennial Blvd 80919 **Location:** I-25 exit 146 (Garden of the Gods Rd), 1 mi w, then just n. Located behind 7-Eleven. **Facility:** 95 kitchen units, some two bedrooms. 3 stories, interior corridors. **Amenities:** high-speed Internet. **Pool(s):** heated outdoor. **Activities:** exercise room. **Guest Services:** valet and coin laundry.

CALL
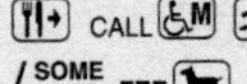 / SOME UNITS FEE

TOWNEPLACE SUITES COLORADO SPRINGS SOUTH
Phone: (719)638-0800 33

Extended Stay Hotel
$119-$139

AAA Benefit:
AAA hotel discounts of 5% or more.

Address: 1530 N Newport Rd 80916 **Location:** I-25 exit 139, 5 mi e on US 24 Bypass, then just n. **Facility:** 97 units, some two bedrooms, efficiencies and kitchens. 4 stories, interior corridors. **Amenities:** high-speed Internet. **Pool(s):** heated indoor. **Activities:** exercise room. **Guest Services:** valet and coin laundry.

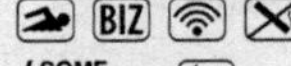 FEE
/ SOME UNITS FEE

TRAVELERS UPTOWN MOTEL
Phone: 719/473-2774 32

Motel
Rates not provided

Address: 220 E Cimarron St 80903 **Location:** I-25 exit 141, 0.8 mi e on US 24. **Facility:** 48 units, some two bedrooms. 2 stories (no elevator), exterior corridors. **Pool(s):** heated outdoor. **Guest Services:** coin laundry.

TRAVELODGE
Phone: (719)632-4600 25

Hotel
$45-$94

Address: 2625 Ore Mill Rd 80904 **Location:** I-25 exit 141, 2.3 mi nw on US 24; entry via 26th St. **Facility:** 49 units. 2 stories (no elevator), interior corridors. **Terms:** cancellation fee imposed. **Amenities:** *Some:* safes. **Pool(s):** heated indoor. **Activities:** limited exercise equipment. **Guest Services:** valet and coin laundry. **Free Special Amenities: expanded continental breakfast and high-speed Internet.**

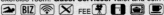

/ SOME UNITS FEE

WHERE TO EAT

THE AIRPLANE RESTAURANT
Phone: 719/570-7656 38

American
$9-$16

AAA Inspector Notes: When I visit this restaurant, I opt to sit on board the Boeing KC-97 rather than in the sports bar. This time the staff had perfected the aviation parlance, noting the flight attendant would be right with me. It's a little cheesy, but absolutely fun. The two gentlemen from the Air Force and the 5-year-old kid in a pilot's outfit were getting a kick out of it, too. The menu features burgers, pastas, steaks and salads. However, the broaster chicken is as good as advertised. **Bar:** full bar. **Address:** 1665 N Newport Rd 80916 **Location:** I-25 exit 139, 4.2 mi e on US 24 Bypass (Fountain Blvd). L D

BIAGGI'S RISTORANTE ITALIANO
Phone: 719/262-9500 3

Italian
$9-$22

AAA Inspector Notes: Cool, upscale decor surrounds diners who savor freshly prepared creations. Delicious combinations of quality, unusual ingredients make for an adventurous dining experience. **Bar:** full bar. **Address:** 1805 Briargate Pkwy 80920 **Location:** I-25 exit 151 (Briargate Pkwy), 0.7 mi e. L D

BIRD DOG BBQ
Phone: 719/599-4655 1

Barbecue
$5-$13

AAA Inspector Notes: I never know what I'll find walking into a Colorado barbecue joint. Bird Dog came highly recommended and has won awards from local papers. I wasn't disappointed. The tender, Oklahoma-style brisket is pure pleasure. House-made sauces add the right amount of sweetness and kick. The baked beans and coleslaw were also quite tasty. I polished off the meal with a chocolate brownie and left completely satisfied. As a dog lover, I enjoyed looking at the dog photos given to the restaurant by patrons. **Bar:** beer only. **Address:** 1645 Briargate Pkwy, Suite 243 80920 **Location:** I-25 exit 151 (Briargate Pkwy), 0.8 mi e. L D

THE BLUE STAR
Phone: 719/632-1086 34

American
$11-$30

AAA Inspector Notes: Mediterranean and Pacific Rim cuisine are highlighted on a weekly changing menu. Entrees, which may feature salmon, pork tenderloin, steak, duck breast and Colorado lamb, are well-complemented by a great wine and port list. Vegetarian options also are available. A loyal local following comes for the bustling, sometimes noisy atmosphere. Parking codes are enforced; the U-Haul lot is a safe bet after 6 pm. **Bar:** full bar. **Reservations:** suggested. **Address:** 1645 S Tejon St 80906 **Location:** I-25 exit 140, just s to Blue Star neon sign.

L D

(See map & index p. 94.)

CASPIAN CAFE MEDITERRANEAN RESTAURANT

Phone: 719/528-1155 (12)

Mediterranean

$9-$27

AAA Inspector Notes: This distinctive restaurant features dishes from throughout the Mediterranean region. Examples include moussaka, gyros, falafel, kebabs, lamb tagine and steak Nicoise. **Bar:** full bar. **Address:** 4375 Sinton Rd 80907 **Location:** I-25 exit 146 (Garden of the Gods Rd), just e, then just s. L D

CHARLES COURT **Phone:** 719/577-5774 (42)

Regional American

$22-$42

AAA Inspector Notes: This fine-dining restaurant delivers elegance and comfort to the discriminating diner. Guests enjoy a sophisticated menu of Colorado-inspired epicurean delights while gazing across the reflective pond, which glitters in the evening lights. Summertime allows the wall of windows to be opened, providing a refreshing open-air experience while remaining fully indoors. A gallery of famous guests' portraits is right around the corner from the entry. **Bar:** full bar. **Reservations:** suggested. **Address:** 1 Lake Ave 80906 **Location:** I-25 exit 138, 3 mi w on Circle Dr (which becomes Lake Ave); in The Broadmoor. **Parking:** on-site (fee) and valet. B D

EDELWEISS RESTAURANT

Menu on AAA.com **Phone:** 719/633-2220 (35)

German

$7-$27

AAA Inspector Notes: In a 100-year-old former schoolhouse, this restaurant has a charming Old World setting. The menu offers Wiener schnitzel, sauerbraten, apple strudel and German beer and wine. Musicians stroll on weekends. A patio is available in summer, while guests are warmed by a fireplace in winter. **Bar:** full bar. **Address:** 34 E Ramona Ave 80906 **Location:** I-25 exit 140 southbound, just s on Nevada Ave, then just w.

L D

EVEREST NEPAL RESTAURANT

Phone: 719/473-3890 (22)

Nepali

$10-$17

AAA Inspector Notes: I arrived for a late lunch and the buffet hadn't been replenished, but the waiter informed me that I also could order from the menu. I chose the latter and sampled the chicken pakoda. The light batter had a nice texture. The saag paneer had the perfect amount of paneer, an Indian-style cheese, and the garlic naan had the puffy texture that I appreciate in tandoori-baked bread. The Tibetan-style décor features Buddha statues and depictions of Ganesha. Lunch is not available on Sundays. **Bar:** beer & wine. **Address:** 28 E Bijou St 80903 **Location:** I-25 exit 142 (Bijou St), 0.5 mi e, just n on Tejon St, then just e. **Parking:** street only. L D

THE FAMOUS "A STEAK HOUSE"

Phone: 719/227-7333 (25)

Steak

$9-$50

AAA Inspector Notes: This steakhouse offers an understated elegance, masculine décor, USDA Prime beef, fresh seafood, classic cocktails and a nightly piano bar. Sandwiches and salads make up much of the lunch menu, and sides on the dinner menu are large. Comfortable booths embrace diners, but the large U-shaped bar is the focus of the restaurant. The place is popular with downtown businessmen and those ready to enjoy an after-work drink by the piano. **Bar:** full bar. **Address:** 31 N Tejon St 80903 **Location:** I-25 exit 142 (Bijou St), just e to Tejon St, then s. **Parking:** street only.

L D CALL &M

FRATELLI RISTORANTE ITALIANO

Menu on AAA.com **Phone:** 719/575-9571 (23)

Italian

$6-$21

AAA Inspector Notes: The family-owned restaurant presents northern and southern Italian meals prepared in the tradition of the Mediterranean countryside. Fine domestic and imported ingredients enhance each recipe of veal, chicken, seafood and pasta dish. Smart casual attire is suggested. **Bar:** full bar. **Reservations:** suggested. **Address:** 124 N Nevada Ave 80903 **Location:** I-25 exit 142 (Bijou St), 0.5 mi e on Kiowa St, then just n. **Parking:** street only. L D

GERTRUDE'S RESTAURANT

Phone: 719/471-0887 (17)

American

$9-$32

AAA Inspector Notes: This intimate restaurant has a sophisticated menu that includes delicious pasta and grilled dishes. Patrons recommend the wild mushroom linguine, the Colorado lamb and the ever-changing steak or game of the day. This restaurant offers both domestic and imported wines, and the staff is professional and knowledgeable. **Bar:** full bar. **Reservations:** suggested. **Address:** 2625 W Colorado Ave 80904 **Location:** I-25 exit 141, 2.1 mi w, just n on 26th St, then just w. **Parking:** street only. B L D

GIUSEPPE'S OLD DEPOT RESTAURANT

Phone: 719/635-3111 (26)

Italian

$8-$33

AAA Inspector Notes: At the historically restored Denver and Rio Grande Railroad Station, this restaurant offers a good view of Pikes Peak. The menu features pasta, pizza and American dishes served in a Victorian atmosphere. This place is a Colorado Springs favorite. **Bar:** full bar. **Address:** 10 S Sierra Madre St 80903 **Location:** I-25 exit 142 (Bijou St), just e over bridge, stay in right lane, then just s. **Historic** L D

IL VICINO WOOD OVEN PIZZA **Phone:** 719/475-9224

Italian

$6-$9

AAA Inspector Notes: Although this is a casual eatery, there is nothing casual about the food, including large calzones, crisp traditional and specialty pizzas, plates overflowing with pasta and hearty salads. The open kitchen enables guests to watch the cooks as they prepare meals around the wood-burning oven. **Bar:** wine only. **Address:** 11 S Tejon St 80903 **Location:** I-25 exit 142 (Bijou St), just e (which becomes Kiowa St), then just s. **Parking:** street only. L D

JAKE AND TELLY'S GREEK TAVERNA

Phone: 719/633-0406 (18)

Greek

$9-$24

AAA Inspector Notes: This restaurant offers quality food in a beautiful Mediterranean atmosphere. Traditional Greek menu options include gyro plate, moussaka, lamb kebabs and shrimp makaronada. The almond, citrus and olive oil cake has a light, savory flavor with a hint of orange and is accompanied by a creamy, sweet homemade vanilla ice cream. The outstanding wine list features more than 40 choices, including quality reds and whites from various regions in Greece as well as wines from around the world. **Bar:** full bar. **Address:** 2616 W Colorado Ave, Suite 24 80904 **Location:** I-25 exit 141, 2.1 mi w, just n on 26th St, then just w. L D

JOSE MULDOON'S **Phone:** 719/636-2311 (21)

Mexican

$7-$17

AAA Inspector Notes: The attractive Southwestern/Mexican décor includes decorative wood beams and ceramic plates. Patio dining is available in season. Offerings on the late-night bar menu go well with the many tequila varieties. The quesadillas have the perfect amount of butter, cheese and grill marks. **Bar:** full bar. **Address:** 222 N Tejon St 80903 **Location:** Between Platte Ave and Bijou St. **Parking:** street only. L D

(See map & index p. 94.)

JUN JAPANESE RESTAURANT

Phone: 719/531-9368 (7)

Japanese
$7-$13

AAA Inspector Notes: This restaurant offers traditional Japanese cuisine in a casual atmosphere. Quick service means guests won't have to wait long to enjoy the flavorful sushi and tempura dishes. **Bar:** full bar. **Address:** 1760 Dublin Blvd 80918 **Location:** I-25 exit 150, 1.8 mi s. [L] [D]

LA BAGUETTE FRENCH BAKERY AND ESPRESSO CAFE

Phone: 719/577-4818 (19)

Breads/Pastries
$6-$9

AAA Inspector Notes: The signature French onion soup draws many patrons into this rustic old town shop, where the breakfast and lunch choices, including coffee delights and pastries, is sure to tempt. **Bar:** beer & wine. **Address:** 2417 W Colorado Ave 80904 **Location:** I-25 exit 141, 1.4 mi w on US 24, just n on 21st St, then just w. **Parking:** street only. [B] [L] [D] CALL [M]

LA BAGUETTE FRENCH BAKERY AND ESPRESSO CAFE

Phone: 719/598-5550 (4)

Breads/Pastries
$6-$9

AAA Inspector Notes: Once guests sample the French onion soup with a fresh baguette, they'll discover this isn't a typical quick-serve restaurant. The bread is made daily and is used for the delicious sandwiches, and the display case is filled with tantalizing pastries. **Bar:** beer & wine. **Address:** 1420 Kelly Johnson Blvd 80920 **Location:** I-25 exit 150, 0.5 mi se on Academy Blvd, then just w; in a strip mall. [B] [L] [D]

LEMONGRASS BISTRO **Phone:** 719/592-1391 (5)

Vietnamese
$7-$13

AAA Inspector Notes: The cheerful yellow walls and modern Asian art pieces help provide a welcoming dining environment. On the menu are various Vietnamese and Chinese dishes, including stir-fries, noodle salads ("bun"), pho, lo mein, chow mein and fried rice. Distinctive desserts incorporate sweet coconut milk, gelatin and tropical fruit. **Bar:** full bar. **Address:** 6840 N Academy Blvd 80918 **Location:** I-25 exit 149 (Woodmen Rd), 0.5 mi e, then just s. [L] [D]

LITTLE NEPAL **Phone:** 719/477-6997 (36)

Indian
$11-$17

AAA Inspector Notes: Although this restaurant is off the main drag, it's worth the drive. The large portions of delicious, aromatic entrées and puffy naan bread satisfy even the heartiest appetite. Friendly staff members get to know their regulars and make newcomers feel at home. Patio seating is available in summer. **Bar:** full bar. **Address:** 1747 S 8th St 80905 **Location:** I-25 exit 140, 0.4 mi s on Tejon St to Cheyenne Blvd, 0.8 mi sw, then just n. [L] [D]

MACKENZIE'S CHOP HOUSE

Phone: 719/635-3536 (29)

Steak
$9-$35

AAA Inspector Notes: The menu at MacKenzie's features flavorful steak, chops, prime rib and seafood. They also have several martinis and an extensive after-dinner drink list. Proper attire is suggested. Private dining rooms are available. **Bar:** full bar. **Reservations:** suggested. **Address:** 128 S Tejon St 80903 **Location:** I-25 exit 142 (Bijou St), e to Tejon St, then 0.5 mi s; between Colorado and Vermijo sts. **Parking:** street only. [L] [D]

MARIGOLD CAFE & BAKERY

Phone: 719/599-4776 (9)

French
$7-$28

AAA Inspector Notes: The popular eatery with an upscale ambience features an eclectic menu and varied wine list. Fresh baked goods, pizza, salads, pasta and rotisserie-cooked meats are just a few of the offerings. Guests heading to the nearby Garden of the Gods might consider a box lunch to go. **Bar:** wine only. **Reservations:** suggested, for dinner. **Address:** 4605 Centennial Blvd 80919 **Location:** I-25 exit 146 (Garden of the Gods Rd), 1.1 mi w, then just n. [L] [D]

THE MASON JAR **Phone:** 719/632-4820 (15)

American
$8-$16

AAA Inspector Notes: This informal, lively family restaurant specializes in chicken-fried steak, real mashed potatoes and traditional American favorites, as well as prime rib, steak, seafood and homemade desserts. Fireside dining is available in winter. **Bar:** full bar. **Address:** 2925 W Colorado Ave 80904 **Location:** I-25 exit 141, 2.5 mi nw on US 24, just n on 31st St, then just e. [L] [D]

MEDITERRANEAN CAFE **Phone:** 719/633-0115 (24)

Mediterranean
$6-$14

AAA Inspector Notes: Delicious food, large portions and reasonable prices make this small cafe a huge hit with the locals. The menu is dominated by traditional Middle Eastern and Greek dishes, including gyro sandwiches, chicken kebabs, falafel, spanakopita, moussaka and hummus. Service is quick and friendly. **Address:** 118 E Kiowa St 80903 **Location:** In historic town center. **Parking:** street only. [L] [D]

MIRCH MASALA-KABAB & CURRY DINING

Phone: 719/599-0003 (10)

Indian
$9-$16

AAA Inspector Notes: The name means "chilies and spices," and guests find plenty of both on the extensive menu. Indian cuisine is presented with understated elegance. The owner recommends rava masala dhosa, saag paneer, navratan korma, baluchi kebab, goan fish vindaloo and lamb rogan josh. Varied preparations of naan include garlic and cilantro, cheddar cheese, and fruit and nut. The daily buffet is a popular offering. Lending to the inviting atmosphere are interesting murals depicting life in India. **Bar:** full bar. **Address:** 5047 N Academy Blvd 80918 **Location:** I-25 exit 146 (Garden of the Gods Rd), 4.5 mi e, then 1 mi n; in Union Square Shopping Plaza. [L] [D]

NOSH **Phone:** 719/634-6674 (30)

American
$9-$23

AAA Inspector Notes: The creatively conceived menu allows patrons the option of ordering multiple tapas-sized items or larger, entrée-sized portions. This flexibility makes Nosh the perfect place to grab a specialty cocktail and a small bite during happy hour or to relax and enjoy a full meal. Menu items include calamari, burgers, steaks, mac 'n' cheese and hand-crafted sausage. Soups, salads and desserts also are featured. The sultry décor features a large mural of a koi fish. **Bar:** full bar. **Address:** 121 S Tejon St, Suite 100 80903 **Location:** I-25 exit 142 (Bijou St), e to Tejon St, 0.5 mi s, then just e on Colorado Ave; in Plaza of the Rockies. [L] [D]

PANINO'S RESTAURANT DOWNTOWN

Phone: 719/635-7452 (20)

Italian
$8-$16

AAA Inspector Notes: Family-owned and –operated since 1974, this popular eatery displays interesting photographs of founder and former Colorado College hockey star Tony Frasca. The menu lists a wide variety of its namesake Paninos, pizzas, pastas, subs, soups and salads. **Bar:** beer & wine. **Address:** 604 N Tejon St 80903 **Location:** Just s of Colorado College, n of downtown; corner of Willamette Ave. **Parking:** street only. [L] [D]

(See map & index p. 94.)

PARAVICINI'S ITALIAN BISTRO

Phone: 719/471-8200 (16)

Italian
$8-$20

AAA Inspector Notes: In a vintage 1895 building, this cozy eatery boasts a neighborhood atmosphere and a menu of Italian favorites as well as creative specialties. Selections from the lengthy wine list complement the pasta, chicken, veal and seafood dishes. **Bar:** full bar. **Address:** 2802 W Colorado Ave 80904 **Location:** I-25 exit 141, 2.5 mi w on US 24, just n on 31st St, then just e.

L D

THE PENROSE ROOM

Phone: 719/577-5773 (40)

Continental
$72-$102

AAA Inspector Notes: The panoramic rooftop view is one splendid element of the restaurant's elegant ambience. Wild game appetizers and entrées are memorable, as is the classic tableside preparation of Caesar salad. The staff is skilled and experienced. Meals are prix fixe, either three or four courses with multiple selections for each course. A seven-course chef's tasting menu, with or without wine pairing, is available. Semi-formal attire. **Bar:** full bar. **Reservations:** suggested. **Address:** 1 Lake Ave 80906 **Location:** I-25 exit 138, 3 mi w on Circle Dr (which becomes Lake Ave); in The Broadmoor. **Parking:** valet only. D

THE PEPPER TREE RESTAURANT

Phone: 719/471-4888 (32)

Continental
$19-$50

AAA Inspector Notes: The Pepper Tree features elegant dining overlooking the downtown skyline. House specialties are served with expert tableside preparation; the waitstaff is attentive and professional. This is the perfect place for a special occasion. Proper attire suggested. **Bar:** full bar. **Reservations:** suggested. **Address:** 888 W Moreno Ave 80905 **Location:** I-25 exit 141, 0.3 mi sw on US 24, 0.3 mi s on 8th St, then just w. D

P.F. CHANG'S CHINA BISTRO

Phone: 719/593-8580 (2)

Chinese
$10-$23

AAA Inspector Notes: Trendy, upscale decor provides a pleasant backdrop for New Age Chinese dining. Appetizers, soups and salads are a meal by themselves. Vegetarian plates and sides, noodles, meins, chicken and meat dishes are created from exotic, fresh ingredients. **Bar:** full bar. **Address:** 1725 Briargate Pkwy 80920 **Location:** I-25 exit 151 (Briargate Pkwy), 0.9 mi e.

L D CALL M

PHANTOM CANYON BREWING CO

Phone: 719/635-2800 (27)

American
$8-$24

AAA Inspector Notes: In a restored 1901 building, the popular restaurant has a bustling atmosphere and massive windows offering great downtown views. Several home brews; appetizers like artichoke with asiago cheese, grilled kielbasa and hot pretzels; and such larger meals as fish 'n' chips, shepherd's pie, pot roast, steak, pasta and daily fresh seafood specials are offered. **Bar:** full bar. **Address:** 2 E Pikes Peak Ave 80903 **Location:** I-25 exit 142 (Bijou St) to Cascade Ave, then just s.

L D LATE

PIZZERIA RUSTICA

Phone: 719/632-8121 (13)

Pizza
$11-$14

AAA Inspector Notes: This rustic bistro imports some ingredients from Italy but also buys fresh vegetables from local farmers. Neapolitan, uncut and regular round pizzas, as well as calzones, are baked in a pecan wood-fired oven. Cured meats, cheeses, marinated vegetables, pickles and olives also are available. Desserts include cookies, gelato, spumoni and sorbetto. Drink selections include artisan Italian beers and wines from Italy and California (some are organic). **Bar:** full bar. **Reservations:** suggested. **Address:** 2527 W Colorado Ave 80904 **Location:** I-25 exit 141, just n, then 0.4 mi w. **Parking:** street only. L D

THE RITZ GRILL

Phone: 719/635-8484 (28)

American
$8-$22

AAA Inspector Notes: Distinctive art deco appointments lend to the restaurant's warm, inviting atmosphere. New American preparations of chicken, steak and fish appeal to both locals and out-of-towners, and delicious breakfast favorites of huevos rancheros and eggs Benedict bring Southwestern and traditional flavors to the table for Sunday brunch. **Bar:** full bar. **Reservations:** suggested. **Address:** 15 S Tejon St 80903 **Location:** I-25 exit 142 (Bijou St), 0.3 mi e, then just s; at Pikes Peak Ave. **Parking:** street only. L D

SALSA BRAVA FRESH MEXICAN GRILL

Phone: 719/266-9244 (6)

Mexican
$9-$18

AAA Inspector Notes: The friendly and inviting hacienda has a staff that makes guests feel right at home. The made-from-scratch salsa gets taste buds dancing, but it's smart to save room for rolled-to-order Baja rolls, fish tacos, enchiladas and fajitas. Some nontraditional items include smoky ribs slathered in a chipotle-fired barbecue sauce, as well as shrimp tossed with Cajun seasonings. **Bar:** full bar. **Address:** 802 Village Center Dr 80919 **Location:** I-25 exit 148 (Rockrimmon Blvd), 1.4 mi w, then just s.

L D

SALSA BRAVA FRESH MEXICAN GRILL

Phone: 719/955-6650

Mexican
$9-$18

AAA Inspector Notes: This popular eatery features flavorful salsas, sauces and dips, in addition to tasty entrees along the lines of enchiladas, Baja fish tacos and rellenos. Warm welcoming decor, friendly staff and delicious food make this place a favorite with locals. **Bar:** full bar. **Address:** 9420 Briar Village Point 80920 **Location:** I-25 exit 151 (Briargate Pkwy), 1.4 mi e, just n on Pine Village Way, then just w; in Pine Creek strip mall. L D

SENOR MANUEL MEXICAN CUISINE

Phone: 719/598-3033 (11)

Mexican
$8-$18

AAA Inspector Notes: Family owned and operated since 1970, the popular eatery prepares menudo, posole, tamales, carnitas and traditional home-style Mexican favorites. The surroundings are unpretentious and the décor is modest. Friendly staffers enhance the experience. **Bar:** full bar. **Address:** 4660 N Nevada Ave 80918 **Location:** I-25 exit 146 (Garden of the Gods Rd), 0.5 mi e to Nevada Ave, then just n. L D CALL M

(See map & index p. 94.)

SHUGA'S RESTAURANT & BAR

Phone: 719/328-1412 (33)

Deli
$8-$9

AAA Inspector Notes: This artful cafe appeals to a diverse clientele, including fashionable hipsters and workers in business casual attire. The unique menu combines flavors from all over the world and offers meat as well as vegetarian dishes. Although the soups and sandwiches are delicious, I absolutely love the almond butter cake and get it every time I eat here. Service tends to be slow, which doesn't matter too much as this is a popular spot to hang out for hours. **Bar:** full bar. **Address:** 702 S Cascade Ave 80903 **Location:** 0.5 mi s of historic downtown; jct Rio Grande Ave. **Parking:** street only. L D LATE

STEAKSMITH **Phone:** 719/596-9300 (14)

Steak
$16-$34

AAA Inspector Notes: In spite of the many nearby new chains, locals continue to frequent this area institution for its attractive Southwestern atmosphere and well-trained, top-notch staff that provides friendly, capable and attentive service. The menu consists of a variety of steaks, hand cut from Choice aged beef, as well as chicken and seafood dishes. **Bar:** full bar. **Reservations:** suggested. **Address:** 3802 Maizeland Rd 80909 **Location:** Jct N Academy Blvd (2500 blk) and Maizeland Rd; in Maizeland Moors Shopping Center. D CALL &M

SUMMIT **Phone:** 719/577-5733 (41)

American
$16-$28

AAA Inspector Notes: More than 2,000 bottles from the vast wine list are displayed in a distinctive glass-enclosed turret designed by international architect Adam D. Tihany. Executive chef Bertrand Bouquin conceives the brasserie's New American dishes, which use seasonal produce found around the country. Upscale presentations add visual punch. **Bar:** full bar. **Reservations:** suggested. **Address:** 1 Lake Ave 80906 **Location:** I-25 exit 138, 3 mi w of Circle Dr (becomes Lake Ave); across from The Broadmoor. **Parking:** valet only. D

THE TAVERN **Phone:** 719/577-5772 (39)

American
$10-$55

AAA Inspector Notes: A gracious atmosphere prevails in a handsome room appointed with Henri de Toulouse-Lautrec prints. Arrangements of steak, prime rib, chicken, seafood and pasta are prepared on the display grill. The front room is intimate, the garden room bright and lush. Nightly dancing contributes to the lively feel of the non-smoking bar. **Bar:** full bar. **Reservations:** suggested. **Address:** 1 Lake Ave 80906 **Location:** I-25 exit 138, 3 mi w on Circle Dr (which becomes Lake Ave); in The Broadmoor. **Parking:** valet only. L D

WALTER'S BISTRO **Phone:** 719/630-0201 (37)

American
$10-$46

AAA Inspector Notes: The cozy but elegant bistro serves artfully presented food, including beef, pork, lamb and seafood selections. Offerings of spirits and wine hail from around the world. **Bar:** full bar. **Reservations:** suggested, weekends. **Address:** 146 E Cheyenne Mountain Blvd 80906 **Location:** I-25 exit 140 (Nevada Ave), 1.7 mi s, then just w; in Country Club Corners retail complex. L D

THE WAREHOUSE
Menu on AAA.com **Phone:** 719/475-8880 (31)

American
$11-$36

AAA Inspector Notes: Owner and chef Lawrence Johnson has received awards from local and national organizations for his innovative cuisine. Many dishes feature ingredients found in the West, such as Rocky Mountain trout, bison, Colorado bass, Colorado lamb and wildflowers. Colorado-produced wines dominate the wine list. In a converted warehouse, the dining room displays oil paintings by local artists. **Bar:** full bar. **Reservations:** suggested. **Address:** 25 W Cimarron St 80903 **Location:** I-25 exit 141, 0.4 mi e. L D

ZIO'S ITALIAN KITCHEN **Phone:** 719/593-9999

Italian
$8-$13

AAA Inspector Notes: The warm, comfortable atmosphere and Old World decor complement the menu. Meals are a good value, and so is the service. This small chain specializes in Italian cuisine, including oven-baked pizzas and pasta dishes. Guests are encouraged to get creative with their pizzas by mixing and matching from a list of 24 toppings. Particularly tempting dishes are Artichoke spinach pasta, chicken parmigiana, and Shrimp Limone. **Bar:** full bar. **Address:** 6650 Corporate Dr 80919 **Location:** I-25 exit 149 (Woodmen Rd), just w, then 0.5 mi s. L D CALL &M

COMMERCE CITY (B-5) pop. 45,913, elev. 5,184'

• **Part of Denver area — see map p. 123**

DICK'S SPORTING GOODS PARK STADIUM TOURS is at 6000 Victory Way. The stadium is the home of Denver's Major League Soccer team, the Rapids. Tours provide visitors a chance to see what goes on behind the scenes at the stadium, park and soccer complex. **Time:** Allow 45 minutes minimum. **Hours:** Tours are given Mon.-Fri. 9-6 (weather permitting). **Cost:** Free; tickets are first-come, first-served, available at box office. **Phone:** (303) 727-3599.

COPPER MOUNTAIN pop. 385

CARBONATE CONDOS **Phone:** (970)968-6854

Resort Condominium
$147-$1575 11/1-4/30
$115-$800 5/1-10/31

Address: 35 Wheeler Pl, #102 80443 **Location:** I-70 exit 195, just s, then just w; corner of Copper Rd and Wheeler Pl. **Facility:** Individually owned condos, some with ski-in/out access, range from studios to four-bedroom units. 65 condominiums. 3-6 stories (no elevator), interior/exterior corridors. **Terms:** office hours 8 am-6 pm, check-in 4 pm, 2 night minimum stay, 45 day cancellation notice-fee imposed. **Amenities:** *Some:* high-speed Internet. **Activities:** saunas, whirlpools, steamrooms, rental bicycles, hiking trails, jogging, playground. *Fee:* golf-18 holes. **Guest Services:** coin laundry.

WHERE TO EAT

C.B. GRILLE Phone: 970/968-3113

American
$18-$33

AAA Inspector Notes: This warm and intimate restaurant's ever-changing menu includes winter and summer tapas such as bacon-and-basil-wrapped lamb chop and saffron-poached shrimp. Entrées may include salmon with smoked wild mushrooms, truffle-scented free-range chicken breast with roasted-beet risotto, elk chop, bison and pan-seared scallops. A wonderful selection of wine flights, specific menu wine pairings and after-dinner drinks are offered. A private fireside dining room is available. **Bar:** full bar. **Address:** 910 Copper Rd, #114 80443 **Location:** I-70 exit 195, just s, then 0.5 mi w; located just inside Copper Mountain Village entrance; park at Beeler Lot.

D AC

CORTEZ (F-1) pop. 8,482, elev. 6,201'

• Restaurants p. 114

Among the mesas and open expanses of land in the Four Corners region, Cortez has been a trading center for more than 2,000 years. Ranching, tourism and light manufacturing support today's economy.

Ten miles east on US 160 is the entrance to Mesa Verde National Park *(see place listing p. 252)*. Hovenweep National Monument *(see place listing p. 227)* is about 48 miles west.

American Indian dances and an outdoor drama are performed at the Cortez Cultural Center, 25 N. Market St., throughout the summer; phone (970) 565-1151. The Mesa Verde Country Indian Arts and Culture Festival takes place in Cortez and the surrounding area, including Mesa Verde National Park, starting Memorial Day weekend. Highlights of the weeklong celebration include an Indian art market, American Indian cultural programs and dances, a featured artist, concerts and archeological tours and exhibits.

Mesa Verde Country Visitor Information: 928 E. Main St., P.O. Box HH, Cortez, CO 81321. **Phone:** (970) 565-8227 or (800) 253-1616. ***(See ad p. 254.)***

CROW CANYON ARCHAEOLOGICAL CENTER is 1.2 mi. w. off US 491 on Rd. L, then 1.4 mi. s. to 23390 Rd. K. The center offers an all-day tour during which visitors examine artifacts and learn about Ancestral Pueblo Indian history, then tour Crow Canyon's archeology laboratory and current excavation site. Lunch is included. Other programs also are available. Allow a full day. **Hours:** Wed.-Thurs. 8:45-4:30, May-Sept. **Cost:** Fee $55; $30 (ages 10-17). Under 10 are not permitted. **Phone:** (970) 565-8975 or (800) 422-8975.

FOUR CORNERS MONUMENT, about 35 mi. s.w., is the only place in the country where four states meet. The juncture of Arizona, Utah, Colorado and New Mexico is marked by a monument bearing each state's seal. The original marker erected in 1912 was a simple concrete pad but is now made of granite and brass. The visitor center features a demonstration center with Navajo artisans. Navajo vendors sell their wares near the site.

Hours: Daily 8 a.m.-8 p.m., May-Aug.; 8-5, rest of year. Closed Jan. 1, Thanksgiving and Christmas. **Cost:** $3. **Phone:** (928) 871-6647.

BAYMONT INN & SUITES Phone: (970)565-3400

Hotel
$94-$117

Address: 2321 E Main St 81321 **Location:** 1.3 mi e on US 160. **Facility:** 145 units. 3 stories, interior/exterior corridors. **Pool(s):** heated indoor. **Activities:** whirlpool, exercise room. **Guest Services:** coin laundry.

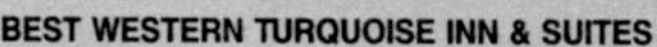

/ SOME UNITS FEE

BUDGET HOST INN Phone: (970)565-3738

Motel
$59-$108 5/1-9/30
$49-$98 10/1-4/30

Address: 2040 E Main St 81321 **Location:** 1.3 mi e of center on US 160 (Main St). **Facility:** 40 units. 1 story, exterior corridors. **Terms:** cancellation fee imposed. **Amenities:** *Some:* high-speed Internet. **Pool(s):** heated outdoor. **Activities:** whirlpool. **Guest Services:** area transportation-casino. **Free Special Amenities: expanded continental breakfast and high-speed Internet.**

SAVE / SOME UNITS FEE

ECONO LODGE Phone: (970)565-3474

Motel
$60-$150

Address: 2020 E Main St 81321 **Location:** 1.3 mi e on US 160. **Facility:** 70 units. 2 stories (no elevator), exterior corridors. **Terms:** cancellation fee imposed. **Pool(s):** heated outdoor. **Guest Services:** coin laundry.

/ SOME UNITS FEE

HOLIDAY INN EXPRESS Phone: (970)565-6000

Hotel

$129-$189 5/1-10/1
$119-$159 10/2-4/30

Address: 2121 E Main St 81321 **Location:** 1.3 mi e on US 160. **Facility:** 100 units. 3 stories, interior corridors. **Amenities:** high-speed Internet. **Dining:** Koko's Friendly Pub, see separate listing. **Pool(s):** heated indoor. **Activities:** sauna, whirlpool, exercise room. **Guest Services:** valet and coin laundry. *(See ad p. 256.)*

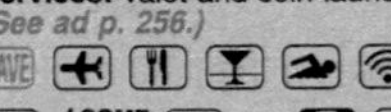

/ SOME UNITS FEE

TOMAHAWK LODGE Phone: (970)565-8521

Motel

$59-$99 5/1-10/31
$49-$79 11/1-4/30

Address: 728 S Broadway 81321 **Location:** 1 mi w of center on US 160. **Facility:** 38 units. 1 story, exterior corridors. **Pool(s):** heated outdoor. **Free Special Amenities: local telephone calls and high-speed Internet.**

/ SOME UNITS FEE

WHITE EAGLE INN & FAMILY LODGE Phone: (970)565-3333

Motel

$49-$99

Address: 2110 S Broadway 81321 **Location:** 1.3 mi s of jct US 160 and 491. **Facility:** 16 units, some houses. 1 story, exterior corridors. **Terms:** cancellation fee imposed. **Activities:** miniature golf, playground. **Guest Services:** area transportation-casino. **Free Special Amenities: local telephone calls and high-speed Internet.**

WHERE TO EAT

DRY DOCK RESTAURANT & PUB
Menu on AAA.com Phone: 970/564-9404

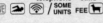

Seafood

$7-$23

AAA Inspector Notes: Patrons can enjoy casual dining with a Southwestern flair, with a menu featuring cuts of aged beef and the freshest seafood available. Seating can be had in several dining rooms or on a garden patio with umbrella tables and a mesmerizing waterfall. **Bar:** full bar. **Address:** 200 W Main St 81321 **Location:** Just w of center. D CALL

KOKO'S FRIENDLY PUB Phone: 970/565-6000

American

$8-$20

AAA Inspector Notes: This friendly Southwest-themed pub is the perfect place to unwind after a long day. Diners sink into comfortable chairs and enjoy specialty margaritas with their meals. Menu choices include grilled romaine heart, homemade white bean chili, tequila-lime chicken, grilled salmon, stuffed trout and brats and burgers, with a Southwestern twist. **Bar:** full bar. **Address:** 2121 E Main St 81321 **Location:** 1.3 mi e on US 160; in Holiday Inn Express. D

LOTSA PASTA & THAT 'ZA PIZZA Phone: 970/564-9131

Italian

$6-$13

AAA Inspector Notes: This restaurant offers fresh, hearty Italian dishes in a casual atmosphere. Friendly servers will make you feel at home. **Bar:** beer & wine. **Address:** 1020 S Broadway 81321 **Location:** 1 mi s of jct US 160 and 491. D

MAIN STREET BREWERY Phone: 970/564-9112

American

$10-$24

AAA Inspector Notes: This casual restaurant offers a variety of traditional pasta, chicken, beef, pizza, burgers, steaks, prime rib and nightly specials. The menu also features 12 microbrews and blends. The friendly, attentive waitstaff will only enhance your dining experience. Their game room includes billiards, video games, foosball and air hockey. A brewery is on the premises. **Bar:** full bar. **Address:** 21 E Main St 81321 **Location:** Center. **Parking:** street only. L D

NERO'S ITALIAN RESTAURANT
Menu on AAA.com Phone: 970/565-7366

Italian

$9-$21

AAA Inspector Notes: The casual and intimate eatery serves Italian dishes prepared with a Southwestern flair. The menu features a popular lasagna, pork loin with apple, duck breast with Grand Marnier, filet mignon with shallots and a Gorgonzola cream sauce, chicken and veal. The house salad and garlic bread are very good, too. Seasonal patio dining is available. **Bar:** full bar. **Address:** 303 W Main St 81321 **Location:** Jct US 160 and 491. **Parking:** street only. D

ONCE UPON A SANDWICH Phone: 970/565-8292

Deli

$7-$9

AAA Inspector Notes: This eatery is a good choice for a quick hearty meal. In addition to sandwiches, comfort food is available. **Address:** 7 W Main St 81321 **Location:** Corner of Main and Market sts; downtown. **Parking:** street only. L

PEPPERHEAD RESTAURANT Phone: 970/565-3303

Mexican

$7-$25

AAA Inspector Notes: Operated by a father-daughter duo, the restaurant specializes in quick lunch plates served with rice and beans, unique platters served with a carafe of red or white wine and special pepperhead margaritas. Signature dishes include chicken mole, carnitas and stuffies-fresh sopaipillas stuffed with chicken, beef or pork and smothered with delicious red or green chili. The attractively presented lemon tart is tasty and made in house. **Bar:** full bar. **Address:** 44 W Main St 81321 **Location:** Center. **Parking:** street only. L D

SHILOH STEAK HOUSE Phone: 970/565-6560

Steak

$9-$29

AAA Inspector Notes: In a small converted residential home on Main Street, the casual restaurant offers a selection of steak and seafood entrées as well as local microbrewery beer and an extensive wine list featuring local wines. **Bar:** full bar. **Address:** 5 S Veach St 81321 **Location:** 0.5 mi e; corner of Sligo and Main sts. L D

COTOPAXI (E-3) pop. 47, elev. 6,364'

RECREATIONAL ACTIVITIES

White-water Rafting

- **Arkansas River Tours** is w. on US 50. **Hours:** Daily 7-7, mid-May through Labor Day. **Phone:** (719) 942-4362 or (800) 321-4352.

CRAIG (C-2) pop. 9,464, elev. 6,186'

In the Yampa River Valley, Craig is a starting point for exploring the meandering canyons of the Yampa and Green rivers. It is the western terminus for the 207-mile scenic stretch of US 40 from Denver. Elk, antelopes, deer and eagles are present in the surrounding mountains.

The Colorado entrance to Dinosaur National Monument *(see place listing in Utah p. 342)* is 90 miles west of Craig on US 40. North of the monument lies Browns Park National Wildlife Refuge. The refuge offers boating, camping and hunting.

Chainsaw artists converge on Craig City Park each June to create elaborate masterpieces from cottonwood logs; visitors are welcome to watch the competition progress. Tours of a private Pullman railroad car once owned by Denver banker David Moffat can be arranged through the chamber of commerce.

Craig Chamber of Commerce/Moffat County Visitor Center: 360 E. Victory Way, Craig, CO 81625. **Phone:** (970) 824-5689 or (800) 864-4405.

MUSEUM OF NORTHWEST COLORADO, in the old State Armory at 590 Yampa (SR 13), contains American Indian artifacts, rock collections and items pertaining to local history. Displays of railroad memorabilia and turn-of-the-20th-century photographs are included. The museum also features one of the largest collections of cowboy and gunfighter memorabilia in the country. **Hours:** Mon.-Fri. 9-5, Sat. 10-4. **Cost:** Donations. **Phone:** (970) 824-6360.

BEST WESTERN PLUS DEER PARK INN & SUITES **Phone:** (970)824-9282

Hotel
$90-$300

AAA Benefit: Members save up to 20%, plus 10% bonus points with Best Western Rewards®.

Address: 262 Commerce St 81625 **Location:** 0.3 mi s of jct US 40 and SR 13. **Facility:** 42 units, some efficiencies and kitchens. 2 stories (no elevator), interior corridors. **Pool(s):** heated indoor. **Activities:** whirlpool. **Guest Services:** valet and coin laundry. **Free Special Amenities: full breakfast and high-speed Internet.**

SAVE BIZ / SOME UNITS FEE

CANDLEWOOD SUITES - CRAIG **Phone:** (970)824-8400

Extended Stay Hotel
$119-$169 5/1-11/19
$89-$139 11/20-4/30

Address: 92 Commerce St 81625 **Location:** 0.4 mi s of jct US 40 and SR 13, just e. **Facility:** 76 efficiencies. 3 stories, interior corridors. **Parking:** winter plug-ins. **Terms:** check-in 4 pm. **Amenities:** high-speed Internet. **Activities:** exercise room. **Guest Services:** complimentary and valet laundry.

BIZ / SOME UNITS FEE

HAMPTON INN & SUITES **Phone:** (970)826-9900

Contemporary Hotel
$109-$149

AAA Benefit: Members save up to 10% everyday!

Address: 377 Cedar Ct 81625 **Location:** 0.4 mi s of jct US 40 and SR 13, just w. **Facility:** 89 units. 4 stories, interior corridors. **Parking:** winter plug-ins. **Terms:** 1-7 night minimum stay, cancellation fee imposed. **Pool(s):** heated indoor. **Activities:** whirlpool, exercise room. **Guest Services:** valet and coin laundry. **Free Special Amenities: expanded continental breakfast and high-speed Internet.**

SAVE CALL BIZ / SOME UNITS

WHERE TO EAT

CARELLI'S ITALIAN RESTAURANT **Phone:** 970/824-6868

Italian
$6-$15

AAA Inspector Notes: The menu lists an array of appetizers, salads, mouthwatering pizzas, hot sandwiches and a variety of pasta dishes. Dinner is offered in the cozy dining room. **Bar:** full bar. **Address:** 465 Yampa Ave 81625 **Location:** Just n of US 40; downtown. **Parking:** street only. L D

THE GALAXY RESTAURANT **Phone:** 970/824-8164

Chinese
$7-$13

AAA Inspector Notes: The well-decorated dining room serves up traditional dishes such as moo goo gai pan and shrimp chow mein, in addition to a few American dishes and an all-you-can-eat lunch buffet. **Bar:** full bar. **Address:** 524 Yampa Ave 81625 **Location:** Just n of US 40; downtown. **Parking:** street only. L D

CREEDE (E-2) elev. 8,838'

A relative latecomer to Colorado's roster of boomtowns—the first silver lode was uncovered in 1889—Creede remained the only silver camp in production during the silver panic of 1893; its mines consistently produced $10 million annually. The industry continued for nearly 100 years until the last mine closed in 1985.

Characters such as Bob Ford (who killed Jesse James), Martha ("Calamity Jane") Cannary and her pal Poker Alice, Bat Masterson and bunco artist "Soapy" Smith gave the town its reputation as one of the wildest camps in the state.

Plays at the nationally acclaimed Creede Repertory Theatre occur from May through September; phone (719) 658-2540. The town also hosts festivals, concerts, bike rallies, mountain runs and art exhibits. The nearby San Juan Mountains and Rio Grande National Forest *(see place listing p. 275)* provide outdoor recreational opportunities throughout the year.

Creede-Mineral County Chamber of Commerce: 907 S. Main St., P.O. Box 580, Creede, CO 81130. **Phone:** (719) 658-2374 or (800) 327-2102.

Self-guiding tours: Brochures outlining a 17-mile driving tour of the historic mining district, as well as walking tours featuring Victorian-era buildings and art galleries, range in price from $1 to $2 at the chamber of commerce.

CREEDE MUSEUM is in the old train depot at 117 Main St. The history of Mineral County is depicted along with the prospectors, miners and entrepreneurs who helped settle the region. Exhibits feature the town's first hand-drawn fire wagon, a horse-drawn hearse, pioneer artifacts, gambling devices, early newspapers, vintage photographs and other memorabilia. **Time:** Allow 30 minutes minimum. **Hours:** Daily 10-4, Memorial Day-Labor Day. **Cost:** $2; $1 (ages 60+); free (ages 0-11); $5 (family). **Phone:** (719) 658-2004.

CREEDE UNDERGROUND MINING MUSEUM, .5 mi. n. of jct. SR 149 and Creede Ave., is housed in rooms blasted out of solid rock. Exhibits trace the history of mining from the 19th century to the present. Cave temperature is 51°F.

A 30-minute narrated CD-ROM is available for self-guiding tours. Retired miners lead guided tours, explaining equipment and methods of mining; reservations are required. Warm clothing is recommended. **Time:** Allow 1 hour minimum. **Hours:** Daily 10-4, Memorial Day to mid-Sept.; Mon.-Fri. 10-3, rest of year. Guided tours are offered Memorial Day to mid-Sept. Closed major holidays. **Cost:** (including CD-ROM) $12.50; $6 (ages 60+); $5 (ages 6-12). Guided tour $15. **Phone:** (719) 658-0811.

RECREATIONAL ACTIVITIES

Fishing

- **South Fork Anglers** departs from 13 S. Main St. **Hours:** Daily dawn-dusk. Phone ahead to confirm schedule. **Phone:** (719) 658-2955 or (877) 656-3474.

CRESTED BUTTE (D-2) pop. 1,487, elev. 8,908'

The Elk Mountain Lodge, dating from 1881, and the Old Town Hall and Union Congregational Church, both built in 1883, are reminders of the town's origins as a supply town and coal-mining camp. Another reminder, a two-story outhouse, is behind the shops of the renovated Company Store building on Third Street. The privy's upper level made it usable during the winters when more than 20 feet of snow fell.

More elegant landmarks from the town's past are found along Elk Avenue, where restored Victorian buildings feature shops, eateries and outfitters. Culturally speaking, the Crested Butte Center for the Arts is the town's destination for music, dance, theater and art; phone (970) 349-7487.

The Gunnison National Forest, Elk Mountains and Raggeds Wilderness surround the town. Jagged peaks, glacial valleys and aspen-covered slopes provide a scenic backdrop for golfing, mountain biking and hiking. Three miles from Crested Butte, the resort community of Mt. Crested Butte has become a center for recreation, especially skiing, snowboarding, tubing, mountain biking, hiking and horseback riding in Gunnison National Forest *(see Grand Mesa-Uncompahgre-Gunnison National Forests p. 219).*

Crested Butte/Mount Crested Butte Chamber of Commerce and Visitor Center: 601 Elk Ave., P.O. Box 1288, Crested Butte, CO 81224. **Phone:** (970) 349-6438 or (800) 851-5929.

Self-guiding tours: A walking tour map of the town's historical attractions is available from the chamber of commerce and the Crested Butte Mountain Heritage Museum.

CRESTED BUTTE MOUNTAIN HERITAGE MUSEUM is at 331 Elk Ave. The front of the museum functioned as a hardware store 1883-1996; a coal stove and original cases filled with goods representing items sold in the past are on display. Exhibits about geology, skiing history, textiles, ranching and domestic life in Crested Butte may be seen as well as a model railroad, a mining diorama and a gondola. The Mountain Bike Hall of Fame features vintage bicycles.

Time: Allow 30 minutes minimum. **Hours:** Daily 10-8, Memorial Day-early Oct.; noon-6, rest of year. **Cost:** $3; free (ages 0-11). **Phone:** (970) 349-1880.

PARAGON GALLERY, 132 Elk Ave. at 2nd St., is in the old town hall. The cooperative gallery displays the works of 14 local artists as well as works by guest artists. Included are fine arts, photographs, ceramics, jewelry, handmade paper, leatherwork, mosaics, stained glass and sculpture. **Hours:** Daily 10-9, mid-June to early Oct.; 11-9, late Nov.-late Apr. Phone ahead to confirm schedule. **Cost:** Free. **Phone:** (970) 349-6484.

GRAND LODGE HOTEL & SUITES

Phone: (970)349-8000

Hotel

$149-$269 11/23-4/30
$95-$169 5/1-11/22

Address: 6 Emmons Loop 81225 **Location:** 2.3 mi n; in Mt. Crested Butte. **Facility:** 218 units, some efficiencies. 5 stories, interior corridors. **Terms:** check-in 4 pm, 1-4 night minimum stay - seasonal, 3 day cancellation notice, 45 day 11/23-4/30-fee imposed. **Amenities:** safes. **Pool(s):** heated indoor/outdoor. **Activities:** whirlpool, steamroom, hiking trails, exercise room, spa. **Guest Services:** coin laundry.

BIZ

/ SOME UNITS FEE

THE LODGE AT MOUNTAINEER SQUARE

Phone: (970)349-4000

Resort Hotel

$169-$309 11/23-4/30
$133-$189 5/1-11/22

Address: 600 Gothic Rd 81225 **Location:** 6 mi n; in Mt Crested Butte. **Facility:** The hotel has studio and one- to four-bedroom suites just steps from ski lifts. All rooms have a humidifier; some feature a gas fireplace and washer and dryer. Underground parking is available. 124 units, some two bedrooms, three bedrooms, efficiencies, kitchens and condominiums. 6 stories, interior corridors. **Parking:** on-site and valet. **Terms:** off-site registration, 1-5 night minimum stay - seasonal, 3 day cancellation notice, 45 day 11/23-4/30-fee imposed. **Amenities:** video games (fee), high-speed Internet, safes. **Dining:** 2 restaurants. **Pool(s):** heated indoor/outdoor. **Activities:** sauna, whirlpool, rental bicycles, hiking trails, jogging, exercise room, spa. *Fee:* downhill & cross country skiing, ice skating. **Guest Services:** area transportation-within 3 mi.

BIZ FEE

/ SOME UNITS

NORDIC INN

Phone: (970)349-5542

Motel

$110-$190 11/22-3/31
$103-$161 6/1-10/8

Address: 14 Treasury Rd 81224 **Location:** 2.7 mi n; in Mt Crested Butte. **Facility:** 27 units, some efficiencies and kitchens. 2 stories (no elevator), exterior corridors. **Terms:** open 6/1-10/8 & 11/22-3/31, check-in 4 pm, 3-5 night minimum stay - seasonal and/or weekends, 30 day cancellation notice-fee imposed. **Activities:** whirlpool. **Free Special Amenities: expanded continental breakfast and high-speed Internet.**

SAVE / SOME UNITS

OLD TOWN INN

Phone: 970/349-6184

Motel

$89-$149

Address: 708 6th St 81224 **Location:** On SR 135, just s of Elk Ave. **Facility:** 33 units. 2 stories (no elevator), interior corridors. **Terms:** office hours 6:30 am-10 pm, 14 day cancellation notice-fee imposed. **Activities:** whirlpool. **Guest Services:** coin laundry. / SOME UNITS FEE

WESTWALL LODGE

Phone: (970)349-1280

Condominium

$350-$2300 11/23-4/30
$250-$1500 5/1-11/22

Address: 14 Hunter Hill Rd 81225 **Location:** 2.2 mi n, then just e; in Mt. Crested Butte. **Facility:** Experience a high degree of luxury and numerous amenities, including an in-room washer and dryer. This ski-in/ski-out residential lodge offers heated underground parking. 20 condominiums. 3-4 stories, interior corridors. **Terms:** office hours 8 am-8 pm, 3-5 night minimum stay - seasonal and/or weekends, 30 day cancellation notice-fee imposed. **Amenities:** high-speed Internet. **Pool(s):** heated outdoor. **Activities:** whirlpool, steamroom. *Fee:* downhill skiing, massage. **Guest Services:** complimentary laundry.

FEE

/ SOME UNITS FEE

CRESTED BUTTE INTERNATIONAL HOSTEL

Phone: 970/349-0588

fyi Not evaluated. **Address:** 615 Teocalli Ave 81224 **Location:** 0.3 mi n of Elk Ave. Facilities, services, and decor characterize an economy property.

THE INN AT CRESTED BUTTE

Phone: 970/349-2111

fyi

Boutique Hotel

Did not meet all AAA rating requirements for locking devices in some guest rooms at time of last evaluation on 08/16/2011. **Address:** 510 Whiterock Ave 81224 **Location:** Just s of Elk Ave, then just w. Facilities, services, and decor characterize a mid-scale property.

WHERE TO EAT

EASTSIDE BISTRO

Phone: 970/349-9699

American

$26-$38

AAA Inspector Notes: This upscale bistro features a breathtaking view of Mt. Crested Butte and serves a fine array of starters and entrées such as baked oysters Rockefeller, scallop chowder, warm spinach salad, seared rack of lamb and grilled strip loin of beef with brie creamed spinach and charred cherry tomatoes. Crème fraîche flan with candied apples and toasted pistachios is among the seasonal desserts. The extensive wine list, dessert martinis and dessert wine and warmed drinks enhance the dining experience. **Bar:** full bar. **Reservations:** suggested. **Address:** 435 Sixth St 81224 **Location:** On SR 135, just s of Elk Ave. D

GINGER CAFE

Phone: 970/349-7291

Asian

$9-$25

AAA Inspector Notes: Among the offerings of authentic, freshly made Pan Asian cuisine are a fiery tom yum goong soup, Vietnamese spring rolls, crab Rangoon, pot stickers served with a green onion soy dipping sauce, green and red curries and krapow, a favorite dish that pairs fresh green cilantro with local vegetables. Beef, chicken, seafood or tofu are available in most dishes. Rich and filling green tea cheesecake or a mango lassi add delicious sweet touches. **Bar:** full bar. **Address:** 425 Elk Ave 81224 **Location:** 0.3 mi w. **Parking:** street only.

L D

THE LAST STEEP BAR & GRILL

Phone: 970/349-7007

American

$9-$17

AAA Inspector Notes: Named for the owner's favorite north-face ski run, this popular eatery serves appetizers such as Ms. Ann's famous crab cakes, which are grilled and then fried; freshly made soups served in hollowed-out bread bowls, salads; veggie, chicken Caesar and crab cake wraps; award-winning burgers; and creative sandwiches such as Kansas City-style pulled pork, Jamaican-style marinated chicken breast, Cajun-grilled ahi, and a Santa Fe veggie burger. **Bar:** full bar. **Address:** 208 Elk Ave 81224 **Location:** 0.3 mi w of center. **Parking:** street only.

L D

LE BOSQUET RESTAURANT FRANCAIS

Phone: 970/349-5808

French

$22-$38

AAA Inspector Notes: This popular restaurant has been offering a warm ambience with tasteful artwork throughout for more than 25 years. Enjoy mountain views as you savor delectable French favorites such as escargot, baked onion soup, rack of lamb and other entrées of beef, pork and fowl. **Bar:** full bar. **Reservations:** suggested. **Address:** 525 Red Lady Ave 81224 **Location:** SR 135 (6th St), just w on Belleview Ave, then just s; in Majestic Plaza. D

LIL'S SUSHI BAR & GRILL

Phone: 970/349-5457

Sushi

$10-$29

AAA Inspector Notes: Lil's is the place to go for seafood, steak, pasta and a prickly pear margarita. Arrive early for the sushi happy hour at the bar only. Choose from the standard menu options anytime. **Bar:** full bar. **Address:** 321 Elk Ave 81224 **Location:** 0.3 mi w. **Parking:** street only. D

LOBAR SUSHI **Phone:** 970/349-0480

Sushi

$10-$35

AAA Inspector Notes: In the heart of downtown, the eatery offers a variety of sushi, sashimi, specialty rolls and desserts. **Bar:** full bar. **Address:** 303 Elk Ave 81224 **Location:** Corner of 3rd St and Elk Ave; downstairs. **Parking:** street only. [D]

MARCHITELLI'S GOURMET NOODLE

Phone: 970/349-7401

Regional Italian

$13-$28

AAA Inspector Notes: This intimate family-owned restaurant offers generations-old recipes such as vegetarian minestrone; wedding soup; and Italian favorites such as ravioli of the day, seafood, veal, chicken, meat and game dishes. Diners can pair pasta choices with Nico's hot sausage, Rocky's vodka sauce, tomato-basil marinara, Alfredo and white clam, pesto Genovese, cilantro and goat cheese, sun-dried tomato or a hearty red sauce. Smaller portions are available. The Italian cream cake is a lovely dessert choice. **Bar:** full bar. **Address:** 411 3rd St 81224 **Location:** 0.3 mi w on Elk Ave, then just s. **Parking:** street only. [D]

MCGILL'S **Phone:** 970/349-5240

American

$9-$12

AAA Inspector Notes: This popular eatery serves delicious breakfasts all day; homemade soups; blackened steak salad; a chicken Cobb sandwich; Mediterranean grilled ham with roasted red pepper, caramelized onion and marinated artichoke hearts; and a popular create-your-own burger. The long, comfortable soda fountain is the perfect spot for an ice cream float, malt, shake or good old-fashioned sundae. **Bar:** full bar. **Address:** 228 Elk Ave 81224 **Location:** 0.3 mi w. **Parking:** street only. [B] [L]

PITAS IN PARADISE **Phone:** 970/349-0897

Greek

$6-$16

AAA Inspector Notes: The uninitiated may not think a falafel and hummus fix exists, but after a meal at this spot, they'll be addicted. Leaving this place without trying the baklava would be criminal. **Bar:** full bar. **Address:** 212 Elk Ave 81224 **Location:** 0.3 mi w on Elk Ave. **Parking:** street only. [L] [D] [AC]

RYCE ASIAN BISTRO **Phone:** 970/349-9888

Asian

$12-$19

AAA Inspector Notes: This charming eatery offers a riverside dining room and seasonal patio. The menu features a wide selection of delicious Chinese, Japanese, Thai and Vietnamese dishes and creative sake concoctions. Vegetarian and gluten-free options are available. **Bar:** full bar. **Address:** 120 Elk Ave 81224 **Location:** 0.5 mi w. **Parking:** street only. [L] [D]

THE SECRET STASH **Phone:** 970/349-6245

Pizza

$9-$19

AAA Inspector Notes: The secret's out on this popular local hangout. After a day of hitting the slopes or exploring the mountains, patrons come to this little gem for great specialty meat or veggie pizzas, calzones, stromboli or pockets. The laid-back, friendly environment means this restaurant comes highly recommended. Settle in with a starter such as stuffed mushrooms or stuffed banana peppers, a fresh salad and a brew (or a fancy drink if you'd prefer). **Bar:** full bar. **Address:** 21 Elk Ave 81224 **Location:** 0.5 mi w; to end of Elk Ave. **Parking:** street only. [L] [D] [AC]

SLOGAR BAR & RESTAURANT **Phone:** 970/349-5765

Comfort Food

$15-$25

AAA Inspector Notes: In an elegant historic Victorian setting, the restaurant is known for skillet-fried chicken dinners and grilled steaks with generous family-style portions of creamed corn and biscuits. **Bar:** full bar. **Address:** 517 2nd St 81225 **Location:** Downtown. **Parking:** street only. [D]

SOUPCON, A FRENCH AMERICAN BISTRO

Phone: 970/349-5448

French

$35-$39

AAA Inspector Notes: Located in an old miner's cabin, this quaint and petite romantic bistro offers appetizers and entrees such as lemon grass- and vodka-braised short ribs, seared day boat sea scallops, crispy striped bass fillet, seared filet mignon and Colorado rack of lamb. The chocolate and Grand Marnier soufflés are to die for. **Bar:** full bar. **Reservations:** suggested. **Address:** 127A Elk Ave 81224 **Location:** 0.3 mi w, then just n on 2nd St. **Parking:** on-site and street. [D] [AC]

TEOCALLI TAMALE **Phone:** 970/349-2005

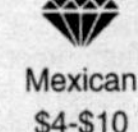

Mexican

$4-$10

AAA Inspector Notes: Teocalli Tamale merits raves for the savory tamales heralded in its name, but you also will find plenty of other Mexican prepared-to-order quick-serve food at the popular spot. **Bar:** full bar. **Address:** 311 1/2 Elk Ave 81224 **Location:** Just w of center. **Parking:** street only. [L] [D] [AC]

WEST END PUBLIC HOUSE **Phone:** 970/349-5662

American

$10-$27

AAA Inspector Notes: This lively gastropub features comfort food, enticing nightly specials and a variety of craft beers as well as innovative cocktails and an eclectic wine list. Seasonal menu items may include a trout BLT, mini duck tacos, club sandwich with chunks of Maine lobster tossed in a creamy tarragon aioli, Colorado rack of lamb with toasted Sardinian couscous and house-brined pork chop served with Boston baked beans, sauteed greens and corn pone. **Bar:** full bar. **Address:** 201 Elk Ave 81224 **Location:** 0.4 mi w, at 2nd St and Elk Ave. **Parking:** street only. [L] [D]

DJANGO'S RESTAURANT & WINE BAR

Phone: 970/349-7574

[fyi] Not evaluated. The cozy eatery features small plates and an extensive wine list. **Address:** 620 Gothic Rd 81225 **Location:** 2.4 mi n of center; at Mt Crested Butte; in Mountaineer Square Courtyard.

CRIPPLE CREEK (D-4) pop. 1,189, elev. 9,508'

Rumors of "color" on the Womack Ranch were largely ignored until the rancher's nephew, Bob, made the first major gold strike in the spring of 1891. Young Womack rode to Colorado City (now Colorado Springs) and went on a binge, celebrating his new wealth. He sold his claim for $500, never dreaming that more than $350 million in gold ultimately would come from it and the claims that followed.

By late 1891 the "$300 million cow pasture" was crawling with prospectors. A town was platted and grew to a population of about 18,000 within 2 years. Town buildings were rebuilt with brick after a fire in 1896; most of the present-day structures date from this period. Although the boom ended in 1904, the shafts that yielded $25 million in a single year were reactivated when gold mining once again became profitable in the 1930s during the Great Depression.

Cripple Creek is reached from Colorado Springs by US 24 and SR 67; the adventurous can take the Gold Camp Road *(see attraction listing p. 91)* over the mountains. The Phantom Canyon Highway runs south from Cripple Creek to US 50, 7 miles east of Cañon City *(see place listing p. 75)*. Only experienced mountain drivers should attempt the Gold Camp and Phantom Canyon routes; check road conditions before starting.

BUTTE THEATER is at 139 E. Bennett Ave. Live performances include traditional melodramas, dramas, musicals and comedies presented in the 1896 opera house that has been restored to its Victorian heyday, complete with grand chandeliers and period wallpaper. Guests enjoy booing the villains and rooting for the heroes at the melodramas, which feature hand-painted sets and era-appropriate costumes.

Time: Allow 2 hours minimum. **Hours:** Matinee and evening performances are offered year-round; phone for schedule. **Cost:** $15.75; $13.75 (ages 62+); $9.75 (ages 0-12). Prices may vary; phone ahead. **Phone:** (719) 689-3247.

CRIPPLE CREEK AND VICTOR NARROW GAUGE RAILROAD, at 520 E. Carr St., offers a 45-minute trip through the mining district of Cripple Creek aboard a 2-foot-gauge, coal-fired steam locomotive. **Hours:** Trains depart daily every 40 minutes 10-5, mid-May to early Oct. Ticket office opens at 9:30. Phone ahead to confirm schedule. **Cost:** Fare $12.25; $11.25 (ages 66+); $7.75 (ages 3-12). Fares may vary; phone ahead. **Phone:** (719) 689-2640.

CRIPPLE CREEK DISTRICT MUSEUM, at Bennett Ave. and Fifth St., is housed in five original historic buildings. The museum includes the original Midland Terminal Railroad Depot, a turn-of-the-20th-century assay office, two Victorian apartments, mining equipment, an art gallery and two fully furnished historic cabins. **Time:** Allow 30 minutes minimum. **Hours:** Daily 10-5, mid-May to mid-Oct.; Sat.-Sun. 10-4, rest of year. **Cost:** $5; $4 (Colorado residents); $3 (ages 60+, 7-12 and military with ID); free (ages 0-6). **Phone:** (719) 689-2634 or (719) 689-9540.

MOLLIE KATHLEEN GOLD MINE, 1 mi. n. of Cripple Creek on SR 67, was discovered by Mollie Kathleen Gortner in 1891 and has been maintained as a mine ever since. Tours 1,000 feet underground allow visitors to understand the lives of the late 19th- and 20th-century hard rock gold miners and the nation's mining legacy. Jackets are supplied.

Time: Allow 1 hour minimum. **Hours:** Daily 10-4, Apr.-Oct. Phone ahead to confirm schedule. **Cost:** Fee $15; $10 (ages 3-12); prices may vary. **Phone:** (719) 689-2466.

THE OLD HOMESTEAD HOUSE MUSEUM is at 353 E. Meyers Ave. Cripple Creek's most famous madam, Pearl DeVere, built the Old Homestead House in 1896. The restored brothel, said to have been the town's finest and most luxurious, features velvet bedspreads and vintage furniture. Guided tours provide information about the house, the lives of the women who lived and worked there, and the gold rush era. **Time:** Allow 30 minutes minimum. **Hours:** Daily 11-5, June-Sept. **Cost:** $4; $2 (ages 7-11). **Phone:** (719) 689-9090.

PIKES PEAK HERITAGE CENTER is at 9283 S. SR 67. Historical and interactive exhibits about the Pikes Peak region are on display at the center, recognizable by a front facade resembling a mine entrance. Visitors also can enjoy a stunning panorama of seven mountain ranges and obtain area information. **Time:** Allow 1 hour minimum. **Hours:** Daily 9-5. **Cost:** Free. **Phone:** (719) 689-3461.

GAMBLING ESTABLISHMENTS

- **Bronco Billy's** is at 233 E. Bennett Ave. **Hours:** Daily 24 hours. **Phone:** (719) 689-2142 or (877) 989-2142.
- **Century Casino Cripple Creek** is at 200-220 E. Bennett Ave. **Hours:** Daily 24 hours. **Phone:** (719) 689-0333 or (888) 966-2257.
- **Gold Rush Casino** is at 209 E. Bennett Ave. **Hours:** Daily 24 hours. **Phone:** (719) 689-2646.
- **J.P. McGills Casino** is at 232 E. Bennett Ave. **Hours:** Daily 8 a.m.-1:45 a.m. **Phone:** (719) 689-2446 or (888) 461-7529.

CARR MANOR **Phone:** 719/689-3709

Historic Bed & Breakfast

$135-$450 5/1-12/31
$110-$450 1/1-4/30

Address: 350 E Carr Ave 80813 **Location:** At E Carr Ave and 4th St; center. **Facility:** Once a high school, the inn has a classroom feel. Blackboards in the rooms feature messages from past guests. Modern amenities include luxurious linens. Call ahead, as winter hours vary. 14 units, some efficiencies. 2 stories (no elevator), interior corridors. **Terms:** office hours 8 am-8 pm, check-in 4 pm, 2-3 night minimum stay - seasonal and/or weekends, age restrictions may apply, 14 day cancellation notice-fee imposed. **Activities:** exercise room. *Fee:* massage.

BIZ / SOME UNITS

GOLD KING MOUNTAIN INN AT WILDWOOD CASINO **Phone:** (719)689-2600

Hotel

$99-$209 5/1-10/12
$79-$177 10/13-4/30

Address: 601 E Galena Ave 80813 **Location:** 0.3 mi e off SR 67. **Facility:** 67 units. 2-3 stories, interior corridors. **Terms:** cancellation fee imposed. **Pool(s):** heated indoor. **Activities:** sauna, whirlpool, exercise room. **Guest Services:** coin laundry, area transportation-within 2 mi. **Free Special Amenities: full breakfast and local transportation.**

SAVE / SOME UNITS FEE

CURECANTI NATIONAL RECREATION AREA (E-2)

The Curecanti National Recreation Area parallels US 50 between Gunnison and Montrose. It contains three reservoirs formed by dams on the Gunnison River—Blue Mesa, Morrow Point and Crystal.

Blue Mesa Reservoir, 20 miles long, offers 10 vehicular-access and four boat-access campgrounds, boat ramps and water sports. Two marinas rent boats and fishing equipment mid-May through September. Boat permits are required. A $4 fee provides boating access at the reservoir for 2 days; for 14 days the fee is $10; an annual pass is $30.

Fishing at Blue Mesa Reservoir yields kokanee salmon and rainbow, brown and Mackinaw trout. The largest brown and Mackinaw trout are caught in April and May. Shore fishing for rainbow trout is best in early spring and late fall. The best salmon fishing is usually late June through August. A Colorado fishing license is required.

Morrow Point and Crystal reservoirs, along SR 92, offer backcountry hiking, fishing and hand-carried boating. Additional summer recreational activities include camping, seven hiking trails through Colorado's high country and a number of scenic overlooks and picnic areas for motorists. Winter recreation offers cross-country skiing, snowmobiling, snowshoeing and ice fishing. Facilities may be limited in winter. Admission to the recreation area is free. Phone (970) 641-2337. *See Recreation Chart.*

CIMARRON VISITOR CENTER, 20 mi. e. of Montrose just off US 50, has a narrow-gauge railroad engine, coal tender, freight car and caboose displayed on an 1895 trestle. Next to the visitor center are sheep- and cattle-loading corrals, a work car, railroad stock cars, a crane car and other historical displays. **Hours:** Daily 9-4, Memorial Day weekend-Labor Day; otherwise varies. **Cost:** Free. Camping fee $12. **Phone:** (970) 641-2337.

ELK CREEK VISITOR CENTER, 16 mi. w. of Gunnison, milepost 142 at 24830 US 50, has seasonal exhibits on natural and cultural history, as well as area information, on summer weekend evenings at the Elk Creek Campground. Occasional ranger-led and Junior Ranger programs are offered. Picnicking is permitted in summer. **Hours:** Daily 8-6, May-Sept.; otherwise days and hours vary. **Cost:** Free. Camping fee $12-$18. **Phone:** (970) 641-2337.

MORROW POINT BOAT TOURS depart from Pine Creek Trail, 26 mi. w. of Gunnison off US 50. A ranger narrates the 90-minute cruise, noting scenic, historical and geological features of the reservoir's canyon setting.

Note: The hike to the boat dock is 1¾ miles and includes 232 stairs. Those with physical limitations should consider their ability to hike this trail before making reservations. Allow at least 1 hour for the hike. **Hours:** Trips depart daily at 10 and 12:30, late May-early Sept. Phone ahead to confirm schedule. **Cost:** Fare $16; $8 (ages 0-12 and Senior/Access Pass holders). Pre-paid reservations are required. **Phone:** (970) 641-2337 for information and reservations.

MORROW POINT DAM, 1.5 mi. off US 50, is reached from the Cimarron turnoff. The dam, 469 feet high, is reputed to be the first double-curvature, thin-arch concrete dam in the country. Footpaths cross along the Crystal Reservoir. Photography is permitted. **Hours:** Daily 24 hours. **Cost:** Free. **Phone:** (970) 641-2337.

DECKERS

LOST VALLEY RANCH **Phone:** (303)647-2311

Resort Ranch
$1400-$3080 5/1-11/30
$910-$1120 3/1-4/30

Address: 29555 Goose Creek Rd 80135 **Location:** From Deckers sign, 3 mi w on CR 126, 9 mi s on gravel road (Forest Service Rd 211), follow signs. Located in a secluded rural area. **Facility:** Nestled in a valley setting, this ranch offers individual and duplex cabins with living rooms, wood-burning fireplaces and ceiling fans. 23 cabins. 1-2 stories, exterior corridors. **Terms:** open 5/1-11/30 & 3/1-4/30, office hours 7 am-7 pm, 7 night minimum stay - seasonal and/or weekends, 60 day cancellation notice-fee imposed. **Pool(s):** heated outdoor. **Activities:** whirlpools, fishing, 2 tennis courts, recreation programs, hiking trails, horseback riding, playground, basketball, horseshoes, volleyball. *Fee:* massage. **Guest Services:** coin laundry. **Free Special Amenities: preferred room (subject to availability with advance reservations) and high-speed Internet.**

SAVE FEE

DEL NORTE (E-3) pop. 1,686, elev. 7,879'

RIO GRANDE COUNTY MUSEUM AND CULTURAL CENTER, a half-blk. s. of US 160 at 580 Oak St., offers visitors a glimpse of the San Luis Valley's cultural and natural history. Artifacts displayed include those of American Indians, pioneers, Hispanic settlers and gold miners. The museum also houses an exhibit about explorer John C. Fremont, a rock art display and changing art exhibits.

Time: Allow 30 minutes minimum. **Hours:** Tues.-Sat. 10-5. Closed major holidays. **Cost:** $1; 50c (ages 6-12); $2.50 (family rate). **Phone:** (719) 657-2847.

DOUBLE SPUR LODGE & RANCH **Phone:** (719)657-2920

Vacation Rental House
$135-$840

Location: 3.2 mi w of town center. **Facility:** Infused with the spirit of the West, this luxurious, rustic-style lodge accommodates families and small groups. At the working ranch up the road, guests can ride through the mountains on horseback. 3 units, some two bedrooms, three bedrooms and kitchens. 1 story, interior/exterior corridors. **Terms:** office hours 9 am-8 pm, 3 night minimum stay - seasonal and/or weekends, cancellation fee imposed. **Activities:** horseshoes. *Fee:* horseback riding.

SAVE

WHERE TO EAT

PEACE OF ART CAFE Phone: 719/657-9042

Natural/Organic $8-$13

AAA Inspector Notes: This eatery offers healthy and delicious soups, salads, sandwiches, quiches, coffee, smoothies and teas. Baked goods include mouthwatering mini scones, muffins and moist carrot cake. The peace keepers menu is just for kids and their meals come with peeled baby carrots or corn chips. The cafe features interesting architecture and one-of-a-kind cordwood construction. The spacious and lovely covered outdoor courtyard features ample seating and a cozy bar made from the front end of a truck. **Bar:** full bar. **Address:** 14475 W Hwy 160 81132 **Location:** Center. B L AC

DELTA (D-1) pop. 8,915, elev. 4,953'

Unlike many Colorado towns, Delta started and stayed small but prosperous. The town owes its stability to agriculture; fruit has always been Delta's economic mainstay. Livestock, mining, lumbering and industry also contribute.

Laid out in 1882 by the Uncompahgre Town Company and named Uncompahgre, the name was later changed to Delta because the shape of the town site resembled that of the Greek letter.

The area is rich in an unusual resource: dinosaur bones. Bones from some of the largest dinosaur skeletons ever found—dubbed supersaurus and brachiosaurus—were unearthed southwest of Delta. The animals are believed to have tipped the scales at nearly 80 tons and to have stood almost five stories tall. The fossilized remains of other prehistoric creatures have been excavated at Dry Mesa Dinosaur Quarry.

Delta is near Grand Mesa, Gunnison and Uncompahgre national forests and the Black Canyon of the Gunnison National Park. It also is the western terminus for the 20-mile scenic stretch of SR 92, which continues northeast as SR 133.

Delta Area Chamber of Commerce & Visitors Center: 301 Main St., Delta, CO 81416. **Phone:** (970) 874-8616.

DELTA COUNTY MUSEUM, 1 blk. e. of US 50 at 251 Meeker St., displays ranching and farming implements, photographs, a collection of nine large bells, household appliances and historical artifacts. The museum's butterfly collection includes examples of species now extinct. A dinosaur exhibit also is featured. **Hours:** Tues.-Sat. 10-4, May-Sept.; Wed. and Sat. 10-4, rest of year. **Cost:** $2; $1 (ages 65+); free (ages 0-11 with an adult). **Phone:** (970) 874-8721.

FORT UNCOMPAHGRE, n. on US 50, then w. on Gunnison River Dr. to Confluence Park, is a history museum consisting of seven re-created cabins on the banks of the Gunnison River. The fort depicts the original 1830s-era civilian trading post. **Time:** Allow 1 hour, 30 minutes minimum. **Hours:** Daily 9-3. Closed major holidays. **Cost:** $3; free (ages 0-2). Cash only. **Phone:** (970) 874-1718.

RECREATIONAL ACTIVITIES

White-water Rafting

- **Wilderness Aware Rafting** departs 14.2 mi. e. on SR 92, passing Milepost 14, s. on LN 2810 (dirt road) to the sign for Gunnison Gorge National Conservation Area, then right into parking lot. **Hours:** Trips depart daily at 9, May-Sept. **Phone:** (719) 395-2112 or (800) 462-7238.

BEST WESTERN SUNDANCE Phone: (970)874-9781

Motel $89-$111

AAA Benefit: Members save up to 20%, plus 10% bonus points with Best Western Rewards®.

Address: 903 Main St 81416 **Location:** 0.5 mi s on US 50. **Facility:** 41 units. 2 stories (no elevator), exterior corridors. **Amenities:** *Some:* high-speed Internet. **Pool(s):** heated outdoor. **Activities:** whirlpool, exercise room. **Guest Services:** coin laundry. **Free Special Amenities: full breakfast and high-speed Internet.**

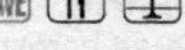  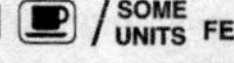 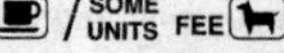 / SOME UNITS FEE

COMFORT INN Phone: 970/874-1000

Hotel

Rates not provided

Address: 180 Gunnison River Dr 81416 **Location:** Just n of jct US 50 and SR 92. Located in shopping center. **Facility:** 47 units. 2 stories (no elevator), interior corridors. **Amenities:** safes (fee). **Guest Services:** coin laundry.

 / SOME UNITS FEE

WHERE TO EAT

DAVETO'S Phone: 970/874-8277

Italian $5-$14

AAA Inspector Notes: Dishes such as baked ravioli, sausage cannoli, Sicilian deep-dish pizza and meatball sandwiches can be ordered in half- or full-size portions. It's hard to go wrong with a half order of the vegetable tray and a dish of Italian spumoni. **Bar:** beer & wine. **Address:** 520 Main St 81416 **Location:** 0.5 mi s of town. **Parking:** street only. L D

FIESTA VALLARTA Phone: 970/874-6877

Mexican $6-$13

AAA Inspector Notes: Fresh whole pinto beans are an example of the ingredients found in this restaurant's tasty dishes. **Bar:** beer only. **Address:** 447 Main St 81416 **Location:** Downtown. **Parking:** street only.

L D

Denver

Then & Now

It's hard not to think of the John Denver song "Rocky Mountain High" in tandem with Colorado. And, when you arrive in the Mile High City, not only will you see "high" in the soaring backdrop of gorgeous, snowcapped peaks, but you may feel it as a result of the temporary shortness of breath that comes with the 5,280-foot altitude. At one time, out-of-state travelers arriving at Denver International Airport typically bypassed the metropolis and headed west for a bout of skiing or an excursion into Rocky Mountain National Park. But these days, Denver itself is a destination for those who wish to explore its culture, beauty and vibrant shopping and nightlife scenes.

In fact, Denver has the best of both worlds—urban sophistication complemented by easy access to a stunning alpine playground. Locals providing directions to lost tourists frequently advise, "If you get turned around, just look for the mountains and you'll know which way is west." Denverites work hard in such industries as aerospace, telecommunications and energy research, but they like to play hard, too. A health-conscious lot, residents are reputed to be among the nation's thinnest according to a federal study. While prime recreational pursuits like skiing, hiking and rock climbing are a short drive away, city dwellers need not leave their own backyard to indulge in outdoor fun—they can play some golf in City Park, bike on the Platte River Greenway Trail, ride horseback in Cherry Creek State Park or fish one of the area's reservoirs.

Today sleek skyscrapers stand in place of the bustling frontier town of Denver City, which once lured prospectors into its saloons. Indeed, vestiges of the Gold Rush days remain in the refurbished Victorian storefronts of Larimer Square. Other Old West legacies are preserved at sites like Buffalo Bill's Grave and Museum; Four Mile House, once a stagecoach stop along the Cherokee Trail; and Civic Center Park, where murals honor wilderness pioneers and bronze sculptures depict such subjects as a bronco buster and a Native American. Just as REI's flagship store holds court for adventurists seeking the latest and greatest in technical outdoor gear, Rockmount Ranch Wear—inventors of the iconic snap-button shirt—has been tantalizing both cowboys and city folk with Western apparel since the 1940s.

Victorian Store Fronts of Larimer Square

Several chic urban pockets in addition to gracious neighborhoods have emerged from Denver's Cowtown beginnings. The LoDo (Lower Downtown) district, once chock-full of dilapidated warehouses and unsavory characters, has been revitalized with loft apartments, galleries, and trendy nightspots and restaurants attracting hipsters, young professionals and baby boomers alike. The upscale Cherry Creek area,

(Continued on p. 124.)

Destination Denver

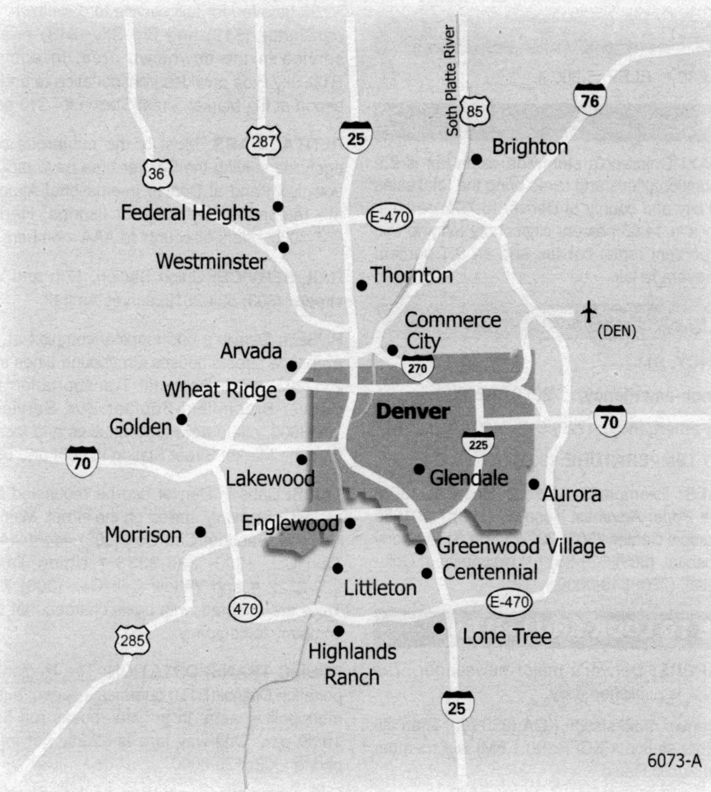

This map shows cities in the Denver vicinity where you will find attractions, hotels and restaurants. Cities are listed alphabetically in this book on the following pages.

Fast Facts

ABOUT THE CITY

POP: 554,636 ▪ **ELEV:** 5,280 ft.

MONEY

SALES TAX: Colorado's statewide sales tax is 2.9 percent. Additional fees and taxes bring the total sales tax for the city and county of Denver to 7.72 percent. There also is a 14.85 percent city/county lodging tax, an 11.35 percent rental car tax and an 8.1 percent food and beverage tax.

WHOM TO CALL

EMERGENCY: 911

POLICE (non-emergency): (720) 913-2000

FIRE (non-emergency): (720) 913-2400

TIME AND TEMPERATURE: (303) 337-2500

HOSPITALS: Exempla St. Joseph Hospital, (303) 837-7111 ▪ Porter Adventist Hospital, (303) 778-1955 ▪ Rose Medical Center, (303) 320-2121 ▪ St. Anthony Central Hospital, (303) 629-3511 ▪ University of Colorado Hospital, (720) 848-0000.

WHERE TO LOOK AND LISTEN

NEWSPAPERS: Denver's major newspaper, *The Denver Post*, is published daily.

RADIO: Denver radio station KOA (850 AM) is an all-news/weather station ▪ KCFR (90.1 FM) is a member of National Public Radio.

VISITOR INFORMATION

VISIT DENVER, The Convention & Visitors Bureau's Visitor Information Center: 1600 California St., Denver, CO 80202. **Phone:** (800) 233-6837.

TRANSPORTATION

AIR TRAVEL: Denver International Airport (DEN) is in northeastern Denver. There is a flat fee of $51 plus a $3.50 gate fee for taxi service to downtown. Both SuperShuttle ($19) and Big Sky ($18) provide van service to the downtown area. In addition, the RTD-Sky Ride provides transportation to and from the airport at the Market Street Station for $10 each way.

RENTAL CARS: Most of the numerous car rental agencies serving the Denver area have facilities both downtown and at Denver International Airport; check the telephone directory for listings. Hertz, (800) 654-3080, offers discounts to AAA members.

RAIL SERVICE: Union Station, 17th and Wynkoop streets, (303) 534-2812, serves Amtrak.

BUSES: Denver's bus terminal complex at 19th and Arapahoe streets houses Greyhound Lines Inc., (800) 231-2222. The Regional Transportation District's Denver-Broomfield-Boulder Bus Service, (303) 299-6000, offers downtown shuttles and local service from the Market Street Station at 16th and Blake.

TAXIS: Cabs in Denver can be requested by phone or, less commonly, hailed on the street. Major companies are Freedom Cab Co., (303) 444-4444 ▪ Metro Taxi Co., (303) 333-3333 ▪ Union Taxi, (303) 922-2222 ▪ and Yellow Cab Co., (303) 777-7777. Taxis are metered, with basic charges that vary from company to company.

PUBLIC TRANSPORTATION: The Regional Transportation District (RTD) operates a fleet of buses in the metropolitan area. In general, buses run 5:30 a.m.-10:30 p.m. One-way fare is $2.25. For information phone (303) 299-6000.

Free shuttle buses known as the 16th Street MallRide traverse the mile-long 16th Street Mall, a pedestrian promenade in downtown Denver.

Light Rail express trains travel from either downtown Denver (D Line/Green) or Union Station (C Line/Orange) to the suburb of Littleton. One-way fare is $2 or $3.50, depending on the route. Another line offers service between downtown Denver and many hotels in the Denver Technological Center area along I-25; one-way fares range from $2-$4.50.

(Continued from p. 122.)

graced by lovely stone mansions, is a high-end retail mecca sure to inspire the savviest shoppers. Denverites delight in Washington Park's Victorian masterpieces and flower gardens.

Denver also celebrates diversity in its neighborhoods, attractions and events. Far East Center is the hub of the Asian population, Hispanic culture prevails in the La Alma/Lincoln Park sector and the black community thrives in Five Points. While the Black American West Museum pays tribute to the black cowboy—a key figure in helping to mold the West—the Museo de las Americas honors Latin-American history and arts. The Colorado Dragon Boat Festival's Asian marketplace and Cinco de Mayo Festival's carnival are ethnic celebrations that captivate all races and religions.

Sports fans find bliss at a variety of venues. Sports Authority Field at Mile High is the hallowed gridiron occupied by Denver's beloved Broncos, and Nuggets basketball sets Pepsi Center on fire. Coors Field, home of the Colorado Rockies baseball team, reigns proudly over LoDo and is credited with its rebirth. A sophisticated classical entertainment scene at the Denver Performing Arts Complex mesmerizes opera, ballet and symphony aficionados, while the metro area's robust selection of innovative restaurants and trendy clubs entertain the masses.

Must Do: AAA Editor's Picks

- Savor a heart-thumping panorama from the Mile High City's **Cheesman Park**—the view extends 150 miles from Pikes Peak to Mount Evans. Enormous shade trees, wide-open grassy areas and meandering walkways make this urban oasis a great spot to have a picnic.
- Relish the excitement of a **Denver Broncos** football game. Fans support their beloved Super Bowl champs by proudly donning orange and blue on game days at Sports Authority Field at Mile High. If you can't snag game tickets, consider a stadium tour to sneak an inside peek at such features as the TV production area, visitor's locker room, press box and playing field.
- Stroll through **LoDo** (Lower Downtown), a vibrant enclave dotted with historic Victorians as well as stylish lofts converted from turn-of-the-20th-century warehouses. Larimer Square serves as a gateway to this bustling hub of restaurants, shops, galleries and nightspots.
- Relax and have a cold one—Denver reputedly brews more **beer** than any other city in the world. Visit the Wynkoop Brewing Company, one of the nation's largest brewpubs, or sidle over to Great Divide Brewing Co., a small outfit with seriously good suds (try the Wild Raspberry Ale). For some education about the brewing process, head out to **Coors Brewing Co.** in nearby Golden to take a guided tour.

Spend an Afternoon on Snowy Trails

- Explore the **Capitol Hill** neighborhood, once home to Titanic survivor Molly Brown and site of opulent Victorian, Tudor and Greek Revival mansions. The **State Capitol** and Governor's Mansion are in this district along with the **Denver Botanic Gardens.**
- Lunch in a quaint outdoor café or peruse upscale specialty boutiques in the tree-shaded **Cherry Creek North** shopping area, southeast of downtown. If you're happiest in a department store, the adjacent Cherry Creek Shopping Center provides such high-end anchors as Saks Fifth Avenue, Neiman Marcus and Nordstrom.
- **Hike, ski, bike or climb**. Cradled in the foothills of the Rockies, Denver offers easy access to recreation areas, ski resorts and trails for an endless supply of year-round fun. And, Rocky Mountain National Park is just an hour-and-a-half drive; in winter, cross-country skiing and snowshoeing are the preferred means of navigating the snowy landscape, while warmer months lure hikers, bikers and anglers eager to perform their sport amid vibrant wildflowers, starkly beautiful alpine tundra and an amazing backdrop of snow-capped peaks.
- sp **Drive a scenic route.** You can stop at any one of a number of parks on **The Lariat Loop National Scenic Byway,** which climbs up the Lariat Trail to stunning mountain vistas and descends into Bear Creek Canyon. If time isn't an issue, take the Colorado Heart of the Rockies drive trip on AAA.com to venture more deeply into the mountains.
- Be entertained in the **Denver Performing Arts Complex**, the second largest events center in the United States—its 10 performance venues seat more than 12,000 people. Home to the Denver Center Theatre Company, Opera Colorado, the Colorado Ballet and the Colorado Symphony, this is also the place to catch a Broadway show, a Vegas act or special holiday performances.
- Hunt for souvenirs downtown along the **16th Street Mall.** A free shuttle transports passengers up and down this nicely decorated thoroughfare, which presents a diverse selection of shops and plentiful dining options. Loaf in a comfy chair and sip a cappuccino at The Tattered Cover, one of the country's largest independent bookstores.

Denver 1-day Itinerary

AAA editors suggest these activities for a great short vacation experience. Those staying in the area for a longer visit can access a 3-day itinerary at AAA.com/TravelGuide.

Morning

- It's best to rent a car in the Mile High City, especially if you have time to explore the nearby Rocky Mountains. Most downtown attractions have parking facilities, and commercial garages and lots are plentiful. While riding the bus is an option, cabs aren't readily available on the street.
- Spend your first day in Denver exploring the Capitol Hill/Civic Center Park area, chock full of attractions all within walking distance. Get a jump-start by breakfasting at **The Delectable Egg,** a couple of blocks north of Civic Center Park and home to everything from decadent Belgian waffles to hearty huevos rancheros. If you'd like to obtain maps, brochures and other tourist information, VISIT DENVER, the Convention & Visitors Bureau's Visitor Information Center is nearby at 1600 California St.
- After breakfast, take a guided tour of the GEM **U.S. Mint** on Colfax near the park's northeast side. Be sure to call first, since fluctuating security levels may restrict access. You'll see the presses in action as they create shiny U.S. coins. One sight that never fails to impress is the stack of glistening gold bars.
- If the Mint is inaccessible, a nice alternative is to visit the **Denver Firefighters Museum,** about a block north on Tremont Place. Kids are enticed by the child-size firefighting gear, while all ages enjoy viewing the display of fire trucks.

Afternoon

- For lunch spots near the park, try **Water Course Foods** for innovative vegetarian selections, or **Pints Pub** for a burger or some robust British fare. You also can have a bite at the café in the GEM **Denver Art Museum,** your next stop at the park's south end. The museum is comprised of the Hamilton Building and the 24-sided, two-towered North Building, a work of art in itself. African, Asian, pre-Columbian, Native American and contemporary art are among the collections represented. Be sure to budget some time—you may wish to linger over some of the pieces, which number close to 60,000.
- If you are running short on time, you may opt to visit a smaller attraction, the **Byers-Evans House Museum,** about a block south of the Denver Art Museum. Guided tours of this 1883 Italianate home provide insight into the lives of the prominent families that lived within over the course of a century.
- Still within walking distance and crowned by a gold-leaf dome, the Colorado GEM **State Capitol** overlooks Civic Center Park. As tour guides usher you across elegant marble floors, you'll notice such impressive architectural details as a grand staircase, rose onyx wainscoting and stained-glass renderings of state leaders.

Take a Guided Tour of the U.S. Mint

Evening

- For an evening of wining and dining, consider the elegant **Palace Arms,** a Denver tradition in the heart of downtown. For a casual, yet cozy approach, try **Ship Tavern** for a buffalo burger or some soul-satisfying seafood.
- There's a plentiful array of casual dining options in LoDo (lower downtown), with pricier establishments holding court in the Larimer Square pocket. A fringe benefit of dining in LoDo is that you will be well positioned for some post-dinner fun in this epicenter of Denver nightlife. Wander through the thriving district and poke into one of the trendy art galleries or sizzling nightspots. LoDo has undergone an urban renaissance of sorts, and many of its businesses are in fashionably restored warehouses. If you're in the mood for a cold one, Denver supposedly brews more beer than any other city in the world and brims with quality brewpubs. Stop by **Wynkoop Brewing Company,** one of the nation's largest. Coors Field also is in LoDo, so baseball fans might be able to catch the Colorado Rockies in action.
- In addition to club hopping, the Mile High City presents other nighttime diversions. The Denver Coliseum is the staging ground for rodeos, circuses and other events. Top-notch indoor concert venues include Fillmore Auditorium and the Denver Performing Arts Complex. Pepsi Center hosts popular entertainers and area sports teams. For some outdoor splendor, GEM **Denver Botanic Gardens** offers summer concerts, while the natural sandstone amphitheater at **Red Rocks Park and Amphitheatre** is an otherworldly place to see a show.

Arriving

By Car

The main access to Denver from either the east or west is via I-70 and US 40/287; from the north I-25 (US 87); from the south I-25 (US 87) and US 85 (all three are the same highway in Denver: the Valley Highway); and from the northeast by I-76.

Other major freeways are 6th Avenue (US 6) in west-central Denver; SR 470 south, east and west of Denver; I-270 northeast of Denver; and I-225, connecting I-70 in the east with I-25 south of the city.

Getting Around

Street System

All avenues run east-west. Streets generally run north-south except those in the downtown area, where arteries are one-way diagonals with *numbered* streets running southeast-northwest and *named* streets, courts and places running southwest-northeast. The Valley Highway (I-25) is the fastest southeast-northwest route, except during rush hours when it is usually congested.

The main east-west arteries are I-70 in north Denver; Colfax Avenue (US 40), 6th Avenue (US 6) and 8th Avenue in central Denver; Alameda and Evans avenues in south Denver; Hampden Avenue (US 285) in the southern suburbs; and Belleview Avenue and Arapahoe Road in the extreme south.

The main north-south highways are Wadsworth (SR 121), Sheridan (SR 95) and Federal (US 287) boulevards in the west; Broadway, from central downtown south to Englewood and Littleton; University Boulevard (which becomes Josephine and York streets, both one-way, north of E. 1st Avenue) in the southeast; Colorado Boulevard and Monaco Parkway in the east; Havana Street in the eastern suburb of Aurora; and Chambers Road in the extreme east.

Diagonal arteries are I-270 northwest to I-76 and US 36 to Boulder from I-25; I-225, east of I-70, from the southeast suburbs to south I-25; Speer Boulevard, from University Boulevard southeast-northwest to Federal Boulevard; and Leetsdale Drive, southeast from Colorado Boulevard and becoming Parker Road (SR 83) to the extreme southeastern suburbs of Denver.

Broadway, which runs north-south through most of the city, is the dividing line for the east and west designations of all cross streets. It is one-way south from the downtown area to I-25. Nearby Lincoln Street is one-way north from I-25 to the downtown area. Ellsworth Avenue, running east-west through most of the city, is the dividing line for the north and south designations of all cross streets.

The speed limit is generally 30 mph in residential districts and 25 mph in business districts. Right turns on red are permitted, unless otherwise posted, as are left turns on red from the extreme left lane of a one-way street into the extreme left lane of another one-way street.

Rush hours are 7 to 9 and 3:30 to 6. Ramp metering signals help control morning rush-hour traffic on the south portion of I-25 (the Valley Highway) in Denver and the south and middle portions of I-225 in Aurora.

Parking

Parking is in accordance with posted signs. Downtown on-street parking is metered and limited; the cost is 25c per quarter-hour. Some meters have a "Tow Away Zone" sign; if you park too long, you are subject to a $25 fine. Commercial garages and lots are plentiful downtown, with rates ranging from $1.50 to $5 per hour or $4 to $12 per day.

Shopping

Denver's prime hunting ground for shoppers is concentrated in LoDo—that's Denverite speak for Lower Downtown. The Mile High City sprang forth from this 23-block district where Gen. William Larimer settled in 1858, and now it's retail history that's being made amid LoDo's hip urban scene.

The 16th Street Mall—a tad touristy, yet a definite to-do on your shopping list—serves as LoDo's hub, a pedestrian thoroughfare brimming with retail opportunities and graced with trees, flowers (in summer) and eclectic sculptures. Free shuttle buses whisk passengers along the mall between Union and Civic Center stations, alleviating the hassle and expense of parking.

Traveling south from the Civic Center, you'll encounter Denver Pavilions at 500 16th St., an outdoor complex that also indulges shoppers with dining and entertainment options. The massive NikeTown here mesmerizes both professional athletes and weekend warriors, while SAVE Hard Rock Cafe offers a collection of rock 'n' roll merchandise. Continuing

Denver Pavilions Offers Shopping and Entertainment

The Churchill Bar in the Brown Palace Hotel

north, the Jeweler's Center in the University Building at 919 16th St. is Denver's "Diamond District," with several floors of jewelry stores and diamond wholesalers that dazzle gem aficionados. The Shops at Tabor Center, Arapahoe and Larimer streets, is a three-level, glass-enclosed galleria flanked by the Westin Hotel. Across the street, brick walkways meander through a hodgepodge of stores and outdoor eateries known as Writer Square. Near the intersection of 16th and Wazee, cowboys and urbanites alike enjoy perusing the racks of spiffy Western duds at Rockmount Ranch Wear. Be sure to stop in the Tattered Cover Bookstore at 16th and Wynkoop, where you can settle into a cozy seat by the fireplace and ponder your book purchase.

As the state's colorful history maintains, LoDo gave birth to modern-day Denver, but it was Larimer Square that gave birth to LoDo. It all started here with Larimer Street being Denver City's main drag in the 1860s, housing the first bank and post office along with saloons and hotels frequented by weary (and sometimes rowdy) pioneers. Renovated storefronts offer a glimpse into the city's Wild West heyday in addition to providing retail recreation; shops tout a nice selection of crafts, Western wear and jewelry.

The Lower Downtown Arts District extends roughly from Larimer to Wynkoop between 14th and 20th streets. Those eager to score that extraordinary conversation piece for their home will have fun browsing the multitude of galleries scattered about, with many situated on Wazee Street. Art objects run the gamut from traditional to modern, including Western-themed paintings, Americana, abstract works, contemporary furnishings and sculpture.

Just south of downtown, art lovers also can check out the ArtDistrict on Santa Fe Drive between 7th and 10th streets. More than 30 galleries are dotted throughout the area, which also contains a smattering of shops and restaurants. During Art Walks, held the first Friday of every month, the galleries host an open-house wine event from 5-9, offering a pleasant evening with a delightful dose of culture. Antique hounds will find bliss in the shops clustered along 1000-2000 South Broadway, referred to as Antique Row. You can spend hours searching for buried treasure in this multiblock enclave, where dealers are often willing to bargain on everything from bric-a-brac to high-quality collectibles.

The Cherry Creek neighborhood, also south of downtown, is Denver's preeminent shopping destination. An outdoor shopping area dubbed Cherry Creek North provides a unique mix of boutiques, galleries, coffeehouses and cafes in a setting perfect for strolling. If scouting an indoor complex is more your style, the Cherry Creek Shopping Center is one of the Mile High City's best—standouts Neiman Marcus, Nordstrom and Saks Fifth Avenue lure those with plenty of cash, but some 150 shops within the posh behemoth usually manage to satisfy all budgets.

The shopping mall is alive and well in Denver's suburbs, and visitors will find no shortage to satisfy their whims. If your top priority is finding great deals, the outlets at Colorado Mills, at Colfax and Indiana near I-70 in Lakewood, are the base of operations for bargain hunters. For novelty's sake, you can explore what is reputedly Colorado's largest shopping center, Park Meadows, on I-25 between SR 470 and County Line Road in Littleton. Striking a perfect balance between high-end and affordable merchandise, its décor reflects a mountain lodge theme, complete with fireplaces, comfy leather sofas and timber ceilings.

Nightlife

Whether your idea of nighttime entertainment is listening to live music, doing some country line dancing or simply sipping a libation while people-watching, the Mile High City delights with a broad spectrum of offerings. Clubs providing entertainment usually charge a cover fee and may require drink minimums; phone ahead to confirm prices, opening hours, scheduled acts and dress codes.

Denver is said to brew more beer than any other city in the world, and individuals from all walks of life enjoy sampling the suds at the area's quality brewpubs. Try one of the handcrafted ales at Bull and Bush (4700 Cherry Creek Dr. S./303-759-0333), a homey neighborhood pub complete with leather sofas and a fireplace, modeled after its namesake in England. If you're interested in learning about the brewing process, take the tour at Great Divide Brewing Company (2201 Arapahoe St./303-296-9460); for connoisseurs, the offer of free samples before ordering offsets the rather sterile digs. At Wynkoop Brewing Company (1634 18th St./303-297-2700), Denver's first microbrewery and one of the nation's largest, you can play darts or pool in addition to savoring such tempting selections as Sagebrush Stout and Patty's Chile Beer—and the pub grub isn't bad, either. Some aficionados define bliss as the Falcon Pale Ale paired with a tasty mound of nachos at Rock Bottom Brewery (1001 16th St./303-534-7616).

Brewpubs aren't the only option for Denver's nightlife scene; a number of comfy spots are perfect for a nightcap or hanging out with friends. Oenophiles looking for a bohemian atmosphere with candlelight and romantic décor reminiscent of a Parisian bistro should drop by Paris Wine Bar (1553 Platte St./303-217-5805), favored by urbanites under 30 in the mood for a quiet chat and a generous pour. Classy yet unpretentious, Trios Enoteca (1730 Wynkoop St./303-293-2887) satisfies the 30 and older set of wine lovers; happy hour is quite the event, with half-price wines by the glass, yummy tapas and hand-tossed pizzas. The Whiskey Bar (2203 Larimer St./303-297-0303) draws an eclectic mix of folks and can be low-key or high-energy, depending on what's happening in downtown that evening; the list of around 115 premium whiskeys has something for every taste. If you prefer to nurse your single-malt scotch—or perhaps an after-dinner brandy or port—in a cigar bar with a more mature, sophisticated clientele, then the Churchill Bar (321 17th St./303-297-3111) in the Brown Palace Hotel is just the ticket.

If you come alive on a crowded dance floor, check out one of Denver's clubs. For the alternative rock/emo scene, head to The Church (1160 Lincoln St. /303-832-8628), where you'll find 18-year-olds in addition to plenty of professionals in their 30s and 40s gyrating to the beat or having a nibble at the sushi bar. A 20s set wooed by hot DJs and techno/trance music moves to the thump of an unrivaled sound system at Beta (1909 Blake St./303-383-1909). All ages with an ear for country music amble up to Grizzly Rose (5450 N. Valley Hwy./303-295-1330) for live acts and the free two-step lessons on Wednesday night.

Up-and-coming indie bands crank out their latest tunes at Hi-Dive (7 S. Broadway/720-570-4500), a friendly, trashy-trendy spot frequented by young, well-behaved hipsters. Herman's Hideaway (1578 S. Broadway/303-777-5840), a bare-bones club with a "come as you are" vibe, appeals to an age-diverse blend who like decent (and loud) rock 'n' roll. The bands are as varied as the customers at Bender's Tavern (314 E. 13th Ave./303-861-7070), a well-worn neighborhood haunt with a loyal local following that offers honest drink prices plus anything from rockabilly to country to heavy metal—Tuesday's karaoke night is a hoot. Bluebird Theater (3317 E. Colfax Ave./303-377-1666), an intimate venue that opened as a movie house in 1913, hosts hometown bands as well as emerging national artists; the audience depends on the gig.

Denver also has a healthy jazz and blues scene. For the stereotypical hole-in-the-wall joint serving up red-hot jazz nightly, visit cozy and usually crowded El Chapultepec (1962 Market St./303-295-9126), appreciated by all ages for its soulful sounds. You can grab a highly touted burrito or some chili if you're hungry. Dazzle (930 Lincoln St. /303-839-5100), a funky retro lounge with a more mature following, offers a relaxed, supper-club setting and top-notch talent. Known for its smokin' house band, Jazz at Jacks (500 16th St./303-433-1000) is another Mile High City favorite, mostly appealing to post-30 Denverites; young professionals patronize Friday's live jazz happy hour.

Big Events

Beginning Denver's roster of annual events is the National Western Stock Show and Rodeo held at the Stockyards and the Coliseum in early January. In honor of Denver's mile-high altitude of 5,280 feet above sea level, the city celebrates its burgeoning culinary scene each February when more than 150 restaurants participate in Denver Restaurant Week; multicourse meals come with the "mile high" price tag of $52.80 for two.

The Denver March Powwow celebrates American Indian culture during the third weekend in March. The Easter Sunrise Service draws thousands to the amphitheater in Red Rocks Park and Amphitheatre *(see Morrison p. 260)* each spring.

Early May brings Cinco de Mayo to Civic Center Park, attracting crowds of more than 500,000 with parades, dancing, mariachi music, food and arts and crafts. The Cherry Creek Arts Festival takes place during the Fourth of July weekend.

In July, African-American visual and performing arts are featured at The Colorado Black Arts Festival, held on the second weekend of July. That

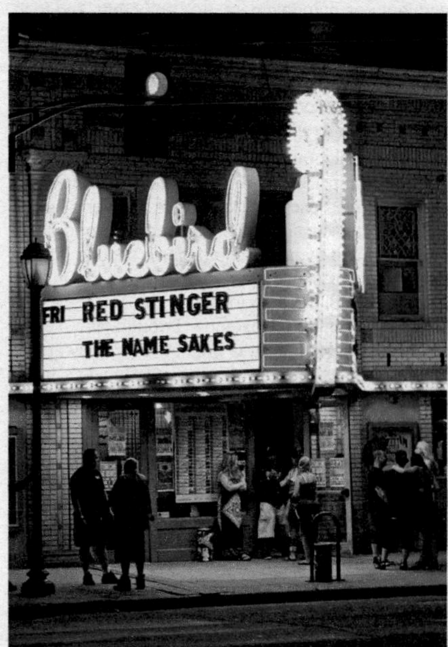

Listen to Live Music at Bluebird Theater

Cheer on Denver Nuggets at the Pepsi Center

same month, the Colorado Dragon Boat Festival is celebrated in Sloan's Lake Park. The event showcases the culture and heritage of the city's Asian Pacific American citizens through performing artists, ethnic cuisine and arts and crafts as well as 2 days of dragon boat races.

A Taste of Colorado is held Labor Day weekend and features entertainment, arts and crafts and food from various restaurants. Additional September events include Oktoberfest, held in Larimer Square, and the Great American Beer Festival, said to be the largest celebration of beer in the nation, with more than 2,000 different brews available for sampling.

Denver celebrates all of the arts—performing to visual—during Denver Arts Week. This November event provides occasion to explore Denver's neighborhood studios and galleries, and its world-class museums and events at the nation's second largest performing arts complex. Downtown Denver Mile High Holidays rounds out the year's event schedule. From late November through New Year's Eve the downtown area is bright with holiday lights; other highlights of the event include Denver's traditional holiday parade and a fireworks display on Dec. 31.

Sports & Rec

With 300 days of sunshine a year, year-round recreational opportunities are almost unlimited in Denver and the surrounding area and include **swimming, boating, golf, tennis, kayaking, hiking, climbing, fishing, sailing, mountain biking, hunting** and **horseback riding.**

Denver has more than 850 miles of paved trails to accommodate bikers, hikers and joggers. Running along the South Platte River for about 30 miles, the Greenway Trail is popular with cyclists—signage depicts the area's history, wildlife and geology. Cherry Creek Bike Path, traveling along the creek for some 40 miles to Franktown, is known for its splendid scenery. The 20-mile-long Clear Creek Bike Path meanders through neighborhoods and countryside as it follows the creek from the South Platte River to Golden, affording views of high buttes as it nears the town. Bear Creek Bike Trail is also 20 miles in length, running along the creek from the South Platte River to Morrison, home to Red Rocks Park and Amphitheatre.

Renowned for its winter sports facilities, Denver offers cold season fun either in the city or just a few minutes away; the closest area for **snow skiing** is within 45 miles. For **ice skating** enthusiasts the Ice Centre, in the Westminster Promenade off US 36 104th Avenue exit in Westminster, offers triple ice sheet facilities. Skate rentals are available. Phone (303) 469-2100 for public skating times.

Auto racing enthusiasts frequent Bandimere Speedway in Morrison and Colorado National Speedway in Erie. **Dog races** are held at Mile High Racing Park in Commerce City.

Note: Policies concerning admittance of children to pari-mutuel betting facilities vary. Phone for information.

At Denver's Coors Field, 2001 Blake St., **baseball** fans can watch the National League Colorado Rockies; phone (303) 762-5437 or (800) 388-7625. **Football** season brings the National Football League's Denver Broncos to Sports Authority Field at Mile High, 1701 Bryant St.; phone (720) 258-3333, or Ticketmaster at (800) 745-3000. The Colorado Rapids, a major league **soccer** team, play at Dick's Sporting Goods Park, 6000 Victory Way in Commerce City; phone (303) 727-3535, or TicketHorse at (866) 461-6556. For **basketball** fans the Pepsi Center, 1000 Chopper Cir., hosts the National Basketball Association's Denver Nuggets; phone TicketHorse at (866) 461-6556.

At the Pepsi Center, **hockey** enthusiasts cheer on the National Hockey League's Colorado Avalanche, and **lacrosse** lovers catch matches for the National Lacrosse League's Colorado Mammoth; for ticket information phone TicketHorse at (866) 461-6556. The area's Major League Lacrosse team, the Denver Outlaws, play their games at Sports Authority Field; phone (303) 688-5297. College sports fans have the opportunity to watch the University of Denver Pioneers play basketball, soccer, lacrosse and hockey at Ritchie Center, 2240 E. Buchtel Blvd.; for ticket information phone (303) 871-2336, or Ticketmaster at (800) 745-3000.

Performing Arts

The Denver Performing Arts Complex, occupying four blocks at Curtis and 14th streets, is the second largest performing arts center in the nation: Its 10 performance venues seat a total of more than 10,000 people. During the main concert season from October through May, the Colorado Symphony

Orchestra usually performs weekly in the Boettcher Concert Hall; Opera Colorado and the Colorado Ballet perform in the Ellie Caulkins Opera House. "The Ellie," as it's called by the locals, features an electronic screen on the back of its seats from which operagoers may view the current performance's text in eight languages.

The Temple Hoyne Buell Theatre features Broadway productions and ballet. The Helen Bonfils Theatre Complex hosts the Denver Center Theatre Company. The 12-acre complex also includes the Galleria Theater.

Free band concerts are held in various city parks during July and August. Comfort Dental Amphitheater, in Greenwood Village south of Denver, also has a summer concert series. A little farther out near Morrison, the natural amphitheater in Red Rocks Park and Amphitheatre *(see Morrison p. 260)* offers summer musical entertainment as well as films.

Family entertainment can be found at the Joseph B. Gould Family Paramount Theatre, downtown at 16th and Glenarm streets. If you prefer drama or comedy while dining, try a dinner theater. Heritage Square Music Hall *(see Golden p. 212)* presents melodramas and other entertainment of the vaudeville era.

ATTRACTIONS

BABI YAR PARK, 1 blk. s. on Havana St. from jct. with Parker Rd. (SR 83), with entry on Yale Ave., is a 26-acre memorial to the 200,000 people killed by the Nazis in Kiev, Ukraine, beginning in 1941. Black granite stones mark the entrance to the park, which serves as a place of remembrance. **Hours:** Daily 5 a.m.-11 p.m. **Cost:** Free. **Phone:** (720) 913-1311.

BLACK AMERICAN WEST MUSEUM, 3091 California St. across from the 30th and Downing Light Rail Station, is in the former home of the first female African-American doctor in Colorado, Justina L. Ford, who began practice in Denver in 1902. This museum houses changing exhibits and displays pertaining to the history of African-American soldiers, pioneers, mountain men, miners and cowboys in the Old West.

Time: Allow 30 minutes minimum. **Hours:** Tues.-Sat. 10-2. Closed Jan. 1, Thanksgiving and Christmas. **Cost:** $8; $7 (ages 65+); $6 (ages 5-12). **Phone:** (303) 482-2242.

BYERS-EVANS HOUSE MUSEUM, near Civic Center Park at 1310 Bannock St., reflects the character of two important Denver families. *Rocky Mountain News* publisher William Byers built the home in 1883 and sold it in 1889 to William Gray Evans, a transportation executive. The elegant two-story Victorian house is restored to reflect the years 1912-24; it contains original Evans family furnishings. The Byers-Evans House Gallery features changing exhibits focused on the history of the city, state and region.

Tours: Guided tours are available. **Time:** Allow 1 hour minimum. **Hours:** Mon.-Sat. 10-4. Guided tours given on the half-hour 10:30-2:30; last tour begins at 2:30. **Cost:** $6; $5 (ages 65+ and students with ID); $4 (ages 6-12). **Phone:** (303) 620-4933.

CHEESMAN PARK, 8th Ave. and Franklin St., offers a panorama that on clear days extends 150 miles from Pikes Peak to Mount Evans. **Hours:** Daily 5 a.m.-11 p.m. **Cost:** Free. **Phone:** (720) 913-1311.

THE CHILDREN'S MUSEUM OF DENVER is at I-25 exit 211 and 23rd Ave. This is a hands-on environment, geared to newborns through age 8 and their grown-ups, where youngsters can dance, act, become an artist or engineer, crawl through an ant tunnel, flash the lights on a real firetruck, shop or play shopkeeper in a marketplace, or enjoy a children's theater performance. Daily and monthly themes are offered focusing on literacy, the arts, creativity, the environment, and scientific and cultural experiences.

Hours: Mon.-Fri. 9-4 (also Wed. 4-7:30), Sat.-Sun. 10-5. Closed Jan. 1, Easter, Thanksgiving, Christmas Eve and Christmas. **Cost:** $8 (ages 2-59); $6 (ages 1 and 60+); free (ages 0-1). **Phone:** (303) 433-7444.

CITY PARK is bounded by 17th and 23rd aves. and York St. and Colorado Blvd. Gardens, pools, fountains and monuments adorn what was a sagebrush flat. Band concerts are presented in the summer. **Hours:** Daily 5 a.m.-11 p.m. **Cost:** Free. **Phone:** (720) 913-1311.

GEM **Denver Museum of Nature & Science,** 2001 Colorado Blvd. in City Park, is one of the largest natural history museums in the country. Hands-on activities in the Expedition Health exhibit demonstrate how the body functions and changes. Prehistoric Journey contains a working fossil lab as well as exhibits of the sights, sounds and vegetation existing on Earth millions of years ago.

Other exhibits feature wildlife dioramas, Egyptian mummies, American Indian cultures, gems and minerals, and sections devoted to the South Pacific islands, Australia and Africa. Explore galaxies at the Space Odyssey exhibit and take a 3-D look at the stars at Gates Planetarium. Traveling exhibits are featured frequently at the three-story museum. The Phipps IMAX Theater and Gates Planetarium present a variety of shows; phone ahead for schedules.

Time: Allow 2 hours minimum. **Hours:** Daily 9-5; Discovery Zone daily 10-4. Closed Christmas. **Cost:** Museum $12; $6 (ages 3-18 and students with ID); $8 (ages 65+). IMAX theater $10; $8 (ages 3-18, 65+ and students with ID). Planetarium $17; $10 (ages 3-18 and students with ID); $12 (ages 65+). Combination ticket for museum and IMAX theater $19; $12 (ages 3-18); $14 (ages 65+). Combination ticket for museum and planetarium $17; $16 (ages 3-18 and students with ID); $18 (ages 65+). All three

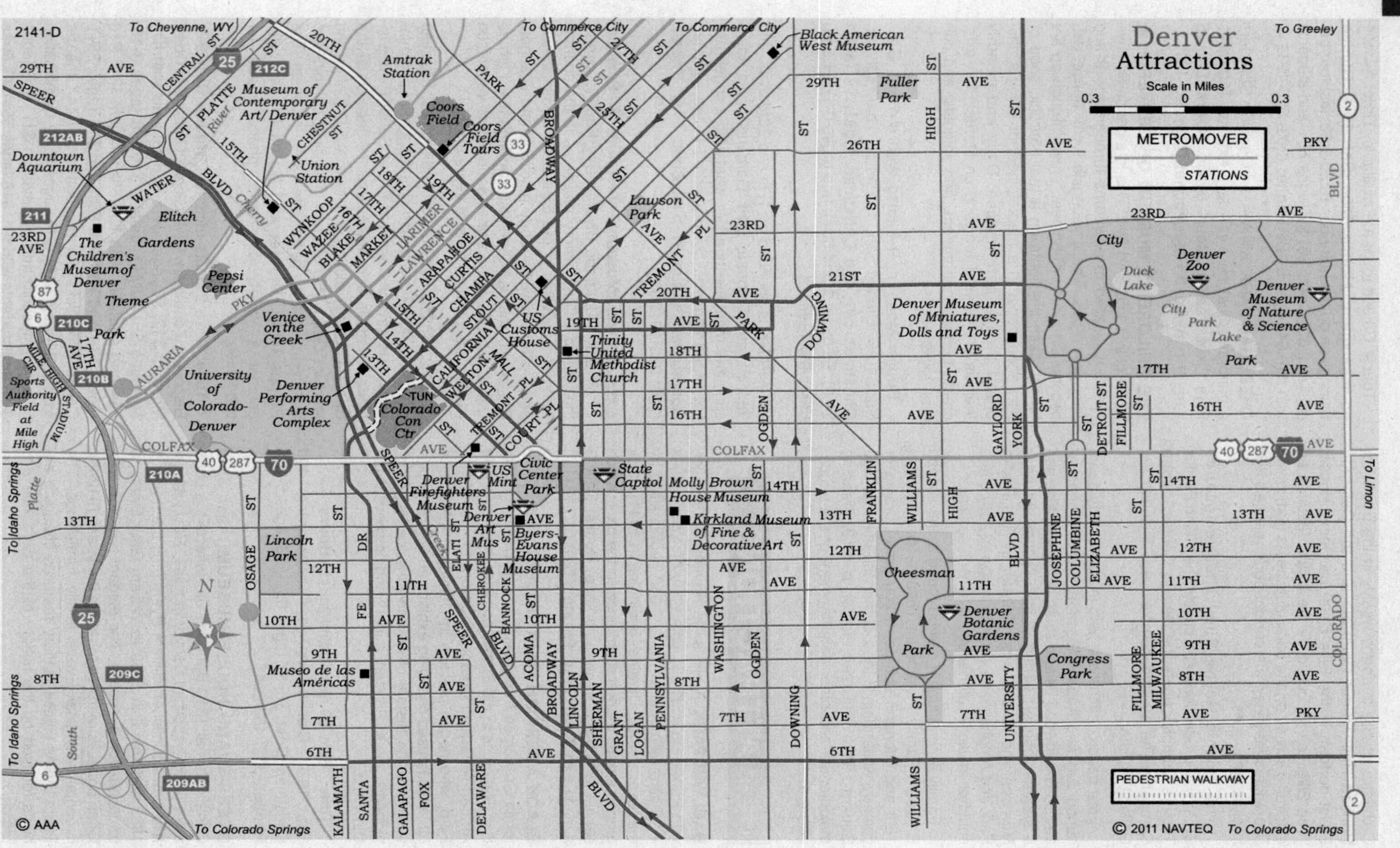
Denver Attractions
Scale in Miles
0.3 0 0.3
METROMOVER
STATIONS
PEDESTRIAN WALKWAY
© 2011 NAVTEQ
© AAA
2141-D
Denver Zoo
Denver Museum of Nature & Science
City Park
Denver Museum of Miniatures, Dolls and Toys
Black American West Museum
Denver Botanic Gardens
Cheesman Park
Congress Park
Molly Brown House Museum
Kirkland Museum of Fine & Decorative Art
State Capitol
Trinity United Methodist Church
US Customs House
Civic Center Park
US Mint
Denver Art Mus
Byers-Evans House Museum
Denver Firefighters Museum
Colorado Con Ctr
Denver Performing Arts Complex
Venice on the Creek
Coors Field
Coors Field Tours
Amtrak Station
Union Station
Museum of Contemporary Art/Denver
Pepsi Center
Elitch Gardens Theme Park
The Children's Museum of Denver
Downtown Aquarium
University of Colorado-Denver
Sports Authority Field at Mile High
Lincoln Park
Museo de las Américas
Fuller Park
Lawson Park
To Greeley
To Limon
To Colorado Springs
To Cheyenne, WY
To Commerce City
To Idaho Springs

attractions $24; $16 (ages 3-18); $18 (ages 65+). Reservations are recommended for IMAX and planetarium shows. **Phone:** (303) 322-7009 or TTY (303) 370-8257.

GEM **Denver Zoo,** in City Park at 2300 Steele St., emphasizes the use of natural habitats to showcase their captivating residents. Rare animals such as Amur tigers, endangered cheetahs and black rhinos thrive in this spacious setting, which represents more than 650 species. Dramatically landscaped special exhibits provide realistic homes for inhabitants, providing an entertaining and educational viewing experience for all ages. Kids are enticed by the Conservation Carousel, featuring wooden animal carvings, and the natural gas-powered Pioneer Train, which takes passengers for a brief spin through a shady stretch of the grounds.

Black and grizzly bears lumber amid replicated craggy boulders at Bear Mountain, while birds fly freely in unencumbered air space at Bird World. Monkeys frolic and climb twisting vines while gorillas lazily nap in swinging hammocks at Primate Panorama, where you'll also spot orangutans, mandrills and lemurs. The curious can wander past settings enhanced with caves, mangroves, waterfalls and coral reefs at Tropical Discovery, also site of one of the world's largest indoor Komodo dragon exhibits.

Predator Ridge provides a glimpse into African wildlife and presents an opportunity to learn about the continent's chief predators—lions, wild dogs and hyenas—with up-close views and educational material. Occasionally, zookeepers can be seen interacting with wild dogs and lions. The Pachyderm Habitat's hippos intrigue zoo visitors, as does the camel exhibit with its one- and two-humped occupants. In addition to observing the nearly 3,500 animals cared for at the zoo, you'll also encounter a variety of bronze sculptures interspersed throughout the grounds. **Time:** Allow 1 hour minimum. **Hours:** Daily 9-6, Mar. 1-Nov. 1; 10-5, rest of year. Last admission 1 hour before closing. **Cost:** Mar. 1-Nov. 1 $13; $10 (ages 65+); $8 (ages 3-11). Rest of year $10; $8 (ages 65+); $6 (ages 3-11). Ages 0-16 must be with an adult. **Phone:** (303) 376-4800.

COLORADO SPORTS HALL OF FAME MUSEUM is at 1701 Bryant St., Suite 500, at Gate 1 on the west side of Sports Authority Field. The Hall of Fame honors the state's leading athletes, coaches and sports leaders. Exhibits include a timeline; photographs; information about sports conditioning; the achievements of sportswomen; and information about the Denver Broncos. **Time:** Allow 1 hour minimum. **Hours:** Tues.-Sat. 10-3, June-Aug.; Thurs.-Sat. 10-3, rest of year. **Cost:** Free. **Phone:** (720) 258-3888.

Sports Authority Field at Mile High Stadium Tours depart from the Colorado Sports Hall of Fame Museum at 1701 Bryant St., Suite 500, at Gate 1 on the west side of the field. A 75-minute, half-mile walking tour of the Denver Broncos' stadium allows participants access to the club level, the visitors' locker room, the field and the press boxes. **Time:** Allow 1 hour, 15 minutes minimum. **Hours:** Tours are given Tues.-Sat. on the hour 10-2, June-Aug.; Thurs.-Sat. on the hour 10-2, rest of year. Closed major holidays and the day before any Broncos home game. **Cost:** $9; $7 (65+ and ages 5-12). **Phone:** (720) 258-3888.

COORS FIELD TOURS is at 2001 Blake St.; tours begin at Gate D. Guided tours offer a behind-the-scenes look at the home of the Colorado Rockies major league baseball team. Highlights of the tour include the dugout, press box, visitors' clubhouse, suite level and club level. The ballpark was built to fit in with the historic downtown area and uses the Rocky Mountain scenery as a backdrop.

Time: Allow 1 hour, 30 minutes minimum. **Hours:** Tours are given Mon.-Sat. at 10, noon and 2, Apr.-Sept.; Mon., Wed. and Fri.-Sat. at noon and 2, rest of year. Tours are not available when afternoon games are scheduled and are limited when evening games take place. **Cost:** Fee $7; $6 (ages 55+); $5 (ages 3-12). Reservations are recommended. **Phone:** (303) 762-5437.

CRANMER PARK, E. 3rd Ave. and Bellaire St., has a Chinese sundial and a terrazzo profile of the Continental Divide. **Hours:** Daily 5 a.m.-11 p.m. **Cost:** Free. **Phone:** (720) 913-1311.

GEM SAVE **DENVER ART MUSEUM** is at the s. end of the Civic Center on 14th Avenue Pkwy., 1 blk. w. of Broadway. More than 1 million faceted glass tiles cover the 24-sided North Building, designed by Gio Ponti. The Frederic C. Hamilton Building, designed by Daniel Libeskind, is clad in titanium and resembles the jagged peaks of the nearby Rocky Mountains. A glass-enclosed bridge stretching across 13th Avenue connects the buildings.

The museum has a collection of more than 69,000 art objects from around the world with exhibits of American, Asian, European, American Indian, Pre-Columbian, Spanish Colonial, Western, African, Oceanic and modern and contemporary works. Additional galleries focus on photography, architecture, design, graphics and textile art. Artists represented include Albert Bierstadt, Alexander Calder, Mary Cassatt, Edgar Degas, Georgia O'Keeffe, Henri Matisse, Claude Monet, Pablo Picasso, Frederic Remington, Charles Russell and Andy Warhol.

The Hamilton Building's modern and contemporary art display includes massive paintings and sculptures enhanced with vibrant hues and composed of a variety of materials, including wood, plaster, fiberglass, steel and vinyl. Masks of all sizes, oils on canvas and enchanting acrylic works characterize the African art collection, while Yipwon spirit, pig and tree-fern figurines capture the imagination in the Oceanic art section.

The North Building's Western American collection entices with works depicting dramatic landscapes, the Gold Rush and the Hispanic West. Buddhist sculptures and bronzes, a Japanese Samurai display and a portion of a wooden palace facade can be discovered in the Asian galleries; the Everyday Traditions exhibit has such captivating features as a monkey god from India, a guardian lion from Thailand and other colorful works. Ceremonial dress, jewelry, basketry, totems, an 1884 tipi, and elaborate pottery and weavings intrigue all ages on the American Indian floor. **Tours:** Guided tours are available. **Hours:** Tues.-Sun. 10-5 (also Fri. 5-8). Closed Thanksgiving and Christmas. **Cost:** $13; $10 (ages 65+ and students with ID); $5 (ages 6-18). Additional tickets may be required during special exhibitions. **Phone:** (720) 865-5000.

GEM **DENVER BOTANIC GARDENS,** 1007 York St. between Cheesman and Congress parks, covers 23 acres. More than 45 formal gardens include rare and endangered plants from around the world, plants native to Colorado, those brought to the state by pioneers, Great Plains grasses and wildflowers, bristlecone and ponderosa pines, an outstanding orchid collection and the Monet Garden, with flowers and water lilies inspired by the French Impressionist.

Rock alpine, herb, romantic and Asian gardens also are displayed. The domed Boettcher Memorial Tropical Conservatory contains thousands of tropical and subtropical plants. A myriad of holiday lights illuminate the gardens during Blossoms of Light from early December to late January.

Time: Allow 1 hour minimum. **Hours:** Daily 9-9, May-Sept.; daily 9-5, rest of year. Blossoms of Light daily 5:30-9:30 p.m., early Dec.-early Jan. Closed Jan. 1, Thanksgiving and Christmas. **Cost:** May 1 to mid-Sept. $12.50; $9.50 (ages 65+); $9 (ages 4-15 and students with ID). Rest of year $11.50; $8.50 (ages 65+); $8 (ages 4-15 and students with ID). Blossoms of Light $9.50; $7.50 (students with ID and 65+); $6.50 (ages 3-12). **Phone:** (720) 865-3500, or (720) 865-3585 for Information Desk.

DENVER FIREFIGHTERS MUSEUM is at 1326 Tremont Pl.; take I-25 exit 210, .5 mi. e. on Colfax Ave., .1 mi. n. on Glenarm St. and s. on 14th St. to Tremont Pl. Presented in a 1909 firehouse, the collection features artifacts, tools and photographs from 1866 to the present that tell the history of the Denver Fire Department.

Hands-on activities for children and adults focus on fire safety and prevention. **Time:** Allow 30 minutes minimum. **Hours:** Mon.-Sat. 10-4. Closed major holidays. **Cost:** $6; $5 (ages 65+ and students with ID); $4 (ages 1-12). **Phone:** (303) 892-1436.

DENVER MUSEUM OF MINIATURES, DOLLS AND TOYS is at 1880 Gaylord St. The museum is in the historic Pearce-McAllister Cottage, built in 1899 and designed in Dutch Colonial Revival style. The collection includes more than 10,000 items from 1680 to the present.

Displays include artisan-created miniature replicas, handmade wooden toys, manufactured metal and plastic cars, historic dollhouses, dolls and teddy bears. Changing exhibits also are featured. **Hours:** Wed.-Sat. 10-4, Sun. 1-4. Closed major holidays. **Cost:** $6; $5 (ages 62+); $4 (ages 5-16). **Phone:** (303) 322-1053.

GEM **DOWNTOWN AQUARIUM,** at 700 Water St. in Qwest Park, is a complex featuring more than 500 species of animals and birds, including lionfish, snakes, otters, sea anemones and Sumatran tigers. Housed in a modern brick building with a striking atrium, the aquarium tells a tale of various ecosystems, including wetlands, oceans, deserts, barrier reefs, beaches, rainforests and mangrove-fringed lagoons.

An aquarium tank is home to sharks, eels, stingrays and other underwater creatures. An interactive touch tank as well as naturalistic sounds and settings complete the experience. For an additional fee, visitors may experience what it's like to be a marine biologist or a zoologist, or snorkel and scuba dive in the large ocean tank.

Time: Allow 1 hour, 30 minutes minimum. **Hours:** Sun.-Thurs. 10-9, Fri.-Sat. 10-9:30. Closed Christmas. **Cost:** $15.99; $14.99 (ages 65+); $9.99 (ages 3-12). **Parking:** $6. **Phone:** (303) 561-4450.

SAVE **ELITCH GARDENS THEME PARK,** downtown off I-25 exit 212A (Speer Blvd. S.), has more than 50 rides, shows and attractions, including roller coasters, family rides, an area dedicated to rides especially for children, the Island Kingdom Water Park, gardens and games. Seasonal festivals include Fright Fest weekends in October.

Hours: Daily 10-9, late May to mid-Aug.; hours vary Sat.-Sun., mid-Aug. through Oct. 31. Phone ahead to confirm schedule. **Cost:** $40.99; $29.99 (under 48 inches tall, 62+ and restricted use); free (ages 0-3). **Parking:** $12 per private vehicle Mon.-Fri., $15 on Sat.-Sun. **Phone:** (303) 595-4386.

FORNEY MUSEUM OF TRANSPORTATION is off I-70 exit 275B (Brighton Blvd.), then 2 blks. s. to 4303 Brighton Blvd., near the Denver Coliseum. The museum features more than 100 antique and classic cars, carriages, bicycles, motorcycles, streetcars, locomotives and other vehicles. Notable exhibits include "Big Boy," said to be the world's largest steam locomotive at 134 feet long and weighing more than 1 million pounds; Amelia Earhart's first car; and a Rolls Royce that once belonged to Prince Aly Khan.

Time: Allow 1 hour minimum. **Hours:** Mon.-Sat. 10-4. Closed Jan. 1, Thanksgiving and Christmas. **Cost:** $8; $6 (ages 62+); $4 (ages 3-15). **Phone:** (303) 297-1113.

FOUR MILE HISTORIC PARK, at 715 S. Forest St. in s.e. Denver, is a 12-acre farm and the site of Denver's oldest standing structure, Four Mile House. Built of hand-hewn pine logs in 1859, the clapboard house reflects the era when it served as a ranch and stage stop along the Cherokee Trail. Barns have been reconstructed to the original design specifications. Horse-drawn wagon rides are offered most weekends while quilters, seamstresses and blacksmiths demonstrate their craft some Sunday afternoons.

Hours: Guided 45-minute tours depart on the half-hour Wed.-Fri. noon-4, Sat.-Sun. 10-4, Apr.-Sept.; Wed.-Sun. noon-4, rest of year. Last tour begins at 2:30. **Cost:** Park free. Tours $5; $4 (ages 65+ and military with ID); $3 (ages 7-17). Stagecoach ride $2; $1 (ages 6-15). **Phone:** (720) 865-0800.

HERITAGE SQUARE—see Golden p. 212.

KIRKLAND MUSEUM OF FINE & DECORATIVE ART, 1311 Pearl St., is housed in an expanded 1911 Arts and Crafts-style building with two windows by Frank Lloyd Wright. An extensive decorative arts collection, including examples from the Arts & Crafts, Art Nouveau, Bauhaus, Art Deco and Modern movements, is on display. Modernistic works by Colorado painters, ceramists, sculptors and furniture designers as well as works by painter Vance Kirkland are featured.

Ages 13-17 must be accompanied by an adult. Ages 0-12 are not permitted. **Hours:** Tues.-Sun. 11-5. Guided tours are given Wed.-Sat. at 1:30. Closed major holidays. **Cost:** $7; $6 (ages 62+ and students or teachers with ID). **Phone:** (303) 832-8576.

LOOKOUT MOUNTAIN PARK—see Golden p. 212.

MOLLY BROWN HOUSE MUSEUM, 2 blks. s. of Colfax Ave. at 1340 Pennsylvania St., was the home of Margaret Tobin Brown, a survivor of the *Titanic*. The socially prominent Mrs. Brown, known for her political activism, was later immortalized in the musical "The Unsinkable Molly Brown." Built in 1889, the house has been restored to its original Victorian splendor.

Hours: Guided 45-minute tours are offered every 30 minutes Mon.-Sat. 10-3:30, Sun. noon-3:30. Closed major holidays. **Cost:** $8; $6 (ages 65+); $4 (ages 6-12). **Phone:** (303) 832-4092.

MUSEO DE LAS AMÉRICAS, 861 Santa Fe Dr., houses changing historical, cultural and visual arts exhibits from Latin America and includes works by regional artists. The museum aims to educate visitors about the diversity of Latin American art and culture, from ancient to contemporary. **Time:** Allow 30 minutes minimum. **Hours:** Tues.-Fri. 10-5, Sat.-Sun. noon-5. Closed major holidays. **Cost:** $5; $4 (ages 66+ and students with ID); free (ages 0-12 and first Fri. 5-9 p.m.). **Phone:** (303) 571-4401.

MUSEUM OF CONTEMPORARY ART/DENVER is at 1485 Delgany St. at jct. with 15th St. Designed by noted architect David Adjaye, the environmentally sustainable glass-walled facility has five exhibition spaces that feature contemporary works by both established and emerging artists. A garden on the roof provides a scenic view of downtown Denver. Guided tours are available.

On-street parking is limited; visitors are encouraged to use public transportation. **Time:** Allow 1 hour minimum. **Hours:** Tues.-Sun. 10-6 (also Fri. 6-10 p.m.). Guided tours depart Tues.-Sun. at 11:30 and 3. Closed Jan. 1 and Christmas. **Cost:** $10; $5 (ages 7-17 and 62+). Guided tours free. **Parking:** $8 daily/$5 evening in the adjacent parking lot. **Phone:** (303) 298-7554.

RED ROCKS PARK AND AMPHITHEATRE—see Morrison p. 260.

GEM **STATE CAPITOL,** between E. 14th and E. Colfax aves. facing Lincoln St., is a 1908 neoclassic building that resembles the U.S. Capitol in Washington, D.C. The imposing structure is built of Colorado granite and topped with a gold-leafed dome, which commemorates the state's mid-19th-century gold rush days. The floors are made of marble from the Yule Marble Quarry in Marble, Colo. On display is the Women's Gold tapestry, honoring 18 Colorado women who were instrumental in the settlement of the state.

The interior wainscoting and pillar facings are of Colorado rose onyx. In keeping with Denver's identity as the Mile High City, the 13th step on the building's west entrance measures exactly 1 mile above sea level. In addition to the above highlights, guided tours provide insights into Colorado's history and the state's legislative process.

Note: Phone ahead for information about security procedures. **Time:** Allow 1 hour minimum. **Hours:** Guided tours of the capitol are given hourly Mon.-Fri. 9-3, Aug.-May; Mon.-Fri. 10-3, rest of year. Last tour begins 30 minutes before closing. Closed major holidays. **Cost:** Free. **Phone:** (303) 866-2604 for information about the capitol and for building tours.

TRINITY UNITED METHODIST CHURCH is at 1820 Broadway opposite the Brown Palace Hotel. The 1888 church, designed by the state's first licensed architect, Robert Roeschlaub, features original stained-glass windows made by Healy and Milet of Chicago. A Roosevelt organ with 4,202 pipes dominates the sanctuary. Sixty-six small lights above the organ symbolize the 66 books of the Bible. The church's congregation was established in 1859 as Denver's first church. Visitors enter through the church office. **Time:** Allow 30 minutes minimum. **Hours:** Mon.-Fri. 8-5. Guided tours are given Sun. at 12:15. **Cost:** Free. **Phone:** (303) 839-1493.

GEM **U.S. MINT** is at 320 W. Colfax Ave.; the tour entrance is on Cherokee St. Built 1898-1904, the building reflects its turn-of-the-20th-century grandeur; the Grand Hallway has murals, nine chandeliers and marble floors and walls. Guided tours enable participants to see the presses that produce 20 million coins each day.

Note: Visitors may only bring a palm-sized wallet or change purse. Handbags, purses, fanny packs, food, drink, strollers, tobacco products, backpacks, personal grooming items and weapons—including pocket knives and personal protective devices—are not permitted. Storage is not available. Pets are not allowed.

Time: Allow 1 hour minimum. **Hours:** Guided tours are offered Mon.-Fri. 8-2. Closed major holidays. **Cost:** Free. Reservations must be made online at the United States Mint website. The U.S. Mint information booth is on Cherokee Street between 14th and Colfax avenues. Reservations are required. **Phone:** (303) 405-4761.

WASHINGTON PARK, extending along Downing St., has tennis, croquet and horseshoe courts, flower gardens, two lakes, lawn bowling, jogging paths, boating, bicycle and walking trails, fishing and a recreation center with a swimming pool. Tennis and basketballs courts as well as a playground also are available. **Hours:** Daily 5 a.m.-11 p.m. **Cost:** Park free. Fees apply to recreational activities. **Phone:** (303) 698-4962 or (720) 913-1311.

WATER WORLD—see Federal Heights p. 196.

WINGS OVER THE ROCKIES AIR & SPACE MUSEUM is .25 mi. e. on 1st Ave., then s. on Roslyn St. to 7711 E. Academy Blvd. (Hangar No. 1 on the former Lowry Air Force Base). The museum displays more than three dozen historic airplanes and space vehicles.

Included are one of only four B-1A bombers ever built, a B-18 Bolo, five Century series fighters, a J-3-65 Piper Cub and an Alexander Eaglerock. Aviation memorabilia as well as exhibits about the science of flight and Lowry history are featured. **Time:** Allow 1 hour minimum. **Hours:** Mon.-Sat. 10-5, Sun. noon-5. Closed Jan. 1, Easter, Thanksgiving, and December 24-25 and 31. Closed major holidays. **Cost:** $11; $9 (ages 65+); $6 (ages 4-12). **Phone:** (303) 360-5360.

Sightseeing

With aspects both Victorian and modern, Denver and its environs offer much to explore. Information about possible sightseeing itineraries can be obtained at VISIT DENVER, The Convention & Visitors Bureau's Visitor Information Center *(see The Fast Facts box)* and from AAA Colorado.

SAVE Gray Line offers a choice of sightseeing tours of Denver and the surrounding area; phone (303) 289-2841 or (800) 348-6877. Blue Moon Carriages, Denver Carriage and Irish Rose Carriages are operators that offer horse-drawn carriage tours of the city; phone (303) 841-0780, (303) 271-1065, or (720) 883-5325, respectively.

Boat Tours

VENICE ON THE CREEK departs from Larimer St. between 14th St. and Speer Blvd. Boats travel a 10-block area between Creekfront Plaza, on Cherry Creek, and Confluence Park on the South Platte River. Guides steer the gondola-style boats and offer narration about local history and landmarks. All rides are 35-45 minutes long.

Time: Allow 45 minutes minimum. **Hours:** Trips Fri.-Sat. 5:30-9 p.m., June-Aug. (weather permitting). **Cost:** Trips must be purchased by the boat. Each boat seats six people. Fare $75 for departures 5:30-7:30 p.m., and $100 for Candlelight tours (8-9 p.m.); reservations required. **Phone:** (303) 893-0750.

Driving Tours

THE LARIAT LOOP NATIONAL SCENIC BYWAY links a number of parks and attractions in the foothills west of Denver. Beginning at US 6 w. of CR 470, the tour passes through Golden and follows the Lariat Trail up Lookout Mountain *(see Golden p. 210)*, then continues south along mountaintops via Lookout Mountain Road. After descending to Evergreen, the route follows Bear Creek Canyon to Morrison, goes north to Red Rocks Park and Amphitheatre and Dinosaur Ridge *(see Morrison p. 260)*, then back to US 6 and Golden. The 40-mile route is marked by blue and white Scenic Byway columbine signs.

Brochures with maps are available at the Golden Visitors Center, the Buffalo Bill Museum on Lookout Mountain, Dinosaur Ridge in Morrison, Hiwan Homestead Museum in Evergreen *(see attraction listings)* and other sites along the Loop. **Phone:** (720) 971-9649.

Industrial Tours

HAMMOND'S CANDIES FACTORY TOURS is n. off I-25 exit 215 (58th Ave.), then 2 blks. e. to the Mapleton Distribution Center at 5735 N. Washington St. This candy factory, founded in 1920, produces old-fashioned handmade hard candy and chocolates. Guided factory tours highlight the production process. **Time:** Allow 30 minutes minimum. **Hours:** Tours are given Mon.-Fri. every 20 minutes 9-3, Sat. 10-3. Closed Jan. 1, Memorial Day, Labor Day, Thanksgiving, Christmas and day after Christmas. **Cost:** Free. **Phone:** (303) 333-5588, ext. 110.

Trolley and Van Tours

THE COLORADO SIGHTSEER adventure tours depart from downtown hotels and Union Station. Adventures range from a 5-hour Foothills Tour that includes stops at the Coors Brewery and Red Rocks Park and Amphitheatre to a 10-hour journey through Rocky Mountain National Park. Other tours include the Ultimate Mountain Trip, Pikes Peak Region Tour, Rocky Mountain Gold Tour and Historic Denver Tour. Ski area tours also are available. Customized tours can be arranged.

Hours: Daily 7-7. Ski tours are available Nov. 15-Apr. 15. **Cost:** Fare $45-$95; $35-$75 (ages 5-12). Reservations are required. **Phone:** (303) 423-8200 or (800) 255-5105.

PLATTE VALLEY TROLLEY can be boarded at Confluence Park, from behind the REI store at 1416 Platte St., the Downtown Aquarium and The Children's Museum of Denver. Narrated tours traverse former railroad tracks on a vintage trolley that is a reproduction of an early 1900s open-sided streetcar. The 3-mile riverfront route travels through parkland along the South Platte River.

Time: Allow 30 minutes minimum. **Hours:** Departures Fri.-Sun. every half-hour noon-3:30 (weather permitting), Memorial Day-Labor Day; Fri.-Sun. noon-3:30 (weather permitting), Apr. 1-day before Memorial Day and day after Labor Day-Oct. 31. **Cost:** Fare $4; $2 (ages 4-12); free (ages 0-3). **Phone:** (303) 458-6255.

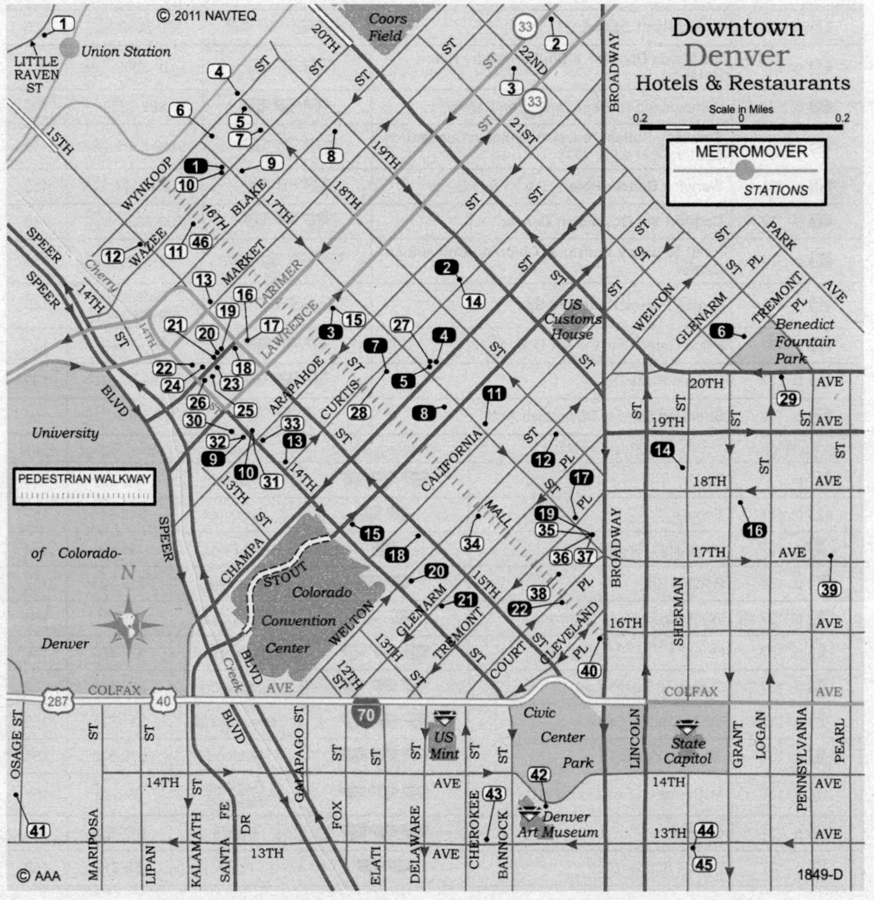

Downtown Denver

This index helps you "spot" where approved hotels and restaurants are located on the corresponding detailed maps. Hotel daily rate range is for comparison only and shows the property's high season. Restaurant rate range is a combination of lunch and/or dinner. Turn to the listing page for more detailed rate information and consult display ads for special promotions.

DOWNTOWN DENVER

Map Page	Hotels	Diamond Rated	High Season	Page
1 p. 137	The Oxford Hotel	◆◆◆	$180-$380	151
2 p. 137	**The Ritz-Carlton, Denver**	◆◆◆◆◆	Rates not provided SAVE	152
3 p. 137	**The Westin Denver Downtown**	◆◆◆◆	$169-$369 SAVE	154
4 p. 137	**Residence Inn by Marriott Denver City Center**	◆◆◆	$107-$319 SAVE	152
5 p. 137	**Hotel Monaco Denver**	◆◆◆◆	$159-$399 SAVE	150
6 p. 137	Queen Anne Urban Bed & Breakfast	◆◆◆	Rates not provided	151
7 p. 137	**Courtyard by Marriott Denver Downtown**	◆◆◆	$107-$309 SAVE	149
8 p. 137	**Magnolia Hotel-Downtown Denver**	◆◆◆	Rates not provided SAVE	151
9 p. 137	**Hotel Teatro** *(See ad p. 151.)*	◆◆◆◆	$159-$1500 SAVE	151
10 p. 137	Four Seasons Hotel Denver	◆◆◆◆	$245-$4000	150
11 p. 137	**Denver Marriott City Center**	◆◆◆◆	$109-$319 SAVE	149
12 p. 137	**Grand Hyatt Denver**	◆◆◆◆	$99-$399 SAVE	150
13 p. 137	**the Curtis Denver - a DoubleTree by Hilton Hotel**	◆◆◆	$119-$309 SAVE	149
14 p. 137	Hampton Inn & Suites Downtown Denver	◆◆◆	$99-$239	150
15 p. 137	**Embassy Suites Denver-Downtown/Convention Center** *(See ad p. 150.)*	◆◆◆	$142-$389 SAVE	149
16 p. 137	**Warwick Denver Hotel** *(See ad p. 153.)*	◆◆◆	$129-$499 SAVE	152
17 p. 137	**Comfort Inn Downtown Denver**	◆◆◆	$99-$299 SAVE	149
18 p. 137	**Hyatt Regency Denver at Colorado Convention Center**	◆◆◆◆	$79-$409 SAVE	151
19 p. 137	**Brown Palace Hotel and Spa**	◆◆◆◆	Rates not provided SAVE	149
20 p. 137	Hilton Garden Inn Denver Downtown	◆◆◆	$95-$366	150
21 p. 137	Crowne Plaza Denver	◆◆◆	$99-$299	149
22 p. 137	**Sheraton Denver Downtown Hotel**	◆◆◆	$119-$369 SAVE	152

Map Page	Restaurants	Diamond Rated	Cuisine	Meal Range	Page
1 p. 137	Zengo	◆◆◆	Fusion	$9-$28	158
2 p. 137	Snooze	◆◆	Breakfast	$10-$15	157
3 p. 137	Biker Jim's Dogs	◆	Hot Dogs	$6-$9	154
4 p. 137	Rodizio Grill	◆◆	Brazilian	$19-$33	157
5 p. 137	Wynkoop Brewing Company	◆◆	American	$9-$21	158
6 p. 137	Morton's The Steakhouse	◆◆◆	American	$27-$58	156
7 p. 137	Sullivan's Steakhouse	◆◆◆	Steak	$25-$60	157
8 p. 137	Vesta Dipping Grill	◆◆◆	International	$11-$36	158
9 p. 137	Jax Fish House	◆◆◆	Seafood	$19-$30	155
10 p. 137	McCormick's Fish House & Bar	◆◆◆	Regional Seafood	$9-$35	156
11 p. 137	Gumbo's	◆◆◆	Creole	$11-$30	155
12 p. 137	Wazee Supper Club	◆◆	Pizza	$6-$11	158

Map Page	Restaurants (cont'd)	Diamond Rated	Cuisine	Meal Range	Page
13 p. 137	**1515 Restaurant**	♦♦♦	American	$8-$29	154
14 p. 137	Elway's Downtown	♦♦♦	Steak	$9-$54	155
15 p. 137	The Palm Restaurant	♦♦♦	Steak	$15-$70	156
16 p. 137	Red Square Euro Bistro	♦♦♦	Russian	$18-$29	157
17 p. 137	Cafe Colore	♦♦	Italian	$9-$19	154
18 p. 137	The Capital Grille	♦♦♦	Steak	$16-$47	154
19 p. 137	The Market	♦	Deli	$6-$10	156
20 p. 137	Osteria Marco	♦♦♦	Italian	$9-$24	156
21 p. 137	TAG	♦♦♦	Fusion	$9-$29	157
22 p. 137	Euclid Hall Bar & Kitchen	♦♦	American	$9-$17	155
23 p. 137	Bistro Vendome	♦♦♦	French	$16-$24	154
24 p. 137	**Rioja**	♦♦♦♦	American	$11-$29	157
25 p. 137	Lime Cantina	♦♦	Mexican	$10-$15	156
26 p. 137	Tamayo Modern Mexican Cuisine	♦♦♦	Mexican	$9-$28	158
27 p. 137	**Panzano**	♦♦♦♦	Northern Italian	$10-$30	156
28 p. 137	Rialto Cafe	♦♦♦	American	$9-$25	157
29 p. 137	Jonesy's EatBar	♦♦	American	$9-$19	155
30 p. 137	Prima Ristorante	♦♦♦	Italian	$10-$28	157
31 p. 137	Edge Restaurant & Bar	♦♦♦♦	Steak	$12-$42	155
32 p. 137	**Restaurant Kevin Taylor**	♦♦♦♦	Regional American	$30-$50	157
33 p. 137	The Oceanaire Seafood Room	♦♦♦	Seafood	$20-$35	156
34 p. 137	Hard Rock Cafe	♦♦	American	$9-$18 SAVE	155
35 p. 137	Ship Tavern	♦♦	American	$15-$38	157
36 p. 137	Palace Arms	♦♦♦♦	Continental	$29-$42	156
37 p. 137	Ellyngton's at the Brown Palace	♦♦♦	American	$11-$26	155
38 p. 137	The Delectable Egg	♦♦	Breakfast	$6-$9	155
39 p. 137	Steuben's	♦♦	American	$4-$16	157
40 p. 137	Green Fine Salad Co.	♦	Natural/Organic	$7-$10	155
41 p. 137	Domo	♦♦	Japanese	$7-$23	155
42 p. 137	Palettes	♦♦♦	American	$10-$29	156
43 p. 137	Pints Pub	♦♦	British	$8-$9	156
44 p. 137	City O' City	♦♦	Pizza	$8-$11	154
45 p. 137	Water Course Foods	♦♦	Vegetarian	$9-$12	158
46 p. 137	ChoLon Modern Asian Bistro	♦♦♦	Asian	$10-$30	154

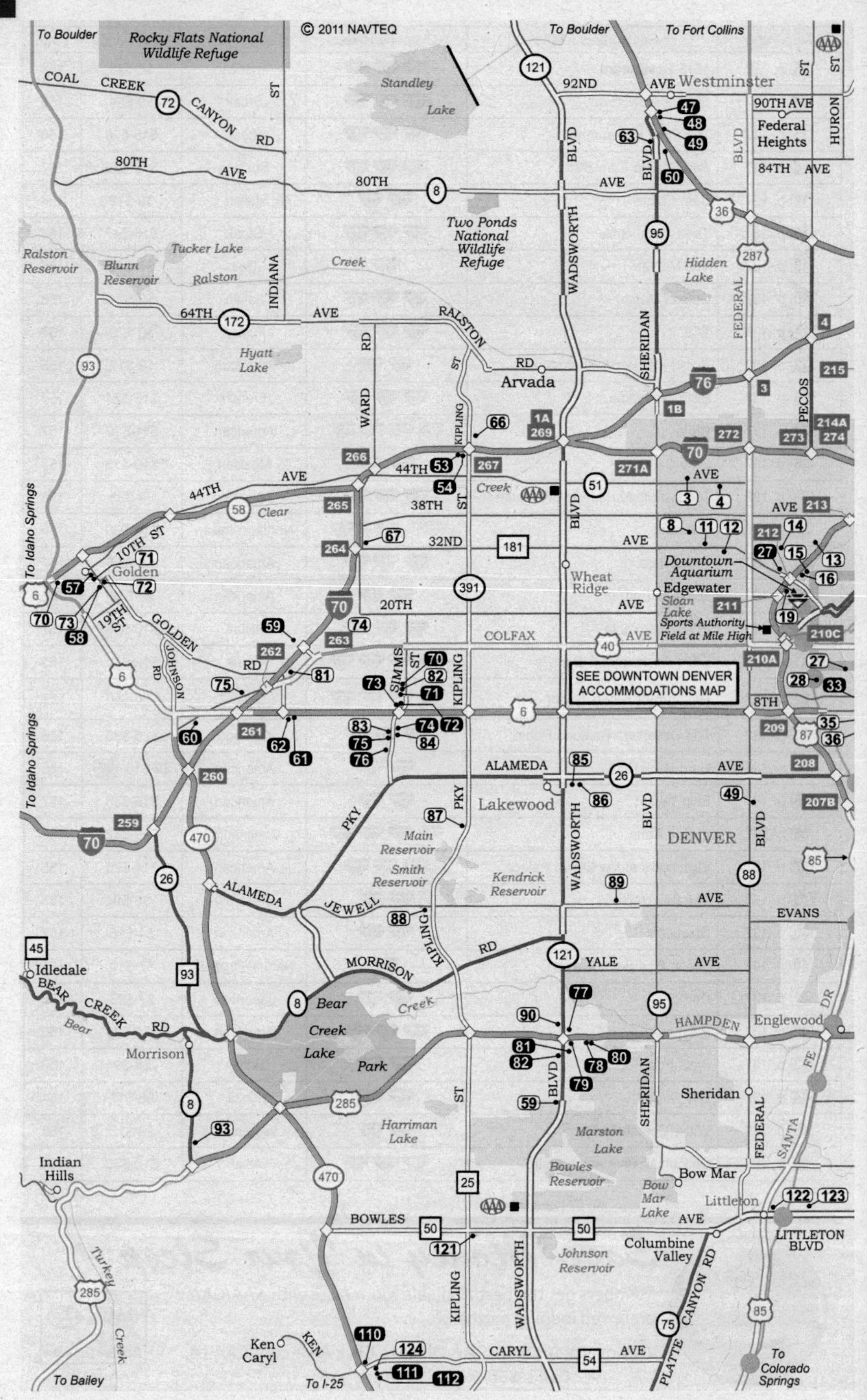

© 2011 NAVTEQ
Rocky Flats National Wildlife Refuge
To Boulder
To Fort Collins
Westminster
Federal Heights
Standley Lake
Two Ponds National Wildlife Refuge
Arvada
Golden
Wheat Ridge
Edgewater
Downtown Aquarium
Sports Authority Field at Mile High
SEE DOWNTOWN DENVER ACCOMMODATIONS MAP
Lakewood
DENVER
Englewood
Sheridan
Morrison
Idledale
Indian Hills
Bear Creek Lake Park
Littleton
Columbine Valley
Ken Caryl
To Idaho Springs
To Bailey
To I-25
To Colorado Springs

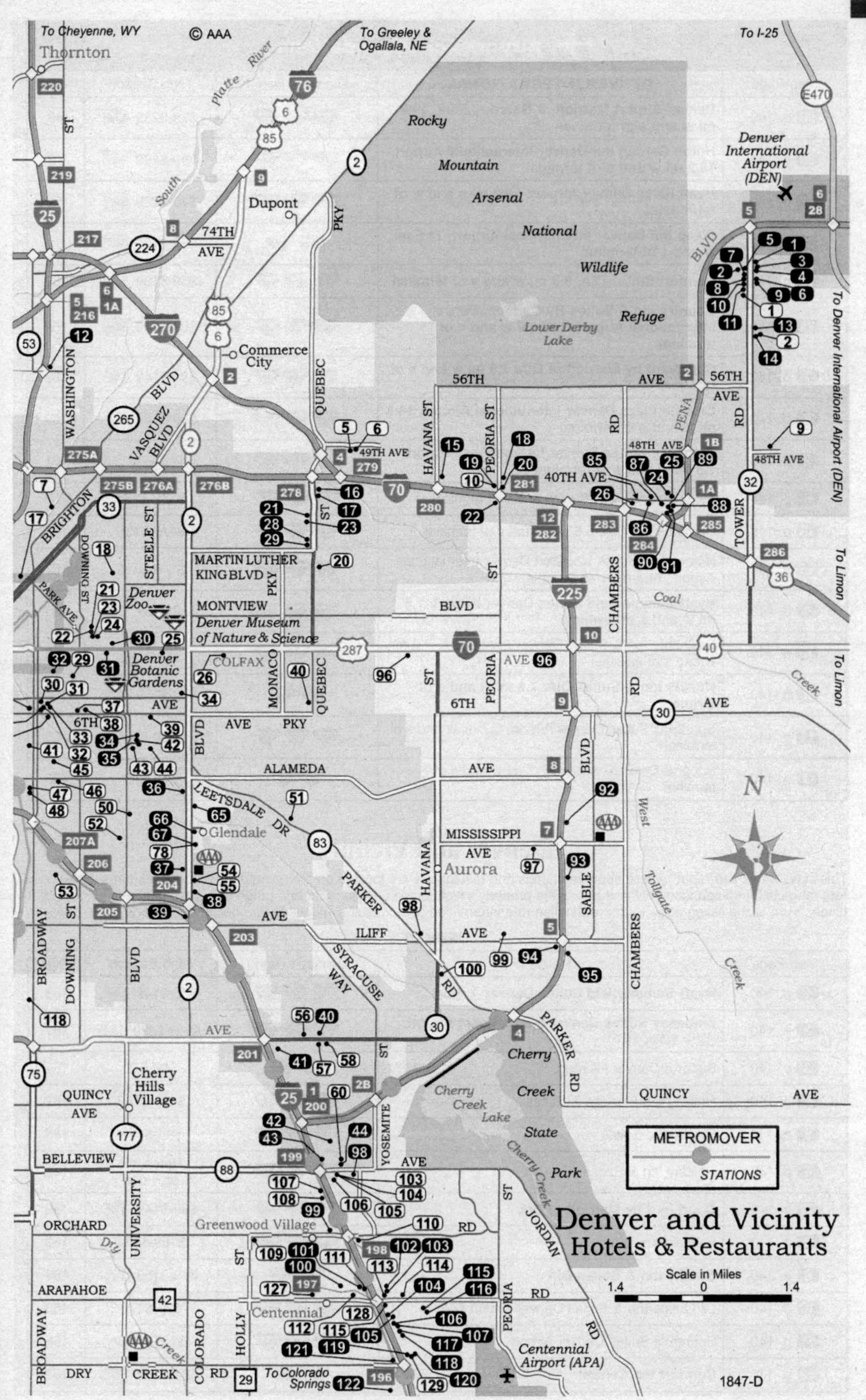

Denver and Vicinity
Hotels & Restaurants
© AAA
To Cheyenne, WY
To Greeley & Ogallala, NE
To I-25
Thornton
Dupont
Commerce City
Rocky Mountain Arsenal National Wildlife Refuge
Lower Derby Lake
Denver International Airport (DEN)
To Denver International Airport (DEN)
To Limon
Denver Zoo
Denver Museum of Nature & Science
Denver Botanic Gardens
Glendale
Aurora
Cherry Hills Village
Cherry Creek State Park
Cherry Creek Lake
Greenwood Village
Centennial
Centennial Airport (APA)
To Colorado Springs
METROMOVER
STATIONS
Scale in Miles
1.4
0
1.4
1847-D

Airport Accommodations

Map Page	DENVER INTERNATIONAL	Diamond Rated	High Season	Page
90 p. 140	**Denver Airport Marriott at Gateway Park, 14.2 mi w and s of terminal**	♦♦♦	$79-$239 SAVE	49
89 p. 140	**Hilton Garden Inn-Denver International Airport, 14.2 mi w and s of terminal**	♦♦♦	$99-$199 SAVE	49
87 p. 140	**Hyatt Place Denver Airport, 14.2 mi s and w of terminal**	♦♦♦	$79-$229 SAVE	51
86 p. 140	**Sleep Inn Denver International Airport, 14.5 mi w and s of terminal**	♦♦	$69-$130 SAVE	51
14 p. 140	**Comfort Suites-DIA, 8.6 mi w and s of terminal**	♦♦♦	$59-$199 SAVE	159
24 p. 140	**Country Inn & Suites By Carlson, Denver International Airport, 14.2 mi w and s of terminal**	♦♦♦	$89-$169 SAVE	159
7 p. 140	**Courtyard by Marriott at DIA, 7.8 mi w and s of terminal**	♦♦♦	$89-$149 SAVE	159
26 p. 140	**Crowne Plaza Denver International Airport, 14.8 mi w and s of terminal**	♦♦♦	$89-$199 SAVE	159
2 p. 140	**Embassy Suites Denver International Airport, 7.8 mi w and s of terminal**	♦♦♦	$119-$229 SAVE	161
8 p. 140	Fairfield Inn-DIA, 7.9 mi w and s of terminal	♦♦♦	$169-$184	162
13 p. 140	Hampton Inn DIA, 8.6 mi w and s of terminal	♦♦♦	$115-$135	162
25 p. 140	Homewood Suites by Hilton Denver International Airport, 14.2 mi w and s of terminal	♦♦♦	$149-$169	162
1 p. 140	**Hyatt Summerfield Suites Denver Airport, 7.6 mi w and s of terminal**	♦♦♦	$89-$149 SAVE	163
10 p. 140	La Quinta Inn & Suites Denver Airport DIA, 7.9 mi w and s of terminal	♦♦♦	$88-$170	163
9 p. 140	**Quality Inn & Suites-DIA, 7.8 mi w and s of terminal**	♦♦	$79-$159 SAVE	164
11 p. 140	SpringHill Suites Denver Airport, 0.7 mi w and s of terminal	♦♦♦	$169-$185	165
3 p. 140	Super 8 Denver - Airport, 7.7 mi w and s of terminal	♦♦	$63-$72	165

Denver and Vicinity

This index helps you "spot" where approved hotels and restaurants are located on the corresponding detailed maps. Hotel daily rate range is for comparison only and shows the property's high season. Restaurant rate range is a combination of lunch and/or dinner. Turn to the listing page for more detailed rate information and consult display ads for special promotions.

DENVER

Map Page	Hotels	Diamond Rated	High Season	Page
1 p. 140	**Hyatt Summerfield Suites Denver Airport**	♦♦♦	$89-$149 SAVE	163
2 p. 140	**Embassy Suites Denver International Airport** *(See ad p. 161.)*	♦♦♦	$119-$229 SAVE	161
3 p. 140	Super 8 Denver - Airport	♦♦	$63-$72	165
4 p. 140	Holiday Inn Express & Suites	♦♦♦	$119-$149	162
5 p. 140	Staybridge Suites	♦♦♦	$94-$179	165
6 p. 140	Holiday Inn & Suites	♦♦♦	Rates not provided	162
7 p. 140	**Courtyard by Marriott at DIA**	♦♦♦	$89-$149 SAVE	159
8 p. 140	Fairfield Inn-DIA	♦♦♦	$169-$184	162
9 p. 140	**Quality Inn & Suites-DIA**	♦♦	$79-$159 SAVE	164
10 p. 140	La Quinta Inn & Suites Denver Airport DIA	♦♦♦	$88-$170	163
11 p. 140	SpringHill Suites Denver Airport	♦♦♦	$169-$185	165
12 p. 140	**Comfort Inn Central**	♦♦	$84-$109 SAVE	158

DENVER (cont'd)

Map Page	Hotels (cont'd)	Diamond Rated	High Season	Page
13 p. 140	Hampton Inn DIA	◆◆◆	$115-$135	162
14 p. 140	**Comfort Suites-DIA**	◆◆◆	$59-$199 SAVE	159
15 p. 140	**Embassy Suites Denver-Aurora**	◆◆◆	$109-$249 SAVE	161
16 p. 140	Courtyard by Marriott Denver Stapleton	◆◆◆	$59-$119	159
17 p. 140	Red Lion Denver Central	◆◆◆	Rates not provided	164
18 p. 140	La Quinta Inn & Suites Denver Gateway Park	◆◆◆	Rates not provided	163
19 p. 140	**Timbers Hotel**	◆◆◆	Rates not provided SAVE	165
20 p. 140	Drury Inn-Denver East	◆◆◆	$85-$139	161
21 p. 140	**Renaissance Denver Hotel**	◆◆◆	$170-$208 SAVE	164
22 p. 140	**Quality Inn Denver East**	◆◆	$62-$119 SAVE	164
23 p. 140	**Best Western Plus Denver Hotel** *(See ad p. 159.)*	◆◆◆	Rates not provided SAVE	158
24 p. 140	**Country Inn & Suites By Carlson, Denver International Airport**	◆◆◆	$89-$169 SAVE	159
25 p. 140	Homewood Suites by Hilton Denver International Airport	◆◆◆	$149-$169	162
26 p. 140	**Crowne Plaza Denver International Airport**	◆◆◆	$89-$199 SAVE	159
27 p. 140	Residence Inn by Marriott Denver Downtown	◆◆◆	$159-$179	164
28 p. 140	Holiday Inn Denver East - Stapleton	◆◆◆	Rates not provided	162
29 p. 140	DoubleTree by Hilton Hotel Denver	◆◆◆	$79-$224	161
30 p. 140	Castle Marne Bed and Breakfast	◆◆◆	$125-$285	158
31 p. 140	**Holiday Chalet A Victorian Bed & Breakfast**	◆◆◆	$94-$160 SAVE	162
32 p. 140	Capitol Hill Mansion Bed & Breakfast Inn	◆◆◆	$119-$219	158
33 p. 140	TownePlace Suites by Marriott Downtown Denver	◆◆	$99-$299	166
34 p. 140	**The Inn at Cherry Creek**	◆◆◆	$199-$425 SAVE	163
35 p. 140	**JW Marriott Denver At Cherry Creek**	◆◆◆◆	$199-$399 SAVE	163
36 p. 140	**Holiday Inn Select Denver-Cherry Creek**	◆◆◆	$89-$159 SAVE	162
37 p. 140	Marriott Courtyard Denver Cherry Creek	◆◆◆	$99-$189	163
38 p. 140	Fairfield Inn & Suites Denver/Cherry Creek	◆◆◆	$69-$219	162
39 p. 140	La Quinta Inn Denver Cherry Creek	◆◆	$78-$170	163
40 p. 140	Embassy Suites Denver Southeast	◆◆◆	$119-$139	161
41 p. 140	**TownePlace Suites by Marriott-Denver Southeast**	◆◆	$69-$149 SAVE	165
42 p. 140	**Hyatt Regency Denver Tech Center**	◆◆◆◆	$69-$319 SAVE	163
43 p. 140	Denver Marriott Tech Center	◆◆◆	$79-$149	159
44 p. 140	Hampton Inn & Suites Denver Tech Center	◆◆◆	$69-$159	162

Map Page	Restaurants	Diamond Rated	Cuisine	Meal Range	Page
1 p. 140	DiCiccio's	◆◆	Italian	$10-$28	167
2 p. 140	Moonlight Diner	◆◆	American	$7-$19	170
3 p. 140	Parisi	◆◆	Italian	$9-$15	170
4 p. 140	Tocabe	◆	Native American	$6-$9	171
5 p. 140	La Sandia	◆◆◆	Mexican	$9-$18	169

Map Page	Restaurants (cont'd)	Diamond Rated	Cuisine	Meal Range	Page
6 p. 140	Ling & Louie's Asian Bar & Grill	◆◆	Asian	$9-$17	169
7 p. 140	Fuel Cafe	◆◆	American	$9-$22	168
8 p. 140	Sabor Latino	◆◆	Latin American	$8-$15	171
9 p. 140	Blue Bay Asian Cafe	◆◆	Asian	$6-$13	166
10 p. 140	Peoria Grill	◆◆	American	$9-$22	170
11 p. 140	Highland's Garden Cafe	◆◆◆	American	$13-$32	168
12 p. 140	Julia Blackbird's	◆◆	Southwestern	$10-$16	169
13 p. 140	Root Down	◆◆◆	Natural/Organic	$8-$27	171
14 p. 140	Duo Restaurant	◆◆◆	American	$17-$24	168
15 p. 140	**Colt & Gray**	◆◆◆◆	American	$14-$35	167
16 p. 140	My Brother's Bar	◆◆	Burgers	$7-$15	170
17 p. 140	Breckenridge Brewery & Pub	◆◆	American	$8-$16	166
18 p. 140	M&D's Cafe	◆◆	American	$8-$22	169
19 p. 140	Aquarium Restaurant	◆◆◆	American	$9-$32 SAVE	166
20 p. 140	Casey's Bistro & Pub	◆◆	American	$8-$18	167
21 p. 140	Hot Cakes Breakfast and Lunch	◆◆	American	$7-$9	168
22 p. 140	Strings	◆◆◆	American	$14-$35	171
23 p. 140	D Bar Desserts	◆◆◆	Desserts	$8-$15	167
24 p. 140	Parallel Seventeen	◆◆◆	Vietnamese	$8-$26	170
25 p. 140	Mezcal	◆◆	Mexican	$9-$17	169
26 p. 140	The Cork House	◆◆◆	American	$14-$29	167
27 p. 140	Cuba Cuba Cafe & Bar	◆◆◆	Cuban	$13-$24	167
28 p. 140	**Buckhorn Exchange**	◆◆	Steak	$10-$43	166
29 p. 140	Potager	◆◆◆	American	$18-$29	170
30 p. 140	Le Central	◆◆	French	$8-$19	169
31 p. 140	Luca d'Italia	◆◆◆	Italian	$14-$36	169
32 p. 140	Mizuna	◆◆◆◆	New American	$28-$43	169
33 p. 140	Bones	◆◆	Asian	$11-$18	166
34 p. 140	Swing Thai	◆◆	Thai	$9-$13	171
35 p. 140	Racines Restaurant	◆◆	American	$8-$20	170
36 p. 140	Little India Restaurant	◆◆	Indian	$9-$16	169
37 p. 140	Table 6	◆◆◆	New World	$18-$26	171
38 p. 140	Fruition Restaurant	◆◆◆	American	$22-$26	168
39 p. 140	Barolo Grill	◆◆◆	Northern Italian	$17-$32	166
40 p. 140	Moongate Asian Grill	◆◆	Asian	$6-$14	170
41 p. 140	El Diablo	◆◆	Mexican	$7-$17	168
42 p. 140	The Cherry Cricket	◆◆	American	$5-$10	167
43 p. 140	Elway's	◆◆◆	Steak	$12-$58	168
44 p. 140	Kona Grill	◆◆◆	Caribbean	$9-$31	169
45 p. 140	Carmine's on Penn	◆◆◆	Italian	$20-$45	167

Map Page	Restaurants (cont'd)	Diamond Rated	Cuisine	Meal Range	Page
46 p. 140	Pete's Central One	◆◆	Greek	$8-$18	170
47 p. 140	Imperial Chinese Seafood Restaurant	◆◆◆	Chinese	$10-$25	168
48 p. 140	The Blue Bonnet Mexican Cafe	◆◆	Mexican	$5-$14	166
49 p. 140	New Saigon Restaurant	◆◆	Vietnamese	$7-$32	170
50 p. 140	**Bonnie Brae Tavern**	◆◆	American	$6-$14	166
51 p. 140	Banzai Sushi	◆◆	Japanese	$7-$25	166
52 p. 140	Devil's Food	◆◆	American	$8-$15	167
53 p. 140	Sushi Den	◆◆◆	Japanese	$15-$28	171
54 p. 140	Saigon Terrace Vietnamese & Chinese Restaurant	◆◆	Vietnamese	$7-$15	171
55 p. 140	Royal India	◆◆	Indian	$9-$17	171
56 p. 140	**New York Deli News**	◆◆	American	$7-$14	170
57 p. 140	**India's Restaurant**	◆◆	Indian	$10-$20	168
58 p. 140	The Fresh Fish Company	◆◆	Seafood	$9-$39	168
59 p. 140	Hanabi Japanese Grill & Sushi Bar	◆◆◆	Japanese	$7-$32	168
60 p. 140	Darcy's Bistro & Pub	◆◆	American	$6-$13	167

WESTMINSTER

Map Page	Hotels	Diamond Rated	High Season	Page
47 p. 140	Hampton Inn by Hilton	◆◆	$79-$129	301
48 p. 140	Residence Inn by Marriott	◆◆◆	$153-$187	302
49 p. 140	**DoubleTree by Hilton Hotel Denver - Westminster**	◆◆◆	$89-$189 SAVE	301
50 p. 140	**Comfort Inn Northwest**	◆◆	$59-$135 SAVE	301

Map Page	Restaurant	Diamond Rated	Cuisine	Meal Range	Page
63 p. 140	Yak & Yeti	◆◆	Indian	$10-$14	302

WHEAT RIDGE

Map Page	Hotels	Diamond Rated	High Season	Page
53 p. 140	Comfort Inn	◆◆	$84-$104	302
54 p. 140	Holiday Inn Express Hotel & Suites	◆◆◆	$110-$129	302

Map Page	Restaurants	Diamond Rated	Cuisine	Meal Range	Page
66 p. 140	Luke's A Steak Place	◆◆	Steak	$20-$37	302
67 p. 140	Abrusci's	◆◆	Italian	$9-$22	302

GOLDEN

Map Page	Hotels	Diamond Rated	High Season	Page
57 p. 140	The Golden Hotel, an Ascend Collection hotel	◆◆◆	$139-$189	213
58 p. 140	**Table Mountain Inn**	◆◆◆	$135-$249 SAVE	213
59 p. 140	Denver Marriott West	◆◆◆	$79-$149	213
60 p. 140	Hampton Inn Denver West/Golden	◆◆◆	$99-$169	213
61 p. 140	Residence Inn by Marriott Denver West/Golden	◆◆◆	$79-$249	213
62 p. 140	Courtyard by Marriott Denver West/Golden	◆◆◆	$69-$209	212

Map Page	Restaurants	Diamond Rated	Cuisine	Meal Range	Page
70 p. 140	The Briarwood Inn	◆◆◆	Continental	$12-$80	213
71 p. 140	Old Capitol Grill	◆◆	American	$7-$23	213

Map Page	Restaurants (cont'd)	Diamond Rated	Cuisine	Meal Range	Page
72 p. 140	Woody's Wood Fired Pizza & Watering Hole	◆◆	Pizza	$7-$11	214
73 p. 140	**Table Mountain Grill & Cantina**	◆◆◆	Southwestern	$8-$26	213
74 p. 140	Tafolino's	◆◆	Mexican	$6-$12	213
75 p. 140	Sushi Uokura	◆◆	Japanese	$8-$20	213

GLENDALE

Map Page	Hotels	Diamond Rated	High Season	Page
65 p. 140	Hilton Garden Inn Denver/Cherry Creek	◆◆◆	$99-$189	206
66 p. 140	Hampton Inn & Suites Denver/Cherry Creek	◆◆◆	$99-$179	206
67 p. 140	**Loews Denver Hotel**	◆◆◆◆	$99-$279 SAVE	206

Map Page	Restaurant	Diamond Rated	Cuisine	Meal Range	Page
78 p. 140	**Tuscany Restaurant**	◆◆◆	Northern Italian	$15-$30	207

LAKEWOOD

Map Page	Hotels	Diamond Rated	High Season	Page
70 p. 140	**Candlewood Suites Lakewood/Golden**	◆◆	Rates not provided SAVE	234
71 p. 140	**TownePlace Suites by Marriott-Denver West/ Federal Center**	◆◆	$79-$169 SAVE	235
72 p. 140	Fairfield Inn Denver West - Federal Center	◆◆	$109-$129	234
73 p. 140	AmericInn Hotel & Suites/Denver West- Federal Center	◆◆	Rates not provided	233
74 p. 140	**Sheraton-Denver West Hotel**	◆◆◆	$89-$279 SAVE	235
75 p. 140	Hampton Inn Denver West/Federal Center	◆◆◆	$99-$139	234
76 p. 140	Homewood Suites by Hilton Denver-West/Lakewood	◆◆◆	$159-$359	234
77 p. 140	**Best Western Denver Southwest**	◆◆	$85-$119 SAVE	234
78 p. 140	Courtyard by Marriott Denver SW/Lakewood	◆◆◆	$69-$189	234
79 p. 140	**Holiday Inn Denver Lakewood** *(See ad p. 235.)*	◆◆◆	$89-$129 SAVE	234
80 p. 140	Residence Inn by Marriott Denver SW/Lakewood	◆◆◆	$79-$219	235
81 p. 140	Lakewood Comfort Suites	◆◆	$100	235
82 p. 140	Hampton Inn-Denver Southwest	◆◆◆	$89-$149	234

Map Page	Restaurants	Diamond Rated	Cuisine	Meal Range	Page
81 p. 140	Blue Sky Cafe	◆◆	Natural/Organic	$6-$11	236
82 p. 140	**Jus Cookin's Restaurant**	◆◆	American	$9-$13	236
83 p. 140	Chad's Grill	◆◆	American	$7-$15	236
84 p. 140	240 Union Restaurant	◆◆◆	American	$9-$29	236
85 p. 140	Wystone's World Teas	◆◆	Coffee/Tea	$9-$16	236
86 p. 140	The Oven Pizza e Vino	◆◆	Pizza	$8-$15	236
87 p. 140	Moose Hill Cantina	◆◆	Mexican	$5-$15	236
88 p. 140	Cafe Jordano	◆◆	Italian	$6-$16	236
89 p. 140	**White Fence Farm Restaurant**	◆◆	American	$9-$23	236
90 p. 140	Pad Thai	◆◆	Thai	$7-$12	236

AURORA

Map Page	Hotels	Diamond Rated	High Season	Page
85 p. 140	Cambria Suites Denver Airport *(See ad p. 103.)*	◆◆◆	$89-$229	49

AURORA (cont'd)

Map Page	Hotels (cont'd)	Diamond Rated	High Season	Page
86 p. 140	**Sleep Inn Denver International Airport**	♦♦	$69-$130 SAVE	51
87 p. 140	**Hyatt Place Denver Airport**	♦♦♦	$79-$229 SAVE	51
88 p. 140	Residence Inn by Marriott	♦♦♦	$98-$152	51
89 p. 140	**Hilton Garden Inn-Denver International Airport** *(See ad p. 50.)*	♦♦♦	$99-$199 SAVE	49
90 p. 140	**Denver Airport Marriott at Gateway Park**	♦♦♦	$79-$239 SAVE	49
91 p. 140	**Aloft Denver International Airport**	♦♦♦	$79-$199 SAVE	49
92 p. 140	**Best Western Plus Gateway Inn & Suites**	♦♦♦	$79-$150 SAVE	49
93 p. 140	Holiday Inn Express & Suites Denver-Aurora	♦♦♦	Rates not provided	51
94 p. 140	**DoubleTree by Hilton Hotel Denver - Aurora** *(See ad p. 50.)*	♦♦♦	$89-$169 SAVE	49
95 p. 140	Fairfield Inn-Denver/Aurora	♦♦♦	$80-$98	49
96 p. 140	**SpringHill Suites by Marriott**	♦♦♦	Rates not provided SAVE	51

Map Page	Restaurants	Diamond Rated	Cuisine	Meal Range	Page
96 p. 140	La Cueva Restaurante	♦♦	Mexican	$8-$16	51
97 p. 140	Café Paprika	♦♦	Moroccan	$7-$18	51
98 p. 140	Caldonia's Barbecue	♦♦	Barbecue	$8-$17	51
99 p. 140	Bent Fork American Grill	♦♦♦	American	$9-$26	51
100 p. 140	Aurora Summit	♦♦♦	Steak	$10-$46	51

GREENWOOD VILLAGE

Map Page	Hotels	Diamond Rated	High Season	Page
98 p. 140	**Hyatt Place Denver Tech Center**	♦♦♦	$79-$219 SAVE	222
99 p. 140	DoubleTree by Hilton Hotel Denver Tech Center	♦♦♦	$80-$229	222
100 p. 140	Wingate by Wyndham	♦♦♦	$67-$152	223
101 p. 140	Residence Inn by Marriott-Denver Tech Center	♦♦♦	$189-$209	222
102 p. 140	Courtyard by Marriott-Denver Tech Center	♦♦♦	$59-$119	222
103 p. 140	Hampton Inn Denver Southeast	♦♦♦	Rates not provided	222
104 p. 140	**Sleep Inn Denver Tech Center**	♦♦	Rates not provided SAVE	223
105 p. 140	**Hyatt Summerfield Suites Denver Tech Center**	♦♦♦	$79-$219 SAVE	222
106 p. 140	**Sheraton Denver Tech Center Hotel**	♦♦♦	$179 SAVE	222
107 p. 140	La Quinta Inn & Suites Denver Tech Center	♦♦♦	$64-$165	222

Map Page	Restaurants	Diamond Rated	Cuisine	Meal Range	Page
103 p. 140	Larkburger	♦	Burgers	$4-$8	224
104 p. 140	Bara Sushi & Grill	♦♦	Sushi	$8-$25	223
105 p. 140	Il Fornaio	♦♦♦	Italian	$10-$35	223
106 p. 140	**Cool River Cafe**	♦♦♦	Steak	$12-$41	223
107 p. 140	Jing	♦♦♦	Asian	$10-$27	224
108 p. 140	Yanni's, A Greek Taverna	♦♦	Greek	$10-$30	224
109 p. 140	Venice Ristorante Italiano	♦♦♦	Italian	$10-$36	224
110 p. 140	Del Frisco's Double Eagle Steak House	♦♦♦	Steak	$11-$50	223
111 p. 140	Brook's Steak House & Cellar	♦♦♦	Steak	$29-$60	223

Map Page	Restaurants (cont'd)	Diamond Rated	Cuisine	Meal Range	Page
112 p. 140	Garbanzo Mediterranean Grill	◆	Mediterranean	$6-$7	223
113 p. 140	Brother's BBQ	◆	Barbecue	$5-$22	223
114 p. 140	Shiraz Fine Persian Cuisine	◆◆	Middle Eastern	$7-$22	224
115 p. 140	Gunther Toody's Diner	◆◆	American	$7-$10	223

LITTLETON

Map Page	Hotels	Diamond Rated	High Season	Page
110 p. 140	**Holiday Inn Express Hotel & Suites**	◆◆◆	$89-$119 SAVE	242
111 p. 140	Hampton Inn & Suites Denver Littleton	◆◆◆	$79-$129	242
112 p. 140	**Homewood Suites by Hilton-Denver Littleton**	◆◆◆	$99-$299 SAVE	242

Map Page	Restaurants	Diamond Rated	Cuisine	Meal Range	Page
121 p. 140	Thai Bistro	◆◆	Thai	$8-$19	243
122 p. 140	Opus Restaurant	◆◆◆	New Continental	$12-$35	243
123 p. 140	Romano's Pizzeria	◆◆	Italian	$7-$15	243
124 p. 140	Lil' Ricci's NY Pizza	◆	Italian	$7-$13	243

CENTENNIAL

Map Page	Hotels	Diamond Rated	High Season	Page
115 p. 140	**Candlewood Suites**	◆◆	$49-$99 SAVE	80
116 p. 140	**Embassy Suites Denver Tech Center**	◆◆◆	$129-$199 SAVE	80
117 p. 140	Staybridge Suites Denver Tech Center	◆◆◆	$85-$105	81
118 p. 140	Extended Stay Deluxe-Denver Tech Center South	◆◆	$80-$90	80
119 p. 140	**Comfort Suites Denver Tech Center**	◆◆◆	$85-$140 SAVE	80
120 p. 140	Holiday Inn Express Hotel & Suites	◆◆◆	$80-$139	81
121 p. 140	Drury Inn & Suites-Denver Near the Tech Center	◆◆◆	$85-$139	80
122 p. 140	**TownePlace Suites Denver Tech Center**	◆◆	$69-$149 SAVE	81

Map Page	Restaurants	Diamond Rated	Cuisine	Meal Range	Page
127 p. 140	Pesce Fresco	◆◆◆	Italian	$8-$26	81
128 p. 140	The Egg & I	◆◆	Breakfast	$6-$9	81
129 p. 140	Maggiano's Little Italy	◆◆◆	Italian	$11-$38	81

MORRISON

Map Page	Restaurant	Diamond Rated	Cuisine	Meal Range	Page
93 p. 140	The Fort	◆◆◆	Steak	$24-$52	260

ENGLEWOOD

Map Page	Restaurant	Diamond Rated	Cuisine	Meal Range	Page
118 p. 140	Twin Dragon Chinese Restaurant	◆◆	Chinese	$8-$30	183

DOWNTOWN DENVER

• Restaurants p. 154
• Hotels & Restaurants map & index p. 137

BROWN PALACE HOTEL AND SPA

Phone: 303/297-3111 19

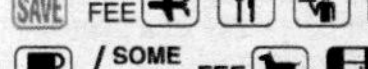

Classic Historic Hotel

Rates not provided

Address: 321 17th St 80202 **Location:** From Broadway and Tremont Pl, just sw. **Facility:** Since opening in 1892, the grande dame has worked hard to keep its character while continuing to modernize. Standard rooms have Victorian-influenced décor with luxurious bedding and flat-screen TVs. 241 units. 9 stories, interior corridors. **Parking:** valet only. **Amenities:** high-speed Internet (fee), safes. **Dining:** 2 restaurants, also, Ellyngton's at the Brown Palace, Palace Arms, Ship Tavern, see separate listings, entertainment. **Activities:** exercise room, spa. **Guest Services:** valet laundry, area transportation-within 5 mi. Affiliated with A Preferred Hotel.

SAVE FEE BIZ FEE / SOME UNITS FEE

COMFORT INN DOWNTOWN DENVER

Phone: (303)296-0400 17

Hotel

$99-$299

Address: 401 17th St 80202 **Location:** From Broadway and Tremont Pl, just sw. **Facility:** 231 units, some two bedrooms. 22 stories, interior corridors. **Parking:** valet only. **Terms:** check-in 4 pm, cancellation fee imposed. **Amenities:** high-speed Internet. **Activities:** exercise room. **Guest Services:** valet laundry. **Free Special Amenities: full breakfast and high-speed Internet.**

SAVE BIZ FEE / SOME UNITS FEE

COURTYARD BY MARRIOTT DENVER DOWNTOWN

Phone: (303)571-1114 7

Hotel

$107-$309

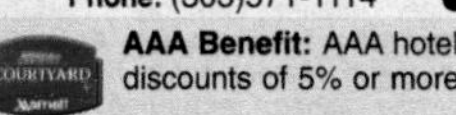

AAA Benefit: AAA hotel discounts of 5% or more.

Address: 934 16th St 80202 **Location:** Jct Curtis St. **Facility:** 177 units. 6 stories, interior corridors. **Parking:** valet only. **Terms:** check-in 4 pm. **Amenities:** high-speed Internet. **Dining:** Rialto Cafe, see separate listing. **Activities:** exercise room. **Guest Services:** valet and coin laundry. **Free Special Amenities: full breakfast and use of on-premises laundry facilities.**

CROWNE PLAZA DENVER

Phone: (303)573-1450 21

Hotel

$99-$299

Address: 1450 Glenarm Pl 80202 **Location:** I-25 exit 210 (W Colfax Ave) to Glenarm Pl, then 0.3 mi n. **Facility:** 364 units. 20 stories, interior corridors. **Parking:** on-site (fee). **Terms:** check-in 4 pm, cancellation fee imposed. **Amenities:** high-speed Internet, safes. **Pool(s):** heated outdoor. **Activities:** exercise room. **Guest Services:** valet laundry.

/ SOME UNITS FEE FEE

THE CURTIS DENVER - A DOUBLETREE BY HILTON HOTEL

Phone: (303)571-0300 13

Boutique Contemporary Hotel

$119-$309

AAA Benefit: Members save 5% or more everyday!

Address: 1405 Curtis St 80202 **Location:** I-25 exit 212 (Speer Blvd S), s to Lawrence St, just ne, just se on 14th St, then just n. **Facility:** The mod-style lobby features a hip toy theme which includes the world's largest Lite-Brite. Each floor has a specific theme with artwork reflecting that theme. Examples include Fun and Games, Sci-Fi Floor, Pedal to the Metal and The Dance Floor. Every room has a flat screen TV and upgraded bedding. 336 units. 30 stories, interior corridors. **Parking:** on-site (fee) and valet. **Terms:** 1-7 night minimum stay, cancellation fee imposed. **Activities:** exercise room. *Fee:* massage. **Guest Services:** valet laundry, area transportation-within 2 mi. **Free Special Amenities: early check-in/late check-out and high-speed Internet.**

FEE / SOME UNITS FEE

DENVER MARRIOTT CITY CENTER

Phone: (303)297-1300 11

Hotel

$109-$319

Marriott HOTELS & RESORTS

AAA Benefit: AAA hotel discounts of 5% or more.

Address: 1701 California St 80202 **Location:** Between 17th and 18th sts. **Facility:** The hotel is one block from the outdoor 16th Street Mall. The well-appointed rooms are on the smaller size but have luxurious bedding, reading lights on the headboards and comfortable seating. 613 units. 20 stories, interior corridors. **Parking:** on-site (fee) and valet. **Terms:** check-in 4 pm. **Amenities:** high-speed Internet (fee), safes. **Pool(s):** heated indoor. **Activities:** sauna, whirlpool, steamroom. **Guest Services:** valet and coin laundry.

SAVE ECO BIZ FEE / SOME UNITS

EMBASSY SUITES DENVER-DOWNTOWN/CONVENTION CENTER

Phone: (303)592-1000 15

Hotel

$142-$389 5/1-10/31
$123-$389 11/1-4/30

AAA Benefit: Members save 5% or more everyday!

Address: 1420 Stout St 80202 **Location:** I-25 exit 212B (Speer Blvd) southbound; exit 212A (Speer Blvd S) northbound, s to Lawrence St, ne to 14th St, just se to Stout St, then just ne. **Facility:** 403 units. 17 stories, interior corridors. **Parking:** valet only. **Terms:** 1-7 night minimum stay, cancellation fee imposed. **Amenities:** high-speed Internet (fee), safes. **Pool(s):** heated indoor. **Activities:** exercise room. *Fee:* massage. **Guest Services:** valet and coin laundry. **Free Special Amenities: early check-in/late check-out and use of on-premises laundry facilities.** *(See ad p. 150.)*

(See map & index p. 137.)

FOUR SEASONS HOTEL DENVER

Phone: (303)389-3000 10

Hotel
$245-$4000

Address: 1111 14th St 80202 **Location:** Between Lawrence and Arapahoe sts. **Facility:** Caramel-colored marble, large windows and modern décor are the hallmarks of this new hotel with a full-service spa. Rooms feature bedding with thick sheets, pillow-top mattresses and down duvets. 239 units, some two bedrooms. 45 stories, interior corridors. **Parking:** valet only. **Terms:** cancellation fee imposed. **Amenities:** safes, honor bars. *Fee:* video games, high-speed Internet. **Dining:** Edge Restaurant & Bar, see separate listing. **Pool(s):** heated outdoor. **Activities:** whirlpools, steamrooms, spa. **Guest Services:** valet laundry, area transportation-within 4 mi.

BIZ FEE / SOME UNITS

GRAND HYATT DENVER **Phone:** (303)295-1234 12

Hotel
$99-$399

HYATT HOTELS & RESORTS

AAA Benefit:
Members save 10% or more everyday.

Address: 1750 Welton St 80202 **Location:** Between 17th and 18th sts. **Facility:** Three blocks from the convention center, the large, downtown hotel features guest rooms with marble-topped furnishings, leather chairs and iHomes. 516 units. 26 stories, interior corridors. **Parking:** on-site (fee) and valet. **Terms:** cancellation fee imposed. **Amenities:** safes. *Fee:* video games, high-speed Internet. **Dining:** 2 restaurants, entertainment. **Pool(s):** heated indoor. **Activities:** whirlpool, exercise room. *Fee:* massage. **Guest Services:** valet laundry. **Free Special Amenities: newspaper and early check-in/late check-out.**

SAVE ECO CALL BIZ FEE / SOME UNITS FEE

Safety tip: Keep a current AAA/CAA Road Atlas in every vehicle

HAMPTON INN & SUITES DOWNTOWN DENVER

Phone: (303)864-8000 14

Hotel
$99-$239

AAA Benefit:
Members save up to 10% everyday!

Address: 1845 Sherman St 80203 **Location:** Between 18th and 19th aves. **Facility:** 148 units. 6 stories, interior corridors. **Parking:** valet only. **Terms:** 1-7 night minimum stay, cancellation fee imposed. **Amenities:** video games (fee), high-speed Internet. **Pool(s):** heated indoor. **Activities:** whirlpool, exercise room. **Guest Services:** valet and coin laundry.

BIZ FEE

HILTON GARDEN INN DENVER DOWNTOWN

Phone: (303)603-8000 20

Hotel
$95-$366

AAA Benefit:
Unparalleled hospitality at a special Member rate.

Address: 1400 Welton St 80202 **Location:** Corner of 14th St. **Facility:** 221 units. 12 stories, interior corridors. **Parking:** valet only. **Terms:** 1-7 night minimum stay, cancellation fee imposed. **Amenities:** video games (fee), high-speed Internet. **Dining:** 2 restaurants. **Pool(s):** heated indoor. **Activities:** whirlpool, exercise room. **Guest Services:** valet and coin laundry.

BIZ FEE

HOTEL MONACO DENVER **Phone:** (303)296-1717 5

Boutique Hotel
$159-$399

Address: 1717 Champa St 80202 **Location:** Between 17th and 18th sts. **Facility:** Whimsical, colorful decor marks this hotel, which offers chair massages during the nightly wine hour and a pet goldfish in the room by request. 189 units. 7 stories, interior corridors. **Parking:** valet only. **Terms:** cancellation fee imposed. **Amenities:** video games (fee), high-speed Internet, safes, honor bars. **Dining:** Panzano, see separate listing. **Activities:** exercise room, spa. **Guest Services:** valet laundry. **Free Special Amenities: high-speed Internet and manager's reception.**

SAVE ECO CALL BIZ FEE / SOME UNITS

▼ See AAA listing p. 149 ▼

(See map & index p. 137.)

HOTEL TEATRO **Phone:** (303)228-1100 9

Historic Boutique Hotel

$159-$1500

Address: 1100 14th St 80202 **Location:** Between Lawrence and Arapahoe sts. **Facility:** Near the theater, elegant rooms at the small boutique hotel have clean lines and original Asian artwork as well as printer/copiers and three phones. 110 units. 9 stories, interior corridors. **Parking:** valet only. **Terms:** cancellation fee imposed. **Amenities:** high-speed Internet, honor bars. **Dining:** Prima Ristorante, Restaurant Kevin Taylor, see separate listings. **Activities:** exercise room. *Fee:* massage. **Guest Services:** valet laundry, area transportation-within 5 mi. **Free Special Amenities: newspaper and high-speed Internet.**

(See ad this page.)

SAVE FEE BIZ FEE

/ SOME UNITS

HYATT REGENCY DENVER AT COLORADO CONVENTION CENTER **Phone:** (303)436-1234 18

Hotel

$79-$409

HYATT HOTELS & RESORTS

AAA Benefit: Members save 10% or more everyday.

Address: 650 15th St 80202 **Location:** Between California and Welton sts. **Facility:** An easy walk from the 16th Street Pedestrian Mall, guest rooms feature an urban, contemporary decor with artwork by talented Colorado artists. 1100 units. 37 stories, interior corridors. **Parking:** on-site (fee) and valet. **Terms:** cancellation fee imposed. **Amenities:** high-speed Internet (fee), safes. **Dining:** 2 restaurants. **Pool(s):** heated indoor. **Activities:** sauna, whirlpool, exercise room, spa. **Guest Services:** valet laundry. **Free Special Amenities: newspaper.**

SAVE ECO CALL BIZ

FEE / SOME UNITS

MAGNOLIA HOTEL-DOWNTOWN DENVER
Phone: 303/607-9000 8

Hotel

Rates not provided

Address: 818 17th St 80202 **Location:** Jct Stout St. **Facility:** 246 units, some kitchens. 12 stories, interior corridors. **Parking:** valet only. **Amenities:** video games (fee), high-speed Internet, safes. **Activities:** steamrooms, exercise room. *Fee:* massage. **Guest Services:** valet and coin laundry. **Free Special Amenities: full breakfast and high-speed Internet.**

SAVE CALL BIZ FEE

/ SOME UNITS

THE OXFORD HOTEL **Phone:** (303)628-5400 1

Historic Hotel

$180-$380

Address: 1600 17th St 80202 **Location:** Corner of 17th and Wazee sts. **Facility:** Antiques and original artwork decorate this restored 1891 hotel, which is near the train station, restaurants, boutiques and event venues in LoDo. The Cruise Room bar has Art Deco décor. 80 units. 5 stories, interior corridors. **Parking:** on-site (fee) and valet. **Terms:** cancellation fee imposed. **Amenities:** high-speed Internet, honor bars. **Dining:** 2 restaurants, also, McCormick's Fish House & Bar, see separate listing. **Activities:** steamrooms, spa. **Guest Services:** valet laundry, area transportation-within 2 mi.

BIZ

/ SOME UNITS

QUEEN ANNE URBAN BED & BREAKFAST
Phone: 303/296-6666 6

Historic Bed & Breakfast

Rates not provided

Address: 2147-51 Tremont Pl 80205 **Location:** Jct Broadway and Colfax Ave, just e to Logan St, 0.5 mi n to 20th Ave, just w, then just ne. Opposite Benedict Fountain Park. **Facility:** Within walking distance of downtown, this B&B is in a residential area of the Clements Historic District. Some rooms have jetted tubs. The rooftop unit has a private deck with a whirlpool and view. 14 units. 2-3 stories (no elevator), interior corridors. **Terms:** office hours 7 am-10 pm. **Activities:** bicycles. **Guest Services:** valet laundry.

FEE / SOME UNITS

▼ *See AAA listing this page* ▼

(See map & index p. 137.)

RESIDENCE INN BY MARRIOTT DENVER CITY CENTER

Phone: (303)296-3444 4

Extended Stay Hotel

$107-$319

AAA Benefit: AAA hotel discounts of 5% or more.

Address: 1725 Champa St 80202 **Location:** Between 17th and 18th sts. **Facility:** 228 units, some two bedrooms, efficiencies and kitchens. 14 stories, interior corridors. **Parking:** on-site (fee). **Terms:** check-in 4 pm. **Amenities:** high-speed Internet. **Activities:** whirlpool, exercise room. **Guest Services:** valet and coin laundry. **Free Special Amenities: full breakfast and high-speed Internet.**

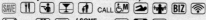

SAVE BIZ / SOME UNITS FEE

THE RITZ-CARLTON, DENVER

Phone: 303/312-3800 2

Hotel

Rates not provided

AAA Benefit: Unequaled service at Special Member Savings.

Address: 1881 Curtis St 80202 **Location:** Between 18th and 19th sts. **Facility:** Luxurious rooms feature hardwood floors in the foyer, bathrooms enhanced with marble, and many amenities including single-serve espresso machines. 202 units. 14 stories, interior corridors. **Parking:** valet and street only. **Amenities:** safes, honor bars. *Fee:* video games, high-speed Internet. **Dining:** Elway's Downtown, see separate listing. **Pool(s):** heated indoor. **Activities:** saunas, whirlpool, steamrooms, basketball, spa. **Guest Services:** valet laundry, area transportation-within 5 mi. **Free Special Amenities: newspaper and preferred room (subject to availability with advance reservations).**

SAVE CALL BIZ

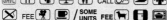

FEE / SOME UNITS FEE

SHERATON DENVER DOWNTOWN HOTEL

Phone: (303)893-3333 22

Hotel

$119-$369 1/1-4/30
$119-$359 5/1-12/31

AAA Benefit: Members get up to 15% off, plus Starwood Preferred Guest® bonuses.

Address: 1550 Court Pl 80202 **Location:** Located near 16th Street Pedestrian Mall. **Facility:** 1231 units. 8-22 stories, interior corridors. **Parking:** on-site (fee) and valet. **Terms:** cancellation fee imposed. **Amenities:** high-speed Internet (fee), safes. **Dining:** 3 restaurants. **Pool(s):** heated outdoor. **Guest Services:** valet laundry. **Free Special Amenities: newspaper.**

SAVE CALL BIZ

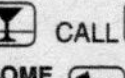
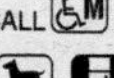

FEE / SOME UNITS FEE

WARWICK DENVER HOTEL

Phone: (303)861-2000 16

Hotel

$129-$499 5/1-10/31
$109-$499 11/1-4/30

Address: 1776 Grant St 80203 **Location:** Between 17th and 18th aves. **Facility:** 219 units. 15 stories, interior corridors. **Parking:** valet only. **Terms:** cancellation fee imposed. **Amenities:** video games (fee), safes, honor bars. *Some:* high-speed Internet (fee). **Pool(s):** heated outdoor. **Activities:** exercise room. **Guest Services:** valet laundry, area transportation-within 2 mi. **Free Special Amenities: preferred room (subject to availability with advance reservations) and local transportation.**

(See ad p. 153.)

SAVE BIZ FEE

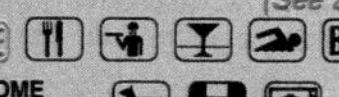

/ SOME UNITS FEE

(See map & index p. 137.)

▼ See AAA listing p. 152 ▼

(See map & index p. 137.)

THE WESTIN DENVER DOWNTOWN
Phone: (303)572-9100 3

Hotel
$169-$369

WESTIN HOTELS & RESORTS **AAA Benefit:** Enjoy up to 15% off your next stay, plus Starwood Preferred Guest® bonuses.

Address: 1672 Lawrence St 80202 **Location:** Between 16th and 17th sts. **Facility:** Find luxurious public areas and city- and mountain-view rooms at this downtown hotel that has made many efforts to reduce its environmental impact. A seasonal poolside bar is open on the weekends. 430 units. 19 stories, interior corridors. **Parking:** on-site (fee) and valet. **Terms:** cancellation fee imposed. **Amenities:** high-speed Internet (fee), safes, honor bars. **Dining:** The Palm Restaurant, see separate listing. **Pool(s):** heated indoor/outdoor. **Activities:** whirlpool, basketball. *Fee:* massage. **Guest Services:** valet laundry. **Free Special Amenities: newspaper.**

SAVE CALL BIZ FEE / SOME UNITS

WHERE TO EAT

1515 RESTAURANT
Menu on AAA.com
Phone: 303/571-0011 13

American
$8-$29

AAA Inspector Notes: I have mixed feelings about the restaurant. Exposed brick walls, historic photos, fresh flowers and light wood wine storage lend a classy, casual atmosphere. The meal started on a bad note with an oddly flavored amuse. The scallops were artfully placed on chopped vegetables. The steak had a nice flavor but an unusual cut, which took too much effort to slice gracefully. I fared better with the escolar; the pea sauce complemented the meaty white fish, and the gnocchi had a light truffle flavor. **Bar:** full bar. **Reservations:** suggested. **Address:** 1515 Market St 80202 **Location:** Just ne of jct 15th and Market sts. L D

BIKER JIM'S DOGS **Phone:** 720/746-9355 3

Hot Dogs
$6-$9

AAA Inspector Notes: The lowly hot dog often is a punchline for jokes about bad food. Luckily, this city has Biker Jim, a man with a mission to elevate street food to gourmet cuisine. I had heard about Jim's street cart but had difficulty tracking it down. Once I found it, I tried the Southwest buffalo dog. It was spicy, meaty and topped with cream cheese and caramelized onions. The homemade ice cream sandwich had a chocolaty, real cookie base and was filled with cinnamon ice cream. Both were delicious. **Bar:** full bar. **Address:** 2148 Larimer St 80205 **Location:** Between 21st and 22nd sts. **Parking:** street only. L D

BISTRO VENDOME **Phone:** 303/825-3232 23

French
$16-$24

AAA Inspector Notes: Bistro Vendome evokes the air of a family-owned Parisian eatery. Skilled staffers knowledgeably explain the French wine choices, which you can appreciate with varied courses of hearty French food. On Sunday, the brunch has an ardent following. Brunch also is offered on Saturday. **Bar:** full bar. **Reservations:** suggested. **Address:** 1420 Larimer St 80202 **Location:** Between 14th and 15th sts. **Parking:** valet and street only. D

CAFE COLORE **Phone:** 303/534-6844 17

Italian
$9-$19

AAA Inspector Notes: The menu centers on wonderful pizza, calzones, panini, salads and pasta; the expanded dinner selection also includes veal and chicken dishes. Patrons can choose among the local draft beers and peruse an ample wine list. The popular patio gives the restaurant, which is located in the Larimer Square outdoor retail area near LoDo (lower downtown), a bit of bistro feel. **Bar:** full bar. **Address:** 1512 Larimer St 80202 **Location:** Corner of 15th and Larimer sts. **Parking:** on-site (fee). L D

THE CAPITAL GRILLE **Phone:** 303/539-2500 18

Steak
$16-$47

AAA Inspector Notes: This is one of the most popular steakhouses in the city. It's a bit spendy but certainly worth a special night on the town. The hot cherry peppers didn't do much for the pan-fried calamari, but they were decent none the less. The tenderloin was tender, juicy and perfectly flavored and well-complemented by butter-poached lobster. The chocolate hazelnut cake was moist and rich. The masculine décor, filled with dark woods, oil paintings and tasteful taxidermy, creates an inviting ambience. **Bar:** full bar. **Address:** 1450 Larimer St 80202 **Location:** Between 14th and 15th sts. **Parking:** valet and street only. L D

CHOLON MODERN ASIAN BISTRO
Phone: 303/353-5223 46

Asian
$10-$30

AAA Inspector Notes: Chef and co-owner, Lon Symensma, traveled to France, Spain, and Asia in order to hone his culinary skills. Luckily for us, he settled in Denver. The exciting menu features fusion at its best. The standout dish for the evening was actually a "small bite", the soup dumplings with sweet onions and Gruyère. Basically, this is the best French onion soup I've ever had. The soup is carefully packaged in dough and steamed in a bamboo basket- a traditional Chinese technique, but with European ingredients. **Bar:** full bar. **Reservations:** suggested. **Address:** 1555 Blake St, Suite 101 80202 **Location:** Between 15th and 16th sts. **Parking:** street only.

L D

CHOPHOUSE & BREWERY **Phone:** 303/296-0800

Steak
$11-$35

AAA Inspector Notes: In a 1923 train depot adjacent to Coors Field, ChopHouse & Brewery carries out a railroad theme in its dining room. When the casually upscale LoDo hot spot is busy, which is often, the restaurant can get noisy. Watch the activity in the open kitchen as the chefs whip up contemporary dishes, including flavorful tenderloin tips with mushrooms, in addition to various cuts of beef, lamb and pork, and wood-oven pizzas, chicken and salads. Beers brewed on site provide just the right refreshment. **Bar:** full bar. **Reservations:** suggested. **Address:** 1735 19th St, Suite 100 80202 **Location:** I-25 exit 212C (20th St), at Wynkoop St. **Parking:** valet only.

L D

CITY O' CITY **Phone:** 303/831-6443 44

Pizza
$8-$11

AAA Inspector Notes: This restaurant is known for its vegetarian pizzas and vegan baked goods, although the menu includes an eclectic range of vegetarian starters, salads and sandwiches, too. The vegan desserts feature crumbly scones and rich chocolate cupcakes, a must for anyone with a sweet tooth. This cafe is a popular hangout for those seeking a dark, hipster coffeehouse during the day. At night, it livens up for late-night drinks. The service is on the slow side. The restroom has excessive graffiti. **Bar:** full bar. **Address:** 206 E 13th Ave 80203 **Location:** Just e of jct Lincoln Ave. **Parking:** street only. B L D LATE

(See map & index p. 137.)

THE DELECTABLE EGG **Phone:** 303/892-5720 (38)

Breakfast
$6-$9

AAA Inspector Notes: In a busy area and with a devoted core of regular patrons, the restaurant is great for a good breakfast. Diners can munch on oversized portions of freshly made Belgian waffles and light, fluffy pancakes smothered in butter. Service is friendly. **Address:** 1625 Court Pl 80202 **Location:** I-25 exit 210A (Colfax Ave), 1.4 mi e, then just ne; just ne of 16th Street Pedestrian Mall. **Parking:** street only. B L

DOMO **Phone:** 303/595-3666 (41)

Japanese
$7-$23

AAA Inspector Notes: The restaurant has the appearance of a traditional Japanese country house complete with padded log stools, stone tables, and tree branch and paper lanterns. Chef/owner Gaku Homma takes authenticity seriously, and guests will not be served additional soy sauce, salt or pepper so they will experience the cuisine as the chef intends it. The menu consists of wanko sushi, nabemono soups, teriyaki, noodle dishes and donburi bowls. A garden and museum are in the back of the restaurant. **Bar:** full bar. **Address:** 1365 Osage St 80204 **Location:** I-25 exit 210A (Colfax Ave), just e, then just s. L D

EDGE RESTAURANT & BAR
Phone: 303/389-3343 (31)

Steak
$12-$42

AAA Inspector Notes: A truly great steakhouse must have high-quality, flavorful, tender beef. That's a given. Edge, however, excels in so many other areas. The crab cake came with a citrus and fennel salad that added a nice tangy flavor to the dish. The spicy rocket greens made the sweet gold and red beet salad pleasurably complex. Dessert was another highlight. The creamy, rich pot de crème with chocolate streusel tasted divine. Staff members were refined and knowledgeable. There were some delays in service. **Bar:** full bar. **Reservations:** suggested. **Address:** 1111 14th St 80202 **Location:** Between Lawrence and Arapahoe sts; in Four Seasons Hotel Denver. **Parking:** valet only.
B L D

ELLYNGTON'S AT THE BROWN PALACE
Phone: 303/297-3111 (37)

American
$11-$26

AAA Inspector Notes: The city's business elite dine here for breakfast and lunch, so guests can expect a lot of suits. Sumptuous breakfasts and lunches with salads, sandwiches, steaks, seafood and pasta are served in elegant surroundings. This place is known for its Dom Perignon Sunday brunch. **Bar:** full bar. **Reservations:** suggested. **Address:** 321 17th St 80202 **Location:** From Broadway and Tremont Pl, just sw; in Brown Palace Hotel and Spa. **Parking:** valet only. B L

ELWAY'S DOWNTOWN **Phone:** 303/312-3107 (14)

Steak
$9-$54

AAA Inspector Notes: Named after former Broncos quarterback John Elway, one of the owners, this restaurant takes the concept of a standard Colorado steakhouse and adds sophisticated decor, refined staff and high-quality ingredients. The menu consists of innovative appetizers, such as lamb chop fondue, and top-quality steaks and seafood. **Bar:** full bar. **Reservations:** suggested. **Address:** 1881 Curtis St 80202 **Location:** Between 18th and 19th sts; in The Ritz-Carlton, Denver. **Parking:** valet only.
B L D

EUCLID HALL BAR & KITCHEN
Phone: 303/595-4255 (22)

American
$9-$17

AAA Inspector Notes: In addition to innovative, quality pub food like hand-cranked sausage, schnitzel, poutine and po' boys, diners will also find an extensive beer and wine list and hand-crafted cocktails. **Bar:** full bar. **Address:** 1317 14th St 80202 **Location:** Jct 14th and Larimer sts, just w; in Larimer Square. **Parking:** street only.
L D LATE

GREEN FINE SALAD CO. **Phone:** 303/629-9127 (40)

Natural/Organic
$7-$10

AAA Inspector Notes: Redefining fast food, this restaurant focuses on quality ingredients, quick service and attractive, modern decor. Patrons may choose from a variety of specialty salads or create their own. Soups, cookies and salads wrapped in a tortilla are also available. **Address:** 110 16th St 80202 **Location:** Jct Broadway; at beginning of 16th Street Pedestrian Mall. **Parking:** street only. L

GUMBO'S **Phone:** 720/956-1490 (11)

Creole
$11-$30

AAA Inspector Notes: A sophisticated contemporary atmosphere and flavorful Cajun food make this a local favorite. When the menu description reads spicy, it means it. Hits include crawfish etouffee and blackened shrimp and tenderloin. Dessert should not be missed. **Bar:** full bar. **Reservations:** suggested. **Address:** 1530 16th St, Suite 103 80202 **Location:** Between Blake and Wazee sts; on 16th Street Pedestrian Mall. **Parking:** street only. L D CALL M

HARD ROCK CAFE **Phone:** 303/623-3191 (34)

American
$9-$18

AAA Inspector Notes: Rock 'n' roll memorabilia decorates the walls of the popular theme restaurant. Live music on the weekends contributes to the bustling atmosphere. On the menu is a wide variety of American cuisine--from burgers and sandwiches to seafood, steaks and pasta. **Bar:** full bar. **Address:** 500 16th St, Suite 120 80202 **Location:** Jct Glenarm St; on 16th Street Pedestrian Mall. **Parking:** street only. SAVE L D

JAX FISH HOUSE **Phone:** 303/292-5767 (9)

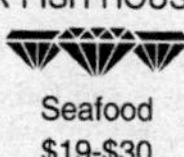

Seafood
$19-$30

AAA Inspector Notes: Popular local chef David Query adds this busy fish house to his successful roster of Boulder eateries, which includes Jax and Zolo Grill. The establishment flies in fresh fish daily. The decor, a collection of eclectic art, adds to the upbeat ambience. It can get noisy when the place is full. **Bar:** full bar. **Reservations:** suggested. **Address:** 1539 17th St 80202 **Location:** Corner of 17th and Wazee sts. **Parking:** valet and street only.
D

JONESY'S EATBAR **Phone:** 303/863-7473 (29)

American
$9-$19

AAA Inspector Notes: The restaurant is very popular, especially on weekends. The pub menu features the perfect wine list and a generous selection of craft beers. Plenty of wines by the glass as well as some low- and high-end bottle options are available. The gastro part of the menu features sliders, mac 'n' cheese and bison Stroganoff and, more unusually, falafel sliders, mussels and an udon noodle bowl. The décor resembles a hipster's closet, a little vintage, a little flea market, with a dash of irony. **Bar:** full bar. **Address:** 400 E 20th Ave 80205 **Location:** Jct Logan St. **Parking:** on-site (fee) and street. D

(See map & index p. 137.)

LIME CANTINA **Phone:** 303/893-5463 (25)

Mexican
$10-$15

AAA Inspector Notes: Down one flight in historic Larimer Square, the upscale eatery presents a menu of traditional appetizers as well as lime shrimp cocktail, tuna al carbon and margarita chicken. Lime is used in the award-winning margaritas, coleslaw and other dishes with vegetarian beans and chili. Beware: The scorpion plate bites back. The cantina gets loud after 8. **Bar:** full bar. **Address:** 1414 Larimer St 80204 **Location:** Between 14th and 15th sts. **Parking:** street only. [D]

THE MARKET **Phone:** 303/534-5140 (19)

Deli
$6-$10

AAA Inspector Notes: The Market draws a diverse crowd. Patrons stop in for a cup of coffee, a quick lunch or dinner from the deli, or a luscious dessert. **Address:** 1445 Larimer St 80202 **Location:** Between 14th and 15th sts. **Parking:** street only. [B] [L] [D]

MCCORMICK'S FISH HOUSE & BAR **Phone:** 303/825-1107 (10)

Regional Seafood
$9-$35

AAA Inspector Notes: The restaurant features a good variety of fresh seafood from both coasts and Victorian-style décor reflecting the building's past. I recommend the Dungeness crab tower, which had the perfect blend of flavors of avocado, mango and crab. Even though seafood is the main attraction, the filet mignon was tender and flavorful. For a before- or after-dinner drink, waltz over to the Art Deco Cruise Room, which is across the corridor but considered part of McCormick's. **Bar:** full bar. **Reservations:** suggested. **Address:** 1659 Wazee St 80202 **Location:** Corner of 17th and Wazee sts; in The Oxford Hotel. **Parking:** valet and street only. [B] [L] [D]

MORTON'S THE STEAKHOUSE **Phone:** 303/825-3353 (6)

American
$27-$58

AAA Inspector Notes: Patrons should make sure to reserve ahead for the popular, well-known steakhouse. Large portions, including huge cuts of fine beef and plentiful seafood, are the norm. Even the vegetables are oversized, with baked potatoes big enough for sharing. **Bar:** full bar. **Reservations:** suggested. **Address:** 1710 Wynkoop St 80202 **Location:** I-25 exit 212C (20th St W) to Blake St, w to 18th St, n to Wynkoop St, then just w; opposite Union Station. **Parking:** on-site (fee) and valet. [D] CALL &M

THE OCEANAIRE SEAFOOD ROOM **Phone:** 303/991-2277 (33)

Seafood
$20-$35

AAA Inspector Notes: Fresh fish and shellfish are flown in daily from around the globe. The sleek, handsomely designed dining room has a raw bar and is tastefully appointed in an Art Deco/nautical theme. The menu notes the seafood available daily and the varied preparation styles, such as broiled, grilled and blackened. **Bar:** full bar. **Reservations:** suggested. **Address:** 1400 Arapahoe St 80202 **Location:** I-25 exit 212C (20th St), 0.8 mi se, just sw on Larimer St, just se on 17th St, then just sw. [D]

OSTERIA MARCO **Phone:** 303/534-5855 (20)

Italian
$9-$24

AAA Inspector Notes: As a cheese lover, I couldn't resist trying the house-made mozzarella accompanied by the sopressata picante. Wow. It was possibly the best cheese-and-salumi combo I've ever tasted. If I had known, I would have just ordered a huge plate of it and skipped the entrée. I'm glad I didn't, though, because the beet salad and scallops were also delicious. You enter at street level, but the restaurant itself is below ground. The casual bistro-style décor is relaxing even when the staff is bustling. **Bar:** full bar. **Address:** 1453 Larimer St 80202 **Location:** Between 14th and 15th sts. **Parking:** street only. [L] [D]

PALACE ARMS **Phone:** 303/297-3111 (36)

Continental
$29-$42

AAA Inspector Notes: Located in the Brown Palace Hotel, the inspired innovations of chef Thanawat Bates make this fine dining experience exceptional. The menu changes seasonally. On my last visit I had the creamy artichoke soup. The crab cake was served with a rich, Thai-influenced sauce with a kick. The beet salad was visually stunning; the beets' sweetness was placated by watercress and olive. Watching the tableside preparation of the bananas Foster is almost as enjoyable as eating it. Jackets are preferred. **Bar:** full bar. **Reservations:** suggested. **Address:** 321 17th St 80202 **Location:** From Broadway and Tremont Pl, just sw; in Brown Palace Hotel and Spa. **Parking:** valet only. **Historic** [D]

PALETTES **Phone:** 303/534-1455 (42)

American
$10-$29

AAA Inspector Notes: The warm, contemporary décor fits well with this restaurant's location in the Denver Art Museum. Diners can gaze at the newest wing of the museum and the sculptures outside it. This artistic theme transcends the walls and appears on your plate. I had the arugula pear salad. The spiciness of the arugula paired well with the sweetness of the pear and the tartness of the fried goat cheese. The walnuts added a nice crunch. The scallops also had a nice flavor. The prix-fixe option is a great deal. **Bar:** full bar. **Address:** 100 W 14th Ave Pkwy 80204 **Location:** 1 blk w of Broadway; at south end of Civic Center; in Denver Art Museum. **Parking:** on-site (fee).

[L] CALL &M

THE PALM RESTAURANT **Phone:** 303/825-7256 (15)

Steak
$15-$70

AAA Inspector Notes: This bustling restaurant is noted for prime, dry-aged steaks and Nova Scotia lobsters, huge portions are delivered by an attentive staff in an atmosphere that is fun and lively. At the end of the meal, servers present tempting pastries tableside. Caricature-lined walls lend to the feeling that patrons are dining in an art gallery. Even if you bring a big appetite you still may leave with a doggy bag. **Bar:** full bar. **Address:** 1672 Lawrence St 80202 **Location:** Between 16th and 17th sts; in The Westin Denver Downtown. **Parking:** valet only. [L] [D] CALL &M

PANZANO **Phone:** 303/296-3525 (27)

Northern Italian
$10-$30

AAA Inspector Notes: Talented, innovative chef Elise Wiggins specializes in Northern Italian cuisine. Focusing on fresh, organic, local and naturally raised ingredients, every dish delights the senses. Her crespelle ai funghi (mushroom-stuffed crepes) whets the appetite for pasta, seasonal fish, Bear Mountain Ranch steak, sea scallops, veal and Colorado lamb entrees. The chocolate cheesecake gelato sandwich is practically divine. The bold décor provides an elegant atmosphere. The staff is knowledgeable and friendly. **Bar:** full bar. **Reservations:** suggested. **Address:** 909 17th St 80202 **Location:** Between 17th and 18th sts; in Hotel Monaco Denver. **Parking:** valet only. [B] [L] [D]

PINTS PUB **Phone:** 303/534-7543 (43)

British
$8-$9

AAA Inspector Notes: Contributing to the pub's good local reputation are 22 draft beers, 200 single-malt scotches and six beers made in the on-site brewery. The menu includes burgers, soup, salad, sandwiches, fish and chips, mashers and chicken choices. **Bar:** full bar. **Address:** 221 W 13th Ave 80204 **Location:** Between Bannock and Cherokee sts; just w of Denver Art Museum. [L] [D]

(See map & index p. 137.)

PRIMA RISTORANTE Phone: 303/228-0770 (30)

Italian
$10-$28

AAA Inspector Notes: The smart location caters to a pre- and post-theater crowd seeking good food and generous portions. Warm cherry-wood tones, industrial tabletops, yellow walls and gothic church lights give this bistro a refined yet casual feel. **Bar:** full bar. **Reservations:** suggested. **Address:** 1106 14th St 80202 **Location:** Between Lawrence and Arapahoe sts; in Hotel Teatro. **Parking:** valet only. L D

RED SQUARE EURO BISTRO Phone: 303/595-8600 (16)

Russian
$18-$29

AAA Inspector Notes: Located in Writer Square, this cozy cafe offers European cuisine with a Russian twist. Entrées include the signature Red Square Stroganoff, grilled N.Y. strip, grilled rack of lamb, seared duck and pan-seared halibut. In true Russian fashion, there are more than 50 different vodkas to sample. Patio dining is available when weather permits. **Bar:** full bar. **Reservations:** suggested. **Address:** 1512 Larimer St, Suite R38 80202 **Location:** Jct 15th and Larimer sts; just e of historic Larimer Square; in Writers Square. **Parking:** on-site (fee). D CALL M

RESTAURANT KEVIN TAYLOR Phone: 303/820-2600 (32)

Regional American
$30-$50

AAA Inspector Notes: The warm, luxurious decor encourages guests to settle in and enjoy an evening of imaginative cuisine. Although popular with the pre-theater crowd, this restaurant caters to anyone appreciative of fresh, flavorful dishes and attentive, amiable service. The menu changes seasonally but usually includes seafood, steaks and wild game. **Bar:** full bar. **Reservations:** suggested. **Address:** 1106 14th St 80202 **Location:** Between Lawrence and Arapahoe sts; in Hotel Teatro. **Parking:** valet only. D

RIALTO CAFE Phone: 303/893-2233 (28)

American
$9-$25

AAA Inspector Notes: Furnished in warm, urban-contemporary décor, the cafe serves flavorful cuisine in the heart of downtown. Steaks, buffalo, salmon and chicken dishes pepper the menu. **Bar:** full bar. **Address:** 934 16th St 80202 **Location:** I-25 Jct Curtis St; in Courtyard by Marriott Denver Downtown. **Parking:** street only. B L D

RIOJA Phone: 303/820-2282 (24)

American
$11-$29

AAA Inspector Notes: Chef Jennifer Jasinski and business partner/ sommelier Beth Gruitch opened Rioja in 2004 and have been receiving accolades ever since. The menu consists of handmade pastas, seafood, Colorado lamb, duck and steak entrées. My most recent visit was the best so far. The Palisade peach spinach salad, featuring lightly battered rosemary-seasoned onions and chanterelle mushrooms, had a nice balance of sweet and savory flavors. Each bite of Jasinki's handmade artichoke tortelloni was a pure delight. **Bar:** full bar. **Reservations:** suggested. **Address:** 1431 Larimer St 80202 **Location:** Between 14th and 15th sts; in historic Larimer Square. **Parking:** valet and street only. L D

RODIZIO GRILL Phone: 303/294-9277 (4)

Brazilian
$19-$33

AAA Inspector Notes: This Brazilian-style restaurant is fun, festive and a meat-eater's paradise. They feature up to 15 types of beef, turkey, pork, chicken, lamb and fish options. Meals are grilled in an open kitchen and removed from the skewer by a server dressed in gaucho attire. An extensive salad bar is included in the meal price. **Bar:** full bar. **Address:** 1801 Wynkoop St 80202 **Location:** Corner of 18th and Wynkoop sts. **Parking:** street only. L D

SHIP TAVERN Phone: 303/297-3111 (35)

American
$15-$38

AAA Inspector Notes: Cape Cod model ships and other nautical accents, as well as closely spaced tables, create a cozy, comfortable ambience. Prime rib is the signature dish. Among other favorite choices are fresh seafood, Kobe Beef burgers, Rocky Mountain trout and French onion soup. Longtime bartenders serve more than 30 microbrews. **Bar:** full bar. **Reservations:** suggested. **Address:** 321 17th St 80202 **Location:** From Broadway and Tremont Pl, just sw; in Brown Palace Hotel and Spa. **Parking:** valet only. L D

SNOOZE Phone: 303/297-0700 (2)

Breakfast
$10-$15

AAA Inspector Notes: Reminiscent of a '50s diner, the popular eatery sports mod decor that appeals to its diverse clientele. It takes only a bite to know why this place is special. Breakfast dishes include the savory and the sweet: Juan's breakfast tacos, steak and eggs Benedict, apple dandy pancakes and churros con chocolate pillow toast. Creative lunch offerings such as the sloppy Josephina, a Southwestern version of the famous comfort food, are also worth sampling. **Bar:** full bar. **Address:** 2262 Larimer St 80205 **Location:** From Market St, just se on 23th St, just sw; jct W Park Ave. **Parking:** street only. B L

STEUBEN'S Phone: 303/830-1001 (39)

American
$4-$16

AAA Inspector Notes: Locals head to this retro, casually upscale diner to indulge in comfort food, decadent desserts and interesting cocktails. Menu options reflect a creative flair enhanced by higher quality ingredients. Fried chicken, macaroni and cheese and barbecue beef brisket saddle up next to cayenne étouffée and trout almandine. Don't skip a milk shake, malt, brownie a la mode or other dessert. The tea-totaler, a nonalcoholic cocktail, combines Earl Grey syrup, mint, lemon and San Pellegrino Limonata. **Bar:** full bar. **Address:** 523 E 17th Ave 80203 **Location:** Corner of Pearl St and 17th Ave. L D

SULLIVAN'S STEAKHOUSE Phone: 303/295-2664 (7)

Steak
$25-$60

AAA Inspector Notes: Named for John L. Sullivan, heavyweight champion of the world in the 1880s, the upscale steak house prepares a wide selection of steaks, chops and seafood. Decorated with black-and-white photographs of Sullivan, Jack Dempsey and other boxing legends. **Bar:** full bar. **Reservations:** suggested. **Address:** 1745 Wazee St 80202 **Location:** Just sw of jct 18th and Wazee sts. **Parking:** valet only. D CALL M

TAG Phone: 303/996-9985 (21)

Fusion
$9-$29

AAA Inspector Notes: Owner and executive chef Troy Guard grew up in Hawaii grilling fish with his father, gained experience at the La Costa Resort in San Diego and later apprenticed under Roy Yamaguchi. Here, Guard blends local and Asian ingredients in dishes like Kobe beef sliders with duck fat fries, Szechwan Colorado rack of lamb, a Surf and Turf sushi roll (Kobe beef and lobster) and an ever-changing selection of fresh fish. The locals seem to love the specialty cocktails such as the jalapeño kumquat mojito. **Bar:** full bar. **Reservations:** suggested. **Address:** 1441 Larimer St 80202 **Location:** Between 14th and 15th sts; in historic Larimer Square. **Parking:** valet and street only. L D

(See map & index p. 137.)

TAMAYO MODERN MEXICAN CUISINE
Phone: 720/946-1433 (26)

Mexican
$9-$28

AAA Inspector Notes: The menu lists a distinctive selection of modern Mexican cuisine, including a great variety of well-prepared and presented specialty dishes. Casual comfort and extraordinary elegance is reflected not only in the food but also in the accomplished staff and the restaurant's chic warehouse setting. **Bar:** full bar. **Reservations:** suggested. **Address:** 1400 Larimer St 80202 **Location:** Corner of 14th and Larimer sts. **Parking:** street only. L D

VESTA DIPPING GRILL **Phone:** 303/296-1970 (8)

International
$11-$36

AAA Inspector Notes: Named after Vesta, the Roman goddess of the hearth, this popular LoDo restaurant exudes a warm, inviting atmosphere. Entrees consist of grilled meats such as beef, lamb, duck, chicken, fish and pork, as well as vegetarian options. Diners pick from numerous sweet, savory and spicy sauces to accompany their meal. **Bar:** full bar. **Reservations:** suggested. **Address:** 1822 Blake St 80202 **Location:** I-25 exit 212C (20th St), 0.7 mi w, then just se. **Parking:** street only. D

WATER COURSE FOODS **Phone:** 303/832-7313 (45)

Vegetarian
$9-$12

AAA Inspector Notes: Popular with omnivores and herbivores alike, the restaurant specializes in vegetarian and vegan cuisine. For an early-morning sugar rush, banana bread French toast is a must. Egg scrambles and breakfast burritos provide more savory options. At lunch and dinner, popular selections range from fresh soups, salads and sandwiches to pasta and Mexican dishes. The vegan baked goods rival anything Grandma whips up (but without the lard). **Bar:** wine only. **Address:** 837 E 17th Ave, Unit 103 80218 **Location:** Jct Broadway, 0.5 mi e. **Parking:** street only. B L D

WAZEE SUPPER CLUB **Phone:** 303/623-9518 (12)

Pizza
$6-$11

AAA Inspector Notes: Built in 1910, the building once housed a plumbing supply house. Reincarnated as a restaurant in 1974, this place now is one of LoDo's weekend hot spots. Locals and visitors descend on this cozy eatery for flavorful thin-crust pizzas and microbrews. The fried Buffalo shrimp basket is a popular lead-in to varied salads, burgers, strombolis and sandwiches. The eclectic décor is distinctive. **Bar:** full bar. **Address:** 1600 15th St 80202 **Location:** Corner of Wazee and 15th sts. **Parking:** street only. L D

WILLIE G'S **Phone:** 303/575-9000

Seafood
$8-$70

AAA Inspector Notes: This restaurant offers a wide selection of seafood and beef dishes. Specialties include bacon-wrapped scallops, trout almondine and dynamite mahi-mahi. The masculine interior, richly accented with dark wood, is reminiscent of the Victorian era. **Bar:** full bar. **Address:** 1585 Lawrence St 80202 **Location:** Corner of Lawrence St and 16th Street Pedestrian Mall. **Parking:** street only. L D

WYNKOOP BREWING COMPANY
Phone: 303/297-2700 (5)

American
$9-$21

AAA Inspector Notes: The casual, unpretentious and sometimes noisy pub features fresh-brewed, European-style ale. Hearty fare such as fish 'n' chips, Denver elk medallions and shepherd's pie is served in a turn-of-the-century building. Billiards can be played upstairs. **Bar:** full bar. **Address:** 1634 18th St 80202 **Location:** Jct Wynkoop St; opposite Union Station. **Parking:** street only. L D

ZENGO **Phone:** 720/904-0965 (1)

Fusion
$9-$28

AAA Inspector Notes: Chef/owner Richard Sandoval went in a new direction with this restaurant by blending Asian and Latin American cuisines, a combination that may sound unusual but is ultimately a bold success. Chef de cuisine Clint Wangsnes artfully fuses the flavors in delicious, delightful dishes such as Thai chicken empanadas, lobster pot stickers, tandoori chicken, Kobe beef churrasco and duck fried rice. The sleek, modern décor enhances the dining experience. **Bar:** full bar. **Reservations:** suggested. **Address:** 1610 Little Raven St 80202 **Location:** Just ne of jct 15th St. **Parking:** street only. D

DENVER

- **Restaurants p. 166**
- **Hotels & Restaurants map & index p. 140**

BEST WESTERN PLUS DENVER HOTEL
Phone: 303/388-6161 (23)

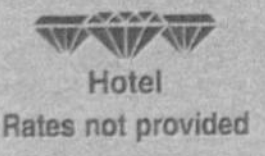

Hotel
Rates not provided

AAA Benefit: Members save up to 20%, plus 10% bonus points with Best Western Rewards®.

Address: 3737 Quebec St 80207 **Location:** I-70 exit 278, just s. **Facility:** 139 units. 4 stories, interior corridors. **Amenities:** safes (fee). *Some:* high-speed Internet. **Pool(s):** heated outdoor. **Activities:** exercise room. **Guest Services:** valet and coin laundry. **Free Special Amenities: full breakfast and high-speed Internet.**

(See ad p. 159.)

SAVE BIZ / SOME UNITS FEE

CAPITOL HILL MANSION BED & BREAKFAST INN
Phone: 303/839-5221 (32)

Historic Bed & Breakfast
$119-$219

Address: 1207 Pennsylvania St 80203 **Location:** Jct 12th Ave. Located in a residential area. **Facility:** Turrets and a balcony add architectural interest to the sandstone mansion in a historic residential neighborhood. Exceptionally well-kept rooms are individually decorated and feature private baths. 8 units, some kitchens. 3 stories (no elevator), interior/exterior corridors. **Terms:** office hours 8 am-10 pm, 14 day cancellation notice-fee imposed. **Guest Services:** valet laundry.

BIZ / SOME UNITS

CASTLE MARNE BED AND BREAKFAST
Phone: 303/331-0621 (30)

Historic Bed & Breakfast
$125-$285

Address: 1572 Race St 80206 **Location:** 1.3 mi e of jct Colfax Ave and Broadway, then just n. Located in Wyman Historic District. **Facility:** Period Victorian furnishings in excellent condition create an elegant, Old World ambience at the 1889 mansion; three rooms include a private hot tub. 9 units. 3 stories (no elevator), interior corridors. **Parking:** on-site and street. **Terms:** check-in 4 pm, age restrictions may apply, 3 day cancellation notice-fee imposed. **Guest Services:** area transportation.

BIZ

COMFORT INN CENTRAL **Phone:** (303)297-1717 (12)

Hotel
$84-$109

Address: 401 E 58th Ave 80216 **Location:** I-25 exit 215, just e, then n on Logan St; connected to Denver Merchandise Mart. **Facility:** 161 units. 9 stories, interior corridors. **Terms:** check-in 4 pm, cancellation fee imposed. **Pool(s):** heated outdoor. **Activities:** exercise room. **Guest Services:** valet and coin laundry. **Free Special Amenities: expanded continental breakfast and high-speed Internet.**

SAVE CALL / SOME UNITS FEE

(See map & index p. 140.)

COMFORT SUITES-DIA **Phone:** (303)371-9300 14

Hotel
$59-$199

Address: 6210 Tower Rd 80249 **Location:** I-70 exit 286 (Tower Rd), 3.4 mi n. **Facility:** 83 units. 3 stories, interior corridors. **Terms:** cancellation fee imposed. **Activities:** whirlpool, exercise room. **Guest Services:** valet and coin laundry. **Free Special Amenities: full breakfast and early check-in/late check-out.**

  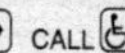 CALL    

COURTYARD BY MARRIOTT DENVER STAPLETON
Phone: (303)333-3303 16

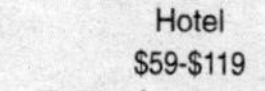

Hotel
$59-$119

AAA Benefit: AAA hotel discounts of 5% or more.

Address: 7415 E 41st Ave 80216 **Location:** I-70 exit 278, s on Quebec St, exit Smith Rd, then e to Frontage Rd; I-270 exit 4. **Facility:** 146 units. 3 stories, interior corridors. **Amenities:** high-speed Internet. **Pool(s):** heated indoor. **Activities:** whirlpool, exercise room. **Guest Services:** valet and coin laundry.

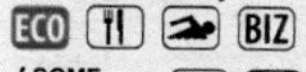

/ SOME UNITS FEE

COUNTRY INN & SUITES BY CARLSON, DENVER INTERNATIONAL AIRPORT **Phone:** (303)375-1105 24

Hotel
$89-$169

Address: 4343 N Airport Way 80239 **Location:** I-70 exit 283 (Chambers Rd), just n to 40th Ave, 0.5 mi e, then just n. **Facility:** 193 units. 6 stories, interior corridors. **Terms:** 7 day cancellation notice. **Amenities:** high-speed Internet. **Pool(s):** heated indoor. **Activities:** whirlpool, exercise room. **Guest Services:** valet and coin laundry. **Free Special Amenities: full breakfast and room upgrade (subject to availability with advance reservations).**

  CALL  FEE

CROWNE PLAZA DENVER INTERNATIONAL AIRPORT
Phone: (303)371-9494 26

Hotel
$89-$199

Address: 15500 E 40th Ave 80239 **Location:** I-70 exit 283 (Chambers Rd), just n, then just e. **Facility:** 255 units. 6 stories, interior corridors. **Terms:** check-in 4 pm. **Pool(s):** heated indoor. **Activities:** whirlpool, exercise room. **Guest Services:** valet laundry. **Free Special Amenities: high-speed Internet and airport transportation.**

 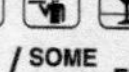 CALL 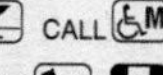 

FEE / SOME UNITS FEE

COURTYARD BY MARRIOTT AT DIA
Phone: (303)371-0300 7

Hotel
$89-$149

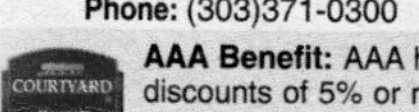

AAA Benefit: AAA hotel discounts of 5% or more.

Address: 6901 Tower Rd 80249 **Location:** I-70 exit 286 (Tower Rd), 4.3 mi n; 0.8 mi s of Pena Blvd. **Facility:** 202 units. 8 stories, interior corridors. **Amenities:** *Some:* high-speed Internet. **Pool(s):** heated indoor. **Activities:** whirlpool, exercise room. **Guest Services:** valet and coin laundry. **Free Special Amenities: local telephone calls and high-speed Internet.**

    CALL  

FEE / SOME UNITS

DENVER MARRIOTT TECH CENTER
Phone: (303)779-1100 43

Hotel
$79-$149

AAA Benefit: AAA hotel discounts of 5% or more.

Address: 4900 S Syracuse St 80237 **Location:** I-25 exit 199, exit Belleview Ave E to Syracuse St, then just n. **Facility:** 628 units. 5-11 stories, interior corridors. **Parking:** on-site (fee) and valet. **Amenities:** high-speed Internet (fee). **Pool(s):** heated outdoor, heated indoor. **Activities:** whirlpool, exercise room. **Guest Services:** valet and coin laundry, area transportation-within 5 mi.

CALL FEE

/ SOME UNITS

▼ *See AAA listing p. 158* ▼

▼ See AAA listing p. 56 ▼

(See map & index p. 140.)

DOUBLETREE BY HILTON HOTEL DENVER
Phone: (303)321-3333 29

Hotel
$79-$224

AAA Benefit: Members save 5% or more everyday!

Address: 3203 Quebec St 80207 **Location:** I-70 exit 278, 0.5 mi s; I-270 exit 4. **Facility:** 561 units. 9 stories, interior corridors. **Terms:** 1-7 night minimum stay, cancellation fee imposed. **Amenities:** video games (fee), high-speed Internet. **Pool(s):** heated indoor. **Activities:** saunas, whirlpool, exercise room. **Guest Services:** valet and coin laundry, area transportation-Northfield Shopping Center.

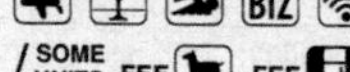

FEE / SOME UNITS FEE FEE

DRURY INN-DENVER EAST
Phone: (303)373-1983 20

Hotel
$85-$139

Address: 4380 Peoria St 80239 **Location:** I-70 exit 281 eastbound; exit 282 westbound, just n. **Facility:** 137 units. 4 stories, interior corridors. **Terms:** cancellation fee imposed. **Amenities:** high-speed Internet. **Pool(s):** heated indoor/outdoor. **Activities:** whirlpool, exercise room. **Guest Services:** valet and coin laundry.

/ SOME UNITS

EMBASSY SUITES DENVER-AURORA
Phone: (303)375-0400 15

Hotel
$109-$249

AAA Benefit: Members save 5% or more everyday!

Address: 4444 N Havana St 80239 **Location:** I-70 exit 280, just n. **Facility:** 210 units. 7 stories, interior corridors. **Terms:** 1-7 night minimum stay, cancellation fee imposed. **Amenities:** video games (fee). **Pool(s):** heated indoor. **Activities:** sauna, whirlpool, exercise room. **Guest Services:** valet and coin laundry, area transportation-within 5 mi.

   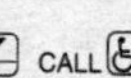  

SAVE CALL

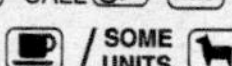

FEE / SOME UNITS

EMBASSY SUITES DENVER INTERNATIONAL AIRPORT
Phone: (303)574-3000 2

Hotel
$119-$229

AAA Benefit: Members save 5% or more everyday!

Address: 7001 Yampa St 80249 **Location:** I-70 exit 286 (Tower Rd), 4.5 mi n, then just w on 71st Ave; 0.8 mi s of Pena Blvd. **Facility:** 174 units. 7 stories, interior corridors. **Terms:** 1-7 night minimum stay, cancellation fee imposed. **Amenities:** *Some:* high-speed Internet. **Pool(s):** heated indoor. **Activities:** whirlpool, exercise room. **Guest Services:** complimentary and valet laundry. **Free Special Amenities: full breakfast and manager's reception.** *(See ad this page.)*

SAVE CALL FEE

EMBASSY SUITES DENVER SOUTHEAST
Phone: (303)696-6644 40

Hotel
$119-$139

AAA Benefit: Members save 5% or more everyday!

Address: 7525 E Hampden Ave 80231 **Location:** I-25 exit 201, 1 mi e. **Facility:** 205 units. 7 stories, interior corridors. **Terms:** 1-7 night minimum stay, cancellation fee imposed. **Amenities:** video games (fee). **Pool(s):** heated indoor. **Activities:** whirlpool, exercise room. **Guest Services:** valet and coin laundry, area transportation-within 5 mi.

FEE / SOME UNITS FEE

Check out our travel blog at AAATravelViews.com

(See map & index p. 140.)

FAIRFIELD INN & SUITES DENVER/CHERRY CREEK
Phone: (303)691-2223 38

Hotel
$69-$219

AAA Benefit:
AAA hotel discounts of 5% or more.

Address: 1680 S Colorado Blvd 80222 **Location:** I-25 exit 204, just n, then just e on Mexico Ave. **Facility:** 134 units. 10 stories, interior corridors. **Amenities:** *Some:* high-speed Internet. **Pool(s):** heated indoor. **Activities:** exercise room. **Guest Services:** valet and coin laundry.

CALL BIZ FEE
/ SOME UNITS

FAIRFIELD INN-DIA **Phone:** (303)576-9640 8

Hotel
$169-$184

AAA Benefit:
AAA hotel discounts of 5% or more.

Address: 6851 Tower Rd 80249 **Location:** I-70 exit 286 (Tower Rd), 4.3 mi n; 0.8 mi s of Pena Blvd. **Facility:** 161 units. 3 stories, interior corridors. **Pool(s):** heated indoor. **Activities:** whirlpool, exercise room. **Guest Services:** valet laundry.

CALL BIZ
/ SOME UNITS

HAMPTON INN & SUITES DENVER TECH CENTER
Phone: (303)804-9900 44

Hotel
$69-$159

AAA Benefit:
Members save up to 10% everyday!

Address: 5001 S Ulster St 80237 **Location:** I-25 exit 199, e to Ulster St, then just n. **Facility:** 123 units, some efficiencies and kitchens. 3 stories, interior corridors. **Terms:** 1-7 night minimum stay, cancellation fee imposed. **Amenities:** video games (fee), high-speed Internet. **Pool(s):** heated outdoor. **Activities:** whirlpool, exercise room. **Guest Services:** valet and coin laundry, area transportation-within 3 mi.

CALL BIZ FEE
/ SOME UNITS

HAMPTON INN DIA **Phone:** (303)371-0200 13

Hotel
$115-$135

AAA Benefit:
Members save up to 10% everyday!

Address: 6290 Tower Rd 80249 **Location:** I-70 exit 286 (Tower Rd), 3.5 mi n. **Facility:** 122 units. 5 stories, interior corridors. **Terms:** 1-7 night minimum stay, cancellation fee imposed. **Amenities:** video games (fee). **Pool(s):** heated indoor. **Activities:** exercise room. **Guest Services:** valet laundry.

CALL BIZ FEE
/ SOME UNITS FEE

HOLIDAY CHALET A VICTORIAN BED & BREAKFAST
Phone: (303)437-8245 31

Historic Bed & Breakfast
$94-$160

Address: 1820 E Colfax Ave 80218 **Location:** Between Williams and High sts. Located on a busy street in Wyman Historic District. **Facility:** Built in 1896, this restored brownstone mansion is furnished with antiques formerly owned by prominent Denver families. 10 units, some kitchens. 3 stories (no elevator), interior corridors. **Parking:** street only. **Terms:** office hours 8 am-10 pm, cancellation fee imposed. **Guest Services:** valet laundry.

SAVE / SOME UNITS FEE

HOLIDAY INN & SUITES **Phone:** 303/574-1300 6

Hotel
Rates not provided

Address: 6900 Tower Rd 80249 **Location:** I-70 exit 286 (Tower Rd), 4.3 mi n. **Facility:** 161 units, some efficiencies. 6 stories, interior corridors. **Amenities:** safes. *Some:* high-speed Internet. **Pool(s):** heated indoor. **Activities:** whirlpools, exercise room. **Guest Services:** valet and coin laundry.

BIZ FEE
/ SOME UNITS

HOLIDAY INN DENVER EAST - STAPLETON
Phone: 303/321-3500 28

Hotel
Rates not provided

Address: 3333 Quebec St 80207 **Location:** I-70 exit 278, 0.3 mi s; I-270 exit 4. **Facility:** 300 units. 11 stories, interior corridors. **Amenities:** video games (fee). **Pool(s):** heated outdoor. **Activities:** whirlpool, exercise room. *Fee:* massage. **Guest Services:** valet and coin laundry.

CALL BIZ FEE
/ SOME UNITS FEE

HOLIDAY INN EXPRESS & SUITES
Phone: (303)373-4100 4

Hotel
$119-$149

Address: 6910 Tower Rd 80249 **Location:** I-70 exit 286 (Tower Rd), 4.3 mi n. **Facility:** 139 units. 4 stories, interior corridors. **Amenities:** high-speed Internet. **Pool(s):** heated indoor. **Activities:** whirlpool, exercise room. **Guest Services:** valet and coin laundry.

BIZ / SOME UNITS

HOLIDAY INN SELECT DENVER-CHERRY CREEK
Phone: (303)388-5561 36

Hotel
$89-$159

Address: 455 S Colorado Blvd 80246 **Location:** I-25 exit 204, 1 mi n. **Facility:** 276 units. 9 stories, interior corridors. **Pool(s):** heated indoor. **Activities:** exercise room. **Guest Services:** valet and coin laundry, area transportation-within 3 mi. **Free Special Amenities: high-speed Internet and local transportation.**

SAVE CALL
/ SOME UNITS

HOMEWOOD SUITES BY HILTON DENVER INTERNATIONAL AIRPORT **Phone:** (303)371-4555 25

Extended Stay Hotel
$149-$169

AAA Benefit:
Contemporary luxury at a special Member rate.

Address: 4210 Airport Way 80239 **Location:** I-70 exit 283 (Chambers Rd), just n to 40th Ave E, 0.5 mi e, then just n. **Facility:** 117 efficiencies, some two bedrooms. 4 stories, interior corridors. **Terms:** 1-7 night minimum stay, cancellation fee imposed. **Amenities:** high-speed Internet. **Pool(s):** heated indoor. **Activities:** whirlpool, sports court, exercise room. **Guest Services:** valet and coin laundry, area transportation-within 5 mi.

CALL BIZ

(See map & index p. 140.)

HYATT REGENCY DENVER TECH CENTER

Phone: (303)779-1234 42

Hotel

$69-$319

AAA Benefit: Members save 10% or more everyday.

Address: 7800 E Tufts Ave 80237 **Location:** I-225 exit 2 (Tamarac St), just s to Tufts Ave; I-25 exit 199 (Belleview Ave), e to S Ulster St, then 0.5 mi n. **Facility:** This luxury hotel caters to families as well as the business traveler. It's a short walk to the Light Rail station, which makes multiple stops in downtown Denver. 451 units. 12 stories, interior corridors. **Parking:** on-site (fee) and valet. **Terms:** cancellation fee imposed. **Amenities:** *Some:* high-speed Internet (fee). **Dining:** 3 restaurants. **Pool(s):** heated indoor. **Activities:** saunas, whirlpool, basketball, horseshoes, volleyball, exercise room. *Fee:* massage. **Guest Services:** valet laundry, area transportation-within 5 mi. **Free Special Amenities: local transportation and children's activities.**

SAVE CALL BIZ FEE / SOME UNITS FEE

HYATT SUMMERFIELD SUITES DENVER AIRPORT

Phone: (303)628-7777 1

Extended Stay Hotel

$89-$149

AAA Benefit: Members save 10% or more everyday.

Address: 18741 E 71st Ave 80249 **Location:** I-70 exit 286 (Tower Rd), 4.6 mi n, then just e; Pena Blvd, exit 5 (Tower Rd/SR 32), just s. **Facility:** 123 units, some two bedrooms, efficiencies and kitchens. 4 stories, interior corridors. *Bath:* shower only. **Parking:** winter plug-ins. **Terms:** cancellation fee imposed. **Amenities:** high-speed Internet. **Pool(s):** heated indoor. **Activities:** whirlpool, exercise room. **Guest Services:** valet and coin laundry. **Free Special Amenities: full breakfast and high-speed Internet.**

SAVE BIZ / SOME UNITS FEE

THE INN AT CHERRY CREEK

Phone: (303)350-4440 34

Boutique Hotel

$199-$425

Address: 233 Clayton St 80206 **Location:** Between 2nd and 3rd aves; in Cherry Creek Village. **Facility:** A short drive from downtown and in the upscale Cherry Creek shopping district, the charming boutique hotel offers a quiet respite from the city. 37 units, some two bedrooms and kitchens. 4 stories, interior corridors. **Parking:** on-site (fee). **Terms:** check-in 4 pm, cancellation fee imposed. **Amenities:** high-speed Internet, safes. **Activities:** exercise room. **Guest Services:** valet laundry. **Free Special Amenities: newspaper and high-speed Internet.**

SAVE BIZ / SOME UNITS

JW MARRIOTT DENVER AT CHERRY CREEK

Phone: (303)316-2700 35

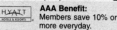

Hotel

$199-$399

AAA Benefit: A deluxe level of comfort and a Member rate.

Address: 150 Clayton Ln 80206 **Location:** I-25 exit 205 (University Blvd), 2.4 mi n to 1st Ave, just e, then just n. **Facility:** Enhanced with modern elegance, the hotel is in the popular, upscale Cherry Creek shopping district. It has the look and feel of a boutique hotel. The spa encourages relaxation and indulgence. 196 units. 11 stories, interior corridors. **Parking:** valet only. **Amenities:** high-speed Internet, safes, honor bars. **Activities:** whirlpools, bicycles, jogging, exercise room, spa. **Guest Services:** valet and coin laundry, area transportation-within 5 mi. **Free Special Amenities: newspaper and high-speed Internet.**

SAVE CALL BIZ FEE / SOME UNITS

LA QUINTA INN & SUITES DENVER AIRPORT DIA

Phone: (303)371-0888 10

Hotel

$88-$170

Address: 6801 Tower Rd 80249 **Location:** I-70 exit 286 (Tower Rd), 4.2 mi n; 0.8 mi s of Pena Blvd. **Facility:** 169 units. 5 stories, interior corridors. **Amenities:** video games (fee), high-speed Internet. **Pool(s):** heated indoor. **Activities:** whirlpool, exercise room. **Guest Services:** valet and coin laundry.

CALL BIZ FEE / SOME UNITS

LA QUINTA INN & SUITES DENVER GATEWAY PARK

Phone: 303/373-2525 18

Hotel

Rates not provided

Address: 4460 Peoria St 80239 **Location:** I-70 exit 281, just n. **Facility:** 81 units. 4 stories, interior corridors. **Amenities:** high-speed Internet. **Pool(s):** heated indoor. **Activities:** whirlpool, exercise room. **Guest Services:** valet and coin laundry.

BIZ   / SOME UNITS

LA QUINTA INN DENVER CHERRY CREEK

Phone: (303)758-8886 39

Hotel

$78-$170

Address: 1975 S Colorado Blvd 80222 **Location:** I-25 exit 204, just s. **Facility:** 130 units. 2 stories (no elevator), exterior corridors. **Amenities:** video games (fee). *Some:* high-speed Internet. **Pool(s):** heated outdoor. **Guest Services:** coin laundry.

FEE / SOME UNITS

MARRIOTT COURTYARD DENVER CHERRY CREEK

Phone: (303)757-8797 37

Hotel

$99-$189

AAA Benefit: AAA hotel discounts of 5% or more.

Address: 1475 S Colorado Blvd 80222 **Location:** I-25 exit 204, 0.5 mi n; entrance on Arkansas St. **Facility:** 240 units. 11 stories, interior corridors. **Amenities:** video games (fee). **Pool(s):** heated indoor. **Activities:** whirlpool, exercise room. **Guest Services:** valet and coin laundry.

(See map & index p. 140.)

QUALITY INN & SUITES-DIA

Phone: (303)371-5300 9

Hotel
$79-$159

Address: 6890 Tower Rd 80249 **Location:** I-70 exit 286 (Tower Rd), 4.2 mi n; 0.8 mi s of Pena Blvd. **Facility:** 122 units. 4 stories, interior corridors. **Terms:** cancellation fee imposed. **Amenities:** high-speed Internet. **Pool(s):** heated indoor. **Activities:** whirlpool, exercise room. **Guest Services:** valet and coin laundry. **Free Special Amenities: expanded continental breakfast and airport transportation.**

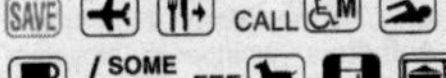

SAVE CALL BIZ FEE / SOME UNITS FEE

QUALITY INN DENVER EAST

Phone: (303)371-5640 22

Hotel
$62-$119

Address: 3975 Peoria Way 80239 **Location:** I-70 exit 281 eastbound; exit 282 westbound, just s. **Facility:** 112 units. 2 stories (no elevator), exterior corridors. **Terms:** cancellation fee imposed. **Amenities:** safes (fee). **Pool(s):** heated outdoor. **Guest Services:** valet and coin laundry.

SAVE BIZ FEE / SOME UNITS FEE

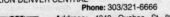

RED LION DENVER CENTRAL

Phone: 303/321-6666 17

Hotel
Rates not provided

Address: 4040 Quebec St 80216 **Location:** I-70 exit 278, s on Quebec St to Smith Rd exit, then e to Frontage Rd. **Facility:** 298 units. 5 stories, interior corridors. **Pool(s):** heated outdoor. **Activities:** exercise room. **Guest Services:** valet and coin laundry, area transportation-The Shops at Northfield & Quebec Square.

BIZ FEE / SOME UNITS FEE

RENAISSANCE DENVER HOTEL

Phone: (303)399-7500 21

Hotel
$170-$208

RENAISSANCE HOTELS & RESORTS

AAA Benefit: AAA hotel discounts of 5% or more.

Address: 3801 Quebec St 80207 **Location:** I-70 exit 278, just s via Smith Rd exit. **Facility:** 400 units. 12 stories, interior corridors. **Amenities:** *Fee:* video games, high-speed Internet. *Some:* safes. **Pool(s):** heated outdoor, heated indoor. **Activities:** whirlpools. **Guest Services:** complimentary and valet laundry. **Free Special Amenities: airport transportation and use of on-premises laundry facilities.**

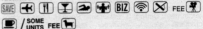

SAVE BIZ FEE / SOME UNITS FEE

RESIDENCE INN BY MARRIOTT DENVER DOWNTOWN

Phone: (303)458-5318 27

Extended Stay Hotel
$159-$179

AAA Benefit:
AAA hotel discounts of 5% or more.

Address: 2777 Zuni St 80211 **Location:** I-25 exit 212B (Speer Blvd) southbound; exit 212A (Speer Blvd S) northbound, just w, then just n. **Facility:** 159 kitchen units. 2 stories (no elevator), exterior corridors. **Terms:** check-in 4 pm. **Amenities:** high-speed Internet. **Pool(s):** heated outdoor. **Activities:** whirlpool, exercise room. **Guest Services:** valet and coin laundry, area transportation-within 3 mi.

BIZ FEE / SOME UNITS FEE

(See map & index p. 140.)

SPRINGHILL SUITES DENVER AIRPORT
Phone: (303)371-9400 11

Hotel
$169-$185

AAA Benefit:
AAA hotel discounts of 5% or more.

Address: 18350 E 68th Ave 80249 **Location:** I-70 exit 286 (Tower Rd), 4.3 mi n, then just w. **Facility:** 124 units. 4 stories, interior corridors. **Amenities:** high-speed Internet, safes. **Pool(s):** heated indoor. **Activities:** whirlpool, exercise room. **Guest Services:** valet and coin laundry, area transportation-within 5 mi.

STAYBRIDGE SUITES **Phone:** (303)574-0888 5

Extended Stay Hotel
$94-$179 5/1-8/31
$79-$159 9/1-4/30

Address: 6951 Tower Rd 80249 **Location:** Just s of jct Pena Blvd. **Facility:** 147 efficiencies, some two bedrooms. 6 stories, interior corridors. **Amenities:** *Some:* high-speed Internet. **Pool(s):** heated indoor. **Activities:** exercise room. **Guest Services:** complimentary and valet laundry, area transportation-within 5 mi.

CALL BIZ

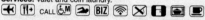

/ SOME UNITS FEE

SUPER 8 DENVER - AIRPORT
Phone: (303)373-5900 3

Hotel
$63-$72

Address: 7010 Tower Rd 80249 **Location:** I-70 exit 286 (Tower Rd), 4.5 mi n. **Facility:** 87 units. 3 stories, interior corridors. **Amenities:** high-speed Internet. *Some:* safes. **Pool(s):** heated indoor. **Activities:** whirlpools, exercise room. **Guest Services:** valet and coin laundry.

CALL BIZ 

TIMBERS HOTEL **Phone:** 303/373-1444 19

Hotel
Rates not provided

Address: 4411 Peoria St 80239 **Location:** I-70 exit 281, just n. **Facility:** 127 units, some efficiencies. 2-3 stories, interior corridors. **Dining:** Peoria Grill, see separate listing. **Activities:** exercise room. **Guest Services:** valet and coin laundry, area transportation-within 5 mi, Children's Hospital & National Jewish Hospital.

SAVE CALL BIZ

/ SOME UNITS FEE

TOWNEPLACE SUITES BY MARRIOTT-DENVER SOUTHEAST **Phone:** (303)759-9393 41

Extended Stay Hotel
$69-$149

AAA Benefit: AAA hotel discounts of 5% or more.

Address: 3699 S Monaco Pkwy 80237 **Location:** I-25 exit 201, just e to Monaco Pkwy, then s. **Facility:** 113 units, some two bedrooms and kitchens. 3 stories, interior corridors. **Amenities:** high-speed Internet. **Pool(s):** heated outdoor. **Activities:** exercise room. **Guest Services:** valet and coin laundry. **Free Special Amenities: continental breakfast and high-speed Internet.**

SAVE BIZ

/ SOME UNITS FEE

Find valuable AAA/CAA member savings at AAA.com/discounts

▼ See AAA listing p. 302 ▼

(See map & index p. 140.)

TOWNEPLACE SUITES BY MARRIOTT DOWNTOWN DENVER **Phone:** (303)722-2322 (33)

Extended Stay Hotel
$99-$299

AAA Benefit:
AAA hotel discounts of 5% or more.

Address: 685 Speer Blvd 80204 **Location:** I-25 exit 209A (6th Ave), 1.4 mi w, then just n on Acoma St. **Facility:** 123 kitchen units, some two bedrooms. 4 stories, interior corridors. **Terms:** check-in 4 pm. **Amenities:** high-speed Internet. **Activities:** exercise room. **Guest Services:** valet and coin laundry.

CALL BIZ / SOME UNITS FEE

WHERE TO EAT

AQUARIUM RESTAURANT **Phone:** 303/561-4450 (19)

American
$9-$32

AAA Inspector Notes: A 150,000-gallon saltwater aquarium dominates the dining room. There is a lot to see with a myriad of fish large and small, including some sharks. Although the menu is varied, I chose to stick with seafood. The salty, creamy clam chowder is made in house. The smoky flavor of the grilled mahi-mahi and shrimp was delicious and the side vegetables were fresh. I also recommend sharing one of the generously sized desserts. The cheesecake is especially fluffy due to the addition of mascarpone. **Bar:** full bar. **Address:** 700 Water St 80211 **Location:** I-25 exit 211, just e; in Downtown Aquarium. **Parking:** on-site (fee) and valet. SAVE L D

BANZAI SUSHI **Phone:** 303/329-3366 (51)

Japanese
$7-$25

AAA Inspector Notes: The restaurant proves sushi doesn't begin and end with the California roll. With more than 100 rolls to choose from, this restaurant aims to please. Patrons who want a combination not on the menu are urged to run it by the staff; most of the roll ideas came from customers. **Bar:** full bar. **Address:** 6655 Leetsdale Dr 80224 **Location:** I-25 exit 201, just e, 3.3 mi n on Monaco Pkwy, then just e. L D

BAROLO GRILL **Phone:** 303/393-1040 (39)

Northern Italian
$17-$32

AAA Inspector Notes: The small, intimate and popular grill showcases the food of Tuscany and Piedmont. Seared, braised duckling is superb. Incorporating vines stenciled on the walls and other distinctly Mediterranean touches, the rustic, elegant décor has a casual sophistication reminiscent of a country inn. Patrons can wait or eat in the bar. **Bar:** full bar. **Reservations:** suggested. **Address:** 3030 E 6th Ave 80206 **Location:** 0.5 mi e of Josephine St. **Parking:** valet only. D

BLUE BAY ASIAN CAFE **Phone:** 303/307-0222 (9)

Asian
$6-$13

AAA Inspector Notes: In a strip mall, this restaurant offers large portions of healthful and tasty dishes made from fresh ingredients. Travelers near the airport frequent this minimally decorated place. **Bar:** beer only. **Address:** 18607 E 48th Ave, Suite 106 80249 **Location:** I-70 exit 286, 1.7 mi n, then just e. L D

THE BLUE BONNET MEXICAN CAFE **Phone:** 303/778-0147 (48)

Mexican
$5-$14

AAA Inspector Notes: One dining room of the popular, well-established cafe has close table spacing, while the other is a bright and picturesque enclosed patio. Reasonably priced entrees include tamales, burritos, menudo and rellenos, which are served in combinations and with side dishes. Margaritas are memorable, and servers are friendly. **Bar:** full bar. **Address:** 457 S Broadway 80209 **Location:** Just s of jct Alameda Ave. L D

BONES **Phone:** 303/860-2929 (33)

Asian
$11-$18

AAA Inspector Notes: Famous for his upscale Italian restaurants, chef Frank Bonanno forages into new territory with this casual Asian-fusion eatery. Lunch consists of appetizers, salads and noodle dishes, while the dinner menu has a few additional offerings. Bonanno might pair ramen noodles with poached lobster, edamame and miso lobster broth, and team soba noodles with seared ahi, summer squash and grapefruit ponzu. Dinner entrees include miso-marinated steak, ahi burgers and shrimp lettuce wraps. **Bar:** full bar. **Address:** 701 Grant St 80203 **Location:** Jct Speer Blvd and 6th Ave, just n on Sherman St, then just e. **Parking:** street only. L D

BONNIE BRAE TAVERN **Phone:** 303/777-2262 (50)

American
$6-$14

AAA Inspector Notes: The family-friendly eatery recalls a bygone era with its vintage, vinyl-upholstered booths. Although such favorites as meatloaf, juicy hamburgers and pork chops with applesauce are a hit, the yummy pizza is what keeps locals coming back. **Bar:** full bar. **Address:** 740 S University Blvd 80209 **Location:** I-25 exit 205 (University Blvd), 1.2 mi n. L D

BRECKENRIDGE BREWERY & PUB **Phone:** 303/297-3644 (17)

American
$8-$16

AAA Inspector Notes: The working brewery is located in a large restored warehouse adjacent to Coors Field. The menu features ribs, brisket, pulled-pork barbecue, salads, burgers and sandwiches in addition to its six homemade brews. The décor is sports-related. **Bar:** full bar. **Address:** 2220 Blake St 80202 **Location:** I-25 exit 212C (20th St); at 22nd St. **Parking:** street only. L D

BUCKHORN EXCHANGE
Menu on AAA.com
Phone: 303/534-9505 (28)

Steak
$10-$43

AAA Inspector Notes: This popular place, first opened in 1893, features Old West memorabilia and a 150-year-old hand carved oak bar. The menu includes an exotic flair. Cowhands may start with a serving of rattlesnake, alligator tail or Rocky Mountain oysters. For the less adventurous, there's grilled duck breast, smoked buffalo sausage and sirloin game tips. Entrees offer more options, including beefsteaks, buffalo, elk, quail, lamb, ribs, Cornish game hen and salmon. There's entertainment Wednesday to Saturday. **Bar:** full bar. **Reservations:** suggested. **Address:** 1000 Osage St 80204 **Location:** I-25 exit 210A (Colfax Ave), 0.4 mi e, then 0.5 mi s. **Historic** L D

(See map & index p. 140.)

CARMINE'S ON PENN **Phone:** 303/777-6443 (45)

Italian
$20-$45

AAA Inspector Notes: In a quiet residential neighborhood, the restaurant offers a warm décor and is a local favorite for flavorful Italian cuisine, including veal, seafood and pasta. All meals are served family-style, which means portions are large enough to be shared among three to four people. Seating is available inside in several dining rooms and on a patio. **Bar:** full bar. **Reservations:** suggested. **Address:** 92 S Pennsylvania St 80209 **Location:** Jct Bayaud Ave and Pennsylvania St; just n of Alameda Ave. **Parking:** valet only. D

CASEY'S BISTRO & PUB **Phone:** 720/974-7350 (20)

American
$8-$18

AAA Inspector Notes: Named for Sean O'Casey, a famous Irish playwright, this great neighborhood eatery is casual but with contemporary, upscale touches. The menu features Irish food, including boxtys (stuffed potato pancakes) and savory pies, along with American fare such as grilled Atlantic salmon and "adult mac 'n' cheese." Beverages abound. **Bar:** full bar. **Address:** 7301 E 29th Ave, Unit 100 80238 **Location:** I-70 exit 278, 1 mi s, then just e. L D LATE CALL

THE CHERRY CRICKET **Phone:** 303/322-7666 (42)

American
$5-$10

AAA Inspector Notes: Patrons have flocked to this restaurant since it opened in 1945. Although it has changed hands many times, the Cricket burger remains at the top of many locals' favorite lists. Besides burgers, the restaurant also has a popular bar and has reasonable prices considering its location in the Cherry Creek shopping district. Other menu items include chicken wings, messy bean nachos, sandwiches and more. **Bar:** full bar. **Address:** 2641 E 2nd Ave 80206 **Location:** Between Columbine and Clayton sts; in Cherry Creek Village.

L D LATE

COLT & GRAY **Phone:** 303/477-1447 (15)

American
$14-$35

AAA Inspector Notes: This intimate restaurant has received much praise in a short time. Each dish exudes artistry, creativity and flavor. The bacon cashew caramel corn and beet burgers redefine bar food. A plate of roasted marrow bones is large enough to share. Entrees feature lamb, chicken, steak, halibut and pork, but the vegetarian house-made cavatelli is not to be missed. The caramelized banana tart with chocolate-hazelnut crust and the sticky toffee pudding with bourbon ice cream are delicious desserts. **Bar:** full bar. **Reservations:** suggested. **Address:** 1553 Platte St, Suite 120 80202 **Location:** Jct 15th St, just ne. **Parking:** on-site and street. D

THE CORK HOUSE **Phone:** 303/355-4488 (26)

American
$14-$29

AAA Inspector Notes: This restaurant specializes in creative American dishes featuring steak, chicken, lamb, duck and seafood. Cheese lovers must try one of the cheese flights, a plate of European and American cheeses served with candied walnuts, apples, grapes, crackers, garlic bread and flavor-infused crème fraîche sauces. The extensive wine list will please fans of both red and white. Depending on the weather, meals may be enjoyed on the spacious outdoor patio. **Bar:** full bar. **Reservations:** suggested. **Address:** 4900 E Colfax Ave 80220 **Location:** I-70 exit 276, s to Colfax Ave, then 0.7 mi e to Eudora St. **Parking:** street only. D

CUBA CUBA CAFE & BAR **Phone:** 303/605-2822 (27)

Cuban
$13-$24

AAA Inspector Notes: Denver finally has a Cuban restaurant and it is muy, muy bueno. The ambience is bright and open with ceiling frond fans, bongo tables in the bar and an outdoor patio. The garlic mojo marinade makes for tasty meat, fish and chicken dishes. The tres leches dessert is fabulous and is reason enough to visit this popular restaurant. **Bar:** full bar. **Address:** 1173 Delaware St 80204 **Location:** I-25 exit 210A (Colfax Ave), just e to Delaware St, then s at U.S. Mint to 12th St. **Parking:** street only. D

DARCY'S BISTRO & PUB **Phone:** 303/770-0477 (60)

American
$6-$13

AAA Inspector Notes: The bistro is a fun place to meet friends for one of the 30 beers on tap or an Irish menu specialty. Representative of the traditional pub fare are fish and chips, shepherd's pie, burgers, sandwiches and an extensive selection of salads. The facility includes a private library room and handsome dark woodwork. Patio seating is available when the weather cooperates. **Bar:** full bar. **Address:** 4955 S Ulster St, Unit 103 80237 **Location:** I-25 exit 199, 3 mi e to Ulster St, then just n. L D

D BAR DESSERTS **Phone:** 303/861-4710 (23)

Desserts
$8-$15

AAA Inspector Notes: Dessert is not the only reason to stop by this casual eatery. I was intrigued by the donut tartar, a savory donut hole filled with Kobe tartar, tomatillo jam and a secret sauce. The presentation was artful, the portion small and the flavor unique. The pizza salad sandwich was a baby green salad with pine nuts wrapped up in a thin-crust pesto, mozzarella and goat cheese pizza. The chocolate cake had a thick, creamy frosting between layers of dense, moist cake. **Bar:** full bar. **Address:** 1475 E 17th Ave 80218 **Location:** Jct Colfax Ave and Humboldt St, just n, then just e. **Parking:** street only. L D

DEVIL'S FOOD **Phone:** 303/733-7448 (52)

American
$8-$15

AAA Inspector Notes: An eclectic neighborhood cafe, Devil's Food tempts with much more than good coffee and charming atmosphere. Start with a perfect pastry or chocolate delicacy, then order challah French toast, salmon Benedict, eggs and corn bread or something more traditional like buttermilk pancakes, an omelet or quiche. Lunch focuses on soups, salads and gourmet sandwiches, while dinner adds an array of comfort foods with a modern twist such as pan-roasted half-chicken, prosciutto and rice stew, and gnocchi. **Bar:** wine only. **Address:** 1020 S Gaylord St 80209 **Location:** Jct University Blvd, just w on Tennessee Ave, then just s; in Gaylord Shopping District; near Washington Park. **Parking:** street only.

B L D

DICICCIO'S **Phone:** 303/574-1956 (1)

Italian
$10-$28

AAA Inspector Notes: The delightful decor is reminiscent of an Italian opera theater. A short drive from Denver International Airport, this spacious restaurant can accommodate large groups as well as parties of one or two. The menu features Italian favorites such as manicotti, veal parmigiana, ravioli and chicken fettuccine. Lighter fare includes sandwiches, salads and pizzas. **Bar:** full bar. **Address:** 6701 Tower Rd 80249 **Location:** I-70 exit 286 (Tower Rd), 4.2 mi n, then 0.8 mi s of Pena Blvd.

L D

(See map & index p. 140.)

DUO RESTAURANT **Phone:** 303/477-4141 (14)

American
$17-$24

AAA Inspector Notes: Locals flock to this restaurant to enjoy chef John Broening and pastry chef Yasmin Lozada-Hissom's artful, flavorful dishes prepared with local and organic ingredients. At the hands of chef Broening, even the humble New York strip tastes divine. Other dishes feature Colorado lamb, striped bass, pork and free-range chicken. Desserts include a delightful brown butter cake, frozen lemon icebox cake and chocolate banana strudel. This casual and inviting restaurant is also a popular brunch spot. **Bar:** full bar. **Address:** 2413 W 32nd Ave 80211 **Location:** I-25 exit 212B (Speer Blvd) southbound; exit 212A (Speer Blvd S) northbound, just w to Zuni St, then 0.5 mi n. **Parking:** street only. D

EL DIABLO **Phone:** 303/954-0324 (41)

Mexican
$7-$17

AAA Inspector Notes: This casual Mexican restaurant goes beyond the standard Tex-Mex fare and serves something creative. The "ramekin" made of corn masa and filled with chopped chorizo, black beans, avocado, cheese and sour cream appealed to me. A lot of flavor is packed into a small package. The puerco de panza tacos were served on unfried corn tortillas filled with rich braised pork belly and lightly seasoned with roasted chile pico de gallo and queso panela, a mild soft cheese. Service and décor are very casual. **Bar:** full bar. **Address:** 101 Broadway St 80203 **Location:** Jct 1st Ave, s of downtown. **Parking:** street only. B L D LATE

ELWAY'S **Phone:** 303/399-5353 (43)

Steak
$12-$58

AAA Inspector Notes: Indeed, the restaurant's name refers to former Broncos star John Elway, who co-owns this upscale steakhouse. Celebrity diners can sometimes be spotted. The other co-owners have extensive restaurant experience and have created a menu of memorable dishes using fresh ingredients. The lunch and dinner menus focus on standard steak and seafood choices, but some creative selections can be found in the "starters" section. The extensive wine list is designed to please even the pickiest connoisseur. **Bar:** full bar. **Reservations:** suggested. **Address:** 2500 E 1st Ave, Suite 101 80206 **Location:** I-25 exit 205 (University Ave), just e. L D CALL &M

THE FRESH FISH COMPANY
Phone: 303/740-9556 (58)

Seafood
$9-$39

AAA Inspector Notes: Fresh seafood-broiled or mesquite-grilled-matches with several microbrews at this restaurant, which is popular and sometimes noisy. Meals are capably served in a nautical atmosphere that includes large aquariums. **Bar:** full bar. **Address:** 7800 E Hampden Ave 80231 **Location:** I-25 exit 201, 1.3 mi e; in Tiffany Square Plaza, east side. L D

FRUITION RESTAURANT **Phone:** 303/831-1962 (38)

American
$22-$26

AAA Inspector Notes: Chef Alex Seidel deserves every accolade he has received and there have been many. His dishes are presented with artistry, and each bite is delicious. The menu changes seasonally, but Seidel's innovation is consistent. His passion for farm-fresh ingredients led him to start his own farm. Entrees feature pork, Colorado lamb, duck, beef, fish and scallops. The heavenly desserts, such as warm vanilla crepes, caramelized banana pudding and lemon meringue pie, make a sweet ending to any meal. **Bar:** full bar. **Reservations:** suggested. **Address:** 1313 E 6th Ave 80218 **Location:** I-25 exit 209A, 2.3 mi e. **Parking:** street only. D

FUEL CAFE **Phone:** 303/296-4642 (7)

American
$9-$22

AAA Inspector Notes: Chef/owner Bob Blair serves casual but creative cuisine featuring fresh, high-quality ingredients. The humble BLT is transformed into a gourmet sandwich when made with heirloom tomatoes, thick slices of bacon and basil aioli on country bread grilled in olive oil. The lunch menu features flavorful dishes such as blackberry mango salad with prosciutto, lamb wrap and banh mi sandwich. Dinner dishes center on hand-made gnocchi and ravioli, red trout, lamb and chicken. **Bar:** full bar. **Address:** 3455 Ringsby Ct, Suite 105 80216 **Location:** I-70 exit 274 to Washington St, just s, then just w; in TAXI development. L D

HANABI JAPANESE GRILL & SUSHI BAR
Phone: 303/979-9298 (59)

Japanese
$7-$32

AAA Inspector Notes: This contemporary hibachi grill offers quite a show. It's all about the preparation and the lighthearted expertise of the chef. There also are two sushi bars and small tables for those craving a quieter experience. **Bar:** full bar. **Address:** 7600 W Quincy Ave 80123 **Location:** US 285 exit Wadsworth Blvd, 0.8 mi s. D

HIGHLAND'S GARDEN CAFE
Phone: 303/458-5920 (11)

American
$13-$32

AAA Inspector Notes: Historic Victorian buildings and lovely gardens establish this restaurant as an exceptional place to enjoy a meal. Tantalizing menu options change to accommodate seasonal ingredients. Accompanied with delightful sauces, beef tenderloin, pheasant, quail, duck, chicken, lamb and scallops make rotating appearances on the menu. **Bar:** full bar. **Reservations:** suggested. **Address:** 3927 W 32nd Ave 80212 **Location:** I-25 exit 212B (Speer Blvd) southbound; exit 212A (Speer Blvd S) northbound, 1 mi nw, then just w. **Parking:** street only. L D

HOT CAKES BREAKFAST AND LUNCH
Phone: 303/832-4351 (21)

American
$7-$9

AAA Inspector Notes: This casual eatery is well known for its delicious, hearty breakfasts. The menu includes innovative variations, as well as traditional morning favorites. Reasonable prices and quick service make this place a hot spot. **Address:** 1400 E 18th Ave 80218 **Location:** Jct Humbolt St; across from St. Joseph's Hospital. **Parking:** on-site and street. B L

IMPERIAL CHINESE SEAFOOD RESTAURANT
Phone: 303/698-2800 (47)

Chinese
$10-$25

AAA Inspector Notes: A local favorite with an appealing atmosphere, the restaurant offers a professional, prompt and attentive staff and colorful presentations of tasty seafood, chicken and beef dishes. **Bar:** full bar. **Address:** 431 S Broadway 80209 **Location:** I-25 exit 6th Ave E to Broadway southbound, 1 mi s; exit Lincoln St northbound, 0.5 mi n, then just w on Dakota Ave; corner of Dakota Ave and Broadway. L D CALL &M

INDIA'S RESTAURANT
Menu on AAA.com **Phone:** 303/755-4284 (57)

Indian
$10-$20

AAA Inspector Notes: The restaurant is known for its Northern Indian cuisine. In addition to a daily lunch buffet, this place offers a menu of tandoori plates, tikka jehangir, naan and vegetarian dishes. Service is casual in the colorful dining room. **Bar:** full bar. **Address:** 7400 E Hampden Ave, Unit F 80231 **Location:** I-25 exit 201, 1.3 mi e; in Tiffany Plaza, east side. L D

(See map & index p. 140.)

JULIA BLACKBIRD'S **Phone:** 303/433-2688 (12)

Southwestern
$10-$16

AAA Inspector Notes: In the popular Highlands neighborhood near downtown, this restaurant specializes in New Mexican cuisine. Entrees include blue corn tortilla enchiladas, tamales, Navajo stew and chiles rellenos. Most entrees come smothered in a choice of green chile, red chile or a combination of both. Beverages include sangria and many flavored margaritas. **Bar:** full bar. **Address:** 3434 W 32nd Ave 80211 **Location:** From Federal Blvd, just nw on Speer Blvd, then just w. **Parking:** street only. L D

KONA GRILL **Phone:** 720/974-1300 (44)

Caribbean
$9-$31

AAA Inspector Notes: The eclectic menu reflects Pacific influences. In addition to noodle dishes and sushi, it lists specialties of macadamia nut chicken and lemon grass-encrusted swordfish. The dining room has a large aquarium, a private area and a sushi bar. The patio opens during warm weather. **Bar:** full bar. **Address:** 3000 E 1st Ave, Suite 184 80206 **Location:** Jct Speer Blvd (turns into 1st Ave) and University Blvd, just e; in Cherry Creek Mall. **Parking:** on-site and valet. L D CALL M

LA SANDIA **Phone:** 303/373-9100 (5)

Mexican
$9-$18

AAA Inspector Notes: While creating La Sandia's menu, acclaimed chef Richard Sandoval found inspiration in his childhood growing up in Acapulco. Local patrons appreciate his talent. Quality ingredients, colorful presentation and bold flavors attract both fans of Mexican cuisine and foodies. The menu lists fajitas, chicken mole and chile relleno capeado, as well as the luscious banana empanadas dessert. Day of the Dead characters and colorful etched glass warm up the metallic, industrial decor. **Bar:** full bar. **Address:** 8340 Northfield Blvd, Unit 1690 80238 **Location:** I-70 exit 278, 0.5 mi n; exit N Field Blvd, just e, just s on Unita St, then just e. **Parking:** street only. L D

LE CENTRAL **Phone:** 303/863-8094 (30)

French
$8-$19

AAA Inspector Notes: Well-prepared courses featuring high-quality ingredients are the focus of this casual French bistro. While the menu changes daily, patrons can always count on exquisite yet unpretentious meals. The rustic Europe-influenced décor lends to an informal, comfortable atmosphere. **Bar:** full bar. **Reservations:** suggested. **Address:** 112 E 8th Ave 80203 **Location:** I-25 exit 207A (Lincoln St/Broadway), 1.6 mi n on Lincoln St, just e on 6th Ave, just n on Sherman St, then just w. **Parking:** street only. L D

LING & LOUIE'S ASIAN BAR & GRILL
Phone: 303/371-4644 (6)

Asian
$9-$17

AAA Inspector Notes: This popular regional chain features creative, accessible Asian dishes. Entrees marked spicy have a kick. Appetizers include lettuce wraps, pan-fried pot stickers, calamari and spring rolls, while teriyaki chicken, sweet and sour pork, orange peel chicken and pad thai are among entrees. This restaurant has a reputation for being kid-friendly. Asia-infused, modern style lends to the comfortable atmosphere. **Bar:** full bar. **Address:** 8354 Northfield Blvd, Suite 1710 80238 **Location:** I-70 exit 278, 0.5 mi n; exit Northfield Blvd, just e, just s on Uinta St, then just e. **Parking:** street only. L D

LITTLE ANITA'S **Phone:** 303/691-3337

Mexican
$5-$11

AAA Inspector Notes: Authentic New Mexican recipes are on the menu at this quaint, quick-serve eatery. A la carte burritos, calabacitas, enchiladas, tacos, quesadillas and tostadas, as well as a variety of combination plates and hamburgers, are available. **Address:** 1550 S Colorado Blvd, Suite 103 80222 **Location:** I-25 exit 204, just n; in Florida Shopping Center. B L D

LITTLE INDIA RESTAURANT
Phone: 303/871-9777 (36)

Indian
$9-$16

AAA Inspector Notes: From the outside, this restaurant doesn't look very special. However, delicious curry, masala, vindaloo, biryani and tandoori dishes continue to win accolades from local critics and patrons. The economical lunch buffet is popular for its cleanliness, variety and price. **Bar:** full bar. **Address:** 330 E 6th Ave 80203 **Location:** Jct Speer Blvd, just e; near downtown. L D

LUCA D'ITALIA **Phone:** 303/832-6600 (31)

Italian
$14-$36

AAA Inspector Notes: The sophisticated menu focuses on contemporary Italian fare along the lines of soft polenta smothered in sautéed wild mushrooms, fresh mozzarella with basil, spicy lobster fra diavolo and wild boar. Other game and seafood dishes also are offered. **Bar:** full bar. **Reservations:** suggested. **Address:** 711 Grant St 80203 **Location:** Jct 7th Ave. **Parking:** valet only. D

M&D'S CAFE **Phone:** 303/296-1760 (18)

American
$8-$22

AAA Inspector Notes: Traditional Texas barbecue is served with a heaping helping of choices such as potato salad, fried okra, coleslaw or even baked beans. Steaming hot peach cobbler and sweet potato pie are delicious finishes. The restaurant has been family owned and operated for three generations. **Address:** 2000 E 28th Ave 80205 **Location:** Jct Race St. L D

MEZCAL **Phone:** 303/322-5219 (25)

Mexican
$9-$17

AAA Inspector Notes: Although relaxed during the day, this restaurant becomes lively at night and is a popular weekend hangout for locals. Savory and flavorful sopes are the perfect way to begin a meal. Entrees include pozole, chicken mole, chiles rellenos, burritos and tacos. The distinctive decor features murals of vintage Mexican movie posters and comic book covers. **Bar:** full bar. **Address:** 3230 E Colfax Ave 80206 **Location:** Jct Broadway, 2 mi e. **Parking:** street only. L D LATE

MIZUNA **Phone:** 303/832-4778 (32)

New American
$28-$43

AAA Inspector Notes: One local food critic calls this hot spot "one of the best restaurants in Denver." It features New American cuisine with emphasis on flavors, a top-notch waitstaff and a classy yet intimate ambience. The lobster macaroni and cheese lives up to the hype-it is truly sensational. The menu changes seasonally, but the ostrich also is not to be missed. **Bar:** full bar. **Reservations:** suggested. **Address:** 225 E 7th Ave 80203 **Location:** I-25 exit 209, e to Sherman St, just n to 7th Ave, then just e. **Parking:** valet and street only. D

(See map & index p. 140.)

MOONGATE ASIAN GRILL **Phone:** 303/329-2921 (40)

Asian
$6-$14

AAA Inspector Notes: Less than 2 miles from the Stapleton hotels, this strip-mall eatery is worth the drive or cab ride. The small, unpretentious dining room is tastefully decorated, and the menu features an interesting variety of Thai, Chinese and Japanese entrees to challenge the American palate. **Bar:** wine only. **Address:** 745 Quebec St 80220 **Location:** 0.7 mi s of Colfax Ave. [L] [D]

MOONLIGHT DINER **Phone:** 303/307-1750 (2)

American
$7-$19

AAA Inspector Notes: A fun place to eat, the diner has 1950s and aircraft décor in the lounge. The menu lists breakfast items, as well as meatloaf, hot and cold sandwiches and burgers. This place provides room service to nearby hotels. **Bar:** full bar. **Address:** 6250 Tower Rd 80249 **Location:** I-70 exit 286 (Tower Rd), 3.5 mi n; 0.7 mi s of Pena Blvd. [B] [L] [D]

MY BROTHER'S BAR **Phone:** 303/455-9991 (16)

Burgers
$7-$15

AAA Inspector Notes: The city's oldest bar has been continuously operating since 1873. I can picture Jack Kerouac and Neal Cassady tossing back a few during a grittier time, as they were reported to do. Hidden behind the humble, unidentified facade are delicious burgers. They're really why people seek out this hard-to-find spot. In the summer, I like to chill on the patio. In the winter, the masculine woodwork feels cozy. Either way, the juicy, made-to-order bison, ground beef and vegetarian burgers hit the spot. **Bar:** full bar. **Address:** 2376 15th St 80202 **Location:** Southwest corner of 15th and Platte sts. [L] [D] [LATE]

NEW SAIGON RESTAURANT
Phone: 303/936-4954 (49)

Vietnamese
$7-$32

AAA Inspector Notes: Although the plain appearance might not suggest much, this well-established family restaurant provides a comfortable setting for relaxed dining. Pleasant pictures of Vietnam decorate the walls of the unpretentious dining room, which has somewhat tight table spacing. The menu's varied dishes, which have won local and national awards, include grilled lamb, duck salad, beef skewers and rice noodles, in addition to chicken and pork concoctions. **Bar:** beer & wine. **Address:** 630 S Federal Blvd 80219 **Location:** 1.4 mi s of jct US 6 and Federal Blvd. [L] [D]

NEW YORK DELI NEWS
Menu on AAA.com **Phone:** 303/759-4741 (56)

American
$7-$14

AAA Inspector Notes: This very popular, authentic New York-style deli offers matzo ball soup, pastrami sandwiches, fish platters and eggs served all day. It also features great variety, ample portions and unlimited refills on soda and pickles. Service is prompt and friendly. **Bar:** beer & wine. **Address:** 7105 E Hampden Ave 80224 **Location:** I-25 exit 201, 0.6 mi e. [B] [L] [D]

PARALLEL SEVENTEEN **Phone:** 303/399-0988 (24)

Vietnamese
$8-$26

AAA Inspector Notes: Although chef Mary Nguyen's menu features some traditional Vietnamese dishes, she is also skilled in traditional French cooking. This diversity pleases the palates of even the pickiest patron. Northern-style pho is delicious, as are tuna taro tacos, lobster dumplings, charcuterie, Tasmanian salmon, lemongrass-roasted poussin and steak. The thoughtful wine list's offerings are compatible with any food choice. The unique decor presents Vietnamese elements in a modern style, much like the food. **Bar:** full bar. **Address:** 1600 E 17th Ave 80218 **Location:** Jct Colfax Ave and Franklin St, just n. **Parking:** street only. [L] [D]

PARISI **Phone:** 303/561-0234 (3)

Italian
$9-$15

AAA Inspector Notes: This casual eatery in the Highlands neighborhood is reminiscent of an Italian bistro. Co-owner Simone Parisi grew up in Italy and was taught to cook by his family. The concept is a little different, as the service is limited. However, the food is delicious. The menu consists of authentic pasta dishes, pizzas and panini. The pizza biancas are free of tomato sauce but are simple and flavorful. Gelato is made in small batches. Other desserts include cannoli, tarts, tiramisu and handmade truffles. **Bar:** full bar. **Address:** 4401 Tennyson St 80212 **Location:** I-70 exit 270, 0.3 mi s on Sheridan Blvd to 44th St, 0.5 mi e, then just n. [L] [D]

PEORIA GRILL **Phone:** 303/375-8080 (10)

American
$9-$22

AAA Inspector Notes: This casual eatery features a varied menu offering everything from barbecue ribs and steak to salmon and shrimp dishes. **Bar:** full bar. **Address:** 4411 Peoria St 80239 **Location:** I-70 exit 281, just n; in Timbers Hotel. [B] [L] [D]

PETE'S CENTRAL ONE **Phone:** 303/778-6675 (46)

Greek
$8-$18

AAA Inspector Notes: The neighborhood cafe serves traditional dishes such as moussaka, souvlaki, dolmades, lamb kebabs, an octopus appetizer and Greek salads in its small dining rooms. Lemon chicken soup is good, and the nice selection of desserts includes yummy baklava. Service is friendly and casual. Pictures of the Mediterranean decorate the small, narrow, bi-level dining room. Window seats offer a view of the street and passers-by. **Bar:** full bar. **Address:** 300 S Pearl St 80209 **Location:** I-25 exit 208 (SR 26/Alameda), 1 mi e to jct Pearl St; on southeast corner. **Parking:** street only. [L] [D]

POTAGER **Phone:** 303/832-5788 (29)

American
$18-$29

AAA Inspector Notes: Acclaimed chef Teri Rippeto strips down her food to the most basic of pleasing elements. The fresh, high-quality ingredients are locally produced and perfectly prepared. A frequent fixture at all the local farmers' markets, Rippeto changes the menu monthly in order to use food that reflects the season. The décor features exposed brick and bistrolike features, giving a rustic, earthy atmosphere that complements the cuisine. I like sitting by the window and watching the street life. **Bar:** wine only. **Address:** 1109 Ogden St 80218 **Location:** From Colfax Ave, 0.4 mi s. **Parking:** on-site and street. [D]

PROTO'S PIZZERIA NAPOLETANA **Phone:** 720/855-9400

Pizza
$6-$17

AAA Inspector Notes: The creator of this small regional chain, Pam Proto, had a simple dream: to bring Neapolitan pizza to Colorado. The original restaurant in Longmont was so successful that Proto and her partner, Rayme Rossello, expanded the business to six locations. This one is on a quiet street a short drive from the more active LoDo area. This cozy restaurant offers delicious gourmet pizzas, flavorful salads and Italy-inspired desserts. **Bar:** full bar. **Address:** 2401 15th St 80202 **Location:** Jct Platte St, just ne. **Parking:** street only. [L] [D]

RACINES RESTAURANT **Phone:** 303/595-0418 (35)

American
$8-$20

AAA Inspector Notes: Diners savor the excellent baked turkey sandwich at this restaurant, which also offers Mexican dishes, pasta, stir-fries and creations from the on-site bakery. Everything can be washed down with terrific margaritas, microbrews and martinis. The youthful, energetic atmosphere is popular with all ages. Brunch is served until 3 pm on weekends. **Bar:** full bar. **Address:** 650 Sherman St 80203 **Location:** Jct Bannock St and Speer Blvd, just n. [B] [L] [D] CALL [&M]

(See map & index p. 140.)

ROOT DOWN Phone: 303/993-4200 (13)

Natural/Organic
$8-$27

AAA Inspector Notes: Located in the Highlands neighborhood, this popular eatery is housed in a former car service station. The menu focuses on global flavors and incorporates fresh, seasonal and mostly organic ingredients. Lighter fare includes small plates such as seared diver scallops, sweet potato "falafel," steamed PEI mussels and interesting interpretations of sliders. Entrees feature lamb, halibut, beef, pork, chicken and tofu. Friendly, knowledgeable servers enhance the dining experience. **Bar:** full bar. **Reservations:** suggested. **Address:** 1600 W 33rd Ave 80211 **Location:** I-25 exit 213 (20th St), just ne on Central St, just n on Osage St, then just w. **Parking:** street only. D

ROYAL INDIA Phone: 303/758-9099 (55)

Indian
$9-$17

AAA Inspector Notes: This restaurant features traditional vegetarian and meat dishes, including chicken tikka masala, biryani, tandoori or grilled meats and saag paneer. Diners can sample a variety during the lunch buffet or order a la carte during dinner. **Bar:** wine only. **Address:** 1550 S Colorado Blvd 80222 **Location:** I-25 exit 204, just n; in Florida Shopping Center. L D

SABOR LATINO Phone: 303/455-8664 (8)

Latin American
$8-$15

AAA Inspector Notes: Reasonably priced Chilean, Peruvian, Mexican and Colombian cuisine is prepared fresh daily. The South American sampler and a flavored mojito are the perfect way to start a meal. Flavorful chicken, beef, seafood, ceviche and vegetarian dishes are served in attractive surroundings that evoke the feeling of a neighborhood cafe. **Bar:** full bar. **Address:** 4340 W 35th Ave 80212 **Location:** Jct Tennyson St. **Parking:** street only. D CALL

SAIGON TERRACE VIETNAMESE & CHINESE RESTAURANT Phone: 303/759-0884 (54)

Vietnamese
$7-$15

AAA Inspector Notes: Fresh Vietnamese creations awaken the palate and satisfy the savvy diner. Ingredients in each dish complement each other and create a unique experience. **Bar:** full bar. **Address:** 1550 S Colorado Blvd, Suite 106 80222 **Location:** I-25 exit 204, just n; in Florida Shopping Center. L D

STRINGS Phone: 303/831-7310 (22)

American
$14-$35

AAA Inspector Notes: Located in a busy residential and hospital area, this attractively designed and appointed restaurant is just over a mile from downtown. It is sophisticated, exciting, inviting, friendly and casual, not to mention popular. Chef Noel Cunningham is known as much for his philanthropic Save Our Strength program as he is for creating beautiful entrees. **Bar:** full bar. **Reservations:** suggested. **Address:** 1700 Humboldt St 80218 **Location:** I-25 exit 210A (Colfax Ave), 2.5 mi e, then just n. **Parking:** valet and street only. L D

SUSHI DEN Phone: 303/777-0826 (53)

Japanese
$15-$28

AAA Inspector Notes: Artistic presentations, fresh ingredients and heavenly flavors contribute to the enjoyable dining experience. In addition to sushi, the menu incorporates choices such as deep-fried crab, sautéed scallops, grilled shrimp and roasted duck breast. Patrons relax while dining in a distinctive Asian-inspired industrial setting. **Bar:** full bar. **Address:** 1487 S Pearl St 80210 **Location:** Jct Florida Ave. **Parking:** street only. L D

SWING THAI Phone: 303/777-1777 (34)

Thai
$9-$13

AAA Inspector Notes: Offering quick-serve Thai cuisine, the menu lists stir-fried, grilled, noodle and curry dishes, including the popular pad thai, drunken noodles and jungle curry entrées. Many choices can be prepared without gluten and in vegetarian or vegan style. The chicken is natural, the beef is from Harris Ranch, and the tofu is organic. **Bar:** full bar. **Address:** 845 Colorado Blvd 80206 **Location:** Jct 8th Ave. L D

TABLE 6 Phone: 303/831-8800 (37)

New World
$18-$26

AAA Inspector Notes: Near the hip Capitol Hill district, the popular, artsy restaurant exudes casual class. Guests watch from their table as the head chef Scott Parker prepares meals from an open kitchen. The menu features innovative cuisine with unique flavor combinations. Parker works magic both with comfort food and more upscale cuisine. Worth extra consideration are the Little Phillie cheese steaks and chicken pot pie. **Bar:** beer & wine. **Address:** 609 Corona St 80218 **Location:** Northwest corner of 6th Ave and Corona St. **Parking:** street only. D

TOCABE Phone: 720/524-8282 (4)

Native American
$6-$9

AAA Inspector Notes: Owners Ben Jacobs and Matt Chandra use family recipes to create popular dishes normally found only on or around American Indian reservations. The modified fry bread, which is flash-fried in corn and canola oil, is amazingly flavorful, puffy, chewy and satisfying. Patrons choose their own toppings-High Plains bison, ground beef, chicken, beans, chicken and vegetables-in an assembly line similar to quick-serve Mexican restaurants. The décor combines American Indian symbolism with modern design. **Address:** 3536 W 44th Ave 80211 **Location:** I-70 exit 272 (US 287/Federal Blvd), 0.5 mi s on Federal Blvd, then 0.4 mi w. L D

DILLON (D-3) pop. 904, elev. 9,087'

• Hotels p. 172 • Restaurants p. 172

Dillon is a resort town. Many year-round recreational activities are available along the Dillon Reservoir's 25-mile shoreline. Mountain scenery of the Arapaho and Roosevelt *(see place listing p. 40)* and White River national forests *(see place listing p. 303)* surrounds the community.

East of Dillon on I-70, the 1.5-mile Eisenhower-Johnson Memorial Tunnel Complex burrows through the heart of Mount Trelease. Besides being a milestone in highway engineering, the tunnel bypasses US 6 and the 11,992-foot Loveland Pass, which is often hazardous in winter.

Summit County Visitor Center: 246 Rainbow Dr., Dillon; P.O. Box 1547, Silverthorne, CO 80498. **Phone:** (970) 468-5780.

BEST WESTERN PTARMIGAN LODGE Phone: (970)468-2341

Hotel

$76-$186

AAA Benefit: Members save up to 20%, plus 10% bonus points with Best Western Rewards®.

Address: 652 Lake Dillon Dr 80435 **Location:** I-70 exit 205, 1.3 mi se on US 6 to Lake Dillon Dr, then 0.3 mi s. Opposite Lake Dillon. **Facility:** 69 units, some efficiencies. 1-2 stories (no elevator), interior/exterior corridors. **Amenities:** *Some:* high-speed Internet. **Activities:** sauna, whirlpool, marina, hiking trails. **Guest Services:** coin laundry. **Free Special Amenities: local telephone calls and high-speed Internet.**

SAVE / SOME UNITS FEE

COMFORT SUITES DILLON Phone: (970)513-0300

Hotel

$80-$300

Address: 276 Dillon Ridge Rd 80435 **Location:** I-70 exit 205, 0.3 mi s, then just e. Located near grocery store and shopping complex. **Facility:** 101 units, some kitchens. 3 stories, interior corridors. **Terms:** check-in 4 pm, cancellation fee imposed. **Amenities:** *Fee:* video games, safes. **Pool(s):** heated indoor. **Activities:** whirlpools, exercise room. **Guest Services:** valet and coin laundry.

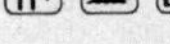

BIZ FEE

DILLON INN Phone: (970)262-0801

Hotel

$60-$135

Address: 708 E Anemone Tr 80435 **Location:** I-70 exit 205, 0.5 mi s on US 6 to 2nd Anemone Tr entrance. **Facility:** 30 units. 2 stories (no elevator), interior corridors. **Pool(s):** heated indoor. **Activities:** sauna, whirlpool, playground, basketball, exercise room.

SUPER 8 DILLON Phone: (970)468-8888

Motel

$49-$136

Address: 808 Little Beaver Tr 80435 **Location:** I-70 exit 205, 0.3 mi s, then just e. **Facility:** 60 units. 3 stories (no elevator), interior corridors. **Terms:** cancellation fee imposed.

/ SOME UNITS FEE

LOOKOUT RIDGE TOWNHOMES Phone: 970/468-6291

fyi Not evaluated. **Address:** 2381 Lodge Pole Cir 80435 **Location:** I-25 exit 205. Facilities, services, and decor characterize a mid-scale property.

WHERE TO EAT

ARAPAHOE CAFE AND PUB Phone: 970/468-0873

American

$6-$16

AAA Inspector Notes: The building was moved from the valley floor to its present location when the Dillon Lake dam was built. Now on the shore of Dillon Lake, the restaurant serves home-style food with flair. The ruby red mountain trout and roast duckling are popular choices. **Bar:** full bar. **Address:** 626 Lake Dillon Dr 80435 **Location:** I-70 exit 205, 1.3 mi se on US 6, then 0.3 mi s.

B L D

DAM BREWERY Phone: 970/262-7777

American

$8-$22

AAA Inspector Notes: Having received countless awards for its hand-crafted ales, lagers and root beer, the casual, light-hearted tavern is proud to serve patrons a pint and takes equal pride in its food. Guests can grab a bowl of hearty stew or slice into one of many succulent chicken dishes. Local bands provide entertainment some evenings. **Bar:** full bar. **Address:** 100 Little Dam St 80435 **Location:** I-70 exit 205, just s to W Anemone Tr, then just w. L D LATE

DOLORES pop. 936

DUNTON HOT SPRINGS Phone: 970/882-4800

fyi Not evaluated. **Address:** 52068 W Fork Rd 38 81323 **Location:** 13.3 mi n of Dolores center via SR 14, 22 mi ne on CR 38 (last 9 mi unpaved); from Telluride, 18 mi s on SR 145, 10.5 mi w on CR 38, follow signs. Facilities, services, and decor characterize an upscale property.

DURANGO (F-2) pop. 16,887, elev. 6,523'

• Hotels p. 174 • Restaurants p. 178

Durango began as a railroad town with a mining and smelting center during the gold and silver booms. It is now a crossroads for local industry, ranching, commerce and culture. Vestiges of the past accent Durango's Victorian downtown, where visitors can still enjoy the spirit of that colorful era.

Durango is a natural gateway to the San Juan Mountains, one of the more scenic sections of the state. Because they are geologically younger than other Colorado mountain ranges, the San Juans present a more jagged, precipitous appearance.

US 550 runs north from Durango to Silverton and Ouray; the part of the road that is known as the Million Dollar Highway includes many overlooks and is cut from nearly vertical cliff sides *(see Ouray p. 262)*. Because the road has steep drop-offs and no guardrails it should be traveled with caution.

Some of the largest and best preserved Ancestral Puebloan cliff dwellings in the Southwest are 36 miles west in Mesa Verde National Park *(see place listing p. 252)*. Tours to these places and into the back country of the San Juan National Forest can be arranged in Durango; contact the tourism office.

A high mountain hamlet and the Tour of Carvings are 22 miles northeast of Durango at Vallecito Lake Reservoir. Ponderosa pines scattered around the reservoir are carved to represent firefighters and animals who perished in a 2002 forest fire; phone (970) 247-1573.

Other activities available in the Durango area include art gallery tours, golfing, hiking, horseback riding, kayaking, mountain and road biking, rafting, rock climbing, skiing and snowboarding. A convenient year-round way to get around in Durango and avoid parking hassles is to ride the trolley-bus that runs along Main Street daily 7 a.m. to 7 p.m. (10 p.m. in summer) and costs $1.

Durango abounds with more than 100 special events during the year, including Snowdown, a wacky celebration of winter held from late January into early February; July's Durango Fiesta Days, which includes a rodeo, parade and street dance; Music in the Mountains, a classical music festival held mid-July to early August; Durango and Silverton Narrow Gauge Railfest in late August; and Durango Cowboy Poetry Gathering in early October.

Durango Area Tourism Office: 111 S. Camino del Rio, P.O. Box 2321, Durango, CO 81302. **Phone:** (970) 247-3500 or (800) 463-8726. ***(See ad on inside front cover, p. 173.)***

AAM'S MILD TO WILD RAFTING & JEEP TOURS INC. is at 50 Animas View Dr. Full- and half-day guided jeep tours explore the surrounding mountains, attractions, ghost towns, waterfalls and nature. A variety of packages combine jeep tours, rafting and railroad excursions.

Hours: Daily 7:30 a.m.-8:30 p.m., Memorial Day-Labor Day; 8-5, mid-April through day before Memorial Day and day after Labor Day-Oct. 31. **Cost:** Full-day jeep fares $125; $99 (children); free (ages 0-4). Half-day jeep fares $71; $57 (children); free (ages 0-4). Rafting full-day $79; $69 (children). Half-day rafting $46; $36 (children). Economy rafting $31; $24 (children). Combination fare with railroad $145; $115 (children); free (ages 0-4). **Phone:** (970) 247-4789 or (800) 567-6745.

BAR D CHUCKWAGON SUPPERS is 6 mi. n. on US 550, 1 mi. e. on Trimble Lane Rd., then 1.5 mi. n. to 8080 CR 250. Chuck wagon suppers are followed by a Western-style stage show with songs and stories performed by the Bar D Wranglers. The Western village also includes shops and a train ride.

Time: Allow 2 hours minimum. **Hours:** Village and ticket booth open at 5:30, Memorial Day weekend-Labor Day. Dinner at 7:30. Stage show at 8:30. **Cost:** (includes dinner and show) $20; $10 (ages 3-8). Reservations are required. **Phone:** (970) 247-5753 or (888) 800-5753.

GEM **THE DURANGO AND SILVERTON NARROW GAUGE RAILROAD & MUSEUM** is at 479 Main Ave. Trains, powered by vintage coal-fired steam locomotives, run through the mountains of the San Juan National Forest following the Animas River to Silverton; the scenery is ruggedly beautiful. The line has been in continuous operation since 1881. Standard-class seating is available in an enclosed coach or open-air car; premium-class cars dating to the 1880s are available on every train.

Least crowded times for the approximately 9-hour round-trip to Silverton are May to early June, late August and in October. The 45-mile trip takes 3 1/2 hours each way and allows 2 1/4 hours in the mining town of Silverton for lunch and shopping. As an upgrade, a bus is available for one direction of the round trip between Durango and Silverton; phone for dates and times. A 5-hour, 52-mile round-trip to Cascade Canyon is offered during the winter. Other themed train rides, such as the Polar Express, are schedule throughout the year; call for information. The museum is in a roundhouse in the Durango yard. Rotating displays include vintage locomotives and cars, 1880s photographs, maps and railroad art.

Note: The coal-fired engines may emit cinders and soot. Dark clothing and sunglasses are recommended. Passengers must be in their seats 30 minutes prior to departure or the seat may be sold to waiting passengers. Food is available onboard. **Hours:** Trips to Silverton depart daily at 8:15 and 9 a.m., early May-late Oct. (also at 9:45, early June to mid-Aug.). The winter train to Cascade Canyon departs daily at 10 a.m., day before Thanksgiving-early May. The Polar Express operates late Nov.-late Dec. Closed Christmas. Phone ahead to confirm schedule.

Cost: Fare to Silverton $79; $49 (ages 4-11); free (ages 0-3 not occupying a seat). Premium-class cars $119-$169. Winter train fare $49; $29 (ages 4-11). Polar Express fare $28-$59; $18-$49 (ages 2-11). Museum $5; $2.50 (ages 5-11). Train fare includes entry to museum. Age requirements for travel in premium-class cars range from 12 to 21; phone ahead for details. Prices may vary, call to confirm. Reservations are recommended. **Parking:** $9 for RVs/trailers, $7 per private vehicle. **Phone:** (970) 247-2733 or (888) 872-4607.

OUTLAW TOURS, 555 Main Ave., offers quarter-, half-, three-quarter- and full-day jeep and Hummer excursions to Colorado's scenic San Juan Mountains, featuring ghost towns, mining camps and American Indian dwellings. Combination packages with The Durango and Silverton Narrow Gauge Railroad & Museum are available. White-water rafting and snowmobile tours also are offered in season.

Hours: Quarter-day tours depart daily at 10 and 1, half-day tours daily at 8 and 1, three-quarter- and full-day tours daily at 8, May-Oct. **Cost:** Quarter-day

▼ *See AAA listing p. 172* ▼

trips $60; $40 (ages 5-11). Half-day trips $80; $60 (ages 5-11). Three-quarter-day trips $100; $75 (ages 5-11). Full-day trips $135; $100 (ages 5-11). **Phone:** (970) 259-1800 or (877) 259-1800.

RECREATIONAL ACTIVITIES

Horseback Riding

- **Rapp Corral** is .75 mi. past Milepost 41 on US 550 at 51 Haviland Lake Rd. Other activities are offered. **Hours:** Daily 8-5, mid-May through Sept. 30; 11-4, mid-Dec. through Feb. 28. **Phone:** (970) 247-8454.

Skiing

- **Purgatory at Durango Mountain Resort** is off US 550 in the San Juan National Forest. Other activities are offered. **Hours:** Daily 9-4, Thanksgiving-early Apr. (weather permitting). **Phone:** (970) 247-9000 or (800) 982-6103.

Snowmobiling

- **Snowmobile Adventures** departs from Purgatory at Durango Mountain Resort on US 550 in the San Juan National Forest. **Hours:** Daily 9-4:30, mid-Dec. to late Mar. (weather permitting). **Phone:** (970) 385-2141, or (970) 259-7293 evenings.

White-water Rafting

- **Mountain Waters Rafting** departs from 643 Camino del Rio in the Albertsons parking lot. **Hours:** Departures daily at 8:15, 8:45, 9:30, 10, noon, 12:45, 1:15, 2:45, 3:30 and 5:15, mid-May through Aug. 31. **Phone:** (970) 259-4191 or (800) 585-8243.

APPLE ORCHARD INN **Phone:** (970)247-0751

Bed & Breakfast
$90-$250

Address: 7758 CR 203 81301 **Location:** 8.5 mi n on US 550, just w at Trimble Ln, then 1.3 mi n. **Facility:** Winding paths and wood bridges lead from the main house through landscaped gardens. Rooms and cottages have feather beds with luxurious comforters, four-poster beds and wraparound porches. 10 units, some cottages. 2 stories (no elevator), interior/exterior corridors. **Terms:** check-in 4 pm, 21 day cancellation notice-fee imposed. **Activities:** whirlpool. **Free Special Amenities: full breakfast and high-speed Internet.**

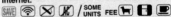

 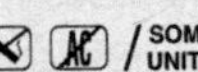 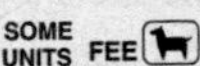 / SOME UNITS FEE 

BEST WESTERN DURANGO INN & SUITES
Phone: (970)247-3251

Motel
$79-$189

AAA Benefit: Members save up to 20%, plus 10% bonus points with Best Western Rewards®.

Address: 21382 US Hwy 160 W 81303 **Location:** On US 160, 1 mi w. **Facility:** 71 units. 2 stories (no elevator), exterior corridors. **Pool(s):** heated outdoor. **Activities:** whirlpool. **Guest Services:** valet and coin laundry. **Free Special Amenities: local telephone calls and high-speed Internet.**

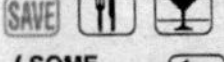  
 / SOME UNITS FEE

BEST WESTERN MOUNTAIN SHADOWS
Phone: (970)247-5200

Motel
$65-$165

AAA Benefit: Members save up to 20%, plus 10% bonus points with Best Western Rewards®.

Address: 3255 Main Ave 81301 **Location:** 2.4 mi n on US 550. **Facility:** 65 units, some two bedrooms. 2 stories (no elevator), exterior corridors. **Amenities:** *Some:* high-speed Internet. **Pool(s):** heated indoor. **Activities:** whirlpool. **Guest Services:** coin laundry. **Free Special Amenities: local telephone calls and high-speed Internet.**

  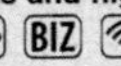   

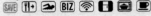

BEST WESTERN PLUS RIO GRANDE INN
Phone: (970)385-4980

Hotel
$109-$199

AAA Benefit: Members save up to 20%, plus 10% bonus points with Best Western Rewards®.

Address: 400 E 2nd Ave 81301 **Location:** Just e of Main Ave; just s of 2nd Ave and 5th St. Located near Durango & Silverton Narrow Gauge Train Depot. **Facility:** 102 units. 3 stories, interior/exterior corridors. **Amenities:** *Some:* high-speed Internet. **Pool(s):** heated indoor. **Activities:** sauna, whirlpool. **Guest Services:** complimentary and valet laundry. **Free Special Amenities: high-speed Internet and manager's reception.** *(See ad p. 175.)*

 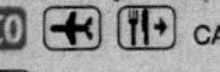 CALL 
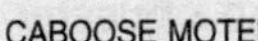

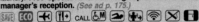

CABOOSE MOTEL **Phone:** (970)247-1191

Motel
$58-$190

Address: 3363 Main Ave 81301 **Location:** 2.5 mi n on US 550. **Facility:** 19 units, some efficiencies and kitchens. 1 story, exterior corridors. **Terms:** cancellation fee imposed. **Activities:** whirlpool.

  / SOME UNITS FEE 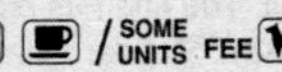

COMFORT INN & SUITES **Phone:** (970)259-7900

Hotel
$79-$300

Address: 455 S Camino Del Rio 81303 **Location:** On US 160 (Frontage Rd), 1.5 mi e of jct US 550. **Facility:** 122 units. 3 stories, interior corridors. **Terms:** cancellation fee imposed. **Amenities:** safes. **Pool(s):** heated indoor. **Activities:** sauna, whirlpool, exercise room. **Guest Services:** coin laundry. **Free Special Amenities: expanded continental breakfast and high-speed Internet.** *(See ad p. 176.)*

CALL 
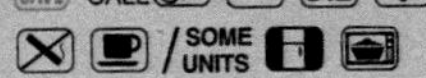 / SOME UNITS

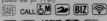

DOUBLETREE BY HILTON HOTEL DURANGO **Phone:** (970)259-6580

Hotel

$209-$269 5/1-10/20
$109-$159 10/21-4/30

AAA Benefit: Members save 5% or more everyday!

Address: 501 Camino Del Rio 81301 **Location:** Jct US 160 and 550. **Facility:** 159 units. 4 stories, interior corridors. **Terms:** 1-7 night minimum stay, cancellation fee imposed. **Amenities:** high-speed Internet. **Dining:** Edgewater Grille, see separate listing. **Pool(s):** heated indoor. **Activities:** saunas, whirlpool, fishing, exercise room. **Guest Services:** valet and coin laundry, area transportation-within 3 mi.

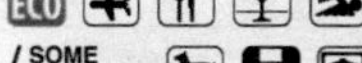 FEE / SOME UNITS FEE 

DURANGO DOWNTOWN INN **Phone:** (970)247-5393

Motel

$109-$189 1/1-4/30
$109-$179 5/1-12/31

Address: 800 Camino Del Rio 81301 **Location:** On US 550, just n of jct US 160. **Facility:** 139 units. 2 stories (no elevator), exterior corridors. **Terms:** check-in 4 pm. **Amenities:** *Some:* high-speed Internet. **Pool(s):** heated indoor. **Activities:** sauna, whirlpool, exercise room. **Guest Services:** valet and coin laundry. **Free Special Amenities: local telephone calls and high-speed Internet.**

SAVE / SOME UNITS FEE

Get pet travel tips and enter the photo contest at AAA.com/PetBook

DURANGO LODGE **Phone:** (970)247-0955

Motel

$85-$160 5/1-11/1
$55-$100 11/2-4/30

Address: 150 E 5th St 81301 **Location:** Just e of 5th St and Main Ave. **Facility:** 39 units. 2 stories (no elevator), interior/exterior corridors. **Terms:** cancellation fee imposed. **Pool(s):** heated outdoor. **Activities:** whirlpool.

ECONO LODGE INN & SUITES **Phone:** 970/247-4242

Motel

Rates not provided

Address: 2002 Main Ave 81301 **Location:** On US 550, 1.3 mi n. **Facility:** 43 units. 2 stories (no elevator), exterior corridors. **Terms:** office hours 7 am-11 pm. **Free Special Amenities: continental breakfast and high-speed Internet.** SAVE / SOME UNITS

GENERAL PALMER HOTEL **Phone:** 970/247-4747

Historic Hotel

$90-$305

Address: 567 Main Ave 81301 **Location:** At Main Ave and College Dr. Next to Durango and Silverton Narrow Gauge Train Depot. **Facility:** This restored 1898 hotel and adjacent annex combine rich Victorian elegance and Southwestern hospitality. Puzzles and other games are available. There is no elevator in the annex. 39 units. 2-3 stories, interior/exterior corridors. **Parking:** winter plug-ins. **Terms:** check-in 4 pm, 7 day cancellation notice-fee imposed. **Guest Services:** valet laundry. **Free Special Amenities: expanded continental breakfast and high-speed Internet.** *(See ad p. 176.)*

SAVE BIZ / SOME UNITS

▼ See AAA listing p. 174 ▼

▼ See AAA listing p. 174 ▼

▼ See AAA listing p. 175 ▼

HAMPTON INN

Phone: (970)247-2600

Hotel

$89-$199

AAA Benefit:
Members save up to 10% everyday!

Address: 3777 Main Ave 81301 **Location:** 2.9 mi n on US 550. **Facility:** 76 units. 3 stories, interior corridors. **Terms:** 1-7 night minimum stay, cancellation fee imposed. **Amenities:** video games (fee). **Pool(s):** heated indoor. **Activities:** whirlpool. **Guest Services:** valet and coin laundry.

 FEE

/ SOME UNITS

LELAND HOUSE BED & BREAKFAST SUITES

Phone: (970)385-1920

Historic Bed & Breakfast

$169-$399 5/1-10/15
$129-$399 10/16-4/30

Address: 721 E 2nd Ave 81301 **Location:** Just e of Main Ave via 7th St, then just n. **Facility:** The restored historic inn offers in-room ceiling fans and cozy, charming décor; three rooms feature a gas fireplace. 11 units, some two bedrooms and kitchens. 2 stories (no elevator), interior/exterior corridors. **Terms:** office hours 7:30 am-10 pm, 14 day cancellation notice-fee imposed. **Activities:** bicycles. **Guest Services:** valet laundry.

/ SOME UNITS FEE

▼ See AAA listing p. 178 ▼

LIGHTNER CREEK INN **Phone:** 970/259-1226

Bed & Breakfast

$99-$199

Address: 999 Lightner Creek Rd, CR 207 81301 **Location:** 3 mi w on US 160, 1 mi n. Located in a quiet area. **Facility:** In a lush valley near a trout stream, the inn offers a peaceful ambience in a beautiful country setting. 9 units, some kitchens. 2 stories (no elevator), interior/exterior corridors. **Terms:** 14 day cancellation notice-fee imposed. **Activities:** whirlpool, fishing, cross country skiing, hiking trails.

/ SOME UNITS FEE

LOGWOOD BED & BREAKFAST **Phone:** 970/259-4396

Bed & Breakfast

$100-$200

Address: 35060 US 550 81301 **Location:** 12 mi n; on east side. **Facility:** 8 units. 3 stories (no elevator), interior corridors. **Terms:** check-in 4 pm, 2 night minimum stay - seasonal and/or weekends, 30 day cancellation notice-fee imposed. **Activities:** game room.

/ SOME UNITS

PURGATORY LODGE & VILLAGE **Phone:** 970/385-2100

Resort Hotel

Rates not provided

Address: 5 Skier Pl 81301 **Location:** 27 mi n on US 550; at Durango Mountain Resort. **Facility:** This mountain resort offers luxury studios as well as two-, three- and four-bedroom condominiums with fireplaces and balconies. Some units are slopeside, providing you with ski-in/ski-out access. 160 units, some houses, cabins and condominiums. 6 stories, interior/exterior corridors. **Terms:** check-in 4 pm. **Amenities:** *Some:* high-speed Internet. **Dining:** 3 restaurants. **Pool(s):** heated outdoor. **Activities:** whirlpool, miniature golf, tennis court, recreation programs, rental bicycles, hiking trails, exercise room. *Fee:* downhill & cross country skiing, snowmobiling, horseback riding, game room, massage. **Guest Services:** coin laundry.

BIZ / SOME UNITS

QUALITY INN **Phone:** (970)259-5373

Motel

$79-$159

Address: 2930 N Main Ave 81301 **Location:** 2 mi n on US 550. Located close to railroad tracks. **Facility:** 48 units. 2 stories (no elevator), exterior corridors. **Terms:** cancellation fee imposed. **Pool(s):** heated outdoor. **Activities:** whirlpools.

/ SOME UNITS FEE

RAMADA LIMITED **Phone:** 970/259-1333

Motel

Rates not provided

Address: 3030 N Main Ave 81301 **Location:** 2.1 mi n on US 550. **Facility:** 48 units. 3 stories (no elevator), interior/exterior corridors. **Amenities:** *Some:* safes. **Pool(s):** heated outdoor. **Activities:** sauna, whirlpool, limited exercise equipment.

BIZ

RESIDENCE INN BY MARRIOTT **Phone:** (970)259-6200

Extended Stay Hotel

$116-$242

AAA Benefit:
AAA hotel discounts of 5% or more.

Address: 21691 Hwy 160 W 81301 **Location:** On US 160, just w. **Facility:** 66 kitchen units, some two bedrooms. 3 stories, interior corridors. **Pool(s):** heated indoor. **Activities:** whirlpool, sports court, exercise room. **Guest Services:** valet and coin laundry.

CALL BIZ / SOME UNITS FEE

THE ROCHESTER HOTEL **Phone:** (970)385-1920

Classic Historic Bed & Breakfast

$169-$399 5/1-10/15
$129-$399 10/16-4/30

Address: 726 E 2nd Ave 81301 **Location:** Just e of Main Ave via 7th St, then just n. **Facility:** Well-appointed guest rooms at the 1892 hotel reflect a Western-theme fashioned after the motion pictures filmed in the local area. 15 units. 2 stories (no elevator), interior corridors. **Terms:** 14 day cancellation notice-fee imposed. **Activities:** bicycles. **Guest Services:** valet laundry.

BIZ / SOME UNITS FEE

SIESTA MOTEL **Phone:** (970)247-0741

Motel

$58-$145

Address: 3475 N Main Ave 81301 **Location:** 2.6 mi n on US 550. **Facility:** 21 units, some efficiencies and kitchens. 1 story, exterior corridors. **Parking:** winter plug-ins. **Activities:** whirlpool.

/ SOME UNITS FEE

STRATER HOTEL **Phone:** (970)247-4431

Classic Historic Hotel

$119-$289

Address: 699 Main Ave 81301 **Location:** Corner of 7th St and Main Ave; historic downtown. Located near Durango and Silverton Narrow Gauge Train Depot. **Facility:** This Victorian-era hotel offers elegant rooms with modern baths, period décor, an old-fashioned lively saloon, and live melodrama and vaudeville at the Henry Strater Theatre. 93 units. 4 stories, interior corridors. **Terms:** check-in 4 pm, cancellation fee imposed. **Dining:** Diamond Belle Saloon, The Mahogany Grille, see separate listings, entertainment. **Activities:** whirlpool. **Guest Services:** valet laundry. **Free Special Amenities: expanded continental breakfast and local telephone calls.**

(See ad p. 177.)

SAVE ECO / SOME UNITS FEE

WHERE TO EAT

BRICKHOUSE CAFÉ & COFFEE BAR **Phone:** 970/247-3760

American

$6-$10

AAA Inspector Notes: The friendly staffers who work in the restored Victorian house serve healthy and delicious homemade meals. The cafe is a great spot to visit for waffles, skillets, soups, salads, sandwiches, fresh-made pastries or a coffee to go. The covered outdoor patio is open seasonally. **Bar:** beer & wine. **Address:** 1849 Main Ave 81301 **Location:** Jct US 160, 1.1 mi n on US 550; at 19th St and Main Ave. B L

COSMO BAR & DINING **Phone:** 970/259-2898

American

$22-$35

AAA Inspector Notes: Enjoy innovative contemporary American cuisine in a warm and inviting atmosphere. Choose from a variety of wines and martinis. Seasonal menu items may include juicy steaks, lobster pot stickers, warm marinated beet salad, prime rib two ways, seared Hawaiian tuna and a crème brûlée trio. Check out the seasonal rooftop patio. **Bar:** full bar. **Reservations:** suggested. **Address:** 919 Main Ave 81301 **Location:** Just n of W 9th St and Main Ave. **Parking:** street only. D

CYPRUS CAFE **Phone:** 970/385-6884

Mediterranean
$9-$29

AAA Inspector Notes: Located in an elegantly restored Victorian house, this cafe serves flavorful, Mediterranean-inspired cuisine. Seasonal menu items may include wild salmon with goat cheese, grape leaves and olive caper tapenade baked in parchment paper; vegetarian specialties; harissa and lemon-marinated lamb chops served with roasted new potatoes; and a wide variety of farmer's market produce. Desserts such as lavender flan, baklava and chocolate pot de crème can be enjoyed on the beautiful garden patio. **Bar:** full bar. **Address:** 725 E 2nd Ave 81301 **Location:** Between 7th and 8th sts; center. **Parking:** street only.
L D

DIAMOND BELLE SALOON **Phone:** 970/247-4431

American
$7-$16

AAA Inspector Notes: Costumed dance hall girls and bartenders transport patrons to the turn of the last century. Diners sip fine wine, creative cocktails and frosty beer as honky-tonk music plays. Menu favorites include Thai marinated chicken and bibb lettuce wraps, green chili pork stew, a delicious caprese sandwich, grilled salmon and juicy steak, while traditional items include meatloaf, pot roast and homemade chicken pot pie. Creative daily lunch specials are delicious and the Sunday gospel brunch is a must. **Bar:** full bar. **Address:** 699 Main Ave 81301 **Location:** Corner of 7th St and Main Ave; historic downtown; in Strater Hotel. **Parking:** street only. L D

DIGS RESTAURANT AT THREE SPRINGS
Phone: 970/259-2344

American
$9-$17

AAA Inspector Notes: This fun and comfortable eatery features a variety of attractively presented appetizers, salads, soups, hand-tossed pizzas, barbecue and Cuban pork sandwiches, buffalo burgers, fried mahi-mahi tacos, grilled salmon and delicious buttermilk-fried chicken served with creamed leeks and corn. The desserts are tempting. **Bar:** full bar. **Address:** 125 Mercado St, Unit 107 81301 **Location:** 6 mi e of jct SR 160 and US 550 to Three Springs Blvd, 1 mi e (1st exit at 1st roundabout, 2nd exit at 2nd roundabout). L D

EAST BY SOUTHWEST **Phone:** 970/247-5533

Japanese
$9-$36

AAA Inspector Notes: Traditional Japanese dishes are prepared with a twist. Some of the chef's innovations include Southwestern spices for added flavor. For the lunch crowd, bento boxes include a sample of many delicious dishes such as California rolls, edamame and teriyaki chicken or beef. Try the artistic sushi boats for small or large dinner parties or a romantic date. Few restaurants serve Japanese desserts, so it's worth saving room for the mochi balls (ice cream with a gelatin coating). **Bar:** full bar. **Address:** 160 E College Dr 81301 **Location:** Corner of College Dr and 2nd Ave; downtown. **Parking:** street only.
L D

EDGEWATER GRILLE **Phone:** 970/259-6580

Regional American
$9-$29

AAA Inspector Notes: This restaurant offers views of the river and mountains along with a menu of seafood, steak, pasta and fresh-baked desserts. There's entertainment during Sunday brunch and music in the lounge on Thursday evenings. A breakfast buffet is also offered. **Bar:** full bar. **Address:** 501 Camino Del Rio 81301 **Location:** Jct US 160 and 550; in DoubleTree by Hilton Hotel Durango. B L D

FRANCISCO'S **Phone:** 970/247-4098

Mexican
$7-$25

AAA Inspector Notes: Reportedly the city's oldest and most respected restaurant, the family-owned establishment serves classic Mexican fare and American dishes, such as Rocky Mountain trout, king salmon and many other steak and seafood delights. **Bar:** full bar. **Address:** 619 Main Ave 81301 **Location:** Corner of Main Ave and College Dr; downtown. **Parking:** street only. **Classic** L D

GAZPACHO NEW MEXICAN RESTAURANT
Phone: 970/259-9494

Mexican
$7-$20

AAA Inspector Notes: Gazpacho's features northern New Mexico cooking with carne adovada, homemade tamales, hot chili and vegetarian dishes. The Southwestern dining rooms display skylights and log beams. This popular place has great service and a loyal local following. **Bar:** full bar. **Address:** 431 E 2nd Ave 81301 **Location:** Just e of Durango and Silverton Narrow Gauge Train Depot. L D

GUIDO'S FAVORITE FOODS **Phone:** 970/259-5028

Italian
$8-$28

AAA Inspector Notes: This authentic Italian trattoria on the corner of 12th and Main has a seasonal outdoor patio and a delicious menu. Patrons can order organic arugula salad with air-cured beef, seared sea scallops with savory lemon-anchovy-garlic white wine sauce on fried polenta cake, sautéed clams or steamed mussels paired with mouthwatering sauces, grilled steak with sautéed mushrooms, fried lemon sole or veal loin scaloppine in a white wine caper sauce. House-made gelato and tiramisu provide a sweet ending. **Bar:** full bar. **Address:** 1201 Main Ave 81301 **Location:** At 12th St and Main Ave. **Parking:** street only. L D

HIMALAYAN KITCHEN **Phone:** 970/259-0956

Tibetan
$9-$19

AAA Inspector Notes: Guests can prepare for a distinctive experience centered on flavorful cuisine. Traditional fare includes Indian curry dishes, hearty soups, salads and preparations of beef, chicken, lamb and exotic yak. **Bar:** full bar. **Address:** 992 Main Ave 81301 **Location:** Corner of 10th St and Main Ave. **Parking:** street only. L D

JEAN-PIERRE BAKERY & CAFE **Phone:** 970/385-0122

French
$8-$24

AAA Inspector Notes: Delicious sandwiches, soups and salads plus heavenly pastries make this eatery a must-stop spot for any visit to Durango. The owners restored the historic Victorian building that houses the restaurant and recently opened a wine bar. Arrive early or late to avoid a long line as the traditional meal hours are quite busy. **Bar:** beer & wine. **Address:** 601 Main Ave 81301 **Location:** Corner of Main Ave and College Dr; downtown. **Parking:** street only. B L D

KEN & SUE'S **Phone:** 970/385-1810

New American
$7-$23

AAA Inspector Notes: This popular restaurant offers an interesting selection of American comfort food and international fusion-style cuisine. Appetizers mainly consist of Asia-influenced dishes such as ginger-chicken pot stickers. Entrées include Aunt Lydia's meatloaf, pistachio-crusted grouper, filet mignon and grilled pork medallions wrapped in smoked bacon. **Bar:** full bar. **Reservations:** suggested. **Address:** 636 Main Ave 81301 **Location:** 6th St and Main Ave; downtown. **Parking:** street only. L D

LADY FALCONBURGH'S **Phone:** 970/382-9664

American
$6-$19

AAA Inspector Notes: Serving handcrafted beer and great food in a family-friendly European pub atmosphere, this lively place features hand-painted murals, an all-brick bar and a sunlit atrium. Favorite dishes include peel-and-eat shrimp, hot chicken Oriental salad, amber ale-battered fish and chips, slow-smoked baby back ribs, grilled salmon with rice and steamed vegetables, and a juicy 10-ounce steak. A tasty black-and-tan soup consists of spicy black bean on one side and creamy cheddar beer on the other. **Bar:** full bar. **Address:** 640 Main Ave 81301 **Location:** Between College Dr and 7th St; downstairs. **Parking:** street only. L D

THE MAHOGANY GRILLE
Menu on AAA.com **Phone:** 970/247-4433

New American
$16-$38

AAA Inspector Notes: Served in an intimate Victorian-themed dining room reminiscent of the 1800s are innovative, cutting-edge New American entrée specialties featuring steak, game, seafood, pasta and gourmet salads followed by "fabulicious" desserts. **Bar:** full bar. **Reservations:** suggested. **Address:** 699 Main Ave 81301 **Location:** At 7th St and Main Ave; in Strater Hotel. **Parking:** on-site and street. **Historic** D

MAMA'S BOY RISTORANTE **Phone:** 970/247-0060

Italian
$12-$21

AAA Inspector Notes: The restaurant offers a good selection of nicely presented pasta dishes, chicken, pork, beef and seafood entrées, as well as pizza, soup and hero sandwiches. Tasty bread and desserts are made on the premises. **Bar:** full bar. **Address:** 2659 N Main Ave 81301 **Location:** On US 550, at 27th St and Main Ave. L D

ORE HOUSE **Phone:** 970/247-5707

Steak
$19-$37

AAA Inspector Notes: The rustic dining room displays Old West décor and works by local artists. Some menu items are Tasmanian sweet crab cakes, fried calamari and artichokes, wild king salmon, Maine lobster, New York strip steak and chateaubriand for two carved tableside. Vegetables such as sweet corn baked in cast iron with a cornbread crust and Brussels sprouts sauteed with bacon, shallots and maple syrup are served family style. Vegetarian and non-red meat options also are available. **Bar:** full bar. **Reservations:** suggested. **Address:** 147 E College Dr 81301 **Location:** Just e of Main Ave and College Dr; downtown. **Parking:** street only. D

PALACE RESTAURANT **Phone:** 970/247-2018

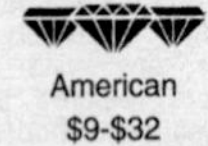

American
$9-$32

AAA Inspector Notes: This restaurant is known for its outdoor patio. The menu features well-prepared pasta, seafood, beef, poultry and pork entrées. Among the specialty dishes are halibut, almond-honey-roasted duck, Colorado lamb and bison rib-eye. The delicious berry crumble dessert is served hot with a scoop of vanilla ice cream. The friendly, attentive staff enhances the dining experience. **Bar:** full bar. **Reservations:** suggested. **Address:** 505 Main Ave 81301 **Location:** Next to Durango and Silverton Narrow Gauge Train Depot. **Parking:** street only. L D

RANDY'S **Phone:** 970/247-9083

American
$16-$28

AAA Inspector Notes: The restaurant is well known for its prime rib entree, however duck, lamb, veal and fish are also featured on the menu. The Crab Rangoon appetizer is a popular dish to share, but remember to save room for the mouthwatering desserts. Attractively presented and garnished with a delicious mango sauce, the key lime pie would give any Florida restaurant stiff competition. For a more private, intimate meal, request one of the curtained booths. **Bar:** full bar. **Reservations:** suggested. **Address:** 152 E College Dr 81301 **Location:** Jct Main Ave, just n. **Parking:** street only. D

THE RED SNAPPER **Phone:** 970/259-3417

Seafood
$9-$39

AAA Inspector Notes: This popular and reputable restaurant is located in a 100-year-old building with an upscale ambience of handsome oak, live plants and nautical décor. Service is friendly and attentive. The menu offers a wide variety of seafood, beef, fowl and pasta meals. **Bar:** full bar. **Address:** 144 E 9th St 81301 **Location:** Between Main and 2nd aves; downtown. **Parking:** street only. D

SEASON'S ROTISSERIE & GRILL **Phone:** 970/382-9790

American
$8-$32

AAA Inspector Notes: You'll enjoy this popular, bustling restaurant with an open-view kitchen. When preparing the food, the chef uses pan-roasted, wood-burning grill and rotisserie cooking methods. Microbrews and California wines are popular, too. Patio seating is available; it's a great place for people-watching. **Bar:** full bar. **Reservations:** suggested. **Address:** 764 Main Ave 81301 **Location:** Between 7th and 8th sts; downtown. **Parking:** street only. L D

SUSHITARIAN **Phone:** 970/382-0001

Japanese
$11-$29

AAA Inspector Notes: This relaxed eatery offers creative appetizers, great lunch (including convenient bento boxes) and dinner choices, and a wide variety of specialty rolls. **Bar:** full bar. **Address:** 601 E 2nd Ave 81301 **Location:** Corner of College Dr and E 2nd Ave. **Parking:** street only. L D

EAGLE pop. 6,508

AMERICINN LODGE & SUITES OF EAGLE
Phone: 970/328-5155

Hotel
Rates not provided

Address: 0085 Pond Rd 81631 **Location:** I-70 exit 147, just n, then w. **Facility:** 54 units. 3 stories, interior corridors. **Amenities:** high-speed Internet, safes (fee). **Pool(s):** heated indoor. **Activities:** sauna, whirlpool, bicycles, exercise room. **Guest Services:** valet and coin laundry, area transportation-within 7 mi.

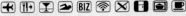

COMFORT INN VAIL VALLEY **Phone:** (970)328-7878

Hotel
$90-$200

Address: 0285 Market St 81631 **Location:** I-70 exit 147, just n, then 0.3 mi e. **Facility:** 60 units. 3 stories, interior corridors. **Terms:** cancellation fee imposed. **Pool(s):** heated indoor. **Activities:** whirlpool. **Guest Services:** coin laundry. **Free Special Amenities: full breakfast and high-speed Internet.**

   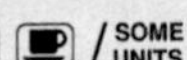   / SOME UNITS 

WHERE TO EAT

GRAND AVE GRILL **Phone:** 970/328-4043

American

$9-$26

AAA Inspector Notes: Listing traditional grill fare, the menu features items such as herb-horseradish-crusted salmon with lemon white wine butter sauce, crab cakes, Mediterranean salad and an unusual roasted meatloaf. Tempting desserts such as the rum raisin bread pudding are sure to please a sweet tooth. Travelers will appreciate viewing a Mike Wolfe photo from American Pickers on the History Channel. **Bar:** full bar. **Address:** 678 Grand Ave 81631 **Location:** I-70 exit 147, 0.3 mi s, take 1st exit at roundabout, then 0.8 mi w. L D

PAZZO'S PIZZERIA **Phone:** 970/337-9900

Italian

$8-$14

AAA Inspector Notes: The menu at this lively eatery includes delicious hand-tossed pizzas, strombolis and calzones with a variety of toppings, lasagna, ravioli, rigatoni, spinach manicotti, and chicken and eggplant Parmigiana. The minestrone soup was very good. **Bar:** full bar. **Address:** 50 Chambers Ave, Suite C 81631 **Location:** I-70 exit 147, just s to Chambers Ave, then just w.

L D

EDWARDS pop. 10,266

DISH RESTAURANT **Phone:** 970/926-3433

Small Plates

$12-$25

AAA Inspector Notes: This eatery offers a variety of seasonal tapas, including adorable appetizers, delicious salads, sauteed mussels, seared wild blue crab, beef Bourguignon and veal scaloppine. The ever-changing desserts are delicious and artistically presented. **Bar:** full bar. **Reservations:** suggested. **Address:** 56 Edwards Village Blvd, Suite 230 81632 **Location:** I-70 exit 167, 0.5 mi s to US 6, then just e (rear entrance). D

EAT! DRINK! **Phone:** 970/926-1393

American

$9-$15

AAA Inspector Notes: The focus of this eatery is gourmet cheese, with most salads and sandwiches featuring a distinct type. The roasted beet salad is made up of artisanal goat cheese, Marcona almonds and fennel, while the California features turkey, Tallegio, pear and fig preserves. The second part of the name refers to the wine shop connected to the restaurant. A variety of wines are available by the glass and by the bottle, but the beer selection is limited. The delicious cupcakes shouldn't be skipped. **Bar:** wine only. **Address:** 56 Edwards Village Blvd 81632 **Location:** I-70 exit 163, 0.6 mi sw, then just e; located in strip mall. L D

THE FRENCH PRESS **Phone:** 970/926-4740

French

$8-$31

AAA Inspector Notes: Perfect for an after-movie meal or early-morning breakfast, this bistro offers a selection of creative American dishes prepared with a definite French accent. The staff assists guests in selecting classic soups such as French onion and entrées such as pan-seared Rocky Mountain trout, roasted Dijon chicken and rack of Colorado lamb. More casual fare is offered for breakfast and lunch. **Bar:** full bar. **Address:** 34295 Hwy 6, C1B 81632 **Location:** I-70 exit 163, 0.5 mi s, then just e; in Riverwalk Plaza. B L D

THE GASHOUSE **Phone:** 970/926-3613

Steak

$9-$32

AAA Inspector Notes: This charming eatery has a rustic log cabin atmosphere and is fun for the whole family. Seasonal selections include hand-cut aged Colorado beef, wild game and a wide array of fresh seafood such as lobster tail, North Atlantic salmon, ruby red trout, soft-shell crab and Blue Point oysters. The seasonal outdoor patio is enclosed and offers umbrella tables, chairs and lush landscaping. **Bar:** full bar. **Address:** 34185 Hwy 6 81632 **Location:** I-70 exit 163, 0.3 mi s; at northwest corner of US 6 and Edwards Village Blvd. L D

JUNIPER RESTAURANT **Phone:** 970/926-7001

American

$30-$39

AAA Inspector Notes: In this wonderful eatery overlooking the Eagle River, contemporary American "comfort-fusion" food is served. The menu includes mouthwatering appetizers and entrees such as maple-braised pork belly with fresh cherry chutney and field greens; lump crab cakes with frisee-cucumber salad and grapefruit aioli; veal scaloppini with angel hair caprese and lemon beurre fondue; apricot granola-crusted wild king salmon with lemon zest couscous and nutmeg creamed spinach; filet mignon with roasted poblano gratin and grilled corn-heirloom tomato salad. Charlie's hot sticky toffee pudding cake is out of this world. **Bar:** full bar. **Reservations:** suggested. **Address:** 97 Main St E, Suite 101 81632 **Location:** I-70 exit 163, 0.5 mi s, then just e; at Riverwalk Plaza. D

LARKBURGER **Phone:** 970/926-9336

Burgers

$4-$8

AAA Inspector Notes: Flavorful burgers, shakes and fries have drawn a large and devoted following to this cozy, quick-serve restaurant. The tasty menu benefits from high-quality, 100 percent natural ingredients, including all-natural turkey, Black Angus beef, Breyers ice cream, Tillamook cheddar and truffle oil. The casual, modern décor features wall panels made from reclaimed timber. Disposable utensils and containers are biodegradable. **Bar:** beer only. **Address:** 105 Edwards Village Blvd 81632 **Location:** I-70 exit 163, 0.6 mi sw; in Edwards Village Center next to post office. L D

SATO SUSHI **Phone:** 970/926-7684

Japanese

$10-$22

AAA Inspector Notes: This popular bistro, with its eclectic, hip and trendy atmosphere, serves a variety of sushi along with Asian-inspired entrees. Chicken pad Thai, spicy beef stir-fry and wasabi pea-crusted halibut are some of the cooked options. **Bar:** full bar. **Address:** 56 Edwards Village Blvd, Suite 120 81632 **Location:** I-70 exit 163, 0.4 mi s; southeast corner of US 6 and Edwards Village Blvd. L D

VISTA AT ARROWHEAD **Phone:** 970/926-2111

American

$8-$33

AAA Inspector Notes: This ever-popular restaurant serves contemporary American cuisine incorporating lamb, beef, chicken and seafood in the menu offerings. This new location has a warm, upscale appearance, yet the staff remains friendly and casual. **Bar:** full bar. **Reservations:** suggested. **Address:** 676 Sawatch Dr 81632 **Location:** I-70 exit 163, 0.4 mi sw, 1.6 mi se on US 6, 0.3 mi s, then just se; in Country Club of the Rockies. **Parking:** valet only. L D

ZINO RISTORANTE **Phone:** 970/926-0777

Italian
$12-$29

AAA Inspector Notes: The spiral staircase leading into the dining room is a focal point of this beautiful restaurant, which also features a large patio overlooking a river. Serving delicious contemporary Italian cuisine, menu items may include skillet-roasted mussels, seasonal soups and salad, crab and mascarpone ravioli in sage butter, prosciutto-wrapped halibut, lamb T-bone in pistachio-mint pesto, wood-fired pizza and traditional Italian desserts. **Bar:** full bar. **Address:** 27 Main St 81632 **Location:** I-70 exit 163, 0.5 mi s, then just e; at Riverwalk Plaza. D

EL JEBEL pop. 3,801

BELLA MIA **Phone:** 970/963-2600

Italian
$10-$30

AAA Inspector Notes: Just off the highway between Carbondale and Aspen, this local favorite has a cozy, bistro feel. The menu revolves around pasta, salads, pizza, veal and homemade desserts. Patio seating is a seasonal option. **Bar:** full bar. **Address:** 60 El Jebel Rd, Unit 108 81623 **Location:** Just n of SR 82; at El Jebel stoplight. D

ZHENG ASIAN BISTRO (EL JEBEL) **Phone:** 970/963-8077

Asian
$9-$15

AAA Inspector Notes: The cozy bistro serves Asia-inspired cocktails and a variety of wok-fired Chinese, Korean and Japanese dishes, as well as a delicious atomic shrimp Thai appetizer. Diners can assemble their own meat or vegetarian stir-fry with a choice of more than 12 vegetables and eight sauces. **Bar:** full bar. **Address:** 400 E Valley Rd 81623 **Location:** On SR 82; in Orchard Plaza.

L D

EMPIRE pop. 282

THE PECK HOUSE
Menu on AAA.com **Phone:** 303/569-9870

Regional American
$15-$29

AAA Inspector Notes: Menu specialties feature delicious Continental dishes, smoked seafood, pates and beef-and-oyster pie. Serving as the dining room of an 1863 hotel, the restaurant offers terrific service, fresh flowers and great mountain views from the porch. **Bar:** full bar. **Reservations:** suggested. **Address:** 83 Sunny Ave 80438 **Location:** I-70 exit 232, 2 mi nw on US 40, then just n on Freeman St. **Parking:** street only. **Historic**

D

ENGLEWOOD pop. 30,255

- **Hotels & Restaurants map & index p. 140**
- **Part of Denver area — see map p. 123**

COURTYARD BY MARRIOTT DENVER PARK MEADOWS
Phone: (720)895-0300

Hotel
$129-$159

AAA Benefit:
AAA hotel discounts of 5% or more.

Address: 8320 S Valley Hwy 80112 **Location:** I-25 exit 195 (County Line Rd), just e, then just s, follow signs. **Facility:** 156 units. 4 stories, interior corridors. **Amenities:** video games (fee), high-speed Internet. **Pool(s):** heated indoor. **Activities:** whirlpool, exercise room. **Guest Services:** valet and coin laundry, area transportation-within 5 mi.

SOME UNITS

HILTON GARDEN INN DENVER SOUTH/MERIDIAN
Phone: (303)824-1550

Hotel
$79-$189

Hilton Garden Inn **AAA Benefit:** Unparalleled hospitality at a special Member rate.

Address: 9290 S Meridian Blvd 80112 **Location:** I-25 exit 193 (Lincoln Ave), e to E Havana St, just n, stay in left lane to Meridian Blvd, then 0.5 mi w. **Facility:** 157 units. 6 stories, interior corridors. **Terms:** 1-7 night minimum stay, cancellation fee imposed. **Amenities:** high-speed Internet. **Pool(s):** heated indoor. **Activities:** whirlpool, jogging, exercise room. **Guest Services:** valet and coin laundry, area transportation-within 10 mi. **Free Special Amenities: newspaper and local transportation.**

SAVE CALL BIZ FEE

HOMEWOOD SUITES BY HILTON - DTC/INVERNESS
Phone: (303)706-0102

Extended Stay Hotel
$89-$209

AAA Benefit:
Contemporary luxury at a special Member rate.

Address: 199 Inverness Dr W 80112 **Location:** I-25 exit 195 (County Line Rd), 0.3 mi ne to traffic light, then just n. **Facility:** 113 efficiencies, some two bedrooms. 4 stories, interior corridors. **Terms:** 1-7 night minimum stay, cancellation fee imposed. **Amenities:** high-speed Internet. **Pool(s):** heated indoor. **Activities:** jogging, sports court, exercise room. **Guest Services:** valet and coin laundry, area transportation-within 5 mi.

BIZ SOME UNITS FEE

THE INVERNESS HOTEL AND CONFERENCE CENTER
Phone: (303)799-5800

Resort Hotel
$89-$249

Address: 200 Inverness Dr W 80112 **Location:** I-25 exit 195 (County Line Rd), 0.3 mi ne to traffic light, then just n. **Facility:** Attractive, spacious rooms overlook the golf course or mountains, giving the hotel a resortlike ambience; an expanded spa provides relaxation. 302 units. 5 stories, interior corridors. **Parking:** on-site and valet. **Terms:** cancellation fee imposed. **Amenities:** video games (fee), high-speed Internet, honor bars. **Dining:** 3 restaurants, also, Baca, see separate listing. **Pool(s):** heated outdoor, heated indoor. **Activities:** saunas, whirlpools, steamrooms, 3 tennis courts, jogging, exercise room, spa. *Fee:* golf-18 holes. **Guest Services:** valet laundry, area transportation-within 5 mi. **Free Special Amenities: high-speed Internet and local transportation.**

SAVE ECO CALL BIZ FEE SOME UNITS

RESIDENCE INN PARK MEADOWS
Phone: (720)895-0200

Extended Stay Hotel
$149-$169

AAA Benefit:
AAA hotel discounts of 5% or more.

Address: 8322 S Valley Hwy 80112 **Location:** I-25 exit 195 (County Line Rd), just e to S Valley Hwy, then just s. **Facility:** 112 units, some two bedrooms, efficiencies and kitchens. 4 stories, interior corridors. **Amenities:** video games (fee), high-speed Internet. **Pool(s):** heated indoor. **Activities:** whirlpool, sports court, exercise room. **Guest Services:** valet and coin laundry, area transportation-within 5 mi.

CALL BIZ FEE SOME UNITS FEE

(See map & index p. 140.)

WHERE TO EAT

BACA **Phone:** 303/799-5800

American
$22-$38

AAA Inspector Notes: Baca is the Inverness Hotel's signature dining venue featuring contemporary cuisine prepared with a Spanish flair. Tapping the region's bounty of Colorado-range bison, stream-fresh fish and locally-raised chicken and beef, chefs prepare dishes in a traditional Spanish manner with lively sauces, spices and indigenous ingredients. Baca offers a medley of tapas and tempting dishes complete with an entire cellar of vintage wines from Spain, Chile and around the globe. **Bar:** full bar. **Reservations:** suggested. **Address:** 200 Inverness Dr W 80112 **Location:** I-25 exit 195 (County Line Rd), 0.3 mi ne to traffic light, then just n; in The Inverness Hotel and Conference Center. **Parking:** on-site and valet. (D)

FLEMING'S PRIME STEAKHOUSE & WINE BAR **Phone:** 303/768-0827

Steak
$28-$46

AAA Inspector Notes: The warm, clubby atmosphere is the ideal setting for perfectly grilled steaks and seafood. Side dishes come in hearty portions, and salads are fresh and crisp. More than 100 wine selections are available. **Bar:** full bar. **Address:** 191 Inverness Dr W 80112 **Location:** I-25 exit 195 (County Line Rd), 0.3 mi ne to traffic light, then just n. (D)

HACIENDA COLORADO **Phone:** 303/858-8588

Mexican
$7-$22

AAA Inspector Notes: Reservations are strongly suggested at the busy restaurant, where the bright colors and comfortable décor remind diners of a welcoming home. Thin chips with fresh, flavorful salsa take the edge off guests' hunger while they await ample portions of reasonably priced Mexican favorites. **Bar:** full bar. **Address:** 10500 Bierstadt Way 80112 **Location:** I-25 exit 193 (Lincoln St), 0.4 mi e to Havana St, n to Meridian Blvd (stay in left lane), 0.5 mi w, then just w. (L) (D)

TWIN DRAGON CHINESE RESTAURANT **Phone:** 303/781-8068 (118)

Chinese
$8-$30

AAA Inspector Notes: This restaurant has been a favorite in the area since 1977. The extensive menu includes spicy (or not) sesame chicken, flavorful Peking duck and distinctive dishes not offered anywhere else. Service is friendly and courteous. Lighting is good enough that diners can read during lunch. **Bar:** full bar. **Address:** 3021 S Broadway 80113 **Location:** 0.7 mi n of jct US 285 and Broadway. (L) (D)

ESTES PARK (A-4) pop. 5,858, elev. 7,522'

• **Hotels p. 189 • Restaurants p. 194**
• **Attractions map p. 279**
• **Hotels & Restaurants map & index p. 186**

Estes Park serves as the eastern gateway to Rocky Mountain National Park *(see place listing p. 276)*, and those not roughing it at a campground frequently seek accommodations here. Just as wildlife viewing opportunities attract tourists today, it was nature's bounty that first lured Native American tribes and Kit Carson and his group of trappers. The area was ultimately named for pioneer Joel Estes, who settled in the mountainous hamlet around 1860.

The town is a pleasant surprise; in addition to offering park enthusiasts the usual creature comforts along with a variety of outfitters and gear shops devoted to recreational pursuits, Estes Park has a charm all its own and is a worthy destination in itself. Elkhorn Avenue is the hub of shopping activity, with stores touting souvenirs, clothes, sports equipment, jewelry and crafts. A number of eateries as well as ice cream and candy stores entice visitors, who often stroll along the Estes Park Riverwalk after indulging in culinary delights—the path runs along the Big Thompson River and past an old-fashioned waterwheel through the town center.

The stately white Stanley Hotel *(see attraction listing)* is an impressive landmark, a gracious presence amid a backdrop of craggy mountain peaks. Figuring prominently in Estes Park's history, the owner of the property—who happened to invent the Stanley Steamer—transported his guests to the lodging via his renowned steam cars. Over the years, many elite guests have booked a room at the Stanley and savored the view from its veranda.

For Western-style fun appealing to all ages, head to the evening Cowboy Sing-Along occurring throughout the summer in Bond Park; phone the Estes Park Convention & Visitors Bureau for specific dates. If you're in town during mid-July, watch modern-day cowboys perform such feats as bronc riding, steer wrestling and barrel racing during the Rooftop Rodeo, a week-long extravaganza including a parade and antique show.

Performance Park, a band shell with great acoustics no doubt aided by its placement below rugged cliffs, entertains locals and visitors like with its Wednesday and Thursday night summer concert series; the sounds of jazz, bluegrass and other genres waft through the air in this lovely mountain setting at 417 W. Elkhorn Ave.

If you're up for a scenic drive, you can take advantage of several stunningly beautiful routes that pass through town. US 34 becomes Trail Ridge Road in Rocky Mountain National Park, linking Estes Park with the western gateway town of Granby. Reputed to be the highest continuous paved road in the nation, the route (closed during winter) should be traveled with caution—you'll see lush forest, vibrant summer wildflowers and wind-swept alpine tundra on this breathtaking mountain drive. The park's Old Fall River Road, also open in summer, provides several pull-offs affording such scenic panoramas as a canyon, waterfall and valley as well as opportunities to spot the park's varied wildlife.

Estes Park Convention and Visitors Bureau: 500 Big Thompson Ave., Estes Park, CO 80517. **Phone:** (970) 577-9900 or (800) 443-7837. ***(See ad p. 278.)***

AERIAL TRAMWAY is 1 blk. s. of the post office at 420 E. Riverside Dr. Enclosed 10-passenger tram cars glide to the summit of 8,700-foot Prospect Mountain. **Time:** Allow 1 hour minimum. **Hours:** Daily 9-6:30, late May-early Sept. (weather permitting). **Cost:** Fare $10; $9(ages 60+); $5 (ages 6-11); free (ages 0-5). **Phone:** (970) 586-3675.

(See map & index p. 186.)

ENOS MILLS CABIN MUSEUM AND GALLERY is 8.5 mi. s. on SR 7, just opposite the brown Longs Peak sign. The 1885 cabin was home to author and conservationist Enos A. Mills, whose efforts to preserve natural lands earned him the nickname "Father of Rocky Mountain National Park." A gallery of photographs taken by Mills and a self-guiding nature trail also are offered.

Time: Allow 30 minutes minimum. **Hours:** Tues.-Wed. 11-4, Memorial Day-Labor Day; additional days by appointment. Phone ahead to confirm schedule. **Cost:** $5; $3 (ages 5-12). **Phone:** (970) 586-4706.

ESTES PARK MUSEUM, 200 4th St., contains exhibits that emphasize the history of Estes Park and the surrounding region. The museum has displays about local American Indians, early settlers, floods, tourism, the arts and outdoor recreation as well as a Stanley Steamer automobile and a homestead cabin. **Hours:** Mon.-Sat. 10-5, Sun. 1-5, May-Oct.; Fri.-Sat. 10-5, Sun. 1-5, rest of year. Closed major holidays. **Cost:** Donations. **Phone:** (970) 586-6256.

HISTORIC FALL RIVER HYDROPLANT is 3 mi. w. on US 34 following signs to 1754 Fish Hatchery Rd. Built on the Fall River in 1909, this plant introduced electricity to the region and made the landmark Stanley Hotel the first in the nation to run entirely on electricity. The plant, which operated until damaged by a 1982 flood, has been restored to period. Original equipment and hands-on museum exhibits depict its operation as well as local history.

Guided tours are available by appointment. **Time:** Allow 30 minutes minimum. **Hours:** Tues.-Sun. 1-4, day after Memorial Day-day before Labor Day; by appointment rest of year. **Cost:** Free. **Phone:** (970) 586-6256.

MacGREGOR RANCH AND MUSEUM, .5 mi. n. of US 34 on MacGregor Ave., is an original 1873 homestead and living-history cattle ranch. The turn-of-the-20th-century ranch house, now a museum, contains furnishings, photographs, clothing, artwork and personal memorabilia from three generations of the MacGregor family. **Hours:** Tues.-Sat. 10-4, June-Aug. **Cost:** $5; free (ages 0-17). **Phone:** (970) 586-3749.

STANLEY HOTEL GHOST TOURS take place at the historic Stanley Hotel, 333 Wonderview Ave. The palatial Georgian-style lodging, which opened in 1909, was built by F.O. Stanley who, with his brother, invented the Stanley Steamer horseless carriage. Guided tours relate the history of the hotel, which claims to be haunted by several ghosts. Author Stephen King's stay at the hotel is said to be the inspiration for his novel "The Shining."

Time: Allow 1 hour, 30 minutes minimum. **Hours:** Tours are given daily 10-5. Phone ahead to confirm schedule. **Cost:** Fee $15. Under 5 are not permitted. Reservations are required. **Phone:** (970) 577-4110.

RECREATIONAL ACTIVITIES

Fishing

- **Trout Haven Ranch Trout Pond** is 1.2 mi. w. on US 36 at 810 Moraine Ave. **Hours:** Daily 9-5, May-Sept. **Phone:** (970) 577-0202 or (800) 794-7857.

Horseback Riding

- **Hi-Country Stables** is at Moraine Park and at Sprague Lake in Glacier Creek within Rocky Mountain National Park. **Hours:** Rides ranging from 2-8 hours are offered daily, mid-May to mid-Sept. (weather permitting). **Phone:** (970) 586-3244 for Glacier Creek, (303) 442-0258 in the off-season, or (970) 586-2327 for Moraine Park.
- **Sombrero Stables** is on US 34E across from Lake Estes Dam. **Hours:** One-hour to all-day rides are offered daily. Reservations required from Labor Day to Memorial Day. **Phone:** (970) 586-4577.

White-water Rafting

- **Rapid Transit Rafting** departs from Estes Park High School. **Hours:** Trips depart daily, Memorial Day weekend-Labor Day. **Phone:** (970) 577-7238 or (800) 367-8523.
- **Rocky Mountain Adventures** is at 380 E. Elkhorn Ave. (US 34). Other activities are offered. **Hours:** Trips depart daily, mid-May through first week in Sept. **Phone:** (970) 586-6191 or (800) 858-6808.

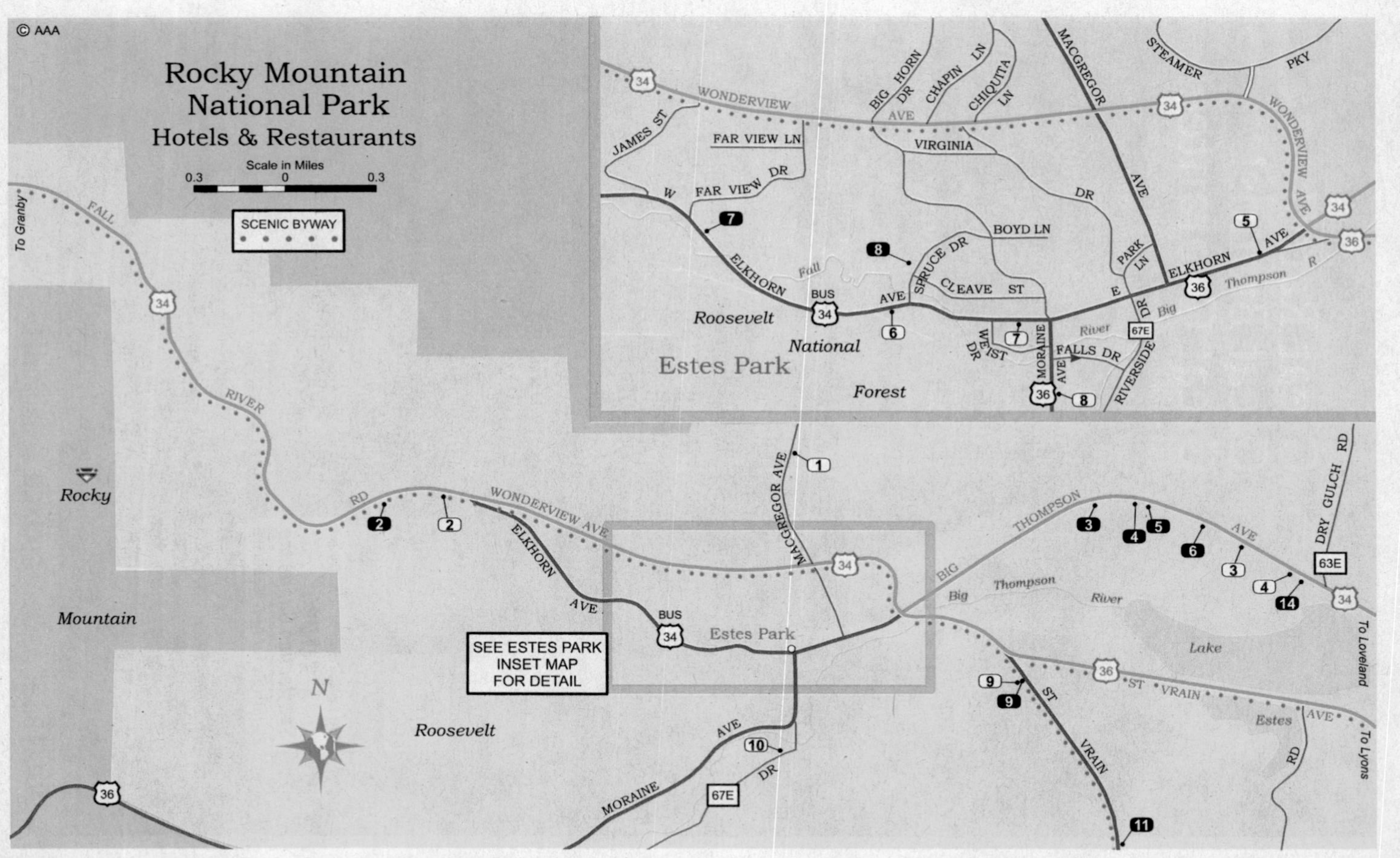
© AAA
Rocky Mountain
National Park
Hotels & Restaurants
Scale in Miles
0.3 0 0.3
SCENIC BYWAY
SEE ESTES PARK INSET MAP FOR DETAIL
To Granby
To Loveland
To Lyons
FALL RIVER RD
WONDERVIEW AVE
ELKHORN AVE
MACGREGOR AVE
BIG THOMPSON AVE
DRY GULCH RD
ST VRAIN AVE
MORAINE AVE
Estes Park
Rocky
Mountain
Roosevelt
Big Thompson River
Lake Estes
Estes Park
Roosevelt
National
Forest
JAMES ST
FAR VIEW LN
W FAR VIEW DR
BIG HORN DR
CHAPIN LN
CHIQUITA LN
VIRGINIA DR
BOYD LN
SPRUCE DR
CLEAVE ST
WEIST DR
MORAINE AVE
FALLS DR
RIVERSIDE DR
PARK LN
STEAMER PKY
Fall River
N

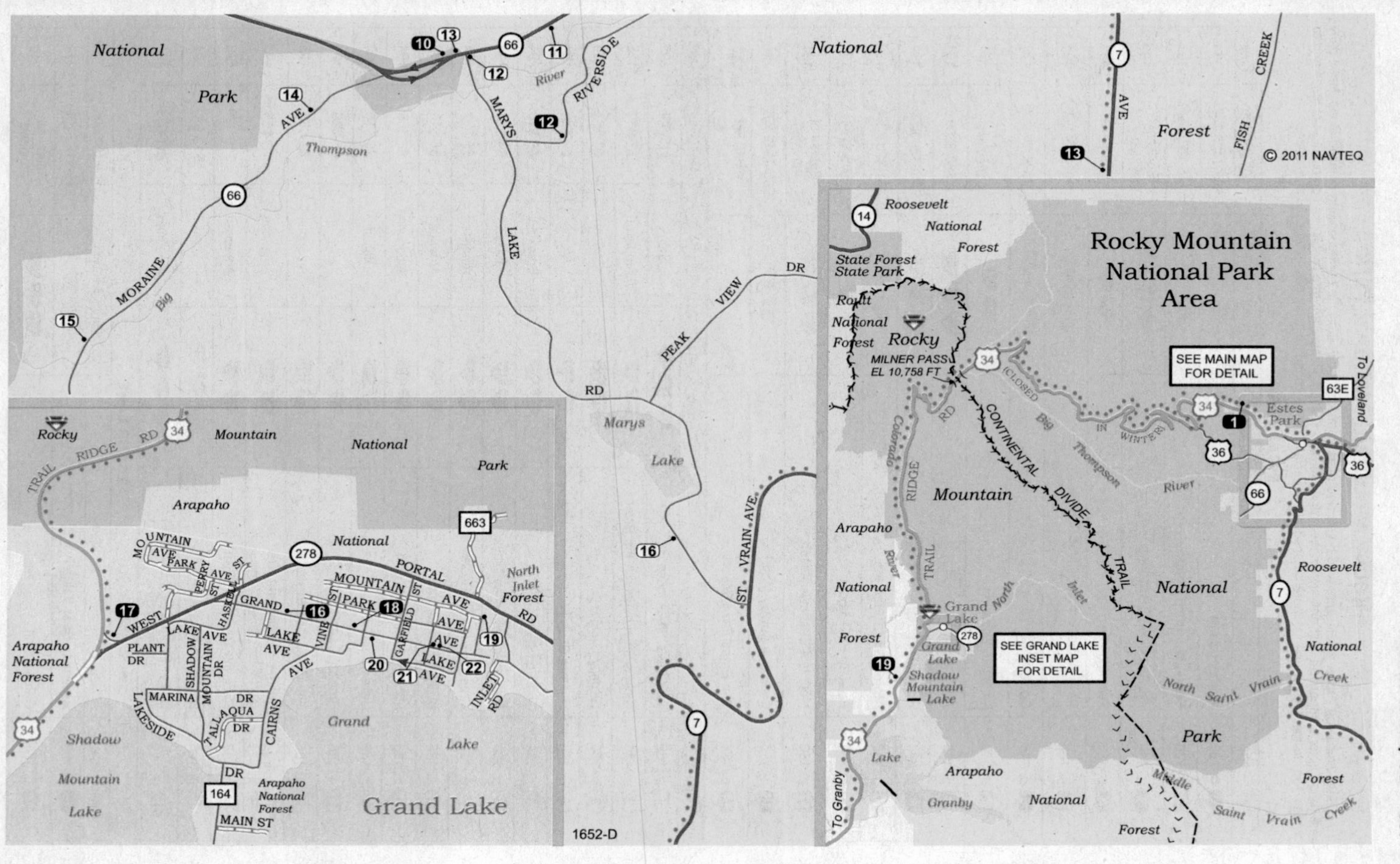
Rocky Mountain National Park Area
SEE MAIN MAP FOR DETAIL
SEE GRAND LAKE INSET MAP FOR DETAIL
To Loveland
Estes Park
CONTINENTAL DIVIDE TRAIL
MILNER PASS EL 10,758 FT
TRAIL RIDGE RD
(CLOSED IN WINTER)
Big Thompson River
Colorado River
North Inlet
North Saint Vrain Creek
Middle Saint Vrain Creek
Roosevelt National Forest
Arapaho National Forest
Routt National Forest
Rocky Mountain National Park
State Forest State Park
Grand Lake
Shadow Mountain Lake
Granby Lake
To Granby
MARYS LAKE RD
PEAK VIEW DR
ST VRAIN AVE
MORAINE AVE
RIVERSIDE
FISH CREEK
Marys Lake
MOUNTAIN AVE
PORTAL AVE
PARK AVE
GRAND AVE
LAKE AVE
VINE ST
GARFIELD ST
HASKELL ST
PERRY ST
WEST
CAIRNS AVE
SHADOW MOUNTAIN DR
TALLAQUA DR
MARINA DR
LAKESIDE
PLANT DR
MAIN ST
INLET RD
North Inlet Forest RD
© 2011 NAVTEQ
1652-D

Rocky Mountain National Park

This index helps you "spot" where approved hotels and restaurants are located on the corresponding detailed maps. Hotel daily rate range is for comparison only and shows the property's high season. Restaurant rate range is a combination of lunch and/or dinner. Turn to the listing page for more detailed rate information and consult display ads for special promotions.

ESTES PARK

Map Page	Hotels	Diamond Rated	High Season	Page
1 p. 186	**Wildwood Inn**	◆◆	$68-$428 SAVE	194
2 p. 186	**Castle Mountain Lodge**	◆◆	$145-$575 SAVE	191
3 p. 186	**Appenzell Inn** *(See ad p. 189.)*	◆◆◆	Rates not provided SAVE	189
4 p. 186	Tyrol Mountain Inn	◆◆	$69-$179	194
5 p. 186	**Best Western Plus Silver Saddle** *(See ad p. 192, p. 276.)*	◆◆◆	$79-$325 SAVE	191
6 p. 186	**Comfort Inn** *(See ad p. 193.)*	◆◆◆	$90-$300 SAVE	191
7 p. 186	Mountain Sage Inn	◆◆	Rates not provided	191
8 p. 186	Silver Moon Inn	◆◆◆	$80-$300	191
9 p. 186	**Rocky Mountain Park Inn**	◆◆◆	$110-$200 SAVE	191
10 p. 186	**Alpine Trail Ridge Inn** *(See ad p. 190.)*	◆◆	$81-$233 SAVE	189
11 p. 186	Peak To Peak Lodge	◆	$55-$199	191
12 p. 186	Mountain Shadows Resort	◆◆◆	Rates not provided	191
13 p. 186	**Saddle & Surrey Motel**	◆◆	$60-$145 SAVE	191
14 p. 186	**The Estes Park Resort**	fyi	Rates not provided SAVE	191

Map Page	Restaurants	Diamond Rated	Cuisine	Meal Range	Page
1 p. 186	Twin Owls Steakhouse	◆◆◆	Steak	$13-$36	195
2 p. 186	Nicky's Steakhouse on the River	◆◆	American	$7-$30	195
3 p. 186	Grumpy Gringo	◆◆	Mexican	$7-$22	194
4 p. 186	Hunters Chop House	◆◆	Steak	$9-$32	194
5 p. 186	The Egg & I	◆◆	Breakfast	$6-$10	194
6 p. 186	Mama Rose's Italian Dining	◆◆	Italian	$9-$23	194
7 p. 186	Grubsteak Family Restaurant	◆◆	American	$6-$32	194
8 p. 186	Molly B Restaurant	◆◆	American	$6-$15	195
9 p. 186	LongZ - A Mountain Grill	◆◆	American	$8-$35	194
10 p. 186	Sweet Basilico	◆◆	Italian	$6-$16	195
11 p. 186	Smokin' Dave's BBQ & Tap House	◆◆	Barbecue	$8-$20	195
12 p. 186	The Other Side Restaurant	◆◆	American	$7-$30	195
13 p. 186	Sundeck Restaurant *(See ad p. 190.)*	◆◆	American	$6-$25	195
14 p. 186	Rock Inn Mountain Tavern	◆◆	American	$10-$29	195
15 p. 186	Dunraven Inn Restaurant	◆◆◆	Italian	$13-$39	194
16 p. 186	Chalet Room & The Tavern at Marys Lake Lodge	◆◆◆	American	$11-$35	194

GRAND LAKE

Map Page	Hotels	Diamond Rated	High Season	Page
16 p. 186	**Americas Best Value Inn Bighorn Lodge**	◆◆	$65-$160 SAVE	219
17 p. 186	Gateway Inn	◆◆◆	Rates not provided	219

GRAND LAKE (cont'd)

Map Page	Hotels (cont'd)	Diamond Rated	High Season	Page
18 p. 186	**Spirit Lake Lodge**	◆◆	$60-$200 SAVE	219
19 p. 186	Black Bear Lodge	◆◆	$88-$135	219

Map Page	Restaurants	Diamond Rated	Cuisine	Meal Range	Page
19 p. 186	**The Historic Rapids Restaurant**	◆◆◆	American	$10-$36	219
20 p. 186	**Fat Cat Cafe**	◆◆	American	$6-$10	219
21 p. 186	**Sagebrush BBQ & Grill**	◆◆	American	$7-$29	219
22 p. 186	Grand Pizza	◆◆	Italian	$6-$15	219

ALPINE TRAIL RIDGE INN

Phone: (970)586-4585 10

◆◆ Motel $81-$233

Address: 927 Moraine Ave 80517 **Location:** 1.5 mi sw of jct Elkhorn and Moraine aves; jct of SR 66 and Marys Lake Rd. **Facility:** 48 units, some two bedrooms and kitchens. 1-2 stories (no elevator), exterior corridors. **Terms:** open 5/1-10/8, office hours 7 am-9 pm, check-in 3:30 pm, 2 night minimum stay - seasonal and/or weekends, 14 day cancellation notice-fee imposed. **Pool(s):** heated outdoor. **Activities:** hiking trails. **Free Special Amenities: local telephone calls and high-speed Internet.**

(See ad p. 190.)

SAVE

APPENZELL INN

Phone: 970/586-2023 3

◆◆◆ Motel Rates not provided

Address: 1100 Big Thompson Ave 80517 **Location:** 0.7 mi e of jct US 34 and 36. **Facility:** 34 units, some two bedrooms. 3 stories, interior/exterior corridors. **Terms:** office hours 8 am-10 pm. **Pool(s):** heated indoor. **Guest Services:** coin laundry. **Free Special Amenities: local telephone calls and high-speed Internet.**

(See ad this page.)

SAVE

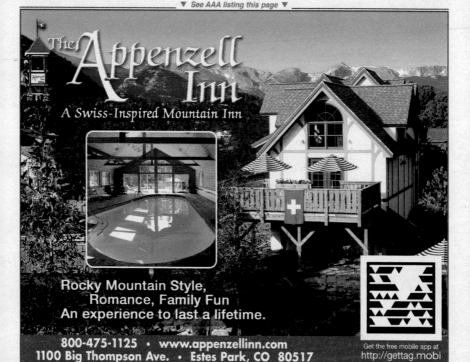

(See map & index p. 186.)

(See map & index p. 186.)

BEST WESTERN PLUS SILVER SADDLE
Phone: (970)586-4476 5

Motel
$79-$325

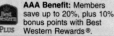

AAA Benefit: Members save up to 20%, plus 10% bonus points with Best Western Rewards®.

Address: 1260 Big Thompson Ave 80517 **Location:** 0.9 mi e of jct US 34 and 36. **Facility:** 55 units, some kitchens. 1-2 stories (no elevator), interior/exterior corridors. **Terms:** office hours 7 am-10 pm, check-in 4 pm, 2-3 night minimum stay - seasonal, 3 day cancellation notice. **Amenities:** high-speed Internet. **Pool(s):** heated outdoor. **Activities:** whirlpool, playground, exercise room. **Guest Services:** coin laundry. **Free Special Amenities: expanded continental breakfast and high-speed Internet.**

(See ad p. 192, p. 276.)

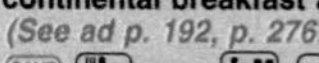 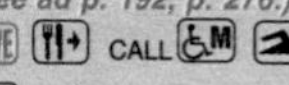    

SAVE CALL

CASTLE MOUNTAIN LODGE
Phone: (970)586-3664 2

Cottage
$145-$575 5/1-10/7
$75-$350 10/8-4/30

Address: 1520 Fall River Rd 80517 **Location:** 1 mi w on US 34. Located on Fall River. **Facility:** 29 units, some cabins and cottages. 1-3 stories (no elevator), exterior corridors. **Terms:** office hours 8 am-9 pm, 2-5 night minimum stay - seasonal and/or weekends, 30 day cancellation notice-fee imposed. **Activities:** fishing, playground, horseshoes, shuffleboard. **Guest Services:** coin laundry. **Free Special Amenities: high-speed Internet.**

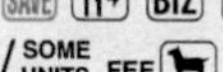

SAVE / SOME UNITS FEE

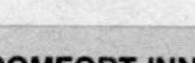

COMFORT INN **Phone:** (970)586-2358 6

Hotel
$90-$300

Address: 1450 Big Thompson Ave 80517 **Location:** 1.5 mi e on US 34. **Facility:** 75 units. 2 stories (no elevator), interior/exterior corridors. **Terms:** office hours 6:30 am-10 pm, check-in 4 pm, 3 day cancellation notice-fee imposed. **Pool(s):** heated outdoor. **Activities:** whirlpool, exercise room. **Guest Services:** coin laundry. **Free Special Amenities: expanded continental breakfast and use of on-premises laundry facilities.**

(See ad p. 193.)

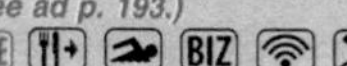

SAVE

THE ESTES PARK RESORT **Phone:** 970/577-6400 14

fyi
Hotel
Rates not provided

Under major renovation, scheduled to be completed March 2012. **Last Rated:** ♦♦ **Address:** 1700 Big Thompson Ave 80517 **Location:** 2 mi e on US 34. Adjacent to a marina. **Facility:** 54 units. 3 stories, interior corridors. **Terms:** check-in 4 pm. **Amenities:** safes. **Pool(s):** heated indoor. **Activities:** saunas, whirlpool, jogging, exercise room. *Fee:* fishing, game room. **Guest Services:** coin laundry. **Free Special Amenities: early check-in/late check-out and high-speed Internet.**

SAVE CALL

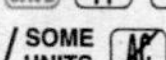

/ SOME UNITS

MOUNTAIN SAGE INN **Phone:** 970/586-2833 7

Motel
Rates not provided

Address: 553 W Elkhorn Ave 80517 **Location:** 1 mi nw of jct US 34 and 36 to James St, just s, then just w. Located in a quiet area. **Facility:** 20 units. 2 stories (no elevator), interior/exterior corridors. **Activities:** whirlpool.

/ SOME UNITS

MOUNTAIN SHADOWS RESORT
Phone: 970/577-0397 12

Cabin
Rates not provided

Address: 871 Riverside Dr 80517 **Location:** Just s of jct Elkhorn and Moraine aves to Riverside Dr, then 1.2 mi sw. **Facility:** These luxury modern duplex cabins feature a whirlpool tub, towel warmer, gas fireplace and well-coordinated furnishings; some units offer nice mountain views. 8 cabins. 1 story, exterior corridors. *Bath:* shower only. **Terms:** age restrictions may apply.

/ SOME UNITS FEE

PEAK TO PEAK LODGE **Phone:** (970)586-4451 11

Motel
$55-$199

Address: 760 S Saint Vrain Ave (Hwy 7) 80517 **Location:** On SR 7, 0.7 mi s of jct US 36. **Facility:** 24 units, some efficiencies and kitchens. 1-2 stories, exterior corridors. **Terms:** open 5/11-10/13, office hours 8 am-10 pm, 14 day cancellation notice-fee imposed. **Pool(s):** heated outdoor. **Activities:** whirlpool.

/ SOME UNITS

ROCKY MOUNTAIN PARK INN
Phone: (970)586-2332 9

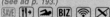

Hotel
$110-$200 5/1-10/13
$100-$150 10/14-4/30

Address: 101 S Saint Vrain Ave 80517 **Location:** 0.4 mi se on US 36 to US 7, then just s. **Facility:** 150 units. 2-4 stories, interior corridors. **Terms:** check-in 4 pm. **Dining:** LongZ - A Mountain Grill, see separate listing. **Pool(s):** heated indoor. **Activities:** whirlpool, exercise room. **Guest Services:** valet and coin laundry. **Free Special Amenities: high-speed Internet and use of on-premises laundry facilities.**

SAVE CALL

/ SOME UNITS FEE

SADDLE & SURREY MOTEL **Phone:** 970/586-3326 13

Motel
$60-$145

Address: 1341 S Saint Vrain Ave 80517 **Location:** 0.4 mi se of jct US 34 and 36 to SR 7, then 1.3 mi s on SR 7 (S Saint Vrain Ave). **Facility:** 26 units, some efficiencies. 1 story, exterior corridors. **Terms:** open 5/4-10/28, office hours 7 am-10 pm, 2-3 night minimum stay - seasonal and/or weekends, 10 day cancellation notice-fee imposed. **Pool(s):** heated outdoor. **Activities:** whirlpool, playground. **Free Special Amenities: local telephone calls and high-speed Internet.**

SAVE / SOME UNITS

SILVER MOON INN **Phone:** 970/586-6006 8

Motel
$80-$300

Address: 175 Spruce Dr 80517 **Location:** Just w of jct Elkhorn and Moraine aves; west end of downtown. **Facility:** 44 units, some two bedrooms, efficiencies and kitchens. 2-3 stories (no elevator), interior/exterior corridors. **Terms:** office hours 7 am-10 pm, 1-3 night minimum stay - seasonal and/or weekends, cancellation fee imposed. **Pool(s):** heated outdoor. **Activities:** whirlpools, fishing, hiking trails, jogging, playground. **Guest Services:** coin laundry.

/ SOME UNITS

▼ See AAA listing p. 191 ▼

▼ See AAA listing p. 191 ▼

(See map & index p. 186.)

TYROL MOUNTAIN INN **Phone:** 970/586-3382 4

Motel
$69-$179

Address: 1240 Big Thompson Ave 80517 **Location:** 0.8 mi e of jct US 34 and 36. **Facility:** 51 units. 2 stories (no elevator), exterior corridors. **Terms:** office hours 7:30 am-8 pm, 2-3 night minimum stay - seasonal and/or weekends, 3 day cancellation notice-fee imposed. **Pool(s):** heated outdoor. **Activities:** whirlpool, playground. **Guest Services:** coin laundry.

FEE

/ SOME UNITS FEE

WILDWOOD INN Phone: 970/586-7804 1
Condominium
$68-$428
Address: 2801 Fall River Rd 80517 Location: 3.5 mi w on US 34. Bordering the Rocky Mountain National Park. Facility: 32 units, some cabins and condominiums. 1-2 stories (no elevator), exterior corridors. Terms: office hours 9 am-7:30 pm, 30 day cancellation notice-fee imposed. Amenities: high-speed Internet. Activities: sauna, whirlpool, hiking trails, playground, horseshoes, spa. Guest Services: valet laundry.
SAVE
/ SOME UNITS
WILDWOOD
Estes Park, Colorado
INN
Offering both Mountain & River locations. Full service Day Spa. Private outdoor & in-room Hot Tubs.

BLACK CANYON INN **Phone:** 970/586-8113

fyi Not evaluated. **Address:** 800 MacGregor Ave 80517 **Location:** 0.5 mi w on US 34, then 0.5 mi n on Devils Gulch Rd. Facilities, services, and decor characterize a mid-scale property.

THE HABER MOTEL **Phone:** 970/449-1660

fyi
Motel

Did not meet all AAA rating requirements for locking devices in some guest rooms at time of last evaluation on 08/05/2011. **Address:** 397 E Elkhorn Ave 80517 **Location:** Jct US 34 and 36; downtown. Facilities, services, and decor characterize a mid-scale property.

THE STANLEY HOTEL **Phone:** 970/586-3371

fyi Not evaluated. **Address:** 333 Wonderview Ave 80517 **Location:** Just n of jct US 34 and 36. Facilities, services, and decor characterize an upscale property.

WHERE TO EAT

CHALET ROOM & THE TAVERN AT MARYS LAKE LODGE **Phone:** 970/586-5958 16

American
$11-$35

AAA Inspector Notes: In a lovely, much-talked-about setting, the Tavern offers rustic charm and serves lunch and dinner daily. Chalet Room is a bit more formal and serves dinner only. Both offer spectacular views and share a menu featuring Prince Edward Island mussels, bacon-wrapped scallops, seafood bisque, pecan-crusted halibut and juicy steaks. Vegetarian items are available. **Bar:** full bar. **Reservations:** suggested. **Address:** 2625 Marys Lake Rd 80517 **Location:** 3.4 mi s of jct US 36 and SR 7, just w. L D

DUNRAVEN INN RESTAURANT **Phone:** 970/586-6409 15

Italian
$13-$39

AAA Inspector Notes: Traditional Italian favorites are on the menu in addition to fresh seafood, charbroiled steaks, veal and chicken entrées. **Bar:** full bar. **Reservations:** suggested. **Address:** 2470 Hwy 66 80517 **Location:** 1.5 mi sw of Elkhorn and Moraine aves to Lake Marys Rd, then 1.3 mi sw on SR 66. D

THE EGG & I **Phone:** 970/586-1173 5

Breakfast
$6-$10

AAA Inspector Notes: The cheerful décor and casual staff create a relaxing environment. Although this restaurant serves lunch, the breakfast menu, served all day, is the main event. **Address:** 393 E Elkhorn Ave 80517 **Location:** Just w of jct US 36 and 34. B L

GRUBSTEAK FAMILY RESTAURANT **Phone:** 970/586-8838 7

American
$6-$32

AAA Inspector Notes: Guests unwind in small, quaint rooms with Western décor or on the covered patio as they peruse a serious menu of steaks, barbecue, ribs, fried or blackened trout, and great burgers prepared with elk, buffalo or beef. Among the other offerings are microbrews and children's dishes. Breakfast is served in the summer only. **Bar:** full bar. **Address:** 134 W Elkhorn Ave 80517 **Location:** Center. **Parking:** street only.

L D

GRUMPY GRINGO **Phone:** 970/586-7705 3

Mexican
$7-$22

AAA Inspector Notes: The restaurant's outstanding house margarita tastes great with the flavorful, build-your-own burritos. The mini rellenos wrapped in egg-roll paper and fried are the perfect way to begin a meal. Delicious sopaipillas please the palate at dessert time. Bright, airy décor lends character to several dining areas that offer great views of Longs Peak, the Continental Divide and Lake Estes. **Bar:** full bar. **Address:** 1560 Big Thompson Ave 80517 **Location:** 1.7 mi e on US 34. L D

HUNTERS CHOP HOUSE **Phone:** 970/586-6962 4

Steak
$9-$32

AAA Inspector Notes: The chophouse welcomes diners to a full Western experience. The décor incorporates taxidermied animals, including a mountain lion standing on the fireplace. Luckier diners will be seated next to a window overlooking Lake Estes. Flavorful steaks, elk, boar, buffalo, lobster and chicken dishes dominate the menu. **Bar:** full bar. **Address:** 1690 Big Thompson Ave 80517 **Location:** 1.9 mi e on US 34.

L D CALL &M

LONGZ - A MOUNTAIN GRILL **Phone:** 970/586-2332 9

American
$8-$35

AAA Inspector Notes: This restaurant features Rocky Mountain-inspired cuisine. The most popular dishes include bison, elk and steak. The casual setting is attractive with upscale décor. **Bar:** full bar. **Address:** 101 S Saint Vrain Ave 80517 **Location:** 0.5 mi se on SR 7 at US 36; in Rocky Mountain Park Inn. B L D

MAMA ROSE'S ITALIAN DINING **Phone:** 970/586-8282 6

Italian
$9-$23

AAA Inspector Notes: This spacious restaurant is in an elegant setting and offers riverside seasonal patio seating. Entrée and dessert items include traditional Italian favorites. **Bar:** full bar. **Reservations:** suggested. **Address:** 342 E Elkhorn Ave 80517 **Location:** On US 36, just e of Elkhorn and Moraine aves; downtown. **Parking:** street only. L D

(See map & index p. 186.)

MOLLY B RESTAURANT **Phone:** 970/586-2766 (8)

American
$6-$15

AAA Inspector Notes: This hot spot fills up quickly and is easy to find with its white picket fence and outdoor patio. The country-style décor creates a laid-back atmosphere. The breakfast menu includes omelets, huevos rancheros, pancakes, waffles and Molly B's famous homemade "outrageous granola." A good variety of appetizers, soup, salads, sandwiches, seafood, pastas, daily specials and vegetarian items also are available. **Bar:** full bar. **Address:** 200 Moraine Ave 80517 **Location:** Just w of Elkhorn and Moraine aves; downtown. **Parking:** street only.
B L D

NICKY'S STEAKHOUSE ON THE RIVER
Phone: 970/586-2123 (2)

American
$7-$30

AAA Inspector Notes: The spacious steakhouse offers a choice of seating in a casual dining room or more upscale space overlooking the river. Menu selections include beef, chicken, seafood and ribs. Large portions leave diners satisfied. **Bar:** full bar. **Address:** 1350 W Fall River Rd 80517 **Location:** 1.4 mi w on US 34. B L D

THE OTHER SIDE RESTAURANT
Phone: 970/586-2171 (12)

American
$7-$30

AAA Inspector Notes: The restaurant serves flavorful prime rib, steaks and seafood, as well as homemade desserts. The comfortable, casual atmosphere offers a nice view of the park and duck pond. Sunday brunch is served from 9 am to 2 pm. **Bar:** full bar. **Reservations:** suggested, in season & holidays. **Address:** 900 Moraine Ave 80517 **Location:** 1.5 mi w on US 36; at Mary's Lake Rd.
B L D

ROCK INN MOUNTAIN TAVERN
Phone: 970/586-4116 (14)

American
$10-$29

AAA Inspector Notes: After a day of exploring at Rocky Mountain National Park, patrons can revive with a microbrew and hearty meal. The innovative menu appeals to those looking for a perfectly prepared steak as well as foodies searching for something more adventurous. The organic quinoa is delicious, and vegan, vegetarian and gluten-free items are available. **Bar:** full bar. **Address:** 1675 Hwy 66 80517 **Location:** 1.6 mi sw of jct Elkhorn and Moraine aves (US 36) to Mary's Lake Rd, then 0.3 mi sw on SR 66. D

SMOKIN' DAVE'S BBQ & TAP HOUSE
Phone: 970/577-7427 (11)

Barbecue
$8-$20

AAA Inspector Notes: Chef/owner "Smokin'" Dave Oehlman prides himself on serving high-quality traditional American barbecue. Generous portions of tender, mouthwatering ribs, pulled pork, beef brisket and sausage quickly made this new restaurant a favorite with locals. **Bar:** full bar. **Reservations:** suggested. **Address:** 820 Moraine Ave 80517 **Location:** Jct Elkhorn Ave, 1.2 mi sw. L D

SUNDECK RESTAURANT **Phone:** 970/586-9832 (13)

American
$6-$25

AAA Inspector Notes: This family-owned operation has been serving diners since 1948. Although the menu is varied, with American offerings as well as a few Mexican dishes, fresh trout is the specialty. The décor is rustic, Western, bright and comfortable. A casually attired waitstaff allows for a relaxing dining experience. **Bar:** full bar. **Reservations:** suggested. **Address:** 915 Moraine Ave 80517 **Location:** 1.7 mi w on US 36; near jct SR 66.
(See ad p. 190.) B L D

SWEET BASILICO **Phone:** 970/586-3899 (10)

Italian
$6-$16

AAA Inspector Notes: This family-owned restaurant serves made-from-scratch Italian cuisine in a casual and relaxed atmosphere. This beloved local favorite moved to a more spacious location on the other side of town, which didn't deter the crowds. The flavors are robust and delightful. Limited seating and booming popularity with both locals and tourists make reservations a good idea. **Bar:** wine only. **Reservations:** suggested. **Address:** 430 Prospect Village 80517 **Location:** 0.3 mi s on Moraine Ave, just s on Riverside Dr. L D

TWIN OWLS STEAKHOUSE
Phone: 970/586-9344 (1)

Steak
$13-$36

AAA Inspector Notes: The rustic restaurant nurtures a romantic mountain atmosphere in an original log building with a fireplace, high beam ceiling and oak floors. The menu offers an array of appetizers and salads, as well as preparations of beef, wild game, seafood, pasta, chicken and pork. **Bar:** full bar. **Reservations:** suggested. **Address:** 800 MacGregor Ave 80517 **Location:** 0.5 mi nw on US 34, then 0.4 mi n. D

EVERGREEN (D-4) pop. 9,038, elev. 7,040'

In the foothills west of Denver, Evergreen is surrounded by the Denver Mountain Park System and Jefferson County open space parks. Alderfer/Three Sisters Open Space Park offers hiking and biking trails that lead to the unusual rock outcropping known as Three Sisters and The Brother.

Bergen Peak's subalpine terrain, grasslands, steep slopes and forests are just outside Elk Meadow Park. Downtown's Evergreen Lake offers boating in summer and ice skating in winter. A 1.5-mile walking path around the lake offers sculptures, picnic areas and wildlife viewing.

Evergreen Area Chamber of Commerce: 28065 SR 74, Suite 201, Evergreen, CO 80439. **Phone:** (303) 674-3412.

HIWAN HOMESTEAD MUSEUM, 4208 S. Timbervale Dr., is a complex of five historic buildings, including a 17-room log lodge. Once the headquarters for the Hiwan Ranch, the buildings are known for their rustic log architecture. Also featured is a collection of Southwestern Indian arts and crafts.

Time: Allow 30 minutes minimum. **Hours:** Tues.-Sun. 11-5, June-Aug.; noon-5, rest of year. Guided tours are offered at 15 minutes before and 15 minutes after the hour. Closed July 4, Thanksgiving and Christmas. **Cost:** Free. **Phone:** (720) 497-7650.

COMFORT SUITES AT EVERGREEN PARKWAY
Phone: (303)526-2000

Hotel
$114-$149

Address: 29300 US Hwy 40 80439 **Location:** I-70 exit 252 (Evergreen Pkwy) westbound; exit 251 eastbound; on west side of El Rancho Restaurant. **Facility:** 85 units. 3 stories, interior corridors. **Terms:** cancellation fee imposed. **Amenities:** safes (fee). **Pool(s):** heated indoor. **Activities:** sauna, whirlpools, exercise room. **Guest Services:** valet and coin laundry.
CALL BIZ

/ SOME UNITS FEE

WHERE TO EAT

EL RANCHO RESTAURANT **Phone:** 303/526-2300

American
$9-$27

AAA Inspector Notes: The restaurant's picturesque setting affords great views of the Continental Divide. Its knotty-pine décor includes seven rustic working fireplaces. The menu features prime rib, fresh trout, burgers and sandwiches. I highly recommend the smoked trout dip. The creamy dill base complemented the flavor of the smoky trout quite nicely. My bison burger was a little overcooked. Servers were attentive. The patio is open seasonally. **Bar:** full bar. **Reservations:** suggested. **Address:** 29260 US Hwy 40 80439 **Location:** I-70 exit 252 (Evergreen Pkwy) westbound; exit 251 (El Rancho) eastbound 0.3 mi s. (L) (D)

FAIRPLAY (D-3) pop. 679, elev. 9,950'

Fairplay was named by prospectors who settled it in 1859 when they were driven from nearby Tarryall by miners who had staked more claims than they could work. Thereafter scorned and referred to as "Grab-all," Tarryall did not survive beyond its boom times.

Fairplay is now a marketing center for the surrounding South Park ranches. More than 20 log houses, all private residences, survive from the 1800s. The scenic portion of US 285, which runs through Pike National Forest between Poncha Springs and Morrison, passes through town.

Town of Fairplay: 400 Front St., P.O. Box 267, Fairplay, CO 80440. **Phone:** (719) 836-2622.

GEM **SOUTH PARK CITY MUSEUM,** at 4th and Front sts., is a restored early Colorado gold-mining town typical of the 1860s to 1900s. Seven of the more than 35 buildings are on their original sites; the remaining structures were moved from deserted mining camps and ghost towns in nearby areas of Park County.

The buildings, all furnished with period articles, include a newspaper office, drugstore, saloon, assay office and general store. Mining machinery also can be seen, and a narrow-gauge train stands at the depot. Special events feature guides dressed in period clothing along with demonstrations of crafts and arts.

Time: Allow 1 hour minimum. **Hours:** Daily 9-7, Memorial Day-Labor Day; 9-5, May 15-day before Memorial Day; 10-6, day after Labor Day-Oct. 15. **Cost:** $7.50; $6 (ages 62+); $4 (ages 6-12). **Phone:** (719) 836-2387.

A RIVERSIDE INN **Phone:** 719/836-0600

Hotel
$99-$149 5/1-9/30
$80-$149 10/1-4/30

Address: 249 Hwy 285 80440 **Location:** Center. **Facility:** 50 units. 2 stories (no elevator), interior corridors. **Parking:** winter plug-ins. **Terms:** cancellation fee imposed. **Pool(s):** heated indoor. **Activities:** whirlpool, fishing, exercise room. **Guest Services:** coin laundry.

FEDERAL HEIGHTS (B-4) pop. 11,467, elev. 5,535'

• Part of Denver area — see map p. 123

WATER WORLD is 1 mi. w. off I-25 exit 219, then 4 blks. n. on Pecos St. to 89th Ave. With 64 acres and more than 45 aquatic attractions, Water World is one of the nation's largest family water theme parks. Thrill rides include Turbo Racer, Revolution, Voyage to the Center of the Earth, Screamin' Mimi, Storm, Zoomerang and Ragin' Colorado as well as multiple slides, two wave pools and a lazy river. Wally World Calypso and Big Top are other highlights.

Time: Allow 4 hours, 30 minutes minimum. **Hours:** Daily 10-6, Memorial Day weekend-Labor Day weekend. Phone ahead to confirm schedule. **Cost:** $34.99; $29.99 (under 48 inches tall); $5.99 (ages 60+); free (under 40 inches tall). **Phone:** (303) 427-7873.

FIRESTONE pop. 10,147

BEST WESTERN FIRESTONE INN & SUITES
Phone: (720)494-1925

Hotel
$90-$130

AAA Benefit: Members save up to 20%, plus 10% bonus points with Best Western Rewards®.

Address: 11228 Business Park Cir 80504 **Location:** I-25 exit 240, just e. **Facility:** 58 units. 3 stories, interior corridors. **Amenities:** high-speed Internet. **Pool(s):** heated indoor. **Activities:** whirlpool, exercise room. **Guest Services:** coin laundry. **Free Special Amenities: full breakfast and room upgrade (subject to availability with advance reservations).**

SAVE CALL / SOME UNITS FEE

COMFORT SUITES **Phone:** 720/864-2970

Hotel
Rates not provided

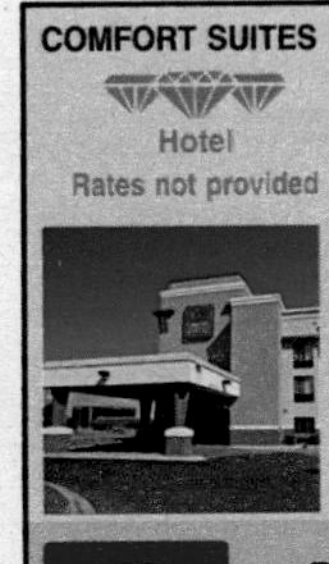

Address: 11292 Business Park Cir 80504 **Location:** I-25 exit 240, just e on Firestone Blvd, just n on Frontage Rd, then just e. **Facility:** 72 units. 3 stories, interior corridors. **Terms:** check-in 4 pm. **Amenities:** high-speed Internet. **Pool(s):** heated indoor. **Activities:** whirlpool, exercise room. **Guest Services:** valet and coin laundry.

SAVE / SOME UNITS FEE

Beautiful view of Rocky Mountains. Comfortable luxury, whether, hiking, skiing or sightseeing.

FLORISSANT FOSSIL BEDS NATIONAL MONUMENT (D-3)

Two miles south of Florissant on Teller CR 1, Florissant Fossil Beds National Monument protects an area once covered by a prehistoric lake. As layer after layer of volcanic ash accumulated some 34 to 35 million years ago, the lake vanished, but its plant and animal life were preserved almost intact in paper-thin layers of shale. It is these fossils, dating from the Eocene period and including standing petrified sequoia stumps, that the 6,000-acre monument protects.

The visitor center houses collections of fossils and offers a variety of interpretive programs during the summer, including talks explaining the geology and paleontology of the area. Tours of an 1878 homestead also are offered. Hiking trails provide access to the back country. Daily 8-6, Memorial Day-Labor Day; 9-5, rest of year. Closed Jan. 1, Thanksgiving and Christmas. Phone ahead to confirm hours. Admission $3; free (ages 0-15). Phone (719) 748-3253.

FORT COLLINS (A-4) pop. 143,986, elev. 5,003'

• **Restaurants p. 199**

After the 1860s conflicts with American Indians ended, the Army garrison abandoned its post on the Cache la Poudre River, leaving its buildings and its name, Fort Collins, to the adjoining settlement. The town's economy initially was supported by commerce along the Overland Trail and nearby farms and ranches. More recently, however, Fort Collins has emerged as an industrial, technological and educational center.

Colorado State University, a land-grant institution established in 1879 as an agricultural college, is known for its forestry, veterinary medicine, biotechnology, computer technology and electronic research programs.

The Fort Collins Municipal Railway runs between the city park and downtown on weekends and holidays during summer. Scenic drive SR 14 leaves US 287 3 miles northwest of Fort Collins. The road follows the Cache la Poudre River through narrow Poudre Canyon—in one place tunneling through solid rock—and traverses the Pawnee National Grassland *(see place listing p. 40)*.

Historic Old Town Square at College and Mountain Avenue is now a retail center. Lincoln Center, a venue for performing and visual arts, hosts plays, musicals, top entertainers and trade shows. Horsetooth Reservoir and Lory State Park *(see Recreation Chart)* offer a variety of recreational activities.

Fort Collins Convention and Visitors Bureau: 19 Old Town Square, Suite 137, Fort Collins, CO 80524. **Phone:** (970) 232-3840.

ANHEUSER-BUSCH BREWERY TOUR CENTER, 2351 Busch Dr., offers tours covering the brewing and packaging of the company's products as well as a visit to the Budweiser Clydesdale Hamlet to see the renowned draft horses. Visits include a stop at the Hospitality Room for product sampling. Close-up photography of the horses is permitted on Clydesdale Camera Days the first Saturday of each month.

The tour contains a considerable amount of walking. Samples available only to ages 21+. **Time:** Allow 1 hour, 30 minutes minimum. **Hours:** Tours are offered daily 10-4, June-Sept.; Thurs.-Mon. 10-4, rest of year. Last tour begins at closing. Closed major holidays. Phone ahead to confirm schedule. **Cost:** Free. **Phone:** (970) 490-4691.

FORT COLLINS MUSEUM & DISCOVERY SCIENCE CENTER, w. off I-25 on SR 14 (Mulberry), then 2.5 blks. n. at 200 Mathews St., specializes in hands-on science exhibits and the history of northern Colorado. Exhibits include local history displays, interactive science exhibits, traveling exhibitions and four historic structures—the Elizabeth Stone Cabin, the Upper Boxelder Schoolhouse, the Franz-Smith Cabin and the Janis Cabin, one of the oldest in the state. A local history archive is available to researchers. **Time:** Allow 30 minutes minimum. **Hours:** Tues.-Sat. 10-5, Sun. noon-5. **Cost:** $4; $3 (ages 60+ and 3-12). Free on the third Sun. of the month. **Phone:** (970) 221-6738.

FORT COLLINS MUSEUM OF CONTEMPORARY ART is at 201 S. College Ave. (US 287) between Olive Street and the Oak Street Plaza. The museum, in the 1912 post office building, features seven to 10 changing exhibitions each year. **Time:** Allow 1 hour minimum. **Hours:** Tues.-Fri. 10-5, Sat. noon-5. **Cost:** $8; $6 (ages 65+ and college students with ID); $5 (ages 7-18); free (ages 0-6 and museum members). **Phone:** (970) 482-2787.

NEW BELGIUM BREWING CO. is off I-25 exit 269B, 3 mi. w. to Riverside, then n.w. to Linden and just n. over the bridge. Several Belgian-style beers are brewed in this alternatively powered plant. Tours include tastings and a behind-the-scenes look at the facility. **Time:** Allow 1 hour minimum. **Hours:** Tours are given Tues.-Sat. 10-6. Phone ahead to confirm schedule. **Cost:** Free. Reservations are recommended. **Phone:** (970) 221-0524 or (888) 622-4044.

BEST WESTERN KIVA INN **Phone:** (970)484-2444

Hotel
$70-$130

AAA Benefit: Members save up to 20%, plus 10% bonus points with Best Western Rewards®.

Address: 1638 E Mulberry St 80524 **Location:** I-25 exit 269B, 1.5 mi w on SR 14. **Facility:** 62 units. 1-2 stories (no elevator), interior/exterior corridors. **Amenities:** *Some:* high-speed Internet. **Pool(s):** heated outdoor. **Activities:** sauna, whirlpools, exercise room. **Guest Services:** valet and coin laundry. **Free Special Amenities: continental breakfast and high-speed Internet.**

SAVE BIZ / SOME UNITS FEE

BEST WESTERN UNIVERSITY INN

Phone: (970)484-1984

Motel
$79-$159

AAA Benefit: Members save up to 20%, plus 10% bonus points with Best Western Rewards®.

Address: 914 S College Ave 80524 **Location:** I-25 exit 268, 4 mi w to College Ave, then just n on US 287. Opposite Colorado State University. **Facility:** 71 units. 2 stories (no elevator), interior/exterior corridors. **Amenities:** high-speed Internet, safes. **Pool(s):** heated indoor. **Activities:** whirlpool, exercise room. **Guest Services:** valet and coin laundry. **Free Special Amenities: local telephone calls and high-speed Internet.**

/ SOME UNITS FEE

BUDGET HOST INN **Phone:** (970)484-0870

Motel

$65-$100 5/1-9/30
$60-$80 10/1-4/30

Address: 1513 N College Ave 80524 **Location:** 1.8 mi n on US 287. **Facility:** 30 units, some two bedrooms and efficiencies. 1-2 stories (no elevator), exterior corridors. **Terms:** office hours 7 am-midnight, cancellation fee imposed. **Activities:** whirlpool. **Free Special Amenities: continental breakfast and local telephone calls.** SAVE

CAMBRIA SUITES **Phone:** (970)267-9000

Contemporary Hotel
$99-$209

Address: 2921 E Harmony Rd 80528 **Location:** I-25 exit 265 (Harmony Rd), 1.5 mi w, then just s on Ziegler. **Facility:** 90 units. 4 stories, interior corridors. **Parking:** winter plug-ins. **Terms:** 3 day cancellation notice-fee imposed. **Amenities:** high-speed Internet. **Pool(s):** heated indoor. **Activities:** whirlpool, exercise room. **Guest Services:** valet and coin laundry, area transportation-within 5 mi. *(See ad p. 103.)*

BIZ

COMFORT INN **Phone:** (970)407-0100

Hotel
$79-$249

Address: 601 SW Frontage Rd 80524 **Location:** I-25 exit 269B, just sw. **Facility:** 62 units. 3 stories, interior corridors. **Terms:** cancellation fee imposed. **Pool(s):** heated indoor. **Activities:** whirlpool, exercise room. *Fee:* game room. **Guest Services:** valet and coin laundry.

CALL BIZ

/ SOME UNITS

COMFORT SUITES FORT COLLINS **Phone:** (970)206-4597

Hotel
$59-$169

Address: 1415 Oakridge Dr 80525 **Location:** I-25 exit 265 (Harmony Rd), 3.3 mi w to McMurry Ave, just s, then w. Located in a quiet area. **Facility:** 66 units. 3 stories, interior corridors. **Terms:** cancellation fee imposed. **Amenities:** safes (fee). **Pool(s):** heated indoor. **Activities:** whirlpool. **Guest Services:** valet laundry.

BIZ

/ SOME UNITS FEE

COURTYARD BY MARRIOTT **Phone:** (970)282-1700

Hotel
$89-$119

AAA Benefit:
AAA hotel discounts of 5% or more.

Address: 1200 Oakridge Dr 80525 **Location:** I-25 exit 265 (Harmony Rd), 3.3 mi w; entry via Lemay Ave. **Facility:** 112 units. 2 stories, interior corridors. **Amenities:** high-speed Internet. **Pool(s):** heated indoor. **Activities:** whirlpool, exercise room. **Guest Services:** valet and coin laundry.

ECO CALL BIZ FEE

/ SOME UNITS FEE

EDWARDS HOUSE BED & BREAKFAST **Phone:** 970/493-9191

Classic Bed & Breakfast
Rates not provided

Address: 402 W Mountain Ave 80521 **Location:** I-25 exit 269B, 4 mi w to Meldrum St, then 0.3 mi n. Located in a residential area. **Facility:** A gas-log fireplace and a shower, claw-foot tub or whirlpool are featured in all guest rooms at this 1904 neoclassical-style home. 8 units. 2-3 stories (no elevator), interior corridors. **Activities:** sauna, limited exercise equipment. BIZ

FORT COLLINS MARRIOTT **Phone:** (970)226-5200

Hotel
$80-$149

AAA Benefit:
AAA hotel discounts of 5% or more.

Address: 350 E Horsetooth Rd 80525 **Location:** I-25 exit 265 (Harmony Rd), 4 mi w to John F Kennedy Pkwy, then n; just beyond Horsetooth Rd. Adjacent to Foothills Fashion Mall. **Facility:** 229 units. 6 stories, interior corridors. **Terms:** check-in 4 pm. **Amenities:** *Fee:* video games, high-speed Internet. **Pool(s):** heated indoor/outdoor. **Activities:** whirlpool, exercise room. **Guest Services:** valet and coin laundry.

ECO CALL BIZ FEE

/ SOME UNITS FEE

HAMPTON INN **Phone:** (970)229-5927

Hotel
$109-$139

AAA Benefit:
Members save up to 10% everyday!

Address: 1620 Oakridge Dr 80525 **Location:** I-25 exit 265 (Harmony Rd), 3.3 mi w, just s on McMurry Ave, then just e. Located in a quiet residential area. **Facility:** 75 units. 3 stories, interior corridors. **Terms:** 1-7 night minimum stay, cancellation fee imposed. **Amenities:** video games (fee). **Pool(s):** heated indoor. **Activities:** whirlpool, exercise room. **Guest Services:** valet and coin laundry.

CALL BIZ FEE

/ SOME UNITS

HILTON FT COLLINS **Phone:** (970)482-2626

Hotel
$109-$189

AAA Benefit:
Members save 5% or more everyday!

Address: 425 W Prospect Rd 80526 **Location:** I-25 exit 268, 4.3 mi w. Located next to the university. **Facility:** 255 units. 9 stories, interior corridors. **Terms:** 1-7 night minimum stay, cancellation fee imposed. **Amenities:** *Some:* high-speed Internet (fee). **Pool(s):** heated indoor. **Activities:** whirlpool, jogging, exercise room. **Guest Services:** valet laundry, area transportation-within 5 mi.

BIZ FEE

/ SOME UNITS FEE FEE FEE

HILTON GARDEN INN **Phone:** (970)225-2900

Hotel
$115-$145

AAA Benefit:
Unparalleled hospitality at a special Member rate.

Address: 2821 E Harmony Rd 80528 **Location:** I-25 exit 265 (Harmony Rd). **Facility:** 120 units. 4 stories, interior corridors. **Parking:** winter plug-ins. **Terms:** 1-7 night minimum stay, cancellation fee imposed. **Amenities:** high-speed Internet, safes. **Pool(s):** heated indoor. **Activities:** whirlpool, exercise room. **Guest Services:** valet and coin laundry, area transportation-within city.

BIZ FEE

HOLIDAY INN EXPRESS & SUITES **Phone:** 970/225-2200

Hotel
Rates not provided

Address: 1426 Oakridge Dr 80525 **Location:** I-25 exit 265 (Harmony Rd), 3 mi w, just s on McMurry Ave, then just w. **Facility:** 89 units. 4 stories, interior corridors. **Amenities:** high-speed Internet. **Pool(s):** heated indoor. **Activities:** whirlpool, exercise room. **Guest Services:** valet and coin laundry.

CALL BIZ

/ SOME UNITS FEE

HOMEWOOD SUITES BY HILTON FORT COLLINS
Phone: (970)225-2400

Extended Stay Hotel
$119-$159

AAA Benefit: Contemporary luxury at a special Member rate.

Address: 1521 Oakridge Dr 80525 **Location:** I-25 exit 265 (Harmony Rd), 3 mi w, just s on McMurry Ave, then just w. **Facility:** 99 units, some two bedrooms, efficiencies and kitchens. 4 stories, interior corridors. **Terms:** 1-7 night minimum stay, cancellation fee imposed. **Amenities:** high-speed internet. **Pool(s):** heated indoor. **Activities:** whirlpool, sports court, game room, exercise room. **Guest Services:** valet and coin laundry, area transportation-within town. **Free Special Amenities: full breakfast and high-speed Internet.**

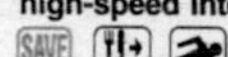     / SOME UNITS FEE 

LA QUINTA INN FORT COLLINS **Phone:** (970)493-7800

Hotel
$76-$149

Address: 3709 E Mulberry St 80524 **Location:** I-25 exit 269B, just w, then just sw on frontage road. **Facility:** 132 units. 2 stories (no elevator), interior corridors. **Pool(s):** heated indoor. **Activities:** sauna, whirlpool, exercise room. **Guest Services:** valet and coin laundry.

  / SOME UNITS

QUALITY INN & SUITES **Phone:** (970)282-9047

Hotel
$89-$199

Address: 4001 S Mason St 80525 **Location:** I-25 exit 265 (Harmony Rd), 4.6 mi w to Mason St, then 0.5 mi n. Adjacent to railroad tracks. **Facility:** 66 units. 3 stories, interior corridors. **Terms:** cancellation fee imposed. **Pool(s):** heated indoor. **Activities:** whirlpool, limited exercise equipment. **Guest Services:** valet and coin laundry.

CALL / SOME UNITS FEE

RESIDENCE INN FORT COLLINS **Phone:** (970)223-5700

Extended Stay Hotel
$89-$209

AAA Benefit: AAA hotel discounts of 5% or more.

Address: 1127 Oakridge Dr 80525 **Location:** I-25 exit 265 (Harmony Rd), 3.3 mi w to Lemay Ave, then s to Oakridge Dr. Located in a residential area. **Facility:** 113 units, some two bedrooms, efficiencies and kitchens. 3 stories, interior corridors. **Terms:** check-in 4 pm. **Amenities:** *Some:* high-speed Internet. **Pool(s):** heated indoor. **Activities:** whirlpool, sports court, exercise room. **Guest Services:** valet and coin laundry.

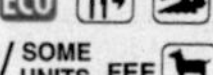

/ SOME UNITS FEE

SUPER 8 **Phone:** (970)493-7701

Hotel
$55-$98

Address: 409 Centro Way 80524 **Location:** I-25 exit 269B, just w. **Facility:** 71 units. 2 stories (no elevator), interior corridors. **Amenities:** safes (fee). **Activities:** sauna, whirlpool, limited exercise equipment. **Guest Services:** valet and coin laundry.

/ SOME UNITS FEE FEE FEE

WHERE TO EAT

BANN THAI **Phone:** 970/797-2707

Thai
$7-$12

AAA Inspector Notes: When I walked into this restaurant, the earth-toned décor struck me as relaxing and attractive. Out of everything I tried, I enjoyed the tom yum koong, a hot and spicy shrimp soup, the best. The ingredients were fresh, and the chef got my medium-spicy request just right. The homemade coconut ice cream was a light, sweet end to my meal. I can't wait to return and try something new; this seems like the perfect place to experiment. **Bar:** wine only. **Address:** 626 S College Ave 80524 **Location:** I-25 exit 269B, 4 mi w, then 0.3 mi s. **Parking:** street only. L D

BEAU JO'S COLORADO STYLE PIZZA **Phone:** 970/498-8898

Pizza
$8-$20

AAA Inspector Notes: The menu features several pizzas, mountain pies and combination dishes. The salad bar is in an old claw-foot bathtub. The casual environment displays several TVs to watch, and service is prompt, friendly and attentive. This pizzeria has an interesting tradition of offering the diners honey to use on the pizza crust. **Bar:** full bar. **Address:** 100 N College Ave 80524 **Location:** Corner of N College and Mountain aves; in Old Town Square. **Parking:** street only. L D

BISETTI'S RISTORANTE **Phone:** 970/493-0086

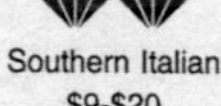

Southern Italian
$9-$20

AAA Inspector Notes: A favorite with local residents for more than 20 years, the family restaurant nurtures a warm, cozy and unusual atmosphere. More than 4,000 personalized wine bottles are on hand. Cheesecake is a specialty. Savory options include pasta favorites such as spaghetti with meatballs or sausage, lasagna, manicotti and fettuccine Alfredo with chicken. The candlelight is popular with couples escaping the chain restaurants. Servers are friendly and capable. **Bar:** full bar. **Address:** 120 S College Ave 80524 **Location:** I-25 exit 269B, just s of Old Town Square; downtown. **Parking:** street only. L D

CHARCO BROILER **Phone:** 970/482-1472

Steak
$5-$50

AAA Inspector Notes: Owner-operated since 1957, the popular steakhouse is just a short distance from nearby motels and I-25. Friendly servers bring around salads, steaks, burgers, sandwiches, seafood and pasta in a rustic Western setting adorned with eclectic art. **Bar:** full bar. **Address:** 1716 E Mulberry St 80524 **Location:** I-25 exit 269B, 1.5 mi w on SR 14. B L D

THE CHOCOLATE CAFE **Phone:** 970/482-2725

Desserts
$5-$8

AAA Inspector Notes: This is a delightful little cafe near the historic center of town. The menu features an eclectic mix of soup, salads, panini, pizza and risotto. The highlight of eating here is, as the name might suggest, dessert. Examples include the sweet ravioli filled with chocolate and hazelnut, the ultimate chocolate cake and key lime pie. **Bar:** full bar. **Address:** 102 W Olive St 80524 **Location:** Jct College Ave. **Parking:** street only. L D

COOPERSMITH'S PUB & BREWING

Phone: 970/498-0483

American
$8-$24

AAA Inspector Notes: Creative names are bestowed on such dishes as fish 'n' chips, pot pies, Mexican dishes and American choices. Various home-brewed beers are available. The seasonal patio offers comfy seating. Garage parking is across the street. The dining room is divided into a lounge with a variety of pictures of hops and typical pub décor and a casual dining room with a view of the open kitchen. **Bar:** full bar. **Address:** 5 Old Town Square 80524 **Location:** Just e of College Ave on Mountain Ave; in Old Town Square. **Parking:** street only. [L] [D]

JEJU SUSHI AND JAPANESE RESTAURANT

Phone: 970/416-7733

Japanese
$7-$18

AAA Inspector Notes: This casual eatery features traditional Japanese and Korean favorites. The menu features sushi, teriyaki, udon noodles, Korean barbecue, tempura and bi bim bob. The lunch sushi special is a great bargain. **Bar:** full bar. **Address:** 238 S College Ave 80524 **Location:** Jct Olive St; downtown. **Parking:** street only. [L] [D]

LA CREPERIE **Phone:** 970/224-2640

French
$7-$12

AAA Inspector Notes: I've had crepes before, but I had yet to experience a savory galette prepared by the hands of a true Frenchman. The thin, buttery, crispy buckwheat pancake, gently folded into a square packet with chopped bacon peeking out from the center, was as delightful to look at as it was to eat. However, the almond croissant was pure ambrosia. This is exactly how I like French food, buttery and decadent. The crepes and galettes take awhile to arrive. Just relax; it's worth the wait. **Bar:** wine only. **Address:** 163 W Mountain Ave 80524 **Location:** Jct Mason St. **Parking:** street only. [B] [L] [AC]

MCCOY'S MORNING GLORY BREAKFAST & LUNCH

Phone: 970/266-0302

American
$7-$9

AAA Inspector Notes: Bright and airy with a wood-beamed ceiling, this restaurant offers a wide variety of coffees, breakfasts, pizzas, soups, salads and sandwiches. In-season patio dining is available. **Bar:** full bar. **Address:** 1003 W Horsetooth Rd 80526 **Location:** I-25 exit 265 (Harmony Rd), 4.5 mi w, 1 mi n on College Ave to Horsetooth Rd, then 1 mi w. [B] [L]

NYALA ETHIOPIAN CUISINE **Phone:** 970/223-6734

Ethiopian
$8-$12

AAA Inspector Notes: If you've never had Ethiopian food, this is the perfect place to try it out. My waitress was patient and informative while explaining the menu items. Both the sambussa, a lentil- or beef-filled pastry, and the chicken alicha, spiced with rosemary and tumeric, were delicious. I enjoyed the spongy texture of the injera pancake, which can be used to scoop up meat and vegetables or be simply eaten by itself. Choose the traditional seating for a more authentic experience. **Bar:** wine only. **Address:** 2900 Harvard St, Suite A 80525 **Location:** Jct Harmony Rd and College Ave, 1.7 mi n, then just e. **Parking:** street only. [D]

RIO GRANDE MEXICAN RESTAURANT

Phone: 970/224-5428

Mexican
$7-$16

AAA Inspector Notes: Tex-Mex and grilled specialties such as tacos de pechuga, enchiladas, tostadas, flautas and plates of flame-broiled meat are offered at the popular, festive restaurant. Breakfast and brunch specials tempt patrons on the weekends, and patio dining is a nice seasonal option. Service is friendly and casual. Although beer and wine are available, cocktails are not. However, some killer margaritas are mixed; the limit is posted on the wall. **Bar:** full bar. **Address:** 143 W Mountain Ave 80524 **Location:** Between Mason St and College Ave; downtown. **Parking:** street only. [L] [D]

SANFORD'S GRUB & PUB **Phone:** 970/206-0400

American
$9-$22

AAA Inspector Notes: Popular with families, this restaurant is adorned with statues of Marilyn Monroe, carousel horses and a cartoonish moose. The $1 domestic beers on tap are a hit. I started with the mild jalapeño hot bites, which were served with a syrupy sauce called berries inferno. The pulled pork sandwich had a sweet sauce with a mild hint of spice. The crunch of the grilled bun provided a nice contrast to the tender meat. The server helped me navigate through the overwhelming menu. Portions are large. **Bar:** full bar. **Address:** 1526 Oakridge Dr 80525 **Location:** I-25 exit 265 (Harmony Rd), 3 mi w, just s on McMurry Ave, then just w. [L] [D]

STAR OF INDIA **Phone:** 970/225-1740

Indian
$10-$19

AAA Inspector Notes: This cozy restaurant may not look like much from the outside, but it's definitely worth the visit. The menu features standard Indian dishes such as tandoori chicken, lamb vindaloo and saag paneer. Prepared to perfection, everything is delicious. The chicken pakora appetizer and naan bread are little treats that should accompany every meal. **Bar:** full bar. **Address:** 2900 Harvard St, Unit B 80525 **Location:** I-25 exit 265 (Harmony Rd), 4.4 mi w, 1.7 mi n on College Ave, then just e. **Parking:** on-site and street. [L] [D]

SUEHIRO **Phone:** 970/482-3734

Japanese
$8-$17

AAA Inspector Notes: The extensive menu includes sushi, teriyaki, hibachi-grilled options, tempura, udon and more. Casual Japanese décor and friendly servers add to the ambience. **Bar:** full bar. **Address:** 223 Linden St 80524 **Location:** Jct College Ave and Walnut St, just se, then just ne. **Parking:** street only. [L] [D]

TAIPAN ASIAN BISTRO **Phone:** 970/472-1167

Asian
$6-$15

AAA Inspector Notes: This bustling restaurant is a favorite spot for locals. Patrons can expect large portions of tasty traditional Chinese cuisine served quickly. **Bar:** full bar. **Address:** 144 N Mason St 80524 **Location:** Jct College and Laporte aves, just w; downtown. **Parking:** on-site (fee). [L] [D]

TAJ MAHAL **Phone:** 970/493-1105

Indian
$9-$17

AAA Inspector Notes: The Taj Mahal features a great variety of delicious lamb, beef and tandoori chicken, which is grilled in a clay oven. Various curries, rice biryanis and fresh tandoori-baked naan bread also are available. They have a very reasonably priced lunch buffet and a nice selection of wine and beer. **Bar:** full bar. **Reservations:** suggested. **Address:** 148 W Oak St 80524 **Location:** Between College Ave and Mason St; downtown. **Parking:** on-site and street. [L] [D]

YOUNG'S CAFE VIETNAMESE CUISINE
Phone: 970/223-8000

Vietnamese
$7-$17

AAA Inspector Notes: A respected restaurant offering delicious dishes such as sesame chicken, seafood delight, tropical island and several desserts in a casual, open and bright atmosphere. The staff is friendly and prompt. A popular spot for lunch with locals and the business crowds. **Bar:** full bar. **Address:** 3307 S College Ave, Suite 114 80525 **Location:** 2.8 mi s on US 287; in Crystal Garden Shopping Center. L D

ZQUILA
Phone: 970/631-8565

Mexican
$8-$16

AAA Inspector Notes: Diners will be pleased with the well-prepared, flavorful Mexican menu, which includes fajitas, burritos, tacos, rellenos, enchiladas, flautas and other favorites. The extensive drink menu is sure to please tequila enthusiasts. A water feature creates a unique focal point on the grand wood bar. **Bar:** full bar. **Address:** 2400 E Harmony Rd, Suite 101 80528 **Location:** I-25 exit 265 (Harmony Rd), 2 mi w. L D

FORT GARLAND (F-4) pop. 433, elev. 7,932'

Fort Garland is a farming community on the eastern edge of the San Luis Valley. Great Sand Dunes National Park and Preserve *(see place listing p. 220)* lies 30 miles north via US 160 and SR 150.

FORT GARLAND MUSEUM is at the s. edge of town at 29477 SR 159. The fort was established in 1858 and served as a supply point, a deterrent to hostilities and to facilitate westward expansion. Col. Kit Carson held his last command at the post 1866-67. Abandoned in 1883, the fort has been restored and contains military memorabilia and folk art from the San Luis Valley.

Time: Allow 30 minutes minimum. **Hours:** Daily 9-5, Apr.-Oct.; Thurs.-Mon. 10-4, rest of year. **Cost:** $5; $4.50 (ages 65+); $3.50 (ages 6-16). **Phone:** (719) 379-3512.

FORT GARLAND MOTOR INN
Phone: 719/379-2993

Motel
$85-$190 5/1-12/31
$80-$160 1/1-4/30

Address: 411 Hwy 160 81133 **Location:** On US 160; west end of town. **Facility:** 17 units, some kitchens. 2 stories (no elevator), interior corridors. **Terms:** 3 day cancellation notice-fee imposed.

/ SOME UNITS

WHERE TO EAT

ALL-GON RESTAURANT & PIZZERIA
Phone: 719/379-2222

Italian
$6-$11

AAA Inspector Notes: The popular neighborhood eatery features a salad bar, freshly-made soups, pizza, calzones, pasta and deli sandwiches. **Address:** 319 Beaubien Ave 81133 **Location:** On US 160; center.

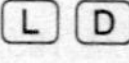

SILVER SAGE STEAKHOUSE
Phone: 719/379-3600

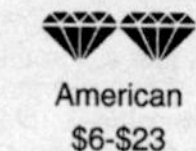

American
$6-$23

AAA Inspector Notes: At this casual restaurant, guests can nibble on peanuts served in an oversize metal measuring cup while they wait for appetizers, pan-seared or broiled U.S. choice reserve steaks, chicken cutlets, jumbo shrimp baskets, slow-roasted pork ribs or liver and onions, an old cowboy favorite. **Bar:** full bar. **Address:** 104 4th St 81133 **Location:** On US 160; center. D

FORT MORGAN (A-6) pop. 11,315, elev. 4,338'

• Restaurants p. 202

Fort Morgan was the childhood home of musician and band leader Glenn Miller. In late June the Dancin' on the Plains festival pays tribute to Miller and his contributions to swing music.

The present city grew out of a military post that was established on the South Platte River in 1864 to protect travelers from hostile American Indians. It later became a station on the Overland Trail from the Missouri River to Denver. A monument on Riverview Avenue marks the site of the fort. Agriculture, manufacturing, cattle ranching and dairy farming are Fort Morgan's leading industries.

Fort Morgan Area Chamber of Commerce: 300 Main St., P.O. Box 971, Fort Morgan, CO 80701. **Phone:** (970) 867-6702 or (800) 354-8660.

FORT MORGAN MUSEUM is in the library-museum complex in City Park at 414 Main St. Exhibits highlight local history. Also featured is a Glenn Miller exhibit and a 1920s soda fountain as well as traveling and temporary exhibits. A research center is on the grounds. **Time:** Allow 30 minutes minimum. **Hours:** Mon. and Fri. 10-5, Tues.-Thurs. 10-8, Sat. 11-5. Closed major holidays. **Cost:** Donations. **Phone:** (970) 542-4010.

CENTRAL MOTEL
Phone: (970)867-2401

Motel
$59-$69 5/1-10/15
$52-$59 10/16-4/30

Address: 201 W Platte Ave 80701 **Location:** I-76 exit 80, 0.6 mi s, then w on US 34. **Facility:** 19 units. 1 story, exterior corridors. **Free Special Amenities: local telephone calls and early check-in/late check-out.**

SAVE / SOME UNITS FEE

CLARION INN FORT MORGAN
Phone: 970/867-8200

Hotel
Rates not provided

Address: 14378 Hwy 34 80701 **Location:** I-76 exit 75, 0.3 mi s. **Facility:** 40 units. 3 stories, interior corridors. **Amenities:** *Some:* high-speed Internet. **Pool(s):** heated indoor. **Activities:** whirlpool, exercise room. **Guest Services:** valet laundry.

BIZ / SOME UNITS FEE

COMFORT INN
Phone: (970)867-6700

Hotel
$80-$170

Address: 1417 Barlow Rd 80701 **Location:** I-76 exit 82 (Barlow Rd), just n. **Facility:** 49 units. 3 stories, interior corridors. **Terms:** cancellation fee imposed. **Amenities:** high-speed Internet. **Pool(s):** heated indoor. **Activities:** whirlpool, exercise room. **Guest Services:** coin laundry.

BIZ

DAYS INN **Phone:** (970)542-0844

Hotel
$70-$138

Address: 1150 Main St 80701 **Location:** I-76 exit 80, just s. **Facility:** 33 units. 2 stories (no elevator), interior corridors. **Amenities:** high-speed Internet. **Pool(s):** heated indoor.

FORT MORGAN SUPER 8 **Phone:** (970)867-9443

Hotel
$58-$70

Address: 1220 N Main St 80701 **Location:** I-76 exit 80, just s, then just e. **Facility:** 37 units. 2 stories (no elevator), interior corridors. **Amenities:** safes. **Guest Services:** coin laundry.

SOME UNITS FEE

RODEWAY INN **Phone:** (970)867-9481

Motel
$60-$120

Address: 1409 Barlow Rd 80701 **Location:** I-76 exit 82 (Barlow Rd), just n. **Facility:** 43 units. 1-2 stories (no elevator), interior/exterior corridors. **Terms:** office hours 6 am-11 pm, cancellation fee imposed. **Dining:** Mavericks Restaurant, see separate listing. **Guest Services:** coin laundry.

SOME UNITS FEE

WHERE TO EAT

COUNTRY STEAK OUT **Phone:** 970/867-7887

Steak
$7-$27

AAA Inspector Notes: Guests appreciate the family-oriented restaurant's menu variety and good value. Prime rib, steaks and chicken are served in a Western-themed dining room. A lunch buffet is set up Tuesday through Friday. Service is capable and pleasant. **Bar:** full bar. **Address:** 19592 E 8th Ave 80701 **Location:** I-76 exit 82 (Barlow Rd), 0.3 mi s, then 0.4 mi w.

B L D

LITTLE BAMBOO **Phone:** 970/867-1827

Asian
$7-$13

AAA Inspector Notes: I started with the wonton soup in a flavorful, dark beef broth. The savory pork wontons were homemade. The crispy tofu wasn't as crispy as I expected, and the sauce was a little bland. On the Healthy Selections side of the menu vegetables are steamed and served with chicken, shrimp or tofu. I tried the chicken with garlicky Yushen sauce. The menu also includes favorites such as Szechuan shrimp, sesame chicken, Mongolian beef, Pad Thai, drunken noodles and Thai curry. Servers were very attentive. **Bar:** wine only. **Address:** 613 W Platte Ave 80701 **Location:** I-76 exit 80, 0.6 mi s, then 0.4 mi w.

L D

MAVERICKS RESTAURANT **Phone:** 970/542-9482

American
$5-$20

AAA Inspector Notes: Specializing in comfort food, the eclectic menu is sure to please most patrons. Burgers, steaks, stuffed potatoes and pizzas are just some of the many offerings. The inviting Western decor, small bar with flat-screen TV and the convenient location enhance the dining experience. **Bar:** full bar. **Address:** 1409 Barlow Rd 80701 **Location:** I-76 exit 82 (Barlow Rd), just n; in Rodeway Inn. L D

FRASER (B-3) pop. 1,224, elev. 8,574'

Fraser, in north-central Colorado just east of Arapaho National Forest *(see place listing p. 40)* and southwest of Rocky Mountain National Park *(see place listing p. 276)*, offers an abundance of nearby recreational opportunities. When snow begins to accumulate, locals and visitors know they can find ample choices for skiing, snowboarding, snowmobiling and sleigh rides, or in summer for hiking, mountain biking, horseback riding, fishing, white-water rafting and hot-air ballooning.

Fraser Visitor Center: 120 Xerex St. (US 40), P.O. Box 120, Fraser, CO 80442. **Phone:** (970) 726-8312.

RECREATIONAL ACTIVITIES

Tubing

- **Fraser Tubing Hill** is .5 mi. n. of jct. US 40 and CR 72 behind the Alco complex. **Hours:** Tues.-Thurs. 2-9, Fri.-Sat. and holidays 10-10, Sun. 10-9, Thanksgiving to mid-Mar. Last tube rental is 1 hour before closing. Phone ahead to confirm schedule. **Phone:** (970) 726-5954.

FRISCO (D-3) pop. 2,683, elev. 9,042'

Although named by European settlers in 1873, the site of Frisco had served as a favored Ute Indian camp for nearly 7,000 years. The town quickly boomed during the late 19th century as gold and silver mines covered the surrounding mountainsides.

Serving the needs of visiting skiers became Frisco's economic mainstay after World War II. In addition to skiing, the area also offers such recreational activities as bicycling, mountain biking, fishing and sailing. The Lake Dillon Water Taxi provides transportation between the marinas in Frisco and Dillon, across the lake. The service is available between Memorial Day and mid-September; phone (970) 486-0250 for information.

FRISCO HISTORIC PARK AND MUSEUM, off I-70 exit 203, then .7 mi. s. on Summit Blvd. to jct. 2nd Ave. and Main St., depicts town history during its mining and logging heydays. Twelve original structures, including furnished homes, depict lifestyles spanning 1880-1930 and include a schoolhouse museum displaying artifacts and photographs, a ranch house, a town house, a jail, a saloon, a post office and a 1943 log chapel.

Other exhibits feature natural history and a coin-operated train diorama. **Time:** Allow 1 hour minimum. **Hours:** Tues.-Sat. 9-5, Sun 9-3, May-Sept.; Tues.-Sat. 10-4, Sun. 10-2, rest of year. **Cost:** Free. **Phone:** (970) 668-3428.

RECREATIONAL ACTIVITIES

Skiing

- **Copper Mountain Resort** is off I-70 exit 195. Other activities are offered year-round. **Hours:** Mon.-Fri. 9-4, Sat.-Sun. and holidays 8:30-4, mid-Nov. to mid-Apr. and June-Sept. **Phone:** (970) 968-2882 or (800) 458-8386.

Skiing (Cross-country)

- **Frisco Nordic Center** is at 18454 SR 9. **Hours:** Daily 9-4, Nov.-Apr. (weather permitting). **Phone:** (970) 668-0866.

White-water Rafting

- **High Side Adventure Tours** picks up guests at area hotels. **Hours:** Daily mid-May to mid-Sept. **Phone:** (970) 453-5559 or (800) 997-3448.
- **Performance Tours** meets at Pioneer Sports, 842 N. Summit Blvd. in Frisco. **Hours:** Daily May 1-Labor Day. **Phone:** (800) 328-7238.

ALPINE INN **Phone:** (970)668-3122

Hotel

$62-$155

Address: 105 Lusher Ct 80443 **Location:** I-70 exit 203, just s, then just w. **Facility:** 37 units. 2 stories (no elevator), interior corridors. **Terms:** office hours 7 am-10 pm, 14 day cancellation notice-fee imposed. **Pool(s):** heated indoor. **Activities:** whirlpool.

/ SOME UNITS

BEST WESTERN LAKE DILLON LODGE **Phone:** (970)668-5094

Hotel

$70-$295

AAA Benefit: Members save up to 20%, plus 10% bonus points with Best Western Rewards®.

Address: 1202 N Summit Blvd 80443 **Location:** I-70 exit 203, just s. **Facility:** 127 units. 4 stories, interior corridors. **Terms:** check-in 4 pm. **Amenities:** *Some:* high-speed Internet. **Pool(s):** heated indoor. **Activities:** whirlpools, rental bicycles, hiking trails, jogging, horseshoes, volleyball. **Guest Services:** valet and coin laundry. **Free Special Amenities: continental breakfast and high-speed Internet.**

/ SOME UNITS

GALENA STREET MOUNTAIN INN **Phone:** 970/668-3224

Bed & Breakfast

$129-$199 11/24-4/30
$109-$169 5/1-11/23

Address: 106 Galena St 80443 **Location:** I-70 exit 201, 0.6 mi e, then just n on 1st Ave. **Facility:** Guest rooms, most with mountain views and some with balconies, are large and stylish. Public areas are beautifully decorated. All rooms have fans. 13 units, some two bedrooms. 2 stories (no elevator), interior corridors. **Terms:** office hours 9 am-6 pm, 2 night minimum stay - seasonal and/or weekends, 7 day cancellation notice-fee imposed. **Activities:** sauna, whirlpool, game room.

HOLIDAY INN FRISCO - SUMMIT COUNTY **Phone:** 970/668-5000

Hotel

Rates not provided

Address: 1129 N Summit Blvd 80443 **Location:** I-70 exit 203, just s, then just e. **Facility:** 217 units. 6 stories, interior corridors. **Terms:** check-in 4 pm. **Pool(s):** heated indoor. **Activities:** sauna, whirlpool, rental bicycles, exercise room. *Fee:* downhill & cross country skiing, snowmobiling, game room. **Guest Services:** valet and coin laundry. ***(See ad p. 103.)***

/ SOME UNITS FEE

HOTEL FRISCO **Phone:** 970/668-5009

Hotel

$99-$319 11/1-4/30
$79-$219 5/1-10/31

Address: 308 Main St 80443 **Location:** I-70 exit 201, 0.7 mi e. **Facility:** 13 units, some two bedrooms. 2 stories (no elevator), interior corridors. **Terms:** office hours 7:30 am-9 pm, 14 day cancellation notice-fee imposed. **Activities:** whirlpool.

NEW SUMMIT INN **Phone:** 970/668-3220

Hotel

$89-$159 12/21-4/30
$49-$109 5/1-12/20

Address: 1205 N Summit Blvd 80443 **Location:** I-70 exit 203, just s, then just e. **Facility:** 31 units. 2 stories (no elevator), interior corridors. **Terms:** office hours 7 am-11 pm, 15 day cancellation notice-fee imposed. **Activities:** sauna, whirlpool. **Guest Services:** coin laundry. **Free Special Amenities: continental breakfast and local telephone calls.**

/ SOME UNITS FEE

RAMADA LIMITED FRISCO **Phone:** (970)668-8783

Hotel

$58-$176

Address: 990 Lakepoint Dr 80443 **Location:** I-70 exit 203, just s, then just e. **Facility:** 51 units. 3 stories, interior corridors. **Terms:** check-in 4 pm. **Activities:** whirlpool. **Free Special Amenities: expanded continental breakfast and high-speed Internet.**

/ SOME UNITS FEE

WOODS INN BED & BREAKFAST **Phone:** 970/668-2255

fyi Not evaluated. **Address:** 205 S 2nd Ave 80443 **Location:** Just s of E Main St and S 2nd Ave. Facilities, services, and decor characterize an economy property.

WHERE TO EAT

BACKCOUNTRY BREWERY **Phone:** 970/668-2337

American

$8-$18

AAA Inspector Notes: On a second story, this huge log and stone brewery offers sweet and sour tater tots, soups and salads, specialty pizza, chicken potpie, several pasta options and barbecue platters. In addition to several dining rooms, there are three pool tables, free Wi-Fi, flat-screen TVs, and a separate cozy sitting area with large windows, cozy leather club chairs and sofas, and majestic views of mountain peaks and mesmerizing sunsets. An elevator is available. **Bar:** full bar. **Address:** 720 Main St 80443 **Location:** I-70 exit 203, 1.3 mi s; southwest corner Main St and Summit Blvd. L D

BAGALI'S **Phone:** 970/668-0601

Italian

$9-$21

AAA Inspector Notes: This handsome and upscale restaurant's interior is offset by a cozy sidewalk patio. The much-talked-about wine bar offers flights, weekly tastings and wine dinners. Menu selections include cioppino, salads, small meat and cheese plates, and scallops with spring pea and red pepper puree. Patrons can choose a pasta and sauce and combine them with chicken, eggplant or veal Parmesan, Italian sausage, salmon, scallops or shrimp. Artisan pizza can be ordered gluten-free. **Bar:** full bar. **Address:** 320 E Main St 80443 **Location:** I-70 exit 203 westbound, 1.3 mi s to Main St, then 0.3 mi w. **Parking:** street only. L D

BLUE SPRUCE INN **Phone:** 970/668-5900

Steak

$9-$33

AAA Inspector Notes: The restaurant offers elegant, intimate dining in an 1880s log cabin. Appetizers include baked brie, blue corn calamari and spinach-artichoke dip. Entrées feature roast duckling, Rocky Mountain trout, king crab legs and steaks. A Western-style saloon is attached and focuses on more casual fare. **Bar:** full bar. **Reservations:** suggested. **Address:** 20 W Main St 80443 **Location:** I-70 exit 201, 0.4 mi e. D

BOATYARD AMERICAN GRILL **Phone:** 970/668-4728

American
$9-$22

AAA Inspector Notes: This former tire store offers an eclectic menu, caters to a diverse set of tastes and moods, and is known for its variety of freshly made entrées, including wood oven-baked penne with chicken, and sauteed shrimp or tofu Asian stir-fry served with soba noodles and fried wonton strips. French onion soup and a delicious tortilla soup are available daily. Many salads, specialty pizza, calzone, sandwiches, burgers and a selection of vegetarian items are available. **Bar:** full bar. **Address:** 304 Main St 80443 **Location:** I-70 exit 201, 0.7 mi e. **Parking:** street only. [L] [D] [AC]

BUTTERHORN BAKERY & CAFE **Phone:** 970/668-3997

American
$4-$10

AAA Inspector Notes: The casual eatery is popular with locals and travelers for the hearty breakfast offerings and the tasty hot and cold sandwiches. The glass cases are attractively lined with homemade bread, dainty treats, thick and crunchy cookies, and yummy muffins. Patrons waiting to be seated tend to stare trancelike at the gooey cinnamon rolls and pecan-caramel sticky buns. **Bar:** full bar. **Address:** 408 E Main St 80443 **Location:** I-70 exit 201, 0.9 mi e. [B] [L] [AC]

FOOD HEDZ WORLD CAFE **Phone:** 970/668-2000

American
$10-$27

AAA Inspector Notes: Chef/owner David Welch began his career washing dishes at the Keystone Resort. After a long apprenticeship, he eventually became executive chef at the resort's restaurant. Nine years later, he opened this place, leaving the formal atmosphere behind. Patrons order at the cashier stand and seat themselves. Some of the innovative dishes include tempura of sea scallops and gulf shrimp, grilled aged beef, steamed mussels and clams, and a steamed cabbage roll filled with lobster, shrimp and crab. **Bar:** wine only. **Address:** 842 Summit Blvd, Suite 19 80443 **Location:** I-70 exit 203, 0.3 mi s; in strip mall. [L] [D] [AC]

HIMALAYAN CUISINE **Phone:** 970/668-3330

Indian
$11-$17

AAA Inspector Notes: Serving authentic Indian and Nepalese cuisine, this charming sidewalk eatery serves traditional favorites such as a delicious daal soup, samosas, pakoras, chicken and lamb tikka kabas and masala and many vegetarian entrées. The homemade mango ice cream is soft and sweet. **Bar:** full bar. **Address:** 409 Main St 80443 **Location:** I-70 exit 203 westbound, 1.2 mi s to Main St, then 0.5 mi w; exit 201 eastbound. **Parking:** street only. [L] [D]

KEMOSABE SUSHI & SAKE **Phone:** 970/668-2100

Sushi
$5-$18

AAA Inspector Notes: The upscale atmosphere combined with relaxing music goes well with chile garlic edamame, tempura jalapeño shooters wrapped in tuna, spicy miso soup, salads and a variety of sashimi, nigiri and specialty rolls. The sweet, fruity Japanese ice cream wrapped in soft fluffy dough is dusted with a white powdery coating. The restaurant also offers more than 20 varieties of sake and Japanese beer along with an innovative cocktail menu. **Bar:** full bar. **Address:** 605 Main St 80443 **Location:** I-70 exit 203 westbound, 1.2 mi s to Main St, then just w; exit 201 eastbound. **Parking:** street only. [D]

LOG CABIN CAFE **Phone:** 970/668-3947

American
$5-$12

AAA Inspector Notes: The 100-plus-year-old log cabin, whose original walls form part of the kitchen, is a quaint spot in which to enjoy a hearty breakfast, grilled burger, sandwich or Mexican special. A nice shaded patio is streetside. **Bar:** full bar. **Address:** 121 Main St 80443 **Location:** I-70 exit 201, 0.7 mi e. [B] [L]

SILVERHEELS BAR & GRILL **Phone:** 970/668-0345

Regional American
$5-$29

AAA Inspector Notes: This popular downtown restaurant's upscale Southwestern atmosphere complements a menu featuring an award-winning green chili stew, seafood chowder, a variety of thick choice steaks, wild game, poultry, sizzling crab empanadas, chicken lettuce wraps, Rocky Mountain trout, caramelized giant Atlantic sea scallops drizzled with spicy Thai sauce, and delicious, creative desserts. **Bar:** full bar. **Address:** 603 Main St 80443 **Location:** I-70 exit 203 westbound, 1.2 mi s to Main St, just w; exit 201 eastbound. **Parking:** street only. [L] [D]

TUSCATO RISTORANTE ITALIANO **Phone:** 970/668-3644

Italian
$12-$29

AAA Inspector Notes: The restaurant focuses on traditional preparations of pasta, chicken, veal and seafood. The lunch menu has lighter fare panini and other Italian sandwiches. The atmosphere is casual both in the dining area and on the patio. **Bar:** full bar. **Address:** 311 Main St 80443 **Location:** I-70 exit 203 westbound, 1.2 mi s to Main St, then 0.3 mi w; exit 201 eastbound. **Parking:** street only. [D]

VINNY'S **Phone:** 970/668-0340

American
$8-$29

AAA Inspector Notes: The Euro-American menu will have you devouring appetizers such as "The Kennedy," featuring fresh Massachusetts baked stuffed clams. Entrées include basil marinated and roasted prosciutto-wrapped pork tenderloin, grass-fed Australian lamb loin with roasted garlic sauce and crispy duck leg confit served with an apple-smoked bacon white bean cassoulet. House-made desserts feature their signature white chocolate bread pudding with sun-dried cherries and a classic tiramisu. **Bar:** full bar. **Address:** 310 Main St, #203 80443 **Location:** I-70 exit 203, 1.3 mi s to Main St, then 0.3 mi e; located upstairs. **Parking:** street only. [L] [D]

SUMMIT EATERY **Phone:** 970/668-8138

[fyi] Not evaluated. The perfect spot for fast casual dining, this eatery features several seasonal soups made daily, flatbreads such as almond peanut with apples, dried cherries and honey, an Angus beef cheese melt, a nice assortment of salads and great luncheon combos. Gluten-free, vegetarian and vegan items are available. **Address:** 842 N Summit Blvd, Suite 38 80443 **Location:** I-70 exit 203, 0.3 mi s; in strip mall.

FRUITA (D-1) pop. 12,646, elev. 4,503'

MUSEUM OF WESTERN COLORADO'S DINOSAUR JOURNEY is 1 blk. s. of I-70 exit 19 (use caution) to 550 Jurassic Ct. This educational and research facility presents animated re-creations of dinosaurs and other prehistoric creatures in natural settings. A working paleontology laboratory and children's dinosaur quarry also are offered. Dinosaur digs are available in summer.

Time: Allow 1 hour minimum. **Hours:** Daily 9-5, May-Sept.; Mon.-Sat. 10-4, Sun. noon-4, rest of year. Closed Jan. 1, Thanksgiving and Christmas. **Cost:** $7; $6 (ages 55+); $4 (ages 3-12); $20 (family rate). Combination ticket with Cross Orchards Historic Farm and the Museum of the West and Sterling T. Smith Educational Tower (both in Grand Junction) $12; $10 (ages 55+); $8 (ages 3-12). **Phone:** (970) 858-7282 or (888) 488-3466.

BALANCED ROCK MOTEL Phone: 970/858-7333

Motel
$55-$65

Address: 126 S Coulson St 81521 **Location:** I-70 exit 19, just n to Aspen Ave, then just w. Located near train tracks. **Facility:** 22 units. 2 stories (no elevator), exterior corridors.

/ SOME UNITS FEE

COMFORT INN **Phone:** (970)858-1333

Hotel
$69-$139

Address: 400 Jurassic Ave 81521 **Location:** I-70 exit 19, 0.3 mi s; just e of Dinosaur Journey Museum. **Facility:** 66 units. 3 stories, interior corridors. **Terms:** cancellation fee imposed. **Pool(s):** heated indoor. **Activities:** whirlpool. **Guest Services:** coin laundry.

/ SOME UNITS

LA QUINTA INN & SUITES FRUITA
Phone: (970)858-8850

Hotel
$116-$189

Address: 570 Raptor Rd 81521 **Location:** I-70 exit 19, 0.3 mi s. Located next to Dinosaur Journey Museum. **Facility:** 64 units. 3 stories, interior corridors. **Amenities:** high-speed Internet. **Pool(s):** heated indoor. **Activities:** whirlpool, exercise room. **Guest Services:** coin laundry. **Free Special Amenities: continental breakfast and high-speed Internet.**

SAVE BIZ / SOME UNITS

SUPER 8 **Phone:** (970)858-0808

Motel
$66-$98

Address: 399 Jurassic Ave 81521 **Location:** I-70 exit 19, 0.3 mi s; just e of Dinosaur Journey Museum. Located near highway. **Facility:** 60 units. 3 stories, interior corridors. **Terms:** cancellation fee imposed. **Pool(s):** heated indoor. **Activities:** whirlpool. **Guest Services:** coin laundry. **Free Special Amenities: continental breakfast and high-speed Internet.**

SAVE / SOME UNITS FEE FEE FEE

WHERE TO EAT

CAMILLA'S KAFFE **Phone:** 970/858-7950

Deli
$4-$9

AAA Inspector Notes: Espresso drinks taste great with items such as the bleu beef panini, freshly made salads, sandwich wraps and homemade baked goods. **Address:** 206 E Aspen Ave 81521 **Location:** I-70 exit 19, 0.3 mi n, then 0.4 mi e. **Parking:** street only.

B L D

DRAGON TREASURE **Phone:** 970/858-8655

Chinese
$8-$15

AAA Inspector Notes: Traditional Chinese cuisine and quick service make this restaurant a local favorite. **Address:** 576 Kokopelli Blvd 81521 **Location:** I-70 exit 19, 0.3 mi s, then just e.

L D

FIESTA GUADALAJARA **Phone:** 970/858-1228

Mexican
$9-$17

AAA Inspector Notes: The attentive and courteous staff at this family restaurant enhances the lively atmosphere. Patrons enjoy cold aguas frescas with made-in-house salsa and chips, sizzling fajitas and other traditional Mexican appetizers, entrees and desserts. **Bar:** full bar. **Address:** 103 Hwy 6 & 50 81521 **Location:** I-70 exit 19, 0.3 mi n, just e, then 0.3 mi s. L D

HOT TOMATO CAFE **Phone:** 970/858-1117

Pizza
$9-$25

AAA Inspector Notes: Patrons gush over the made-to-order calzones, Stromboli, sausage rolls, handcrafted pizza dough, fresh-grated mozzarella and the specialty pizzas, which include a white-sauce variety and a mouth-watering basil. The homemade hot and chewy breadsticks go well with the eight different carefully prepared and layered salads. Beers on tap and craft beers from the New Belgium Brewery are to be enjoyed inside or outside on the cozy covered patio. **Bar:** beer only. **Address:** 124 N Mulberry St 81521 **Location:** I-70 exit 19, 0.3 mi n to W Aspen Ave, just e (2nd exit at roundabout), then just n. **Parking:** street only.

L D CALL M

RIB CITY **Phone:** 970/858-6566

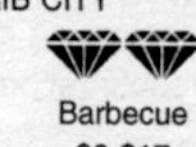

Barbecue
$6-$17

AAA Inspector Notes: A local favorite, the grill serves Southern-style barbecue and claims its ribs are the best. It's difficult to argue otherwise. The menu also lists barbecue chicken, pork, riblets and beef dinners presented with all the fixings. **Bar:** beer & wine. **Address:** 455 Kokopelli Blvd, Suite 5 81521 **Location:** I-70 exit 19, just s to Frontage Rd, just e, then just s. L D

GATEWAY

GATEWAY CANYONS RESORT **Phone:** 970/931-2458

fyi Not evaluated. **Address:** 43200 Hwy 141 81522 **Location:** On SR 141, 42.5 mi w of US 50; 48.5 mi n of CR 90. Facilities, services, and decor characterize an upscale property.

GEORGETOWN (B-3) pop. 1,034, elev. 8,512'

• **Restaurants p. 206**

Within 2 years of George and Dave Griffith's gold strike at the head of Clear Creek in 1859, the "bust" part of the familiar boom-and-bust story had begun to affect Georgetown. One by one its buildings emptied as the gold ran out and prospectors went elsewhere. In 1864, however, the first large silver discovery in Colorado was made about 5 miles northwest, and Georgetown was in business again.

Until the great strike at Leadville in 1878, Georgetown and its sister camp of Silver Plume, 2 miles up the canyon, comprised the premier silver district. Aptly nicknamed the "Silver Queen of the Rockies," Georgetown blossomed into the third largest city in Colorado.

Unlike other mining towns of the day, it escaped destruction by fire. More than 200 original buildings still stand. Shops now occupy many of the historic downtown structures and the city has been designated the Georgetown/Silver Plume National Historic Landmark District. Outdoor recreational options include fishing, mountain biking and hiking.

Gateway Visitor Center: 1491 Argentine St., Georgetown, CO 80444. **Phone:** (303) 569-2405.

GEORGETOWN LOOP RAILROAD departs from the Devil's Gate station (I-70 Georgetown exit 228) and Silver Plume station (I-70 Silver Plume exit 226). Passengers travel on a historic train over Devil's Gate High Bridge and through silver mining country with views of the Rocky Mountains. A tour of the Lebanon Silver Mine is available. Tickets may be purchased at the Silver Plume station or the Devil's Gate station. Mine tours are only accessible by train and are only available with the train ride.

Allow 2 hours, 30 minutes for train ride and mine tour. **Hours:** Trains depart from Silver Plume station daily at 9:45, 11:15, 12:45, 2:15 and 3:45 and from Georgetown Devil's Gate station at 10:25, 11:55, 1:25 and 2:55, Memorial Day weekend-early Oct.; Sat-Sun. only, first weekend in May-day before Memorial Day weekend and early Oct.-Dec. 30. Hours may vary, day after Labor Day-Dec. 30; phone ahead. Mine tours are available daily Memorial Day-Labor Day; Sat-Sun. in Sept. **Cost:** Train fare $22.50; $16.50 (ages 3-15). Mine tour $8.50; $5.50 (ages 3-15). Train reservations are strongly recommended. **Phone:** (888) 456-6777.

HAMILL HOUSE, 305 Argentine St., was built in 1879. The restored home of silver mine owner William Arthur Hamill demonstrates the wealth and opulence of the late-19th-century silver boom in Colorado. The home had central heating, gaslights and running water before most of the community had heard of such things. It also has a six-seat, cupola-topped privy, a granite-constructed stable, a carriage house and an office building. Guided walking tours are available.

Time: Allow 30 minutes minimum. **Hours:** Daily 10-4, Memorial Day-Sept. 30; Sat.-Sun. 10-4, Oct. 1-Dec. 19. **Cost:** $4; $3 (ages 65+ and students with ID); free (ages 0-12). Guided walking tour $8; $10 (family of up to 10 people); free children's tour available. Combination ticket with Hotel de Paris Museum $7. **Phone:** (303) 569-2840.

HOTEL DE PARIS MUSEUM, 409 6th St., was founded by Frenchman Louis Dupuy in 1875 and became internationally renowned for its architecture, appointments, wine cellar, cuisine and intellectual ambience. A museum since 1954, the hotel retains its Victorian atmosphere, wine cellar, courtyard and diamond-dust mirrors. The hotel displays original furnishings.

A 9-minute video about the building and a 30-minute tour are available. **Time:** Allow 1 hour minimum. **Hours:** Daily 10-4, Memorial Day-Labor Day; Sat.-Sun. 10-4, day after Labor Day-late Dec. Last tour 30 minutes before closing. **Cost:** $5; $3 (ages 5-17); free (ages 0-4, Georgetown residents and museum members). Combination ticket with Hamill House $7. **Phone:** (303) 569-2311.

RECREATIONAL ACTIVITIES

Skiing

- **Loveland Ski Area** is at I-70 exit 216. **Hours:** Mon.-Fri. 9-4, Sat.-Sun. and holidays 8:30-4, mid-Dec. to early Apr. **Phone:** (303) 569-3203 or (800) 736-3754.

THE HAPPY COOKER

Menu on AAA.com

Phone: 303/569-3166

American

$6-$9

AAA Inspector Notes: In a renovated 1920s Victorian home, this well-established and popular eatery nurtures a charming ambience. With an emphasis on healthy cooking, the menu offers homemade breads, chili, daily soups and specials, a large vegetarian selection and home-baked desserts. Patrons can unwind on the umbrella-shaded wood patio and sip a glass of fine local Colorado wine, a mimosa, beer, screwdriver, Bloody Mary, cappuccino, latte or hot spiced cider. **Bar:** beer & wine. **Address:** 412 6th St 80444 **Location:** I-70 exit 228, just e, 0.5 mi s, just e; at 6th and Taos sts, follow signs. **Parking:** street only.

B L AC

GLENDALE pop. 4,184

• **Hotels & Restaurants map & index p. 140**
• **Part of Denver area — see map p. 123**

HAMPTON INN & SUITES DENVER/CHERRY CREEK

Phone: (303)692-1800 66

Hotel

$99-$179

AAA Benefit: Members save up to 10% everyday!

Address: 4150 E Kentucky Ave 80246 **Location:** I-25 exit 204, 1 mi n on Colorado Blvd, just e; between Ohio Way and Mississippi Ave, set back from Colorado Blvd. **Facility:** 133 units, some efficiencies. 6 stories, interior corridors. **Terms:** 1-7 night minimum stay, cancellation fee imposed. **Amenities:** video games (fee). **Pool(s):** heated indoor. **Activities:** whirlpool, exercise room. **Guest Services:** valet and coin laundry.

CALL 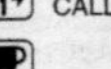 BIZ  FEE  

HILTON GARDEN INN DENVER/CHERRY CREEK

Phone: (303)754-9800 65

Hotel

$99-$189

AAA Benefit: Unparalleled hospitality at a special Member rate.

Address: 600 S Colorado Blvd 80246 **Location:** I-25 exit 204, 1.6 mi n. **Facility:** 210 units. 7 stories, interior corridors. **Terms:** 1-7 night minimum stay, cancellation fee imposed. **Amenities:** high-speed Internet. **Pool(s):** heated indoor. **Activities:** whirlpool, exercise room. **Guest Services:** valet and coin laundry.

CALL BIZ  

LOEWS DENVER HOTEL **Phone:** (303)782-9300 67

Hotel

$99-$279 5/1-10/2
$89-$259 10/3-4/30

Address: 4150 E Mississippi Ave 80246 **Location:** I-25 exit 204, 0.8 mi n on Colorado Blvd, then just e. **Facility:** The hotel features Italian-style decor, a shoeshine station and a lobby newsstand. 183 units. 11 stories, interior corridors. **Parking:** on-site and valet. **Terms:** check-in 4 pm, cancellation fee imposed. **Amenities:** video games (fee), safes. **Dining:** Tuscany Restaurant, see separate listing. **Activities:** exercise room. **Guest Services:** valet laundry, area transportation-within 6 mi. **Free Special Amenities: newspaper and local transportation.**

SAVE CALL BIZ FEE

/ SOME UNITS FEE

(See map & index p. 140.)

WHERE TO EAT

TUSCANY RESTAURANT Phone: 303/639-1600 (78)

Northern Italian
$15-$30

AAA Inspector Notes: Guests revel in Tuscany's regal decor and enjoy the friendly, Western hospitality and warm, intimate ambience. The cuisine includes a nice mix of Northern Italian and popular American entrees. **Bar:** full bar. **Reservations:** suggested. **Address:** 4150 E Mississippi Ave 80246 **Location:** I-25 exit 204, 0.8 mi n on Colorado Blvd, then just e; in Loews Denver Hotel. **Parking:** on-site and valet. B L D

GLENWOOD SPRINGS (D-2) pop. 9,614, elev. 5,763'

• Hotels p. 208 • Restaurants p. 209

Hot mineral springs and natural vapor caves have made Glenwood Springs popular since the days of the Ute Indians. During the mining boom the newly rich from Aspen and other bonanza towns came by special train to enjoy the waters at this fashionable spa and stay at the elegant Hotel Colorado. A memorial to Doc Holliday, a dentist with a sideline as a gunslinger, is in nearby Linwood Cemetery.

Ten miles east on I-70 through Glenwood Canyon is a 1.7-mile trail to Hanging Lake, a water-filled rocky bowl literally clinging to the face of a cliff 1,200 feet above the floor of the canyon. Spouting Rock Creek, which feeds the lake, creates Bridal Veil Falls.

Glenwood Springs, at the confluence of the Colorado and Roaring Fork rivers, is a popular rafting and trout fishing destination. The city lies along the scenic stretches of two highways: I-70 from Grand Junction to Georgetown and SR 82 from Glenwood Springs to Aspen, over Independence Pass (the pass is closed in winter).

Glenwood Springs Chamber Resort Association: 1102 Grand Ave., Glenwood Springs, CO 81601. **Phone:** (970) 945-6589 or (888) 445-3696.

FRONTIER HISTORICAL MUSEUM is at 1001 Colorado Ave. The museum features exhibits pertaining to the history of Glenwood Springs and Garfield County. Included in the collection are portraits of Doc Holliday, an ornate pump organ, a kitchen with period articles, a mineral case, and children's books and toys. **Time:** Allow 30 minutes minimum. **Hours:** Mon.-Sat. 11-4, May-Sept.; Mon. and Thurs.-Sat. 1-4, rest of year. **Cost:** $3; $2 (ages 60+); $1 (ages 3-12). **Phone:** (970) 945-4448.

GLENWOOD CAVERNS ADVENTURE PARK is off I-70 exit 116, .3 mi. w. on 6th St., then s. on Devereux Rd. to 51000 Two Rivers Plaza Rd. The Iron Mountain Tramway carries visitors to the caves and adventure park. The 70-minute cave tour features soda straws and other crystalline formations as well as Exclamation Point, a cliff-side balcony that offers panoramic views. Longer, more adventurous cave tours also are available. The park also offers thrill rides including an alpine coaster and a giant swing as well as a 4-dimensional theater, laser tag arena, bungee trampolines, gemstone sluice box mining, a maze and a climbing wall.

Time: Allow 2 hours minimum. **Hours:** Daily 9-9, Memorial Day-Labor Day. Schedule varies rest of year; phone ahead. **Cost:** Tram ride $12; $11 (ages 65+); $8 (ages 3-12). Cave tour $10; $9 (ages 65+); $8 (ages 3-12). Ride tickets $3 (thrill rides and attractions use 1 to 3 tickets each). Day pass (includes tram ride and unlimited thrill rides) Memorial Day-Labor Day $39. **Phone:** (970) 945-4228, ext. 111 or (800) 530-1635.

The Iron Mountain Tramway departs from Iron Mountain Station at 51000 Two Rivers Plaza Rd. Visitors travel 4,300 feet to the top of Iron Mountain in glass-enclosed gondolas. An observation area at the top of the mountain offers a panoramic view of Mount Sopris and the Colorado River Valley.

Time: Allow 1 hour minimum. **Hours:** Daily 9-9, Memorial Day-Labor Day. Schedule varies rest of year; phone ahead. **Cost:** Fare $12; $11 (ages 65+); $8 (ages 3-12). Combination ticket for tram and cave tour $22; $20 (ages 65+); $18 (ages 3-12). **Phone:** (970) 945-4228, ext. 111 or (800) 530-1635.

GEM **GLENWOOD HOT SPRINGS POOL** is off I-70 exit 116 to 401 N. River St. Measuring 2 blocks long, this is one of the world's largest outdoor thermal pools. The pool's mineral-rich waters come from Yampah Springs, once considered sacred by the Ute Indians (Yampah means "big medicine"), and are maintained between 90 and 93 degrees Fahrenheit. By the late 19th century the springs had been developed into a resort containing a hot springs pool, bath house and a lodge, which soon became a popular getaway for movie stars and other dignitaries.

Exercise lap lanes, a children's wading area, diving boards and two waterslides are featured. A smaller therapy pool is maintained at 104 degrees Fahrenheit. An athletic club, spa and miniature golf also are offered.

Lockers, towels and bathing suits are available for a small fee. **Time:** Allow 1 hour minimum. **Hours:** Pool daily 7:30 a.m.-10 p.m., Memorial Day weekend-Labor Day; 9 a.m.-10 p.m., rest of year. Waterslides and miniature golf available daily Memorial Day-Labor Day, Sat.-Sun., May 1-day before Memorial Day and day after Labor Day-Sept. 30. Pool closed 1-2 days in Jan., Mar., Apr., Sept. and Nov.; phone for schedule.

Cost: Memorial Day weekend-Labor Day: Mon.-Fri. $17.25; $11 (ages 3-12). Sat.-Sun. $18.75; $11.50 (ages 3-12). Rest of year: $13.75; $9.50 (ages 3-12). Additional fees apply to athletic club, spa, waterslides and miniature golf. **Phone:** (970) 947-2955 or (800) 537-7946.

RECREATIONAL ACTIVITIES

Skiing

- **Sunlight Mountain Resort** is at 10901 CR 117. Other activities are offered. **Hours:** Daily 9-4, early Dec.-early Apr. **Phone:** (970) 945-7491 or (800) 445-7931.

White-water Rafting

- **Blue Sky Adventures Inc.** departs from Hotel Colorado, 319 6th St. **Hours:** Daily 8-8, late May-early Sept. **Phone:** (970) 945-6605 or (877) 945-6605.
- **Rock Gardens Rafting** is at 1308 CR 129. **Hours:** Daily Apr.-Sept. (weather permitting). **Phone:** (970) 945-6737 or (800) 958-6737.
- **Whitewater Rafting** is off I-70 exit 114 at 2000 Devereux Rd. **Hours:** Daily 8-7, mid-Apr. to early Oct. **Phone:** (970) 945-8477 or (800) 993-7238.

AMERICAS BEST VALUE INN **Phone:** (970)945-6279

Motel
$53-$159

Address: 51871 Hwy 6 & 24 81601 **Location:** I-70 exit 114, 0.8 mi ne. **Facility:** 23 units. 1-2 stories (no elevator), exterior corridors. **Terms:** office hours 7:30 am-10 pm, cancellation fee imposed.

FEE / SOME UNITS

BEST WESTERN ANTLERS **Phone:** (970)945-8535

Motel
$96-$176

AAA Benefit: Members save up to 20%, plus 10% bonus points with Best Western Rewards®.

Address: 171 W 6th St 81601 **Location:** I-70 exit 116, just n, then just w. **Facility:** 99 units. 2 stories (no elevator), exterior corridors. **Pool(s):** heated outdoor. **Activities:** whirlpool, jogging, playground, horseshoes, volleyball. **Guest Services:** coin laundry, area transportation-train station. **Free Special Amenities: expanded continental breakfast and high-speed Internet.**

/ SOME UNITS FEE

CEDAR LODGE MOTEL **Phone:** (970)945-6579

Motel
$59-$200

Address: 2102 Grand Ave 81601 **Location:** I-70 exit 116, 1.5 mi s on SR 82. **Facility:** 76 units, some two bedrooms and kitchens. 2 stories (no elevator), exterior corridors. **Terms:** office hours 7 am-11 pm. **Pool(s):** heated outdoor, heated indoor. **Activities:** sauna, whirlpool, exercise room. **Guest Services:** coin laundry.

/ SOME UNITS

COURTYARD BY MARRIOTT **Phone:** (970)947-1300

Contemporary Hotel
$99-$179

AAA Benefit: AAA hotel discounts of 5% or more.

Address: 105 Wulfsohn Rd 81601 **Location:** I-70 exit 114, 2nd exit at roundabout, 1.5 mi e on Midland Ave, then just s. **Facility:** 101 units. 3 stories, interior corridors. **Amenities:** high-speed Internet. **Pool(s):** heated indoor. **Activities:** whirlpool, exercise room. **Guest Services:** valet and coin laundry.

/ SOME UNITS

FRONTIER LODGE **Phone:** (970)945-5496

Motel
$59-$149

Address: 2834 S Glen Ave 81601 **Location:** I-70 exit 116, 2 mi s on SR 82. **Facility:** 27 units. 1-2 stories (no elevator), exterior corridors. **Terms:** cancellation fee imposed. **Activities:** whirlpool. **Guest Services:** coin laundry.

/ SOME UNITS

GLENWOOD HOT SPRINGS **Phone:** (970)945-6571

Hotel
$189-$329 5/1-9/6
$139-$309 9/7-4/30

Address: 415 E 6th St 81601 **Location:** I-70 exit 116, just ne. Across from Hot Springs Pool. **Facility:** 107 units. 5 stories, interior corridors. **Terms:** check-in 4 pm, 2 night minimum stay - seasonal, cancellation fee imposed. **Amenities:** video games (fee), high-speed Internet, safes. **Pool(s):** heated outdoor. **Activities:** spa. *Fee:* waterslide, miniature golf. **Guest Services:** coin laundry, area transportation-train & bus stations. **Free Special Amenities: full breakfast and high-speed Internet.**

SAVE FEE BIZ

/ SOME UNITS

GLENWOOD SUITES, AN ASCEND COLLECTION HOTEL **Phone:** (970)384-4700

Hotel
$89-$199

Address: 2625 Gilstrap Ct 81601 **Location:** I-70 exit 114, just s, then w. **Facility:** 57 units, some two bedrooms and kitchens. 3 stories, interior corridors. **Terms:** cancellation fee imposed. **Amenities:** high-speed Internet, safes (fee). **Activities:** exercise room. **Guest Services:** valet and coin laundry.

FEE

HAMPTON INN **Phone:** (970)947-9400

Hotel
$169 5/1-9/30
$139 10/1-4/30

AAA Benefit: Members save up to 10% everyday!

Address: 401 W First St 81601 **Location:** I-70 exit 116, just w on US 6. **Facility:** 70 units. 3 stories, interior corridors. **Terms:** 1-7 night minimum stay, cancellation fee imposed. **Amenities:** video games (fee). **Pool(s):** heated indoor. **Activities:** whirlpool, exercise room. **Guest Services:** valet and coin laundry.

BIZ

HOLIDAY INN EXPRESS **Phone:** 970/928-7800

Hotel
Rates not provided

Address: 501 W First St 81601 **Location:** I-70 exit 116, just w on US 6 and 24. **Facility:** 65 units. 3 stories, interior corridors. **Parking:** winter plug-ins. **Amenities:** *Some:* high-speed Internet. **Pool(s):** heated outdoor. **Activities:** whirlpool. **Guest Services:** coin laundry.

HOTEL COLORADO

Phone: 970/945-6511

Historic Hotel

Rates not provided

Address: 526 Pine St 81601 **Location:** I-70 exit 116, just ne. **Facility:** This hotel was built in 1893 and has lodged such guests as President Theodore Roosevelt, Al Capone and Molly Brown. 130 units, some two and three bedrooms. 6 stories, interior corridors. **Terms:** check-in 4 pm. **Dining:** 2 restaurants. **Activities:** rental bicycles, spa. **Guest Services:** valet and coin laundry, area transportation-within 2 mi. **Free Special Amenities: high-speed Internet and local transportation.**

SAVE / SOME UNITS FEE

THE HOTEL DENVER

Phone: (970)945-6565

Historic Hotel

$124-$339

Address: 402 7th St 81601 **Location:** I-70 exit 116; across from historic train station; in town center. **Facility:** Although the hotel boasts the ambience of bygone days, you'll find the luxury of today's conveniences throughout; cozy quilts adorn each guest room. 72 units. 3 stories, interior corridors. **Terms:** cancellation fee imposed. **Amenities:** high-speed Internet. **Dining:** Glenwood Canyon Brew Pub, see separate listing. **Guest Services:** valet and coin laundry.

BIZ / SOME UNITS

THE HOTEL GLENWOOD SPRINGS

Phone: (970)928-8188

Hotel

$99-$235

Address: 52000 Two Rivers Plaza Rd 81601 **Location:** I-70 exit 116, 0.3 mi w on US 6 and 24. **Facility:** 72 units. 5 stories, interior corridors. **Terms:** check-in 4 pm, cancellation fee imposed. **Amenities:** video games (fee), high-speed Internet. **Pool(s):** heated indoor. **Activities:** whirlpool, waterslide, exercise room. **Guest Services:** valet and coin laundry.

BIZ FEE

/ SOME UNITS FEE

QUALITY INN & SUITES

Phone: (970)945-5995

Hotel

$79-$149

Address: 2650 Gilstrap Ct 81601 **Location:** I-70 exit 114, just s, then just w. **Facility:** 60 units, some efficiencies. 3 stories, interior corridors. **Terms:** cancellation fee imposed. **Amenities:** safes (fee). **Pool(s):** heated indoor. **Activities:** whirlpool, exercise room. **Guest Services:** valet and coin laundry.

BIZ / SOME UNITS FEE

RESIDENCE INN BY MARRIOTT

Phone: (970)928-0900

Extended Stay Hotel

$152-$186

AAA Benefit:
AAA hotel discounts of 5% or more.

Address: 125 Wulfsohn Rd 81601 **Location:** I-70 exit 114, 2nd exit at roundabout, 1.5 mi e on Midland Ave, then just s. **Facility:** 124 units, some two bedrooms, efficiencies and kitchens. 4 stories, interior corridors. **Terms:** check-in 4 pm. **Amenities:** high-speed Internet. **Pool(s):** heated indoor. **Activities:** whirlpool, sports court, basketball, exercise room. **Guest Services:** valet and coin laundry.

BIZ / SOME UNITS FEE

RODEWAY INN

Phone: 970/945-8817

Motel

Rates not provided

Address: 52039 Hwy 6 & 24 81601 **Location:** I-70 exit 114, 1 mi ne; exit 116, 1 mi nw. **Facility:** 42 units. 3 stories (no elevator), exterior corridors. **Activities:** whirlpool. **Guest Services:** coin laundry. **Free Special Amenities: continental breakfast and high-speed Internet.**

SAVE

WHERE TO EAT

19TH STREET DINER

Phone: 970/945-9133

American

$7-$16

AAA Inspector Notes: A touch of nostalgia characterizes this breakfast, lunch and dinner spot, which has a full bar and courteous servers. The eclectic menu features burgers, sandwiches, fajitas, burritos, chicken-fried steak and meatloaf. **Bar:** full bar. **Address:** 1908 Grand Ave 81601 **Location:** I-70 exit 116, just ne, then 1.4 mi s to 19th St. B L D

DOUBLE DOG PUB

Phone: 970/945-7827

American

$8-$16

AAA Inspector Notes: This dog-themed English-style pub and gathering place features menu items such as the dog house Caesar, the mutt Cobb salad and a double dog chicken club. Pub fare features mom's meatloaf with Irish Whiskey sauce and beef and Guinness stew with mashed potatoes. The puppy chow menu is for the kids. **Bar:** full bar. **Address:** 30 Market St, Suite A 81601 **Location:** I-70 exit 114, 2nd exit at roundabout (Midland Ave); 0.4 mi e to Wulfsohn Rd, 0.7 mi e to Market St; in Glenwood Meadows Mall. L D

FIESTA GUADALAJARA

Phone: 970/947-1670

Mexican

$9-$15

AAA Inspector Notes: The family restaurant features attractive hand-carved wooden booths, attentive service, traditional Mexican fare and delicious chips and salsa. **Bar:** full bar. **Address:** 503 Pine St 81601 **Location:** I-70 exit 116, just ne to Pine St, then just n. L D

FIN'S GRILLE & RAW BAR

Phone: 970/945-4771

Seafood

$14-$49

AAA Inspector Notes: Overlooking the street and overpass, this popular downtown eatery offers a variety of fresh seafood, pasta and steak dishes, which are served by the cordial staff. **Bar:** full bar. **Address:** 710 Grand Ave 81601 **Location:** I-70 exit 116; downtown. **Parking:** street only. D

FLORINDO'S ITALIAN CUISINE **Phone:** 970/945-1245

Italian
$12-$25

AAA Inspector Notes: Traditional pasta dishes, veal chops, steak and fresh seafood are featured at this cozy eatery. Paintings by local artists and some black-and-white photos of Italy add to the popular restaurant's décor. **Bar:** full bar. **Address:** 721 Grand Ave 81601 **Location:** I-70 exit 116, just s over bridge on Grand Ave (SR 82). **Parking:** street only. D

GLENWOOD CANYON BREW PUB **Phone:** 970/945-1276

American
$8-$22

AAA Inspector Notes: Featuring award-winning seasonal hand-crafted beers, the friendly eatery serves pita pizzas, beef stroganoff, steak and potato pie, and homemade root beer. **Bar:** full bar. **Address:** 402 7th St 81601 **Location:** I-70 exit 116; across from historic train station; in The Hotel Denver. **Parking:** on-site and street.

L D

HAUTE PLATE BISTRO **Phone:** 970/945-5011

American
$7-$9

AAA Inspector Notes: This popular locals' eatery has a coffee bar and offers healthy breakfasts and a wide variety of specialty items, including Greek dolmades, Mediterranean salad, lamb, chicken and falafel gyros, seared ahi tuna with wasabi mayonnaise and Asian slaw, and traditional cold and hot sandwiches. **Bar:** beer & wine. **Address:** 205 8th St 81601 **Location:** Just w on 8th St; downtown. **Parking:** street only. B L

ITALIAN UNDERGROUND RESTAURANT
Phone: 970/945-6422

Italian
$12-$16

AAA Inspector Notes: Downtown under the Grand Avenue Bridge, this best-kept secret features authentic Italian food, including cannoli, escargots in pesto butter, pasta, rotisserie chicken and a delightful selection of desserts and wine. **Bar:** full bar. **Address:** 715 Grand Ave 81601 **Location:** I-70 exit 116; downtown.

D

JH CHEN ASIAN BISTRO **Phone:** 970/945-9898

Sushi
$8-$17

AAA Inspector Notes: Examples of the popular bistro's Szechuan Chinese and Japanese fare include sushi and sashimi, special rolls, a menu sampler and daily lunch specials. **Bar:** full bar. **Address:** 730 Cooper Ave 81601 **Location:** I-70 exit 116, just e on 8th St, then just n.

L D

JUICY LUCY'S STEAKHOUSE **Phone:** 970/945-4619

Steak
$7-$38

AAA Inspector Notes: Downtown below the bridge, the restaurant employs casual, efficient servers who glide through the dining room with appetizers, varied steaks, fresh seafood, salads and sides. **Bar:** full bar. **Address:** 308 7th St 81601 **Location:** I-70 exit 116, just e off SR 82; downtown. **Parking:** street only. L D

THE PULLMAN FOOD & DRINK **Phone:** 970/230-9234

American
$9-$19

AAA Inspector Notes: Appropriately named, The Pullman is across the street from the train station. This chic neighborhood eatery serves up a wonderful array of snacks such as chicken liver pâté with homemade wheat thins; small plates, including rabbit hash and a grilled duck relleno; small and large salads such as a crisp sweet pork served with watermelon and arugula. The grass-fed beef burger is a popular sandwich, as is the roasted Rocky Mountain trout. Mouthwatering seasonal desserts are a treat to behold. **Bar:** full bar. **Address:** 330 7th St 81601 **Location:** I-70 exit 113, at 7th St and Cooper Ave; downtown. **Parking:** street only. L D

RIVERS RESTAURANT
Menu on AAA.com **Phone:** 970/928-8813

American
$15-$29

AAA Inspector Notes: There often is a wait to take advantage of the restaurant's above-the-river dining deck, which affords nice views of the nearby cliff. Diners get a feel for the Southeast in a setting evocative of a Southern plantation and veranda. On the menu are creative appetizers, salads, ruby red trout, elk medallions, prime rib and pistachio creme brulee. **Bar:** full bar. **Reservations:** suggested, weekends. **Address:** 2525 S Grand Ave 81601 **Location:** I-70 exit 116, 1.5 mi s; next to 27th St Bridge.

D

RIVIERA RESTAURANT **Phone:** 970/945-7692

New American
$15-$28

AAA Inspector Notes: The trendy supper club serves creatively prepared and tasty steaks and seafood along the lines of bacon-wrapped filet, and halibut encrusted with crab and Parmesan. Attentive service contributes to a wonderful dining experience. **Bar:** full bar. **Reservations:** suggested. **Address:** 702 Grand Ave 81601 **Location:** I-70 exit 116, just ne, then just s. **Parking:** street only. D

RUSSO'S NEW YORK PIZZA **Phone:** 970/945-7437

Pizza
$9-$12

AAA Inspector Notes: The friendly, family-operated eatery features more than 15 specialty pizzas, Italian sandwiches, several selections of pasta and eight family-style salads. You will not be able to resist the warm and chewy garlic knots. **Bar:** beer & wine. **Address:** 40 Market St, Suite D 81601 **Location:** I-70 exit 114, just s, take 2nd exit at roundabout; 1 mi e on Midland Ave to W Meadows Dr, then just s to Meadow Ln. L D

ZHENG ASIAN BISTRO **Phone:** 970/928-9077

Asian
$7-$15

AAA Inspector Notes: This cozy and comfortable bistro prepares a variety of Chinese, Korean and Japanese menu items, most notably the atomic shrimp Thai appetizer. **Bar:** full bar. **Address:** 35 Market St 81601 **Location:** I-70 exit 114, in Glenwood Meadows Mall.

L D

NEPAL INDIAN RESTAURANT **Phone:** 970/945-8803

fyi Not evaluated. Recipes at this eatery offer a delightful Nepali experience. Menu offerings include an array of appetizers, breads, poultry, lamb, seafood and vegetarian entrées. **Address:** 6824 Hwy 82 81601 **Location:** 5.5 mi s of center to CR 114; 5 mi n of Carbondale.

GOLDEN (B-4) pop. 18,867, elev. 5,674'

• Hotels p. 212 • Restaurants p. 213
• Hotels & Restaurants map & index p. 140
• Part of Denver area — see map p. 123

Golden was settled in 1859 among the glacial deposits on Clear Creek. Its name recalls an early miner and the local preoccupation with gold prospecting. Golden rivaled Denver in importance for several years. From 1862 to 1867 it served as capital of the Colorado Territory.

The Colorado School of Mines, founded in 1874, is among the oldest institutions devoted to mineral sciences and engineering. The school enrolls more than 3,000 students. The National Earthquake Information Center is on the campus; appointments for weekday guided tours of this facility may be arranged with at least 48 hours' advance notice by phoning (303) 273-8500, option 2.

(See map & index p. 140.)

The Lariat Trail, the first 7 miles of The Lariat Loop National Scenic Byway *(see attraction listing p. 136)*, begins at US 6 and 19th Street and winds into the Denver Mountain Parks, ending near the Buffalo Bill Museum and Grave and Lookout Mountain Park *(see attraction listings)*.

Red Rocks Park and Amphitheatre *(see Morrison p. 260)*, south of Golden, and Hogback Park, off I-70 near the US 40 exit, contain interesting geological formations. Golden Gate Canyon State Park *(see Recreation Chart)* and White Ranch Park, 9 miles northwest of Golden, offer recreational facilities. Golden celebrates the spirit of the Old West with Buffalo Bill Days in late July; highlights include a parade, bands and crafts.

Greater Golden Chamber of Commerce and Visitors Center: 1010 Washington Ave., Golden, CO 80401. **Phone:** (303) 279-3113.

Self-guiding tours: Literature outlining a self-guiding walking tour of Golden's historic district and a separate Golden Walk tour, featuring the Colorado School of Mines, Foothills Art Center, downtown and the Twelfth Street Historic District, is available from the chamber of commerce.

ASTOR HOUSE MUSEUM, 822 12th St., was built in 1867 as a hotel where territorial lawmakers stayed when Golden City was the capitol of the Colorado territory. After the capitol moved to Denver, the Astor House became a boarding house for laborers, miners, students and immigrants. Known at the time as the finest stone hotel west of the Mississippi, its Victorian furnishings and exhibits of the 1867-1908 era tell the stories of its former occupants.

Hours: Tues.-Sat. 10-4:30 (also Sun. 11-3, June-Aug.). Closed major holidays. **Cost:** $4; $3 (ages 65+); $2 (ages 6-16). Combination ticket with Clear Creek History Park $4.50; $4 (ages 65+); $3 (ages 6-16). **Phone:** (303) 278-3557.

BRADFORD WASHBURN AMERICAN MOUNTAINEERING MUSEUM is at 710 10th St. Devoted to mountains, rock climbing and mountaineering, the museum features interactive exhibits, multimedia presentations, historic mountaineering and rock climbing gear, and a scale model of Mount Everest. Mountain cultures, safety, conservation and the achievements of mountaineers also are depicted. **Hours:** Tues.-Fri. 10-5, Sat. 10-6, Sun. 11-4. Hours may vary. Closed major holidays. Phone ahead to confirm schedule. **Cost:** $6.50; $5 (students with ID and 65+); $4.50 (ages 0-11). **Phone:** (303) 996-2755.

BUFFALO BILL MUSEUM AND GRAVE is at the top of Lookout Mountain at 987 1/2 Lookout Mountain Rd. The museum displays artifacts of the Old West and depicts the life of William F. Cody, from his job as a Pony Express rider and buffalo hunter to the world's greatest showman. Exhibits include American Indian artifacts, antique firearms and Wild West show posters. Hands-on activities for children and Wild West videos also are offered. A large observation deck provides a spectacular view of the Denver metropolitan area and the Colorado Rockies. Changing exhibits are presented.

Note: The park is best approached from Golden along the Lariat Trail. **Hours:** Daily 9-5, May-Oct.; Tues.-Sun. 9-4, rest of year. Closed Christmas. **Cost:** $5; $4 (ages 65+); $1 (ages 6-15). **Phone:** (303) 526-0747.

CLEAR CREEK HISTORY PARK is 1 blk. w. of Washington Ave. on 11th St. Costumed interpreters depict 19th-century Colorado pioneer life in living history demonstrations, including presentations about foods grown by the pioneers. Historic buildings, originally homesteaded in a nearby canyon, include 1870s cabins, a blacksmith shop and an 1876 one-room schoolhouse.

Time: Allow 1 hour minimum. **Hours:** Park open daily dawn-dusk. Buildings open for paid tours, events and programs on occasion; call for schedule. Closed major holidays. **Cost:** Free. Some programs and events charge a fee. **Phone:** (303) 278-3557.

COLORADO RAILROAD MUSEUM, off I-70W exit 265 to 17155 W. 44th Ave., houses records and artifacts of early Colorado railroads. More than 100 locomotives and train cars, some of which can be boarded, are displayed. The main museum building, modeled after an 1880s depot, also contains an extensive model railroad collection and two floors of photographs and artifacts. A coin-operated HO-scale model train layout is on the lower level. A train restoration center in the roundhouse is open for viewing. Rides aboard a 19th-century passenger car are available during special events.

Tours: Guided tours are available. **Time:** Allow 30 minutes minimum. **Hours:** Daily 9-6, June-Aug.; daily 9-5, rest of year; also first Thurs. of month 5-9 p.m. Ninety-minute guided tours are offered daily, May-Sept. Closed Jan. 1, Thanksgiving and Christmas. **Cost:** $8; $7 (ages 61+); $5 (ages 2-16); $18 (family, two adults and ages 2-16). During special events $12; $10 (ages 60+); $5 (ages 2-16); $25 (family, two adults and ages 2-16). **Phone:** (303) 279-4591 or (800) 365-6263.

COLORADO SCHOOL OF MINES GEOLOGY MUSEUM, 1310 Maple St., contains extensive displays of minerals, mining artifacts, meteorites, fossils and gemstones as well as a walk-through mine. Highlights include an introductory video on area geology as well as interactive displays on radioactivity and ultraviolet minerals. An Apollo 17 moon rock, collected in December 1972, can also be viewed. Murals originally exhibited at the Golden Gate International Exposition in 1939 by artist Irwin Hoffman depict the history of mining and can be seen in the main gallery.

An outdoor geologic trail features outcrops containing fossilized dinosaur tracks, logs and leaves.

(See map & index p. 140.)

Guided tours are available by appointment. **Hours:** Mon.-Sat. 9-4, Sun. 1-4; closed certain legal and school holidays. Phone ahead to confirm schedule. **Cost:** Free. **Phone:** (303) 273-3815.

COORS BREWING CO., 13th and Ford sts., offers 30-minute self-guiding tours of traditional brewing methods used in the Rocky Mountains since 1873. Visitors learn about the malting, brewing and packaging processes and then may sample products in the hospitality lounge. Nonalcoholic beverages also are available.

Note: Product samples are limited in quantity and are available only to those age 21 or older with a valid ID. **Time:** Allow 1 hour, 30 minutes minimum. **Hours:** Mon. and Thurs.-Sat. 10-4, Sun. noon-4; extended hours in summer, call for schedule. Closed major holidays. **Cost:** Free. Ages 0-17 must be accompanied by an adult. **Phone:** (303) 277-2337 or (866) 812-2337.

GOLDEN HISTORY CENTER, 923 10th St., presents the history of Golden from pioneer to modern times. Collections include clothing, guns, and American Indian dolls and artifacts. The Harmsen Gallery of Western Art includes sculptures and paintings. Old-time pharmacy and mercantile displays also are offered. Changing exhibits are featured. A research library contains genealogical and historical records. Guided tours are available by appointment.

Hours: Tues.-Sat. 10-4:30, Sun. 11-3, June-Aug.; Tues.-Sat. 10-4:30, rest of year. Closed major holidays. **Cost:** $4; $3 (ages 65+); $2 (ages 6-16). **Phone:** (303) 278-7151.

HERITAGE SQUARE is 1 mi. n. of I-70 exit 259 at 18301 W. Colfax Ave. (US 40). A re-created Victorian village, Heritage Square includes amusement rides, go-carts, miniature golf, an alpine slide, a train, street performers and numerous shops. Family dinner theater, children's shows and melodramas are presented in the Music Hall.

Hours: Mon.-Sat. 10-8, Sun. 11-8, Memorial Day-Labor Day; Mon.-Sat. 10-5, Sun. noon-5, rest of year. Music Hall performances and hours vary; phone ahead. Rides open daily Memorial Day-Labor Day; hours vary rest of year. **Cost:** Fees for amusements vary. Music Hall shows start at $27.50; $35.50 with meal. **Phone:** (303) 279-7800 for the Music Hall, (303) 277-0040 for general information, (303) 279-1661 for alpine slide, or (303) 727-8437 for ride information.

LOOKOUT MOUNTAIN NATURE CENTER AND PRESERVE is off I-70E exit 254 or I-70W exit 256, following signs to 910 Colorow Rd. The 110-acre preserve includes 1.4 miles of trails through forest and meadow. The nature center features exhibits about bird migration as well as indigenous plants and animals. Naturalist-led programs are available.

Time: Allow 30 minutes minimum. **Hours:** Preserve daily 8-dusk. Nature center Tues.-Fri. 10-4, Sat.-Sun. 9-5, Memorial Day-Labor Day, Tues.-Sun. 10-4, rest of year. **Cost:** Free. **Phone:** (720) 497-7600.

LOOKOUT MOUNTAIN PARK, 5 mi. w. off US 6, occupies 66 acres atop Lookout Mountain. It affords a view of snowcapped mountains and Denver's skyline. Buffalo-hunter turned Wild West show entrepreneur William F. Cody—"Buffalo Bill"—is buried here. Picnic pavilions are available. **Phone:** (303) 526-0744.

MOTHER CABRINI SHRINE is 1.5 mi. off I-70E exit 256 at 20189 Cabrini Blvd. A 22-foot statue of Christ at the head of a gradual 373-step stairway is the setting for a panorama of the Denver area. **Time:** Allow 1 hour minimum. **Hours:** Daily 7-7, Memorial Day weekend-Labor Day; 7-5, rest of year. Last admission is 30 minutes before closing. **Cost:** Donations. **Phone:** (303) 526-0758.

NATIONAL RENEWABLE ENERGY LABORATORY VISITORS CENTER, off I-70 exit 263, following signs to 15013 Denver West Pkwy., offers an interactive exhibit hall and showcases renewable energy and energy efficiency technologies that lower energy costs. A docent-guided tour of the visitor center includes a virtual view of the lab, an exploration of new technology developments, a "Science on a Sphere" presentation, a narrated tour of the exhibit hall and tips for conserving energy.

The U.S. Department of Energy Public Records Center has additional information about currently available renewable energy and energy efficiency resources. **Time:** Allow 30 minutes minimum. **Hours:** Mon.-Fri. 9-5. Closed major holidays. **Cost:** Free. **Phone:** (303) 384-6565.

THE ROCKY MOUNTAIN QUILT MUSEUM, 1213 Washington Ave., explores the art and history of American quilts and how they are made. The museum's gallery features four changing exhibitions each year. **Tours:** Guided tours are available. **Time:** Allow 30 minutes minimum. **Hours:** Mon.-Sat. 10-4. Closed Jan. 1, July 4, Thanksgiving and Christmas. **Cost:** $6; $5 (ages 65+); $3 (ages 6-12). **Phone:** (303) 277-0377.

(See map & index p. 140.)

DENVER MARRIOTT WEST Phone: (303)279-9100 59

Hotel
$79-$149

AAA Benefit:
AAA hotel discounts of 5% or more.

Address: 1717 Denver West Blvd 80401 **Location:** I-70 exit 263, just n, then w. **Facility:** 305 units. 6 stories, interior corridors. **Amenities:** *Fee:* video games, high-speed Internet. **Dining:** 2 restaurants. **Pool(s):** heated outdoor, heated indoor. **Activities:** whirlpool, exercise room. *Fee:* massage. **Guest Services:** valet and coin laundry, area transportation-within 2 mi.

ECO CALL FEE / SOME UNITS

THE GOLDEN HOTEL, AN ASCEND COLLECTION HOTEL Phone: (303)279-0100 57

Hotel
$139-$189

Address: 800 11th St 80401 **Location:** At 11th St and Washington Ave; downtown. **Facility:** 62 units. 4 stories, interior corridors. **Terms:** 1-2 night minimum stay - seasonal, cancellation fee imposed. **Amenities:** high-speed Internet. **Activities:** jogging, exercise room. **Guest Services:** valet laundry, area transportation-within 5 mi.

BIZ / SOME UNITS FEE

HAMPTON INN DENVER WEST/GOLDEN
Phone: (303)278-6600 60

Hotel
$99-$169

AAA Benefit:
Members save up to 10% everyday!

Address: 17150 W Colfax Ave 80401 **Location:** I-70 exit 262 (Colfax Ave), 1.2 mi w. **Facility:** 121 units. 4 stories, interior corridors. **Terms:** 1-7 night minimum stay, cancellation fee imposed. **Amenities:** high-speed Internet. **Pool(s):** heated indoor. **Activities:** whirlpool, exercise room. **Guest Services:** valet and coin laundry.

CALL BIZ FEE

RESIDENCE INN BY MARRIOTT DENVER WEST/ GOLDEN Phone: (303)271-0909 61

Extended Stay Hotel
$79-$249

AAA Benefit:
AAA hotel discounts of 5% or more.

Address: 14600 W 6th Ave, Frontage Rd 80401 **Location:** US 6 exit Indiana Ave, just s to frontage road, then just e. **Facility:** 88 units, some two bedrooms, efficiencies and kitchens. 4 stories, interior corridors. **Terms:** check-in 4 pm. **Pool(s):** heated indoor. **Activities:** whirlpool, sports court, exercise room. **Guest Services:** valet and coin laundry.

CALL FEE / SOME UNITS FEE

TABLE MOUNTAIN INN Phone: (303)277-9898 58

Boutique Hotel
$135-$249

Address: 1310 Washington Ave 80401 **Location:** US 6 exit 19th St, 0.5 mi n to Washington Ave, 0.5 mi w; downtown, just s of arch. **Facility:** With comfortable, modern rooms featuring Southwestern decor, this hotel has remained one of Golden's most popular lodgings since it opened in 1925. 74 units. 5 stories, interior corridors. **Terms:** cancellation fee imposed. **Dining:** Table Mountain Grill & Cantina, see separate listing. **Activities:** exercise room. **Guest Services:** valet laundry.

SAVE CALL BIZ / SOME UNITS FEE

WHERE TO EAT

THE BRIARWOOD INN Phone: 303/279-3121 70

Continental
$12-$80

AAA Inspector Notes: This special-occasion dining spot boasts elegant decor and an informal European country atmosphere; appetizers and dessert are included with dinner. **Bar:** full bar. **Reservations:** suggested. **Address:** 1630 8th St 80401 **Location:** 1 mi e of jct US 6, SR 58 and 93, exit s on Washington Ave, w on 8th St, then 1 mi to end of street. L D

OLD CAPITOL GRILL Phone: 303/279-6390 71

American
$7-$23

AAA Inspector Notes: Located in the territory's capitol building dating to 1862, this restaurant features large portions of flavorful steaks, chicken, seafood and a few Mexican offerings. Visitors especially enjoy the Western décor and the old artifacts on display. Patio dining is available. **Bar:** full bar. **Address:** 1122 Washington Ave 80401 **Location:** Corner of Washington Ave and 12th St; in historic downtown. **Parking:** on-site and street.

L D CALL

SUSHI UOKURA Phone: 303/278-8000 75

Japanese
$8-$20

AAA Inspector Notes: Although a bit hidden, this restaurant is worth seeking out. It is near the Colorado Mills Outlet Mall and about a 10-minute drive from downtown. The owner grew up in Japan, the son of a fisherman, and began training as a sushi chef at the age of 12. This is clearly evident in the freshness of the fish and the flavorful rolls Mr. Ogi creates. In addition to sushi and sashimi, patrons may sample chicken teriyaki, gyoza dumplings and tempura dishes. **Bar:** full bar. **Address:** 815 Nile Ct 80401 **Location:** I-70 exit 262 (Colfax Ave), just sw, then just n. L D

TABLE MOUNTAIN GRILL & CANTINA
Phone: 303/216-8040 73

Southwestern
$8-$26

AAA Inspector Notes: Specializing in Southwestern cuisine, this restaurant offers tortilla-encrusted trout, hand-cut steak and fresh fish specials, in addition to a nice variety of draft microbrews and numerous margaritas and tequila drinks. The décor has a Santa Fe flair, and the staff is prompt and attentive. This locals' favorite is just a stone's throw from the Coors brewery. **Bar:** full bar. **Address:** 1310 Washington Ave 80401 **Location:** US 6 exit 19th St, 0.5 mi n to Washington Ave, 0.5 mi w; downtown, just s of arch; in Table Mountain Inn. **Parking:** on-site and street.

B L D CALL

TAFOLINO'S Phone: 303/232-5118 74

Mexican
$6-$12

AAA Inspector Notes: This family-owned restaurant focuses on quality, flavorful Mexican dishes. Popular entrees include tamales, fajitas, burritos, soft tacos, enchiladas and rellenos. Those who can't decide on one item should check out the list of combination plates. Creamy flan is the perfect ending to a meal. **Bar:** full bar. **Address:** 2001 Youngfield St 80401 **Location:** I-70 exit 264, 0.8 mi s. L D

WESTFALEN HOF Phone: 303/642-3180

German
$10-$29

AAA Inspector Notes: Patrons can take a journey through the fine cuisines of Germany and other regions in Europe. Traditional dishes include frikadellan, rindsroulade, sauerbraten, stroganoff, spierogis and goulash, while a few American and seafood dishes appeal to less adventurous diners. Tastefully decorated in German style with steins, plates and pictures, the dining rooms offer views of the foothills. **Bar:** full bar. **Reservations:** required. **Address:** 32138 Hwy 72 W 80403 **Location:** 7 mi n on SR 93, 9.3 mi w on SR 72; up Coal Creek Canyon. D AC

(See map & index p. 140.)

WOODY'S WOOD FIRED PIZZA & WATERING HOLE
Phone: 303/277-0443 (72)

Pizza
$7-$11

AAA Inspector Notes: Traditional and specialty pizzas made in a wood-burning oven share a spot on the menu with sandwiches, pasta dishes, calzones and salad bar offerings. Pool and air hockey tables contribute to the sports-oriented atmosphere, as do eight TVs tuned to sports broadcasts. **Bar:** full bar. **Address:** 1305 Washington Ave 80401 **Location:** US 6 exit 19th St, 0.5 mi n to Washington Ave, then 0.5 mi w; downtown. (L) (D)

GOLD HILL pop. 230

• Restaurants p. 214

GOLD HILL INN **Phone:** 303/443-6461

American
$33

AAA Inspector Notes: This family-owned restaurant, which is listed in the National Register of Historic Places, has been in business since 1962. The menu offers a popular six-course dinner, and the décor is handsome and rugged. Checks are accepted and there is occasional live entertainment. **Bar:** full bar. **Reservations:** suggested. **Address:** 401 Main St 80302 **Location:** US 36 (28th St), 1.3 mi w on Canyon Ave, 0.3 mi n on 9th St, 6 mi w on Mapleton Ave and CR 52, then 4 mi on dirt road. **Historic** (D) (AC)

GRANADA (E-6) pop. 517, elev. 3,494'

Less than a half-mile south of US 50 in Granada are the remains of a Japanese-American internment camp. From August 1942 to October 1945 the Granada Relocation Center housed more than 7,000 Japanese-Americans, removed by executive order from the West Coast during World War II. A couple of small monuments, a cemetery, building foundations and roads are all that remain of the camp. An information kiosk and walking trail with picnic tables are onsite.

GRANBY (A-3) pop. 1,864, elev. 7,939'

Granby began as a railroad center serving cattle ranching and lumbering industries; it is now home to many dude ranches and golf courses. The town also is the western gateway to the Arapaho National Recreation Area *(see place listing p. 40)* and Rocky Mountain National Park *(see place listing p. 276)*.

Lake Granby, 6 miles north on US 34 within the recreation area, is an installation of the Colorado-Big Thompson project, which provides irrigation water for portions of northeastern Colorado; it's also a popular fishing spot. Granby lies at the junction of two portions of scenic highway: US 40 from Denver to Craig and US 34 north to Estes Park.

Greater Granby Area Chamber of Commerce: 365 E. Agate Ave., Suite B, P.O. Box 35, Granby, CO 80446. **Phone:** (970) 887-2311 or (800) 325-1661.

RECREATIONAL ACTIVITIES

Skiing

- **SolVista Basin** is 2 mi. s. on US 40, then 2.5 mi. e. following signs. Other activities are offered.

Hours: Daily 9-4, mid-Dec. to late Mar. (weather permitting). **Phone:** (970) 887-3384 or (888) 283-7458.

C LAZY U RANCH **Phone:** 970/887-3344

(fyi) Not evaluated. **Address:** 3640 Colorado Hwy 125 80446 **Location:** 4 mi w on US 40, 3.5 mi n. Facilities, services, and decor characterize a mid-scale property.

DROWSY WATER GUEST RANCH **Phone:** 970/725-3456

(fyi) Not evaluated. **Address:** 1454 County Road 219 80446 **Location:** 3 mi w of jct US 40 and SR 34, 1.3 mi n on CR 219 (unpaved road in front of red chuck wagon). Facilities, services, and decor characterize a mid-scale property.

GRAND JUNCTION (D-1) pop. 58,566, elev. 4,597'

• Restaurants p. 217

Two junctions made Grand Junction what it is: that of the Grand—now called the Colorado—and Gunnison rivers, whose waters brought to life the fertile soils of the surrounding valley, and the linking of the railroads from Denver and Salt Lake City.

The surrounding Grand Valley, a major producer of cherries, peaches, grapes and a variety of other crops, is bordered on the east by the Grand Mesa, said to be the largest flat-topped mountain in the world, and the sandstone beauty of the Colorado National Monument on the west. There are more than 18 wineries in the Grand Junction area.

The Colorado Riverfront Trail System consists of a series of trails for biking or walking along the Colorado River; for more information contact the visitor and convention bureau. From US 50 south of the city, a road climbs eastward via a series of spectacular switchbacks to Lands End, the westernmost projection of Grand Mesa. From the summit much of western Colorado is visible.

The Grand Junction Symphony Orchestra offers a concert series August through May as well as a December Christmas program; phone (970) 243-6787. In addition, various performances are presented throughout the year at Mesa State College Theater, (970) 248-1604.

Grand Junction Visitor & Convention Bureau: 740 Horizon Dr., Grand Junction, CO 81506. **Phone:** (970) 244-1480 or (800) 962-2547.

ADVENTURE BOUND RIVER EXPEDITIONS picks up guests at the Grand Vista Hotel at 2790 Crossroads Blvd. Professional guides lead 1- and 2-day float trips and white-water rafting expeditions along the Westwater Canyon of the Colorado River. Rafters may elect to enjoy the scenery while the guides do all the paddling or use an inflatable kayak if they choose to participate. Longer trips also are available.

Hours: One-and 2-day trips depart several times weekly at 8 a.m., May-Sept.; phone for schedule. **Cost:** One-day fare $155; $145 (ages 0-15). Two-day fare $350; $330 (ages 0-15). **Phone:** (970) 245-5428 or (800) 423-4668.

THE ART CENTER: WESTERN COLORADO CENTER FOR THE ARTS, w. off I-70 Horizon Dr. exit to 7th St., then .7 mi. s. to 1803 N. 7th St., features a permanent collection of some 300 historic and contemporary works by Western artists, including Paul Pletka lithographs and more than 50 Navajo weavings from the early 1900s. Changing exhibits also are presented including oil, watercolor and pastel pieces as well as clay art. **Time:** Allow 30 minutes minimum. **Hours:** Tues.-Sat. 9-4. Closed major holidays. **Cost:** $3; free (Tues., and ages 0-11). **Phone:** (970) 243-7337.

GEM **COLORADO NATIONAL MONUMENT**— see place listing p. 83.

CROSS ORCHARDS HISTORIC FARM, 3073 Patterson (F) Rd., is a turn-of-the-20th-century apple orchard providing interpretation of the early social and agricultural heritage of western Colorado. Guides in period clothing give tours of the orchard and farm buildings. Also on the grounds are the Uintah Narrow Gauge Railway exhibit, a collection of road-building and related equipment and an agricultural exhibit building.

Special events and workshops are held periodically. **Time:** Allow 1 hour minimum. **Hours:** Tues.-Sat. 9-4, Apr.-Oct. Phone ahead to confirm schedule. **Cost:** $4; $3 (ages 55+); $2.50 (ages 3-12); $10 (family rate). Combination ticket with the Museum of the West and Sterling T. Smith Educational Tower and the Museum of Western Colorado's Dinosaur Journey (in Fruita) $12; $10 (ages 60+); $8 (ages 3-12). **Phone:** (970) 434-9814 or (970) 242-0971.

MUSEUM OF THE WEST AND STERLING T. SMITH EDUCATIONAL TOWER, 462 Ute Ave., presents regional history from prehistoric times to the present. Exhibits include Southwestern pottery, Old West artifacts and a collection of antique firearms. An 1890s schoolhouse and an interactive exhibit about uranium mining also are featured. The 75-foot-tall Sterling T. Smith Educational Tower offers panoramic views of the surrounding mountains and contains a working weather station.

Time: Allow 1 hour minimum. **Hours:** Mon.-Sat. 9-5, Sun. noon-4, May-Sept.; Tues.-Sat. 10-3, rest of year. Closed major holidays. **Cost:** $5.50; $4.50 (ages 55+); $3 (ages 3-12); $16 (family rate). Combination ticket with the Cross Orchards Historic Farm and the Museum of Western Colorado's Dinosaur Journey (in Fruita) $12; $10 (ages 60+); $8 (ages 3-12). **Phone:** (970) 242-0971 or (888) 488-3466.

WESTERN COLORADO BOTANICAL GARDENS is at 655 Struthers Ave. A variety of native and tropical plants is featured in indoor and outdoor settings. The Butterfly House contains butterflies in various stages of development. Outdoor plantings include cacti, herbs, roses and native turf grasses. Orchids and water gardens are featured within the tropical greenhouse. A castle and moat are focal points in the children's garden.

Time: Allow 1 hour minimum. **Hours:** Tues.-Sun. 10-4. Phone ahead to confirm winter schedule. **Cost:** $5; $4 (students and 62+); $3 (ages 3-12). **Phone:** (970) 245-9030.

WINERIES

- **Two Rivers Winery** is 5.3 mi. w. on SR 340. **Hours:** Mon.-Sat. 10:30-6, Sun. noon-5. Tours available on request. **Phone:** (970) 255-1471.

AMERICAS BEST VALUE INN **Phone:** (970)245-1410

Motel
$62-$120

Address: 754 Horizon Dr 81506 **Location:** I-70 exit 31, just n. **Facility:** 97 units. 2 stories (no elevator), exterior corridors. **Pool(s):** heated outdoor. **Activities:** whirlpool, playground. **Guest Services:** coin laundry. **Free Special Amenities: expanded continental breakfast and high-speed Internet.**
(See ad this page.)

SAVE

/ SOME UNITS FEE

Get pet travel tips
and enter the photo contest
at AAA.com/PetBook

BEST WESTERN SANDMAN MOTEL

Phone: (970)243-4150

Motel
$70-$125

AAA Benefit: Members save up to 20%, plus 10% bonus points with Best Western Rewards®.

Address: 708 Horizon Dr 81506 **Location:** I-70 exit 31, 0.3 mi s. **Facility:** 80 units. 2 stories (no elevator), exterior corridors. **Pool(s):** heated outdoor. **Activities:** whirlpool. **Guest Services:** coin laundry, area transportation-bus & train stations. **Free Special Amenities: continental breakfast and high-speed Internet.**

 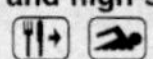   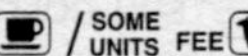 / SOME UNITS FEE

CANDLEWOOD SUITES GRAND JUNCTION

Phone: 970/255-8093

Extended Stay Hotel
Rates not provided

Address: 654 Market St 81506 **Location:** I-70 exit 28 (24 Rd), 1.3 mi s to F Rd, just e, then just n. **Facility:** 97 efficiencies. 4 stories, interior corridors. **Amenities:** high-speed Internet. **Activities:** exercise room. **Guest Services:** complimentary laundry.

  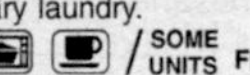 / SOME UNITS FEE

CLARION INN

Phone: (970)243-6790

Hotel
$84-$109

Address: 755 Horizon Dr 81506 **Location:** I-70 exit 31, just n. **Facility:** 239 units. 2 stories (no elevator), interior/exterior corridors. **Terms:** check-in 4 pm, cancellation fee imposed. **Amenities:** video games (fee), high-speed Internet. **Pool(s):** heated outdoor, heated indoor. **Activities:** whirlpools, exercise room. **Guest Services:** valet and coin laundry, area transportation-within 5 mi, train & bus stations. **Free Special Amenities: expanded continental breakfast and high-speed Internet.** *(See ad this page.)*

 FEE / SOME UNITS

COMFORT INN

Phone: (970)245-3335

Hotel
$80-$170

Address: 750 3/4 Horizon Dr 81506 **Location:** I-70 exit 31, just n. **Facility:** 57 units. 2 stories (no elevator), interior corridors. **Terms:** cancellation fee imposed. **Pool(s):** heated indoor. **Activities:** whirlpool, exercise room. **Guest Services:** valet and coin laundry.

COURTYARD BY MARRIOTT

Phone: (970)263-4414

Hotel
$89-$139

AAA Benefit:
AAA hotel discounts of 5% or more.

Address: 765 Horizon Dr 81506 **Location:** I-70 exit 31, 0.3 mi n. **Facility:** 136 units. 5 stories, interior corridors. **Amenities:** video games (fee), high-speed Internet. **Pool(s):** heated indoor. **Activities:** whirlpool, exercise room. **Guest Services:** valet and coin laundry, area transportation-within 5 mi.

 FEE / SOME UNITS

DOUBLETREE BY HILTON HOTEL GRAND JUNCTION

Phone: (970)241-8888

Hotel
$114-$169 5/1-9/30
$95-$129 10/1-4/30

AAA Benefit:
Members save 5% or more everyday!

Address: 743 Horizon Dr 81506 **Location:** I-70 exit 31, just s. **Facility:** 273 units. 8 stories, interior corridors. **Terms:** 1-7 night minimum stay, cancellation fee imposed. **Dining:** Bistro 743, see separate listing. **Pool(s):** heated outdoor. **Activities:** whirlpool, putting green, 3 tennis courts, playground, basketball, horseshoes, volleyball, exercise room. **Guest Services:** valet laundry, area transportation-within 5 mi, bus & train stations.

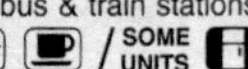 / SOME UNITS 

FAIRFIELD INN & SUITES GRAND JUNCTION
Phone: (970)242-2525

Extended Stay Hotel
$99-$199

AAA Benefit:
AAA hotel discounts of 5% or more.

Address: 225 Main St 81501 **Location:** At 2nd and Main sts; downtown. **Facility:** 70 units, some efficiencies. 4 stories, interior corridors. **Amenities:** high-speed Internet. **Pool(s):** heated indoor. **Activities:** whirlpool, exercise room. **Guest Services:** valet and coin laundry.

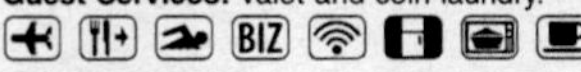
/ SOME UNITS FEE

HAMPTON INN **Phone:** (970)243-3222

Hotel
$84-$94

AAA Benefit:
Members save up to 10% everyday!

Address: 205 Main St 81501 **Location:** At 2nd and Main sts; downtown. **Facility:** 80 units. 3 stories, interior corridors. **Terms:** 1-7 night minimum stay, cancellation fee imposed. **Amenities:** high-speed Internet. **Pool(s):** heated outdoor. **Activities:** exercise room. **Guest Services:** valet laundry.

/ SOME UNITS

HOLIDAY INN & SUITES **Phone:** (970)424-5888

Hotel
$159-$209 5/1-10/1
$109-$169 10/2-4/30

Address: 2751 Crossroads Blvd 81506 **Location:** I-70 exit 31, 0.3 mi n, then 0.5 mi w. **Facility:** 119 units. 4 stories, interior corridors. **Amenities:** high-speed Internet. **Pool(s):** heated indoor. **Activities:** whirlpool, exercise room. **Guest Services:** valet and coin laundry, area transportation-within 5 mi.

/ SOME UNITS

HOLIDAY INN EXPRESS & SUITES
Phone: (970)245-8164

Hotel
$99-$189 5/1-10/31
$89-$159 11/1-4/30

Address: 625 Raelynn St 81505 **Location:** I-70 exit 28 (24 Rd), 1.1 mi s. **Facility:** 89 units, some kitchens. 4 stories, interior corridors. **Amenities:** high-speed Internet. **Pool(s):** heated indoor. **Activities:** whirlpool, exercise room. **Guest Services:** valet and coin laundry.

LA QUINTA INN & SUITES GRAND JUNCTION
Phone: (970)241-2929

Hotel
$88-$192

Address: 2761 Crossroads Blvd 81506 **Location:** I-70 exit 31, 0.3 mi n, then 0.3 mi w. **Facility:** 108 units. 5 stories, interior corridors. **Amenities:** video games (fee). *Some:* high-speed Internet. **Pool(s):** heated outdoor. **Activities:** whirlpool, exercise room. **Guest Services:** valet and coin laundry, area transportation-within 5 mi.

CALL FEE
/ SOME UNITS

LOS ALTOS BED & BREAKFAST **Phone:** 970/256-0964

Bed & Breakfast
$119-$215 5/1-10/31
$102-$185 11/1-4/30

Address: 375 Hill View Dr 81503 **Location:** I-70 exit 28 (Redlands Pkwy), 3.4 mi s to SR 340 (Broadway Rd), 2 mi w to Ridges Blvd, 0.5 mi to Ridge Cir Dr, 0.8 mi to Ridge View Dr, then just sw. **Facility:** The hilltop island in the sky affords spectacular views from the wraparound porch of the many mountains and natural wonders surrounding the property. Each room has a balcony or porch. 7 units, some efficiencies. 2 stories (no elevator), interior/exterior corridors. **Terms:** check-in 4 pm, 2 night minimum stay - seasonal and/or weekends, 21 day cancellation notice-fee imposed.

/ SOME UNITS

QUALITY INN OF GRAND JUNCTION
Phone: (970)245-7200

Hotel
$70-$129

Address: 733 Horizon Dr 81506 **Location:** I-70 exit 31, just s. **Facility:** 107 units, some two bedrooms. 3 stories, interior corridors. **Terms:** cancellation fee imposed. **Pool(s):** heated outdoor. **Guest Services:** coin laundry. **Free Special Amenities: full breakfast and high-speed Internet.**

SAVE / SOME UNITS FEE

RESIDENCE INN BY MARRIOTT **Phone:** (970)263-4004

Extended Stay Hotel
$99-$149

AAA Benefit:
AAA hotel discounts of 5% or more.

Address: 767 Horizon Dr 81506 **Location:** I-70 exit 31, 0.3 mi n. **Facility:** 104 units, some efficiencies and kitchens. 4 stories, interior corridors. **Amenities:** high-speed Internet. **Pool(s):** heated indoor. **Activities:** whirlpool, sports court, exercise room. **Guest Services:** valet and coin laundry, area transportation-within 5 mi.

/ SOME UNITS FEE

SPRINGHILL SUITES GRAND JUNCTION DOWNTOWN/ HISTORIC MAIN STREET **Phone:** (970)424-5777

Hotel
$99-$199

AAA Benefit:
AAA hotel discounts of 5% or more.

Address: 236 Main St 81501 **Location:** At 3rd and Main sts; west end of Main St. **Facility:** 100 units. 5 stories, interior corridors. **Amenities:** high-speed Internet. **Pool(s):** heated indoor. **Activities:** whirlpool, exercise room. **Guest Services:** valet and coin laundry.

CALL
/ SOME UNITS FEE

SUPER 8 **Phone:** (970)248-8080

Motel
$58-$80

Address: 728 Horizon Dr 81506 **Location:** I-70 exit 31, just s. **Facility:** 130 units. 3 stories, interior corridors. **Pool(s):** heated outdoor. **Activities:** limited exercise equipment. **Guest Services:** coin laundry. **Free Special Amenities: continental breakfast and high-speed Internet.**

SAVE / SOME UNITS FEE

WHERE TO EAT

626 ON ROOD RESTAURANT & WINE BAR
Phone: 970/257-7663

Seafood
$9-$58

AAA Inspector Notes: Mediterranean- and Latin-influenced modern cuisine can be paired with interesting wine flights from around the world. Fresh seafood is flown in overnight from Hawaii and may include sashimi-grade hamachi, which is served with an Asian salad; sea scallops with watercress-ginger dressing; spiced crab and black rice; or butter-poached lobster tail with smoked paprika green lentils, risotto and white truffle oil garnish. Fresh, local, organic ingredients are used in all items, including desserts. **Bar:** full bar. **Reservations:** suggested. **Address:** 626 Rood Ave 81501 **Location:** From Main St, just n on 6th St, then just e. **Parking:** street only.

L D

BIN 707 FOODBAR **Phone:** 970/243-4543

American
$7-$22

AAA Inspector Notes: On the ground floor of a bank building, this urban restaurant features appetizers, soups and entrées such as blistered shishito peppers, braised pork belly steamed buns, a tasty watermelon, heirloom tomato gazpacho, lager braised short ribs, seared wild salmon, and shrimp and grits. Seasonal bread puddings, crème brûle and pineapple upside down cake are a few of the popular desserts. **Bar:** full bar. **Address:** 225 N 5th St, Suite 105 81501 **Location:** At Rood Ave and N 5th St; downtown. **Parking:** street only. L D CALL M

BISTRO 743 **Phone:** 970/241-8888

American
$6-$25

AAA Inspector Notes: This restaurant presents a three-meal menu. Among dinner choices are steak and seafood dishes, pizza and items lined on a small salad bar. **Bar:** full bar. **Address:** 743 Horizon Dr 81506 **Location:** I-70 exit 31, just s; in DoubleTree by Hilton Hotel Grand Junction. B L D

BLUE MOON BAR & GRILLE **Phone:** 970/242-4506

American
$5-$22

AAA Inspector Notes: The busy eatery and watering hole is a great place for lunch in the Main Street area. Generously portioned burgers, sandwiches and salads are popularly priced. **Bar:** full bar. **Address:** 120 N 7th St 81501 **Location:** Corner of 7th and Main sts. **Parking:** street only. L D

DOLCE VITA **Phone:** 970/242-8482

Italian
$8-$20

AAA Inspector Notes: Friendly staff members provide attentive service at this downtown eatery, which serves salads, sandwiches with hand-cut fries, and a variety of traditional chicken, beef and seafood pasta dishes. **Bar:** full bar. **Address:** 336 Main St 81501 **Location:** Just e of 3rd St; downtown. L D

DOS HOMBRES (THE REDLANDS)
Phone: 970/242-8861

Mexican
$8-$13

AAA Inspector Notes: This restaurant features a relaxed, family-dining atmosphere and appealing surroundings. The menu offers authentic dishes such as fajitas, tamales, chicken tacos, chiles rellenos, fried ice cream and sopaipillas. Servers are friendly, prompt and efficient. **Bar:** full bar. **Address:** 421 Brach Dr 81507 **Location:** 1 mi w on Grand Ave, 0.3 mi w of entrance to Colorado National Monument. L D

ENZO'S PIZZERIA & ITALIAN CAFE
Phone: 970/255-8500

Italian
$8-$19

AAA Inspector Notes: This place offers a nice selection. The Cordon Bleu sub is addictive, and skilled pizza tossers make specialty pies and made-to-order slices. Favorite appetizers include asparagus wraps and Gorgonzola cheese bruschetta. I opted for the caprese skewer made with imported mozzarella and wanted seconds. Be prepared for a wait as the pasta selections, chicken dishes, smoked salmon Alfredo and Parmesan-breaded eggplant with prosciutto are made from scratch. Traditional desserts are available. **Bar:** full bar. **Address:** 759 Horizon Dr, Suite N 81506 **Location:** I-70 exit 31, 0.3 mi n; in strip mall. L D

NEPAL RESTAURANT, NEPALI & INDIAN CUISINE
Phone: 970/242-2233

Nepali
$9-$19

AAA Inspector Notes: The cozy eatery features authentic Indian and Nepali cuisine such as crispy lentil wafers, ample selections of traditional tandoor-baked flat breads, a nonvegetarian sampler and a variety of chicken, lamb and seafood biryani and curry dishes. Typical Nepalese desserts include basmati rice cooked in milk, raisins and nuts, and Indian-style mango or pistachio ice cream. **Bar:** beer & wine. **Address:** 356 Main St 81501 **Location:** Just e of S 4th and Main sts; downtown. **Parking:** street only. L D

THE WINERY RESTAURANT **Phone:** 970/242-4100

Seafood
$17-$49

AAA Inspector Notes: Tucked away in a beautifully landscaped breezeway, patrons appreciate the fresh seafood specialties and flavorful prime rib, steak, rack of lamb and elegant desserts. Rough woods, hand-made clay dishware, intimate lighting and stained glass create a comfortable ambience. Dinners include salad, potato or rice and seasonal vegetables. **Bar:** full bar. **Reservations:** suggested. **Address:** 642 Main St 81501 **Location:** Just w of 7th and Main sts, down the breeze way; downtown. **Parking:** street only. D

WW PEPPERS **Phone:** 970/245-9251

Steak
$8-$35

AAA Inspector Notes: Diners may experience a wait at night in the summer, as this is a very popular dining spot. It has an ideal location for those staying in the nearby hotels. One can enjoy a cocktail on the outdoor patio before entering the ambience of handsome woodwork and a very nice Southwestern art collection. While steaks are a specialty here, there is a full page of Southwestern cuisine. **Bar:** full bar. **Address:** 753 Horizon Ct 81506 **Location:** I-70 exit 31, 0.3 mi n. L D

GRAND LAKE (A-3) pop. 471, elev. 8,437'

• Attractions map p. 279
• Hotels & Restaurants map & index p. 186

The resort community of Grand Lake owes its name, as well as its claim as one of the world's highest yacht clubs, to the lake nearby. One mile long and three-quarters of a mile wide, this deep, clear glacial lake is the largest natural body of water in the state. Mount Baldy, with its 12,007-foot-high peak, and the snowcapped Never Summer Range also are nearby.

Adjacent to the Arapaho National Recreation Area *(see place listing p. 40)*, the town is the western gateway to Rocky Mountain National Park *(see place listing p. 276)*. Traversing Trail Ridge Road, the highest continually paved road in the United States, it is just a 48-mile drive to Estes Park *(see place listing p. 183)*, a resort community on the opposite side of the Continental Divide from Grand Lake. Activities popular in Grand Lake include boating, hiking, fishing, cross-country skiing, shopping, horseback riding and attending the Rocky Mountain Repertory Theatre.

Winter Carnival, held in early February, features bed sled races, human bowling, a snow sculpture contest and other events. The Grand Lake Regatta and Lipton Cup Races are held in early August.

(See map & index p. 186.)

Grand Lake Area Chamber of Commerce: 14700 SR 34, P.O. Box 429, Grand Lake, CO 80447. **Phone:** (970) 627-3402 or (800) 531-1019.

KAUFFMAN HOUSE MUSEUM, 407 Pitkin Ave., is a restored log hotel built in 1892. It houses a museum of early Grand Lake memorabilia. **Hours:** Daily 11-5, Memorial Day weekend-Labor Day; Sat.-Sun. 11-5, day after Labor Day-Sept. 30; by appointment rest of year. **Cost:** Donations. **Phone:** (970) 627-9644.

AMERICAS BEST VALUE INN BIGHORN LODGE

Phone: (970)627-8101 16

Motel

$65-$160 5/1-10/11
$65-$125 10/12-4/30

Address: 613 Grand Ave 80447 **Location:** 0.3 mi e to Grand Ave, then just e. **Facility:** 20 units. 2 stories (no elevator), exterior corridors. **Terms:** office hours 8 am-9 pm, cancellation fee imposed. **Activities:** whirlpool. **Free Special Amenities: continental breakfast and high-speed Internet.**

BLACK BEAR LODGE **Phone:** 970/627-3654 19

Motel

$88-$135

Address: 12255 US Hwy 34 80447 **Location:** On US 34, 2 mi s of center. **Facility:** 17 units, some efficiencies. 1 story, exterior corridors. **Terms:** office hours 7:30 am-8 pm, 7 day cancellation notice-fee imposed. **Pool(s):** heated outdoor. **Activities:** sauna, whirlpool, horseshoes.

/ SOME UNITS

GATEWAY INN **Phone:** 970/627-2400 17

Hotel

Rates not provided

Address: 200 W Portal Rd 80447 **Location:** Jct US 34 and CR 278. **Facility:** 32 units, some kitchens. 3 stories (no elevator), interior corridors. **Terms:** office hours 8 am-9 pm, check-in 4 pm. **Activities:** sauna, whirlpool, putting green, shuffleboard, exercise room. *Fee:* massage.

SPIRIT LAKE LODGE **Phone:** 970/627-3344 18

Motel

$60-$200 5/1-10/15
$55-$160 10/16-4/30

Address: 829 Grand Ave 80447 **Location:** 0.3 mi e to Grand Ave, then 0.4 mi e. **Facility:** 19 units, some efficiencies. 1-2 stories (no elevator), exterior corridors. **Terms:** office hours 8 am-9 pm, 2-3 night minimum stay - weekends, 7 day cancellation notice-fee imposed. **Activities:** whirlpool. *Fee:* snowmobiling. **Free Special Amenities: local telephone calls and high-speed Internet.**

/ SOME UNITS FEE

WHERE TO EAT

FAT CAT CAFE

Menu on AAA.com **Phone:** 970/627-0900 20

American

$6-$10

AAA Inspector Notes: The owners of this bustling eatery want you to be as satisfied as a fat cat after leaving their cafe. Patrons don't mind waiting for the fresh eggs, thick slices of bacon, large English sausages and flavorful quiches. They also won't leave without sampling one of the freshly baked pastries; the reasonable portions and matching prices make it easy to end a meal with one of these small indulgences. **Address:** 916 Grand Ave 80447 **Location:** In historic town center. **Parking:** street only.

B L

GRAND PIZZA **Phone:** 970/627-8390 22

Italian

$6-$15

AAA Inspector Notes: This quaint eatery is known for its friendly staff and specialty pizzas. Many patrons begin their meals with one of the unusual salads, which can be served in an individual portion or in a family-style serving large enough for the table to share. Gluten and nut-free items are available. **Bar:** beer & wine. **Address:** 1131 Grand Ave 80447 **Location:** In historic town center. **Parking:** street only.

L D

THE HISTORIC RAPIDS RESTAURANT

Menu on AAA.com **Phone:** 970/627-3707 19

American

$10-$36

AAA Inspector Notes: This restaurant's log structure, built in 1903, was the first in town to have electricity and running water. The menu offers pasta, beef, fish, elk, lamb and chicken dishes, and the patio by the river is the perfect place to enjoy dessert. **Bar:** full bar. **Reservations:** suggested, for dinner. **Address:** 209 Rapids Ln 80447 **Location:** South end of Grand Ave, just e. **Historic**

L D

SAGEBRUSH BBQ & GRILL

Menu on AAA.com **Phone:** 970/627-1404 21

American

$7-$29

AAA Inspector Notes: Formerly an 1800s jailhouse, this restaurant hangs artifacts from that era on its walls. Barbecue platters consist of pork ribs, smoked pork, beef brisket, buffalo or sausage and come with two sides. The extensive menu also includes steaks, game and seafood, as well as many traditional and Southwest-influenced breakfasts. A full-service bar is adjacent to the dining area. Gluten-free and vegetarian items also are available. **Bar:** full bar. **Address:** 1101 Grand Ave 80447 **Location:** At Grand Ave and Pitkin St; downtown. **Parking:** street only.

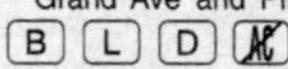

GRAND MESA—UNCOMPAHGRE—GUNNISON NATIONAL FORESTS (D-1)

Elevations in the forests range from 6,600 ft. at Dominguez Canyon in Uncompahgre National Forest to 14,309 ft. at Uncompahgre Peak, also in Uncompahgre National Forest. Refer to AAA maps for additional elevation information.

In west-central Colorado three separate national forests—Grand Mesa, Uncompahgre and Gunnison—form a multitude of scenic vistas and mountainous terrain. The three combined forests total 2,952,549 acres, including a half-million acres of wilderness.

The Grand Mesa, one of the world's highest flattop mountains with an average elevation of 10,000 feet, is dotted with about 300 lakes and reservoirs. Crag Crest National Recreation Trail, a 10-mile circular trail, provides scenic views from an elevation of more than 11,000 feet.

The Grand Mesa Scenic and Historic Byway, a 55-mile trip between Cedaredge and the junction of I-70 and SR 65, crosses the Grand Mesa, climbing from the valley to its 11,000-foot crest. Along the way, opportunities exist for fishing, hiking, scenic views, cross-country skiing, snowmobiling and sightings of mountain lions, coyotes, red foxes, elk and deer. The forests are noted for outstanding deer and elk hunting.

The Uncompahgre comprises the Uncompahgre Plateau; the San Juan Mountains, with more than 100 peaks topping 13,000 feet; and the Big Blue, Mount Sneffels and Lizard Head wilderness areas.

The Gunnison includes 22 peaks of more than 13,000 feet in elevation as well as the Fossil Ridge, La Garita, Collegiate Peaks, Maroon Bells-Snowmass, Powderhorn, Raggeds and West Elk wilderness areas. About 130 miles of the Continental Divide National Scenic Trail and 100 miles of the Colorado Trail wind through the forest.

For additional information contact the Forest Supervisor, Grand Mesa-Uncompahgre-Gunnison National Forests, 2250 US 50, Delta, CO 81416; phone (970) 874-6600. *See Recreation Chart.*

TAYLOR RESERVOIR, 30 mi. n.e. of Gunnison at the foot of the Sawatch Range, is one of Colorado's largest lakes. The road to the reservoir follows the Taylor River through a 20-mile canyon where the walls reach up to 1,000 feet high. **Phone:** (970) 874-6600.

GEM GREAT SAND DUNES NATIONAL PARK AND PRESERVE (E-3)

Great Sand Dunes National Park and Preserve is 38 miles northeast of Alamosa via US 160 and SR 150. Too heavy to rise over the mountains with the winds that carry it northeastward across the flat, semiarid floor of the San Luis Valley, sand settles at the foot of the Sangre de Cristo Range. Deposits accumulating over the course of thousands of years have created a 30-square-mile, stark yet ever-changing sandscape that forms a vaguely eerie foreground for the rugged mountains.

Local legends maintain that wagon trains vanished among the dunes, some of which are 750 feet high, and that strange creatures inhabit the area's inner reaches.

Two self-guiding nature trails and camping and picnicking facilities are available. Naturalist-conducted walks and nightly amphitheater programs are held in summer. Visitor center exhibits depict the region's natural and cultural history.

Allow 1 hour minimum for the park. Park open daily 24 hours. Visitor center daily 8:30-6, Memorial Day weekend-Labor Day; 8:30-4:30, rest of year. Closed Jan. 1, Thanksgiving and Christmas. Hours may vary; phone ahead. Admission $3 per person; free (ages 0-15). Phone (719) 378-6399.

GREAT SAND DUNES LODGE **Phone:** 719/378-2900

Motel
$89-$100

Address: 7900 Hwy 150 N 81146 **Location:** From Alamosa, 16 mi e on US 160, then 16 mi n. Located in a quiet area. **Facility:** 12 units. 1 story, exterior corridors. **Terms:** open 5/1-10/21, 3 day cancellation notice. **Pool(s):** heated indoor.

/ SOME UNITS

GREELEY (A-5) pop. 92,889, elev. 4,664'

Greeley was founded by a group of visionaries who responded to New York publisher Horace Greeley's renowned exhortation, "Go West, young man!" Greeley's dream to establish an agricultural community in Colorado grew from his visit in 1859. Given power by his newspaper, the *New York Tribune*, and leadership by his agricultural editor, Nathan Meeker, the dream became a reality with the arrival of the first colonists in 1870.

The location, near the confluence of the Cache la Poudre and South Platte rivers, was well chosen. By 1875 the colony had constructed one of the first large irrigation systems in the territory, and hay and barley were waving in the fields not occupied by cattle. Cattle and crops remain agricultural mainstays.

Many of Greeley's cultural activities are hosted by the University of Northern Colorado and the city's Union Colony Civic Center. The century-old Greeley Philharmonic Orchestra continues to perform concerts throughout the year. Featuring one of the largest outdoor rodeos in the nation, the GEM Greeley Stampede is held each year from late June to early July and includes—in addition to rodeos—a carnival, concerts, a parade and fireworks on the Fourth of July.

Greeley Convention and Visitors Bureau: 902 7th Ave., Greeley, CO 80631-4603. **Phone:** (970) 352-3567 or (800) 449-3866.

Self-guiding tours: Literature describing a walking tour that includes some of Greeley's historic homes and buildings is available at the Greeley History Museum.

CENTENNIAL VILLAGE MUSEUM, 1475 A St., is a museum of architectural and cultural history. Victorian and adobe houses surrounded by flower beds, a church, a train depot, operational blacksmith and print shops, a fire station, a homesteader's shack, a one-room schoolhouse and the first county courthouse are among more than 45 structures on the landscaped 8-acre site. Programs and festivals are held throughout the year.

Time: Allow 2 hours minimum. **Hours:** Tues.-Sat. 10-4, May-Sept. Closed July 4. Phone ahead to confirm schedule. **Cost:** $7; $5 (ages 60+); $3 (ages 6-11). **Phone:** (970) 350-9220.

GREELEY FREIGHT STATION MUSEUM is at 680 10th St. This model railroad museum is based on the Oregon, California and Eastern Railroad, a defunct logging railway. It features more than 22.5 scale miles of single track mainline, enhanced by mountain scenes and details such as lakes, bridges, tunnels, towns and miniature people. Visitors can also view railroad-related articles and explore a caboose. **Time:** Allow 45 minutes minimum. **Hours:** Wed.-Sat. 10-4, Sun. 1-4, first Fri. of month 6 p.m.-9 p.m., Memorial Day-Labor Day; first Fri. of month 6 p.m.-9 p.m., Sat. 10-4, rest of year. **Cost:** $6; $5 (ages 62+); $3 (ages 2-11). **Phone:** (970) 392-2934.

GREELEY HISTORY MUSEUM, 714 8th St., features permanent and changing exhibits in a renovated 1929 building. The Hazel E. Johnson Research Center contains historical documents and more than 30,000 photographs. Special events and programs are offered. **Time:** Allow 30 minutes minimum. **Hours:** Tues.-Fri. 8:30-4:30, Sat. 10-4. Closed major holidays. **Cost:** Free. **Phone:** (970) 350-9220.

COMFORT INN-GREELEY **Phone:** (970)330-6380

Hotel
$90-$120

Address: 2467 W 29th St 80631 **Location:** US 34 Bypass exit 23rd Ave, just sw. **Facility:** 54 units. 3 stories, interior corridors. **Terms:** cancellation fee imposed. **Amenities:** safes (fee). **Pool(s):** heated indoor. **Activities:** whirlpool, exercise room. **Guest Services:** valet and coin laundry. **Free Special Amenities: full breakfast and high-speed Internet.**

SAVE / SOME UNITS FEE

COUNTRY INN & SUITES BY CARLSON
Phone: (970)330-3404

Hotel
$95-$180

Address: 2501 W 29th St 80631 **Location:** US 34 Bypass exit 23rd Ave, just s, then w. **Facility:** 63 units. 3 stories, interior corridors. **Terms:** 3 day cancellation notice-fee imposed. **Pool(s):** heated indoor. **Activities:** whirlpool. **Guest Services:** valet and coin laundry.

CALL BIZ / SOME UNITS FEE

FAIRFIELD INN BY MARRIOTT **Phone:** (970)339-5030

Hotel
$99-$129

AAA Benefit:
AAA hotel discounts of 5% or more.

Address: 2401 W 29th St 80631 **Location:** US 34 Bypass exit 23rd Ave, just s, then just w. **Facility:** 62 units. 3 stories, interior corridors. **Pool(s):** heated indoor. **Activities:** whirlpool. **Guest Services:** valet and coin laundry.

CALL BIZ

GREELEY HAMPTON INN & SUITES
Phone: (970)339-5525

Hotel
$119-$149

AAA Benefit:
Members save up to 10% everyday!

Address: 2350 W 29th St 80631 **Location:** US 34 Bypass exit 23rd Ave, just s, then just w. **Facility:** 74 units. 3 stories, interior corridors. **Parking:** winter plug-ins. **Terms:** 1-7 night minimum stay, cancellation fee imposed. **Amenities:** video games (fee), high-speed Internet. **Pool(s):** heated indoor. **Activities:** whirlpool, exercise room. **Guest Services:** valet and coin laundry.

/ SOME UNITS

HOLIDAY INN EXPRESS **Phone:** (970)330-7495

Hotel
$99-$159

Address: 2563 W 29th St 80631 **Location:** US 34 Bypass exit 23rd Ave, just s, then just w. **Facility:** 64 units. 3 stories, interior corridors. **Pool(s):** heated indoor. **Activities:** whirlpool. **Guest Services:** valet and coin laundry.

CALL BIZ / SOME UNITS

WHERE TO EAT

THE ARMADILLO **Phone:** 970/304-9024

Mexican
$7-$14

AAA Inspector Notes: Downtown in the Plaza, the family-owned restaurant nurtures a festive atmosphere amid Southwestern décor. On the menu are homemade and traditional recipes and flavorful daily specials. Servers are friendly and attentive. **Bar:** full bar. **Address:** 819 9th St 80631 **Location:** On US 85 business route; corner of 8th Ave and 9th St; downtown. **Parking:** street only. L D

COYOTE'S SOUTHWESTERN GRILL
Phone: 970/336-1725

Southwestern
$8-$17

AAA Inspector Notes: The popular eatery prepares a selection of innovative Southwest-inspired foods, such as Southwestern crab rolls, steak poblano and tequila-lime chicken. The awesome coconut brownie with caramel is just one of the luscious, great-for-sharing desserts. **Bar:** full bar. **Address:** 5250 W 9th Street Dr 80634 **Location:** 0.5 mi w of 47th Ave on US 34 (10th St), just n on 52nd Ave, then just w. L D

THE EGG & I **Phone:** 970/353-7737

Breakfast
$7-$9

AAA Inspector Notes: This restaurant serves only breakfast and lunch and has earned the city newspaper's "best breakfast in town" nod. Creative dishes emphasize quality. The colorful dining room evokes an inviting garden-like setting, and during the warmer months, the shaded patio affords a nice seating alternative. **Address:** 3830 W 10th St 80634 **Location:** Jct 39th Ave and 10th St; in Market Square Shopping Center. B L

THE EGG & I **Phone:** 970/392-1191

Breakfast
$7-$9

AAA Inspector Notes: This small chain specializes in hearty breakfasts that incorporate fresh ingredients. A to-go cup lets guests pick up freshly brewed coffee, including seasonal flavors. The lunch menu lists popular sandwiches, soups, varied juices and teas and numerous sides. **Address:** 2305 W 27th St, Unit 509A 80634 **Location:** US 34 Bypass exit 23rd Ave, just n, then just e; in Willow Station. B L CALL

FAT ALBERT'S FOOD & DRINK
Menu on AAA.com **Phone:** 970/356-1999

American
$7-$16

AAA Inspector Notes: The casual restaurant presents a wide selection of sandwiches, croissants, interesting salads, full dinners and mouthwatering desserts. Diners who are too late for the outdoor seating in summer might find an adequate substitute amid the plants and fresh flowers inside. **Bar:** full bar. **Address:** 1717 23rd Ave 80634 **Location:** At 17th St and 23rd Ave; in Cottonwood Square. L D

GREENWOOD VILLAGE pop. 13,925

• Hotels & Restaurants map & index p. 140
• Part of Denver area — see map p. 123

COURTYARD BY MARRIOTT-DENVER TECH CENTER

Phone: (303)721-0300 102

Hotel
$59-$119

AAA Benefit:
AAA hotel discounts of 5% or more.

Address: 6565 S Boston St 80111 **Location:** I-25 exit 197 (Arapahoe Rd), e to Boston St, then n. **Facility:** 155 units. 3 stories, interior corridors. **Amenities:** high-speed Internet. **Pool(s):** heated indoor. **Activities:** whirlpool, exercise room. **Guest Services:** valet and coin laundry, area transportation-within 5 mi.

ECO CALL BIZ
/ SOME UNITS

DOUBLETREE BY HILTON HOTEL DENVER TECH CENTER

Phone: (303)779-6161 99

Hotel
$80-$229

AAA Benefit:
Members save 5% or more everyday!

Address: 7801 E Orchard Rd 80111 **Location:** I-25 exit 198, just w; 1 blk from Denver Tech Center. **Facility:** 305 units. 6 stories, interior/exterior corridors. **Terms:** 1-7 night minimum stay, cancellation fee imposed. **Amenities:** safes. *Some:* high-speed Internet (fee). **Dining:** 2 restaurants. **Pool(s):** heated outdoor, heated indoor. **Activities:** exercise room. **Guest Services:** valet laundry, area transportation-within 5 mi.

CALL BIZ FEE
/ SOME UNITS

HAMPTON INN DENVER SOUTHEAST

Phone: 303/792-9999 103

Hotel
Rates not provided

AAA Benefit:
Members save up to 10% everyday!

Address: 9231 E Arapahoe Rd 80112 **Location:** I-25 exit 197 (Arapahoe Rd), just e. **Facility:** 149 units. 5 stories, interior corridors. **Amenities:** video games (fee). **Pool(s):** heated outdoor. **Activities:** exercise room. **Guest Services:** valet and coin laundry, area transportation-within 5 mi.

CALL BIZ FEE

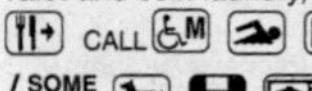

HYATT PLACE DENVER TECH CENTER

Phone: (303)804-0700 98

HYATT PLACE

AAA Benefit: Members save 10% or more everyday.

Address: 8300 E Crescent Pkwy 80111 **Location:** I-25 exit 199, 0.4 mi e to Crescent Pkwy, then just s. **Facility:** 126 units. 6 stories, interior corridors. **Terms:** cancellation fee imposed. **Amenities:** safes. *Some:* high-speed Internet. **Pool(s):** heated indoor. **Activities:** exercise room. **Guest Services:** valet laundry, area transportation-within 5 mi. **Free Special Amenities: expanded continental breakfast and high-speed Internet.**

HYATT SUMMERFIELD SUITES DENVER TECH CENTER

Phone: (303)706-1945 105

Extended Stay
Hotel
$79-$219

HYATT SUMMERFIELD SUITES

AAA Benefit: Members save 10% or more everyday.

Address: 9280 E Costilla Ave 80112 **Location:** I-25 exit 197 (Arapahoe Rd), e to Clinton St, then just s. **Facility:** 135 kitchen units, some two bedrooms. 3 stories, interior corridors. **Terms:** cancellation fee imposed. **Amenities:** *Some:* high-speed Internet. **Pool(s):** heated outdoor. **Activities:** whirlpool, exercise room. **Guest Services:** valet and coin laundry, area transportation-within 5 mi. **Free Special Amenities: full breakfast and high-speed Internet.**

SAVE CALL BIZ
/ SOME UNITS FEE

LA QUINTA INN & SUITES DENVER TECH CENTER

Phone: (303)649-9969 107

Hotel
$64-$165

Address: 7077 S Clinton St 80112 **Location:** I-25 exit 197 (Arapahoe Rd), e to Clinton St, then 0.5 mi s. **Facility:** 149 units. 4 stories, interior corridors. **Amenities:** *Some:* high-speed Internet. **Pool(s):** heated outdoor. **Activities:** whirlpool, exercise room. **Guest Services:** valet and coin laundry, area transportation-within 5 mi.

CALL BIZ
/ SOME UNITS

RESIDENCE INN BY MARRIOTT-DENVER TECH CENTER

Phone: (303)740-7177 101

Extended Stay
Hotel
$189-$209

AAA Benefit:
AAA hotel discounts of 5% or more.

Address: 6565 S Yosemite St 80111 **Location:** I-25 exit 197 (Arapahoe Rd), just w, then n. **Facility:** 128 kitchen units. 2 stories (no elevator), exterior corridors. **Terms:** check-in 4 pm. **Pool(s):** heated outdoor. **Activities:** whirlpool, sports court, exercise room. **Guest Services:** valet and coin laundry, area transportation-within 5 mi.

BIZ
/ SOME UNITS FEE

SHERATON DENVER TECH CENTER HOTEL

Phone: (303)799-6200 106

Hotel
$179 5/1-11/15
$149 11/16-4/30

Sheraton HOTELS & RESORTS

AAA Benefit:
Members get up to 15% off, plus Starwood Preferred Guest® bonuses.

Address: 7007 S Clinton St 80112 **Location:** I-25 exit 197 (Arapahoe Rd), just e, then s. **Facility:** 262 units. 10 stories, interior corridors. **Amenities:** *Fee:* video games, high-speed Internet. **Pool(s):** heated outdoor. **Activities:** whirlpool, exercise room. **Guest Services:** valet and coin laundry, area transportation-within 5 mi.

SAVE CALL BIZ FEE
/ SOME UNITS FEE FEE

(See map & index p. 140.)

SLEEP INN DENVER TECH CENTER

Phone: 303/662-9950 (104)

Hotel

Rates not provided

Address: 9257 Costilla Ave 80112 **Location:** I-25 exit 197 (Arapahoe Rd), just e to Clinton St, s to Costilla Ave, then w. **Facility:** 118 units. 3 stories, interior corridors. *Bath:* shower only. **Amenities:** video games (fee). **Pool(s):** heated indoor. **Activities:** exercise room. **Guest Services:** valet and coin laundry. **Free Special Amenities: continental breakfast and high-speed Internet.**

SAVE CALL FEE

/ SOME UNITS 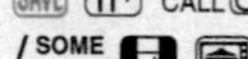

WINGATE BY WYNDHAM

Phone: (303)221-0383 (100)

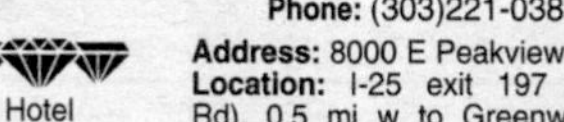

Hotel

$67-$152

Address: 8000 E Peakview Ave 80111 **Location:** I-25 exit 197 (Arapahoe Rd), 0.5 mi w to Greenwood Plaza Blvd, then just n. **Facility:** 86 units. 3 stories, interior corridors. **Terms:** check-in 4 pm, cancellation fee imposed. **Amenities:** video games (fee), high-speed Internet, safes. **Pool(s):** heated indoor. **Activities:** whirlpool, exercise room. **Guest Services:** valet and coin laundry, area transportation-within 6 mi.

WHERE TO EAT

BARA SUSHI & GRILL **Phone:** 720/489-5509 (104)

Sushi

$8-$25

AAA Inspector Notes: The eatery specializes in decorative rolls, grilled meat and seafood, which patrons enjoy at the sushi bar or in the dining area. Those traveling with children will be pleased with the kid's plate, a smaller version of a bento box. The elegant décor and attentive servers enhance the dining experience. **Bar:** full bar. **Address:** 8000 E Belleview Ave, Suite D-50 80111 **Location:** I-25 exit 199, just e; in strip mall. L D

BROOK'S STEAK HOUSE & CELLAR

Phone: 303/770-1177 (111)

Steak

$29-$60

AAA Inspector Notes: This popular purveyor of beef accents Old World décor with polished dark wood, shiny brass and a lounge above the large dining room. Dog pictures along one wall are an amusing incongruity. As is the case in most other local beef palaces, big food translates into big prices. **Bar:** full bar. **Reservations:** suggested. **Address:** 6538 S Yosemite Cir 80111 **Location:** I-25 exit 197 (E Arapahoe Rd), just w, just n on S Yosemite St to S Yosemite Cir, then just e. D

BROTHER'S BBQ **Phone:** 303/799-9777 (113)

Barbecue

$5-$22

AAA Inspector Notes: The popular barbecue eatery presents a menu that includes Kansas City-style beef brisket, Memphis-style pork shoulder and St. Louis-style pork spare ribs. Among other offerings are the usual sides of slaw, beans and potato salad, as well as chicken, hot links, sandwiches and family platters. This place is great for guests of nearby hotels, as it delivers. The colorful atmosphere emphasizes automobiles. **Bar:** full bar. **Address:** 9069 E Arapahoe Rd 80112 **Location:** I-25 exit 197 (Arapahoe Rd), just e to Boston St, just n to Southtech Dr, then just w to frontage road. L D CALL

COOL RIVER CAFE **Phone:** 303/771-4117 (106)

Steak

$12-$41

AAA Inspector Notes: This popular, upscale steakhouse features Angus beefsteak, fresh seafood and poultry. An extensive selection of wine and spirits is available, and live bands play Friday and Saturday nights. Be sure and make reservations, as this is one of the city's most in-style restaurants. **Bar:** full bar. **Reservations:** suggested. **Address:** 8000 E Belleview Ave, Suite C-10 80111 **Location:** I-25 exit 199, just e. **Parking:** on-site and valet. L D

Steak, seafood, Southwestern fare, world-class bar

DEL FRISCO'S DOUBLE EAGLE STEAK HOUSE

Phone: 303/796-0100 (110)

Steak

$11-$50

AAA Inspector Notes: This restaurant continues to win awards for its flavorful steaks. The menu also features fresh seafood, veal and lamb. After dinner, guests can relax by the fire in the beautiful cigar lounge, which features nightly live entertainment. **Bar:** full bar. **Reservations:** suggested. **Address:** 8100 E Orchard Rd 80111 **Location:** I-25 exit 198, just e, then just s on South Willow Dr. **Parking:** on-site and valet. L D

GARBANZO MEDITERRANEAN GRILL

Phone: 303/694-7777 (112)

Mediterranean

$6-$7

AAA Inspector Notes: The fresh-baked puffy pitas alone are worth the visit to this quick-serve eatery. The menu features raw, unprocessed, high-quality Middle Eastern options such as hummus, chicken shwarma, beef shwarma, falafel and a variety of salads. Baklava is a must for dessert. The modern décor encourages diners to eat in, yet, many people opt to take their meals to go. **Address:** 8547 E Arapahoe Rd 80112 **Location:** I-25 exit 197 (Arapahoe Rd), just w, then just n; in Arapahoe Marketplace Shopping Center. L D

GUNTHER TOODY'S DINER

Phone: 303/799-1958 (115)

American

$7-$10

AAA Inspector Notes: This fun 1950s-style family-oriented diner offers salads, burgers, sandwiches, fries, blue-plate specials, shakes and malts. The décor is clean, bright and infused with energy and golden oldies music. A 1956 Corvette hangs above the bar. **Bar:** full bar. **Address:** 9220 E Arapahoe Rd 80112 **Location:** I-25 exit 197 (Arapahoe Rd), just e, then s on Clinton St.

B L D

IL FORNAIO **Phone:** 303/221-8400 (105)

Italian

$10-$35

AAA Inspector Notes: Accomplished servers begin guests' experiences with crisp, crusty bread hot from the oven. Pasta and flavorful sauces enhance the roasted meats and vegetables. The spacious restaurant thoughtfully replicates the trattorias of Italy. **Bar:** full bar. **Address:** 8000 E Belleview Ave 80111 **Location:** I-25 exit 199, just e; corner of Belleview Ave and Ulster St. L D CALL

(See map & index p. 140.)

JING

Phone: 303/779-6888 (107)

Asian
$10-$27

AAA Inspector Notes: A friend invited me to this restaurant and we enjoyed it so much that I went back to evaluate it for AAA. A small plate that is consistently delicious is the ahi Napoleon, a mix of chopped raw ahi tuna and avocado tiered between layers of deep-fried wonton squares. The Kobe on the rock consists of raw Kobe (or Wagyu) beef that you grill yourself on a hot rock. Watch it or you'll overcook it. The lounge has a dark velvet interior. An outdoor patio is an enjoyable place to people-watch. **Bar:** full bar. **Address:** 5370 Greenwood Plaza Blvd 80111 **Location:** I-25 exit 199, just w, just s on Quebec St, just e on Berry Ave, then just n; in strip mall. **Parking:** on-site and valet.

L D LATE

LARKBURGER

Phone: 303/779-0093 (103)

Burgers
$4-$8

AAA Inspector Notes: This story began when chef Thomas Salamunovich put his gourmet Larkburger on the menu at Larkspur, his fine dining restaurant in Vail. The burger became so popular Salamunovich created a fast-food restaurant around it; now it's a small chain. The juicy, all-natural Angus beef and turkey burgers are heavenly. Fries seasoned with Parmesan and truffle oil are the perfect accompaniment. The creamy $5 shakes are made with Breyers ice cream. Reclaimed wood panels complement the modern décor. **Bar:** beer only. **Address:** 8000 E Belleview Ave, B45 80111 **Location:** I-25 exit 199, just e. L D

PAPPADEAUX SEAFOOD KITCHEN

Phone: 303/740-9449

Regional Seafood
$9-$32

AAA Inspector Notes: A seafood lover's delight, the restaurant taps into a little bit of New Orleans with its Cajun dishes and elaborate menu selections. Patrons might start off with a creative choice of blackened oyster and shrimp fondeaux with crayfish and let the feast begin. While music plays in the background, patrons can dig into dirty rice or spicy gumbo loaded with seafood. Well-seasoned shrimp and fish are prepared in varied ways. **Bar:** full bar. **Address:** 7520 E Progress Pl 80111 **Location:** I-25 exit 199, just w to Quebec St, just s to Progress Pl, then just e.

L D CALL &M

SHIRAZ FINE PERSIAN CUISINE

Phone: 303/792-5000 (114)

Middle Eastern
$7-$22

AAA Inspector Notes: Kebabs are tender with juicy vegetables, salads are nicely spiced with herbs, and the homemade pita is excellent. Heavenly baklava or gourmet ice cream are a perfect end to any meal. This casual eatery is a must for fine Persian cuisine. **Bar:** beer only. **Address:** 9625 E Arapahoe Rd, Unit H 80112 **Location:** I-25 exit 197 (Arapahoe Rd), 0.4 mi e to Dayton St, then just n.

L D

VENICE RISTORANTE ITALIANO

Phone: 720/482-9191 (109)

Italian
$10-$36

AAA Inspector Notes: The degree of Italian charm is somewhat surprising in this strip-mall location. Authentic music, fresco-painted walls and dim lighting envelop patrons in soothing comfort. The expert waitstaff serves artistic, well-seasoned food. **Bar:** full bar. **Reservations:** suggested, weekends. **Address:** 5946 S Holly St 80111 **Location:** I-25 exit 198, 1.5 mi w, then just s; in Orchards strip mall. L D

YANNI'S, A GREEK TAVERNA

Phone: 303/692-0404 (108)

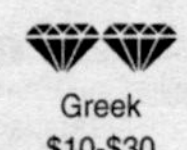

Greek
$10-$30

AAA Inspector Notes: This local favorite moved to the Landmark Theatre shopping complex. The cheerful décor features artful photos of life in Greece, while the menu offers traditional favorites such as dolmades, kalamaria, spanakopita, tzatziki, gyro, mousaka and baklava. Other options include saganaki (flaming cheese), oktapodi (marinated charbroiled octopus), jumbo sinagrida (grilled red snapper) and a variety of delectable desserts including creme caramel and Kefalonian key lime pie. **Bar:** full bar. **Reservations:** suggested. **Address:** 5425 S Landmark Pl, D109 80111 **Location:** I-25 exit 199, just w, just s on Quebec St, just e on Berry Ave, then just n; in strip mall.

L D

GUNNISON (E-2) pop. 5,854, elev. 7,681'

In the broad, fertile valley of the Gunnison River, Gunnison was settled in 1874; the town was founded in 1880 as a mining supply camp. Operating as a trade center for the area's ranching operations as well as home to Western State College, Gunnison serves as a gateway to the Gunnison National Forest *(see Grand Mesa-Uncompahgre-Gunnison National Forests p. 219)* and the Curecanti National Recreation Area *(see place listing p. 120)*.

Summer activities include fishing, horseback riding, camping, mountain biking, kayaking, rafting and boating. Winter offers hockey, snowmobiling, skating, snowshoeing and cross-country skiing. The Gunnison Arts Center features cultural events such as music productions, art exhibits and classes, and theatrical performances.

Gunnison Country Chamber of Commerce and Visitor Center: 500 E. Tomichi Ave., P.O. Box 36, Gunnison, CO 81230. **Phone:** (970) 641-1501 or (800) 274-7580.

PIONEER MUSEUM, jct. S. Adams St. and Tomichi Ave., occupies several buildings, including two restored schoolhouses and an 1876 post office. A car barn holds 64 antique vehicles; another building houses antique ranch wagons and buggies, a horse-drawn hearse, a taxi, printing presses, a telephone display and cowboy paraphernalia.

A narrow-gauge railroad engine and 1881 rail cars are on the grounds. Dolls, china and a mineral and arrowhead collection are among other items displayed. **Time:** Allow 1 hour minimum. **Hours:** Mon.-Sat. 9-5, Sun. 11-5, Memorial Day-Sept. 30. **Cost:** $7; $3 (ages 6-12). **Phone:** (970) 641-4530.

ALPINE INN

Phone: (970)641-2804

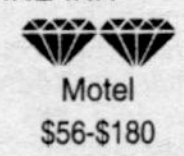

Motel
$56-$180

Address: 1011 W Rio Grande 81230 **Location:** 1.1 mi w of center, then just s. **Facility:** 36 units. 2 stories (no elevator), interior corridors. **Parking:** winter plug-ins. **Terms:** cancellation fee imposed. **Pool(s):** heated indoor. **Activities:** whirlpool, limited exercise equipment.

/ SOME UNITS FEE

COMFORT INN **Phone:** (970)642-1000

Hotel

$70-$120 5/1-9/4
$70-$100 9/5-4/30

Address: 911 N Main St 81230 **Location:** 0.7 mi n of center, then just w. **Facility:** 58 units, some two bedrooms. 3 stories, interior corridors. **Parking:** winter plug-ins. **Amenities:** *Some:* high-speed Internet. **Pool(s):** heated indoor. **Activities:** whirlpool, exercise room. **Guest Services:** coin laundry.

/ SOME UNITS

HOLIDAY INN EXPRESS HOTEL & SUITES
Phone: (970)641-1288

Hotel

$95-$169

Address: 910 E Tomichi Ave 81230 **Location:** 0.5 mi e of center. **Facility:** 107 units. 3 stories, interior corridors. **Terms:** check-in 4 pm, 3 day cancellation notice. **Amenities:** high-speed Internet. **Pool(s):** heated indoor. **Activities:** whirlpools, exercise room. **Guest Services:** valet and coin laundry, area transportation-within 5 mi. **Free Special Amenities: full breakfast and high-speed Internet.**

(See ad this page.)

RODEWAY INN **Phone:** 970/641-0500

Motel

Rates not provided

Address: 37760 W Hwy 50 81230 **Location:** 2.3 mi w of center. **Facility:** 38 units. 1 story, exterior corridors. **Activities:** whirlpool, limited exercise equipment. **Guest Services:** coin laundry.

  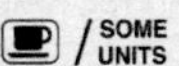  
/ SOME UNITS FEE

THE SEASONS INN **Phone:** 970/641-0700

Motel

Rates not provided

Address: 412 E Tomichi Ave 81230 **Location:** 0.3 mi e of center. **Facility:** 24 units. 2 stories (no elevator), exterior corridors. **Parking:** winter plug-ins. **Terms:** office hours 7 am-11 pm. **Activities:** whirlpool, horseshoes. **Guest Services:** coin laundry. **Free Special Amenities: continental breakfast and use of on-premises laundry facilities.**

/ SOME UNITS FEE

SUPER 8 **Phone:** (970)641-3068

Motel

$40-$149

Address: 411 E Tomichi Ave 81230 **Location:** 0.3 mi e of center. **Facility:** 52 units. 2 stories (no elevator), interior corridors. **Parking:** winter plug-ins. **Terms:** cancellation fee imposed. **Activities:** whirlpool. **Guest Services:** area transportation-within 3 mi.

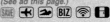

/ SOME UNITS FEE

WATER WHEEL INN **Phone:** (970)641-1650

Hotel

$69-$109

Address: 37478 W Hwy 50 81230 **Location:** On US 50, 2.5 mi w. **Facility:** 52 units, some efficiencies and condominiums. 2 stories (no elevator), interior/exterior corridors. **Terms:** office hours 6:30 am-10 pm, cancellation fee imposed. **Activities:** whirlpools, exercise room. *Fee:* massage. **Guest Services:** coin laundry. **Free Special Amenities: expanded continental breakfast and early check-in/late check-out.**

  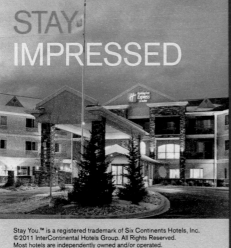 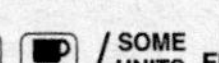
/ SOME UNITS FEE  

▼ *See AAA listing this page* ▼

WHERE TO EAT

GARLIC MIKE'S **Phone:** 970/641-2493

Italian
$12-$29

AAA Inspector Notes: This locally popular restaurant has menu offerings such as small or bigger salads; three soup choices; fried green tomatoes; traditional steak, veal, seafood and chicken dishes; thin-crust pizza, and tasty desserts that are meant to be shared. The fireplace and open kitchen add to the comfortable log cabin atmosphere. Dining on the deck with its view of the Gunnison River through the willows is offered in the summer. **Bar:** full bar. **Reservations:** suggested. **Address:** 2674 N Hwy 135 81230 **Location:** 3 mi n of center. D

GUNNISACK COWBOY BISTRO **Phone:** 970/641-5445

Southwestern
$8-$19

AAA Inspector Notes: The restaurant serves a wide array of appetizers, sandwiches, and lunch and dinner entrées, all with a Southwestern flair. Favorites include the jalapeño beer cheese soup, grilled salmon salad, a grilled wild red yellowfin tuna sandwich with Havarti dill cheese, a large selection of vegetarian items, fresh-ground Angus burgers and their award-winning chicken-fried rib-eye. Granny's recipe for the apple and cherry baked cobbler is the real deal. **Bar:** full bar. **Address:** 142 N Main St 81230 **Location:** Just n of center. **Parking:** street only.
L D

MARIO'S PIZZA & RISTORANTE **Phone:** 970/641-1374

Italian
$6-$15

AAA Inspector Notes: This cozy, family-run Italian eatery features a wide variety of handmade items, including appetizers, calzones, pizza, strombolis, soup, salad and sandwiches. Pasta includes manicotti, cannelloni, eggplant or chicken parmigiana, ravioli, ziti and a nine-layer lasagna. The "pick your pasta and pick your sauce" is a favorite. The cozy booth for one is fun, and the service is prompt and friendly. **Bar:** beer & wine. **Address:** 213 W Tomichi Ave 81230 **Location:** Just w of center. **Parking:** street only. L D

OL' MINER STEAKHOUSE **Phone:** 970/641-5153

Steak
$8-$29

AAA Inspector Notes: Most entrée selections start with the salad bar and feature USDA Choice steaks with clever names such as silver cup mine steak, blistered horn flat iron and gold cup mine bone-in rib-eye. Other choices include roaring Judy wild salmon, El Capitan Mine tuna steak and a half or full slab of Robert E. Lee Mine pork ribs. **Bar:** full bar. **Address:** 139 N Main St 81230 **Location:** Just n on Main St. **Parking:** street only.
B L D

THE TROUGH
Menu on AAA.com **Phone:** 970/641-3724

Steak
$13-$35

AAA Inspector Notes: This well-established eatery has attractive woodwork and candlelight that contribute to a more intimate dining experience. A distinctive salad presentation precedes the arrival of the entrée, typically a steak or seafood favorite, or perhaps barbecue ribs or chicken. Service is friendly and efficient. **Bar:** full bar. **Reservations:** suggested. **Address:** 37550 W Hwy 50 81230 **Location:** 2.4 mi w of center. D

HESPERUS

KENNEBEC CAFE **Phone:** 970/247-5674

Mediterranean
$11-$29

AAA Inspector Notes: Mediterranean and American cuisine is served during lunch, dinner and at a weekend brunch in this casually elegant atmosphere. The ever-changing seasonal menu may feature fried artichokes, crab cake salad, beef Bourguignon, chicken potpie with shiitake mushrooms, and made-fresh-daily desserts such as a chocolate mousse cake covered with cherries. An extensive wine list is sure to please. The spectacular mountain views from inside and on the outdoor courtyard patio are delightful. **Bar:** full bar. **Reservations:** suggested. **Address:** 4 CR 124 81326 **Location:** 10 mi w on US 160 (north side). L D

HIGHLANDS RANCH

• Part of Denver area — see map p. 123

COMFORT SUITES-DENVER SOUTH
Phone: (303)770-5400

Hotel
$69-$199

Address: 7060 E County Line Rd 80126 **Location:** SR 470 exit Quebec St, just n to County Line Rd, just w, then just s; at Quebec Highlands Center. **Facility:** 73 units. 4 stories, interior corridors. **Terms:** cancellation fee imposed. **Amenities:** high-speed Internet, safes (fee). **Activities:** whirlpool, exercise room. **Guest Services:** valet and coin laundry. **Free Special Amenities: full breakfast and high-speed Internet.**

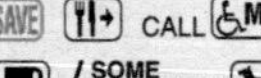

SAVE CALL BIZ FEE / SOME UNITS FEE

FAIRFIELD INN & SUITES DENVER TECH SOUTH
Phone: (303)290-6700

Hotel
$83-$101

AAA Benefit:
AAA hotel discounts of 5% or more.

Address: 7056 E County Line Rd 80126 **Location:** SR 470 exit Quebec St, just n to County Line Rd, just w, then just s; at Quebec Highlands Center. **Facility:** 61 units. 3 stories, interior corridors. **Amenities:** *Some:* high-speed Internet. **Pool(s):** heated indoor. **Activities:** whirlpool, exercise room. **Guest Services:** valet and coin laundry.

CALL BIZ FEE / SOME UNITS

HILTON GARDEN INN DENVER/HIGHLANDS RANCH
Phone: (303)683-4100

Hotel
$64-$153

AAA Benefit:
Unparalleled hospitality at a special Member rate.

Address: 1050 Plaza Dr 80126 **Location:** SR 470 exit Lucent Blvd, just s to Plaza Dr, then 0.4 mi e. **Facility:** 128 units. 5 stories, interior corridors. **Terms:** 1-7 night minimum stay, cancellation fee imposed. **Amenities:** video games (fee), high-speed Internet. **Pool(s):** heated indoor. **Activities:** whirlpool, exercise room. **Guest Services:** valet and coin laundry, area transportation-within 5 mi.

BIZ FEE

RESIDENCE INN BY MARRIOTT DENVER HIGHLANDS RANCH **Phone:** (303)683-5500

Extended Stay Hotel
$159-$179

AAA Benefit:
AAA hotel discounts of 5% or more.

Address: 93 Centennial Blvd 80126 **Location:** SR 470 exit Broadway, just s, then w. **Facility:** 117 units, some two bedrooms, efficiencies and kitchens. 4 stories, interior corridors. **Amenities:** video games (fee). **Pool(s):** heated outdoor. **Activities:** whirlpool, sports court, exercise room. **Guest Services:** valet and coin laundry.

CALL FEE / SOME UNITS FEE

WHERE TO EAT

LODO'S BAR AND GRILL **Phone:** 303/346-2930

American
$9-$22

AAA Inspector Notes: The hopping sports bar is best known for its 2,500-square-foot rooftop terrace, which affords panoramic views of the front range. Guests often can enjoy live music under the Colorado blue sky as they dine. **Bar:** full bar. **Address:** 8545 S Quebec St 80126 **Location:** SR 470 exit Quebec St, just s, then w.

HOT SULPHUR SPRINGS (A-3) pop. 663, elev. 7,680'

HOT SULPHUR SPRINGS RESORT AND SPA, off US 40 and across the Colorado River, following signs to 5609 CR 20, offers 24 terraced natural hot springs pools. These mineral waters, used since the days of the Ute Indians, have temperatures of 98 to 112 degrees Fahrenheit. The resort contains 19 outdoor pools and four indoor cave pools; included are a summer swimming pool, four children's pools and a full spa.

Time: Allow 3 hours minimum. **Hours:** Daily 8 a.m.-10 p.m. **Cost:** Outdoor pools $17.50; $11.50 (ages 3-12). Indoor pools $15 per hour. **Phone:** (970) 725-3306.

PIONEER VILLAGE MUSEUM, .2 mi. e. on US 40 at CR 55, is in a 1924 schoolhouse. Exhibits about the skiing industry, pioneer families, transportation development and the Windy Gap archeological site are presented. Other exhibits highlight the history and construction of a P.O.W. camp and the Moffat Tunnel, a railroad tunnel running through James Peak. Restored buildings on the grounds include a ranch house, a blacksmith shop, a schoolhouse, a courthouse and a jail. **Hours:** Tues.-Sat. 10-5. **Cost:** $5; $4 (ages 60+); $3 (ages 6-18). **Phone:** (970) 725-3939.

CANYON MOTEL **Phone:** (970)725-3395

Motel
$59-$139

Address: 221 Byers Ave 80451 **Location:** Just e on US 40. **Facility:** 14 units, some efficiencies. 1 story, exterior corridors. **Terms:** office hours 7:30 am-10 pm, cancellation fee imposed. **Free Special Amenities: local telephone calls and high-speed Internet.**

SAVE / SOME UNITS FEE

HOVENWEEP NATIONAL MONUMENT (F-1)

Hovenweep National Monument lies in both Colorado and Utah and can be reached from either state. There are two Colorado entrances to the monument. One is the Pleasant View turnoff 18 miles north of Cortez on US 491; the other is the McElmo Canyon Road accessible south of Cortez on US 160.

The Utah approach begins by turning off US 191 onto SR 262 midway between the towns of Blanding and Bluff. Go 14 miles to Hatch Trading Post and continue 16 miles to the Square Tower unit and visitor center.

The name Hovenweep, a Ute Indian word meaning "deserted valley," seems well-suited for the remote mesas and canyons north of the San Juan River. The presence of many standing, structured and tumbled piles of masonry—the remains of many-roomed pueblos, small cliff dwellings and towers—and scattered refuse over canyon slopes tells the story of the sizable population that once lived in this now desolate country.

The early inhabitants of Hovenweep were part of the large group of Ancestral Pueblo Indians who once occupied the Four Corners region of Utah, Colorado, Arizona and New Mexico. For centuries they lived in small villages as peaceful and secure farmers, hunters and gatherers.

Extended droughts in the 12th and 13th centuries gradually reduced their resources. Erosion, failing crops, diminishing water supplies, and perhaps warfare forced the people to abandon their homes by A.D. 1300 and move south and east, never to return.

The Hovenweep National Monument consists of six separate prehistoric village sites: In Utah there are Square Tower, the best preserved and most impressive, and Cajon. Colorado sites include Holly, Hackberry Canyon, Cutthroat Castle and Horseshoe. These landmarks are all noted for their square, oval, circular and D-shaped towers.

The Square Tower visitor center offers interpretive displays as well as maps and brochures for self-guiding tours. With the exception of Square Tower, all the sites are difficult to locate; obtain directions at the visitor center before attempting to find them. Tours are given at Square Tower when staff is available.

The monument is open year-round. The visitor center is open daily 8-6, Apr.-Sept.; 8-5, rest of year. Admission $6 per private vehicle or $3 per person arriving by other means (valid for 7 days). For more information write the Superintendent, Hovenweep National Monument, McElmo Route, Cortez, CO 81321; phone (970) 562-4282.

HUDSON pop. 2,356

PEPPER POD RESTAURANT **Phone:** 303/536-4736

American
$7-$24

AAA Inspector Notes: This popular family-owned roadside eatery features an extensive menu of buffalo steak, burgers, chicken-fried steak and homemade pies. The Old West artwork and wall-mounted buffalo heads are just a part of the country-casual charm. Restaurants come and go, but this place has been in continuous operation for more than 80 years. **Bar:** full bar. **Address:** 530 Fir St 80642 **Location:** I-76 exit 31, just s, then immediately w. B L D

IDAHO SPRINGS (B-4) pop. 1,717, elev. 7,524'

As had the Ute Indians before them, bone-weary miners from the nearby diggings soothed their aches in the mineral springs of Idaho Springs. Known particularly for its radium hot springs, the town has been a popular spa since the 1880s. It retains many Victorian buildings and structures characteristic of the brick and stone architecture of the 1880s.

The first major gold strike in Colorado was made in early 1859 at the juncture of Chicago and Clear creeks; a monument less than one-quarter mile southwest on Chicago Creek Road marks the spot. More than 200 mines in the vicinity once produced silver, uranium, tungsten, zinc, molybdenum, gold and lead.

A relic of the early mining days is "Locomotive 60," which, along with a coal tender and a passenger coach of the Colorado and Southern Railroad, stands on a section of the original narrow-gauge track in the downtown business district. The train made its first run in 1886.

A popular scenic loop is provided by SR 103 south through Chicago Creek Canyon to Echo Lake, then east over Squaw Pass to SR 74 to Bergen Park and Fillius Mountain Park. Follow the highway north to I-70, which returns to Idaho Springs. Another scenic route starts on SR 5 at Echo Lake and goes to the top of 14,260-foot Mount Evans.

Idaho Springs Visitor Center: 2060 Miner St., P.O. Box 1318, Idaho Springs, CO 80452-1318. **Phone:** (303) 567-4382.

ARGO GOLD MINE AND MILL is off I-70 exit 241A to 2350 Riverside Dr. Self-guiding 45-minute tours begin at the Double Eagle Mine (a hand-dug gold mine), continue through the gold- and silver-processing levels of this late 19th-century mill and conclude in the Clear Creek Mining Museum. The museum displays ore and mineral samples, equipment and early photographs.

Visitors can pan for gold or gemstones. **Hours:** Daily 9-6, mid-Apr. to mid-Oct. (weather permitting). **Cost:** $15; $7.50 (ages 7-12). **Phone:** (303) 567-2421.

"OH MY GAWD" ROAD—see Central City p. 81.

PHOENIX MINE, off I-70 exit 239, 1 mi. s.w. on Stanley Rd., then 1 mi. s. on Trail Creek Rd., offers underground guided tours of a working hard-rock gold mine; tours include gold panning. **Time:** Allow 30 minutes minimum. **Hours:** Daily 10-6 (weather permitting). **Cost:** Fee $15; $8 (ages 65+); $5 (ages 5-11). Gold panning only, $8. **Phone:** (303) 567-0422.

SAINT MARY'S GLACIER is accessible by a .7-mile hike from Fall River Rd., .75 mile n. of the ghost town of Alice, which is 12 miles n.w. via I-70 and Fall River Rd. exit 238. St. Mary's Lake is at the foot of the glacier on the flank of James Peak. Parking at the glacier is limited to a small pay lot, north of the glacier trailhead. No parking is permitted on Fall River Rd. or nearby subdivisions. **Cost:** Free. **Parking:** $5. **Phone:** (303) 567-4660.

RECREATIONAL ACTIVITIES

Hiking

- **Mount Goliath Wildflower Hike** departs from the entrance to the Mount Evans Scenic Byway. **Hours:** Tues. and Thurs. (also some Sat.) at 8:45, late June-early Aug. Phone ahead to confirm schedule. **Phone:** (720) 865-3539.

Skiing

- **Echo Mountain** is at 19285 SR 103. **Hours:** Wed.-Sat. 9-9, Sun.-Mon. 9-5, early Dec.-late Mar. **Phone:** (303) 325-7347.

White-water Rafting

- **Clear Creek Rafting Co.** is at 350 Whitewater Rd. **Hours:** Daily 7 a.m.-9 p.m., May-Aug. **Phone:** (303) 567-1000 or (800) 353-9901.
- **Raft Masters** is at 2804 Colorado Blvd. **Hours:** Daily 8-6, mid-May through Labor Day. **Phone:** (303) 567-2044 or (800) 568-7238.

BEAU JO'S COLORADO STYLE PIZZA **Phone:** 303/567-4376

Pizza
$10-$30

AAA Inspector Notes: The original location for this small regional chain has been a local favorite for more than 35 years. Patrons may choose a specialty pizza or design their own from crust to toppings. The menu also features sandwiches, pasta dishes and calzones. Locals know to save their crusts and drizzle honey on them for dessert. The city's mining-town history inspires the decor. **Bar:** full bar. **Address:** 1517 Miner St 80452 **Location:** I-70 exit 240, just n, then just e. **Parking:** on-site and street. L D AC

THE BUFFALO RESTAURANT & BAR **Phone:** 303/567-2729

American
$8-$23

AAA Inspector Notes: This fun, popular and well-established place is in an intriguing old mining town. The cuisine features an interesting mix of buffalo, pizza, barbecue and Mexican dishes. Built in 1906, the restaurant's Western décor includes skylights. **Bar:** full bar. **Address:** 1617 Miner St 80452 **Location:** I-70 exit 240, just e; exit 241A, just w. **Historic** L D AC

MANGIA! CASUAL ITALIAN **Phone:** 303/567-4371

Italian
$15-$29

AAA Inspector Notes: In the historic center of the city, this restaurant features stylish decor, knowledgeable servers and classic Italian fare. Patrons may choose from a variety of pizzas, grinders and pasta and meat dishes. **Bar:** full bar. **Address:** 1446 Miner St 80452 **Location:** I-70 exit 240, just n, then just e. **Parking:** street only. L D

SUGAR PLUM RESTAURANT
Menu on AAA.com **Phone:** 303/567-4470

American
$4-$33

AAA Inspector Notes: The Sugar Plum serves meals in a parlor originally built in the 1880s and a dining room with country decor and a nice view of the beautiful garden. The menu includes oven-roasted rib-eye and fresh, boneless baked trout. Expect terrific service. **Bar:** full bar. **Address:** 1845 Miner St 80452 **Location:** Jct Soda Creek and Miner sts; e of Miner St bridge; near downtown.

IGNACIO pop. 697

SKY UTE CASINO RESORT **Phone:** (970)563-3000

Hotel
$100-$300 10/1-4/30
$130-$275 5/1-9/30

Address: 14324 Hwy 172 N 81137 **Location:** Jct US 172 and CR 517. **Facility:** Convenient to Durango, Farmington and Pagosa Springs, this new luxury hotel offers you plenty to do, including bowling in a 24-lane center, dining in multiple eateries and an array of events. 140 units. 5 stories, interior corridors. **Amenities:** high-speed Internet, safes. **Dining:** 3 restaurants. **Pool(s):** heated indoor. **Activities:** whirlpool, hiking trails, jogging, playground, exercise room. **Guest Services:** coin laundry, area transportation (fee)-Durango. **Free Special Amenities:** continental breakfast and children's activities.

 BIZ FEE

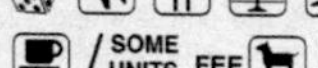 / SOME UNITS FEE

JULESBURG (B-6) pop. 1,225, elev. 3,477'

FORT SEDGWICK MUSEUM is at 114 E. 1st St. Three buildings, all part of the Fort Sedgwick Historical Society, are dedicated to local history. Fort Sedgwick Museum houses exhibits about the history of the fort and the four incarnations of Julesburg as well as temporary exhibits. The Depot Museum, at 201 W. 1st St., has Pony Express and Union Pacific Railroad memorabilia, period clothing, barbed wire and buggies. The Old Ford Garage, at 112 E. 1st St., features historic photographs, antique cars and gasoline pumps.

Time: Allow 1 hour minimum. **Hours:** Fort Sedgwick Museum and Old Ford Garage Tues.-Sat. 10-4, Sun. 1-4, Memorial Day-Labor Day; Tues.-Fri. 9-1, rest of year. Depot Museum Tues.-Sat. 10-4, Sun. 1-4, Memorial Day-Labor Day. **Cost:** (includes Fort Sedgwick and Depot museums) $1; 50c (ages 6-12). Old Ford Garage free. **Phone:** (970) 474-2061.

KEYSTONE (D-3) pop. 1,079, elev. 9,166'

• Hotels p. 230 • Restaurants p. 230

A Pennsylvania prospector searching for gold in the 1880s named the town after his home state's nickname. Great skiing on three mountains—the Outback, Dercum Mountain and North Peak—lure today's visitors. Summer recreation includes boating on Lake Dillon, biking, golfing and hiking.

RECREATIONAL ACTIVITIES

Skiing

- **Arapahoe Basin** is at 28194 US 6. **Hours:** Mon.-Fri. 9-4, Sat.-Sun. and holidays 8:30-4, mid-Oct. to early June. **Phone:** (888) 272-7246.
- **Keystone Resort** is at I-70 exit 205. Other activities are offered. **Hours:** Daily 8:30-8:30, early Nov.-early Apr. **Phone:** (970) 496-4386 or (800) 842-8072.

THE INN AT KEYSTONE Phone: (970)496-4825

Hotel

$119-$249

Address: 23044 Hwy 6 80435 **Location:** I-70 exit 205, 6.5 mi e (on south side of US 6). **Facility:** 103 units. 6 stories, interior corridors. **Parking:** on-site and valet. **Terms:** check-in 4 pm, 1-5 night minimum stay - seasonal, 21 day cancellation notice-fee imposed. **Amenities:** safes. **Activities:** whirlpools, bicycle trails, hiking trails. *Fee:* downhill & cross country skiing. **Guest Services:** valet and coin laundry.

BIZ / SOME UNITS FEE

KEYSTONE LODGE & SPA Phone: (970)496-2316

Resort Hotel

$159-$369

Address: 22101 Hwy 6 80435 **Location:** I-70 exit 205, 6 mi e. **Facility:** The lodge, offering hotel rooms and condominiums each with a humidifier and fan, is bordered by ski slopes and a national forest. In ski season, entertainment is presented on site. 152 units. 6 stories, interior corridors. **Parking:** on-site and valet. **Terms:** check-in 4 pm, 1-5 night minimum stay - seasonal, 21 day cancellation notice-fee imposed. **Amenities:** safes. **Dining:** Bighorn Steakhouse, see separate listing. **Pool(s):** heated outdoor. **Activities:** sauna, whirlpools, steamroom, rental canoes, rental paddleboats, fishing, recreation programs, rental bicycles, hiking trails, jogging, playground, basketball, horseshoes, volleyball, spa. *Fee:* golf-36 holes, 5 tennis courts (1 lighted), downhill & cross country skiing, snowmobiling, ice skating, horseback riding, game room. **Guest Services:** valet laundry, area transportation-within 5 mi. **Free Special Amenities: newspaper and high-speed Internet.** Affiliated with A Preferred Hotel. *(See ad this page.)*

SAVE FEE CALL BIZ / SOME UNITS

Safety tip: Keep a current AAA/CAA Road Atlas in every vehicle

RIVER RUN CONDOMINIUMS AT KEYSTONE
Phone: (970)496-3390

Resort Condominium

$165-$769 11/7-4/30
$139-$409 5/1-11/6

Address: 100 Dercum Dr 80435 **Location:** I-70 exit 205, 7.5 mi e on US 6; at base of ski area. **Facility:** Modern and luxury 1-bedroom studio to 4-bedrooms units located near the gondola; guests have access to Keystone Resort activities. 340 condominiums. 4-6 stories, interior corridors. **Terms:** office hours 8 am-8 am, off-site registration, check-in 4 pm, 21 day cancellation notice-fee imposed. **Amenities:** high-speed Internet, safes. **Dining:** 8 restaurants. **Pool(s):** 2 heated outdoor. **Activities:** whirlpools, fishing, rental bicycles, hiking trails, jogging, playground. *Fee:* paddleboats, golf-36 holes, miniature golf, downhill & cross country skiing, snowmobiling, ice skating, horseback riding, massage. **Guest Services:** valet and coin laundry, area transportation-within resort. **Free Special Amenities: high-speed Internet and local transportation.**

SAVE FEE BIZ

SKI TIP LODGE BED & BREAKFAST
Phone: 970/496-4950

fyi Not evaluated. **Address:** 764 Montezuma Rd 80435 **Location:** I-70 exit 205, 8 mi se on US 6, then 0.8 mi s. Facilities, services, and decor characterize a mid-scale property.

WHERE TO EAT

ALPENGLOW STUBE
Menu on AAA.com
Phone: 970/496-4386

Regional American

$32-$99

AAA Inspector Notes: Diners looking for a once-in-a-lifetime dining experience will find a memorable one here. Two gondola rides take guests to the highest restaurant in the United States at 11,444 feet. The view from the front deck is as spectacular as the one talented servers deliver to the table. Winter lunches and rotisserie duck dinners are prepared in the wood-fired oven of the open kitchen. **Bar:** full bar. **Reservations:** required, for dinner. **Address:** 22101 Hwy 6 80435 **Location:** I-70 exit 205, 7 mi se to the Keystone Gondola, follow directions to North Peak (2 gondola rides). L D

▼ *See AAA listing this page* ▼

BIGHORN STEAKHOUSE **Phone:** 970/496-4386

Steak
$20-$39

AAA Inspector Notes: Although a large portion of the menu consists of high-quality beef steaks, many dishes feature local game such as venison, pheasant, elk, antelope and buffalo. Adventurous diners should try the Rocky Mountain oysters, a culinary experience unique to Colorado. The warm, inviting décor combines elegance with a hint of Western flair. **Bar:** full bar. **Reservations:** suggested. **Address:** 22101 Hwy 6 80435 **Location:** I-70 exit 205, 6 mi e; in Keystone Lodge & Spa. **Parking:** on-site and valet.

DOS LOCOS MEXICAN RESTAURANT & CANTINA **Phone:** 970/262-9185

Mexican
$6-$15

AAA Inspector Notes: The restaurant provides a varied menu consisting of everything from popular chile rellenos and fajitas to harder-to-find fish tacos and chicken mole. While the large bar is suitable for lively groups, the dining rooms provide a quieter backdrop for laid-back dining. **Bar:** full bar. **Address:** 22869 Hwy 6 80435 **Location:** I-70 exit 205, 7.4 mi e; in Mountain View Plaza (north side of US 6).

KEYSTONE RANCH RESTAURANT **Phone:** 970/496-4386

Western American
$30-$45

AAA Inspector Notes: This restaurant features an expertly prepared six-course dinner set in a refined, rustic dining room. After finishing the main course, diners are escorted into a living room area for after-dinner beverages and dessert. This area is comfortably furnished with overstuffed furniture and a stone fireplace, lending to a nice, relaxed environment. **Bar:** full bar. **Reservations:** suggested. **Address:** 1437 Keystone Ranch Rd 80435 **Location:** I-70 exit 205, 6 mi e, then 3 mi sw on Keystone Ranch Rd; follow signs to Ranch Golf Course. **Historic**

SKI TIP LODGE RESTAURANT **Phone:** 970/496-4950

Regional American
$69

AAA Inspector Notes: Creative cuisine is expertly and beautifully presented in a rustic former stagecoach stop. Rotating four-course dinners are offered in quaint and inviting surroundings, and diners may retreat to the cabin sitting room or outdoor patio for dessert. While the setting is ideal for couples, the talented waitstaff will make the single diner and groups feel right at home. **Bar:** full bar. **Reservations:** suggested. **Address:** 764 Montezuma Rd 80435 **Location:** I-70 exit 205, 8 mi se on US 6, then 0.8 mi s; in Ski Tip Lodge Bed & Breakfast. **Historic**

SNAKE RIVER SALOON **Phone:** 970/468-2788

American
$23-$36

AAA Inspector Notes: The Snake River Saloon offers steak, chicken, chops and pasta in a quite-cozy, knotty pine-paneled dining room. This place also has great bands in the lounge, so guests should check the daily paper for the schedule. **Bar:** full bar. **Address:** 23074 Hwy 6 80435 **Location:** I-70 exit 205, 6 mi e.

DER FONDUE CHESSEL **Phone:** 970/496-4386

fyi Not evaluated. Enjoy four-course traditional Swiss and Bavarian fondue dinners at 11,444 feet. There are seven beers on tap and Bavarian entertainment. **Address:** 22010 Hwy 6 80435 **Location:** I-70 exit 205, 6 mi e; at The Outpost atop North Peak, take River Run and Outpost gondolas.

KREMMLING (C-3) pop. 1,444, elev. 7,362'

RECREATIONAL ACTIVITIES

White-water Rafting

- **Wilderness Aware Rafting** trips depart from the Pumphouse Recreation Area; go s. on SR 9 crossing the Colorado River to a dirt road (watch for the Pumphouse sign), w. 10.5 mi. to the next Pumphouse sign, then n. 1.3 mi. **Hours:** Trips depart daily at 9:30, mid-June to mid-Sept. **Phone:** (719) 395-2112 or (800) 462-7238.

ALLINGTON INN & SUITES **Phone:** (970)724-9800

Hotel
$97-$117

Address: 215 W Central Ave 80459 **Location:** Just n on 2nd St. **Facility:** 46 units. 2 stories, interior corridors. **Amenities:** high-speed Internet. **Pool(s):** heated indoor. **Activities:** whirlpool, limited exercise equipment. **Guest Services:** coin laundry.

SAVE BIZ / SOME UNITS FEE

LAFAYETTE (B-4) pop. 24,453, elev. 5,236'

Lafayette was founded in 1888 by Mary Miller, a prosperous widow who named the town after her husband. In 1884 she discovered coal on her farm; within several years the coal mining industry spurred the town's rapid growth. Mrs. Miller established the Lafayette Bank in 1900, reputedly becoming the only female bank president in the world at the time.

With 20 neighborhood parks, recreational opportunities such as boating, swimming, tennis and picnicking abound. Community events include the Lafayette Quaker Oatmeal Festival in January, the Peach Festival in August and Celebrate Lafayette in September.

Lafayette Chamber of Commerce: 1290 S. Public Rd., P.O. Box 1018, Lafayette, CO 80026. **Phone:** (303) 666-9555.

WORLD OF WONDER CHILDREN'S MUSEUM is at 110 N. Harrison Ave. Children's activities focus on the arts, music and science. Play areas include a stage, a pirate ship, a grocery store and a bank. **Time:** Allow 1 hour minimum. **Hours:** Tues.-Wed. 9-5, Thurs.-Sat. 10-6, Memorial Day weekend to mid-Aug.; Tues.-Wed. 9-5, Thurs.-Sat. 10-6, Sun. noon-4, rest of year. Closed Jan. 1, Thanksgiving and Christmas. **Cost:** $7 (ages 15 months-11 years); free (all other ages). **Phone:** (303) 604-2424.

LA JUNTA (E-5) pop. 7,077, elev. 4,052'

• Hotels p. 232 • Restaurants p. 232

This was once *la junta*—the junction—where the main and southern routes of the old Santa Fe Trail divided. Bent's Fort, a major trading post, was just to the east. In 1875, with the arrival of the Santa Fe Railroad, La Junta (HUN-ta) became a major hub on the route, and the hoot of the locomotive replaced the rumble of wagon wheels.

La Junta is still a junction, but the term now refers to the numerous state and federal highways that converge in the town. One of these, US 50, is part of the scenic and historic Santa Fe Trail route that continues on as US 350 heading southwest out of La Junta. La Junta also is a major cattle- and produce-shipping center for the lower Arkansas Valley.

Nearby Holbrook Lake provides a setting for water skiing, fishing, boating and camping. The northern unit of Comanche National Grassland lies southwest of town. Vogel Canyon, 13 miles south on SR 109, then following signs, is within the grassland. Several trails beginning at the parking lot lead to scenic overlooks and rock art.

Also part of the grassland is Picketwire Canyonlands where, in addition to rock art, one of the nation's largest known set of dinosaur tracks (more than 1,300 footprints) can be seen. Picketwire Canyon is about 13 miles past Vogel Canyon. **Note:** Only experienced hikers in good physical condition should attempt the trek to Picketwire Canyon. Guided full-day auto tours are offered on Saturdays in May, June, September and October; participants must have their own high-clearance, four-wheel-drive vehicle. These tours are the only way cars may be taken into the canyon. Contact the Comanche National Grasslands office, 1420 E. 3rd. St. in La Junta, (719) 384-2181, for information and reservations.

La Junta Chamber of Commerce: 110 Santa Fe Ave., La Junta, CO 81050. **Phone:** (719) 384-7411.

BENT'S OLD FORT NATIONAL HISTORIC SITE, 6 mi. e. on SR 194E, is a reconstruction of an adobe fur trading post that operated here 1833-49. It figured prominently in westward expansion and maintained friendly relations with many American Indian tribes. Kit Carson once worked here as a hunter and trader. The rooms, restored to the 1846 era, include a kitchen, blacksmith shop and trade room. Guides in period dress demonstrate life in the 1840s. An orientation film is available.

Time: Allow 1 hour minimum. **Hours:** Daily 8-5:30, June-Aug.; 9-4, rest of year. Guided tours are given daily at 9:30, 11, 1 and 2:30, June-Aug.; at 10:30 and 1, rest of year. Tour schedule may vary; phone ahead. Closed Jan. 1, Thanksgiving and Christmas. **Cost:** $3; $2 (ages 6-12). **Phone:** (719) 383-5010.

KOSHARE INDIAN MUSEUM, 18th St. and Santa Fe Ave., is patterned after the American Indian ceremonial kivas of the Southwest. The museum houses fine art and sculpture, pottery, bead and quill work, baskets, rugs and kachinas. The Koshare Indian Dancers perform interpretive American Indian dances, preserving the Pueblo and Plains heritage and culture.

Hours: Daily 10-5, June-Aug.; daily noon-5, in Dec.; Fri.-Mon. and Wed. noon-5, rest of year. Winter hours vary; phone ahead. Dances are performed June-July at 7:30, and the week after Christmas to mid-Jan. at 7 p.m. Closed major holidays. Phone ahead to confirm schedule. **Cost:** Museum $5; $3 (ages 7-17 and 55+). Museum and dance performances $10; $5 (ages 3-17). **Phone:** (719) 384-4411.

OTERO MUSEUM is at 218 Anderson Ave. Guides take visitors through the museum, which has memorabilia from La Junta and the surrounding lower Arkansas Valley area dating from 1875-1945. Displays focus on transportation, including an 1867 Old Overland Stage and early fire engines; a home and grocery store furnished in the early 20th-century style; a 19th-century wood-framed structure formerly used as a boarding house; La Junta's first schoolhouse; a mini post office; and a mustache cup collection. **Time:** Allow 1 hour minimum. **Hours:** Mon.-Sat. 1-5, June-Sept.; by appointment, rest of year. **Cost:** Free. **Phone:** (719) 384-7500.

HAMPTON INN LA JUNTA **Phone:** (719)384-4444

Hotel
$79-$149

AAA Benefit:
Members save up to 10% everyday!

Address: 27800 US Hwy 50 81050 **Location:** On US 50 frontage road, 0.9 mi w. **Facility:** 62 units. 3 stories, interior corridors. **Terms:** 1-7 night minimum stay, cancellation fee imposed. **Amenities:** high-speed Internet. **Pool(s):** heated indoor. **Activities:** whirlpool, exercise room. **Guest Services:** valet and coin laundry.

HOLIDAY INN EXPRESS **Phone:** (719)384-2900

Hotel
$109-$119 5/1-10/1
$99-$109 10/2-4/30

Address: 27994 US Hwy 50 Frontage Rd 81050 **Location:** On US 50, 0.8 mi w. **Facility:** 59 units. 2 stories, interior corridors. **Parking:** winter plug-ins. **Amenities:** high-speed Internet. **Pool(s):** heated indoor. **Activities:** whirlpool, exercise room. **Guest Services:** valet and coin laundry.

SOME UNITS FEE

STAGECOACH MOTEL **Phone:** (719)384-5476

Motel
$55-$70 5/1-9/30
$50-$65 10/1-4/30

Address: 905 W 3rd St 81050 **Location:** US 50 and 350. **Facility:** 31 units. 2 stories (no elevator), exterior corridors. **Parking:** winter plug-ins. **Terms:** cancellation fee imposed. **Pool(s):** heated outdoor. **Guest Services:** area transportation-train depot. **Free Special Amenities: continental breakfast and high-speed Internet.**

SOME UNITS FEE

WHERE TO EAT

BOSS HOGG'S SALOON & RESTAURANT **Phone:** 719/384-7879

American
$6-$29

AAA Inspector Notes: This restaurant features flavorful, freshly cut steaks and hickory-smoked barbecue. **Bar:** full bar. **Address:** 808 E 3rd St 81050 **Location:** On SR 109, 0.5 mi e of center.

FELISA'S MEXICAN RESTAURANT **Phone:** 719/384-4814

Mexican
$5-$10

AAA Inspector Notes: A local favorite, the restaurant offers typical Mexican fare such as burritos, enchiladas and tacos. **Bar:** full bar. **Address:** 27948 Frontage Rd 81050 **Location:** On US 50, 0.8 mi w.

NEW CHINA RESTAURANT **Phone:** 719/384-8504

Chinese
$5-$13

AAA Inspector Notes: Family-owned and -operated, this casual eatery offers an extensive list of standard Chinese rice and meat dishes. Patrons can expect efficient service and large portions packed with flavor. **Bar:** wine only. **Address:** 414 W 1st St 81050 **Location:** On US 50.

L D

LAKE CITY (E-2) pop. 408, elev. 8,658'

Lake City was named for nearby Lake San Cristobal, the second largest natural lake in Colorado. Hidden Treasure and Golden Fleece—the names of local mines—attest to Lake City's early preoccupation. One of the earliest settlements in western Colorado, Lake City served as a supply center for the gold and silver mines of the surrounding San Juan Mountains.

Today the town is a starting point for enjoying two of Colorado's most scenic and historic byways, the Alpine Backcountry Loop and the Silver Thread Scenic Byway. The Alpine Loop's 65 miles of dirt and gravel roads connect the former mining towns of Lake City, Ouray and Silverton. Depending on snowfall, it's open late May to late October; four-wheel-drive, high-clearance vehicles are recommended for some portions, including Engineer and Cinnamon passes.

Weaving over the Continental Divide for some 120 miles, the fully paved Silver Thread (SR 149) links Blue Mesa Reservoir to Creede and South Fork and is open year-round. Mountain peaks, river valleys and the Gunnison and Rio Grande national forests provide outstanding scenery at nearly every turn.

Five 14,000-foot peaks provide plenty of hiking, biking, fishing, camping, boating, wildlife viewing and horseback riding opportunities; backcountry skiing, snowmobiling, ice climbing, ice fishing and a family ski hill round out the year's recreational activities.

Lake City also is known for its Victorian architecture; most of the town's old buildings have been restored and preserved within a National Historic District.

Lake City/Hinsdale County Chamber of Commerce: 800 N. Gunnison Ave., P.O. Box 430, Lake City, CO 81235. **Phone:** (970) 944-2527 or (800) 569-1874.

Self-guiding tours: A map detailing a walking tour of Lake City is available at the chamber of commerce.

HARD TACK MINE TOURS & MUSEUM is 2.5 mi. w. on CR 20 (Engineer Pass Rd.). The mine, owned and operated by a former hard rock miner, offers 35-minute walking tours that show how hand tools and dynamite were used to blast through the mine's rock. The Hard Tack Mine tunnel was begun more than 100 years ago by employees of the Hidden Treasure Mine, which produced more than $1.5 million in silver ore. Minerals, crystals and gold panning items are displayed. A light jacket is recommended, as the mine temperature is 45 F. **Time:** Allow 45 minutes minimum. **Hours:** Tues.-Sat. 10-5, Memorial Day-Labor Day. **Cost:** $10; $9 (senior citizens); $6 (ages 1-14). **Phone:** (970) 944-2506.

HINSDALE COUNTY MUSEUM, 130 N. Silver St., traces the history of Lake City and Hinsdale County. Displays include medical equipment, an 1878 hook and ladder truck, old-fashioned gardens utilizing vintage plants, a restored Denver & Rio Grande caboose and a small home depicting late 19th-century family life. Exhibits in the Transportation Building include early transportation memorabilia and a blacksmith shop. In summer, cemetery, ghost and historic home tours are offered. **Time:** Allow 30 minutes minimum. **Hours:** Mon.-Sat. 10-5, Sun. 1-4:30, late May to mid-Sept. **Cost:** $4; $3 (ages 8-15); free (ages 0-7). Tours $8-$10. **Phone:** (970) 944-2050.

POKER ALICE PIZZA **Phone:** 970/944-4100

Pizza
$5-$12

AAA Inspector Notes: Patrons can dine inside or outside on the covered front porch or at a picnic table. Salads, hearty sandwiches, fresh-baked breads, hand-rolled calzones, pasta and stone-baked pizza are offered at this fun eatery. Cake, cookies, pie and good coffee are always available. **Bar:** beer & wine. **Address:** 188 S Gunnison Ave 81235 **Location:** On SR 149, south end of town.

L D

LAKE GEORGE

MULE CREEK OUTFITTERS/M LAZY C RANCH
Phone: 719/748-3398

Ranch
$75-$110

Address: 801 CR 453 80827 **Location:** 5 mi w on US 24, then 1 mi n on dirt road. **Facility:** 7 cabins. 1 story, exterior corridors. *Bath:* some shared. **Terms:** office hours 8:30 am-5:30 pm, 2 night minimum stay, 30 day cancellation notice-fee imposed. **Activities:** whirlpool, cross country skiing, hiking trails, jogging, playground, horseshoes, volleyball. *Fee:* fishing, horseback riding. **Free Special Amenities: full breakfast and high-speed Internet.**

SAVE

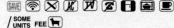

/ SOME UNITS FEE

LAKEWOOD pop. 142,980

- **Restaurants p. 236**
- **Hotels & Restaurants map & index p. 140**
- **Part of Denver area — see map p. 123**

AMERICINN HOTEL & SUITES/DENVER WEST-FEDERAL CENTER **Phone:** 303/231-9929 73

Hotel
Rates not provided

Address: 11909 W 6th Ave 80401 **Location:** US 6 exit Simms St/Union Blvd, westbound turn right at traffic light, but do not use right turn lane, follow signs to frontage road. **Facility:** 62 units. 2 stories (no elevator), interior corridors. **Amenities:** safes (fee). **Pool(s):** heated indoor. **Activities:** sauna, whirlpool, exercise room. **Guest Services:** valet and coin laundry.

CALL BIZ

/ SOME UNITS FEE

(See map & index p. 140.)

BEST WESTERN DENVER SOUTHWEST

Phone: (303)989-5500 77

Hotel

$85-$119

AAA Benefit: Members save up to 20%, plus 10% bonus points with Best Western Rewards®.

Address: 3440 S Vance St 80227 **Location:** Just ne of jct US 285 (Hampden Ave) and S Wadsworth Blvd, e on Girton Dr, then just s. **Facility:** 117 units. 2 stories (no elevator), interior corridors. **Amenities:** *Some:* high-speed Internet. **Pool(s):** heated outdoor. **Activities:** limited exercise equipment. **Guest Services:** valet and coin laundry. **Free Special Amenities: expanded continental breakfast and high-speed Internet.**

SAVE BIZ

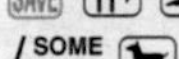

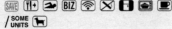

/ SOME UNITS

CANDLEWOOD SUITES LAKEWOOD/GOLDEN

Phone: 303/232-7171 70

Extended Stay Hotel

Rates not provided

Address: 895 Tabor St 80401 **Location:** US 6 exit Simms St/Union Blvd, just n to 8th St, then just w. **Facility:** 122 efficiencies. 3 stories, interior corridors. **Amenities:** high-speed Internet. **Activities:** exercise room. **Guest Services:** complimentary and valet laundry. **Free Special Amenities: local telephone calls and high-speed Internet.**

COURTYARD BY MARRIOTT DENVER SW/LAKEWOOD

Phone: (303)985-9696 78

Hotel

$69-$189

AAA Benefit: AAA hotel discounts of 5% or more.

Address: 7180 W Hampden Ave 80227 **Location:** Just se of jct US 285 (W Hampden Ave) and S Wadsworth Blvd, e on Jefferson Ave, then n on Frontage Rd. Located in a business park. **Facility:** 90 units. 3 stories, interior corridors. **Amenities:** *Some:* high-speed Internet. **Pool(s):** heated indoor. **Activities:** whirlpool, exercise room. **Guest Services:** valet and coin laundry.

CALL BIZ FEE

/ SOME UNITS

FAIRFIELD INN DENVER WEST - FEDERAL CENTER

Phone: (303)231-9939 72

Hotel

$109-$129

AAA Benefit: AAA hotel discounts of 5% or more.

Address: 11907 W 6th Ave 80401 **Location:** US 6 exit Simms St/Union Blvd, westbound travelers turn right at traffic light, but do not use right lane, follow signs to frontage road. **Facility:** 63 units. 3 stories, interior corridors. **Pool(s):** heated indoor. **Activities:** whirlpool. **Guest Services:** valet laundry.

BIZ

HAMPTON INN-DENVER SOUTHWEST

Phone: (303)989-6900 82

Hotel

$89-$149

AAA Benefit: Members save up to 10% everyday!

Address: 3605 S Wadsworth Blvd 80235 **Location:** Just sw of jct US 285 (Hampden Ave) and S Wadsworth Blvd; entry on frontage road. **Facility:** 150 units. 4 stories, interior corridors. **Terms:** 1-7 night minimum stay, cancellation fee imposed. **Amenities:** video games (fee). **Pool(s):** heated outdoor. **Activities:** exercise room. **Guest Services:** valet and coin laundry, area transportation-within 3 mi.

CALL BIZ FEE

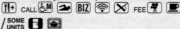

/ SOME UNITS

HAMPTON INN DENVER WEST/FEDERAL CENTER

Phone: (303)969-9900 75

Hotel

$99-$139

AAA Benefit: Members save up to 10% everyday!

Address: 137 Union Blvd 80228 **Location:** 0.8 mi s of US 6. **Facility:** 170 units. 6 stories, interior corridors. **Terms:** 1-7 night minimum stay, cancellation fee imposed. **Amenities:** video games (fee), high-speed Internet. **Pool(s):** heated outdoor. **Activities:** exercise room. **Guest Services:** valet and coin laundry, area transportation-within 5 mi.

CALL BIZ FEE

HOLIDAY INN DENVER LAKEWOOD

Phone: (303)980-9200 79

Hotel

$89-$129

Address: 7390 W Hampden Ave 80227 **Location:** US 285 (W Hampden Ave) exit S Wadsworth Blvd, just e on Jefferson Ave, then n on Vance St. **Facility:** 188 units. 6 stories, interior corridors. **Terms:** check-in 4 pm. **Amenities:** high-speed Internet. **Pool(s):** heated outdoor. **Activities:** sauna, whirlpool, exercise room. **Guest Services:** valet and coin laundry, area transportation-within 5 mi. **Free Special Amenities: high-speed Internet and local transportation.** *(See ad p. 235.)*

SAVE BIZ

/ SOME UNITS FEE

HOMEWOOD SUITES BY HILTON DENVER-WEST/ LAKEWOOD

Phone: (303)716-5737 76

Extended Stay Hotel

$159-$359

AAA Benefit: Contemporary luxury at a special Member rate.

Address: 139 Union Blvd 80228 **Location:** US 6 exit Simms St/Union Blvd, 0.6 mi s on Union Blvd to 2nd Pl, just w, then just s on Van Gordon St. **Facility:** 110 units, some efficiencies. 4 stories, interior corridors. **Terms:** 1-7 night minimum stay, cancellation fee imposed. **Amenities:** high-speed Internet, safes. **Pool(s):** heated indoor. **Activities:** whirlpool, basketball, exercise room. **Guest Services:** valet and coin laundry.

BIZ

(See map & index p. 140.)

LAKEWOOD COMFORT SUITES

Phone: (303)988-8600 **81**

Hotel
$100

Address: 7260 W Jefferson Ave 80235 **Location:** Just se of US 285 (W Hampden Ave) and S Wadsworth Blvd, then e. **Facility:** 71 units. 3 stories, interior corridors. **Terms:** cancellation fee imposed. **Pool(s):** heated indoor. **Activities:** whirlpools, exercise room. **Guest Services:** valet and coin laundry.

BIZ

/ SOME UNITS FEE

RESIDENCE INN BY MARRIOTT DENVER SW/LAKEWOOD

Phone: (303)985-7676 **80**

Extended Stay Hotel
$79-$219

AAA Benefit:
AAA hotel discounts of 5% or more.

Address: 7050 W Hampden Ave 80227 **Location:** Just se of jct US 285 (W Hampden Ave) and Wadsworth Blvd, e on Jefferson Ave, then n on frontage road. Located in a business park. **Facility:** 102 units, some two bedrooms, efficiencies and kitchens. 3 stories, interior corridors. **Amenities:** *Some:* high-speed Internet. **Pool(s):** heated indoor. **Activities:** whirlpool, sports court, exercise room. **Guest Services:** valet and coin laundry.

CALL BIZ FEE  

/ SOME UNITS FEE

SHERATON-DENVER WEST HOTEL

Phone: (303)987-2000 **74**

Hotel
$89-$279

Sheraton

AAA Benefit:
Members get up to 15% off, plus Starwood Preferred Guest® bonuses.

Address: 360 Union Blvd 80228 **Location:** US 6 exit Simms St/Union Blvd, just s on Union Blvd; 3 mi e of jct I-70 exit 261. **Facility:** 242 units. 12 stories, interior corridors. **Terms:** cancellation fee imposed. **Amenities:** video games (fee). **Pool(s):** heated indoor. **Activities:** whirlpool, steamroom, spa. **Guest Services:** valet laundry, area transportation-within 5 mi. **Free Special Amenities: high-speed Internet and local transportation.**

SAVE BIZ FEE

/ SOME UNITS

TOWNEPLACE SUITES BY MARRIOTT-DENVER WEST/ FEDERAL CENTER

Phone: (303)232-7790 **71**

Extended Stay Hotel
$79-$169

TownePlace Suites

AAA Benefit: AAA hotel discounts of 5% or more.

Address: 800 Tabor St 80401 **Location:** US 6 exit Simms St/Union Blvd, just n to 8th St, then w. **Facility:** 107 kitchen units, some two bedrooms. 3 stories, interior corridors. **Amenities:** high-speed Internet. **Pool(s):** heated outdoor. **Activities:** exercise room. **Guest Services:** valet and coin laundry. **Free Special Amenities: continental breakfast and high-speed Internet.**

SAVE CALL BIZ

/ SOME UNITS FEE

▼ See AAA listing p. 234 ▼

(See map & index p. 140.)

WHERE TO EAT

240 UNION RESTAURANT Phone: 303/989-3562 (84)

American
$9-$29

AAA Inspector Notes: This bustling, well-known restaurant features an open kitchen, a wood-burning oven and a large, whimsical and flawlessly food-friendly wine list. Creative appetizers, pasta, pizza and other entrées get better every season. The well-trained waitstaff offers friendly and attentive service. **Bar:** full bar. **Reservations:** suggested. **Address:** 240 Union Blvd 80228 **Location:** US 6, 0.3 mi s on Union Blvd; I-70 exit 261, 3 mi e. L D CALL &M

BLUE SKY CAFE Phone: 303/216-2670 (81)

Natural/Organic
$6-$11

AAA Inspector Notes: Set in a strip mall, this cozy cafe features menu options that are designed to promote good health as well as good taste. Vegetarian options are available as well as wheat-free pancakes, soy milk and freshly made juices and smoothies. **Address:** 14403 W Colfax Ave 80401 **Location:** I-70 exit Colfax Ave, 0.4 mi ne; in Denver West Village strip mall; n of Colorado Mills Mall.
B L

CAFE JORDANO Phone: 303/988-6863 (88)

Italian
$6-$16

AAA Inspector Notes: The delectable Italian cuisine served at this popular eatery can be summed up in a few words: fresh, flavorful and authentic. Scrumptious, colorful dishes made from scratch and attentive, friendly servers are staples of this unassuming strip-mall restaurant. Patrons should expect to wait for a table, but they won't regret it. **Bar:** full bar. **Address:** 11068 W Jewell Ave 80232 **Location:** US 285 exit Kipling Pkwy, 2 mi nw; in strip mall.
L D

CHAD'S GRILL Phone: 303/988-5666 (83)

American
$7-$15

AAA Inspector Notes: A good stop for lunch, dinner or weekend brunch, the restaurant has been a local favorite since 1982. Hearty breakfasts include crab Benedict, huevos rancheros and pecan cream cheese French toast. The lunch and dinner menus line up pizzas, pasta, rotisserie chicken dishes, burgers and sandwiches. More elaborate options include pistachio- and pumpkin seed-crusted halibut, spicy Cajun jambalaya and fire-grilled rib-eye steak. When the weather permits, the covered patio is a nice option. **Bar:** full bar. **Address:** 275 Union Blvd 80228 **Location:** 6th Ave exit Union Blvd, just s.
L D CALL &M

HACIENDA COLORADO Phone: 303/932-0272

Mexican
$7-$17

AAA Inspector Notes: The spacious, comfortable hacienda welcomes all who enter the door with its homey and upscale décor. Fresh, flavorful salsa is served with thinner-than-usual chips. Grilled items and juicy fajitas are included on the menu. Portions are large and plentiful in this bustling, popular restaurant. **Bar:** full bar. **Address:** 5056 S Wadsworth Way 80123 **Location:** US 285 exit Wadsworth Blvd, 1.9 mi s. L D

JUS COOKIN'S RESTAURANT
Menu on AAA.com
Phone: 303/205-0123 (82)

American
$9-$13

AAA Inspector Notes: This family-owned and -operated restaurant features very good, wholesome, home-cooked meals such as meatloaf, turkey, herb-roasted chicken and real mashed potatoes. The fried chicken is famous in these parts, and the cobblers and other desserts are homemade. **Bar:** beer & wine. **Address:** Simms St & 8th Pl 80401 **Location:** US 6 exit Simms St/Union Blvd, just n to 8th St, then w. L D

MOOSE HILL CANTINA Phone: 303/989-2875 (87)

Mexican
$5-$15

AAA Inspector Notes: The Moose Hill Cantina serves up a good variety of well-prepared and ample-portioned Tex-Mex food in a festive, lively, family-oriented atmosphere. Next to the Green Mountain Bowling Center, this restaurant offers an excellent overall value as well as inviting décor and friendly service. **Bar:** full bar. **Address:** 955 S Kipling Pkwy 80226 **Location:** US 6 exit Kipling Pkwy, 1.7 mi s, just w on Kentucky Dr, then just s on private road.
L D

THE OVEN PIZZA E VINO Phone: 303/934-7600 (86)

Pizza
$8-$15

AAA Inspector Notes: When an average pizza just won't do, hungry folks can head to this spot for an elevated dining experience. Chef Mark Tarbell carefully prepares gourmet pizzas from scratch using organic and local ingredients. Fresh salads, bowls of soup and homemade desserts are fitting accompaniments. Devoted patrons swear by the fresh mozzarella appetizer, and wine lovers delight in the short but tasteful wine list. The patio is a comfortable alternative to the stylish dining room. **Bar:** full bar. **Address:** 7167 W Alaska Dr 80226 **Location:** Jct S Teller St; in Bel-Mar shopping district. L D CALL &M

PAD THAI Phone: 303/985-3344 (90)

Thai
$7-$12

AAA Inspector Notes: The small kitchen produces amazing amounts of sweet and spicy Thai classics. Pad thai, curries and other stir-fried entrées share menu space with some traditional Chinese offerings. Diners might finish with a bowl of homemade custard or sticky rice topped with mango. **Bar:** wine only. **Address:** 3333 S Wadsworth Blvd, Suite A101 80227 **Location:** Just nw of jct US 285 (W Hampden Ave) and S Wadsworth Blvd.
L D

WHITE FENCE FARM RESTAURANT
Menu on AAA.com
Phone: 303/935-5945 (89)

American
$9-$23

AAA Inspector Notes: This delightful Colonial farmhouse restaurant and American barn comes complete with an adjacent animal corral. The famous fried chicken has a crispy batter that stays on the chicken rather than the clumpy type that crumbles off. Every meal comes with sweet pickled beets, a vinegary coleslaw, and, my favorite, the sweet corn fritter. Order the mashed potatoes purely for the gravy flavored with thyme. **Bar:** full bar. **Address:** 6263 W Jewell Ave 80232 **Location:** US 6 exit Sheridan Blvd, 3 mi s, then 0.5 mi w; between Sheridan and Wadsworth blvds.
D CALL &M

WYSTONE'S WORLD TEAS
Phone: 303/663-5775 (85)

Coffee/Tea
$9-$16

AAA Inspector Notes: The chef at the cozy eatery uses tea to infuse flavors into food. It's not unusual to see rooibus added to a salad dressing or a chicken breast poached in lapsang souchong. Of course, not all of the menu items include tea. I had a sweet and tart pear salad and a standard turkey panini. The chocolate petits fours were delicious. The variety of British-style high teas, which include a pot of tea and a sampling of sweet and savory treats, looks like a fun adventure. Service was a bit spotty. **Address:** 7323 W Alaska Dr 80226 **Location:** From jct Wadsworth Blvd, just e. **Parking:** street only.
B L D

(See map & index p. 140.)

YARD HOUSE

Phone: 303/278-9273

American

$10-$30

AAA Inspector Notes: Draft beer flows from 250 taps in the noisy restaurant, in which the state-of-the-art sound system shakes the walls while keeping the vivacious vibe alive. Guests can scan an extensive menu. The restaurant, while very popular, may be too loud for some guests. **Bar:** full bar. **Address:** 14500 W Colfax Ave, Suite 341 80401 **Location:** I-70 exit 262 (Colfax Ave), 0.9 mi e; in Colorado Mills Outlet Mall. L D CALL

LAMAR (E-6) pop. 7,804, elev. 3,610'

The town of Lamar was born May 24, 1886, when the railroad depot in Blackwell, 3 miles to the east, was surreptitiously moved to the new town site.

"The Madonna of the Trail" monument, at the corner of S. Main and Beech streets, is one of 12 Madonna monuments, each in a different state, which mark one of the old national trails—in this case, the Santa Fe Trail (US 50). It was decided that the "Big Timbers" location in Colorado would be the most appropriate place for that state's monument.

Big Timbers refers to a dense grove of cottonwood trees growing along both banks of the Arkansas River. The trees provided shelter from the heat of summer and from cold winter winds, initially for the Plains Indians and later for pioneers heading west over the Santa Fe Trail.

A state welcome center is in a renovated Santa Fe Railroad Depot next to the Madonna of the Trail monument. About 2 miles north of the chamber of commerce on US 50/287 is a marker commemorating the location of the Santa Fe Trail. Willow Creek Park offers opportunities for bird-watching.

Lamar Chamber of Commerce: 109A E. Beech St., Lamar, CO 81052. **Phone:** (719) 336-4379.

BIG TIMBERS MUSEUM, at jct. US 50/287 and SR 196, contains dresses, photographs, dolls and musical instruments as well as household and farm implements representing the period from the late 1800s to the present. Included among the collection of dresses is an 1893 lace wedding gown. A firearms collection, cowboy gear and American Indian relics also are exhibited, as are 39 framed World War I posters and a rare Civil War flag.

Time: Allow 30 minutes minimum. **Hours:** Mon.-Sat. 10-5, June-Aug.; Mon.-Sat. 1-4, rest of year. Closed county and major holidays. Phone ahead to confirm schedule. **Cost:** $3; $5 (family rate). **Phone:** (719) 336-2472.

BLUE SPRUCE MOTEL

Phone: (719)336-7454

Motel

$55-$85

Address: 1801 S Main St 81052 **Location:** 1.3 mi s on US 287 and 385. **Facility:** 30 units, some efficiencies. 1 story, exterior corridors. **Parking:** winter plug-ins. **Terms:** cancellation fee imposed. **Pool(s):** outdoor. **Activities:** playground. **Guest Services:** coin laundry, area transportation-bus & train stations. **Free Special Amenities: expanded continental breakfast and high-speed Internet.**

SAVE / SOME UNITS FEE

CHEK INN

Phone: (719)336-4331

Motel

$50-$75

Address: 1210 S Main St 81052 **Location:** 1 mi s on US 287 and 385. **Facility:** 40 units, some kitchens. 1 story, exterior corridors. **Parking:** winter plug-ins. **Terms:** office hours 6:30 am-10 pm, cancellation fee imposed. **Pool(s):** outdoor. **Guest Services:** area transportation-bus & train stations. **Free Special Amenities: early check-in/late check-out and high-speed Internet.**

SAVE / SOME UNITS FEE

DAYS INN

Phone: 719/336-5340

Hotel

Rates not provided

Address: 1302 N Main St 81052 **Location:** 0.8 mi n on US 50 and 287. **Facility:** 37 units. 2 stories (no elevator), interior corridors. **Parking:** winter plug-ins. **Pool(s):** heated indoor. **Activities:** whirlpool, exercise room.

BIZ / SOME UNITS FEE

HOLIDAY INN EXPRESS & SUITES

Phone: 719/931-4010

Hotel

Rates not provided

Address: 1304 N Main St 81052 **Location:** 0.8 mi n on US 50 and 287. **Facility:** 75 units. 3 stories, interior corridors. **Amenities:** high-speed Internet. **Pool(s):** heated indoor. **Activities:** whirlpool, exercise room. **Guest Services:** valet and coin laundry.

CALL BIZ / SOME UNITS FEE

WHERE TO EAT

GREEN GARDEN RESTAURANT

Phone: 719/336-3264

Chinese

$7-$12

AAA Inspector Notes: This eatery has a new location and offers traditional Chinese dishes at reasonable prices. **Bar:** beer & wine. **Address:** 1301 S Main St 81052 **Location:** 1 mi s on US 287 and 385.

L D

THAI SPICY BASIL ASIAN GRILL

Phone: 719/336-0688

Thai

$6-$11

AAA Inspector Notes: Attractive contemporary décor and delicious Thai dishes make the restaurant an oasis of hip in this rural locale. **Address:** 10 N Main St 81052 **Location:** Town center.

L D

LARKSPUR (D-4) pop. 183, elev. 6,720'

Larkspur hosts the Colorado Renaissance Festival, held weekends in June and July. Drawing inspiration from 16th-century England, festivities include jousting, 10 stages of continuous entertainment, fine arts, crafts and food; for information phone (303) 688-6010.

LAS ANIMAS (E-5) pop. 2,410, elev. 3,886'

• Hotels p. 238

In taking the name of the river that flows into the nearby Arkansas River, town founders thought it expedient to shorten the name, since the original title of the Purgatoire River was *Río de las Animas Perdidas en Purgatorio* (River of Souls Lost in Purgatory).

Las Animas flourishes as a trading center for the stock ranches and irrigated farms of the surrounding high plains and as a destination for vacationers at

John Martin Reservoir State Park *(see Recreation Chart)*. Two murals highlighting the Western heritage of the Santa Fe Trail can be seen from US 50.

Las Animas-Bent County Chamber of Commerce: 332 Ambassador Thompson Blvd., Las Animas, CO 81054. **Phone:** (719) 456-0453.

BENT'S FORT INN **Phone:** 719/456-0011

Motel

Rates not provided

Address: 10950 E US 50 81054 **Location:** On US 50, 1.5 mi e on frontage road. **Facility:** 38 units. 2 stories (no elevator), interior corridors. **Amenities:** high-speed Internet. **Pool(s):** heated outdoor. **Guest Services:** area transportation-within 5 mi.

/ SOME UNITS FEE

SANTA FE TRAIL INN **Phone:** 719/456-0303

fyi Not evaluated. **Address:** 638 Bent Ave 81054 **Location:** On US 50, just n of 7th St. Facilities, services, and decor characterize an economy property.

LA VETA (F-4) pop. 800, elev. 7,013'

La Veta is a quaint town nestled in the Upper Cuchara Valley. In 1859, John M. Francisco purchased land here and constructed Fort Francisco; the adobe structure soon became the commercial center of the area. The fort now serves as the Francisco Fort Museum *(see attraction listing)*.

Twin mountains known as the Spanish Peaks, visible from 100 miles away, serve as landmarks for all who pass this way. The Apache, Cheyenne, Comanche, Navajo and Ute tribes hunted and camped there often. The Comanche Indians named the Spanish Peaks "Wahatoya," meaning "breasts of the world." Giant rock walls (dikes) radiate out from these peaks.

The town, now known for its art galleries and shops, is on the Scenic Highway of Legends (SR 12), which follows the Cucharas River past ranches, aspen groves, clear lakes and the small town of Cuchara. Recreational options include fishing, biking, hiking and hunting. The Rio Grande Scenic Railroad *(see attraction listing p. 38)* schedules daily trips to and from La Veta in the summer and fall seasons over the scenic La Veta Pass.

La Veta-Cuchara Chamber of Commerce Information Center: P.O. Box 32, La Veta, CO 81055. **Phone:** (719) 742-3676.

FRANCISCO FORT MUSEUM, off US 160 to SR 12, following signs to 306 S. Main St., is within an 1862 fort and features seven buildings surrounding an original Spanish-style adobe plaza. The fort contains 11 display rooms, including a kitchen, bedroom, parlor and country store. Fossils, American Indian pottery, 19th-century farm equipment, an Edison phonograph and weapons are featured.

Other historic buildings include an 1800s saloon, blacksmith shop and log schoolhouse. Living-history programs are presented on Saturday. Guided tours depart from 123 W. Francisco St. **Time:** Allow 1 hour minimum. **Hours:** Tues.-Sat. 10-4, Sun. 1-4, Memorial Day weekend-first Sat. in Oct. **Cost:** $6; $4 (ages 60+); $3 (ages 6-18). **Phone:** (719) 742-5501.

LEADVILLE (D-3) pop. 2,602, elev. 10,152'

• Restaurants p. 240

Said to be the highest incorporated city in the country, Leadville lies at an altitude that makes its climate rigorous even by Rocky Mountain standards. No less heady is its history, which condenses all the dramatic elements of the mining era into one compact package.

The discovery of gold in California Gulch in 1860 triggered the usual stampede of prospectors; within 4 months of the initial find, Oro City had more than 5,000 miners working a half-mile segment of the gulch. While there was plenty of gold, extracting it was hampered by heavy black sand that clogged sluice boxes. When the easily obtainable ore dwindled, so did Oro City.

By 1870 only a few residents remained. One of these was H.A.W. Tabor, who, in league with the heavy black sand, was to provide the necessary ingredients for a great American saga—the tale of fabulous wealth and flamboyant romance that has been immortalized in the opera "The Ballad of Baby Doe."

The black sand was carbonate of lead, and it was full of silver. By 1880 Leadville—formerly Oro City—was a booming town of 30,000 with storekeeper Tabor as mayor. It was Tabor's financing of a pair of German shoemakers that catapulted him to incredible wealth. He bought up as many claims as he could in the district, including the Matchless, which yielded up to $100,000 a month at its peak.

Drunk with money and generosity, Tabor spent so freely that he alienated his wife, Augusta. He met young, beautiful Baby Doe, whose zest for the pleasures of life matched his own. Tabor divorced Augusta, married Baby Doe and moved to Denver to begin a career as a public servant.

Since the beginning of the silver boom, Leadville district mines have produced nearly $2 billion in gold, silver, lead, zinc, copper, iron, bismuth, manganese and molybdenum.

Colorado's highest peak, 14,433-foot Mount Elbert, is 9 miles south via US 24. The 82-mile Top of the Rockies scenic and historic byway passes through the area. Leadville also is the northern gateway to the Arkansas Headwaters Recreation Area *(see Recreation Chart)*.

Leadville/Lake County Chamber of Commerce: 809 Harrison Ave., P.O. Box 861, Leadville, CO 80461. **Phone:** (719) 486-3900 or (888) 532-3845.

Self-guiding tours: Maps of historic areas and mountain biking, hiking and skiing trails are available from the chamber of commerce for a donation.

GEM **HEALY HOUSE MUSEUM AND DEXTER CABIN,** 912 Harrison Ave., depict Western life in a booming 19th-century silver mining town.

Built as a private home in 1878, the three-story, clapboard Greek Revival Healy House is restored to its original Victorian style. Lavish furnishings and collections, including items belonging to silver magnate Horace Tabor and his wife Augusta, depict the late 1800s bonanza mining period. Gardens include heritage plants and native wildflowers.

The 1879 Dexter Cabin—built by James V. Dexter, one of the state's early millionaires— looks like a rustic log cabin from the outside but is finished inside with fine woodwork and hardwood floors.

Guided tours are available by reservation year-round. **Time:** Allow 1 hour minimum. **Hours:** Daily 10-4:30, late May-early Oct. Last tour begins at 3:45. **Cost:** $6; $5.50 (ages 65+); $4.50 (ages 6-16). **Phone:** (719) 486-0487.

HERITAGE MUSEUM, 9th St. and Harrison Ave., depicts Leadville's history with a series of dioramas and mining-era memorabilia. An art gallery, a replica of the town's 19th-century ice palace and an exhibit about the U.S. Army's 10th Mountain Division also are featured.

Time: Allow 30 minutes minimum. **Hours:** Daily 10-6, Memorial Day-Labor Day; 10-4, mid-May through day before Memorial Day and day after Labor Day-Oct. 31. **Cost:** $6; $5 (ages 62+); $3 (ages 6-16). **Phone:** (719) 486-1878.

THE HISTORIC TABOR HOME is at 116 E. 5th St. This was the first home of entrepreneur Horace Tabor, perhaps the most famous of the Silver Kings. Guided tours of the renovated home tell the life story of the Tabor family. **Time:** Allow 45 minutes minimum. **Hours:** Daily 8-5 (also 5-8 Sat.-Sun.). Limited winter hours; phone ahead to confirm schedule. **Cost:** $6; $5 (ages 63+); $2 (ages 6-12). **Phone:** (719) 486-7368.

LEADVILLE, COLORADO & SOUTHERN RAILROAD COMPANY, 3 blks. e. on 7th St., offers scenic narrated railroad trips through the Colorado Rocky Mountains from Leadville to Climax. Wildflowers and wildlife may be seen along the way.

Time: Allow 2 hours, 30 minutes minimum. **Hours:** Trips depart daily at 10 and 2, mid-June to mid-Aug.; Mon.-Fri at 1, Sat.-Sun. at 10 and 2, mid-Aug. to early Oct.; daily at 1, Memorial Day weekend to mid-June. Phone ahead to confirm schedule. **Cost:** Fare $32.50; $19.50 (ages 4-12). **Phone:** (719) 486-3936 or (866) 386-3936.

LEADVILLE NATIONAL FISH HATCHERY is 2 mi. w. off US 24 on SR 300. Established in 1889, this hatchery is one of the oldest in the federal system. It propagates cutthroat and rainbow trout. A visitor center offers educational information and a historic perspective on hatchery operations. Hiking, snowshoeing, cross-country skiing and fish feeding are offered. **Hours:** Grounds dawn-dusk. Hatchery daily 7-3:30. **Cost:** Free. **Phone:** (719) 486-0189.

THE MATCHLESS MINE CABIN is 1.2 mi. e. on E. 7th St. Sen. H.A.W. Tabor earned his wealth from the Matchless Mine in the 1880s but lost it when the repeal of the Sherman Purchase Act of 1893 dealt the final blow to his fortune. Legend says that on his deathbed in 1899 he instructed his second wife, Baby Doe, to "hang onto the Matchless." She did, living in poverty until her death in 1935. The museum has exhibits of Baby Doe memorabilia.

Hours: Daily 9-4, May-Sept.; by appointment, rest of year. **Cost:** $7; $6 (ages 63+); $3 (ages 6-11). Combination ticket with The National Mining Hall of Fame and Museum $10; $9 (ages 63+); $5 (ages 6-11). **Phone:** (719) 486-1229.

GEM **THE NATIONAL MINING HALL OF FAME AND MUSEUM,** 120 W. 9th St., is housed in a 70,000-square-foot Victorian school built during the 19th-century silver boom. It offers 17 exhibit rooms portraying the history of mining from the Bronze Age through the present.

Visitors may walk through a replicated underground hard rock mine complete with ore cars and drills. The Gold Rush Room exhibits gold samples, mining artifacts and dioramas depicting early prospecting days. Illuminated crystals from around the world are presented in the Crystal Room.

Murals and sculptures highlight historic mining developments. The Hall of Fame contains plaques honoring individuals who made significant contributions to the industry. **Time:** Allow 1 hour minimum. **Hours:** Daily 9-5, May-Oct.; 11-6, rest of year. **Cost:** $7; $6 (ages 65+); $5 (ages 13-18); $3 (ages 6-12). Combination ticket with The Matchless Mine Cabin $10; $9 (ages 65+); $8 (ages 13-18); $5 (ages 6-11). **Phone:** (719) 486-1229.

TABOR OPERA HOUSE, 308 Harrison Ave., opened in 1879. It retains the decor of its "last show," when miners spent huge sums to be entertained by celebrated New York and Chicago artists. A museum on the second floor features opera house memorabilia and traces area history. **Hours:** Mon.-Sat. 10-5, Memorial Day-Labor Day; by appointment rest of year. **Cost:** $5; $4 (military with ID); $2.50 (ages 6-13); free (ages 0-6). **Phone:** (719) 486-8409.

RECREATIONAL ACTIVITIES

Skiing

- **Ski Cooper** is 9 mi. n. of Leadville at 1101 Poplar St. **Hours:** Daily 9-4, mid-Dec. to mid-Apr. **Phone:** (719) 486-2277 or (800) 707-6114.

MCGINNIS COTTAGE INN BED & BREAKFAST

Phone: 719/486-3110

Historic Bed & Breakfast

$130-$160

Address: 809 Spruce St 80461 **Location:** Just w of US 24 and 8th St, then just n. **Facility:** Built in 1898, this painted lady near downtown features a cozy living room with a carved wood fireplace and a flat-screen TV. Guest rooms feature comfortable bedding and individually decorated rooms. 4 units. 3 stories (no elevator), interior/exterior corridors. **Parking:** street only. **Terms:** 15 day cancellation notice-fee imposed.

SUPER 8

Phone: (719)486-3637

Motel

$54-$112

Address: 1128 S Hwy 24 80461 **Location:** On US 24, 1 mi s. **Facility:** 58 units. 3 stories (no elevator), interior corridors. **Parking:** winter plug-ins. **Terms:** office hours 7 am-11 pm, cancellation fee imposed. **Activities:** sauna. **Free Special Amenities: expanded continental breakfast and high-speed Internet.**

SAVE CALL / SOME UNITS

WHERE TO EAT

QUINCY'S

Phone: 719/486-9765

Steak

$8-$17

AAA Inspector Notes: In an age when people feel overwhelmed by too many choices, Quincy's offers relief. On Friday and Saturday, it serves a prime rib dinner. The rest of the week is devoted to filet mignon. Although there's just one option, patrons know what to expect. Meals come with salad, baked potato and bread, and dessert options change nightly. A vegetarian lasagna also is offered. **Bar:** full bar. **Address:** 416 Harrison Ave 80461 **Location:** In historic town center. **Parking:** street only.

D CALL

TENNESSEE PASS CAFE

Phone: 719/486-8101

International

$6-$14

AAA Inspector Notes: The brightly painted cafe presents an eclectic menu that picks up on influences from Asia, Mexico, Italy and America. For a light meal, guests might try a flavorful salad or sandwich. Pizza, pasta, stir-fry and Mexican favorites make for a heartier stomach-filler. In summer, patrons head for the patio to enjoy the temperate Leadville weather while dining. **Bar:** full bar. **Address:** 222 Harrison Ave 80461 **Location:** South end of historic town center. **Parking:** street only.

B L D

ZICHITTELLA'S

Phone: 719/486-1298

Italian

$9-$15

AAA Inspector Notes: This family-owned restaurant offers traditional Italian fare in a relaxed atmosphere. **Bar:** full bar. **Address:** 422 Harrison Ave 80461 **Location:** In historic town center. **Parking:** street only.

L D

LIMON (D-5) pop. 1,880, elev. 5,365'

Limon was named after railroad crew boss John Limon. The town is rich in railroad history; the Union Pacific Railroad and Kyle Railroad in Phillipsburg, Kan., still use the railyards. Near downtown is the historic Smoky Hill Trail, established in the mid-1800s by gold prospectors seeking a quick route to the Rockies.

Limon Chamber of Commerce: 205 E Ave., P.O. Box 101, Limon, CO 80828. **Phone:** (719) 775-9418.

LIMON HERITAGE MUSEUM, 1 mi. w. of I-70 exit 361, then 2 blks. s. on E Ave., is housed in the restored Union Pacific and Rock Island depot, and an

▼ See AAA listing this page ▼

exhibit building featuring a two-room prairie house, a mercantile store, geology displays, a radar weather station, plows, wagons and an 11-foot-high bronze sculpture, "Prairie Odyssey." An extensive Native American collection is a major highlight of the museum. Five rail cars, including a restored dining car and caboose, contain permanent and changing exhibits about area history. **Time:** Allow 30 minutes minimum. **Hours:** Mon.-Sat. 1-8, Memorial Day-Labor Day. **Cost:** Free. **Phone:** (719) 775-8605. ***(See ad p. 240.)***

HOLIDAY INN EXPRESS HOTEL & SUITES
Phone: (719)775-9033

Hotel
$129-$199 5/1-10/31
$99-$159 11/1-4/30

Address: 803 Hwy 24 80828 **Location:** I-70 exit 359, just s. **Facility:** 69 units. 3 stories, interior corridors. **Terms:** check-in 4 pm. **Amenities:** high-speed Internet. **Pool(s):** heated indoor. **Activities:** whirlpool, exercise room. **Guest Services:** coin laundry.

CALL / SOME UNITS

LIMON COMFORT INN **Phone:** (719)775-2752

Hotel
$80-$150

Address: 2255 9th St 80828 **Location:** I-70 exit 359, just s. **Facility:** 50 units. 2 stories (no elevator), interior corridors. **Terms:** cancellation fee imposed. **Amenities:** high-speed Internet. **Pool(s):** heated indoor. **Activities:** whirlpool, limited exercise equipment. **Guest Services:** coin laundry. **Free Special Amenities: full breakfast and high-speed Internet.**

SAVE / SOME UNITS

SAFARI INN **Phone:** 719/775-2363

Motel
$48-$130 5/1-9/30
$45-$120 10/1-4/30

Address: 637 Main St 80828 **Location:** I-70 exit 361, 0.8 mi w. **Facility:** 28 units. 1-2 stories (no elevator), exterior corridors. **Parking:** winter plug-ins. **Pool(s):** heated outdoor. **Activities:** playground. **Guest Services:** coin laundry, area transportation-bus station. **Free Special Amenities: continental breakfast and high-speed Internet.**

SAVE   / SOME UNITS FEE

WHERE TO EAT

RUBY'S **Phone:** 719/775-9564

American
$4-$8

AAA Inspector Notes: Locals congregate in this cheerful eatery to enjoy comfort food and friendly conversation. Most of the tables are large, and patrons often share with other parties when it's busy. Menu items include hamburgers, sandwiches, steaks and even some Mexican dishes. **Address:** 197 E Ave 80828 **Location:** I-70 exit 361, 1.2 mi w, then just s. **Parking:** street only.

B L

LITTLETON (D-4) pop. 41,737, elev. 5,389'

• **Hotels p. 242 • Restaurants p. 243**
• **Hotels & Restaurants map & index p. 140**
• **Part of Denver area — see map p. 123**

On the southern edge of metropolitan Denver, Littleton was settled in the 1860s by farmers homesteading the fertile land along the South Platte River. The arrival of Martin Marietta Corp. in the late 1950s brought rapid growth and economic vitality to this small town.

The city's more than 1,477 acres of parks and open space afford opportunities for picnicking, fishing, hiking and biking. Chatfield State Park *(see Recreation Chart)*, a few miles south, is a popular summer recreation spot. Roxborough State Park offers scenic hiking trails that allow for cross-country skiing in winter, opportunities for wildlife viewing and a visitor center featuring historical and geological exhibits; pets are not permitted. Cyclists enjoy riding along the scenic Mary Carter Greenway, with the South Platte River flowing adjacent to the trail. Pedestrians can take a self-guiding walking tour of the historic downtown area with its charming Main Street.

The Columbine Memorial in Clement Park remembers the innocent victims of the 1999 shootings at nearby Columbine High School. It is configured around an inner Ring of Remembrance and an outer Ring of Healing, honoring all those whose lives were affected by the tragedy.

Western Welcome Week, held in mid-August, is an 11-day celebration that includes concerts, fireworks, a parade, an arts and crafts fair, fishing and sports competitions.

South Metro Denver Chamber of Commerce: 6840 S. University Blvd., Centennial, CO 80122. **Phone:** (303) 795-0142.

DENVER BOTANIC GARDENS AT CHATFIELD is at 8500 Deer Creek Canyon Rd. Encompassing 750 acres along Deer Creek, this preserve includes native flora and fauna, wetlands and several distinct ecosystems. A restored 19th-century ranch, farm and one-room schoolhouse also are presented. A children's play area includes a treehouse and water features. Nature trails afford views of native wildlife, including coyotes, deer and birds. The Corn Maze is a popular event held in September and October.

Time: Allow 30 minutes minimum. **Hours:** Daily 9-5; closed Jan. 1, Thanksgiving, day after Thanksgiving, Christmas Eve and Christmas. **Cost:** $5 per passenger vehicle. **Phone:** (303) 973-3705.

THE HUDSON GARDENS & EVENT CENTER is at 6115 S. Santa Fe Dr., 3 mi. n. of jct. SR 470 and US 85, or .5 mi. s. of Bowles Ave. The gardens' 30 acres offer beauty and tranquility, and its grounds feature a multitude of plants, trees and flowers that thrive in Colorado. The setting is complemented by ponds, sculpture, fountains, a miniature railroad and wildlife.

Seasonal events, educational forums and summer picnic concerts also are offered. **Hours:** Gardens Mon.-Sat. 9-5 (also Sun. 9-3, June-Aug.). **Cost:** May-Oct. $5; $3 (ages 60+); $2 (ages 3-12). Rest of year, free. **Phone:** (303) 797-8565.

LITTLETON MUSEUM is at 6028 S. Gallup St. The museum has a permanent gallery that tells the story of Littleton from its settlement days to the present, a gallery that displays traveling exhibitions, a gallery featuring fine arts and photographs, and a children's area with hands-on exhibits.

The 15-acre complex also has two living-history farms with costumed interpreters, historic buildings

(See map & index p. 140.)

furnished in period, livestock typical of the 19th century, gardens, a blacksmith shop, an 1860s schoolhouse and an icehouse. **Time:** Allow 1 hour minimum. **Hours:** Tues.-Fri. 8-5, Sat. 10-5, Sun. 1-5. Closed major holidays. **Cost:** Donations. **Phone:** (303) 795-3950.

RECREATIONAL ACTIVITIES

Hot Air Ballooning

- **Balloon Rides of the Rockies** meets and departs from Chatfield State Park. **Hours:** Flights depart at dawn (weather permitting). **Phone:** (866) 606-7433.
- **Colorado Balloon Rides** departs from Chatfield State Park, .5 mi. s. of SR 470 and Wadsworth Blvd. **Hours:** Flights depart daily at dawn (weather permitting). **Phone:** (303) 978-1813 or (866) 606-7433.

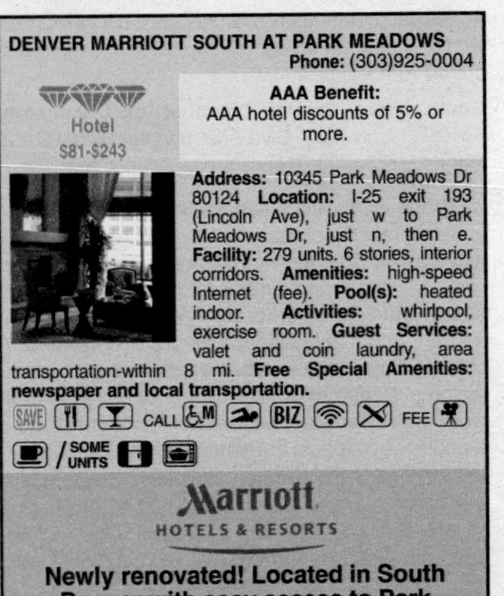

DENVER MARRIOTT SOUTH AT PARK MEADOWS
Phone: (303)925-0004

Hotel
$81-$243

AAA Benefit:
AAA hotel discounts of 5% or more.

Address: 10345 Park Meadows Dr 80124 **Location:** I-25 exit 193 (Lincoln Ave), just w to Park Meadows Dr, just n, then e. **Facility:** 279 units. 6 stories, interior corridors. **Amenities:** high-speed Internet (fee). **Pool(s):** heated indoor. **Activities:** whirlpool, exercise room. **Guest Services:** valet and coin laundry, area transportation-within 8 mi. **Free Special Amenities: newspaper and local transportation.**

SAVE CALL BIZ FEE / SOME UNITS

Marriott
HOTELS & RESORTS

Newly renovated! Located in South Denver with easy access to Park Meadows Mall.

HAMPTON INN & SUITES
Phone: (303)794-1800

Hotel
$69-$139

AAA Benefit:
Members save up to 10% everyday!

Address: 3095 W County Line Rd 80129 **Location:** SR C470 exit Santa Fe Dr, just n, then 0.3 mi e. **Facility:** 118 units. 7 stories, interior corridors. **Terms:** 1-7 night minimum stay, cancellation fee imposed. **Amenities:** high-speed Internet. **Pool(s):** heated indoor. **Activities:** whirlpool, exercise room. **Guest Services:** valet and coin laundry, area transportation-within 5 mi.

BIZ / SOME UNITS

HAMPTON INN & SUITES DENVER LITTLETON
Phone: (303)973-2400 111

Hotel
$79-$129

AAA Benefit:
Members save up to 10% everyday!

Address: 7611 Shaffer Pkwy 80127 **Location:** SR 470 exit Ken Caryl Ave, just e, then just s. **Facility:** 89 units. 4 stories, interior corridors. **Terms:** 1-7 night minimum stay, cancellation fee imposed. **Amenities:** video games (fee), high-speed Internet. **Pool(s):** heated indoor. **Activities:** whirlpool, exercise room. **Guest Services:** valet and coin laundry.

CALL BIZ FEE / SOME UNITS FEE

HOLIDAY INN EXPRESS HOTEL & SUITES
Phone: (720)981-1000 110

Hotel
$89-$119

Address: 12683 W Indore Pl 80127 **Location:** I-70 to SR 470 and Ken Caryl Ave; I-25 to SR 470 and Ken Caryl Ave, to Shaffer Ave, just n, then w. **Facility:** 76 units. 3 stories, interior corridors. **Amenities:** video games (fee). **Pool(s):** heated indoor. **Activities:** whirlpool, exercise room. **Guest Services:** valet and coin laundry. **Free Special Amenities: expanded continental breakfast and high-speed Internet.**

SAVE CALL BIZ FEE / SOME UNITS FEE

HOMEWOOD SUITES BY HILTON-DENVER LITTLETON
Phone: (720)981-4763 112

Extended Stay Hotel
$99-$299

HOMEWOOD SUITES Hilton

AAA Benefit:
Contemporary luxury at a special Member rate.

Address: 7630 Shaffer Pkwy 80127 **Location:** SR 470 exit Ken Caryl Ave, just e, then just s. **Facility:** 84 efficiencies, some two bedrooms. 4 stories, interior corridors. **Parking:** winter plug-ins. **Terms:** 1-7 night minimum stay, cancellation fee imposed. **Amenities:** high-speed Internet. **Pool(s):** heated indoor. **Activities:** whirlpool, sports court, exercise room. **Guest Services:** valet and coin laundry. **Free Special Amenities: full breakfast and manager's reception.**

SAVE CALL BIZ / SOME UNITS FEE

TOWNEPLACE SUITES BY MARRIOTT-LITTLETON DENVER SOUTHWEST
Phone: (303)972-0555

Extended Stay Hotel
$149-$164

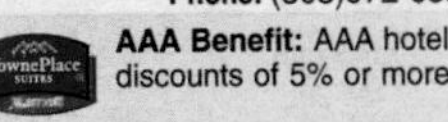

AAA Benefit: AAA hotel discounts of 5% or more.

Address: 10902 W Toller Dr 80127 **Location:** SR 470 exit Kipling Pkwy, just s then 0.4 mi w on Ute St. **Facility:** 99 kitchen units, some two bedrooms. 3 stories, interior corridors. **Parking:** winter plug-ins. **Amenities:** high-speed Internet. **Pool(s):** heated outdoor. **Activities:** exercise room. **Guest Services:** valet and coin laundry.

SAVE BIZ / SOME UNITS FEE

(See map & index p. 140.)

WHERE TO EAT

LIL' RICCI'S NY PIZZA **Phone:** 303/948-0274 (124)

Italian
$7-$13

AAA Inspector Notes: Although this restaurant offers a few pasta dishes, most patrons opt for the famous New York-style pizzas. The menu also features calzones, sandwiches and salads. This is the perfect place to stop for a slice and a brew after a long day. **Bar:** full bar. **Address:** 12652 W Ken Caryl Ave 80127 **Location:** SR 470 exit Ken Caryl Ave, just e, then just s; in strip mall.

L D

LUIGI'S ITALIAN RESTAURANT **Phone:** 303/694-9357

Italian
$8-$17

AAA Inspector Notes: This casual Italian eatery offers generous portions of traditional favorites. The diverse menu appeals to those seeking the comfort of ravioli or baked ziti, as well as those craving the sophistication of lamb osso buco or veal piccata. **Bar:** full bar. **Address:** 8130 S University Blvd 80122 **Location:** SR 470 exit University Blvd, just n. L D

NO NO'S CAFE **Phone:** 303/738-8330

American
$9-$18

AAA Inspector Notes: The cafe specializes in home-style Southern cooking, including lighter dishes and vegetarian selections for particular diets. People return for comfort foods such as shepherd's pie, gumbo and flank steak. Mayme's macaroni and cheese, which makes a delicious side dish or entree, exemplifies the menu items, which are credited to their actual creators. The all-year signature menu is complemented by features that change frequently. **Bar:** full bar. **Address:** 3005 W County Line Rd 80129 **Location:** SR 470 exit Santa Fe, just n, then just e.

B L D

OPUS RESTAURANT **Phone:** 303/703-6787 (122)

New Continental
$12-$35

AAA Inspector Notes: Located in the charming historic area of what was once Little Town, this upscale spot is worth seeking out. Chef Michael Long pairs innovative sauces with meat and seafood. The menu, featuring locally inspired ingredients, includes a Colorado lamb duo (petite rack in pomegranate glaze and a Guinness-braised shank). The yellowfin tuna served with spicy miso lobster broth, Asian pear kimchi relish and baby bok choy reflects international influences. The artisanal cheese plate is easily shared. **Bar:** full bar. **Reservations:** suggested. **Address:** 2575 W Main St 80120 **Location:** Just e of Santa Fe Dr; historic town center. **Parking:** street only. L D

ROMANO'S PIZZERIA **Phone:** 303/798-4944 (123)

Italian
$7-$15

AAA Inspector Notes: It's rare to find a restaurant that's been open for more than 40 years, not to mention owned and operated by the same family. There's a clear reason why the Romano family has been so successful; it's their friendly staff and flavorful Italian American dishes. The extensive menu features sandwiches, pizza and pasta dishes, including stuffed shells, ravioli, spaghetti, tortellini and more. The quaint storefront location hearkens back to a time before the town grew up around it. **Bar:** full bar. **Address:** 5655 S Windermere St 80123 **Location:** From jct Littleton Blvd, just n. **Parking:** on-site and street. L D

THAI BISTRO **Phone:** 720/981-7600 (121)

Thai
$8-$19

AAA Inspector Notes: Featuring robustly flavored recipes from southern Thailand, the restaurant has won numerous awards. Exotic herbs and spices help create unmistakable flavors. The restaurant's exterior is deceiving, as it belies the spacious, tranquil dining room inside. **Bar:** full bar. **Address:** 5924 S Kipling Pkwy, Unit G 80127 **Location:** US 285 exit Kipling Pkwy, 3.2 mi s.

L D

LONE TREE pop. 10,218

- **Restaurants p. 244**
- **Part of Denver area — see map p. 123**

ELEMENT DENVER PARK MEADOWS
Phone: (303)790-2100

Contemporary Hotel
$89-$199

AAA Benefit: Experience element, get up to 15% off + Starwood Preferred Guest® bonuses.

Address: 9985 Park Meadows Dr 80124 **Location:** SR 470 exit Yosemite St, just s, then 0.4 mi e. **Facility:** 123 units, some efficiencies. 4 stories, interior corridors. *Bath:* shower only. **Amenities:** high-speed Internet, safes. **Pool(s):** heated indoor. **Activities:** exercise room. **Guest Services:** valet and coin laundry, area transportation-within 5 mi. **Free Special Amenities: expanded continental breakfast and high-speed Internet.**

SAVE ECO BIZ

/ SOME UNITS

HYATT PLACE DENVER - SOUTH/PARK MEADOWS
Phone: (303)662-8500

Hotel
$79-$189

HYATT PLACE

AAA Benefit: Members save 10% or more everyday.

Address: 9030 E Westview Rd 80124 **Location:** I-25 exit 195 (County Line Rd), 0.5 mi w to Yosemite St, just s to Parkland Rd, then just w; SR 470 exit Yosemite St, 0.5 mi nw, just n on Parkland Rd, then just w. Adjacent to Park Meadows. **Facility:** 127 units. 6 stories, interior corridors. **Terms:** cancellation fee imposed. **Amenities:** safes. *Some:* high-speed Internet. **Pool(s):** heated indoor. **Activities:** exercise room. **Guest Services:** valet laundry, area transportation-within 5 mi. **Free Special Amenities: expanded continental breakfast and high-speed Internet.**

SAVE BIZ

STAYBRIDGE SUITES DENVER SOUTH-LONE TREE
Phone: (303)649-1010

Extended Stay Hotel
$79-$189

Address: 7820 Park Meadows Dr 80124 **Location:** I-25 exit 195 (County Line Rd), w to Acres Green Dr, s to E Park Meadows Dr, then just w; SR 470 exit Quebec St, just s, then just e. **Facility:** 115 efficiencies, some two bedrooms. 3 stories, interior corridors. **Terms:** cancellation fee imposed. **Amenities:** high-speed Internet. **Pool(s):** heated outdoor. **Activities:** sports court, exercise room. **Guest Services:** complimentary and valet laundry, area transportation-within 5 mi.

CALL BIZ

/ SOME UNITS FEE

WHERE TO EAT

CALIFORNIA CAFE **Phone:** 303/649-1111

American
$10-$25

AAA Inspector Notes: Executive chef Scott Hybbeneth takes inspiration from his travels to the Piedmont region of Italy and other areas of Europe. Using high-quality, seasonal ingredients, he creates appetizers such as crab cakes, steamed mussels, lamb lollipops and crispy chicken ginger spring rolls. Entrees feature scallops, Wagyu beef, salmon and Rocky Mountain trout. The menu should please those looking for a flavorful pizza or something more elaborate. The friendly service lacks pretension. **Bar:** full bar. **Reservations:** suggested. **Address:** 8505 Park Meadows Center Dr, Suite 2184 80124 **Location:** I-25 exit 195 (County Line Rd), just w, then s; at south end of Park Meadows Mall.

L D CALL

JOHN HOLLY'S ASIAN BISTRO **Phone:** 303/768-9088

Chinese
$6-$20

AAA Inspector Notes: This unpretentious yet alluring eatery serves an imaginative and tempting variety of Asian dishes. The dining area has a flair for casual elegance with its contemporary style and excellent service, while the streamlined sushi bar also offers seating. The creative menu appeals to discriminating palates. **Bar:** full bar. **Address:** 9232 Park Meadows Dr 80124 **Location:** I-25 exit 195 (County Line Rd), 0.5 mi w to Yosemite St, then s. L D

VIA BACI **Phone:** 303/790-0828

Italian
$8-$16

AAA Inspector Notes: Although well-known for its gourmet pizzas, this popular restaurant also offers flavorful pasta dishes such as pumpkin ravioli, chicken cavatappi and three-meat lasagna. In addition to pasta, patrons can choose from a list of sandwiches, salads and oven-fired meat entrees. The cheerful decor matches the personality of the friendly staff. **Bar:** full bar. **Address:** 10005 Commons St, Bldg A 80124 **Location:** I-25 exit 193, 0.7 mi w on E Lincoln Ave, then just s; in shopping complex. L D

LONGMONT (A-4) pop. 86,270, elev. 4,942'

Before Longmont was established at the foot of the Rocky Mountains, the area was the haunt of gold seekers, fur traders and adventurers. However, in the mid-19th century, Longmont—in the fertile St. Vrain River Valley—attracted a more stable type of pioneer. The farming community established in 1871 as the Chicago-Colorado Colony was named for Colorado explorer Maj. Steven H. Long, who explored the valley in 1820.

The Golden Rule Store was a Longmont retailer credited with launching JCPenney into the dry goods business; the name was changed accordingly in 1912. Today, the town is an important agricultural center, with sugar beets a chief crop. An appreciation of the arts has resulted in a growing collection of public art pieces placed around town. Outdoor recreational opportunities are plentiful and include hiking, bicycling, horseback riding, hot air balloon rides and skiing.

Longmont Area Visitors Association: 630 Coffman St., Longmont, CO 80501. **Phone:** (303) 776-9011.

LONGMONT MUSEUM & CULTURAL CENTER is 1 mi. s. on US 287, then e. to 400 Quail Rd. Regional history is exhibited in several galleries, including the Longs Peak Room, which offers panoramic views of the Rocky Mountains and Great Plains. Front Range Rising is an interactive exhibit that guides visitors through 14,000 years of area history featuring maps, re-created habitations and photographs.

A research archive is available. Special exhibits about art and history are offered. **Time:** Allow 1 hour minimum. **Hours:** Tues.-Sat. 9-5 (also Wed. 5-8), Sun. 1-5. **Cost:** Free. **Phone:** (303) 651-8374.

COURTYARD BY MARRIOTT BOULDER/LONGMONT **Phone:** (303)682-1166

Hotel
$95-$200

AAA Benefit: AAA hotel discounts of 5% or more.

Address: 1410 Dry Creek Dr 80503 **Location:** I-25 exit 235 (SR 52), 8 mi w to 95th (Hover Rd), 3.8 mi n to Clover Basin, just w, then s. **Facility:** 78 units. 3 stories, interior corridors. **Pool(s):** heated indoor. **Activities:** whirlpool, exercise room. **Guest Services:** valet and coin laundry.

CALL BIZ / SOME UNITS

HAMPTON INN **Phone:** (303)772-2554

Hotel
$92-$180

AAA Benefit: Members save up to 10% everyday!

Address: 850 S Main St 80501 **Location:** Just s of jct US 287 and Ken Pratt Blvd (SR 119). **Facility:** 62 units. 3 stories, interior corridors. **Terms:** 1-7 night minimum stay, cancellation fee imposed. **Amenities:** video games (fee). **Pool(s):** heated indoor. **Activities:** whirlpool, exercise room. **Guest Services:** valet and coin laundry.

BIZ FEE / SOME UNITS

HOLIDAY INN EXPRESS & SUITES **Phone:** (303)684-0404

Hotel
$133-$169 5/1-10/31
$133-$159 11/1-4/30

Address: 1355 Dry Creek Dr 80503 **Location:** Jct Main St and Ken Pratt Blvd (SR 119), 2.2 mi w, just n, then just ne. **Facility:** 75 units. 3 stories, interior corridors. **Amenities:** high-speed Internet. **Pool(s):** heated indoor. **Activities:** whirlpool, exercise room. **Guest Services:** valet and coin laundry.

BIZ / SOME UNITS FEE

PLAZA HOTEL LONGMONT **Phone:** (303)776-2000

Hotel
$100-$170

Address: 1900 Ken Pratt Blvd 80501 **Location:** Jct US 287, 1.3 mi sw on Ken Pratt Blvd (SR 119). **Facility:** 210 units. 2 stories, interior corridors. **Amenities:** video games (fee), safes. **Pool(s):** heated outdoor. **Activities:** sauna, exercise room. **Guest Services:** complimentary and valet laundry. **Free Special Amenities: full breakfast and high-speed Internet.**

SAVE BIZ FEE / SOME UNITS

RESIDENCE INN BY MARRIOTT BOULDER/LONGMONT

Phone: (303)702-9933

Extended Stay Hotel

$105-$210

AAA Benefit:
AAA hotel discounts of 5% or more.

Address: 1450 Dry Creek Dr 80503 **Location:** Jct Main St and Ken Pratt Blvd (SR 119), 2.2 mi w, just n, then just ne; jct Hoover Rd and SR 119. **Facility:** 84 units, some two bedrooms, efficiencies and kitchens. 3 stories, interior corridors. **Pool(s):** heated indoor. **Activities:** whirlpool, sports court, exercise room. **Guest Services:** valet and coin laundry.

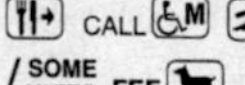

CALL BIZ / SOME UNITS FEE

SPRINGHILL SUITES BY MARRIOTT BOULDER/LONGMONT

Phone: (303)682-2894

Hotel

$95-$200

AAA Benefit:
AAA hotel discounts of 5% or more.

Address: 1470 Dry Creek Dr 80503 **Location:** Jct Ken Pratt Blvd (SR 119) and Hover Rd, just n to Clover Basin Dr, then just w to Dry Creek Dr. **Facility:** 90 units. 3 stories, interior corridors. **Amenities:** video games (fee). **Pool(s):** heated indoor. **Activities:** whirlpool, exercise room. **Guest Services:** valet and coin laundry.

CALL BIZ FEE

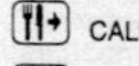

SUPER 8 TWIN PEAKS, LONGMONT

Phone: (303)772-8106

Hotel

$57-$89

Address: 2446 N Main St 80501 **Location:** I-25 exit 240, 6.9 mi w to US 287, then 3.5 mi n; jct SR 66. **Facility:** 64 units. 2 stories (no elevator), interior corridors. **Terms:** cancellation fee imposed. **Amenities:** safes (fee). **Guest Services:** coin laundry. **Free Special Amenities: expanded continental breakfast and high-speed Internet.**

SAVE / SOME UNITS FEE

WHERE TO EAT

3 MARGARITAS

Phone: 303/682-0888

Mexican

$4-$17

AAA Inspector Notes: This family-owned place is part of a popular local chain. The menu features a variety of burritos, enchiladas and fajitas, as well as more creative items such as steak tampiquena, pollo culichi and camarones jarochos. Patrons wash down their food with one of the many specialty margaritas. **Bar:** full bar. **Address:** 2350 Main St 80501 **Location:** 2.5 mi n on US 287 at SR 66. L D

FLAVOR OF INDIA

Phone: 303/682-9010

Indian

$9-$26

AAA Inspector Notes: In addition to the buffet, patrons may order off an extensive menu that includes traditional Indian dishes featuring lamb, chicken, vegetables and seafood. The paneer pakoras and vegetable samosas are popular appetizers. There are a variety of naan breads to choose from, ranging from garlic to dried fruit and nuts. **Bar:** full bar. **Address:** 516 Main St 80501 **Location:** Jct US 287 and Ken Pratt Blvd (SR 119), 1 mi n. **Parking:** street only. L D

MARTINI'S BISTRO

Phone: 303/651-2772

American

$9-$19

AAA Inspector Notes: Although I went for lunch, I could see myself grabbing some friends for nighttime martinis at the small, swanky bar or outside on the wicker patio furniture. The bruschetta was quite good. It was served not in the traditional way but more like a tomato, basil, mozzarella salsa with a side of grilled bread soaked in garlic-infused olive oil. I also had the sea of hearts, a take on shrimp scampi. The white wine lobster butter sauce was as good as it sounds and one of the lighter pasta sauces. **Bar:** full bar. **Address:** 543 Terry St 80501 **Location:** Just w of US 287 on 3rd St, then 0.3 mi n. **Parking:** street only.

L D

MIKE O'SHAYS RESTAURANT & ALE HOUSE

Phone: 303/772-0252

American

$8-$20

AAA Inspector Notes: Patrons don't have to be Irish to appreciate the good food and pub atmosphere of this local favorite. The diversified menu includes salads, sandwiches, fresh fish, scampi and pasta entrées. A city parking lot is in the back. **Bar:** full bar. **Address:** 512 Main St 80501 **Location:** Just n on US 287; downtown. **Parking:** street only. L D LATE

THE RIB HOUSE BY CHEF EXTRAORDINAIRE

Phone: 303/485-6988

Barbecue

$4-$23

AAA Inspector Notes: Located in "New Town Prospect" (which is worth seeing as it looks like a set from a Disney movie), this barbecue restaurant is worth finding. It features Kansas City-style 'que with pork, brisket, chicken, links and smoked turkey. But the ribs are what live up to the menu's claim of "the best baby back ribs in Colorado" as they are smoked for 12 hours and are tender, lean and delicious. **Bar:** wine only. **Address:** 1920 S Coffman St 80504 **Location:** Jct Ken Pratt Blvd (SR 119) and US 287, 1 mi s on US 287 to Pike Rd, 0.3 mi w to Coffman St, then s. **Parking:** on-site and street. L D

SUGARBEET

Phone: 303/651-3330

American

$22-$27

AAA Inspector Notes: In a quiet warehouse area close to the historic part of town, this restaurant quickly fills up at night. Chef/owner Seth Witherspoon prefers to work with local ranchers, dairies and farmers, which means the menu features fresh, seasonal ingredients. Knowledgeable staff members, artwork from local artists and a relaxed atmosphere complement the meal. **Bar:** full bar. **Reservations:** suggested. **Address:** 101 Pratt St, Unit A 80501 **Location:** Jct Ken Pratt Blvd (SR 119) and Main St, just n to 2nd Ave, just w, then just s. D

SUSHI HANA

Phone: 303/485-1055

Japanese

$9-$30

AAA Inspector Notes: Although the building formerly housed a fast-food joint, the remodeled inside leaves little trace of Sushi Hana's previous incarnation. As the name implies, the menu consists of many sushi and sashimi dishes. Tempura, noodle and teriyaki entrées also are offered. I especially enjoyed the panko-crusted fried oysters. The salmon sushi was competently executed. I was less impressed by the Kobe beef sushi, as it was on the tough side and hard to chew. This made me suspect it wasn't Kobe beef. **Bar:** full bar. **Address:** 2065 Main St 80501 **Location:** 2.2 mi n on US 287 at SR 66. L D

TERROIR Phone: 303/651-0630

American

$16-$25

AAA Inspector Notes: Owners Timothy Payne and Melissa Newell bring their extensive wine and culinary knowledge to the table at this popular, intimate restaurant. The weekly changing menu focuses on local, organic and seasonal ingredients. Pork, beef, duck and vegetable entrees are creatively prepared with flavorful sauces. Knowledgeable servers provide the perfect wine pairing for every course. **Bar:** full bar. **Address:** 246 Main St 80501 **Location:** Jct Ken Pratt Blvd (SR 119), just n. **Parking:** street only. D

LOUISVILLE (B-4) pop. 18,376, elev. 5,394'

Although a statue of a miner outside City Hall pays tribute to the coal industry that Louisville was built upon, all traces of the mines have vanished and high-tech and health care now fuel the economy. Situated just east of Boulder and a half-hour from Denver, Louisville embodies small-town charm and is graced with a backdrop of majestic peaks looming in the distance.

The downtown area's rustic early 1900s buildings along Main and Front streets house pubs, thrift stores, boutiques and eateries with a family-friendly vibe, like the occasional ice cream parlor or sandwich shop. During summer Saturdays, a farmer's market takes place on Front and Walnut streets from 9-2; in addition to fresh produce, meats and baked goods, vendors tout such specialty items as chiles, Colorado wildflowers and homemade tamales.

Summer evenings bring the Downtown Street Faire, which runs from 5 to 9. Music, food, arts and crafts displays, fun activities for the kids, and a beer and wine garden are all part of the agenda at this free event. And there's a strong sense of community during winter, too, as the WinterSkate—an old-time ice skating rink—swings into action with the onset of the holidays, when traditional tunes entertain those gliding across the ice.

Louisville holds allure for the outdoor enthusiast, with Estes Park—the gateway to Rocky Mountain National Park—just over an hour's drive and the ski resorts of Summit County about 2 hours away. Coal Creek Golf Course, 585 W. Dillon Rd., offers 18 holes along with spectacular views of the Rockies; phone (303) 666-7888. Cyclists like to follow Coal Creek Trail, a diverse 7-mile trek extending from the golf course to Lafayette that travels through open spaces, cottonwood groves, ranch land and neighborhoods. The area is blessed with an abundance of biking and hiking trails, with most routes originating in nearby Boulder.

Louisville Chamber of Commerce: 901 Main St., Louisville, CO 80027. **Phone:** (303) 666-5747.

LOUISVILLE HISTORICAL MUSEUM is at 1001 Main St. Two historic buildings constructed between 1904 and 1908 feature artifacts and historic photographs reflecting the area's coal mining heritage. The Tomeo House is representative of a coal miner's home during the town's mining heyday. **Time:** Allow 30 minutes minimum. **Hours:** Wed. and first Sat. of month 10-3; other times by appointment. Closed major holidays. **Cost:** Free. **Phone:** (303) 665-9048.

BEST WESTERN PLUS LOUISVILLE INN & SUITES Phone: 303/327-1215

Hotel

Rates not provided

AAA Benefit: Members save up to 20%, plus 10% bonus points with Best Western Rewards®.

Address: 960 W Dillon Rd 80027 **Location:** US 36 (Boulder Tpke) exit Superior (SR 170), just n on McCaslin Blvd to Dillon Rd, then just e. **Facility:** 61 units, some cabins. 2 stories, interior corridors. **Amenities:** safes. **Pool(s):** heated outdoor. **Activities:** whirlpool, exercise room. **Guest Services:** valet and coin laundry. **Free Special Amenities: full breakfast and high-speed Internet.**

SAVE BIZ FEE

/ SOME UNITS FEE

HAMPTON INN BOULDER/LOUISVILLE Phone: (303)666-7700

Hotel

$89-$150

AAA Benefit: Members save up to 10% everyday!

Address: 912 W Dillon Rd 80027 **Location:** US 36 (Boulder Tpke) exit Superior (SR 170), ne on McCaslin Blvd, then e. **Facility:** 80 units. 3 stories, interior corridors. **Terms:** 1-7 night minimum stay, cancellation fee imposed. **Amenities:** video games (fee). **Pool(s):** heated indoor. **Activities:** whirlpool, exercise room. **Guest Services:** valet and coin laundry.

CALL BIZ FEE

QUALITY INN IN BOULDER COUNTY Phone: (303)604-0181

Hotel

$59-$159

Address: 1196 Dillon Rd 80027 **Location:** US 36 (Boulder Tpke) exit Superior (SR 170), just n on McCaslin Blvd, then just w. Located next to cinemas. **Facility:** 68 units. 2 stories, interior corridors. **Terms:** cancellation fee imposed. **Activities:** exercise room. **Guest Services:** valet and coin laundry.

CALL BIZ

/ SOME UNITS FEE

RESIDENCE INN BY MARRIOTT-BOULDER/LOUISVILLE Phone: (303)665-2661

Extended Stay Hotel

$100-$200

AAA Benefit: AAA hotel discounts of 5% or more.

Address: 845 Coal Creek Cir 80027 **Location:** US 36 (Boulder Tpke) exit Superior (SR 170), n on McCaslin Blvd to Dillon Rd, then 0.6 mi e. **Facility:** 88 units, some two bedrooms, efficiencies and kitchens. 2 stories, interior corridors. **Amenities:** video games (fee). **Pool(s):** heated indoor. **Activities:** whirlpool, jogging, sports court, exercise room. **Guest Services:** valet and coin laundry.

CALL BIZ FEE

/ SOME UNITS FEE

WHERE TO EAT

THE HUCKLEBERRY **Phone:** 303/666-8020

American

$8-$15

AAA Inspector Notes: This cheerfully decorated restaurant is located in a building built in the late 1800s. Tea lovers will appreciate the extensive beverage menu and the traditional British afternoon tea service. Scrumptious breakfasts, innovative sandwiches and hearty entrees dominate the menu. The decadent, house-made desserts are a real treat. **Bar:** full bar. **Address:** 700 Main St 80027 **Location:** Corner of Pine and Main sts; in historic downtown. **Parking:** street only. B L D

LOVELAND (A-4) pop. 66,859, elev. 4,982'

• **Restaurants p. 248**

Hundreds of thousands of valentines from around the world are sent to Loveland each year to be hand-stamped by volunteers with the town's postmark and a special poem, which changes annually, and then re-mailed in February from the Sweetheart City.

The town, nestled in the valley at the mouth of Big Thompson Canyon, was named for W.A.H. Loveland, who supervised the building of the Colorado Central Railroad through the valley in 1877. Many who did not strike it rich in the gold fields struck it rich selling vegetables grown in this fertile area. Rocky Mountain National Park *(see place listing p. 276)* is 30 miles west of Loveland.

Several lakes and reservoirs offer water sports. Golf, hiking, bicycling, camping and horseback riding also are popular pastimes. Boyd Lake State Recreation Area *(see Recreation Chart)* is 2 miles east.

Loveland Chamber of Commerce and Visitors Center: 5400 Stone Creek Cir., Loveland, CO 80538. **Phone:** (970) 667-6311 or (800) 258-1278.

DESIGNS BY RICKER MUSEUM/SHOWROOM, 6868 N. Franklin Ave., features pewter castings by noted artist and sculptor Michael Anthony Ricker. Staff members provide a detailed tour of the showroom and museum, explaining the process of how the pewter figures are made and giving information about the creations. **Time:** Allow 30 minutes minimum. **Hours:** Mon.-Fri. 8-5:30, Sat. 10-2. Closed Jan. 1, Memorial Day, July 4, Labor Day, Thanksgiving and Christmas. **Cost:** Free. **Phone:** (970) 593-6950 or (800) 373-9837.

LOVELAND MUSEUM/GALLERY, 503 N. Lincoln Ave. at Fifth St., contains exhibits relating to town history, including a 40- by 50-foot topographic map of the Colorado-Big Thompson water project and a display about Loveland's Great Western Sugar Factory. Objects from the museum's historical collection and private collections are displayed in the Fireside Gallery, and works by regional, national and international artists are exhibited in the art galleries.

Special events take place throughout the year. **Time:** Allow 30 minutes minimum. **Hours:** Tues.-Fri. 10-5 (also Thurs. 5-7), Sat. 10-4, Sun. noon-4. **Cost:** Free. **Phone:** (970) 962-2410.

RECREATIONAL ACTIVITIES

Horseback Riding

- **Sylvan Dale Guest Ranch** is off US 34 at 2939 N. CR 31-D. Other activities are offered. **Hours:** Daily 9-4:30 (weather permitting). **Phone:** (970) 667-3915 or (877) 667-3999.

BEST WESTERN PLUS CROSSROADS INN & CONFERENCE CENTER **Phone:** (970)667-7810

Hotel

$80-$200

AAA Benefit: Members save up to 20%, plus 10% bonus points with Best Western Rewards®.

Address: 5542 E US Hwy 34 80537 **Location:** I-25 exit 257B, just w. **Facility:** 89 units, some kitchens. 2 stories (no elevator), interior/exterior corridors. **Terms:** cancellation fee imposed. **Amenities:** high-speed Internet. **Pool(s):** heated outdoor. **Guest Services:** valet and coin laundry. **Free Special Amenities: expanded continental breakfast and high-speed Internet.**

/ SOME UNITS FEE

COMFORT INN **Phone:** (970)593-0100

Hotel

$90-$140

Address: 1500 N Cheyenne Ave 80538 **Location:** I-25 exit 257B, 3 mi w on US 34. **Facility:** 62 units. 3 stories, interior corridors. **Terms:** cancellation fee imposed. **Amenities:** safes (fee). **Pool(s):** heated indoor. **Activities:** whirlpool, exercise room. **Guest Services:** valet and coin laundry.

CALL BIZ

EMBASSY SUITES LOVELAND **Phone:** (970)593-6200

Hotel

$129-$159

AAA Benefit: Members save 5% or more everyday!

Address: 4705 Clydesdale Pkwy 80538 **Location:** I-25 exit 259, just e, then just n. **Facility:** 263 units. 8 stories, interior corridors. **Terms:** 1-7 night minimum stay, cancellation fee imposed. **Amenities:** high-speed Internet (fee), safes. **Pool(s):** heated indoor. **Activities:** whirlpool, exercise room, spa. *Fee:* steamrooms. **Guest Services:** valet and coin laundry, area transportation-within 5 mi.

/ SOME UNITS FEE

FAIRFIELD INN & SUITES - LOVELAND/FORT COLLINS **Phone:** (970)461-1000

Hotel

$149-$164

AAA Benefit: AAA hotel discounts of 5% or more.

Address: 1710 Foxtrail Dr 80538 **Location:** I-25 exit 257B, 0.5 mi to outlet mall entry, just n, then just e. **Facility:** 82 units. 3 stories, interior corridors. **Pool(s):** heated indoor. **Activities:** whirlpool, exercise room. **Guest Services:** valet and coin laundry.

CALL BIZ FEE

/ SOME UNITS

HAMPTON INN LOVELAND **Phone:** (970)593-1400

Hotel

$139-$169

AAA Benefit:
Members save up to 10% everyday!

Address: 5500 Stone Creek Cir 80538 **Location:** I-25 exit 257B, 0.5 mi to outlet mall entry, just n, then just e. **Facility:** 80 units. 3 stories, interior corridors. **Terms:** 1-7 night minimum stay, cancellation fee imposed. **Amenities:** video games (fee). *Some:* high-speed Internet. **Pool(s):** heated indoor. **Activities:** whirlpool, exercise room. **Guest Services:** valet and coin laundry.

CALL BIZ FEE

LA QUINTA INN & SUITES LOVELAND **Phone:** (970)622-8600

Hotel

$116-$179 5/1-10/31
$79-$109 11/1-4/30

Address: 1450 Cascade Ave 80538 **Location:** I-25 exit 257B, 7.3 mi w. **Facility:** 69 units. 3 stories, interior corridors. **Amenities:** high-speed Internet. **Pool(s):** heated indoor. **Activities:** whirlpool, exercise room. **Guest Services:** valet and coin laundry.

BIZ / SOME UNITS

RESIDENCE INN BY MARRIOTT LOVELAND **Phone:** (970)622-7000

Extended Stay Hotel

$149-$164

AAA Benefit:
AAA hotel discounts of 5% or more.

Address: 5450 McWhinney Blvd 80538 **Location:** I-25 exit 257B, 0.5 mi w to outlet mall entry, just n, then just e. **Facility:** 103 kitchen units, some two bedrooms. 3 stories, interior corridors. **Amenities:** high-speed Internet. **Pool(s):** heated indoor. **Activities:** whirlpool, sports court, exercise room. **Guest Services:** valet and coin laundry.

BIZ FEE / SOME UNITS FEE

WHERE TO EAT

3 MARGARITAS **Phone:** 970/669-4441

Mexican

$7-$16

AAA Inspector Notes: This family-owned place is part of a popular local chain. The menu features a variety of burritos, enchiladas and fajitas, as well as more creative items such as steak tampiquena, pollo culichi and camarones jarochos. Patrons wash down their food with one of the many specialty margaritas. **Bar:** full bar. **Address:** 1417 Cheyenne Ave 80538 **Location:** I-25 exit 257B, 3 mi w. L D

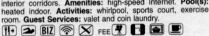

THE BLACK STEER **Phone:** 970/667-6679

Steak

$6-$25

AAA Inspector Notes: Pleasing locals since 1966, the downtown eatery employs friendly servers. The rustic, Western atmosphere incorporates supper club touches. On the menu are traditional appetizers, soups, salads, burgers, chicken, steaks and seafood. **Bar:** full bar. **Address:** 436 N Lincoln Ave 80537 **Location:** Jct US 287 and 34, 0.8 mi s on Cleveland Ave, just e, then just n. L D

BOHEMIAN COTTAGE **Phone:** 970/667-3718

Czechoslovakian

$17-$22

AAA Inspector Notes: The charming cottage has walls covered in art, postcards, stuffed animal heads and artifacts from Central Europe. The chef/owner freshly prepares each dish, and the classic presentations are hearty and tasteful. It's open for lunch on Sundays. **Bar:** full bar. **Address:** 8039 W Hwy 34 80537 **Location:** Jct US 287, 6.8 mi w. D

LOVELAND BREAKFAST CLUB **Phone:** 970/461-1261

American

$5-$8

AAA Inspector Notes: Hearty breakfasts served all day, a friendly waitstaff and a cheerful atmosphere have earned this casual eatery a devoted local following. The extensive breakfast options leave little out. Patrons can fill up on omelets, steak, eggs Benedict, pancakes, waffles, breakfast burritos and much more. A variety of sandwiches, burgers and burritos also are offered. Senior and kids menus are available. **Bar:** wine only. **Address:** 1451 N Boise Ave 80538 **Location:** I-25 exit 257B, 3.1 mi w on US 34, then just n. B L

MCGRAFF'S AMERICAN GRILL **Phone:** 970/669-8847

American

$7-$17

AAA Inspector Notes: Although the dining room is large, it maintains a warm, friendly feel. Pleasant staffers assist with meals ranging from grilled steak and tender ribs to such comfort foods as meatloaf. **Bar:** full bar. **Address:** 1602 E Eisenhower Blvd 80537 **Location:** I-25 exit 257B, 3.1 mi w. L D

LYONS (A-4) pop. 2,033, elev. 5,362'

LYONS REDSTONE MUSEUM, 1 blk. n. of US 36 and SR 66 on 3rd Ave., then 1 blk. w. to 340 High St. in the town's 1881 schoolhouse, contains local artifacts, photographs and memorabilia. Brochures are available for a driving tour of the historic district. **Time:** Allow 30 minutes minimum. **Hours:** Mon.-Sat. 9:30-4:30, Sun. 12:30-4:30, June-Oct.; by appointment rest of year. **Cost:** Donations. **Phone:** (303) 823-5271 or (303) 823-6692.

MANASSA (F-3) pop. 991, elev. 7,683'

THE JACK DEMPSEY MUSEUM, 3 mi. e. of US 285 on SR 142 at 412 Main St., is in the restored home of Jack Dempsey, who earned worldwide fame after winning the 1919 heavyweight boxing championship. Photographs and other memorabilia depicting his life and boxing career are displayed. **Time:** Allow 30 minutes minimum. **Hours:** Tues.-Sat. 9-5, Memorial Day weekend-Labor Day. **Cost:** Free. **Phone:** (719) 843-5207 (town hall).

MANCOS pop. 1,336

MESA VERDE MOTEL **Phone:** 970/533-7741

Motel

$55-$108

Address: 191 W Railroad Ave 81328 **Location:** On US 160 at SR 184; 7 mi e of Mesa Verde National Park entrance. **Facility:** 16 units, some two bedrooms. 1 story, exterior corridors. **Terms:** 3 day cancellation notice. **Activities:** whirlpool. **Free Special Amenities:** early check-in/late check-out and high-speed Internet.

SAVE / SOME UNITS FEE

MANITOU SPRINGS (D-4) pop. 4,992, elev. 6,320'

- **Restaurants p. 251**
- **Attractions map p. 89**
- **Hotels & Restaurants map & index p. 94**
- **Part of Colorado Springs area — see map p. 85**

Sitting at the foot of Pikes Peak, Manitou Springs is perhaps best known for the naturally carbonated mineral springs that bubble from the earth. Acknowledging the source of the curative power of the mineral waters, American Indians named the springs for the Great Spirit Manitou.

Dr. William Bell, an English physician who was convinced that the springs provided "miracle cures," envisioned spas that rivaled those in Europe. He encouraged health seekers, many suffering from consumption, to drink the waters and his patients did, indeed, recover. Little did he or his patients realize, however, that the reason for their cures had more to do with the dry mountain air than the water. Nonetheless, the springs made Manitou a leading spa area and contributed greatly to the successful development of Colorado Springs.

Behind the mineral springs, resort developments and vacation attractions, quaint houses and narrow lanes clamber up the steep hillsides. The town retains an art-colony atmosphere while serving thousands of vacationers each year.

Although once a "summer-only" vacation destination, Manitou Springs draws visitors year-round. The historic district offers numerous shops, eateries and art galleries. Special events include the Pikes Peak International Auto Hill Climb race held in July; the race begins west of Manitou Springs. Halloween weekend the town celebrates with the Emma Crawford Memorial Coffin Races and Festival.

Manitou Springs Chamber of Commerce and Visitors Bureau: 354 Manitou Ave., Manitou Springs, CO 80829. **Phone:** (877) 626-4808.

GEM **CAVE OF THE WINDS,** 6 mi. w. of I-25 exit 141 on US 24, offers cave tours through lighted chambers. On the Discovery Tour, a half-mile walking tour, visitors see chambers containing stalactites, stalagmites, helictites and other natural cave formations. On the Lantern Tour visitors light their own way with handheld candle lanterns while guides tell tales of early cave exploration, ghosts and the history of the cave's first owners. Cave temperature is 54 F; jackets are recommended.

Food is available in summer. **Hours:** Daily 9-9, Memorial Day-Labor Day; 10-5, rest of year. Closed Christmas. Phone ahead to confirm schedule. **Cost:** Discovery Tour $18; $14 (military with ID); $9 (ages 6-11). Lantern Tour $24; $20 (military with ID); $14 (ages 6-11); $11 (children of the military). Ages 5 and under are not permitted on the Lantern Tour. **Phone:** (719) 685-5444.

MANITOU CLIFF DWELLINGS is w. on US 24 bypass above Manitou Springs. These dwellings, built in Southern Colorado during the Great Pueblo Period, A.D. 1100-1300, depict the lives, culture and architectural achievements of Southwestern American Indians. The ruins were moved to this site in 1892 in an effort to preserve them. Two museums feature artifacts and exhibits. American Indian dances are performed daily June through August. **Hours:** Daily 9-6, May-Sept.; 9-5, Mar.-Apr. and Oct.-Nov.; 10-4, rest of year. Closed Thanksgiving and Christmas. **Cost:** $9.50; $8.50 (ages 60+); $7.50 (ages 7-11). **Phone:** (719) 685-5242 or (800) 354-9971.

MIRAMONT CASTLE is at 9 Capitol Hill Ave. off Ruxton Ave. Nine types of architecture are incorporated into the design of the 46-room mansion. Built of now-rare hand-quarried greenstone into a mountainside in 1895, it "stair-steps" up the mountain with the front door on the first level and the rear door on the fourth. Victorian gardens, a 16-sided room and a tearoom offering lunch and afternoon tea by reservation are featured.

Hours: Daily 9-5, Memorial Day weekend-Labor Day; Tues.-Sun. 10-4, rest of year. **Cost:** $8; $7 (ages 60+); $2 (ages 6-15); free (active military with ID). **Phone:** (719) 685-1011, (719) 884-4109 for the tea room or (888) 685-1011.

PIKES PEAK—see Pikes Peak and Pike National Forest p. 269.

PIKES PEAK COG RAILWAY leaves from 515 Ruxton Ave. and runs to the summit of Pikes Peak. On a clear day Denver is visible 75 miles to the north, and the Sangre de Cristo Mountains in southern Colorado and New Mexico can be seen on the horizon 100 miles away. During the ride to the top, visitors view cascading streams, aspen and pine forests, and one of the state's largest herds of bighorn sheep.

Note: Distinct altitude and temperature changes from base to peak may cause discomfort for persons with heart or respiratory problems, and for infants under 3 months. Wear warm clothing as temperatures at the 14,100-foot summit are approximately 30 degrees colder than at the base. **Time:** Allow 3 hours, 30 minutes minimum. **Hours:** Train operates year-round, with daily departure times varying; phone ahead. **Cost:** Fare $33; $18 (ages 3-12). Fares may vary; phone ahead. Reservations are required. **Phone:** (719) 685-5401 or (800) 745-3773.

AMERICAS BEST VALUE INN VILLA MOTEL

Phone: (719)685-5492 57

Motel
$77-$129

Address: 481 Manitou Ave 80829 **Location:** I-25 exit 141, 4 mi w on US 24, then 0.8 mi sw on US 24 business route. Opposite Memorial Park. **Facility:** 47 units, some efficiencies. 1-2 stories (no elevator), exterior corridors. **Terms:** office hours 8 am-9 pm. **Amenities:** high-speed Internet. **Pool(s):** heated outdoor. **Activities:** whirlpool. **Guest Services:** coin laundry. **Free Special Amenities: continental breakfast and high-speed Internet.**

SAVE / SOME UNITS

(See map & index p. 94.)

BED AND BREAKFAST AT HISTORIC ONALEDGE

Phone: (719)685-4515 53

Bed & Breakfast

$100-$200 5/1-10/31
$100-$175 11/1-4/30

Address: 336 El Paso Blvd 80829 **Location:** I-25 exit 141, 4 mi w on US 24, just sw on US 24 business route, just w on Garden of the Gods Pl, then just s. **Facility:** The large Arts and Crafts Tudor Revival mansion has an English lodge feel, thanks to hardwood floors, a copper fireplace hood, wall tapestries and plush red velvet furnishings. 6 units. 3 stories (no elevator), interior corridors. **Terms:** office hours 7 am-6 pm, 2 night minimum stay - seasonal and/or weekends, 14 day cancellation notice-fee imposed. **Activities:** whirlpool, bicycles, hiking trails. *Fee:* massage. / SOME UNITS

BEST WESTERN SKY WAY INN & SUITES

Phone: (719)685-5991 63

Hotel

$89-$139

AAA Benefit: Members save up to 20%, plus 10% bonus points with Best Western Rewards®.

Address: 311 Manitou Ave 80829 **Location:** I-25 exit 141, 4 mi w on US 24, then just sw. **Facility:** 38 units. 2 stories (no elevator), exterior corridors. **Terms:** open 5/1-11/1 & 3/1-4/30. **Amenities:** *Some:* high-speed Internet. **Pool(s):** heated indoor. **Activities:** whirlpool. **Guest Services:** coin laundry. **Free Special Amenities: local telephone calls and high-speed Internet.**

SAVE BIZ / SOME UNITS

THE CLIFF HOUSE AT PIKES PEAK

Phone: (719)685-3000 52

Historic Country Inn

$117-$370 5/1-10/31
$100-$234 11/1-4/30

Address: 306 Canon Ave 80829 **Location:** I-25 exit 141, 4 mi w on US 24, 1.2 mi sw on US 24 business route/Manitou Ave, then just w. Opposite post office. **Facility:** Antique furnishings, reproductions and soft colors help create an atmosphere of elegance at this country inn, where Clark Gable was once a guest. 54 units. 5 stories, interior corridors. **Parking:** valet only. **Terms:** cancellation fee imposed. **Amenities:** high-speed Internet, safes. **Dining:** The Cliff House Dining Room, see separate listing. **Activities:** rental bicycles, hiking trails, exercise room. *Fee:* massage. **Guest Services:** valet laundry, area transportation (fee)-within 10 mi. **Free Special Amenities: expanded continental breakfast and high-speed Internet.**

COMFORT INN

Phone: (719)685-5455 61

Hotel

$89-$149

Address: 45 Manitou Ave 80829 **Location:** I-25 exit 141, 4 mi w on US 24 to Manitou Ave, then just e. **Facility:** 46 units. 2 stories, interior corridors. **Terms:** 3 day cancellation notice-fee imposed. **Amenities:** high-speed Internet. **Pool(s):** heated indoor. **Activities:** whirlpool. **Guest Services:** coin laundry. BIZ

EAGLE MOTEL

Phone: (719)685-5467 58

Motel

$64-$89

Address: 423 Manitou Ave 80829 **Location:** I-25 exit 141, 4 mi w, then 0.5 mi w on US 24 business route. **Facility:** 25 units. 1-2 stories (no elevator), exterior corridors. **Terms:** open 5/1-10/12, office hours 7 am-10 pm, cancellation fee imposed. **Activities:** whirlpool.

/ SOME UNITS FEE FEE

EL COLORADO LODGE

Phone: (719)685-5485 64

Historic Cabin

$90-$175 5/1-9/8
$56-$153 9/9-4/30

Address: 23 Manitou Ave 80829 **Location:** I-25 exit 141, 4 mi w on US 24, then just ne on US 24 business route. **Facility:** This historic 1926 property features Santa Fe decor, and various on-site activities and a modern meeting room make it a great spot for a family reunion. 27 cabins. 1 story, exterior corridors. **Terms:** office hours 9 am-9 pm, 14 day cancellation notice-fee imposed. **Amenities:** high-speed Internet. **Pool(s):** heated outdoor. **Activities:** whirlpool, playground, basketball, horseshoes, shuffleboard, volleyball. **Free Special Amenities: local telephone calls and high-speed Internet.**

SAVE / SOME UNITS FEE

PARK ROW LODGE

Phone: (719)685-5216 60

Motel

$59-$89 5/1-10/1
$49-$69 10/2-4/30

Address: 54 Manitou Ave 80829 **Location:** I-25 exit 141, 4 mi w on US 24, then just ne on US 24 business route. **Facility:** 20 units, some kitchens and cottages. 1 story, exterior corridors. **Terms:** office hours 7 am-11 pm, 2 night minimum stay - seasonal. **Activities:** playground. **Guest Services:** coin laundry. **Free Special Amenities: continental breakfast and high-speed Internet.**

SAVE / SOME UNITS FEE

RED CRAGS BED & BREAKFAST INN

Phone: (719)685-4515 56

Historic Bed & Breakfast

$100-$200 5/1-10/31
$75-$200 11/1-4/30

Address: 302 El Paso Blvd 80829 **Location:** I-25 exit 141, 4 mi nw on US 24, just sw on US 24 business route/Manitou Ave, just w on Garden of the Gods Pl, then just n. **Facility:** On a hill, the 1875 Victorian mansion has flower and herb gardens, mountain views and stylish rooms with fireplaces and king-size feather beds. 8 units, some two bedrooms. 3 stories (no elevator), interior/exterior corridors. **Terms:** office hours 7 am-6 pm, 2 night minimum stay - seasonal and/or weekends, age restrictions may apply, 14 day cancellation notice-fee imposed. **Activities:** whirlpool, bicycles, hiking trails. *Fee:* massage. / SOME UNITS

RED WING MOTEL

Phone: 719/685-9547 54

Motel

Rates not provided

Address: 56 El Paso Blvd 80829 **Location:** I-25 exit 141, 4 mi w on US 24, just ne on US 24 business route/Manitou Ave, then just w on Beckers Ln. **Facility:** 27 units, some two bedrooms and kitchens. 2 stories (no elevator), exterior corridors. **Terms:** office hours 8 am-8 pm. **Pool(s):** heated outdoor. **Guest Services:** coin laundry.

/ SOME UNITS FEE

ROCKLEDGE COUNTRY INN

Phone: (719)685-4515 55

Historic Bed & Breakfast

$185-$355 5/1-10/31
$150-$275 11/1-4/30

Address: 328 El Paso Blvd 80829 **Location:** I-25 exit 141, 4 mi w on US 24, just sw on US 24 business route, just w on Garden of the Gods Pl, then just s. **Facility:** A two-story copper fireplace and hardwood floors distinguish this Arts and Crafts-style 1912 mansion above the town center with views of Pikes Peak. Complimentary afternoon wine service is offered. 7 units. 2 stories (no elevator), interior/exterior corridors. **Terms:** office hours 7 am-6 pm, 2 night minimum stay - seasonal and/or weekends, 14 day cancellation notice-fee imposed. **Activities:** whirlpool, bicycles, hiking trails. *Fee:* massage. / SOME UNITS

(See map & index p. 94.)

RODEWAY INN AT THE CASTAWAYS

Phone: (719)685-3300 59

Hotel

$60-$190

Address: 103 Manitou Ave 80829 **Location:** I-25 exit 141, 4 mi w on US 24 to Manitou Ave, then just e. **Facility:** 47 units. 2 stories (no elevator), exterior corridors. **Terms:** seasonal, office hours 7 am-10 pm, 2 night minimum stay - seasonal, 3 day cancellation notice-fee imposed. **Pool(s):** heated outdoor. **Activities:** whirlpool. **Guest Services:** valet and coin laundry. **Free Special Amenities: expanded continental breakfast and high-speed Internet.**

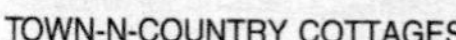

SILVER SADDLE MOTEL **Phone:** (719)685-5611 62

Motel

$59-$129 5/1-10/15
$59-$99 3/1-4/30

Address: 215 Manitou Ave 80829 **Location:** I-25 exit 141, 4 mi w on US 24, then just sw on US 24 business route. **Facility:** 53 units, some two bedrooms. 1-3 stories (no elevator), exterior corridors. **Terms:** open 5/1-10/15 & 3/1-4/30, cancellation fee imposed. **Pool(s):** heated outdoor. **Guest Services:** coin laundry. **Free Special Amenities: expanded continental breakfast and high-speed Internet.**

SOME UNITS

TOWN-N-COUNTRY COTTAGES

Phone: 719/685-5427 65

Cottage

$85-$145 5/1-9/6
$75-$125 9/7-4/30

Address: 123 Crystal Park Rd 80829 **Location:** I-25 exit 141, 4 mi w on US 24 business route exit Manitou Ave, just sw to Crystal Park Rd, then 0.3 mi (curve at entry). **Facility:** 10 cottages, some kitchens. 1 story, exterior corridors. **Terms:** 3 night minimum stay - seasonal and/or weekends, 14 day cancellation notice-fee imposed. **Amenities:** high-speed Internet. **Pool(s):** heated outdoor. **Activities:** whirlpool, playground, basketball, volleyball. *Fee:* game room. **Guest Services:** coin laundry.

WHERE TO EAT

ADAM'S MOUNTAIN CAFE **Phone:** 719/685-1430 47

Vegetarian

$8-$17

AAA Inspector Notes: Asian, Mediterranean and Southwestern influences punctuate dishes on the restaurant's eclectic menu. Breakfasts and healthy cuisine are casually served in a charming atmosphere. An acoustic-guitar player entertains on Tuesdays and Thursdays. **Bar:** beer & wine. **Address:** 934 Manitou Ave 80829 **Location:** I-25 exit 141, 4 mi w on US 24, then 1.3 mi sw on US 24 business route. **Parking:** street only.

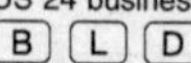

BRIARHURST MANOR **Phone:** 719/685-1864 51

Regional American

$20-$45

AAA Inspector Notes: This fine-dining restaurant is located in an intriguing 1878 stone mansion with nine dining rooms. It is known for regional Colorado cuisine, which includes Rocky Mountain elk, Colorado bison steak, chateaubriand, steak Diane, seared sea scallops, Atlantic salmon and Rocky Mountain trout. Hardwood flooring throughout, soft lighting and antiques set one back in time. Classical music playing lightly and the sound of clinking wine glasses make for a romantic evening. **Bar:** full bar. **Reservations:** suggested. **Address:** 404 Manitou Ave 80829 **Location:** I-25 exit 141, 5 mi w on US 24 exit Manitou Ave; west side of Manitou Chamber of Commerce. **Historic** D

THE CLIFF HOUSE DINING ROOM

Phone: 719/785-2415 45

New Continental

$16-$26

AAA Inspector Notes: The chefs' creative lamb, duck, veal and trout dishes incorporate a wealth of regional ingredients and cross-cultural techniques to provide a distinctive Colorado culinary experience. Oil paintings done by local legend C.H. Rockey as well as Riedel crystal wine glasses, Christofle flatware and damask linens typify high quality. The inn was established in 1873 on the stage line to Leadville. Service is refined but not pretentious. Desserts are works of art. **Bar:** full bar. **Reservations:** suggested. **Address:** 306 Canon Ave 80829 **Location:** I-25 exit 141, 4 mi w on US 24, 1.2 mi sw on US 24 business route/Manitou Ave, then just w; in The Cliff House at Pikes Peak. **Parking:** valet only.

B L D

CRAFTWOOD INN **Phone:** 719/685-9000 48

Regional American

$20-$35

AAA Inspector Notes: This fine-dining restaurant is noted for its Colorado cuisine centered on elk, venison, wild boar, pheasant, duck, quail, antelope, caribou, steak, seafood and braised herbal chicken. Distinctive desserts include jalapeño white chocolate mousse and prickly pear sorbet. Patrons can soak up a cozy, romantic feel in a setting that started as a coppersmith workshop in 1912. The inn has beamed ceilings, stained glass and a copper-hood fireplace. **Bar:** full bar. **Reservations:** suggested. **Address:** 404 El Paso Blvd 80829 **Location:** I-25 exit 141, 4 mi w on US 24 to Manitou Ave, just n to Garden of the Gods Pl, then just w. **Historic** D

THE LOOP **Phone:** 719/685-9344 46

Mexican

$8-$15

AAA Inspector Notes: This perennial favorite among locals and tourists alike offers delicious Mexican fare such as burritos, fajitas, enchiladas and more, as well as award-winning margaritas, in a casual setting in the heart of downtown. **Bar:** full bar. **Address:** 965 Manitou Ave 80829 **Location:** I-25 exit 141, 4 mi w on US 24, then 1.3 mi sw on US 24 business route. **Parking:** street only.

L D

THE MONA LISA FONDUE RESTAURANT

Phone: 719/685-0277 49

Fondue

$17-$30

AAA Inspector Notes: At this restaurant, guests choose from a selection of shareable four-course fondue meals. For the entree, pieces of beef, chicken, seafood and wild game are dipped in a variety of flavorful sauces. It's easy to get carried away with the first few courses, but leaving room for the decadent dessert course is a must. **Bar:** beer & wine. **Reservations:** suggested. **Address:** 733 Manitou Ave 80829 **Location:** In historic downtown. **Parking:** street only. D

SAVELLI'S **Phone:** 719/685-3755 52

Italian

$7-$13

AAA Inspector Notes: Near several motels and just off US 24, the popular pizza place also prepares reasonably priced pasta dishes that appeal to families. Smoking is permitted on the patio. **Bar:** wine only. **Address:** 301 Manitou Ave 80829 **Location:** I-25 exit 141, 4 mi w on US 24 business route, then just w. L D

(See map & index p. 94.)

STAGECOACH INN Phone: 719/685-9400 (50)

Regional American
$8-$25

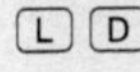

AAA Inspector Notes: Cozy mountain charm envelops the former stage stop and inn, which has two creekside decks for outdoor dining and inviting fireplaces in various dining rooms. The menu features preparations of slow-roast buffalo, choice beef, seafood, pasta and chicken. Past patrons include President Dwight Eisenhower and the Cartwrights from Bonanza. **Bar:** full bar. **Reservations:** suggested. **Address:** 702 Manitou Ave 80829 **Location:** I-25 exit 141, 4.2 mi nw on Manitou Ave, then 1 mi sw.

MEEKER (C-2) pop. 2,475, elev. 6,239'

In 1868 explorer John Wesley Powell led a 20-person contingent to the area and established winter quarters; that site is now known as Powell Park. Ten years later Nathan C. Meeker arrived at the same site to serve as the agent of the White River Agency of the Bureau of Indian Affairs. The Ute Indians, resentful of Meeker's attempt to make them farmers, ambushed Meeker and 10 agency employees. After the U.S. Army arrived and established a camp on the White River, the Indians were banished to a reservation in eastern Utah.

The town of Meeker, the county seat of Rio Blanco County, is near White River National Forest *(see place listing p. 303)* and the Flat Tops Wilderness Area. As a result, recreation opportunities are plentiful and include biking, boating, camping, cross-country skiing, fishing, hiking, horseback riding and snowmobiling.

Meeker Chamber of Commerce: 710 Market St., P.O. Box 869, Meeker, CO 81641. **Phone:** (970) 878-5510.

WHITE RIVER MUSEUM, 2 blks. n. of SR 13 at 565 Park Ave., occupies the original 1880 log U.S. Army officers' quarters used by the soldiers who came to assist troops pinned down at Milk Creek Battlefield who were helping Bureau of Indian Affairs agent Nathan Meeker, killed in an 1879 Indian uprising. Artifacts, pictures and records document the rich Ute and pioneer history of the White River area. **Tours:** Guided tours are available. **Hours:** Mon.-Fri. 9-5, Sat.-Sun. 10-5, Nov. 1 to mid-Apr.; daily 10-4, rest of year. Closed Jan. 1, Thanksgiving and Christmas. Phone ahead to confirm schedule. **Cost:** Donations. **Phone:** (970) 878-9982.

MESA (D-1) elev. 5,639'

RECREATIONAL ACTIVITIES

Skiing

- **Powderhorn Ski Resort** is 35 mi. e. on SR 65. **Hours:** Daily 9-4, mid-Dec. to late Mar. **Phone:** (970) 268-5700.

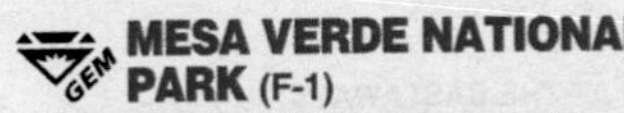

MESA VERDE NATIONAL PARK (F-1)

• Hotels p. 256 • Restaurants p. 256

Elevations in the park range from 6,954 ft. at Chapin Mesa to 8,572 ft. at Park Point. Refer to AAA maps for additional elevation information.

In southwestern Colorado, 9 miles east of Cortez, Mesa Verde National Park is one of the nation's major archeological preserves. The park consists of nearly 5,000 archeological sites, which include 600 cliff dwellings. Mesa Verde, Spanish for "green table," is so called because of its comparatively level top, forested with juniper and pinyon trees. It encompasses 80 square miles, rises 1,800 to 2,000 feet above the valley along the north side and slopes gradually down to the cliffs bordering the Mancos River Canyon on the south.

A score of large canyons seam the mesa, and in the shelter of the hundreds of alcoves eroded in the cliffs are some of the world's largest and best preserved cliff dwellings. Archeologists have stabilized only a few of the sites; asphalt roads lead to overlooks above the main ones.

The earliest known inhabitants of Mesa Verde were the Modified Basket Makers, descendants of a people who lived in the Four Corners region. They built subterranean pit houses about A.D. 500-750. From A.D. 750 to 1100 these cliff dwellers perfected their living quarters, building kivas (ceremonial rooms) and masonry houses around open courts (pueblos).

From A.D. 1100 to 1300 arts and crafts reached their peak; pottery and cloth were often elaborately decorated. Around 1200 they moved into the alcoves for reasons that remain unknown and built cliff dwellings. Sometime about 1276 a drought struck and lasted 24 years. The resulting crop failures, depletion of resources, other environmental problems and possible conflict may have driven the people from Mesa Verde in search of a more reliable water supply and improved living conditions.

Some of the Pueblo people living in the Rio Grande pueblos in northwestern New Mexico and on the Hopi mesas in northern Arizona are descendants of the former occupants of Mesa Verde.

General Information and Activities

Mesa Verde National Park is open all year but on a limited basis in winter. Interpretive activities are held throughout the year (weather permitting). The Chapin Mesa Archeological Museum, with exhibits, artifacts of the Ancestral Puebloans, tour information and campfire schedules, is open daily 8-6:30, mid-Apr. to mid-Oct.; 8-5, rest of year. A free 25-minute park video can also be viewed; phone (970) 529-4465. The Far View Visitor Center is open daily 8-5, mid-Apr. to mid-Oct.

Half-day guided tours are available for a fee April through October. For prices and schedules, phone (800) 449-2288. During summer and fall special events, Hopi dances, cultural demonstrations and lectures are presented. Visitors arriving at other times can inspect the museum, visit mesa-top sites, take a guided trip to a cliff dwelling and, when weather permits, drive along some of the scenic routes.

From Memorial Day through Labor Day visitors can drive along a 12-mile access road to Wetherill Mesa, where two cliff dwellings date from the 12th and 13th centuries and four mesa-top villages date from the seventh through 12th centuries.

Phone (970) 529-4465 for the latest information about schedules, weather and road conditions. *See Recreation Chart.*

ADMISSION to the park is $15 per private vehicle, Memorial Day-Labor Day; $10 per private vehicle, rest of year. Admission $8 per person arriving by other means, Memorial Day-Labor Day; $5, rest of year. All admission fees are valid for 7 days.

PETS are permitted in the park only if they are on a leash, crated or otherwise physically restricted at all times. They are not permitted on trails, in public buildings or in the archeological sites.

LODGING is available from mid-April to mid-October at Far View. For reservations write the ARAMARK Far View Lodge, Mesa Verde National Park, 34879 US 160, Mancos, CO 81328; phone (970) 529-4421 or (800) 449-2288.

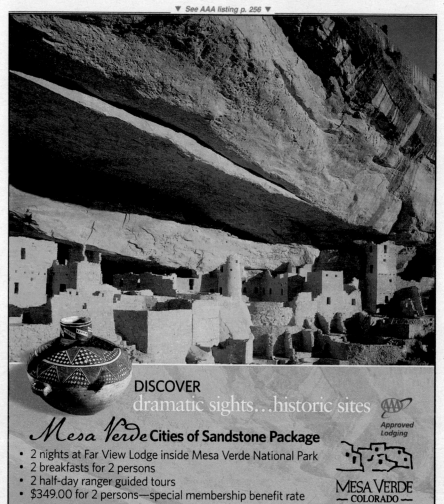

▼ See AAA listing p. 256 ▼

ADDRESS inquiries to the Superintendent, Mesa Verde National Park, P.O. Box 8, Mesa Verde National Park, CO 81330; phone (970) 529-4465.

ANASAZI HERITAGE CENTER—see Canyons of the Ancients National Monument p. 78.

BALCONY HOUSE, in a high alcove in the west wall of Soda Canyon, is a site that can be reached only by a 32-foot ladder. Careful attention to detail and the skill necessary to construct a village in this particular alcove make Balcony House a classic example of Pueblo architecture. It can be visited only on ranger-guided trips that fill quickly in summer months.

Time: Allow 1 hour minimum. **Hours:** Tours are offered daily every 30 minutes 9-5:30, late May-Labor Day; every hour 9-5:30, in early May and day after Labor Day to mid-Oct.; at 9:30, noon, 2 and 3:30, late Apr.-early May (weather permitting). **Cost:** Fee $3. Tickets are sold at the Far View Visitor Center and the Colorado Welcome Center in Cortez. **Phone:** (970) 529-4465.

CLIFF PALACE is in an alcove in the east wall of Cliff Canyon. Though visible from the Sun Temple or the Sun Point overlook directly opposite on the west rim, access is permitted only on ranger-guided tours. Arrive early for tours during summer months.

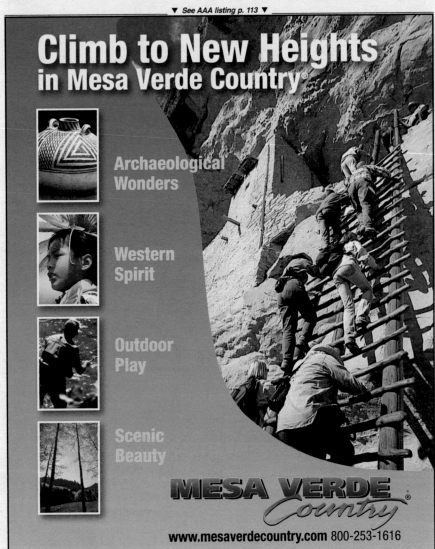

▼ *See AAA listing p. 113* ▼

Time: Allow 1 hour minimum. **Hours:** Tours are given daily every 30 minutes 9-6, late May-Labor Day; 9-5, early May-late May and day after Labor Day to early Nov. (weather permitting). **Cost:** Fee $3. Tickets are sold at the Far View Visitor Center and the Colorado Welcome Center in Cortez. **Phone:** (970) 529-4465.

FAR VIEW SITES, on the entrance highway 4 mi. n. of Chapin Mesa Archeological Museum, exemplify pueblos that were built on the mesa tops during the Developmental and Classic Pueblo periods. The site had been used for centuries before the existing walls were constructed. Self-guiding tours are permitted. **Time:** Allow 1 hour minimum.

FEWKES CANYON SITES are visible from Mesa Top Dr. Consisting of four interesting cliff dwellings, the sites cannot be entered due to deterioration. Near the head of the canyon is Fire Temple, one of the most remarkable of the sites. Nearby is New Fire House, composed of two alcoves. In the upper alcove are a number of living rooms; the lower one contains a few living rooms and three kivas.

Down the canyon a short distance in a deep, arched alcove is Oak Tree House, with about 55 living rooms and seven kivas. South of this building and directly under Sun Temple is Mummy House, so called because of the discovery of a child's mummified body. With the exception of one small, well-preserved room high on the face of the cliff, this dwelling is badly deteriorated.

LONG HOUSE is in a small side canyon off Rock Canyon on Wetherill Mesa. The second largest cliff dwelling in Mesa Verde National Park, Long House can be visited only on ranger-guided trips. The round-trip hike is 3/4 mile, with a 130-foot gain in elevation upon exiting. During the tour, visitors climb two 15-foot ladders within the site. The tours can be strenuous due to the elevation, steepness and summer heat. **Tours:** Guided tours are available. **Time:** Allow 1 hour, 30 minutes minimum. **Hours:** Tours are offered daily 10-4, Memorial Day-Labor Day. Schedule varies; phone ahead for times.. **Cost:** $3. Tickets must be purchased in advance at the Far View Visitor Center. **Phone:** (970) 529-4465.

MESA TOP LOOP ROAD covers two 6-mi. loops and provides views of about 40 cliff dwellings from canyon-rim lookout points. Two pit houses and six pueblos illustrate the architectural sequence of the Mesa Verde structures. Several cliff dwellings can be viewed at close range from lookout points along the cliff edge. **Hours:** Daily 8-dusk (weather permitting).

PARK POINT FIRE LOOKOUT, 9 mi. inside the park entrance, has the highest elevation—8,572 feet—within the park. From this point portions of Colorado, Arizona, New Mexico and Utah are visible. **Time:** Allow 30 minutes minimum.

PETROGLYPH POINT TRAIL starts at the Chapin Mesa Archeological Museum. Nearly a 3-mile round-trip, the trail follows the base of the cliff on the east side of Spruce Tree and Navajo canyons to Petroglyph Point and returns via the mesa top. To use this trail, register at the trailhead near the museum. **Time:** Allow 2 hours minimum. **Hours:** Open mid-May to mid-Oct.

SPRUCE CANYON TRAIL branches off from the Spruce Tree House Trail. The 2.5-mile round-trip follows the bottom of Spruce Tree Canyon and ends in a picnic area around the headquarters. To use this trail, register at the trailhead near the museum. **Time:** Allow 1 hour, 30 minutes minimum. **Hours:** Open mid-May to mid-Oct.

SPRUCE TREE HOUSE is in an alcove in Spruce Tree Canyon, just behind the museum at park headquarters. It is one of the largest and best preserved cliff dwellings in the park and is easily accessible to visitors. **Time:** Allow 1 hour minimum. **Hours:** Self-guiding tours daily 8:30-6:30, Memorial Day-Labor Day; 9-5, mid-Mar. through day before Memorial Day and day after Labor Day-Oct. 31. Guided tours are given daily at 10, 1 and 3:30, rest of year.

SQUARE TOWER HOUSE is in a shallow alcove in the east wall of Navajo Canyon, opposite Echo Cliff. Its four-story tower stands against the rear wall of the alcove. The square tower cannot be entered, but Mesa Top Loop Road provides a close-up look.

SUN TEMPLE is across the canyon from Cliff Palace on Mesa Top Loop Rd., on the promontory formed by the confluence of Cliff and Fewkes canyons. There is no evidence showing how this site was used, but its construction was probably never completed. **Time:** Allow 30 minutes minimum.

Safety tip: Keep a current AAA/CAA Road Atlas in every vehicle

FAR VIEW LODGE **Phone:** (970)529-4421

Motel
$110-$153

Address: 1 Navajo Hill, MM 15 81330 **Location:** 14 mi from park gate. **Facility:** 150 units. 1-2 stories (no elevator), exterior corridors. **Terms:** open 5/1-10/22 & 4/21-4/30, 3 day cancellation notice-fee imposed. **Dining:** Metate Room, see separate listing. **Activities:** hiking trails.

(See ad p. 257, p. 253.)

SAVE BIZ

SOME UNITS FEE

WHERE TO EAT

METATE ROOM **Phone:** 970/529-4422

Southwestern
$13-$32

AAA Inspector Notes: The contemporary Southwestern cuisine is inspired by regional heritage foods and flavorings and features prickly pear red pepper shrimp cocktail, bison shepherd's pie, buffalo rib-eye, hatch green chiles and asadero cheese in a chicken breast breaded in corn tortillas, cinnamon chili pork tenderloin dusted with cinnamon, and decadent house-made desserts. **Bar:** full bar. **Address:** 1 Navajo Hill, MM15 81330 **Location:** 14 mi from park gate; in Far View Lodge.

B D

▼ See AAA listing p. 114 ▼

▼ See AAA listing p. 256 ▼

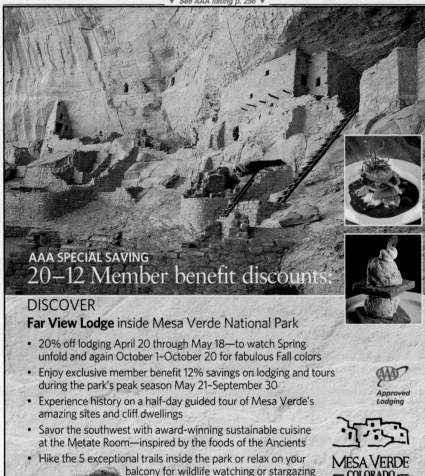

MONARCH (E-3)

MONARCH CREST TRAM is 15 mi. w. on US 50. An enclosed tram car ascends to a height of 12,012 feet for a view of the Rocky Mountains and Pikes Peak, 72 miles to the east. **Hours:** Daily 8:30-5:30, May 15-Sept. 15 (weather permitting). **Cost:** Fare $7; $6 (ages 55+); $4 (ages 3-12). **Phone:** (719) 539-4091.

RECREATIONAL ACTIVITIES

Skiing

- **Monarch Mountain** is 17 mi. w. on US 50 at 23715 W. US 50. Other activities are offered. **Hours:** Daily 9-4, late Nov.-early Apr. **Phone:** (719) 530-5000 or (888) 996-7669.

MONTE VISTA (E-3) pop. 4,444, elev. 7,663'

Monte Vista thrives on the shipping of potatoes and other crops from the surrounding San Luis Valley and on its proximity to the recreational lands of the Rio Grande National Forest *(see place listing p. 275)* to the west.

Monte Vista Chamber of Commerce: 947 1st Ave., Monte Vista, CO 81144. **Phone:** (719) 852-2731.

MONTE VISTA NATIONAL WILDLIFE REFUGE, 6 mi. s. on SR 15, is a 14,800-acre refuge for migratory birds. Ducks, geese, shorebirds and water birds nest in the area, and mallards and geese visit in winter. Sandhill cranes can be seen February through April and mid-September through October; bald eagles are abundant November through March. A 2.5-mile driving route and short walking trail are available. **Hours:** Daily dawn-dusk. **Cost:** Free. **Phone:** (719) 589-4021.

BEST WESTERN MOVIE MANOR **Phone:** (719)852-5921

Hotel

$85-$150

AAA Benefit: Members save up to 20%, plus 10% bonus points with Best Western Rewards®.

Address: 2830 W Hwy 160 81144 **Location:** On US 160, 2 mi w. Drive-in theater on site. **Facility:** 59 units. 2 stories (no elevator), exterior corridors. **Parking:** winter plug-ins. **Activities:** playground, exercise room. **Free Special Amenities: local telephone calls and high-speed Internet.**

SAVE / SOME UNITS FEE

WHERE TO EAT

NINO'S MEXICAN RESTAURANT **Phone:** 719/852-0101

Mexican

$6-$12

AAA Inspector Notes: The quick service and tasty burritos make this casual eatery a favorite with locals. Mixing past and present, one brick wall of this historic building has been left exposed to reveal a Victorian-era advertisement. **Bar:** beer & wine. **Address:** 118 Adams St 81144 **Location:** Just s from 1st Ave (US 160).

L D

MONTROSE (E-2) pop. 19,132, elev. 5,806'

Developed in the 1880s as a supply point for miners following the Uncompahgre River into the silver-laden San Juan Mountains, Montrose now serves a similar purpose for the ranching, farming, mining and recreational interests in the area.

Orchard and truck crops flourish using water diverted from the Gunnison River; the lower portal of the diversion tunnel is 7.5 miles east of Montrose off US 50. The city is headquarters for the power operations segment of the Colorado River storage project.

Black Canyon of the Gunnison National Park *(see place listing p. 55)* is northeast via US 50 and SR 347. In addition to opportunities for a variety of recreational pursuits, the Curecanti National Recreation Area *(see place listing p. 120)* and the Grand Mesa-Uncompahgre-Gunnison National Forests *(see place listing p. 219)* offer beautiful scenery.

Montrose is the western terminus of a scenic stretch of US 50 extending 126 miles from Poncha Springs; it also is the northern end of scenic US 550, which includes the Million Dollar Highway *(see attraction listing p. 262)*, from Durango.

Montrose Association of Commerce & Tourism: 1519 E. Main St., Montrose, CO 81401. **Phone:** (970) 249-5000 or (800) 873-0244.

MONTROSE COUNTY HISTORICAL MUSEUM, at Main St. and Rio Grande Ave. in the 1912 D&RG Depot building, displays dolls, toys, quilts, clothing, railroad and mining memorabilia, a stage coach, a Union Pacific caboose and farm equipment from the 18th and 19th centuries. Black and white photographs and documents chronicle town history. A furnished homesteader's cabin and a cowboy cabin are on the grounds.

Hours: Mon.-Sat. 10-4, mid-May to mid-Oct.; by appointment rest of year. Closed major holidays. **Cost:** $6; $4 (ages 56+); $2 (ages 0-17). **Phone:** (970) 249-2085.

UTE INDIAN MUSEUM, 3 mi. s. on US 550, highlights the Ute Indians and early explorers, including the Franciscan missionaries who mapped and named many rivers, valleys and mountains in western Colorado. Medicinal plants are featured in a botanical garden. A monument honors Chief Ouray, peacemaker between the Utes and the settlers, upon whose farm the museum now stands. The grave of his wife, Chipeta, and her brother Chief John McCook, also are on the grounds.

Time: Allow 30 minutes minimum. **Hours:** Tues.-Sat. 9-4. **Cost:** $4.50; $4 (ages 66+); $2 (ages 6-16). **Phone:** (970) 249-3098.

RECREATIONAL ACTIVITIES

Horseback Riding

- **Deb's Livery** is at 31268 US 550S. **Hours:** Daily 9-5. **Phone:** (970) 626-5587 or (970) 729-1266.

BEST WESTERN RED ARROW **Phone:** (970)249-9641

Hotel
$69-$129

AAA Benefit: Members save up to 20%, plus 10% bonus points with Best Western Rewards®.

Address: 1702 E Main St 81401 **Location:** 1 mi e on US 50. **Facility:** 58 units. 2 stories (no elevator), interior/exterior corridors. **Amenities:** *Some:* high-speed Internet. **Pool(s):** heated outdoor. **Activities:** whirlpool, playground, exercise room. **Guest Services:** valet and coin laundry. **Free Special Amenities: local telephone calls and high-speed Internet.**

SAVE BIZ / SOME UNITS FEE

DAYS INN **Phone:** (970)249-4507

Hotel
$68-$125

Address: 1417 E Main St 81401 **Location:** 0.8 mi e on US 50. **Facility:** 70 units. 2 stories (no elevator), exterior corridors. **Terms:** check-in 4 pm. **Pool(s):** heated outdoor. **Activities:** whirlpool. **Guest Services:** coin laundry.

BIZ / SOME UNITS FEE

ECONO LODGE **Phone:** (970)240-8000

Hotel
$62-$109

Address: 2100 E Main St 81401 **Location:** 1.3 mi e on US 50. **Facility:** 51 units. 2 stories (no elevator), interior corridors. **Terms:** cancellation fee imposed. **Pool(s):** heated indoor. **Activities:** whirlpool. **Guest Services:** coin laundry.

BIZ / SOME UNITS

HAMPTON INN **Phone:** (970)252-3300

Hotel
$109-$159

AAA Benefit: Members save up to 10% everyday!

Address: 1980 N Townsend Ave 81401 **Location:** 1.5 mi n on US 550. **Facility:** 64 units. 3 stories, interior corridors. **Terms:** 1-7 night minimum stay, cancellation fee imposed. **Amenities:** video games (fee). **Pool(s):** heated indoor. **Activities:** whirlpool, exercise room. **Guest Services:** valet and coin laundry.

BIZ / SOME UNITS

QUALITY INN & SUITES **Phone:** (970)249-1011

Hotel
$80-$159

Address: 2751 Commercial Way 81401 **Location:** 2 mi s on US 550, just w on O'Delle Rd. **Facility:** 52 units. 3 stories, interior corridors. **Terms:** cancellation fee imposed. **Amenities:** high-speed Internet, safes (fee). **Pool(s):** heated indoor. **Activities:** whirlpool, exercise room. **Guest Services:** valet and coin laundry.

BIZ / SOME UNITS FEE

UNCOMPAHGRE BED & BREAKFAST **Phone:** (970)240-4000

Historic Bed & Breakfast
$110-$150 5/1-10/31
$90-$125 11/1-4/30

Address: 21049 Uncompahgre Rd 81401 **Location:** 8 mi s on US 550 (east side). **Facility:** This spacious white mansion was once a school. The large welcoming common area, with lots of puzzles, board and card games, is the former auditorium and gymnasium. 8 units. 1 story, interior corridors. **Activities:** basketball, horseshoes.

CALL / SOME UNITS

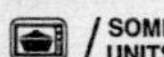

WESTERN MOTEL **Phone:** 970/249-3481

Motel
Rates not provided

Address: 1200 E Main St 81401 **Location:** 0.8 mi e on US 50. **Facility:** 27 units, some two bedrooms. 1-2 stories (no elevator), exterior corridors. **Terms:** office hours 7 am-9 pm. **Pool(s):** heated outdoor. **Activities:** whirlpool.

/ SOME UNITS FEE

WHERE TO EAT

ASII THAI RESTAURANT **Phone:** 970/240-4567

Thai
$7-$19

AAA Inspector Notes: This inviting eatery offers lovely presentations of traditional appetizers, soups, Thai curries, noodles and fried-rice entrées, duck and elk specials. A nice selection of lunch specials is offered. Vegan and vegetarian entrées also are available. **Bar:** beer & wine. **Address:** 1015 S Townsend Ave 81401 **Location:** 0.7 mi s of jct US 50 and 550. L D

CAMP ROBBER **Phone:** 970/240-1590

Southwestern
$9-$22

AAA Inspector Notes: With a charming outdoor patio and fireplace as well as a kids' menu, this restaurant offers diners an eclectic selection of Southwestern cuisine for lunch, dinner and its Champagne Sunday brunch. The green chili chicken potato soup is a must to start. Other favorites include Asian barbecue chicken salad, chile rellenos, prime rib, vegetarian delight and green chili pistachio-crusted pork medallions. Photo art adorns the dining rooms, where friendly servers attend to their patrons' needs. **Bar:** full bar. **Reservations:** suggested. **Address:** 1515 Ogden Rd 81401 **Location:** 2.1 mi s from US 50; corner of US 550 and Ogden Rd. L D

DAMIANO'S ON MAIN, AN ITALIAN GASTRO PUB **Phone:** 970/249-4446

Italian
$9-$19

AAA Inspector Notes: Have dinner in the separate cozy dining room of this new gastropub or in the social area, which offers a variety of upscale seating and table arrangements, a bar and a coal-fired oven used for mouthwatering pizza. A nice selection of traditional Italian appetizers, salads and entrées is available, as are attractively presented homemade desserts. I enjoyed the penne Bolognese made with Black Angus beef and the delicious garlic knots. **Bar:** full bar. **Address:** 1135 E Main St 81401 **Location:** 0.8 mi e of jct US 550, on US 50. D

GARLIC MIKE'S **Phone:** 970/249-4381

Italian
$12-$29

AAA Inspector Notes: The family eatery pleases a broad range of patrons with fried green tomatoes; three nightly choices of soup, steak and veal; and favorite pasta dishes such as lasagna, manicotti and seafood cannelloni crepes. Among the Italian desserts are whipped silky custard served over warm fresh berries and vanilla gelato. **Bar:** full bar. **Address:** 103 Rose Ln 81401 **Location:** 1.3 mi e on US 550. D

GURU'S RESTAURANT & BAR **Phone:** 970/252-8777

Nepali
$7-$19

AAA Inspector Notes: The restaurant serves a traditional menu of items that have been carefully prepared and seasoned with an exotic blend of curry spices. Options include chicken tikka masala, lamb kawab, shrimp bhuteko and vegetarian fire-roasted eggplant curry. The lunch buffet is a popular local favorite. **Bar:** full bar. **Address:** 448 E Main St 81401 **Location:** 0.3 mi e of US 550. **Parking:** street only. L D

PAHGRE'S PIZZA, PASTA & SALAD **Phone:** 970/249-6442

Pizza
$8-$25

AAA Inspector Notes: Locally grown and produced ingredients are used whenever possible in the good selection of panini, pastas, small and entrée-size creative salads, stone-baked signature pizza pies and campfire calzones. You can build your own pizza, select a sauce and choose from more than 40 toppings. Gluten-free crust, pasta and beer are available. **Address:** 1541 Oxbow Dr, Suite 1800 81401 **Location:** 2.3 mi s of jct US 50 and 550; in Oxbow Crossing. L D

RED BARN RESTAURANT **Phone:** 970/249-9202

Steak
$7-$29

AAA Inspector Notes: The large cow sign perched on the roof is a giveaway that you've arrived at the Red Barn, where down-home Western cooking is served in a laid-back atmosphere. **Bar:** full bar. **Address:** 1413 E Main St 81401 **Location:** 0.8 mi e on US 50. L D

THE STONE HOUSE **Phone:** 970/240-8899

American
$9-$25

AAA Inspector Notes: The upscale bar and cozy sitting area in front of a fireplace are ideal spots to enjoy a cocktail before or after lunch or dinner. In addition to soup, salads and burgers, a wide variety of steaks, seafood and pasta is offered, including pan-seared sea scallops on crab cakes, Blue Point oysters, baked Caribbean lobster tail and coffee-rubbed rib-eye. There is a nice selection of desserts. **Bar:** full bar. **Address:** 1415 Hawk Pkwy 81401 **Location:** 2.2 mi s on US 550. L D

MORRISON (C-4) pop. 428, elev. 5,766'

• Hotels & Restaurants map & index p. 140
• Part of Denver area — see map p. 123

DINOSAUR RIDGE is w. of SR 470 at 16831 W. Alameda Pkwy. Dinosaur Ridge is the site of such paleontological discoveries as dinosaur bones and tracks, plant and animal fossils, and rock formations from the Jurassic and Cretaceous periods. Twenty interpretive signs help visitors identify these features along the ridge. The visitor center has large murals and interactive exhibits. Shuttle bus tours of the grounds are available.

Time: Allow 1 hour, 30 minutes minimum. **Hours:** Mon.-Sat. 10-4:30, Sun. 11-4:30. Forty-minute shuttle bus tours board hourly (half-hourly June-Aug.) at 10 a.m. at the visitor center; last bus leaves at 4 p.m. (May-Oct.) and 3 p.m. (Nov.-Apr.). Closed Jan. 1, Thanksgiving and Christmas. **Cost:** Free. Shuttle bus tour $4; free (ages 0-5); boarding is first come, first served. **Phone:** (303) 697-3466.

MORRISON NATURAL HISTORY MUSEUM is .25 mi. s. at 501 SR 8 (Morrison Rd.). This museum offers interactive exhibits highlighting historic dinosaur discoveries. Displays include hatchling Jurassic dinosaur fossils from the Denver area. Visitors may help prepare dinosaur bones and encounter live reptiles during tours.

Time: Allow 1 hour minimum. **Hours:** Daily 10-5. Guided tours hourly, starting at 10:30 a.m.; final tour and tickets sold half-hour before closing. **Cost:** $5; $4 (ages 4-12 and 65+). Guided tours included with admission. **Phone:** (303) 697-1873.

RED ROCKS PARK AND AMPHITHEATRE, I-70W exit 259, then 1.5 mi. s., is an 868-acre park laced with hiking trails at the foot of the Rocky Mountains. The red sandstone formations were created 250 to 300 million years ago and gain their color from varying levels of iron oxide.

Red Rocks Amphitheatre's 9,450-seats are flanked on either side by striking 400-foot-high red sandstone formations. The amphitheater is well-known as one of the nation's finest outdoor concert venues. The Burnham Hoyt Visitor Center has interactive displays about the history of Red Rocks, and a state welcome center provides area maps and guides.

Concerts and Easter sunrise services are held seasonally. **Time:** Allow 30 minutes minimum. **Hours:** Park daily 5 a.m.-11 p.m. State welcome center daily 9-4. Visitor center daily 8-7, May-Sept.; 9-4, rest of year. Guided tours of the amphitheater depart from the visitor center daily at 10, June-Oct. The visitor center closes 4 hours before show time on concert dates and reopens at gate time for patrons with tickets. Closed Thanksgiving and Christmas. **Cost:** Park free. Tour $6; $3 (seniors); $2 (children). **Phone:** (720) 865-2474 for the amphitheater, (303) 697-2048 for the state welcome center, or (303) 697-4939 for the visitor center.

TINY TOWN AND RAILROAD is off US 285 at 6249 Turkey Creek Rd. The 10-acre Tiny Town is a miniature children's village begun in 1915. More than 100 buildings in rural, town and mountain settings are featured, including a toy store, grocery, saloon, church, ice cream shop, newspaper office and bank. Town houses are Victorian-style reproductions. Visitors can ride an authentic miniature open-air train through the town, and children can enter some of the buildings.

Time: Allow 1 hour minimum. **Hours:** Daily 10-5, Memorial Day-Labor Day; Sat.-Sun. 10-5, May 1-day before Memorial Day and day after Labor Day-Sept. 30. **Cost:** $5; $3 (ages 2-12). Train $1. **Phone:** (303) 697-6829.

THE FORT **Phone:** 303/697-4771 93

Steak
$24-$52

AAA Inspector Notes: The unique building housing this restaurant is a replica of historic Bent's Old Fort. Influenced by the early American West, the menu focuses on wild game such as buffalo, quail and elk. Hearty steaks, poultry and seafood dishes also are available. The atmosphere of the attractively decorated dining room is warm and inviting, and its Western-attired staff is outgoing. **Bar:** full bar. **Reservations:** suggested. **Address:** 19192 Hwy 8 80465 **Location:** 2 mi s on SR 8; 0.3 mi n of jct US 285.
D

MOSCA (E-3) elev. 7,562'

COLORADO GATORS, 17 mi. n. on SR 17, features alligators lolling in the Colorado sun with snowcapped mountain peaks in the background. The unusual nature of this farm grew out of a need to keep the fish hatchery at the site clean of fish remains. The waters of the artesian well are 87 F and allow the alligators to thrive in the otherwise inhospitable Colorado climate. The farm also serves as a refuge for rescued reptiles.

Time: Allow 30 minutes minimum. **Hours:** Daily 9-7, Memorial Day-Labor Day; 9-5, rest of year. Closed Thanksgiving and Christmas. **Cost:** $15; $7.50 (ages 6-15 and 65-79). **Phone:** (719) 378-2612.

MOUNT CRESTED BUTTE (D-2) pop. 801

RECREATIONAL ACTIVITIES

Skiing

- **Crested Butte Mountain Resort** is at 500 Gothic Rd. Other activities are offered. **Hours:** Daily 9-4, mid-Nov. to early Apr. **Phone:** (800) 544-8448.

NATHROP (D-3) elev. 7,690'

RECREATIONAL ACTIVITIES

White-water Rafting

- **Bill Dvorak Rafting & Kayak Expeditions** is at 17921 US 285. **Hours:** Daily 7 a.m.-9 p.m., May-Sept. **Phone:** (719) 539-6851 or (800) 824-3795.
- **Four Corners Rafting** is at 22565 US 285S. **Hours:** Daily 7-7, mid-May through Aug. 31. **Phone:** (719) 395-4137.

NEDERLAND (B-4) pop. 1,445, elev. 8,233'

RECREATIONAL ACTIVITIES

Skiing

- **Eldora Mountain Resort** is 4 mi. w. of CR 119 at 2861 Eldora Ski Rd. **Hours:** Daily 9-4, mid-Nov. to mid-Apr. (weather permitting). **Phone:** (303) 440-8700.

BEST WESTERN LODGE AT NEDERLAND
Phone: 303/258-9463

Hotel
Rates not provided

AAA Benefit: Members save up to 20%, plus 10% bonus points with Best Western Rewards®.

Address: 55 Lakeview Dr 80466 **Location:** SR 119; across from Visitor's Center. Located below shopping center. **Facility:** 23 units. 2 stories (no elevator), interior corridors. **Terms:** office hours 7 am-10 pm. **Amenities:** *Some:* high-speed Internet. **Activities:** whirlpool. **Guest Services:** coin laundry. **Free Special Amenities: local telephone calls and high-speed Internet.**

 / SOME UNITS FEE

WHERE TO EAT

BLACK FOREST RESTAURANT
Menu on AAA.com
Phone: 303/279-2333

German
$8-$27

AAA Inspector Notes: Diners will enjoy the homey, comfy décor at this restaurant, which has been serving guests since 1957. The menu features traditional dishes such as sauerbraten, as well as wild game and fowl specialties and American entrees. Entertainment is provided on weekends. **Bar:** full bar. **Reservations:** suggested. **Address:** 24 Big Springs Dr 80466 **Location:** SR 119 to Peak Hwy, just s of roundabout; above The Village Shopping Center. L D

NEW CASTLE pop. 4,518

RODEWAY INN
Phone: 970/984-2363

Motel
Rates not provided

Address: 781 Burning Mountain Ave 81647 **Location:** I-70 exit 105, just n, then w. **Facility:** 51 units. 2 stories (no elevator), interior corridors. **Pool(s):** heated indoor. **Activities:** whirlpool. **Guest Services:** coin laundry.

 / SOME UNITS FEE

WHERE TO EAT

ELK CREEK MINING CO
Phone: 970/984-0828

American
$8-$24

AAA Inspector Notes: Soups, salads, pasta, burgers, sandwiches, steak, prime rib and "border grub" make up the restaurant's menu. **Bar:** full bar. **Address:** 502 W Main St 81647 **Location:** I-70 exit 105, just n, then 1.1 mi w. **Parking:** on-site and street. L D

NIWOT pop. 4,006

COLTERRA
Phone: 303/652-0777

New Continental
$10-$32

AAA Inspector Notes: Chef Bradford Heap honed his skills under Alain Ducasse, Georges Blanc and Carlo Cioni and received accolades from the James Beard Foundation. His menu, inspired by Northern Italy and Southern France, features seasonal ingredients from local purveyors. Meals start with rustic bread with a soft middle and a crunchy crust. Flavorful appetizers include buffalo carpaccio, an artisanal cheese plate and PEI mussels. Entrees feature duck, Wagyu beef, pork, lamb, mahi-mahi and vegetarian options. **Bar:** full bar. **Address:** 210 Franklin St 80504 **Location:** I-25 exit 235, 6.6 mi w to US 287, 1 mi n, then w on Niwot Rd to 2nd Ave; in historic downtown area. **Parking:** street only. L D

LEFTY'S GOURMET PIZZA & ICE CREAM
Phone: 303/652-3100

Pizza
$2-$26

AAA Inspector Notes: A small facility with big ideas, the restaurant offers gourmet pizza prepared according to guests' preferences, tasty chicken wings and fresh-flavored homemade ice cream. **Address:** 364 2nd Ave 80503 **Location:** I-25 exit 235, 6.6 mi w to US 287, 1 mi n, then w on Niwot Rd to 2nd Ave; in historic downtown area. **Parking:** street only. L D

NORWOOD pop. 518

HAPPY BELLY DELI
Phone: 970/327-0208

Deli
$6-$9

AAA Inspector Notes: Tasty, freshly made sandwiches on homemade bread, soups and salads make up the deli's menu. For dessert, an array of freshly baked pastries tempts. **Address:** 1610 Grand Ave 81423 **Location:** Town center. **Parking:** street only. B L

OAK CREEK (C-2) pop. 884

TRACKS AND TRAILS MUSEUM is at 129 E. Main St. The museum's collection pertains to the history of coal mining, the railroad and diverse immigration. An outdoor mining display features an 83,000 pound drag-line bucket, while indoor exhibits focus on local railroad and mining artifacts. A rotating art exhibit also is on the premises. **Time:** Allow 1 hour minimum. **Hours:** Mon.-Sat. 9-4, Apr. 1-Oct. 15.; by appointment, rest of year. **Cost:** Free. **Phone:** (970) 736-8245.

OURAY (E-2) pop. 1,000, elev. 7,811'

• Restaurants p. 265

The town draws its name from the Ute chieftain Ouray (you-RAY). Before the miners arrived, the Indians came to the area to enjoy the hot springs. The first silver strike was made in 1875. The politics, foibles and personalities of the mining camps were lambasted in the *Solid Muldoon;* the paper became one of the most widely quoted of the time—even Queen Victoria of England was a subscriber.

Not silver but gold stabilized the community after the Panic of 1893. The wealth that poured from Tom Walsh's Camp Bird Mine amounted to $24 million 1896-1902. The fortune bought the family a place in Washington, D.C., society and daughter Evalyn the Hope Diamond. Mining has long since given way to year-round tourism as the leading factor in Ouray's economy.

The springs once enjoyed by the Indians now feed the outdoor Ouray Hot Springs Pool; for more information phone (970) 325-7073.

At the end of 8th Avenue is Cascade Falls Park, which features a nature trail and a lovely 300-foot waterfall. Another noteworthy local feature is Ouray Ice Park, one of the only parks in the world dedicated to the sport of ice climbing.

Ouray is the halfway point along the San Juan Skyway, Colorado's first scenic byway. The town also marks the northern terminus of the byway known as the Million Dollar Highway *(see attraction listing)*. The surrounding San Juan and Uncompahgre national forests are popular with four-wheel-drive enthusiasts and feature hundreds of hiking trails.

Ouray Chamber Resort Association: 1230 Main St., P.O. Box 145, Ouray, CO 81427. **Phone:** (970) 325-4746 or (800) 228-1876. ***(See ad this page.)***

Self-guiding tours: Information about a self-guiding historic walking tour of Ouray is available from the visitor information center at the resort association.

BACHELOR-SYRACUSE MINE is 1 mi. n. on US 550, then 1.2 mi. e. on CR 14, following signs. A mine train transports visitors 1,800 feet horizontally into Gold Hill, where some $90 million worth of silver and $8 million worth of gold have been removed. The mine temperature is 52 F. Gold panning is available.

Warm clothing is recommended. **Time:** Allow 1 hour minimum. **Hours:** Tours are given daily on the hour 9-5, in July; 9-4, May 20-June 15 and Aug. 20-Sept. 15. **Cost:** Fare $16.95; $14.95 (ages 60+); $8.95 (ages 4-11). Gold panning $6.95. Combination ticket $20.95; $19.95 (ages 60+); $12.95 (ages 4-11). **Phone:** (970) 325-0220.

BOX CAÑON FALLS AND PARK is s. on US 550 to CR 361, following signs. The canyon is 20 feet wide and 285 feet high. Its perpendicular granite walls are roofed by stone. Canyon Creek rushes through the narrow gorge, which is spanned by a high bridge. Interpretive exhibits highlight the canyon's diverse ecosystems. A trail leads from the parking area to a point from which the falls can be seen. **Time:** Allow 30 minutes minimum. **Hours:** Daily 8-8, Memorial Day-Labor Day; 8-7, day after Labor Day to mid-Oct.; 9-5, May 1-day before Memorial Day. **Cost:** $3; $2.50 (ages 65+); $1.50 (ages 5-12). **Phone:** (970) 325-7080.

MILLION DOLLAR HIGHWAY is a name often given to all of US 550 s. from Ouray to Silverton, but it technically applies only to the 6-mile section south of Ouray that follows Otto Mears' original toll road. Ranked among the nation's most spectacular automobile routes, it features chasms so deep that neither cliff tops nor canyon bottoms are visible on either side. Bear Creek Falls cascades under the highway into the canyon below and can be viewed from one of the many scenic overlooks along the road.

A few miles from Ouray, a backward look from the portal of a tunnel provides a magnificent view of pyramidal Mount Abrams. Whether the "million dollar" label refers to the cost of rebuilding the road, to the value of the gold in the mine tailings or to the views is uncertain. **Note:** Drivers unfamiliar with mountain roads should use caution.

OURAY COUNTY MUSEUM is at 420 6th Ave. The building that houses this museum was the town's hospital for 77 years. Some 27 rooms contain individual displays about the county's history. Hospital memorabilia remain along with mining relics, ranching and merchant exhibits, Ute Indian artifacts, a replica of the old jail and two restored log cabins.

Time: Allow 1 hour minimum. **Hours:** Mon.-Sat. 10-4:30, Sun. noon-4:30, mid-May through Sept. 30; Thurs.-Sat. 10-4:30, Oct.-Nov.; Thurs.-Sat. 1-4:30, mid-Apr. to mid-May. Phone ahead to confirm schedule. **Cost:** $5; $1 (ages 6-12). **Phone:** (970) 325-4576.

SWITZERLAND OF AMERICA TOURS, 226 7th Ave., offers guided off-road scenic tours of the back country in four-wheel-drive vehicles; sights include ghost towns, mining camps, wildflowers, waterfalls and the San Juan Mountains. Jeep rentals, horseback riding, rafting and hot air balloon rides also are available.

Hours: Daily 7:30-7, mid-June through Labor Day; 8-6, May 1 to mid-June and day after Labor Day to mid-Oct. **Cost:** Half-day off-road tours $60; $35 (ages 4-12). Full-day off-road tours $120-$130; $65-$70 (ages 4-12). Reservations are recommended. **Phone:** (970) 325-4484 or (866) 990-5337.

RECREATIONAL ACTIVITIES

Climbing

- **San Juan Mountain Guides** departs from 636 Main St. and various area locations. **Hours:** Daily 7 a.m.-9 p.m. **Phone:** (970) 325-4925.

ALPENGLOW CONDOMINIUMS **Phone:** 970/325-4664

Condominium
$150-$500

Address: 215 5th Ave 81427 **Location:** Just w of US 550 (Main St) via 5th Ave. **Facility:** 15 condominiums. 4 stories (no elevator), exterior corridors. **Terms:** off-site registration, 2 night minimum stay, 40 day cancellation notice-fee imposed. **Activities:** sauna, whirlpool. **Guest Services:** coin laundry.

/ SOME UNITS

BEAUMONT HOTEL & SPA **Phone:** (970)325-7000

Classic Historic Hotel
$120-$260

Address: 505 Main St 81427 **Location:** Just s on US 550 (Main St). **Facility:** A modern, comfortable property offering charming guest rooms and elegant public areas. 12 units. 3 stories, interior corridors. **Terms:** open 5/15-10/31 & 12/1-4/30, office hours 7 am-10 pm, check-in 4 pm, age restrictions may apply, 14 day cancellation notice-fee imposed. **Dining:** Bulow's Bistro, see separate listing. **Activities:** sauna, whirlpool, spa.

/ SOME UNITS

BEST WESTERN PLUS TWIN PEAKS LODGE & HOT SPRINGS **Phone:** (970)325-4427

Hotel
$100-$399

Best Western PLUS

AAA Benefit: Members save up to 20%, plus 10% bonus points with Best Western Rewards®.

Address: 125 3rd Ave 81427 **Location:** Just s on US 550 (Main St), then just w on 3rd Ave. **Facility:** 56 units. 2 stories (no elevator), exterior corridors. **Terms:** office hours 7:30 am-9:30 pm, cancellation fee imposed. **Amenities:** *Some:* high-speed Internet, safes. **Pool(s):** heated outdoor. **Activities:** whirlpools, hiking trails, jogging, shuffleboard, exercise room. **Guest Services:** coin laundry. **Free Special Amenities: full breakfast and high-speed Internet.** *(See ad p. 264.)*

SAVE

/ SOME UNITS FEE

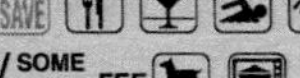

BOX CANYON LODGE & HOT SPRINGS **Phone:** (970)325-4981

Hotel
$99-$180 5/1-10/17
$99-$150 10/18-4/30

Address: 45 3rd Ave 81427 **Location:** Just s on US 550 (Main St) to 3rd Ave, then just w. **Facility:** 39 units, some efficiencies and kitchens. 2 stories (no elevator), exterior corridors. **Terms:** office hours 7:30 am-10 pm, 3 day cancellation notice-fee imposed. **Guest Services:** coin laundry. **Free Special Amenities: continental breakfast and high-speed Internet.**

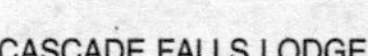

CASCADE FALLS LODGE **Phone:** 970/325-4394

Motel
$66-$165

Address: 120 6th Ave 81427 **Location:** Just w of US 550 (Main St) via 6th Ave. **Facility:** 19 units. 2 stories (no elevator), exterior corridors. **Terms:** open 5/10-10/18, 7 day cancellation notice-fee imposed. **Activities:** whirlpool.

CHINA CLIPPER INN **Phone:** 970/325-0565

Bed & Breakfast
Rates not provided

Address: 525 2nd St 81427 **Location:** Just w of US 550 (Main St) via 6th Ave, then just s on 2nd St. **Facility:** This Victorian-style inn features luxurious, nautically decorated rooms, many of which afford dramatic views of the San Juan Mountains. 13 units. 2 stories (no elevator), interior/exterior corridors. **Terms:** office hours 7 am-8 pm, check-in 4 pm. **Activities:** whirlpool.

/ SOME UNITS

COMFORT INN **Phone:** (970)325-7203

Motel
$69-$149 5/1-10/7
$64-$109 10/8-4/30

Address: 191 5th Ave 81427 **Location:** Just w of US 550 (Main St) via 5th Ave. **Facility:** 33 units. 2 stories (no elevator), exterior corridors. **Terms:** office hours 7 am-9 pm, cancellation fee imposed. **Activities:** whirlpool. **Guest Services:** coin laundry.

CALL

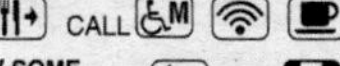

/ SOME UNITS FEE FEE FEE

HOT SPRINGS INN — Phone: (970)325-7277

Hotel
$72-$190

Address: 1400 Main St 81427 **Location:** 1 mi n of center on US 550 (Main St). **Facility:** 42 units. 2 stories (no elevator), exterior corridors. *Bath:* shower only. **Terms:** open 5/15-10/20, office hours 7 am-9 pm, 3 day cancellation notice. **Amenities:** safes. **Activities:** whirlpools. **Guest Services:** coin laundry.

MATTERHORN MOTEL — Phone: 970/325-4938

Motel
$75-$120

Address: 201 6th Ave 81427 **Location:** Just w of US 550 (Main St), at 6th Ave and 2nd St. **Facility:** 25 units, some two bedrooms. 2 stories (no elevator), exterior corridors. **Terms:** office hours 8 am-10 pm, 6 day cancellation notice-fee imposed.

/ SOME UNITS

OURAY CHALET INN — **Phone:** (970)325-4331

Motel
$56-$119 5/11-10/20
$60-$70 12/7-3/23

Address: 510 Main St 81427 **Location:** Just s of center on US 550 (Main St). **Facility:** 32 units. 2 stories (no elevator), interior/exterior corridors. **Terms:** open 5/11-10/20 & 12/7-3/23, office hours 7:30 am-10 pm, cancellation fee imposed. **Activities:** whirlpool. **Guest Services:** coin laundry. **Free Special Amenities: local telephone calls and high-speed Internet.**

SAVE

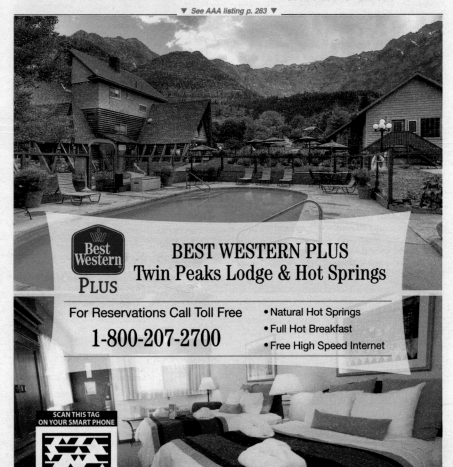

▼ See AAA listing p. 263 ▼

OURAY RIVERSIDE INN & CABINS

Phone: 970/325-4061

Motel

$62-$212

Address: 1804 N Main St 81427 **Location:** 1 mi n of center on US 550 (Main St). **Facility:** 21 units, some two bedrooms, efficiencies, kitchens and cabins. 2 stories (no elevator), exterior corridors. **Terms:** office hours 7 am-8 pm, 3 day cancellation notice-fee imposed. **Activities:** whirlpool, hiking trails, jogging. **Guest Services:** coin laundry. **Free Special Amenities: local telephone calls and high-speed Internet.**

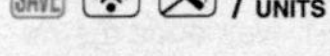

OURAY VICTORIAN INN **Phone:** (970)325-7222

Motel

$81-$199 5/1-10/31

$72-$150 12/15-3/31

Address: 50 3rd Ave 81427 **Location:** Just w of US 550 (Main St) via 3rd Ave. **Facility:** 38 units. 2 stories (no elevator), exterior corridors. **Terms:** open 5/1-10/31 & 12/15-3/31, office hours 7:30 am-9 pm, cancellation fee imposed. **Activities:** whirlpools, playground. **Free Special Amenities: full breakfast and high-speed Internet.**

RIVER'S EDGE MOTEL **Phone:** 970/325-4621

Motel

$51-$150

Address: 110 7th Ave 81427 **Location:** Just w of US 550 (Main St) via 7th Ave. **Facility:** 18 units, some efficiencies. 2 stories (no elevator), exterior corridors. **Terms:** cancellation fee imposed. **Activities:** whirlpool. **Guest Services:** coin laundry. **Free Special Amenities: expanded continental breakfast and use of on-premises laundry facilities.**

SOME UNITS FEE

ST. ELMO HOTEL **Phone:** (970)325-4951

Historic Country Inn

$110-$190 5/1-10/8

$85-$150 10/9-4/30

Address: 426 Main St 81427 **Location:** Just s of center on US 550 (Main St). **Facility:** This property's individually decorated rooms feature lovely Victorian antiques and furnishings. 9 units. 2 stories (no elevator), interior corridors. **Parking:** on-site and street. **Terms:** age restrictions may apply, 7 day cancellation notice-fee imposed. **Dining:** Bon Ton Restaurant, see separate listing. **Activities:** sauna, whirlpool.

WHERE TO EAT

ARTISAN BAKERY & CAFE **Phone:** 970/325-4677

Breads/Pastries

$6-$10

AAA Inspector Notes: This cafe offers a variety of sandwiches, quiche, soups and pastries. Perfect for breakfast or lunch, dine in or takeout. **Address:** 460 Main St 81427 **Location:** Just s of center on US 550 (Main St). **Parking:** street only. B L

BISTRO AT BILLY GOAT GRUFF'S **Phone:** 970/325-4370

American

$7-$27

AAA Inspector Notes: The casual bistro serves creative seasonal appetizers; entrées such as tender red wine-braised pork shank with buttered asparagus and potato-wrapped, pan-seared salmon; as well as petite sweets of creamy mousses and layered delights in martini or tulip glasses. A Little Goats children's menu is available. **Bar:** full bar. **Address:** 400 Main Ave 81427 **Location:** South end of US 550. **Parking:** street only. D

BON TON RESTAURANT **Phone:** 970/325-4951

American

$14-$34

AAA Inspector Notes: In the basement of the St. Elmo Hotel, the warm and inviting restaurant is surrounded by rock walls, hardwood floors and an elegant martini bar. Menu selections include escargot and crawfish tails, beef Wellington, prime Angus steak, veal piccata, fresh seafood, chicken and pasta dishes. Decadent desserts such as the Galloping Goose Caboose and the Black Nasty, a chocolate fudge pie with a graham cracker crust, enhance the dining experience. **Bar:** full bar. **Reservations:** suggested. **Address:** 426 Main St 81427 **Location:** Just s of center on US 550 (Main St); in St Elmo Hotel. **Parking:** street only. D

BUEN TIEMPO RESTAURANT & CANTINA

Phone: 970/325-4544

Mexican

$10-$24

AAA Inspector Notes: The local favorite prepares Mexican food with flair. Distinctive sauces flavor family-pleasing preparations of fish, chicken and beef. **Bar:** full bar. **Address:** 515 Main St 81427 **Location:** Just s of center on US 550 (Main St). **Parking:** street only. L D

▼ *See AAA listing p. 274* ▼

BULOW'S BISTRO **Phone:** 970/325-7050

American
$8-$22

AAA Inspector Notes: The bistro offers unique, flavorful entrées in a casual, yet elegant, atmosphere. Although the menu changes seasonally, entrées typically include steak, chicken, pasta and seafood. In summer, mountain views can be enjoyed from the patio. **Bar:** full bar. **Address:** 505 Main St 81427 **Location:** Just s on US 550 (Main St); in Beaumont Hotel & Spa. **Parking:** street only. L D

COACHLIGHT RESTAURANT & TAVERN
Phone: 970/325-4361

American
$16-$39

AAA Inspector Notes: Patrons sit down to appetizers, chicken, seafood, steak, ribs and homemade mountain bread in the dining room. Specialty pizzas are served in the upstairs tavern, where seasonal outdoor decks afford beautiful mountain views. **Bar:** full bar. **Address:** 118 W 7th Ave 81427 **Location:** Just w of US 550 (Main St). **Parking:** street only. D

GOLDBELT BAR & GRILL **Phone:** 970/325-7242

Sandwiches
$5-$16

AAA Inspector Notes: Sweet potato fries with curry mayonnaise are addicting, as are the pesto chicken melt sandwich and East Coast-style steak and cheese sub. Popular homemade soup is served daily and patrons can build their own hand-tossed pizzas with homemade sauce, fresh dough and fine, quality cheeses. Postcard-perfect scenery can be viewed from the tall windows inside or from the wrap-around outdoor patio with umbrellas. Veggie burgers and gluten-free pizza also are available. **Bar:** full bar. **Address:** 800 Main St 81427 **Location:** Just n of center on US 550 (Main St). L D

OUTLAW STEAKHOUSE **Phone:** 970/325-4366

Steak
$15-$29

AAA Inspector Notes: In the heart of town, this is the longest-operating restaurant run by Ouray natives. Guests are treated to spectacular mountain views as they sit down to well-prepared steak, prime rib, chicken, ribs, crab legs and seafood. Old West atmosphere fills the tavern-style setting, which displays Western artwork, cowboy hats and wagon wheel overhead lighting. Great service is a hallmark. **Bar:** full bar. **Reservations:** suggested, in summer. **Address:** 610 Main St 81427 **Location:** On US 550 (Main St); center. **Parking:** street only. D

PAGOSA SPRINGS (F-2) pop. 1,727, elev. 7,105'

Pagosa (healing water) Springs, aptly named by the Ute Indians who vied for possession of the area's thermal springs, became a lumbering center and popular spa in the late 19th century. Bursting from the earth at 140 degrees Fahrenheit, the waters are used to heat some of the community's buildings. Today's bathers enjoy the waters at a variety of pools open to the public.

Numerous lakes and the surrounding lands of the San Juan National Forest *(see place listing p. 282)* and the Weminuche Wilderness Area offer a wide variety of year-round recreational opportunities, including fishing, hiking, horseback riding, bicycling, rafting, hot air ballooning, hunting, alpine and cross-country skiing, ice skating and snowmobiling. Just 17 miles west of the city is the 3,160-acre Chimney Rock Archaeological Area, set atop a high mesa that contains hundreds of Ancestral Puebloan sites. Tours and interpretive events are offered May 15 through September 30; phone (970) 883-5359 or (970) 264-2268, Oct. 1-May 14.

Pagosa Springs Area Visitor Center: 402 San Juan St., P.O. Box 787, Pagosa Springs, CO 81147. **Phone:** (970) 264-2360.

FRED HARMAN ART MUSEUM is at 85 Harman Park Dr. The work of Western painter and illustrator Fred Harman is displayed. Harman's cowboy comic strip "Red Ryder," drawn 1938-64, was once the nation's most widely syndicated print cartoon. The museum features Harman's studio as well as the oil paintings, pen and ink drawings, and bronze sculptures created in his later years. **Hours:** Mon.-Sat. 10:30-5, mid-May through Labor Day; Mon.-Fri. 10:30-5, day after Labor Day- Oct. 2. **Cost:** $3; $1 (ages 6-12). **Phone:** (970) 731-5785.

THE SPRINGS, 165 Hot Springs Blvd., offers 23 outdoor naturally hot, therapeutic mineral pools, a salt-water swimming pool and a freshwater whirlpool bath. The pools are arranged in a parklike setting, terraced along the San Juan River. A bath house with towels, robes and lockers is available.

Hours: Daily 7 a.m.-1 a.m., Memorial Day weekend-Labor Day; daily 7 a.m.-11 p.m. (also Fri.-Sat. 11 p.m.-1 a.m.), rest of year. **Cost:** Single visit $20; $17 (senior citizens); $12 (ages 2-10). Day pass $43 (locker included). Ages 0-13 must be with an adult. **Phone:** (970) 264-4168 or (800) 225-0934.

RECREATIONAL ACTIVITIES

Fishing

- **Wolf Creek Anglers** departs from 169 Pagosa St. **Hours:** Daily dawn-dusk. Phone ahead to confirm schedule. **Phone:** (719) 873-1414 or (970) 264-1415.

Skiing

- **Wolf Creek Ski Area** is 23 mi. e. on US 160 at the top of Wolf Creek Pass. **Hours:** Daily 8:30-4, early Nov.-early Apr. **Phone:** (970) 264-5639 or (800) 754-9653.

White-water Rafting

- **AAM's Mild to Wild Rafting & Jeep Tours Inc.** departs from the Piedra River Store 15 mi. w. on US 160. **Hours:** Full-day trips depart Wed., Fri. and Sun. at 9:15, mid-Apr. through July 4. **Phone:** (970) 247-4789 or (800) 567-6745.

ALPINE INN OF PAGOSA SPRINGS
Phone: 970/731-4005

Motel
Rates not provided

Address: 8 Solomon Dr 81147 **Location:** 2.5 mi w on US 160, just w on Piedra Rd. **Facility:** 28 units. 2 stories (no elevator), interior/exterior corridors. **Free Special Amenities: expanded continental breakfast and local telephone calls.**

SAVE / SOME UNITS FEE

FIRESIDE INN CABINS **Phone:** 970/264-9204

Cabin
$105-$194

Address: 1600 E Hwy 160 81147 **Location:** 1.3 mi e on US 160. **Facility:** 15 cabins. 1 story, exterior corridors. **Terms:** 30 day cancellation notice-fee imposed. **Activities:** whirlpool, fishing, horseshoes. **Guest Services:** coin laundry.

BIZ / SOME UNITS FEE

FIRST INN OF PAGOSA **Phone:** 970/264-4161

Motel
$66-$115

Address: 260 E Pagosa St 81147 **Location:** 0.5 mi e on US 160; on frontage road. **Facility:** 34 units. 2 stories (no elevator), interior corridors. **Terms:** cancellation fee imposed. **Activities:** sauna, whirlpool, fishing. *Fee:* ice skating. **Guest Services:** coin laundry. **Free Special Amenities: continental breakfast and high-speed Internet.**

SAVE

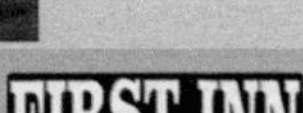

American owned, great rates, wake up to fresh cinnamon rolls, non-smoking facility, no pets allowed

HIGH COUNTRY LODGE & CABINS
Phone: (970)264-4181

Motel
$79-$210

Address: 3821 E Hwy 160 81147 **Location:** On US 160, 3 mi e. **Facility:** 32 units, some efficiencies, kitchens and cabins. 1-2 stories (no elevator), exterior corridors. **Terms:** cancellation fee imposed. **Activities:** whirlpools, fishing, horseshoes, limited exercise equipment. **Guest Services:** coin laundry.

/ SOME UNITS FEE

HILLSIDE INN **Phone:** 970/731-5101

Hotel
$80-$100

Address: 2 Solomon Dr 81147 **Location:** 2 mi w on US 160. **Facility:** 60 units. 2 stories (no elevator), interior corridors. **Pool(s):** heated indoor. **Activities:** whirlpool. **Guest Services:** coin laundry.

BIZ / SOME UNITS

PAGOSA LODGE **Phone:** 970/731-4141

Hotel
Rates not provided

Address: 3505 W Hwy 160 81147 **Location:** On US 160, 3.5 mi w. **Facility:** 100 units. 2 stories, interior corridors. **Amenities:** *Some:* high-speed Internet. **Pool(s):** heated indoor. **Activities:** sauna, whirlpools, limited exercise equipment.

/ SOME UNITS FEE

PAGOSA SPRINGS INN & SUITES **Phone:** 970/731-3400

Motel
$65-$189

Address: 519 Village Dr 81147 **Location:** 3.8 mi w on US 160. **Facility:** 90 units. 3 stories, interior corridors. **Terms:** cancellation fee imposed. **Pool(s):** heated indoor. **Activities:** whirlpool, exercise room. **Guest Services:** coin laundry.

    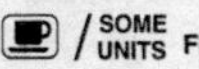   

/ SOME UNITS FEE

WHERE TO EAT

ALLEY HOUSE GRILLE **Phone:** 970/264-0999

American
$13-$27

AAA Inspector Notes: Guests can enjoy global cuisine served in a casually elegant atmosphere. Regular selections may include out-of-the-ordinary appetizers such as calamari with wasabi dipping sauce, a tempting Thai Caesar salad, gourmet pizza served on Belgian beer-based sourdough and scrumptious seasonal dessert selections. **Bar:** full bar. **Reservations:** suggested. **Address:** 214 Pagosa St 81147 **Location:** 0.3 mi e of center. **Parking:** street only. D

FARRAGO MARKET CAFE **Phone:** 970/264-4600

Deli
$7-$18

AAA Inspector Notes: Build-your-own pizzas with organic crust are a specialty at this cozy and colorful eatery. Among additional selections are Asian barbecue wings, fish tacos, Moroccan chicken salad, mango Gorgonzola quesadilla, daily made special salads, sandwiches and a good selection of gourmet coffees and tea. Cookies, brownies and pastries make great travel companions. **Bar:** beer & wine. **Address:** 175 Pagosa St 81147 **Location:** 0.3 mi e of center; corner of US 160 and 2nd St. L D

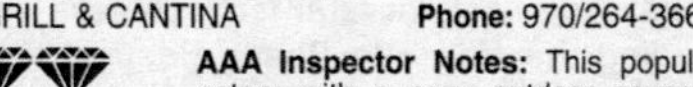

KIP'S GRILL & CANTINA **Phone:** 970/264-3663

Mexican
$7-$11

AAA Inspector Notes: This popular eatery with a cozy outdoor covered patio features delicious Baja tacos served with salsa fresca, cabbage and lime; chicken breast marinated in a cayenne garlic sauce; and beef and buffalo burgers. The Key lime pie is absolutely mouthwatering. **Bar:** full bar. **Address:** 121 Pagosa St 81147 **Location:** 0.4 mi e of center on US 160.

L D

MONTOYA'S ELK HORN CAFE **Phone:** 970/264-2146

Southwestern
$6-$10

AAA Inspector Notes: There's no doubt about it. This low-key restaurant is where loyal locals congregate for a hearty Southwestern meal such as Navajo tacos, a stuffed beef or chicken sopaipillas and daily specials. **Bar:** beer only. **Address:** 438C Pagosa St 81147 **Location:** On US 160; center. **Parking:** street only.

B L D

SAN JUAN ROADHOUSE **Phone:** 970/264-4545

Steak
$13-$36

AAA Inspector Notes: The rustic and romantic gold-mining setting invites a casual meal of savory appetizers, freshly cut steak or seasonal game selections, then one of the homemade desserts. Friendly, efficient servers enhance the dining experience. **Bar:** full bar. **Address:** 3825 Hwy 160 E 81147 **Location:** On US 160, 3 mi e; next to High Country Lodge & Cabins. D

VICTORIA'S CAFE & GRILL **Phone:** 970/264-0204

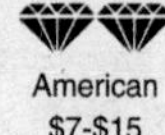

American

$7-$15

AAA Inspector Notes: The attractively decorated eatery offers delicious homemade soup, a wide variety of Her Majesty's salads, sandwiches fit for the lord of the manor, and nightly pasta, seafood and steak specials. For breakfast, tempting choices include Lady Caroline's ham and cheese quiche and King Louis' French toast. **Bar:** full bar. **Address:** 274 Pagosa St 81147 **Location:** Just e of historic downtown.

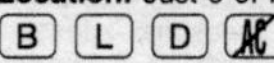

PALISADE (D-1) pop. 2,692, elev. 4,724'

A fruit-growing region for more than a century, the East Grand Valley area along the Colorado River at the base of the Book Cliffs and Grand Mesa is known in particular for its peaches. Apples, apricots, cherries and plums also are plentiful, and roadside fruit stands are common sights in season. Vineyards also flourish here. Palisade is home to several wineries producing traditional grape wines as well as those made from other fruits. Bicycling, river floats and hiking are popular choices for outdoor recreation.

Palisade hosts several festivals each year, including the Palisade Peach Festival the third weekend in August, which offers an ice cream social, street dance, orchard tours, a pancake breakfast, a recipe contest, a car show and a parade. The Colorado Mountain Winefest celebrates the grape with 4 days of tastings, seminars, jazz, grape stomping, winery tours and an amateur winemaker's competition in mid-September. In mid-December the Olde-Fashioned Christmas entertains attendees with horse-drawn wagon rides, a soup challenge, music, caroling, arts and crafts and wine tastings.

Palisade Chamber of Commerce: 319 S. Main St., P.O. Box 729, Palisade, CO 81526. **Phone:** (970) 464-7458.

WINERIES

- **Canyon Wind Cellars** is off I-70 exit 44, then .5 mi. s.w. following signs to 3907 North River Rd. **Hours:** Tastings daily 10-5. Guided tours are offered Sat.-Sun. at 11, 1 and 3, June-Aug. **Phone:** (970) 464-0888.
- **Carlson Vineyards** is at 461 35 Rd. **Hours:** Daily 10-6. Closed Jan. 1, Thanksgiving and Christmas. **Phone:** (970) 464-5554 or (888) 464-5554.
- **Garfield Estates Vineyard & Winery** is at 3572 G Rd. **Hours:** Tastings daily 11-5, Mar.-Dec.; Mon.-Fri. noon-5, rest of year. Tours available by appointment. Closed Easter, Thanksgiving and Christmas. **Phone:** (970) 464-0941.
- **Grande River Vineyards** is off I-70 exit 42, then .75 mi. s. to 787 N. Elberta Ave. **Hours:** Daily 9-5. Closed Jan. 1, Thanksgiving and Christmas. **Phone:** (970) 464-5867 or (800) 264-7696.
- **Plum Creek Cellars** is off I-70 exit 42, s. to US 6, then 5 mi. w. to 3708 G Rd. **Hours:** Sun.-Thurs. 10-5, Fri.-Sat. 10-6, Apr.-Oct.; daily 10-5, rest of year. Closed Jan. 1, Thanksgiving and Christmas. Phone ahead to confirm schedule. **Phone:** (970) 464-7586.

WINE COUNTRY INN **Phone:** (970)464-5777

Hotel

$145-$275 5/1-10/31
$105-$275 11/1-4/30

Address: 777 Grande River Dr 81526 **Location:** I-70 exit 42, 0.3 mi w. **Facility:** 80 units, some two bedrooms and kitchens. 2-3 stories, interior corridors. **Terms:** check-in 4 pm, cancellation fee imposed. **Amenities:** high-speed Internet. **Pool(s):** heated outdoor. **Activities:** whirlpool, exercise room. **Guest Services:** valet and coin laundry.

SAVE CALL BIZ

/ SOME UNITS FEE

WHERE TO EAT

INARI'S, A PALISADE BISTRO **Phone:** 970/464-4911

American

$13-$19

AAA Inspector Notes: Located in a quaint neighborhood, the bistro's salads, appetizers, small plates and entrées lead up to the yummy indulgence of decadent seasonal desserts. **Bar:** beer & wine. **Reservations:** suggested. **Address:** 336 Main St 81526 **Location:** I-70 exit 42, 0.5 mi s, 0.5 mi e on W 1st St, then 0.3 mi s. **Parking:** on-site and street. D

RED ROSE CAFE **Phone:** 970/464-7673

Specialty

$8-$25

AAA Inspector Notes: Patrons feast on a mix of Italian, Asian, Vietnamese and American cuisine. Rose often stops at tables to demonstrate how to wrap the lettuce, bean sprouts, cucumber and mint around the egg roll. Appetizers may include mussels or deep-fried Rocky Mountain oysters. Specialty steaks include steak Diane, pizziola and twin medallions pressed with black pepper and finished with a Jack Daniels whiskey sauce. The wine bar offers an assortment of local wines. **Bar:** full bar. **Reservations:** suggested. **Address:** 235 Main St 81526 **Location:** I-70 exit 42, 0.3 mi s to W 1st St, 0.5 mi e, then just s. L D

PAONIA pop. 1,451

BROSS HOTEL BED & BREAKFAST
Phone: (970)527-6776

Historic Bed & Breakfast

$125-$138

Address: 312 Onarga Ave 81428 **Location:** Corner of 3rd St and Onarga Ave; just n of downtown. **Facility:** This 1906 B&B combines lovely landscaping and Western charm with modern conveniences, including private baths. 10 units. 3 stories (no elevator), interior corridors. **Terms:** office hours 4 pm-8 pm, check-in 4 pm, cancellation fee imposed. **Activities:** whirlpool.

WHERE TO EAT

FLYING FORK CAFE & BAKERY **Phone:** 970/527-3203

Italian

$7-$23

AAA Inspector Notes: Simple elegance describes both the cuisine and ambience. The lunch menu may include an open-faced chicken Parmigiana sandwich, grilled lemon ginger chicken salad or a creamy pesto pasta with garlic toast. Among elegant dinner entrées are pasta, beef tenderloin, daily fresh fish or homemade lasagna or ravioli. In the summer, the best seating is in the outdoor garden under the fruit trees. Patrons can choose from a very nice selection of wines and beers from Colorado and Italy. **Bar:** full bar. **Reservations:** suggested. **Address:** 103 3rd St 81428 **Location:** From SR 133, 0.7 mi e.

L D

PARKER (D-4) pop. 45,297, elev. 5,868'

THE WILDLIFE EXPERIENCE is 1 mi. n. on Parker Rd., then 4 mi. w. on Lincoln Ave. to jct. S. Peoria St. The center is dedicated to the preservation and appreciation of wildlife and their habitats. Permanent and traveling interactive exhibits of natural history, film and fine art are featured. Natural history exhibits showcase animals in natural environments. The 315-seat Extreme Screen Theater presents large-screen format adventure films. Education and conservation programs and two interactive children's galleries are available.

Time: Allow 1 hour minimum. **Hours:** Tues.-Sun. and Mon. holidays 9-5. Closed Thanksgiving and Christmas. **Cost:** Museum $10; $9 (ages 65+); $6 (ages 3-12). Extreme Screen Theater $9; $8 (ages 65+); $6 (ages 3-12). Combination ticket $14; $13 (ages 65+); $9 (ages 3-12). **Phone:** (720) 488-3300.

HAMPTON INN & SUITES **Phone:** (303)841-2977

Hotel
$98-$104

AAA Benefit: Members save up to 10% everyday!

Address: 19010 E Cottonwood Dr 80138 **Location:** E470 toll road exit 5 (Parker Rd/SR 83), 0.4 mi se on Crown Crest Blvd, then just e. **Facility:** 84 units. 4 stories, interior corridors. **Terms:** 1-7 night minimum stay, cancellation fee imposed. **Amenities:** video games (fee), high-speed Internet. **Pool(s):** heated indoor. **Activities:** whirlpool, exercise room. **Guest Services:** valet laundry.

BIZ FEE / SOME UNITS

HOLIDAY INN **Phone:** (303)248-2147

Hotel
$127-$147

Address: 19308 Cottonwood Dr 80138 **Location:** E470 toll road exit 5 (Parker Rd/SR 83) eastbound, straight at light, follow signs to Cottonwood Dr; exit westbound, just s to Crown Crest Blvd, follow signs to Cottonwood Dr. **Facility:** 100 units. 4 stories, interior corridors. **Terms:** check-in 4 pm. **Amenities:** high-speed Internet, safes. **Dining:** 2 restaurants. **Pool(s):** heated indoor. **Activities:** whirlpool, exercise room. **Guest Services:** valet and coin laundry.

BIZ FEE / SOME UNITS FEE

SUPER 8-PARKER **Phone:** (720)851-2644

Hotel
$71-$98

Address: 6230 E Pine Ln 80138 **Location:** E470 toll road exit 5 (Parker Rd/SR 83), 0.4 mi se, then just e. **Facility:** 74 units. 3 stories, interior corridors. **Terms:** cancellation fee imposed. **Guest Services:** valet and coin laundry.

BIZ / SOME UNITS FEE

WHERE TO EAT

ARMANDO'S RISTORANTE ITALIANO **Phone:** 720/851-6770

Italian
$7-$23

AAA Inspector Notes: The first time I tried the double-crust pizza filled with spinach, black olives and mozzarella, I fell in love. This was at their fast-food-style eatery near my old high school. This new location has a more formal dining area and expanded menu. The Italian owners still assist in the kitchen and occasionally sing opera with the staff. This time I tried the calamari, which had a savory crust and was easy to bite into. When I had a bite of the eggplant Parmigiana I knew what to order next time. **Bar:** full bar. **Address:** 9964 S Twenty Mile Rd 80134 **Location:** E470 toll road exit 5 (Parker Rd/SR 83), 1.2 mi s, just w on Lincoln Ave, then just s on Dransfeldt Rd. L D

JUNZ **Phone:** 720/851-1005

Japanese
$8-$24

AAA Inspector Notes: Chef Jun combines elements of French and Japanese cooking to create his own innovative dishes. The eclectic menu lists delicious tempura, sushi and teriyaki dishes, as well as filet mignon, lamb chops and pasta. Lobster salad makes a delightful light lunch. **Bar:** full bar. **Address:** 11211 S Dransfeldt Rd, Suite 100 80134 **Location:** E470 toll road exit 5 (Parker Rd/SR 83), 2.3 mi s, just w on Main St, then 0.4 mi s; in Parker Valley Center strip mall. L D

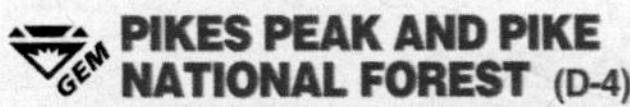

PIKES PEAK AND PIKE NATIONAL FOREST (D-4)

Elevations in the forest range from 7,000 ft. near Colorado Springs to 14,110 ft. at Pikes Peak. Refer to AAA maps for additional elevation information.

West of Denver and Colorado Springs, the 14,110-foot summit of Pikes Peak is visible from a long distance on the Great Plains. The view from the peak inspired poet Katherine Lee Bates in 1893 to write "America the Beautiful." The sentinel of the Front Range is the prime attraction of 1,105,704-acre Pike National Forest. The summit is reached by highway or cog railway; hikers can climb the 11.7-mile Barr National Recreation Trail.

Pike's proximity to the Denver-Colorado Springs corridor makes it one of the most heavily used national forests in the state. The forest has many developed campgrounds and ample opportunities for fishing, hunting, hiking and winter sports. Scenic drives include the Rampart Range Road and the Pikes Peak Highway. Lost Creek and Mount Evans wildernesses are accessible only by foot or horseback.

The Devil's Head Lookout Tower, the last operational fire lookout along the Front Range, stands atop the highest point in the Rampart Range; it is accessible by a 1.3-mile hiking trail. Remnants of early mining activities are evident near Fairplay *(see place listing p. 196)* in the South Park Valley.

For more information write the Forest Supervisor, Pike National Forest, 2840 Kachina Dr., Pueblo, CO 81008; phone (719) 553-1400. *See Recreation Chart.*

PIKES PEAK COG RAILWAY—
see Manitou Springs p. 249.

PIKES PEAK HIGHWAY starts at Cascade, 10 mi. w. of Colorado Springs off US 24. This scenic 19-mile toll road leads to the 14,110-foot summit of one of the nation's tallest mountains. From the gateway at an elevation of 7,400 feet, visitors travel above the timberline and encounter scenic vistas, alpine forests, mountain reservoirs and wildlife habitats. The historic Glen Cove Inn, the North Slope Recreation Area, the Crystal Reservoir Gift Shop and the Summit House offer visitor services.

Caution: Excessive automotive braking is dangerous; use low gear for ascent and descent. An informational handout provides safe driving tips. High altitudes may be hazardous to infants or those with respiratory problems. Fishing and hiking are permitted; a state fishing permit is required. Allow 2 hours, 30 minutes for round-trip travel. **Hours:** Uphill gate open daily 7:30-6, Memorial Day weekend-Labor Day; 7:30-5, day after Labor Day-Sept. 30; 9-3, rest of year (weather permitting).

Cost: $12; $5 (ages 6-15). Maximum charge per private vehicle $40 (up to five people). A fee is charged for fishing. **Phone:** (719) 385-7325 or (800) 318-9505.

PINEWOOD SPRINGS

VILLA TATRA **Phone:** 303/823-6819

Polish
$9-$30

AAA Inspector Notes: This charming restaurant offers Eastern European dishes prepared from scratch, homemade pastry, smoked fish and sausage dishes. Smoked salmon and trout are available by mail. Macrobiotic and vegetarian dinners are available with a two-day reservation. It's open for lunch on Saturday and Sunday. **Bar:** full bar. **Reservations:** suggested. **Address:** 729 Pinewood Dr 80540 **Location:** 12.5 mi se of Estes Park on US 36; town center. D

PLACERVILLE (E-1) elev. 7,316'

RECREATIONAL ACTIVITIES

White-water Rafting

- **AAM's Mild to Wild Rafting & Jeep Tours Inc.** departs from Placerville City Park on SR 145. **Hours:** One, 2 and 3-day trips depart Wed.-Thurs. and Sat.-Sun. at 9:30, May 1-late July. **Phone:** (970) 247-4789 or (800) 567-6745.

PLATTEVILLE (A-5) pop. 2,485, elev. 4,825'

FORT VASQUEZ MUSEUM AND VISITOR INFORMATION CENTER, 13412 US 85, features a full-size reconstruction of an early adobe fur-trading post. Built by Louis Vasquez and Andrew Sublette in 1835 to trade with the Cheyenne and Arapaho people, the fort was abandoned in 1842 and eventually worn down by wind, rain and snow. Works Progress Administration (WPA) workers rebuilt the adobe walls 1935-36.

A modern museum features exhibits about the fur-trade era, American Indian culture and archeological work completed at the fort in the 1960s. **Hours:** Daily 9:30-4:30, Memorial Day-Labor Day; Wed.-Sat. 9:30-4:30, Sun. 1-4:30, rest of year. **Cost:** $2. **Phone:** (970) 785-2832.

PONCHA SPRINGS (E-3) pop. 737

GRIMO'S ITALIAN RESTAURANT **Phone:** 719/539-2903

Italian
$11-$20

AAA Inspector Notes: For a taste of New York Italian cuisine, this is the place to try, especially for those travelers staying in nearby Salida. **Bar:** full bar. **Address:** 146 S Main St 81242 **Location:** Just s of jct US 50 and 285. D

PUEBLO (E-4) pop. 106,595, elev. 4,662'

• Restaurants p. 272

Trader Jim Beckwourth knew a good location when he saw one. He and his party of trappers constructed an adobe fortress at the confluence of Fountain Creek and the Arkansas River in autumn 1842. By the following spring a thriving community had developed and Beckwourth dubbed it Pueblo, meaning "town."

Mountain men, trappers, traders, American Indians and immigrants convened at this crossroads post. Until a Ute massacre on Christmas Day 1854, Pueblo was the largest settlement in the region. The arrival of the railroad in 1872 and the discovery of coal near Trinidad *(see place listing p. 295)* made the town a booming workshop for the mines. Foundries manufactured mining equipment; smelters processed the ores.

By 1880 Pueblo's population had increased eightfold, and its present status as Colorado's major industrial center was well established. One of the industrial pioneers of this period was Colorado Coal & Iron Co., now Rocky Mountain Steel, Inc.

Downtown's revitalized waterfront includes the Historic Arkansas Riverwalk of Pueblo, a favorite place for walking, renting paddleboats or enjoying guided boat tours; phone (719) 595-1589 for information and events.

Just west of the city, Lake Pueblo State Park *(see Recreation Chart)* impounds 17,000-acre Pueblo Reservoir, which is part of the Fryingpan-Arkansas irrigation project. Within the city limits 279 acres of municipal parks provide recreational facilities. Many nature and bicycle trails are available. The Arkansas River is popular for white-water rafting.

The Colorado State Fair is held at the fairgrounds in late August. The third weekend after Labor Day the Chile & Frijoles Festival features cooking contests, a jalapeño-eating competition, a farmers market and live entertainment.

Greater Pueblo Chamber of Commerce: 302 N. Santa Fe Ave., Pueblo, CO 81003. **Phone:** (719) 542-1704 or (800) 233-3446.

Shopping areas: The Union Avenue Historic District features shopping, galleries, cafés and entertainment in restored brick buildings.

EL PUEBLO HISTORY MUSEUM is off I-25 exit 98B, then 3 blks. w. to 301 N. Union Ave. The museum depicts the history of the region's varied cultures. Permanent exhibits focus on American Indians, European explorers, trade and settlement, agriculture, industry and natural history. Murals and a hall of international flags also are presented. The museum functions as a visitor information center and a gateway to the city's Historic Arkansas Riverwalk and Union Avenue historic district.

Time: Allow 1 hour minimum. **Hours:** Tues.-Sat. 10-4. Closed Jan. 1, Thanksgiving and Christmas. **Cost:** $5; $4 (ages 6-12, ages 65+ and students with ID); free (ages 0-5). Free to ages 0-12 on Sat. **Phone:** (719) 583-0453.

THE NATURE AND RAPTOR CENTER OF PUEBLO, 5200 Nature Center Rd., provides a variety of educational and recreational activities set along the Arkansas River with miles of paved and unpaved trails, xeriscape demonstration gardens, fishing, a watercraft launch, and a raptor rehabilitation center, home to numerous species of predatory birds including eagles, hawks, owls and falcons. **Hours:** Grounds dawn-dusk. Raptor Center Tues.-Sun. 11-4. **Cost:** Free. **Parking:** $3. **Phone:** (719) 549-2414, or (719) 549-2327 for the raptor center.

PUEBLO ZOO, in Pueblo City Park, 4 mi. s. of US 50 on SR 45 (Pueblo Blvd.) at jct. Goodnight Ave., houses a collection of animals from around the world, including some threatened or endangered species. Visitors can experience a rainforest, visit the underwater penguin and otter observation areas or view the African lion and Asian monkey exhibits. Wonders of the natural world are explored in the White Discovery Room.

Time: Allow 1 hour, 30 minutes minimum. **Hours:** Daily 9-5, Memorial Day-Labor Day; Mon.-Fri. 9-4, Sat.-Sun. 9-5, May 1-day before Memorial Day; Mon.-Sat. 9-4, Sun. noon-4, rest of year. Last admission is 1 hour before closing. Closes at noon on Christmas Eve and Dec. 31. Closed Jan. 1, Thanksgiving and Christmas. **Cost:** $8; $7 (ages 13-17, 65+ and military with ID); $5 (ages 3-12). **Phone:** (719) 561-1452.

ROSEMOUNT MUSEUM is off I-25 exit 99B, w. on 13th St., then 1 blk. n. on Greenwood to 419 W. 14th St. The 37-room, 1893 Victorian mansion contains original antique furnishings and depicts gracious life in the late 1800s. Built by a wealthy Pueblo entrepreneur, the house is constructed of pink rhyolite stone. **Hours:** Tues.-Sat. 10-3:30, Feb.-Dec. Closed major holidays. **Cost:** $6; $5 (ages 60+); $4 (ages 6-18). **Phone:** (719) 545-5290.

SANGRE DE CRISTO ARTS AND CONFERENCE CENTER, 210 N. Santa Fe Ave., is the scene of cultural and civic events. Six galleries feature changing art exhibits; a children's museum has hands-on activities. **Hours:** Tues.-Sat. 11-4. Closed major holidays. **Cost:** (includes Buell Children's Museum) $4; $3 (ages 3-13). **Phone:** (719) 295-7200.

Buell Children's Museum is at 210 N. Santa Fe Ave. Interactive exhibits for children focus on the arts, history and science. Children may put on a theatrical show, create works of art and participate in a multisensory exhibit. The Buell Baby Barn presents activities for children ages 0-3. **Time:** Allow 2 hours minimum. **Hours:** Tues.-Sat. 11-4 (also Fri. 9-11 a.m.). Closed major holidays. **Cost:** (includes Sangre de Cristo Arts and Conference Center) $4; $3 (ages 3-13). **Phone:** (719) 295-7200.

STEELWORKS MUSEUM OF INDUSTRY AND CULTURE is at 215 Canal St. The museum provides an overview of some 120 years of operations of the Colorado Fuel & Iron Company, which controlled the Western steel and mining industry for many years. The primary exhibit covers the period 1915-1936; topics include the steel mill, coal mines and the C&W Railway. The Mine Rescue Car, just outside the building, is a train car once used as a first-aid training station and rescue car to aid trapped or injured miners. **Tours:** Guided tours are available. **Time:** Allow 45 minutes minimum. **Hours:** Mon.-Sat. 10-4. Closed Jan. 1, July 4, Thanksgiving and Christmas. **Cost:** $5; $3 (ages 4-12). **Phone:** (719) 564-9086.

BEST WESTERN EAGLERIDGE INN & SUITES
Phone: (719)543-4644

Hotel
$89-$100

AAA Benefit: Members save up to 20%, plus 10% bonus points with Best Western Rewards®.

Address: 4727 N Elizabeth St 81008 **Location:** I-25 exit 102, just w, then just n. **Facility:** 59 units. 3 stories, interior corridors. **Parking:** winter plug-ins. **Amenities:** high-speed Internet. **Pool(s):** heated indoor. **Activities:** sauna, whirlpool, exercise room. **Guest Services:** valet and coin laundry. **Free Special Amenities: full breakfast and local telephone calls.**

/ SOME UNITS FEE

CAMBRIA SUITES **Phone:** (719)546-1234

Contemporary Hotel
$99-$163

Address: 150 S Santa Fe Ave 81003 **Location:** I-25 exit 98B, just w, then 0.3 mi s. **Facility:** 105 units. 4 stories, interior corridors. **Terms:** cancellation fee imposed. **Amenities:** high-speed Internet. **Pool(s):** heated indoor. **Activities:** whirlpool, exercise room. **Guest Services:** valet and coin laundry.

COMFORT INN **Phone:** 719/542-6868

Hotel
Rates not provided

Address: 4645 N Freeway 81008 **Location:** I-25 exit 102, just w. **Facility:** 60 units. 2 stories (no elevator), interior corridors. **Pool(s):** heated indoor. **Guest Services:** valet and coin laundry.

FEE

ECONO LODGE **Phone:** (719)542-9933

Hotel
$54-$120

Address: 4615 N Elizabeth St 81008 **Location:** I-25 exit 102, just w, just s. **Facility:** 53 units. 2 stories (no elevator), interior corridors. **Terms:** cancellation fee imposed. **Pool(s):** heated indoor. **Activities:** whirlpool. **Guest Services:** coin laundry.

HAMPTON INN & SUITES NORTH **Phone:** (719)543-6606

Hotel
$98-$116

AAA Benefit: Members save up to 10% everyday!

Address: 4790 Eagleridge Cir 81008 **Location:** I-25 exit 102, just w, then just n. **Facility:** 100 units. 4 stories, interior corridors. **Terms:** 1-7 night minimum stay, cancellation fee imposed. **Amenities:** high-speed Internet. **Pool(s):** heated indoor. **Activities:** whirlpool, exercise room. **Guest Services:** valet and coin laundry.

BIZ

HAMPTON INN & SUITES SOUTH **Phone:** (719)566-1726

Hotel
$89-$98

AAA Benefit: Members save up to 10% everyday!

Address: 3315 Gateway Dr 81004 **Location:** I-25 exit 94, just w. **Facility:** 81 units, some efficiencies. 5 stories, interior corridors. **Terms:** 1-7 night minimum stay, cancellation fee imposed. **Pool(s):** heated indoor/outdoor. **Activities:** whirlpool, exercise room. **Guest Services:** valet and coin laundry.

CALL BIZ / SOME UNITS

HOLIDAY INN & SUITES **Phone:** (719)542-8888

Hotel
$79-$159

Address: 4530 Dillon Dr 81008 **Location:** I-25 exit 102, just e, then just s. **Facility:** 89 units. 4 stories, interior corridors. **Parking:** winter plug-ins. **Amenities:** high-speed Internet. **Pool(s):** heated indoor. **Activities:** whirlpool, exercise room. **Guest Services:** valet and coin laundry.

CALL BIZ / SOME UNITS FEE

LA QUINTA INN & SUITES PUEBLO **Phone:** (719)542-3500

Hotel
$88-$174

Address: 4801 N Elizabeth St 81008 **Location:** I-25 exit 102, just nw. **Facility:** 101 units. 4 stories, interior corridors. **Amenities:** video games (fee). *Some:* high-speed Internet. **Pool(s):** heated outdoor. **Activities:** whirlpool, exercise room. **Guest Services:** valet and coin laundry.

FEE / SOME UNITS

MICROTEL INN & SUITES **Phone:** (719)242-2020

Hotel
$44-$71

Address: 3343 Gateway Dr 81004 **Location:** I-25 exit 94, just w, then just s. **Facility:** 63 units. 3 stories, interior corridors. **Guest Services:** valet and coin laundry.

/ SOME UNITS FEE

PUEBLO MARRIOTT AT THE CONVENTION CENTER **Phone:** (719)542-3200

Hotel
$161-$197

Marriott HOTELS & RESORTS **AAA Benefit:** AAA hotel discounts of 5% or more.

Address: 110 W 1st St 81003 **Location:** I-25 exit 98B, just w. **Facility:** 163 units. 7 stories, interior corridors. **Amenities:** *Some:* high-speed Internet. **Pool(s):** heated indoor. **Activities:** whirlpool, exercise room. **Guest Services:** valet and coin laundry.

/ SOME UNITS FEE

WHERE TO EAT

CACTUS FLOWER RESTAURANT **Phone:** 719/545-8218

Mexican
$5-$12

AAA Inspector Notes: This restaurant prepares traditional Mexican-American fare in a Southwestern setting. Those seeking the perfect margarita have an extensive array of choices. **Bar:** full bar. **Address:** 4610 N Elizabeth St 81008 **Location:** I-25 exit 102, just w. L D

THE CARRIAGE HOUSE AT ROSEMOUNT MUSEUM **Phone:** 719/543-4192

American
$9-$19

AAA Inspector Notes: Pueblo's premier lunch venue offers creatively prepared savory dishes, soups, sandwiches, fresh salads and more served in the dramatic Victorian interior of a century-old building. **Bar:** full bar. **Address:** 406 W 15th St 81003 **Location:** I-25 exit 99B, 0.3 mi w to Grand Ave, then 0.6 mi n. **Parking:** street only. L

DC'S ON B STREET **Phone:** 719/584-3410

American
$7-$28

AAA Inspector Notes: The restaurant is a must-stop for visitors. The fresh, attractively presented food, including gourmet sandwiches, salads and pasta dishes, tastes delicious, and staff members make guests feel at home. The seasonal dinner menu features beef tenderloin, fresh fish, Colorado lamb and a nice selection of wines. **Bar:** full bar. **Address:** 115 W B St 81003 **Location:** I-25 exit 98B, just w on 1st St, 0.5 mi s on Union Ave, then just w. **Parking:** street only. L D

HOPSCOTCH BAKERY **Phone:** 719/542-4467

Breads/Pastries
$4-$10

AAA Inspector Notes: Patrons grab gourmet panini sandwiches, salads and desserts to go, then picnic nearby, especially along the Riverfront area. Bakery cases beckon with delicious croissants, cakes, cookies and pastries, which pair great with yummy ice cream. **Address:** 333 S Union Ave 81003 **Location:** Corner of W B St and S Union Ave; in historic downtown. **Parking:** street only.

B L

LA RENAISSANCE
Menu on AAA.com **Phone:** 719/543-6367

American
$14-$25

AAA Inspector Notes: In a renovated church building dating back to 1886, you'll enjoy a five-course dinner accompanied by a selection from a very good wine list. Tasty appetizers, soup, salad and dessert are served tableside by a very good staff. **Bar:** full bar. **Reservations:** suggested. **Address:** 217 E Routt Ave 81004 **Location:** I-25 exit 97B (Abriendo Ave), 0.5 mi w, then just s; corner of Michigan St and Routt Ave. **Historic** D

MAGPIES **Phone:** 719/542-5522

American
$7-$23

AAA Inspector Notes: In historic Holden Block, which was built in 1883 by Delos Holden, the city's first mayor, the restaurant features warm wood accents that evoke this earlier era. The menu features gourmet sandwiches, soup and quiches for lunch. On Friday evening only, more upscale offerings are featured such as teriyaki-glazed salmon, grilled lamb chops and rib-eye steak. **Bar:** full bar. **Address:** 229 S Union Ave 81003 **Location:** I-25 exit 98B, 0.3 mi w, then 0.5 mi sw. **Parking:** street only.

L

MANHATTAN'S PIZZA PARLOR **Phone:** 719/545-3400

Italian
$6-$18

AAA Inspector Notes: A smaller-scale replica of the Statue of Liberty greets visitors at the entry of the New York-style pizza parlor. After a while, murals of the Big Apple's famous landmarks might make diners start believing they're actually in the city that never sleeps. Folks looking for a traditional pizza will find it, but a list of creative pies satisfies adventurous folks who want to try something new. **Bar:** beer & wine. **Address:** 1110 W Hwy 50 81008 **Location:** I-25 exit 101, just s on Club Manor Dr, then w on frontage road. L D

MO MO JAPANESE RESTAURANT **Phone:** 719/542-8500

Japanese
$7-$15

AAA Inspector Notes: Patrons of this quaint restaurant who can't decide what to eat can try a bento box: a sample of sushi, tempura, teriyaki chicken and more. Exotic-flavored ice cream ends the meal on a sweet note. **Bar:** beer & wine. **Address:** 716 N Santa Fe Ave 81003 **Location:** I-25 exit 99B, just w, then just s. **Parking:** on-site and street. L D

NACHO'S **Phone:** 719/544-0733

Mexican
$5-$13

AAA Inspector Notes: The local favorite offers up the usual suspects: tacos, enchiladas, fajitas and more in a hacienda-style setting. **Bar:** full bar. **Reservations:** suggested, weekends. **Address:** 409 N Santa Fe Ave 81001 **Location:** I-25 exit 99A, just w on 6th St, then s; downtown. B L D

ROSARIO'S ITALIAN RESTAURANT
Phone: 719/583-1822

Italian
$9-$28

AAA Inspector Notes: Family-owned and –operated, the restaurant serves traditional, attractively presented Italian dishes, seafood, and USDA Prime aged beef in an elegant atmosphere. **Bar:** full bar. **Address:** 2930 N Elizabeth St 81008 **Location:** I-25 exit 101, just s. L D

SHAMROCK BREWING CO. **Phone:** 719/542-9974

Irish
$8-$19

AAA Inspector Notes: This pub features hearty portions, flavorful beers and Irish-theme décor. The menu lines up traditional Irish favorites such as shepherd's pie, fish and chips, and boxties (fluffy potato crepes stuffed with a variety of fillings). **Bar:** full bar. **Address:** 108 W 3rd St 81003 **Location:** I-25 exit 98B, just w to Santa Fe Ave, just n to 3rd St, then just w. **Parking:** street only. L D

PUEBLO WEST pop. 29,637

COMFORT INN WEST **Phone:** (719)547-9400

Motel
$76-$81 5/1-9/9
$70-$76 9/10-4/30

Address: 77 S Radnor Dr 81007 **Location:** I-25 exit 101 (US 50 W), 7.5 mi w to McCulloch Blvd, just s to Spaulding Ave, then just e. **Facility:** 49 units. 2 stories (no elevator), interior corridors. **Pool(s):** heated indoor. **Activities:** whirlpool, exercise room. **Guest Services:** coin laundry. **Free Special Amenities: expanded continental breakfast and local telephone calls.**

RANGELY pop. 2,365

BLUE MOUNTAIN INN & SUITES **Phone:** 970/675-8888

Hotel
Rates not provided

Address: 37 Park St 81648 **Location:** 0.3 mi w of center. **Facility:** 50 units. 2 stories, interior corridors. **Pool(s):** heated indoor. **Activities:** whirlpool. **Guest Services:** valet and coin laundry.

FEE

WHERE TO EAT

GIOVANNI'S ITALIAN GRILL **Phone:** 970/675-2670

Italian
$8-$16

AAA Inspector Notes: In a convenient Main Street location, this colorfully decorated restaurant serves a variety of salads and pasta entrees. **Bar:** beer & wine. **Address:** 855 E Main St 81648 **Location:** East end of town. L D

RED FEATHER LAKES (B-3) pop. 343, elev. 8,342'

THE GREAT STUPA is 5 mi. e. on CR 68C (gravel road) to the Shambhala Mountain Center. Rising out of a ponderosa pine forest, this Buddhist shrine is the centerpiece of a 600-acre meditation retreat center. The shrine, said to be one of the world's most significant examples of Buddhist architecture, features a 108-foot-tall gold dome and brightly painted facade. The interior features inlaid marble floors, an intricately painted ceiling and a towering gold statue of Buddha.

Note: Since visitors must walk two-thirds of a mile from the parking lot to the shrine, comfortable shoes are recommended. **Tours:** Guided tours are available. **Time:** Allow 1 hour minimum. **Hours:** Daily 9-6. Guided tours are offered Sat.-Sun. at 2. **Cost:** $10; $8 (senior citizens). **Phone:** (888) 788-7221.

REDSTONE (D-2) pop. 130, elev. 7,190'

At the turn of the 20th century, John Cleveland Osgood—cousin to President Grover Cleveland and one of the wealthiest industrialists of his day—created a utopian village in the Crystal River Valley to house the men who worked his coal mines and coke ovens.

Taking its name from the valley's red sandstone cliffs, Redstone was filled with cottages for miners and their families and an inn for bachelors. For his own home Osgood built a magnificent 25,000-square-foot mansion he named Cleveholm Manor, which rivaled some of the finest estates in Europe. The estate is known today as Redstone Castle, and tours recount its history; phone (970) 963-9656 for information. As the mines declined and the workers moved away, the cottages were sold as residences. Many now contain unique shops and boutiques.

Redstone retains much of its Craftsman-era character. A small museum preserves photographs and relics from Redstone's past, and several shops exhibit pottery, jewelry and paintings by local artists.

Carbondale Chamber of Commerce: 981 Cowen Dr., Suite C, P.O. Box 1645, Carbondale, CO 81623. **Phone:** (970) 963-1890.

RIDGWAY (E-2) pop. 924, elev. 6,988'

Ridgway is nestled between the verdant San Juan and Uncompahgre national forests with the rugged San Juan Mountains serving as a dramatic backdrop. Recreational activities, including boating, fishing, cross-country skiing, swimming and hiking, abound at Ridgway State Park *(see Recreation Chart)*. The San Juan Skyway begins its southerly route on US 550 in Ridgway, offering scenic views of emerald pine and golden aspen forests at every turn.

Ridgway Area Chamber of Commerce and Visitors Information Center: 150 Racecourse Rd., Ridgway, CO 81432. **Phone:** (970) 626-5181 or (800) 220-4959.

Self-guiding tours: Historic buildings and homes from the late 19th and the early 20th centuries may be seen on a walking tour of Ridgway. Maps can be picked up at the visitors information center.

RIDGWAY RAILROAD MUSEUM, 150 Racecourse Rd., educates visitors about narrow-gauge railroad history in southwestern Colorado. Featured railroads include the Rio Grande Southern, Silverton Railroad and Ouray Branch Denver and Rio Grande. Indoor and outdoor exhibits include rolling stock and portray the history of the famous RGS "Galloping Geese." Self-guiding tour brochures are contained in a box at the entrance. **Time:** Allow 30 minutes minimum. **Hours:** Daily 9-4, May-Oct.; Mon.-Fri. 10-3, rest of year. Closed July 4, Thanksgiving and Christmas. **Cost:** Free. **Phone:** (970) 626-5181.

RECREATIONAL ACTIVITIES

Hot Air Ballooning

- **San Juan Balloon Adventures** departs from various locations in Ridgway. **Hours:** Tours depart daily at dawn (weather permitting). **Phone:** (970) 626-5495.

RIDGWAY LODGE & SUITES **Phone:** (970)626-5444

Hotel
$79-$99

Address: 373 Palomino Tr 81432 **Location:** Jct US 550 and SR 62, just e, just s. **Facility:** 52 units. 2 stories (no elevator), interior corridors. **Parking:** winter plug-ins. **Pool(s):** heated indoor. **Activities:** sauna, whirlpool, exercise room. **Guest Services:** coin laundry. *(See ad p. 265.)*

/ SOME UNITS FEE

WHERE TO EAT

THE ADOBE INN RESTAURANT **Phone:** 970/626-5939

Mexican
$13-$16

AAA Inspector Notes: This restaurant offers homemade salsa with corn and flour chips, and entrées made from scratch. The healthy cuisine emphasizes flavors from Northern Mexico and New Mexico. The adobe decor provides a comfortable, relaxing ambiance. **Bar:** full bar. **Address:** 251 Liddell Dr 81432 **Location:** 0.3 mi w of jct US 550 and SR 62, then just s. D

DRAKES RESTAURANT **Phone:** 970/626-3113

American
$13-$27

AAA Inspector Notes: The eclectic menu lists choices such as pear, walnut and blue cheese salad; grilled salmon over linguine; tender pork loin topped with maple-bourbon sauce; seafood étouffée simmered in a mild Cajun sauce; and delicious chicken Tuscany. Representative of the nightly house desserts are deep-dish apple pie and cheesecake with a Bailey's and sour cream topping. When orders are ready to be served, you'll hear a "quack." Many stop by for martini hour. **Bar:** full bar. **Address:** 220 S Lena St 81432 **Location:** 0.3 mi w of jct US 550 and SR 62, then just s. D

KATE'S PLACE **Phone:** 970/626-9800

American
$8-$11

AAA Inspector Notes: Focusing on cuisine from the heart and soul, this charming eatery serves breakfast and lunch and takes pride in using the finest ingredients available. The garden patio features cozy square picnic tables. Service is efficient and friendly. **Address:** 615 W Clinton St 81432 **Location:** 0.5 mi w of jct US 550 and SR 82 to N Cora St, just n, then just w. **Parking:** street only.

B L

THAI PARADISE **Phone:** 970/626-2742

Thai
$8-$24

AAA Inspector Notes: Warm, trendy decor complements the spicy and tasty dishes, including classics such as green or red curry and pad thai. Sticky rice pudding with mango for dessert is a palate-delighting indulgence. **Bar:** beer & wine. **Address:** 146 N Cora St 81432 **Location:** 0.5 mi w; corner of SR 82 and N Cora St.

L D

RIFLE pop. 9,172

COMFORT INN & SUITES RIFLE Phone: (970)625-9912

Hotel
$71-$166

Address: 301 S 7th St 81650 **Location:** I-70 exit 90, just s, then just w. **Facility:** 82 units. 3 stories, interior corridors. **Parking:** winter plug-ins. **Amenities:** *Some:* high-speed Internet. **Pool(s):** heated indoor. **Activities:** whirlpool, playground, exercise room. **Guest Services:** valet and coin laundry.

/ SOME UNITS FEE

HAMPTON INN & SUITES RIFLE
Phone: (970)625-1500

Hotel
$89-$119

AAA Benefit: Members save up to 10% everyday!

Address: 499 Airport Rd 81650 **Location:** I-70 exit 90, just s, then just e. **Facility:** 92 units. 4 stories, interior corridors. **Terms:** 1-7 night minimum stay, cancellation fee imposed. **Amenities:** high-speed Internet. **Pool(s):** heated indoor. **Activities:** exercise room. **Guest Services:** valet and coin laundry, area transportation-within 15 mi.

(See ad this page.)

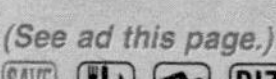

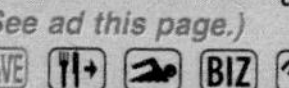

/ SOME UNITS FEE

LA QUINTA INN & SUITES RIFLE Phone: (970)625-2676

Hotel
$82-$148

Address: 600 Wapiti Ct 81650 **Location:** I-70 exit 90, just s, then just e. **Facility:** 114 units. 3 stories, interior corridors. **Amenities:** *Some:* high-speed Internet. **Pool(s):** heated indoor. **Activities:** whirlpool, exercise room. **Guest Services:** valet and coin laundry.

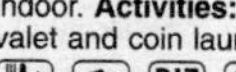

/ SOME UNITS FEE

RUSTY CANNON MOTEL Phone: (970)625-4004

Motel
$76-$129

Address: 701 Taughenbaugh Blvd 81650 **Location:** I-70 exit 90, just s of roundabout. **Facility:** 88 units. 1-2 stories (no elevator), exterior corridors. **Pool(s):** heated indoor/outdoor. **Activities:** sauna. **Guest Services:** coin laundry, area transportation-within 4 mi. **Free Special Amenities: continental breakfast and high-speed Internet.**

/ SOME UNITS FEE

WHERE TO EAT

CREEKBEND BISTRO & COFFEE Phone: 970/625-3131

Natural/Organic
$8-$18

AAA Inspector Notes: Stop in at this cozy downtown bistro for baby organic salads, grilled salmon, French country quiche, sesame Thai pasta or jumbo shrimp scampi. There are lots of specialty sandwiches and wraps to choose from. Call ahead for times for weekend dinners. **Address:** 121 E 3rd St 81650 **Location:** Just e of Railroad Ave (SR 13) and 3rd St; downtown. **Parking:** street only.

B L

SAMMY'S ON PARK AVENUE Phone: 970/625-8008

Seafood
$8-$40

AAA Inspector Notes: The downtown restaurant grabs guests' interest with a selection of appetizers, soups, light dinners and house specials such as filet mignon, Colorado lamb T-bones, Alaskan king crab legs, twin lobster tails, Rocky Mountain trout, schnitzel, pasta and delicious desserts. Colorado microbrews go down easy with the fare. **Bar:** full bar. **Address:** 412 Park Ave 81650 **Location:** I-70 exit 90, 0.3 mi n, w on 3rd St, then just n. D

RIO GRANDE NATIONAL FOREST (F-3)

Elevations in the forest range from 7,500 ft. at the low end of the Rio Grande to 14,345 ft. at Mount Blanca. Refer to AAA maps for additional elevation information.

Rio Grande National Forest, at the headwaters of the Rio Grande, is characterized by mountain waterways and rugged high country. The 1,851,792-acre

▼ See AAA listing this page ▼

forest surrounds the San Luis Valley; its southern tip is along the Colorado-New Mexico boundary.

A majority of the forest lies west of US 285 and is bisected by SR 149 and US 160. The Sangre de Cristo mountain range, now designated a federal wilderness area, lies between SRs 17 and 69. Parts of the San Juan and Sangre de Cristo mountain ranges lie within the forest. The Silver Thread Highway, a 75-mile scenic highway, winds through the San Juan Mountains on SR 149.

Saddle and pack trips can be made into La Garita, Sangre de Cristo, South San Juan and Weminuche wilderness areas. Scenic drives over Wolf Creek Pass on US 160 and Cumbres Pass on SR 17 also are popular. Big-game hunting is allowed in season. Wolf Creek Winter Sports Area is near Wolf Creek Pass on US 160.

For more information write Visitor Information Services, Rio Grande National Forest, 1803 US 160W, Monte Vista, CO 81144; phone (719) 852-5941. *See Recreation Chart.*

GEM ROCKY MOUNTAIN NATIONAL PARK (A-3)

• **Attractions map p. 279**

Elevations in the park range from 7,840 ft. at the park headquarters to 14,259 ft. at Longs Peak. Refer to AAA maps for additional elevation information.

Rocky Mountain National Park is accessible from the east via SR 7, US 34 and US 36 and from the west via US 34. The park includes about 265,800 acres of the Front Range of the Rocky Mountains. This particular section, one of the highest regions in the country, is truly representative of the grandest in American mountain scenery.

The 240-mile grand loop from Denver via Boulder, Estes Park, Grand Lake and Idaho Springs offers one of the most impressive circular trips in the nation. It cuts across the Continental Divide over one of the country's highest continuous roads, reaches Grand Lake, crosses the Divide again at Berthoud Pass, traverses the Denver Mountain Parks and returns to Denver.

The park's valleys are about 8,000 feet above sea level, with the peaks rising thousands of feet higher. Longs Peak attains a height of 14,259 feet. Within the park, 60 named peaks reach elevations of 12,000 feet or higher. The range lies north and south, with the gentler slope on the west. On the east side the descent can be extremely precipitous, with sheer drops of 2,000 and 3,000 feet into rock-bound gorges.

Seen from the eastern valleys, the range rises in bold relief, rugged in outline and crowned with snow. The west side, lush with wet meadowland, has many streams and natural lakes. The park is surrounded by the Arapaho and Roosevelt National Forests *(see place listing p. 40)*, while the southwest corner adjoins the Arapaho National Recreation Area *(see place listing p. 40)*.

The records of glacial action on these mountains are so clear that even the untrained eye recognizes them. This is particularly true on the eastern side, where the moraines are enormous. Four of the park's many small alpine cirque glaciers—Tyndall, Andrews, Rowe and Taylor—can be seen at the heads of some of the high mountain canyons at about 12,000 feet.

The park is a wildlife sanctuary. The lofty rocks are the natural home of the Rocky Mountain bighorn sheep. Elk and deer are numerous, and coyotes are often seen by park visitors. Black bears reside in the park and are sometimes seen. Mountain lions, bobcats and smaller carnivores, however, are seldom seen by visitors. Birds also can be observed.

Those bizarre sounds you may hear echoing throughout autumn evenings are more than likely elk calling to each other during rutting, or mating season. During this time of year, elk descend from the higher elevations to valleys and meadows, and you'll usually see them at dawn and dusk at such locations as Moraine Park, Horseshoe Park and the Kawuneeche Valley. Observe these animals from a distance, and do not make loud noises in their presence.

Wildflower viewing is spectacular from April to September and can be found at varying elevations, with dozens of varieties contributing to a vibrant palette of blue, yellow, pink, purple and white. The Tundra World Nature Trail presents the opportunity to view colorful plants and wildflowers unique to the alpine tundra during a half-hour walk.

General Information and Activities

The park is never closed, although many facilities are open only June through October. Trail Ridge Road generally remains open for through travel from late May until the first heavy snowfall, usually in mid-October.

Because Rocky Mountain National Park is primarily a scenic park, motoring, horseback riding, camping, hiking, snowshoeing and mountain climbing are the most popular activities. Horses and camping equipment can be rented in Estes Park and at Grand Lake. There are no accommodations in the park other than camping.

Many beautiful trails of varying lengths and difficulties traverse these mountains, with stunning mountains, lakes, waterfalls and vistas. Dramatic weather changes can occur rapidly at higher elevations so plenty of water and food, plus gloves, hats, appropriate footwear, rain gear and layers of clothing are recommended. Altitude sickness can be a problem; it helps to drink at least a gallon of water a day, and assess how you are feeling as you climb in elevation.

Information about trails and routes is available at all park visitor centers, or by phoning (970) 586-1206. The park has several easy hikes: Bear Lake Trail is a half-mile loop, Adams Falls and Alberta Falls lead to picturesque waterfalls, and Deer Mountain, while more moderate, is a popular summit hike with beautiful panoramas. Those seeking more challenge will have no trouble finding mid-range and strenuous routes.

Fans of winter recreation also can take advantage of several trails geared toward cold-weather sports. Snowshoe enthusiasts will want to check out the Bear Lake area—the invigorating Emerald Lake Trail is a wonderland in winter, with snowy drifts, frozen lakes and glistening peaks. Cross-country skiers gravitate to the Glacier Basin Campground area, where there are several novice trails to choose from. Black Lake offers a more strenuous trek for advanced skiers.

A permit is required for overnight backcountry trips and bivouac climbs; visitors must obtain a permit at the backcountry office near Beaver Meadows Visitor Center (phone (970) 586-1242), the Kawuneeche Visitor Center or the Longs Peak and Wild Basin ranger stations (summer only). Special regulations apply to fishing; inquire at any of the visitor centers. A Colorado fishing license is required.

Free ranger-led programs are conducted year-round; see the park newspaper for schedules. An orientation film is shown every half-hour in summer and by request in winter at Beaver Meadows Visitor Center and Kawuneeche Visitor Center.

Illustrated talks and campfire programs are presented nightly in the major campgrounds during the summer. Five campgrounds are available within the park. The fee is $20 per night in summer and $14 per night in winter. Reservations for the Moraine Park, Aspenglen and Glacier Basin campgrounds can be made up to 6 months in advance through Recreation.gov; phone (877) 444-6777.

There are lots of sites and activities within the park that mesmerize kids. Short trails like Moraine Park and Sprague Lake captivate youngsters, as does the Beaver Boardwalk near the foot of Trail Ridge Road. Glimpses of wandering elk, scurrying beavers and bighorn sheep also entice children, as does scrambling across boulders on Gem Lake Trail, gazing at flowers near Cub Lake or saddling up on a gentle horse for a trail ride. The Junior Ranger program offers a variety of hikes and talks that focus on the park's environment, geology and wildlife—during one talk, kids can touch the skulls and skins of such animals as bighorn sheep, moose and elk. For details about ranger-led programs geared toward youngsters, pick up a park newspaper or inquire at one of the visitor centers.

Schedules of activities are available at ranger stations and visitor centers. *See Recreation Chart.*

ADMISSION to the park is $20 per private vehicle or $10 per person arriving by other means (valid for 7 days).

PETS are prohibited in all areas of the park not accessible by motor vehicles, including all trails and meadows.

ADDRESS inquiries and information requests to the Superintendent, Rocky Mountain National Park, 1000 US 36, Estes Park, CO 80517-8397; phone (970) 586-1206.

ALPINE VISITOR CENTER, at Fall River Pass, features exhibits about the alpine tundra environment, its related safety issues, and mountain weather and climate. Information and park literature are available. **Hours:** Open daily 9-5, mid-June through Labor Day; daily 10:30-4:30, Memorial Day weekend to mid-June and day after Labor Day to mid-Oct. (weather permitting). Phone ahead to confirm schedule. **Cost:** Free with park admission. **Phone:** (970) 586-1206, or (970) 586-1222 for road information.

BEAR LAKE ROAD leads from the Beaver Meadows entrance through Moraine Park. It then follows the valley of Glacier Creek to Bear Lake. Several trails offering a range of hiking opportunities begin at Bear Lake, including trails to Dream Lake (1.1 mi.), Emerald Lake (1.8 mi.) and Lake Haiyaha (2.1 mi.). Elk herd sightings are common in the spring and fall in Moraine Park. Horseback riding is available at Sprague Lake and Moraine Park.

BEAVER MEADOWS VISITOR CENTER, 3 mi. w. of Estes Park on US 36, has a large, 3-D topographical map and an orientation film about the park. Programs are presented nightly in summer and Saturdays the rest of the year. **Hours:** Open daily 8-4:30 (also daily 8-9 p.m., mid-June through Aug. 31). Phone ahead to confirm schedule. **Cost:** Free. **Phone:** (970) 586-1206.

FALL RIVER VISITOR CENTER, 5 mi. w. of Estes Park on US 34, contains life-size wildlife displays and a discovery room with exhibits for children. **Hours:** Daily 9-5, late Apr.-Oct. 31; daily 9-4, rest of year. Phone ahead to confirm schedule. **Cost:** Free. **Phone:** (970) 586-1206.

KAWUNEECHE VISITOR CENTER is on the w. side of the park on US 34, 1 mi. n. of the town of Grand Lake. The visitor center has exhibits about the plants and animals native to the western portion of the park. **Hours:** Daily 8-5 (also 5-6, mid-June through Labor Day). Phone ahead to confirm schedule. **Cost:** Free. **Phone:** (970) 627-3471 or (970) 586-1206.

MORAINE PARK VISITOR CENTER, 1 mi. s. of the Beaver Meadows entrance, contains exhibits that interpret the story of the park environment and the natural elements that shaped it. Park literature, maps and ranger-led activities are available; a half-mile self-guiding nature trail starts at the museum. **Hours:** Daily 9-5, mid-June through Labor Day; 9-4:30, May 1 to mid-June and day after Labor Day-Columbus Day. Phone ahead to confirm schedule.

▼ *See AAA listing p. 183* ▼

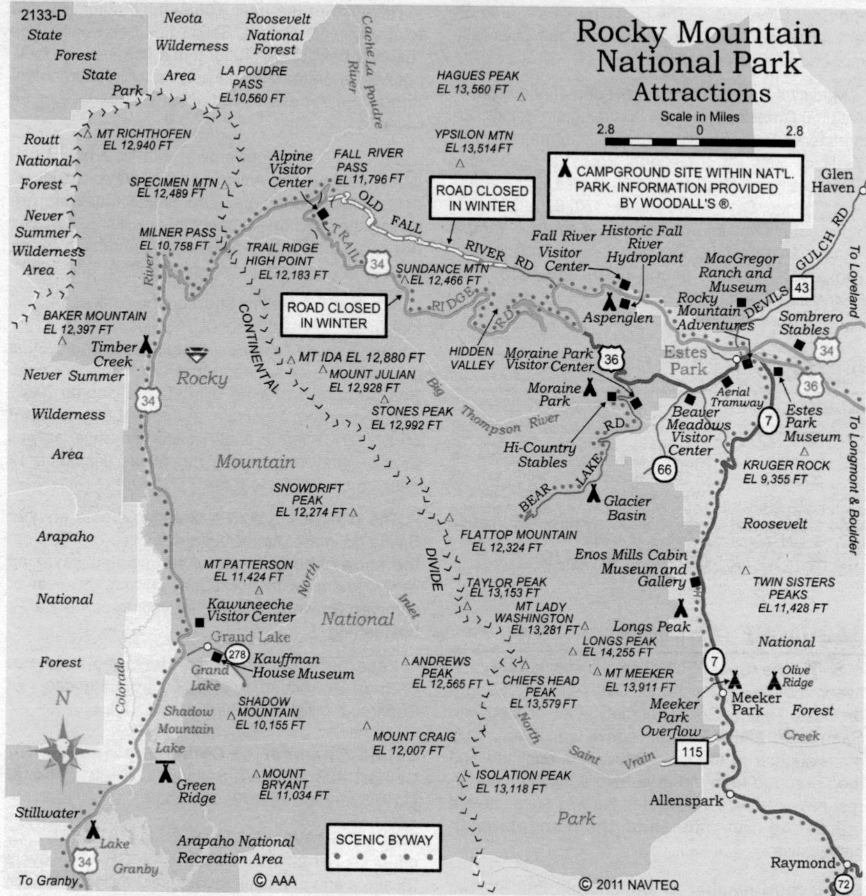

Cost: Free with park admission. **Phone:** (970) 586-1206.

TRAIL RIDGE ROAD, (US 34) between Estes Park and Grand Lake, climbs to the crest of the range and crosses the Continental Divide. The 48-mile route reaches elevations of more than 12,000 feet.

Note: The route should be driven with caution by anyone unfamiliar with mountain driving. Rapid weather changes also can occur; dress appropriately. **Time:** Allow 3 hours minimum. **Hours:** Road open late May to mid-Oct. **Cost:** Free with park admission. **Phone:** (970) 586-1222, or (970) 586-1206 for road conditions.

ROUTT NATIONAL FOREST (B-2)

Elevations in the forest range from 6,750 ft. at the Elk River to 12,940 ft. at Mount Richthofen. Refer to AAA maps for additional elevation information.

Accessible via US 40, Routt National Forest lies astride the Continental Divide. The 1.26 million-acre forest offers many scenic areas. Totally within Routt are the 160,000-acre Mount Zirkel Wilderness, surrounding the rugged Park Range, and the 45,190 acres of Sarvis Creek Wilderness.

Other wilderness areas partially within Routt include Flat Tops Wilderness, its 235,214 acres coadministered with the White River National Forest *(see place listing p. 303)*. A portion of the 23,492-acre Platte River Wilderness falls into Routt, while the rest is part of Medicine Bow National Forest.

In Routt's eastern section, the 21,090 acres of Never Summer Wilderness spill into the Arapaho and Roosevelt National Forests *(see place listing p. 40)*.

In the northeastern section are the 9,924 acres of the Neota Wilderness and the 73,068 acres of the Rawah Wilderness, both part of the Arapaho and Roosevelt National Forests. Pack and saddle trips can be arranged.

Facilities for camping and picnicking are available in the summer; there are recreation areas at Big Creek Lake and Dumont Lake, and along the Elk and Bear River areas. The Fish Creek Falls area offers hiking and picnicking, a trail for the physically impaired and other facilities.

Medicine Bow National Forest and Thunder Basin National Grassland, both in Wyoming, are jointly administered with Routt. For more information write Medicine Bow-Routt National Forest and Thunder Basin National Grassland, 925 Weiss Dr., Steamboat Springs, CO 80487; phone (970) 870-2299. Another source for information is the forest's Yampa Ranger District, 300 Roselawn Ave., P.O. Box 7, Yampa, CO 80483; phone (970) 638-4516. *See Recreation Chart.*

RUSTIC

BIGHORN CABINS **Phone:** 970/881-2142

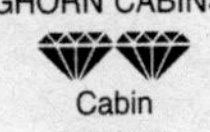

Cabin

$83-$160

Address: 31635 Poudre Canyon (SR 14) 80512 **Location:** On SR 14 between MM 90 and 91. **Facility:** 5 kitchen cabin units. 1 story, exterior corridors. *Bath:* shower only. **Terms:** open 5/1-10/31, office hours 9 am-9 pm, 2-7 night minimum stay - seasonal and/or weekends, 30 day cancellation notice-fee imposed. **Activities:** fishing, basketball.

SAGUACHE (E-3) pop. 485, elev. 7,694'

Saguache (Sa-WATCH) lies in a scenic valley between the great Continental Divide and the Sangre de Cristo Range. Some notoriety is associated with Saguache; Alferd Packer, convicted of voluntary manslaughter in the late 1800s, was confined and then escaped from the area before his eventual arrest in Wyoming 9 years later. He was suspected of murdering five men and then engaging in cannibalism.

Saguache Chamber of Commerce: 309 4th St., P.O. Box 53, Saguache, CO 81149. **Phone:** (719) 850-1249.

SAGUACHE COUNTY MUSEUM, on US 285, depicts life in the mid- to late 1800s. The Memorial Room contains early medical equipment, an antique gun collection and vintage saddles. Other exhibits include a pioneer kitchen, a school, Spanish and American Indian artifacts, a parlor and a mineral collection. An old jail features a likeness of the area's infamous killer, Alferd Packer.

Time: Allow 30 minutes minimum. **Hours:** Daily 10-4, Memorial Day weekend-third weekend in Sept. **Cost:** $5; $1 (ages 1-11). **Phone:** (719) 655-2805.

SALIDA (E-3) pop. 5,236, elev. 7,080'

The thoroughfare provided by the Arkansas River and several passes cutting through the nearby mountain ranges insured that a settlement would develop in this region. Aided by the arrival of the railroad in 1880, Salida (sa-LYE-da)—meaning "exit"—served as an outlet for mines in the Leadville area.

Because of the cool, comfortable summers and relatively mild winters, Salida has been called the "banana belt" of Colorado. It is a fine area for rockhounds; aquamarine, garnet, sapphire, turquoise, topaz and American Indian arrowheads can be found in the vicinity.

Salida's historic downtown, with its array of galleries, studios and antique shops, draws art lovers and antique collectors. The Salida Museum, adjoining the chamber of commerce building, contains displays pertaining to pioneer and American Indian life, railroading and mining; phone (719) 539-7483.

In spring the melting snow on the flank of 14,239-foot Mount Shavano, about 14 miles northwest, assumes a shape called the "Angel of Shavano." It is said that the angel appeared when the Ute chief Shavano prayed for his dying friend George Beckwith. Tenderfoot Mountain, at the east edge of town off SR 291, offers a good view of the angel as well as the valley and nearby mountains, including 12 peaks over 14,000 feet tall.

The diminishing snows of spring create another Salida hallmark. As the Arkansas River swells from the snowmelt, a variety of rafting and kayaking races are held in mid-June. During the rest of summer, Browns Canyon offers some of the state's best rafting.

Less turbulent are the waters at Salida Hot Springs Swimming Pool piped from Poncha Hot Springs, 5 miles southwest.

Salida Chamber of Commerce and Visitor Center: 406 US 50W, Salida, CO 81201. **Phone:** (719) 539-2068 or (877) 772-5432.

MOUNT SHAVANO STATE FISH HATCHERY, .2 mi. n. on SR 291, then 1 mi. w. on CR 154, covers 25 acres and produces more than 2 million fish each year, including cutthroat and rainbow trout. **Hours:** Daily 7:30-4. Guided tours are given daily 10-4, June-Aug. **Cost:** Donations. **Phone:** (719) 539-6877.

SALIDA MUSEUM, US 50 and I St., adjoins the chamber of commerce building. Displays pertain to pioneer and American Indian life, railroading and mining. **Time:** Allow 30 minutes minimum. **Hours:** Daily 11-5, Memorial Day-Labor Day. Phone ahead to confirm schedule. **Cost:** $3; $1.50 (ages 12-18); $1 (ages 7-11). **Phone:** (719) 539-7483.

RECREATIONAL ACTIVITIES

White-water Rafting

- **Canyon Marine Whitewater** is at 5620 E. US 50. **Hours:** Trips depart daily at 8:30 and 1:30, mid-May to late Sept. **Phone:** (719) 539-4444 or (800) 539-4447.

WINERIES

- **Mountain Spirit Winery** is 13 mi. w. at 15750 CR 220. **Tours:** Guided tours are available. **Hours:** Daily 10-5, Memorial Day-Labor Day; Mon.-Sat. 10-5, rest of year. **Phone:** (719) 539-7848.

ASPEN LEAF LODGE Phone: 719/539-6733

Motel
$45-$99

Address: 7350 W Hwy 50 81201 **Location:** 0.3 mi w of Hot Springs Pool. **Facility:** 17 units. 1 story, exterior corridors. **Activities:** whirlpool.

 / SOME UNITS FEE

CHALETS AT TUDOR ROSE Phone: (719)539-2002

Vacation Rental House
$200-$300

Location: Just e on US 50, just s on CR 104, 0.5 mi up the hill, follow signs. **Facility:** Surrounded by the Sangre de Cristo mountains, the luxury mountain chalets have fireplaces, full kitchens, great rooms and remote-controlled skylights. 5 houses. 2 stories (no elevator), exterior corridors. **Terms:** check-in 4 pm, 2 night minimum stay, 30 day cancellation notice-fee imposed. **Activities:** hiking trails, jogging.

CALL / SOME UNITS

COMFORT INN Phone: (719)539-5000

Hotel
$89-$159

Address: 315 E Rainbow Blvd 81201 **Location:** On US 50; east end of town. **Facility:** 45 units, some kitchens. 2 stories (no elevator), interior corridors. **Terms:** cancellation fee imposed. **Pool(s):** heated indoor. **Activities:** whirlpool. **Guest Services:** coin laundry.

DAYS INN Phone: (719)539-6651

Motel
$58-$135

Address: 407 E Hwy 50 81201 **Location:** East end of town. **Facility:** 28 units. 2 stories (no elevator), interior corridors. **Parking:** winter plug-ins. **Terms:** cancellation fee imposed. **Activities:** whirlpool.

 / SOME UNITS 

SILVER RIDGE LODGE Phone: (719)539-2553

Motel
$50-$100

Address: 545 W Rainbow Blvd 81201 **Location:** On US 50. Opposite Hot Springs Pool. **Facility:** 39 units, some two bedrooms. 1-2 stories (no elevator), exterior corridors. **Terms:** office hours 7 am-10 pm, cancellation fee imposed. **Pool(s):** heated outdoor. **Activities:** sauna, whirlpool. **Free Special Amenities: expanded continental breakfast and high-speed Internet.**

 / SOME UNITS FEE

SUPER 8 Phone: (719)539-6689

Motel
$85-$126

Address: 525 W Rainbow Blvd 81201 **Location:** On US 50. Opposite Hot Springs Pool. **Facility:** 52 units. 1-3 stories (no elevator), exterior corridors. **Terms:** office hours 6:30 am-10 pm, cancellation fee imposed. **Pool(s):** heated indoor. **Activities:** whirlpools. **Guest Services:** coin laundry.

 / SOME UNITS

THOMAS HOUSE BED & BREAKFAST Phone: 719/539-7104

Historic Bed & Breakfast
$89-$179

Address: 307 E 1st St 81201 **Location:** Just e of historic downtown. **Facility:** Near downtown with roomy decks, patios, a hot tub and flower garden, these individually decorated, well-appointed rooms have terry robes, handmade log cabin quilts and antique claw-foot tubs. 7 units, some efficiencies and cottages. 2 stories (no elevator), interior/exterior corridors. **Parking:** street only. **Terms:** check-in 4 pm, 2 night minimum stay - seasonal and/or weekends, 14 day cancellation notice-fee imposed.

/ SOME UNITS

TUDOR ROSE BED & BREAKFAST Phone: (719)539-2002

Bed & Breakfast
$90-$185 5/1-10/31
$81-$167 11/1-4/30

Address: 6720 CR 104 81201 **Location:** Just e on US 50, s on CR 104, 0.5 mi up the hill, follow signs. **Facility:** Nestled on a hilltop with scenic mountain views, the B&B offers guest rooms characteristic of a country manor. A walking trail loops the property. 6 units. 2 stories (no elevator), interior corridors. **Terms:** check-in 4 pm, age restrictions may apply, 7 day cancellation notice. **Activities:** whirlpool, hiking trails, horseshoes.

/ SOME UNITS

WOODLAND MOTEL Phone: (719)539-4980

Motel
$55-$165

Address: 903 W 1st St 81201 **Location:** 0.5 mi w on 1st St (SR 291); just w of historic district. Across from a ballpark. **Facility:** 18 units, some two bedrooms and kitchens. 1-2 stories (no elevator), exterior corridors. **Amenities:** high-speed Internet. **Activities:** whirlpool. **Free Special Amenities: local telephone calls and high-speed Internet.**

SAVE / SOME UNITS

HAMPTON INN & SUITES Phone: 719/539-0800

fyi

Contemporary Hotel

AAA Benefit: Members save up to 10% everyday!

Did not meet all AAA rating requirements for locking devices in some guest rooms at time of last evaluation on 03/29/2011. **Address:** 785 E US 50 81201 **Location:** On US 50, east end of town. Facilities, services, and decor characterize a mid-scale property.

WHERE TO EAT

AMICA'S PIZZA, MICROBREWS & MORE Phone: 719/539-5219

Italian
$5-$11

AAA Inspector Notes: Located in historic downtown, this warm and inviting local favorite specializes in gourmet pizzas, salads, calzones and more. Microbrews are made on site. Their desserts are irresistible. **Bar:** beer & wine. **Address:** 136 E 2nd St 81201 **Location:** Between E and F sts; in historic district. **Parking:** street only.

L D 

COUNTRY BOUNTY RESTAURANT Phone: 719/539-3546

American
$7-$18

AAA Inspector Notes: The best way to describe this restaurant is to say that it's very popular, not only with the locals but also with the many tourists who drive by. It continues to draw customers thanks to a good variety of traditional American dishes and delicious desserts. **Bar:** beer & wine. **Address:** 413 W Rainbow Blvd 81201 **Location:** On US 50, opposite Hot Springs Pool. B L D

FIRST STREET CAFE
Menu on AAA.com Phone: 719/539-4759

American
$7-$25

AAA Inspector Notes: The menu at this locally popular eatery is varied and includes lunch and dinner specials as well as a salad bar. **Bar:** full bar. **Address:** 137 E 1st St 81201 **Location:** From US 50, 1 mi n on F St, then just e on 1st St; in historic district. **Parking:** street only. B L D

LAUGHING LADIES RESTAURANT
Menu on AAA.com
Phone: 719/539-6209

American
$8-$23

AAA Inspector Notes: The 1905 building offers Victorian-era charm with hardwood floors and patterned tin ceiling tiles. The fresh seafood and other creative entrées are served in a dining room with an art-gallery ambience or on the outdoor patio. Colorado-brewed beers and fine wines are offered. **Bar:** full bar. **Reservations:** suggested. **Address:** 128 W 1st St 81201 **Location:** US 50, 0.8 mi n on F St; in historic district. **Parking:** street only. **Historic** L D

MOONLIGHT PIZZA
Phone: 719/539-4277

Pizza
$6-$18

AAA Inspector Notes: Mouthwatering pizzas and calzones are served in a cozy, easygoing atmosphere. Patrons can choose from the inventive combinations on the menu or create their own masterpiece. Microbrews also are popular here. **Bar:** beer & wine. **Address:** 242 F St 81201 **Location:** Corner of F and 3rd sts; in historic district.
L D

TWISTED CORK CAFE
Phone: 719/539-7384

International
$7-$24

AAA Inspector Notes: Distinctive contemporary décor helps create an inviting atmosphere in the spacious cafe. The diverse menu features Asia- and Italy-inspired dishes, which pair nicely with wine selections from the local Mountain Spirit Winery. **Bar:** full bar. **Address:** 8048 W US Hwy 50 81201 **Location:** 1 mi w of Hot Springs Pool.
L D

SAN ISABEL NATIONAL FOREST (E-4)

Elevations in the forest range from 5,860 ft. in the grasslands area to 14,433 ft. at Mount Elbert. Refer to AAA maps for additional elevation information.

Reached via US 24, 50 and 285, and SRs 82, 91 and 165, San Isabel National Forest includes scenic and recreational features within its 1,109,782 acres. A network of roads makes most of the forest easily accessible. The Highway of Legends, starting at Trinidad and traveling through the Cucharas Pass, offers 82 miles of scenic driving on SR 12.

More than 700 miles of trails are available for backpacking and saddle trips into the back country. Twin Lake and Turquoise Lake recreation areas, near Leadville, and the Spanish Peaks National Natural Landmark, near La Veta, provide opportunities for summer activities and camping. Many easy, family-friendly hikes are available in the forest, including the San Carlos Trail near Beulah and the Wachob Trail near Colorado City.

Holy Cross, Mount Massive and Collegiate Peaks wildernesses are accessible by foot or horseback. Numerous ghost towns from Colorado's mining heyday dot the region.

Among the 17 peaks that exceed 14,000 feet in San Isabel National Forest is 14,433-foot Mount Elbert, highest in the state. The high mountain reaches afford summer range for deer, bears, elk, grouse, mountain sheep and turkeys.

For more information write the Forest Superintendent, San Isabel National Forest, 2840 Kachina Dr., Pueblo, CO 81008; phone (719) 553-1400. *See Recreation Chart.*

SAN JUAN NATIONAL FOREST (E-1)

Elevations in the forest range from 6,800 ft. at Junction Creek to 14,246 ft. at Mount Wilson in the Lizard Head Wilderness. Refer to AAA maps for additional elevation information.

West of the Continental Divide in southwestern Colorado, US 550 bisects the forest north/south; US 160 is a major east/west route that borders the southern region. Mountains, canyons, waterfalls, unusual landforms and wide variations in elevation and vegetation characterize the forest, which encompasses 1,881,586 acres.

The Durango and Silverton Narrow Gauge Railroad *(see attraction listing p. 173)* passes through the spectacular canyon of the Rio de Las Animas.

The area around Durango is popular for winter sports; McPhee Reservoir, Vallecito Reservoir, Lemon Reservoir and Williams Creek Reservoir are summer recreation sites. Hunting and fishing are permitted in season. Saddle and pack trips can be made into such backcountry areas as the Lizard Head, South San Juan and Weminuche wildernesses. The San Juan Skyway offers 232 miles of scenic driving through the San Juan and Uncompahgre national forests.

For further information write the San Juan Public Lands Center, 15 Burnett Ct., Durango, CO 81301; phone (970) 247-4874. *See Recreation Chart.*

SAN LUIS (F-4) pop. 629, elev. 7,965'

San Luis was founded in 1851 and is one of the oldest towns in Colorado. The area is popular with anglers; nearby Mountain Home Reservoir has trout and Sanchez Reservoir contains pike, walleye and trout.

San Luis Visitor Center: 408 1/2 Main St.; P.O. Box 200, San Luis, CO 81152. **Phone:** (719) 672-3002.

SHRINE OF THE STATIONS OF THE CROSS, jct. SRs 159 and 142, features two-thirds life-size bronze statues depicting the stations of the cross. The statues, created by sculptor Huberto Maestas, are situated on a .7-mile trail overlooking the community. The Chapel of All Saints is at the end of the trail. **Time:** Allow 30 minutes minimum. **Hours:** Daily dawn-dusk. **Cost:** Free. **Phone:** (719) 672-3685.

SEDALIA pop. 206

GABRIEL'S **Phone:** 303/688-2323

Northern Italian
$30-$55

AAA Inspector Notes: In a conspicuous location in a Victorian-style home at the center of the foothills in the tiny town of Sedalia, this restaurant offers an intimate dining experience. The menu features flavorful four-course meals served by a polished, attentive waitstaff. The wine list is excellent. **Bar:** full bar. **Reservations:** suggested. **Address:** 5450 Manhart Ave 80135 **Location:** SR 67, just w of jct US 85. **Historic**

SILT pop. 2,930

HOLIDAY INN EXPRESS & SUITES SILT **Phone:** (970)876-5100

Hotel
$99-$119 5/1-9/3
$89-$119 9/4-4/30

Address: 1535 River Frontage Rd 81652 **Location:** I-70 exit 97, just s, then just e. **Facility:** 80 units. 3 stories, interior corridors. **Pool(s):** heated indoor. **Activities:** whirlpool, exercise room. **Guest Services:** valet and coin laundry.

 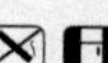 

WHERE TO EAT

STEFFIE'S PLACE **Phone:** 970/876-0499

American
$6-$19

AAA Inspector Notes: Menu items include traditional breakfast favorites; burgers; hot and cold sandwiches; turkey, roast beef and steak platters and baskets; and south-of-the-border lunches and dinners. Homemade pie wraps up meals deliciously. **Bar:** full bar. **Address:** 1290 E Main St 81652 **Location:** I-70 exit 97, just n, then just e.

B L D

SILVERTHORNE (C-3) pop. 3,887, elev. 8,751'

RECREATIONAL ACTIVITIES

Fishing

- **Cutthroat Anglers** departs from 400 Blue River Pkwy. A variety of full- and half-day trips are available. Rod and gear are provided. **Hours:** Daily 7-7, May-Oct.; Mon.-Fri. 8-6, Sat.-Sun.10-6, rest of year. **Phone:** (970) 262-2878 or (888) 876-8818.

QUALITY INN & SUITES **Phone:** (970)513-1222

Hotel
$129-$189

Address: 530 Silverthorne Ln 80498 **Location:** I-70 exit 205, just n on SR 9, just e on Rainbow Dr, then just e on Tanglewood Ln. **Facility:** 57 units, some efficiencies. 3 stories, interior corridors. **Terms:** cancellation fee imposed. **Amenities:** safes (fee). **Pool(s):** heated indoor. **Activities:** whirlpools, exercise room. **Guest Services:** valet and coin laundry.

BIZ / SOME UNITS FEE

SILVER INN **Phone:** 970/513-0104

Hotel
Rates not provided

Address: 675 Blue River Pkwy 80498 **Location:** I-70 exit 205, 1 mi n on SR 9, then just w. **Facility:** 30 units. 2 stories (no elevator), interior corridors. **Activities:** sauna, whirlpool.

CALL

TIMBER RIDGE CONDOMINIUMS **Phone:** 970/468-6291

fyi Not evaluated. **Address:** 91100 Ryan Gulch Rd 80498. Facilities, services, and decor characterize an economy property.

WHERE TO EAT

MOUNTAIN LYON CAFE **Phone:** 970/262-6229

American
$6-$10

AAA Inspector Notes: Popular with the locals, the cafe serves hearty breakfast items made from fresh ingredients. Eggs Benedict, steak and eggs, shrimp, spinach and Swiss omelets, and banana-nut pancakes are a few of the samplings. The lunch menu centers on burgers, hot entrées and delicatessen sandwiches. **Address:** 381 Blue River Pkwy 80498 **Location:** I-70 exit 205, just n.

B L

SILVERTON (E-2) pop. 637, elev. 9,305'

• **Hotels p. 284** • **Restaurants p. 284**

After the first major silver strike in 1871, Silverton became a prosperous mining community. Between 1882 and 1918, the Las Animas district mines produced $65 million in ore. The Grand Imperial Hotel, an 1880s showplace for silver kings, and the gold-domed San Juan County Courthouse are evidence of the opulence of Silverton's bonanza years.

Blair Street and its assorted 24-hour bordellos thrived. The infamous thoroughfare, with its false-fronted buildings recalling the Wild West, is a tourist attraction and was often used as a movie set.

Other remnants of yesteryear are several ghost towns, including Animas Forks, 12 miles northeast on CR 2. **Note:** CR 2 is mostly a gravel road, passable by two-wheel-drive vehicles. Past Animas Forks a four-wheel-drive vehicle is required.

The rugged San Juan Mountain Range, one of the most scenic parts of the state, is crossed by US 550 through Silverton and is part of the San Juan Skyway, a scenic byway. The section leading from Silverton to Ouray includes the spectacular Million Dollar Highway *(see Ouray p. 262)*. San Juan County is a top destination for off-road adventurers; jeep tours and rentals are available.

Silverton is the terminus of the Durango and Silverton Narrow Gauge Railroad, a historic coal-burning passenger train *(see attraction listing p. 173)*. Much of the surrounding region lies within the San Juan National Forest *(see place listing p. 282)*.

To help recall the Old West, gunfights are staged at 12th and Blair streets, Memorial Day-Labor Day (weather permitting).

Silverton Chamber of Commerce: 414 Greene St., P.O. Box 565, Silverton, CO 81433. **Phone:** (970) 387-5654 or (800) 752-4494.

Self-guiding tours: Maps for a walking tour of historic Silverton as well as jeep road maps are available at the chamber of commerce. Gallery and studio literature also is available.

MAYFLOWER GOLD MILL TOUR, 2 mi. e. on CR 2, operates in the Sunnyside Mill, which was one of the town's major employers 1929-91. Former miners demonstrate the mill's original equipment, which remains unchanged since operations ceased. A 30-minute video about the mill's history is shown. **Tours:** Guided tours are available. **Hours:** Daily 10-5, Memorial Day weekend-Labor Day. **Cost:** $8; $7.50 (ages 60+); free (ages 0-12). Guided tours $10; $9 (ages 60+); free (ages 0-12). Reservations are required for guided tours. **Phone:** (970) 387-5838 or (970) 387-0294.

OLD HUNDRED GOLD MINE TOUR is 5 mi. e. on CR 2, following signs. An electric mine train takes visitors into the heart of 13,257-foot-tall Galena Mountain. Narrated 1-hour tours through the mine's tunnels provide geological and historical insights as well as demonstrations of early and modern-day mining equipment. Gold panning on the surface is included.

Warm clothing is recommended. **Time:** Allow 1 hour minimum. **Hours:** Tours are given daily on the hour 10-4, mid-May to early Oct. **Cost:** Fee (includes gold panning) $16.95; $14.95 (ages 60+); $7.95 (ages 5-12). **Phone:** (970) 387-5444 or (800) 872-3009.

SAN JUAN BACKCOUNTRY, 1119 Greene St., offers guided jeep and ATV tours of the San Juan Mountains. Knowledgeable drivers take passengers on back roads to see mountain views, old mines, wildflowers and wild animals. Rental jeeps and recreational vehicles are available for self-guiding tours. **Time:** Allow 2 hours minimum. **Hours:** Daily 8-6, May-Oct. **Cost:** Two-hour tour $55; $40 (ages 5-17). Four-hour tour $75; $50 (ages 5-17). All-day tour $150; $90 (ages 5-17). **Phone:** (970) 387-5565 or (800) 494-8687.

SAN JUAN COUNTY HISTORICAL SOCIETY MUSEUM, 1559 Greene St., is in a 1902 county jail. Displays include artifacts from early mining and railroading days. The upper floor still has all the old jail cells used at the turn of the 20th century. The Mining Heritage Center also includes displays about mining as well as printing and early transportation. **Hours:** Daily 10-4, Memorial Day weekend to mid-Oct. **Cost:** $5; $4.50 (ages 62+); free (ages 0-12). **Phone:** (970) 387-5838.

RECREATIONAL ACTIVITIES

Jeep Tours (Self-driving)

- **Silver Summit Jeep Rentals** is at 640 Mineral St. **Hours:** Daily 8-5, May 15 to mid-Oct. **Phone:** (970) 387-0240 or (800) 352-1637.

BENT ELBOW HOTEL **Phone:** 970/387-5775

Historic Motel
$60-$140

Address: 1114 Blair St 81433 **Location:** Jct 11th and Blair sts. **Facility:** Themed rooms are individually appointed in Old World décor and have modern amenities. 6 units, some kitchens. 2 stories (no elevator), interior corridors. **Terms:** office hours 11 am-8:30 pm, 4 day cancellation notice-fee imposed. **Dining:** Bent Elbow Restaurant & Bar, see separate listing.

/ SOME UNITS

SILVERTON'S INN OF THE ROCKIES AT THE HISTORIC ALMA HOUSE **Phone:** (970)387-5336

Address: 220 E 10th St 81433 **Location:** Just se of 10th and Main sts. **Facility:** Built in 1898, this charming B&B offers well-appointed guest rooms with down comforters, feather mattresses and Victorian claw-foot tubs. Personalized back-country adventure planning is available. 9 units. 3 stories (no elevator), interior corridors. *Bath:* some shared. **Parking:** street only. **Terms:** open 5/15-10/15 & 12/15-4/15, 7 day cancellation notice-fee imposed. **Activities:** whirlpool. **Free Special Amenities: full breakfast and high-speed Internet.**

/ SOME UNITS FEE

TRIANGLE MOTEL **Phone:** 970/387-5780

Address: 848 Greene St 81433 **Location:** On Main St, north end of town. **Facility:** 16 units, some two bedrooms, efficiencies and kitchens. 2 stories (no elevator), exterior corridors. **Terms:** office hours 7:30 am-8 pm, 14 day cancellation notice-fee imposed.

/ SOME UNITS

VILLA DALLAVALLE INN **Phone:** 970/387-5555

Historic Bed & Breakfast
$109-$125

Address: 1257 Blair St 81433 **Location:** Corner of 13th and Blair sts. **Facility:** Built in 1901, the décor of each guest room depicts a different period in the town's history. 7 units. 2 stories (no elevator), interior corridors. **Parking:** street only. **Activities:** whirlpool. *Fee:* massage.

/ SOME UNITS FEE

THE WYMAN HOTEL & INN **Phone:** 970/387-5372

Historic Bed & Breakfast
Rates not provided

Address: 1371 Greene St 81433 **Location:** Corner of 14th and Main sts. **Facility:** Ceiling fans and feather beds are featured in each well-appointed room. A converted candlelight caboose car features a two-person whirlpool tub with a cozy sitting area and fireplace stove. 17 units, some two bedrooms. 2 stories (no elevator), interior corridors. **Parking:** street only. **Terms:** office hours 7 am-9 pm. **Activities:** recreation programs, rental bicycles. *Fee:* downhill & cross country skiing, snowmobiling, ice skating, massage.

/ SOME UNITS FEE

WHERE TO EAT

BENT ELBOW RESTAURANT & BAR **Phone:** 970/387-5775

American
$7-$22

AAA Inspector Notes: Patrons try menu items such as fresh salmon with a lightly smoked tomato, carrot and curry sauce, delicious shepherd meat pie served with warm cornbread, grilled onion-crusted chicken drizzled with wasabi-honey vinaigrette or slow-roasted prime rib. Fresh daily soups are available, as are the popular seasonal fruit and cream pies. **Bar:** full bar. **Address:** 1114 Blair St 81433 **Location:** Jct 11th and Blair sts; in Bent Elbow Hotel. **Parking:** on-site and street. **Historic** L D

HANDLEBARS FOOD & SALOON **Phone:** 970/387-5395

American
$7-$21

AAA Inspector Notes: The casual, rustic décor of this popular restaurant is reminiscent of bygone days. Menu selections include salads, sandwiches, steak, prime rib, poultry and burgers-each made from scratch, just like at grandma's. **Bar:** full bar. **Address:** 117 E 13th St 81433 **Location:** Corner of Greene (Main St) and 13th sts. **Parking:** street only. L D

PICKLE BARREL

Phone: 970/387-5713

American
$8-$23

AAA Inspector Notes: In a historic downtown building reminiscent of an Old West saloon, the Pickle Barrel is located within walking distance of the Narrow-Gauge Train Station. Cuisine features include chicken, beef, salads, soups and sandwiches. **Bar:** full bar. **Address:** 1304 Greene St 81433 **Location:** Center. **Parking:** street only. **Historic**

L D

SNOWMASS VILLAGE (D-2) pop. 2,826, elev. 9,100'

- Restaurants p. 286
- Hotels & Restaurants map & index p. 43

Founded in 1967, the ski resort at Snowmass Village was originally dubbed Snowmass-at-Aspen, presumably to distinguish the town from its better-known neighbor. The ski area and all-year resort has since come into its own, however, and lures vacationers from around the world.

First-timers often confuse Snowmass Village with Snowmass, an unincorporated assemblage of ranches and houses on the back side of the ski area's principal mountain. Snowmass Village, incorporated as a town in 1977, is one of several thriving resort communities in the area, as is Aspen *(see place listing p. 41)*, just 9 miles east.

Snowmass Village's 3,100 acres of ski terrain sit within the White River National Forest *(see place listing p. 303)*, a ruggedly mountainous area renowned for spectacular scenery and year-round outdoor recreation. The ski slopes stretch across Baldy and Burnt mountains. The core of Snowmass Village, including lodgings, condominiums, restaurants and boutiques, is centered around the Snowmass Mall and the base village, which both border the beginner slope Fanny Hill.

For those who think ski resorts are only worth visiting in the winter, Snowmass Village has a full slate of warm-weather activities. From June to mid-September, guided nature hikes, free weekly concerts and outdoor theater, golfing, spas, jeep tours, fly-fishing clinics, mountainboarding, horseback riding, mountain biking, chairlift rides, disc golf, white-water rafting and campfire storytelling are popular pastimes. The Anderson Ranch Arts Center, housed on a former sheep ranch, presents workshops and free lectures in painting, ceramics, photography, woodworking and furniture design.

Warm weather also brings with it a host of festivals and special events. The Snowmass Chili Pepper and Brew Fest kicks off the summer season in early June with popular music acts and chili and microbrew competitions. From late June to late August the Snowmass Summer of Free Music Series presents weekly evening concerts by well-known performers at the resort's slopeside amphitheater on Fanny Hill. The Snowmass Rodeo hosts Wednesday rodeos with calf roping, bronco and bull riding, family activities and a Western barbecue, also from late June through August.

Labor Day weekend brings the JazzAspen Snowmass Labor Day Festival featuring nationally known acts that attract music connoisseurs. Oktoberfest takes place in mid-September, as does the Snowmass Balloon Festival, a wine and jazz festival with 3 days of hot air balloon competitions set against the backdrop of the Elk Mountain Range at sunrise.

Snowmass Village Visitor Information: 130 Kearns Rd., P.O. Box 5566, Snowmass Village, CO 81615. **Phone:** (970) 922-2297 or (800) 766-9627.

RECREATIONAL ACTIVITIES

Skiing

- **Snowmass** is 6 mi. s.w. of SR 82 on Brush Creek Rd. **Hours:** Daily 9-3:30, late Nov. to mid-Apr. (weather permitting). **Phone:** (970) 925-1220 or (800) 525-6200.

SNOWMASS MOUNTAIN CHALET

Phone: (970)923-3900 **18**

Hotel
$150-$364 11/26-3/31
$99-$139 6/1-10/12

Address: 115 Daly Ln 81615 **Location:** 4 mi sw of SR 82 via Brush Creek and Lower Village rds; Lot 5. **Facility:** 64 units. 4 stories, interior/exterior corridors. **Parking:** on-site (fee). **Terms:** open 6/1-10/12 & 11/26-3/31, office hours 7 am-11 pm, check-in 4 pm, 45 day cancellation notice-fee imposed. **Pool(s):** heated outdoor. **Activities:** saunas, whirlpool, bicycle trails, hiking trails, jogging, exercise room. **Guest Services:** coin laundry, area transportation-within 5 mi.

BIZ

STONEBRIDGE INN

Phone: 970/923-2420 **17**

Hotel
Rates not provided

Address: 300 Carriage Way 81615 **Location:** 3.9 mi sw of SR 82 via Brush Creek and Lower Village rds; Lot 2. **Facility:** 92 units. 7 stories, interior corridors. **Parking:** street only. **Terms:** check-in 4 pm. **Pool(s):** heated outdoor. **Activities:** whirlpools, hiking trails, jogging, exercise room. *Fee:* massage. **Guest Services:** valet and coin laundry, area transportation-Snowmass Village.

BIZ

TIMBERLINE CONDOMINIUMS

Phone: (970)923-4000 **20**

Condominium
$150-$1220 11/24-4/30
$105-$280 5/1-11/23

Address: 690 Carriage Way 81615 **Location:** 4 mi sw off SR 82 via Brush Creek and Snowmelt rds; Lot 13. Located in Upper Village. **Facility:** Some of the apartment-style units of this ski-in/ski-out facility include a loft and fireplace; phone ahead for seasonal closures. 89 condominiums. 3 stories (no elevator), interior/exterior corridors. **Parking:** on-site (fee). **Terms:** office hours 7 am-11 pm, check-in 4 pm, 3 night minimum stay - seasonal, 14 day cancellation notice, 45 day 11/24-4/30-fee imposed. **Amenities:** safes. **Dining:** Garnish Cafe, see separate listing. **Pool(s):** heated outdoor. **Activities:** steamroom, exercise room. *Fee:* downhill skiing. **Guest Services:** valet and coin laundry, area transportation-Snowmass Village.

BIZ

(See map & index p. 43.)

VILLAS AT SNOWMASS CLUB

Phone: (970)923-0391 16

Condominium

$200-$1100 12/1-4/5
$150-$400 5/25-10/7

Address: 160 Snowmass Club Cir Dr 81615 **Location:** 2.6 mi n up Brush Creek Rd to roundabout, 2nd exit, 0.3 mi s on Highline Rd, then just w to Welcome Center. **Facility:** This family-friendly resort offers manicured landscaping and individually decorated condominiums with one to three bedrooms, lofts and skylights. 47 kitchen units, some two and three bedrooms. 2-3 stories, interior/exterior corridors. **Terms:** open 5/25-10/7 & 12/1-4/5, check-in 4 pm, 3 night minimum stay - weekends, 30 day cancellation notice-fee imposed. **Amenities:** high-speed Internet. **Dining:** Sage Restaurant & Patio, see separate listing. **Pool(s):** 3 heated outdoor. **Activities:** saunas, whirlpools, steamrooms, recreation programs, bicycle trails, hiking trails, jogging. *Fee:* golf-18 holes, 13 tennis courts (2 indoor, 2 lighted), massage. **Guest Services:** valet and coin laundry, area transportation-Snowmass Village.

BIZ

POKOLODI LODGE **Phone:** 970/923-4310

fyi Not evaluated. **Address:** 25 Daly Ln 81615 **Location:** 4 mi sw of SR 82 via Brush Creek and Lower Village rds; Lot 5. Facilities, services, and decor characterize an economy property.

VICEROY SNOWMASS **Phone:** 970/923-8000

fyi Not evaluated. **Address:** 130 Wood Rd 81615 **Location:** 6 mi sw of SR 82 via Brush Creek Rd, then 0.3 mi to lower Carriage Way. Facilities, services, and decor characterize an upscale property.

WHERE TO EAT

ARTISAN RESTAURANT & BAR

Phone: 970/923-2427 28

American

$12-$29

AAA Inspector Notes: Representative of the restaurant's innovative and hand-crafted cuisine are dishes such as jumbo lump blue crab with grilled avocado and yellow tomato salad, seasonal soups, risotto of the day and a fun tapas menu. The indoor and patio seating both have a casually sophisticated feel. **Bar:** full bar. **Reservations:** suggested. **Address:** 300 Carriage Way 81615 **Location:** 6 mi sw of SR 82 via Brush Creek Rd, then 0.3 mi to lower Carriage Way; across from Lot 2.

B D AC

GARNISH CAFE **Phone:** 970/923-4004 27

American

$19-$32

AAA Inspector Notes: This New England-style restaurant serves Maine lobster-steamed, baked or grilled-as well as steak, pasta and other East Coast seafood specialties. **Bar:** full bar. **Reservations:** suggested. **Address:** 690 Carriage Way 81615 **Location:** 4 mi sw off SR 82 via Brush Creek and Snowmelt rds; Lot 13; in Timberline Condominiums. D AC

KRABLOONIK RESTAURANT

Phone: 970/923-3953 29

Regional American

$8-$62

AAA Inspector Notes: Specializing in wild mushroom soup, fresh fish and preparations of seasonal wild game such as caribou, pheasant, wild boar and elk, this restaurant has a log cabin dining room with magnificent mountain views, an intimate sunken fire pit, a warm atmosphere and an excellent wine list. **Bar:** full bar. **Reservations:** suggested. **Address:** 4250 Divide Rd 81615 **Location:** 5.3 mi w of SR 82 on Brush Creek Rd, 1 mi on Divide Rd; 40 steps, high altitude. L D AC

SAGE RESTAURANT & PATIO

Phone: 970/923-0923 26

American

$10-$36

AAA Inspector Notes: Colorado bistro fare is served in a gracious setting that includes a dining room appointed in rustic décor and an expansive seasonal patio that offers breathtaking views of Mount Daly. The menu and homemade ice creams and sorbets change seasonally. **Bar:** full bar. **Reservations:** suggested. **Address:** 0239 Snowmass Club Cir 81615 **Location:** 2.6 mi n up Brush Creek Rd to roundabout, 2nd exit, 0.3 mi s on Highline Rd, then just w to Welcome Center; in Villas at Snowmass Club. **Parking:** valet only. L D AC

SOUTH FORK (E-3) pop. 386, elev. 8,208'

The town of South Fork is named for its proximity to the south fork of the Rio Grande. Since its beginnings as a stagecoach stop in the 1880s, timber processing, agriculture, mining and ranching as well as tourism and recreation have contributed to the town's economy.

South Fork serves as the southern gateway to the Silver Thread Scenic Byway on US 149 as it winds its way 117 miles westward through the San Juan Mountains to Blue Mesa Reservoir. Interpretive signs along the highway give details about the region's history, geology and wildlife.

The area's many lakes and 47 Rio Grande tributaries allow for plentiful fishing and river rafting opportunities. Other recreational activities include hiking, horseback riding, snowmobiling, hunting and skiing.

South Fork Visitors Center: 28 Silver Thread Ln., P.O. Box 1030, South Fork, CO 81154. **Phone:** (719) 873-5512 or (800) 571-0881.

RECREATIONAL ACTIVITIES

Fishing

- **South Fork Anglers** departs from 30359 US 160. **Hours:** Daily dawn-dusk. Phone ahead to confirm schedule. **Phone:** (719) 658-2955 or (877) 656-3474.

Horseback Riding

- **Wolf Creek Ranch Ski Lodge** is at 177022 W. US 160. Other activities are available. **Hours:** Trail rides are offered daily, Memorial Day weekend to mid-Oct. Phone ahead to confirm schedule. **Phone:** (719) 873-5371, or (719) 873-5998 for trail ride information.

White-water Rafting

- **Cottonwood Cove** is at 13046 SR 149. Other activities are available. **Hours:** Daily May-Aug. Phone ahead to confirm schedule. **Phone:** (719) 658-2242.

UTE BLUFF LODGE & CABINS **Phone:** 719/873-5595

Motel

$49-$208

Address: 27680 W Hwy 160 81154 **Location:** Jct US 160 and SR 149, 2.7 mi e. **Facility:** 29 units, some kitchens and cabins. 1-2 stories (no elevator), exterior corridors. **Terms:** 14 day cancellation notice-fee imposed. **Activities:** whirlpools, horseshoes. **Guest Services:** coin laundry.

AC / SOME UNITS FEE

WHERE TO EAT

FEELIN' GOOD COFFEEHOUSE & CAFE

Phone: 719/873-5150

Coffee/Tea
$6-$8

AAA Inspector Notes: This is the perfect spot to take a break from the road, check e-mail and enjoy a delicious breakfast that includes homemade biscuits and muffins. A nice selection of salads is available for lunch along with a freshly made daily soup. Sandwich options include a Reuben, chicken salad and a hand-patted burger, all of which are served with fresh cucumber and tomato salad, cottage cheese or chips. **Bar:** full bar. **Address:** 0076 Hwy 149 81154 **Location:** Jct SR 112 and 149.

B L

STEAMBOAT SPRINGS (C-2) pop. 12,088, elev. 6,728'

• Restaurants p. 289

Ute Indians, drawn by valuable resources and hot springs, were the area's first inhabitants, but it was French fur trappers who gave Steamboat Springs its name. Legend has it that the rhythmic chugging of the hot spring near the river, from which mineral water spewed 15 feet into the air, sounded like a steamboat chugging down the river.

In the immediate vicinity there are more than 150 mineral springs, both medicinal and recreational. Today Old Town Hot Springs is built on the site of the original Heart Springs; phone (970) 879-1828. Strawberry Park Hot Springs, 7 miles northwest on CR 36, offers rejuvenation in a more natural setting; phone (970) 879-0342.

In addition to the thermal waters, Steamboat Springs has gained prominence as a winter sports playground. Norwegian Carl Howelsen, dubbed the Flying Norseman by Barnum & Bailey, introduced skiing and ski jumping in 1913; by the 1930s Steamboat Springs was internationally known. A number of world ski jump records were set on Howelsen Hill, one of the state's oldest ski areas still in use. Howelsen Ice Arena features an Olympic-size ice rink, which offers hockey and public ice skating July through May; phone (970) 879-0341.

Howelsen also organized the first Winter Carnival in 1914. Held in February, this ski festival—along with some 69 winter Olympians who have called the town home and the popularity of the Steamboat Ski Area—perpetuate Steamboat Spring's reputation as "Ski Town, U.S.A."

June through August the Strings Music Festival features string ensembles, chamber music, bluegrass, jazz and youth and family concerts at Strings Festival Park. The Steamboat Springs Arts Council hosts a number of cultural events, featuring the Emerald City Opera in August and the Summer Concert Series from June through Labor Day, which features national acts.

The Yampa River Core Trail, a 7-mile route that runs the length of the town, provides scenic opportunities for walking, jogging, bicycling and skating. The path winds beside the Yampa River through city parks and wetlands. Kayakers and tubers enjoy the rushing waters of the Yampa River created by the spring snowmelt; tamer currents later in the season lure anglers.

Spectacular Fish Creek Falls, which plunge 283 feet through a geologic fault, is just minutes away. The falls are reached from the parking lot by a footpath along the creek. A footbridge at the bottom of the falls provides an excellent view of the cascades. The overlook trail is paved and is accessible for the physically impaired. Picnic facilities are available.

South of town a scenic route follows SR 131 to Toponas, turns east on SR 134, crosses 9,570-foot Gore Pass and rejoins US 40 at a point 6 miles north of Kremmling. The headquarters for the Routt National Forest *(see place listing p. 279)*, which encompasses much of the neighboring mountain country, is in town. Steamboat Lake State Park lies 25 miles north via CR 129 *(see Recreation Chart)*.

Steamboat Springs Chamber Resort Association: 125 Anglers Dr., P.O. Box 774408, Steamboat Springs, CO 80477. **Phone:** (970) 879-0880.

TREAD OF PIONEERS MUSEUM, 8th and Oak sts., reflects the history and heritage of the Steamboat Springs area. Set in a furnished 1908 Queen Anne-style home, the collection includes early household items; skiing, ranching and mining memorabilia; an extensive collection of firearms; and American Indian arts. Educational programs and tours are available. **Hours:** Tues.-Sat. 11-5. **Cost:** $5; $4 (ages 62+); $1 (ages 6-12). **Phone:** (970) 879-2214.

YAMPA RIVER BOTANIC PARK, 1 mi. s. on US 40, then w. on Trafalgar Ln. to Pamela Ln., following signs to 1000 Pamela Ln., contains plants, flowers, ornamentals and trees native to the Yampa River basin. Among the gardens are those devoted to day lilies, irises, roses, native plants, spring bulbs and medicinal herbs. A pond complements the surroundings. Pets are not permitted. **Time:** Allow 30 minutes minimum. **Hours:** Daily dawn-dusk, May-Oct. **Cost:** Donations. **Phone:** (970) 846-5172.

RECREATIONAL ACTIVITIES

Fishing

- **Bucking Rainbow Outfitters** is at 730 Lincoln Ave. Other activities are offered. **Hours:** Daily 8-8. Phone ahead to confirm schedule. **Phone:** (970) 879-8747 or (888) 810-8747.

Skiing

- **Howelsen Hill** is at 845 Howelsen Pkwy. Other activities are offered. **Hours:** Tues.-Fri. 1-8, Sat.-Sun. 10-4, early Dec.-late Mar. Phone ahead to confirm schedule. **Phone:** (970) 879-8499.
- **Steamboat Ski Resort** is 2.3 mi. e. on US 40 in the Routt National Forest. Other activities are offered. **Hours:** Daily 8:30-3:30, mid-Nov. to mid-Apr. **Phone:** (970) 879-6111 for information, or (800) 922-2722 for reservations.

BUNKHOUSE LODGE **Phone:** (970)871-9121

Hotel

$59-$128

Address: 3155 S Lincoln Ave 80487 **Location:** 3 mi se on US 40, then just e. **Facility:** 38 units. 2 stories (no elevator), interior corridors. **Terms:** office hours 7 am-10 pm, off-site registration, cancellation fee imposed. **Activities:** whirlpool, fishing, hiking trails. **Guest Services:** complimentary laundry.

CALL

CANYON CREEK AT EAGLE RIDGE **Phone:** 970/879-6606

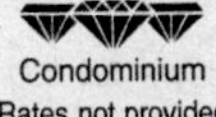

Condominium

Rates not provided

Address: 2740 Eagle Ridge Dr 80487 **Location:** US 40 W, 2.8 mi se on Walton Creek Rd, then n at Eagle Ridge Dr. **Facility:** Located in a residential area near the ski area, these modern two- to four-bedroom condo units offer fireplaces, fans and balconies. 44 condominiums. 3 stories, interior/exterior corridors. **Terms:** office hours 7 am-11 pm, check-in 4 pm. **Pool(s):** heated outdoor. **Activities:** whirlpool, exercise room. **Guest Services:** complimentary and valet laundry, area transportation-within 5 mi.

FAIRFIELD INN & SUITES BY MARRIOTT **Phone:** (970)870-9000

Hotel

$143-$175

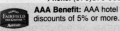

AAA Benefit: AAA hotel discounts of 5% or more.

Address: 3200 S Lincoln Ave 80477 **Location:** 3 mi s on US 40. **Facility:** 66 units. 3 stories, interior corridors. **Pool(s):** heated indoor. **Activities:** whirlpool, exercise room. **Guest Services:** valet and coin laundry. **Free Special Amenities: expanded continental breakfast and high-speed Internet.**

SOME UNITS FEE

HAMPTON INN & SUITES **Phone:** (970)871-8900

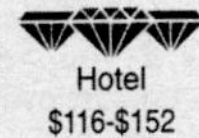

Hotel

$116-$152

AAA Benefit: Members save up to 10% everyday!

Address: 725 S Lincoln Ave 80487 **Location:** 1.1 mi e on US 40. Located near railroad tracks. **Facility:** 73 units. 3 stories, interior corridors. **Terms:** check-in 4:30 pm, 1-7 night minimum stay, cancellation fee imposed. **Pool(s):** heated outdoor. **Activities:** whirlpools, exercise room. **Guest Services:** valet and coin laundry.

CALL

SOME UNITS FEE

HOLIDAY INN STEAMBOAT SPRINGS **Phone:** (970)879-2250

Hotel

$109-$199 1/1-4/30
$99-$199 5/1-12/31

Address: 3190 S Lincoln Ave 80487 **Location:** 3 mi e on US 40. **Facility:** 117 units. 2 stories, interior corridors. **Terms:** check-in 4 pm, 3 day cancellation notice. **Amenities:** high-speed Internet. **Pool(s):** heated outdoor, heated indoor. **Activities:** whirlpools, exercise room. *Fee:* game room. **Guest Services:** valet and coin laundry, area transportation-ski shuttle.

CALL

SOME UNITS FEE

INN AT STEAMBOAT **Phone:** (970)879-2600

Hotel

$99-$269 11/22-4/30
$79-$149 5/1-11/21

Address: 3070 Columbine Dr 80487 **Location:** 2.7 mi s of center on US 40, 0.8 mi e on Walton Creek Rd, then just s. **Facility:** 34 units, some two bedrooms, kitchens and condominiums. 3 stories (no elevator), interior corridors. **Terms:** check-in 4 pm, 1-2 night minimum stay - seasonal, 10 day cancellation notice-fee imposed. **Pool(s):** heated outdoor. **Activities:** sauna, whirlpool, exercise room. **Guest Services:** valet and coin laundry, area transportation-within 2 mi.

LA QUINTA INN STEAMBOAT SPRINGS **Phone:** (970)871-1219

Hotel

$89-$189

Address: 3155 Ingles Ln 80487 **Location:** 3 mi s on US 40, then just e. **Facility:** 29 units. 2 stories (no elevator), interior corridors. **Amenities:** high-speed Internet. **Pool(s):** heated indoor. **Activities:** whirlpool. **Guest Services:** coin laundry.

SOME UNITS FEE

LEGACY VACATION CLUB **Phone:** 970/879-2900

Condominium

Rates not provided

Address: 1000 High Point Dr 80477 **Location:** 1.5 mi se from center on US 40 to High Point Dr, then 0.4 mi ne. **Facility:** 77 units, some kitchens. 5 stories, interior corridors. **Terms:** check-in 4 pm. **Amenities:** safes. **Pool(s):** heated indoor. **Activities:** saunas, whirlpools, miniature golf, 2 tennis courts. *Fee:* game room. **Guest Services:** complimentary and valet laundry, area transportation-within 3 mi.

THE LODGE AT STEAMBOAT SPRINGS **Phone:** (970)879-6000

Condominium

$175-$850

Address: 2700 Village Dr 80487 **Location:** Off US 40, 0.5 mi e on Walton Creek Rd to Village Dr, then just n. **Facility:** 115 condominiums. 3 stories (no elevator), exterior corridors. **Terms:** office hours 7 am-11 pm, check-in 4 pm, 2-6 night minimum stay - seasonal and/or weekends, 10 day cancellation notice-fee imposed. **Pool(s):** heated outdoor. **Activities:** whirlpools, 2 tennis courts, shuffleboard. **Guest Services:** valet and coin laundry, area transportation-within 3 mi.

NORDIC LODGE **Phone:** 970/879-0531

Motel

Rates not provided

Address: 1036 Lincoln Ave 80477 **Location:** Between 10th and 11th sts; downtown. **Facility:** 29 units. 1-2 stories (no elevator), exterior corridors. **Parking:** winter plug-ins. **Terms:** office hours 7 am-11 pm. **Pool(s):** heated outdoor. **Activities:** whirlpool, hiking trails, jogging. **Guest Services:** coin laundry.

SOME UNITS FEE

PTARMIGAN HOUSE **Phone:** 970/879-6278

Condominium

Rates not provided

Address: 2322 Apres Ski Way 80487 **Location:** 2.3 mi e from center on US 40, 0.8 mi n on Mt. Werner Rd, then take Apres Ski Way. **Facility:** 22 condominiums. 3 stories, interior corridors. **Terms:** office hours 7 am-8 pm, off-site registration, check-in 4 pm. **Activities:** sauna, whirlpool. **Guest Services:** valet and coin laundry, area transportation-within 3 mi.

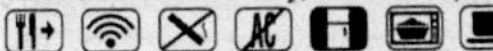

QUALITY INN & SUITES Phone: (970)879-6669

Hotel
$80-$200

Address: 1055 Walton Creek Rd 80487 **Location:** 2.8 mi e on US 40. **Facility:** 52 units, some two bedrooms. 2 stories (no elevator), interior corridors. **Terms:** check-in 4 pm, cancellation fee imposed. **Pool(s):** heated indoor. **Activities:** whirlpool, fishing. **Guest Services:** valet and coin laundry. **Free Special Amenities: full breakfast and high-speed Internet.**

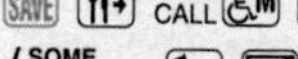

SAVE CALL BIZ / SOME UNITS FEE

RABBIT EARS MOTEL Phone: (970)879-1150

Motel
$89-$189

Address: 201 Lincoln Ave 80477 **Location:** Just e on US 40. Opposite Municipal Hot Springs Pool and next to park. **Facility:** 65 units. 2 stories (no elevator), exterior corridors. **Terms:** 3 day cancellation notice-fee imposed. **Activities:** hiking trails, jogging. **Guest Services:** coin laundry.

BIZ / SOME UNITS FEE

RESORTQUEST TRAPPEUR'S CROSSING RESORT Phone: (970)879-0720

Condominium
$379-$1259 11/25-4/30
$307 5/1-11/24

Address: 2800 Village Dr 80487 **Location:** Off US 40, take Walton Creek Rd, 0.5 mi e to Village Dr, just n to Medicine Springs Dr, then just e. **Facility:** These large two-, three- and four-bedroom condos all have a humidifier and well-appointed guest rooms and amenities. Gas grills are by the outdoor pool. 120 condominiums. 3 stories, interior corridors. **Terms:** check-in 4 pm, 3-5 night minimum stay - seasonal, cancellation fee imposed. **Pool(s):** 3 heated outdoor, heated indoor/outdoor. **Activities:** sauna, whirlpools, 2 tennis courts, exercise room. *Fee:* massage. **Guest Services:** complimentary and valet laundry.

/ SOME UNITS

SHERATON STEAMBOAT RESORT Phone: (970)879-2220

Resort Hotel
$149-$519

Sheraton **AAA Benefit:** Members get up to 15% off, plus Starwood Preferred Guest® bonuses.

Address: 2200 Village Inn Ct 80487 **Location:** 2.3 mi s from center on US 40 to Mt. Werner Rd exit, 0.8 mi e, 0.3 mi ne on Mt. Werner Cir, just ne at Ski Time Sq, then just s. **Facility:** All rooms in the resort are handsomely furnished and feature a balcony with a village, valley or ski slope view. 207 units, some kitchens and condominiums. 8 stories, interior corridors. **Parking:** on-site (fee) and valet. **Terms:** open 5/25-4/7, check-in 4 pm, 2-3 night minimum stay - seasonal, 30 day cancellation notice-fee imposed. **Amenities:** safes. *Fee:* video games, high-speed Internet. **Dining:** 3 restaurants. **Pool(s):** heated outdoor. **Activities:** whirlpools, steamrooms, hiking trails, jogging, spa. *Fee:* golf-18 holes, downhill & cross country skiing, snowmobiling. **Guest Services:** valet and coin laundry, area transportation-within 3 mi.

SAVE BIZ FEE / SOME UNITS FEE

SKI INN CONDOMINIUMS Phone: (970)879-4477

Condominium
$175-$720 11/24-4/30
$175-$245 5/1-11/23

Address: 2350 Ski Trail Ln 80487 **Location:** Jct US 40 and Walton Creek Rd, 0.5 mi e to Village Dr, 0.3 mi n, just e on Apres Ski Way, then just ne. **Facility:** 44 condominiums. 3 stories (no elevator), interior corridors. **Terms:** office hours 7:30 am-10 pm, check-in 4 pm, 2 night minimum stay - seasonal, 30 day cancellation notice-fee imposed. **Amenities:** high-speed Internet. **Activities:** saunas, whirlpools. **Guest Services:** valet and coin laundry, area transportation-within 3 mi.

BIZ

STEAMBOAT HOTEL Phone: (970)879-5230

Hotel
$59-$115

Address: 3195 S Lincoln Ave 80487 **Location:** 3 mi e on US 40. **Facility:** 60 units. 3 stories (no elevator), interior corridors. **Terms:** office hours 7 am-11 pm, cancellation fee imposed. **Pool(s):** heated outdoor. **Activities:** whirlpool, fishing, hiking trails. **Guest Services:** coin laundry.

/ SOME UNITS FEE

TIMBER RUN CONDOMINIUMS Phone: 970/879-7000

Condominium
Rates not provided

Address: 2015 Walton Creek Rd 80487 **Location:** Jct US 40, 0.6 mi e. **Facility:** 74 condominiums. 2 stories (no elevator), exterior corridors. **Terms:** office hours 7 am-11 pm, check-in 4 pm. **Pool(s):** heated outdoor. **Activities:** sauna, whirlpools, tennis court. **Guest Services:** valet and coin laundry, area transportation-within 4 mi.

BIZ

ANTLERS AT CHRISTIE BASE Phone: 970/879-8000

fyi Not evaluated. **Address:** 2085 Ski Time Square Dr 80487 **Location:** Se on US 40 to Mt. Werner Cir, e to Ski Time Square Dr, then just e. Facilities, services, and decor characterize a mid-scale property.

EAGLERIDGE LODGE & TOWNHOMES Phone: 970/879-5555

fyi
Condominium

Did not meet all AAA rating requirements for locking devices in some guest rooms at time of last evaluation on 04/11/2011. **Address:** 1463 Flat Top Cir 80487 **Location:** From US 40 and Mt. Werner Rd, 0.7 mi e to Mt. Werner Cir, 0.3 mi s to Eagle Ridge Dr, then just e. Facilities, services, and decor characterize a mid-scale property.

THE HIGHMARK STEAMBOAT SPRINGS Phone: 970/879-8744

fyi Not evaluated. **Address:** 2525 Village Dr 80487 **Location:** Off US 40, 0.5 mi e on Walton Creek Rd to Village Dr, then just n. Facilities, services, and decor characterize an upscale property.

HOTEL BRISTOL Phone: 970/879-3083

fyi Not evaluated. **Address:** 917 Lincoln Ave 80477 **Location:** In historic downtown. Facilities, services, and decor characterize a mid-scale property.

KUTUK CONDOMINIUMS Phone: 970/879-6605

fyi Not evaluated. **Address:** 2000 Ski Time Square Dr 80487 **Location:** In Ski Time Square. Facilities, services, and decor characterize an upscale property.

SHADOW RUN CONDOMINIUMS Phone: 970/879-2118

fyi Not evaluated. **Address:** 2900 Whistler Rd 80487 **Location:** Jct US 40 and Walton Creek Rd, 0.3 mi e, just s. Facilities, services, and decor characterize an economy property.

VILLAS AT WALTON CREEK Phone: 970/879-0517

fyi Not evaluated. **Address:** 2910 Whistler Rd 80487 **Location:** Jct US 40 and Walton Creek Rd, 0.3 mi e, just s. Facilities, services, and decor characterize an economy property.

WHERE TO EAT

AZTECA TAQUERIA Phone: 970/870-9980

Mexican
$5-$9

AAA Inspector Notes: This casual eatery features burritos, enchiladas, chimichangas, tacos, quesadillas and salads prepared quickly and made to order. Patrons, who can dine in or take their food to go, can choose their toppings and sauces. **Bar:** beer only. **Address:** 116 9th St 80488 **Location:** Just n of Lincoln Ave and 9th St; downtown. **Parking:** street only. L D

BEAU JO'S COLORADO STYLE PIZZA **Phone:** 970/870-6401

Pizza
$8-$16

AAA Inspector Notes: Part of a popular local chain, this restaurant prepares delicious pizzas, calzones and sandwiches. Mountain pies have large crusts, which patrons save for the end of the meal, when they'll drizzle the puffy, crusty dough with honey. **Address:** 704 Lincoln Ave 80487 **Location:** Corner of 7th St and Lincoln Ave; downtown. **Parking:** street only. L D AC

BISTRO C.V. **Phone:** 970/879-4197

Regional American
$23-$39

AAA Inspector Notes: This upscale bistro adds a touch of class to ski town dining. Sample items may include a popular grilled Caesar salad with truffle-garlic dressing, steak tartare with fried quail egg, Humboldt Fog grilled cheese, mussels in piquillo pepper broth, Wagyu steak and braised short ribs with baby golden beets, and rib-eye with chanterelle mushrooms. The wine list includes local, regional and international selections. **Bar:** full bar. **Reservations:** suggested. **Address:** 345 Lincoln Ave 80487 **Location:** Corner of Lincoln Ave and 4th St; downtown. **Parking:** street only. D AC

CAFÉ DIVA **Phone:** 970/871-0508

American
$21-$39

AAA Inspector Notes: This luxurious restaurant at the base of the mountain offers an elegant yet relaxed atmosphere. It's known for its imaginative menu, which includes crab tomato bisque and a taste of Colorado with elk tenderloin and other dishes with out-of-this-world flavors. The accomplished staff can make suggestions from the vast wine list. **Bar:** full bar. **Reservations:** suggested. **Address:** 1855 Ski Time Square 80487 **Location:** At the base of Steamboat Ski Area; in Torian Plum Plaza. D

CANTINA FRESH MEXICAN GRILL & TEQUILA BAR **Phone:** 970/879-0826

Mexican
$7-$17

AAA Inspector Notes: Flavorful Mexican fare and tasty margaritas draw large crowds to this popular hangout. Menu items include a nice selection of appetizers and tapas, pork tamales, buffalo carne asada, chiles rellenos, chicken enchiladas and sizzling tequila-fired fajitas prepared tableside. The cheerful, festive décor enhances the lively atmosphere. **Bar:** full bar. **Address:** 818 Lincoln Ave 80487 **Location:** Just s of center; corner of Lincoln Ave and 8th St; downtown. **Parking:** street only. L D AC

CREEKSIDE CAFE & GRILL **Phone:** 970/879-4925

American
$8-$12

AAA Inspector Notes: Popular with locals and tourists alike, this casual eatery offers hearty breakfasts and lunches. Breakfast choices include many variations on traditional eggs Benedict, French toast, pancakes, waffles, breakfast burritos and more, while the lunch menu features creative, flavor-filled sandwiches, wraps, soups and salads. The atmosphere indoors has a bistro feel, and the patio overlooking Soda Creek has a breezier atmosphere. **Bar:** full bar. **Address:** 131 11th St 80487 **Location:** Corner of Lincoln Ave and 11th St, then just n; downtown. **Parking:** street only. B L AC

DRUNKEN ONION GET & GO KITCHEN **Phone:** 970/879-8423

Deli
$7-$11

AAA Inspector Notes: Chef/owner Ben Stroock redefines quick serve with a variety of heat-and-serve meals that patrons can take to go. Options include blackened chicken with lemon chive aioli, mac 'n' cheese, pan-fried pork chops and applesauce, and rotisserie chicken enchiladas. This is an excellent option for members who want a high-quality home-cooked meal but also want to relax on vacation. Those wanting to dine in can choose among freshly made soups, sandwiches, salads and desserts. **Address:** 685 Marketplace Plaza, Suite 5 80487 **Location:** 2.6 mi s to Mt. Werner Rd, 0.3 mi e; in Wildhorse Marketplace. L

FRESHIES RESTAURANT **Phone:** 970/879-8099

American
$8-$13

AAA Inspector Notes: Well known for its breakfasts, Freshies also offers a wonderful lunch menu filled with tasty soups, sandwiches and salads. As the name implies, fresh ingredients are the key to this eatery's success. Cheerful décor and upbeat staff complete the experience. **Bar:** full bar. **Address:** 595 S Lincoln Ave 80477 **Location:** 0.6 mi e on US 40. B L

LA MONTANA **Phone:** 970/879-5800

Mexican
$12-$36

AAA Inspector Notes: This popular restaurant's specialty is creative Southwestern cuisine, including camarones de La Montana, in which jumbo shrimp are stuffed with crab, poblano chilies and jack cheese and wrapped in hickory-smoked bacon. Other favorites include enchiladas, fajitas, braised chicken mole and pecan-topped grilled buffalo medallions. Artful presentations enhance the meal. The inviting décor has intimate, open dining areas and a patio. **Bar:** full bar. **Reservations:** suggested. **Address:** 2500 Village Dr, Suite 102 80487 **Location:** 2.3 mi e on US 40, 1 mi n on Mt. Werner Rd, just e on Apres Ski Way; corner of Village Dr. D CALL &M

L'APOGEE **Phone:** 970/879-1919

International
$27-$40

AAA Inspector Notes: Creative French and Continental cuisine is served in candlelit ambience. An excellent wine list enhances the menu. Although they change seasonally, entrées often feature Colorado lamb, line-caught fish, duck, chicken, beef and venison. Innovative flavor combinations and artful presentations add to the experience. Lighter fare and more casual dining is offered in Harwigs in a building dating to 1886. **Bar:** full bar. **Reservations:** suggested. **Address:** 911 Lincoln Ave 80487 **Location:** On US 40; downtown. **Parking:** street only. D

MAHOGANY RIDGE BREWERY & GRILL **Phone:** 970/879-3773

Fusion
$10-$28

AAA Inspector Notes: Not your ordinary brewpub, the restaurant gives guests a choice of creative and artistic Asian and Latin-fusion dishes and American comfort food such as a build-your-own satay platter, pork tenderloin, chipotle chicken potpie, sandwiches, salads and soups, as well as 21 dipping sauces to flavor many of the options. The cozy seasonal outdoor patio is popular in the summer. **Bar:** full bar. **Address:** 435 Lincoln Ave 80487 **Location:** Corner of 5th St and Lincoln Ave; downtown. **Parking:** street only. D

MAMBO ITALIANO **Phone:** 970/870-0500

Italian
$15-$30

AAA Inspector Notes: In the historic downtown area, this restaurant features specialty pizzas and flavorful pasta dishes. When the weather permits, the outdoor patio is the perfect place to dine. The atmosphere is low-key during the day but amps up to become lively at night. **Bar:** full bar. **Address:** 521 Lincoln Ave 80477 **Location:** Corner of 5th St and Lincoln Ave; downtown. **Parking:** street only. D

MAZZOLA'S MAJESTIC ITALIAN DINER **Phone:** 970/879-2405

Italian
$10-$25

AAA Inspector Notes: The established family-friendly restaurant, which locals call the "pizza-pasta place," prepares delicious ravioli and scampi calzone, as well as other Italian entrées, sandwiches and designer pizza pies. The Mazzola salad is tossed tableside with lemon-garlic vinaigrette. Look for the red awning. **Bar:** full bar. **Address:** 917 Lincoln Ave 80487 **Location:** Corner of Lincoln Ave and 9th St; downtown. **Parking:** street only. D LATE

OLD WEST STEAK HOUSE **Phone:** 970/879-1441

Steak
$11-$40

AAA Inspector Notes: The restaurant prepares a good variety of beef, wild game and fresh seafood dishes, which pair with selections, including several by-the-glass choices, from a good wine list. The staff is friendly, and the stylish atmosphere has a Western bent. **Bar:** full bar. **Reservations:** suggested. **Address:** 1104 Lincoln Ave 80477 **Location:** US 40, at 11th St and Lincoln Ave; downtown; in Old West Bldg; entrance on 11th St. **Parking:** street only. D

ORE HOUSE AT THE PINE GROVE **Phone:** 970/879-1190

American
$16-$45

AAA Inspector Notes: Western charm abounds in this popular restaurant's converted 100-year-old barn, which is between the town and the mountain. Specialties include steak, prime rib, wild game and fresh seafood selections. The walls are adorned with historic pictures, and the dining rooms have stone fireplaces and Western appointments such as spurs, chaps and old wagon wheels. **Bar:** full bar. **Reservations:** suggested. **Address:** 1465 Pine Grove Rd 80487 **Location:** 1.5 mi e on US 40. **Historic** D

STEAMBOAT SMOKEHOUSE **Phone:** 970/879-7427

American
$7-$19

AAA Inspector Notes: The floor is covered with peanut shells, and a few peanuts are lodged in mounted animal heads at this quirky haunt. Good barbecue results from a blend of Texas pit, Oklahoma hickory and Colorado beef and pork. **Bar:** full bar. **Address:** 912 Lincoln Ave 80487 **Location:** West end on US 40; downtown; in Thiesen Mall. **Parking:** street only. L D

TRUFFLE PIG **Phone:** 970/879-7470

American
$10-$39

AAA Inspector Notes: Literally steps from the gondola, magnificent views can be seen from the upscale bar, spacious dining room and the slopeside patio. Hot and cold appetizers, salads, flatbreads, sandwiches and entrées may include smoked onion soup, bouillabaisse, mussels and fries served in white wine and confit garlic in a cast-iron skillet, braised Colorado lamb, day boat cod or scallops, and the popular Truffle Pig bacon burger with aged cheddar and tomato jam. Tempting seasonal desserts vary. **Bar:** full bar. **Reservations:** suggested. **Address:** 2250 Apres Ski Way 80487 **Location:** 3 mi s of center on US 40 to Walton Creek Rd, 0.5 mi e to Village Dr, 0.3 mi n, then just e; at One Steamboat Place. **Parking:** on-site and valet. L D

WINONA'S **Phone:** 970/879-2483

Breads/Pastries
$7-$11

AAA Inspector Notes: Large, thick and covered with tons of gooey white frosting, the homemade cinnamon buns alone have people lining up. The cheerful eatery also offers flavorful fresh sandwiches, soups and hearty breakfasts. **Bar:** full bar. **Address:** 617 Lincoln Ave 80488 **Location:** Just e of 7th St; in historic downtown. **Parking:** street only. B L

STERLING (C-5) pop. 14,777, elev. 3,940'

• Restaurants p. 292

Cattle ranchers began arriving in the area in the 1860s, and since then Sterling has grown into a trade center for northeastern Colorado. Agriculture, educational institutions and light industry contribute to its diversified economy.

Fishing, boating, a full-service marina, picnicking, water skiing, swimming and hunting are available at North Sterling State Park *(see Recreation Chart)*, 12 miles north via N. 7th Avenue; phone (970) 522-3657. Types of wildlife that may be found in the area include deer, eagles, pelicans, coyotes, rabbits and many species of waterfowl and shorebirds.

The City of Living Trees is a collection of 12 trees that have been carved into sculptures; some have been bronzed. Located throughout town, the collection includes Skygrazers, a group of five giraffes looking upward.

Tourist Information Center: 12510 CR 370, Sterling, CO 80751. **Phone:** (970) 522-8962 or (800) 544-8609.

OVERLAND TRAIL MUSEUM, e. of the Platte River Bridge at jct. I-76 and US 6, contains historical exhibits including an Evangelical church, blacksmith shop, house, print shop, one-room schoolhouse, barn, general store, barber shop, a 1930s gas station, household goods and American Indian artifacts. The Dave Hamil Rural Electric Association building demonstrates how electricity changed rural America. Fossils from northeastern Colorado also are displayed.

Time: Allow 1 hour, 30 minutes minimum. **Hours:** Mon.-Sat. 9-5, Sun. 1-5, holidays 10-5, Apr.-Oct.; Mon.-Sat. 10-4, rest of year. **Cost:** $3; $1.50 (ages 4-17); $7.50 (family rate). **Phone:** (970) 522-3895.

BEST WESTERN SUNDOWNER **Phone:** (970)522-6265

Motel
$90-$140

AAA Benefit: Members save up to 20%, plus 10% bonus points with Best Western Rewards®.

Address: 125 Overland Trail St 80751 **Location:** I-76 exit 125, just w. **Facility:** 58 units. 2 stories (no elevator), interior/exterior corridors. **Amenities:** *Some:* high-speed Internet. **Pool(s):** heated outdoor, heated indoor. **Activities:** whirlpool, exercise room. **Guest Services:** valet and coin laundry. **Free Special Amenities: expanded continental breakfast and high-speed Internet.**

SAVE BIZ / SOME UNITS FEE

RAMADA INN **Phone:** (970)522-2625

Hotel
$71-$109

Address: 22140 E Hwy 6 80751 **Location:** I-76 exit 125, 0.5 mi e on US 6. **Facility:** 102 units. 2 stories (no elevator), interior/exterior corridors. **Pool(s):** heated indoor. **Activities:** whirlpool, exercise room. *Fee:* game room. **Guest Services:** valet and coin laundry.

/ SOME UNITS FEE

STERLING COMFORT INN **Phone:** (970)522-3700

Hotel
$75-$150

Address: 2020 Leisure Ln 80751 **Location:** I-76 exit 125, just e. **Facility:** 54 units. 3 stories, interior corridors. **Terms:** cancellation fee imposed. **Amenities:** high-speed Internet, safes (fee). **Pool(s):** heated indoor. **Activities:** whirlpool, exercise room. **Guest Services:** coin laundry. **Free Special Amenities: full breakfast and high-speed Internet.**

   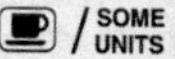  

SAVE BIZ / SOME UNITS

WHERE TO EAT

T. J. BUMMER'S **Phone:** 970/522-8397

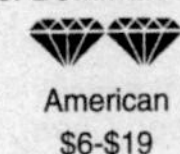

American
$6-$19

AAA Inspector Notes: Specializing in good ol' American comfort food, this family-friendly restaurant is a favorite among locals and tourists alike. **Bar:** wine only. **Address:** 203 Broadway St 80751 **Location:** I-76 exit 125, 1.8 mi w, then 0.5 mi n on 3rd St. (B) (L) (D) (AC)

STRASBURG (B-6) pop. 2,447, elev. 5,386'

Near Strasburg on Aug. 15, 1870, the Kansas Pacific Railroad completed laying the tracks that formed part of a continuous chain of railways connecting the Atlantic and Pacific coasts. A sign and obelisk mark the site of the rail hookup.

COMANCHE CROSSING MUSEUM, 1 blk. n. and 3 blks. w. of I-70 exit 310, portrays the history of the Strasburg area. Exhibits include a doctor's office, cobbler's shop, two relocated school buildings, a railroad station, caboose, antique vehicles, fossils, meteorites and American Indian artifacts. **Hours:** Daily 1-4, June-Aug; grounds open dawn-dusk. **Cost:** Donations. **Phone:** (303) 622-4322 or (303) 622-4345.

STRATTON pop. 658

BEST WESTERN GOLDEN PRAIRIE INN
Phone: (719)348-5311

Hotel
$96-$120

AAA Benefit: Members save up to 20%, plus 10% bonus points with Best Western Rewards®.

Address: 700 Colorado Ave 80836 **Location:** I-70 exit 419, just n. **Facility:** 40 units. 2 stories (no elevator), exterior corridors. **Amenities:** high-speed Internet. **Pool(s):** heated outdoor. **Guest Services:** coin laundry. **Free Special Amenities: local telephone calls and high-speed Internet.**

SAVE   BIZ

/ SOME UNITS FEE

TELLURIDE (E-2) pop. 2,325, elev. 8,792'

• **Restaurants p. 294**

It seemed logical that the gold and silver veins that were yielding fortunes in Ouray on the east slope of the Uncompahgre Range also would show on the west side. The claims staked in 1875 on the mountainsides above the headwaters of the San Miguel proved the premise. Columbia, the supply camp at the bottom of the narrow gorge, soon changed its name to Telluride after tellurium, the non-metallic matrix in which the precious metals appeared.

Efforts to lend respectability to the brawling camp led to the construction around 1891 of the luxurious Sheridan Hotel and adjacent opera house; the preservation of these structures contributes to the town's Victorian atmosphere.

Although such luminaries as Sarah Bernhardt, William Jennings Bryan and Lillian Gish appeared at the Sheridan Opera House, in 1889 a star of another sort also impressed Telluride: Butch Cassidy "withdrew" $30,000 from a local bank, unauthorized.

In its heyday the mining town boasted a population of 5,000 and included a bowling alley, tennis courts and the highest-altitude YMCA in the country. Once an 1870s mining camp of 250 people, the ghost town of Alta is 5 miles south on SR 145.

A free gondola ride provides a spectacular view of the town and the surrounding mountains. Gondolas stop at Station St. Sophia before continuing on to Mountain Village, where the St. Sophia Nature Center is located a short walk away. Visitors may explore the town's mining past by visiting the Tomboy Mine located near the 13,000-foot summit of Imogene Pass. To get to the mine, take Oak Street north, then continue 6 miles east on Tomboy Road; a four-wheel-drive vehicle is required.

Many local guide services are available. Dave's Mountain Tours provides guided scenic tours of the San Juan Mountains via snowmobile in winter or four-wheel-drive vehicles in the summer; phone (970) 728-9749.

About 2.5 miles east of town Bridal Veil Falls, the longest free-falling waterfall in Colorado, drops 365 feet to become the headwaters of the San Miguel River. Precariously perched at the edge of a cliff above the falls is a renovated 1907 structure that housed one of the oldest Westinghouse generators in the country. The building's machinery has been restored to provide hydroelectric power for Telluride. Hikers, mountain bikers and four-wheelers can take a mining road that dates from the late 1800s up the canyon to the power station and falls. **Note:** The power station is privately owned and not open to the public.

Another dramatic canyon walk begins at the edge of town and climbs 1,040 feet over 2.5 miles to Bear Creek Falls. The hiking and biking trail leads to the waterfall canyon and mining ruins. With more than 350 forested acres, Bear Creek Canyon offers cross-country and back-country skiing during the winter months.

Major summer festivals include Mountainfilm, Memorial Day weekend; the Telluride Jazz Celebration, the first weekend in June; the Telluride Bluegrass Festival, the third weekend in June; the Telluride Chamber Music Festival in mid-August; the Telluride Film Festival, Labor Day weekend; and the Telluride Blues & Brews Festival, the third weekend in September.

Telluride Tourism Board: 700 W. Colorado Ave., Box 1009, Telluride, CO 81435. **Phone:** (970) 728-3041 or (888) 605-2578.

Self-guiding tours: Maps for self-guiding walking tours are available at the visitor information center at the entrance to town.

TELLURIDE HISTORICAL MUSEUM is at 201 W. Gregory St. The history of Telluride from the 1800s to the present is told through exhibits about mining, railroads, home life and healthcare. **Time:** Allow 45 minutes minimum. **Hours:** Tues.-Sat. 11-5 (also Thurs. 5-7), Sun. 1-5, June-Oct.; Tues.-Sat. 11-5, rest of year. **Cost:** $5; $3 (ages 5-18 and 66+). **Phone:** (970) 728-3344.

TELLURIDE OUTSIDE, 121 W. Colorado Ave., offers several guided off-road 4 x 4 tours of the San Juan mountains. Guides are well-versed in local history, flora and fauna, and geology. The Imogene Pass tour passes through mining camps en route to a summit of more than 13,000 feet. Fly fishing, river rafting, mountain bike and photography tours also are offered as well as tours of ghost towns and Ouray. Half- and full-day tours are available.

Time: Allow 4 hours minimum. **Hours:** Departures require a minimum of 2 people. Daily 8-5, May-Oct. **Cost:** Fare $85-$245; $70-$105 (ages 0-12). Reservations are required. **Phone:** (970) 728-3895 or (800) 831-6230.

RECREATIONAL ACTIVITIES

Skiing

- **Telluride Ski Resort** is at 565 Mountain Village Blvd. Other activities are offered. **Hours:** Daily 9-4, Thanksgiving to mid-Apr. **Phone:** (970) 728-6900 or (800) 778-8581.

FAIRMONT HERITAGE PLACE FRANZ KLAMMER LODGE **Phone:** (970)728-3318

Resort Condominium
$750-$2200 11/20-4/7
$250-$750 5/23-10/14

Address: 567 Mountain Village Blvd 81435 **Location:** 2.3 mi e; in Mountain Village. **Facility:** Huge guest rooms are on the Plaza Center with two gondolas just feet away. The sky ride to downtown takes about 15 minutes. Transportation is provided to and from the Montrose and Telluride airports. 63 condominiums. 5 stories, interior corridors. **Parking:** valet only. **Terms:** open 5/23-10/14 & 11/20-4/7, check-in 4:30 pm, 45 day cancellation notice-fee imposed. **Amenities:** high-speed Internet. **Pool(s):** heated indoor/outdoor. **Activities:** sauna, whirlpools, steamroom, recreation programs, hiking trails, jogging, game room, exercise room, spa. *Fee:* downhill & cross country skiing, snowmobiling, ice skating. **Guest Services:** valet laundry.

ECO BIZ / SOME UNITS FEE

HOTEL COLUMBIA **Phone:** (970)728-0660

Contemporary Hotel
$215-$1625 11/20-4/7
$175-$1245 5/22-10/14

Address: 301 W San Juan Ave 81435 **Location:** At Aspen St and San Juan Ave; opposite gondola. **Facility:** 21 units, some two bedrooms, three bedrooms, efficiencies and kitchens. 4 stories, interior corridors. **Parking:** on-site (fee) and valet. **Terms:** open 5/22-10/14 & 11/20-4/7, office hours 7 am-11 pm, 30 day cancellation notice-fee imposed. **Amenities:** high-speed Internet, honor bars. **Dining:** Cosmopolitan - Telluride, see separate listing. **Activities:** *Fee:* massage. **Guest Services:** valet laundry. **Free Special Amenities: expanded continental breakfast and high-speed Internet.**

SAVE / SOME UNITS FEE

HOTEL MADELINE TELLURIDE **Phone:** (970)369-0880

Hotel
$150-$1675

Address: 568 Mountain Village Blvd 81435 **Location:** 2.2 mi e; in Mountain Village. **Facility:** Richly appointed in classic European alpine design, the hotel features the finest hand-picked furnishings and ultra-luxurious finishes. Ski valets will ready your equipment and warm your boots. 106 units, some efficiencies, kitchens and condominiums. 7 stories, interior corridors. **Parking:** on-site (fee) and valet. **Terms:** check-in 4 pm, 30 day cancellation notice-fee imposed. **Amenities:** safes. **Dining:** M's Restaurant at Hotel Madeline Telluride, see separate listing. **Pool(s):** heated indoor. **Activities:** whirlpool, rental bicycles, hiking trails, jogging, exercise room, spa. *Fee:* downhill & cross country skiing, snowmobiling, ice skating. **Guest Services:** valet laundry, area transportation-within Mountain Village.

/ SOME UNITS FEE

THE HOTEL TELLURIDE **Phone:** 970/369-1188

Boutique Hotel
Rates not provided

Address: 199 N Cornet St 81435 **Location:** Just s of roundabout, then just e. **Facility:** This upscale hotel features a spacious, lodge-style lobby with comfortable seating areas and a fireplace. Guest rooms feature luxurious bedding and a private balcony or patio. 59 units. 3 stories, interior corridors. **Parking:** on-site (fee) and street. **Terms:** check-in 4 pm. **Amenities:** safes. **Activities:** whirlpools, steamroom, bicycles, hiking trails, jogging, exercise room. *Fee:* massage. **Guest Services:** valet and coin laundry, area transportation-within town.

CALL BIZ / SOME UNITS FEE

ICE HOUSE LODGE & CONDOMINIUMS **Phone:** (970)728-6300

Hotel
$185-$595

Address: 310 S Fir St 81435 **Location:** Just s of SR 145 (Colorado Ave); end of Fir St. **Facility:** 22 units, some two bedrooms and condominiums. 4 stories, interior corridors. **Parking:** on-site and street. **Terms:** office hours 7 am-11 pm, check-in 4 pm, 30 day cancellation notice-fee imposed. **Pool(s):** heated indoor/outdoor. **Activities:** whirlpool, steamroom, hiking trails, jogging. *Fee:* massage.

/ SOME UNITS FEE

NEW SHERIDAN HOTEL **Phone:** (970)728-4351

Classic Boutique Hotel
$129-$399 11/21-4/6
$129-$349 5/18-10/13

Address: 231 W Colorado Ave 81435 **Location:** SR 145 (Colorado Ave) and Oak St. **Facility:** The hotel offers well-appointed rooms with heated tile floors in the bathrooms. A billiard room, rooftop sundeck with whirlpools and a lounge with a fireplace enhance this restored 1891 hotel. 26 units. 3 stories, interior corridors. **Parking:** street only. **Terms:** open 5/18-10/13 & 11/21-4/6, check-in 4 pm, 30 day cancellation notice-fee imposed. **Amenities:** high-speed Internet, safes. **Dining:** 2 restaurants, also, New Sheridan Chop House, see separate listing. **Activities:** whirlpools. *Fee:* massage. **Guest Services:** valet laundry.

THE PEAKS, A GRAND HERITAGE RESORT & SPA **Phone:** 970/728-6800

Resort Hotel
Rates not provided

Address: 136 Country Club Dr 81435 **Location:** 2.5 mi e; in Mountain Village. **Facility:** Enticing features include a full-service spa, styling salon, tanning facilities, oxygen room, ski-in/ski-out access, a three-lane lap pool and an on-site helipad for heli-skiing. 161 units. 8 stories, interior corridors. **Parking:** valet only. **Terms:** check-in 4 pm. **Amenities:** safes. **Dining:** 3 restaurants. **Pool(s):** heated indoor, heated indoor/outdoor. **Activities:** saunas, whirlpools, steamrooms, waterslide, recreation programs, hiking trails, jogging, playground, sports court, exercise room, spa. *Fee:* golf-18 holes, 6 tennis courts, downhill & cross country skiing, snowmobiling, game room. **Guest Services:** valet laundry, area transportation-within 2 mi.

FEE BIZ / SOME UNITS FEE

RIVER CLUB CONDOMINIUMS **Phone:** 970/728-3388

fyi Not evaluated. **Address:** 550 W Depot Ave 81435. Facilities, services, and decor characterize an upscale property.

VICTORIAN INN **Phone:** 970/728-6601

fyi Not evaluated. **Address:** 401 W Pacific Ave 81435. Facilities, services, and decor characterize an economy property.

WHERE TO EAT

221 SOUTH OAK ST BISTRO
Phone: 970/728-9507

American
$29-$42

AAA Inspector Notes: Eliza H.S. Gavin serves creative, quality food in a tastefully furnished historic home just steps from the gondola. Her intimate bistro features delicious salads and mouthwatering dishes such as pistachio-stuffed risotto cakes with shaved fennel, yellow pepper tapenade and fig jam, and a sausage plate. The to-die-for desserts include espresso and pistachio ice cream cake with white chocolate blueberry crust and brûleed lemon cheesecake with strawberries and mango. **Bar:** full bar. **Address:** 221 S Oak St 81435 **Location:** Just s of Colorado Ave (SR 145). **Parking:** street only. D

ALLRED'S RESTAURANT
Phone: 970/728-7474

Steak
$24-$46

AAA Inspector Notes: To enjoy one of Colorado's most unique dining experiences, patrons ride the free gondola up to 10,551 feet. The restaurant, with exquisite views and impressive décor, is open nightly through summer and winter. Offerings include steamed mussels and crawfish; black-pearl organic salmon with black-olive pine nut tapenade, Chilean sea bass; steak; Colorado lamb chops; and sides such as macaroni and cheese with Kurobuta ham. The award-winning wine list and elegant desserts are sure to please. **Bar:** full bar. **Reservations:** suggested. **Address:** 565 Mountain Village Blvd 81435 **Location:** Gondola Station Saint Sophia. D

BROWN DOG PIZZA
Phone: 970/728-8046

Pizza
$6-$16

AAA Inspector Notes: Although specialty pizzas make the sports bar a popular city institution, the menu also lists pasta, burgers, salads and many other options. Patrons can stop in for a drink or quick meal. **Bar:** full bar. **Address:** 110 E Colorado Ave 81435 **Location:** Just e of historic downtown. **Parking:** street only.

L D AC

COSMOPOLITAN - TELLURIDE
Phone: 970/728-1292

American
$25-$42

AAA Inspector Notes: Next to the gondola, the classy yet casual restaurant affords wonderful views of the nearby mountains. On the menu is a selection of sushi, steak, seafood, lamb and pasta entrées, which are individually prepared and colorfully presented. For a quiet dinner, be sure to make reservations in the dining room. The climate-controlled wine cellar is richly decorated. **Bar:** full bar. **Reservations:** suggested. **Address:** 300 W San Juan Ave 81435 **Location:** At Aspen St and San Juan Ave; in Hotel Columbia. **Parking:** street only. D AC

EMILIO'S GRILL & BAR
Phone: 970/369-1101

Mexican
$8-$15

AAA Inspector Notes: This family-friendly restaurant is attractively decorated and features traditional Mexican appetizers, daily luncheon specials and dinner combinations to please everyone. **Bar:** full bar. **Address:** 226 W Colorado Ave 81435 **Location:** Center; downstairs. **Parking:** street only. L D AC

HONGA'S LOTUS PETAL
Phone: 970/728-5134

Asian
$14-$25

AAA Inspector Notes: This local favorite serves delectable Asian-fusion cuisine in a warm, friendly atmosphere. Enjoy hearty appetizers, innovative entrées and exotic teas. **Bar:** full bar. **Address:** 135 E Colorado Ave 81435 **Location:** East end of town. **Parking:** street only. D AC

LA COCINA DE LUZ
Phone: 970/728-9355

Mexican
$7-$15

AAA Inspector Notes: The restaurant provides fresh, mostly organic Mexican dishes for locals and travelers on the go. You can take your meal to a picnic table outside or to your favorite Telluride destination. **Bar:** beer & wine. **Address:** 123 E Colorado Ave 81435 **Location:** Just e of historic downtown. **Parking:** street only.

B L D AC

LA MARMOTTE
Phone: 970/728-6232

French
$20-$49

AAA Inspector Notes: Guests can savor a cozy, intimate meal in the French country-style cottage. Professionally prepared, modern French dishes may include lamb, seafood, pork, venison or veal choices. For dessert, try the creatively presented crème brûle or chocolate molten cake. The attentive, professional staff enhances the dining experience. **Bar:** full bar. **Address:** 150 W San Juan Ave 81435 **Location:** Just e of San Juan Ave and Fir St. **Parking:** street only. D AC

M'S RESTAURANT AT HOTEL MADELINE TELLURIDE
Phone: 970/369-8989

American
$23-$38

AAA Inspector Notes: The inviting brasserie-style setting offers creative cuisine, including fresh seafood with a focus on local and seasonal products. Game, stews, wild alpine mushroom cappuccino soup, pretzel-crusted Colorado lamb chops and crispy phyllo-wrapped Rocky Mountain buffalo short rib are available. Free-range Colorado beef is dry aged on the premises. **Bar:** full bar. **Reservations:** suggested. **Address:** 568 Mountain Village Blvd 81435 **Location:** 2.2 mi e; in Mountain Village; in Hotel Madeline Telluride. **Parking:** on-site and valet.

B D

NEW SHERIDAN CHOP HOUSE
Phone: 970/728-4351

Steak
$17-$33

AAA Inspector Notes: Diners appreciate the convivial ambience and stylish décor of the chophouse, which presents a menu of excellent-quality beef, wild game, pasta, seafood and nicely presented side dishes. The serving staff is friendly, hospitable and knowledgeable. **Bar:** full bar. **Reservations:** suggested. **Address:** 233 W Colorado Ave 81435 **Location:** SR 145 (Colorado Ave) and Oak St; in New Sheridan Hotel. **Parking:** street only.

B L D AC

RUSTICO RISTORANTE
Phone: 970/728-4046

Italian
$9-$49

AAA Inspector Notes: Italian dishes are served in an elegant setting. Wine lovers will delight in sampling something from the extensive list of Italian wines. In summer, guests can enjoy their meal on the patio, a popular spot to watch passers-by or enjoy the mountain view. **Bar:** full bar. **Address:** 114 E Colorado Ave 81435 **Location:** Just e of historic downtown. **Parking:** street only.

D AC

SIAM
Phone: 970/728-6886

Thai
$14-$29

AAA Inspector Notes: Warm, trendy decor complements the spicy and tasty Thai cuisine, including red or green curry and pad thai, and mouthwatering sweet sticky rice with mango. **Bar:** full bar. **Address:** 200 S Davis St 81435 **Location:** At Davis St and W Pacific Ave, just s of SR 145 (Colorado Ave). **Parking:** street only.

D AC

THORNTON pop. 118,772

• Part of Denver area — see map p. 123

HAMPTON INN BY HILTON **Phone:** (303)451-7900

Hotel
$89-$130 5/1-8/31
$89-$117 9/1-4/30

AAA Benefit: Members save up to 10% everyday!

Address: 243 E 120th Ave 80233 **Location:** I-25 exit 223, e to Grant St on 120th Ave, then just n, follow signs; use caution entering Grant St due to median. **Facility:** 78 units. 4 stories, interior corridors. **Terms:** 1-7 night minimum stay, cancellation fee imposed. **Pool(s):** heated indoor. **Activities:** whirlpool, exercise room. **Guest Services:** valet laundry.

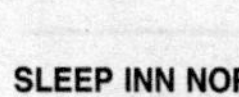
CALL / SOME UNITS

SLEEP INN NORTH DENVER **Phone:** (303)280-9818

Hotel
$70-$75

Address: 12101 Grant St 80241 **Location:** I-25 exit 223, e to Grant St, then n. **Facility:** 100 units. 4 stories, interior corridors. *Bath:* shower only. **Terms:** cancellation fee imposed. **Amenities:** high-speed Internet. **Pool(s):** heated indoor. **Activities:** whirlpool, exercise room. **Guest Services:** coin laundry. **Free Special Amenities: high-speed Internet and manager's reception.**

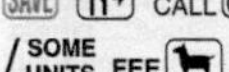
CALL / SOME UNITS FEE

TRINIDAD (F-4) pop. 9,096, elev. 6,019'

Trinidad, below the Santa Fe Trail's landmark Fisher's Peak, began as a supply center for the westward trail. The historic downtown area, designated *Corazon de Trinidad* (Heart of Trinidad), is known for its Victorian architecture, brick streets, shops and restaurants. The town was shaped by the influence of the Spanish, who came from the Southwest, and by the ranching and mining interests to the east and north. An early visitor was scout Kit Carson, whose name and statue mark a park on Kansas Street.

Leading west from the city, SR 12 travels about 35 miles through the Purgatoire Valley to 1,200-acre Monument Lake Park, part of Trinidad's city park system. The route then crosses 9,941-foot Cucharas Pass in a portion of the San Isabel National Forest *(see place listing p. 282)* and passes through La Veta, joining US 160 west of Walsenburg.

Trinidad & Las Animas County Chamber of Commerce: 136 W. Main St., Trinidad, CO 81082. **Phone:** (719) 846-9285 or (866) 480-4750.

ARTHUR ROY MITCHELL MEMORIAL MUSEUM OF WESTERN ART is at 150 E. Main St. in the center of the *Corazon de Trinidad* National Historic District. The museum features the work of Arthur Roy Mitchell, known as the "king" of western pulp magazine illustration, as well as works by illustrators Harvey Dunn and Harold Von Schmidt.

Other displays include a collection of early Hispanic religious folk art, Western memorabilia, historic photographs by Ben Wittick, American Indian artifacts and early photographs of Trinidad. **Time:** Allow 1 hour minimum. **Hours:** Tues.-Sat. 10-4, Sun. noon-4, May 1-early Oct. **Cost:** $3; free (ages 0-11). **Phone:** (719) 846-4224.

TRINIDAD HISTORY MUSEUM, 312 E. Main St., is comprised of several properties that illustrate early settlers' lives. The museum complex includes the Bloom Mansion, Baca House and Santa Fe Trail Museum as well as gardens. **Tours:** Guided tours are available. **Hours:** Museums Mon.-Sat. 10-4, gardens 9-4, May-Sept. **Cost:** (includes Baca House, Bloom Mansion and Santa Fe Trail Museum) $8; $6 (ages 65+); $3 (ages 6-16). **Phone:** (719) 846-7217.

Baca House, 312 E. Main St., is a restored 1870s territorial-style adobe structure that was home to two influential pioneer families. Its Hispanic folk art and Victorian furnishings reflect the lifestyle of Dolores and Felipe Baca, who were among the earliest settlers of Trinidad. The two-story home features a widow's walk and Greek architectural details.

Bloom Mansion, 312 E. Main St., was built in 1882 as a family home for banker and cattle baron Frank G. Bloom. The mansion, built in the French style with locally manufactured bricks, is filled with ornate furnishings, including a horn chair and porcelain figures.

Heritage Gardens, 312 E. Main St., surround the Baca House and Bloom Mansion. They contain century-old trees, native plants, herbs, flowers, vegetables and heirloom roses.

Santa Fe Trail Museum, 120 S. Chestnut St., is a one-story adobe building that originally served as living quarters for the Baca family's domestic workers. It contains exhibits that depict the heydays of the Santa Fe Trail through the 1920s. Historic photographs, commercial goods, family heirlooms and a buckskin coat that belonged to Kit Carson are among the items presented. Tickets can be purchased directly at the museum or at the main ticket office at 312 E. Main St.

BEST WESTERN TRINIDAD INN **Phone:** (719)846-2215

Motel
$59-$119

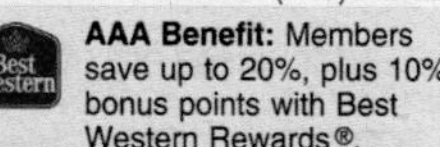

AAA Benefit: Members save up to 20%, plus 10% bonus points with Best Western Rewards®.

Address: 900 W Adams St 81082 **Location:** I-25 exit 13A northbound; exit Cross Bridge southbound, just ne. **Facility:** 55 units, some kitchens. 2 stories (no elevator), exterior corridors. **Parking:** winter plug-ins. **Amenities:** *Some:* high-speed Internet. **Pool(s):** heated outdoor. **Activities:** whirlpool, exercise room. **Guest Services:** coin laundry. **Free Special Amenities: local telephone calls and high-speed Internet.**

/ SOME UNITS FEE

HOLIDAY INN HOTEL & SUITES **Phone:** (719)845-8400

Hotel
$79-$159

Address: 3130 Santa Fe Trail Dr 81082 **Location:** I-25 exit 11, just e, then 1.2 mi n. **Facility:** 86 units. 3 stories, interior corridors. **Amenities:** high-speed Internet. **Pool(s):** heated indoor. **Activities:** whirlpool, exercise room. **Guest Services:** valet and coin laundry.

CALL / SOME UNITS FEE

LA QUINTA INN & SUITES TRINIDAD
Phone: (719)845-0102

Hotel
$116-$179 5/1-9/30
$79-$109 10/1-4/30

Address: 2833 Toupal Dr 81082 **Location:** I-25 exit 11, just w, then n. **Facility:** 100 units. 3 stories, interior corridors. **Amenities:** high-speed Internet. **Pool(s):** heated outdoor, heated indoor. **Activities:** whirlpool, exercise room. *Fee:* game room, massage. **Guest Services:** valet and coin laundry.

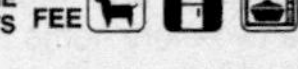

/ SOME UNITS FEE

SUPER 8
Phone: (719)846-8280

Motel
$63-$85

Address: 1924 Freedom Rd 81082 **Location:** I-25 exit 15, just ne. **Facility:** 42 units. 2 stories (no elevator), interior corridors. **Amenities:** safes (fee). **Guest Services:** coin laundry.

/ SOME UNITS FEE

WHERE TO EAT

BLACK JACK'S SALOON, STEAKHOUSE & INN
Phone: 719/846-9501

Steak
$9-$36

AAA Inspector Notes: Diners can take a trip back to the Victorian West with dinner at this laid-back spot, a favorite with locals and tourists alike. Hearty steaks earn pride of place on the menu. **Bar:** full bar. **Address:** 225 W Main St 81082 **Location:** I-25 exit 13B, just e. **Parking:** street only. D

THE CAFE
Phone: 719/846-7119

Breads/Pastries
$4-$11

AAA Inspector Notes: The gourmet sandwiches, salads and baked goods from this humble cafe draw locals and visitors from surrounding towns. Fresh ingredients, flavorful food combinations and decadent desserts please even the toughest critic. The unique decor mixes exposed brick with enchanting glass chandeliers. **Address:** 135 E Main St 81082 **Location:** Historic town center. **Parking:** street only. B L

CHEF LIU'S CHINESE RESTAURANT & LOUNGE
Phone: 719/846-3333

Chinese
$4-$19

AAA Inspector Notes: This restaurant's extensive menu features traditional entrées, vegetarian dishes and family dinners, including garlic pork, a triple delight of shrimp, beef and chicken, and fried apples and banana for desserts. The pleasing décor is comfortable and casual. **Bar:** full bar. **Address:** 1423 Santa Fe Trail Dr 81082 **Location:** I-25 exit 13A, 0.5 mi se. L D

MISSION AT THE BELL RESTAURANT
Phone: 719/845-1513

Mexican
$9-$13

AAA Inspector Notes: The entrance to the Bell building might give first-timers the wrong impression, but a trip down the stairs leads to a pleasant surprise. Tasty Mexican entrées and friendly servers do not disappoint; in fact, this should be a must stop on any travel itinerary. **Bar:** full bar. **Address:** 134 W Main St, Suite 14 81082 **Location:** I-25 exit 13B, just e; in Bell Block Building, downstairs. **Parking:** street only. L D

RINO'S ITALIAN RESTAURANT & STEAKHOUSE
Phone: 719/845-0949

Italian
$10-$28

AAA Inspector Notes: Owner and head chef Frank Cordova clearly loves entertaining and sharing fine food with his patrons. Although born and raised in this city, he spent 25 years in Las Vegas, singing and waiting tables at his brother's Italian restaurant. The Cordovas brought this family tradition back to Colorado, where Frank and his waitstaff still burst into song every evening and Frank makes every effort to befriend his patrons. The menu features classic Italian cuisine as well as steaks. **Bar:** full bar. **Address:** 400 E Main St 81082 **Location:** In historic downtown. **Parking:** street only. D

TWIN LAKES pop. 171

TWIN LAKES ROADHOUSE LODGE
Phone: 719/486-9345

Historic Bed & Breakfast
$82-$165

Address: 6411 Hwy 82 81251 **Location:** Center. **Facility:** This quaint lodge offers intimate and elegant rooms overlooking glacial lakes, an adorable cottage, a cabin and a carriage house with a fireplace and front porch. Local artwork is on display. 6 units, some kitchens. 1 story, interior/exterior corridors. **Terms:** open 5/10-10/20, check-in 4 pm, 14 day cancellation notice-fee imposed. **Activities:** boating, fishing, cross country skiing, rental bicycles, hiking trails, jogging. *Fee:* canoes. **Guest Services:** coin laundry. **Free Special Amenities: expanded continental breakfast and high-speed Internet.**

SAVE / SOME UNITS

VAIL (D-3) pop. 5,305, elev. 8,380'

• **Restaurants p. 299**

Vail is one of Colorado's flourishing resort centers. Internationally known for its extensive winter sports facilities, the Bavarian-style town also offers year-round access to recreation in the surrounding White River National Forest *(see place listing p. 303)*. The resort was founded in 1962 by members of the 10th Mountain Division who trained near Vail at Camp Hale.

Athletes, art and music converge in Vail each June for the annual Teva Mountain Games, which feature trail running, rock climbing, kayaking, adventure racing and mountain biking competitions. Prima! is a summer long celebration of music, theater and dance that includes the Bravo! Vail Valley Music Festival and the Vail International Dance Festival. In mid-September the town gets an early start on Oktoberfest with traditional German food, music and beer.

Vail Valley Partnership, the Chamber and Tourism Bureau: Vail Village, 101 Fawcett Rd., Ste. 240, Avon, CO 81620; P.O. Box 1130, Vail, CO 81658. **Phone:** (970) 476-4790.

BETTY FORD ALPINE GARDENS is off I-70 exit 176 to 530 S. Frontage Rd. in Ford Park. An alpine rock garden showcases a 120-foot cascading waterfall and hundreds of native plants that depict alpine and subalpine habitats. A perennial garden features more than 1,500 varieties of plants, and a meditation garden combines Asian design and philosophy with Rocky Mountain plantings. Prime viewing season is May through September. A children's garden features an adventure hike and a schoolhouse museum. Children's programs also are offered.

Time: Allow 30 minutes minimum. **Hours:** Daily dawn-dusk. Guided tours are offered Mon., Thurs. and Sat. at 10:30, mid-June through Labor Day. Hours and dates may vary; phone ahead. Children's programs Wed. at 10:30, mid-June to mid-Aug. **Cost:** Donations. **Phone:** (970) 476-0103.

COLORADO SKI AND SNOWBOARD MUSEUM AND HALL OF FAME is 2 blks. e. of I-70 exit 176 at 231 S. Frontage Rd. E., in the Vail Village parking structure. The Hall of Fame honors those who have made significant contributions to skiing and snowboarding in Colorado. Museum exhibits commemorate milestones in Colorado's skiing history and the winter Olympics. A replica of the 10th Mountain Division's Camp Hale is also on display. Videotapes about skiing are shown.

Time: Allow 30 minutes minimum. **Hours:** Daily 10-6, June-Mar.; 10-5, rest of year. Closed Thanksgiving and Christmas. **Cost:** Free. **Phone:** (970) 476-1876 or (800) 950-7410.

RECREATIONAL ACTIVITIES

Skiing

- **Vail Ski Resort** is off I-70 exit 176 in White River National Forest. Other activities are offered. **Hours:** Daily 9-3:30, mid-Nov. to mid-Apr. **Phone:** (970) 476-9090 or (800) 525-2257.

THE ARRABELLE AT VAIL SQUARE, A ROCKRESORT **Phone:** 970/754-7777

Resort Hotel
Rates not provided

Address: 675 Lionshead Pl 81657 **Location:** I-70 exit 176, 1 mi w on S Frontage Rd, then just e. **Facility:** The Arrabelle is a grand and elegant ski-in/ski-out hotel. Drapery above the beds hide two reading lights. Other features include a bar area with cocktail and wine glasses as well as a bartender kit. 90 units, some kitchens and condominiums. 4-6 stories, interior corridors. **Parking:** valet only. **Terms:** check-in 4 pm. **Amenities:** safes. **Pool(s):** heated outdoor. **Activities:** sauna, whirlpools, steamrooms, recreation programs, rental bicycles, hiking trails, jogging, spa. *Fee:* downhill & cross country skiing, ice skating, horseback riding. **Guest Services:** valet laundry, area transportation-within 5 mi. **Free Special Amenities: newspaper and high-speed Internet.**

FEE / SOME UNITS FEE

AUSTRIA HAUS HOTEL **Phone:** 970/754-7850

Boutique Hotel
Rates not provided

Address: 242 E Meadow Dr 81657 **Location:** I-70 exit 176, just s to roundabout, just e on S Frontage Rd to Village Center Rd, then just s; in Vail Village. **Facility:** The hotel's large rooms have excellent appointments, including baths with upscale amenities and marble accents. Some rooms have a fireplace. 25 units. 4 stories, interior corridors. **Parking:** on-site (fee) and valet. **Terms:** check-in 4 pm. **Amenities:** safes. **Pool(s):** heated outdoor. **Activities:** whirlpool, exercise room. **Guest Services:** valet laundry. **Free Special Amenities: continental breakfast and high-speed Internet.**

EAGLE POINT RESORT **Phone:** 970/476-6905

Condominium
$120-$448

Address: 1500 Matterhorn Cir 81657 **Location:** I-70 exit 176, just s, 2 mi w on S Frontage Rd, then 0.4 mi se. **Facility:** In a quiet residential area, the property offers spacious, attractively appointed units with modern, fully equipped kitchens. Only one parking space is available per unit. 54 condominiums. 3 stories (no elevator), exterior corridors. **Terms:** office hours 7:30 am-10 pm, check-in 4 pm, 3 night minimum stay - seasonal and/or weekends, 60 day cancellation notice-fee imposed. **Amenities:** video games. **Pool(s):** heated indoor/outdoor. **Activities:** sauna, whirlpools, fishing, recreation programs, horseshoes. *Fee:* massage. **Guest Services:** coin laundry, area transportation-Lionshead gondola (winter only).

EVERGREEN LODGE AT VAIL **Phone:** (970)476-7810

Hotel
$230-$570 11/16-4/30
$120-$219 5/1-11/15

Address: 250 S Frontage Rd W 81657 **Location:** I-70 exit 176, just w on Frontage Rd. **Facility:** 128 units. 7 stories, interior corridors. **Terms:** check-in 4 pm, 30 day cancellation notice-fee imposed. **Amenities:** high-speed Internet. **Pool(s):** heated outdoor. **Activities:** saunas, whirlpool, exercise room. *Fee:* game room. **Guest Services:** valet laundry, area transportation-within 5 mi.

/ SOME UNITS FEE

FOUR SEASONS RESORT VAIL **Phone:** 970/477-8600

Contemporary Resort Hotel
Rates not provided

Address: One Vail Rd 81657 **Location:** I-70 exit 176, just w of roundabout. **Facility:** The rustic yet luxurious alpine hotel and ski resort offers well-appointed rooms, some with a balcony, all with humidifiers. The concierge desk can arrange recreational adventures for the family. 131 units, some two bedrooms, three bedrooms, kitchens and condominiums. 10 stories, interior corridors. **Parking:** valet only. **Terms:** check-in 4 pm. **Amenities:** high-speed Internet, safes. **Dining:** 2 restaurants. **Pool(s):** heated outdoor. **Activities:** sauna, whirlpools, steamrooms, rental bicycles, hiking trails, jogging, game room, spa. *Fee:* fishing, downhill & cross country skiing, ice skating. **Guest Services:** valet laundry, area transportation-within 5 mi.

FEE
FEE / SOME UNITS

HOLIDAY INN APEX VAIL **Phone:** (970)476-2739

Hotel
$129-$249 12/16-4/30
$99-$149 5/1-12/15

Address: 2211 N Frontage Rd 81657 **Location:** I-70 exit 173, just nw, then 0.3 mi ne. **Facility:** 115 units, some kitchens and condominiums. 4 stories, interior corridors. **Terms:** check-in 4 pm, cancellation fee imposed. **Amenities:** high-speed Internet, safes. **Dining:** 2 restaurants, also, Westside Cafe & Market, see separate listing. **Pool(s):** heated outdoor. **Activities:** whirlpool, steamroom, exercise room. *Fee:* massage. **Guest Services:** valet and coin laundry, area transportation-within 2.5 mi.

/ SOME UNITS FEE

LION SQUARE LODGE AT THE GONDOLA **Phone:** 970/476-2281

Condominium
Rates not provided

Address: 660 W Lionshead Pl 81657 **Location:** I-70 exit 176, 0.5 mi w, then just s on Lionshead Cir. Located at base of gondola. **Facility:** Accommodations include four- to six-bedroom units, some with lofts, grills and fireplaces. The pool and hot tubs overlook the mountains. Covered and underground parking are available. 133 condominiums. 4-7 stories, interior/exterior corridors. **Parking:** on-site and valet. **Terms:** seasonal, check-in 4 pm. **Amenities:** high-speed Internet, safes. **Pool(s):** heated outdoor. **Activities:** sauna, whirlpools, fishing, rental bicycles, hiking trails, exercise room. **Guest Services:** valet and coin laundry, area transportation-within 5 mi.

THE LODGE AT VAIL, A ROCKRESORT & SPA **Phone:** 970/476-5011

Hotel

Rates not provided

Address: 174 E Gore Creek Dr 81657 **Location:** I-70 exit 176, 0.3 mi s on Vail Rd to Gore Creek Dr. **Facility:** 165 units, some two bedrooms, three bedrooms, kitchens and condominiums. 5 stories, interior/exterior corridors. **Parking:** valet only. **Terms:** check-in 4 pm. **Amenities:** video games (fee), safes. **Pool(s):** 2 heated outdoor. **Activities:** saunas, whirlpools, steamrooms, hiking trails, jogging, spa. **Guest Services:** valet and coin laundry, area transportation-within 5 mi. Affiliated with A Preferred Hotel.

/ SOME UNITS FEE

MANOR VAIL LODGE **Phone:** (970)476-5000

Hotel

$119-$3499

Address: 595 E Vail Valley Dr 81657 **Location:** I-70 exit 176, just s; take 3rd exit at roundabout to S Frontage Rd E, 0.4 mi e to Vail Valley Dr, then 0.3 mi s. **Facility:** 110 units, some two bedrooms, three bedrooms, kitchens and condominiums. 4 stories, interior/exterior corridors. **Parking:** on-site (fee). **Terms:** check-in 5 pm, 30 day cancellation notice-fee imposed. **Pool(s):** 2 heated outdoor. **Activities:** sauna, whirlpools, steamroom, hiking trails, jogging, exercise room, spa. **Guest Services:** valet and coin laundry, area transportation-within 10 mi.

MARRIOTT'S STREAMSIDE AT VAIL **Phone:** (970)476-6000

Resort Condominium

$512-$879

AAA Benefit:
AAA hotel discounts of 5% or more.

Address: 2284 S Frontage Rd W 81657 **Location:** I-70 exit 173, 2nd exit at roundabout, south side. **Facility:** These condos feature a variety of guest rooms, including a studio and a loft unit. Each room has a gas or wood-burning fireplace, fan and humidifier. 90 condominiums. 3-5 stories, interior corridors. **Terms:** check-in 4 pm, 14 day cancellation notice. **Amenities:** safes. **Pool(s):** heated indoor/outdoor. **Activities:** sauna, whirlpools, steamroom, racquetball court, recreation programs, hiking trails, jogging, playground, game room, horseshoes, exercise room. *Fee:* downhill skiing, snowmobiling. **Guest Services:** complimentary laundry, area transportation-Vail Village & Lionshead.

MONTANEROS CONDOMINIUMS **Phone:** (970)476-2491

Condominium

$159-$2300

Address: 641 W Lionshead Cir 81657 **Location:** I-70 exit 176, just s, just w on S Frontage Rd, then just s. **Facility:** The comfortable, homey condos are located close to the ski lift and within easy walking distance of Vail Village restaurants and shops. There's a fan and humidifier in every unit. 36 condominiums. 4 stories, exterior corridors. **Terms:** open 5/25-4/30, office hours 8 am-9 pm, check-in 4 pm, 1-7 night minimum stay - seasonal, 14 day cancellation notice-fee imposed. **Amenities:** safes. **Pool(s):** heated outdoor. **Activities:** sauna, whirlpool. **Guest Services:** valet and coin laundry.

THE SEBASTIAN VAIL **Phone:** (970)477-8000

Boutique Resort Hotel

$199-$1800

Address: 16 Vail Rd 81657 **Location:** I-70 exit 176, 2nd exit at roundabout (Vail Rd); just s of S Frontage and Vail rds. **Facility:** The luxury hotel features stellar, tastefully appointed one- to three-bedroom suites with fireplaces and Bose speakers. It also has a private ski valet and cafe at the base of the mountain. 107 units, some two bedrooms, three bedrooms, kitchens and condominiums. 6 stories, interior corridors. **Parking:** valet only. **Terms:** check-in 4 pm, 2-3 night minimum stay - seasonal and/or weekends, 31 day cancellation notice-fee imposed. **Amenities:** video games (fee), high-speed Internet, safes. **Dining:** 2 restaurants. **Pool(s):** heated outdoor. **Activities:** saunas, whirlpools, steamrooms, recreation programs in season, rental bicycles, hiking trails, jogging, spa. **Guest Services:** valet laundry. **Free Special Amenities: newspaper and room upgrade (subject to availability with advance reservations).**

SAVE CALL BIZ FEE / SOME UNITS FEE

SONNENALP RESORT OF VAIL **Phone:** (970)476-5656

Boutique Resort Hotel

$160-$3500

Address: 20 Vail Rd 81657 **Location:** I-70 exit 176, 2nd exit at the roundabout, then just s. **Facility:** An international staff strives to pamper and please guests at this resort, which is situated at the entry to Vail Village. Public areas are handsomely appointed with distinct European touches. 128 units, some two bedrooms. 4-5 stories, interior corridors. **Parking:** valet only. **Terms:** check-in 4 pm, 4-7 night minimum stay - seasonal and/or weekends, 30 day cancellation notice-fee imposed. **Amenities:** video games (fee), high-speed Internet, safes, honor bars. **Dining:** 3 restaurants, entertainment. **Pool(s):** heated indoor/outdoor. **Activities:** saunas, whirlpools, steamrooms, recreation programs, rental bicycles, hiking trails, jogging, exercise room, spa. *Fee:* downhill & cross country skiing. **Guest Services:** valet laundry, area transportation-within 3 mi. **Free Special Amenities: early check-in/late check-out and room upgrade (subject to availability with advance reservations).**

SAVE ECO FEE BIZ FEE / SOME UNITS FEE

VAIL CASCADE RESORT & SPA **Phone:** (970)476-7111

Resort Hotel

$99-$659

Address: 1300 Westhaven Dr 81657 **Location:** I-70 exit 176, 1.3 mi w via S Frontage Rd; 1 mi e of exit 173. **Facility:** Some of the well-coordinated guest rooms have a fireplace and balcony. The saline pools are heated. 292 units. 5 stories, interior corridors. **Parking:** on-site (fee) and valet. **Terms:** check-in 4 pm, 3 day cancellation notice, 14 day in season-fee imposed. **Amenities:** video games (fee), high-speed Internet, safes. **Dining:** 2 restaurants. **Pool(s):** 2 heated outdoor. **Activities:** whirlpools, steamrooms, fishing, 6 tennis courts (3 indoor), racquetball court, recreation programs, rental bicycles, hiking trails, jogging, basketball, volleyball, spa. *Fee:* downhill skiing, snowmobiling, game room. **Guest Services:** valet laundry, area transportation-within 3 mi.

SAVE FEE CALL BIZ FEE / SOME UNITS FEE

VAIL MARRIOTT MOUNTAIN RESORT & SPA
Phone: (970)476-4444

Resort Hotel
$459-$599

Marriott HOTELS & RESORTS **AAA Benefit:** AAA hotel discounts of 5% or more.

Address: 715 W Lionshead Cir 81657 **Location:** I-70 exit 176, take first exit at roundabout, 0.8 mi w on Frontage Rd, then just s. **Facility:** Ski lodge-style common areas and handsomely decorated rooms enhance this large-scale resort. 344 units, some condominiums. 7 stories, interior corridors. **Parking:** valet only. **Terms:** check-in 4 pm, 60 day cancellation notice. **Amenities:** safes. *Fee:* video games, high-speed Internet. **Dining:** 2 restaurants. **Pool(s):** heated outdoor, heated indoor. **Activities:** whirlpools, steamrooms, fishing, rental bicycles, hiking trails, jogging, exercise room, spa. *Fee:* downhill & cross country skiing, snowmobiling, game room. **Guest Services:** valet and coin laundry, area transportation-within 5 mi. **Free Special Amenities: local telephone calls and newspaper.**

 FEE   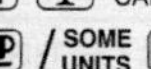 CALL 

FEE / SOME UNITS

SIMBA RUN CONDOMINIUMS **Phone:** 970/476-0344

fyi Not evaluated. **Address:** 1100 N Frontage Rd 81657 **Location:** I-70 exit 176, just n, then 1.2 mi w. Facilities, services, and decor characterize an economy property.

VAIL SPA CONDOMINIUMS **Phone:** 970/476-0882

fyi Not evaluated. **Address:** 710 W Lionshead Cir 81657 **Location:** I-70 exit 176, 0.4 mi w on S Frontage Rd. Facilities, services, and decor characterize a mid-scale property.

WILLOWS CONDOMINIUMS **Phone:** 970/476-2233

fyi Not evaluated. **Address:** 74 Willow Rd 81657 **Location:** I-70 exit 176, just s toward village on Vail Rd, then e. Facilities, services, and decor characterize a mid-scale property.

WHERE TO EAT

KELLY LIKEN **Phone:** 970/479-0175

American
$35-$42

AAA Inspector Notes: Hand your keys over to the valet, and prepare for an experience you won't soon forget. Chef Kelly Liken guides you on a journey through food that takes advantage of seasonally available artisan cheeses, lamb and other products. Experience bold flavors in such innovative dishes as elk carpaccio with bulgur tabbouleh, and consider wine flights to accompany each course. For dessert, you'll be amazed by the pastry chef's sublime creations such as chocolate semifreddo, poached peaches and their signature sticky bun sundae. **Bar:** full bar. **Reservations:** suggested. **Address:** 12 Vail Rd, Suite 100 81657 **Location:** I-70 exit 176, just past south roundabout; in The Gateway Building. **Parking:** valet only. D

LA TOUR RESTAURANT & BAR **Phone:** 970/476-4403

French
$29-$52

AAA Inspector Notes: This elegant fine dining restaurant features contemporary French cuisine and an excellent selection of both American and French wines. The chef/proprietor attained his expertise at famous Chicago restaurants. **Bar:** full bar. **Reservations:** suggested. **Address:** 122 E Meadow Dr 81657 **Location:** I-70 exit 176, just s, just e on S Frontage Rd, then just s; across from Vail Village parking deck. **Parking:** on-site (fee). D AC

THE LEFT BANK **Phone:** 970/476-3696

French
$24-$49

AAA Inspector Notes: The chef/owner of the restaurant, who has served guests since 1970, prepares delicious favorites that include lamb and fresh seafood, as well as homemade pastries and breads. The staff is professional and the wine list is terrific. **Bar:** full bar. **Reservations:** suggested. **Address:** 183 Gore Creek Dr 81657 **Location:** I-70 exit 176, s on Vail Rd to center of village through guard check point; in Sitzmark Lodge. **Parking:** no self-parking. D

THE LITTLE DINER **Phone:** 970/476-4279

Breakfast
$9-$13

AAA Inspector Notes: This hidden little gem serves made-from-scratch breakfast and lunch items. Highlights include build-your-own omelets, eggs Benedict, incredibly tasty corned beef hash, huevos rancheros, savory and sweet crepes, hot and cold sandwiches and juicy burgers. **Address:** 616 W Lionshead Cir 81657 **Location:** I-70 exit 176, just s, take 1st exit at roundabout to S Frontage Rd W, then 0.7 mi w; park at Visitor Parking; west end of Lionshead Plaza. **Parking:** no self-parking. B L AC

SAPPHIRE RESTAURANT AND OYSTER BAR
Phone: 970/476-2828

American
$8-$34

AAA Inspector Notes: Overlooking Gore Creek, the sophisticated and fun-spirited seafood restaurant has attentive servers and a pleasant atmosphere. Influences from both Asian and Mexican cuisine are evident in American preparations, including appetizers such as lobster spring rolls, poblano chiles rellenos and sesame-seared tuna nachos. Among tempting entrees are ground lamb kebab, miso-marinated ahi tuna and roasted Alaskan halibut. Menu changes seasonally. **Bar:** full bar. **Reservations:** suggested. **Address:** 223 Gore Creek Dr 81657 **Location:** Just n of Children's Fountain; in Vail Village. **Parking:** no self-parking. L D CALL

SWEET BASIL **Phone:** 970/476-0125

American
$25-$40

AAA Inspector Notes: This contemporary restaurant serves creative cuisine made from the freshest available ingredients. An upscale casual ambience pervades the dining room, which affords a view of the creek. From the patio, diners can watch the passers-by at Vail Village. The wine list features more than 500 selections from around the world. **Bar:** full bar. **Reservations:** suggested. **Address:** 193 E Gore Creek Dr, Suite 201 81657 **Location:** I-70 exit 176, just e on south frontage road to public parking; in Vail Village. **Parking:** no self-parking. L D AC

UP THE CREEK **Phone:** 970/476-8141

American
$8-$38

AAA Inspector Notes: The popular restaurant enjoys a great location next to the creek and near the pedestrian mall. **Bar:** full bar. **Reservations:** suggested. **Address:** 223 Gore Creek Dr, Suite 103 81657 **Location:** I-70 exit 176, s on Vail Rd to center of village; along Gore Creek. **Parking:** no self-parking. L D AC

WESTSIDE CAFE & MARKET **Phone:** 970/476-7890

American
$8-$23

AAA Inspector Notes: A friendly staff, tasty food plated in sizable portions, and décor featuring photos and relics from Vail's past combine to make this a favorite among locals. The relatively inexpensive meals draw crowds during breakfast and lunch, but diners are usually seated quickly. **Bar:** full bar. **Address:** 2211 N Frontage Rd 81657 **Location:** I-70 exit 273, just e; in Holiday Inn Apex Vail.

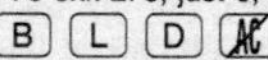

BOL VAIL **Phone:** 970/476-5300

fyi Not evaluated. At Bol, each custom white bowling lane comes with a lounge area and oversize couches. A wide variety of seasonal menu items may include pan-roasted artichokes, grilled steak skewers, spicy honey-glazed ribs, a selection of salads, personal pizzas, all-natural beef burgers and a two-tier platter of fresh seafood. Colorado peach fried pie and hot chocolate with spiced biscotti are a few of the delicious desserts. **Address:** 141 E Meadow Dr 81657 **Location:** I-70 exit 176, just s, take 3rd exit at roundabout, 0.3 mi e to Vail Center Rd, just s, then just w; in Solaris.

MATSUHISA VAIL **Phone:** 970/476-6628

fyi Not evaluated. Created by noted celebrity chef Nobu Matsuhisa, this popular eatery draws locals and tourists alike. Attractively presented, delicious dishes and flavors from around the world are sure to please and surprise. The extensive beverage menu offers various wines and cocktails and even a variety of cocktails with shochu, a Japanese distilled alcohol. **Address:** 141 E Meadow Dr 81657 **Location:** I-70 exit 176, just s, take 3rd exit at roundabout, 0.3 mi e to Vail Center Rd, just s, then just w; in Solaris.

VICTOR (D-4) pop. 397, elev. 9,695'

Victor was founded in 1893 at the base of Battle Mountain, one of the world's richest sources of gold. Some 475 mines in the Cripple Creek-Victor district extracted more than $800 million in gold 1891-1961. In the prime of its mining heyday at the turn of the 20th century, the town's population topped 12,000, and dozens of trains rolled through daily.

More than 300 houses and buildings from Victor's early days still stand, including city hall, where Jack Dempsey once trained, and the *Victor Record* newspaper building, where well-known journalist Lowell Thomas worked as a young man.

Several trails wind past remnants of the 1890s gold mines and millsites. Hikers, bicyclists and those on horseback take advantage of the sights in summer, while those on skis and snowshoes take over when the weather turns frosty.

Victor can be reached from Colorado Springs via US 24 and SR 67 through Cripple Creek, or by turning southeast onto CR 81 just before reaching Cripple Creek and following the roadbed of the old Midland Terminal Railroad.

Scenic access in summer is by the Gold Camp Road (CR 4) from Colorado Springs or the Phantom Canyon Highway (SR 67) from US 50 west of Pueblo. Only experienced drivers should attempt the Gold Camp and Phantom Canyon routes. Neither one is suitable for trailers and some RVs. Call for road conditions before starting. For Gold Camp Road, phone (719) 636-1602; for Phantom Canyon Highway, phone (719) 275-2331 or (800) 876-7922.

Southern Teller County Focus Group: P.O. Box 328, Victor, CO 80860. **Phone:** (719) 689-2675.

Self-guiding tours: Brochures for a self-guiding walking tour of downtown Victor's historic buildings are available at the Victor Lowell Thomas Museum and at the Victor Hotel, 4th Street and Victor Avenue.

VICTOR LOWELL THOMAS MUSEUM, at jct. 3rd St. and Victor Ave., offers glimpses into the gold rush days of the 1890s as well as the life of the noted journalist, who grew up in Victor. Exhibits also feature World War II memorabilia, a local doctor's office and Victor's mining history. Gold panning and gold mine tours are available.

Time: Allow 30 minutes minimum. **Hours:** Museum Wed.-Sun. 9:30-5:30, Memorial Day-Labor Day; Sat.-Sun. 9:30-5:30, day after Labor Day to mid-Oct. Mine tours Wed. and Fri. at 10 and 1, early June-late Aug. Gold panning Wed.-Sun. 9:30-5:30, Memorial Day-Labor Day. **Cost:** $4; $3 (ages 60+); $2 (ages 4-12). Gold panning $4; $3 (ages 60+); $2 (ages 4-12). Combination gold panning and museum $5; $4 (ages 60+); $3 (ages 4-12). Mine tours (includes museum admission) $5. **Phone:** (719) 689-5509.

WALDEN (B-3) pop. 608, elev. 8,099'

RECREATIONAL ACTIVITIES

White-water Rafting

- **Wilderness Aware Rafting** departs from 4.4 mi. n. of jct. SRs 125 and 127, then e. on first road past the North Platte River to parking area. **Hours:** Trips depart daily at 9:30, late May-late June. **Phone:** (719) 395-2112 or (800) 462-7238.

WALSENBURG (E-4) pop. 3,068, elev. 6,182'

Walsenburg is a trade and distribution center for an area devoted to farming, ranching and tourism. It began as the Spanish village of Plaza de los Leones, and now bears the name of Fred Walsen, a German merchant who operated the town's first coal mine and general store during the 1870s. Grateful residents showed their gratitude by renaming the town in his honor.

Nearby Lathrop State Park *(see Recreation Chart)* provides water sports, fishing, camping, hiking, skiing and a visitor center. A popular scenic drive along the Highway of Legends follows US 160 and SR 12 west and south through former coal mining towns and the Cucharas Pass area *(see Trinidad p. 295)*.

Huerfano County Chamber of Commerce: 400 Main St., Walsenburg, CO 81089. **Phone:** (719) 738-1065.

WALSENBURG MINING MUSEUM, 112 W. 5th St. in the 1896 Huerfano County Jail, depicts coal mining history and the lives of workers who populated camps throughout the region. A mine office, jail cells, vintage photographs, maps, gear, tools and memorabilia are presented. **Tours:** Guided tours are available. **Time:** Allow 30 minutes minimum. **Hours:** Mon.-Fri. 10-4, Sat. 10-1, Sun. 1-4, early May-Sept. 30. **Cost:** $2; $1 (ages 13-19). **Phone:** (719) 738-1992.

ANCHOR MOTEL **Phone:** 719/738-2800

Motel

$40-$90 5/1-9/30
$35-$80 10/1-4/30

Address: 1001 Main St 81089 **Location:** I-25 exit 49, 0.5 mi nw. **Facility:** 14 units. 1 story, exterior corridors. **Parking:** winter plug-ins. **Terms:** office hours 9 am-11 pm, cancellation fee imposed. **Free Special Amenities: local telephone calls and high-speed Internet.**

SAVE / SOME UNITS

BEST WESTERN RAMBLER **Phone:** (719)738-1121

Hotel

$94-$112

AAA Benefit: Members save up to 20%, plus 10% bonus points with Best Western Rewards®.

Address: 457 US Hwy 85-87 81089 **Location:** I-25 exit 52, just w. **Facility:** 59 units, some kitchens. 1-2 stories (no elevator), interior/exterior corridors. **Terms:** 3 day cancellation notice. **Amenities:** high-speed Internet. **Pool(s):** heated indoor. **Activities:** whirlpool, exercise room. **Guest Services:** coin laundry. **Free Special Amenities: expanded continental breakfast and high-speed Internet.**

SAVE BIZ / SOME UNITS FEE

WESTMINSTER (B-4) pop. 106,114, elev. 5,300'

- **Restaurants p. 302**
- **Hotels & Restaurants map & index p. 140**
- **Part of Denver area — see map p. 123**

BUTTERFLY PAVILION is e. off US 36 to 6252 W. 104th Ave. Science education combines with hands-on fun to teach visitors about invertebrates and conservation. The invertebrate zoo offers five interactive exhibits including a 7,000-square-foot tropical rainforest filled with 1,200 free-flying butterflies.

Time: Allow 1 hour, 30 minutes minimum. **Hours:** Daily 9-5. Last admission at 4:15. Closed Thanksgiving and Christmas. **Cost:** $8.50; $6.50 (ages 65+); $5.50 (ages 2-12). **Phone:** (303) 469-5441.

COMFORT INN NORTHWEST
Phone: (303)428-3333 50

Hotel

$59-$135

Address: 8500 Turnpike Dr 80031 **Location:** US 36 (Boulder Tpke) exit Sheridan Ave, just s, left on Turnpike Dr at 87th Ave, then 0.4 mi. **Facility:** 66 units. 3 stories, interior corridors. **Terms:** cancellation fee imposed. **Amenities:** safes (fee). **Pool(s):** heated indoor. **Activities:** whirlpool, exercise room. **Guest Services:** valet and coin laundry. **Free Special Amenities: expanded continental breakfast and high-speed Internet.**

SAVE CALL BIZ / SOME UNITS FEE

COMFORT SUITES DENVER NORTH
Phone: (303)429-5500

Hotel

$69-$124

Address: 12085 Delaware St 80234 **Location:** I-25 exit 223, just w. **Facility:** 77 units. 3 stories, interior corridors. **Terms:** cancellation fee imposed. **Amenities:** safes. **Pool(s):** heated indoor. **Activities:** whirlpool, exercise room. **Guest Services:** valet and coin laundry. **Free Special Amenities: full breakfast and room upgrade (subject to availability with advance reservations).**

SAVE BIZ / SOME UNITS FEE

DOUBLETREE BY HILTON HOTEL DENVER - WESTMINSTER **Phone:** (303)427-4000 49

Hotel

$89-$189

AAA Benefit: Members save 5% or more everyday!

Address: 8773 Yates Dr 80031 **Location:** US 36 (Boulder Tpke) exit Sheridan Ave, n to 92nd Ave, e to Yates Dr, then 0.5 mi s. **Facility:** 180 units. 7 stories, interior corridors. **Terms:** 1-7 night minimum stay, cancellation fee imposed. **Amenities:** *Some:* high-speed Internet. **Pool(s):** heated indoor. **Activities:** whirlpool, exercise room. **Guest Services:** valet and coin laundry, area transportation-within 6 mi. **Free Special Amenities: high-speed Internet and local transportation.**

SAVE BIZ / SOME UNITS FEE

FAIRFIELD INN & SUITES-DENVER NORTH
Phone: (303)255-3100

Hotel

$109-$129

AAA Benefit: AAA hotel discounts of 5% or more.

Address: 12080 Melody Dr 80234 **Location:** I-25 exit 223, just w to Melody Dr, then n. **Facility:** 82 units. 3 stories, interior corridors. **Pool(s):** heated indoor. **Activities:** whirlpool, exercise room. **Guest Services:** valet and coin laundry.

CALL BIZ / SOME UNITS

HAMPTON INN BY HILTON **Phone:** (303)427-0700 47

Hotel

$79-$129

AAA Benefit: Members save up to 10% everyday!

Address: 5030 W 88th Pl 80030 **Location:** US 36 (Boulder Tpke) exit Sheridan Ave, 0.3 mi n to 92nd Ave, e to Yates Dr, 0.4 mi s, then just w. **Facility:** 106 units. 3 stories, interior corridors. **Terms:** 1-7 night minimum stay, cancellation fee imposed. **Pool(s):** heated indoor. **Activities:** whirlpool, exercise room. **Guest Services:** valet laundry.

CALL BIZ

(See map & index p. 140.)

RESIDENCE INN BY MARRIOTT
Phone: (303)427-9500 48

Extended Stay Hotel
$153-$187

AAA Benefit:
AAA hotel discounts of 5% or more.

Address: 5010 W 88th Pl 80031 **Location:** US 36 (Boulder Tpke) exit Sheridan Ave, n to 92nd Ave, e to Yates Dr, then s. **Facility:** 94 units, some two bedrooms, efficiencies and kitchens. 4 stories, interior corridors. **Parking:** winter plug-ins. **Terms:** check-in 4 pm. **Pool(s):** heated indoor. **Activities:** whirlpool, sports court, exercise room. **Guest Services:** valet and coin laundry.

CALL / SOME UNITS FEE

SPRINGHILL SUITES BY MARRIOTT DENVER/WESTMINSTER **Phone:** (303)464-1999

Hotel
$90-$190

AAA Benefit:
AAA hotel discounts of 5% or more.

Address: 6845 W 103rd Ave 80021 **Location:** US 36 (Boulder Tpke) exit Church Ranch Blvd W, just s, then just e. **Facility:** 164 units. 6 stories, interior corridors. **Amenities:** video games (fee), high-speed Internet, safes. **Pool(s):** heated indoor. **Activities:** whirlpool, sports court, exercise room. **Guest Services:** valet and coin laundry.

CALL FEE

THE WESTIN WESTMINSTER **Phone:** (303)410-5000

Hotel
$109-$329

WESTIN® HOTELS & RESORTS **AAA Benefit:** Enjoy up to 15% off your next stay, plus Starwood Preferred Guest® bonuses.

Address: 10600 Westminster Blvd 80020 **Location:** US 36 (Boulder Tpke) exit 104th Ave, just n. Opposite a movie plex. **Facility:** Inspired by the state's canyons and wheat fields, the hotel is decorated in natural colors. Guests have activities at their fingertips. Original artwork reflects a modern take on the area's character. 369 units. 13 stories, interior corridors. **Parking:** on-site and valet. **Terms:** 3 day cancellation notice-fee imposed. **Amenities:** safes, honor bars. *Fee:* video games, high-speed Internet. **Pool(s):** heated indoor. **Activities:** saunas, whirlpool, bicycle trails, jogging, exercise room. *Fee:* massage. **Guest Services:** valet laundry, area transportation-within 5 mi. **Free Special Amenities: newspaper and local transportation.** *(See ad p. 165.)*

SAVE CALL FEE / SOME UNITS

WHERE TO EAT

KABOB STATION **Phone:** 303/451-1595

Mediterranean
$6-$13

AAA Inspector Notes: Patrons should be sure to arrive early to be seated promptly during the popular eatery's hectic lunch hour. Among the Syrian favorites are kebabs, shawarma (marinated and grilled meat), curry, gyros and falafel. The baklava is delicious. **Address:** 12041 Pecos St 80234 **Location:** I-25 exit 223, 0.8 mi w, then just n. L D

QUE BUENO! MEXICAN GRILL **Phone:** 303/464-1171

Mexican
$9-$22

AAA Inspector Notes: The walls of this attractive eatery are adorned with Mayan figures etched in glass that are lit from behind with changing neon lights. Expect to find traditional Mexican cuisine artistically presented in a casual but elegant atmosphere. I enjoyed the chile relleno, which was grilled instead of deep fried. The house salad's dressing had a slightly sweet, tart flavor. **Bar:** full bar. **Address:** 10633 Westminster Blvd, Unit 600 80031 **Location:** US 36 (Boulder Tpke) exit 104th Ave, just n; in Westminster Promenade Shopping Complex. **Parking:** on-site and valet. L D

YAK & YETI **Phone:** 303/426-1976 63

Indian
$10-$14

AAA Inspector Notes: This casual eatery specializes in savory, flavorful Indian and Nepalese dishes. Patrons may choose from the lunch or dinner buffet or order a la cart. Entrees feature salmon, shrimp, chicken, lamb and vegetables prepared in a variety of techniques, including tandoori, masala, korma, saag, vindaloo, biryani, makhani and Rogan Josh. The cheerful staff and colorful décor enhance the experience. **Bar:** full bar. **Address:** 8665 N Sheridan Blvd 80031 **Location:** US 36 exit SR 95/Sheridan Blvd, 0.5 mi s; located in a strip mall. L D

WHEAT RIDGE pop. 30,166

- **Hotels & Restaurants map & index p. 140**
- **Part of Denver area — see map p. 123**

COMFORT INN **Phone:** (303)422-6346 53

Hotel
$84-$104

Address: 10200 S I-70 Service Rd 80033 **Location:** I-70 exit 267, just s, then w. Adjacent to city park. **Facility:** 65 units. 3 stories, interior corridors. **Pool(s):** heated indoor. **Activities:** whirlpool, exercise room. **Guest Services:** valet and coin laundry.

CALL / SOME UNITS

HOLIDAY INN EXPRESS HOTEL & SUITES
Phone: (303)424-8300 54

Hotel
$110-$129 5/1-9/15
$105-$129 9/16-4/30

Address: 10101 W 48th Ave 80033 **Location:** I-70 exit 267, just sw. **Facility:** 104 units, some two bedrooms. 3 stories, interior corridors. **Amenities:** *Some:* high-speed Internet. **Pool(s):** heated outdoor. **Activities:** whirlpool, exercise room. **Guest Services:** valet and coin laundry.

/ SOME UNITS

WHERE TO EAT

ABRUSCI'S **Phone:** 303/232-2424 67

Italian
$9-$22

AAA Inspector Notes: At this casual spot, the waiters and waitresses may sit down at the tables to take the orders. The restaurant offers individual and family-style classic Italian cuisine, including pastas and pizza. Great sandwiches and pasta lunch values also are offered, as are extensive gluten-free choices. **Bar:** full bar. **Address:** 3244 Youngfield St, Suite G 80033 **Location:** I-70 exit 264 (32nd Ave), just n. L D

LUKE'S A STEAK PLACE **Phone:** 303/422-3300 66

Steak
$20-$37

AAA Inspector Notes: Just a short hop off I-70 in a strip mall, the eatery has the feel of a friendly neighborhood tavern. The décor is pleasant, with sports-themed items and autographed coach and athlete pictures. **Bar:** full bar. **Address:** 4990 Kipling St 80033 **Location:** I-70 exit 267, just n, then just e to Independence Square. D

WHITE RIVER NATIONAL FOREST (C-2)

Elevations in the forest range from 5,345 ft. near the town of Rifle to 14,265 ft. at Castle Peak. Refer to AAA maps for additional elevation information.

The White River National Forest is composed of 2.3 million acres of northwestern and north-central Colorado mountains on both sides of I-70; it is entered via US 24 and SRs 13, 82, 131 and 133. The forest was once a favorite hunting ground of the Ute Indians and later of settlers. Highlights include Mount of the Holy Cross, southwest of Vail; Glenwood Canyon; the mountains known as Maroon Bells *(see attraction listing p. 42)*; Ruedi, Dillon and Green Mountain reservoirs; and Trappers Lake.

The Flat Tops, Eagles Nest, Hunter-Fryingpan, Collegiate Peaks, Holy Cross, Ptarmigan Peak, Raggeds and Maroon Bells-Snowmass wildernesses provide opportunities for pack trips, backpacking and mountain climbing. Fishing and big-game hunting also are popular. The forest is home to one of the world's largest elk herds. Camping is available at a number of areas throughout the forest. Some of the world's best-known winter sports areas are found at Aspen, Breckenridge, Copper Mountain, Keystone and Vail.

The following district ranger stations can offer assistance: Aspen, (970) 925-3445; Blanco, (970) 878-4039; Dillon, (970) 468-5400; Eagle, (970) 328-6388; Holy Cross, (970) 827-5715; Rifle, (970) 625-2371; or Sopris, (970) 963-2266. *See Recreation Chart.*

WINDSOR pop. 18,644

PORTER HOUSE BED & BREAKFAST INN
Phone: (970)686-5793

Historic Bed & Breakfast
$95-$165

Address: 530 Main St 80550 **Location:** I-25 exit 262, 4.5 mi e; center. Located in a commercial area. **Facility:** A hot, gourmet breakfast, lush flower gardens and antique furnishings distinguish this restored 1898 Victorian inn. 4 units. 2 stories (no elevator), interior/exterior corridors. **Parking:** street only. **Terms:** office hours 7 am-9 pm, check-in 4 pm, 14 day cancellation notice-fee imposed. **Guest Services:** valet laundry.

SUPER 8 MOTEL
Phone: (970)686-5996

Hotel
$63-$72

Address: 1265 Main St 80550 **Location:** I-25 exit 262, 3.8 mi e; in shopping and restaurant complex. **Facility:** 40 units. 2 stories (no elevator), interior corridors. **Terms:** cancellation fee imposed. **Amenities:** safes (fee). **Activities:** exercise room. **Guest Services:** coin laundry.

CALL / SOME UNITS FEE

WHERE TO EAT

CHIMNEY PARK RESTAURANT & BAR
Phone: 970/686-1477

American
$19-$31

AAA Inspector Notes: The pesto dumplings were recommended by the waiter as one of the chef's signature dishes, but I found the flavor a bit overpowering. I enjoyed the sweet, tangy and savory watermelon and beet salad. The cool watermelon crunch complemented the silky beets. The buttery sauce added a lot of flavor to the halibut. The décor features floral themed art, hardwood floors and fresh flowers. My server was attentive but seemed reluctant to give recommendations. A chef's menu with wine pairings is available. **Bar:** full bar. **Address:** 406 Main St 80550 **Location:** Downtown. **Parking:** street only. D

OKOLE MALUNA
Phone: 970/686-8844

Hawaiian
$9-$18

AAA Inspector Notes: This cheerful little restaurant brings a touch of the tropics to northern Colorado. The menu features traditional Hawaiian dishes including smoked pork, lomi-lomi salmon and Pulehu sirloin steak. Given that Asia heavily influences Hawaiian cuisine, the menu also lists Korean barbecue beef ribs, Japanese udon noodles and seaweed-crusted ahi tuna. On the dessert menu are pineapple, cheesecake, mango sorbet and haupia, which is made from coconuts. **Bar:** full bar. **Address:** 431 Main St 80550 **Location:** I-25 exit 262, 5 mi e on SR 392. **Parking:** street only. L D

WINTER PARK (B-3) pop. 999, elev. 9,040'

• Hotels p. 304 • Restaurants p. 304

Winter Park and the surrounding Fraser Valley offer an extensive network of groomed trails for cross-country skiing, snowshoeing, dog sledding, snow tubing and snowmobiling. One of Colorado's major ski resorts, Winter Park Resort offers three interconnected mountains that cater to a wide variety of skiing abilities.

Summer presents equally diverse activities. More than 600 miles of marked hiking, biking and horseback riding trails offer challenges ranging from novice loops to back-country excursions. The ski resort features some 50 miles of trails that crisscross the mountains.

Visitors can golf at four championship courses, zoom down one of Colorado's longest alpine slides or fish in streams where President Dwight D. Eisenhower once cast a line. White-water rafting on the Colorado River and hiking in the surrounding Arapaho and Roosevelt National Forests *(see place listing p. 40)* present their own fun and adventure.

A major railroad link between the east and west coasts in the early 1900s, Moffat Road was built over 11,600-foot Corona Pass in Winter Park. The Moffat Tunnel, a 6.2-mile-long railroad tunnel, replaced this route in 1927 and still is a major rail route through the Continental Divide.

Winter Park-Fraser Valley Chamber of Commerce: 78841 US 40, P.O. Box 3236, Winter Park, CO 80482. **Phone:** (970) 726-4118, (303) 422-0666 or (800) 903-7275.

RECREATIONAL ACTIVITIES

Skiing

- **Winter Park Resort** is on US 40 in the Arapaho National Forest. Other activities are offered.

Hours: Mon.-Fri. 9-4, Sat.-Sun. and holidays 8:30-4, mid-Nov. to mid-Apr. **Phone:** (970) 726-5514 for information, or (800) 453-2525 for reservations.

Snowmobiling

- **Grand Adventures Snowmobiling** is behind the Beaver Village Lodge at 79303 US 40. Other activities are available. **Hours:** Daily 8-6, late Nov. to mid-Apr. **Phone:** (970) 726-9247 or (800) 726-9247.

AMERICAS BEST VALUE SUNDOWNER MOTEL

Phone: (970)726-9451

Motel

$70-$190 12/1-4/30
$50-$150 5/1-11/30

Address: 78869 US Hwy 40 80482 **Location:** On US 40; downtown. Across from Cooper Creek Square. **Facility:** 34 units, some two bedrooms and kitchens. 2 stories (no elevator), exterior corridors. **Terms:** office hours 7 am-11 pm, check-in 4 pm, 3 night minimum stay - seasonal, 20 day cancellation notice. **Pool(s):** heated indoor. **Activities:** whirlpool. **Guest Services:** coin laundry, area transportation-train station. **Free Special Amenities: continental breakfast and local telephone calls.**

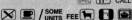

BEST WESTERN ALPENGLO LODGE

Phone: (970)726-8088

Hotel

$79-$167

AAA Benefit: Members save up to 20%, plus 10% bonus points with Best Western Rewards®.

Address: 78665 US Hwy 40 80482 **Location:** 0.3 mi n of center. **Facility:** 58 units. 3 stories, interior corridors. **Terms:** check-in 4 pm, 2-3 night minimum stay - seasonal. **Activities:** whirlpool. **Free Special Amenities: local telephone calls and high-speed Internet.**

(See ad this page.)

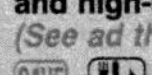

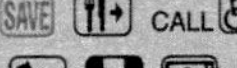

/ SOME UNITS FEE

OLYMPIA MOTOR LODGE

Phone: (970)726-8843

Motel

$74-$179

Address: 78572 US Hwy 40 80482 **Location:** 0.4 mi n of center. **Facility:** 40 units, some kitchens and condominiums. 1-2 stories (no elevator), interior/exterior corridors. **Terms:** open 5/13-4/21, office hours 7 am-10:30 pm, 1-5 night minimum stay - seasonal and/or weekends, 30 day cancellation notice-fee imposed. **Pool(s):** heated indoor. **Activities:** whirlpool. **Guest Services:** area transportation-train station. **Free Special Amenities: continental breakfast and high-speed Internet.**

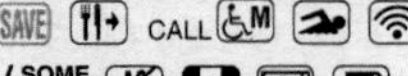

CALL / SOME UNITS

ZEPHYR MOUNTAIN LODGE

Phone: 970/726-8400

Resort Condominium

Rates not provided

Address: 201 Zephyr Way 80482 **Location:** 3 mi s of center on US 40 to Winter Park Dr, then 0.5 mi w to gate check. Located in Winter Park Resort - The Village. **Facility:** Each nicely appointed condo at this rustic and contemporary lodge has an outdoor deck, cozy gas fireplace, fan and humidifier. Slopeslide units and underground parking are available. 150 condominiums. 7-8 stories, interior corridors. **Parking:** on-site (fee). **Terms:** check-in 4 pm. **Amenities:** high-speed Internet. **Activities:** whirlpools, ice skating, rental bicycles, hiking trails, jogging, playground, exercise room. *Fee:* miniature golf, downhill skiing, game room. **Guest Services:** coin laundry.

CALL

WHERE TO EAT

ALBERTO'S

Phone: 970/726-4747

Southwestern

$18-$33

AAA Inspector Notes: Enjoy a variety of appetizers, soups, salads, entrées and gourmet pizza, most with a Southwestern flair. Popular menu items include lobster mac 'n' cheese, salmon tournedo, dry-aged steaks and ahi tuna tempura. The views from this third-level corner eatery are spectacular. **Bar:** full bar. **Reservations:** suggested. **Address:** 78930 US 40 80482 **Location:** Corner of Cooper Creek Square; Third Level. **Parking:** street only.

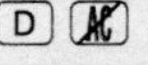

▼ See AAA listing this page ▼

CARVERS **Phone:** 970/726-8202

American
$7-$10

AAA Inspector Notes: The local favorite serves artisan hearth breads, bagels, a wide variety of breakfasts, soups, stews, sandwiches and burgers, as well as vegetarian options. Guests can request seating in the cozy dining room, which is paneled in knotty pine, or out on the patio. **Bar:** beer & wine. **Address:** 93 Cooper Creek Way 80482 **Location:** Just off US 40; downtown; behind Cooper Creek Square. B L AC

DENO'S MOUNTAIN BISTRO **Phone:** 970/726-5332

Seafood
$8-$26

AAA Inspector Notes: This former pharmacy and barber shop offers sports, music and good food. With nine TVs, an HD projection screen and satellite coverage, you can watch your favorite sports event while enjoying wine, specialty cocktails or microbrews. The pub menu features hearty soups, sandwiches, pizza, quesadillas and burgers. The dining room menu offers seared sesame-crusted ahi tuna, Alaskan king crab legs, rosemary- and sea salt-crusted rib-eye, and St. Louis fall-off-the-bone barbecue pork ribs. **Bar:** full bar. **Address:** 78911 US Hwy 40 80482 **Location:** South end of town. **Parking:** on-site and street. L D

SMOKIN MOE'S RIBHOUSE & SALOON
Phone: 970/726-4600

American
$8-$20

AAA Inspector Notes: Diners can enjoy their favorite games or sporting events while feasting on grilled meats smoked over hickory wood from Osage County, Oklahoma. The menu also includes sandwiches, salads and typical barbecue side dishes. **Bar:** full bar. **Address:** 65 Cooper Creek Way 80482 **Location:** Just off US 40; downtown; at Cooper Creek Square; lower level of courtyard. L D

STAR OF INDIA **Phone:** 970/726-5991

Indian
$10-$19

AAA Inspector Notes: The extensive menu offers popular Indian dishes such as tandoori chicken, as well as lesser known dishes such as lamb Mughlai. The puffy naan bread alone is worth a visit. Patrons may choose from the daily lunch and dinner buffets or order a la carte from the menu. **Bar:** full bar. **Address:** 47 Cooper Creek Square 80482 **Location:** Just off US 40; downtown; at Cooper Creek Square. D AC

WOODLAND PARK (D-4) pop. 7,200, elev. 8,437'

Incorporated in 1891, Woodland Park's primary industry first took place in its sawmills, where railroad ties and other wood products were made. Nearby Manitou Lake and Rampart Reservoir provide trout and ice fishing. Other leisure activities include biking, camping, hiking and horseback riding.

The Greater Woodland Park Chamber of Commerce: 210 E. Midland Ave., P.O. Box 9022, Woodland Park, CO 80866. **Phone:** (719) 687-9885 or (800) 551-7886.

ROCKY MOUNTAIN DINOSAUR RESOURCE CENTER is at 201 S. Fairview St. More than 30 skeletons and life restorations of dinosaurs and other reptiles are on display, including one of the largest Cretaceous sea monster collections in North America. Interactive exhibits, fossils, a viewable fossil laboratory, a children's educational area and theater presentations also are offered.

Tours: Guided tours are available. **Time:** Allow 30 minutes minimum. **Hours:** Mon.-Sat. 9-6, Sun. 10-5. Closed Jan. 1, Easter, Thanksgiving and Christmas. **Cost:** $11.50; $10.50 (ages 66+); $7.50 (ages 5-12). **Phone:** (719) 686-1820.

BRISTLECONE LODGE **Phone:** 719/687-9518

Cottage
$89-$140

Address: 510 N Hwy 67 80863 **Location:** 0.5 mi n. **Facility:** These four duplex units nestled between the pines offer overhead fans and front porches. 8 cottages. 1 story, exterior corridors. **Terms:** office hours 8 am-8 pm, 14 day cancellation notice-fee imposed. **Activities:** whirlpool, horseshoes. **Guest Services:** coin laundry.

/ SOME UNITS FEE

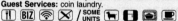

WHERE TO EAT

SWISS CHALET RESTAURANT **Phone:** 719/687-2001

Continental
$10-$35

AAA Inspector Notes: This family restaurant offers creative menu choices of Continental cuisine and flambé specialties. A fireplace and candlelight evoke a cozy and charming ambience. Patio dining is available, weather permitting. This well-established restaurant is a favorite with locals and tourists alike. **Bar:** full bar. **Reservations:** suggested, weekends. **Address:** 19263 E US Hwy 24 80863 **Location:** 1.8 mi e of jct SR 67. L D

YAMPA pop. 429

OAK TREE INN **Phone:** (970)638-1000

Motel
$76-$125

Address: 98 Moffat Ave 80483 **Location:** 0.3 mi w of SR 131. **Facility:** 37 units. 3 stories, interior corridors. **Terms:** cancellation fee imposed. **Activities:** exercise room. **Guest Services:** coin laundry.

BIZ / SOME UNITS

Grand Staircase-Escalante National Monument

Utah

Utah's spectacular scenery—which ranges from lush Rocky Mountain valleys to desolate, red rock canyons—routinely elicits gasps and exclamations from visitors.

The southern half of the state features terrain carved by wind and water into surreal shapes arrayed in dramatic vistas. Large portions of this many-colored land are preserved within a dozen national parks and monuments.

An area with stunning vistas but little else may seem an unlikely place to establish a homeland, but it suited 19th-century Mormon pioneers who came to the valley of the Great Salt Lake seeking religious freedom. Their hard work transformed a near desert into productive farm country, earning Utah the apt nickname, "The Beehive State."

Today vacationers flock to Utah to admire stately Mormon landmarks and enjoy the urban amenities of fast-growing Salt Lake City, or to explore the canyons, buttes and natural arches of the south or the snow-capped peaks of the east.

"The Beehive State," Salt Lake City Mural

Tales Told in Stone

Due to a seismically active past and a scarcity of terrain-obscuring vegetation, Utah's landscape provides scientists with a remarkable record of the Earth's geologic history. Throughout the state, exposed rock strata billions of years old tell stories of dramatic upheaval. At Dinosaur National Monument on the Colorado-Utah border, the sandstone has yielded thousands of dinosaur bones now displayed in museums around the country.

With fanciful monikers like the Watchman, the Castle, Court of the Patriarchs, Queen Victoria and Fairyland, the countless unusual rock formations obviously inspire human imagination as well. In Capitol Reef National Park, rainbow-hued cliffs form a 100-mile-long barrier reminiscent of an ocean reef, while at Cedar Breaks National Monument, natural columns thrusting upward from the floor of a bowl-shaped valley recall Rome's Coliseum.

And in addition to Bryce Canyon's hoodoos—strangely shaped rock formations that inspired Paiute Indian legends—Utah is graced by colorful arches, pinnacles, precipices and gorges. Watch sandstone chimneys change color with the daylight in Kodachrome Basin State Park or marvel at the myriad shades of red as the sun sets on the buttes of Monument Valley Navajo Tribal Park.

"This is the Right Place"

Upon first seeing the Great Salt Lake Valley in 1847, Brigham Young, leader of the Mormon church's westward exodus, proclaimed, "This is the right place." As befitting a man regarded by his followers as a prophet, he was correct.

Salt Lake City is the result of Mormon pioneers' dream to establish a community where adherents could practice their religion free from persecution. Today the city's magnificent six-spired, cathedral-like temple is a symbol and center of Mormonism, a belief system formally referred to as The Church of Jesus Christ of Latter-day Saints.

Though immigration has altered state demographics in recent decades, still more than 70 percent of Utah's citizens are Mormon. Church buildings around Temple Square top Salt Lake City's list of tourist attractions. As an added reminder of the city's spiritual orientation, the central tower of the temple is capped by a nearly 13-foot-tall golden statue of an angel. According to Mormon doctrine, an angel named Moroni appeared to church founder Joseph Smith Jr. and led him to a cache of gold plates etched with text from which the Book of Mormon was translated.

From his lofty setting, Moroni looks out over a state that manages to encompass scenes both ordinary and considerably outside the ordinary—a land of ethereal beauty seemingly poised between this world and the next.

Recreation

The Mormon State boasts five national parks, more than a half-dozen national monuments, and too many state and local parks to mention.

Spectacular views can be had along hiking and backpacking trails. Standouts include Delicate Arch Trail in Arches National Park, Watchman Viewpoint Trail in Zion National Park, the trail to Hickman Bridge in Capitol Reef National Park, and Queens Garden and Fairyland Loop trails in Bryce Canyon National Park.

East of Salt Lake City, Brighton Lakes Trail ascends 2.5 miles to three lovely lakes and then continues up the summit of Catherine Pass. Near Provo, a 6-mile hike to the top of 11,788-foot Mt. Timpanogos offers dramatic vistas. The High Uintas Wilderness features several trails that wind below the peaks of Utah's tallest mountains.

You can easily arrange an equestrian journey through Utah's unforgettable terrain; plus, the state serves up some of the most challenging bike trails in the country.

At the end of the scenic drive through Salt Lake City's Mill Creek Canyon, Wasatch Crest Trail, a 10-mile section of the Great Western Trail that runs from Canada to Mexico, attracts bikers with its gorgeous alpine views. Nearby Antelope Island, the largest of the ten Great Salt Lake islands, features nearly 20 miles of trails. The 4-mile ride to Powell Point, 23 miles northeast of Bryce Canyon National Park, culminates with a precipitous drop and an awesome view of Grand Staircase-Escalante National Monument. Near Nephi, there's the 66-mile Mt. Nebo Loop, while Moab's Slickrock Bike Trail draws hard-core bikers from all over.

Those who know snow perennially place Utah powder at the top of their lists. Four miles north of Park City stands Utah Olympic Park, the world-class training facility that played host to the bobsled, luge and ski jumping competitions for the 2002 Olympic Winter Games. Minutes away from Park City nightlife, The Canyons ski resort features 155 runs. The Alta Ski Area also has a reputation for being a die-hard skiers' retreat. And nearby Snowbird Ski and Summer Resort offers expert slopes wisely avoided by the fainthearted.

Expert Slopes at Snowbird Ski and Summer Resort

Historic Timeline

1776 Franciscan priests Escalante and Dominguez explore Utah in their search for a route from New Mexico to California.

1824 Trapper James Bridger reaches the Great Salt Lake.

1847 Mormons led by Brigham Young reach the Salt Lake Valley.

1848 The United States gains the region from Mexico through the Treaty of Guadalupe Hidalgo.

1850 The Territory of Utah is created, with Brigham Young serving as governor.

1869 The Union Pacific and Central Pacific rails meet at Promontory to form the nation's first transcontinental railroad.

1896 Utah becomes the 45th state.

1952 Uranium deposits are discovered near Moab.

1964 Two dams—Flaming Gorge and Glen Canyon—are completed.

1998 The state of Utah and the federal government conclude one of the largest U.S. land exchanges since the acquisition of Alaska.

2002 Salt Lake City hosts the Winter Olympics.

What To Pack

Temperature Averages Maximum/Minimum	JANUARY	FEBRUARY	MARCH	APRIL	MAY	JUNE	JULY	AUGUST	SEPTEMBER	OCTOBER	NOVEMBER	DECEMBER
Cedar City	43/20	46/24	52/29	60/35	70/44	81/54	86/60	83/58	76/50	64/38	53/29	42/20
Delta	39/14	46/20	56/27	65/33	74/41	86/49	94/56	92/55	82/45	68/34	52/23	40/14
Mexican Hat	42/17	51/23	62/30	70/36	79/45	90/51	95/60	92/59	84/49	71/36	55/25	44/17
Moab	41/16	50/23	62/31	72/39	81/47	91/54	96/61	93/59	84/50	71/38	57/27	43/19
Salt Lake City	37/20	42/24	51/30	62/37	72/45	82/52	92/61	90/59	80/50	66/39	49/28	40/23
Vernal	29/5	36/11	49/23	62/32	72/39	83/46	88/52	85/51	76/41	62/30	48/22	31/7

From the records of The Weather Channel Interactive, Inc.

Good Facts To Know

ABOUT THE STATE

POPULATION: 2,763,885.

AREA: 84,990 square miles; ranks 11th.

CAPITAL: Salt Lake City.

HIGHEST POINT: 13,528 ft., Kings Peak.

LOWEST POINT: 2,200 ft., Beaver Wash Dam.

TIME ZONE(S): Mountain. DST.

REGULATIONS

TEEN DRIVING LAWS: No passengers under 21 except family members are permitted for the first 6 months. Driving is not permitted daily midnight-5 a.m. The minimum age for an unrestricted driver's license is 17. Phone (801) 965-4437 for more information about Utah driver's license regulations.

SEAT BELT/CHILD RESTRAINT LAWS: Seat belts are required for driver and all passengers ages 16 and older. Children ages 8 until 16 and more than 57 inches tall must use a child restraint or seat belt; child restraints are required for under age 8 and less than 57 inches tall.

CELL PHONE RESTRICTIONS: All drivers are prohibited from text messaging while driving. In addition Utah has a law against careless driving; a person can be charged if they commit a moving violation other than speeding while using a handheld cell phone or engaging in other distracting activities.

HELMETS FOR MOTORCYCLISTS: Required for all riders under age 18.

RADAR DETECTORS: Permitted.

MOVE OVER LAW: Driver is required to slow down and vacate the lane nearest stopped police, fire and rescue vehicles using audible or flashing signals. The law also includes tow trucks.

FIREARMS LAWS: Vary by state and/or county. Contact Firearms Laws Bureau of Criminal Investigation, 3888 West 5400 South, Taylorsville, UT 84118; phone (801) 965-4445.

HOLIDAYS

HOLIDAYS: Jan. 1 ■ Martin Luther King Jr. Day, Jan. (3rd Mon.) ■ Washington's Birthday, Feb. (3rd Mon.) ■ Memorial Day, May (last Mon.) ■ July 4 ■ Pioneer Day, July 24 ■ Labor Day, Sept. (1st Mon.) ■ Columbus Day, Oct. (2nd Mon.) ■ Veterans Day, Nov. 11 ■ Thanksgiving, Nov. (4th Thurs.) ■ Christmas, Dec. 25.

MONEY

TAXES: Utah's statewide general sales tax is 4.7 percent. Local options allow additional increments up to 1.5 percent. Qualified localities may add an additional resort sales tax of 1 percent. Counties are authorized to levy a lodgings tax of up to 4.25 percent.

VISITOR INFORMATION

INFORMATION CENTERS: State welcome centers are off I-15 southbound 1.5 mi. n. of Brigham City ■ on I-80 westbound at Echo, 6 mi. e. of Coalville ■ in Jensen at jct. US 40 and SR 149 ■ off I-15 northbound 4 mi. s. of exit 6 near St. George ■ and on I-70 westbound 26 mi. e. of Green River at Thompson Springs.

FURTHER INFORMATION FOR VISITORS:

Utah Office of Tourism
300 N. State St.
Salt Lake City, UT 84114
(801) 538-1030
(800) 200-1160

NATIONAL FOREST INFORMATION:

Intermountain Region, USDA Forest Service
324 25th St.
Ogden, UT 84401
(801) 625-5306
(877) 444-6777 (reservations)
(877) 833-6777 (TTY)

FISHING AND HUNTING REGULATIONS:

Utah Division of Wildlife Resources
P.O. Box 146301
Salt Lake City, UT 84114-6301
(801) 538-4700

RECREATION INFORMATION:

Utah Division of Parks and Recreation
1594 W. North Temple
Salt Lake City, UT 84116-3156
(801) 538-7220
(877) 887-2757

Utah Annual Events

Please call ahead to confirm event details.

JANUARY	FEBRUARY	MARCH
■ Hof Winterfest German Festival / Ogden 801-399-8711 ■ Sundance Film Festival Park City 801-907-4050 ■ Bluff International Balloon Festival / Bluff 435-672-2360	■ Utah Boat Show and Watersports Expo / Sandy 801-485-7399 ■ Art in Kayenta Festival Ivins 435-231-2246 ■ FIS Freestyle World Cup International / Park City 435-645-6504	■ St. Patrick's Day Celebration and Spring Festival / Springdale 888-518-7070 ■ Red, White and Snow Park City 435-658-3992 ■ St. Patrick's Day Parade Salt Lake City 801-573-5580
APRIL	**MAY**	**JUNE**
■ St. George Art Festival St. George 435-634-5850 ■ April Action Car Show Moab 435-259-5858 ■ Baby Animal Days Wellsville 435-245-6050	■ Scandinavian Heritage Festival / Ephraim 435-283-4621 ■ The Great Salt Lake Bird Festival / Farmington 801-451-3286 ■ Moab Arts Festival / Moab 435-259-2742	■ Groovefest American Music Festival / Cedar City 435-867-9800 ■ Mormon Miracle Pageant Manti 888-255-8860 ■ Canyonlands PRCA Rodeo Moab 435-259-8825
JULY	**AUGUST**	**SEPTEMBER**
■ American Fork Steel Days American Fork 801-763-3000 ■ Utah Mid-Summer Renaissance Faire Cedar City 435-896-6757 ■ America's Freedom Festival at Provo / Provo 801-818-1776	■ Bear Lake Raspberry Festival / Garden City 435-946-2901 ■ Park City Kimball Arts Festival / Park City 435-649-8882 ■ Western Legends Roundup Kanab 800-733-5263	■ Utah State Fair / Salt Lake City 801-538-8440 ■ Peach Days Celebration Brigham City 435-723-3931 ■ Oktoberfest Bavarian Bash Brian Head 888-677-2810
OCTOBER	**NOVEMBER**	**DECEMBER**
■ Pumpkin Chuckin' Festival Moab 435-259-2326 ■ Cedar City Livestock and Heritage Festival Cedar City 800-354-4849 ■ Utah Humanities Book Festival / Salt Lake City 801-359-9670	■ Navajo Rug and Jewelry Show / Park City 435-649-0535 ■ Moab Folk Music Festival Moab 435-260-2488 ■ Cowboy Poetry and Buckaroo Fair / Heber City 435-654-1339	■ ZooLights / Salt Lake City 801-584-1750 ■ Dickens' Christmas Festival St. George 435-688-2990 ■ A Midway Christmas Midway 435-654-3666

Slickrock Cafe, Moab

Downtown Mural, Salt Lake City

Cathedral of the Madeleine, Salt Lake City

Bonneville Salt Flats, Great Salt Lake

Salt Lake Tabernacle on Temple Square Pipe Organ, Salt Lake City

Great Experience for Members

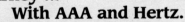

AAA editor's picks of exceptional note

Rainbow Bridge National Monument

Utah Shakespeare Festival

Bryce Canyon National Park

Ogden Union Station Museums

Arches National Park (E-6)
Arches National Park *(See p. 321.)*

Bingham Canyon (C-3)
Kennecott's Bingham Canyon Mine *(See p. 324.)*

Bryce Canyon National Park (F-3)
Bryce Canyon National Park *(See p. 332.)*

Canyonlands National Park (E-5)
Canyonlands National Park *(See p. 334.)*

Capitol Reef National Park (E-4)
Capitol Reef National Park *(See p. 335.)*

Cedar Breaks National Monument (F-2)
Cedar Breaks National Monument *(See p. 336.)*

Cedar City (F-2)
Utah Shakespeare Festival *(See p. 337.)*

Dinosaur National Monument (B-5)
Dinosaur National Monument *(See p. 342.)*

Farmington (B-3)
Lagoon *(See p. 345.)*

Glen Canyon National Recreation Area (F-4)
Glen Canyon National Recreation Area *(See p. 347.)*

Lehi (C-3)
Children's Discovery Garden *(See p. 359.)*

Museum of Ancient Life *(See p. 359.)*

Thanksgiving Point *(See p. 359.)*

Moab (E-6)
Dead Horse Point State Park *(See p. 367.)*

Monument Valley Navajo Tribal Park (G-5)
Monument Valley Navajo Tribal Park *(See p. 379.)*

Natural Bridges National Monument (F-5)
Natural Bridges National Monument *(See p. 380.)*

Ogden (B-3)
Ogden Union Station Museums *(See p. 382.)*

Rainbow Bridge National Monument (G-4)
Rainbow Bridge National Monument *(See p. 401.)*

St. George (G-1)
Rosenbruch Wildlife Museum *(See p. 403.)*

Salt Lake City (B-3)
Salt Lake Tabernacle on Temple Square *(See p. 419.)*

Salt Lake Temple *(See p. 420.)*

State Capitol *(See p. 419.)*

Temple Square *(See p. 419.)*

Tracy Aviary *(See p. 419.)*

Visitor Centers *(See p. 420.)*

Zion National Park (F-2)
Zion National Park *(See p. 461.)*

Utah

Atlas Section

ROADS/HIGHWAYS

- INTERSTATE
- CONTROLLED ACCESS
- CONTROLLED ACCESS TOLL
- TOLL ROAD
- PRIMARY DIVIDED
- PRIMARY UNDIVIDED
- SECONDARY DIVIDED
- SECONDARY UNDIVIDED
- LOCAL DIVIDED
- LOCAL UNDIVIDED
- UNPAVED ROAD
- UNDER CONSTRUCTION
- TUNNEL
- PEDESTRIAN ONLY
- AUTO FERRY
- PASSENGER FERRY
- SCENIC BYWAY
- 10 DISTANCE BETWEEN MARKERS
- EXIT NUMBER-FREE/TOLL
- INTERCHANGE FULL/PARTIAL
- WELCOME CENTER
- REST AREA/ SERVICE CENTER

BOUNDARIES

- INTERNATIONAL
- STATE
- COUNTY
- TIME ZONE
- >>>>>>>> CONTINENTAL DIVIDE

ROAD SHIELDS

- 95 95 INTERSTATE/BUSINESS
- 22 22 22 U.S./STATE/COUNTY
- 22 22 FOREST/INDIAN
- TRANS- CANADA
- 1 PROVINCIAL AUTOROUTE
- 1 MEXICO
- 66 HISTORIC ROUTE 66
- VT 41 REFERENCE PAGE INDICATOR

AREAS OF INTEREST

- INDIAN
- MILITARY
- PARK
- FOREST
- GRASSLANDS
- HISTORIC
- INT'L/REGIONAL AIRPORT
- INCORPORATED CITY

POINTS OF INTEREST

- TOWN
- NATIONAL CAPITAL
- STATE/PROVINCIAL CAPITAL
- AAA/CAA CLUB LOCATION
- FEATURE OF INTEREST
- COLLEGE/UNIVERSITY
- CAMPGROUND
- CUSTOMS STATION
- HISTORIC
- LIGHTHOUSE
- MONUMENT/MEMORIAL
- STATE/PROVINCIAL PARK
- NATIONAL WILDLIFE REFUGE
- SKI AREA
- SPORTS COMPLEX

CITIES/TOWNS are color-coded by size, showing where to find AAA Approved and Diamond rated lodgings or restaurants listed in the AAA TourBook guides and on AAA.com:

- RED - major destinations and capitals; many listings
- Black - destinations; some listings
- Grey - no listings

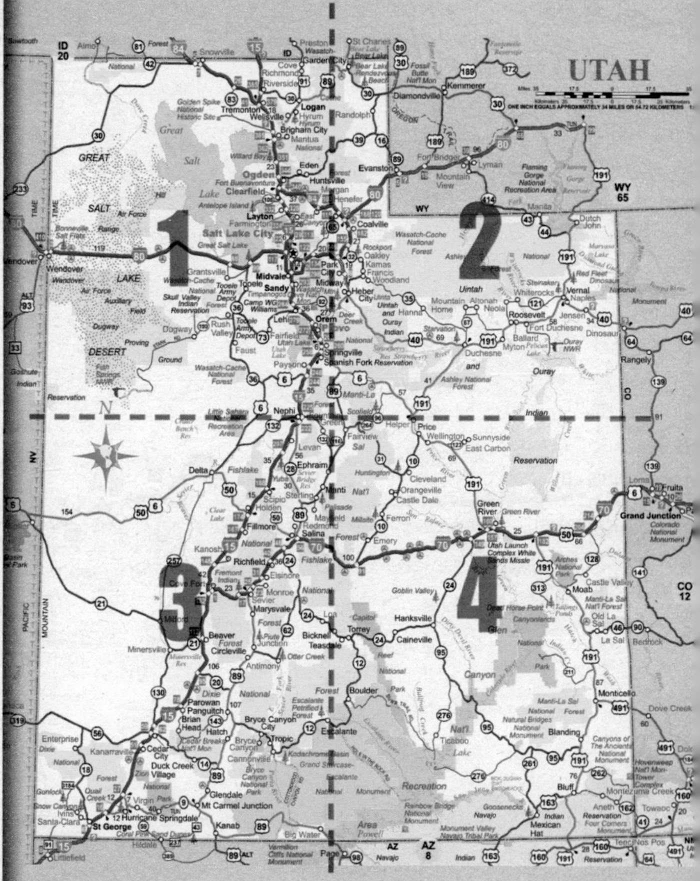

UTAH

ONE INCH EQUALS APPROXIMATELY 34 MILES OR 54.72 KILOMETERS

Use driving maps from the AAA Road Atlas to plan your itinerary and route. Purchase the complete 2012 AAA Road Atlas at participating AAA/CAA offices, retail stores and online booksellers.

AAA ROAD Atlas
Travel With Someone You Trust
2012
CANADA
UNITED STATES
MEXICO

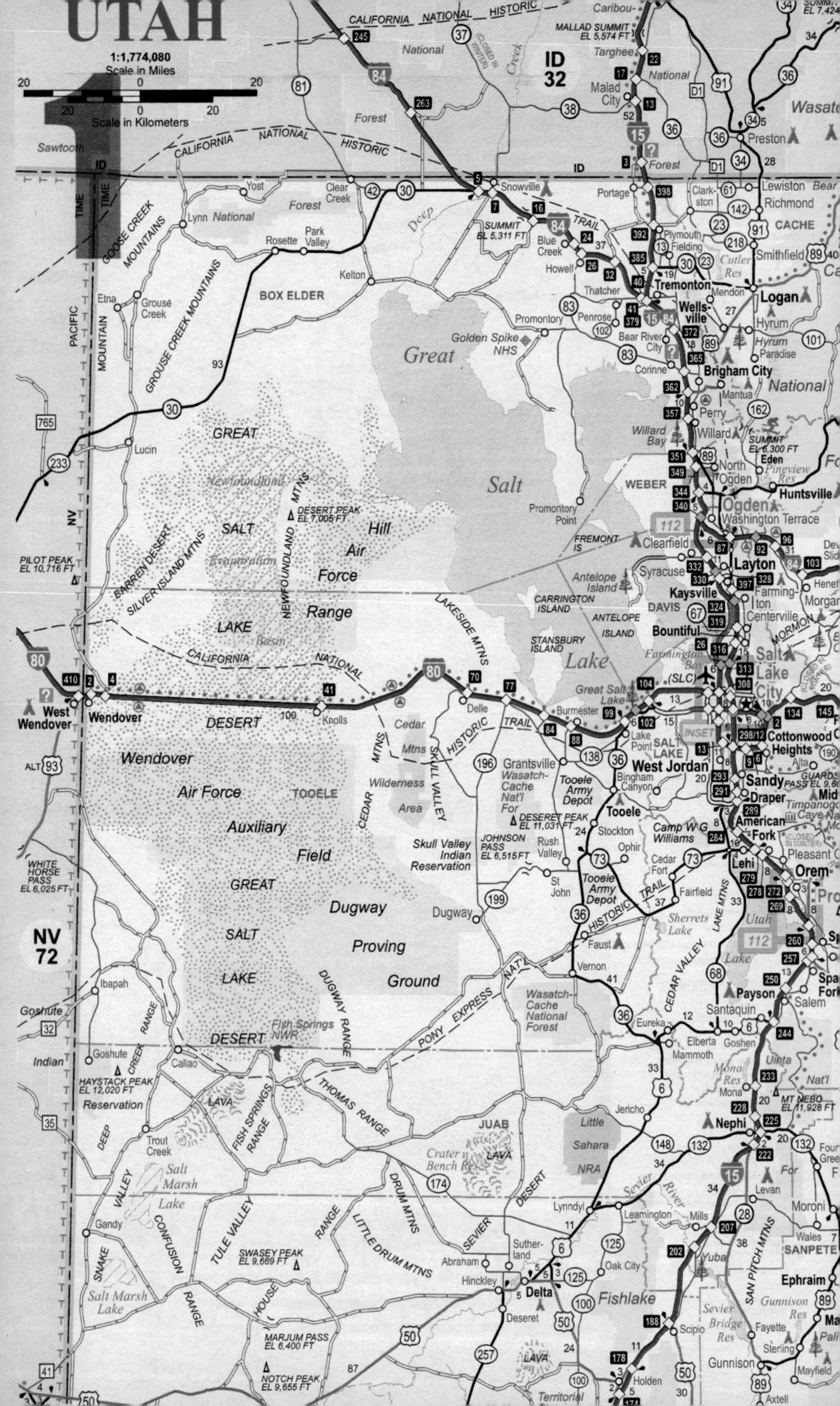
UTAH
1:1,774,080
Scale in Miles
Scale in Kilometers
ID 32
NV 72
Great Salt Lake
Great Salt Lake Desert
Hill Air Force Range
Wendover Air Force Auxiliary Field
Dugway Proving Ground
Skull Valley Indian Reservation
Goshute Indian Reservation
Wasatch-Cache National Forest
Sawtooth National Forest
BOX ELDER
TOOELE
JUAB
WEBER
DAVIS
CACHE
SANPETE
Salt Lake City
Ogden
Logan
Brigham City
Tremonton
Layton
Kaysville
Bountiful
West Jordan
Sandy
Draper
American Fork
Lehi
Orem
Tooele
Grantsville
Payson
Nephi
Delta
Wendover
West Wendover
Snowville
Huntsville
Ephraim
Gunnison
Fishlake
Little Sahara NRA
Golden Spike NHS
Fish Springs NWR
CALIFORNIA NATIONAL HISTORIC TRAIL
PONY EXPRESS NAT'L HISTORIC TRAIL
PILOT PEAK EL 10,716 FT
DESERT PEAK EL 7,005 FT
DESERET PEAK EL 11,031 FT
HAYSTACK PEAK EL 12,020 FT
SWASEY PEAK EL 9,669 FT
NOTCH PEAK EL 9,655 FT
MARJUM PASS EL 6,400 FT
JOHNSON PASS EL 6,515 FT
WHITE HORSE PASS EL 6,025 FT
SUMMIT EL 5,311 FT
SUMMIT EL 6,300 FT
MALLAD SUMMIT EL 5,574 FT
MT NEBO EL 11,928 FT
GOOSE CREEK MOUNTAINS
GROUSE CREEK MOUNTAINS
SILVER ISLAND MTNS
NEWFOUNDLAND MTNS
LAKESIDE MTNS
CEDAR MTNS
DUGWAY RANGE
THOMAS RANGE
FISH SPRINGS RANGE
HOUSE RANGE
CONFUSION RANGE
DRUM MTNS
LITTLE DRUM MTNS
SAN PITCH MTNS
LAKE MTNS
ANTELOPE ISLAND
STANSBURY ISLAND
CARRINGTON ISLAND
FREMONT IS
PACIFIC TIME
MOUNTAIN TIME

2
Montpelier
GENEVA SUMMIT EL 7,461 FT
Ovid
Paris
OREGON NATIONAL
Cokeville
St Charles
Bear Lake
Garden City
RICH
BEAR LAKE SUMMIT EL 7,810 FT
Laketown
Round Valley
Cache
HISTORIC
OREGON TRAIL
Randolph
Big Creek
Woodruff
WY 125
Woodruff Narrows Res
MONTE CRISTO SUMMIT EL 9,000 FT
Neponset Reservoir
Forest
Evanston
TRAIL
SUMMIT EL 6,850 FT
MORGAN
PIONEER NATL HIST
Devils Slide
Croydon
Coalville
Upton
SUMMIT
Hoytsville
Wanship
East Canyon
Rockport
Wasatch-
Cache
National
Forest
High
Uintas
SOUTH BURRO PEAK EL 12,726 FT
MT LOVENIA EL 13,227 FT
KINGS PEAK EL 13,528 FT
MARSH PEAK EL 12,240 FT
HAYDEN PASS EL 10,347 FT
Oakley
Kamas
Francis
Park City
Wilderness
UINTA MOUNTAINS
Lake Fork River
Rock Creek
Moon Lake
National
Uintah
Whiterocks
Forest
Jordanelle
Heber City
Provo River
WOLF CREEK SUMMIT EL 9,480 FT
Ashley
and
Ouray
Mountain Home
DUCHESNE
Hanna
Tabiona
Deer Creek
Walls-burg
Uintah
Indian
WASATCH
and
DANIELS PASS EL 7,980 FT
Ouray
Currant Creek
Duchesne
Altamont
Neola
Roosevelt
Fort Duchesne
Ballard
Upalco
Starvation Res
Starvation
Fruitland
Strawberry Res
Strawberry River
Duchesne
Bridge-land
Myton
Randlett
Pelican L
Leota
Ouray NWR
Ouray
Indian
Res
Flaming Gorge Res
Manila
DAGGETT
Flaming Gorge
NRA
Green Lake
Dutch John
Green River
Henrys Fork
WY
SUMMIT EL 8,428 FT
Red Fleet
Vernal
Maeser
Naples
Tridell
White-rocks
Lapoint
Jensen
Nat'l
Dinosaur
Yampa
Mo
CO
Bonanza
UINTAH
White River
CO 20
PROVO PEAK EL 11,068 FT
Provo
Uinta
Springville
Mapleton
Spanish Fork
UTAH
Nat'l
Forest
Indian
Res
Uintah
and
Ouray
Ashley
National
Forest
Thistle
SOLDIER SUMMIT EL 7,477 FT
Soldier Summit
WEST TAVAPUTS
SUMMIT EL 9,100 FT
Colton
Manti-
La
Indianola
Scofield
Scofield Res
Milburn
Clear Creek
Helper
Kenilworth
Price River
Nine Mile Creek
PLATEAU
CARBON
PATMOS MOUNTAINS
DESOLATION CANYON
Uintah and Ouray Indian Reservation
EAST TAVAPUTS PLATEAU
Fairview
Mt Pleasant
Spring City
Sal
Price
Sunnyside
East Carbon
Wellington
Range Creek
Hiawatha
Huntington
Elmo
Cleveland
SOUTH TENT MTN EL 11,285 FT
SUMMIT EL 10,200 FT
Huntington
Lawrence
Joe's Valley Res
National
Orangeville
Manti
Castle Dale
Clawson
Ferron Creek
Ferron
TRAIL
LAVA
GRAY CANYON
Green River
GRAND
BOOK CLIFFS
RIVER VALLEY
BAXTER PASS EL 8,422 FT
TRAIL

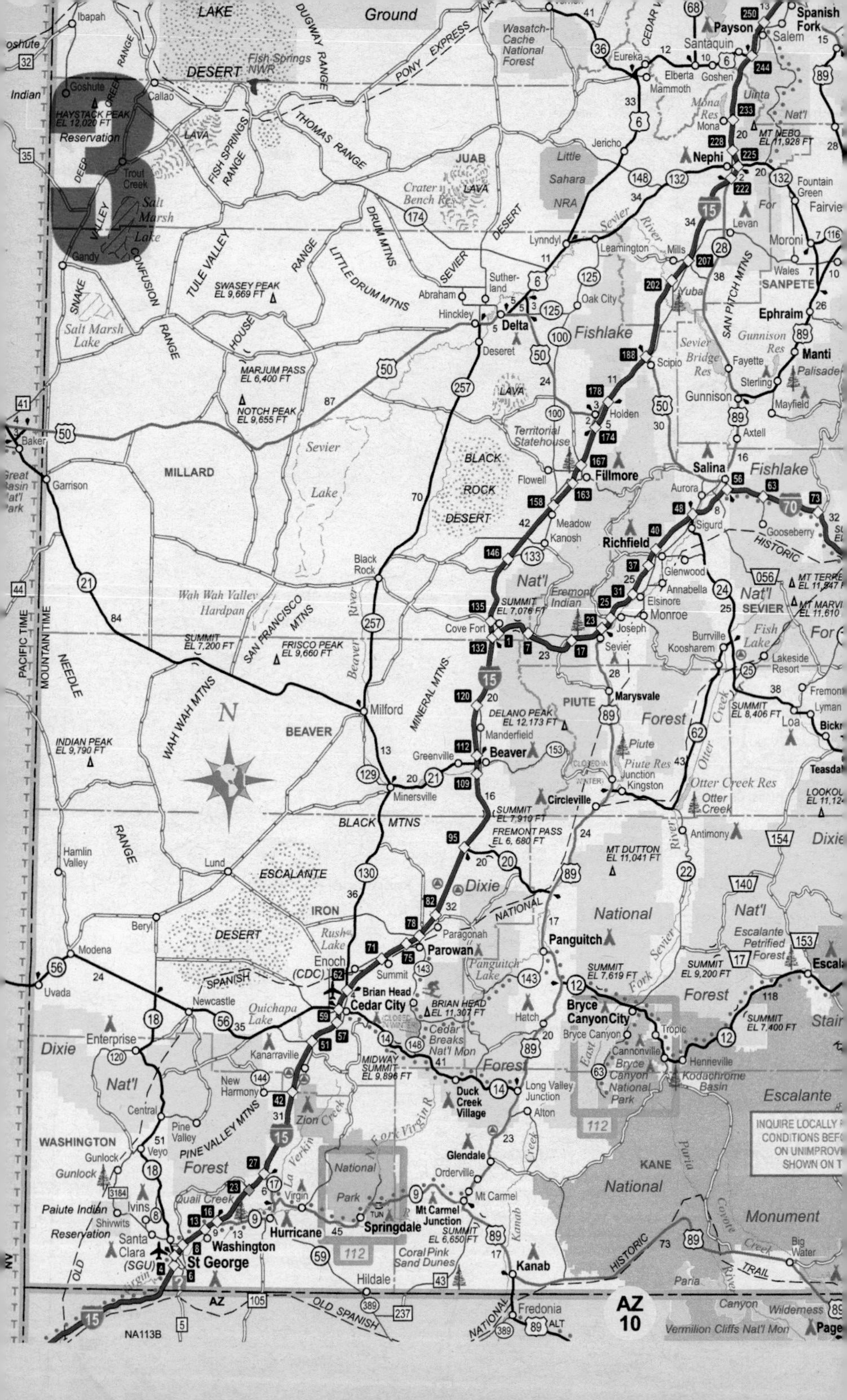
3
Ibapah
LAKE
Ground
DUGWAY RANGE
PONY EXPRESS
Wasatch-Cache National Forest
Payson
Spanish Fork
Salem
Santaquin
Eureka
Elberta
Goshen
Mammoth
CEDAR V
Goshute
Fish Springs NWR
DESERT
Indian
HAYSTACK PEAK EL 12,020 FT
Reservation
Callao
THOMAS RANGE
LAVA
FISH SPRINGS RANGE
DEEP CREEK RANGE
Trout Creek
Salt Marsh Lake
VALLEY
Gandy
Jericho
Little Sahara NRA
Nephi
Mona Res
Mona
Uinta Nat'l
MT NEBO EL 11,928 FT
JUAB
LAVA
Crater Bench Res
DRUM MTNS
LITTLE DRUM MTNS
SEVIER DESERT
Lynndyl
Leamington
Mills
Sevier River
Levan
Fountain Green
Fairview
Moroni
Wales
SANPETE
TULE VALLEY
CONFUSION RANGE
SNAKE
SWASEY PEAK EL 9,669 FT
HOUSE RANGE
Abraham
Sutherland
Hinckley
Delta
Oak City
Yuba
SAN PITCH MTNS
Ephraim
Salt Marsh Lake
Deseret
Fishlake
Scipio
Sevier Bridge Res
Gunnison Res
Fayette
Manti
Sterling
Palisade
Gunnison
Mayfield
Axtell
MARJUM PASS EL 6,400 FT
NOTCH PEAK EL 9,655 FT
LAVA
Holden
Territorial Statehouse
Baker
Great Basin Nat'l Park
Garrison
MILLARD
Sevier Lake
BLACK ROCK DESERT
Flowell
Fillmore
Salina
Fishlake
Aurora
Sigurd
Meadow
Kanosh
Richfield
Gooseberry
HISTORIC
Glenwood
Annabella
Elsinore
Monroe
Nat'l
Fremont Indian
Black Rock
Wah Wah Valley Hardpan
SAN FRANCISCO MTNS
FRISCO PEAK EL 9,660 FT
SUMMIT EL 7,200 FT
SUMMIT EL 7,076 FT
Cove Fort
Joseph
Sevier
Koosharem
Burrville
Fish Lake
Lakeside Resort
MT TERRE EL 11,547 FT
MT MARVI EL 11,610
SEVIER
PACIFIC TIME
MOUNTAIN TIME
NEEDLE
WAH WAH MTNS
Beaver River
Milford
MINERAL MTNS
DELANO PEAK EL 12,173 FT
PIUTE
Marysvale
Manderfield
Forest
Piute
Piute Res
Junction
Kingston
Otter Creek Res
Otter Creek
SUMMIT EL 8,406 FT
Loa
Lyman
Fremont
Teasdale
LOOKOUT EL 11,124
INDIAN PEAK EL 9,790 FT
BEAVER
Greenville
Beaver
Minersville
Circleville
SUMMIT EL 7,910 FT
FREMONT PASS EL 6,680 FT
BLACK MTNS
Antimony
MT DUTTON EL 11,041 FT
Dixie
RANGE
Hamlin Valley
Lund
ESCALANTE DESERT
Dixie
NATIONAL
National
IRON
Paragonah
Parowan
Panguitch
Nat'l
Escalante Petrified Forest
Beryl
Modena
Uvada
Rush Lake
Enoch (CDC)
Summit
SPANISH
Brian Head
Cedar City
BRIAN HEAD EL 11,307 FT
Panguitch Lake
SUMMIT EL 7,619 FT
SUMMIT EL 9,200 FT
Forest
Escalante
Newcastle
Quichapa Lake
Enterprise
Dixie
Nat'l
Kanarraville
Cedar Breaks Nat'l Mon
Hatch
Bryce Canyon City
Bryce Canyon
Tropic
SUMMIT EL 7,400 FT
Stair
MIDWAY SUMMIT EL 9,896 FT
New Harmony
Duck Creek Village
Forest
Long Valley Junction
Cannonville
Bryce Canyon National Park
Henrieville
Kodachrome Basin
Escalante
Central
PINE VALLEY MTNS
Zion
Pine Valley
Alton
INQUIRE LOCALLY CONDITIONS BEFO ON UNIMPROVE SHOWN ON T
WASHINGTON
Veyo
Gunlock
Forest
National Park
N Fork Virgin R
Glendale
KANE
National
Orderville
Paria
Monument
La Verkin
Virgin
Quail Creek
Springdale
Mt Carmel
Mt Carmel Junction
Paiute Indian Reservation
Ivins
Shivwits
Santa Clara (SGU)
Washington
Hurricane
St George
SUMMIT EL 6,650 FT
Coral Pink Sand Dunes
Kanab
HISTORIC
Big Water
TRAIL
Hildale
Paria
Canyon
OLD SPANISH
AZ
Fredonia
NATIONAL
AZ 10
Wilderness
Vermilion Cliffs Nat'l Mon
Page
NA113B
OLD
NV

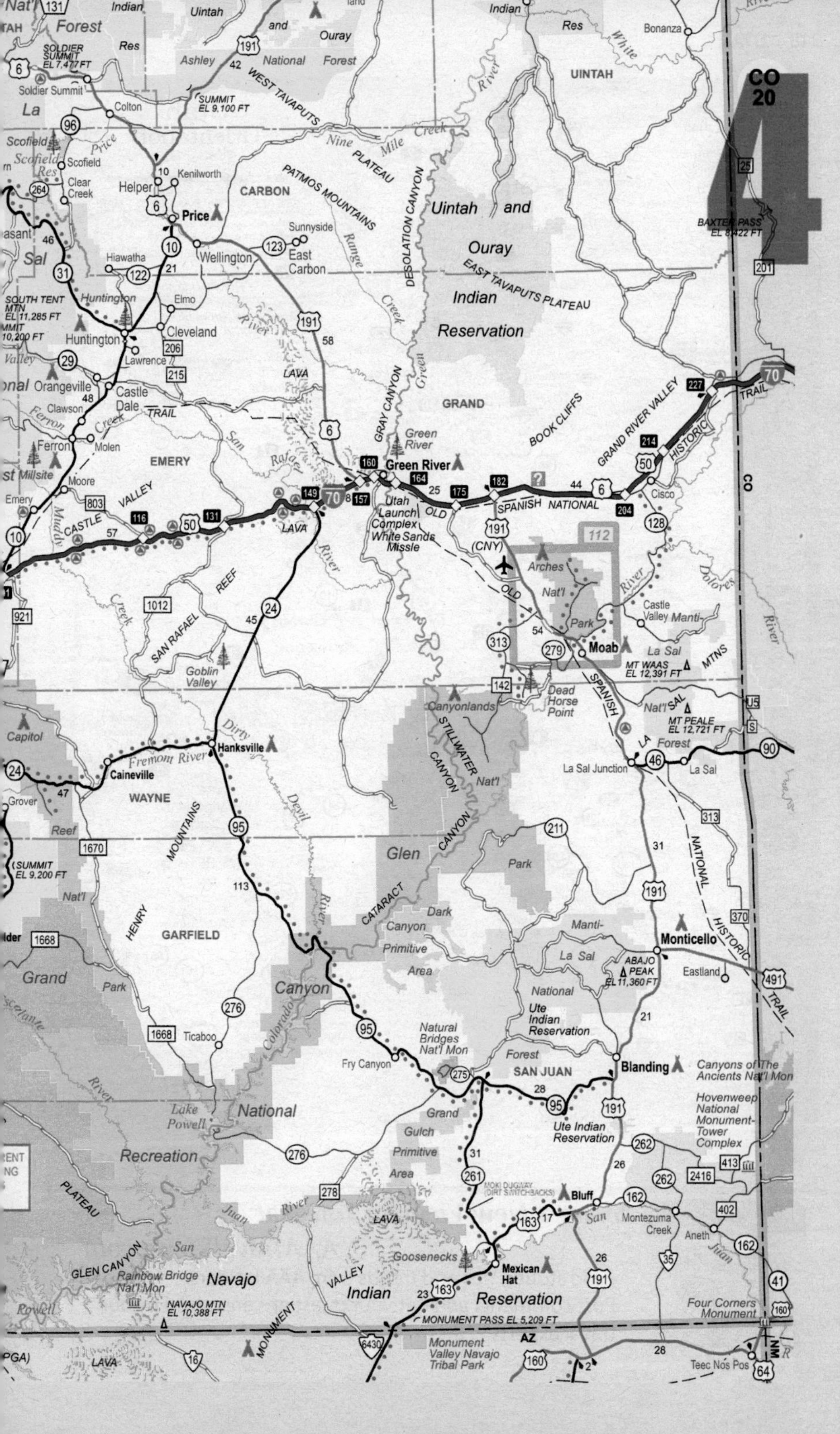

4
CO 20
Green River
Moab
Price
Hanksville
Monticello
Blanding
Bluff
Mexican Hat
Uintah and Ouray Indian Reservation
Arches Nat'l Park
Canyonlands Nat'l Park
Glen Canyon National Recreation Area
Navajo Indian Reservation
Natural Bridges Nat'l Mon
Monument Valley Navajo Tribal Park
Four Corners Monument
Canyons of The Ancients Nat'l Mon
Hovenweep National Monument-Tower Complex
Rainbow Bridge Nat'l Mon

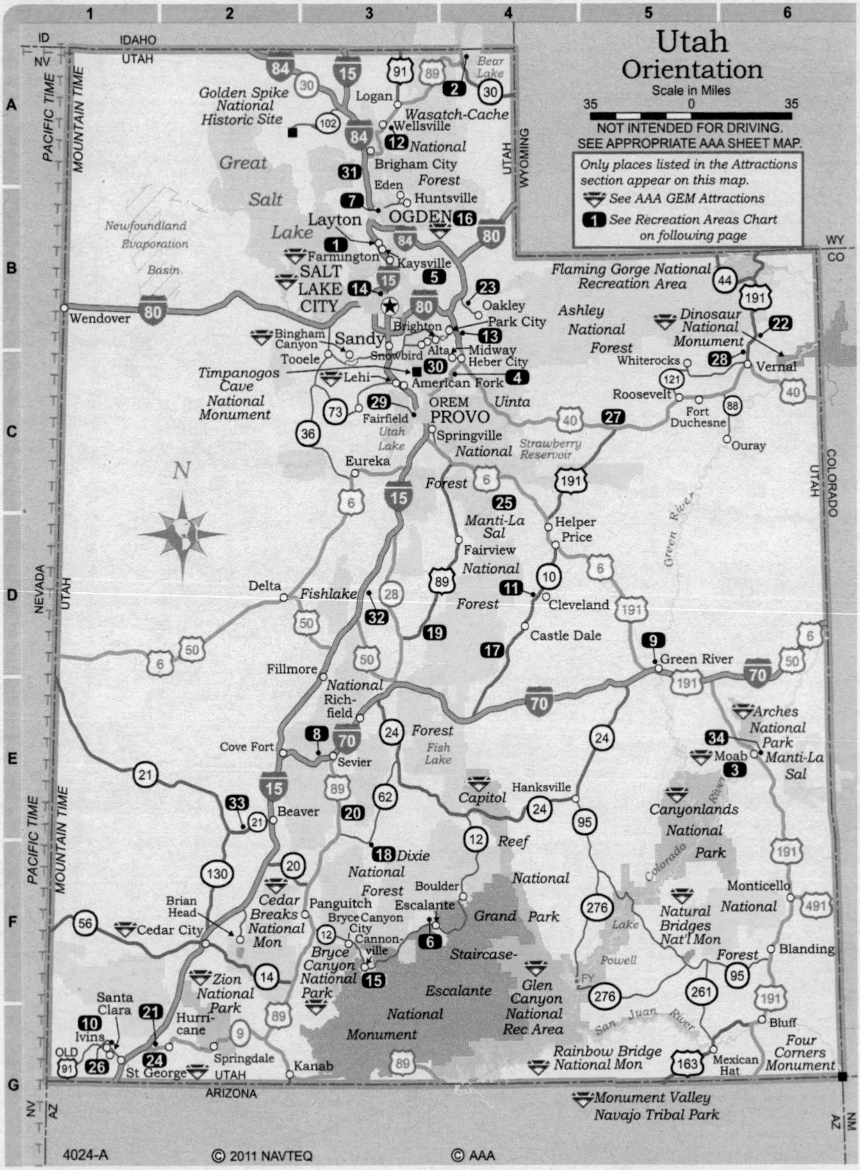

Utah Orientation

Scale in Miles

35 0 35

NOT INTENDED FOR DRIVING.
SEE APPROPRIATE AAA SHEET MAP.

Only places listed in the Attractions section appear on this map.

See AAA GEM Attractions

1 See Recreation Areas Chart on following page

4024-A

Recreation Areas Chart

The map location numerals in column 2 show an area's location on the preceding map.

	MAP LOCATION	CAMPING	PICNICKING	HIKING TRAILS	BOATING	BOAT RAMP	BOAT RENTAL	FISHING	SWIMMING	PETS ON LEASH	BICYCLE TRAILS	NATURE PROGS.	VISITOR CENTER	LODGE/CABINS	FOOD SERVICE
NATIONAL PARKS *(See place listings.)*															
Arches (E-6) 76,519 acres. Rock climbing; guided tours.		●	●	●						●		●	●		
Bryce Canyon (F-3) 35,835 acres. Horse and mule rental, interpretive programs.		●	●	●						●		●	●	●	●
Canyonlands (E-5) 337,598 acres. Canoeing, horseback riding, kayaking, mountain biking, river running, rock climbing.		●	●	●						●		●	●		
Capitol Reef (F-4) 241,904 acres. Historic. Scenic. Horseback riding, rock climbing; interpretive programs.		●	●	●				●		●	●	●	●		
Zion (F-2) 147,551 acres. Bird-watching; guided walks.		●	●	●						●	●	●	●	●	●
NATIONAL FORESTS *(See place listings.)*															
Ashley (B-4) 1,384,132 acres in northeastern Utah. Hunting, kayaking, rock climbing, skiing; horse rental.		●	●	●	●	●	●	●	●	●	●	●	●	●	●
Dixie (F-3) 1,700,000 acres in southwestern Utah. All-terrain vehicle trails, horse rental.		●	●	●	●	●	●	●	●	●	●	●	●	●	●
Fishlake (D-3) 1,434,599 acres in south-central Utah. Hunting, ice fishing, scuba diving, snowmobiling.		●	●	●	●	●	●	●		●	●	●	●	●	●
Manti-La Sal (D-4) 1,413,111 acres in southeastern Utah. Cross-country skiing, horseback riding, hunting, snowmobiling; all-terrain vehicle trails.		●	●	●	●	●	●	●		●	●	●		●	●
Uinta (C-4) 949,848 acres in central Utah. Horseback riding, hunting, skiing, snowmobiling, snowshoeing.		●	●	●	●	●		●	●	●	●	●	●		
Wasatch-Cache (A-3) 1,259,160 acres in north-central and northeastern Utah. Rock climbing, skiing, snowmobiling; all-terrain vehicle trails, horse rental.		●	●	●	●	●	●	●	●	●	●	●	●		
NATIONAL MONUMENTS *(See place listings.)*															
Dinosaur (B-5) 204,000 acres.		●	●	●				●		●	●	●	●		
NATIONAL RECREATION AREAS *(See place listings.)*															
Flaming Gorge (B-5) 207,363 acres. Cross-country skiing, horseback riding, hunting, ice fishing, parasailing, rafting, snowmobiling, water skiing.		●	●	●	●	●	●	●	●	●	●	●	●	●	●
Glen Canyon (F-4) 1,250,000 acres.		●	●	●	●	●	●	●	●	●		●	●	●	●
STATE															
Antelope Island (B-3) 28,022 acres in the Great Salt Lake 9.8 mi. w. of Syracuse via West 1700 South and the 7-mi.-long Davis County Cswy. Bird-watching, kayaking; American bison herd. *(See Great Salt Lake p. 350.)*	1	●	●	●	●	●			●	●	●		●		●
Bear Lake (A-4) 69,760 acres 1.5 mi. n. of Garden City on US 89. Scuba diving, water skiing.	2	●	●		●	●	●	●	●	●		●	●		●
Dead Horse Point (E-6) 5,362 acres 9 mi. n. of Moab via US 191, then 18 mi. s.w. on SR 313. Scenic. *(See Moab p. 367.)*	3	●	●	●						●	●	●	●		
Deer Creek (C-4) 3,000 acres 9 mi. s.w. of Heber City on US 189. Sailing, water skiing, windsurfing.	4	●	●		●	●	●	●	●	●		●			●
East Canyon (B-3) 950 acres 25 mi. n.e. of Salt Lake City on SR 65. Water skiing.	5	●	●		●	●	●	●	●	●		●			●
Escalante Petrified Forest (F-3) 1,784 acres 1 mi. w. of Escalante on SR 12, then .5 mi. on an unnamed road, following signs. Historic. *(See Escalante p. 344.)*	6	●	●	●	●	●	●	●	●	●		●	●		
Fort Buenaventura (B-3) 84 acres at 2450 A Ave. in Ogden. Historic. Canoeing. *(See Ogden p. 381.)*	7	●	●	●				●				●	●		
Fremont Indian (E-3) 1,784 acres 5 mi. s.w. of Sevier off I-70 exit 17. Historic. Archeological site, interpretive trails, museum. *(See Sevier p. 448.)*	8	●	●	●				●		●	●		●		●
Green River (D-5) 53 acres 1 mi. s. of Green River off Main St. Golf (nine holes).	9	●	●		●	●		●		●					
Gunlock Lake (G-1) 600 acres 1 mi. s. of Gunlock, then n. on Old US 91. Water skiing, wildlife viewing.	10	●	●		●	●		●	●	●					
Huntington (D-4) 350 acres 2 mi. n. of Huntington on SR 10. Bird-watching, ice fishing, water skiing.	11	●	●		●	●		●	●	●					

Recreation Areas Chart

The map location numerals in column 2 show an area's location on the preceding map.

Area	MAP LOCATION	CAMPING	PICNICKING	HIKING TRAILS	BOATING	BOAT RAMP	BOAT RENTAL	FISHING	SWIMMING	PETS ON LEASH	BICYCLE TRAILS	NATURE PROGS.	VISITOR CENTER	LODGE/CABINS	FOOD SERVICE
Hyrum (A-3) 450 acres s.w. of Hyrum on the n. shore of Hyrum Reservoir. Ice fishing, water skiing, wildlife viewing.	12	•	•	•	•	•	•	•	•	•		•			
Jordanelle (B-4) 4,000 acres n. of Heber City on US 40, then 6 mi. s.e. on SR 248. Scenic. Canoeing, ice fishing, kayaking, sailing, wildlife viewing; beaches, interpretive trails, nature center, playground.	13	•	•	•	•	•	•	•	•	•	•	•	•		•
Jordan River (B-3) 500 acres along an 8.5 mi. corridor of the Jordan River from 1700 South in Salt Lake City to the Davis County line. Golf (nine holes), jogging; exercise course, model airplane and helicopter ports, off-highway vehicle and motocross tracks.	14		•	•	•			•		•	•				•
Kodachrome Basin (F-3) 4,000 acres 9 mi. s.e. of Cannonville on Kodachrome Rd. Wildlife viewing; horse rental. *(See Cannonville p. 334.)*	15	•	•	•						•	•		•		•
Lost Creek (B-4) 415 acres 10 mi. n.e. of Croydon on Lost Creek Rd. Ice fishing, water skiing. Non-motorized boats only.	16		•		•	•		•	•	•					
Millsite (D-4) 435 acres w. of Ferron off SR 10. Water skiing; all-terrain vehicle and mountain biking trails.	17	•	•		•	•		•	•	•	•	•			
Otter Creek (F-3) 3,120 acres 5 mi. n.w. of Antimony on SR 22.	18	•	•		•	•	•	•	•	•	•	•	•		•
Palisade (D-3) 62 acres 10 mi. s. of Manti off US 89. Canoeing, golf (18 holes), ice fishing, water skiing.	19	•	•		•	•		•	•	•		•			•
Piute (E-3) 3,360 acres 12 mi. s. of Marysvale off US 89. Canoeing, ice fishing, kayaking, rock hounding, waterfowl hunting. Electric boats only.	20	•	•		•	•	•	•	•	•		•			•
Quail Creek (G-1) 1,000 acres 14 mi. n.e. of St. George on SR 9. Canoeing, kayaking, winter fishing.	21	•	•		•	•		•	•	•					
Red Fleet (B-6) 1,963 acres 13 mi. n. of Vernal on US 191. Canoeing, ice fishing, kayaking.	22	•	•	•	•	•		•	•	•		•			
Rockport (B-4) 550 acres 45 mi. e. of Salt Lake City just off I-80. Cross-country skiing, ice fishing, mountain biking, snowshoeing, water skiing.	23	•	•	•	•	•	•	•	•	•	•	•			•
Sand Hollow (G-1) 20,000 acres 7 mi. e. off I-15 exit 16 (SR 9) near Hurricane. Canoeing, kayaking, mountain biking; sand dunes.	24	•	•	•	•	•		•	•	•	•		•		
Scofield (C-4) 2,815 acres 35 mi. w. of Price on SR 96. Canoeing, cross-country skiing, ice fishing, kayaking, snowmobiling.	25	•	•		•	•	•	•	•	•		•			
Snow Canyon (G-1) 7,100 acres 3.7 mi. n. of Ivins on SR 8. Mountain biking, rock climbing, wildlife viewing; horseback riding trails. *(See Ivins p. 353.)*	26	•	•	•						•	•				
Starvation (C-5) 3,500 acres 4 mi. n.w. of Duchesne. Ice fishing, water skiing.	27	•	•		•	•	•	•	•	•		•			•
Steinaker (C-6) 750 acres 6 mi. n. of Vernal off SR 191. Ice fishing, water skiing.	28	•	•		•	•		•	•	•		•			
Utah Lake (C-3) 295 acres 4 mi. w. of Provo off I-15. Ice fishing, water skiing; ice-skating rink. *(See American Fork p. 321.)*	29	•	•		•	•		•	•	•		•	•		•
Wasatch Mountain (C-3) 21,592 acres 2 mi. w. of Midway. Historic. Cross-country skiing, golf (54 holes), horseback riding, inline skating, mountain biking, snowmobiling, wildlife viewing; off-highway vehicle trails.	30	•	•	•						•	•	•	•		•
Willard Bay (A-3) 2,673 acres 15 mi. n. of Ogden. Ice fishing, water skiing; interpretive trails.	31	•	•		•	•	•	•	•	•		•			•
Yuba (D-3) 660 acres 25 mi. w. of Nephi off I-15. Ice fishing, mountain biking, water skiing.	32	•	•		•	•		•	•	•			•		
OTHER															
Minersville Lake (E-2) 1,130 acres 12 mi. s.w. of Beaver on SR 21.	33	•	•		•	•		•	•	•					•
Sand Flats Recreation Area (E-5) 7,320 acres .5 mi. e. of Moab on Mill Creek Dr., then 2.5 mi. n.e. on Sand Flats Rd. to entrance booth. *(See Moab p. 367.)*	34	•	•	•						•	•				

ALTA (B-3) pop. 383, elev. 8,583'

• Part of Salt Lake City area — see map p. 412

Alta ballooned into a raucous mining town of 5,000 people with the 1865 discovery of silver. The presence of six breweries and 26 saloons did little to cool the tempers that resulted in more than 100 killings in the town's first few years. The 1873 devaluation of silver put an end to Alta's heyday, and the town languished until the first ski lodge was built in 1940.

The Alta area is now known for many excellent ski areas, all of which offer snow skiing November through May. It also is where the U.S. Forest Service began its avalanche control program, which eliminates such hazards through the use of artillery shells or explosives. The canyon road to the town has alternate routes that avoid these areas.

RECREATIONAL ACTIVITIES

Skiing

- **Alta Ski Area** is off I-215 exit 6 to SR 210, following signs. **Hours:** Daily 9:15-4:30, mid-Nov. to mid-Apr. **Phone:** (801) 572-3939 or (801) 359-1078.

AMERICAN FORK (C-3) pop. 26,263, elev. 4,563'

At the foot of the Wasatch Mountains, American Fork lies in the shadow of 11,750-foot Mount Timpanogos. Utah Lake State Park *(see Recreation Chart)*, at the southern edge of town, has the largest body of fresh water in the intermountain region. The lake offers boating, fishing and skiing. Duck hunting is permitted on the lake beyond the state park boundaries.

The Alpine Scenic Loop, a paved highway, encircles Mount Timpanogos; it is especially popular for its spectacular autumn foliage. Points of interest along the 45-minute drive include Bridal Veil Falls, Timpanogos Cave National Monument *(see place listing p. 452)* and American Fork Canyon. This road is narrow and not recommended for RVs.

American Fork Chamber of Commerce: 51 E. Main St., American Fork, UT 84003. **Phone:** (801) 756-5110.

HOLIDAY INN EXPRESS & SUITES AMERICAN FORK - NORTH PROVO **Phone:** (801)763-8500

Hotel

$89-$159

Address: 712 S Utah Valley Dr 84003 **Location:** I-15 exit 276, 0.3 mi n on S 500 E, just e on E 620 S, then just s. **Facility:** 80 units. 3 stories, interior corridors. **Pool(s):** heated indoor. **Activities:** whirlpool, exercise room. **Guest Services:** valet laundry.

    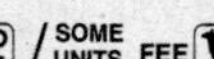 / SOME UNITS FEE

VALUE PLACE **Phone:** 801/492-1600

Extended Stay Motel

Rates not provided

Address: 57 N 900 W 84003 **Location:** I-15 exit 278, just w. **Facility:** 123 efficiencies. 4 stories, interior corridors. **Terms:** office hours 9 am-6 pm. **Amenities:** high-speed Internet (fee). **Guest Services:** coin laundry.

ARCHES NATIONAL PARK (E-6)

Elevations in the park range from 4,500 ft. at the visitor center to 5,200 ft. at Devils Garden. Refer to AAA maps for additional elevation information.

Arches National Park lies 5 miles northwest of Moab on US 191. The rugged area contains the largest number of natural stone arches in the country. Along with more than 2,000 arches are many red rock canyons, spires, fins and balancing rocks. The erosion of the Entrada Sandstone, a 300-foot-thick layer of rock that was deposited as sand 150 million years ago, created these formations.

The arches were formed by the weathering of openings in vertical slabs of sandstone. Opinions vary as to how big an opening must be before it can be classified as an arch, but park officials consider arches to be any opening extending at least 3 feet in any one direction.

General Information and Activities

The park is open year-round. It is particularly photogenic in the morning and evening light, when the sandstone formations take on a fiery glow. Many highlights can be seen from the road, but short foot trails lead to some of the most impressive features. A few trails entail strenuous climbs, and hikers must carry water.

Two miles past the visitor center at the park's entrance, the main road passes the Park Avenue viewpoint. Park Avenue offers an easy 1-mile hike through a red rock canyon whose walls resemble a city skyline. Those who have taken the hike can be picked up farther along the road at the end of the trail.

One of the most accessible areas is the Windows section, where visitors can study the basic geology of arches. Grouped together at the end of a side road 12 miles from the visitor center are Double Arch, Turret Arch, the North Window and the South Window. The route to this area leaves the main road 9 miles past the visitor center.

A paved road passing the Wolfe Ranch and ending at a viewpoint for Delicate Arch *(see attraction listing)* leaves the main road 2.5 miles farther. From the Wolfe Ranch a strenuous, one-way 1.5-mile trail leads to Delicate Arch. At the ranch are the weathered remnants of a homesteader's 20-year sojourn in this barren land in the late 1800s.

The Devils Garden section extends from the end of the paved road 18 miles from the visitor center. Only Skyline Arch is visible from the road, but many more arches, including Landscape Arch *(see attraction listing)*, can be reached by a 1.6-mile round-trip trail. Camping spaces can be reserved March through October and are on a first-come, first-served basis the rest of the year; phone (877) 444-6777, or TTY (877) 833-6777 for reservations. *See Recreation Chart.*

ADMISSION is $10 (per private vehicle); $5 (per person arriving by other means). The above fees permit entrance to the park for 7 calendar days from date of purchase. An annual pass is $25. The annual permit also is valid for Canyonlands National Park *(see place listing p. 334)* and Natural Bridges *(see place listing p. 380)* and Hovenweep *(see place listing in Colorado p. 227)* national monuments. The camping fee is $20. Fees also are charged for some interpretive programs and ranger-guided walks March through October.

PETS are permitted in parking areas or on roads only if they are on a leash no longer than 6 feet, crated or otherwise physically restricted at all times. Pets are not allowed on trails or in the backcountry areas.

ADDRESS inquiries to the Superintendent, Arches National Park, P.O. Box 907, Moab, UT 84532-0907; phone (435) 719-2100. The superintendent's office is open Mon.-Fri. 8-4:30.

DELICATE ARCH is 15 mi. n.e. from the Arches National Park entrance. Set amid cliffs and slickrock domes, the freestanding arch, with an opening of nearly 35 feet, can be seen from a distant viewpoint 1 mile to the southeast. The viewpoint is accessible by a short hike from the Delicate Arch Viewpoint parking area. The arch is reached by a strenuous 1.5-mile one-way trail starting at the Wolfe Ranch parking area. During the morning the arch is silhouetted against the sun; afternoon is the best time to take close-up pictures, but it also is the hottest and most crowded part of the day.

LANDSCAPE ARCH is in the Devils Garden section of Arches National Park. With a span of 306 feet and a height of 105 feet, it is one of the longest natural stone arches in the world; at one point it is only 6 feet thick. The arch can be reached by a 2-mile round-trip trail starting at the Devils Garden trailhead parking area.

VISITOR CENTER is just inside the Arches National Park entrance. The center offers exhibits about the park's cultural and natural history and presents an orientation film. Campfire talks and guided trips take place March through October. **Hours:** Daily 7:30-6:30, Apr.-Oct.; 8-4:30, rest of year. Closed Christmas. **Phone:** (435) 719-2299.

ASHLEY NATIONAL FOREST (B-4)

Elevations in the forest range from 6,000 ft. at Antelope Canyon to 13,528 ft. at Kings Peak. Refer to AAA maps for additional elevation information.

In the northeast corner of Utah, Ashley National Forest includes the only major mountain range in the lower 48 states with an east-west alignment—the Uintas. Ashley National Forest embraces this area and the pinion-juniper and ponderosa pine-covered benchland along the Green River. One of the major water-producing areas in the state of Utah, the forest was established by President Theodore Roosevelt in 1908.

The forest contains most of the High Uintas Wilderness *(see attraction listing)*, the spectacular Red Canyon of the Green River, and 13,528-foot Kings Peak, the highest of Utah's mountains. Flaming Gorge Dam and National Recreation Area *(see place listing p. 346)* provides many recreational and scenic opportunities. This 502-foot-high dam is 1,180 feet long and contains water for 91 miles. Hunting for pronghorn antelopes, mule deer, elk, mountain lions and black bears is allowed in the forest.

Several drives provide access to areas of scenic and geological interest. The Flaming Gorge-Uintas National Scenic Byway (US 191), Utah's first national forest scenic byway, extends from Vernal to the Wyoming border, traversing an area in which a billion years of Earth's history lie exposed. The Sheep Creek Canyon Geological Area, north and west of the byway, is reached via US 191 and another paved road. The Red Cloud Loop, a dirt and gravel road that is rough in spots, is a scenic forest drive that can be accessed near Vernal.

Camping is available in improved sites and backcountry areas throughout the forest. For camping reservations contact the National Recreation Reservation System, P.O. Box 900, Cumberland, MD 21501-0900; phone (877) 444-6777, or TTY (877) 833-6777.

For further information contact the Forest Supervisor, Ashley National Forest, 355 N. Vernal Ave., Vernal, UT 84078; phone (435) 789-1181. *See Recreation Chart.*

INSIDER INFO:
Mountain Driving

Driving through scenic mountains in the western United States can be the high point of your long-awaited vacation—or it can be disastrous. The trick is to know what to expect and to be prepared. By taking a little time before you leave, you can eliminate most potential problems before they happen.

Many tips for safe mountain driving are purely common sense and apply to driving in general: Before you begin your trip, check the weather and road conditions along the way and at your destination; let a member of your family or a friend know where you're going and the route you plan on taking, including stops along the way; consider taking a cellular phone with you; keep your gas tank near full, as service stations may be far apart; make sure your car and your tires are in tip-top shape; observe posted speed limits, especially on narrow, winding roads; keep a first-aid kit in your car; and stop every 2-3 hours to stretch and help prevent fatigue.

Remember that high elevations can mean changing weather and road conditions. If you are traveling in winter, make sure you have the following items in your vehicle: a scraper, tire chains, booster cables, shovel, flashlight, blanket, warm clothing and nonperishable food. Be aware that high altitudes (usually above 8,000 feet) can cause headaches, shortness of breath or a lack of energy.

Downshifting to a lower gear when going up or down steep grades will lessen engine and brake stress. Leaving your air conditioner off while ascending a steep hill will also help eliminate strain on your engine. On downhill slopes tap your brakes instead of applying full pressure in order to avoid overheating and possible brake failure. Consider changing to a brake fluid listed as DOT 4; this grade has a higher boiling point and is recommended for mountain driving conditions.

Experts advise that it is best to maintain a steady speed whenever possible when driving mountain roads in winter; it is also best not to engage your cruise control in wintery driving situations. Try to avoid starting or stopping suddenly. If you encounter slippery or icy roads, remember the technique of applying gentle pressure on your brakes; this will help avoid skidding or spinning. If you do find yourself in a skid, stay calm, take your foot off the accelerator or brake and steer in the direction you want the front of the car to go. Be aware that it takes longer to stop on snow or ice, so give yourself plenty of time. And when you do stop, be sure to set your emergency brake.

HIGH UINTAS WILDERNESS extends from Mirror Lake eastward beyond Kings Peak to North Pole Pass. It encompasses approximately 456,705 mountainous acres of forests and lakes and offers 545 miles of trails. Ridges divide the region into large scenic basins interspersed with high glacial moraines and drifts. The floors of these basins are a spectacular contrast to the abrupt ridges rising several thousand feet. Many of the hundreds of lakes are stocked with trout.

Backpacking is the most popular way to visit the High Uintas; no motor vehicles are allowed. Visitors should register at a trailhead before entering the area. **Hours:** The wilderness is accessible late June to mid-Sept. **Cost:** Free. **Phone:** (435) 789-1181.

RED CANYON VISITOR CENTER is 40 mi. n. of Vernal via US 44. The center contains exhibits about natural and cultural history. An observation deck overlooks the Flaming Gorge National Recreation Area *(see place listing p. 346)* and the Uinta Mountains. **Hours:** Daily 8-6, mid-May to mid-Sept. **Cost:** Free. **Phone:** (435) 889-3713.

BEAVER (E-2) pop. 3,112, elev. 5,898'

BEAVER COURTHOUSE MUSEUM is at 90 E. Center St. The courthouse, destroyed by fire in 1882, was rebuilt and used through 1975. Now strictly a museum, it contains the U.S. flag that flew on the USS *Utah,* which sank during the attack on Pearl Harbor. Also displayed are re-created judges' chambers, court recorder's and sheriff's offices, and several 19th-century items. The jail in the basement was used through 1976. **Hours:** Tues.-Sat. and holidays 11-5, June 1-Labor Day. **Cost:** Donations. **Phone:** (435) 438-5727.

BEAVER DAYS INN **Phone:** (435)438-7800

Motel
$55-$100

Address: 646 W 1400 N 84713 **Location:** I-15 exit 112, just w. Across from travel center and truck stop. **Facility:** 29 units. 2 stories (no elevator), interior corridors. **Terms:** cancellation fee imposed. **Guest Services:** coin laundry. **Free Special Amenities: full breakfast and high-speed Internet.**

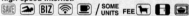

BEST WESTERN BUTCH CASSIDY INN
Phone: (435)438-2438

Motel
$80-$86

AAA Benefit: Members save up to 20%, plus 10% bonus points with Best Western Rewards®.

Address: 161 S Main St 84713 **Location:** I-15 exit 112, 1.8 mi e. **Facility:** 35 units, some two bedrooms. 2 stories (no elevator), exterior corridors. **Terms:** cancellation fee imposed. **Amenities:** *Some:* high-speed Internet. **Pool(s):** heated outdoor. **Free Special Amenities: full breakfast and high-speed Internet.**

  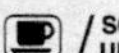 / SOME UNITS FEE 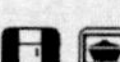

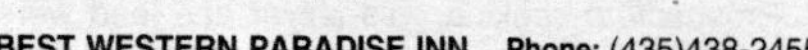

BEST WESTERN PARADISE INN **Phone:** (435)438-2455

Hotel
$80

AAA Benefit: Members save up to 20%, plus 10% bonus points with Best Western Rewards®.

Address: 314 W 1425 N 84713 **Location:** I-15 exit 112, just e. **Facility:** 53 units, some two bedrooms. 2 stories (no elevator), exterior corridors. **Pool(s):** heated indoor. **Activities:** whirlpool. **Free Special Amenities: local telephone calls and high-speed Internet.**

/ SOME UNITS FEE

COMFORT INN & SUITES **Phone:** (435)438-6283

Hotel
$65-$90

Address: 1540 S Main St 84713 **Location:** I-15 exit 109, just e. **Facility:** 46 units. 2 stories (no elevator), interior corridors. **Pool(s):** heated indoor. **Activities:** whirlpool, limited exercise equipment. **Guest Services:** coin laundry.

  / SOME UNITS 

QUALITY INN **Phone:** 435/438-5426

Hotel
Rates not provided

Address: 781 W 1800 S 84713 **Location:** I-15 exit 109, just w. **Facility:** 52 units. 2 stories (no elevator), interior corridors. **Pool(s):** heated indoor. **Activities:** whirlpool.

   / SOME UNITS FEE

WHERE TO EAT

ARSHEL'S CAFE **Phone:** 435/438-2977

American
$5-$13

AAA Inspector Notes: Cozy and friendly, family-owned and operated since 1944, the cafe specializes in fresh homemade pies, country-fried chicken and steak. **Address:** 711 N Main St 84713 **Location:** I-15 exit 112, 0.8 mi se. B L D

HUNAN GARDEN CHINESE RESTAURANT
Phone: 435/438-5070

Chinese
$6-$12

AAA Inspector Notes: This very basic place offers typical Chinese items in a simple wood dining room. It's the only Chinese restaurant in town. **Address:** 1425 N 400 W 84713 **Location:** I-15 exit 112, just e.

L D

TIMBERLINE INN **Phone:** 435/438-2474

American
$9-$20

AAA Inspector Notes: Since 1983, the restaurant has been a favorite among families. All day long, guests can order food like Mom used to make, including anytime breakfast items. Servers are friendly. **Address:** 1542 S 450 W 84713 **Location:** I-15 exit 109, just w.

B L D

BICKNELL pop. 327

AQUARIUS MOTEL & RESTAURANT
Phone: 435/425-3835

fyi Not evaluated. **Address:** 240 W Main St 84715 **Location:** 0.4 mi w of center on SR 24. Facilities, services, and decor characterize a mid-scale property.

BINGHAM CANYON (C-3) elev. 6,280'

• Part of Salt Lake City area — see map p. 412

Prospectors seeking gold, silver and lead were active in Bingham Canyon as early as 1863, but until the late 1800s they neglected the most promising mineral: copper. Nearly 320,000 tons a year of the nation's refined-grade copper, as well as quantities of gold and silver, come from the open pit mine of Kennecott Utah Copper Corporation's Bingham Canyon Mine.

GEM **KENNECOTT'S BINGHAM CANYON MINE** is w. on SR 48, following signs. Mining began here in 1906 in what was to become one of the largest open pit mines in the world. The mine currently provides 15 percent of the nation's copper needs. The terraced pit is three-quarters of a mile deep and about 2.5 miles wide; the working area covers 1,900 acres.

The site contains a visitor center with interactive exhibits, 3-D models of the mine and photographs. A 16-minute videotape presentation explains how the mineral is produced and used in our daily lives. An overlook provides a panoramic view of live mining operations; a multilingual narration explains the operations. Motorcycles are not permitted. **Hours:** Daily 8-8, Apr.-Oct. Last admission 1 hour before closing. **Cost:** $5 (per private vehicle). **Phone:** (801) 204-2025.

BLANDING (F-6) pop. 3,375, elev. 6,000'

Originally a trading center for the surrounding stock ranches, Blanding was settled in 1905 as a result of an irrigation project that still waters abundant crops of hay and grain. Several trading posts deal in Native American arts and crafts.

The town borders some of southeastern Utah's most dramatic canyon country. Natural Bridges National Monument *(see place listing p. 380)* and Glen Canyon National Recreation Area *(see place listing p. 347)* are west via SR 95.

Beginning just southwest of town is the 100-mile loop known as the Trail of the Ancients, along which can be seen many remnants of the Anasazi Indian culture that flourished A.D. 300-1300. The trail begins at Edge of the Cedars State Park *(see attraction listing)* and follows US 191 and US 163 east to Mexican Hat *(see place listing p. 363)*, then north on SR 261 and east again on SR 95. Some sections of SR 261 are unpaved and not recommended for RVs or trailers. Trail of the Ancients also takes a side trip on SR 262 to Hovenweep National Monument *(see place listing in Colorado p. 227)*.

Blanding Visitor Center: 12 N. Grayson Pkwy., Blanding, UT 84511. **Phone:** (435) 678-3662.

THE DINOSAUR MUSEUM is at 754 South 200 West. The museum displays a 360-pound meteorite, dinosaur skeletons and life-size models, a living fossils exhibit and fossil trees that are more than 275 million years old. Exhibits are arranged chronologically. The History Hall of Hollywood Dinosaur Movies features original movie posters. **Time:** Allow 1 hour minimum. **Hours:** Mon.-Sat. 9-5, Apr. 15-Oct. 15. **Cost:** $3; $2 (ages 65+); $1.50 (ages 3-12). **Phone:** (435) 678-3454.

EDGE OF THE CEDARS STATE PARK, just off US 191 at 660 West 400 North, is the site of a Puebloan Indian village, inhabited A.D. 825-1125, and a museum. The museum features a fine Puebloan pottery collection and exhibits about the cultures that influenced the area. The site has a prehistoric Great House and Great Kiva surrounded by unit pueblos and changing exhibits on a ridge overlooking Westwater Canyon. A solstice sculpture is just west of the Puebloan ruin.

Videotape presentations cover area ruins, rock art and Puebloan life. **Hours:** Mon.-Sat. 9-5. Closed Jan. 1, Thanksgiving and Christmas. **Cost:** $5; $3 (ages 6-17); $20 (family, maximum eight people). **Phone:** (435) 678-2238.

BLUE MOUNTAIN INN **Phone:** 435/678-3271

Hotel
Rates not provided

Address: 711 S Main St 84511 **Location:** On US 191. **Facility:** 52 units, some efficiencies. 2 stories (no elevator), interior corridors. **Pool(s):** heated outdoor. **Activities:** whirlpool, limited exercise equipment. **Guest Services:** coin laundry.

GATEWAY INN **Phone:** (435)678-2278

Motel
$61-$85 5/1-10/20
$55-$69 10/21-4/30

Address: 88 E Center St 84511 **Location:** On US 191. **Facility:** 55 units. 2 stories (no elevator), exterior corridors. **Terms:** cancellation fee imposed. **Amenities:** *Some:* high-speed Internet. **Pool(s):** heated outdoor.

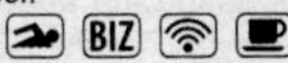

/ SOME UNITS

SUPER 8 **Phone:** (435)678-3880

Motel
$60-$129

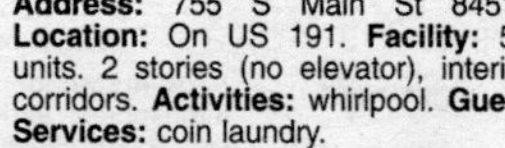

Address: 755 S Main St 84511 **Location:** On US 191. **Facility:** 59 units. 2 stories (no elevator), interior corridors. **Activities:** whirlpool. **Guest Services:** coin laundry.

BIZ / SOME UNITS FEE

WHERE TO EAT

HOMESTEAD STEAK HOUSE **Phone:** 435/678-3456

American
$6-$20

AAA Inspector Notes: Patrons enjoy favorite home-cooked meals in a casual family-friendly setting. **Address:** 121 E Center 84511 **Location:** Downtown. L D

OLD TYMER RESTAURANT **Phone:** 435/678-2122

American
$4-$13

AAA Inspector Notes: Home-style dishes served with corn bread, including Mexican items, steaks, chicken and prime rib dinners, appeal to families. **Address:** 733 S Main St 84511 **Location:** On US 191; next to Comfort Inn of Blanding. B L D

BLUFF (G-6) pop. 258, elev. 4,320'

Bluff lies in the shadow of the Navajo Twins, two massive sandstone turrets towering over the valley of the San Juan River. Nearby ruins include the Pioneer Cemetery, off US 191 following signs, and the 14-Window Ruin, on a marked trail in the Navajo reservation.

St. Christopher's Mission, a small chapel on SR 162, affords a spectacular view of the surrounding red rock cliffs. Bluff is at the northern end of scenic US 191, which runs southwest through Mexican Hat *(see place listing p. 363)* and continues as US 163 into Arizona.

Bluff Fort Visitors Center: 55 North 600 East, Bluff, UT 84512. **Phone:** (435) 672-9995.

RECREATIONAL ACTIVITIES

Hiking

- **Far Out Expeditions** picks up at area lodgings. Other activities are offered. **Hours:** Half-day, full-day and multi-day trips are offered. **Phone:** (435) 672-2294.

White-water Rafting

- **Wild Rivers Expeditions, LLC** is 1 blk. w. of the post office on US 191 at 101 Main St. Other activities are offered. **Hours:** One-day trips on the San Juan River are offered daily, Mar.-Oct. Departure times vary; phone ahead. **Phone:** (435) 672-2244, (435) 672-2200 or (800) 422-7654.

DESERT ROSE INN & CABINS **Phone:** (435)672-2303

Hotel
$115-$179 5/1-10/31
$80-$179 11/1-4/30

Address: 701 W Main St 84512 **Location:** On US 191 (Main St), west end of town. **Facility:** 36 units, some cabins. 1-2 stories (no elevator), exterior corridors. **Terms:** office hours 6:30 am-10:30 pm, check-in 4 pm. **Guest Services:** coin laundry. **Free Special Amenities: local telephone calls and high-speed Internet.**

KOKOPELLI INN **Phone:** (435)672-2322

Motel
$65-$75

Address: 160 E Main St 84512 **Location:** On US 191 (Main St). **Facility:** 26 units. 1 story, interior corridors. *Bath:* shower only. **Terms:** office hours 7 am-11 pm, check-in 3:30 pm. **Free Special Amenities: local telephone calls and early check-in/late check-out.**

SAVE / SOME UNITS FEE

RECAPTURE LODGE **Phone:** 435/672-2281

Motel
$75

Address: 220 E Main St 84512 **Location:** On US 191 (Main St). **Facility:** 29 units, some efficiencies, kitchens and houses. 2 stories (no elevator), exterior corridors. **Terms:** open 5/1-12/20 & 2/1-4/30. **Pool(s):** heated outdoor. **Activities:** whirlpool, recreation programs, hiking trails, jogging, playground, game room. **Guest Services:** coin laundry. **Free Special Amenities: continental breakfast and children's activities.**

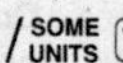
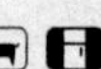

WHERE TO EAT

COMB RIDGE COFFEE **Phone:** 435/672-9931

Coffee/Tea
$4-$8

AAA Inspector Notes: This special coffeehouse is the perfect spot to take a well-deserved reprieve from driving, biking, hiking-you name it-to check e-mail and enjoy tasty blue corn pancakes and a variety of breads and pastries. **Address:** 680 S Hwy 191 84512 **Location:** On US 191 (Main St), west end of town. B

COTTONWOOD STEAKHOUSE **Phone:** 435/672-2282

Steak
$13-$25

AAA Inspector Notes: Indoor dining in an Old West atmosphere can't get more relaxing, but guests also can enjoy dinner in covered booths beneath a beautiful cottonwood tree beside an evening campfire in the outside courtyard. Entrées are grilled to order over an open flame. In addition to steaks such as the marshal, the deputy and the maverick, the menu lists half and full racks of barbecue ribs, barbecue chicken and grilled salmon. The vegetable stir-fry in spicy Thai peanut sauce is delicious. **Bar:** beer & wine. **Address:** 409 W Main St 84512 **Location:** Just s of center. D

SAN JUAN RIVER KITCHEN **Phone:** 435/672-9956

Specialty
$9-$18

AAA Inspector Notes: The cuisine changes each year, but fresh, locally grown foods are the focus here. Patrons will always find a fresh soup of the day, baked bread, wonderful salads, sandwiches, entrées and creative desserts, all skillfully prepared. **Bar:** beer & wine. **Address:** 281 E Main St 84512 **Location:** On US 191 (Main St). D

TWIN ROCKS CAFE & GIFT SHOP **Phone:** 435/672-2341

American
$6-$22

AAA Inspector Notes: Beneath scenic red rock towers, this eatery features indigenous Native American dishes, including fry bread and chicken soup with homemade noodles, Navajo tacos and burgers, smoked meats, vegetarian entrées such as the sauteed vegetable medley or spicy peanut stir-fry, and microbrewed beer. Desserts include an apple puff pastry and the famous fruits of the forest pie. The attractive covered patio with many plants and bird feeders for the hummingbirds is inviting. **Bar:** beer only. **Address:** 913 E Navajo Twins Dr 84512 **Location:** On US 191 (Main St), east end of town.

B L D

BOULDER (F-4) pop. 226, elev. 6,640'

Boulder lies on SR 12, a particularly scenic route that runs through Escalante and Cannonville to Panguitch. For 5 miles south of Boulder unusual formations of white slickrock are shot with bursts of red hues.

ANASAZI STATE PARK MUSEUM is on SR 12. The park is the site of an Anasazi Indian village that may have been occupied A.D. 1160-1235. One hundred structures have been excavated; a self-guiding trail leads visitors through the site. A life-size six-room replica of an Anasazi dwelling depicts village life almost 800 years ago. Artifacts are displayed in a glass-enclosed area. **Hours:** Daily 8-6, May-Sept.; Mon.-Sat. 9-5, rest of year. Closed Jan. 1, Thanksgiving and Christmas. **Cost:** $5; $10 (family, maximum eight people). **Phone:** (435) 335-7308.

BOULDER MOUNTAIN LODGE **Phone:** (435)335-7460

Hotel
$79-$200

Address: 20 N Hwy 12 84716 **Location:** Just s on SR 12. **Facility:** 20 units, some two bedrooms. 2 stories (no elevator), interior/exterior corridors. **Terms:** 30 day cancellation notice-fee imposed. **Dining:** Hell's Backbone Grill, see separate listing. **Activities:** whirlpool, hiking trails, horseshoes, volleyball. **Guest Services:** valet laundry.

BIZ / SOME UNITS FEE

WHERE TO EAT

BOULDER MESA RESTAURANT **Phone:** 435/335-7447

American
$6-$18

AAA Inspector Notes: The eatery offers meticulously prepared meals including sandwiches, hand-pressed hamburgers, fresh salads and soup; an extensive vegetarian menu is also available as well as breakfast. **Bar:** beer & wine. **Address:** 155 E Burr Trail Rd 84716 **Location:** Just e at Burr Trail Rd. B L D

HELL'S BACKBONE GRILL **Phone:** 435/335-7464

Natural/Organic
$17-$32

AAA Inspector Notes: A rugged frontier look gives this place its interesting character. The Western-range menu changes weekly and features locally raised meats and vegetables from an on-site organic garden. **Bar:** beer & wine. **Reservations:** suggested. **Address:** 20 N Hwy 12 84716 **Location:** Just s on SR 12; at Boulder Mountain Lodge. B D

BOUNTIFUL pop. 42,552

• **Hotels & Restaurants map & index p. 426**
• **Part of Salt Lake City area — see map p. 412**

COUNTRY INN & SUITES BY CARLSON BOUNTIFUL
Phone: (801)292-8100 25

Hotel
$89-$149

Address: 999 N 500 W 84010 **Location:** I-15 exit 317 (500 W), just e, then 0.7 mi n. **Facility:** 87 units. 4 stories, interior corridors. **Pool(s):** heated indoor. **Activities:** whirlpool, exercise room. **Guest Services:** valet and coin laundry, area transportation-within 6 mi.

BIZ / SOME UNITS 

WHERE TO EAT

ROBINTINO'S **Phone:** 801/298-1515 28

Italian
$7-$15

AAA Inspector Notes: With a great atmosphere and location, the eatery serves traditional Italian entrées, pizza, steak and seafood. **Bar:** beer only. **Address:** 1385 S 500 W 84010 **Location:** I-15 exit 316 (S 500), just e, then 0.6 mi s. L D

BRIAN HEAD (F-2) pop. 83, elev. 9,800'

RECREATIONAL ACTIVITIES

Skiing

- **Brian Head Resort** is at 329 S. SR 143. Other activities are offered. **Hours:** Open daily, early Nov.-late Apr. Hours vary; phone ahead. **Phone:** (435) 677-2035 or (866) 930-1010. ***(See ad p. 337.)***

CEDAR BREAKS LODGE **Phone:** (435)677-3000

Resort Hotel
$85-$375

Address: 223 Hunter Ridge Rd 84719 **Location:** On SR 143. **Facility:** At 9,600 feet, many rooms feature forest views; accommodations vary from studios to suites. 118 units, some two bedrooms, efficiencies and kitchens. 3 stories, interior corridors. **Terms:** check-in 4 pm, 3 night minimum stay - seasonal, 3 day cancellation notice-fee imposed. **Amenities:** safes. **Dining:** 3 restaurants. **Pool(s):** heated indoor. **Activities:** sauna, whirlpools, steamrooms, hiking trails, playground, basketball, horseshoes, volleyball, exercise room, spa. *Fee:* downhill & cross country skiing, game room. **Guest Services:** coin laundry. **Free Special Amenities: local transportation and children's activities.**

SAVE BIZ

THE GRAND LODGE AT BRIAN HEAD
Phone: 435/677-9000

Resort Hotel
Rates not provided

Address: 314 Hunter Ridge Rd 84719 **Location:** On SR 143. **Facility:** This rustic and elegant hotel has beautifully appointed rooms with mountain views, upscale bathrooms and a deck with fire pits. 100 units, some two bedrooms. 3 stories, interior corridors. **Terms:** check-in 4 pm. **Amenities:** high-speed Internet, safes. **Dining:** 2 restaurants. **Pool(s):** heated indoor. **Activities:** whirlpools, rental bicycles, hiking trails, jogging, exercise room, spa. *Fee:* downhill skiing, snowmobiling, game room, horseshoes. **Guest Services:** coin laundry. **Free Special Amenities: high-speed Internet.**

SAVE CALL BIZ / SOME UNITS FEE

BRIGHAM CITY (A-3) pop. 17,899, elev. 4,310'

The Wasatch Range is a towering backdrop for the busy agricultural and manufacturing center of Brigham City. The city began in 1851 as Box Elder.

In 1856 it was renamed for Brigham Young, who delivered his last public address in the town in 1877. Relics of the early days of Mormon settlement can be seen in the Community Center, the Brigham City Museum-Gallery *(see attraction listing)* and the Golden Spike Display. The Golden Spike National Historic Site *(see place listing p. 349)* is 32 miles west.

The city's foundation is a fertile alluvial delta that produces some of Utah's finest peaches as well as apricots, cherries and other crops. From July to mid-September fruit stands flank the 10-mile section of SR 89 known as the Golden Spike Fruitway.

Brigham City Area Chamber of Commerce: 6 N. Main St., P.O. Box 458, Brigham City, UT 84302. **Phone:** (435) 723-3931.

BEAR RIVER MIGRATORY BIRD REFUGE AND JAMES V. HANSEN WILDLIFE EDUCATION CENTER is 15 mi. w. off I-15 exit 363 (Forest St.) and at 2155 W. Forest St., respectively. The 80,000-acre refuge, which consists of pristine marshes, uplands and open water, attracts migrating bald eagles, falcons, hawks and swans and is an important breeding and stopover site for several species of waterfowl.

A 12-mile-long auto tour loop follows a dike road and allows for wildlife viewing. Boasting a modern architectural design, the education center features interactive exhibits as well as a wetland diorama, a video presentation and a .5-mile walking trail. Various activities, including those geared toward children, are offered.

Time: Allow 1 hour minimum. **Hours:** Refuge auto loop accessible daily dawn-dusk (weather permitting). Education center open Mon.-Fri. 8-5, Sat. 10-4. Guided refuge tours are offered seasonally. Closed major holidays. **Cost:** Free. **Phone:** (435) 723-6422, or (435) 734-6425 for recorded information.

BRIGHAM CITY MUSEUM-GALLERY, 24 North 300 West, displays settlement artifacts and furnishings, items relating to the history of Brigham City 1850-1900, and rotating art exhibits. **Hours:** Tues.-Fri. 11-6, Sat. 1-5. Closed most holidays. **Cost:** Free. **Phone:** (435) 723-6769.

BRIGHAM CITY TABERNACLE is at 251 S. Main St. The tabernacle of The Church of Jesus Christ of Latter-day Saints is an effective blend of Gothic and neoclassic architecture. Begun in 1868, it was rebuilt after a fire in 1896. **Hours:** Guided tours Tues.-Sun. noon-8, Mon. noon-6, Memorial Day-Labor Day; Tues.-Sun. noon-8, rest of year. **Cost:** Free. **Phone:** (435) 723-5376.

INSPIRATION POINT is near the top of Willard Peak (Mount Baldy). The site offers a view that extends into Idaho and, on a clear day, Nevada. The point is reached by a 16-mile drive from Brigham City; the narrow mountain road from Mantua is hazardous.

CRYSTAL INN — **Phone:** (435)723-0440

Hotel
$75-$119

Address: 480 Westland Dr 84302 **Location:** I-15 exit 362, 1 mi e. **Facility:** 52 units. 2 stories (no elevator), interior corridors. **Terms:** office hours 6 am-11 pm. **Pool(s):** heated indoor. **Activities:** whirlpool, exercise room. **Guest Services:** coin laundry. ***(See ad p. 361.)***

/ SOME UNITS FEE

DAYS INN — **Phone:** (435)723-3500

Hotel
$59-$124

Address: 1033 S 1600 W 84302 **Location:** I-15 exit 362, just w. **Facility:** 63 units. 3 stories, interior corridors. **Amenities:** high-speed Internet. **Pool(s):** heated outdoor. **Activities:** whirlpool, limited exercise equipment. **Guest Services:** coin laundry.

BIZ

WHERE TO EAT

IDLE ISLE CAFE — **Phone:** 435/734-2468

American
$7-$12

AAA Inspector Notes: Beautiful fresh flowers adorn the tables and original handcrafted booths year-round at this lovely eatery. The menu includes delicious hearty soups, healthy seafood, chicken and chef's salads, fettuccine with grilled salmon or chicken breast, moist roasted pot roast and other favorites. Root beer floats and malts are served at a marble-and-onyx soda fountain that contributes to the 1920s family atmosphere. **Address:** 24 S Main St 84302 **Location:** I-15 exit 363 (Forest St), 2.5 mi e, then just s.

L D

MADDOX RANCH HOUSE — **Phone:** 435/723-8545

American
$6-$26

AAA Inspector Notes: Guests are treated like family at this genuine ranch house serving aged beef that's hand cut on the premises. Bison is a specialty, and the menu also includes chicken, seafood and homemade cream pies. Seating is available in several dining rooms. **Address:** 1900 S Hwy 89 84302 **Location:** I-15 exit 362, 2 mi e, then 1 mi s. L D

BRIGHTON (B-3) elev. 8,730'

• Part of Salt Lake City area — see map p. 412

A year-round mountain resort at an elevation of more than 8,700 feet, Brighton is at the head of Big Cottonwood Canyon, 25 miles southeast of Salt Lake City.

RECREATIONAL ACTIVITIES

Skiing

- **Brighton Resort** is off I-215 exit 6, following signs to Big Cottonwood Canyon. **Hours:** Daily 9-4, mid-Nov. to late Apr. (also Mon.-Sat. 4-9, early Dec.-Mar. 31). **Phone:** (801) 532-4731 or (800) 873-5512.
- **Solitude Mountain Resort** is at 12000 Big Cottonwood Canyon. Other activities are offered. **Hours:** Winter activities daily 9-4, mid-Nov. to late Apr. Schedule varies rest of year; phone ahead. **Phone:** (801) 534-1400 or (800) 748-4754.

BRYCE CANYON CITY (F-3)

• Restaurants p. 332

BRYCE MUSEUM AND WILDLIFE ADVENTURE is at 1945 W. SR 12. The museum features more than 450 mounted animals indigenous to North America as well as exotic game from Africa, India and Europe in lifelike dioramas. In addition displays of rare birds and fossils; a collection of Native American artifacts, pottery, tools and weapons; and a large group of butterfly specimens are exhibited. Visitors also can see a live herd of fallow deer. **Time:** Allow 30 minutes minimum. **Hours:** Daily 9-9, Apr. 1-Nov. 15. **Cost:** $8. **Phone:** (435) 834-5555.

BEST WESTERN PLUS BRYCE CANYON GRAND HOTEL Phone: (435)834-5700

Hotel
$79-$180

AAA Benefit: Members save up to 20%, plus 10% bonus points with Best Western Rewards®.

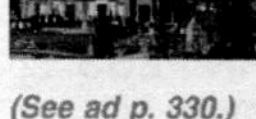

Address: 30 N 100 E 84764 **Location:** On SR 63, 1 mi s of SR 12. **Facility:** 164 units. 4 stories, interior corridors. **Terms:** check-in 4 pm. **Pool(s):** heated outdoor. **Activities:** whirlpool, exercise room. **Guest Services:** coin laundry, area transportation-within 2 mi. **Free Special Amenities: local telephone calls and high-speed Internet.**

(See ad p. 330.)

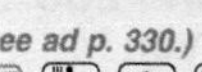   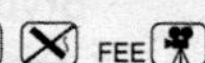 FEE  

Create complete trip routings and custom maps with the TripTik® Travel Planner on AAA.com or CAA.ca

BEST WESTERN PLUS RUBY'S INN Phone: (435)834-5341

Hotel
$65-$150

AAA Benefit: Members save up to 20%, plus 10% bonus points with Best Western Rewards®.

Address: 26 S Main St 84764 **Location:** On SR 63, 1 mi s of SR 12. **Facility:** 370 units. 1-3 stories (no elevator), interior/exterior corridors. **Terms:** check-in 4 pm. **Dining:** Ruby's Cowboy's Buffet & Steak House, see separate listing, entertainment. **Pool(s):** heated outdoor, heated indoor. **Activities:** whirlpools, rental bicycles, hiking trails, jogging, playground, sports court, basketball. *Fee:* cross country skiing, horseback riding. **Guest Services:** coin laundry. **Free Special Amenities: local telephone calls and high-speed Internet.** *(See ad p. 331.)*

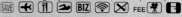

   FEE  / SOME UNITS FEE

BRYCE CANYON PINES Phone: 435/834-5441

Motel
$95-$130 5/1-10/31
$55-$110 11/1-4/30

Address: 2476 W Hwy 12, MM 10 84764 **Location:** On SR 12, at MM 10. **Facility:** 50 units, some two bedrooms, three bedrooms, kitchens and cottages. 1-2 stories (no elevator), exterior corridors. **Terms:** check-in 4 pm, 3 day cancellation notice-fee imposed. **Dining:** restaurant, see separate listing. **Pool(s):** heated outdoor. **Activities:** whirlpool, cross country skiing, hiking trails. *Fee:* horseback riding. **Free Special Amenities: room upgrade (subject to availability with advance reservations) and high-speed Internet.**

(See ad this page.)

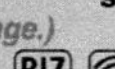    / SOME UNITS 

▼ See AAA listing p. 329 ▼

BRYCE VIEW LODGE **Phone:** (435)834-5180

Motel
$60-$110

Address: 991 S SR 63 84764 **Location:** 1 mi s of SR 12. **Facility:** 160 units. 2 stories (no elevator), exterior corridors. **Terms:** open 5/1-10/31 & 4/1-4/30, check-in 4 pm, cancellation fee imposed. **Activities:** fishing, hiking trails, jogging, playground, sports court, basketball. *Fee:* cross country skiing, bicycles, horseback riding. **Free Special Amenities: local telephone calls and high-speed Internet.** *(See ad p. 330.)*

  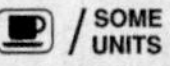  / SOME UNITS FEE  

WHERE TO EAT

BRYCE CANYON PINES RESTAURANT **Phone:** 435/834-5441

American
$4-$20

AAA Inspector Notes: This restaurant offers comfort food for hungry guests. Patrons unwind in a rustic setting with many antiques along the walls. The menu lists choices such as large cowboy steaks, fresh trout, chicken-fried steak and homemade pies. **Bar:** beer & wine. **Address:** 2476 W Hwy 12, MM 10 84764 **Location:** On SR 12, MM 10; next to Bryce Canyon Pines.

B L D

CANYON DINER **Phone:** 435/834-8030

Burgers
$4-$10

AAA Inspector Notes: Adjacent to the Best Western Plus Ruby's Inn, this place caters to on-the-go diners. Basic items, including burgers, nachos and personal pizzas, are served quickly. Everything here is self-service, making it an appealing place to grab a quick bite before or after a hike through the park. **Address:** 25 N Main St 84764 **Location:** On SR 63, 1 mi s of SR 12; 1 mi n of Bryce Canyon National Park entrance. B L D

FOSTER'S FAMILY STEAK HOUSE **Phone:** 435/834-5227

Steak
$6-$28

AAA Inspector Notes: This casual steak house serves fresh steaks, seafood and sandwiches. The western décor features wooden walls and booths along with wildlife art. The boneless grilled chicken is very moist. Desserts are made in the adjacent bakery. **Address:** 1150 Hwy 12 84759 **Location:** Jct SR 63, 1.7 mi w.

B L D

RUBY'S COWBOY'S BUFFET & STEAK HOUSE
Menu on AAA.com **Phone:** 435/834-5341

American
$7-$25

AAA Inspector Notes: Steak and seafood specialties are among the choices on the varied menu. Boxed lunches are favorite to-go orders. **Bar:** full bar. **Address:** 26 S Main St 84764 **Location:** On SR 63, 1 mi s of SR 12; in Best Western Plus Ruby's Inn. B L D

BRYCE CANYON NATIONAL PARK (F-3)

• Hotels p. 334

Elevations in the park range from 6,600 ft. at the bottom of the canyon to 9,120 ft. at Rainbow Point. Refer to AAA maps for additional elevation information.

Bryce Canyon National Park is 26 miles southeast of Panguitch via US 89 and SRs 12 and 63. The park includes some of Earth's most colorful rocks, which have been sculpted by erosion into pillars called "hoodoos," and other fantastic forms. Iron oxides give red, yellow and brown tints to the limestone, while manganese oxides lend a lavender hue.

The area's difficult topography led Mormon settler Ebenezer Bryce, whose cattle grazed in the maze-like twists of the canyons' stream beds, to declare it "a hell of a place to lose a cow." Bryce is not a true canyon but a series of horseshoe-shaped amphitheaters carved in the edge of the Paunsaugunt Plateau by tributaries of the Paria River. A Native American name for the area translates as "red rocks standing like men in a bowl-shaped canyon."

General Information and Activities

The park is open all year. The main geological features of the park are easily seen from numerous roadside viewing areas. **Note:** Visitors are advised to avoid using Cottonwood Road to access the park; the road is dangerous and inclement weather may further impair driving conditions. Visitors can take a 37-mile round-trip on a road that follows the high rim to many major vantage points, such as Bryce Point, Inspiration Point, the Natural Bridge, Paria View, Sunrise Point, Sunset Point, and Rainbow Point, at

the park's end. A free shuttle service with 13 designated stops is available throughout the park late May through September.

Hiking trails descend below the rim, affording close views of colorful formations. Horseback tours provide another way of seeing the park's geology up-close. The most brilliant hues in the park come alive with the rising and setting of the sun. Since the park is on an 8,000- to 9,000-foot plateau, hikers should allow for adjustment to the altitude. Camping is available in improved sites and backcountry areas throughout the park; for reservations phone the National Recreation Reservation System at (877) 444-6777, or TTY (877) 833-6777. *See Recreation Chart.*

ADMISSION is $25 (per private vehicle); $12 (per person arriving by other means). Generally, the above fees permit entrance to the park for 7 calendar days from date of purchase. An annual pass is $30. A backcountry permit, available at the visitor center, is $5. The camping fee is $15.

PETS are permitted in the park only if they are on a leash, crated or otherwise physically restricted at all times. Pets are not allowed on trails or viewpoints or in any of the public buildings.

ADDRESS inquiries to the Superintendent, Bryce Canyon National Park, P.O. Box 170001, Bryce

Canyon, UT 84717; phone (435) 834-5322. The superintendent's office is open Mon.-Fri. 8-4:30. To request an information packet write Bryce Canyon National Park, P.O. Box 640201, Bryce Canyon, UT 84764-0201.

BRYCE AMPHITHEATER is s. of the visitor center off Bryce Canyon National Park Rd. (SR 63). Within 3 miles of the park entrance, Bryce Amphitheater is a semicircular area of the canyon filled with the park's signature hoodoo limestone formations. Four overlooks offer some of the park's best views: Sunrise, Sunset, Inspiration and Bryce points. The Rim Trail follows the edge of the canyon, connecting all four overlooks.

BRYCE CANYON NATIONAL PARK VISITOR CENTER is at the park headquarters 1 mi. from the entrance off SR 63. The visitor center contains exhibits pertaining to the geology, biology, archeology and history of the region. Park rangers conduct free hikes and illustrated talks daily Memorial Day through Labor Day. A video presentation is offered every 30 minutes. **Hours:** Daily 8-8, May-Sept.; 8-6 in Apr. and Oct.; 8-4:30, rest of year. Closed Thanksgiving and Christmas. **Phone:** (435) 834-5322.

PARK ROAD is the portion of SR 63 stretching 18 mi. s. from the Bryce Canyon National Park entrance to Rainbow Point. Bryce's main access road runs along a forested plateau near the canyon's edge offering glimpses of the canyon. Drivers can reach 15 viewpoints along the way with either pullouts or parking lots. Since the overlooks are on the east side of the road, it is easier and safer to drive south first and then visit the overlooks on the return trip back to the park entrance.

RECREATIONAL ACTIVITIES

Horseback Riding

- **Canyon Trail Rides** departs from The Lodge at Bryce Canyon off SR 63. **Hours:** Two-hour and half-day trips are offered daily, Apr.-Oct. Departure times vary; phone ahead. **Phone:** (435) 679-8665 or (435) 834-5500.

THE LODGE AT BRYCE CANYON **Phone:** 435/834-8700

Address: Hwy 63 84764 **Location:** In Bryce Canyon National Park; at 8000 feet elevation. **Facility:** Built in 1924, the lodge is within walking distance of a rim overlook. Motel units with a balcony and duplex cabins with a fireplace are available. 114 units, some cabins. 1-2 stories (no elevator), interior/exterior corridors. **Terms:** open 5/1-11/10 & 4/1-4/30, check-in 4 pm, 3 day cancellation notice-fee imposed. **Dining:** 2 restaurants. **Activities:** hiking trails. *Fee:* horseback riding. **Guest Services:** coin laundry. **Free Special Amenities: high-speed Internet and use of on-premises laundry facilities.**

SAVE

CAINEVILLE

RODEWAY INN CAPITOL REEF **Phone:** (435)456-9900

Address: 25 E SR 24 84775 **Location:** West end of town. **Facility:** 16 units. 2 stories (no elevator), exterior corridors. **Pool(s):** heated outdoor. **Activities:** whirlpool. **Guest Services:** coin laundry. **Free Special Amenities: expanded continental breakfast and high-speed Internet.**

SAVE FEE / SOME UNITS FEE

CANNONVILLE (F-3) pop. 167, elev. 5,913'

At one time Cannonville was called Gunshot by its residents, who maintained that it was too small to qualify as a cannon.

Irrigation brings water to the farms and orchards surrounding this quiet hamlet on the Paria River. Bryce Canyon National Park *(see place listing p. 332)* is 12 miles northwest. Cannonville is one of several villages along SR 12, a particularly scenic route that connects Panguitch *(see place listing p. 385)* and Boulder *(see place listing p. 326)*.

KODACHROME BASIN STATE PARK is 9 mi. s.e. on Kodachrome Rd. The 4,000-acre park contains striking, unusual rock formations that change in color—depending on the time of day and weather conditions—from gray and white to various shades of red. About 10 miles beyond the park entrance via Cottonwood Wash, a dirt road, is Grosvenor Arch. *See Recreation Chart.*

Riding trails are available. **Hours:** Daily 6 a.m.-10 p.m. **Cost:** $6 (per private vehicle, maximum eight people). Annual pass $75. Camping $16. **Phone:** (435) 679-8562, (801) 322-3770, or (800) 322-3770 for camping reservations.

CANYONLANDS NATIONAL PARK (E-5)

Elevations in the park range from 3,720 ft. at Cataract Canyon to 6,987 ft. in the Needles District. Refer to AAA maps for additional elevation information.

In southeastern Utah, Canyonlands National Park encompasses deeply eroded canyons interspersed with sheer-sided mesas and a variety of spires, arches and unusual rock formations. The Green and Colorado rivers join and continue in a series of powerful rapids through the multicolored recesses of Cataract Canyon. The rivers' confluence divides the park into three districts reached by separate accesses.

To reach the entrance to the Island in the Sky District (the easiest district to reach), travel 9 miles north from Moab on US 191, then 26 miles south on SR 313. The entrance to the Needles District is 41 miles south of Moab on US 191, then 34 miles west on SR 211; the entrance to the Maze District is 46 miles from the SR 24 turnoff to the Hans Flat Ranger Station via a rough dirt road.

The northernmost district, Island in the Sky, is a huge, level mesa featuring Upheaval Dome and Grand View Point. Southeast of the rivers' junction lies the Needles District, where multicolored rock spires overshadow meadowlands and natural parks. The Maze District, a remote and rugged section at the western edge of the park, encompasses the Land of Standing Rocks, the Maze and Horseshoe Canyon. The Native American pictograph panels in this area are considered to be among the finest in North America.

General Information and Activities

Although much of the park is backcountry territory, Canyonlands provides paved roads to several of its most scenic areas. The entrance roads to the Needles and the Island in the Sky districts are fully paved, as are the park roads to Grand View Point and Upheaval Dome. The road to the Maze District is passable to high clearance two-wheel-drive vehicles in good weather conditions; most of the roads within the park are limited to high clearance four-wheel-drive vehicles. Water is not available in most areas.

The park has many opportunities for backcountry hiking and travel by four-wheel-drive vehicle, mountain bike, horse, canoe, kayak or white-water raft. Permits for overnight backcountry travel must be obtained at a ranger station, visitor center or by mail. River permits for any overnight canoe, kayak or white-water excursions must be obtained from the national park office in Moab or by mail at least 2 weeks in advance. Phone (435) 259-4351 for information about land- or water-based tours. Local tour services provide a variety of guided jeep, air and river tours. Many of these services operate out of Green River *(see place listing p. 350)*, and Moab *(see place listing p. 365)*.

Visitor centers in the Island in the Sky and Needles districts distribute brochures, information and maps daily 9-4:30. The Hans Flat Ranger Station in the Maze District is open daily 8-4:30. All three visitor centers have extended hours March through October and are closed on some federal holidays. Guided walks and evening programs are available during the summer. *See Recreation Chart.*

ADMISSION is $10 (per private vehicle); $5 (per person arriving by other means). Generally, the above fees permit entrance to the park for 7 calendar days from date of purchase. Annual local passes are available for $25 (per private vehicle) and permit entrance into Canyonlands and Arches *(see place listing p. 321)* national parks as well as Natural Bridges *(see place listing p. 380)* and Hovenweep *(see place listing in Colorado p. 227)* national monuments. Backcountry camping fees are $10-$15.

PETS are permitted only if on a leash, crated or otherwise physically restricted at all times. Pets are not allowed in the backcountry, on trails, or in or on rivers within the park.

ADDRESS inquiries to the Superintendent, Canyonlands National Park, 2282 S.W. Resource Blvd., Moab, UT 84532-8000; phone (435) 719-2313.

ISLAND IN THE SKY VISITOR CENTER, 22 mi. s.w. of jct. US 191 and SR 313, offers exhibits and brochures about Canyonlands National Park. An orientation video also is available. From March through October, rangers highlight the area's features through various interpretive programs. **Hours:** Visitor center daily 9-4:30, with extended hours some days. Closed major holidays. Phone ahead to confirm schedule. **Cost:** Visitor center free. **Phone:** (435) 259-4712.

CAPITOL REEF NATIONAL PARK (E-4)

Elevations in the park range from 4,000 ft. near Halls Creek to 9,000 ft. at Thousand Lake Mountain. Refer to AAA maps for additional elevation information.

Five miles east of Torrey on SR 24, Capitol Reef National Park was named for reef-like cliffs capped by white Navajo sandstone formations that have eroded and now resemble the dome of the U.S. Capitol. The park contains a spectacular section of the Waterpocket Fold. The fold extends some 100 miles southeastward from Thousand Lake Mountain to Lake Powell and graphically illustrates the way the Earth's surface was built, folded and eroded. Numerous eroded basins or "pockets" can hold critical rainwater necessary to maintain desert life—hence the term "waterpocket fold."

Near the visitor center, brightly colored tiered cliffs rise 1,000 feet above the Fremont River. Pre-Columbian Indian petroglyphs can be seen on the surrounding canyon walls. Amid Capitol Reef's red rock are orchards where fruit may be picked in season. Visitors also can see the remains of Fruita, an early Mormon pioneer settlement.

General Information and Activities

The park is open daily 24 hours; services are reduced in winter. Many hiking trails and drives provide scenic views of the park; a backcountry use permit is required for overnight trips. A trail near the campground leads to Cohab Canyon, where another trail continues to the canyon rim. A nature trail along SR 24 about 2 miles east of the visitor center goes to Hickman Natural Bridge. A scenic drive to Capitol Gorge leaves SR 24 at the visitor center. The Ripple Rock Nature Center, just south of the visitor center, is open Tues.-Sat. noon-5, Memorial Day-June 30; Tues.-Sat. 10-3, July 1-Labor Day. *See Recreation Chart.*

ADMISSION to the park is free. Admission to the Capitol Gorge scenic drive is $5 (per private vehicle or motorcycle); $3 (per person arriving by other means). The above fees permit entrance for 7 calendar days from date of purchase. The camping fee is $10.

PETS are not permitted on park trails; they are allowed in specific areas only if on a leash, crated or otherwise physically restricted at all times.

ADDRESS inquiries to the Superintendent, Capitol Reef National Park, HC 70, Box 15, Torrey, UT 84775; phone (435) 425-3791.

GIFFORD HOMESTEAD MUSEUM is in Capitol Reef National Park, 1 mi. s. of the visitor center on SR 24. The homestead features a renovated farmhouse, barn, smokehouse, garden and pasture. The site depicts the lifestyle of early 20th-century Mormon settlers in the Fruita Valley. Antiques on display include a spinning wheel, treadle sewing machine, Hoosier cupboard and Monarch cookstove. **Time:** Allow 45 minutes minimum. **Hours:** Daily 8-5, Mar.-Oct. Phone ahead to confirm schedule. **Cost:** Donations. **Phone:** (435) 425-3791.

VISITOR CENTER is 6 mi. from Capitol Reef National Park's western entrance on SR 24 at the park's north end. The visitor center offers exhibits about the park's geology and history as well as an orientation program. **Hours:** Daily 8-6, Memorial Day-Labor Day; 8-4:30, rest of year. Closed Jan. 1, Thanksgiving and Christmas. **Phone:** (435) 425-3791, ext. 4111.

RECREATIONAL ACTIVITIES

Horseback Riding

- **Hondoo Rivers & Trails** departs from 90 E. Main St. Other activities are offered. **Hours:** Trips are offered daily with advance reservations. **Phone:** (435) 425-3519 or (800) 332-2696.

CASTLE DALE (D-4) pop. 1,630, elev. 5,771'

The pinnacles and spires of the San Rafael Swell south of Castle Dale were the site of Robbers Roost, the hideout from which Butch Cassidy and other outlaws launched their holdups and rustling activities. The town was settled in 1875 by Orange Seely, a cattleman who gave medical attention to other settlers and was known for weighing more than 300 pounds.

Although the lowlands around Castle Dale eventually became a prosperous farming region, Mrs. Seely allegedly said, "The first time I ever swore was when we arrived ... and I said, 'Damn a man who would bring a woman to such a Godforsaken country.'"

No longer forsaken, the Castle Dale area became industrialized with the building of a Utah Power and Light plant and the development of many coal-mining operations.

MUSEUM OF THE SAN RAFAEL, 64 North 100 East, has artifacts found in Emery County's caves and rock ledges. Visitors can see dinosaur skeletons, a replica of a fossilized dinosaur egg and rocks from throughout Utah. Also displayed are mounted animals depicted in their natural habitat and such Native American artifacts as the Sitterud Bundle, a knapsack dating from 1250 that was used to hold berries, knives and tools. **Time:** Allow 1 hour minimum. **Hours:** Mon.-Fri. 10-4, Sat. 10-2. Closed major holidays. **Cost:** Donations. **Phone:** (435) 381-5252.

PIONEER MUSEUM is in the city hall at 64 East 100 North. The museum includes pioneer artifacts as well as re-creations of a pioneer law office, schoolroom and general store. Changing exhibits feature historical items loaned by local residents. **Time:** Allow 30 minutes minimum. **Hours:** Tues.-Fri. 10-4, second and fourth Sat. noon-2. Closed Jan. 1, Thanksgiving and Christmas. Phone ahead to confirm schedule. **Cost:** Donations. **Phone:** (435) 381-5154.

GEM CEDAR BREAKS NATIONAL MONUMENT (F-2)

Cedar Breaks National Monument is off SR 14 between Bryce Canyon National Park *(see place listing p. 332)* and Cedar City *(see place listing)*. The park encompasses a 5-mile-wide natural limestone amphitheater eroded to a depth of nearly 2,500 feet. Settlers mistook the junipers at the base of the rock layers for cedars, thus coining the name.

Below the amphitheater's 10,000-foot rim the slopes fall sharply away in ragged walls, spires, columns and arches tinted shades of red, yellow and purple by the manganese and iron oxides in the rock. Bristlecone pines, among the oldest plants on Earth, cling to the windswept ridges above the rim. Hiking trails can be found around the rim.

In summer the meadows and slopes are resplendent wildflower gardens. The area also is a wildlife habitat; mule deer often can be seen grazing in the meadows in the early morning or evening. A self-guiding trail leads from the Chessman Meadow parking area to Alpine Pond, a good spot to take in the view. Guided tours of Spectra Point Trail depart from the trailhead Saturday and Sunday afternoons (phone ahead for tour times); guided tours of Alpine Pond Trail depart from the trailhead Saturdays and Sundays at 10.

A visitor center 1 mile from the south entrance is open daily 9-6, late May to mid-Oct. Camping and picnic facilities are near Point Supreme. The high season is early June-late Oct. (weather permitting). The road may be closed due to snow, rest of year; phone (435) 586-9451 to check conditions.

Admission late May to mid-October is $4 (per person arriving by car, motorcycle, bicycle or foot); free (ages 0-16). Admission rest of year is free. Generally, the above fees permit entrance to the park for 7 calendar days from date of purchase.

For further information contact the Superintendent, Cedar Breaks National Monument, 2390 W. SR 56, Suite 11, Cedar City, UT 84720-4151; phone (435) 586-0787.

CEDAR CITY (F-2) pop. 28,857, elev. 5,840'

• Hotels p. 338 • Restaurants p. 339

An abundance of iron ore west of the site of Cedar City induced English, Scottish and Welsh Mormon converts, who were skilled miners, to settle the area. But floods, harsh winters, poor harvests and cheap iron transported by the transcontinental railroad closed the mines, so most of the settlers turned to raising livestock. Since 1920 tourists have been attracted by the town's proximity to scenic areas, making it a prosperous community.

Cedar City-Brian Head Tourism & Convention Bureau: 581 N. Main St., Suite A, Cedar City, UT 84720. **Phone:** (435) 586-5124 or (800) 354-4849. ***(See ad this page.)***

BRAITHWAITE FINE ARTS GALLERY is on the Southern Utah University campus at 351 W. Center St. The gallery presents changing exhibitions of works by state and national artists. The gallery's permanent collection consists of 19th-century and contemporary paintings. Pottery and textile objects also are displayed. **Time:** Allow 30 minutes minimum. **Hours:** Mon.-Sat. 11-8, June-Aug.; Tues.-Sat. noon-7, rest of year. Closed major holidays and between monthly exhibits. **Cost:** Free. **Phone:** (435) 586-5432.

FRONTIER HOMESTEAD STATE PARK MUSEUM is n.w. of Coal Creek Bridge on SR 91 at 635 N. Main St. The first iron foundry west of the Mississippi River was begun here in 1851 by a group of Mormons who answered Brigham Young's call to settle the area and process its extensive iron deposits. A diorama based on descriptions of the foundry; a collection of horse-drawn vehicles such as stagecoaches, surreys and sleighs; and a display of farm machinery can be seen.

The horse-drawn vehicle collection also includes a Stanhope Phaeton and a Studebaker White Top Wagon. One of the stagecoaches, from Utah's Four Corners region, dates from the Butch Cassidy era and is scarred by bullets. **Hours:** Mon.-Sat. 9-5. Closed Jan. 1, Thanksgiving and Christmas. **Cost:** $3. Annual pass $75. **Phone:** (435) 586-9290.

GEM **UTAH SHAKESPEARE FESTIVAL,** held on the Southern Utah University campus off I-15, presents three Shakespearean plays in rotation in the Adams Shakespearean Theatre, a near replica of London, England's, open-air Globe Theatre, and the works of at least three noted playwrights, also in rotation, in the Randall L. Jones Theater. Evening performances are preceded by a complimentary Greenshow featuring Elizabethan music, dance of Merrie Olde England, juggling, magic or storytelling. Offerings in 2012 include "The Merrie Wives of Windsor," "Titus Andronicus" and "Hamlet."

Day-care services are available on the festival grounds. **Hours:** Performances Mon.-Sat., June 21-Oct. 20. Evening performances start at 8 p.m. following the 7 p.m. pre-performance Greenshow entertainment held mid-June through Sept. 1. Matinees begin at 2 p.m. Evening performances after Sept. 1 start at 7:30 p.m. Backstage tours are given Tues.-Wed. and Fri.-Sat. at 10:15, July-Aug.; Thurs. and Sat. at 11, late Sept.- late Oct. **Cost:** Tickets \$22-\$71. Gallery seats \$16-\$20 (available after 10 a.m. on day of performance). Backstage tour \$8. Under 6 are not permitted at performances. Reservations are recommended. **Phone:** (435) 586-7878 or (800) 752-9849. *(See ad p. 337.)*

ABBEY INN OF CEDAR CITY **Phone:** (435)586-9966

Motel
\$76-\$129

Address: 940 W 200 N 84720 **Location:** I-15 exit 59, just e. **Facility:** 83 units, some two bedrooms and kitchens. 2 stories, exterior corridors. **Terms:** cancellation fee imposed. **Amenities:** high-speed Internet. **Pool(s):** heated indoor. **Activities:** whirlpool, exercise room. **Guest Services:** valet and coin laundry. **Free Special Amenities: full breakfast and high-speed Internet.**
(See ad this page.)

SAVE BIZ

AMERICAS BEST VALUE INN **Phone:** (435)867-4700

Motel
\$43-\$95

Address: 333 N 1100 W 84720 **Location:** I-15 exit 59, just e. **Facility:** 50 units. 2 stories (no elevator), interior corridors. **Terms:** cancellation fee imposed. **Pool(s):** heated outdoor. **Activities:** whirlpool. **Guest Services:** coin laundry, area transportation-Utah Shakespeare Festival.

/ SOME UNITS FEE

BEST WESTERN EL REY INN & SUITES
Phone: (435)586-6518

Hotel
\$60-\$100

AAA Benefit: Members save up to 20%, plus 10% bonus points with Best Western Rewards®.

Address: 80 S Main St 84720 **Location:** I-15 exit 57, 2 mi n; center. **Facility:** 70 units, some two bedrooms. 2 stories (no elevator), exterior corridors. **Parking:** winter plug-ins. **Pool(s):** heated outdoor. **Activities:** sauna, whirlpool, exercise room. **Guest Services:** area transportation-within 5 mi. **Free Special Amenities: local telephone calls and high-speed Internet.**

SAVE BIZ

/ SOME UNITS FEE

BEST WESTERN TOWN & COUNTRY INN
Phone: (435)586-9900

Hotel
\$79-\$149

AAA Benefit: Members save up to 20%, plus 10% bonus points with Best Western Rewards®.

Address: 189 N Main St 84720 **Location:** I-15 exit 59. **Facility:** 156 units, some two bedrooms. 2 stories (no elevator), interior/exterior corridors. **Dining:** 2 restaurants. **Pool(s):** heated outdoor, heated indoor. **Activities:** whirlpools. **Guest Services:** coin laundry. **Free Special Amenities: full breakfast and high-speed Internet.**

SAVE ECO FEE BIZ

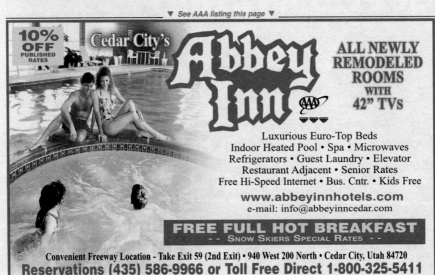

THE BIG YELLOW INN **Phone:** (435)586-0960

Bed & Breakfast
\$99-\$199

Address: 234 S 300 W 84720 **Location:** Jct Main St, 0.6 mi n; downtown. **Facility:** This Georgian revival home, located a block from the Shakespeare festival, features a grand staircase, eight fireplaces, sitting rooms and balconies. 11 units. 4 stories (no elevator), interior corridors. **Terms:** age restrictions may apply, 14 day cancellation notice-fee imposed. BIZ / SOME UNITS

▼ *See AAA listing this page* ▼

COMFORT INN & SUITES **Phone:** (435)865-0003

Hotel
$79-$169

Address: 1288 S Main St 84720 **Location:** I-15 exit 57, just e, then just n. **Facility:** 85 units, some two bedrooms. 3 stories, interior corridors. **Terms:** cancellation fee imposed. **Amenities:** high-speed Internet, safes (fee). **Pool(s):** heated indoor. **Activities:** whirlpool, exercise room. *Fee:* massage. **Guest Services:** valet and coin laundry.

CALL BIZ / SOME UNITS FEE

CRYSTAL INN CEDAR CITY **Phone:** (435)586-8888

Hotel
$69-$119

Address: 1575 W 200 N 84720 **Location:** I-15 exit 59, just w. **Facility:** 100 units. 2 stories (no elevator), interior/exterior corridors. **Dining:** Bard's Food and Drink Establishment & Oddfellows Pub, see separate listing. **Pool(s):** heated outdoor. **Activities:** sauna, whirlpool, exercise room. **Guest Services:** valet and coin laundry, area transportation-Utah Shakespeare Festival.
(See ad p. 408.)

BIZ / SOME UNITS FEE

DAYS INN **Phone:** (435)867-8877

Motel
$45-$111

Address: 1204 S Main St 84720 **Location:** I-15 exit 57, 0.4 mi ne. **Facility:** 71 units. 2 stories (no elevator), exterior corridors. **Terms:** 3 night minimum stay - seasonal, cancellation fee imposed. **Pool(s):** heated indoor. **Activities:** whirlpool. **Guest Services:** coin laundry. **Free Special Amenities: continental breakfast and high-speed Internet.**

SAVE / SOME UNITS FEE

HAMPTON INN CEDAR CITY **Phone:** (435)586-5000

Hotel
$79-$99

AAA Benefit:
Members save up to 10% everyday!

Address: 1145 S Bentley Blvd 84720 **Location:** I-15 exit 57, just w of off-ramp via Cross Hollow and Royal Hunt. **Facility:** 58 units. 3 stories, interior corridors. **Terms:** 1-7 night minimum stay, cancellation fee imposed. **Amenities:** video games (fee), high-speed Internet. **Pool(s):** heated indoor. **Activities:** exercise room. **Guest Services:** valet and coin laundry.

BIZ FEE / SOME UNITS

HOLIDAY INN EXPRESS HOTEL & SUITES
Phone: (435)865-7799

Hotel
$99-$139 5/1-8/31
$89-$129 9/1-4/30

Address: 1555 S Old Hwy 91 84720 **Location:** I-15 exit 57, just e, then s. **Facility:** 80 units. 3 stories, interior corridors. **Terms:** cancellation fee imposed. **Amenities:** high-speed Internet. **Pool(s):** heated indoor. **Activities:** whirlpool, exercise room. **Guest Services:** valet and coin laundry.

CALL BIZ / SOME UNITS FEE

KNIGHTS INN **Phone:** (435)586-9916

Motel
$45-$90

Address: 281 S Main St 84720 **Location:** I-15 exit 57, just e. **Facility:** 47 units, some two bedrooms. 2 stories (no elevator), exterior corridors. **Terms:** cancellation fee imposed. **Pool(s):** heated outdoor. **Activities:** sauna. **Guest Services:** coin laundry.

MOTEL 6 OF CEDAR CITY - 4041 **Phone:** 435/586-9200

Motel
Rates not provided

Address: 1620 W 200 N 84720 **Location:** I-15 exit 59, just w. **Facility:** 79 units. 3 stories, interior corridors. **Guest Services:** coin laundry.

CALL / SOME UNITS

QUALITY INN **Phone:** (435)586-2082

Motel
$59-$129

Address: 250 N 1100 W 84720 **Location:** I-15 exit 59, just e. **Facility:** 88 units, some efficiencies. 2 stories (no elevator), exterior corridors. **Terms:** 7 day cancellation notice-fee imposed. **Pool(s):** heated indoor. **Activities:** whirlpool. **Guest Services:** coin laundry, area transportation-Utah Shakespeare Festival.

/ SOME UNITS FEE

SPRINGHILL SUITES BY MARRIOTT CEDAR CITY
Phone: (435)586-1685

Hotel
$99-$169

AAA Benefit:
AAA hotel discounts of 5% or more.

Address: 1477 S Old Hwy 91 84720 **Location:** I-15 exit 57, just e, then just s. **Facility:** 72 units. 3 stories, interior corridors. **Amenities:** high-speed Internet. **Pool(s):** heated indoor. **Activities:** whirlpool, exercise room. **Guest Services:** valet and coin laundry.

BIZ

STRATFORD COURT HOTEL **Phone:** (435)586-2433

Motel
$69-$139

Address: 18 S Main St 84720 **Location:** I-15 exit 57, 2 mi n; center. **Facility:** 50 units. 3 stories (no elevator), interior corridors. **Pool(s):** heated outdoor. **Activities:** whirlpool. **Guest Services:** valet and coin laundry, area transportation-within 5 mi. **Free Special Amenities: full breakfast and high-speed Internet.**

SAVE BIZ

SUPER 8 **Phone:** (435)586-8880

Motel
$43-$85

Address: 145 N 1550 W 84720 **Location:** I-15 exit 59, just w. **Facility:** 53 units. 3 stories, interior corridors. **Guest Services:** coin laundry.

CALL BIZ / SOME UNITS FEE

WILLOW GLEN INN **Phone:** (435)586-3275

Bed & Breakfast
$79-$225

Address: 3308 N Bulldog Rd 84720 **Location:** I-15 exit 62, 1.5 mi sw via 3000 N. **Facility:** 9 units, some two bedrooms, three bedrooms and efficiencies. 1-2 stories (no elevator), exterior corridors. **Terms:** 5 day cancellation notice-fee imposed.

WHERE TO EAT

BARD'S FOOD AND DRINK ESTABLISHMENT & ODDFELLOWS PUB **Phone:** 435/865-7645

English
$7-$20

AAA Inspector Notes: This casually upscale spot is nicely decorated with rustic colors, inlaid rock columns, heavy ceiling beams and warm, woodsy décor. Examples of the pub's English-style cuisine include scones, fish and chips, and liver and onions. **Bar:** full bar. **Address:** 1575 W 200 N 84720 **Location:** I-15 exit 59, just w; in Crystal Inn Cedar City. L D

THE GARDEN HOUSE OF CEDAR CITY

Phone: 435/586-6110

American
$10-$23

AAA Inspector Notes: The charming, two-story Victorian-style home serves upscale American cuisine. This is a great place for a romantic date. **Address:** 164 S 100 W 84720 **Location:** I-15 exit 59, 1 mi e to 100 W, then just s. **Parking:** on-site and street. L D

LA CASA DON MIGUEL **Phone:** 435/586-6855

Mexican
$6-$15

AAA Inspector Notes: This small, basic and cramped restaurant serves authentic Mexican cuisine with great flavor. The owner serves the tables herself with only one back server, so it can take awhile for dishes to arrive. The line sometimes winds out the door, so it's wise to show up early. **Bar:** full bar. **Address:** 453 S Main St 84720 **Location:** Center. L D

LA FIESTA **Phone:** 435/586-4646

Mexican
$6-$15

AAA Inspector Notes: Colorful tropical décor incorporating birds, flowers, monkeys and a large collection of masks lends character to the setting, where guests sit down to delicious homemade cuisine. **Bar:** full bar. **Address:** 890 N Main St 84720 **Location:** I-15 exit 62 eastbound, 2 mi s via Main St, then just n of Center St.

L D

LEFTY'S HIDEOUT MEXICAN RESTAURANT

Phone: 435/586-4741

Mexican
$6-$13

AAA Inspector Notes: The friendly staff at this casual and small restaurant serves Mexican favorites. The salsa and guacamole are both made in house. **Address:** 2107 N Main St 84720 **Location:** I-15 exit 62, 1 mi sw. L D

MAIN STREET GRILL **Phone:** 435/586-8389

Breakfast
$6-$8

AAA Inspector Notes: Families sit down together for home-style breakfast and lunch dishes in this relaxed and friendly spot. The locally owned restaurant has a great location. **Address:** 155 N Main St 84720 **Location:** Downtown. **Parking:** on-site and street.

B L

MARKET GRILL **Phone:** 435/586-9325

American
$6-$17

AAA Inspector Notes: A well-rounded menu is presented in an Old West setting. The cordial staff adds to the enjoyable dining experience. **Address:** 2290 W 400 N 84720 **Location:** I-15 exit 59, 0.5 mi w.

B L D

NINJA JAPANESE STEAKHOUSE & SUSHI

Phone: 435/867-5577

Japanese
$14-$38

AAA Inspector Notes: In a small shopping center, the restaurant lets guests enjoy Japanese favorites right at the hibachi grills, at regular tables and even at the sushi bar. The décor is fun and contemporary. **Bar:** beer & wine. **Address:** 1180 S Sage Dr, Unit A 84720 **Location:** I-15 exit 57, just w via Cross Hollow Rd and Royal Hunt Dr.

L D

THE PASTRY PUB **Phone:** 435/867-1400

American
$4-$9

AAA Inspector Notes: A younger crowd frequent this pub, where diners can choose from bistro tables on the sidewalk, seats on the seasonal patio or spots in the spacious dining room. Specialty drinks, house-brewed tea and coffee complement salads, sandwiches, wraps and croissants. **Address:** 86 W Center St 84720 **Location:** Downtown. B L

RUSTY'S RANCH HOUSE **Phone:** 435/586-3839

American
$12-$22

AAA Inspector Notes: Not far from Main Street, the restaurant is surrounded by beautiful mountain scenery. American dishes are served in a rustic ranch house setting. **Bar:** full bar. **Address:** 2275 E Hwy 14 84720 **Location:** Jct Main St, 1.5 mi e. D

SONNY BOY'S BARBECUE **Phone:** 435/867-8010

Barbecue
$5-$10

AAA Inspector Notes: Ribs smoking on the large grill in the parking lot draw guests off the street. Patrons also can enjoy fresh chicken and pulled pork. A special is offered daily, and the owner smokes and cuts the meat for everyone to see. This kind of great barbecue is a rare find in this part of the country. **Address:** 126 N Main St 84720 **Location:** Center. **Parking:** on-site and street.

L D

CIRCLEVILLE pop. 547

BUTCH CASSIDY'S HIDEOUT **Phone:** 435/577-2008

Motel
Rates not provided

Address: 339 S Hwy 89 84723 **Location:** Just s of center. **Facility:** 11 units. 1 story, exterior corridors.

CLEVELAND (D-4) pop. 464, elev. 5,735'

CLEVELAND-LLOYD DINOSAUR QUARRY is 14 mi. s. following signs. Some 12,000 bones representing at least 70 different animals have been recovered from the quarry, which provides bones and complete skeletons to museums throughout the world. The exact reason why the dinosaurs perished here has not been determined. About two-thirds of the bones are from the large carnivore allosaurus. The quarry has a visitor center as well as a nature trail and two hiking trails.

The road to the quarry is graded and unpaved and may be hazardous when wet. Pets on a leash are permitted on trails. **Hours:** Mon.-Sat. 10-5, Sun. noon-5, Memorial Day-Labor Day; Fri.-Sat. 10-5, Sun. noon-5, mid-Mar. through day before Memorial Day and day after Labor Day-late Oct. Phone ahead to confirm schedule. **Cost:** $5; free (ages 0-15). **Phone:** (435) 636-3600.

COALVILLE pop. 1,363

BEST WESTERN HOLIDAY HILLS

Phone: (435)336-4444

Hotel
$80-$90

AAA Benefit: Members save up to 20%, plus 10% bonus points with Best Western Rewards®.

Address: 200 S 500 W 84017 **Location:** I-80 exit 162, just w. **Facility:** 60 units. 3 stories, interior corridors. **Amenities:** high-speed Internet. **Pool(s):** heated indoor. **Activities:** whirlpool, hiking trails, jogging, exercise room. **Guest Services:** coin laundry. **Free Special Amenities: expanded continental breakfast and high-speed Internet.**

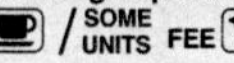

/ SOME UNITS FEE

COTTONWOOD HEIGHTS pop. 33,433

- **Hotels & Restaurants map & index p. 426**
- **Part of Salt Lake City area — see map p. 412**

CANDLEWOOD SUITES FORT UNION

Phone: 801/567-0111 54

Extended Stay Hotel
Rates not provided

Address: 6990 S Park Centre Dr 84121 **Location:** I-15 exit 297 (7200 S), 2.6 mi e to Park Centre Dr, then just s. **Facility:** 98 efficiencies. 3 stories, interior corridors. **Amenities:** high-speed Internet. **Activities:** exercise room. **Guest Services:** complimentary and valet laundry. / SOME UNITS FEE

WHERE TO EAT

CAFE TRIO COTTONWOOD

Phone: 801/944-8746 47

Italian
$8-$24

AAA Inspector Notes: This spacious neighborhood restaurant offers a seasonally changing, eclectic menu of simple, fresh Italian cuisine served in a smart and warm contemporary setting. The menu is complemented by a great wine list, decadent desserts such as bittersweet chocolate pudding and Toll House pie, scrumptious sweet martinis and great, personalized service. **Bar:** full bar. **Address:** 6405 S 3000 E 84121 **Location:** I-215 exit 6 (6200 S), 0.3 mi e, then just s. L D

MARKET STREET GRILL COTTONWOOD

Phone: 801/942-8860 48

Seafood
$11-$37

AAA Inspector Notes: The menu comprises fresh seafood, certified Angus beef, poultry, lamb and pasta dishes. Patio seating is offered seasonally. **Bar:** full bar. **Address:** 2985 E Cottonwood Pkwy 84121 **Location:** I-215 exit 6 (6200 S), 0.8 mi se. L D

PISTOL PETE'S **Phone:** 801/944-1833 50

Tex-Mex
$8-$17

AAA Inspector Notes: This restaurant serves up crowd-pleasers such as their special mesa beans, fajitas, seafood tacos, enchiladas, combination plates, kids meals and healthy salads with an excellent variety of mixed greens, not to mention great chips and salsa. **Address:** 2477 E Fort Union Blvd 84121 **Location:** I-15 exit 297 (7200 S), 4 mi e via 7200 S and E Fort Union Blvd. L D

PORCUPINE PUB & GRILLE

Phone: 801/942-5555 51

American
$8-$24

AAA Inspector Notes: Themed dinner specials are served on holidays, with a special emphasis on St. Patrick's Day and Oktoberfest. From November through May, skiers race to their tables for the much-talked-about hot chicken soup for the soul. Salad specials rotate Monday through Friday. Made-in-house desserts include Toll House pie and peanut butter cheesecake, but the chocolate porcupine served with vanilla bean ice cream is a treat above all others. **Bar:** full bar. **Address:** 3698 E Fort Union Blvd 84121 **Location:** I-215 exit 6 (6200 S), 2 mi se. L D

PRIMO RESTAURANT **Phone:** 801/947-0025 49

Northern Italian
$15-$36

AAA Inspector Notes: Attractively framed reproduction pieces adorn the walls of this charming restaurant. Service is attentive and gracious. The steamed clams and cold antipasto plate with melon and prosciutto are popular appetizers, while entrée selections may feature filet mignon garnished with asparagus, clams, shrimp and lobster over linguine, and several chicken and veal dishes. Regulars stop in for wine and homemade desserts such as sabayon with fresh berries, tiramisu, crème brûlée or German chocolate cake. **Bar:** full bar. **Address:** 2350 W 7000 S 84047 **Location:** I-15 exit 297 (7200 S), 2.8 mi w on 7200 S (becomes 7000 S), then just n; in shopping plaza. D

COVE FORT (E-2) elev. 5,998'

COVE FORT HISTORIC SITE is 1 mi. n. off I-70 exit 1, or 2 mi. s off I-15 exit 135. This volcanic rock and limestone fort served as a way station for settlers and travelers in the late 1800s and as a pickup and delivery site for the Pony Express. Period furnishings and artifacts are displayed throughout the restored 12-room fort. **Tours:** Guided tours are available. **Time:** Allow 30 minutes minimum. **Hours:** Daily 8-dusk, Apr.-Oct.; 9-dusk, rest of year. **Cost:** Free. **Phone:** (435) 438-5547.

DELTA (D-2) pop. 3,436, elev. 4,635'

GREAT BASIN MUSEUM is 1 blk. n. of US 6/50 at 328 West 100 North. The museum features exhibits about area history, including mining and pioneer artifacts, photographs, documents and a collection of beryllium. Arrowheads, minerals and fossils also are displayed, as is an exhibit about the Topaz Relocation Center, an internment camp for Japanese Americans during World War II.

Note: At press time, the museum at 328 West 100 North was open; however, a new facility being built on Main Street was scheduled to open sometime in 2012. Phone ahead for updates and to confirm the museum's location and hours. **Time:** Allow 30 minutes minimum. **Hours:** Mon.-Sat. 10-5, mid-Mar. to mid-Nov. Winter hours vary. **Cost:** Donations. **Phone:** (435) 864-5013.

DAYS INN **Phone:** (435)864-3882

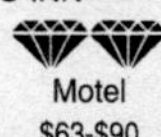

Motel
$63-$90

Address: 527 E Topaz Blvd 84624 **Location:** Jct US 6 and 50. **Facility:** 82 units. 2 stories (no elevator), exterior corridors. **Amenities:** *Some:* high-speed Internet. **Pool(s):** heated outdoor. **Guest Services:** coin laundry.

BIZ / SOME UNITS FEE

DINOSAUR NATIONAL MONUMENT (B-5)

Dinosaur National Monument's Utah section is reached via SR 149, which joins US 40 at Jensen. One of the world's largest concentrations of fossilized dinosaur bones is found in the park, which encompasses about 325 square miles in Utah and Colorado. Fossilized bones of allosaurs and other prehistoric creatures have been revealed in a single sandstone cliff. Several of the region's exhumed skeletons are exhibited in the Carnegie Museum of Natural History in Pittsburgh.

Among the exceptional natural features of the national monument are deep, narrow gorges with strangely carved and delicately tinted sheer sandstone cliffs along the Green and Yampa rivers. The Canyon of Lodore, cut by the Green River, ranges from 1,000 to 3,300 feet deep.

More than 1,500 fossilized bones are on display at the Quarry Exhibit Hall just north of Jensen; shuttles to the cliff face run from the Quarry Visitor Center *(see attraction listing)*. Located a half a mile away from the quarry, the visitor center offers exhibits as well as information about recreational activities and ranger-led interpretive programs. A mostly paved 10-mile road that begins nearby leads to petroglyph panels, overlooks and a historic cabin. Several established hiking trails, including Sound of Silence, Desert Voices and Hog Canyon, are accessed from this road.

From the Canyon Area Visitor Center in Dinosaur, Colo., a 31-mile paved road leads north into the heart of the canyon country. There are no fossil bones in this section, but scenic overlooks and a 2-mile-long trail at Harpers Corner provide spectacular views of the Green and Yampa rivers and their confluence at Steamboat Rock 2,500 feet below.

One- to 5-day river trips through the monument can be arranged by contacting private companies mid-May to mid-September. Camping, hiking and fishing are available within the monument.

Admission is $10 (per private vehicle); $5 (per person arriving by other means). Camping fees are $8-$25. Backcountry camping is free with permit. For further information contact the Superintendent, Dinosaur National Monument, 4545 US 40, Dinosaur, CO 81610-9724; phone (435) 781-7700. *See Recreation Chart.*

CANYON AREA VISITOR CENTER is at jct. Harpers Corner Rd. and US 40, 2 mi. e. of Dinosaur, Colo. The center offers exhibits about the area's canyon country and an audiovisual program. **Time:** Allow 30 minutes minimum. **Hours:** Daily 8:30-4:30, May 1-early Sept.; Wed.-Sun. 8:30-4:30, early Sept.-early Oct. Closed major holidays. Phone ahead to confirm schedule. **Cost:** Free. **Phone:** (970) 374-3000.

QUARRY VISITOR CENTER, 7 mi. n. of Jensen on SR 149, serves as the gateway to the Quarry Exhibit Hall, which showcases more than 1,500 dinosaur bones embedded in rock. Shuttles departing from the visitor center offer access to the cliff face. Displays at the visitor center illustrate the park's geological and cultural history as well as the nature of the dinosaurs that once roamed the area. An auditorium features educational films.

Time: Allow 1 hour minimum. **Hours:** Visitor center open daily 9-5. Last trip to the Quarry Exhibit Hall is at 4:15. Closed Jan. 1, Thanksgiving, Christmas and day after Christmas. Phone ahead to confirm schedule. **Cost:** Free. **Phone:** (435) 781-7700.

DIXIE NATIONAL FOREST (F-3)

Elevations in the forest range from 2,800 ft. near the town of St. George to 11,310 ft. at Brian Head Peak on Cedar Mountain. Refer to AAA maps for additional elevation information.

In southwestern Utah, Dixie National Forest's warm climate reminded early Mormon settlers of the Deep South, thus its name. The forest, which is the largest in the state, covers approximately 1,700,000 acres. The state's largest trees—predominantly ponderosa pine and spruce—grow in the forest. Bryce Canyon *(see place listing p. 332)*, Capitol Reef *(see place listing p. 335)* and Zion *(see place listing p. 461)* national parks and Cedar Breaks *(see place listing p. 336)* and Grand Staircase-Escalante *(see place listing p. 349)* national monuments are all adjacent to or within the forest.

The Markagunt Plateau, about 9 miles southeast of Cedar City via SR 14, offers many recreational facilities. A fish hatchery west of Hatch raises the fish stocked in the streams and lakes; rainbow trout predominate. Duck Creek Recreation Area has a pond stocked several times yearly. Spring-fed Navajo Lake has outlets in Cascade Falls and Duck Creek, and Panguitch Lake offers excellent fishing. Boat rentals, cabins and camping facilities are available late May to early October.

Brian Head Peak, Strawberry Point and Zion Overlook provide scenic views. Bristlecone pine, one of the oldest forms of plant life on Earth, can be seen on a self-guiding nature trail at Midway Summit.

The Pine Valley Mountains are about 24 miles north of St. George via SR 18 to the town of Central, then east on CR 035 for about 8 miles. The tops of the mountains, which rise some 3,000 feet above the valley floor, are designated as a wilderness area. The cool air at these elevations contrasts sharply with the higher temperatures of the valley. Camping and fishing are available in the valley. More than 100 miles of trails exist for hiking and horseback riding.

The Paunsaugunt and Sevier plateaus parallel SR 89 for 60 miles from Circleville south. The area is known for its panoramic views and distinctive rock formations. Red Canyon along SR 12 affords views, in the heart of the forest, of the pink and red rocks and cliffs. The canyon can be seen by car or by hiking one of the nature trails. Red Canyon Visitor Center and a campground are in the canyon.

Tropic Reservoir, just off SR 12 to the south, is a popular recreation spot that has lake and stream fishing. The reservoir provides a source of water for agricultural land at lower elevations. Additional campsites are at Kings Creek Campground near Kings Creek Lake.

The Boulder Mountain-Aquarius Plateau is a high mountain plateau that lies about 10 miles north of Escalante. SR 12 winds through spectacular slickrock formations, mountain passes and large areas of aspen that burst with color in the fall. Views from the road take in Capitol Reef National Park and many distant mountain ranges. Small campgrounds are scattered along the way.

Visitor centers Duck Creek, (435) 682-2432, and Red Canyon, (435) 676-2676, are open daily 10-5, Memorial Day-Labor Day; Sat.-Sun. 10-5, day after Labor Day-Sept. 30.

For further information contact the Forest Supervisor, Dixie National Forest, 1789 N. Wedgewood Ln., Cedar City, UT 84721; phone (435) 865-3700, or TTY (435) 865-3719. *See Recreation Chart.*

DRAPER pop. 42,274

• Part of Salt Lake City area — see map p. 412

FAIRFIELD INN BY MARRIOTT **Phone:** (801)572-1200

Hotel
$84-$132

AAA Benefit:
AAA hotel discounts of 5% or more.

Address: 12117 S State St 84020 **Location:** I-15 exit 291, just e, then just n on frontage road. Across from interstate. **Facility:** 66 units. 2 stories (no elevator), interior corridors. **Pool(s):** heated indoor. **Activities:** whirlpool, exercise room. **Guest Services:** valet and coin laundry, area transportation-within 5 mi.

BIZ / SOME UNITS

SPRINGHILL SUITES BY MARRIOTT
Phone: (801)572-1800

fyi
Hotel
$132-$156

AAA Benefit: AAA hotel discounts of 5% or more.

Too new to rate, opening scheduled for February 2012. **Address:** 12111 S State St 84020 **Location:** I-15 exit 292. **Amenities:** 124 units, coffeemakers, microwaves, refrigerators, pool, exercise facility.

WHERE TO EAT

GUADALAHONKY'S RESTAURANT **Phone:** 801/571-3838

Mexican
$8-$16

AAA Inspector Notes: The restaurant serves made-from-scratch Mexican entrées, including chiles rellenos. Warm tortilla chips and fresh salsa are served with every meal. **Bar:** full bar. **Address:** 136 E 12300 S 84020 **Location:** I-15 exit 291, 0.3 mi e. L D

DUCK CREEK VILLAGE

PINEWOODS RESORT RESTAURANT
Phone: 435/682-2512

American
$6-$27

AAA Inspector Notes: The restaurant offers the charm and warm ambiance of a rustic country inn and the soul-satisfying cuisine that will leave you fulfilled. **Bar:** beer & wine. **Address:** 121 Duck Creek Ridge Rd 84762 **Location:** Just s of SR 14 via Cedar Mountain Rd, 31 mi e of Cedar City in Cedar Mountain Village; 10 mi w of jct US 89; in Pinewoods Resort. D

EDEN (B-3) pop. 600

RECREATIONAL ACTIVITIES

Skiing

- **Powder Mountain Resort** is approximately 7 mi. n. on SR 158, which becomes Powder Mountain Rd. **Hours:** Open daily, mid-Nov. to mid-Apr. Hours vary; phone ahead. **Phone:** (801) 745-3772, or (801) 745-3771 for the snow line.
- **Wolf Mountain Ski Resort** is 1.9 mi. n. on SR 162, then 1 mi. s. on Nordic Valley Dr. **Hours:** Open daily, mid-Dec. to mid-Mar. Hours vary; phone ahead. **Phone:** (801) 745-3511.

RED MOOSE LODGE **Phone:** 801/745-6667

Hotel
Rates not provided

Address: 2547 N Valley Junction Dr 84310 **Location:** I-15 exit 344 (12th St), 10 mi e to Pineview Reservoir bridge, 4.3 mi n, then just nw of jct SR 158 and SR 162. **Facility:** 27 units. 1 story, interior corridors. **Terms:** office hours 8 am-8 pm. **Pool(s):** heated outdoor. **Activities:** whirlpool, exercise room. *Fee:* massage.

/ SOME UNITS FEE

SNOWBERRY INN BED & BREAKFAST
Phone: (801)745-2634

Bed & Breakfast
$99-$159

Address: 1315 N Hwy 158 84310 **Location:** I-15 exit 344 (12th St), 10 mi e to Pineview Reservoir bridge, then 2.6 mi n on SR 158. **Facility:** 8 units, some kitchens. 3 stories (no elevator), interior corridors. **Terms:** check-in 4 pm, 14 day cancellation notice-fee imposed. **Activities:** whirlpool.

/ SOME UNITS

WHERE TO EAT

CARLOS & HARLEY'S FRESH-MEX CANTINA
Phone: 801/745-8226

Mexican
$10-$19

AAA Inspector Notes: Menu favorites at this eatery include thin masa pork tamales steamed in the husk; Texas-style chili; beef, chicken, shrimp and vegetarian fajitas; and a fun make-your-own plate. Sugar-coated flour tortilla chips topped with fresh berries, chocolate and caramel sauce and fresh whipped cream are hard to pass up, but mega chocolate cake and homemade Key lime pie also tempt. **Bar:** full bar. **Address:** 2429 N Hwy 158 84310 **Location:** I-15 exit 344 (12th St), 10 mi e to Pineview Reservoir bridge, then 4 mi n on SR 158. L D

HARLEY & BUCKS GRILL **Phone:** 801/745-2060

American
$7-$28

AAA Inspector Notes: This restaurant is in a fabulous new location offering spectacular views of the sunset and illuminated ski runs. Choices such as crab cakes, beef brisket, barbecue ribs, Kona steak, chicken and prime rib lead up to desserts such as apple walnut cobbler a la mode. **Bar:** full bar. **Address:** 3900 N Wolf Creek Dr 84310 **Location:** I-15 exit 344 (12th St), 10 mi e to Pineview Reservoir bridge, 4.3 mi n on SR 158 to jct SR 162, then 2 mi n; at Wolf Creek Resort. D

EPHRAIM pop. 6,135

WILLOW CREEK INN **Phone:** (435)283-4566

Motel
$82-$114

Address: 450 S Main St 84627 **Location:** On US 89; south end of town. **Facility:** 58 units. 3 stories, interior corridors. **Activities:** whirlpool, game room, exercise room. **Guest Services:** coin laundry. / SOME UNITS

WHERE TO EAT

ROY'S PIZZA & TIN PLATE PASTA **Phone:** 435/283-4222

Italian
$5-$11

AAA Inspector Notes: Patrons enjoy pizza combinations, Alfredo pizza and calzones in the pizzeria, while right next door, the restaurant serves up pasta varieties including spinach fettuccine, cavatappi, angel hair, spaghetti, bow-tie, garden spiral or penne with a choice of sauce. Breadsticks, dipping sauces, sandwiches and salads are also available. The exit is through an old-fashioned ice cream parlor, where offerings include malts, milk shakes and banana splits. **Address:** 81 S Main St 84627 **Location:** Center of town. **Parking:** street only. L D

ESCALANTE (F-3) pop. 797, elev. 5,812'

Although Francisco Silvestre Vélez de Escalante came no closer than 150 miles to the present site of Escalante, the town was named for the Spanish priest, who explored sections of Utah in 1776. The Mormons, who settled in Escalante in 1875 because of its mild climate, called it "Potato Valley" for a local wild species of that vegetable.

The town is near the Kaiparowits Plateau, a sparsely settled area of highly eroded rock formations that extends east to the Colorado River and south to Arizona. The nearby Grand Staircase-Escalante National Monument *(see place listing p. 349)* provides recreational opportunities. Highlights of the Escalante Canyons Art Festival, held in late September, include a plein air painting competition, lectures, films and gallery open houses.

Escalante Chamber of Commerce: P.O. Box 175, Escalante, UT 84726. **Phone:** (435) 826-4810.

Self-guiding tours: A brochure describing a walking tour of Escalante's pioneer homes and barns is available at many locations throughout the town.

ESCALANTE PETRIFIED FOREST STATE PARK is 1 mi. w. on SR 12, then .5 mi. on an unnamed road, following signs. The 1,784-acre park contains colorful mineralized wood and fossilized logs. A visitor center has dinosaur bones, specimens of petrified wood and Native American artifacts that were found in the area. Wide Hollow Reservoir, a freshwater lake, provides many recreational opportunities. A self-guiding nature trail leads through a section of the reserve. *See Recreation Chart.*

Hours: Daily 7 a.m.-10 p.m., June-Aug.; 8 a.m.-10 p.m., rest of year. Closed Jan. 1 and Christmas. **Cost:** $6 (per private vehicle, maximum eight people). Annual pass $75. Camping fees $16-$20. **Phone:** (435) 826-4466, (801) 322-3770, or (800) 322-3770 for camping reservations.

ESCALANTE'S GRAND STAIRCASE BED & BREAKFAST INN **Phone:** 435/826-4890

Bed & Breakfast
Rates not provided

Address: 280 W Main St 84726 **Location:** West end of town. **Facility:** This B&B features large rooms featuring Native American drums, beautiful throws, skylights and rocking chairs; the gourmet breakfasts are pleasing. 8 units. 1-2 stories (no elevator), exterior corridors. **Terms:** age restrictions may apply. **Amenities:** *Some:* high-speed Internet.

RAINBOW COUNTRY BED & BREAKFAST **Phone:** (435)826-4567

Bed & Breakfast
$79-$109

Address: 585 E 300 S 84726 **Location:** Just s of SR 12; east end of town. **Facility:** 4 units. 2 stories (no elevator), interior corridors. **Terms:** check-in 4 pm, 3 day cancellation notice. **Activities:** whirlpool.
/ SOME UNITS FEE

WHERE TO EAT

KIVA KOFFEEHOUSE **Phone:** 435/826-4550

Natural/Organic
$7-$10

AAA Inspector Notes: An oasis for travelers, hikers and bikers, this oversize restaurant uses organic ingredients whenever feasible in its salads, muffins, wraps, sandwiches, baked goods and great breakfasts. Many of the seasonal vegetables come right from the on-site organic garden. Wide windows offer views of the Escalante River, and words can't describe the feeling experienced from taking advantage of them from the patio. **Address:** Hwy 12, MM 73-74 84726 **Location:** SR 12, MM 73-74.
B L

EUREKA (C-3) pop. 669, elev. 6,430'

You'll find a hodgepodge of wooden and squat brick structures along the once-bustling Main Street of Eureka. Though still an active community, the vicissitudes of more than a century of mining lend the place an air of past glory. Slag heaps, tailings and abandoned mines dot the landscape, and the surrounding mountains, long ago stripped of their forests, look careworn with their cloak of scrub juniper.

Prospectors arrived in the area in 1869. The first mine claim was filed in 1870, triggering a rush. Eureka, straddling an easy east-west pass through the mountains, soon became the focal point of a cluster of rough camps known as the East Tintic Mining District. Mining continued through the 1950s, and some small-scale mining operations remain operational. Since 1870, area mines have produced nearly half a billion dollars in gold, silver, lead, zinc, copper and uranium.

Containing historical photos and newspapers, minerals and mining equipment, the Tintic Mining Museum, on Main Street in the former city hall built in 1899, is open Sat.-Sun. 10-5, May-Sept.; otherwise by appointment. Phone (435) 433-6842.

LITTLE SAHARA RECREATION AREA, 27020 Sand Mountain Rd., is a 60,000-acre tract of shifting dunes, juniper-dotted hills and sagebrush flats inhabited by a wide range of animals. Off-road vehicles traverse 124 square miles of dune fields, which were created when strong winds picked up sand from the Sevier Desert and deposited them here.

Sand Mountain, a challenging, nearly 700-foot wall of sand, is Little Sahara's focal point. Attracting riders of all abilities, the White Sand Dunes offer numerous bowls. The Black Mountain includes a network of dirt trails. There also are fenced sand play areas at the White Sands Campground and the Jericho Picnic Area. The Rockwell Outstanding Natural Area is a 9,000-acre unit reserved for non-vehicle use.

Time: Allow 1 hour minimum. **Hours:** Recreation area daily dawn-dusk. Visitor center Wed.-Mon. 10-7; closed Thanksgiving and Christmas. Phone ahead to confirm visitor center hours. **Cost:** (valid for 2 consecutive days) $18 (per private vehicle). **Phone:** (435) 433-5960, or (435) 433-5961 for weather information.

FAIRFIELD (C-3) pop. 119, elev. 4,866'

Fairfield flourished during a brief boom 1858-59 when Gen. Albert Sidney Johnston's army forces were at nearby Camp Floyd. The population at that time swelled to about 7,000. About 2,500 of these were soldiers; the rest were camp followers, gamblers and Mormon settlers. Johnston's men were stationed in Fairfield until the beginning of the Civil War, and supplying them with food and goods provided the settlers with a steady cash income, a rarity in pioneer Utah.

CAMP FLOYD/STAGECOACH INN STATE PARK AND MUSEUM, .5 mi. s.w. on SR 73, then .2 mi. s. on North 18150 West following signs, was the site of the largest army encampment in the United States 1858-61. More than 3,500 troops were stationed there to suppress a Mormon rebellion that never materialized.

Of its 400 structures, only the commissary (now a museum) and the Johnston Army Cemetery, .5 miles west on SR 73, remain. The nearby Stagecoach Inn served as a rest stop for Pony Express riders; it houses period items. **Hours:** Mon.-Sat. 9-5. Closed Jan. 1, Thanksgiving and Christmas. **Cost:** $2; $6 (family, maximum eight people). **Phone:** (801) 768-8932.

FAIRVIEW (D-4) pop. 1,247, elev. 6,033'

Settled in 1859, Fairview was named for its impressive view of the Sanpete Valley. Just east of the city on SR 31 is the central point of Skyline Drive, an unpaved road that winds along the Wasatch Plateau for nearly 100 miles. The road is open July through October.

FAIRVIEW MUSEUM OF HISTORY AND ART is at 85 North 100 East. The museum contains Native American and pioneer relics and thousands of miniature woodcarvings. Early farm equipment is displayed on the grounds. The Natural History Building houses a replica of a Columbian mammoth unearthed nearby in 1988. Changing exhibits feature paintings and sculptures by local and regional artists. **Time:** Allow 30 minutes minimum. **Hours:** Mon.-Sat. 10-6, Sun. 2-6, May-Oct.; Mon.-Sat. 10-5, Sun. 2-5, rest of year. **Cost:** Donations. **Phone:** (435) 427-9216.

FARMINGTON (B-3) pop. 18,275, elev. 4,231'

• Part of Salt Lake City area — see map p. 412

The Farmington area is no longer in the shape William Chandless found it in "A Visit to Salt Lake," published in 1857. Chandless wrote that "though the Mormons are certainly a hospitable people, they have a prodigious number of savage inhospitable dogs about their houses, and worse still, almost impassible ditches, so that the benighted traveler has pretty well as much work to find his way into a house to inquire, as to find the one he is inquiring for without information . . ."

Bountiful/Farmington Loop, a 24-mile loop connecting Farmington and Bountiful, offers views of alpine scenery, the Great Salt Lake and Antelope Island. From Bountiful take 400 North east to 1300 East, then north on Ward Canyon Road. Facilities for camping, picnicking and hiking are along the road, which is open May through October.

Note: This route should not be attempted by anyone unfamiliar with mountain driving. Four-wheel-drive vehicles are recommended. Visitors are advised to drive slowly, as the gravel road is rough and washboarded and the road grades are steep. Inclement weather may further impair road conditions.

GEM **LAGOON** is off I-15 at 375 N. Lagoon Dr. The amusement park features Pioneer Village, a re-created frontier settlement of the 19th century, where exhibits provide a living-history atmosphere. Two music theaters are available, along with a variety of entertainment and the Wild Kingdom Train. The park includes a wild animal area as well as Lagoon-A-Beach, a water park featuring several waterslides, a swimming pool and a lazy river. Seven roller coasters are among the park's more than 40 rides.

Time: Allow 3 hours minimum. **Hours:** Amusement park open Sun.-Fri. at 11, Sat. at 10, early June-late Aug.; Sat. at 10, Sun. at 11 (also Memorial

Day and Labor Day), early Apr.-early June and late Aug.-late Sept. Lagoon-A-Beach open daily at 11, Memorial Day weekend to mid-Sept. (weather permitting). Frightmares! takes place at the amusement park Fri.-Sun., late Sept.-late Oct. Phone ahead to confirm schedule and closing times for both amusement and water parks.

Cost: $43.95; $38.95 (ages 65+ and under 51 inches tall); $27.95 (ages 0-3). Prices may vary. A photo ID is required for payment by credit card. **Parking:** $8. **Phone:** (801) 451-8000 or (800) 748-5246.

FILLMORE (E-3) pop. 2,435, elev. 5,700'

Fillmore was selected as the seat of government by the territorial legislature in 1851 and served as the territorial capital until 1856. The city and surrounding Millard County were named for President Millard Fillmore. The town is in generally flat country west of the Pavant Mountains and is a trading center for the surrounding farm and livestock region.

Fillmore Area Chamber of Commerce: 460 N. Main St., P.O. Box 164, Fillmore, UT 84631-5504. **Phone:** (435) 743-7803.

TERRITORIAL STATEHOUSE STATE PARK is on US 91 at 50 W. Capitol Ave. The park was the site of Utah's first territorial government headquarters. Isolation and lack of funds prevented completion of more than one wing of the 1851 statehouse. Pioneer relics, Native American artifacts and early documents are displayed. The American Rose Society Trial Gardens are next to the park grounds. **Hours:** Statehouse Mon.-Sat. 9-5. Closed Jan. 1, Thanksgiving and Christmas. **Cost:** $2; $1 (ages 6-11). **Phone:** (435) 743-5316.

BEST WESTERN PARADISE INN & RESORT
Phone: (435)743-6895

Motel
$80-$90

AAA Benefit: Members save up to 20%, plus 10% bonus points with Best Western Rewards®.

Address: 905 N Main St 84631 **Location:** I-15 exit 167, just e. **Facility:** 76 units. 2 stories (no elevator), exterior corridors. **Amenities:** *Some:* high-speed Internet. **Dining:** Garden of Eat'n, see separate listing. **Pool(s):** heated indoor. **Activities:** whirlpool. *Fee:* golf-9 holes. **Free Special Amenities: local telephone calls and high-speed Internet.**

SAVE / SOME UNITS

COMFORT INN & SUITES **Phone:** (435)743-4334

Hotel
$90-$140

Address: 940 S Hwy 99 84631 **Location:** I-15 exit 163, just e. **Facility:** 53 units, some kitchens. 2 stories (no elevator), interior corridors. **Terms:** cancellation fee imposed. **Pool(s):** heated indoor. **Activities:** whirlpool. **Guest Services:** coin laundry.

WHERE TO EAT

GARDEN OF EAT'N **Phone:** 435/743-5414

American
$5-$16

AAA Inspector Notes: The eatery offers American cuisine, daily specials and plenty of homemade fruit and cream pies. Breakfast is available all day. **Bar:** full bar. **Address:** 915 N Main St 84631 **Location:** I-15 exit 167, just e; next to Best Western Paradise Resort.

B L D

FISHLAKE NATIONAL FOREST (D-3)

Elevations in the forest range from 5,500 ft. near the town of Kanosh to 12,173 ft. at Delano Peak. Refer to AAA maps for additional elevation information.

In south-central Utah, Fishlake National Forest is divided into four segments by intervening valleys. It covers 1,434,599 acres and includes 76 streams and more than 60 lakes. The forest contains a wide variety of environments, from the alpine of the Tushar Mountains to the red desert of Wayne Wonderland.

The scenic Fish Lake-Johnson Valley area in the southeast includes 2,600-acre Fish Lake and 670-acre Johnson Reservoir, camping and picnicking areas, a boat launch site and three resorts. Another picturesque area is Beaver Mountain in the southwest. The highway to Fish Lake is paved.

Scenic drives from Fish Lake to Salina Canyon and from Beaver to Junction can be taken in good weather; high-clearance vehicles are recommended on most of the forest's 1,700 miles of road. Hunting for deer and elk is permitted, and several species of trout, splake and large mackinaw provide challenging fishing throughout the year. Other possible recreational pursuits include traversing 1,100 miles of trail by foot, horse or mountain bike and ATV. Camping is possible at 29 developed campgrounds and nine undeveloped campgrounds at elevations ranging from 5,500 to 9,300 feet.

For additional information contact the Forest Supervisor, Fishlake National Forest, 115 East 900 North, Richfield, UT 84701; phone (435) 896-9233. *See Recreation Chart.*

FLAMING GORGE NATIONAL RECREATION AREA (B-5)

Reached by SR 530 or US 191 from I-80 in Wyoming or US 191 from Utah, Flaming Gorge National Recreation Area straddles the border between Wyoming and Utah. The area includes a 91-mile-long reservoir and the Flaming Gorge and Red canyons, which were carved through the Uinta Mountains by the Green River.

Lake Flaming Gorge is bounded primarily by Red Canyon to the south and by rolling hills and occasional abrupt cliffs and promontories to the north. Of geologic interest are the exposed strata in Firehole Canyon and the Sheep Creek Geological Loop.

Once belonging to Mexico, Wyoming's portion of the Flaming Gorge region was annexed to the United States after the Mexican War. John Wesley Powell, a one-armed Army major and professor, mapped the area on his way down the Green River in the late 1860s and early 1870s, naming Flaming Gorge and many other prominent landmarks.

I-80 is connected to SR 530 and US 191. In Utah, US 191 joins with SRs 43 and 44, which then link with SR 530 again, to form a complete 160-mile loop around the recreation area. Along the route are the Flaming Gorge Dam and Visitor Center, off US 191 adjacent to the Bureau of Reclamation offices; the Red Canyon Visitor Center and Overlook, which offers a spectacular view from 1,400 feet above Red Canyon and Flaming Gorge Reservoir off SR 44; the Sheep Creek Geological Loop; and Flaming Gorge.

Known for its bountiful fishing waters, Lake Flaming Gorge also is a popular setting for swimming, boating and water skiing. Large boat ramps are found near campgrounds at convenient access points along the western and eastern sides of the lake.

The western shore, accessible from Buckboard, Wyo., and Lucerne Valley, Utah, has campsites and two marinas that provide boat rentals and supplies. Cedar Springs to the southeast is similarly equipped; the latter has a dock and marina. Other campgrounds are scattered throughout the Utah and Wyoming sections.

The reservoir contains a broad sampling of fish, including German brown, lake, rainbow and cutthroat trout; small-mouth bass; and kokanee salmon. Fishing is permitted all year. A license from either Utah or Wyoming is required.

Seasonal hunting is permitted except near public-use facilities. Cross-country skiing, snowmobiling and ice fishing are popular winter activities. For further information, contact the Flaming Gorge Ranger District, Flaming Gorge National Recreation Area, P.O. Box 279, Manila, UT 84046.

The recreation area is open all year, but most developed facilities are closed during the winter. The Red Canyon Visitor Center is open daily 8-6, Memorial Day weekend-Labor Day. The Flaming Gorge Dam Visitor Center is open daily 8-6, Memorial Day-Labor Day; daily 9-5, Apr. 1-day before Memorial Day and day after Labor Day-Oct. 14; Fri.-Mon. 10-4, rest of year. Guided tours of the dam depart from the visitor center daily 9-3, Memorial Day-Labor Day; phone ahead to confirm schedule.

A use fee pass is required for all facilities. Passes are $5 (1-day), $15 (7-day) and $35 (annual), beginning from the date of purchase. America the Beautiful–National Parks and Federal Recreational Lands Pass holders enter free. Phone (435) 784-3445 for the ranger district, (435) 889-3713 for the Red Canyon Visitor Center, or (435) 885-3135 for the Flaming Gorge Dam and Visitor Center. *See Recreation Chart.*

FLAMING GORGE DAM is off US 191 near Dutch John, Utah. The dam is a concrete arch structure rising 502 feet above bedrock. **Hours:** Guided 1-hour tours are offered daily 9-3, mid-Mar. to mid-Oct. Phone ahead to confirm schedule. **Cost:** Free. **Phone:** (435) 885-3135.

JOHN JARVIE HISTORIC RANCH is about 8 mi. n.w. of Dutch John, Utah, on US 191, then 22 mi. e. on a gravel road, following signs to Browns Park. A haven for outlaws around the turn of the 20th century, Browns Park formerly was the site of a successful ranching operation started by Scottish immigrant John Jarvie in the 1880s. The ranch today includes a replica of the general store originally built in 1881, a blacksmith shop, a corral, and a two-room dugout that was once Jarvie's residence.

A 15-minute orientation video is shown in a historical stone house that now serves as a museum. **Tours:** Guided tours are available. **Time:** Allow 1 hour minimum. **Hours:** Daily 10-5, May-Oct.; Mon.-Sat. 10-5, rest of year. **Cost:** Donations. **Phone:** (435) 885-3307 or (435) 781-4400.

FORT DUCHESNE (C-5) pop. 714, elev. 4,988'

Fort Duchesne (doo-SHAYN) is headquarters for the Ute Indian Reservation, home of 1,600 members of the Uinta, White River and Uncompaghre tribes. The tribal organization has encouraged many educational and business enterprises to develop and employ its members. Industry makes use of the vast landholdings.

The Ute Fish and Game Committee runs stocking and conservation programs to ensure supplies of fish. Upland game bird, waterfowl and big game hunting also are available. For further information contact the Ute Indian Tribe Complex at (435) 722-5141.

FOUR CORNERS MONUMENT—See Colorado p. 113.

GARDEN CITY pop. 562

GLEN CANYON NATIONAL RECREATION AREA (F-4)

Along the Colorado River from Grand Canyon National Park in far north-central Arizona to Canyonlands National Park in southeastern Utah, Glen Canyon National Recreation Area is home to one of the highest dams in the United States. Part of the Colorado River storage project, the Glen Canyon

Dam generates hydroelectric power that is distributed to cities and industries throughout the West; the dam's main purpose is water storage.

Reaching out to hidden canyons, sandy coves and inlets, and winding through towering red cliffs, 186-mile-long Lake Powell presents an ever-changing array of scenery and such recreational opportunities as water skiing, boating and fishing. Amenities include campsites, marinas, and boat rentals and tours. A copy of fishing regulations can be obtained at park ranger stations, the Carl Hayden Visitor Center, the Navajo Bridge Interpretive Center, the Bullfrog Visitor Center or at the administration offices in Page, Ariz.; phone (928) 355-2319.

The Bullfrog Visitor Center, at the Bullfrog Marina in Utah, exhibits the natural and cultural history of Glen Canyon and includes a life-size slot canyon model. The Navajo Bridge Interpretive Center, on US 89A near Lees Ferry, Ariz., features a historic pedestrian bridge over the Colorado River at Marble Canyon and outdoor exhibits highlighting the early river crossings. The interpretive center is open daily 9-5, Apr.-Oct., as staffing allows; phone (928) 355-2319 or (435) 684-7420.

Exhibits in the Carl Hayden Visitor Center, next to US 89, Glen Canyon Dam and Glen Canyon Bridge in Page illustrate the construction of the dam and bridge and include a relief model of the canyon country. Guided tours of the dam are available throughout the year. The center is open daily 8-6, Memorial Day-Labor Day; 8-5, Mar. 1-day before Memorial Day; 8:30-4:30, rest of year. Closed Jan. 1, Thanksgiving and Christmas. Phone (928) 608-6404.

Free evening programs are given at Wahweap campground, 7 miles northwest of Page off US 89, Memorial Day through Labor Day; phone or stop by the visitor center for a list of scheduled performance days and times.

Arrangements for boat tours on Lake Powell can be made at Wahweap Lodge and Marina; facilities, including public launching ramps, boat rentals, camping and boat and automobile fuel, are provided at Wahweap and at four other marinas on the lake. A boat ramp providing access to 15 miles of the Colorado River below Glen Canyon Dam is available at Lees Ferry, 5 miles north of Marble Canyon.

Boat excursions, which last from 4 to 6.5 hours, are available through Colorado River Discovery; phone (928) 645-9175 or (888) 522-6644. The tours begin near the Glen Canyon Dam and conclude at Lees Ferry. One-day raft trips on the Colorado River below the dam can be arranged in Page. Half-day and full-day trips are available to Rainbow Bridge National Monument, Utah, which is about 50 miles from Wahweap. Trips on the San Juan River leave from Mexican Hat and Bluff, Utah.

Park admission, valid for up to 7 days, is $15 (per private vehicle); $7 (per person arriving by foot or bicycle). An annual pass is $30. An additional use fee of $16 is charged for one motorized water vessel and is valid for up to 7 days; a use fee of $8 is charged for each additional water vessel on the same trailer.

For further information contact the Superintendent, Glen Canyon National Recreation Area, P.O. Box 1507, Page, AZ 86040; phone (928) 608-6404 or (928) 608-6200. *See Recreation Chart.*

GLENDALE pop. 381

HISTORIC SMITH HOTEL BED & BREAKFAST

Phone: (435)648-2156

Bed & Breakfast
$78-$98 5/1-10/31
$48-$74 11/1-4/30

Address: 295 N Main St 84729 **Location:** US 89; north end of town. **Facility:** 7 units. 2 stories (no elevator), interior corridors. **Terms:** 4 day cancellation notice. **Guest Services:** coin laundry.

/ SOME UNITS FEE

GOLDEN SPIKE NATIONAL HISTORIC SITE (A-2)

Thirty-two miles west of Brigham City via SRs 13 and 83, the site marks Promontory Summit, the place where the Union Pacific and Central Pacific rails met to form the nation's first transcontinental railroad on May 10, 1869. A golden spike was the last one driven to make this connection.

The culmination of the nation's dream to unite the East and West coasts brought major changes to the country. The new railroad provided the first practical means of round-trip travel. New opportunities for commerce brought buffalo hunters, who depleted the great bison herds that roamed the plains. The railroad also advanced the settlement of California, Colorado, Nebraska, Nevada, Wyoming and Utah.

Working replicas of the 1869 steam locomotives "119" and "Jupiter" are displayed. Steam demonstrations are given, though no rides are available. A self-guiding driving tour over the old railroad grade is possible spring through fall. The Big Fill Loop Trail is a 1.5 mile walk on the original Central and Union Pacific railroad grades. Films and museum exhibits are offered daily throughout the year. A reenactment of the driving of the golden spike ceremony is held Saturdays and holidays at 11 and 1, May through October.

Allow 2 hours minimum for the historic site and visitor center. The visitor center is open daily 9-5. Steam locomotives are displayed daily, May 1-Labor Day (schedule varies; phone the visitor center to confirm hours). Closed Jan. 1, Thanksgiving and Christmas. Admission is $5-$7 (per private vehicle); $3-$4 (per person arriving by other means). Phone (435) 471-2209 for park information or for the visitor center.

GRAND STAIRCASE-ESCALANTE NATIONAL MONUMENT (F-4)

Between Bryce Canyon National Park and Glen Canyon National Recreation Area, Grand Staircase-Escalante National Monument consists of 1.9 million acres in southern Utah. Established by presidential proclamation in September 1996, the national monument's name is derived from the series of multi-colored cliffs and mesas extending from Bryce Canyon to the Grand Canyon in Arizona. The Escalante and Paria rivers and their tributaries, which run through this area, have created two major canyon systems as well as natural bridges and arches. The majority of monument land remains rugged, remote and undeveloped.

Geological formations found within the monument include red rock canyons, cliffs, rock formations and natural bridges and arches. Highlights include Escalante Natural Bridge, which measures 100 feet across and 130 feet high, and Grosvenor Arch, which are actually two arches reachable from a dirt road off SR 12. Reaching Escalante Natural Bridge entails a 2-mile hike up the Escalante River. Lower Calf Creek Falls, requiring a 6-mile round-trip hike, and Devils Garden are other popular features.

The monument also contains major paleontological and archeological sites, including numerous examples of fossils and petrified wood. Also of significance is the knowledge to be gained from the remains of the area's earliest inhabitants. Prehistoric dwellings and rock art attest to early settlement within the monument's boundaries by antediluvian cultures. Anasazi and Fremont cultures were followed by settlements of Southern Paiutes and Navajos.

The monument's vast acreage, which embraces both deserts and forests, is populated by mountain lions, bighorn sheep, mule deer, coyotes, foxes and more than 200 species of birds, including bald eagles and peregrine falcons.

Access to the monument is by two routes: Scenic SR 12 leads to the monument from the north, and US 89 provides access from the south. Other roads within the monument are partially surfaced or are of gravel, sand or clay; these may present difficult driving conditions in inclement weather.

The monument encompasses one of the country's most remote regions. Driving in the backcountry requires preparation for emergencies and all weather conditions, including flash floods. Services and rescue capabilities are limited. Permits are required for overnight camping or backpacking visitors; these can be obtained for free at trailheads or at the Escalante Interagency Visitor Center.

There are four visitor centers and one information desk within the national monument. Visitor centers are in Kanab, (435) 644-4680, site of the monument's headquarters; in Escalante, (435) 826-5499; in Cannonville, (435) 826-5640; and in Big Water, (435) 675-3200. A contact station is 44 miles east of Kanab at Paria on US 89. The Kanab and Escalante centers are open daily 8-4:30. The Cannonville center is open daily 8-4:30, mid-Mar. to mid-Nov. The Big Water center is open daily 8:30-5:30, Apr.-Oct.; 8:30-4:30, rest of year. Each visitor center offers exhibits and a DVD presentation about the monument. Exhibits vary and range from ecology, biology and archeology to geology, human geography and paleontology.

The monument is open all year (weather permitting), but the best time to visit is March through May and September 1 to early November. Visitors should phone ahead to confirm that weather conditions within the monument are favorable. Closed Jan. 1, Thanksgiving and Christmas.

For additional information contact the Grand Staircase-Escalante National Monument, Kanab Visitor Center, 745 E. US 89, Kanab, UT 84741, (435) 644-4680, or the Escalante Interagency Visitor Center, 755 W. Main St., Escalante, UT 84726, (435) 826-5499.

GREAT SALT LAKE (B-2)

• Part of Salt Lake City area — see map p. 412

With the exception of the Dead Sea, the Great Salt Lake is the saltiest body of water on Earth. Occupying a large part of the northern portion of Utah, the lake is 72 miles long and as wide as 30 miles but only 10 to 28 feet deep. The only crossing over the lake is the 102-mile Southern Pacific Railroad cutoff between Ogden and Lucin.

Centuries ago the northwestern quarter of Utah was covered by Lake Bonneville, a great freshwater lake 10 times the size of the Great Salt Lake. Covering more than 20,000 square miles in Utah, Nevada and Idaho, the lake was 1,000 feet deep where the Great Salt Lake now lies and 900 feet deep at the site of Salt Lake City.

The lake's weight was so great that the Earth's crust in the middle of the basin was depressed more than 150 feet, leaving a shoreline that is still visible. Because of a change in climate or a volcanic diversion of contributing streams, the huge lake fell below its lowest outlet and shrank to what is now known as the Great Salt Lake.

The Great Salt Lake's salinity varies from 15 to 25 percent (at least six times saltier than the ocean) according to the water level. This salt content can only be tolerated by blue-green algae and brine shrimp.

The lake owes its extreme saltiness to the mineral-laden freshwater streams that feed into it and find no outlet. The evaporation of the streams' waters leaves so much salt behind that the lake will buoy a human body. The water trapped in open, diked lakes near the shores of the larger lake leaves inches of almost pure salt, which is harvested annually for commercial purposes.

On the north side of the lake, at Promontory Summit, the Golden Spike National Historic Site *(see place listing p. 349)* commemorates the place where the first transcontinental railroad linked the East and West coasts in 1869. In the lake itself is Antelope Island State Park *(see attraction listing)*, where visitors can float effortlessly in the lake as well as take advantage of the park's recreational activities.

Great Salt Lake State Park, 16 miles west of Salt Lake City off I-80 exit 104, provides access to the south shore of the lake. The park's marina is a good spot for watching the sun set over the lake. For additional information phone (801) 250-1898.

The Great Salt Lake Desert to the west of the lake is part of the bed of extinct Lake Bonneville and is composed of silt washed into the huge lake hundreds of years ago. Highways crossing the desert follow trails blazed by some of the first Mormon settlers. Also in this region are the Bonneville Salt Flats, where many land speed records have been set on the 10-mile, circular Bonneville Speedway.

For additional information contact the Salt Lake Field Office of the Bureau of Land Management at (801) 977-4300.

ANTELOPE ISLAND STATE PARK, within the Great Salt Lake 9.8 mi. w. of Syracuse via West 1700 South and the 7-mi.-long Davis County Cswy., has sand beaches; trails for hiking, horseback riding, mountain biking and cross-country skiing; and a marina. A herd of more than 500 bison as well as mule deer, pronghorn antelopes, bighorn sheep, coyotes and waterfowl are full-time residents.

The Fielding Garr Ranch, Utah's oldest, also can be toured, and the visitor center has a video and information about the island's geology, biology and history. Kayaking, bird-watching, and horseback and wagon rides are available. *See Recreation Chart.*

Time: Allow 2 hours minimum. **Hours:** Park open daily 7 a.m.-10 p.m., May-Sept.; 7 a.m.-9 p.m., in Apr.; 7 a.m.-8 p.m., in Oct.; 7-7, in Mar.; 7-6, rest of year. Visitor center and ranch open daily 9-6, mid-Apr. to mid-Sept.; 9-5, rest of year. Closed Thanksgiving and Christmas. **Cost:** $9 (per private vehicle); $3 (per person arriving by other means). Camping $13. **Phone:** (801) 773-2941 for park information, or (800) 322-3770 for camping reservations.

GREEN RIVER (D-5) pop. 952, elev. 4,080'

Green River was settled as a mail relay station in 1878 on the site where it was easiest to ford the river. Today it is the center of a melon-growing region.

Crystal Geyser is 5 miles east via US 6/50 to the I-70 overpass, then 7 miles south on a gravel road. The unpredictable eruptions of this rare cold-water geyser generally occur twice daily and reach as high as 100 feet. The gravel road to the geyser is in good condition but is not well marked.

About 45 miles west of Green River on I-70, Wedge Overlook affords a view of the San Rafael River 1,000 feet below. The panorama across the San Rafael Swell consists of an impressive 30- by 60-mile hollowed-out red dome marked with buttes, gorges and canyons.

Emery County Travel Center: 1765 E. Main St., Green River, UT 84525. **Phone:** (435) 564-3427.

JOHN WESLEY POWELL RIVER HISTORY MUSEUM is at 1765 E. Main St. The museum features photographs, artifacts, models, displays and maps that describe the exploration of the Green and Colorado rivers as well as the geological formation of the rivers' gorges and mountains. Some exhibits focus on the accomplishments of 19th-century explorer John Wesley Powell, whose expeditions contributed to the development of the Colorado Plateau. An art gallery and a visitor center are on the premises.

Hours: Daily 8-7, Apr.-Oct.; Tues.-Sat. 9-5, rest of year. Closed Jan. 1, Thanksgiving and Christmas. Phone ahead to confirm schedule. **Cost:** $6; $2 (ages 5-12); $15 (family). **Phone:** (435) 564-3427.

RECREATIONAL ACTIVITIES

White-water Rafting

- **Holiday Expeditions** departs from the company's headquarters on the e. side of the Green River Bridge behind the Comfort Inn on E. Main St. Other activities and multi-day trips are offered. **Hours:** One-day trips on the Green River depart daily at 9, Memorial Day-Labor Day. **Phone:** (801) 266-2087 or (800) 624-6323.
- **Moki Mac River Expeditions** offers passenger pickups at local lodgings. **Hours:** Departures require a minimum of six people. Rafting trips are offered daily, early May-early Oct. Departure times vary; phone ahead. **Phone:** (801) 268-6667 or (800) 284-7280.

COMFORT INN — **Phone:** (435)564-3300

Hotel
$80-$170

Address: 1975 E Main St 84525 **Location:** I-70 exit 160 eastbound, 3 mi n; exit 164 westbound, 1.5 mi n. **Facility:** 57 units. 2 stories (no elevator), interior corridors. **Terms:** cancellation fee imposed. **Pool(s):** heated indoor. **Activities:** whirlpool, exercise room. **Guest Services:** coin laundry.

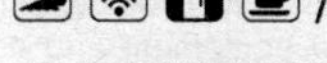

SOME UNITS

HOLIDAY INN EXPRESS — **Phone:** (435)564-4439

Hotel
$99-$199 5/1-10/10
$69-$119 10/11-4/30

Address: 1845 E Main St 84525 **Location:** I-70 exit 160 eastbound, 3 mi e; exit 164 westbound, 1.7 nw. **Facility:** 60 units. 2 stories, interior corridors. **Pool(s):** heated indoor. **Activities:** whirlpool. **Guest Services:** coin laundry.

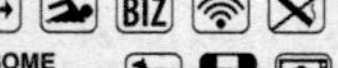

SOME UNITS FEE

RIVER TERRACE INN — **Phone:** (435)564-3401

Hotel
$90-$116

Address: 1740 E Main St 84525 **Location:** I-70 exit 160 eastbound, 3 mi e; exit 164 westbound, 1.7 mi nw. **Facility:** 50 units. 2-3 stories (no elevator), interior corridors. **Terms:** office hours 7 am-10 pm, cancellation fee imposed. **Pool(s):** heated outdoor. **Activities:** whirlpool.

SUPER 8 — **Phone:** (435)564-8888

Motel
$58-$90

Address: 1248 E Main St 84525 **Location:** I-70 exit 164, 1.3 mi n. **Facility:** 67 units. 2 stories (no elevator), interior corridors. **Pool(s):** heated indoor. **Activities:** whirlpool, limited exercise equipment. **Guest Services:** coin laundry. **Free Special Amenities: continental breakfast and high-speed Internet.**

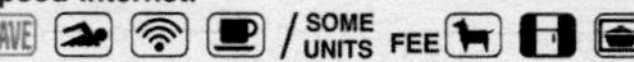

WHERE TO EAT

RAY'S TAVERN — **Phone:** 435/564-3511

American
$6-$20

AAA Inspector Notes: Highly recommended by the locals, this no-frills restaurant specializes in juicy steaks and burgers but also serves pizza, chicken and veggie burgers. Pool tables keep patrons busy in the back room. **Bar:** beer only. **Address:** 25 S Broadway 84525 **Location:** Downtown. **Parking:** street only. L D

TAMARISK RESTAURANT — **Phone:** 435/564-8109

American
$7-$20

AAA Inspector Notes: Overlooking a bridge over the Green River, which is surrounded by tamarisk trees and bushes, this restaurant is the perfect stop for breakfast, lunch or dinner. Favorites such as charbroiled steak, fettuccine Alfredo and Navajo tacos share menu space with soups, salads and sandwiches. The seasonal triple-berry pie is delicious. Service is friendly. **Bar:** beer only. **Address:** 1710 E Main St 84525 **Location:** I-70 exit 160 eastbound, 3 mi e; exit 164 westbound, 1.7 mi nw. B L D

HANKSVILLE (E-4) pop. 219, elev. 4,288'

GOBLIN VALLEY STATE PARK is 20 mi. n. on SR 24, then 12 mi. w. via Temple Mountain Rd., following signs. The reserve contains thousands of colorful rock formations that resemble gnomes. Hiking facilities are available. **Hours:** Daily dawn-dusk. **Cost:** $7 (per private vehicle). Camping $16. **Phone:** (435) 275-4584, (801) 322-3770, or (800) 322-3770 for camping reservations.

HATCH pop. 133

MOUNTAIN RIDGE MOTEL — **Phone:** 435/735-4300

Motel
$59-$139

Address: 106 S Main St 84735 **Location:** On US 89; center. **Facility:** 8 units, some kitchens. 1 story, exterior corridors. **Terms:** open 5/1-11/1, 7 day cancellation notice-fee imposed.

SOME UNITS

HEBER CITY (C-4) elev. 5,595'

• Hotels p. 352 • Restaurants p. 352

Founded in 1859 and named for Heber C. Kimball, counselor to Mormon leader Brigham Young, Heber City is the farming and livestock center of the pastoral Heber Valley. Glider and sailplane rides are available spring through fall. Snowmobile and dog sled races are popular winter events.

Heber Valley Chamber of Commerce and Visitor Center: 475 N. Main St., Heber City, UT 84032. **Phone:** (435) 654-3666.

HEBER VALLEY RAILROAD, at 450 South 600 West, offers scenic, narrated 3-hour Provo Canyon Limited tours aboard historic diesel or steam-powered trains. Passengers see Provo Canyon, Deer Creek Lake and the farmlands of Heber Valley. Other scenic, seasonal and one-way trips also are offered.

Hours: Provo Canyon Limited trips depart Tues.-Sun. at 11, early June to mid-Oct.; Fri.-Sun. at 11, mid-Oct. through Oct. 30. Phone ahead to confirm schedule. **Cost:** Provo Canyon Limited trip $30; $25 (ages 60+); $20 (ages 3-12). Prices may vary. Reservations are recommended. **Phone:** (435) 654-5601, or (800) 888-8499 for tickets.

DANIELS SUMMIT LODGE **Phone:** (435)548-2300

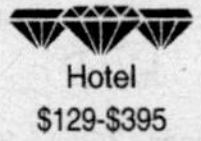

Hotel

$129-$395

Address: 17000 S Hwy 40 84032 **Location:** I-80 exit 146 (US 40), 34 mi se. **Facility:** 48 units, some cabins. 2 stories, interior/exterior corridors. **Terms:** check-in 4 pm, 3 day cancellation notice-fee imposed. **Amenities:** *Some:* high-speed Internet. **Pool(s):** heated indoor. **Activities:** whirlpool, cross country skiing, bicycles, hiking trails, jogging, horseshoes, volleyball, exercise room. *Fee:* snowmobiling, horseback riding, game room, massage.

HOLIDAY INN EXPRESS HEBER CITY
Phone: 435/654-9990

Hotel

Rates not provided

Address: 1268 S Main St 84032 **Location:** I-80 exit 146 (US 40), 17 mi s. **Facility:** 75 units, some kitchens. 3 stories, interior corridors. **Pool(s):** heated indoor. **Activities:** whirlpool. **Guest Services:** coin laundry.

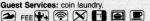

THE LODGE AT STILLWATER **Phone:** (435)940-3800

Condominium

$159-$329 12/21-4/30
$109-$306 5/1-12/20

Address: 1364 W Stillwater Dr 84032 **Location:** I-80 exit 146 (US 40), 8 mi s to exit 8 (Mayflower), then just e. **Facility:** The condominium hotel is convenient to skiing. Studios and one- and two-bedroom suites are offered. 40 condominiums. 3 stories, interior corridors. **Terms:** office hours 10 am-9 pm, check-in 4 pm, 3 day cancellation notice. **Amenities:** high-speed Internet. **Pool(s):** heated outdoor. **Activities:** whirlpools, exercise room. *Fee:* game room. **Guest Services:** valet and coin laundry, area transportation-ski shuttle.

SWISS ALPS INN **Phone:** (435)654-0722

Motel

$70-$110 5/1-8/31
$60-$90 9/1-4/30

Address: 167 S Main St 84032 **Location:** I-80 exit 146 (US 40), 15 mi s. **Facility:** 14 units, some two bedrooms. 1 story, exterior corridors. **Terms:** office hours 10 am-midnight. **Amenities:** high-speed Internet. **Pool(s):** heated outdoor. **Activities:** sauna, whirlpool, playground, basketball. **Free Special Amenities: early check-in/late check-out and high-speed Internet.**

WHERE TO EAT

DAIRY KEEN HOME OF THE TRAIN
Phone: 435/654-5336

American

$5-$9

AAA Inspector Notes: This is a fun place to bring the family for award-winning shakes and burgers along with soups made in house fresh daily. Not looking for a burger? Then choose chicken, salad, fish or tacos. While the food is quickly prepared, take a moment to enjoy all of the operating trains and railroad memorabilia located throughout the restaurant. The place can really rock during the local school's short lunch break. **Address:** 199 S Main 84032 **Location:** I-80 exit 146 (US 40), 15 mi s; downtown. L D

SNAKE CREEK GRILL **Phone:** 435/654-2133

American

$15-$29

AAA Inspector Notes: Unpretentious cuisine, including creative nightly steak specials and yummy black-bottom banana pie, are served at this spot along the historic Heber Creeper railway line. **Bar:** full bar. **Reservations:** suggested. **Address:** 650 W 100 S 84032 **Location:** I-80 exit 146 (US 40), 16.5 mi s to 100 S, then 0.6 mi w. D

SPIN CAFE **Phone:** 435/654-0251

American

$7-$19

AAA Inspector Notes: At this hip and fun eatery, patrons enjoy Asian pork lettuce wraps, tasty sandwiches and burgers, slow-cooked pulled pork and specialties such as Key West Caesar salad, pork spare ribs and cedar-plank salmon. In addition to great coffee and hot chocolate, tasty homemade gelato and decadent desserts leave guests hooked. **Bar:** full bar. **Address:** 220 N Main St 84032 **Location:** I-80 exit 146 (US 40), 16 mi s. L D

HELPER (D-4) pop. 2,201, elev. 5,840'

Helper was settled in 1870 by a coal prospector who later sold his property to the Denver & Rio Grande Railroad. The extra engines required to push the heavily laden coal trains to Soldier Summit gave the town its name.

WESTERN MINING AND RAILROAD MUSEUM is at 294 S. Main St. in the historic district. The museum depicts area railroad and mining operation history. Exhibits include historical photographs, a videotape room, 19th-century coal-mining tools, railroad equipment, a hand press used to print payrolls and the wooden steps on which Butch Cassidy robbed the Pleasant Valley Coal Co. in 1897.

The museum also hosts rotating art exhibitions and boasts one of the largest collections of WPA artwork from the Great Depression era. The grounds feature a native plant garden as well as two outdoor display lots showcasing mining equipment and a 1917 railroad caboose. **Time:** Allow 30 minutes minimum. **Hours:** Mon.-Sat. 10-5, mid-May to mid-Sept.; Tues.-Sat. 11-4, rest of year. **Cost:** Donations. **Phone:** (435) 472-3009.

HOLLADAY pop. 26,472

• **Hotels & Restaurants map & index p. 426**
• **Part of Salt Lake City area — see map p. 412**

CAFE MADRID **Phone:** 801/273-0837 (36)

Spanish

$22-$28

AAA Inspector Notes: Authentic Spanish cuisine, including tapas and full entrées, is served at this distinctive and elegant European bistro. The seasonal outdoor seating area has a romantic feel. **Bar:** full bar. **Reservations:** suggested. **Address:** 5244 S Highland Dr 84117 **Location:** I-15 exit 301 (4500 S), 3.2 mi e to Highland Dr, then 1.3 mi s. D

FRANCK'S **Phone:** 801/274-6264 (38)

French

$22-$36

AAA Inspector Notes: This intimate setting goes perfect with the restaurant's French-inspired cuisine with some twists. Unusual presentations of meatloaf and fried chicken are offered in addition to more traditional fare. **Bar:** full bar. **Address:** 6263 S Holladay Blvd 84121 **Location:** I-215 exit 6 (6200 S), just w. **Parking:** on-site and valet. D

(See map & index p. 426.)

TUSCANY Phone: 801/277-9919 (37)

Northern Italian
$15-$29

AAA Inspector Notes: Former Utah Jazz star Mark Eaton and his partners bring tempting Italian fare to their alpine chalet. The detail-rich décor is very dramatic and inviting. **Bar:** full bar. **Address:** 2832 E 6200 S 84121 **Location:** I-215 exit 6 (6200 S), just w. **Parking:** on-site and valet. (D)

HOVENWEEP NATIONAL MONUMENT—See Colorado p. 227.

HUNTSVILLE (B-3) pop. 608, elev. 4,929'

RECREATIONAL ACTIVITIES

Skiing

- **Snowbasin** is 2 mi. s. on SR 39 to SR 167, 6 mi. s. to SR 226 (Snowbasin Rd.), then 3 mi. e. Other activities are offered. **Hours:** Open for winter activities daily, Thanksgiving-early Apr. (weather permitting). Hours vary; phone ahead. **Phone:** (801) 620-1000 or (888) 437-5488.

JACKSON FORK INN **Phone:** (801)745-0051

Motel
$85-$160

Address: 7345 E 900 S 84317 **Location:** I-15 exit 344 (12th St), 12 mi e. **Facility:** 7 units. 2 stories (no elevator), interior corridors. **Terms:** check-in 4 pm, 3 day cancellation notice. / SOME UNITS FEE

HURRICANE (G-2) pop. 13,748, elev. 3,254'

Named for the Hurricane Fault, a jagged escarpment rising 7,000 feet above the town, Hurricane is the center of Utah's fruit-raising region.

Hurricane Valley Chamber of Commerce: 1155 W. State St., Suite 202, P.O. Box 101, Hurricane, UT 84737. **Phone:** (435) 635-3402.

HURRICANE VALLEY HERITAGE PARK, PIONEER AND INDIAN MUSEUM, at the corner of Main and State sts., contains artifacts relating to settlers and Native Americans, displays about local architecture, and an exhibit about the building of the Hurricane Canal. On the grounds are early wagons, farm machinery and a large sculpture of a pioneer family. Across Main Street, the 1906 Bradshaw House was Hurricane's first residence; it contains a doll collection and early medical equipment. **Hours:** Mon.-Sat. 9-5. **Cost:** Donations. **Phone:** (435) 635-3245.

COMFORT INN ZION **Phone:** 435/635-3500

Motel
Rates not provided

Address: 43 N 2600 W 84737 **Location:** 1 mi w on SR 9. **Facility:** 53 units. 2 stories (no elevator), interior corridors. **Pool(s):** heated outdoor. **Activities:** whirlpool. *Fee:* miniature golf. **Guest Services:** coin laundry.

SUPER 8 **Phone:** (435)635-0808

Motel
$40-$99

Address: 65 S 700 W 84737 **Location:** Just s of SR 9. **Facility:** 50 units. 2 stories (no elevator), exterior corridors. **Terms:** cancellation fee imposed. **Pool(s):** heated outdoor. **Activities:** whirlpool. **Guest Services:** coin laundry.

/ SOME UNITS FEE

TRAVELODGE **Phone:** (435)635-4647

Motel
$40-$89

Address: 280 W State St 84737 **Location:** Just w on SR 9. **Facility:** 62 units. 2 stories (no elevator), exterior corridors. **Pool(s):** heated outdoor. **Activities:** whirlpool. **Guest Services:** coin laundry. **Free Special Amenities: continental breakfast and high-speed Internet.**

SAVE

WHERE TO EAT

TED & ALLEN'S SPORTS GRILL **Phone:** 435/635-3264

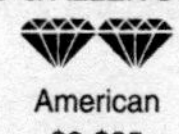

American
$8-$25

AAA Inspector Notes: In the middle of town, this sports grill is the place to go for televised sports action. Diners appreciate the large menu and personable service. **Bar:** beer & wine. **Address:** 980 W State St 84737 **Location:** Center. (L) (D)

IVINS (G-1) pop. 6,753

Tuacahn Amphitheatre and Center for the Arts, off SR 91, presents original productions and its Broadway in the Desert series from June through October in a 2,000-seat outdoor venue surrounded by the towering red rock cliffs of *Tuacahn,* the Canyon of the Gods; phone (435) 652-3200, or (800) 746-9882 for tickets.

SNOW CANYON STATE PARK is 3.7 mi. n. on SR 8. Black lava rock formations contrast with the red sandstone walls and white sandstone formations in this canyon. Pictographs still survive on the walls. *See Recreation Chart.* **Hours:** Daily 6 a.m.-10 p.m. **Cost:** $6 (per private vehicle, maximum eight people); $3 (per person arriving by other means). Camping $16-$20. **Phone:** (435) 628-2255, (801) 322-3770, or (800) 322-3770 for camping reservations.

KANAB (G-2) pop. 4,312, elev. 4,925'

• Hotels p. 354 • Restaurants p. 355

Kanab lies south of Bryce Canyon National Park *(see place listing p. 332)* and southeast of Zion National Park *(see place listing p. 461)* in a region of exceptional scenery. Fort Kanab was built in 1864 on the east bank of Kanab Creek for defense and as a base for exploration. Indian attacks forced its abandonment in 1866, but a group of Mormon missionaries reoccupied it and founded the present town in 1870.

Hundreds of movies and TV episodes have been filmed in the area. A favorite set was the Coral Pink Sand Dunes State Park, a windswept area of coral-colored dunes 23 miles northwest of Kanab. The park has camping and picnic facilities as well as a recreation area for off-road vehicles; phone (435) 648-2800.

Kane County Office of Tourism: 78 South 100 East, Kanab, UT 84741. **Phone:** (435) 644-5033 or (800) 733-5263.

Self-guiding tours: Brochures detailing a self-guiding walking tour of Kanab's historic homes are available at Heritage House and at the office of tourism.

BEST FRIENDS ANIMAL SOCIETY SANCTUARY is 5 mi. n. on US 89 to 5001 Angel Canyon Rd., following signs. The sanctuary is one of the country's largest shelters for abused, abandoned and neglected animals. Van tours of the 3,000-acre facility include a visit to Dogtown, where canines are housed, and WildCats Village, home to felines. Birds, horses and rabbits also are among the 2,000 domestic animals at the sanctuary.

Time: Allow 1 hour, 30 minutes minimum. **Hours:** Tours are given daily at 9, 10:30, 1:30 and 3. Closed Christmas. **Cost:** Donations. Reservations are recommended. **Phone:** (435) 644-2001.

CRESCENT MOON THEATER, 150 South 100 East, presents traditional western music and comedy in a relaxed, comfortable setting. Classic movies also are featured year-round. **Time:** Allow 1 hour, 30 minutes minimum. **Hours:** Music and comedy performances are offered once a month. Classic western movies are screened Mon. night. Schedules vary; phone ahead. **Cost:** Music and comedy performance $5-$15; $3-$12 (ages 56+); $2-$6 (ages 6-12). Classic movie $2. **Phone:** (435) 644-2350.

FRONTIER MOVIE TOWN, 297 W. Center St., features a Western town consisting of original movie sets from a variety of local and big-screen productions filmed in the area. **Hours:** Daily 9-9, Mar.-Oct.; 9-5, Nov.-Dec. Phone ahead to confirm schedule. **Cost:** Free. **Phone:** (435) 644-5337.

HERITAGE HOUSE, at the corner of East 100 South and Main St., was built in 1894 for Henry Bowman, one of Kanab's first settlers. The Victorian structure exemplifies human ingenuity in using local resources: Rocks for the foundation and cellar walls were quarried from the red ledges just north of town, the lumber was milled locally and the brick was made by a local kiln operator. Inside is a collection of items from the original owners and neighborhood residents.

Guided tours are available by appointment. **Time:** Allow 30 minutes minimum. **Hours:** Mon.-Fri. 1-5, May-Sept.; by appointment rest of year. Phone ahead to confirm schedule. **Cost:** Donations. **Phone:** (435) 644-3506.

MOQUI CAVE is 5.5 mi. n. on US 89. The cave has collections of dinosaur tracks, which were removed from their original site and brought to the cave; fluorescent minerals; Native American artifacts; and foreign currency. A replica of nearby cliff dwellings that were inhabited about A.D. 900 is displayed. **Hours:** Mon.-Sat. 9-7, Memorial Day-Labor Day; 10-4, rest of year. **Cost:** $5; $4.50 (ages 60+); $3.50 (ages 13-17); $3 (ages 6-12). **Phone:** (435) 644-8525.

AIKENS LODGE **Phone:** (435)644-2625

Motel

$62-$100

Address: 79 W Center St 84741 **Location:** On US 89. **Facility:** 31 units, some two bedrooms. 1-2 stories (no elevator), exterior corridors. **Terms:** open 5/1-11/29 & 4/1-4/30. **Pool(s):** heated outdoor. **Guest Services:** coin laundry.

BIZ

BEST WESTERN RED HILLS **Phone:** (435)644-2675

Hotel

$60-$130

AAA Benefit: Members save up to 20%, plus 10% bonus points with Best Western Rewards®.

Address: 125 W Center St 84741 **Location:** Center. **Facility:** 75 units, some two bedrooms. 2 stories (no elevator), interior/exterior corridors. **Amenities:** *Some:* high-speed Internet. **Pool(s):** heated outdoor. **Activities:** whirlpool. **Guest Services:** coin laundry. **Free Special Amenities: full breakfast and high-speed Internet.**

SAVE BIZ / SOME UNITS FEE

BOB-BON INN **Phone:** 435/644-3069

Motel

Rates not provided

Address: 236 Hwy 89 N 84741 **Location:** On US 89. **Facility:** 16 units. 1-2 stories (no elevator), exterior corridors. **Terms:** office hours 7:30 am-midnight. **Pool(s):** heated outdoor. **Guest Services:** valet and coin laundry. **Free Special Amenities: continental breakfast and local telephone calls.**

SAVE / SOME UNITS FEE

COMFORT INN KANAB **Phone:** 435/644-8888

Hotel

Rates not provided

Address: 815 E 300 S 84741 **Location:** On US 89, just e. **Facility:** 71 units. 3 stories, interior corridors. **Pool(s):** heated outdoor. **Activities:** whirlpool. *Fee:* golf-9 holes. **Guest Services:** coin laundry.

CALL BIZ

/ SOME UNITS FEE

HOLIDAY INN EXPRESS HOTEL & SUITES **Phone:** (435)644-3100

Hotel

$119-$154 5/1-10/31
$89-$119 11/1-4/30

Address: 217 S 100 E 84741 **Location:** On US 89; jct 200 S. **Facility:** 80 units. 3 stories, interior corridors. **Terms:** cancellation fee imposed. **Amenities:** high-speed Internet. **Pool(s):** heated indoor. **Activities:** whirlpool, exercise room. **Guest Services:** coin laundry. **Free Special Amenities: full breakfast and high-speed Internet.**

SAVE BIZ

/ SOME UNITS FEE

PARRY LODGE Phone: 435/644-2601

Motel

$70-$115 5/1-10/31
$49-$69 11/1-4/30

Address: 89 E Center St 84741 **Location:** On US 89; corner of 100 E; center. **Facility:** 89 units, some two bedrooms, efficiencies and kitchens. 1-2 stories (no elevator), interior/exterior corridors. **Terms:** cancellation fee imposed. **Dining:** restaurant, see separate listing. **Pool(s):** heated outdoor. **Guest Services:** coin laundry.

 / SOME UNITS FEE

QUAIL PARK LODGE Phone: (435)215-1447

Motel

$79-$149 5/1-10/31
$69-$119 11/1-4/30

Address: 125 N 300 W (Hwy 89) 84741 **Location:** On US 89. **Facility:** 13 units, some two bedrooms. 1 story, exterior corridors. **Terms:** cancellation fee imposed. **Pool(s):** heated outdoor. **Free Special Amenities: continental breakfast and high-speed Internet.**

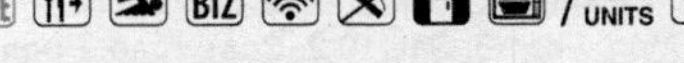 / SOME UNITS

SHILO INN SUITES-KANAB Phone: (435)644-2562

Hotel

$69-$199

Address: 296 W 100 N 84741 **Location:** On US 89; north of downtown. **Facility:** 116 units. 2-3 stories, interior corridors. **Terms:** check-in 4 pm, cancellation fee imposed. **Amenities:** video games (fee). **Pool(s):** heated outdoor. **Activities:** whirlpool. **Guest Services:** coin laundry. **Free Special Amenities: continental breakfast and high-speed Internet.**

(See ad this page.)

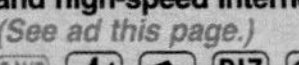

FEE 

/ SOME UNITS FEE

VICTORIAN INN Phone: (435)644-8660

Hotel

$109-$199 5/1-11/1
$89-$159 11/2-4/30

Address: 190 N 300 W 84741 **Location:** North end of town. **Facility:** 28 units. 2 stories (no elevator), interior corridors. **Terms:** check-in 4 pm.

 / SOME UNITS FEE

WHERE TO EAT

CANYONLANDS CAFE Phone: 435/644-8404

American

$8-$15

AAA Inspector Notes: This small family-owned and –operated dining room has minimal décor. Flavorful favorites include burgers, fish tacos and sandwiches. **Address:** 198 S 100 E 84741 **Location:** On US 89; jct 200 S. 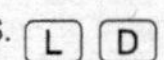

ESCOBAR'S MEXICAN RESTAURANT Phone: 435/644-3739

Mexican

$8-$18

AAA Inspector Notes: This small restaurant is always packed due to the friendly owners and fresh authentic Mexican cuisine. It's not fancy, but the food tastes great. **Address:** 373 E 300 S 84741 **Location:** Just e.

HOUSTON'S TRAIL'S END RESTAURANT Phone: 435/644-2488

American

$8-$20

AAA Inspector Notes: Steak and seafood, as well as some Mexican specialties, are served in the Western-style dining room. **Bar:** beer only. **Address:** 32 E Center St 84741 **Location:** On US 89.

LUO'S CAFE Phone: 435/644-5592

Chinese

$10-$22

AAA Inspector Notes: In the center of town, the family-run restaurant offers casual Chinese fare such as chicken fried rice, tempura shrimp, kung pao chicken and mu shu pork. To-go orders are welcomed. **Bar:** beer only. **Address:** 365 S 100 E 84741 **Location:** Jct US 89 and 89A, just s. L D

▼ *See AAA listing this page* ▼

NEDRA'S TOO **Phone:** 435/644-2030

Mexican
$4-$17

AAA Inspector Notes: This second location is just like the first with great Southwestern charm and fresh Mexican food. Friendly servers bring simple dishes to guests in a small dining room whose walls are covered with Mexican art, old movie pictures and NASCAR collectibles. Any of the staff here can reel off a list of celebrities who have dined here over the years. **Bar:** beer & wine. **Address:** 310 S 100 E 84741 **Location:** Jct US 89 and SR 89A. B L D

PARRY LODGE RESTAURANT **Phone:** 435/644-2601

American
$6-$18

AAA Inspector Notes: Attractive, reserved dining room. **Bar:** beer & wine. **Address:** 89 E Center St 84741 **Location:** On US 89; corner of 100 E center; in Parry Lodge. B L D

ROCKING V CAFE **Phone:** 435/644-8001

International
$8-$36

AAA Inspector Notes: Casual, elegant food is served in the 1892 historic cafe. The varied menu offers made-from-scratch enchiladas, wraps, fresh fish and fine steaks, as well as vegan and vegetarian selections. **Bar:** full bar. **Reservations:** suggested. **Address:** 97 W Center St 84741 **Location:** Downtown. D

THE THREE BEARS CREAMERY COTTAGE
Phone: 435/644-3300

Sandwiches
$4-$10

AAA Inspector Notes: In a city nicknamed "Little Hollywood" for the many old movies that were filmed there, the small restaurant doesn't look like much from outside. Inside, however, is a comfortable setting decorated with bears and a small waterfall. Fresh soups, sandwiches and sundaes make up the menu. The fresh wheat bread is homemade. **Address:** 210 S 100 E 84741 **Location:** On US 89; jct 200 S. L D

KAYSVILLE (B-3) pop. 27,300, elev. 4,357'

• Part of Salt Lake City area — see map p. 412

UTAH BOTANICAL CENTER is at 725 S. Sego Lily Dr. (South 50 West). The 100-acre site features a wildflower meadow; a variety of themed gardens, including butterfly and teaching gardens; walking and bicycling trails; and an arboretum. Wetlands shelter such wildlife as great blue herons and terns.

Ponds are stocked with largemouth bass, bluegill and channel catfish, and fishing is permitted. At the Utah House, a demonstration and education center, visitors can learn about sustainable living, which aims to reduce an individual's or society's use of the Earth's natural resources. **Time:** Allow 2 hours minimum. **Hours:** Grounds daily dawn-dusk. Utah House Mon.-Fri. 1-5, Sat. 10-2. **Cost:** Free. **Phone:** (801) 593-8969.

PEPPERBELLY'S **Phone:** 801/444-3132

Mexican
$7-$12

AAA Inspector Notes: The eatery serves favorite Mexican dishes in a dining room filled with automotive memorabilia celebrating yesteryear and a love of the road. **Address:** 141 N Main St 84037 **Location:** I-15 exit 328, just e, then just s. L D

Safety tip: Keep a current AAA/CAA Road Atlas in every vehicle

LAKE POWELL—See Glen Canyon National Recreation Area p. 347.

LAYTON (B-3) pop. 67,311, elev. 4,350'
• Restaurants p. 358

Davis Area Convention & Visitors Bureau: 1572 N. Woodland Park Dr., Suite 510, Layton, UT 84041. **Phone:** (801) 774-8200 or (888) 777-9771.

HERITAGE MUSEUM OF LAYTON is .4 mi. e. on W. Gentile St., then .3 mi. n. to 403 N. Wasatch Dr. The historical museum displays Native American and pioneer artifacts, documents, newspapers and photographs that tell the story of the cultural, recreational and economic development of northern Davis County. Many displays depict the area at the turn of the 20th century when it was predominately rural and agricultural.

Wheelchairs are available. **Tours:** Guided tours are available. **Time:** Allow 30 minutes minimum. **Hours:** Tues.-Fri. 11-6, Sat. 1-5. Closed major holidays. **Cost:** Free. **Phone:** (801) 336-3930.

COMFORT INN **Phone:** (801)544-5577

Hotel
$69-$149

Address: 877 N 400 W 84041 **Location:** I-15 exit 331, just e. **Facility:** 122 units. 3 stories, interior corridors. **Terms:** cancellation fee imposed. **Amenities:** high-speed Internet, safes (fee). **Pool(s):** heated indoor. **Activities:** whirlpool, exercise room. **Guest Services:** valet and coin laundry.

SAVE BIZ / SOME UNITS FEE

COURTYARD BY MARRIOTT **Phone:** (801)217-2300

Hotel
$89-$169

AAA Benefit:
AAA hotel discounts of 5% or more.

Address: 1803 Woodland Park Dr 84041 **Location:** I-15 exit 332 (Antelope Dr), 0.3 mi se. **Facility:** 110 units. 3 stories, interior corridors. **Pool(s):** heated indoor. **Activities:** whirlpool, exercise room. **Guest Services:** valet and coin laundry, area transportation-within 5 mi.

BIZ / SOME UNITS

HAMPTON INN **Phone:** (801)775-8800

Hotel
$89-$139

AAA Benefit:
Members save up to 10% everyday!

Address: 1700 Woodland Park Dr 84041 **Location:** I-15 exit 332 (Antelope Dr), 0.3 mi e, then just s. **Facility:** 98 units. 3 stories, interior corridors. **Terms:** 1-7 night minimum stay, cancellation fee imposed. **Amenities:** video games (fee). **Pool(s):** heated indoor. **Activities:** whirlpool, exercise room. **Guest Services:** valet and coin laundry.

BIZ / SOME UNITS

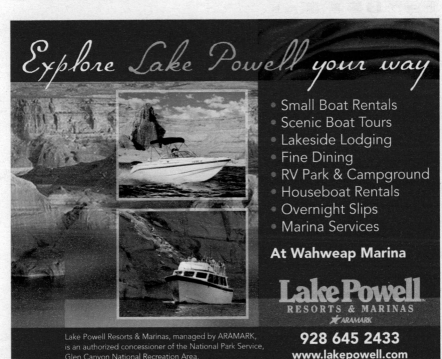

HILTON GARDEN INN **Phone:** (801)416-8899

Hotel
$79-$149

AAA Benefit:
Unparalleled hospitality at a special Member rate.

Address: 762 W Heritage Park Blvd 84041 **Location:** I-15 exit 332 (Antelope Dr), 0.5 mi e to 700 W, then 0.5 mi s. **Facility:** 147 units. 3 stories, interior corridors. **Terms:** 1-7 night minimum stay, cancellation fee imposed. **Amenities:** high-speed Internet. **Pool(s):** heated indoor. **Activities:** whirlpool, exercise room. **Guest Services:** valet and coin laundry. BIZ

HOLIDAY INN EXPRESS LAYTON **Phone:** (801)773-3773

Hotel
$99-$139

Address: 1695 Woodland Park Dr 84041 **Location:** I-15 exit 332 (Antelope Dr), 0.3 mi se. **Facility:** 102 units. 4 stories, interior corridors. **Amenities:** video games (fee). **Pool(s):** heated indoor. **Activities:** whirlpool, exercise room. **Guest Services:** valet and coin laundry.

BIZ

HOME2 SUITES BY HILTON LAYTON
Phone: (801)820-9222

Hotel
$99-$119

AAA Benefit:
AAA members can save up to 10% everyday.

Address: 803 W Heritage Park Blvd 84041 **Location:** I-15 exit 331, 0.6 mi n to Heritage Blvd, then 0.4 mi w. **Facility:** 107 units. 4 stories, interior corridors. *Bath:* shower only. **Terms:** 1-7 night minimum stay, cancellation fee imposed. **Amenities:** *Fee:* video games, high-speed Internet. **Pool(s):** heated indoor. **Activities:** whirlpool, exercise room. **Guest Services:** coin laundry.

LA QUINTA INN & SUITES SALT LAKE CITY LAYTON
Phone: (801)776-6700

Hotel
$72-$148

Address: 1965 N 1200 W 84041 **Location:** I-15 exit 332 (Antelope Dr), just e. **Facility:** 100 units. 3 stories, interior corridors. **Amenities:** video games (fee). *Some:* high-speed Internet. **Pool(s):** heated indoor. **Activities:** whirlpool, exercise room. **Guest Services:** coin laundry.

FEE / SOME UNITS

TOWNEPLACE SUITES BY MARRIOTT
Phone: (801)779-2422

Extended Stay Hotel
$116-$142

AAA Benefit:
AAA hotel discounts of 5% or more.

Address: 1743 Woodland Park Dr 84041 **Location:** I-15 exit 332 (Antelope Dr), 0.3 mi se. **Facility:** 95 kitchen units, some two bedrooms. 3 stories, interior corridors. **Pool(s):** heated outdoor. **Activities:** exercise room. **Guest Services:** valet and coin laundry.

BIZ

/ SOME UNITS FEE

WHERE TO EAT

CORBIN'S GRILLE **Phone:** 801/825-2502

Steak
$8-$29

AAA Inspector Notes: Specializing in wood-fired steaks and fresh seafood from around the world, the restaurant tempts with choices such as surf and turf, seafood martini shakers and pork saltimbocca. Last but not least, the chocolate fondue and made-in-house desserts satisfy. **Bar:** full bar. **Reservations:** suggested. **Address:** 748 W Heritage Park Blvd 84041 **Location:** I-15 exit 332 (Antelope Dr), 0.5 mi e, then 0.3 mi s. L D

IGGY'S SPORTS GRILL **Phone:** 801/525-1515

American
$7-$18

AAA Inspector Notes: Every seat has a view of the sports action on the multiple TVs. There are plenty of choices on the menu, including burgers, pizza, pasta, ribs, chicken and seafood. **Bar:** full bar. **Address:** 802 W 1425 N 84041 **Location:** I-15 exit 331, 0.7 mi n on Hill Field Rd, then 0.4 mi w. L D

MACCOOL'S PUBLIC HOUSE **Phone:** 801/728-9111

Irish
$6-$18

AAA Inspector Notes: Families enjoy an authentic Irish dining experience in this friendly pub, which has 7-foot-high carved wooden chairs, stenciled Irish blessings and darts in the game room. Traditional favorites include Guinness stew, corned beef and cabbage, shepherd's pie and chicken potpie. **Bar:** full bar. **Address:** 855 W Heritage Park Blvd 84041 **Location:** I-15 exit 332 (Antelope Dr), 0.5 mi se.
L D

ROOSTER'S BREWING CO **Phone:** 801/774-9330

American
$8-$22

AAA Inspector Notes: Cordial service enhances visits to this inviting brewpub. Menu selections include a wide variety of starters, pizza, specialty salads, sandwiches and entrées such as baked chicken Milano, broiled salmon, Angus rib-eye topped with Cambozola butter and herb-crusted rack of lamb. The center-cut beef tenderloin is delicious. **Bar:** full bar. **Address:** 748 W Heritage Park Blvd 84041 **Location:** I-15 exit 332 (Antelope Dr), 0.5 mi e to 700 W, then just s. L D

LEHI (C-3) pop. 47,407, elev. 4,550'

Lehi was named for an individual in the Book of Mormon. The polygamous practices of the area's Mormons were vigorously prosecuted by the federal government in the 1870s and '80s; many church members went into hiding. Local legend claims that when federal officers ordered a small boy to take them to a polygamist, he cautiously led them to a chicken run and pointed out a rooster.

JOHN HUTCHING'S MUSEUM OF NATURAL HISTORY is at 55 N. Center St. The museum contains pioneer and Native American artifacts, fossils, an extensive mineral collection, seashells and bird specimens. Among the highlights are Butch Cassidy's sawed-off shotgun, military items and Anasazi Indian artifacts. **Time:** Allow 2 hours minimum. **Hours:** Tues.-Sat. 11-5. Closed major holidays. **Cost:** $4; $3 (ages 3-12 and 60+); $12 (family, maximum six people). **Phone:** (801) 768-7180.

THANKSGIVING POINT is off I-15 exit 284 to Ashton Blvd. The more than 700-acre complex, a dairy farm for close to a century, includes extensive flower and vegetable gardens, museums and learning centers, an animal farm, a golf course designed by Hall of Fame golfer Johnny Miller, a farmers market, a dinosaur exhibit, shops, restaurants, a megaplex theater and a 5,000-seat amphitheater.

Farm Country—a working farm that is home to chickens, cows, horses, llamas and peacocks—also has educational displays and pony and wagon rides. Fifty-five acres of themed gardens available for strolling include the Children's Discovery Garden, Rose Garden, Italianate Garden, Butterfly Garden, Monet Garden, Waterfall Garden and Fragrance Garden.

Hours: Grounds Mon.-Sat. and holidays 10-8. Gardens Mon.-Sat. 10-8, late Mar.-late Oct. Farm Country Mon.-Sat. 10-8, Apr.-Oct.; 10-6, rest of year. Closed Thanksgiving and Christmas. **Cost:** Gardens $10; $9 (ages 65+); $6 (ages 3-12). Farm Country (includes pony and wagon ride) $5. **Phone:** (801) 768-2300, (801) 768-7401 for golf course or (888) 672-6040.

Children's Discovery Garden is off I-15 exit 284 at Thanksgiving Point, adjacent to the botanical gardens. The manicured grounds feature acres of colorful botanical gardens. Nearly 2 miles of walking paths wind throughout the bright landscape. Of particular interest to children are the Noah's Ark exhibit, a maze constructed from hedges, and bear caves ready for exploration; Noah's Ark also has water features. Educational programs are offered. **Time:** Allow 1 hour minimum. **Hours:** Mon.-Sat. 10-8, late Mar.-late Oct. **Cost:** $6; $4 (ages 3-12). **Phone:** (801) 768-2300.

Museum of Ancient Life is off I-15 exit 284 at Thanksgiving Point. The museum features 60 mounted skeletons, hundreds of large and small fossils, various paleontology displays and more than 50 hands-on exhibits geared toward children. The Mammoth Screen Theater features large format 3-D movies. A seasonal farmers market provides produce, arts and crafts, and entertainment.

Hours: Museum Mon.-Sat. and holidays 10-8; closed Thanksgiving and Christmas. Theater Mon.-Sat. 10:30-7:30. Farmers market Fri. 3-7, early Aug.-early Oct. **Cost:** Museum $10; $8 (ages 3-12 and 65+). Theater $7.50; $5.50 (ages 3-12 and 65+). Combination ticket $15; $12 (ages 3-12 and 65+). **Phone:** (801) 768-2300.

BEST WESTERN PLUS TIMPANOGOS INN
Phone: 801/768-1400

Hotel
Rates not provided

AAA Benefit: Members save up to 20%, plus 10% bonus points with Best Western Rewards®.

Address: 195 S 850 E 84043 **Location:** I-15 exit 279, just w, then just s. **Facility:** 59 units. 2 stories (no elevator), interior corridors. **Amenities:** safes (fee). **Pool(s):** heated indoor. **Activities:** whirlpool, limited exercise equipment. **Guest Services:** valet and coin laundry. **Free Special Amenities: full breakfast and high-speed Internet.**

SAVE BIZ / SOME UNITS FEE

HAMPTON INN LEHI THANKSGIVING POINT
Phone: (801)766-1186

Contemporary Hotel
$89-$109

AAA Benefit: Members save up to 10% everyday!

Address: 3576 N Maple Loop 84043 **Location:** I-15 exit 284 (Highland), just w. **Facility:** 75 units. 3 stories, interior corridors. **Terms:** 1-7 night minimum stay, cancellation fee imposed. **Pool(s):** heated indoor. **Activities:** whirlpool, exercise room. **Guest Services:** valet and coin laundry.

BIZ

SPRINGHILL SUITES BY MARRIOTT LEHI AT THANKSGIVING POINT
Phone: (801)341-6970

Hotel
$125-$153

AAA Benefit: AAA hotel discounts of 5% or more.

Address: 2447 W Executive Pkwy 84043 **Location:** I-15 exit 284 (Highland), just w, then 0.5 mi s. **Facility:** 94 units. 4 stories, interior corridors. **Amenities:** high-speed Internet. **Pool(s):** heated indoor. **Activities:** whirlpool, exercise room. **Guest Services:** valet and coin laundry.

BIZ

SUPER 8
Phone: (801)766-8800

Motel
$54-$130

Address: 125 S 850 E 84043 **Location:** I-15 exit 279, just w, then just s. **Facility:** 64 units. 3 stories, interior corridors. **Amenities:** high-speed Internet. **Pool(s):** heated indoor. **Activities:** whirlpool, exercise room. **Guest Services:** coin laundry.

BIZ / SOME UNITS FEE

WHERE TO EAT

HARVEST RESTAURANT
Phone: 801/768-4990

Continental
$11-$29

AAA Inspector Notes: Seasonal contemporary American and classical French-inspired dishes incorporate fresh, regional ingredients that are either locally grown or from the restaurant's own gardens and greenhouses. **Address:** 3003 N Thanksgiving Way 84043 **Location:** I-15 exit 284 (Highland), just w, then 0.6 mi s; at Thanksgiving Point. L D

LOGAN (A-3) pop. 48,174, elev. 4,507'

• Hotels p. 360 • Restaurants p. 362

Built on the terraces of prehistoric Lake Bonneville, Logan lies in the fertile Cache Valley by the Logan River. A monument to Logan's past and present is its Mormon Temple. Finished in 1884, the temple overlooks the town and is one of the state's earliest and finest; it is not open to visitors.

The Logan, Utah Regional Family History Center, on the lower level of the Logan Tabernacle at 50 N. Main, is available for research. The tabernacle has been described as an excellent example of an early Mormon meeting house. The history center contains computers, microfilm, microfiche, books, periodicals and manuscripts for reference use; phone (435) 755-5594. The tabernacle is open for tours in summer. Logan also is the home of Utah State University.

The Logan area is well known for its Jardine Juniper, believed to be the planet's largest and oldest juniper tree. An easy 4.4-mile trail to the 1,500-year-old tree begins 12 miles up Logan Canyon. To the west are the Wellsville Mountains, said to be the world's tallest mountains on the narrowest base.

Hardware Ranch, 15 miles up Blacksmith Fork Canyon on SR 101, is an elk feeding station where the animals can be viewed during sleigh rides on fall weekends and in winter (weather permitting) or from the visitor center *(see Wasatch-Cache National Forest p. 458)*; phone (435) 753-6168 or (435) 753-6206.

Logan also is the southeastern terminus of the Logan Canyon National Scenic Byway (US 89), which ends at Bear Lake State Park. This road runs through Logan Canyon beneath cliffs, along a river and through forests.

Nearby Bear Lake is a turquoise-colored lake with white sandy beaches. It is 20 miles long, 8 miles wide and 208 feet deep. Four state parks offer boating, jet skiing, sailboarding, fishing, swimming, picnicking and camping facilities. Equipment rentals are available at the beach or in Garden City. North of the Bear Lake Marina is a marker along the Oregon Trail. Skiing is available nearby off US 89. A guide detailing 15 scenic area hiking trails is available at the visitors bureau.

Cache Valley Visitors Bureau: 199 N. Main St., Logan, UT 84321. **Phone:** (435) 755-1890 or (800) 882-4433.

Self-guiding tours: A brochure describing a walking tour of 19th- and early 20th-century buildings along and near Logan's historic Main Street is available at the visitors bureau.

Shopping areas: Dillard's and JCPenney are the anchor stores at Cache Valley Mall, 1300 N. Main St.

AMERICAN WEST HERITAGE CENTER—see Wellsville p. 459.

DAUGHTERS OF UTAH PIONEERS CACHE MUSEUM is at 160 N. Main St. The museum exhibits Mormon pioneer relics and a collection of musical instruments, including a melodeon. The museum also provides wool-dyeing, carding and spinning demonstrations. **Time:** Allow 30 minutes minimum. **Hours:** Tues.-Fri. 10-4, June-Aug.; by appointment rest of year. **Cost:** Donations. **Phone:** (435) 752-5139, or (435) 753-1635 in the off-season.

ELLEN ECCLES THEATRE is at 43 S. Main St. Completed in 1923, the ornate theater began as a vaudeville house. Managed and restored in the early 1990s to its former beauty by the Cache Valley Center for the Arts (CVCA), the theater boasts an opulent interior and a graceful shape. In addition to year-round performances by such regional groups as the Utah Festival Opera & Musical Theatre, Cache Valley Civic Ballet and Music Theatre West, CVCA presents dozens of touring productions September to May.

Guided tours are available by appointment. **Time:** Allow 2 hours minimum. **Hours:** Ticket office open Mon.-Fri. 10-5:30 and 1 hour prior to curtain. Closed major holidays. Phone ahead to confirm schedule. **Cost:** Guided tour $5 (July-Aug.); free (rest of year). Performance ticket prices vary. **Phone:** (435) 752-0026.

NORA ECCLES HARRISON MUSEUM OF ART is on the Utah State University campus at 650 North 1100 East. The museum contains changing exhibitions of ceramics, paintings, sculpture, photographs and prints. It also features a permanent collection of 20th-century American ceramics and paintings. **Hours:** Tues.-Sat. 11-4. Closed major holidays. **Cost:** Free. **Parking:** $5; free (after 3:45 p.m. and on weekends). **Phone:** (435) 797-0163.

UTAH STATE UNIVERSITY MUSEUM OF ANTHROPOLOGY is in Utah State University's Old Main building, 1.5 mi. e. on US 89/East 400 North, .1 mi. n. on North 1100 East, then .2 mi. w. on East 550 North to 730 Old Main Hill. Through exhibits, teaching guides and special programs, the museum allows visitors to explore various cultures, including those of the Great Basin Indians, Egyptians, Africans and Peruvians. **Tours:** Guided tours are available. **Time:** Allow 30 minutes minimum. **Hours:** Mon.-Fri. 8-5, Sat. 10-4. Closed major holidays. **Cost:** Free. **Phone:** (435) 797-7545.

BEST WESTERN BAUGH MOTEL **Phone:** (435)752-5220

Motel
$80-$160

AAA Benefit: Members save up to 20%, plus 10% bonus points with Best Western Rewards®.

Address: 153 S Main St 84321 **Location:** Just s of center. **Facility:** 76 units, some two bedrooms. 1-2 stories (no elevator), exterior corridors. **Terms:** 3 day cancellation notice. **Amenities:** *Some:* high-speed Internet. **Pool(s):** heated outdoor. **Activities:** whirlpool. **Guest Services:** valet laundry. **Free Special Amenities: local telephone calls and high-speed Internet.**

  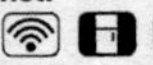  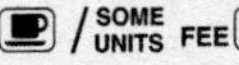

BEST WESTERN WESTON INN **Phone:** (435)752-5700

Hotel
$90-$130

AAA Benefit: Members save up to 20%, plus 10% bonus points with Best Western Rewards®.

Address: 250 N Main St 84321 **Location:** 0.3 mi n of center. **Facility:** 89 units. 2 stories (no elevator), exterior corridors. **Amenities:** high-speed Internet. **Pool(s):** heated indoor. **Activities:** sauna, whirlpool, exercise room. **Guest Services:** coin laundry. **Free Special Amenities: local telephone calls and high-speed Internet.**

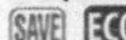     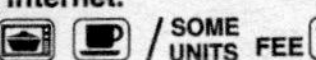

CRYSTAL INN **Phone:** (435)752-0707

Hotel
$73-$129

Address: 853 S Hwy 89 and 91 84321 **Location:** 2 mi s of center. **Facility:** 86 units, some kitchens. 3 stories, interior corridors. **Pool(s):** heated indoor. **Activities:** whirlpool, exercise room. **Guest Services:** coin laundry. ***(See ad this page.)***

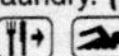   

HAMPTON INN **Phone:** (435)713-4567

Hotel
$82-$109

AAA Benefit:
Members save up to 10% everyday!

Address: 1665 N Main St 84341 **Location:** 1.5 mi n of center. **Facility:** 58 units. 3 stories, interior corridors. **Terms:** 1-7 night minimum stay, cancellation fee imposed. **Amenities:** high-speed Internet. **Pool(s):** heated indoor. **Activities:** whirlpool, exercise room. **Guest Services:** valet and coin laundry.

HOLIDAY INN EXPRESS & SUITES
Phone: (435)752-3444

Contemporary Hotel
$95-$299

Address: 2235 N Main St 84341 **Location:** 2.8 mi n of center. **Facility:** 75 units. 3 stories, interior corridors. **Amenities:** high-speed Internet. **Pool(s):** heated indoor. **Activities:** whirlpool, exercise room. **Guest Services:** valet and coin laundry.

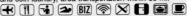

SPRINGHILL SUITES BY MARRIOTT
Phone: (435)750-5180

Hotel
$109-$299

AAA Benefit:
AAA hotel discounts of 5% or more.

Address: 625 S Riverwoods Pkwy 84321 **Location:** 0.8 mi s of center. Located at Riverwoods Conference Center. **Facility:** 115 units. 4 stories, interior corridors. **Amenities:** high-speed Internet. **Dining:** Elements Restaurant at Riverwoods, see separate listing. **Pool(s):** heated indoor. **Activities:** whirlpool, exercise room. **Guest Services:** valet and coin laundry, area transportation-within 35 mi.

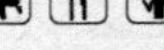 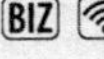   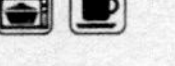

SUPER 8 **Phone:** (435)753-8883

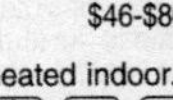

Motel
$46-$86

Address: 865 S Hwy 89/91 84321 **Location:** 2 mi s of center. **Facility:** 59 units, some two bedrooms. 3 stories (no elevator), interior corridors. **Parking:** winter plug-ins. **Pool(s):** heated indoor. **Activities:** whirlpool.

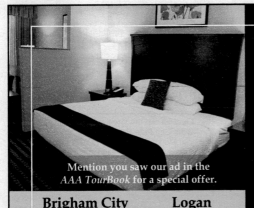

UNIVERSITY GUEST HOTEL & CONFERENCE CENTER **Phone:** 435/797-0017

Hotel

$79-$129 5/1-10/31
$65-$109 11/1-4/30

Address: 860 E 700 N 84322 **Location:** E of US 89 and 91; on Utah State University campus. **Facility:** 74 units. 5 stories, interior corridors. **Guest Services:** valet and coin laundry.

WHERE TO EAT

ANGIE'S RESTAURANT **Phone:** 435/752-9252

American
$7-$21

AAA Inspector Notes: Guests can stop in at this established spot for three meals a day seven days a week. On the extensive menu are dishes served in good-size portions. Friendly servers make their way among the booths, tables and counter. **Address:** 690 N Main 84321 **Location:** 0.3 mi n of center. B L D

BEEHIVE GRILL **Phone:** 435/753-2600

American
$7-$19

AAA Inspector Notes: Home of a namesake root beer, this pub features hand-crafted sodas, fine ales and large-screen televisions in the lounge. The varied menu includes chili, soup, pub burgers, plenty of poultry favorites, pork ribs, smoked salmon wraps and beer-battered fish and chips. **Bar:** full bar. **Address:** 255 S Main St 84321 **Location:** I-15 exit 362, 0.5 mi s of center. L D

CAFE SABOR **Phone:** 435/752-8088

Mexican
$6-$12

AAA Inspector Notes: The eatery, with a comfortable, authentic Mexican atmosphere, serves large, reasonably priced dishes for both lunch and dinner. **Bar:** full bar. **Address:** 600 W Center St 84321 **Location:** Just w of downtown; in Old Rail Depot. L D

COPPER MILL **Phone:** 435/752-0647

American
$9-$21

AAA Inspector Notes: Families can unwind in this relaxed space as they savor prime rib, chicken, steak, ribs and seafood dishes. **Bar:** beer & wine. **Address:** 55 N Main St, Suite 408 84321 **Location:** Center of Main St; 3rd Level. L D

ELEMENTS RESTAURANT AT RIVERWOODS **Phone:** 435/750-5171

American
$8-$28

AAA Inspector Notes: The upscale restaurant features sleek décor and gracious staff. The extensive menu includes a colorful Thai lettuce wrap, mouthwatering wood-fired pizza, sugar-spiced pork baguette, roasted-chicken fettuccine, turkey chop, Alaskan halibut, kamikaze salmon served with roasted pineapple-ginger coulis, sweet cola-glazed meatloaf and wood-fired roast tenderloin. Desserts include lemon carrot cake, peanut butter cup and layered s'mores semifreddo. The outdoor patio offers awesome river views. **Bar:** full bar. **Address:** 35 E 640 S 84321 **Location:** 0.8 mi s of center; in SpringHill Suites by Marriott. L D

EL SOL **Phone:** 435/752-5743

Mexican
$6-$11

AAA Inspector Notes: Fast, friendly, upbeat service can be expected at this colorful eatery, which prepares favorites such as nachos, quesadillas, enchiladas, chimichangas, tostadas, chile verde, chiles rellenos and burritos, in addition to a nice selection of value combination entrées and delicious marinated mahi-mahi tacos. The attractively garnished fried ice cream is delicious. **Address:** 871 N Main St 84321 **Location:** 1.1 mi n of center.

L D

FREDRICO'S PIZZA **Phone:** 435/752-0130

Pizza
$6-$15

AAA Inspector Notes: Enjoy pizza, pasta, a salad or a sandwich at this popular eatery that has been around since the 1950s. **Address:** 1349 E 700 N 84321 **Location:** E of Utah State University.

L D

HAMILTONS STEAK & SEAFOOD **Phone:** 435/787-8450

Steak
$9-$29

AAA Inspector Notes: The impressive stone structure and inviting lobby add to the ambience of the warm and cozy dining areas and lounge. The vast menu features a wide variety of appetizers, Caesar and wedge salads, soups, sandwiches, clam linguine, seafood Alfredo, blackened ahi tuna, cedar-plank salmon, beef Wellington, herb-roasted rack of lamb, pineapple-glazed chicken and a rack of ribs. Delicious side dishes are available. The carving station is a favorite, and the creative seasonal dessert menu is plentiful. **Bar:** full bar. **Address:** 2427 N Main St 84341 **Location:** 3 mi n. L D

KAMIN THAI CUISINE **Phone:** 435/755-6543

Thai
$8-$16

AAA Inspector Notes: With a pleasant atmosphere and charming garden patio, diners sit down to preparations of meat, seafood, rice and noodles with varied wines and beers. **Bar:** beer & wine. **Address:** 51 W 200 S 84321 **Location:** 0.3 mi s of Center St, then just w.

B L D

LE NONNE RISTORANTE ITALIANO **Phone:** 435/752-9577

Italian
$8-$23

AAA Inspector Notes: The charming home turned upscale ristorante serves classic Italian entrées inspired by the Tuscan Alps and the rest of country. Choices include grapefruit salad with asparagus and bay shrimp, tagliatelle and crème brûle. Patrons can relax in the comfortable dining room or on a lovely tree-shaded patio. **Bar:** full bar. **Reservations:** suggested. **Address:** 129 N 100 E 84321 **Location:** Just e of 100 N, then just n; downtown. **Parking:** street only. L D

MANTI pop. 3,276

MANTI COUNTRY VILLAGE MOTEL **Phone:** 435/835-9300

Motel
$69-$99

Address: 145 N Main St 84642 **Location:** On US 89; just n of center. **Facility:** 23 units, some two bedrooms. 2 stories (no elevator), exterior corridors. **Terms:** cancellation fee imposed. **Activities:** whirlpool.

/ SOME UNITS FEE

MANTI-LA SAL NATIONAL FOREST (D-4)

Elevations in the forest range from 5,320 ft. at the San Pete Ranger District to 12,721 ft. at Mount Peale. Refer to AAA maps for additional elevation information.

In southeastern Utah, Manti-La Sal National Forest encompasses 1,413,111 acres in three sections. The largest portion, the Manti Division, is characterized by narrow canyons, mountain meadows and broad rolling ridges covered with aspen and spruce. It lies in central Utah and is part of the Wasatch Plateau.

The La Sal Division, in the spectacular natural bridge and red rock canyon country of southeastern

Utah, is made up of two isolated mountain ranges, the La Sals east of Moab and the Blue Mountains west of Monticello. Cross-country skiing and snowmobiling are popular. The forest's La Sal and Abajo mountain ranges provide opportunities for hiking and climbing. Hunting for grouse, waterfowl, turkeys, mule deer, elk, black bears and mountain lions, and fishing for trout are permitted in the forest. A variety of campsites is available.

Skyline Drive Scenic Backway, an 87-mile-long scenic route through the high mountains along the crest of the Wasatch Plateau, affords spectacular views of Nevada to the west and Colorado to the east. Animals are abundant and include elk, deer, bears and moose. Prehistoric animals that once inhabited the area include mammoths, mastodons and short-faced bears.

The narrow, rough, unpaved road, which is open mid-July through September 30, should be attempted only in good weather. Some sections are open to four-wheel-drive, high clearance vehicles only. Contact a ranger for road conditions before making the drive.

For further information contact the Forest Supervisor, Manti-La Sal National Forest, 599 W. Price River Dr., Price, UT 84501; phone (435) 637-2817. *See Recreation Chart.*

MARYSVALE pop. 408

MOORE'S OLD PINE INN **Phone:** 435/326-4565

Bed & Breakfast

$65-$125

Address: 60 S Hwy 89 84750 **Location:** Center. **Facility:** Guests of this 1882 inn can choose a room or suite in the B&B or stay out back in one of the Old West-style cabins. A creek runs through the property. 14 units, some efficiencies and cabins. 1-2 stories (no elevator), interior/exterior corridors. *Bath:* some shared. **Terms:** 2-14 night minimum stay - seasonal and/or weekends, 30 day cancellation notice. **Activities:** horseshoes. **Guest Services:** coin laundry.

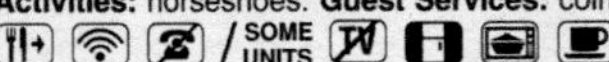

MEXICAN HAT (G-5) pop. 31, elev. 4,400'

Mexican Hat is named for a 2,500-ton boulder that resembles a sombrero. The formation, 60 feet wide and 12 feet thick, balances on a 200-foot cliff and can be seen from a 17-mile looping dirt road.

GOOSENECKS STATE PARK is 9 mi. n.w. off SR 261. The park provides a cliff-top overlook into the scenic "gooseneck" canyons of the San Juan River. The deep loops are entrenched meanders dug by the silt-laden river. The distance across the goosenecks is 1 mile; the river's course covers 6 miles.

At one point the river makes a 3-mile curve around a ridge only 100 yards wide. Eventually some of the necks will be breached, creating new natural bridges. **Hours:** Daily dawn-dusk. **Cost:** Free. **Phone:** (435) 678-2238.

THE VALLEY OF THE GODS is 10 mi. n.e. via SR 261. Nature, by way of water, wind and ice erosion, has carved spectacular, brilliantly colored sandstone monoliths and rock formations over millions of years. A scenic, 17-mile loop road that connects SRs 163 and 261 winds its way through the valley. The dirt road is bumpy and steep in some parts but is suitable for driving during favorable weather.

Note: Visitors should inquire about road conditions during inclement weather. **Time:** Allow 1 hour minimum. **Hours:** Daily dawn-dusk (weather permitting). **Cost:** Free. **Phone:** (435) 587-1500.

SAN JUAN INN & TRADING POST **Phone:** 435/683-2220

Motel

Rates not provided

Address: Hwy 163 & San Juan River 84531 **Location:** Center. **Facility:** 36 units. 2 stories (no elevator), exterior corridors. **Activities:** fishing, exercise room. **Guest Services:** coin laundry.

BIZ / SOME UNITS FEE

MIDVALE pop. 27,964

- **Restaurants p. 364**
- **Hotels & Restaurants map & index p. 426**
- **Part of Salt Lake City area — see map p. 412**

HOLIDAY INN EXPRESS SALT LAKE CITY SOUTH – MIDVALE **Phone:** 801/352-8100 51

Contemporary Hotel

Rates not provided

Address: 7134 S 700 E 84047 **Location:** I-15 exit 297 (7200 S), 1.7 mi e to 700 E, then just n. **Facility:** 66 units. 3 stories, interior corridors. **Amenities:** high-speed Internet, safes. **Pool(s):** heated indoor. **Activities:** whirlpool, exercise room. **Guest Services:** valet and coin laundry. BIZ

LA QUINTA INN SALT LAKE CITY MIDVALE **Phone:** (801)566-3291 49

Hotel

$68-$126

Address: 7231 S Catalpa St 84047 **Location:** I-15 exit 297 (7200 S), just e, then just s. Close to interstate. **Facility:** 122 units. 2 stories (no elevator), interior corridors. **Amenities:** video games (fee). **Pool(s):** heated indoor. **Activities:** whirlpool. **Guest Services:** coin laundry.

FEE / SOME UNITS

MAGNUSON HOTEL SALT LAKE - MIDVALE **Phone:** (801)566-4141 48

Hotel

$59-$90

Address: 280 W 7200 S 84047 **Location:** I-15 exit 297 (7200 S), just e. **Facility:** 91 units. 2 stories (no elevator), interior corridors. **Pool(s):** heated outdoor. **Activities:** whirlpool, exercise room. **Guest Services:** coin laundry. **Free Special Amenities: expanded continental breakfast and high-speed Internet.**

SAVE / SOME UNITS FEE

SUPER 8 MIDVALE **Phone:** (801)255-5559 50

Motel

$49-$62

Address: 7048 S 900 E 84047 **Location:** I-15 exit 297 (7200 S), 1.8 mi e to 900 E, then just n. **Facility:** 65 units. 2 stories, interior corridors. **Amenities:** *Some:* safes. **Activities:** whirlpool. **Guest Services:** coin laundry. **Free Special Amenities: expanded continental breakfast and high-speed Internet.**

SAVE / SOME UNITS

(See map & index p. 426.)

WHERE TO EAT

BOHEMIAN BREWERY **Phone:** 801/566-5474 (41)

American
$8-$24

AAA Inspector Notes: This cozy brewery serves aged-to-perfection specialty beers alongside such authentic Czech and Bohemian pub-style cuisine as beef goulash, bread dumplings with sauerkraut, schnitzels and blackberry brandy breast of chicken. **Bar:** full bar. **Address:** 94 E 7200 S 84047 **Location:** I-15 exit 297 (7200 S), 1 mi e.

EPIC CASUAL DINING **Phone:** 801/748-1300 (43)

American
$14-$24

AAA Inspector Notes: The popular eatery features a variety of gourmet brick-oven flat breads such as the three-olive tapenade and hummus, and Kobe skirt steak with grilled portobello mushrooms. Seasonal appetizers, salads named after friends and family, and creative entrées such as steamed clams, Dungeness crab cake with balsamic remoulade and sweet bell pepper slaw, sautéed pork medallions, seared salmon with tomato-caper butter and shallot-herb mashers, and angel hair pasta also are on the menu. Seasonal desserts vary nightly. **Bar:** beer & wine. **Address:** 707 E Fort Union Blvd 84047 **Location:** I-215 exit 9 (Union Park Ave), 0.7 mi s, then 0.7 mi w.

HOPPERS GRILL & BREWING CO
Phone: 801/566-0424 (42)

American
$7-$18

AAA Inspector Notes: Friends often meet at this fun spot after work or on weekends to watch the big game. Seafood selections are dominant on a menu that also lists a few chicken and beef choices. The handcrafted beers, brewed on site, have won awards. **Bar:** full bar. **Address:** 890 E Fort Union Blvd 84047 **Location:** I-15 exit 297 (7200 S), 1.6 mi e; southwest corner of 900 E and Fort Union Blvd.

KNEADERS BAKERY & CAFE
Phone: 801/563-1991 (44)

Breads/Pastries
$6-$7

AAA Inspector Notes: This bakery serves up hearty soups, fresh salads and sandwiches. The aromatic breads, homemade pastries and luscious desserts are made in the Italian hearth-stone oven. Friendly servers carry out their responsibilities with enthusiasm. **Address:** 742 E Fort Union Blvd 84047 **Location:** I-15 exit 297 (7200 S), 1.5 mi e.

MIDWAY (C-4) pop. 3,845, elev. 5,640'

HOMESTEAD CRATER is at 700 N. Homestead Dr. at Homestead Resort. The crater, which began forming 10,000 years ago, is filled with warm mineral waters now enjoyed by swimmers, snorkelers and scuba divers. Sunlight enters through a large hole at the top of the hollowed out 55-foot-tall, beehive-shaped limestone rock. After checking in at the Activity Center, visitors enter through a short, lighted tunnel that was dug through the rock wall at ground level. Decks, a soaking area and dressing rooms are available.

Hours: Mon.-Thurs. noon-8, Fri.-Sat. 10-8, Sun. 10-6. Phone ahead to confirm schedule. **Cost:** Forty-minute access to the crater and mineral springs $16 (Sat.-Sun.) or $11 (Mon.-Fri.). Snorkeling equipment $5. Under 5 are not permitted. **Phone:** (435) 657-3840 for the activity center, (435) 654-1102 for the resort or (888) 327-7220.

RECREATIONAL ACTIVITIES

Skiing (Cross-country)

- **Soldier Hollow** is at 2002 Olympic Dr. in Wasatch Mountain State Park. **Hours:** Daily 9-4:30, mid-Dec. to late Mar. **Phone:** (435) 654-2002.

BLUE BOAR INN **Phone:** 435/654-1400

Country Inn
$175-$295

Address: 1235 Warm Springs Rd 84049 **Location:** I-80 exit 146 (US 40), 13 mi s to River Rd traffic light, 2.9 mi w to roundabout, follow signs. **Facility:** On the edge of beautiful Heber Valley, the European château has elegant rooms and is in a quiet area yet close to the nightlife in Park City. 12 units. 2 stories, interior corridors. **Terms:** office hours 7 am-11 pm, 14 day cancellation notice-fee imposed. **Dining:** restaurant, see separate listing.

HOMESTEAD RESORT **Phone:** (435)654-1102

Classic Historic Resort Hotel
$99-$769 12/1-4/30
$89-$769 5/1-11/30

Address: 700 N Homestead Dr 84049 **Location:** I-80 exit 146 (US 40), 13 mi s to River Rd traffic light, 2.9 mi w to roundabout, 1.2 mi w, follow signs to Homestead Dr, then 0.4 mi s. Located in a quiet area. **Facility:** The resort has a range of room styles. Guests can play basketball and volleyball, or take a seasonal sleigh ride or horse-drawn buggy ride. 145 units, some efficiencies, houses and condominiums. 1-2 stories (no elevator), interior/exterior corridors. **Terms:** check-in 4 pm, 7 day cancellation notice-fee imposed. **Amenities:** high-speed Internet. *Some:* safes. **Pool(s):** heated outdoor, heated indoor. **Activities:** sauna, whirlpools, 2 lighted tennis courts, recreation programs, rental bicycles, hiking trails, jogging, playground, basketball, horseshoes, shuffleboard, volleyball, spa. *Fee:* scuba diving, snorkeling, golf-18 holes, cross country skiing, game room. **Guest Services:** valet and coin laundry.

SOME UNITS FEE

INVITED INN BED & BREAKFAST **Phone:** (435)654-7075

Bed & Breakfast
$135-$275

Address: 1045 N Homestead Dr 84049 **Location:** I-80 exit 146 (US 40), 13 mi s to River Rd traffic light, 2.9 mi w to roundabout, follow signs. **Facility:** The Swiss-style home with a lovely gazebo overlooks mountains and the Heber Valley. Rooms have fireplaces, steam showers, whirlpools and saunas. 5 units. 2 stories (no elevator), interior corridors. **Terms:** office hours 8 am-10 pm, age restrictions may apply, 30 day cancellation notice-fee imposed. **Amenities:** high-speed Internet. **Activities:** basketball.

JOHNSON MILL BED & BREAKFAST
Phone: 435/654-4466

Historic Bed & Breakfast
Rates not provided

Address: 100 N Johnson Mill Rd 84049 **Location:** I-80 exit 146 (US 40), 16.5 mi s to 100 S traffic light, 2.1 mi w, then just n. **Facility:** Built in 1893, the 14-acre property is a perfect getaway. Guests can stroll along the lake at sunset, fish, or borrow canoes or paddleboats. 10 units. 4 stories (no elevator), interior/exterior corridors. **Terms:** office hours 10 am-7 pm. **Amenities:** high-speed Internet. **Activities:** canoeing, paddleboats, fishing, hiking trails, jogging. **Free Special Amenities: full breakfast and high-speed Internet.**

ZERMATT RESORT & SPA **Phone:** (435)657-0180

Resort Hotel
$179-$599

Address: 784 W Resort Dr 84049 **Location:** I-80 exit 146 (US 40), 13 mi s to River Rd traffic light, 2.9 mi w to roundabout, 1.2 mi w, follow signs to Homestead Dr, then 0.3 mi s. **Facility:** An array of amenities offer endless recreational and relaxation possibilities at this Alpine village complex, which boasts outstanding mountain views. 255 units, some condominiums. 3-5 stories, interior corridors. **Terms:** check-in 4 pm, 30 day cancellation notice-fee imposed. **Amenities:** video games (fee), high-speed Internet, safes. **Dining:** 3 restaurants, also, Schneitter's Restaurant, see separate listing. **Pool(s):** heated indoor/outdoor. **Activities:** saunas, whirlpools, steamrooms, putting green, hiking trails, jogging, shuffleboard, volleyball, spa. *Fee:* downhill & cross country skiing, snowmobiling, bicycles. **Guest Services:** valet and coin laundry, area transportation-local ski resorts.

SAVE FEE BIZ

FEE / SOME UNITS

WHERE TO EAT

BLUE BOAR INN RESTAURANT **Phone:** 435/654-1400

Continental
$8-$36

AAA Inspector Notes: An elegant spot for dignified European/Swiss dining, this restaurant specializes in wild boar, bison and seasonal cheese and chocolate fondues. **Bar:** full bar. **Reservations:** suggested. **Address:** 1235 Warm Springs Rd 84049 **Location:** I-80 exit 146 (US 40), 13 mi s to River Rd traffic light, 2.9 mi w to roundabout, follow signs; in Blue Boar Inn. B L D

CAFE GALLERIA **Phone:** 435/657-2002

Pizza
$5-$11

AAA Inspector Notes: Manicured grounds and beautiful foliage surround this quaint eatery that oozes old-school charm. Patrons dine on wood fired oven-baked bagels and pizza, a variety of fresh salads and spaghetti with huge homemade meatballs. The locally named sundaes and homemade cheesecake are sure to please. Outdoor seating is available. **Bar:** beer only. **Address:** 101 W Main St 84049 **Location:** West end of Main St.

B L D AC

SCHNEITTER'S RESTAURANT **Phone:** 435/657-0180

American
$16-$32

AAA Inspector Notes: The restaurant offers a fine dining experience with creative appetizers, salads, soups and entrées. **Bar:** full bar. **Address:** 784 W Resort Dr 84049 **Location:** I-80 exit 146 (US 40), 13 mi to River Rd light, 2.9 mi w to roundabout, 1.2 mi w to Homestead Dr, follow signs, then 0.3 mi s; in Zermatt Resort & Spa.

D

MOAB (E-6) pop. 5,046, elev. 4,000'

• **Hotels p. 371** • **Restaurants p. 376**
• **Hotels & Restaurants map & index p. 369**

Tucked into a valley at the foot of red cliffs and the La Sal Mountains, Moab enjoys unusually mild weather because of its lower elevation. The town, which overlooks the Colorado River, was familiar to Butch Cassidy's Wild Bunch and other outlaw gangs. Zane Grey made Moab the scene of many of his novels, and it has been used frequently as a setting for movies.

The discovery of uranium in the 1950s changed Moab from a quiet agricultural town into a bustling center for mining and prospecting. Although the uranium boom has passed, the area is still rich in oil and potash. Tourism, however, has become the main industry.

Moab is the starting point for four-wheel-drive, airplane, white-water rafting, canoe, cross-country skiing, hiking, horseback and mountain biking trips into Arches *(see place listing p. 321)* and Canyonlands *(see place listing p. 334)* national parks. Local tour companies provide hiking, rafting, bicycling, boating, scenic flights, photography and four-wheel-drive tours; other companies provide equipment for such trips. Golf, tennis and fishing in stocked lakes round out the recreational opportunities.

Redtail Aviation offers scenic flight tours of Canyonlands National Park, Monument Valley and the Colorado River; phone (435) 259-7421 or (800) 842-9251. Moab Adventure Center *(see listing p. 367)* makes sightseeing flights over Canyonlands National Park, the Colorado and Green rivers, Moab and Island in the Sky; phone (435) 259-7019 or (866) 904-1163.

Canyonlands by Night & Day offers boat trips on the Colorado River. The night trip features illuminated cliff and rock formations and a narrative about the area's history and geology, while the day trip allows visitors to see arches, balanced rocks, birds and wildlife; phone (435) 259-5261 or (800) 394-9978.

The monumental red rock spires of Fisher Towers are 24 miles northeast of Moab off SR 128. Used for many movies and television commercials, the area is accessible via a 3-mile gravel road. Travelers who want a closer look at the towers can make the 2-mile hike from the rest area at the end of the road.

Affording spectacular and contrasting views of the desert floor and the mountain range, the La Sal Mountain Loop Road connects with SR 128 and winds through Castle Valley and up into the La Sal Mountains, returning to the lower end of Moab Valley. SR 128 between Moab and I-70 offers a particularly scenic drive as it parallels the rugged canyons of the Colorado River.

The Slickrock Bike Trail in Moab is prized by mountain bikers; the technically difficult 10.5-mile trail is geared toward skilled riders. Part of the Sand Flats Recreation Area *(see attraction listing)*, the trail is known for its sandpaper-like surface that grips rubber bicycle tires. Geographical features include petrified sand dunes, colorful cliff walls and steep ledges.

In addition to its bounty of outdoor activities, Moab is home to a thriving arts community. Photographers and painters find inspiration in the area's natural beauty; local art is displayed in galleries, cafés and bookstores. The Moab Arts Festival in late May draws attention to local art.

Other festivals of note in Moab include the April Action Car Show in late April, which showcases more than 750 hot rods, classic cars and muscle cars; Canyonlands PRCA Rodeo in June; the Moab Music Festival, a chamber music festival held for several weeks in September; and November's Moab Folk Music Festival.

(See map & index p. 369.)

Moab Area Travel Council: P.O. Box 550, Moab, UT 84532. **Phone:** (435) 259-8825 or (800) 635-6622.

A visitor information center at Main and Center streets is open Mon.-Sat. 8-8, Sun. 9-7, Mar. 31-late Oct.; daily 9-5, late Oct.-Dec. 31. ***(See ad this page.)***

BAR M CHUCKWAGON LIVE WESTERN SHOW & COWBOY SUPPER lies 7 mi. n. on US 191. This is a small re-creation of a Western town where visitors can wander or watch a gunfight until it is time for their "cowboy supper," which is followed by a live Western stage show. **Time:** Allow 2 hours, 30 minutes minimum. **Hours:** Operates several nights per week, early Apr. to mid-Oct. Grounds open at 6:30. Gunfight takes place at 7. Supper takes place at 7:30; music show follows. Phone ahead to confirm schedule. **Cost:** $27.95; $13.98 (ages 4-12). Prices may vary. Reservations are recommended. **Phone:** (435) 259-2276 or (800) 214-2085.

CANYONLANDS FIELD INSTITUTE tours depart from the Moab Information Center, at Main and Center streets, and from local hotels. A naturalist leads and narrates the guided half-day van tours or hikes through Arches National Park. Other educational tours and river trips also are offered. **Hours:**

(See map & index p. 369.)

Half-day tours depart Fri.-Sun. at 8:30 and 4, Apr.-Oct. **Cost:** Arches tour $45 (per person). Ancient Past Rock Art tour $40 (per person). Reservations are required. **Phone:** (435) 259-7750 or (800) 860-5262.

DAN O'LAURIE MUSEUM OF MOAB is at 118 E. Center St. The museum has displays about the archeology, geology, mineralogy and history of southeastern Utah. **Hours:** Mon.-Fri. 10-5, Sat. noon-5, Mar.-Oct.; Mon.-Sat. noon-5, rest of year. Closed Jan. 1, Thanksgiving and Christmas. **Cost:** $5; free (ages 0-7 and to all Mon.); $10 (family). **Phone:** (435) 259-7985.

GEM **DEAD HORSE POINT STATE PARK** is 9 mi. n. via US 191, then 18 mi. s.w. on SR 313. A band of wild mustangs was once herded into the natural corral formed by the rock formations and inadvertently left to die of thirst in view of the Colorado River—hence the name Dead Horse Point.

The point provides a striking panorama of the pinnacles, buttes and sandstone cliffs of the Colorado River's 2,000-foot canyons. The sun and changing weather conditions produce a range of colors on these cliffs. The park offers an interpretive trail, hiking and a visitor center. *See Recreation Chart.*

Hours: Park open 6 a.m.-10 p.m. Visitor center open daily 8-6, mid-May to mid-Sept.; 8-5, rest of year. Closed Jan. 1, Thanksgiving and Christmas. **Cost:** $10 (per private vehicle, maximum eight people). Camping $20. **Phone:** (435) 259-2614, (801) 322-3770 or (800) 322-3770.

HOLE 'N THE ROCK is 15 mi. s. via US 191. This 14-room home excavated from solid sandstone by Albert and Gladys Christensen beginning in the early 1940s and continuing for 20 years looks much as it did when the couple lived there; a rock and cactus garden are outside. Mr. Christensen also completed several paintings, including "Sermon on the Mount." A likeness of Franklin D. Roosevelt is carved on the outside face of the home.

A petting zoo has sheep, goats, pigs, wallabies, emus, alpacas, and miniature donkeys and horses. **Hours:** Tours begin daily every 15-20 minutes 9-5. Closed Thanksgiving and Christmas. **Cost:** $5; $3.50 (ages 5-10). **Phone:** (435) 686-2250.

MOAB MUSEUM OF FILM AND WESTERN HERITAGE is in the Red Cliffs Lodge at Milepost 14 on SR 128. The museum—part of Red Cliffs Ranch, a working ranch since the late 19th century—houses memorabilia detailing Moab's involvement in the film industry, along with displays relating cowboy culture. Since the late 1940s, numerous movies have been shot on location in the region. Its rugged terrain made it an ideal spot to film Westerns, especially in the eyes of director John Ford, a pioneer of on-location shooting who made "Wagon Master" and "Rio Grande" here.

"Taza, Son of Cochise," with Rock Hudson; "Warlock," which featured Henry Fonda and Anthony Quinn; and "The Comancheros," starring John Wayne, were filmed in and around Moab. In addition to more than 100 commercials, such '90s cinematic productions as "City Slickers" and "Thelma & Louise" also were shot in Moab. The museum's collection includes early pioneer relics as well as photographs of such actors as Maureen O'Hara, Lee Marvin and James Stewart, all of whom worked on motion pictures at the ranch. **Time:** Allow 45 minutes minimum. **Hours:** Daily 8 a.m.-10 p.m. **Cost:** Free. **Phone:** (435) 259-2002 or (866) 812-2002.

SAND FLATS RECREATION AREA is .5 mi. e. on Mill Creek Dr., then 2.5 mi. n.e. on Sand Flats Rd. to entrance booth. At the Colorado Plateau's core lies this 7,320-acre recreation area, home to the Slickrock and Porcupine Rim bicycle trails; nearly 40 miles of jeep trails; and varied fauna and flora, including desert cottontail rabbits, bats, mule deer, pinyon pine and cliff rose shrubs.

The site's spectacular geological features also lure visitors; exposures of Jurassic-aged sedimentary rock layers are encountered by visitors traversing Sand Flats' multitude of foot and vehicle paths. *See Recreation Chart.*

Hours: Daily 24 hours. **Cost:** One-day pass $5 (per private vehicle); $2 (per person arriving by other means). Seven-day pass $10 (per private vehicle); $5 (per person arriving by other means). Vehicle trailer fee $2. **Phone:** (435) 259-2444.

RECREATIONAL ACTIVITIES

Climbing

- **Moab Cliffs & Canyons** is at 253 N. Main St. **Hours:** Departure days and times vary; phone ahead. **Phone:** (435) 259-3317 or (877) 641-5271.

White-water Rafting

- **AAM's Mild to Wild Rafting & Jeep Trail Tours Inc.** departs from local hotels and campgrounds. **Hours:** One- to 3-day trips on the Colorado River are offered daily, Apr. 1-early Oct. Departure times vary; phone ahead. **Phone:** (970) 247-4789 or (800) 567-6745.
- **Adrift Adventures** is at 378 N. Main St. Other activities are offered. **Hours:** Rafting trips are offered daily, Mar.-Oct. Departure times vary; phone ahead. **Phone:** (435) 259-8594 or (800) 874-4483.
- **Canyon Voyages Adventure Co.** is at 211 N. Main St. Other activities are offered. **Hours:** Rafting trips are offered daily, Mar.-Oct. Departure times vary; phone ahead. **Phone:** (435) 259-6007 or (800) 733-6007.
- **Moab Adventure Center** is at 225 S. Main St. Other activities are offered. **Hours:** Open daily, mid-Mar. through Oct. 31. Hours vary; phone

(See map & index p. 369.)

ahead. **Phone:** (435) 259-7019 or (866) 904-1163.

- **NAVTEC Expeditions** is at 321 N. Main St. Other activities are offered. **Hours:** Rafting trips are offered daily, Mar.-Oct. Departure times vary; phone ahead. **Phone:** (435) 259-7983 or (800) 833-1278.
- **O.A.R.S. Canyonlands Tours** departs from several locations in Moab. Other activities are offered. **Hours:** Rafting trips are offered daily, Apr.-Oct. Departure times vary; phone ahead. **Phone:** (435) 259-5865 or (800) 346-6277.
- **Sheri Griffith Expeditions Inc.** is at 2231 S. US 191. Other activities are offered. **Hours:** Rafting trips are offered daily, Mar.-Oct. Departure times vary; phone ahead. **Phone:** (435) 259-8229 or (800) 332-2439.
- **Tag-A-Long Expeditions** is at 452 N. Main St. Other activities are offered. **Hours:** Rafting trips are offered daily, mid-Apr. to mid-Oct. Departure times vary; phone ahead. **Phone:** (435) 259-8946 or (800) 453-3292. ***(See ad this page.)***

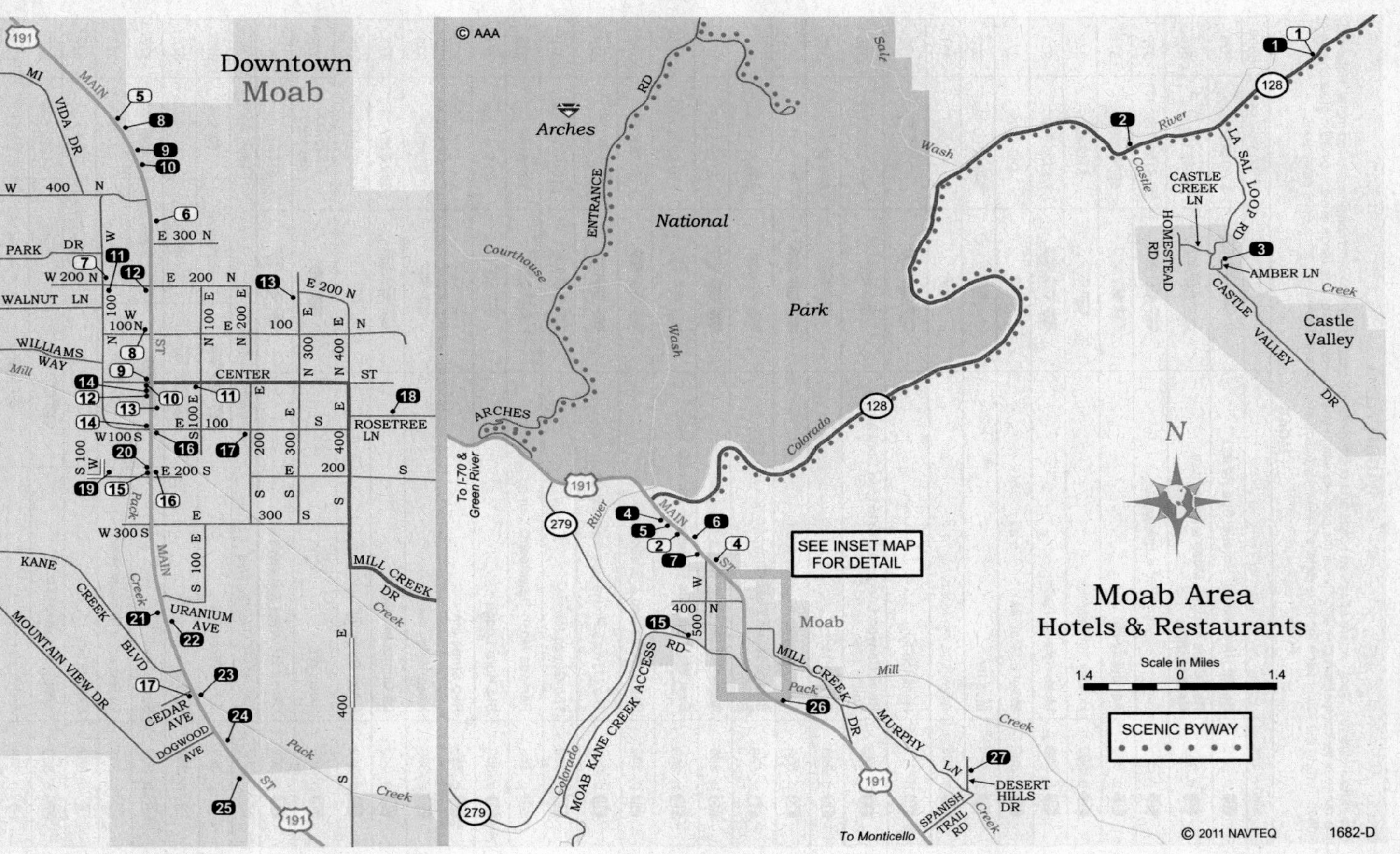
Downtown Moab
Moab Area
Hotels & Restaurants
SEE INSET MAP FOR DETAIL
SCENIC BYWAY
Scale in Miles
1.4
0
1.4
N
© AAA
© 2011 NAVTEQ
1682-D
Arches
National
Park
Castle Valley
Moab
LA SAL LOOP RD
CASTLE VALLEY DR
AMBER LN
CASTLE CREEK LN
HOMESTEAD RD
ARCHES ENTRANCE RD
MOAB KANE CREEK ACCESS RD
MILL CREEK DR
MURPHY LN
SPANISH TRAIL RD
DESERT HILLS DR
To I-70 & Green River
To Monticello
Colorado River
Castle River
Salt Wash
Courthouse Wash
Mill Creek
Pack Creek
MAIN ST
MI VIDA DR
PARK DR
WALNUT LN
WILLIAMS WAY
CENTER ST
ROSETREE LN
URANIUM AVE
CEDAR AVE
DOGWOOD AVE
KANE CREEK BLVD
MOUNTAIN VIEW DR
128
191
279

Moab Area

This index helps you "spot" where approved hotels and restaurants are located on the corresponding detailed maps. Hotel daily rate range is for comparison only and shows the property's high season. Restaurant rate range is a combination of lunch and/or dinner. Turn to the listing page for more detailed rate information and consult display ads for special promotions.

MOAB

Map Page	Hotels	Diamond Rated	High Season	Page
1 p. 369	**Sorrel River Ranch Hotel & Spa Resort**	◆◆◆◆	$399-$699 SAVE	376
2 p. 369	**Red Cliffs Lodge - Moab's Adventure Headquarters**	◆◆◆	$99-$320 SAVE	375
3 p. 369	Castle Valley Inn Bed & Breakfast	◆◆◆	$105-$190	372
4 p. 369	**Aarchway Inn**	◆◆◆	$60-$230 SAVE	371
5 p. 369	Holiday Inn Express	◆◆	$119-$209	372
6 p. 369	Moab Springs Ranch	◆◆◆	$125-$340	373
7 p. 369	Motel 6 Moab #4119 *(See ad p. 374.)*	◆	$59-$199	374
8 p. 369	**Inca Inn**	◆	$49-$100 SAVE	373
9 p. 369	Adventure Inn Moab	◆	$60-$95	371
10 p. 369	Hampton Inn	◆◆◆	Rates not provided	372
11 p. 369	**River Canyon Lodge, An Extended Stay Inn & Suites** *(See ad p. 376.)*	◆◆	$69-$290 SAVE	375
12 p. 369	**Bowen Motel**	◆◆	$50-$134 SAVE	371
13 p. 369	Sunflower Hill, A Luxury Inn	◆◆◆	$175-$245	376
14 p. 369	**Best Western Plus Canyonlands Inn** *(See ad p. 372.)*	◆◆◆	$99-$399 SAVE	371
15 p. 369	Adobe Abode Moab Bed & Breakfast	◆◆◆	$139-$149	371
16 p. 369	**Best Western Plus Greenwell Inn** *(See ad p. 373.)*	◆◆◆	$79-$299 SAVE	371
17 p. 369	Cali Cochitta Bed & Breakfast	◆◆◆	$135-$175	371
18 p. 369	The Mayor's House Bed & Breakfast	◆◆◆	Rates not provided	373
19 p. 369	**The Gonzo Inn**	◆◆◆	$101-$329 SAVE	372
20 p. 369	**Ramada Moab Downtown** *(See ad p. 375.)*	◆◆	$69-$199 SAVE	375
21 p. 369	**Big Horn Lodge**	◆◆	$50-$130 SAVE	371
22 p. 369	**Red Stone Inn**	◆◆	$90-$125 SAVE	375
23 p. 369	Moab Valley Inn	◆◆	$69-$199	373
24 p. 369	**La Quinta Inn Moab**	◆◆◆	$89-$209 SAVE	373
25 p. 369	**Silver Sage Inn**	◆	$45-$100 SAVE	375
26 p. 369	Sleep Inn	◆◆	Rates not provided	376
27 p. 369	Desert Hills Bed & Breakfast	◆◆◆	$119-$189	372

Map Page	Restaurants	Diamond Rated	Cuisine	Meal Range	Page
1 p. 369	Sorrel River Grill	◆◆◆	American	$8-$36	377
2 p. 369	Buck's Grill House	◆◆◆	Steak	$10-$26	376
4 p. 369	Sunset Grill	◆◆	Steak	$14-$24	377
5 p. 369	La Hacienda Mexican Restaurant	◆◆	Mexican	$7-$18	377
6 p. 369	**EklectiCafe**	◆	Natural/Organic	$5-$10	377
7 p. 369	Jeffrey's Steakhouse	◆◆◆	Steak	$22-$39	377
8 p. 369	Jailhouse Cafe	◆◆	Breakfast	$8-$10	377

Map Page	Restaurants (cont'd)	Diamond Rated	Cuisine	Meal Range	Page
9 p. 369	Slickrock Cafe	2	American	$7-$19	377
10 p. 369	Pasta Jay's	2	Italian	$7-$16	377
11 p. 369	Singha Thai Cuisine	2	Thai	$11-$18	377
12 p. 369	Peace Tree Juice Cafe	1	Natural/Organic	$5-$9	377
13 p. 369	Eddie McStiff's	2	American	$7-$21	376
14 p. 369	Zax Restaurant and Watering Hole	2	American	$6-$19	377
15 p. 369	Pancake Haus	1	Breakfast	$6-$10	377
16 p. 369	Moab Diner	1	American	$6-$15	377
17 p. 369	Moab Brewery	2	American	$8-$19	377

AARCHWAY INN **Phone:** (435)259-2599 4

Hotel
$60-$230

Address: 1551 N Hwy 191 84532 **Location:** 2 mi n. **Facility:** 97 units, some kitchens. 2 stories (no elevator), interior corridors. **Terms:** cancellation fee imposed. **Pool(s):** heated outdoor. **Activities:** whirlpool, hiking trails, playground, horseshoes, volleyball, exercise room. **Guest Services:** coin laundry. **Free Special Amenities: full breakfast and high-speed Internet.** SAVE BIZ

ADOBE ABODE MOAB BED & BREAKFAST **Phone:** 435/259-7716 15

Bed & Breakfast
$139-$149

Address: 778 Kane Creek Blvd 84532 **Location:** 0.4 mi s to Kane Creek Blvd, 1.1 mi nw. Located in a quiet area. **Facility:** Surrounded by red cliffs, these elegant rooms have unusual furnishings made by the creative innkeeper; common areas include secluded spaces. 6 units. 1-2 stories (no elevator), interior corridors. **Terms:** open 5/1-11/20 & 3/1-4/30, 2 night minimum stay - weekends, age restrictions may apply, 7 day cancellation notice-fee imposed. **Activities:** whirlpool, hiking trails. / SOME UNITS

ADVENTURE INN MOAB **Phone:** 435/259-6122 9

Motel
$60-$95

Address: 512 N Main St 84532 **Location:** 0.4 mi n. **Facility:** 21 units. 1 story, exterior corridors. **Terms:** open 5/1-10/26 & 3/10-4/30, office hours 7 am-11 pm, cancellation fee imposed. **Guest Services:** coin laundry.

/ SOME UNITS

BEST WESTERN PLUS CANYONLANDS INN **Phone:** (435)259-2300 14

Hotel
$99-$399

AAA Benefit: Members save up to 20%, plus 10% bonus points with Best Western Rewards®.

Address: 16 S Main St 84532 **Location:** Just s of Main and W Center sts. **Facility:** 79 units. 2 stories, interior corridors. **Terms:** check-in 4 pm. **Amenities:** *Some:* high-speed Internet. **Pool(s):** heated indoor/outdoor. **Activities:** whirlpool, playground, exercise room. **Guest Services:** coin laundry. **Free Special Amenities: full breakfast and high-speed Internet.** *(See ad p. 372.)*

SAVE ECO BIZ

BEST WESTERN PLUS GREENWELL INN **Phone:** (435)259-6151 16

Hotel
$79-$299

AAA Benefit: Members save up to 20%, plus 10% bonus points with Best Western Rewards®.

Address: 105 S Main St 84532 **Location:** Just s. **Facility:** 72 units. 2 stories (no elevator), exterior corridors. **Pool(s):** heated outdoor. **Activities:** whirlpool, exercise room. **Guest Services:** coin laundry. **Free Special Amenities: local telephone calls and high-speed Internet.** *(See ad p. 373.)*

SAVE / SOME UNITS FEE

BIG HORN LODGE **Phone:** (435)259-6171 21

Motel
$50-$130

Address: 550 S Main St 84532 **Location:** 0.5 mi s. **Facility:** 58 units. 2 stories (no elevator), exterior corridors. **Terms:** office hours 6 am-1 am, cancellation fee imposed. **Amenities:** high-speed Internet. **Pool(s):** heated outdoor. **Free Special Amenities: local telephone calls and high-speed Internet.**

SAVE / SOME UNITS FEE

BOWEN MOTEL **Phone:** 435/259-7132 12

Motel
$50-$134

Address: 169 N Main St 84532 **Location:** Just n. **Facility:** 41 units, some three bedrooms and kitchens. 1-2 stories (no elevator), exterior corridors. **Terms:** cancellation fee imposed. **Pool(s):** heated outdoor. **Free Special Amenities: local telephone calls and high-speed Internet.**

SAVE / SOME UNITS FEE

CALI COCHITTA BED & BREAKFAST **Phone:** (435)259-4961 17

Bed & Breakfast
$135-$175 5/1-10/31
$90-$140 11/1-4/30

Address: 110 S 200 E 84532 **Location:** Corner of 100 S and 200 E. **Facility:** Guests can admire the Victorian B&B's rosebushes and flowers from an oversize hammock or on a rocker or swing on the covered front porch. 6 units, some two bedrooms. 2 stories (no elevator), interior/exterior corridors. **Terms:** check-in 4 pm, 2 night minimum stay - weekends, 15 day cancellation notice-fee imposed. **Activities:** whirlpool.

/ SOME UNITS

(See map & index p. 369.)

CASTLE VALLEY INN BED & BREAKFAST
Phone: 435/259-6012 **3**

Bed & Breakfast
$105-$190

Address: 424 Amber Ln 84532 **Location:** From jct US 191 and SR 128, 15.5 mi ne to LaSal Mountain Loop Rd, 1.7 mi se to Castle Valley Dr, 0.7 mi sw to Meadow Ln, just e, then just n. Located in a quiet secluded area. **Facility:** Deer come by to sample the rich grass of this 5-acre property in a secluded green valley surrounded by impressive buttes, mountains and fruit trees. 7 units, some two bedrooms and cabins. 1-2 stories (no elevator), interior/exterior corridors. **Terms:** office hours 10 am-10 pm, 14 day cancellation notice-fee imposed. **Activities:** whirlpool, horseshoes.

DESERT HILLS BED & BREAKFAST
Phone: 435/259-3568 **27**

Bed & Breakfast
$119-$189

Address: 1989 Desert Hills Ln 84532 **Location:** 4.1 mi s to Spanish Trail Rd, then 1 mi e to roundabout, take Murphy Ln just n to Desert Hills Ln, then just e. **Facility:** At this B&B in a quiet neighborhood, guests can enjoy beautiful mountain views while relaxing in the hot tub or sitting on the garden patio. 5 units, some two bedrooms. 2 stories (no elevator), interior/exterior corridors. **Terms:** 2 night minimum stay - weekends, 14 day cancellation notice-fee imposed. **Activities:** whirlpool, playground.

Explore the Travel Guides on AAA.com/Travel or CAA.ca/Travel

THE GONZO INN
Phone: (435)259-2515 **19**

Boutique Hotel
$101-$329

Address: 100 W 200 S 84532 **Location:** Just w of 200 S and S Main St. **Facility:** This boutique hotel successfully blends Southwest architecture and contemporary décor to create a distinctive lodging option. A bicycle wash/repair station and secure storage are available. 43 units, some two bedrooms. 2 stories (no elevator), interior/exterior corridors. **Terms:** check-in 4 pm, cancellation fee imposed. **Pool(s):** heated outdoor. **Activities:** whirlpool. **Guest Services:** coin laundry. **Free Special Amenities: continental breakfast and high-speed Internet.**

SAVE BIZ / SOME UNITS FEE

HAMPTON INN
Phone: 435/259-3030 **10**

Hotel
Rates not provided

AAA Benefit:
Members save up to 10% everyday!

Address: 488 N Main St 84532 **Location:** 0.5 mi n. **Facility:** 79 units. 3 stories, interior corridors. **Pool(s):** heated outdoor. **Activities:** whirlpool, exercise room. **Guest Services:** coin laundry.

CALL BIZ / SOME UNITS FEE FEE

HOLIDAY INN EXPRESS
Phone: (435)259-1150 **5**

Hotel
$119-$209 5/1-10/31
$109-$199 11/1-4/30

Address: 1515 N Main St 84532 **Location:** 2 mi n. **Facility:** 79 units. 3 stories, interior corridors. **Terms:** 14 day cancellation notice. **Amenities:** high-speed Internet. **Pool(s):** heated indoor. **Activities:** whirlpool. **Guest Services:** coin laundry.

/ SOME UNITS

▼ See AAA listing p. 371 ▼

(See map & index p. 369.)

INCA INN **Phone:** (435)259-7261 8

Motel

$49-$100

Address: 570 N Main St 84532 **Location:** 0.6 mi n. **Facility:** 24 units. 1 story, exterior corridors. **Terms:** open 5/1-12/1 & 2/13-4/30, office hours 7 am-10 pm, cancellation fee imposed. **Amenities:** high-speed Internet. **Pool(s):** heated outdoor. **Free Special Amenities: expanded continental breakfast and local telephone calls.**

  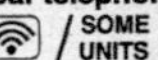  / SOME UNITS

INN OF MOAB **Phone:** 435/259-6869

fyi

Motel

Under construction, scheduled to open May 2012. **Address:** 41 W 100 N 84532 **Location:** Just w of Main St and 100 N. **Planned Amenities:** 91 units, restaurant, coffeemakers, microwaves, refrigerators, pool, exercise facility. ***(See ad p. 374.)***

LA QUINTA INN MOAB **Phone:** (435)259-8700 24

Hotel

$89-$209

Address: 815 S Main St 84532 **Location:** 0.8 mi s. **Facility:** 99 units. 3 stories, interior corridors. **Pool(s):** heated outdoor. **Activities:** whirlpool, exercise room. **Guest Services:** coin laundry. **Free Special Amenities: expanded continental breakfast and high-speed Internet.**

     / SOME UNITS

Download eTourBook guides for ereaders and smartphones at AAA.com/ebooks

THE MAYOR'S HOUSE BED & BREAKFAST **Phone:** 435/259-6015 18

Bed & Breakfast

Rates not provided

Address: 505 Rosetree Ln 84532 **Location:** 0.4 mi e on Center St, just s on 400 S, then just e. **Facility:** Once owned by the town's mayor, this B&B has a lovely, shaded yard and garden with a pool; one very large family room with multiple beds is available. 6 units. 2 stories (no elevator), interior/exterior corridors. **Terms:** seasonal, age restrictions may apply. **Pool(s):** heated outdoor. **Activities:** whirlpool.

   / SOME UNITS 

MOAB SPRINGS RANCH **Phone:** 435/259-7891 6

Condominium

$125-$340

Address: 1266 N Hwy 191 84532 **Location:** 1.5 mi n. **Facility:** Enter a shady oasis with flowing water, huge trees and a spacious grassy campus; the condo's floor plan has been called the smartest in town. 15 condominiums. 2 stories (no elevator), exterior corridors. **Terms:** check-in 4 pm, 2 night minimum stay - weekends, 31 day cancellation notice-fee imposed. **Pool(s):** heated outdoor. **Activities:** hiking trails. **Guest Services:** complimentary laundry.

MOAB VALLEY INN **Phone:** (435)259-4419 23

Hotel

$69-$199

Address: 711 S Main St 84532 **Location:** 0.7 mi s. **Facility:** 126 units. 3 stories, interior corridors. **Pool(s):** heated indoor/outdoor. **Activities:** whirlpool, exercise room. *Fee:* game room. **Guest Services:** coin laundry.

BIZ / SOME UNITS FEE

▼ *See AAA listing p. 371* ▼

MOTEL 6 MOAB #4119 **Phone:** (435)259-6686 7

Motel
$59-$199

Address: 1089 N Main St 84532 **Location:** 1.5 mi n. **Facility:** 66 units. 3 stories, interior corridors. **Pool(s):** heated outdoor. **Activities:** whirlpool. **Guest Services:** coin laundry.

(See ad this page.) / SOME UNITS

▼ *See AAA listing p. 373* ▼

▼ *See AAA listing this page* ▼

(See map & index p. 369.)

RAMADA MOAB DOWNTOWN
Phone: (435)259-7141 20

Motel
$69-$199

Address: 182 S Main St 84532 **Location:** Just s. **Facility:** 81 units, some two bedrooms. 2 stories (no elevator), exterior corridors. **Terms:** office hours 7 am-11 pm. **Pool(s):** heated outdoor. **Activities:** whirlpool. **Free Special Amenities: early check-in/late check-out and high-speed Internet.**
(See ad this page.)

SAVE BIZ

RED CLIFFS LODGE - MOAB'S ADVENTURE HEADQUARTERS
Phone: (435)259-2002 2

Resort Ranch
$99-$320

Address: Milepost 14 Hwy 128 84532 **Location:** 2.3 mi n to jct US 191 and SR 128, then 14 mi e to MM 14. **Facility:** Creekside and riverfront cabins and a wonderful selection of spacious rooms, all with large secluded patios, overlook the Colorado River. A barbecue lunch is served daily on the cowboy river deck. 110 units, some two bedrooms and cabins. 1 story, exterior corridors. **Terms:** open 5/1-12/1 & 3/1-4/30, 30 day cancellation notice-fee imposed. **Amenities:** high-speed Internet, safes. **Pool(s):** heated outdoor. **Activities:** whirlpool, 2 lighted tennis courts, recreation programs in summer, bicycle trails, hiking trails, jogging, playground, horseshoes, volleyball, exercise room. *Fee:* horseback riding. **Guest Services:** coin laundry. **Free Special Amenities: local telephone calls and high-speed Internet.**

 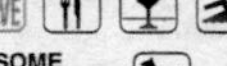    

/ SOME UNITS FEE

RED STONE INN
Phone: (435)259-3500 22

Motel
$90-$125 5/1-11/30
$45-$125 12/1-4/30

Address: 535 S Main St 84532 **Location:** 0.5 mi s. **Facility:** 50 units. 1 story, interior corridors. **Terms:** office hours 7 am-11:30 pm, cancellation fee imposed. **Amenities:** high-speed Internet. **Activities:** whirlpool. **Guest Services:** coin laundry. **Free Special Amenities: local telephone calls and high-speed Internet.**

SAVE / SOME UNITS FEE

RIVER CANYON LODGE, AN EXTENDED STAY INN & SUITES
Phone: (435)259-8838 11

Extended Stay Motel
$69-$290 5/1-11/30
$59-$290 2/28-4/30

Address: 71 W 200 N 84532 **Location:** Just w of 200 N and Main St. **Facility:** 80 units, some two bedrooms and kitchens. 3 stories, interior corridors. **Terms:** open 5/1-11/30 & 2/28-4/30, cancellation fee imposed. **Pool(s):** heated outdoor. **Activities:** whirlpool. **Free Special Amenities: room upgrade (subject to availability with advance reservations) and high-speed Internet.**
(See ad p. 376.)

SAVE 

/ SOME UNITS FEE

SILVER SAGE INN
Phone: (435)259-4420 25

Motel
$45-$100

Address: 840 S Main St 84532 **Location:** 0.9 mi s. **Facility:** 17 units. 1 story, interior corridors. **Free Special Amenities: local telephone calls and high-speed Internet.**

SAVE / SOME UNITS FEE

(See map & index p. 369.)

SLEEP INN Phone: 435/259-4655 26

Hotel

Rates not provided

Address: 1051 S Main St 84532 **Location:** 1.3 mi s. **Facility:** 61 units. 2 stories (no elevator), interior corridors. *Bath:* shower only. **Pool(s):** heated outdoor. **Activities:** whirlpool. **Guest Services:** coin laundry.

SOME UNITS FEE

SORREL RIVER RANCH HOTEL & SPA RESORT

Phone: (435)259-4642 1

Resort Hotel

$399-$699 5/1-10/31
$329-$549 11/1-4/30

Address: Hwy 128 at MM 17 84532 **Location:** 17 mi e of jct US 191 and SR 128; at MM 17. **Facility:** On the Colorado River and surrounded by red rocks, this resort offers upscale rooms and family suites with designer details in a "rich ranch" style. Guests can enjoy the new riverfront beach. 55 units. 1-2 stories (no elevator), exterior corridors. **Parking:** on-site and valet. **Terms:** check-in 4 pm, 45 day cancellation notice-fee imposed. **Amenities:** high-speed Internet. **Dining:** Sorrel River Grill, see separate listing. **Pool(s):** heated outdoor. **Activities:** sauna, whirlpool, steamroom, limited beach access, 2 tennis courts, hiking trails, jogging, playground, basketball, horseshoes, volleyball, exercise room, spa. *Fee:* bicycles, horseback riding. **Guest Services:** valet and coin laundry.

SOME UNITS FEE

SUNFLOWER HILL, A LUXURY INN

Phone: 435/259-2974 13

Bed & Breakfast

$175-$245 5/1-10/31
$130-$245 11/1-4/30

Address: 185 N 300 E 84532 **Location:** 0.3 mi e of Main St via 100 N, then just n. Located in a residential area. **Facility:** Guests stay in either a historic farmhouse or a two-story garden cottage, both situated on an acre of wooded pathways and flower gardens. 12 units. 2 stories (no elevator), interior/exterior corridors. **Terms:** office hours 9 am-6 pm, age restrictions may apply, 14 day cancellation notice-fee imposed. **Pool(s):** heated outdoor. **Activities:** whirlpool. **Guest Services:** complimentary laundry.

SOME UNITS

WHERE TO EAT

BUCK'S GRILL HOUSE Phone: 435/259-5201 2

Steak

$10-$26

AAA Inspector Notes: Guests get a taste of the West at this warm and attractive cowboy-themed restaurant. Varied steak and chicken dishes share menu space with preparations of buffalo, elk, duck, lamb and trout. A decorative waterfall lends to the relaxed feel on the patio. **Bar:** full bar. **Address:** 1393 N US 191 84532 **Location:** 1.7 mi n. D

EDDIE MCSTIFF'S Phone: 435/259-2337 13

American

$7-$21

AAA Inspector Notes: The eatery features handcrafted ales with menu items ranging from steaks to pasta and pizza, all served by a friendly staff. **Bar:** full bar. **Address:** 57 S Main St 84532 **Location:** Just s of center. L D

▼ See AAA listing p. 375 ▼

(See map & index p. 369.)

EKLECTICAFE

Menu on AAA.com **Phone:** 435/259-6896 (6)

Natural/Organic

$5-$10

AAA Inspector Notes: An ideal stop for a quick healthful meal, this cafe focuses on fresh, organic dishes. Pancakes, eggs, tofu, granola and bagels dominate the breakfast menu, while the lunch menu has a more international flair. Highlights include Indonesian satay, hummus plates, curry wraps and Southwestern veggie burgers. Only breakfast is available on Sunday. **Address:** 352 N Main St 84532 **Location:** 0.3 mi n. B L

JAILHOUSE CAFE **Phone:** 435/259-3900 (8)

Breakfast

$8-$10

AAA Inspector Notes: This restaurant serves only breakfast, but it's done exceptionally well with a sophisticated twist. The motto is "good enough for a last meal." Options include a spinach, feta and mushroom omelet, old-fashioned ginger pancakes and Southwestern eggs Florentine. **Address:** 101 N Main St 84532 **Location:** Just n. **Parking:** street only. B

JEFFREY'S STEAKHOUSE **Phone:** 435/259-3588 (7)

Steak

$22-$39

AAA Inspector Notes: This elegant new restaurant features a popular lobster, crab and shrimp appetizer, Wagyu steaks, lollipop lamb chops and decadent desserts. **Bar:** full bar. **Address:** 218 N 100 W 84532 **Location:** Just n to W 200 N, just w, then just n. D

LA HACIENDA MEXICAN RESTAURANT

Phone: 435/259-6319 (5)

Mexican

$7-$18

AAA Inspector Notes: This family-owned eatery whips up Mexican dishes such as enchiladas, chiles rellenos, burritos and tacos. Margarita fans won't be disappointed with the many tasty varieties. The daily specials provide great value for those dining on a budget. **Bar:** full bar. **Address:** 574 N Main St 84532 **Location:** 0.6 mi n; next to Inca Inn. L D

MOAB BREWERY **Phone:** 435/259-6333 (17)

American

$8-$19

AAA Inspector Notes: Warehouse walls laden with sports regalia surround an enclosed pub in the town's only brewery/restaurant. Seating is available in a large inside dining room or on the patio in season. Standard pub fare goes down easy with the eight hand-crafted ales on tap, which are enough to quench any thirst on a hot Utah day. **Bar:** full bar. **Address:** 686 S Main St 84532 **Location:** 0.7 mi s. L D

MOAB DINER **Phone:** 435/259-4006 (16)

American

$6-$15

AAA Inspector Notes: Step back in time to the fabulous era of the diner and ice cream shoppe in this establishment, which specializes in Kokopelli chicken and world famous green chili. **Address:** 189 S Main St 84532 **Location:** 0.3 mi s. B L D

PANCAKE HAUS **Phone:** 435/259-7141 (15)

Breakfast

$6-$10

AAA Inspector Notes: Serving only breakfast, the eatery specializes in banana and walnut pancakes, fruit-topped French toast and crepes, stuffed omelets and country-fried steak with eggs. **Address:** 196 S Main St 84532 **Location:** Just s; next to Ramada Moab Downtown. B

PASTA JAY'S **Phone:** 435/259-2900 (10)

Italian

$7-$16

AAA Inspector Notes: A nice selection of pasta, pizza, salads, sandwiches and wine is served on red-and-white-checkered tablecloths. The large covered patio, which is open year-round, surrounds the attractively landscaped exterior, which runs along two downtown sidewalks. **Bar:** beer & wine. **Address:** 4 S Main St 84532 **Location:** At Main and W Center sts. **Parking:** street only. L D

PEACE TREE JUICE CAFE **Phone:** 435/259-0101 (12)

Natural/Organic

$5-$9

AAA Inspector Notes: Specializing in fresh juices, delicious smoothies, healthful salads, chips and hummus, wraps and tasty ice cream, this brightly colored cafe lifts guests' moods. Fresh coffee also is available. **Bar:** beer & wine. **Address:** 20 S Main St 84532 **Location:** Just s of center. **Parking:** street only. B L D

SINGHA THAI CUISINE **Phone:** 435/259-0039 (11)

Thai

$11-$18

AAA Inspector Notes: Well-prepared traditional entrées are served in this charming eatery. The menu includes spring rolls, stuffed angel wings, authentic Thai curry, soups, and house specials such as tamarind duck and volcano shrimp. Gluten-free dishes are available upon request. **Bar:** beer & wine. **Address:** 92 E Center St 84532 **Location:** Just e. **Parking:** street only. L D

SLICKROCK CAFE **Phone:** 435/259-8004 (9)

American

$7-$19

AAA Inspector Notes: An island adventure awaits at this Caribbean-themed cafe. The menu consists of meat, fish and chicken dishes infused with mango, spiced pecans, chili verde and other international flavors. **Bar:** full bar. **Address:** 5 N Main St 84532 **Location:** At W Center St. **Parking:** street only. B L D

SORREL RIVER GRILL **Phone:** 435/259-4642 (1)

American

$8-$36

AAA Inspector Notes: The restaurant offers sensational dishes made from local ingredients in a riverfront setting with covered decks. Patrons might start with grilled marinated shrimp then move on to Colorado wild duck or grilled salmon steak with creamy truffle sauce. The service is excellent. **Bar:** full bar. **Reservations:** required, dinner. **Address:** Hwy 128, MM 17 84532 **Location:** 17 mi e of jct US 191 and SR 128 at MM 17; in Sorrel River Ranch Resort & Spa. B L D

SUNSET GRILL **Phone:** 435/259-7146 (4)

Steak

$14-$24

AAA Inspector Notes: The grill occupies the historic former home of Uranium King Charlie Steen. The menu emphasis is on seafood, prime rib, filet mignon and pasta. Patrons will enjoy watching the sunset by candlelight at this cliff-side spot, which affords a million-dollar panoramic view. **Bar:** full bar. **Address:** 900 N Hwy 191 84532 **Location:** 1.1 mi n, then 0.3 mi e up to bluff; rough road to top of bluff. D

ZAX RESTAURANT AND WATERING HOLE

Phone: 435/259-6555 (14)

American

$6-$19

AAA Inspector Notes: This restaurant offers much more than delicious pizzas, including a variety of burgers, sandwiches, steaks and pasta dishes. Attractive murals reflect the adventurous spirit of the city and its surroundings. **Bar:** full bar. **Address:** 96 S Main St 84532 **Location:** At W Center and Main sts. **Parking:** street only. B L D

MONTICELLO (F-6) pop. 1,972, elev. 7,050'

Named for Thomas Jefferson's Virginia home, Monticello is on the edge of the Manti-La Sal National Forest *(see place listing p. 362)* and 14 miles south of the southern entrance to Canyonlands National Park *(see place listing p. 334)*. The surrounding Abajo Mountains (also known as the Blue Mountains) provide many opportunities for backpacking, camping, off-road driving, snowmobiling and cross-country skiing.

Harts Draw Road is a 22-mile scenic drive that connects Monticello to SR 211, passing lakes and pine forests and offering views of Canyonlands National Park.

San Juan County Travel Council: 117 S. Main St., P.O. Box 490, Monticello, UT 84535. **Phone:** (435) 587-3235 or (800) 574-4386.

NEWSPAPER ROCK is near Indian Creek Canyon, 14 mi. n. on US 191, then 12 mi. w. on SR 211. Newspaper Rock is a large cliff mural consisting of ancient Native American petroglyphs and pictographs from three distinctive periods. **Cost:** Free. **Phone:** (435) 587-1500.

INN AT THE CANYONS **Phone:** (435)587-2458

Motel

$40-$150

Address: 533 N Main St 84535 **Location:** On US 191; north end of town. **Facility:** 43 units. 2 stories (no elevator), interior corridors. **Terms:** open 5/1-11/1, cancellation fee imposed. **Amenities:** high-speed Internet. **Pool(s):** heated indoor. **Activities:** whirlpool. **Free Special Amenities: expanded continental breakfast and room upgrade (subject to availability with advance reservations).**

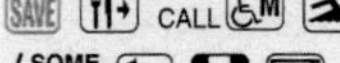

/ SOME UNITS

RODEWAY INN & SUITES **Phone:** (435)587-2489

Hotel

$76-$120

Address: 649 N Main St 84535 **Location:** On US 191; north end of town. **Facility:** 40 units. 2 stories (no elevator), interior corridors. **Terms:** cancellation fee imposed. **Pool(s):** heated indoor.

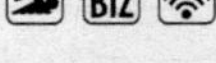

/ SOME UNITS FEE

WAYSIDE INN **Phone:** 435/587-2261

Motel

Rates not provided

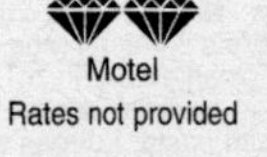

Address: 197 E Central St 84535 **Location:** On US 491, just e of US 191. **Facility:** 37 units. 1 story, exterior corridors. **Terms:** seasonal. **Pool(s):** heated outdoor. **Activities:** whirlpool.

/ SOME UNITS FEE

WHERE TO EAT

LAMPLIGHT RESTAURANT **Phone:** 435/587-2170

American

$7-$28

AAA Inspector Notes: The relaxed family restaurant treats patrons to home-baked bread and desserts, as well as all-you-can-eat prime rib and seafood each Saturday night. The salad bar lines up more than a dozen house-made choices. **Address:** 655 E Central 84535 **Location:** Jct US 191 and 491, 0.5 mi e.

B L D

PEACE TREE JUICE CAFE **Phone:** 435/587-5063

Deli

$5-$9

AAA Inspector Notes: Specializing in fresh juice, healthful wraps and tasty ice cream, this brightly colored cafe lifts guests' moods as they sip on delicious smoothies. **Address:** 516 N Main St 84535 **Location:** Jct US 191 and 491, 0.5 mi n. **Parking:** street only. B L

MONUMENT VALLEY (G-5)

GOULDING'S MONUMENT VALLEY MUSEUM is 2 mi. w. of US 163 in Goulding's Lodge at 1000 Main St. The first floor is a re-creation of the original 1920s trading post and contains items pertaining to local history. The Gouldings' living quarters on the second floor has displays of photographs and personal items.

The Movie Days Film Gallery has area film memorabilia. Earth Spirit and Among the Monuments, 20-minute multimedia presentations that capture the beauty of Monument Valley, are shown nightly. **Hours:** Daily 8-8. Multimedia shows are offered nightly at 6:10, 7:10 and 8:10. **Cost:** Donations. **Phone:** (435) 727-3231.

GOULDING'S MONUMENT VALLEY TOURS departs from Goulding's Lodge at 1000 Main St. All-day, half-day, and 3.5- and 2.5-hour tours are conducted by Navajo Indian guides in four-wheel-drive vehicles. Monument Valley sights include pictographs and petroglyphs, natural arches and windows, monoliths and pueblo-style cliff dwellings built by Anasazi Indians about A.D. 1250. Sunset and full moon tours also are available.

Hours: Full-day tours and tours lasting 3.5 hours depart daily at 9, year-round. Half-day tours depart daily at 9 and 4, year-round. Tours lasting 2.5 hours depart daily at 1:30, late Mar.-early Oct. Winter tour times vary; phone ahead. **Cost:** Full-day tour $90; $70 (ages 0-8). Half-day tour $70; $55 (ages 0-8). Tour lasting 3.5 hours $50; $30 (ages 0-8). Tour lasting 2.5 hours $40; $27 (ages 0-8). **Phone:** (435) 727-3231.

GOULDING'S TRADING POST & LODGE **Phone:** (435)727-3231

Hotel

$160-$218 5/1-10/31

$85-$182 11/1-4/30

Address: 1000 Main St 84536 **Location:** 2 mi w of US 163; 0.5 mi n of Arizona border. **Facility:** 62 units, some efficiencies and cabins. 2 stories (no elevator), exterior corridors. **Terms:** 3 day cancellation notice. **Pool(s):** heated indoor. **Activities:** exercise room. **Guest Services:** coin laundry. **Free Special Amenities: local telephone calls and high-speed Internet.**

SAVE / SOME UNITS FEE

MONUMENT VALLEY NAVAJO TRIBAL PARK (G-5)

Reached via scenic US 163, Monument Valley Navajo Tribal Park is a colorful region covering several thousand square miles within the Navajo Indian Reservation. The park contains Mystery Valley, where isolated monoliths of red sandstone tower as much as 1,000 feet above the valley floor.

The visitor center, 4 miles southeast of US 163, provides information about self-guiding tours. Guided tours from the center are offered daily; primitive camping and picnicking are permitted.

Horseback and four-wheel-drive trips through the vicinity can be arranged through agencies in Arizona at Kayenta and in Utah at Bluff, Mexican Hat and Monument Valley. Overnight accommodations also are available in Kayenta, Mexican Hat and Monument Valley; reservations are recommended.

Visitors should not photograph the Navajo people, their homes or their possessions without asking permission; a gratuity is usually requested. Other restrictions apply. For more information contact Monument Valley Navajo Tribal Park, P.O. Box 360289, Monument Valley, UT 84536.

The park is open daily 6 a.m.-8:30 p.m., May-Sept.; 8-5, rest of year (weather permitting). Closed Thanksgiving and Christmas. Last admission 30 minutes before closing. Recreational vehicles more than 25 feet long are not permitted on the self-guiding tour. Admission is $5; free (ages 0-9). Primitive camping fee is $10. Phone (435) 727-5870.

VISITOR CENTER, 4 mi. s.e. of US 163 near the Arizona/Utah border, offers an impressive panorama of the Mitten and Merrick buttes; exhibits about Native Americans; an auditorium; an outdoor amphitheater; a patio; a library; and a Navajo hogan, the traditional housing structure of the Navajo people.

Departing from the center are various guided tours led by Navajo tour operators, who take visitors down into the valley. Food is available in summer. **Time:** Allow 2 hours, 30 minutes minimum. **Hours:** Daily 6 a.m.-8 p.m., May-Sept.; 8-7, Mar.-Apr.; 8-5, rest of year. Closed Thanksgiving and Christmas. **Cost:** Visitor center $5; free (ages 0-9). **Phone:** (435) 727-5870 or (435) 727-5875.

MOUNT CARMEL JUNCTION

BEST WESTERN EAST ZION THUNDERBIRD LODGE
Phone: 435/648-2203

Hotel
Rates not provided

AAA Benefit: Members save up to 20%, plus 10% bonus points with Best Western Rewards®.

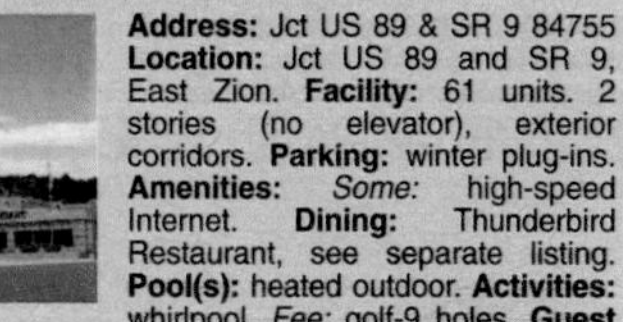

Address: Jct US 89 & SR 9 84755 **Location:** Jct US 89 and SR 9, East Zion. **Facility:** 61 units. 2 stories (no elevator), exterior corridors. **Parking:** winter plug-ins. **Amenities:** *Some:* high-speed Internet. **Dining:** Thunderbird Restaurant, see separate listing. **Pool(s):** heated outdoor. **Activities:** whirlpool. *Fee:* golf-9 holes. **Guest Services:** coin laundry. **Free Special Amenities: local telephone calls and high-speed Internet.**
(See ad p. 464.)

    / SOME UNITS 

WHERE TO EAT

GOLDEN HILLS RESTAURANT **Phone:** 435/648-2602

American
$6-$19

AAA Inspector Notes: Long a staple in area dining, the restaurant is a great stop for travelers on their way to or from Zion National Park. The salad bar is an option at lunch or dinner. **Address:** 4475 S State St 84755 **Location:** US 89, jct SR 9. B L D

THUNDERBIRD RESTAURANT **Phone:** 435/648-2262

American
$6-$21

AAA Inspector Notes: Right off the lobby, the three-meal-a-day restaurant has something to offer everyone. Breads and desserts all are homemade. **Bar:** beer & wine. **Address:** Jct US 89 & SR 9 84755 **Location:** Jct US 89 and SR 9, East Zion; in Best Western East Zion Thunderbird Lodge. B L D

MURRAY pop. 46,746

- **Hotels & Restaurants map & index p. 426**
- **Part of Salt Lake City area — see map p. 412**

CRYSTAL INN MIDVALLEY MURRAY
Phone: (801)685-9300 

Hotel
$79-$139

Address: 818 E Winchester St 84107 **Location:** I-215 exit 9 (Union Park Ave), 1.2 mi nw via 6600 S. **Facility:** 128 units. 4 stories, interior corridors. **Pool(s):** heated indoor. **Activities:** whirlpool, exercise room. **Guest Services:** valet and coin laundry.
(See ad p. 432.)

(See map & index p. 426.)

FAIRFIELD INN BY MARRIOTT MURRAY
Phone: (801)265-9600 43

Hotel
$107-$131

AAA Benefit:
AAA hotel discounts of 5% or more.

Address: 594 W 4500 S 84123 **Location:** I-15 exit 301 (4500 S), 0.3 mi w. **Facility:** 60 units. 3 stories, interior corridors. **Pool(s):** heated indoor. **Activities:** whirlpool, exercise room. **Guest Services:** complimentary and valet laundry. BIZ

HAMPTON INN MURRAY **Phone:** (801)293-1300 42

Hotel
$89-$129

AAA Benefit:
Members save up to 10% everyday!

Address: 606 W 4500 S 84123 **Location:** I-15 exit 301 (4500 S), just w. **Facility:** 64 units. 3 stories, interior corridors. **Terms:** 1-7 night minimum stay, cancellation fee imposed. **Pool(s):** heated indoor. **Activities:** whirlpool, exercise room. **Guest Services:** valet and coin laundry.
/ SOME UNITS

HOLIDAY INN EXPRESS MURRAY
Phone: 801/268-2533 41

Hotel
Rates not provided

Address: 4465 S Century Dr 84123 **Location:** I-15 exit 301 (4500 S), just w to 4500 S, then just n. **Facility:** 130 units. 2 stories (no elevator), interior corridors. **Amenities:** video games (fee). **Pool(s):** heated outdoor. **Activities:** exercise room. **Guest Services:** valet and coin laundry.
BIZ FEE
/ SOME UNITS FEE

PAVILION INN **Phone:** 801/506-8000 44

Hotel
Rates not provided

Address: 5335 S College Dr 84123 **Location:** I-15 exit 300 (5300 S), 0.3 mi w. **Facility:** 98 units. 3 stories, interior corridors. **Pool(s):** heated indoor. **Activities:** whirlpool, exercise room. **Guest Services:** complimentary laundry.
/ SOME UNITS FEE

GEM NATURAL BRIDGES NATIONAL MONUMENT (F-5)

Natural Bridges National Monument is 42 miles west of Blanding via SR 95. The park has a scenic 7,780 acres. Within the winding corridors of White and Armstrong canyons, water has eroded the stone walls to form three massive bridges. The natural bridges remained known only to the Anasazi and other Native American tribes until 1883, when Cass Hite, a gold prospector, first entered the area from a remote mining camp on the Colorado River.

All three bridges can be viewed from overlooks accessible by short walks from a scenic 9-mile loop drive. Trails lead down to each bridge, and an 8.6-mile round-trip trail connects the bridges.

The three natural bridges were named after Hopi Indian terms that relate to their characteristics. The Sipapu Bridge, the longest and highest, is 268 feet long, 31 feet wide, 53 feet thick and 220 feet high. The second largest natural bridge in the world, Sipapu represents a mature stage in the evolution of a natural bridge.

Kachina Bridge, 2.5 miles away at the junction of Armstrong and White canyons, crosses the stream bed at a height of 210 feet. The most massive bridge, Kachina is 204 feet long, 44 feet wide and 93 feet thick. Owachomo Bridge, the smallest and oldest, is a narrow strip of rock only 9 feet thick in the center and 27 feet wide. Spanning 180 feet, Owachomo is in a late stage of erosion and is approaching the day when weather and gravity will bring it crashing to the canyon floor.

Bridge View Drive, a scenic, 9-mile-long, one-way loop starting and ending near the visitor center has overlooks for each of the three bridges. Horse Collar Ruin, an ancestral Puebloan cliff dwelling, is visible from the Bridge View Drive overlook. Pets and bicycles are not permitted on trails or off-road areas. Hiking on bridges is not allowed.

Camping is permitted. Visitors should note that there is a 26-foot limit for RVs and any vehicles pulling them and that the closest gas stations are some 20 miles away at Fry Canyon from the west, 44 miles away in Mexican Hat from the south and 38 miles away in Blanding from the east.

A visitor center at the monument headquarters presents a slide show and a museum with historical and geological exhibits. The monument is open all year (weather permitting), but the best time to visit is late April to late October. The visitor center is open daily 8-6, Apr.-Sept.; 8-5, rest of year. Closed Jan. 1, Thanksgiving and Christmas. Admission is $6 (per private vehicle); $3 (per person arriving by other means). The above fees permit entrance to the park for 7 calendar days from date of purchase. Annual local passes are available for $25 and permit entrance into Arches *(see place listing p. 321)* and Canyonlands *(see place listing p. 334)* national parks as well as Hovenweep National Monument *(see place listing in Colorado p. 227)*. The camping fee is $10.

For additional information contact the Superintendent, Natural Bridges National Monument, HC-60, Box 1, Lake Powell, UT 84533; phone (435) 692-1234.

NEPHI pop. 5,389

BEST WESTERN PARADISE INN OF NEPHI
Phone: (435)623-0624

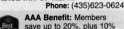

Motel
$81-$130

AAA Benefit: Members save up to 20%, plus 10% bonus points with Best Western Rewards®.

Address: 1025 S Main St 84648 **Location:** I-15 exit 222, 0.5 mi n. Across from train tracks. **Facility:** 40 units. 2 stories (no elevator), exterior corridors. **Pool(s):** heated indoor. **Activities:** whirlpool, playground. **Free Special Amenities: local telephone calls and high-speed Internet.**
SAVE / SOME UNITS FEE

WHERE TO EAT

JC MICKELSON'S RESTAURANT **Phone:** 435/623-0152

American
$7-$17

AAA Inspector Notes: Old-fashioned cooking and country-friendly service are to be expected at this eatery. Favorites include homemade soups and pies, as well as made-from-scratch dinner rolls. **Address:** 2100 S Main St, Suite 7 84648 **Location:** I-15 exit 222, just s.

B L D

NORTH SALT LAKE pop. 16,322

• **Hotels & Restaurants map & index p. 426**
• **Part of Salt Lake City area — see map p. 412**

BEST WESTERN PLUS COTTONTREE INN
Phone: (801)292-7666 22

Hotel
$105-$155

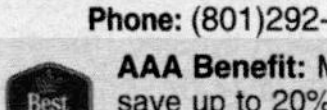
AAA Benefit: Members save up to 20%, plus 10% bonus points with Best Western Rewards®.

Address: 1030 N 400 E 84054 **Location:** I-15 exit 315 (Woods Cross) northbound, just e to Onion St, then just s; southbound, 0.3 mi e to 500 E, just s, then just w. **Facility:** 116 units. 2 stories (no elevator), interior corridors. **Amenities:** *Some:* safes. **Pool(s):** heated indoor. **Activities:** whirlpool. **Guest Services:** valet and coin laundry, area transportation-within 5 mi. **Free Special Amenities: full breakfast and airport transportation.**

SAVE FEE

/ SOME UNITS FEE

OAKLEY (B-4) pop. 1,470, elev. 6,434'

ROCKY MOUNTAIN SLEIGH CO. is 10.7 mi. n.e. on Weber Canyon Rd. from jct. SR 32, then just n.w., following signs to the Stillman Ranch. Half-hour sleigh rides in a two-horse sled take passengers along the Weber River and through meadows and woods. The sleigh's destination is a rustic log cabin at the ranch where a sumptuous, homey dinner is served before a huge, roaring fireplace.

Time: Allow 2 hours, 30 minutes minimum. **Hours:** Trips depart daily at 5 and 7 p.m., mid-Nov. through Apr. 30. **Cost:** Mid-Dec. to early Jan. sleigh ride with dinner $89; $69 (ages 3-11). Rest of season sleigh ride with dinner $79; $59 (ages 3-11). Sleigh ride only $45; $30 (ages 3-11). Reservations are required. **Phone:** (435) 645-7256 or (800) 303-7256.

OGDEN (B-3) pop. 82,825, elev. 4,300'

• **Hotels p. 382 • Restaurants p. 383**

Ogden is one of the largest cities in Utah and an important railroad distribution center for products destined for the West Coast. The city's importance as a rail center dates from 1869, when the golden spike uniting the nation by rail was driven at Promontory, northwest of Ogden. The main rail junction was moved to Ogden soon afterward.

Mormon pioneers arrived at the confluence of the Weber and Ogden rivers soon after reaching the Great Salt Lake Valley on July 24, 1847. Named for a noted fur trapper and designed by Brigham Young, Ogden's layout incorporates broad, straight streets lined with box elder, elm and poplar trees. Late July is highlighted by the Pioneer Days Rodeo and Celebration.

The Ogden Tabernacle and Temple is at 2133 Washington Blvd. The temple is not open to visitors, but strolling the grounds is encouraged. Also of interest in the city is Weber State University's Ott Planetarium, which presents free planetarium shows; phone (801) 626-6871 for the schedule.

Municipal Gardens is at 25th Street and Washington Boulevard. The park contains 5 acres of gardens, gaslit paths and picnic facilities. Between Thanksgiving and Christmas a Santa's village and an international Christmas display are presented.

The Willard Bay State Recreation Area *(see Recreation Chart)*, north of Ogden, offers a number of recreational activities March through November. Ogden Canyon, east on 12th Street, is known for numerous faults and erosion patterns that are of interest to both expert and novice explorers.

Golden Spike Events Center, 1000 North 1200 West, hosts rodeos horse racing, the county fair, outdoor concerts and soccer and softball games; phone (801) 399-8798 or (800) 442-7362.

Ogden/Weber Convention and Visitors Bureau: 2438 Washington Blvd., Ogden, UT 84401. **Phone:** (801) 778-6250 or (866) 867-8824.

DAUGHTERS OF UTAH PIONEERS MUSEUM AND MILES GOODYEAR CABIN is at 2148 Grant Ave. The site contains furnishings, clothing and handicrafts reminiscent of pioneer days. Miles Goodyear, a mountain man trapper, established the first permanent settlement in the Basin in 1836. Built in 1845, the cabin is said to be the oldest homestead in Utah. **Time:** Allow 30 minutes minimum. **Hours:** Mon.-Fri. 1-5. **Cost:** Free. **Phone:** (435) 623-5202.

ECCLES COMMUNITY ART CENTER is at 2580 Jefferson Ave. The center displays visual works in various media by Utah artists. **Hours:** Mon.-Fri. 9-5, Sat. 9-3. Closed major holidays. **Cost:** Free. **Phone:** (801) 392-6935.

FORT BUENAVENTURA STATE PARK is off I-15, then e. to 2450 A Ave. The park contains a replica of the 1836 stockade and cabins built by trapper Miles Goodyear. Wooden pegs and mortise and tenon joints were used instead of nails in the construction of the stockade. Fishing and canoeing are permitted. Hiking trails are available. *See Recreation Chart.*

Time: Allow 30 minutes minimum. **Hours:** Park open daily 8-8, Apr.-Nov. Visitor center open daily 9-5, Apr.-Nov. **Cost:** $1; free (ages 0-5). Camping $18. Canoe rental $5 (1 hour); $3 (half-hour). **Phone:** (801) 399-8099.

GEORGE S. ECCLES DINOSAUR PARK is at 1544 E. Park Blvd. The park features replicas of prehistoric creatures such as crawlers, dinosaurs, flying reptiles and marine animals from the Permian through the Jurassic and Cretaceous eras. An exhibit hall displays dinosaur bones and other prehistoric objects.

Time: Allow 1 hour, 30 minutes minimum. **Hours:** Mon.-Sat.10-8, Sun. noon-6, Memorial Day-Labor Day; Mon.-Sat. and holidays 10-6, rest of year. Last admission 1 hour before closing. Closed major holidays. **Cost:** $7; $6 (ages 13-17 and 62+); $5 (ages 2-12). **Phone:** (801) 393-3466.

HILL AEROSPACE MUSEUM, e. of I-15 exit 338 on Hill Air Force Base, displays aircraft, missiles, engines, bombs and other weapons in more than 100 indoor and outdoor exhibits. Over 80 military aircraft, including a B-1 bomber, B-17 bomber, B-29 Superfortress, B-52 bomber, C-47 cargo plane, C-119 Flying Boxcar, HH-3 Jolly Green Giant helicopter and an SR71 Blackbird, are showcased.

Changing films include the story of the recovery and restoration of a P-38 airplane that crashed in Alaska. **Time:** Allow 2 hours minimum. **Hours:** Daily 9-4:30. Closed Jan. 1, Thanksgiving and Christmas. **Cost:** Donations. **Phone:** (801) 777-6818 or (801) 777-6868.

OGDEN NATURE CENTER, 966 W. 12th St., is a 152-acre wildlife sanctuary and nature center. Its grounds, gardens and ponds provide shelter and a natural habitat for birds, insects and small animals. A visitor center houses non-releasable raptors as well as hands-on and educational exhibits, including an observation beehive. The center also has 1.5 miles of trails. **Time:** Allow 1 hour minimum. **Hours:** Mon.-Fri. 9-5, Sat. 9-4. Closed major holidays. **Cost:** $4; $3 (ages 62+); $2 (ages 2-11). **Phone:** (801) 621-7595.

GEM **OGDEN UNION STATION MUSEUMS,** 2501 Wall Ave., houses four museums and two art galleries in Ogden's former 1924 train station.

The John M. Browning Firearms Museum displays the well-known handguns, rifles and machine guns created by Ogden's Browning family. The Utah State Railroad Museum interprets the state's railroad history and includes the Wattis-Dumke Model Railroad Museum featuring model trains that highlight the transcontinental line from California to Wyoming. The Eccles Rail Center outdoor exhibit features vintage engines and cars. The Browning-Kimball Classic Car Museum exhibits a collection of elegant early 20th-century automobiles. Gallery at the Station showcases fine art, and the Myra Powell Gallery features the station's permanent art collection.

Tours: Guided tours are available. **Time:** Allow 1 hour, 30 minutes minimum. **Hours:** Mon.-Sat. 10-5. Closed Jan. 1, Thanksgiving, Christmas and Dec. 31. **Cost:** $5; $4 (ages 62+); $3 (ages 2-12); $12 (family, two adults and up to four children). **Phone:** (801) 393-9886 or (866) 379-9599.

TREEHOUSE CHILDREN'S MUSEUM is at 347 22nd St. The hands-on museum offers the younger set interactive exhibits with an emphasis on language and literacy. There also is a tree house to climb, a storybook village to explore and a chance to travel back in time to experience Utah's history. **Time:** Allow 2 hours minimum. **Hours:** Mon.-Sat. 10-5 (also Fri. 5-8), June-Aug. and holidays; Tues.-Sat. 10-5 (also Fri. 5-8), Mon. 10-3, rest of year. Closed Jan. 1, July 4 and 24, 12 days in mid-Sept., Thanksgiving and Christmas. **Cost:** $6 (ages 1-12); $5 (adults). **Phone:** (801) 394-9663.

WEBER STATE MUSEUM OF NATURAL SCIENCE is at 1551 Edvalson St. on the Weber State University campus. The museum contains an exhibit based on the diary of 19th-century geologist and ethnologist John Wesley Powell's river explorations. Other exhibits include dinosaur fossils, rocks, minerals, geologic specimens and a valley glaciation display. **Hours:** Mon.-Fri. 8-5, late Aug.-early May. Closed campus holidays. Phone ahead to confirm schedule. **Cost:** Free. **Phone:** (801) 626-6000.

ALASKAN INN — **Phone:** 801/621-8600

Bed & Breakfast
Rates not provided

Address: 435 Ogden Canyon Rd 84401 **Location:** I-15 exit 344 (12th St), 7.5 mi e. **Facility:** Located in Ogden Canyon among lofty pines and granite-crested mountains, this inn features Arctic-inspired suites and cozy cabins. 23 units, some cabins. 1-2 stories (no elevator), interior/exterior corridors. **Terms:** check-in 4 pm, age restrictions may apply.

BEST WESTERN PLUS CANYON PINES
Phone: (801)675-5534

Hotel
$96-$120

Best Western Plus — **AAA Benefit:** Members save up to 20%, plus 10% bonus points with Best Western Rewards®.

Address: 6650 S Hwy 89 84405 **Location:** I-84 exit 87 (US 89/South Ogden), 0.6 mi n. Located near train tracks. **Facility:** 52 units. 3 stories, interior corridors. **Amenities:** high-speed Internet. **Pool(s):** heated indoor. **Activities:** whirlpool, exercise room. **Guest Services:** valet and coin laundry. **Free Special Amenities: full breakfast and high-speed Internet.**

SAVE BIZ

BEST WESTERN PLUS HIGH COUNTRY INN
Phone: (801)394-9474

Hotel
$82-$139

Best Western Plus — **AAA Benefit:** Members save up to 20%, plus 10% bonus points with Best Western Rewards®.

Address: 1335 W 12th St 84404 **Location:** I-15 exit 344 (12th St), just e. Located near train tracks. **Facility:** 109 units. 2 stories (no elevator), interior/exterior corridors. **Amenities:** video games (fee). *Some:* high-speed Internet. **Dining:** Jeremiah's Restaurant, see separate listing. **Pool(s):** heated outdoor. **Activities:** whirlpool, exercise room. **Guest Services:** valet and coin laundry. **Free Special Amenities: newspaper and room upgrade (subject to availability with advance reservations).**

SAVE FEE

/ SOME UNITS

COMFORT INN FARR WEST **Phone:** 801/737-5660

Hotel

Rates not provided

Address: 1776 W 2550 N 84404 **Location:** I-15 exit 349 (Farr West), 0.3 mi e to 1850 W, then just s. **Facility:** 72 units. 3 stories, interior corridors. **Pool(s):** heated indoor. **Activities:** waterslide, exercise room. **Guest Services:** valet and coin laundry.

   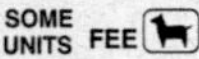

/ SOME UNITS FEE

COMFORT SUITES **Phone:** (801)621-2545

Hotel

$88-$135

Address: 2250 S 1200 W 84401 **Location:** I-15 exit 343 (21st St), just se. **Facility:** 142 units. 3 stories, interior corridors. **Terms:** cancellation fee imposed. **Amenities:** high-speed Internet. **Pool(s):** heated indoor. **Activities:** whirlpool, playground, sports court, basketball, exercise room. **Guest Services:** valet and coin laundry.

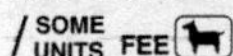

/ SOME UNITS FEE

HAMPTON INN & SUITES **Phone:** (801)394-9400

Hotel

$89-$159

AAA Benefit: Members save up to 10% everyday!

Address: 2401 Washington Blvd 84401 **Location:** I-15 exit 342 (24th St), 1.5 mi e; corner of 24th St and Washington Blvd. **Facility:** 124 units. 8 stories, interior corridors. **Terms:** 1-7 night minimum stay, cancellation fee imposed. **Amenities:** high-speed Internet. **Activities:** whirlpool, exercise room. **Guest Services:** valet and coin laundry.

  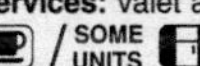  

/ SOME UNITS

HOLIDAY INN EXPRESS & SUITES **Phone:** (801)392-5000

Hotel

$95-$118

Address: 2245 S 1200 W 84401 **Location:** I-15 exit 343 (21st St), 0.3 mi e. **Facility:** 75 units. 3 stories, interior corridors. **Terms:** 3 day cancellation notice. **Pool(s):** heated indoor. **Activities:** whirlpool, exercise room. **Guest Services:** valet and coin laundry.

/ SOME UNITS FEE

OGDEN MARRIOTT **Phone:** (801)627-1190

Hotel

$170-$208

Marriott HOTELS & RESORTS **AAA Benefit:** AAA hotel discounts of 5% or more.

Address: 247 24th St 84401 **Location:** I-15 exit 342 (24th St), 1.5 mi e. **Facility:** 292 units. 8 stories, interior corridors. **Amenities:** *Some:* high-speed Internet. **Pool(s):** heated indoor. **Activities:** whirlpool, exercise room. **Guest Services:** valet and coin laundry, area transportation-within 5 mi. **Free Special Amenities: full breakfast and high-speed Internet.**

FEE

/ SOME UNITS FEE

SLEEP INN **Phone:** (801)731-6500

Motel

$70-$100

Address: 1155 S 1700 W 84404 **Location:** I-15 exit 344 (12th St), just w. **Facility:** 66 units. 2 stories (no elevator), interior corridors. **Terms:** cancellation fee imposed. **Guest Services:** coin laundry. **Free Special Amenities: continental breakfast and high-speed Internet.**

/ SOME UNITS FEE

VALUE PLACE **Phone:** 801/334-8628

Extended Stay Motel

Rates not provided

Address: 2160 S 1200 W 84401 **Location:** I-15 exit 343 (21st St), 0.3 mi e. **Facility:** 124 efficiencies. 4 stories, interior corridors. **Terms:** office hours 9 am-6 pm. **Amenities:** high-speed Internet (fee). **Guest Services:** coin laundry.

WHERE TO EAT

ATHENIAN RESTAURANT **Phone:** 801/621-4911

Greek

$6-$16

AAA Inspector Notes: Friendly service adds to the warm and casual atmosphere at this cozy eatery. Combination platters combine samples of traditional Greek specialties such as dolmades, beeftekia and spanakopita. Lemon rice is delicious, and yummy Greek wedding cookies can be taken home or snacked on while traveling. **Bar:** full bar. **Address:** 252 25th St 84401 **Location:** I-15 exit 342 (24th St), 1.5 mi e to Grant Ave, just s, then just w. **Parking:** street only. L D

BISTRO 258 **Phone:** 801/394-1595

American

$8-$27

AAA Inspector Notes: Tucked in along historic 25th Street, the bistro serves certified Angus steak, trendy pasta, chicken and seafood entrées in a cozy dining room and on an outdoor patio. **Bar:** full bar. **Address:** 258 25th St 84401 **Location:** I-15 exit 343 (21st St), 2.3 mi e, 0.6 mi s on Wall Ave, then just e. **Parking:** on-site and street.

L D

GOLDEN DYNASTY **Phone:** 801/621-6789

Chinese

$6-$11

AAA Inspector Notes: Lunch and dinnertime favorites are savored in a comfortable, friendly setting. Service is attentive yet unobtrusive. **Address:** 3433 Washington Blvd 84401 **Location:** I-15 exit 341A (31st St), 1.5 mi e, then 0.5 mi s. L D

GRAY CLIFF LODGE RESTAURANT **Phone:** 801/392-6775

American

$15-$39

AAA Inspector Notes: People travel for miles to enjoy the ride up breathtaking Ogden Canyon and to experience the cozy atmosphere in this historic 1912 grand old house. Made-from-scratch traditional dinners include a fruit cup or tomato juice, salad or soup, baked potato, cinnamon rolls and a choice of chicken, prime rib, filet mignon, lamb chops, Alaskan king crab legs, fresh local trout filleted at the table and more. Although varied desserts are offered, the oatmeal pie is a favorite. **Bar:** full bar. **Address:** 508 Ogden Canyon Rd 84401 **Location:** I-15 exit 344 (12th St), 9 mi e. D

THE GREENERY RESTAURANT **Phone:** 801/392-1777

American

$8-$15

AAA Inspector Notes: At the mouth of Ogden Canyon, this bright eatery with black-and-white tile and red cafe chairs is famous for its Mormon muffin and gabby-crabby sandwich. Children have their own menu, and everyone can feast on appetizers and dishes such as chicken penne pesto, salads and soups. **Bar:** beer & wine. **Address:** 1875 Valley Dr 84401 **Location:** I-15 exit 344 (12th St), 4.8 mi e; at mouth of Ogden City Canyon. L D

JEREMIAH'S RESTAURANT **Phone:** 801/394-3273

American

$7-$17

AAA Inspector Notes: Known for its all-day breakfast menu, the restaurant also serves good-size lunches and dinners to appreciative locals and tourists. **Bar:** full bar. **Address:** 1307 W 12th St 84404 **Location:** I-15 exit 344 (12th St), just e; next to Best Western Plus High Country Inn. B L D

LA FERROVIA RISTORANTE Phone: 801/394-8628

Italian
$7-$18

AAA Inspector Notes: The charming eatery offers a variety of authentic Italian options along the lines of cannelloni, sausage and ground beef lasagna, breaded grilled chicken breast and rib-eye steak in a mouthwatering house marinade. The daily specials can't be beat. **Bar:** beer & wine. **Address:** 234 25th St 84401 **Location:** I-15 exit 341 (31st St), just e of Lincoln Ave and 25th St. **Parking:** street only. L D

PRAIRIE SCHOONER STEAK HOUSE Phone: 801/621-5511

Steak
$16-$50

AAA Inspector Notes: Patrons dine in a covered wagon next to an open prairie fire as they enjoy fresh seafood, hand-cut steaks, chicken, prime rib and signature desserts. **Bar:** full bar. **Reservations:** suggested. **Address:** 445 Park Blvd 84401 **Location:** I-15 exit 342 (24th St), 1.5 mi e to Washington Blvd, 0.3 mi n, then just e. L D

RICKENBACKER'S BISTRO Phone: 801/627-4100

Seafood
$9-$38

AAA Inspector Notes: Guests can take in amazing mountain views and watch airplanes take off and land as they enjoy shepherd's pie, pistachio-crusted halibut, prime-grade bone-in-tenderloin or a creative take on chicken-n-waffles. Several vegetarian and pasta selections also are available, and the list of wine has been carefully chosen to compliment the cuisine. **Bar:** full bar. **Address:** 4282 S 1650 W 84405 **Location:** I-15 exit 341 (31st St), 0.3 mi w, 2 mi s on Airport Rd, 1st exit at roundabout, then just w. D

ROOSTERS 25TH STREET BREWING CO & RESTAURANT Phone: 801/627-6171

American
$7-$22

AAA Inspector Notes: Located on historic 25th Street, this friendly pub features specialty beers brewed on-site along with chicken, seafood, steak, pasta and beer-battered fish and chips. **Bar:** full bar. **Address:** 253 25th St 84401 **Location:** I-15 exit 342 (24th St), 1.5 mi e; downtown. L D

RUBY RIVER STEAKHOUSE Phone: 801/622-2320

Steak
$8-$37

AAA Inspector Notes: Guests can nibble on peanuts from the shell before their meal or while watching the game in the lounge. Menu choices range from steaks and ribs to chicken and pasta. The atmosphere is fun. **Bar:** full bar. **Address:** 4286 Riverdale Rd 84405 **Location:** I-15 exit 339 (Riverdale Rd), 2.2 mi e. L D

SONORA GRILL Phone: 801/393-1999

Mexican
$9-$20

AAA Inspector Notes: Patrons will enjoy the comfortable upscale ambiance in this eatery where watching the delicious guacamole made tableside is part of the fun. Menu offerings feature a variety of ceviche, lettuce wrap tacos, mouth-watering fajitas, achiote salmon, all made with truly authentic Mexican ingredients. **Bar:** full bar. **Address:** 2310 S Kiesel Ave 84401 **Location:** I-15 exit 342 (24th St), 1.5 mi e, then just n; corner of Kiesel Ave and 23rd St. L D

UNION GRILL RESTAURANT Phone: 801/621-2830

American
$8-$19

AAA Inspector Notes: The cross-cooking restaurant offers soups, salads, sandwiches, seafood, pastas and specialty dishes seasoned with American, Cajun, Greek, Italian or Mexican spices. The bread pudding is highly recommended. **Bar:** full bar. **Address:** 2501 Wall Ave 84401 **Location:** I-15 exit 341 (31st St), west end of 25th St; downtown; in Union Station. L D

ZUCCA TRATTORIA Phone: 801/475-7077

Italian
$8-$22

AAA Inspector Notes: Among the varied menu items are rigatoni with house-made fennel sausage sugo; grilled pork loin with Marsala and porcini mushroom sauce; antipasti of Italian sopressata, pistachio mortadella, prosciutto or pancetta; and Neapolitan-style pizza made in a wood-fired oven. Diners can add chicken, New York steak or shrimp to any of the salads. Tiramisu soaked in organic bean espresso and the El Rey Icoa white chocolate Italian crème brûlée are great for sharing. **Bar:** full bar. **Address:** 1479 E 5600 S 84403 **Location:** I-15 exit 341, just w of Harrison Blvd. L D

OREM pop. 88,328

HAMPTON INN & SUITES OREM Phone: (801)426-8500

Hotel
$79-$199

AAA Benefit: Members save up to 10% everyday!

Address: 851 W 1250 S 84058 **Location:** I-15 exit 269 (University Pkwy), 0.3 mi e, then just s. **Facility:** 129 units, some kitchens. 4 stories, interior corridors. **Terms:** 1-7 night minimum stay, cancellation fee imposed. **Amenities:** video games (fee). **Pool(s):** heated indoor. **Activities:** whirlpool, exercise room. **Guest Services:** valet and coin laundry.

HOLIDAY INN EXPRESS & SUITES OREM - NORTH PROVO Phone: (801)655-1515

Hotel
$99-$179

Address: 1290 W University Pkwy 84058 **Location:** I-15 exit 269 (University Pkwy), 0.5 mi w. **Facility:** 122 units. 4 stories, interior corridors. **Terms:** cancellation fee imposed. **Amenities:** high-speed Internet. **Pool(s):** heated indoor. **Activities:** whirlpool, exercise room. **Guest Services:** valet and coin laundry.

BIZ / SOME UNITS FEE

LA QUINTA INN & SUITES OREM UNIVERSITY PARKWAY Phone: (801)226-0440

Hotel
$78-$163

Address: 521 W University Pkwy 84058 **Location:** I-15 exit 269, 0.4 mi e. **Facility:** 130 units. 4 stories, interior corridors. **Amenities:** video games (fee). *Some:* high-speed Internet. **Pool(s):** heated indoor. **Activities:** whirlpool, exercise room. **Guest Services:** valet and coin laundry, area transportation-within 3 mi.

FEE / SOME UNITS

LA QUINTA INN OREM Phone: (801)235-9555

Hotel
$64-$139

Address: 1100 W 780 N 84057 **Location:** I-15 exit 272 (800 N), 0.3 mi e. **Facility:** 54 units. 3 stories, interior corridors. **Pool(s):** heated indoor. **Activities:** whirlpool, exercise room. **Guest Services:** valet and coin laundry. **Free Special Amenities: full breakfast and high-speed Internet.**

SAVE / SOME UNITS

TOWNEPLACE SUITES BY MARRIOTT OREM

Phone: (801)225-4477

Extended Stay Hotel

$89-$139

AAA Benefit: AAA hotel discounts of 5% or more.

Address: 873 N 1200 W 84057 **Location:** I-15 exit 272 (800 N), just e. **Facility:** 100 units, some two bedrooms, efficiencies and kitchens. 4 stories, interior corridors. **Terms:** check-in 4 pm. **Amenities:** high-speed Internet. **Pool(s):** heated indoor. **Activities:** whirlpool, exercise room. **Guest Services:** valet and coin laundry.

WHERE TO EAT

BANGKOK GRILL THAI RESTAURANT

Phone: 801/434-8424

Thai

$9-$15

AAA Inspector Notes: This treat of a restaurant is just off State Street in a small strip mall. The menu is diverse and lengthy and features affordable lunch specials. The Thai meatballs from the barbecue section are recommended, as is the fried banana with mango ice cream for dessert. The booths are cozy. **Address:** 338 E 800 S 84097 **Location:** I-15 exit 269 northbound, 1.5 mi e, then 0.6 mi n; exit 271 southbound, 1.6 mi e, then 0.3 mi s.

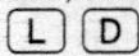

CHEF'S TABLE **Phone:** 801/235-9111

Continental

$9-$35

AAA Inspector Notes: This small romantic castle, nestled on a hill with excellent views, has private dining rooms. The creative menu, which changes seasonally, features elegant, handcrafted American dishes such as beef tenderloin, chicken, rack of lamb and seafood. **Bar:** full bar. **Reservations:** suggested. **Address:** 2005 S State St 84097 **Location:** I-15 exit 269 (University Pkwy), 2.5 mi e, then 1.5 mi s. L D

KNEADERS BAKERY & CAFE **Phone:** 801/764-9451

Breads/Pastries

$6-$9

AAA Inspector Notes: Prompt, pleasant servers buzz through the dining room with great cups of soup, quality sandwiches on artisan breads and a wide selection of tempting pastries and other desserts. **Address:** 1990 N State St 84057 **Location:** I-15 exit 273 (1600 N), 1.3 mi e, then 0.5 mi n; corner of E 200 S and N State St.

L D

P.F. CHANG'S CHINA BISTRO **Phone:** 801/426-0900

Chinese

$8-$22

AAA Inspector Notes: Trendy, upscale decor provides a pleasant backdrop for New Age Chinese dining. Appetizers, soups and salads are a meal by themselves. Vegetarian plates and sides, noodles, meins, chicken and meat dishes are created from exotic, fresh ingredients. **Bar:** full bar. **Address:** 575 E University Pkwy 84097 **Location:** I-15 exit 269 (University Pkwy), 2.3 mi e; south side of University Mall. L D

PIZZERIA SEVEN TWELVE **Phone:** 801/623-6712

Pizza

$9-$16

AAA Inspector Notes: Seasonal small plates highlight a menu that may include crunchy polenta beneath tender short ribs that have been braised low and slow in a cooler part of the wood-fired oven, or wood-roasted Brussels sprouts with toasted hazelnuts, bacon and vinegar. A wide selection of high-end ingredients are available as toppings on thin-crust pizza. Pomegranate panna cotta and Amano chocolate pudding are among the dessert choices. **Bar:** beer & wine. **Reservations:** suggested. **Address:** 320 S State St, #185 84058 **Location:** I-15 exit 272 (800 N), 1.3 m e to State St, then 1.5 mi s (on west side). L D

OURAY (C-6) elev. 4,650'

Off SR 88 near Ouray is the Ouray National Wildlife Refuge. This largely undeveloped refuge along the Green River is home to large numbers of waterfowl as well as eagles, hawks, pheasants and deer. Visitors can walk or drive through the area, which is open daily; phone (435) 545-2522.

PANGUITCH (F-3) pop. 1,520, elev. 6,560'

The name Panguitch comes from the Paiute Indian word for "big fish," many of which were caught at nearby Panguitch Lake. This ranching community offers access to the colorful and remote "Inner Utah" of the Kaiparowits Plateau region. The city's historic district is peppered with shops and museums as well as historic homes, which feature red bricks fired in the community kiln years ago.

Garfield County Travel Council: 740 N. Main St., P.O. Box 200, Panguitch, UT 84759. **Phone:** (435) 676-1102 or (800) 444-6689. ***(See ad p. 333.)***

Self-guiding tours: A self-guiding, 45-minute walking tour of the area, featuring the Garfield County Courthouse, the Social Hall and the Panguitch Playhouse among other notable sights, is available from the travel council.

PANGUITCH-ESCALANTE-BOULDER SCENIC DRIVE begins off US 89 at SR 12 and traverses Bryce Canyon for 122 miles. SR 12 borders a large, unsurveyed wilderness area. The Kaiparowits Plateau's vividly colored canyons and rock formations contrast with the heavy forest of the Aquarius Plateau; Native American ruins and pictographs can be seen. Near Escalante are extensive deposits of colorful petrified wood. Hells Backbone, between Escalante and Boulder, offers spectacular views.

BLUE SPRINGS LODGE AT PANGUITCH LAKE

Phone: 435/676-2277

Cabin

$85-$205

Address: 120 W Hwy 143 84759 **Location:** Jct US 89, 18 mi sw on SR 143. **Facility:** 6 cabins. 1 story, exterior corridors. *Bath:* shower only. **Terms:** 2 night minimum stay - seasonal and/or weekends, 14 day cancellation notice-fee imposed. **Activities:** fishing, bicycles, hiking trails, playground, volleyball. *Fee:* canoes.

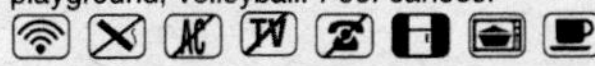

COLOR COUNTRY MOTEL **Phone:** (435)676-2386

Motel

$39-$84

Address: 526 N Main St 84759 **Location:** 0.3 mi n of center. **Facility:** 26 units, some two bedrooms. 1-2 stories (no elevator), exterior corridors. **Parking:** winter plug-ins. **Terms:** cancellation fee imposed. **Activities:** basketball, volleyball. **Free Special Amenities: continental breakfast and high-speed Internet.** SAVE / SOME UNITS FEE

HAROLD'S PLACE CABINS **Phone:** (435)676-2350

Cabin

$85-$95

Address: 3066 Hwy 12 84759 **Location:** Jct US 89 and SR 12, 0.5 mi e. **Facility:** 20 cabins. 1 story, exterior corridors. *Bath:* shower only. **Terms:** open 5/1-11/15. **Dining:** Harold's Place Restaurant, see separate listing.

HAROLD'S PLACE INN **Phone:** (435)676-2350

Motel

$75-$95

Address: 3090 Hwy 12 84759 **Location:** Jct US 89 and SR 12, 0.5 mi e. **Facility:** 32 units. 2 stories (no elevator), interior corridors. **Terms:** open 5/1-11/15. **Dining:** Harold's Place Restaurant, see separate listing.

/ SOME UNITS

HORIZON MOTEL **Phone:** 435/676-2651

Motel

Rates not provided

Address: 730 N Main St 84759 **Location:** 0.4 mi n of center. **Facility:** 16 units, some two bedrooms. 1 story, exterior corridors. **Terms:** seasonal. **Activities:** playground.

/ SOME UNITS FEE

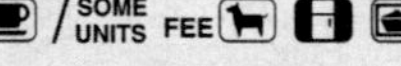

WHERE TO EAT

COWBOY'S SMOKEHOUSE CAFE' **Phone:** 435/676-8030

Barbecue

$6-$20

AAA Inspector Notes: A cowboy style, complete with Western artifacts and game trophies, characterizes the restaurant's dining room. On the menu are mesquite-barbecued beef brisket, pork ribs, chicken, turkey and steak. **Bar:** beer only. **Address:** 95 N Main St 84759 **Location:** Just n. B L D

FLYING M RESTAURANT **Phone:** 435/676-8008

American

$6-$17

AAA Inspector Notes: The restaurant offers a down-home American menu with specialties of homemade turkey potpie and buttermilk pancakes, in addition to made-from-scratch pastries, breads and sauces. **Bar:** beer & wine. **Address:** 614 N Main St 84759 **Location:** 0.5 mi n. B L D

FOY'S COUNTRY CORNER **Phone:** 435/676-8851

American

$5-$13

AAA Inspector Notes: In the center of town, the small restaurant has a diner feel and welcomes families. Among the basic items that make up the menu are burgers, chicken, ham steaks and fish and chips. **Address:** 80 N Main St 84759 **Location:** Just n. **Parking:** street only. B L D

HAROLD'S PLACE RESTAURANT **Phone:** 435/676-2350

American

$10-$15

AAA Inspector Notes: The rustic setting evokes a casual feel. After sampling an entrée from the varied menu, guests can enjoy great-great-grandma's strawberry shortcake. **Bar:** beer only. **Address:** 3066 Hwy 12 84759 **Location:** Jct US 89 and SR 12, 0.5 mi e; in Harold's Place Cabins. B D

PARK CITY (B-4) pop. 7,558, elev. 6,911'

• Hotels p. 390 • Restaurants p. 393
• Hotels & Restaurants map & index p. 388

When three off-duty soldiers discovered silver in the mountains above Park City in the 1870s, they started a rush that produced millions of dollars worth of the metal from mines in the surrounding area. Since the early 1960s, another natural resource has made Park City a popular destination for skiers: snow, and lots of it. In 2002 this small town became part of Olympic Winter Games history. Fourteen Olympic medal events, including bobsledding, luge and ski jumping, thrilled more than 300,000 spectators at Utah Olympic Park *(see attraction listing)*. Park City, or P.C. as it's known to locals, also is the home of the U.S. Ski and Snowboard Association.

Park City is a year-round recreational community as well as a resort town. Winter sports include cross-country and downhill skiing, snowboarding and snowshoeing. Horseback riding, mountain biking, golf and hiking are popular in snow-free months. The 28-mile Historic Union Pacific Rail Trail winds its way along I-80 through Coalville and Wanship and is open year-round for hikers, mountain bikers, joggers, skiers and equestrians; phone (435) 649-6839.

A variety of festivals to please many tastes are scattered throughout the year. The Sundance Institute premieres the works of independent filmmakers at the GEM Sundance Film Festival in late January.

▼ *See AAA listing p. 387* ▼

(See map & index p. 388.)

The Winterfest Celebration, usually held in February, features ice sculpture contests, fireworks, dog sled races and skiing competitions. Wine, culinary and ski festivals are combined in March's Red, White and Snow. From late March to early April The Canyons resort hosts Spring Gruv, a weeklong festival offering free rock, reggae and R&B concerts.

The Deer Valley Music Festival in July brings a blend of performances by the Utah Symphony and the Utah Opera. Celebrate the arts at the Park City Kimball Art Festival in August. The Miner's Day Parade and Celebration in September pays tribute to Park City's beginnings; mucking and drilling competitions showcase 19th-century mining techniques.

The year ends with a flurry of holiday festivals in December, including Santa on the Slopes; Christmas Eve at Park City Mountain Resort, featuring caroling, synchronized skiing, torchlight parades and sleigh rides; Deer Valley Celebrity Skifest; and a New Year's Celebration.

In a city where a car can be more of a hindrance than a help, a leisurely walk is a stress-free way to while away some time. Head down to Main Street, where a stroll past its shops of brightly painted 19th-century facades that harken to the Old West provides a pleasant interlude between or prelude to lunch or dinner.

Park City Chamber and Visitors Bureau: 1885 W. Ute Blvd., P.O. Box 1630, Park City, UT 84060. **Phone:** (435) 649-6100 or (800) 453-1360. ***(See ad p. 386.)***

Shopping areas: SAVE Tanger Factory Outlet Center, 6699 N. Landmark Dr., offers more than 60 outlet stores including Ann Taylor, Banana Republic, Gap and Tommy Hilfiger.

KIMBALL ART CENTER is at 638 Park Ave. The center features three galleries and displays the works of local, regional and national professional artists. Changing exhibits are presented every 6 to 8 weeks. **Time:** Allow 30 minutes minimum. **Hours:** Mon.-Fri. 10-5, Sat.-Sun. noon-5. **Cost:** Free. **Phone:** (435) 649-8882.

PARK CITY MUSEUM is at 518 Main St. Housed in the old city hall, the museum depicts the town's history, with displays chronicling the local silver boom, the town's days as a mining camp and Utah's skiing history. A territorial jail in the basement has been preserved; the dungeon once held several of the nation's early labor leaders.

Interactive exhibits and movies are offered, and groups with children may check out educational backpacks filled with hands-on activities. **Time:** Allow 1 hour minimum. **Hours:** Mon.-Sat. 10-7, Sun. noon-6. Closed Thanksgiving and Christmas. Phone ahead to confirm schedule. **Cost:** $10; $8 (ages 65+ and students and military with ID); $5 (ages 7-17). **Phone:** (435) 649-7457.

UTAH OLYMPIC PARK, 3419 Olympic Pkwy., served as the 2002 Olympic Winter Games venue for bobsled, skeleton, luge and Nordic ski jumping. National and international competitions are held at the 389-acre park, and athletes train here year-round. Self-guiding tours include Olympic competition sites, a ski museum and a museum devoted to the 2002 games. A guided bus tour also includes access to the ski jump and bobsled track. Depending on the season, visitors can see freestyle aerial shows and experience ziplines, an alpine slide and bobsled rides.

Time: Allow 1 hour minimum. **Hours:** Daily 9-6, July 1-Oct. 1; 10-6, rest of year. Guided tours are given daily on the hour 10-4. Closed Jan. 1, Easter, Thanksgiving and Christmas. **Cost:** Park and self-guiding tour free. Guided tour $7; $5 (ages 3-17 and 65+); $25 (family, maximum five people). Seasonal aerial shows, ziplines and bobsled rides are additional; phone for schedules, rates and reservations. **Phone:** (435) 658-4200 or (800) 659-7275.

2002 Eccles Winter Olympic Museum is at 3000 Bear Hollow Dr. in Utah Olympic Park. The museum showcases every officially licensed 2002 Olympic pin as well as the 2002 Winter Olympics equipment, uniforms and medals, many donated by the athletes. Videos and touch screens also are featured. **Time:** Allow 30 minutes minimum. **Hours:** Daily 10-6. Closed Jan. 1, Easter, Thanksgiving and Christmas. **Cost:** Free. **Phone:** (435) 658-4200 or (866) 659-7275.

Alf Engen Ski Museum is in Utah Olympic Park at the Joe Quinney Winter Sports Center. Utah's ski history is highlighted through interactive displays, videos, virtual reality theaters, games and topographical maps. The museum also features ski equipment from the past as well as trophies and awards. Pictures depicting the skiing prowess of Alf Engen, a Utah native and ski pioneer, are displayed. **Time:** Allow 1 hour minimum. **Hours:** Daily 10-6. Closed Jan. 1, Easter, Thanksgiving and Christmas. **Cost:** Free. **Phone:** (435) 658-4233.

RECREATIONAL ACTIVITIES

Alpine Slides

- **Alpine Slide** is at 1310 Lowell Ave. in the Park City Mountain Resort. **Hours:** Open daily, late May to mid-Oct. Hours vary; phone ahead. **Phone:** (435) 649-8111 or (800) 222-7275.

Skiing

- **The Canyons** is at 4000 The Canyons Resort Dr. Other activities are offered. **Hours:** Open daily, early Dec.-early Apr. Hours vary; phone ahead. **Phone:** (435) 649-5400, or (888) 226-9667 for reservations.
- **Deer Valley Resort** is at 2250 Deer Valley Dr. S. Other activities are offered. **Hours:** Open daily, early Dec.-early Apr. Hours vary; phone ahead. **Phone:** (435) 649-1000 or (800) 424-3337.
- **Park City Mountain Resort** is at 1345 Lowell Ave. Other activities are offered. **Hours:** Open daily, mid-Nov. to mid-Apr. Hours vary; phone ahead. **Phone:** (435) 649-8111 or (800) 222-7275.

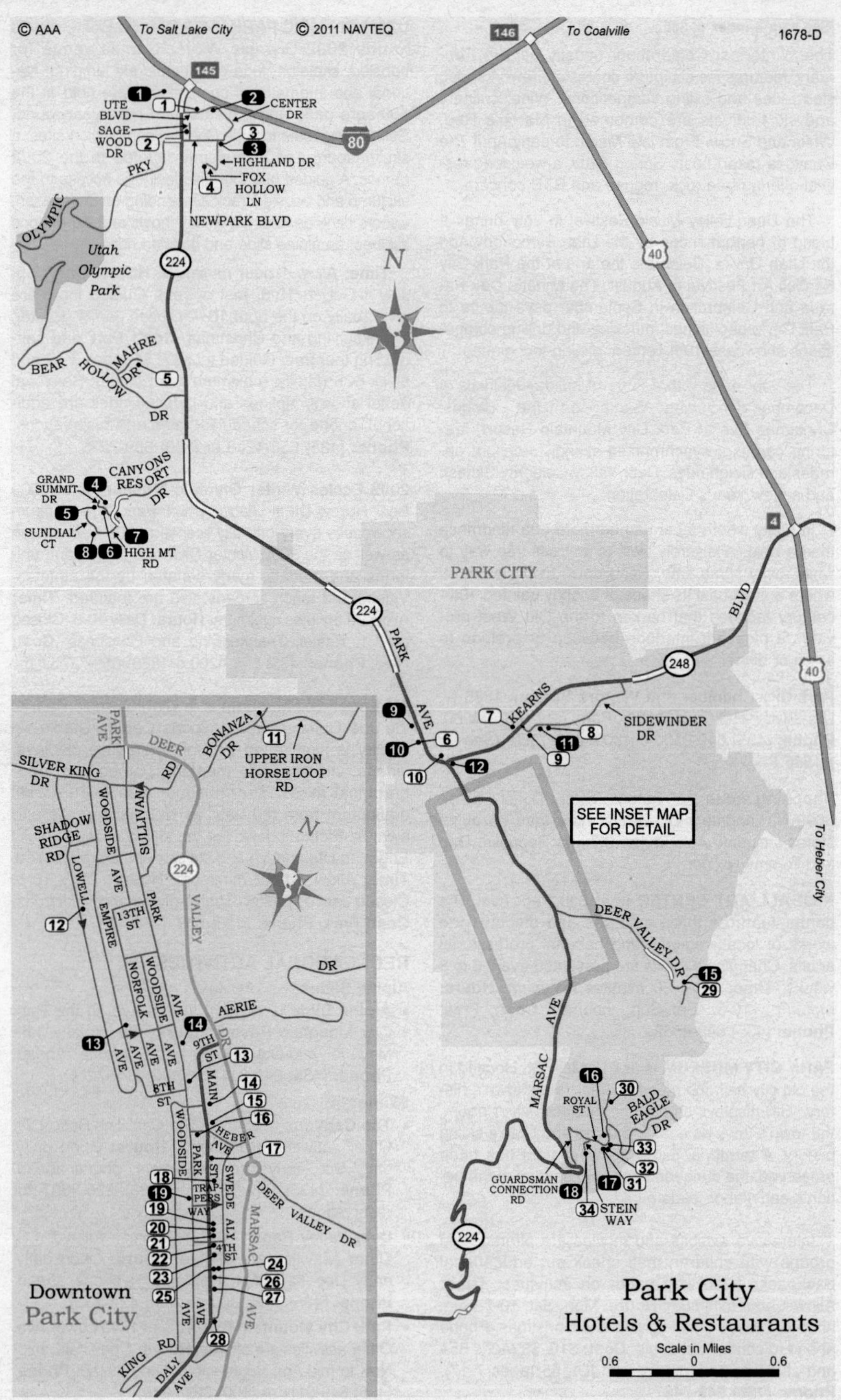
© AAA
To Salt Lake City
© 2011 NAVTEQ
To Coalville
1678-D
UTE BLVD
SAGE WOOD DR
CENTER DR
HIGHLAND DR
FOX HOLLOW LN
NEWPARK BLVD
PKY
OLYMPIC
Utah Olympic Park
BEAR HOLLOW DR
MAHRE DR
GRAND SUMMIT DR
CANYONS RESORT DR
SUNDIAL CT
HIGH MT RD
PARK CITY
PARK AVE
KEARNS BLVD
SIDEWINDER DR
SEE INSET MAP FOR DETAIL
To Heber City
DEER VALLEY DR
MARSAC AVE
ROYAL ST
BALD EAGLE DR
GUARDSMAN CONNECTION RD
STEIN WAY
Park City
Hotels & Restaurants
Scale in Miles
0.6 0 0.6
SILVER KING DR
DEER VALLEY DR
BONANZA DR
UPPER IRON HORSE LOOP RD
SHADOW RIDGE RD
LOWELL AVE
WOODSIDE AVE
SULLIVAN RD
EMPIRE AVE
13TH ST
NORFOLK AVE
AERIE DR
9TH ST
8TH ST
MAIN ST
HEBER AVE
SWEDE ALY
TRAPPERS WAY
4TH ST
KING RD
DALY AVE
Downtown
Park City

Park City

This index helps you "spot" where approved hotels and restaurants are located on the corresponding detailed maps. Hotel daily rate range is for comparison only and shows the property's high season. Restaurant rate range is a combination of lunch and/or dinner. Turn to the listing page for more detailed rate information and consult display ads for special promotions.

PARK CITY

Map Page	Hotels	Diamond Rated	High Season	Page
1 p. 388	**Best Western Plus Landmark Inn & Pancake House** *(See ad p. 391.)*	◆◆◆	$59-$299 SAVE	390
2 p. 388	Holiday Inn Express Hotel & Suites	◆◆	$169-$199	391
3 p. 388	Newpark Hotel	◆◆◆	Rates not provided	391
4 p. 388	**Grand Summit Resort Hotel**	◆◆◆◆	$159-$3629 SAVE	390
5 p. 388	Sundial Lodge at The Canyons	◆◆◆	$125-$1715	393
6 p. 388	**Westgate Park City Resort & Spa**	◆◆◆	$99-$1369 SAVE	393
7 p. 388	Silverado Lodge at The Canyons	◆◆◆	$99-$1599	393
8 p. 388	**Hyatt Escala Lodge at Park City**	◆◆◆◆	$99-$549 SAVE	391
9 p. 388	Park City Peaks Hotel	◆◆◆	Rates not provided	392
10 p. 388	**Hotel Park City**	◆◆◆◆	Rates not provided SAVE	391
11 p. 388	**Park City Marriott**	◆◆◆	$104-$484 SAVE	392
12 p. 388	Yarrow Hotel & Conference Center	◆◆	$99-$589	393
13 p. 388	Old Town Guest House	◆◆	Rates not provided	392
14 p. 388	Park Station Condos	◆◆	Rates not provided	392
15 p. 388	**St. Regis Deer Valley Resort**	◆◆◆◆	$649-$3449 SAVE	392
16 p. 388	**The Chateaux at Silver Lake**	◆◆◆	$259-$669 SAVE	390
17 p. 388	**Goldener Hirsch Inn**	◆◆◆◆	$299-$1399 SAVE	390
18 p. 388	**Stein Eriksen Lodge** *(See ad p. 392.)*	◆◆◆◆◆	$235-$850 SAVE	393
19 p. 388	Washington School House	fyi	Rates not provided	393

Map Page	Restaurants	Diamond Rated	Cuisine	Meal Range	Page
1 p. 388	Loco Lizard Cantina	◆◆	Mexican	$8-$18	395
2 p. 388	Good Thymes Bistro	◆◆	American	$9-$24	395
3 p. 388	Maxwell's East Coast Eatery	◆◆	Italian	$9-$21	395
4 p. 388	Ghidotti's Classic Italian Restaurant	◆◆◆	Italian	$17-$37	394
5 p. 388	The Viking Dinner Yurt	◆◆◆	Norwegian	$157-$219	396
6 p. 388	Ruth's Chris Steak House	◆◆◆	Steak	$35-$70	396
7 p. 388	Adolph's Restaurant	◆◆◆	Swiss	$23-$39	393
8 p. 388	Fuego Bistro & Pizzeria	◆◆	Italian	$8-$20	394
9 p. 388	Blind Dog Restaurant	◆◆◆	American	$16-$32	394
10 p. 388	Squatters Roadhouse Grill & Pub	◆◆	American	$8-$19	396
11 p. 388	Windy Ridge Cafe & Bakery	◆◆	American	$9-$24	396
12 p. 388	Baja Cantina	◆◆	Mexican	$7-$15	394
13 p. 388	Flying Sumo Sushi Bar & Grill	◆◆	Sushi	$15-$22	394
14 p. 388	Reef's Kitchen	◆◆	Middle Eastern	$11-$29	395
15 p. 388	Zoom Roadhouse Grill	◆◆	American	$11-$38	396

Map Page	Restaurants (cont'd)	Diamond Rated	Cuisine	Meal Range	Page
16 p. 388	Jean Louis Restaurant & Bar	◆◆◆	French	$19-$36	395
17 p. 388	Wahso, An Asian Grill	◆◆◆	Asian	$27-$37	396
18 p. 388	**Riverhorse on Main**	◆◆◆◆	American	$29-$50	396
19 p. 388	Shabu	◆◆◆	Asian	$26-$45	396
20 p. 388	Cafe Terigo	◆◆◆	American	$10-$30	394
21 p. 388	Bistro 412	◆◆◆	French	$12-$38	394
22 p. 388	Chimayo	◆◆◆	Southwestern	$32-$46	394
23 p. 388	350 Main New American Brasserie	◆◆◆	International	$22-$39	393
24 p. 388	Red Banjo Pizza Parlor	◆	Italian	$6-$12	395
25 p. 388	The Eating Establishment	◆◆	American	$9-$25	394
26 p. 388	Cisero's Ristorante & Nightclub	◆◆	Italian	$11-$28	394
27 p. 388	Wasatch Brew Pub	◆◆	American	$9-$24	396
28 p. 388	Grappa Italian Restaurant	◆◆◆◆	Northern Italian	$24-$36	395
29 p. 388	J & G Grill at St. Regis Deer Valley	◆◆◆◆	American	$12-$44	395
30 p. 388	High West Distillery & Saloon	◆◆◆	American	$9-$35	395
31 p. 388	**Goldener Hirsch Restaurant**	◆◆◆◆	Continental	$10-$38	395
32 p. 388	Royal Street Cafe	◆◆	American	$10-$32	396
33 p. 388	Mariposa	◆◆◆◆	Continental	$38-$48	395
34 p. 388	**The Glitretind at Stein Eriksen Lodge** *(See ad p. 392.)*	◆◆◆◆	Continental	$12-$38	394

BEST WESTERN PLUS LANDMARK INN & PANCAKE HOUSE **Phone:** (435)649-7300 1

Hotel
$59-$299

AAA Benefit: Members save up to 20%, plus 10% bonus points with Best Western Rewards®.

Address: 6560 N Landmark Dr 84098 **Location:** I-80 exit 145 (Kimball Jct), 0.3 mi s, then 0.3 mi nw. **Facility:** 106 units, some two bedrooms and kitchens. 3 stories, interior corridors. **Amenities:** high-speed Internet, safes (fee). **Pool(s):** heated indoor. **Activities:** whirlpool, basketball, horseshoes, volleyball, exercise room. *Fee:* game room. **Guest Services:** valet and coin laundry. **Free Special Amenities: full breakfast and high-speed Internet.** *(See ad p. 391.)*

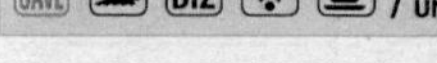
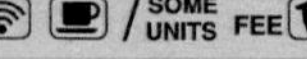
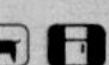

THE CHATEAUX AT SILVER LAKE **Phone:** (435)658-9500 16

Hotel
$259-$669 12/1-4/30
$109-$189 5/1-11/30

Address: 7815 Royal St E 84060 **Location:** I-80 exit 145 (Kimball Jct), 6 mi se to Deer Valley Dr, 1 mi e via SR 224 to roundabout, take Marsac Ave exit, 2 mi s to Guardsman Connection, then 0.3 mi n, follow signs. **Facility:** 150 units, some two bedrooms, three bedrooms and kitchens. 4 stories, interior corridors. **Terms:** 2-4 night minimum stay - seasonal and/or weekends, 7 day cancellation notice-fee imposed. **Amenities:** high-speed Internet. **Pool(s):** heated outdoor. **Activities:** whirlpools, rental bicycles, hiking trails, jogging, exercise room. *Fee:* downhill skiing, massage. **Guest Services:** complimentary and valet laundry, area transportation-within 5 mi. **Free Special Amenities: high-speed Internet and local transportation.**

GOLDENER HIRSCH INN **Phone:** 435/649-7770 17

Boutique Hotel
$299-$1399 12/1-4/14
$155-$300 6/29-9/23

Address: 7570 Royal St E 84060 **Location:** I-80 exit 145 (Kimball Jct), se on Deer Valley Rd to roundabout, take 2nd exit (Marsac Ave), then 2.5 mi to Silver Lake Village sign, follow signs. Located in Deer Valley. **Facility:** Nestled high in the village, the inn offers an idyllic blend of quality, refinement and comfort, including in-room fireplaces. 20 units. 4 stories, interior corridors. **Terms:** open 6/29-9/23 & 12/1-4/14, check-in 4 pm, 4 night minimum stay - seasonal and/or weekends, 60 day cancellation notice, 14 day 6/1-10/31-fee imposed. **Amenities:** high-speed Internet, safes, honor bars. **Dining:** restaurant, see separate listing. **Activities:** sauna, whirlpools, hiking trails, jogging, limited exercise equipment. *Fee:* fishing, downhill skiing, bicycles, massage. **Guest Services:** valet laundry, area transportation-downtown. **Free Special Amenities: expanded continental breakfast and high-speed Internet.**

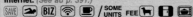

GRAND SUMMIT RESORT HOTEL **Phone:** (435)615-8040 4

Resort Hotel
$159-$3629 11/23-4/30
$99-$916 5/1-11/22

Address: 4000 Canyons Resort Dr 84098 **Location:** I-80 exit 145 (Kimball Jct), 3 mi sw via SR 224, then 0.7 mi w; at The Canyons. **Facility:** The resort offers a combination of a ski-in/ski-out location, beautiful design, attentive service, luxury guest quarters and panoramic views. 350 units, some two bedrooms, three bedrooms and kitchens. 7 stories, interior corridors. **Parking:** on-site (fee) and valet. **Terms:** check-in 5 pm, 2-7 night minimum stay - seasonal and/or weekends, 45 day cancellation notice-fee imposed. **Amenities:** high-speed Internet, safes. **Dining:** 2 restaurants. **Pool(s):** heated outdoor. **Activities:** sauna, whirlpools, steamroom, rental bicycles, hiking trails, jogging, exercise room, spa. *Fee:* fishing, downhill & cross country skiing. **Guest Services:** valet and coin laundry, area transportation-within 5 mi.

(See map & index p. 388.)

HOLIDAY INN EXPRESS HOTEL & SUITES

Phone: (435)658-1600 2

Hotel

$169-$199 12/18-4/30
$89-$129 5/1-12/17

Address: 1501 W Ute Blvd 84098 **Location:** I-80 exit 145 (Kimball Jct), just s, then 0.3 mi e. **Facility:** 76 units. 3 stories, interior corridors. **Amenities:** *Some:* high-speed Internet, safes. **Pool(s):** heated indoor. **Activities:** sauna, whirlpool, exercise room. **Guest Services:** coin laundry.

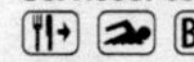 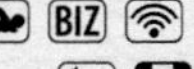 FEE 

/ SOME UNITS FEE

HOTEL PARK CITY **Phone:** 435/200-2000 10

Resort Hotel

Rates not provided

Address: 2001 Park Ave 84068 **Location:** I-80 exit 145 (Kimball Jct), 5.6 mi s to corner of Thaynes Canyon Dr and Park Ave. **Facility:** This ski, golf and spa retreat is close to three ski resorts. All units are well-appointed and have a fireplace. Guests can expect great service. 100 units, some two bedrooms, efficiencies, kitchens and cottages. 1-3 stories, interior corridors. **Terms:** check-in 4 pm. **Amenities:** high-speed Internet, safes. **Dining:** Ruth's Chris Steak House, see separate listing. **Pool(s):** heated outdoor. **Activities:** saunas, whirlpools, exercise room, spa. *Fee:* golf-18 holes, downhill & cross country skiing. **Guest Services:** complimentary and valet laundry.

CALL

Learn about AAA/CAA Diamond Ratings at AAA.com/Diamonds

HYATT ESCALA LODGE AT PARK CITY

Phone: (435)940-1234 8

Hotel

$99-$549

AAA Benefit: Members save 10% or more everyday.

Address: 3551 N Escala Ct 84098 **Location:** I-80 exit 145 (Kimball Jct), 3 mi sw via SR 224, then 0.8 mi w; at The Canyons. **Facility:** The mountainside ski-in/ski-out lodge's residential accommodations are filled with Old World charm and luxury amenities. 153 units, some two bedrooms, three bedrooms and kitchens. 6 stories, interior corridors. **Parking:** on-site and valet. **Terms:** check-in 4 pm, 7 day cancellation notice-fee imposed. **Amenities:** safes. **Pool(s):** heated outdoor. **Activities:** saunas, whirlpools, steamrooms, rental bicycles, hiking trails, jogging, exercise room. *Fee:* downhill & cross country skiing. **Guest Services:** complimentary and valet laundry, area transportation-within 5 mi. **Free Special Amenities: local telephone calls and early check-in/late check-out.**

 FEE 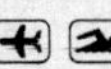    

NEWPARK HOTEL **Phone:** 435/649-3600 3

Hotel

Rates not provided

Address: 1456 Newpark Blvd 84098 **Location:** I-80 exit 145 (Kimball Jct), 0.3 mi s to Newpark Blvd, then just e. **Facility:** 160 two-bedroom units, some kitchens and condominiums. 4 stories, interior corridors. **Terms:** check-in 4 pm. **Amenities:** high-speed Internet, safes. **Dining:** Maxwell's East Coast Eatery, see separate listing. **Pool(s):** heated indoor/outdoor. **Activities:** sauna, whirlpool, steamroom, hiking trails, jogging, exercise room. *Fee:* cross country skiing. **Guest Services:** complimentary and valet laundry.

FEE

/ SOME UNITS

▼ See AAA listing p. 390 ▼

(See map & index p. 388.)

OLD TOWN GUEST HOUSE

Phone: 435/649-2642 13

Bed & Breakfast

Rates not provided

Address: 1011 Empire Ave 84060 **Location:** I-80 exit 145 (Kimball Jct), 6 mi s, then 0.7 mi w. Located in a residential area. **Facility:** 4 units, some two bedrooms. 2 stories (no elevator), interior corridors. *Bath:* some shared. **Parking:** street only. **Terms:** office hours 9 am-9 pm. **Amenities:** high-speed Internet, safes. **Activities:** whirlpool. **Guest Services:** complimentary laundry. BIZ

PARK CITY MARRIOTT Phone: (435)649-2900 11

Hotel

$104-$484

Marriott HOTELS & RESORTS **AAA Benefit:** AAA hotel discounts of 5% or more.

Address: 1895 Sidewinder Dr 84060 **Location:** I-80 exit 145 (Kimball Jct), 6 mi s to Kearns Blvd, then 0.6 mi ne to Sidewinder Dr; in Prospector Square. **Facility:** 199 units. 4 stories, interior corridors. **Amenities:** high-speed Internet (fee), safes. **Pool(s):** heated indoor. **Activities:** whirlpool, steamroom, exercise room. *Fee:* downhill & cross country skiing. **Guest Services:** valet and coin laundry, area transportation-ski shuttle.

SAVE BIZ FEE

PARK CITY PEAKS HOTEL

Phone: 435/649-5000 9

Hotel

Rates not provided

Address: 2121 Park Ave 84060 **Location:** I-80 exit 145 (Kimball Jct), 5.5 mi s; corner of SR 224 (Park Ave) and Saddle View Way. **Facility:** 131 units. 3 stories, interior corridors. **Amenities:** safes. **Pool(s):** heated indoor/outdoor. **Activities:** sauna, whirlpools. **Guest Services:** valet and coin laundry.

BIZ / SOME UNITS FEE

PARK STATION CONDOS Phone: 435/649-7717 14

Condominium

Rates not provided

Address: 950 Park Ave 84060 **Location:** I-80 exit 145 (Kimball Jct), 6.3 mi s on SR 224 (Park Ave). **Facility:** 40 condominiums. 3 stories, interior corridors. **Terms:** office hours 8 am-9 pm, check-in 4 pm. **Pool(s):** heated outdoor. **Activities:** sauna, whirlpools. **Guest Services:** coin laundry.

/ SOME UNITS

ST. REGIS DEER VALLEY RESORT

Phone: (435)940-5700 15

Resort Hotel

$649-$3449 12/7-4/30

$199-$1559 5/1-12/6

ST. REGIS HOTELS & RESORTS **AAA Benefit:** Legendary stays at a preferred rate.

Address: 2300 Deer Valley Dr E 84060 **Location:** I-80 exit 145 (Kimball Jct), 6 mi se to Deer Valley Dr/SR 224, 1 mi e to roundabout, exit Deer Valley Dr, then 1.2 mi se; I-40 exit 4, 2.7 mi sw on SR 248/Kearns Blvd to Bonanza Dr, 0.5 mi to Deer Valley Dr/SR 224, then 1 mi se to roundabout. **Facility:** Featuring luxurious guest rooms, this ski-in, ski-out resort offers upscale services and amenities, including three outdoor fire pits and a ski beach. 170 units, some two bedrooms, three bedrooms and kitchens. 11 stories, interior corridors. **Parking:** valet only. **Terms:** check-in 4 pm, 2-8 night minimum stay - seasonal, cancellation fee imposed. **Amenities:** high-speed Internet (fee), safes, honor bars. **Dining:** J & G Grill at St. Regis Deer Valley, see separate listing. **Pool(s):** heated outdoor. **Activities:** whirlpools, bicycles, hiking trails, game room, exercise room, spa. *Fee:* downhill skiing. **Guest Services:** valet laundry, area transportation-within 6 mi. **Free Special Amenities: newspaper and local transportation.**

SAVE FEE BIZ

/ SOME UNITS FEE

▼ See AAA listing p. 393 ▼

(See map & index p. 388.)

SILVERADO LODGE AT THE CANYONS

Phone: (435)655-7400 7

Hotel

$99-$1599

Address: 2669 Canyons Resort Dr 84098 **Location:** I-80 exit 145 (Kimball Jct), 3 mi s, then 0.5 mi w. **Facility:** 180 units, some two bedrooms, three bedrooms and kitchens. 5 stories, interior corridors. **Terms:** check-in 5 pm, 7 day cancellation notice-fee imposed. **Pool(s):** heated outdoor. **Activities:** sauna, whirlpool, steamroom, exercise room. *Fee:* downhill skiing, snowmobiling. **Guest Services:** valet laundry, area transportation-downtown.

FEE / SOME UNITS

STEIN ERIKSEN LODGE

Phone: (435)649-3700 18

Resort Hotel

$235-$850

Address: 7700 Stein Way 84060 **Location:** I-80 exit 145 (Kimball Jct), 6 mi se to Deer Valley Dr, 1 mi e via SR 224 to roundabout, take Marsac Ave exit, 2 mi s to Guardsman Connection, then 0.3 mi n, follow signs. Located in Deer Valley. **Facility:** A picturesque, secluded setting is the premier feature of this mountain lodge, which offers exceptional service and elegant, well-appointed rooms. 180 units, some two bedrooms, three bedrooms and kitchens. 3 stories (no elevator), interior/exterior corridors. **Parking:** valet only. **Terms:** check-in 4 pm, 4 night minimum stay - seasonal, 7 day cancellation notice-fee imposed. **Amenities:** high-speed Internet, safes. **Dining:** 2 restaurants, also, The Glitretind at Stein Eriksen Lodge, see separate listing. **Pool(s):** heated outdoor. **Activities:** saunas, whirlpools, recreation programs in winter, rental bicycles, hiking trails, jogging, game room, exercise room, spa. *Fee:* downhill skiing. **Guest Services:** complimentary and valet laundry, area transportation-within 5 mi. **Free Special Amenities: local telephone calls and newspaper.** Affiliated with A Preferred Hotel.

(See ad p. 392.)

SUNDIAL LODGE AT THE CANYONS

Phone: (435)615-8070 5

Hotel

$125-$1715 11/23-4/30
$99-$406 5/1-11/22

Address: 3720 Sundial Ct 84098 **Location:** I-80 exit 145 (Kimball Jct), 3 mi s via SR 224, then 0.5 mi w. **Facility:** 163 units, some two bedrooms, efficiencies and kitchens. 6 stories, interior corridors. **Terms:** check-in 5 pm, 45 day cancellation notice, 7 day off season-fee imposed. **Amenities:** high-speed Internet. **Pool(s):** heated outdoor. **Activities:** whirlpools, rental bicycles, hiking trails, jogging, exercise room. *Fee:* fishing, downhill skiing, snowmobiling, game room. **Guest Services:** complimentary and valet laundry, area transportation-within 5 mi.

FEE BIZ

WASHINGTON SCHOOL HOUSE

Phone: 435/649-3800 19

fyi

Historic Country Inn

Rates not provided

Under major renovation, scheduled to be completed December 2011. **Last Rated:** **Address:** 543 Park Ave 84060 **Location:** I-80 exit 145 (Kimball Jct), 5.8 mi se to Kearns Blvd and SR 224 (Park Ave), then 1.2 mi s. **Facility:** A renovated stone schoolhouse dating to the turn of the 19th century, the charming inn has modern baths and elegant rooms; the suites have fireplaces. 12 units. 3 stories (no elevator), interior corridors. **Terms:** office hours 7 am-7 pm, age restrictions may apply. **Pool(s):** heated outdoor. **Activities:** sauna, whirlpool. *Fee:* massage. **Guest Services:** valet laundry.

/ SOME UNITS

WESTGATE PARK CITY RESORT & SPA

Phone: (435)655-2240 6

Hotel

$99-$1369

Address: 3000 Canyons Resort Dr 84098 **Location:** I-80 exit 145 (Kimball Jct), 3 mi s, then 0.5 mi w up Canyons Resort Dr. **Facility:** 351 units, some two bedrooms, three bedrooms, efficiencies and kitchens. 5-9 stories, interior corridors. **Terms:** check-in 4 pm, 3 day cancellation notice-fee imposed. **Amenities:** high-speed Internet, safes. **Pool(s):** heated outdoor, heated indoor, heated indoor/outdoor. **Activities:** saunas, whirlpools, steamrooms, tennis court, hiking trails, playground, basketball, exercise room, spa. *Fee:* downhill skiing, bicycles, game room. **Guest Services:** complimentary and valet laundry, area transportation-within 5 mi.

SAVE FEE BIZ

YARROW HOTEL & CONFERENCE CENTER

Phone: (435)649-7000 12

Hotel

$99-$589 11/16-4/30
$79-$589 5/1-11/15

Address: 1800 Park Ave 84060 **Location:** I-80 exit 145 (Kimball Jct), 6 mi s; corner of SR 224 (Park Ave) and Kearns Blvd. **Facility:** 181 units, some efficiencies. 2 stories, interior corridors. **Terms:** check-in 4 pm, 3 day cancellation notice-fee imposed. **Amenities:** high-speed Internet, safes. **Pool(s):** heated outdoor. **Activities:** whirlpool, exercise room. **Guest Services:** valet and coin laundry.

BIZ / SOME UNITS

MONTAGE DEER VALLEY **Phone:** 435/604-1300

fyi Not evaluated. **Address:** 9100 Marsac Ave 84060 **Location:** I-80 exit 145 (Kimball Jct), 6 mi se to Deer Valley Dr, 1 mi e via SR 224 to roundabout, take Marsac Ave exit, 2 mi s to Guardsman Connection, then 2 mi sw on SR 224. Facilities, services, and decor characterize an upscale property.

WALDORF ASTORIA PARK CITY **Phone:** 435/647-5500

fyi

AAA Benefit: Unparalleled hospitality at a special Member rate.

Not evaluated. **Address:** 2100 W Frostwood Blvd 84098 **Location:** I-80 exit 145 (Kimball Jct), 3 mi sw via SR 224, then 0.3 mi w; at The Canyons. Facilities, services, and decor characterize an upscale property.

WHERE TO EAT

350 MAIN NEW AMERICAN BRASSERIE

Phone: 435/649-3140 23

International

$22-$39

AAA Inspector Notes: An innovative menu features naturally or organically grown ingredients whenever possible. Diners sit under a copper and tin stamped roof to enjoy flavorful dishes, the likes of which might be the tower of ahi and hamachi appetizer and such entrées as black pepper-crusted venison medallions, wasabi-seared Pacific ono, black sesame sea scallops and grilled Rocky Mountain red trout. The lemon-mint angel food cake is a must. **Bar:** full bar. **Reservations:** suggested. **Address:** 350 Main St 84060 **Location:** Center of historic Main St. D

ADOLPH'S RESTAURANT **Phone:** 435/649-7177 7

Swiss

$23-$39

AAA Inspector Notes: The menu lines up specialties such as escargot, ahi tuna sashimi, table-side-served Chateaubriand for two, salmon, fondue for two and the chef's nightly specials. Eye-catching made-in-house desserts are beautifully presented. **Bar:** full bar. **Reservations:** suggested. **Address:** 1500 Kearns Blvd 84060 **Location:** I-80 exit 145 (Kimball Jct), 6 mi se to Kearns Blvd, then 0.5 mi e. **Parking:** on-site and valet.

D

(See map & index p. 388.)

BAJA CANTINA **Phone:** 435/649-2252 (12)

Mexican
$7-$15

AAA Inspector Notes: Colorful décor contributes to the restaurant's lively atmosphere. Seafood specialties stand out on a menu of nicely varied dishes. Patio seating can be requested in summer. **Bar:** full bar. **Address:** 1284 Lowell Ave 84060 **Location:** I-80 exit 145 (Kimball Jct), 5.5 mi s on SR 224 (Park Ave) to Empire Ave, 0.3 mi w to Shadow Ridge Rd, just w to Lowell Rd, then just s; upstairs at the base of ski lift. [L] [D] [AC]

BISTRO 412 **Phone:** 435/649-8211 (21)

French
$12-$38

AAA Inspector Notes: Efficient servers bring dishes prepared with fresh ingredients and rich sauces at this American-style sidewalk bistro. Specialties include fresh Idaho red trout and French dishes such as braised lamb shank. The oversize crème brûlée is a great ending. **Bar:** full bar. **Address:** 412 Main St 84060 **Location:** Center of historic Main St. **Parking:** street only. [L] [D]

BLIND DOG RESTAURANT
Phone: 435/655-0800 (9)

American
$16-$32

AAA Inspector Notes: Named for the owner's beloved pet, the restaurant displays accolades to canines throughout its décor. Signature dishes such as the hearty "dreamloaf" with creamed spinach, the lobster bisque and delicate crab cakes are served by polished waitstaff. **Bar:** full bar. **Reservations:** suggested. **Address:** 1251 Kearns Blvd 84060 **Location:** I-80 exit 145 (Kimball Jct), 6 mi s to Kearns Blvd, then 0.3 mi e; at The Yard. [D]

CAFE TERIGO **Phone:** 435/645-9555 (20)

American
$10-$30

AAA Inspector Notes: Whimsical sayings etched on the walls lend to the light, fresh décor of this casual eatery, which has a large patio. Innovative combinations such as roasted pork tenderloin with grilled polenta and seafood choices along the lines of trout and diver scallops are expertly prepared. This place is known for its bread pudding. **Bar:** full bar. **Address:** 424 Main St 84060 **Location:** I-80 exit 145 (Kimball Jct), center of historic Main St. **Parking:** street only. [L] [D]

CHIMAYO **Phone:** 435/649-6222 (22)

Southwestern
$32-$46

AAA Inspector Notes: This restaurant serves distinctive gourmet Southwestern fare in surroundings of terra cotta and blue and white tiles, suggestive of a hacienda. **Bar:** full bar. **Reservations:** suggested. **Address:** 368 Main St 84060 **Location:** Upper historic Main St. **Parking:** street only. [D]

CISERO'S RISTORANTE & NIGHTCLUB
Phone: 435/649-5044 (26)

Italian
$11-$28

AAA Inspector Notes: Open for dinner, this street-level spot puts forth a menu of cioppino, steak, chicken, veal and pasta. The lounge dining area, which serves lighter fare, has live entertainment and is popular for dancing. **Bar:** full bar. **Address:** 306 Main St 84060 **Location:** On upper historic Main St. **Parking:** street only. [D]

THE EATING ESTABLISHMENT
Phone: 435/649-8284 (25)

American
$9-$25

AAA Inspector Notes: Known by locals as the "Double E," this cozy eatery has nourished many skiers since 1972 and offers traditional American fare with a Western flair. Menu items include daily hearty soups, burgers, sandwiches, steaks and slowly smoked barbecue beef, pork and chicken. The two cozy dining rooms have plenty of sunlight and warm fires, while an outside patio is available seasonally. **Bar:** full bar. **Address:** 317 Main St 84060 **Location:** I-80 exit 145 (Kimball Jct), On upper historic Main St. **Parking:** street only. [B] [L] [D]

FLYING SUMO SUSHI BAR & GRILL
Phone: 435/649-5522 (13)

Sushi
$15-$22

AAA Inspector Notes: Tucked under a ski lift, this tiny restaurant with a large sumo heart serves great sushi along with delicate wok-seared fish, chicken and steak. **Bar:** beer & wine. **Address:** 838 Park Ave 84060 **Location:** I-80 exit 145 (Kimball Jct), 7 mi se on SR 224 (Park Ave). **Parking:** street only. [D]

FUEGO BISTRO & PIZZERIA
Phone: 435/645-8646 (8)

Italian
$8-$20

AAA Inspector Notes: This brightly colored eatery features more than 13 types of gourmet pizza; Italian grilled sandwiches; traditional entrées such as handmade baked lasagna, shrimp and clam linguine; and large house-made meatballs. The daily lunch special is very affordable. **Bar:** full bar. **Address:** 2001 Sidewinder Dr 84068 **Location:** I-80 exit 145 (Kimball Jct), 6 mi se, 0.7 mi ne on Kearns Blvd, then just e. [L] [D]

GHIDOTTI'S CLASSIC ITALIAN RESTAURANT
Phone: 435/658-0669 (4)

Italian
$17-$37

AAA Inspector Notes: Large fires burn at the entrance to this elegant restaurant where the New World ambience features large linen-covered round tables that are meant to be shared family-style. With menus that change with the seasons, classics include minestrone soup with house-made Italian sausage, clams casino, veal Marsala and cannoli with toasted pistachios and amarena cherries. **Bar:** full bar. **Reservations:** suggested. **Address:** 6030 N Market St, Suite 100 84098 **Location:** I-80 exit 145 (Kimball Jct), just s; in Redstone Village. [D]

THE GLITRETIND AT STEIN ERIKSEN LODGE
Phone: 435/649-3700 (34)

Continental
$12-$38

AAA Inspector Notes: Contemporary gourmet cuisine prepared with a European flair by chef Zane Holmquist is served in a warm and elegant setting. The Sunday jazz brunch is lavish. **Bar:** full bar. **Reservations:** suggested. **Address:** 7700 Stein Way 84060 **Location:** 6 mi se via SR 224 to Deer Valley Rd, 1 mi e to roundabout exit Marsac Ave, 2.5 mi s to Guardsman Connection, 0.3 mi n, follow signs; in Stein Eriksen Lodge. **Parking:** valet only. *(See ad p. 392.)* [B] [L] [D]

(See map & index p. 388.)

GOLDENER HIRSCH RESTAURANT
Phone: 435/649-7770 (31)

Continental
$10-$38

AAA Inspector Notes: Chef Michael Showers' seasonal menu of Austrian classics includes a signature fondue of Swiss and French cheeses, house-cured meats and charcuterie served with pickles and cherry mustard, wiener schnitzel with crispy capers, Rocky Mountain elk flank and Wagyu bavette with chimichurri. Decadent desserts include Bavarian apple strudel, Amano milk chocolate fondue, and beignets and blueberry preserve served with a candied citrus mascarpone. Skiers will feast on the elaborate apres ski. **Bar:** full bar. **Reservations:** suggested. **Address:** 7570 Royal St E 84060 **Location:** I-80 exit 145 (Kimball Jct), 6 mi se to Deer Valley Rd, 1 mi e on SR 224 exit Marsac Ave at roundabout, 2 mi s, then 0.3 mi n at Guardsman Connection, follow signs; in Goldener Hirsch Inn. [D] [AC]

GOOD THYMES BISTRO **Phone:** 435/615-7090 (2)

American
$9-$24

AAA Inspector Notes: Good food, good friends and good service are what patrons can expect here. Among the choices are house chop salad with crispy fried corn, Mom's meatloaf, chicken potpie and s'mores. **Bar:** full bar. **Address:** 1456 N New Park Blvd, Suite 15 84098 **Location:** I-80 exit 145 (Kimball Jct), 0.3 mi s to New Park Blvd, then 0.3 mi e. **Parking:** on-site and street.
[B] [L] [D]

GRAPPA ITALIAN RESTAURANT
Phone: 435/645-0636 (28)

Northern Italian
$24-$36

AAA Inspector Notes: The romantic restaurant serves favorites such as osso buco and risotto-stuffed chicken involtini in its dining room, on a seasonal patio and on a private balcony in a lovely garden setting. **Bar:** full bar. **Address:** 151 Main St 84060 **Location:** At the top of historic Main St. **Parking:** street only. [D]

HIGH WEST DISTILLERY & SALOON
Phone: 435/649-8300 (30)

American
$9-$35

AAA Inspector Notes: Menu items feature a sauce, herb or grain directly related to products of High West distilled spirits. Vegetarian items are available. Children are welcome and have their own menu. **Bar:** full bar. **Address:** 703 Park Ave 84060 **Location:** I-80 exit 146 (US 40), 6.5 mi s. **Parking:** street only. [L] [D]

J & G GRILL AT ST. REGIS DEER VALLEY
Phone: 435/940-5760 (29)

American
$12-$44

AAA Inspector Notes: Diners ride up the mountain in an upscale funicular to this slopeside restaurant with amazing views. With Jean-Georges Vongerichten at the helm, the kitchen prepares seasonal creations such as charred corn ravioli in basil fondue, lime juice-and-basil-roasted Maine lobster and melt-in-your-mouth glazed short ribs. Decadent desserts may include macerated strawberries with poppy sorbet and meringue, and crème fraîche cheesecake with roasted plum and lavender. The wine vault has to be seen. **Bar:** full bar. **Address:** 2300 Deer Valley Dr E 84060 **Location:** I-80 exit 145 (Kimball Jct), 6 mi se to Deer Valley Dr/SR 224, 1 mi e to roundabout, exit Deer Valley Dr, then 1.2 mi se; I-40 exit 4, 2.7 mi sw on SR 248/Kearns Blvd to Bonanza Dr, 0.5 mi to Deer Valley Dr/SR 224, then 1 mi se to roundabout; in St. Regis Deer Valley Resort. **Parking:** valet only. [B] [L] [D]

JEAN LOUIS RESTAURANT & BAR
Phone: 435/200-0260 (16)

French
$19-$36

AAA Inspector Notes: The seasonal menu features attractively presented classic French dishes, including Burgundy snails with lemony herb butter, Mediterranean fish soup served with crouton and olive oil aioli, a classic Caesar salad, pepper-encrusted filet mignon, white bean stew with duck, sausage and bacon, and pan-roasted halibut served with Asian noodles and julienne of vegetables in a white wine broth. Some patrons drop in just for an after-dinner drink and the signature chocolate or Grand Marnier soufflé. **Bar:** full bar. **Address:** 136 Heber Ave, #107 84060 **Location:** I-80 exit 145 (Kimball Jct), 6.8 mi s on SR 224 (Park Ave) to Heber Ave, then just e; corner of Main St and Heber Ave; historic downtown. **Parking:** on-site (fee) and street. [D]

LOCO LIZARD CANTINA **Phone:** 435/645-7000 (1)

Mexican
$8-$18

AAA Inspector Notes: The family-friendly Mexican cantina serves good food at reasonable prices. The menu consists of some non-traditional touches such as rellenos that are baked, not fried. **Bar:** full bar. **Address:** 1612 Ute Blvd, Suite 101 84098 **Location:** I-80 exit 145 (Kimball Jct), just s, then just e. [L] [D]

MARIPOSA **Phone:** 435/645-6715 (33)

Continental
$38-$48

AAA Inspector Notes: The seasonal menu in this rustic lodge features Japanese and French-influenced cuisine such as tamari-glazed sablefish, free-raised veal in a lemon-wine-caper sauce and a chef's vegetarian tasting. **Bar:** full bar. **Reservations:** suggested. **Address:** 7600 Royal St 84060 **Location:** I-80 exit 145 (Kimball Jct), in Deer Valley; in Silver Lake Lodge. [D]

MAXWELL'S EAST COAST EATERY
Phone: 435/647-0304 (3)

Italian
$9-$21

AAA Inspector Notes: After a starter of caprese salad, crispy calamari or steamed mussels, diners can savor homemade pasta with a choice of meat (grilled chicken, sauteed shrimp, Italian sausage or meatball) and sauce (marinara, Alfredo, tomato basil cream or brown butter sage with pine nuts). House specialties include pizza, risotto, chicken piccata, eggplant parmigiana and veal sauteed with pancetta, shallots, spinach and sun-dried tomatoes. Scrumptious cannoli or cookie pizza satisfy a sweet tooth. **Bar:** full bar. **Address:** 1456 Newpark Blvd 84098 **Location:** I-80 exit 145 (Kimball Jct), 0.3 mi s to Newpark Blvd, then 0.3 mi e; in Newpark Hotel. **Parking:** on-site and valet.
[L] [D] [LATE]

RED BANJO PIZZA PARLOR
Phone: 435/649-9901 (24)

Italian
$6-$12

AAA Inspector Notes: This eatery on historic Main Street has a lovely upper-level patio that offers spectacular mountain views. The root beer floats are worth the splurge. **Bar:** beer & wine. **Address:** 322 Main St 84060 **Location:** On upper historic Main St. **Parking:** street only. [L] [D]

REEF'S KITCHEN **Phone:** 435/658-0323 (14)

Middle Eastern
$11-$29

AAA Inspector Notes: The intimate and distinctive restaurant serves an appetizer sampler featuring hummus, baba ghanoush, tahini, falafel and roasted eggplant. Also featured are delicious salads; Moroccan salmon; filet mignon; poached walu in tomato stew; beef, lamb or fish kebabs; and mouthwatering semolina and coconut cake. Several tiers of interesting prix fixe options also are available. **Bar:** beer & wine. **Address:** 710 Main St 84098 **Location:** On lower historic Main St; behind Village Shopping Plaza. **Parking:** street only. [D]

(See map & index p. 388.)

RIVERHORSE ON MAIN Phone: 435/649-3536 (18)

American
$29-$50

AAA Inspector Notes: The appetizer trilogy of smoked salmon and potato pancake, goat cheese wontons and chicken satay served on lovely logoed china is a start, while roasted tomato bisque and heirloom beet and baby arugula salad is a good following. Colorful entrées may include Chardonnay-poached scallops and lobster tail or slow-roasted Berkshire pork ribs. A creative dessert with a fine wine is the only way to finish the evening. Views through the floor-to-ceiling windows are postcard-picture perfect. **Bar:** full bar. **Reservations:** suggested. **Address:** 540 Main St 84060 **Location:** On historic Main St, 2nd Floor. **Parking:** street only. D

ROYAL STREET CAFE **Phone:** 435/645-6724 (32)

American
$10-$32

AAA Inspector Notes: The seasonal menu features a wide variety of appetizers and entrées such as a shrimp and lobster margarita, Asian cured duck confit spring rolls, iceberg wedges, specialty veggie and meat panini, and slow-roasted chili- and coffee-rubbed duck breast. Frozen lemon meringue pie and fresh thyme maple ice cream are among the scrumptious desserts offered daily. **Bar:** full bar. **Address:** 7600 Royal St 84060 **Location:** I-80 exit 145 (Kimball Jct); in Deer Valley. **Parking:** street only.
L D

RUTH'S CHRIS STEAK HOUSE
Phone: 435/940-5070 (6)

Steak
$35-$70

AAA Inspector Notes: The main fare is steak, which is prepared from several cuts of prime beef and cooked to perfection, but the menu also lists lamb, chicken and seafood dishes. Guests should come hungry because the side dishes, which are among the a la carte offerings, could make a meal in themselves. **Bar:** full bar. **Reservations:** suggested. **Address:** 2001 Park Ave 84068 **Location:** I-80 exit 145 (Kimball Jct), 5.5 mi s; corner of Park Ave and Thaynes Canyon Dr; in Hotel Park City. **Parking:** on-site and valet. D

SHABU **Phone:** 435/645-7253 (19)

Asian
$26-$45

AAA Inspector Notes: They call it "freestyle" Asian food, although the well-balanced blend of tastes and textures are designed to delight any palate. From sushi hand rolls to wok-seared diver scallops with mango fried rice, patrons will be tantalized by the flavors. **Bar:** full bar. **Reservations:** suggested. **Address:** 442 Main St 84060 **Location:** On upper historic Main St; downstairs. **Parking:** street only. L D LATE

SQUATTERS ROADHOUSE GRILL & PUB
Phone: 435/649-9868 (10)

American
$8-$19

AAA Inspector Notes: At this grill and pub, award-winning beers are paired with a large selection of appetizers, soups, salads, sandwiches and pub favorites. It's a great choice for breakfast, lunch or dinner. Vegetarian and low-carb items are available. **Bar:** full bar. **Address:** 1900 Park Ave 84060 **Location:** I-80 exit 145 (Kimball Jct), 6 mi se; corner of Kearns Blvd and Park Ave (SR 224).
B L D

THE VIKING DINNER YURT
Phone: 435/615-9878 (5)

Norwegian
$157-$219

AAA Inspector Notes: Dinner starts with a 25-minute meandering ride in a heated cab (seats eight) or an open sleigh (seats 32) to the 8,000-foot top of the Park City Mountain Resort ski runs. The views of the valley below and the stars above are stunning. More adventurous types can strap on skis or snowshoes and hike in for lunch. To ease the chill, diners warm themselves in front of a fire with hot Norwegian spiced glögg before digging into a six-course gourmet meal complete with fine wine and Scandinavian fare. **Bar:** full bar. **Reservations:** required. **Address:** Top of Canyons Resort Dr 84098 **Location:** I-80 exit 145 (Kimball Jct), 6.3 mi se to corner of Empire and Park aves, 0.3 mi sw to Shadow Ridge Rd, just w to Lowell Ave, then just se; take stairs up to Legacy Lodge at Park City Mountain Resort.
D AC

WAHSO, AN ASIAN GRILL **Phone:** 435/615-0300 (17)

Asian
$27-$37

AAA Inspector Notes: Guests who unwind in the 1930s Shanghai Deco-Victorian setting can savor traditional Oriental meals prepared in a French-cooking-style. Flavors and textures blend for a true culinary delight. **Bar:** full bar. **Reservations:** suggested. **Address:** 577 Main St 84060 **Location:** On lower historic Main St. **Parking:** street only. D

WASATCH BREW PUB **Phone:** 435/649-0900 (27)

American
$9-$24

AAA Inspector Notes: This eatery serves up a wide variety of award-winning brews in the dining room and on a seasonal patio. Menu items include a healthy Cobb salad, fire-fried Monterey Bay calamari, roasted chicken and mussels paella, fish and chips with creole coleslaw, shrimp tacos, house-made pizza and decadent desserts. Children will be pleased with their own menu. **Bar:** full bar. **Address:** 250 S Main St 84060 **Location:** I-80 exit 145 (Kimball Jct), Top of historic Main St. **Parking:** street only. L D

WINDY RIDGE CAFE & BAKERY
Phone: 435/647-0880 (11)

American
$9-$24

AAA Inspector Notes: Gourmet influences enhance the lunch and dinner options at this comfortable eatery. **Bar:** full bar. **Address:** 1250 Iron Horse Dr 84060 **Location:** I-80 exit 145 (Kimball Jct), 6 mi s, then 0.5 mi e. L D

ZOOM ROADHOUSE GRILL
Phone: 435/649-9108 (15)

American
$11-$38

AAA Inspector Notes: In a historic railroad depot, the bar and dining room have a rustic character that speaks to days gone by. Notice the original wood floors that have survived two major fires as you slide into your private booth or sit at the copper-topped show kitchen counter. Choose several small plates of Asian beef skewers, spicy buffalo onion rings, seafood ceviche and white cheddar mac 'n' cheese that are perfect for sharing or a full rack of baby back pork ribs served with cornbread and poppyseed coleslaw. **Bar:** full bar. **Reservations:** suggested. **Address:** 660 Main St 84060 **Location:** Corner of Main St and Heber Ave. **Parking:** street only. L D

PAROWAN pop. 2,790

DAYS INN PAROWAN Phone: 435/477-3326

Motel

Rates not provided

Address: 625 W 200 S 84761 **Location:** I-15 exit 75, 1.5 mi e. **Facility:** 44 units. 2 stories (no elevator), exterior corridors. **Pool(s):** heated indoor. **Activities:** whirlpool. **Guest Services:** coin laundry.

/ SOME UNITS FEE

PRICE (D-4) pop. 8,715, elev. 5,547'

Originally settled as a farming area, Price grew with the coming of the railroad in the early 1880s. The discovery of coal brought new wealth and new residents to the town but also made it popular with such outlaws as the Brown's Hole Gang and Butch Cassidy and his Wild Bunch. The Price Mural, painted by native Lynn Fausett, details the history of Carbon County and covers 800 square feet in the Price Municipal Building.

Price is in a large coal-mining and farming district. Uranium, helium and natural gas deposits have been discovered in the area. The Manti-La Sal National Forest *(see place listing p. 362)* headquarters is in town.

Castle Country Travel Region: 81 North 200 East, #2, Price, UT 84501. **Phone:** (435) 636-3701 or (800) 842-0789.

Self-guiding tours: Maps and information about self-guiding tours to Native American dwellings and several areas of geological interest—including the San Rafael Desert, Little Grand Canyon and Nine Mile Canyon, with its extensive array of petroglyphs and pictographs—are available from the travel office.

COLLEGE OF EASTERN UTAH PREHISTORIC MUSEUM is at 155 E. Main St. The museum contains a raptor display, an 11,500-year-old mammoth skeleton and exhibits of Fremont Indian artifacts, including the Pilling figurine collection—unbaked clay ornaments believed to be 800 to 900 years old. The museum also has collections of minerals and fossils and a Hall of Dinosaurs, featuring several full-size dinosaur skeletons. Information about self-guiding tours to Native American petroglyphs in Nine Mile Canyon also is available.

Hours: Mon.-Sat. 9-5. Closed Jan. 1, Thanksgiving, Christmas Eve, Christmas and Dec. 31. **Cost:** $5; $4 (ages 65+); $2 (ages 2-12); $15 (family). **Phone:** (435) 613-5060 or (800) 817-9949.

BEST WESTERN CARRIAGE HOUSE INN

Phone: (435)637-5660

Motel

$76-$100

AAA Benefit: Members save up to 20%, plus 10% bonus points with Best Western Rewards®.

Address: 590 E Main St 84501 **Location:** Cross streets 600 E and Main St; downtown. **Facility:** 40 units. 2 stories (no elevator), interior corridors. **Pool(s):** heated indoor. **Activities:** whirlpool. **Free Special Amenities: local telephone calls and high-speed Internet.**

GREENWELL INN & CONVENTION CENTER

Phone: 435/637-3520

Hotel

Rates not provided

Address: 655 E Main St 84501 **Location:** Corner of 600 E and Main St. **Facility:** 128 units. 2 stories (no elevator), interior/exterior corridors. **Parking:** winter plug-ins. **Dining:** Ricardo's Restaurant, see separate listing. **Pool(s):** heated indoor. **Activities:** whirlpool, exercise room. **Guest Services:** valet and coin laundry.

BIZ / SOME UNITS FEE

HOLIDAY INN & SUITES Phone: (435)637-8880

Hotel

$89-$149 11/1-4/30

$89-$139 5/1-10/31

Address: 838 Westwood Blvd 84501 **Location:** US 6 exit 240, just e. Located near Castleview Hospital. **Facility:** 151 units, some efficiencies. 2 stories (no elevator), interior corridors. **Terms:** cancellation fee imposed. **Amenities:** video games (fee), high-speed Internet. **Pool(s):** heated indoor. **Activities:** exercise room. **Guest Services:** valet and coin laundry.

CALL M BIZ FEE

/ SOME UNITS

LEGACY INN Phone: 435/637-2424

Motel

$59-$125

Address: 145 N Carbonville Rd 84501 **Location:** US 6 exit 240 (Business Loop), 0.6 mi se, then just e on N Carbonville Rd (at traffic light). **Facility:** 31 units, some two bedrooms and efficiencies. 1 story, exterior corridors. **Terms:** office hours 6:30 am-midnight, cancellation fee imposed. **Guest Services:** coin laundry. **Free Special Amenities: expanded continental breakfast and high-speed Internet.**

SAVE / SOME UNITS FEE

SUPER 8 Phone: (435)637-8088

Motel

$56-$113

Address: 180 N Hospital Dr 84501 **Location:** US 6 exit 240, just e. Located near Castle Valley-Price Hospital. **Facility:** 40 units. 2 stories (no elevator), interior corridors. **Pool(s):** heated indoor. **Activities:** whirlpool. **Guest Services:** coin laundry.

SAVE BIZ

WHERE TO EAT

GROGG'S PINNACLE BREWING CO

Phone: 435/637-2924

American

$5-$16

AAA Inspector Notes: Informal, laid-back dining is the norm at this pine-walled brewing company. Menu items include house-smoked meats, baked salmon, steamed clams, burgers, wraps and pizza. The delicious gourmet sandwich offerings include a cheese steak made with cream cheese; baked pork roast; chicken, mushroom and avocado; and an Italian dip, all served with a choice of potato salad, broccoli slaw, chips and salsa, oven-baked fries, soup or salad. **Bar:** beer only. **Address:** 1653 N Carbonville Rd 84526 **Location:** SR 6 exit 240, 0.3 mi e to W 600 St, then 2 mi n; 1.5 mi se from jct SR 6 and Carbonville Rd. L D

RICADO'S RESTAURANT **Phone:** 435/637-2020

Mexican
$5-$14

AAA Inspector Notes: This casual family restaurant serves made-from-scratch Mexican food, along with a good selection of American items. **Bar:** full bar. **Address:** 655 E Main St 84501 **Location:** Cross streets 600 E and Main St; next to Greenwell Inn Convention Center.

B L D

SILVER STEAKHOUSE **Phone:** 435/637-4393

Steak
$11-$30

AAA Inspector Notes: This cozy local favorite in the heart of downtown offers a wide variety of steaks, including filet mignon, seafood, scrumptious desserts and signature side dishes such as twice-baked potatoes. **Bar:** full bar. **Address:** 40 W Main St 84501 **Location:** Center. **Parking:** street only. D

PROVO (C-3) pop. 112,488, elev. 4,549'

• Restaurants p. 400

Provo, on a shelf along the former shoreline of prehistoric Lake Bonneville, is nurtured by the Provo River. Etienne Provost, a French-Canadian, explored this area with a trapping expedition in 1825, found it suitable for settlement and gave the river his name. Encouraged by his reports, a colony from Salt Lake City settled in 1849 on the river's south bank, which is overshadowed by Provo Peak, Mount Timpanogos and the Wasatch Range.

By 1851 the village was well established, and irrigation was being used successfully. The railroad came to Provo in 1875, linking the settlement to Salt Lake City. Brigham Young University, which was organized by the Mormon colonizer, was established 2 years later to supply trained teachers for the public schools. The area is important industrially for the production of steel, pig iron and foundry products.

The gold-spired Provo Mormon Temple, completed in 1972, overlooks the city from the northeast; it is open to Mormons only.

Various water sports are permitted at Deer Creek Reservoir in Provo Canyon, which irrigates a vast area. Provo is at the southern terminus of scenic US 189, which passes through Uinta National Forest *(see place listing p. 456)* and joins scenic SR 92 just southeast of Deer Creek State Park *(see Recreation Chart)*. SR 92 then runs west, passing through Timpanogos Cave National Monument *(see place listing p. 452)* before terminating at the junction with I-15, 19 miles northwest of Provo.

Between February and November, numerous patriotic events that are part of GEM America's Freedom Festival at Provo take place in the city. Independence Day highlights include the Grand Parade; the Freedom Run, which encompasses a 1-mile Fun Run as well as 10- and 5-kilometer races; and the Stadium of Fire, a popular extravaganza boasting fireworks, concerts and dance performances.

Utah Valley Convention and Visitors Bureau: 111 S. University Ave., Provo, UT 84601. **Phone:** (801) 851-2100 or (800) 222-8824.

BRIGHAM YOUNG UNIVERSITY, at the base of the Wasatch Mountains, is one of the largest church-related private universities in the nation. Its 634-acre campus is dominated by the 112-foot Centennial Carillon Tower, where 52 bells ring at intervals throughout the day. The Hosting Center offers free 45-minute guided riding tours of the campus. Appointments are recommended, though walk-in visitors can be accommodated, based on availability. **Hours:** Tours are given Mon.-Fri. on the hour 9-4. **Phone:** (801) 422-4678 for tour information.

Monte L. Bean Life Science Museum is on the campus of Brigham Young University at 645 East 1430 North. The museum displays wildlife from around the world; collections of mounted birds, fish, insects, plants, reptiles also can be seen. Free live animal shows are presented. **Time:** Allow 1 hour minimum. **Hours:** Museum Mon.-Fri. 10-9, Sat. 10-5. Animal show is given Mon.-Fri. at 7:30 p.m. (also Mon. at 6:30 p.m.), Sat. at 1 and 3. **Cost:** Free. **Phone:** (801) 422-5051.

Museum of Art is on the n.e. corner of the Brigham Young University campus on N. Campus Dr. The museum houses galleries of European, local and 19th-century American paintings. Additional galleries house ceramics, paintings, pottery and sculpture by faculty and students. The center's theaters offer theatrical and musical performances; ticket prices vary by performance. **Time:** Allow 1 hour minimum. **Hours:** Mon.-Sat. 10-6 (also Thurs.-Fri. 6-9 p.m.). **Cost:** Free. A fee may be charged for some traveling exhibitions. **Phone:** (801) 422-8287.

Museum of Paleontology is directly w. of Cougar Stadium on the n.w. edge of the Brigham Young University campus at 1683 N. Canyon Rd. The museum displays what is said to be one of the top five collections of Jurassic dinosaur fossils in the world. **Time:** Allow 1 hour minimum. **Hours:** Mon.-Fri. 9-5. Closed university holidays. **Cost:** Free. **Phone:** (801) 422-3680.

Museum of Peoples and Cultures is at 100 East 700 North at 105 Allen Hall (off campus). The archeology museum has annually rotating exhibitions that feature the cultures of the Great Basin, Mesoamerica, ancient Peru and Polynesia and Southwest. Brigham Young University students serve as curators. **Time:** Allow 1 hour minimum. **Hours:** Mon.-Fri. 9-5 (also Tues. and Thurs. 5-7, Sept.-Apr.). Closed major holidays. **Cost:** Donations. **Phone:** (801) 422-0020.

SEVEN PEAKS WATERPARK is .5 mi. e. on East 100 North, .1 mi. s. on North 600 East, .4 mi. e. on E. Center St., then .3 mi. n. on N. Seven Peaks Blvd. to 1330 East 300 North. The park contains tube runs, speed slides, activity pools, a wave pool, a zero-depth entry pool, a 500,000-gallon lazy river, a bowl slide and a 100-foot free-fall drop slide. Also featured are carnival games, a children's play area, a game area, a tadpole pond and a beach volleyball sand pit.

Note: The facility is not wheelchair accessible. Towels are not provided. Cabana, tube, lounge chair, umbrella and barbecue rentals are available. **Time:** Allow 2 hours minimum. **Hours:** Mon.-Sat. 11-8, Memorial Day-Labor Day (weather permitting). Phone ahead to confirm schedule. **Cost:** $24.95; $19.95 (under 48 inches tall); $7.95 (nonparticipants); free (ages 0-3 and 65+). After 4 p.m. $15.95; free (ages 0-3 and 65+). After 6 p.m. $9.95 (under 48 inches tall); free (ages 0-3 and 65+). Life jacket requires a driver's license or refundable season pass deposit. **Parking:** $5 (full day); $3 (half-day). **Phone:** (801) 377-4386.

RECREATIONAL ACTIVITIES

Skiing

- **Sundance Resort** is off I-15 exit 272; take US 189 7 mi. n.e., then SR 92 2.3 mi. n.w. Other activities are offered. **Hours:** Open for winter activities daily, mid-Dec. to early Apr. Hours vary; phone ahead. **Phone:** (801) 225-4107 or (866) 259-7468.

BEST WESTERN PLUS COTTONTREE INN
Phone: (801)373-7044

Hotel
$89-$112

AAA Benefit: Members save up to 20%, plus 10% bonus points with Best Western Rewards®.

Address: 2230 N University Pkwy 84604 **Location:** I-15 exit 269 (University Pkwy), 3.2 mi e, then just n; in CottonTree Square. **Facility:** 80 units. 2 stories (no elevator), interior corridors. **Terms:** 30 day cancellation notice-fee imposed. **Amenities:** video games (fee). **Pool(s):** heated outdoor, heated indoor. **Activities:** whirlpool. **Guest Services:** valet and coin laundry, area transportation-within 4 mi. **Free Special Amenities: full breakfast and local transportation.**

SAVE FEE / SOME UNITS FEE

COURTYARD BY MARRIOTT **Phone:** (801)373-2222

Hotel
$89-$179

AAA Benefit:
AAA hotel discounts of 5% or more.

Address: 1600 N Freedom Blvd 84604 **Location:** I-15 exit 269 (University Pkwy), 3.9 mi e to N Freedom Blvd, then just s. **Facility:** 100 units. 5 stories, interior corridors. **Dining:** Magleby's Grill & Oyster Bar, see separate listing. **Pool(s):** heated indoor. **Activities:** whirlpool, exercise room. **Guest Services:** valet and coin laundry, area transportation-within 10 mi. / SOME UNITS

DAYS INN **Phone:** (801)375-8600

Motel
$41-$113

Address: 1675 N 200 W 84604 **Location:** I-15 exit 269 (University Pkwy), 3.7 mi e, then just s at Freedom Blvd; in Village Green Square. **Facility:** 48 units. 2 stories (no elevator), exterior corridors. **Pool(s):** heated outdoor. **Free Special Amenities: continental breakfast and newspaper.**

SAVE / SOME UNITS FEE

ECONO LODGE **Phone:** (801)373-0099

Motel
$59-$89

Address: 1625 W Center St 84601 **Location:** I-15 exit 265 (Center St), just w. **Facility:** 27 units. 2 stories (no elevator), exterior corridors. **Terms:** cancellation fee imposed.

/ SOME UNITS FEE

FAIRFIELD INN BY MARRIOTT **Phone:** (801)377-9500

Hotel
$79-$129

AAA Benefit:
AAA hotel discounts of 5% or more.

Address: 1515 S University Ave 84601 **Location:** I-15 exit 263 (University Ave), just e. **Facility:** 72 units. 3 stories, interior corridors. **Pool(s):** heated indoor. **Activities:** whirlpool. **Guest Services:** valet and coin laundry.

CALL / SOME UNITS

HINES MANSION BED & BREAKFAST
Phone: (801)374-8400

Historic Bed & Breakfast
$142-$270

Address: 383 W 100 S 84601 **Location:** I-15 exit 265 (Center St), 1.2 mi e to 500 W, just s to 100 S, then just e. **Facility:** Pass some peaceful time by this B&B's imported Italian marble fireplace or play games in the restored Victorian parlor. 9 units. 3 stories (no elevator), interior/exterior corridors. **Terms:** check-in 4 pm, 8 day cancellation notice-fee imposed.

LA QUINTA INN PROVO TOWN CENTER
Phone: (801)374-9750

Hotel
$80-$140

Address: 1460 S University Ave 84601 **Location:** I-15 exit 263 (University Ave), 0.5 mi e. **Facility:** 78 units. 2 stories (no elevator), interior corridors. **Pool(s):** heated outdoor. **Activities:** exercise room. **Guest Services:** valet and coin laundry, area transportation-within 4 mi.

BIZ / SOME UNITS

PROVO MARRIOTT HOTEL & CONFERENCE CENTER
Phone: (801)377-4700

Hotel
$89-$169

Marriott HOTELS & RESORTS

AAA Benefit: AAA hotel discounts of 5% or more.

Address: 101 W 100 N 84601 **Location:** I-15 exit 265 (Center St), 1.2 mi e, just n at 500 W, then 0.3 mi e. **Facility:** 330 units. 9 stories, interior corridors. **Amenities:** high-speed Internet (fee). *Some:* safes. **Dining:** 2 restaurants. **Pool(s):** heated outdoor, heated indoor. **Activities:** whirlpool, exercise room. **Guest Services:** valet and coin laundry, area transportation (fee)-within 10 mi. **Free Special Amenities: newspaper and local transportation.**

RESIDENCE INN BY MARRIOTT PROVO
Phone: (801)374-1000

Extended Stay Hotel
$152-$186

AAA Benefit:
AAA hotel discounts of 5% or more.

Address: 252 W 2230 N 84604 **Location:** I-15 exit 269 (University Pkwy), 3.2 mi e, then just n. **Facility:** 114 units, some two bedrooms, efficiencies and kitchens. 3 stories, interior corridors. **Amenities:** video games (fee). *Some:* high-speed Internet. **Pool(s):** heated indoor. **Activities:** whirlpool, sports court, exercise room. **Guest Services:** valet and coin laundry.

CALL FEE

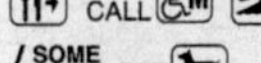

SLEEP INN
Phone: 801/377-6597

Hotel
Rates not provided

Address: 1505 S 40 E 84606 **Location:** I-15 exit 263 (University Ave), just e. Located near Town Centre Mall. **Facility:** 82 units. 3 stories, interior corridors. **Terms:** check-in 4 pm. **Pool(s):** heated indoor. **Activities:** whirlpool, exercise room. **Guest Services:** coin laundry.

BIZ

/ SOME UNITS FEE

SPRINGHILL SUITES BY MARRIOTT
Phone: (801)373-0073

Hotel
$99-$199

AAA Benefit:
AAA hotel discounts of 5% or more.

Address: 1580 N Freedom Blvd 84604 **Location:** I-15 exit 269 (University Pkwy), 3.9 mi e to N Freedom Blvd, then just s. **Facility:** 82 units. 4 stories, interior corridors. **Amenities:** high-speed Internet. **Pool(s):** heated indoor. **Activities:** exercise room. **Guest Services:** valet and coin laundry, area transportation-within 10 mi.

SUNDANCE RESORT
Phone: 801/225-4107

fyi Not evaluated. **Address:** 8841 N Alpine Loop Rd 84604 **Location:** I-15 exit 272 (800 N/Sundance). Facilities, services, and decor characterize a mid-scale property.

WHERE TO EAT

BOMBAY HOUSE CUISINE OF INDIA
Phone: 801/373-6677

Indian
$11-$19

AAA Inspector Notes: Patrons feel like they've stepped into India when they pass through the doors of one of Provo's most authentic and outstanding ethnic restaurants. **Bar:** beer & wine. **Address:** 463 N University Ave 84601 **Location:** I-15 exit 265 (Center St), 1.8 mi e to University Ave, then 0.3 mi n. D

COMMUNAL
Phone: 801/373-8000

American
$8-$24

AAA Inspector Notes: Introverts can sit at a set table, while extroverts are welcome to join the communal table at this small and elegant eatery. The a la carte menu is meant for sharing, too. Seasonal items, which incorporate fresh, local ingredients, may include Berkshire pork chop in persimmon sauce, pan-roasted salmon in a warm leek vinaigrette, gnocchi in lemon-thyme cream, creamy farro and chanterelles, and winter squash gratin. Desserts include steamed maple pudding with local berries and ice cream. **Bar:** beer & wine. **Reservations:** suggested. **Address:** 102 N University Ave 84601 **Location:** I-15 exit 265 (Center St), 1.2 mi e, just n on 500 W, 0.4 mi e on 100 N, then just s on University Ave; historic downtown. **Parking:** street only.

L D

GURU'S CAFE
Phone: 801/375-4878

Continental
$6-$13

AAA Inspector Notes: This eclectic eatery serves fresh, healthy pastas, soups, rice bowls, wraps, salads, tacos, burritos and elegant desserts. **Address:** 45 E Center St 84606 **Location:** I-15 exit 265 (Center St), 2 mi e. **Parking:** on-site and street. B L D

LA DOLCE VITA RISTORANTE
Phone: 801/373-8482

Italian
$7-$16

AAA Inspector Notes: Patrons stop in this local's favorite restaurant for lunch and dinner specials and to enjoy the homemade garlic bread, crisp salads, cannelloni, lasagna, halibut, tortellini, tasty calzones, house-made pizza and decadent desserts. **Bar:** beer & wine. **Address:** 61 N 100 E 84606 **Location:** I-15 exit 265 (Center St), 2 mi e to 100 E, then just n. L D

LA JOLLA GROVES
Phone: 801/224-5111

New American
$10-$19

AAA Inspector Notes: Diners eat under a lemon grove with a yellow rose and lemon linen napkins at their tables. The menu features organically grown vegetables from the restaurant's own garden and from local greenhouses. Popular choices include slow-roasted portobello and crimini mushroom soup finished with chicken stock, caprese salad and oven-fired salmon with cilantro-lime butter. Lemon cake is served with a sour cream glaze under a caramel dome with raspberries and mint. **Bar:** full bar. **Reservations:** suggested. **Address:** 4801 N University Ave, Suite 610 84604 **Location:** I-15 exit 271, 3 mi e; in The Shops at Riverwoods (east courtyard). L D

MAGLEBY'S GRILL & OYSTER BAR
Phone: 801/374-6249

Seafood
$8-$29

AAA Inspector Notes: No alcohol is served, but guests of this cozy restaurant can savor tasty dishes such as oysters on the half shell, lump crab, gourmet shrimp, hazelnut-encrusted chicken topped with rosemary sauce, pasta and an outstanding center-cut filet mignon. The bottomless homemade soup and famous asiago breadsticks merit many return visits. Children have their own menu. Desserts include a to-die-for buttermilk pie. **Address:** 1600 N Freedom Blvd 84604 **Location:** I-15 exit 269 (University Pkwy), 3.9 mi e to N Freedom Blvd, then just s; in Courtyard by Marriott. B L D

MALAWI'S PIZZA
Phone: 801/225-2800

Pizza
$9-$11

AAA Inspector Notes: Guests can go for a more healthy pizza by choosing honey-wheat or gluten-free crust. Signature pies include the popular herb-roasted chicken and pesto cream with asparagus, spinach and Gorgonzola cheese. Pasta, paired with a choice of sauce, vegetables and other toppings, also are available. Mixed berries and cream, Oreo cookie crumble, and cinnamon-roasted apples and cream are among the dessert pizzas. **Address:** 4801 N University Pkwy, Suite 110 84604 **Location:** I-15 exit 271, 3 mi e; in The Shops at Riverwoods; east side. L D

NICOLITALIA PIZZERIA Phone: 801/356-7900

Italian
$6-$18

AAA Inspector Notes: This eatery serves hand-tossed, East Coast-style pizza baked in a hearth brick oven, calzones, soups, salads, sides of meatballs and sausage, chicken and eggplant Parmesan and a small selection of pasta with marinara or Alfredo sauce. The Boston Italian cream pie and cannoli are yummy. **Address:** 2295 N University Pkwy 84604 **Location:** I-15 exit 269 (University Pkwy), 3 mi e, just s of Carterville Rd; in shopping plaza (west side). L D

RUBY RIVER STEAKHOUSE **Phone:** 801/371-0648

Steak
$8-$37

AAA Inspector Notes: The restaurant serves great steaks along with pasta, seafood and chicken, too. The atmosphere is casual and fun with a lively lounge; a pail of peanuts in the shell is on every table. **Bar:** full bar. **Address:** 1454 S University Ave 84601 **Location:** I-15 exit 263 (University Ave), 0.5 mi e. L D

SPARKS RESTAURANT LOUNGE **Phone:** 801/701-6780

American
$12-$33

AAA Inspector Notes: The refreshing drink menu includes seasonal fruit mojitos, appletinis and peartinis rimmed with cinnamon sugar, but all are non-alcoholic. The food menu changes often and may include wonton-wrapped ground pork skewers served with jalapeno aioli, orange sweet chili and lemon soy vinegar dipping sauces; Cajun shrimp risotto with sauteed prosciutto and green onions; pan-roasted filet mignon; or pan-seared salmon. Dessert doesn't get much better than the house-made mousse. **Reservations:** suggested. **Address:** 86 N University Ave 84601 **Location:** I-15 exit 265 (Center St), 1.3 mi e, just n on 500 W, 0.4 mi e on 100 N, then just s; in Wells Fargo Bank Building. **Parking:** street only.
L D LATE

TREE ROOM AT SUNDANCE RESORT
Phone: 801/223-4200

American
$28-$46

AAA Inspector Notes: American Indian and Old West artifacts decorate the restaurant's rustic and elegant interior. Serving seasonal mountain cuisine, the menu features a selection of chicken, seafood, steak and elegant desserts, including a warm chocolate cherry truffle cake. **Bar:** full bar. **Reservations:** suggested. **Address:** 8841 N Alpine Loop Rd 84604 **Location:** I-15 exit 272 (800 N/Sundance), 4 mi e, 6 mi n on US 189, then 2 mi w on US 92. D

GEM RAINBOW BRIDGE NATIONAL MONUMENT (G-4)

Just north of the Arizona-Utah border within Glen Canyon National Recreation Area *(see place listing p. 347)*, Rainbow Bridge is the largest known natural bridge in the world—standing 290 feet above the stream bed and stretching 275 feet wide. It has an enormous and almost perfectly formed arch below and a curved surface above, giving the effect of a rainbow. Rainbow Bridge is considered a sacred place by many Native American tribes.

The bridge is reached by a 14-mile hike over rugged terrain or by boat and, depending on the lake's water level, a 1- to 1.5-mile hike. Backpackers must obtain a permit to hike the 14-mile trail from the Navajo Nation Parks and Recreation Department, P.O. Box 2520, Window Rock, AZ 86515; phone (928) 871-6647 or (928) 871-6592.

Regularly scheduled boat tours on Lake Powell provide access to Rainbow Bridge. Tours provided by Lake Powell Resorts & Marina depart from the Wahweap Marina in Arizona; phone (888) 896-3829 for schedule, prices and reservations. Camping and swimming are not permitted within the monument grounds.

For information contact the Superintendent, Rainbow Bridge National Monument, c/o Glen Canyon National Recreation Area, P.O. Box 1507, Page, AZ 86040; phone (928) 608-6200.

RICHFIELD (E-3) pop. 7,551, elev. 5,308'

• **Restaurants p. 402**

Big Rock Candy Mountain, 24 miles south on US 89, has multicolored rock formations. Six miles north of the mountain on US 89 are canyons with Native American petroglyphs that predate the birth of Christ. Nearby, Fremont Indian State Park comprises archeological sites, rock art and a museum that houses exhibits relating to the Fremont Anasazi Indian culture *(see attraction listing in Sevier p. 448)*.

Richfield Area Chamber of Commerce: 250 N. Main, Suite B42, Richfield, UT 84701. **Phone:** (435) 896-4241.

BEST WESTERN RICHFIELD INN **Phone:** (435)893-0100

Motel
$80-$90

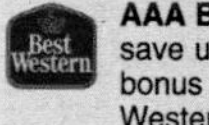

AAA Benefit: Members save up to 20%, plus 10% bonus points with Best Western Rewards®.

Address: 1275 N Main St 84701 **Location:** I-70 exit 40, just s. **Facility:** 42 units. 2 stories (no elevator), interior corridors. **Terms:** cancellation fee imposed. **Amenities:** *Some:* high-speed Internet. **Pool(s):** heated indoor. **Activities:** whirlpool, exercise room. **Guest Services:** coin laundry. **Free Special Amenities: continental breakfast and high-speed Internet.**
SAVE / SOME UNITS FEE

COMFORT INN **Phone:** 435/893-0119

Hotel
Rates not provided

Address: 1070 W 1250 S 84701 **Location:** I-70 exit 37, just e. **Facility:** 63 units. 3 stories, interior corridors. **Amenities:** high-speed Internet. **Pool(s):** heated indoor. **Activities:** whirlpool, limited exercise equipment. **Guest Services:** valet and coin laundry.
BIZ / SOME UNITS

FAIRFIELD INN & SUITES BY MARRIOTT
Phone: (435)896-9191

Hotel
$89-$104

AAA Benefit:
AAA hotel discounts of 5% or more.

Address: 990 W 1350 S 84701 **Location:** I-70 exit 37, just e. **Facility:** 65 units. 3 stories, interior corridors. **Amenities:** high-speed Internet. **Pool(s):** heated indoor. **Activities:** whirlpool, exercise room. **Guest Services:** valet and coin laundry. BIZ / SOME UNITS

HAMPTON INN Phone: (435)896-6666

Hotel
$80-$119

AAA Benefit:
Members save up to 10% everyday!

Address: 1100 W 1350 S 84701 **Location:** I-70 exit 37, just e. **Facility:** 52 units. 3 stories, interior corridors. **Terms:** 1-7 night minimum stay, cancellation fee imposed. **Amenities:** video games (fee). **Pool(s):** heated indoor. **Activities:** whirlpool, exercise room. **Guest Services:** valet and coin laundry.

BIZ FEE / SOME UNITS

HOLIDAY INN EXPRESS & SUITES Phone: (435)896-8552

Hotel
$89-$189

Address: 20 W 1400 N 84701 **Location:** I-70 exit 40, just s. **Facility:** 64 units. 3 stories, interior corridors. **Terms:** cancellation fee imposed. **Amenities:** high-speed Internet. **Pool(s):** heated indoor. **Activities:** whirlpool, exercise room. **Guest Services:** coin laundry.

BIZ / SOME UNITS FEE

SUPER 8 Phone: (435)896-9204

Motel
$50-$64

Address: 1377 N Main St 84701 **Location:** I-70 exit 40, just s. **Facility:** 42 units. 2 stories (no elevator), interior/exterior corridors. **Terms:** 7 day cancellation notice. **Guest Services:** coin laundry.

/ SOME UNITS FEE

WHERE TO EAT

IDEAL DAIRY Phone: 435/896-5061

American
$5-$9

AAA Inspector Notes: In the center of town, the mom-and-pop creamery offers fresh sandwiches, homemade ice cream, fresh milk and freshly baked bread. It's a great stop for any meal, great dessert or even a gallon of milk to go. **Address:** 490 S Main St 84701 **Location:** I-70 exit 40, 0.9 mi s on US 89. B L D

LITTLE WONDER CAFE Phone: 435/896-8960

American
$6-$14

AAA Inspector Notes: Down-home cooking has been going on at the cafe since 1929. A comfortable country look brightens the interior, and the staff goes out of its way to make patrons feel welcome. **Address:** 101 N Main St 84701 **Location:** At center; on Main St (SR 120).

B L D

PEPPERBELLY'S Phone: 435/896-2097

Mexican
$7-$12

AAA Inspector Notes: The casual restaurant serves Mexican favorites in a dining room filled with memorabilia celebrating yesteryear and a love of the road. **Address:** 680 S Cove View Rd 84701 **Location:** I-70 exit 37, 0.4 mi e, then 0.8 mi ne. L D

STEVE'S STEAKHOUSE Phone: 435/893-8880

American
$12-$27

AAA Inspector Notes: Those not in the mood for steak can contemplate several choices of chicken and seafood at this Western-themed spot on the main street through town. Servers are friendly and attentive. **Bar:** beer & wine. **Address:** 647 S Main St 84701 **Location:** I-70 exit 37, 0.3 mi e to Cove View Rd, then 0.7 mi ne.

D

ROOSEVELT (C-5) pop. 6,046, elev. 5,100'

The area south of Roosevelt was the site of the discovery of Gilsonite, a brittle asphalt used in the manufacture of pipe insulation and ink. The Uinta Basin deposit was discovered in 1885 by Samuel H. Gilson, who was told by Native Americans of a substance that would not burn.

Duchesne County Area Chamber of Commerce: 50 East 200 South, P.O. Box 1417, Roosevelt, UT 84066. **Phone:** (435) 722-4598.

Self-guiding tours: Brochures outlining self-guiding tours of the area, including Indian petroglyphs, a 30-mile Rock Creek tour and a 60-mile Elkhorn Loop trip, are available from the chamber of commerce.

AMERICAS BEST VALUE INN Phone: (435)722-4644

Motel
$110-$150

Address: 2203 E Hwy 40 84066 **Location:** On US 40, 1 mi e. **Facility:** 40 units. 2 stories (no elevator), exterior corridors. **Terms:** office hours 7 am-10 pm. **Amenities:** high-speed Internet. **Pool(s):** heated outdoor. **Activities:** whirlpool. **Guest Services:** coin laundry. **Free Special Amenities: continental breakfast and high-speed Internet.**

ST. GEORGE (G-1) pop. 72,897, elev. 2,840'

• Hotels p. 404 • Restaurants p. 409

St. George is in Utah's "Dixie," where summers are warm and winters are mild. The area was settled during the Civil War by Mormons sent by Brigham Young to raise cotton. A textile mill was built and production continued until the South was once again able to supply Utah with cotton.

The St. George Mormon Temple, built 1869-77, was the first Mormon temple built in Utah. The temple and several other early buildings still stand. The red sandstone 1863 tabernacle at Main and Tabernacle streets supports a 140-foot steeple that serves as a town landmark; the tabernacle is open to visitors. Although the temple is not open to the public, guided tours offered by the St. George Temple Visitors Center, 490 South 300 East (on the temple grounds), explain the temple's functions and Mormon beliefs; phone (435) 673-5181.

St. George's temperate weather makes it ideal for all sorts of outdoor recreation, including boating, water skiing, fishing and camping. The area also is popular with golfers and offers a variety of courses that can be played throughout the year.

St. George Area Chamber of Commerce: 97 E. St. George Blvd., St. George, UT 84770. **Phone:** (435) 628-1658. ***(See ad p. 333, p. 403.)***

Self-guiding tours: Many of St. George's late 19th-century buildings can be seen on a walking tour that begins at the chamber of commerce's visitor center at 100 East and St. George Boulevard; a map describing the route and each building is available at the visitor center.

Shopping areas: Among the more than 65 stores at Red Cliffs Mall, 1770 E. Red Cliffs Dr., are the anchor stores Dillard's, JCPenney and Sears. The Outlets at Zion, off I-15 exit 8, has more than 33 outlet shops, including Eddie Bauer, Izod, Levi's, OshKosh B'Gosh and Polo Ralph Lauren.

BRIGHAM YOUNG WINTER HOME is at 67 West 200 North. Built around 1873, the restored house contains 19th-century furnishings. **Hours:** Guided tours are offered daily 10-7, Apr.-Oct.; 10-5, rest of year. Last tour begins 30 minutes before closing. **Cost:** Free. **Phone:** (435) 673-5181.

DAUGHTERS OF UTAH PIONEERS MUSEUM is in the McQuarrie Memorial Building at 145 North 100 East. The museum contains memorabilia from the pioneer days 1847-70. Clothing, pictures of early settlers and pioneer implements are among the items exhibited. **Time:** Allow 30 minutes minimum. **Hours:** Mon.-Tues. and Thurs.-Sat. 10-5, Mar.-May and Sept.-Oct.; 10:30-2, June-Aug.; 12:30-4, Jan.-Feb. and in Nov. Closed major holidays. **Cost:** Free. **Phone:** (435) 628-7274.

GEM SAVE **ROSENBRUCH WILDLIFE MUSEUM** is off I-15 exit 6 to 1835 Convention Center Dr. Visitors encounter realistic representations of wildlife habitats that resemble those in Africa, Australia, the Arctic, Europe and Asia as well as

▼ See AAA listing p. 402 ▼

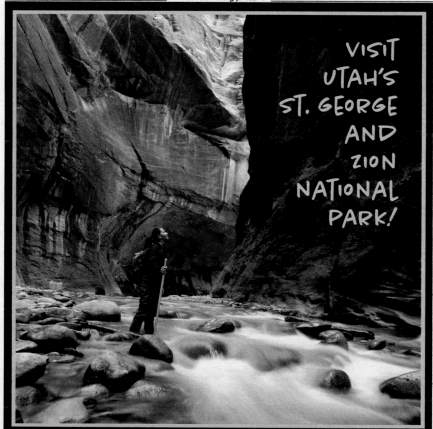

North America. Replicas of wildlife are created using fiberglass or foam forms and real animal skin and fur. Among animals represented are several types of antelopes, bears, camels, caribous, cats, crocodiles and deer as well as elk, foxes, kangaroos, monkeys, sheep and wolves.

The museum features an interactive children's area, an exotic insect collection and an art gallery. Videotaped presentations and rotating exhibits also are available. **Time:** Allow 1 hour, 30 minutes minimum. **Hours:** Mon.-Sat. 10-6 (also Mon. 6-8 p.m.). Closed Jan. 1, Thanksgiving and Christmas. **Cost:** $8; $6 (ages 55+); $4 (ages 3-12). **Phone:** (435) 656-0033.

ST. GEORGE ART MUSEUM is at 47 East 200 North. The museum's permanent collection consists of approximately 500 items that include photographs, ceramics and bronze sculptures. Paintings are featured in such media as oil, acrylic and watercolor. A Family Discovery Center and the Adult Study Center also are offered. Changing exhibits are offered throughout the year. Children's cultural classes are available in summer. **Time:** Allow 30 minutes minimum. **Hours:** Mon.-Sat. 10-5 (also third Thurs. of the month 5-9). **Cost:** $3; $1 (ages 3-11). **Phone:** (435) 627-4525.

ST. GEORGE DINOSAUR DISCOVERY SITE AT JOHNSON FARM is at 2180 E. Riverside Dr. Visitors can see 200-million-year-old dinosaur tracks that were uncovered when the property was being cleared for commercial development. Other exhibits include fossils of dinosaur and fish bones, shells of marine animals, and imprints of leaves and seeds. **Time:** Allow 1 hour minimum. **Hours:** Mon.-Sat. 10-6. Closed Thanksgiving and Christmas. **Cost:** $6; $3 (ages 4-11). **Phone:** (435) 574-3466.

ST. GEORGE TABERNACLE is at 18 S. Main St. Guided tours offer visitors insight into the history of the church as well as the people who contributed to its development. **Time:** Allow 1 hour minimum. **Hours:** Daily 10-5. Closed Jan. 1, Thanksgiving and Christmas. **Cost:** Free. **Phone:** (435) 673-5181.

AMERICA'S BEST INN & SUITES **Phone:** (435)652-3030

Motel
$54-$145

Address: 245 N Red Cliffs Dr 84790 **Location:** I-15 exit 8, just e. **Facility:** 49 units. 2 stories (no elevator), exterior corridors. **Terms:** 2-3 night minimum stay, 3 day cancellation notice-fee imposed. **Pool(s):** heated outdoor. **Activities:** whirlpool. **Guest Services:** coin laundry.

/ SOME UNITS FEE

AMERICAS BEST VALUE INN **Phone:** 435/688-8383

Motel
Rates not provided

Address: 915 S Bluff St 84770 **Location:** I-15 exit 6 (Bluff St), just w. **Facility:** 78 units. 2 stories (no elevator), interior corridors. **Pool(s):** heated outdoor. **Guest Services:** coin laundry. **Free Special Amenities: continental breakfast and newspaper.**

FEE / SOME UNITS FEE

BEST WESTERN CORAL HILLS **Phone:** (435)673-4844

Motel
$70-$126

AAA Benefit: Members save up to 20%, plus 10% bonus points with Best Western Rewards®.

Address: 125 E St. George Blvd 84770 **Location:** I-15 exit 8, 1 mi w. **Facility:** 98 units, some two bedrooms. 2 stories (no elevator), interior/exterior corridors. **Amenities:** *Some:* high-speed Internet. **Pool(s):** heated outdoor, heated indoor. **Activities:** whirlpools, putting green, exercise room. **Guest Services:** valet and coin laundry. **Free Special Amenities: expanded continental breakfast and high-speed Internet.**

(See ad p. 405.)

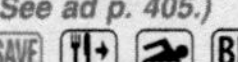

BEST WESTERN PLUS ABBEY INN
Phone: (435)652-1234

Motel
$80-$140

AAA Benefit: Members save up to 20%, plus 10% bonus points with Best Western Rewards®.

Address: 1129 S Bluff St 84770 **Location:** I-15 exit 6 (Bluff St), just n. **Facility:** 154 units. 3 stories, interior corridors. **Amenities:** *Some:* high-speed Internet. **Pool(s):** heated outdoor. **Activities:** whirlpool, exercise room. **Guest Services:** valet and coin laundry. **Free Special Amenities: full breakfast and high-speed Internet.**

(See ad p. 405.)

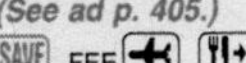
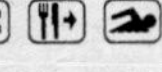

FEE

BEST WESTERN TRAVEL INN **Phone:** (435)673-3541

Motel
$60-$115

AAA Benefit: Members save up to 20%, plus 10% bonus points with Best Western Rewards®.

Address: 316 E St. George Blvd 84770 **Location:** I-15 exit 8, 0.8 mi w; downtown. **Facility:** 30 units, some two bedrooms. 1 story, exterior corridors. **Amenities:** high-speed Internet. **Pool(s):** heated outdoor. **Activities:** whirlpool. **Free Special Amenities: expanded continental breakfast and high-speed Internet.**

(See ad p. 405.)

BUDGET INN & SUITES **Phone:** (435)673-6661

Hotel
$89-$120

Address: 1221 S Main St 84770 **Location:** I-15 exit 6 (Bluff St), just w. **Facility:** 143 units, some efficiencies. 2 stories (no elevator), exterior corridors. **Pool(s):** heated outdoor, heated indoor. **Activities:** whirlpools, playground, exercise room. **Guest Services:** coin laundry.

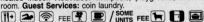

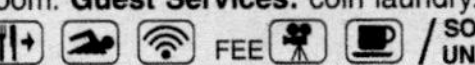

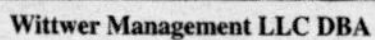

BEST WESTERN PLUS Abbey I[illegible] Suites

Complimentary Full Hot Breakfast

- Elegant Rooms with Euro-Top Beds and 42" Flat Screen TVs
- Large Indoor Spa & Heated Outdoor Pool • Guest Laundry
- Fridges & Microwaves • Free High Speed Internet • Bus. Cntr.

Toll Free **1-888-222-3946**

(435) 652-1234

1129 South Bluff Street • St. George, Utah 84770

www.abbeyinnhotels.com

E-mail: bwabbey@infowest.com

BEST WESTERN Coral Hills & Suites

Free Deluxe Breakfast w/Belgian Waffles

- All Newly Remodeled Rooms w/42" TVs • Bus. Cntr.
- Heated Indoor & Outdoor Pools & Spas • Guest Laundry
- Fridges & Microwaves • Free High Speed Internet

Toll Free **1-800-542-7733**

(435) 673-4844

125 East St. George Blvd. • St. George, Utah 84770

www.abbeyinnhotels.com

E-mail: bwcoral@infowest.com

BEST WESTERN Travel Inn

Free Deluxe Breakfast w/Belgian Waffles

- Heated Outdoor Pool & Indoor Spa • All 37" TVs
- All Non-Smoking Rooms • Microwaves
- Free High Speed Internet • Voice Mail • Fridges
- Large Family Rooms up to 5-6 Persons • Business Center

Toll Free **1-888-590-2835**

(435) 673-3541

316 East St. George Blvd. • St. George, Utah 84770

www.abbeyinnhotels.com

E-mail: travelinn@infowest.com

...e: (435)673-7000

...1239 S Main St 84770 ...ion: I-15 exit 6 (Bluff St), just ...w. **Facility:** 122 units. 2 stories, exterior corridors. **Terms:** cancellation fee imposed. **Amenities:** video games (fee), high-speed Internet. **Pool(s):** heated outdoor. **Activities:** whirlpool, exercise room. **Guest Services:** valet and coin laundry. **Free Special Amenities: full breakfast and high-speed Internet.**

(See ad this page.)

FEE

COMFORT INN

Hotel

Rates not provided

Phone: 435/628-8544

Address: 138 E Riverside Dr 84790 **Location:** I-15 exit 6 (Bluff St), just e. **Facility:** 122 units. 3 stories, interior corridors. **Pool(s):** heated outdoor. **Activities:** whirlpools, exercise room. **Guest Services:** coin laundry.

FEE

/ SOME UNITS FEE

Learn about AAA/CAA Diamond Ratings at AAA.com/Diamonds

▼ *See AAA listing this page* ▼

COUNTRY INN & SUITES BY CARLSON

Phone: (435)251-9600

Hotel

$79-$299 5/1-11/30
$99-$249 12/1-4/30

Address: 974 N 2720 E 84790 **Location:** I-15 exit 10, just e, then just s. **Facility:** 60 units, some two bedrooms. 4 stories, interior corridors. **Terms:** 2 night minimum stay - seasonal, 3 day cancellation notice-fee imposed. **Amenities:** high-speed Internet. **Pool(s):** heated indoor. **Activities:** sauna, whirlpool, exercise room. **Guest Services:** coin laundry.

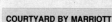

 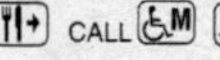 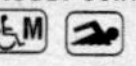    

COURTYARD BY MARRIOTT **Phone:** (435)986-0555

Hotel

$109-$159

AAA Benefit: AAA hotel discounts of 5% or more.

Address: 185 S 1470 E 84790 **Location:** I-15 exit 8, just e, just s, then just e. **Facility:** 131 units. 4 stories, interior corridors. **Amenities:** high-speed Internet. **Pool(s):** heated outdoor, heated indoor. **Activities:** whirlpools, exercise room. **Guest Services:** valet and coin laundry, area transportation-within 3 mi. **Free Special Amenities: newspaper and high-speed Internet.** *(See ad this page.)*

 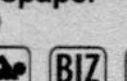  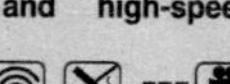 

CRYSTAL INN ST. GEORGE **Phone:** (435)688-7477

Hotel

$79-$139

Address: 1450 S Hilton Dr 84770 **Location:** I-15 exit 6 (Bluff St), just w. **Facility:** 101 units. 2 stories, interior corridors. **Pool(s):** heated outdoor. **Activities:** sauna, whirlpool, 3 lighted tennis courts, basketball, exercise room. **Guest Services:** valet and coin laundry. ***(See ad p. 408.)***

 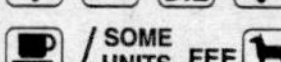

DIXIE PALM MOTEL **Phone:** (435)673-3531

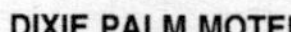

Motel

$29-$89

Address: 185 E St. George Blvd 84770 **Location:** I-15 exit 8, 0.9 mi w; downtown. **Facility:** 15 units, some two bedrooms and kitchens. 1 story, exterior corridors. **Free Special Amenities: high-speed Internet.**

GREEN GATE VILLAGE HISTORIC INN

Phone: (435)628-6999

Historic Bed & Breakfast

$99-$259

Address: 76 W Tabernacle St 84770 **Location:** I-15 exit 8, 2 mi w to Main St, just left, then just right. **Facility:** Eight 1800s-era houses make up this property, which features many antique furnishings; smoking is permitted outdoors only. 12 units, some two bedrooms, efficiencies, cabins and cottages. 2 stories (no elevator), interior/exterior corridors. **Terms:** 7 day cancellation notice-fee imposed. **Pool(s):** heated outdoor. **Activities:** whirlpool.

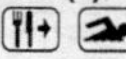     

THE GREEN VALLEY SPA & RESORT

Phone: (435)628-8060

Resort Hotel

$149-$650

Address: 1871 W Canyon View Dr 84770 **Location:** Jct Bluff and S Main sts, 4 mi sw via Hilton Dr to Dixie Dr, then just w to Canyon View Dr. **Facility:** A refuge from the outside world, the rooms are designed with the luxury and comfort of the guest in mind. 50 units, some two bedrooms, efficiencies and kitchens. 1 story, exterior corridors. **Parking:** on-site and valet. **Terms:** check-in 5 pm, 3 night minimum stay - weekends, 3 day cancellation notice-fee imposed. **Amenities:** safes. **Pool(s):** 6 heated outdoor, heated indoor. **Activities:** sauna, whirlpools, putting green, 14 tennis courts (4 indoor, 6 lighted), racquetball courts, recreation programs, hiking trails, jogging, playground, basketball, game room, horseshoes, shuffleboard, volleyball, spa. *Fee:* miniature golf. **Guest Services:** valet laundry, area transportation (fee)-within 15 mi. **Free Special Amenities: full breakfast and high-speed Internet.**

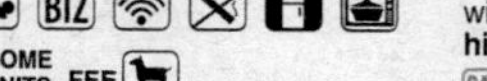  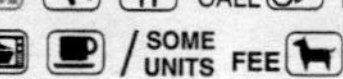

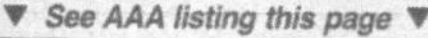

▼ *See AAA listing this page* ▼

HAMPTON INN **Phone:** 435/652-1200

Motel

Rates not provided

AAA Benefit: Members save up to 10% everyday!

Address: 53 N River Rd 84790 **Location:** I-15 exit 8, just e. **Facility:** 124 units. 4 stories, interior corridors. **Amenities:** video games (fee). **Pool(s):** heated outdoor, heated indoor. **Activities:** whirlpools, exercise room. **Guest Services:** valet and coin laundry, area transportation-within city.

CALL     FEE 

HILTON GARDEN INN **Phone:** 435/634-4100

Hotel

Rates not provided

AAA Benefit: Unparalleled hospitality at a special Member rate.

Address: 1731 S Convention Center Dr 84790 **Location:** I-15 exit 6 (Bluff St), just e, then s. **Facility:** 150 units, some two bedrooms. 5 stories, interior corridors. **Amenities:** video games (fee), high-speed Internet. **Pool(s):** heated outdoor. **Activities:** whirlpool, exercise room. **Guest Services:** valet and coin laundry.

CALL FEE

HOWARD JOHNSON INN Phone: (435)628-8000

Motel
$44-$113

Address: 1040 S Main St 84770 **Location:** I-15 exit 6 (Bluff St), just w, then just e. **Facility:** 52 units, some two bedrooms and kitchens. 2 stories (no elevator), exterior corridors. **Terms:** cancellation fee imposed. **Amenities:** safes. **Pool(s):** heated outdoor. **Activities:** whirlpool. **Guest Services:** valet and coin laundry. **Free Special Amenities: expanded continental breakfast and high-speed Internet.**

SAVE FEE / SOME UNITS FEE

LA QUINTA INN & SUITES - ST. GEORGE Phone: (435)674-2664

Hotel
$71-$179

Address: 91 E 2680 S 84790 **Location:** I-15 exit 4, just e on Brigham Rd. **Facility:** 104 units. 3 stories, interior corridors. **Amenities:** high-speed Internet. **Pool(s):** heated outdoor. **Activities:** whirlpool, exercise room. **Guest Services:** valet and coin laundry.

CALL FEE / SOME UNITS

LEXINGTON HOTEL Phone: (435)628-4235

Hotel
$79-$199

Address: 850 S Bluff St 84770 **Location:** I-15 exit 6 (Bluff St), just w. **Facility:** 164 units. 2 stories, interior/exterior corridors. **Terms:** cancellation fee imposed. **Pool(s):** heated indoor/outdoor. **Activities:** whirlpool, playground, game room, exercise room. **Guest Services:** valet and coin laundry, area transportation-within 5 mi.

BIZ / SOME UNITS FEE

QUALITY INN ST. GEORGE Phone: 435/628-4481

Motel
Rates not provided

Address: 1165 S Bluff St 84770 **Location:** I-15 exit 6 (Bluff St), just w. **Facility:** 96 units. 2 stories (no elevator), exterior corridors. **Pool(s):** heated outdoor. **Activities:** whirlpool. **Guest Services:** coin laundry.

BIZ / SOME UNITS FEE

RAMADA Phone: (435)628-2828

Motel
$69-$139

Address: 1440 E St. George Blvd 84790 **Location:** I-15 exit 8, just e. Adjacent to factory outlet stores. **Facility:** 136 units. 2-3 stories, interior corridors. **Pool(s):** heated outdoor. **Activities:** whirlpool. **Guest Services:** valet laundry.

/ SOME UNITS FEE

RED CLIFFS INN & SUITES Phone: 435/673-3537

Hotel
Rates not provided

Address: 912 W Red Cliffs Dr 84780 **Location:** I-15 exit 10, just e. **Facility:** 75 units. 2 stories (no elevator), interior/exterior corridors. **Amenities:** *Some:* high-speed Internet. **Pool(s):** heated outdoor. **Activities:** whirlpool. **Guest Services:** coin laundry.

/ SOME UNITS FEE

SEVEN WIVES INN Phone: (435)628-3737

Historic Bed & Breakfast
$99-$195

Address: 217 N 100 W 84770 **Location:** I-15 exit 8, 2.1 mi w, then n. **Facility:** The property consists of two adjacent two-story homes, both with historic status. 13 units, some cottages. 3 stories (no elevator), interior/exterior corridors. **Terms:** 7 day cancellation notice-fee imposed. **Pool(s):** outdoor. **Activities:** *Fee:* massage.

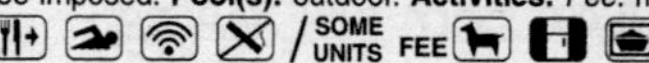

TOWNEPLACE SUITES BY MARRIOTT
Phone: (435)986-9955

Extended Stay Hotel
$109-$159

AAA Benefit: AAA hotel discounts of 5% or more.

Address: 251 S 1470 E 84790 **Location:** I-15 exit 8, just e. **Facility:** 84 kitchen units, some two bedrooms. 3 stories, interior corridors. **Amenities:** high-speed Internet. **Pool(s):** heated outdoor. **Activities:** whirlpool, exercise room. **Guest Services:** valet and coin laundry. **Free Special Amenities: continental breakfast and high-speed Internet.**

SAVE CALL BIZ / SOME UNITS FEE

WINGATE BY WYNDHAM Phone: (435)673-9608

Hotel
$89-$161

Address: 144 W Brigham Rd, Bldg G 84790 **Location:** I-15 exit 4, just w. **Facility:** 77 units. 4 stories, interior corridors. **Amenities:** high-speed Internet, safes. **Pool(s):** heated outdoor. **Activities:** whirlpool, exercise room. **Guest Services:** valet and coin laundry, area transportation-within 6 mi.

CALL BIZ FEE

WHERE TO EAT

AHI'S "TASTE OF ASIA" Phone: 435/673-6604

Asian
$6-$12

AAA Inspector Notes: In a small shopping center, this little Asian restaurant has its guests order food and pay at the same time. They then grab a seat in the contemporary dining area and wait for items to be brought to the table. Offerings include sesame scallops, orange chicken and beef fried rice. **Address:** 157 Riverside Dr, Unit 2E 84790 **Location:** I-15 exit 6 (Bluff St), just e.

L D

ANASAZI STEAKHOUSE & GALLERY
Phone: 435/674-0095

Steak
$10-$34

AAA Inspector Notes: Guests enjoy great steaks cooked on stones at the table, as well as cheese and dessert fondues, in an art gallery setting. In the dining area are photographs by William Carr and metal works by Darrick Phallon, all of which are available for purchase. **Bar:** beer & wine. **Address:** 1234 W Sunset Blvd 84770 **Location:** Jct N Bluff St, 0.5 mi w. D

BEAR PAW COFFEE CO Phone: 435/634-0126

Breakfast
$7-$11

AAA Inspector Notes: Gourmet coffees and teas are offered at this popular local place. Food specialties include homemade soup, sandwiches and early dinner specials, all served in large portions. **Address:** 75 N Main St 84770 **Location:** Downtown. B L

BENJA THAI & SUSHI Phone: 435/628-9538

Asian
$12-$18

AAA Inspector Notes: Diners savor many sushi items and Thai dishes prepared with fresh herbs in the calm and peaceful dining room. The staff is helpful and friendly. **Bar:** beer & wine. **Address:** 2 W St. George Blvd, Suite 12 84770 **Location:** Jct Main St. L D

FAIRWAY GRILL **Phone:** 435/656-4448

American
$8-$21

AAA Inspector Notes: The restaurant is open every day for breakfast, lunch and dinner. An extensive menu is offered, as is some patio seating. **Bar:** beer & wine. **Address:** 430 E St. George Blvd 84770 **Location:** I-15 exit 8, 0.6 mi w. B L D

THE GUN BARREL STEAK & GAME HOUSE **Phone:** 435/652-0550

Steak
$8-$35

AAA Inspector Notes: The sister restaurant of the original Wyoming restaurant, this place originally functioned as a wild game museum. Lending to the log cabin décor are deer, hog, buffalo and other trophies along the walls. Before a meal of juicy steak or game, diners may wish to visit the large lounge to grab a drink. **Bar:** full bar. **Address:** 1091 N Bluff St, Suite 1400 84770 **Location:** I-15 exit 8, 1.8 mi w, then 1.2 mi n. D

IGGY'S SPORTS GRILL **Phone:** 435/673-3344

American
$7-$18

AAA Inspector Notes: A lively atmosphere, good casual food and large-screen TVs make outposts of this small chain great places to watch the game. The menu consists mostly of pub grub burgers, BLTs and rib-eye steaks. **Bar:** full bar. **Address:** 148 S 1470 E 84770 **Location:** I-15 exit 8, just e. L D

MADE IN BRAZIL BRAZILIAN STEAKHOUSE **Phone:** 435/688-2026

Brazilian
$11-$20

AAA Inspector Notes: The comfortable restaurant has a buffet in the center where guests gather salads and sides. A team of servers then come to the table with long skewers of steak, top sirloin, pork tenderloin, chicken and even grilled pineapple. This is the perfect place for meat lovers. **Bar:** beer & wine. **Address:** 929 W Sunset Blvd 84770 **Location:** Jct Bluff St, just w. L D

MONGOLIAN BBQ **Phone:** 435/656-1880

Asian
$5-$12

AAA Inspector Notes: At this unusual restaurant, guests choose their own noodles and the ingredients to go along with it before the chef stir-fries it in front of them. The décor is basic, but the staff is friendly and helpful. **Address:** 250 N Red Cliffs Dr, Suite 3 84790 **Location:** I-15 exit 6 (Bluff St), just e, then just n; in The Outlets at Zion. L D

OSAKA JAPANESE BISTRO **Phone:** 435/656-1314

Japanese
$8-$17

AAA Inspector Notes: Small, with contemporary décor, the bistro serves many fresh sushi items, teriyaki, tofu and tempura veggie dishes. Guests can sit at the small sushi bar or in the main dining room. **Bar:** beer & wine. **Address:** 42 S River Rd, Suite 11 84790 **Location:** I-15 exit 8, just e, then just s. L D

PAINTED PONY RESTAURANT **Phone:** 435/634-1700

American
$9-$35

AAA Inspector Notes: The restaurant is adorned with contemporary Southwestern art and fresh flowers. The menu blends fresh ingredients and delicate flavorings. A simple but varied wine list is available. **Bar:** full bar. **Reservations:** suggested. **Address:** 2 W St. George Blvd 84770 **Location:** I-15 exit 8, at Main St; in Ancestor Square. L D

THE PASTA FACTORY **Phone:** 435/674-3753

Italian
$6-$14

AAA Inspector Notes: Downtown in Ancestor's Square, this popular restaurant offers such traditional pasta choices as spaghetti, chicken fettuccine and bow-tie pasta with shrimp. Patrons also can make their own varieties. Those who prefer pizza to pasta can bring over a pie from the pizza factory just next door. **Address:** 2 W St. George Blvd 84770 **Location:** Jct Main St; downtown; in Ancestor Square. L D

PAULA'S CAZUELA MEXICAN FOOD **Phone:** 435/673-6568

Mexican
$6-$18

AAA Inspector Notes: Views of the city are nice from the casual restaurant, where patrons gather to enjoy attentive, friendly service and traditional Mexican cuisine, including daily lunch specials. **Bar:** beer & wine. **Address:** 745 Ridgeview Dr 84770 **Location:** I-15 exit 6 (Bluff St), 2.5 mi nw. L D

PLAYERS SPORTS GRILL **Phone:** 435/634-9211

American
$8-$20

AAA Inspector Notes: The upscale sports grill offers a range of pub grub, pasta dishes, steaks and specialty items. Guests can watch the big-game action on many large flat-screen TVs as the friendly staff does its thing. **Bar:** full bar. **Address:** 1688 S Convention Center Dr 84770 **Location:** I-15 exit 6 (Bluff St), just e. L D

SAMURAI 21 **Phone:** 435/656-8628

Japanese
$8-$24

AAA Inspector Notes: In a busy shopping center, this restaurant employs talented chefs who prepare Japanese food in front of guests at hibachi tables. On the other side of the dining room, patrons can experience a more Americanized style of dining. **Bar:** beer & wine. **Address:** 245 N Red Cliff Dr, Suite 11 84790 **Location:** I-15 exit 8, just e; in Promenade at Red Cliffs Plaza. L D

SALINA pop. 2,489

SCENIC HILLS SUPER 8 **Phone:** (435)529-7483

Motel
$54-$90

Address: 375 E 1620 S 84654 **Location:** I-70 exit 56, just n. Adjacent to a truck stop. **Facility:** 69 units, some two bedrooms and kitchens. 2 stories (no elevator), exterior corridors. **Parking:** winter plug-ins. **Pool(s):** heated outdoor. **Guest Services:** coin laundry. **Free Special Amenities: expanded continental breakfast and high-speed Internet.**

SAVE / SOME UNITS FEE

WHERE TO EAT

EL MEXICANO **Phone:** 435/529-2132

Mexican
$5-$13

AAA Inspector Notes: Although it may take 15 minutes for the soup to arrive, it's worth the wait at this attractively decorated place. The authentic taste of Mexico can be found in the steak, chicken, shrimp or pork fajitas and tamales. Beans and fresh rice are served with the more than 25 specialty dinners and 30 combination platters, including mole poblano, carne asada, chili verde, crab enchiladas and coconut shrimp. The sampler appetizer offers plenty of flavors to take the edge off a party's hunger. **Address:** 1425 S State St 84654 **Location:** I-70 exit 56, just n. L D

Salt Lake City

Then & Now

Founded by Mormons in 1847, Salt Lake City—today the cultural and ecclesiastical as well as the political capital of Utah—lies in a spectacular setting at the foot of the Wasatch Mountains, with the Great Salt Lake visible to the northwest and the Great Salt Lake Desert to the west.

Like many earlier American settlers, adherents of The Church of Jesus Christ of Latter-day Saints (who often are referred to as Mormons) traveled across the country in search of a place where they could practice their religion without persecution. As these Mormon pioneers approached the Salt Lake Valley for the first time, their leader, Brigham Young, proclaimed, "This is the right place."

In 1850, following a failed petition by the settlers for their "State of Deseret" to be recognized by the U.S. government, Congress established the Utah Territory, with Salt Lake City later named as its capital. A few years after Utah joined the Union in 1896, the decorous Corinthian-style State Capitol was built. Set on a lush site showcasing plants native to the region, the seat of government spotlights Utah's history, people and values in its masterful design.

Still, many of the city's finest buildings are ecclesiastical, and some of its most striking houses were once occupied by Young and his family. With streets designed to be "wide enough for a team of four oxen and a covered wagon to turn around," Salt Lake was laid out in a grid pattern fanning out from what is now known as Temple Square.

The three-block area is home to the most prominent LDS Church edifices. Today, both clued-in and inexperienced sightseers have this square on their list of must-sees, as evidenced by the two visitor centers located here. Most trip itineraries include a tour of the dome-shaped Salt Lake Tabernacle on Temple Square. Outside the Salt Lake Temple, amateur photographers feverishly snap pictures of the dazzling multi-spired edifice, an active and highly revered place of worship whose interior is closed to the public.

The Dazzling Exterior of Salt Lake Temple

South Temple Street has a large concentration of 19th- and early 20th-century designs, including the Gothic-style Cathedral of the Madeleine, completed in 1909, and the 1901 Thomas Kearns Mansion. Architectural evidence of Salt Lake City's mining wealth around the turn of the 20th century can be seen during guided tours at the latter, now the governor's mansion; phone (801) 538-1005.

The Brigham Young Monument, a tribute to the second president of the Mormon Church and the first territorial

(Continued on p. 413.)

Destination Salt Lake City

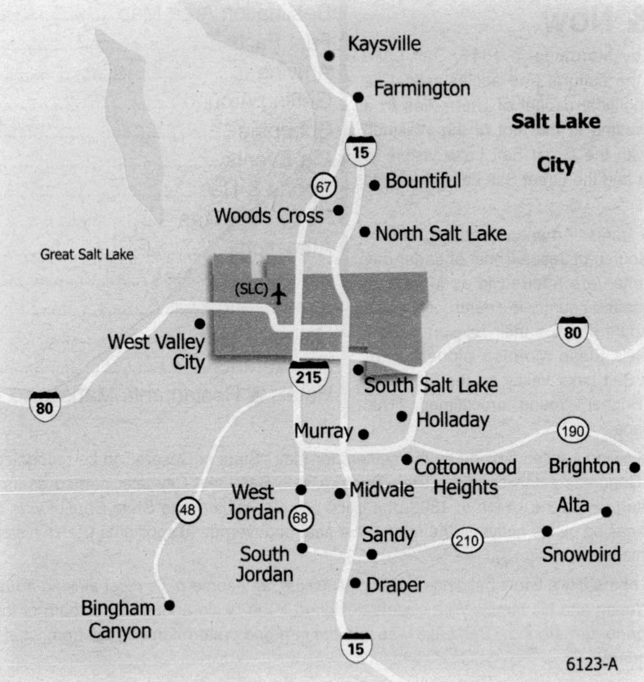

This map shows cities in the Salt Lake City vicinity where you will find attractions, hotels and restaurants. Cities are listed alphabetically in this book on the following pages.

Fast Facts

ABOUT THE CITY

POP: 186,440 ▪ **ELEV:** 4,390 ft.

MONEY

SALES TAX: The sales tax in Salt Lake County is 6.85 percent. There also is a 4.75 percent tax on lodgings in Salt Lake County, 9.5 percent levied on automobile rentals and a 1 percent restaurant tax.

WHOM TO CALL

EMERGENCY: 911

POLICE (non-emergency): (801) 799-3000

HOSPITALS: LDS Hospital, (801) 408-1100 ▪ Salt Lake Regional Medical Center, (801) 350-4111 ▪ University Health Care, (801) 581-2121.

WHERE TO LOOK AND LISTEN

NEWSPAPERS: The *Salt Lake Tribune* and the *Deseret News* are the city's daily morning newspapers.

RADIO: Salt Lake City radio station KSL (1160 AM/102.7 FM) is an all-news radio station ▪ KCPW (88.3 FM) and KUER (90.1 FM) are members of National Public Radio.

VISITOR INFORMATION

Salt Lake City Visitor Information Center: 90 S. West Temple, Salt Lake City, UT 84101-1406. **Phone:** (801) 534-4900 or (800) 541-4955.

TRANSPORTATION

AIR TRAVEL: Salt Lake City International Airport (SLC), 7 miles west of the downtown area, is accessible from I-80. Driving time is approximately 10 minutes. Most Salt Lake City hotels offer free shuttle service to and from the airport. Average taxi fare from the airport to the city is $17; limousine fare averages $35 per person.

Canyon Transportation provides car and van service from Salt Lake International Airport to hotels and resorts in Alta, Brighton, Park City, Sundance and other destinations throughout the Salt Lake Valley; phone (801) 255-1841 or (800) 255-1841.

RENTAL CARS: Hertz, 775 N. Terminal Dr. at the airport, offers discounts to AAA members; phone (801) 575-2683 or (800) 654-3080. For listings of other agencies check the telephone directory.

RAIL SERVICE: The Amtrak station is at 340 South 600 West; phone (800) 872-7245.

BUSES: The Greyhound Lines Inc. terminal is at 300 South 600 West; phone (801) 355-9579 or (800) 231-2222 or TTY (800) 345-3109.

TAXIS: Taxis are on the meter system. Cab companies include City Cab, (801) 363-8400 ▪ Ute Cab, (801) 359-7788 ▪ and Yellow Cab, (801) 521-1862.

PUBLIC TRANSPORTATION: Utah Transit Authority (UTA) provides bus service for Salt Lake City as well as transportation to nearby ski areas. Salt Lake City's light rail system, TRAX, also is operated by UTA. The SLC/Sandy Line (blue line) runs from downtown south to Sandy; a one-way trip takes approximately 38 minutes. The Mid-Jordan/University Line (red line) connects downtown with Jordan and the University of Utah campus. The West Valley Line (green line) connects downtown with West Valley City. TRAX arrives at stations within 10-30 minutes. In addition, the FrontRunner commuter rail line connects downtown with Ogden, and a high-speed MAX bus links the Millcreek TRAX station with the town of Magna.

One-way fare, valid on buses and light rail, is $2.25 (ages 6-64); $1.10 (ages 65+). Round-trip fare is $4.50. A 1-day pass is $5.50. A round-trip group pass is $12 (up to four people). All fares include a fuel surcharge. Exact change is required.

When traveling within the Free Ride Zone, located downtown from North Temple to 500 South and 400 West to 200 East and including the TRAX library station and the bus stops between 200 East and 300 East on 400 South, passengers may use either the buses or light rail for free, but boarding and unloading must occur within the defined area. Phone (801) 287-4636 for information about either system.

(Continued from p. 411.)

governor of Utah, is on the corner of South Temple and Main streets. On its north face, a bronze plaque lists the Mormon pioneers who arrived here on July 24, 1847; their predecessors, Native Americans and enterprising fur trappers, also are commemorated with two bronze figures at the monument's base.

One of Salt Lake City's most interesting structures is the Eagle Gate, erected in 1859 as the entrance to Young's private farm. Spanning State Street in front of the Beehive House, the giant four-legged arch is surmounted by a 4,000-pound bronze statue of an eagle with a wingspread of 20 feet. The gate has been remodeled several times; the original copper-plated eagle, which has a wingspread of 16 feet, is in the Pioneer Memorial Museum on Main Street.

A more modern architectural showpiece is the Salt Palace, an integral part of the city's cultural scene. Officially the Calvin L. Rampton Salt Palace Convention Center, the complex at 90 S. West Temple St. includes Abravanel Hall, the home of the Utah Symphony, and the Salt Lake Art Center.

Arriving

By Car

Salt Lake City is sometimes called the "Crossroads of the West" due to its easy access. I-15 crosses through Salt Lake City in a north-south direction, while I-80 cuts through the city carrying traffic east and west. I-215 provides a loop around all but the northeastern quadrant of the city. US 89 (State Street) is a major north-south thoroughfare, with the State Capitol as its northern terminus. An alternate east-west route through the city is 2100 South Street.

Getting Around

Street System

Getting around Salt Lake City is not difficult once you know how the street system works. Salt Lake City is based on a grid system. Temple Square in downtown Salt Lake is the center of the grid and is the point at which all numbering begins. Addresses in Salt Lake City usually consist of two numbers. For example, the AAA office is at 560 East 500 South. This means that the office is 5 blocks south of the temple and slightly more than 5 blocks east of the temple. Another way of stating this is 560 East on 500 South. Locals tend to drop the last two zeros when giving directions; thus 500 South becomes 5th South. Some streets have a name as well as a number, but most have numbers only.

Parking

Metered parking is available throughout the city, with a 2-hour limit at most meters. After 6 p.m. metered parking is free. Parking is available at the Firestone Building, 175 West 200 South and through Ampco System Parking at various locations; phone (801) 364-7275. Fees range from $3-$5 (hourly rate) to $5-$10 (daily rate).

Spend an Afternoon Shopping at The Gateway

Shopping

Downtown shopping mainstays Crossroads Plaza, bounded by S. Main, South Temple and West Temple streets, and ZCMI Center Mall, across from Temple Square on S. State Street, closed in early 2007 to make way for the creation of a new mixed-use downtown district, City Creek Center, which will combine retail, office and residential development. The malls' anchor stores, Macy's and Nordstrom, will reopen as part of the new area in 2013.

The Gateway, located on South 400 West, features a restored 1908 Union Pacific Depot with French Renaissance architecture and original artwork. In addition to more than 130 stores and restaurants, the area also offers the "dancing waters" of the Olympic Snowflake Fountain at the Olympic Legacy Plaza; phone (801) 456-2000.

Gardner Village, 1100 West 7800 South in West Jordan, consists of historic cabins and homes from sites throughout Utah that now house old-time stores offering furniture, accessories and collectibles; phone (801) 566-8903. The Old Gardner Mill also is featured.

Trolley Square, on 700 East between 500 and 600 South streets, is in a 1908 trolley barn built by railroad magnate E.H. Harriman. The plants, trolley cars, stained-glass windows and antique lighting fixtures create a nostalgic atmosphere. Shops, restaurants and theaters line the mall; some of the businesses are housed in refurbished trolley cars, while the exteriors of others resemble Victorian mansions; phone (801) 521-9877. Self-guiding walking tours are available.

Area malls include Fashion Place Mall, with 110 stores and restaurants at 6191 S. State St. in Murray, counts Dillard's, Macy's, Nordstrom and Sears as its anchors. South Towne Center, with a carousel in the mall's center, claims the title of largest mall in the state. At 10450 S. State St. in Sandy, its 130 stores include Dillard's, JCPenney and Macy's; phone (801) 572-1516. Valley Fair Mall, 3601 South 2700 West, lists JCPenney and Macy's among its 100 retailers; phone (801) 969-6211.

Big Events

Proud of their heritage, Salt Lake City residents celebrate it throughout the year. The Days of '47 Celebration in July commemorates the arrival of the Mormon pioneers in the Salt Lake Valley. A week of community festivities, which includes a rodeo and a fireworks display, ends with floats, bands, horse brigades, clowns and dignitaries marching down Main Street in the Days of '47 Parade.

Other events include the Utah Arts Festival in late June; the Salt Lake City International Jazz Festival in early July; the Utah State Fair and the Greek Festival, both in September; the GEM Christmas Lighting of Temple Square after Thanksgiving; and Pioneer

Calvin L. Rampton Salt Palace Convention Center

Christmas Days over 2 weekends in early December. The New Year's Eve First Night Celebration of the Arts concludes the year's festivities as residents of all ages join to usher in the new year.

Sports & Rec

Salt Lake City is known for its variety of year-round sports and recreational opportunities. Perhaps most prominent are the major **ski** resorts located within 45 minutes of the Salt Lake City airport. Little Cottonwood and Big Cottonwood canyons are home to Snowbird, Alta, Brighton and Solitude Mountain ski resorts. Parleys Canyon is where snow falls on the Park City Resort. With snowfall in excess of 400 inches per year, snow is fresh and falls often. **Snowmobiling** and **cross-country skiing** also are abundant along the Wasatch Front. Nearby local mountains also offer **mountain biking.**

Summer activities include both indoor and outdoor sports. Favorite **golf** courses include Bonneville, Bountiful Ridge, The Country Club, Davis Park, Eaglewood, Glendale, Glenmoor, Jordan River, Mountain Dell, Nibley Park, Old Mill, Rose Park, University of Utah, West Ridge and Wingpointe. Information and reservations for most of these courses can be made by phoning the Utah Golf Association at (801) 563-0400.

Bicycling in the mountains or valleys is a popular activity; trails follow the Jordan River, which runs through Salt Lake County. **Hiking, camping** and **fishing** in and around the city also are favorite pastimes. Along Canyon Road in the northeast section of the city is City Creek Canyon, a favorite recreational area for hikers, joggers, picnickers and bicyclists. Reservations must be made to drive through or to picnic beyond the main gate, and a fee for picnicking is charged; phone the Watershed Management Division, (801) 483-6797. On even-numbered days the park is closed to cyclists and joggers; on odd-numbered days the park is closed to all motorized vehicles.

Three large reservoirs provide opportunities for **boating** and water sports. Public **tennis** courts are available in many parks, including Liberty and Murray. Antelope Island State Park offers sand beaches and **swimming.** The park, about a 30-minute drive north of Salt Lake City, is reachable via a causeway.

The 20,500-seat EnergySolutions Arena at 300 West and South Temple streets is the home of the NBA's Utah Jazz; phone (801) 325-2500. **Baseball** is represented by the Salt Lake Bees, the AAA farm team of the Los Angeles Angels of Anaheim. Games are played at Spring Mobile Ballpark at 77 West 1300 South; phone (801) 350-6900. **Hockey** fans attend the games of the Utah Grizzlies of the ECHL. Their rink, the Maverik Center, is at 3200 S. Decker Lake Dr. in West Valley City; phone (801) 988-7825, or (801) 988-8000 for the box office.

Performing Arts

The Salt Palace (officially the Calvin L. Rampton Salt Palace Convention Center), 90 S. West Temple, serves as Salt Lake City's cultural center; phone (801) 534-4777. Performances of the Utah Symphony are held in Abravanel Hall, located within the Salt Palace complex at 123 W. South Temple. Self-guiding tours of the Salt Palace and related buildings are available, as are guided tours of Abravanel Hall; phone (801) 534-6324.

Capitol Theater, nearby at 50 West 200 South, is the home of Ballet West, which stages both classical and modern works. The theater, which has been restored to its original turn-of-the-20th-century opulence, also is the home of Utah Opera productions. Phone ArtTix at (801) 355-2787; or (888) 451-2787 or TTY (801) 328-8202 for symphony, ballet or opera tickets. The Mormon Tabernacle Choir presents free weekly performances of inspirational music and thought in the acoustically unique Salt Lake Tabernacle on Temple Square *(see attraction listing p. 419).*

Pioneer Theatre Company, Utah's resident professional theater, is located on the University of Utah campus. The company presents musicals as well as classical and contemporary plays; for ticket information phone (801) 581-6961.

Dance in Salt Lake City is represented by Repertory Dance Theatre, which stages American modern dance classics and contemporary masterpieces at 138 West 300 South, and the Ririe-Woodbury Dance Company, a modern dance touring company performs at the Rose Wagner Performing Arts Center and Capitol Theater. Phone the Repertory Dance Theater at (801) 534-1000 or ArtTix at (801)

355-2787, (888) 451-2787 or TTY (801) 328-8202 for Rose Wagner Performing Arts Center tickets.

INSIDER INFO:
Mormonism

Joseph Smith Jr., the son of a poor upstate New York farmer, is said to have received a visit in 1827 from the angel Moroni. Smith said the angel, who was the son of the prophet Mormon, entrusted him with golden plates inscribed with symbols, which Smith translated into the Book of Mormon.

The name of the church, which began in 1830, is The Church of Jesus Christ of Latter-day Saints, or LDS Church; "Mormon" is a nickname. Mormons believe that Jesus Christ is the son of God and that divine revelation did not end with the disciples, but continues today. They place strong emphasis on the family and rely on the leadership of lay members rather than professional clergy.

Smith advocated polygamy and was plurally married himself. Although no more than 4 percent of the Mormon population practiced polygamy at any time, advocacy of it led to strife with non-Mormons wherever the Mormons settled. Smith had designated Missouri as Zion, but persecution there forced the Mormons to move to Illinois, where they established the city of Nauvoo. Smith was arrested and jailed in neighboring towns; in 1844 he was shot to death by a mob which stormed Carthage City Jail.

Soon after Smith's death the church split into two factions. Mormons who rejected polygamy formed a "Reorganized Church" and returned to Missouri. A larger group followed Brigham Young to Utah in 1847, establishing Salt Lake City. Although Utah Mormons applied for statehood as early as 1849, their request was not granted until 1896, after the church abolished polygamy.

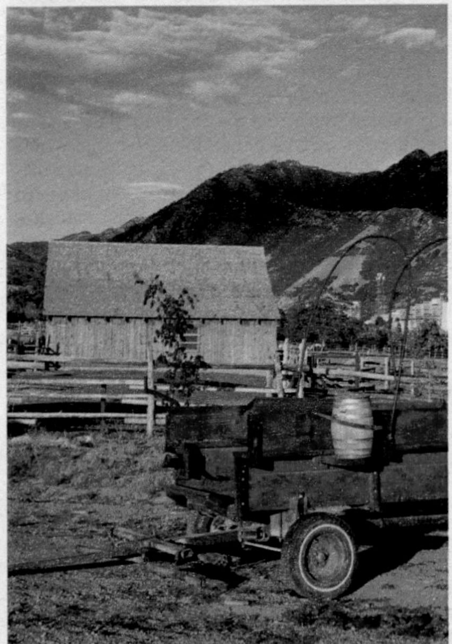

Experience Living History at "This Is The Place" Heritage Park

ATTRACTIONS

BEEHIVE HOUSE is at 67 E. South Temple St. The 1854 house, the restored official residence of Brigham Young, the second president of the Mormon Church, is decorated with period furnishings. A beehive, the symbol of industry and a reference to Young's work ethic, sits on top of the house. **Hours:** Half-hour guided tours are given Mon.-Sat. 9:30-8:30. Last tour begins 15 minutes before closing. Closed Christmas. **Cost:** Free. **Phone:** (801) 240-2681.

BRIGHAM YOUNG'S GRAVE is on First Ave. between State and A sts. The Mormon leader died in 1877. Others buried in the small plot include several family members and Eliza R. Snow, a pioneer songwriter. The Mormon Pioneer Memorial Monument, honoring the 6,000 pioneers who perished during their 1847-69 journey to Utah, also is at the site.

CATHEDRAL OF THE MADELEINE is at 331 E. South Temple St. The cathedral was built by the first bishop of Salt Lake City, Bishop Lawrence Scanlon. Begun in 1900, the cathedral is 190 feet long, 100 feet wide and has two towers 220 feet high. The Gothic interior has Venetian mosaics and Tennessee marble, three main altars of Utah marble and wall niches with oak statues. Above each altar is a painting of St. Mary Magdalene. **Time:** Allow 1 hour minimum. **Hours:** Mon.-Fri. 7:30 a.m.-9 p.m., Sat.-Sun. 7:30-7:30. Guided tours are given Sun. at 12:30. Phone ahead to confirm schedule. **Cost:** Free. **Phone:** (801) 328-8941.

CHURCH HISTORY MUSEUM is at 45 N. West Temple St. Parking is available at 103 N. West Temple St. The museum chronicles the history of Mormonism from 1820 to the present through interpretive exhibits, films and demonstrations. Displays include memorabilia, sculpture and paintings from around the world as well as changing exhibits. Guided tours are available by appointment.

Time: Allow 30 minutes minimum. **Hours:** Mon.-Fri. 9-9, Sat.-Sun. 10-7, holidays 9-5. Closed Jan. 1, Easter, Thanksgiving, Christmas Eve and Christmas. **Cost:** Free. **Phone:** (801) 240-3310 for recorded information, or (801) 240-4615 for tour reservations.

THE CHURCH OFFICE BUILDING, 50 E. North Temple St., houses the Mormon Church's administrative, communications and missionary departments. A mural of Christ and the Apostles occupies a lobby wall. Guided tours include an explanation of the mural and a visit to the 26th-floor observation deck, which offers a panoramic view of the Salt Lake

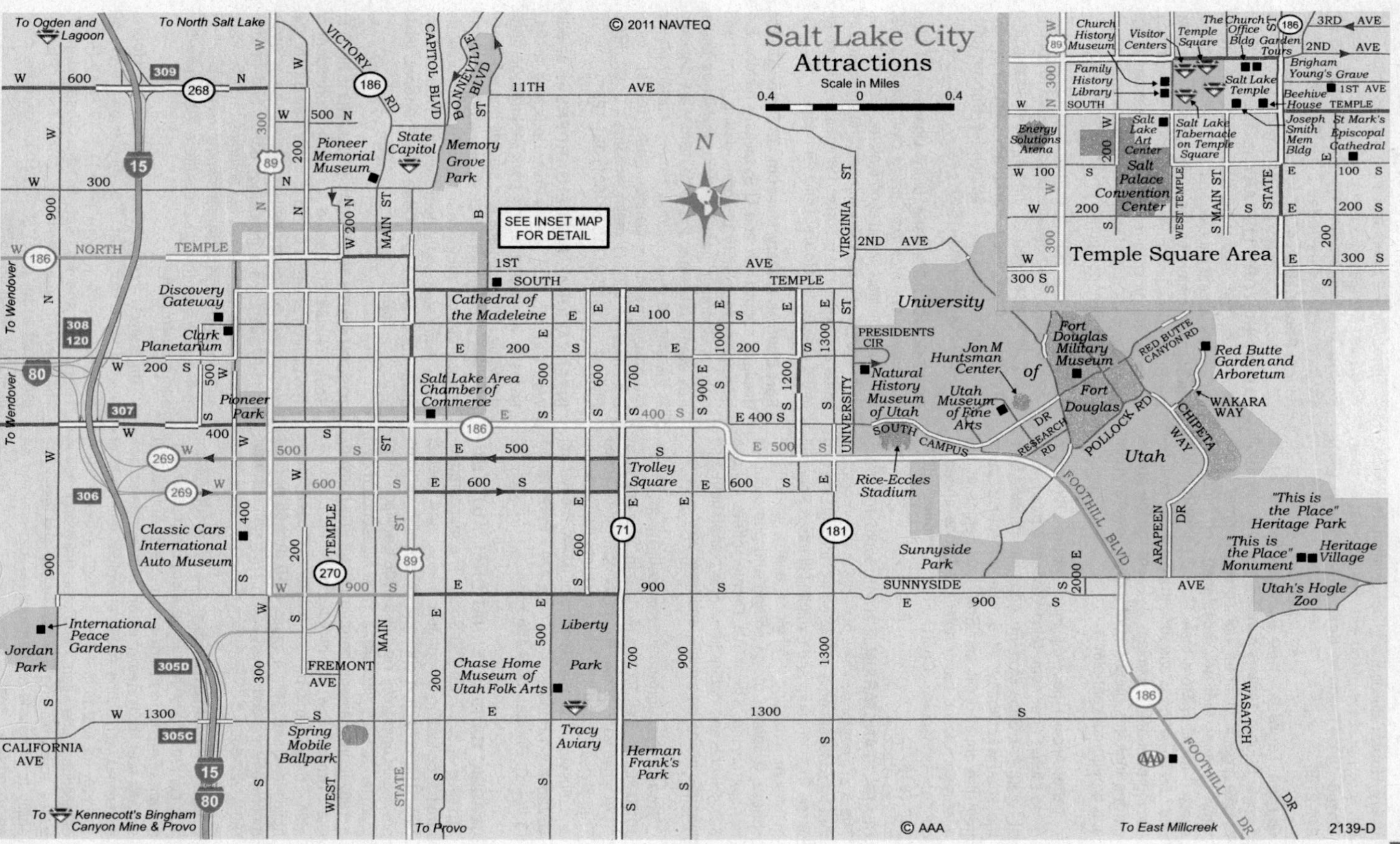

Salt Lake City
Attractions
Scale in Miles
0.4 0 0.4
© 2011 NAVTEQ
© AAA
2139-D
N
SEE INSET MAP FOR DETAIL
Temple Square Area
Church History Museum
Family History Library
Visitor Centers
Temple Square
The Church Office Bldg
Garden Tours
Brigham Young's Grave
Beehive House
Salt Lake Temple
Joseph Smith Mem Bldg
St Mark's Episcopal Cathedral
Salt Lake Tabernacle on Temple Square
Salt Lake Art Center
Salt Palace Convention Center
Energy Solutions Arena
State Capitol
Pioneer Memorial Museum
Memory Grove Park
Cathedral of the Madeleine
Salt Lake Area Chamber of Commerce
Discovery Gateway
Clark Planetarium
Pioneer Park
Classic Cars International Auto Museum
International Peace Gardens
Jordan Park
Spring Mobile Ballpark
Chase Home Museum of Utah Folk Arts
Liberty Park
Tracy Aviary
Herman Frank's Park
Trolley Square
University of Utah
Natural History Museum of Utah
Jon M Huntsman Center
Utah Museum of Fine Arts
Rice-Eccles Stadium
Fort Douglas Military Museum
Fort Douglas
Red Butte Garden and Arboretum
Sunnyside Park
"This is the Place" Heritage Park
"This is the Place" Monument
Heritage Village
Utah's Hogle Zoo
To Ogden and Lagoon
To North Salt Lake
To Wendover
To Kennecott's Bingham Canyon Mine & Provo
To Provo
To East Millcreek
VICTORY RD
CAPITOL BLVD
BONNEVILLE BLVD
11TH AVE
2ND AVE
1ST AVE
3RD AVE
VIRGINIA ST
SOUTH TEMPLE
NORTH TEMPLE
MAIN ST
STATE ST
WEST TEMPLE
PRESIDENTS CIR
UNIVERSITY ST
SOUTH CAMPUS
FOOTHILL BLVD
FOOTHILL DR
WASATCH DR
SUNNYSIDE AVE
ARAPEEN DR
CHIPETA WAY
WAKARA WAY
RED BUTTE CANYON RD
POLLOCK RD
RESEARCH RD
FREMONT AVE
CALIFORNIA AVE

Valley. **Hours:** Building and observation deck Mon.-Fri. 9-5, Apr.-Sept.; Mon.-Fri. 9-4:30, rest of year. Closed major holidays. **Cost:** Free. **Phone:** (801) 240-2190.

Garden Tours is at 50 E. North Temple St. in Temple Square. Visitors may enjoy a leisurely stroll or take a guided tour through spring, summer or autumn gardens that are redesigned and replanted every 6 months. More than 16,500 bedding plants and 250 flower beds surround the plaza, an oval reflecting pool and a fountain. A 4-acre rooftop prairie garden includes hundreds of native flowers, trees and drought-tolerant plants.

Time: Allow 1 hour minimum. **Hours:** Tours are given Mon.-Fri. at noon (also Wed. at 7 p.m.), Sun. at 10:30, Apr.-Sept. Mon.-Fri. noon tour departs from the southwest lobby; Wed. evening tour departs from the south door; and Sun. tour begins at the east gate. Closed major holidays. Phone ahead to confirm schedule. **Cost:** Free. **Phone:** (801) 240-5916.

CLARK PLANETARIUM is at 110 South 400 West. The Star Theater contains high-resolution projectors that take visitors on a simulated trip through the universe. The Museum and Exhibit Hall has a Foucault pendulum, a rotating relief globe, a large lunar hemisphere, a sphere movie screen and photographic transparencies. The IMAX Theater offers various 3-D science and nature films. The planetarium also features hands-on exhibits and laser concerts.

Hours: Planetarium and museum Sun.-Thurs. 10:30-10, Fri.-Sat. 10:30 a.m.-11 p.m. Star and laser show times vary; phone ahead for schedule. Closed Thanksgiving and Christmas. **Cost:** Planetarium and museum free. Star Theater or IMAX Theater $8; $6 (ages 0-12 and to all at matinees). **Parking:** $1 (3 hours). **Phone:** (801) 456-7827.

CLASSIC CARS INTERNATIONAL AUTO MUSEUM is at 355 West 700 South. The museum features a collection of antique, classic and special cars. The collection changes continually; vehicles previously on display include a 1906 Cadillac "Tulip" roadster, a 1936 Packard, a 1929 Duesenberg and a 1957 Ford Fairlane hardtop retractable convertible. **Time:** Allow 30 minutes minimum. **Hours:** Mon.-Fri. 9-3 and by appointment. Closed major holidays. **Cost:** $6; $4 (ages 0-10 and 66+). Free (police officers and emergency personnel). **Phone:** (801) 322-5509.

DISCOVERY GATEWAY is at 444 West 100 South. The contemporary interactive discovery center, encompassing four floors and more than 60,000 square feet, provides children with hands-on exhibits and workshops. Visitors explore the world of science, art and humanities through activities such as piloting a Life Flight helicopter, delivering mail in a kids' town, building a model house and testing its ability to withstand an earthquake, and creating an animated film.

Time: Allow 2 hours minimum. **Hours:** Mon.-Sat. 10-6 (also Fri.-Sat. 6-8 p.m.), Sun. noon-6. Closed Easter, Thanksgiving and Christmas. **Cost:** $8.50; $6 (ages 65+); free (ages 0-1). **Parking:** $1 (3 hours). **Phone:** (801) 456-5437.

FAMILY HISTORY LIBRARY is at 35 N. West Temple St. The library, founded in 1894, is one of the world's largest genealogical libraries. The collection focuses mainly on the United States, Canada, the British Isles and Europe, including Scandinavia, but there are growing records for other areas of the world. Records date 1550-1920. Research tools include microfilm, computers and reference books.

Hours: Tues.-Sat. 8 a.m.-9 p.m., Mon. 8-5. Closes early some holidays; phone ahead to confirm schedule. Closed Jan. 1, July 4, Thanksgiving and Christmas. **Cost:** Free. **Parking:** Available at several lots in the area for $3-$6 per day. **Phone:** (801) 240-2584 or (866) 406-1830.

FORT DOUGLAS is just e. of the University of Utah campus on Wasatch Dr. Spread over 9,000 acres, the former military installation was founded in 1862. Its buildings embrace five architectural styles and include an impressive group of 19th-century red sandstone structures. **Hours:** Daily 24 hours.

Fort Douglas Military Museum, 32 Potter St., has displays about Utah and U.S. military history. Exhibits include military uniforms dating from 1858 through Operation Iraqi Freedom as well as tanks. Key events relating to the fort's history are depicted in the stained glass window panels. Artillery pieces are on display in the Cannon Park. **Hours:** Tues.-Sat. noon-5. Closed major holidays. **Cost:** Free. **Phone:** (801) 581-1710 or (801) 581-1251.

INTERNATIONAL PEACE GARDENS is at 900 West 1000 South in Jordan Park. Dedicated in 1947 to foster world peace, the park features gardens dotted by buildings, flags and statues that reflect the heritage and culture of 26 countries. Among the statues located throughout the park are miniature Eiffel Tower and Matterhorn replicas. **Hours:** Daily dawn-dusk, May-Sept. **Cost:** Free. **Phone:** (801) 938-5326.

JOSEPH SMITH MEMORIAL BUILDING is at 15 E. South Temple St. Named for the first president of The Church of Jesus Christ of Latter-day Saints, the renovated building, which served as a hotel 1911-87, contains a genealogy center and decorative features such as marble columns, art glass and an elegant staircase. Gardens surround the building, and a 500-seat theater presents a 70-minute film about Smith's life.

Time: Allow 1 hour, 30 minutes minimum. **Hours:** Guided tours Mon.-Sat. 9-9. Film shown every 90 minutes. Gardens Mon.-Sat. 11-3:30 (also Mon.-Thurs. 5-9 and Fri.-Sat. 5-10). Closed Jan. 1, Thanksgiving and Christmas. **Cost:** Free. **Phone:** (801) 539-3130, (801) 539-1911 for gardens information or (800) 881-5762.

LIBERTY PARK stretches from 500 to 700 East St. and 900 to 1300 South St. The 100-acre park contains an aviary, a museum featuring Utah folk art, a playground, a pool, tennis courts, the Seven Canyons Fountain, and a seasonal children's amusement park and garden. Paddleboat rentals are available Memorial Day weekend through Labor Day.

Hours: Park open daily 6 a.m.-11 p.m. Pool open daily, June-Aug.; phone ahead for hours. Tennis courts open daily 7-6. Amusement park open daily 11-8, Memorial Day weekend-Labor Day. **Cost:** Park free. Pool $4.50; $3.50 (ages 60+); $3 (ages 3-15); $2 (ages 0-2). Amusement park ride prices vary. **Phone:** (801) 521-0962 for concessions, rides and boats, (801) 328-4711 for the tennis courts, or (801) 486-5867 for the pool.

Chase Home Museum of Utah Folk Arts is in the middle of Liberty Park. In a two-story, 1853 adobe Greek-Revival house, the museum showcases traditional folk art crafted by Utahns. Native art such as baskets, cradleboards and jewelry; ethnic pieces, including origami and piñatas; items that are occupational in nature, such as saddles and spurs; and handmade objects from rural areas, such as rugs and furniture help depict Utah's history and culture.

In addition to its exhibits, the museum also has a collection of recordings and photographs and presents concerts and dances in the park. **Hours:** Mon.-Fri. 8-5. Closed major holidays. **Cost:** Free. **Phone:** (801) 533-5760.

GEM **Tracy Aviary** is at 589 East 1300 South in the s.w. corner of Liberty Park; access is via the park's north entrance off 900 South between 500 East and 700 East. One of the world's oldest public aviaries, it was begun in 1938 by banker Russell Tracy. More than 400 birds from around the world can be seen, including 135 species (some endangered). A free-flying bird show, offered May through August, explains how these creatures live.

Tours: Guided tours are available. **Time:** Allow 2 hours minimum. **Hours:** Daily 9-5. Closed Thanksgiving and Christmas. **Cost:** $7; $6 (ages 65+ and students and military with ID); $5 (ages 3-12). **Phone:** (801) 596-8500.

PIONEER MEMORIAL MUSEUM is w. of the Capitol at 300 N. Main St. The museum is a replica of the old Salt Lake Theater. Displays include doll collections, handmade textiles and 19th-century furniture. The adjacent carriage house contains historic vehicles and antique farm machinery. **Hours:** Mon.-Sat. 9-5, Sun. 1-5, June-Aug.; Mon.-Sat. 9-5, rest of year. **Cost:** Donations. **Phone:** (801) 532-6479.

ST. MARK'S EPISCOPAL CATHEDRAL is at 231 East 100 South. The small 1870 cathedral has thick native sandstone walls and heavy wooden roof trusses. Exquisite stained-glass windows by Louis Comfort Tiffany and painted glass creations by artist Charles Connick are highlights. The 1857 Mirrlees chamber organ, said to be the oldest pipe organ in Utah, was built in Glasgow, Scotland. An Opus 35 tracker organ with three manuals and 40 ranks was installed in 2011. **Hours:** Mon.-Fri. 10-3. **Cost:** Donations. **Phone:** (801) 322-3400.

SALT LAKE ART CENTER is at 20 S. West Temple St. This venue for contemporary art offers five galleries featuring changing exhibitions. **Hours:** Tues.-Sat. 11-6 (also Fri. 6-9 p.m.). Closed major holidays. **Cost:** Donations. **Phone:** (801) 328-4201.

SEVEN PEAKS WATERPARK is at 1200 West 1700 South. The 17-acre water park has heated pools, a water roller coaster, waterslides, a lazy river and the Wild Wave pool. A special children's area offers activities for toddlers. **Hours:** Mon.-Sat. 11-8, Memorial Day-Labor Day. **Cost:** $24.95; $19.95 (under 48 inches tall); $7.95 (nonparticipants); free (ages 0-3 and 65+). After 4 p.m. $15.95. After 6 p.m. $9.95. **Parking:** $5 (full day); $3 (half-day). **Phone:** (801) 972-3300.

GEM **STATE CAPITOL** is at 350 N. Main St. on Capitol Hill. The Corinthian-style structure was built in 1916 of Georgia marble and Utah granite. The top consists of a huge copper-covered dome. Inside are a main hall and rotunda, wall and ceiling murals, a state reception area and exhibits about Utah's 29 counties.

Time: Allow 45 minutes minimum. **Hours:** Capitol open Mon.-Fri. 8-8, Sat.-Sun. 8-6. Guided tours are given on the hour Mon.-Fri. 9-4 (also Wed. at 6 and 7 p.m. by appointment). Closed Jan. 1-2, Easter, Thanksgiving, Christmas Eve, Christmas, day after Christmas and state holidays. **Cost:** Free. **Phone:** (801) 538-1800.

GEM **TEMPLE SQUARE** is bounded by North Temple, South Temple, West Temple and Main sts. This 35-acre, three-block area contains the most prominent buildings of The Church of Jesus Christ of Latter-day Saints, the Seagull Monument and several other memorials and statues, including the Handcart Monument. The 1877 Gothic-style Assembly Hall is the site of free 60-minute concerts; phone ahead for schedule.

Hours: Grounds 9-9. Guided 30-minute tours of the square begin at the north and south gates every 15 minutes daily 9:15-8:15; hours vary for tours on Jan. 1, Mormon Conference days (first Sun. in Apr. and Oct.), Thanksgiving and Christmas. **Cost:** Free. Under 8 are not permitted at Assembly Hall concerts. **Phone:** (801) 240-1245, (801) 240-2534 for Assembly Hall, (801) 240-4872 or (800) 537-9703.

GEM **Salt Lake Tabernacle on Temple Square** is in Temple Square at 50 W. North Temple St. Completed in 1867, the tabernacle seats 6,500 under one of the world's largest domed roofs without center supports. The building has remarkable acoustics, and its 11,623-pipe organ is said to be one of the finest in existence.

The tabernacle has been the home of the renowned Mormon Tabernacle Choir since the group's inception in the mid-19th century. The choir's 360 volunteer singers, all members of The Church of Jesus Christ of Latter-day Saints, practice and perform weekly.

Hours: Tours are given daily 9-8:15; hours vary for tours on Jan. 1, Thanksgiving and Christmas. The choir's public rehearsals are Thurs. 8-9:30 p.m. The choir's weekly live broadcast is Sun. 8:15-10 a.m.; guests for the broadcast must be seated by 9:15 a.m. Organ recitals are held Mon.-Sat. at noon and 2, May.-Sept.; at noon, rest of year. **Cost:** Free. **Phone:** (801) 240-2534.

Salt Lake Temple, in Temple Square, is the symbol of The Church of Jesus Christ of Latter-day Saints and holds the ordinances sacred to the Mormon faith. Begun in 1853 when Brigham Young laid the cornerstone and completed in 1893, the neo-Gothic temple cost $4 million to build. Atop the 210-foot east tower is a gold leaf-covered statue of the Angel Moroni, an angel that Joseph Smith Jr. said visited him on numerous occasions. **Note:** The building is closed to the public.

Visitor Centers are located in the n.w. and s.e. corners of Temple Square. The starry dome of the North Visitor Center is highlighted by an 11-foot-tall statue of Jesus Christ. Exhibits include Old and New Testament murals, a scale model of Jerusalem as it likely appeared during Jesus' lifetime and examples of the church's humanitarian efforts. Three films are shown on a daily basis.

The South Visitor Center features exhibits and artifacts about the construction of the temple and the importance the religion places on the family. **Tours:** Guided tours are available. **Hours:** Both visitor centers open daily 9-9. **Cost:** Free. **Phone:** (801) 240-2534 for the South Visitor Center, or (801) 240-4872 for the North Visitor Center.

"THIS IS THE PLACE" HERITAGE PARK is e. at the mouth of Emigration Canyon at 2601 E. Sunnyside Ave. The 430-acre park includes the This Is The Place Monument commemorating the Mormons' entrance into the valley; the National Pony Express Monument; a number of sculptures that recall Western expansion; and Heritage Village, a recreated 19th-century pioneer settlement. A visitor center has a videotape presentation. **Hours:** Park open Mon.-Sat. 9-5, Sun. 10-5. Visitor center open Mon.-Sat. 9-6, Sun. 10-5. **Cost:** Free. **Phone:** (801) 582-1847.

Heritage Village, e. at the mouth of Emigration Canyon at "This Is The Place" Heritage Park, is a living-history village with more than 40 original and replica structures typical of the 1847-98 Utah pioneer era. Staff and tradesmen in period costumes demonstrate pioneer crafts, trades and homemaking skills. Also included are the Pioneer Playground, the Petting Corral and pony rides. Small-scale trains representing those that completed the transcontinental railroad in Utah in 1869 provide access to the village's facilities.

Time: Allow 1 hour minimum. **Hours:** Daily 9-5. Limited facilities are available on Sun. Phone ahead to confirm schedule. **Cost:** Mon.-Sat., May-Sept., $10; $7 (ages 3-11 and 55+). Daily, Oct.-Apr., and Sun., May-Sept., $5; $3 (ages 3-11 and 55+). Additional fees may be charged during special events. **Phone:** (801) 582-1847.

UNIVERSITY OF UTAH, e. on 400 South to 13th East, then 1 blk. e. to the campus at University St., occupies 1,494 acres overlooking the city. **Tours:** Guided tours are available. **Hours:** The Park Building, which houses the university's administrative offices, is open Mon.-Fri. 8-5. **Phone:** (801) 581-6773, or (800) 685-8856 for guided tour information.

Natural History Museum of Utah is on the University of Utah campus in the Rio Tinto Center at 301 Wakara Way. An active research institution, the museum presents the natural and cultural history of the Great Basin region. Ten themed galleries contain such exhibits as dinosaur skeletons, live insect specimens, and gems and minerals. Hands-on displays, wall murals and multimedia presentations enhance visitors' understanding of Utah's landscapes and people.

On the fourth level of the facility is an indoor-outdoor interpretive space featuring dazzling views of the surrounding Salt Lake Valley. In addition, the museum is located on the Bonneville Shoreline Trail, a developing hiking and biking route that, when complete, will stretch from Nephi to the Idaho border.

Time: Allow 1 hour, 30 minutes minimum. **Hours:** Daily 10-5 (also Wed. 5-9). Last admission 1 hour before closing. Closed Thanksgiving and Christmas. **Cost:** $9; $7 (ages 13-24 and 65+); $6 (ages 3-12); free (ages 0-2 and University of Utah students, faculty and staff with ID). **Phone:** (801) 581-4303 or (801) 581-6927.

Olympic Cauldron Park is at 451 South 1400 East on the University of Utah campus. The park showcases the authentic 2002 Hoberman Arch and glass-and-steel Olympic cauldron. An 8.5-minute cinematic film featuring memorable images and sounds of the opening ceremonies and athletes in action is shown every 15 minutes. An art gallery contains more than 50 photographs of the 2002 Olympics.

Time: Allow 30 minutes minimum. **Hours:** Mon.-Fri. 10-6. Closed university holidays and during major stadium events. Phone ahead to confirm schedule. **Cost:** Park and visitor center free. Film by donation. **Phone:** (801) 581-8849.

Red Butte Garden and Arboretum, 300 Wakara Way on the University of Utah campus, has hiking trails and garden paths, wildlife, a waterfall garden, a floral walk, a children's garden and a terraced garden with herbs and fragrant plants. The 150-acre botanical garden features more than 9,000 tree and shrub specimens collected since 1931 from all over the world. Morning bird-watching tours, evening garden tours and wildflower hikes are available seasonally.

Time: Allow 1 hour minimum. **Hours:** Daily 9-9, May-Aug.; daily 9-7:30, in Apr.; daily 9-7, in Sept.; daily 9-5 in Mar. and Oct. 1-Dec. 23; Mon.-Sat. 9-5, rest of year. Closed Thanksgiving and Christmas Eve-Jan. 1. **Cost:** $8; $6 (ages 3-17 and 65+). **Phone:** (801) 585-0556.

Utah Museum of Fine Arts is on the University of Utah campus in the Marcia and John Price Museum Building at 410 Campus Center Dr. The permanent collection encompasses some 18,000 paintings, photographs, sculpture and other art objects from around the world—from Egyptian antiquities to contemporary art. A variety of public programs are scheduled year-round. Special exhibitions also are offered.

Tours: Guided tours are available. **Time:** Allow 1 hour minimum. **Hours:** Tues.-Fri. 10-5 (also Wed. 5-8), Sat.-Sun. 11-5. Closed major holidays. **Cost:** $7; $5 (ages 6-18, ages 65+ and students with ID); free (ages 0-5 and military with ID and their dependents). **Phone:** (801) 581-5163.

UTAH'S HOGLE ZOO, 2600 E. Sunnyside Ave. (840 South) near the entrance to Emigration Canyon, contains a large collection of birds, mammals and reptiles in natural settings as well as the Tropical Garden, where visitors can view the colorful creatures up close.

Elephant Encounter offers an up-close look at three African elephants and white rhinoceros. Asian Highlands is home to tigers, leopards, lynx and Pallas' cats. The Conservation Carousel features 42 hand-carved wooden animals and two stationary chariots. A miniature locomotive offers rides through part of the zoo March through October (weather permitting).

Stroller and wheelchair rentals are available. **Time:** Allow 2 hours minimum. **Hours:** Daily 9-5, Mar.-Oct.; 9-4, rest of year. Closed Jan. 1 and Christmas. **Cost:** $9; $7 (ages 3-12 and 65+). Carousel ride $2. Train ride $1; free (ages 0-1). **Phone:** (801) 582-1631.

WHEELER HISTORIC FARM is at 6351 South 900 East; from I-215 exit 9 take Union Park Ave. n. via 6400 South and 900 East. This 75-acre living-history dairy farm is operated using animal and manual labor just as it was at the end of the 19th and beginning of the 20th centuries. Visitors can tour the outbuildings, farm grounds and nature preserve and help milk the cows. Guided tours of the 1898 house are available. Wagon rides are available all day (weather permitting). Special activities are held periodically; phone for schedule.

Hours: Grounds daily dawn-dusk. House tours are given Mon.-Sat. on the hour 10-4, in summer; at 3, rest of year. Cow milking takes place Mon.-Sat. at 4:15 and 5. **Cost:** Free. House and grounds tour $2. Wagon ride $2. Cow milking 50c. **Phone:** (801) 264-2241.

Sightseeing

Carriage Tours

Carriage rides, which begin at Temple Square, are a popular way to see the downtown area. Reservations are suggested; check the telephone directory for vendors or inquire at your hotel for recommendations.

Walking and Driving Tours

A free brochure covering self-guiding walking and driving tours is available at the Salt Lake City Visitor Information Center *(see Fast Facts)* and at major area hotels and motels. The Utah Heritage Foundation also provides information about self-guiding tours of the area; phone (801) 533-0858.

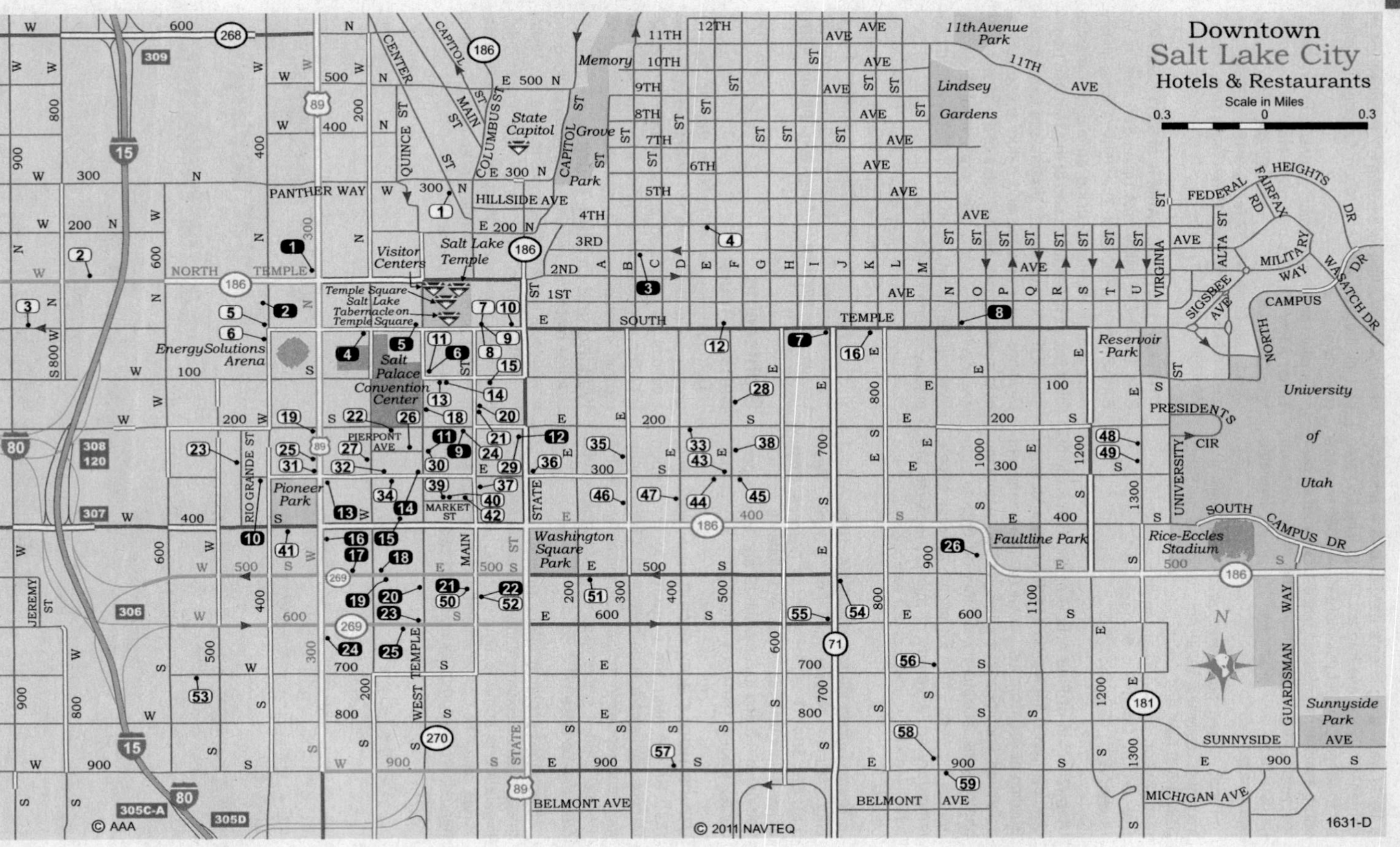

Downtown
Salt Lake City
Hotels & Restaurants
Scale in Miles
0.3
0
0.3
University of Utah
Rice-Eccles Stadium
Reservoir Park
Faultline Park
Sunnyside Park
Washington Square Park
Pioneer Park
Salt Palace Convention Center
EnergySolutions Arena
Salt Lake Temple
Temple Square
Salt Lake Tabernacle on Temple Square
Visitor Centers
State Capitol
Memory Grove Park
Lindsey Gardens
11th Avenue Park
© 2011 NAVTEQ
© AAA
1631-D

Downtown Salt Lake City

This index helps you "spot" where approved hotels and restaurants are located on the corresponding detailed maps. Hotel daily rate range is for comparison only and shows the property's high season. Restaurant rate range is a combination of lunch and/or dinner. Turn to the listing page for more detailed rate information and consult display ads for special promotions.

DOWNTOWN SALT LAKE CITY

Map Page	Hotels	Diamond Rated	High Season	Page
1 p. 422	**Howard Johnson Express Inn Downtown**	2	$58-$107 SAVE	433
2 p. 422	**Hyatt Place Salt Lake City Downtown/The Gateway**	3	$89-$279 SAVE	434
3 p. 422	Ellerbeck Mansion Bed & Breakfast	3	$119-$169	431
4 p. 422	**Radisson Hotel Salt Lake City Downtown** *(See ad p. 434.)*	3	$79-$299 SAVE	434
5 p. 422	**Salt Lake Plaza Hotel at Temple Square** *(See ad p. 436.)*	3	$79-$129 SAVE	436
6 p. 422	Salt Lake City Marriott Downtown	3	$109-$249	436
7 p. 422	Anniversary Inn South Temple	3	Rates not provided	431
8 p. 422	Haxton Manor Bed & Breakfast	3	Rates not provided	431
9 p. 422	**Hotel Monaco**	4	Rates not provided SAVE	433
10 p. 422	Homewood Suites by Hilton Downtown	3	$99-$199	432
11 p. 422	**Hilton Salt Lake City Center**	3	$99-$249 SAVE	432
12 p. 422	**Salt Lake City Marriott City Center**	4	$109-$349 SAVE	436
13 p. 422	Residence Inn by Marriott City Center	3	$99-$329	435
14 p. 422	**Peery Hotel**	3	Rates not provided SAVE	434
15 p. 422	Courtyard by Marriott Downtown	3	$89-$299	431
16 p. 422	Hampton Inn Downtown	3	$89-$179	431
17 p. 422	Crystal Inn Downtown *(See ad p. 432.)*	2	$89-$199	431
18 p. 422	**Sheraton Salt Lake City Hotel**	3	$219-$359 SAVE	436
19 p. 422	Comfort Inn Downtown	2	$80-$310	431
20 p. 422	Metropolitan Inn Downtown	2	Rates not provided	434
21 p. 422	**Little America Hotel** *(See ad p. 435.)*	4	$79-$229 SAVE	434
22 p. 422	**The Grand America Hotel** *(See ad p. 433.)*	5	$189-$5000 SAVE	431
23 p. 422	Embassy Suites Hotel Downtown	3	$109-$239	431
24 p. 422	SpringHill Suites by Marriott Downtown	3	$152-$186	436
25 p. 422	**Red Lion Hotel Salt Lake Downtown**	3	$80-$170 SAVE	435
26 p. 422	Anniversary Inn Fifth South	3	Rates not provided	431

Map Page	Restaurants	Diamond Rated	Cuisine	Meal Range	Page
1 p. 422	Em's Restaurant	2	American	$7-$24	438
2 p. 422	Red Iguana	2	Mexican	$9-$18	440
3 p. 422	Red Iguana 2	2	Mexican	$9-$18	440
4 p. 422	Cafe Shambala	1	Tibetan	$7-$9	437
5 p. 422	Thaifoon, Taste of Asia	2	Asian	$9-$19	441

Map Page	Restaurants (cont'd)	Diamond Rated	Cuisine	Meal Range	Page
6 p. 422	Fleming's Prime Steakhouse & Wine Bar		Steak	$20-$40	438
7 p. 422	The Roof Restaurant		American	$38	440
8 p. 422	The Garden Restaurant		American	$9-$19	438
9 p. 422	Nauvoo Cafe		American	$6-$8	440
10 p. 422	The Lion House Pantry		American	$6-$11	439
11 p. 422	Elevations		American	$10-$25	438
12 p. 422	Wild Grape Bistro		New American	$10-$32	441
13 p. 422	Naked Fish Japanese Bistro		Sushi	$9-$24	440
14 p. 422	Caffe Molise		Italian	$16-$26	437
15 p. 422	Martine Cafe & Tapas		Provincial Mediterranean	$18-$28	439
16 p. 422	Sawadee Thai Restaurant		Thai	$7-$15	440
18 p. 422	Blue Iguana Downtown		Mexican	$7-$14	437
19 p. 422	Cafe Trang		Chinese	$8-$17	437
20 p. 422	Bayleaf Cafe		Comfort Food	$7-$15	437
21 p. 422	Lamb's Grill Cafe		American	$6-$25	439
22 p. 422	J. Wong's Asian Bistro		Asian	$9-$19	439
23 p. 422	Rio Grande Cafe		Mexican	$8-$13	440
24 p. 422	**Bambara**		New American	$9-$35	437
25 p. 422	Cucina Toscana Tuscan Trattoria		Italian	$18-$29	437
26 p. 422	Christopher's Prime Steak House & Grill		Seafood	$10-$47	437
27 p. 422	Settebello Pizzeria Napoletana		Pizza	$7-$13	440
28 p. 422	Oasis Cafe		Vegetarian	$9-$22	440
29 p. 422	La Bella Piastra		Italian	$9-$28	439
30 p. 422	Spencer's for Steaks and Chops		Steak	$11-$49	441
31 p. 422	Tony Caputo's Market & Deli		Regional Deli	$6-$8	441
32 p. 422	P.F. Chang's China Bistro		Chinese	$10-$21	440
33 p. 422	Vinto		Pizza	$7-$11	441
34 p. 422	Squatter's Pub Brewery		American	$9-$15	441
35 p. 422	Gourmandise The Bakery		Breads/Pastries	$6-$9	438
36 p. 422	The Copper Onion		Regional American	$9-$19	437
37 p. 422	Eva		Small Plates	$5-$15	438
38 p. 422	Al Forno's Ristorante		Italian	$9-$20	436
39 p. 422	The New Yorker		American	$10-$48	440
40 p. 422	Market Street Grill Downtown		Seafood	$11-$39	439
41 p. 422	Tin Angel Bistro		Regional Natural/Organic	$7-$21	441
42 p. 422	Takashi		Sushi	$9-$24	441

Map Page	Restaurants (cont'd)	Diamond Rated	Cuisine	Meal Range	Page
43 p. 422	Sage's Cafe	♦♦	Natural/Organic	$7-$14	440
44 p. 422	Faustina	♦♦♦	Continental	$8-$25	438
45 p. 422	Su Casa Mexican Restaurant	♦♦	Mexican	$6-$10	441
46 p. 422	Cinegrill	♦♦	American	$7-$16	437
47 p. 422	Ichiban Sushi	♦♦♦	Sushi	$12-$33	438
48 p. 422	Aristo's Greek Restaurant & Cafe	♦♦♦	Greek	$10-$29	437
49 p. 422	Market Street Grill University	♦♦♦	Seafood	$10-$28	439
50 p. 422	Little America Dining Room	♦♦♦	Steak	$14-$49	439
51 p. 422	Les Madeleines Cafe & Patisserie	♦♦	Breads/Pastries	$6-$11	439
52 p. 422	Garden Café at Grand America	♦♦♦	American	$8-$32	438
53 p. 422	Frida Bistro	♦♦♦	Regional Mexican	$9-$30	438
54 p. 422	Tucci's Cucina Italiana	♦♦	Italian	$7-$18	441
55 p. 422	Rodizio Grill	♦♦	Brazilian	$17-$25	440
56 p. 422	Cafe Trio Downtown	♦♦♦	Italian	$9-$25	437
57 p. 422	Forage Restaurant	♦♦♦♦	Regional American	$39-$65	438
58 p. 422	Pago	♦♦♦	Natural/Organic	$8-$37	440
59 p. 422	Mazza Cafe at 9th	♦♦	Middle Eastern	$7-$21	439

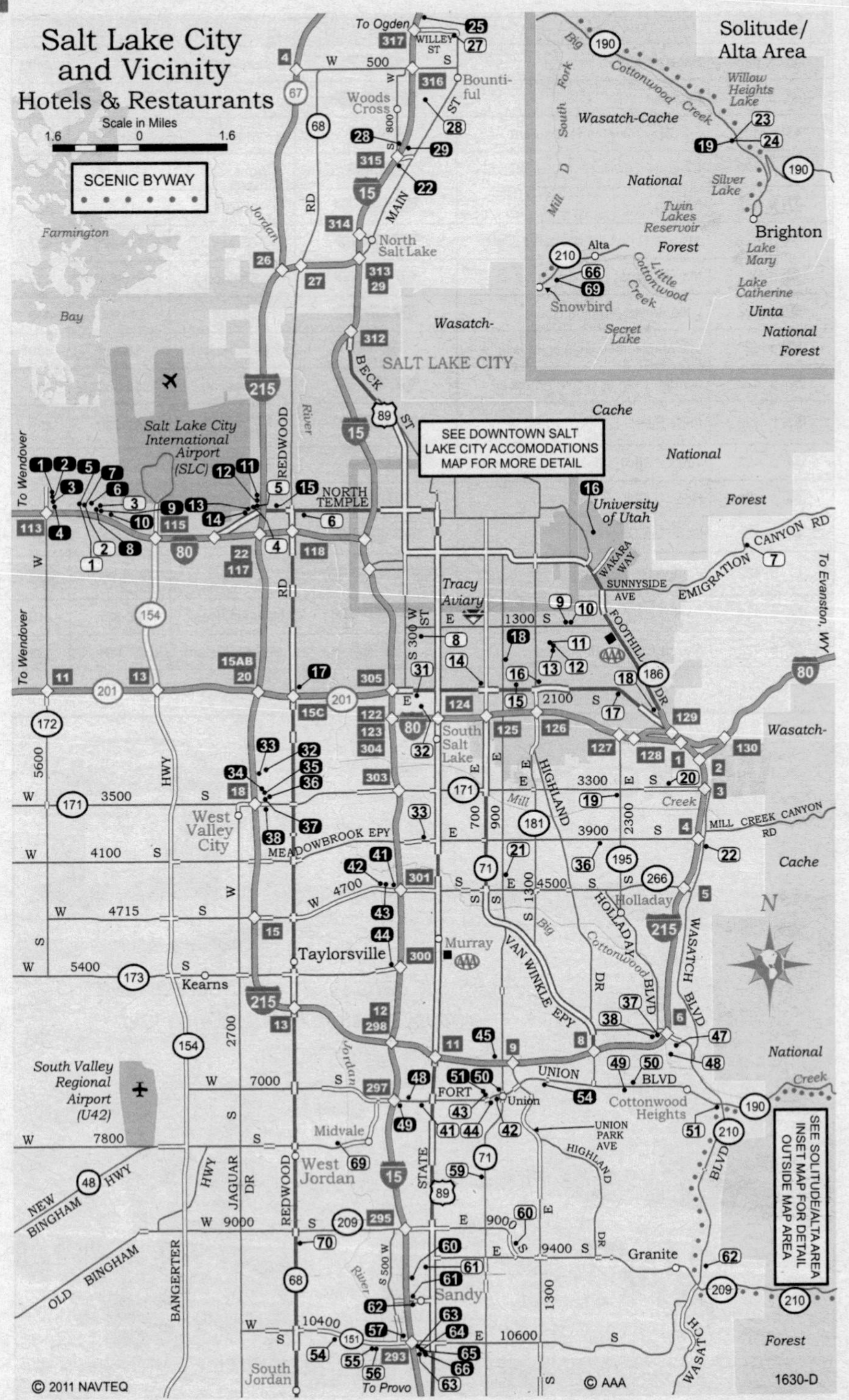
Salt Lake City and Vicinity
Hotels & Restaurants
Scale in Miles
1.6 0 1.6
SCENIC BYWAY
Solitude/ Alta Area
SEE DOWNTOWN SALT LAKE CITY ACCOMODATIONS MAP FOR MORE DETAIL
SEE SOLITUDE/ALTA AREA INSET MAP FOR DETAIL OUTSIDE MAP AREA
SALT LAKE CITY
Salt Lake City International Airport (SLC)
South Valley Regional Airport (U42)
University of Utah
West Valley City
Taylorsville
Murray
South Salt Lake
Holladay
Kearns
Midvale
West Jordan
Sandy
South Jordan
Cottonwood Heights
Granite
Brighton
Alta
Snowbird
North Salt Lake
Woods Cross
Bountiful
Farmington
To Ogden
To Provo
To Wendover
To Evanston, WY
© 2011 NAVTEQ
© AAA
1630-D

Airport Accommodations

Map Page	SALT LAKE CITY INT'L	Diamond Rated	High Season	Page
13 p. 426	Candlewood Suites Airport, 2.5 mi e of airport		$109-$159	441
4 p. 426	**Comfort Inn Airport, 3.4 mi w of airport**		$79-$179 SAVE	441
12 p. 426	Comfort Suites, 2.5 mi e of airport		$79-$199	442
9 p. 426	Courtyard by Marriott Airport, 3 mi w of airport		$69-$160	442
3 p. 426	Fairfield Inn & Suites Airport, 3.7 mi w of airport		$67-$123	442
2 p. 426	**Hampton Inn & Suites Airport, 3.7 mi w of airport**		$99-$169 SAVE	442
5 p. 426	**Hilton Salt Lake City Airport, 3.5 mi w of airport**		$79-$232 SAVE	442
7 p. 426	Holiday Inn & Suites Airport West, 3.5 mi w of airport		$75-$219	442
11 p. 426	Holiday Inn Express Airport East, 2.5 mi e of airport		$159-$209	442
10 p. 426	**Hyatt Place Salt Lake City Airport, 3 mi w of airport**		$79-$189 SAVE	442
1 p. 426	Quality Inn & Suites Airport, 3.7 mi w of airport		Rates not provided	443
14 p. 426	Radisson Hotel Salt Lake City Airport, 2.4 mi e of airport		Rates not provided	443
8 p. 426	Residence Inn by Marriott Airport, 3 mi w of airport		$79-$149	443
15 p. 426	**Sky Harbor Suites, 3 mi e of airport**		$79-$164 SAVE	444
6 p. 426	SpringHill Suites by Marriott Airport, 3 mi w of airport		$69-$139	444

Salt Lake City and Vicinity

This index helps you "spot" where approved hotels and restaurants are located on the corresponding detailed maps. Hotel daily rate range is for comparison only and shows the property's high season. Restaurant rate range is a combination of lunch and/or dinner. Turn to the listing page for more detailed rate information and consult display ads for special promotions.

SALT LAKE CITY

Map Page	Hotels	Diamond Rated	High Season	Page
1 p. 426	Quality Inn & Suites Airport		Rates not provided	443
2 p. 426	**Hampton Inn & Suites Airport**		$99-$169 SAVE	442
3 p. 426	Fairfield Inn & Suites Airport		$67-$123	442
4 p. 426	**Comfort Inn Airport**		$79-$179 SAVE	441
5 p. 426	**Hilton Salt Lake City Airport**		$79-$232 SAVE	442
6 p. 426	SpringHill Suites by Marriott Airport		$69-$139	444
7 p. 426	Holiday Inn & Suites Airport West		$75-$219	442
8 p. 426	Residence Inn by Marriott Airport		$79-$149	443
9 p. 426	Courtyard by Marriott Airport		$69-$160	442
10 p. 426	**Hyatt Place Salt Lake City Airport**		$79-$189 SAVE	442
11 p. 426	Holiday Inn Express Airport East		$159-$209	442
12 p. 426	Comfort Suites		$79-$199	442
13 p. 426	Candlewood Suites Airport		$109-$159	441
14 p. 426	Radisson Hotel Salt Lake City Airport		Rates not provided	443
15 p. 426	**Sky Harbor Suites** *(See ad p. 444.)*		$79-$164 SAVE	444
16 p. 426	University Guest House & Conference Center		$89-$120	444

SALT LAKE CITY (cont'd)

Map Page	Hotels (cont'd)	Diamond Rated	High Season	Page
17 p. 426	Hampton Inn Central	◆◆◆	Rates not provided	442
18 p. 426	Wildflowers Bed & Breakfast	◆◆	$90-$145	444
19 p. 426	The Inn at Solitude	◆◆◆	$209-$449	443

Map Page	Restaurants	Diamond Rated	Cuisine	Meal Range	Page
1 p. 426	Grill 114	◆◆	American	$10-$25	445
2 p. 426	Wing Tips	◆◆	American	$9-$19	446
3 p. 426	Roberts Restaurant	◆◆	American	$6-$18	446
4 p. 426	Lofte's Pizzeria & Restaurant	◆◆	Italian	$8-$13	445
5 p. 426	Encore Grill	◆◆	American	$6-$16	445
6 p. 426	Diamond Lil's Steak House	◆◆	Steak	$6-$25	444
7 p. 426	Ruth's Diner	◆◆	American	$7-$20	446
8 p. 426	Meditrina Small Plates & Wine Bar	◆◆◆	Small Plates	$7-$12	445
9 p. 426	Eggs in the City	◆◆	Breakfast	$6-$11	445
10 p. 426	Sea Salt	◆◆◆	Southern Italian	$8-$19	446
11 p. 426	The Paris Bistro	◆◆◆◆	New American	$15-$30	446
12 p. 426	Fresco Italian Cafe	◆◆◆	Italian	$19-$29	445
13 p. 426	Mazza Cafe' at 15th	◆◆	Middle Eastern	$7-$17	445
14 p. 426	Sampan	◆◆	Chinese	$8-$12	446
15 p. 426	Salt Lake Pizza & Pasta	◆◆	Italian	$7-$17	446
16 p. 426	DoDo Restaurant	◆◆	American	$10-$27	445
17 p. 426	Rino's Italian Ristorante	◆◆◆	Italian	$13-$30	446
18 p. 426	Bombay House Cuisine of India	◆◆	Indian	$9-$17	444
19 p. 426	Lugano Restaurant	◆◆◆	Northern Italian	$11-$27	445
20 p. 426	Citris Grill at 33rd	◆◆	American	$5-$19	444
21 p. 426	Stella Grill	◆◆	American	$8-$20	446
22 p. 426	Rocky Mountain Pizza Co	◆	Pizza	$6-$19	446
23 p. 426	St. Bernard's at Solitude	◆◆◆	French	$26-$32	446
24 p. 426	Kimi's Mountainside Bistro at Solitude	◆◆◆	European	$8-$29	445

NORTH SALT LAKE

Map Page	Hotel	Diamond Rated	High Season	Page
22 p. 426	**Best Western Plus CottonTree Inn**	◆◆◆	$105-$155 SAVE	381

BOUNTIFUL

Map Page	Hotel	Diamond Rated	High Season	Page
25 p. 426	Country Inn & Suites By Carlson Bountiful	◆◆◆	$89-$149	326

Map Page	Restaurants	Diamond Rated	Cuisine	Meal Range	Page
28 p. 426	Robintino's	◆◆	Italian	$7-$15	326

WOODS CROSS

Map Page	Hotels	Diamond Rated	High Season	Page
28 p. 426	Hampton Inn Salt Lake City North - Woods Cross	◆◆◆	$79-$99	461

WOODS CROSS (cont'd)

Map Page	Hotels (cont'd)	Diamond Rated	High Season	Page
29 p. 426	**Comfort Inn & Suites Salt Lake City North - Woods Cross**	◆◆	Rates not provided SAVE	461

WEST VALLEY CITY

Map Page	Hotels	Diamond Rated	High Season	Page
32 p. 426	Staybridge Suites West Valley	◆◆◆	$99-$169	460
33 p. 426	Holiday Inn Express Waterpark West Valley	◆◆◆	$90-$150	460
34 p. 426	Crystal Inn West Valley *(See ad p. 432.)*	◆◆	$79-$139	460
35 p. 426	Baymont Inn & Suites West Valley	◆◆	$44-$89	460
36 p. 426	Country Inn & Suites By Carlson West Valley	◆◆	$89-$129	460
37 p. 426	Sleep Inn West Valley	◆◆	$69-$139	460
38 p. 426	La Quinta Inn Salt Lake City West	◆◆	$84-$144	460

MURRAY

Map Page	Hotels	Diamond Rated	High Season	Page
41 p. 426	Holiday Inn Express Murray	◆◆◆	Rates not provided	380
42 p. 426	Hampton Inn Murray	◆◆◆	$89-$129	380
43 p. 426	Fairfield Inn by Marriott Murray	◆◆	$107-$131	380
44 p. 426	Pavilion Inn	◆◆	Rates not provided	380
45 p. 426	Crystal Inn Midvalley Murray *(See ad p. 432.)*	◆◆	$79-$139	379

MIDVALE

Map Page	Hotels	Diamond Rated	High Season	Page
48 p. 426	**Magnuson Hotel Salt Lake - Midvale**	◆◆	$59-$90 SAVE	363
49 p. 426	La Quinta Inn Salt Lake City Midvale	◆◆	$68-$126	363
50 p. 426	**Super 8 Midvale**	◆◆	$49-$62 SAVE	363
51 p. 426	Holiday Inn Express Salt Lake City South – Midvale	◆◆◆	Rates not provided	363

Map Page	Restaurants	Diamond Rated	Cuisine	Meal Range	Page
41 p. 426	Bohemian Brewery	◆◆	American	$8-$24	364
42 p. 426	Hoppers Grill & Brewing Co	◆◆	American	$7-$18	364
43 p. 426	Epic Casual Dining	◆◆	American	$14-$24	364
44 p. 426	Kneaders Bakery & Cafe	◆	Breads/Pastries	$6-$7	364

COTTONWOOD HEIGHTS

Map Page	Hotel	Diamond Rated	High Season	Page
54 p. 426	Candlewood Suites Fort Union	◆◆	Rates not provided	341

Map Page	Restaurants	Diamond Rated	Cuisine	Meal Range	Page
47 p. 426	Cafe Trio Cottonwood	◆◆◆	Italian	$8-$24	341
48 p. 426	Market Street Grill Cottonwood	◆◆◆	Seafood	$11-$37	341
49 p. 426	Primo Restaurant	◆◆◆	Northern Italian	$15-$36	341
50 p. 426	Pistol Pete's	◆◆	Tex-Mex	$8-$17	341
51 p. 426	Porcupine Pub & Grille	◆◆	American	$8-$24	341

SOUTH JORDAN

Map Page	Hotel	Diamond Rated	High Season	Page
57 p. 426	**Country Inn & Suites By Carlson, South Salt Lake City South Towne**	◆◆◆	$109-$149 SAVE	449

Map Page	Restaurants	Diamond Rated	Cuisine	Meal Range	Page
54 p. 426	Madelines Steakhouse & Grill	2	Steak	$7-$28	449
55 p. 426	Gecko's Mexican Grill	2	Mexican	$8-$15	449
56 p. 426	Market Street Grill South Jordan	3	Seafood	$14-$38	449

SANDY

Map Page	Hotels	Diamond Rated	High Season	Page
60 p. 426	**Hyatt Summerfield Suites Salt Lake City Sandy**	3	$89-$329 SAVE	447
61 p. 426	Residence Inn by Marriott Sandy	3	$99-$279	447
62 p. 426	Hilton Garden Inn Sandy	3	$99-$209	447
63 p. 426	Hampton Inn Sandy	3	$79-$149	447
64 p. 426	Courtyard by Marriott Sandy	3	$161-$197	447
65 p. 426	Holiday Inn Express & Suites Sandy	3	Rates not provided	447
66 p. 426	**Best Western Plus CottonTree Inn**	2	$99-$124 SAVE	447

Map Page	Restaurants	Diamond Rated	Cuisine	Meal Range	Page
59 p. 426	Tiburon Fine Dining	3	New American	$27-$38	448
60 p. 426	Fratelli Ristorante	2	Italian	$7-$26	448
61 p. 426	Mi Ranchito Grill	2	Mexican	$8-$17	448
62 p. 426	La Caille	4	Continental	$36-$68	448
63 p. 426	Carvers Steaks & Seafood	3	Steak	$19-$34	447

SNOWBIRD

Map Page	Hotel	Diamond Rated	High Season	Page
69 p. 426	The Cliff Lodge, Spa & Conference Center	3	Rates not provided	449

Map Page	Restaurant	Diamond Rated	Cuisine	Meal Range	Page
66 p. 426	Aerie Restaurant at Snowbird	3	New American	$21-$48	449

SOUTH SALT LAKE

Map Page	Restaurants	Diamond Rated	Cuisine	Meal Range	Page
31 p. 426	Pat's Barbecue	2	Barbecue	$9-$15	449
32 p. 426	Vertical Diner	1	Vegan	$6-$11	449
33 p. 426	Left Fork Grill	2	Comfort Food	$7-$14	449

HOLLADAY

Map Page	Restaurants	Diamond Rated	Cuisine	Meal Range	Page
36 p. 426	Cafe Madrid	3	Spanish	$22-$28	352
37 p. 426	Tuscany	3	Northern Italian	$15-$29	353
38 p. 426	Franck's	3	French	$22-$36	352

WEST JORDAN

Map Page	Restaurants	Diamond Rated	Cuisine	Meal Range	Page
69 p. 426	Archibald's Restaurant at Gardner Village	2	American	$7-$19	460
70 p. 426	Salsa Leedos Mexican Grill	2	Mexican	$8-$15	460

DOWNTOWN SALT LAKE CITY

- Restaurants p. 436
- Hotels & Restaurants map & index p. 422

ANNIVERSARY INN FIFTH SOUTH

Phone: 801/363-4900 26

Historic Bed & Breakfast

Rates not provided

Address: 460 S 1000 E 84102 **Location:** Just e of 900 E and 500 S; top of hill. **Facility:** In a quiet residential area, the inn offers elegant rooms. Popular themed suites include the Lighthouse, Romeo and Juliet, and Treasure Island. 36 units. 3 stories (no elevator), interior corridors. **Terms:** check-in 5 pm, age restrictions may apply.

ANNIVERSARY INN SOUTH TEMPLE

Phone: 801/363-4950 7

Historic Bed & Breakfast

Rates not provided

Address: 678 E South Temple Dr 84102 **Location:** 1 mi e of Temple Square; corner of E South Temple and 700 E. **Facility:** Choose from several uniquely themed rooms, all wonderfully appointed and comfortable. 13 units. 4 stories (no elevator), interior/exterior corridors. **Terms:** check-in 5 pm, age restrictions may apply.

COMFORT INN DOWNTOWN

Phone: (801)325-5300 19

Hotel

$80-$310

Address: 171 W 500 S 84101 **Location:** Cross streets 100 W and 500 S. **Facility:** 85 units. 2 stories, interior/exterior corridors. **Terms:** cancellation fee imposed. **Activities:** whirlpool, exercise room. **Guest Services:** valet and coin laundry.

BIZ / SOME UNITS FEE

COURTYARD BY MARRIOTT DOWNTOWN

Phone: (801)531-6000 15

Hotel

$89-$299

AAA Benefit:
AAA hotel discounts of 5% or more.

Address: 130 W 400 S St 84101 **Location:** Cross streets 100 W and 400 S. **Facility:** 121 units. 3 stories, interior corridors. **Pool(s):** heated indoor. **Activities:** whirlpool, exercise room. **Guest Services:** valet and coin laundry.

BIZ / SOME UNITS

CRYSTAL INN DOWNTOWN

Phone: (801)328-4466 17

Hotel

$89-$199

Address: 230 W 500 S 84101 **Location:** Cross streets 500 S and 200 W. **Facility:** 175 units. 4 stories, interior corridors. **Pool(s):** heated indoor. **Activities:** sauna, whirlpool, exercise room. **Guest Services:** valet and coin laundry. *(See ad p. 432.)*

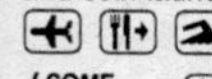

/ SOME UNITS FEE

ELLERBECK MANSION BED & BREAKFAST

Phone: (801)355-2500 3

Historic Bed & Breakfast

$119-$169

Address: 140 B St 84103 **Location:** 0.6 mi e of Temple Square via E North Temple (2nd Ave), then just n; corner of B St and 3rd Ave. **Facility:** The home, recently renovated and restored to its earlier charm, boasts hardwood floors, original molding and stained glass with a period-theme décor. 6 units. 2 stories (no elevator), interior corridors. *Bath:* shower only. **Terms:** office hours 8 am-10 pm, check-in 4 pm, age restrictions may apply, 7 day cancellation notice-fee imposed.

EMBASSY SUITES HOTEL DOWNTOWN

Phone: (801)359-7800 23

Extended Stay Hotel

$109-$239

AAA Benefit:
Members save 5% or more everyday!

Address: 110 W 600 S 84101 **Location:** Corner of S West Temple and 600 S. **Facility:** 241 efficiencies, some two bedrooms. 9 stories, interior corridors. **Terms:** 1-7 night minimum stay, cancellation fee imposed. **Amenities:** video games (fee). **Pool(s):** heated indoor. **Activities:** sauna, whirlpool, exercise room. **Guest Services:** valet and coin laundry, area transportation-downtown.

BIZ

THE GRAND AMERICA HOTEL

Phone: (801)258-6000 22

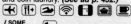

Hotel

$189-$5000

Address: 555 S Main St 84111 **Location:** 1 mi s of Temple Square; just s of Main St and 500 S. **Facility:** Inspired by the charm of Europe's classic hotels, this family-friendly place was crafted from exquisite materials and offers an exceptional experience. 775 units, some kitchens. 24 stories, interior corridors. **Parking:** on-site (fee) and valet. **Amenities:** video games (fee), high-speed Internet, safes, honor bars. **Dining:** Garden Café at Grand America, see separate listing. **Pool(s):** heated outdoor, heated indoor. **Activities:** saunas, whirlpools, steamrooms, spa. **Guest Services:** valet laundry. **Free Special Amenities: newspaper and high-speed Internet.** *(See ad p. 433.)*

SAVE CALL BIZ

FEE / SOME UNITS

HAMPTON INN DOWNTOWN

Phone: (801)741-1110 16

Hotel

$89-$179

AAA Benefit:
Members save up to 10% everyday!

Address: 425 S 300 W 84101 **Location:** Corner of 400 S and 300 W. **Facility:** 158 units. 5 stories, interior corridors. **Terms:** 1-7 night minimum stay, cancellation fee imposed. **Amenities:** video games (fee). **Pool(s):** heated indoor. **Activities:** whirlpool, exercise room. **Guest Services:** valet and coin laundry.

BIZ FEE / SOME UNITS

HAXTON MANOR BED & BREAKFAST

Phone: 801/363-4646 8

Historic Bed & Breakfast

Rates not provided

Address: 943 E South Temple 84102 **Location:** 1.5 mi e of Temple Square; corner of E South Temple and N St. **Facility:** The circa-1906 English country inn is tucked in the heart of the Salt Lake Valley, minutes away from many world-famous ski areas. 7 units. 3 stories (no elevator), interior corridors. **Terms:** office hours 7 am-9 pm, check-in 4 pm.

(See map & index p. 422.)

HILTON SALT LAKE CITY CENTER

Phone: (801)328-2000 **11**

Hotel

$99-$249

AAA Benefit: Members save 5% or more everyday!

Address: 255 S W Temple 84101 **Location:** Just s of cross streets 200 S and S W Temple. **Facility:** 499 units, some kitchens. 18 stories, interior corridors. **Parking:** on-site (fee) and valet. **Terms:** 1-7 night minimum stay, cancellation fee imposed. **Amenities:** safes. *Fee:* video games, high-speed Internet. **Dining:** 2 restaurants, also, Spencer's for Steaks and Chops, see separate listing. **Pool(s):** heated indoor. **Activities:** saunas, whirlpool, exercise room. *Fee:* massage. **Guest Services:** valet laundry.

 FEE   FEE

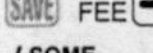 FEE

HOMEWOOD SUITES BY HILTON DOWNTOWN

Phone: (801)363-6700 **10**

Extended Stay Contemporary Hotel

$99-$199

AAA Benefit: Contemporary luxury at a special Member rate.

Address: 423 W Broadway (300 S) 84101 **Location:** Just w of 400 W and 300 S; close to Gateway Mall. **Facility:** 124 efficiencies, some two bedrooms. 6 stories, interior corridors. **Terms:** 1-7 night minimum stay, cancellation fee imposed. **Amenities:** safes. **Pool(s):** heated outdoor. **Activities:** whirlpool, exercise room. **Guest Services:** valet and coin laundry.

(See map & index p. 422.)

HOTEL MONACO **Phone:** 801/595-0000 9

Boutique Hotel

Rates not provided

Address: 15 W 200 S 84101 **Location:** Cross streets 200 S and Main St. **Facility:** French-inspired architecture with rich décor embody the comfortable guest rooms. 225 units. 15 stories, interior corridors. **Parking:** on-site (fee) and valet. **Amenities:** safes, honor bars. *Fee:* video games, high-speed Internet. **Dining:** Bambara, see separate listing. **Activities:** exercise room. *Fee:* massage. **Guest Services:** valet laundry. **Free Special Amenities: high-speed Internet and manager's reception.**

SAVE ECO BIZ FEE

/ SOME UNITS

HOWARD JOHNSON EXPRESS INN DOWNTOWN **Phone:** (801)521-3450 1

Motel

\$58-\$107

Address: 121 N 300 W 84103 **Location:** 0.4 mi w of Temple Square; corner of W North Temple and 300 W. **Facility:** 96 units. 3 stories, interior/exterior corridors. **Terms:** cancellation fee imposed. **Amenities:** safes (fee). **Pool(s):** heated outdoor. **Activities:** exercise room. **Guest Services:** valet and coin laundry, area transportation-train and bus stations. **Free Special Amenities: high-speed Internet and airport transportation.**

SAVE BIZ

/ SOME UNITS FEE

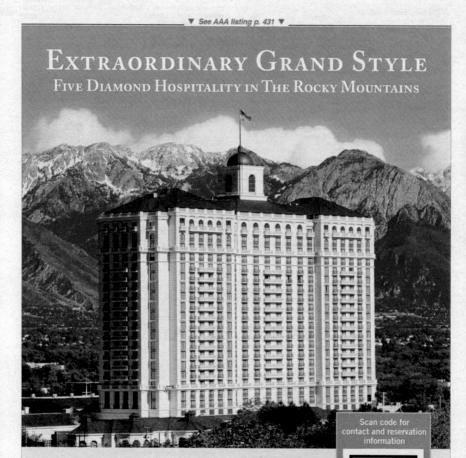

▼ See AAA listing p. 431 ▼

(See map & index p. 422.)

HYATT PLACE SALT LAKE CITY DOWNTOWN/THE GATEWAY Phone: (801)456-6300 2

Hotel
$89-$279

AAA Benefit: Members save 10% or more everyday.

Address: 55 N 400 W 84101 **Location:** 0.5 mi w of Temple Square via W South Temple to 400 W, then just n. **Facility:** 128 units. 6 stories, interior corridors. **Parking:** on-site (fee). **Terms:** check-in 4 pm, cancellation fee imposed. **Pool(s):** heated outdoor. **Activities:** whirlpool, exercise room. **Guest Services:** valet and coin laundry. **Free Special Amenities: expanded continental breakfast and high-speed Internet.**

SAVE BIZ

LITTLE AMERICA HOTEL
Phone: (801)363-6781 21

Hotel
$79-$229

Address: 500 S Main St 84101 **Location:** 1 mi s of Temple Square; just s of Main St and 500 S. **Facility:** The tower units and two-story buildings are surrounded by fountains and manicured grounds. 849 units. 2-17 stories, interior/exterior corridors. **Parking:** on-site and valet. **Terms:** cancellation fee imposed. **Amenities:** high-speed Internet, safes. **Dining:** 2 restaurants, also, Little America Dining Room, see separate listing. **Pool(s):** heated outdoor, heated indoor. **Activities:** saunas, whirlpool, exercise room. *Fee:* massage. **Guest Services:** valet laundry. **Free Special Amenities: newspaper and high-speed Internet.**

(See ad p. 435.)

SAVE BIZ FEE

/ SOME UNITS FEE

Explore the Travel Guides on AAA.com/Travel or CAA.ca/Travel

METROPOLITAN INN DOWNTOWN
Phone: 801/531-7100 20

Motel
Rates not provided

Address: 524 S W Temple 84101 **Location:** Cross streets 500 S and S West Temple. **Facility:** 60 units. 3 stories, exterior corridors. **Activities:** whirlpool. **Guest Services:** valet laundry.

/ SOME UNITS FEE FEE FEE

PEERY HOTEL Phone: 801/521-4300 14

Historic Boutique Hotel
Rates not provided

Address: 110 W Broadway (300 S) 84101 **Location:** Cross streets W Temple and 300 S. **Facility:** The boutique-style hotel offers a variety of rooms and modern baths. 73 units. 3 stories, interior corridors. **Parking:** valet and street only. **Activities:** exercise room. **Guest Services:** valet laundry.

SAVE

/ SOME UNITS FEE FEE FEE

RADISSON HOTEL SALT LAKE CITY DOWNTOWN
Phone: (801)531-7500 4

Hotel
$79-$299

Address: 215 W South Temple 84101 **Location:** Cross streets 200 S and W South Temple. Located near Energy Solutions Arena and Salt Palace. **Facility:** 381 units. 3-15 stories, interior corridors. **Parking:** on-site (fee) and valet. **Terms:** cancellation fee imposed. **Amenities:** high-speed Internet. *Some:* safes. **Pool(s):** heated indoor. **Activities:** sauna, whirlpool, exercise room. **Guest Services:** valet laundry. **Free Special Amenities: early check-in/late check-out and high-speed Internet.**

(See ad this page.)

SAVE ECO BIZ FEE

/ SOME UNITS FEE FEE

(See map & index p. 422.)

RED LION HOTEL SALT LAKE DOWNTOWN

Phone: (801)521-7373 25

Hotel
$80-$170

Address: 161 W 600 S 84101 **Location:** Cross streets S West Temple and 600 S. **Facility:** 392 units. 12 stories, interior corridors. **Terms:** cancellation fee imposed. **Dining:** 2 restaurants. **Pool(s):** heated outdoor. **Activities:** whirlpool, exercise room. **Guest Services:** valet and coin laundry, area transportation-downtown. **Free Special Amenities: high-speed Internet and airport transportation.**

SAVE / SOME UNITS FEE FEE FEE

RESIDENCE INN BY MARRIOTT CITY CENTER

Phone: (801)355-3300 13

Extended Stay Hotel
$99-$329

AAA Benefit:
AAA hotel discounts of 5% or more.

Address: 285 W Broadway (300 S) 84101 **Location:** Corner of 300 W and 300 S. **Facility:** 178 units, some two bedrooms, efficiencies and kitchens. 3-4 stories, interior corridors. **Amenities:** safes. **Pool(s):** heated outdoor. **Activities:** whirlpool, sports court, exercise room. **Guest Services:** valet and coin laundry.

/ SOME UNITS FEE

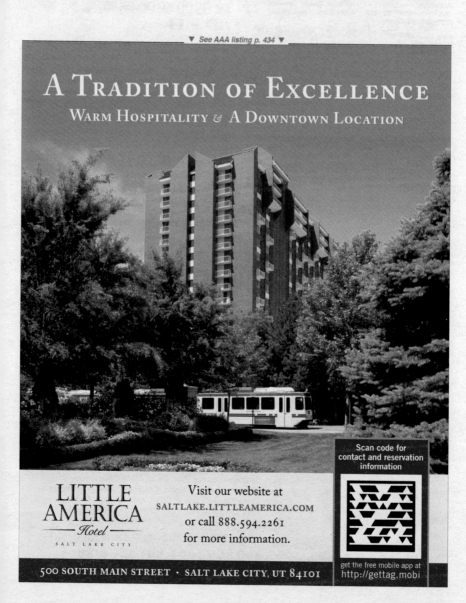

▼ See AAA listing p. 434 ▼

(See map & index p. 422.)

SALT LAKE CITY MARRIOTT CITY CENTER

Phone: (801)961-8700 12

Hotel

$109-$349

Marriott HOTELS & RESORTS **AAA Benefit:** AAA hotel discounts of 5% or more.

Address: 220 S State St 84111 **Location:** Cross streets State and 200 S. **Facility:** Located in the heart of the city's cultural and business center, the hotel sits adjacent to the Gallivan Center. Rooms are well-appointed. 359 units. 12 stories, interior corridors. **Parking:** on-site (fee) and valet. **Amenities:** high-speed Internet, safes. **Dining:** La Bella Piastra, see separate listing. **Pool(s):** heated indoor. **Activities:** whirlpool. *Fee:* massage. **Guest Services:** valet laundry. **Free Special Amenities:** newspaper and high-speed Internet.

SAVE BIZ FEE

/ SOME UNITS

SALT LAKE CITY MARRIOTT DOWNTOWN

Phone: (801)531-0800 6

Hotel

$109-$249

AAA Benefit: AAA hotel discounts of 5% or more.

Address: 75 S West Temple 84101 **Location:** Cross streets 100 S and S W Temple. **Facility:** 515 units. 16 stories, interior corridors. **Parking:** on-site (fee) and valet. **Amenities:** *Fee:* video games, high-speed Internet. *Some:* safes. **Dining:** Elevations, see separate listing. **Pool(s):** heated indoor/outdoor. **Activities:** saunas, whirlpool, exercise room. *Fee:* massage. **Guest Services:** valet and coin laundry.

FEE BIZ FEE

/ SOME UNITS

SALT LAKE PLAZA HOTEL AT TEMPLE SQUARE

Phone: (801)521-0130 5

Hotel

$79-$129

Address: 122 W S Temple 84101 **Location:** Cross streets W Temple and S Temple. Across from Salt Palace and near Energy Solutions Arena. **Facility:** 150 units. 13 stories, interior corridors. **Parking:** on-site (fee) and street. **Terms:** 3 day cancellation notice-fee imposed. **Amenities:** high-speed Internet, safes (fee). **Pool(s):** heated outdoor. **Activities:** whirlpool, exercise room. **Guest Services:** valet and coin laundry. *(See ad this page.)*

SAVE BIZ

SHERATON SALT LAKE CITY HOTEL

Phone: (801)401-2000 18

Hotel

$219-$359

Sheraton **AAA Benefit:** Members get up to 15% off, plus Starwood Preferred Guest® bonuses.

Address: 150 W 500 S 84101 **Location:** Cross streets 200 W and 500 S. **Facility:** 362 units. 2-10 stories, interior corridors. **Parking:** on-site and valet. **Terms:** 4 day cancellation notice-fee imposed. **Amenities:** high-speed Internet (fee). **Dining:** 3 restaurants. **Pool(s):** heated outdoor. **Activities:** whirlpool, exercise room. *Fee:* massage. **Guest Services:** valet laundry, area transportation-within 10 mi. **Free Special Amenities: local transportation and airport transportation.**

SAVE BIZ

/ SOME UNITS

SPRINGHILL SUITES BY MARRIOTT DOWNTOWN

Phone: (801)238-3000 24

Contemporary Hotel

$152-$186

AAA Benefit: AAA hotel discounts of 5% or more.

Address: 625 S 300 W 84101 **Location:** I-15 exit 306 (600 S) northbound; exit 307 (400 S) southbound. **Facility:** 86 units. 4 stories, interior corridors. **Pool(s):** heated indoor. **Activities:** whirlpool, exercise room. **Guest Services:** valet and coin laundry.

BIZ

WHERE TO EAT

AL FORNO'S RISTORANTE

Phone: 801/359-6040 38

Italian

$9-$20

AAA Inspector Notes: The eatery offers reasonably priced eggplant tortellini, veal linguine, ravioli and a delicious signature lasagna. **Bar:** full bar. **Address:** 239 S 500 E 84102 **Location:** Cross street 200 S.

L D

▼ See AAA listing this page ▼

(See map & index p. 422.)

ARISTO'S GREEK RESTAURANT & CAFE

Phone: 801/581-0888 (48)

Greek
$10-$29

AAA Inspector Notes: Traditional soups, salads and entrées are made using generations-old family recipes and served in a warm, elegant dining room and on a lovely landscaped patio. Assortment platters offer a taste of many of the specialties. Homemade desserts taste great with a demitasse cup of strong Greek coffee. **Bar:** full bar. **Address:** 224 S 1300 E 84102 **Location:** 1.8 mi e on S Temple, 0.4 mi s. **Parking:** street only. L D

BAMBARA **Phone:** 801/363-5454 (24)

New American
$9-$35

AAA Inspector Notes: Located in a former bank lobby, this beautifully renovated bistro serves artistic and colorful creations of local and regional products from an open-air kitchen in a vibrant atmosphere. Diners can enjoy a before- or after-dinner cocktail in the lounge. The weekday lunch is popular, as is the 3 for $33 dinner special. **Bar:** full bar. **Address:** 202 S Main St 84101 **Location:** Cross streets 200 S and Main St; in Hotel Monaco. **Parking:** on-site (fee) and valet. B L D

BAYLEAF CAFE **Phone:** 801/359-8490 (20)

Comfort Food
$7-$15

AAA Inspector Notes: Traditional comfort food blended with Asian fare can be found at this downtown eatery, which is open 24 hours a day on weekends. Menu items include pineapple fried rice, chicken 'n' waffles, shepherd's pie, beef short ribs cooked in red wine sauce and a meatloaf platter prepared from a 150-year-old family recipe. Sides might include collard greens, mac 'n' cheese and fried corn on the cob. Old-fashioned Southern desserts such as apple brown Betty, warm peach cobbler, nanner puddin' and fried sweet plantains are sure to please. **Bar:** beer & wine. **Address:** 159 S Main St 84111 **Location:** 0.3 mi s of Temple Square. **Parking:** street only.
L D

BLUE IGUANA DOWNTOWN

Phone: 801/533-8900 (18)

Mexican
$7-$14

AAA Inspector Notes: Off a courtyard in midtown, the restaurant whips up authentic Mexican food, including classic enchiladas and burritos, with tasty mole sauces and other great flavor-enhancers. **Bar:** full bar. **Address:** 165 S W Temple 84101 **Location:** Just n of S West Temple and 200 S; in Arrow Press Square Shopping Center. **Parking:** street only. L D

CAFE SHAMBALA **Phone:** 801/364-8558 (4)

Tibetan
$7-$9
L D

AAA Inspector Notes: This cafe focuses on interesting Tibetan preparations. **Address:** 382 E 4th Ave N 84103 **Location:** Between D and E sts; in The Avenues. **Parking:** street only.

CAFE TRANG **Phone:** 801/539-1638 (19)

Chinese
$8-$17

AAA Inspector Notes: Warm, inviting service is what diners experience at this family-operated restaurant, which serves tasty traditional poultry, beef, pork and seafood entrées; mouthwatering appetizers; and fire-pot or broth soups. **Bar:** beer & wine. **Address:** 307 W 200 S 84101 **Location:** Jct 300 W. **Parking:** street only.
L D

CAFE TRIO DOWNTOWN **Phone:** 801/533-8746 (56)

Italian
$9-$25

AAA Inspector Notes: This upbeat and energetic neighborhood spot features a menu of specialty flatbreads, mouthwatering organic salads, cedar-plank wild salmon and a wide variety of appetizers and pastas. Patrons can expect great service. The decadent desserts include bittersweet chocolate pudding, seasonal cobblers and a tollhouse pie with roasted walnuts. **Bar:** full bar. **Address:** 680 S 900 E 84102 **Location:** Corner of 700 S and 900 E.
L D

CAFFE MOLISE **Phone:** 801/364-8833 (14)

Italian
$16-$26

AAA Inspector Notes: Featuring fresh Italian cuisine and attentive service, this downtown cafe is the perfect location for dining before or after a theater, concert, opera or sporting event. The garden patio affords intimate seating. **Bar:** full bar. **Reservations:** suggested. **Address:** 55 W 100 S 84101 **Location:** Just e of 100 S and West Temple. **Parking:** street only.
L D

CHRISTOPHER'S PRIME STEAK HOUSE & GRILL

Phone: 801/519-8515 (26)

Seafood
$10-$47

AAA Inspector Notes: Selections include seafood, which is flown in daily, slow-roasted prime rib, free-range chicken and New Zealand lamb. **Bar:** full bar. **Address:** 134 W Pierpont Ave 84101 **Location:** Just n of 300 S and 200 W, then just e on Pierpont Ave. **Parking:** valet and street only. L D

CINEGRILL **Phone:** 801/328-4900 (46)

American
$7-$16

AAA Inspector Notes: A Salt Lake institution, this restaurant is as suitable for a first date as it is for a night out with the kids. Checkered tablecloths drape tables in the dining room, where a pianist plays on weekends. The menu offers a mouthwatering, lean, Kosher-style corned beef sandwich, salads made with secret ingredients, pizza, pasta and Armenian-style shish kebabs. **Bar:** full bar. **Address:** 344 S 300 E 84111 **Location:** Just n of 400 S and 300 E. **Parking:** street only. L D

THE COPPER ONION **Phone:** 801/355-3282 (36)

Regional American
$9-$19

AAA Inspector Notes: This trendy downtown bistro offers well-prepared seasonal dishes such as melt-in-your-mouth ricotta dumplings, pork belly salad, sauteed mushrooms topped with a farm fresh egg, roasted heirloom chicken and Wagyu tri-tip steak with watercress salad. Cured meat and cheese plates and flavorful and creative sides are served family-style on long wooden platters with insets for bowls of Brussels sprouts, sauteed spinach with cashews and raisins. **Bar:** full bar. **Reservations:** suggested. **Address:** 111 E 300 S, Suite 170 84111 **Location:** Just e of State St and 300 S; 0.4 mi e of Temple Square; next to Broadway Theatre. **Parking:** on-site (fee).
L D

CUCINA TOSCANA TUSCAN TRATTORIA

Phone: 801/328-3463 (25)

Italian
$18-$29

AAA Inspector Notes: Located in the arts and entertainment district and serving authentic Tuscan fare, the chef's special reserve menu includes carefully prepared salads, soups, chicken, veal, seafood and steak, as well as an excellent selection of wine. The Caesar salad and risotto del giorno are served table side. The knowledgeable staff provides personalized, attentive service. **Bar:** full bar. **Reservations:** suggested. **Address:** 307 W Pierpont Ave 84101 **Location:** Just n of 300 S and 300 W. D

(See map & index p. 422.)

ELEVATIONS **Phone:** 801/531-0800 (11)

American
$10-$25

AAA Inspector Notes: Set within a rustic yet refined ambiance, the restaurant serves a menu with Southwest flavors and anchored in American classics such as steaks, chops, flatbread pizza, piled-high sandwiches and home cooked pot pies. **Bar:** full bar. **Address:** 75 S West Temple 84101 **Location:** Cross streets 100 S and S W Temple; in Salt Lake City Marriott Downtown. **Parking:** valet and street only. B L D

EM'S RESTAURANT **Phone:** 801/596-0566 (1)

American
$7-$24

AAA Inspector Notes: This lovely neighborhood restaurant is casual and comfortable. Selections, which incorporate local and organic ingredients, may include potato pancakes, phyllo stuffed with goat cheese and duck confit, pear and walnut greens salad, red wine-braised short ribs, rib-eye with blue cheese and caramelized onions, leek-stuffed wild salmon and free-range chicken. Seasonal dessert selections always include crème brûlée, ice cream and sorbet. A gallery-like dining room and shaded patio are available. **Bar:** beer & wine. **Address:** 271 N Center St 84103 **Location:** Just n on State St to W North Temple, just w to N Main St, just n to Center St, then just nw; located in The Avenues. **Parking:** street only.

L D AC

EVA **Phone:** 801/359-8447 (37)

Small Plates
$5-$15

AAA Inspector Notes: The sautéed Brussels sprouts with toasted hazelnuts and cider vinegar are addictive, as are other delicious and attractively presented tapas, salads, breads, wood-fired pizzas, pastas and specialized entrées and drinks. **Bar:** full bar. **Address:** 317 S Main St 84111 **Location:** 0.6 mi s of Temple Square. **Parking:** street only. D LATE

FAUSTINA **Phone:** 801/746-4441 (44)

Continental
$8-$25

AAA Inspector Notes: This hip restaurant serves a variety of appetizers, salads, soups, sandwiches and pasta, not to mention creative seasonal chicken, seafood and steak entrées prepared with fresh ingredients. Lunch and dinner selections may include an addictive salmon BLT, shrimp bisque poured tableside, crab cake sliders, lobster ravioli and oven-roasted filet mignon. Seasonal homemade desserts may include blueberry soufflé with honey-lavender cream sauce. Dining is available on a seasonal outdoor patio. **Bar:** full bar. **Address:** 300 S 454 E 84111 **Location:** Cross streets 300 S and 500 E. **Parking:** on-site and street. L D

FLEMING'S PRIME STEAKHOUSE & WINE BAR
Phone: 801/355-3704 (6)

Steak
$20-$40

AAA Inspector Notes: The warm, clubby atmosphere is the ideal setting for perfectly grilled steaks and seafood. Side dishes come in hearty portions, and salads are fresh and crisp. More than 100 wine selections are available. **Bar:** full bar. **Reservations:** suggested. **Address:** 20 S 400 W 84101 **Location:** I-15 exit 306 (600 S), 0.4 mi e, then 1 mi n on S 400 W; exit 309 (600 N) southbound, 0.4 mi e, then 1 mi s on S 400 W; across from Energy Solutions Arena. **Parking:** on-site and street.

D

FORAGE RESTAURANT **Phone:** 801/708-7834 (57)

Regional American
$39-$65

AAA Inspector Notes: This place presents carefully and artistically prepared and seasonal fixed-prices menus. Utilizing the best local ingredients available, courses may include butter-poached scallops, braised shellfish, olive oil-poached beef, roast Colorado lamb, tasting of rabbit, brown butter-poached apricots and chilled passion fruit soup. **Bar:** beer & wine. **Reservations:** suggested. **Address:** 370 E 900 S 84111 **Location:** I-15 exit 307 (400 S), 0.9 mi e, 0.3 mi s on 300 W, 1 mi e on 600 S, 0.4 mi s on 300 E, then just e; 1.3 mi s of Temple Square via S State St to 900 S, then 0.4 mi e. D

FRIDA BISTRO **Phone:** 801/983-6692 (53)

Regional Mexican
$9-$30

AAA Inspector Notes: Flavorful courses of modern Mexican fare may include three-cheese fondue with poblano rajas and Mexican chorizo, mole negro turkey tamale steamed in a banana leaf, or pan-seared duck quesadilla with orange reduction and menonita cheese. The poblano stuffed with organic Utah beef, peaches and apples resting in walnut cream, garnished with pomegranate seeds and served with tres verdes rice is very good. The warm, handmade corn tortillas melt in the mouth. Desserts are artistically presented. **Bar:** full bar. **Reservations:** suggested. **Address:** 545 W 700 S 84101 **Location:** I-15 exit 306 (600 S) northbound, 0.5 mi e to 400 W, just s to 700 S, then just w; exit 307 (400 S) southbound, 0.5 mi e over ramp to 500 W, 0.5 mi s to 700 S, then just w. L D

GARDEN CAFÉ AT GRAND AMERICA
Phone: 801/258-6000 (52)

American
$8-$32

AAA Inspector Notes: The elegant décor incorporates spun-glass chandeliers and windows overlooking floral gardens. The friendly, attentive staff brings out such delicious dishes as cilantro-lime-marinated free-range chicken and pepper-crusted beef tenderloin. **Bar:** full bar. **Address:** 555 S Main St 84111 **Location:** Cross street 500 S; in The Grand America Hotel. **Parking:** on-site and valet.

B L D

THE GARDEN RESTAURANT
Phone: 801/539-3170 (8)

American
$9-$19

AAA Inspector Notes: With stunning views of downtown and Temple Square, the restaurant features a retractable glass roof and offers local favorites such as fried dill pickles, spinach salad, several pasta dishes, gourmet sandwiches and oven-roasted Pacific salmon drizzled with Thai peanut sauce. Scrumptious desserts include the restaurant's famous chocolate cinnamon cake. **Address:** 15 E S Temple 84150 **Location:** In Joseph Smith Memorial Bldg, 10th Floor. L D

GOURMANDISE THE BAKERY
Phone: 801/328-9022 (35)

Breads/Pastries
$6-$9

AAA Inspector Notes: The menu lists a plentiful array of grilled panini sandwiches, daily quiches with flaky and buttery, made-from-scratch crust, hearty soups and traditional or vegetable lasagna. Sweet diversions include feuilletee, English bread pudding and baba au rum tartlet. A children's menu also is available. **Address:** 250 S 300 E 84111 **Location:** Between 200 S and 300 S.

L D

ICHIBAN SUSHI **Phone:** 801/532-7522 (47)

Sushi
$12-$33

AAA Inspector Notes: Fresh sushi and sashimi, as well as traditional Japanese dishes, are prepared by skillfully trained chefs in this beautiful historic restaurant, which was once a cathedral. The saltwater aquarium is mesmerizing. **Bar:** full bar. **Address:** 336 S 400 E 84111 **Location:** I-15 exit 307 (400 S), 1 mi e, then just n.

D

(See map & index p. 422.)

IGGY'S SPORTS GRILL **Phone:** 801/532-9999

American
$7-$19

AAA Inspector Notes: Patrons seeking hearty food in a fun atmosphere will find it at the upbeat sports grill. Among diverse offerings are chicken teriyaki, barbecue ribs, pizza, macadamia nut salmon, Sicilian lasagna, burgers and rib-eye steak. Iggy's Tin Lid is great for a pre-game snack along the lines of coconut shrimp, onion straws, Southwest egg rolls or hot wings. Beer lovers will delight in a variety of microbrews on tap. **Bar:** full bar. **Address:** 423 W 300 S 84101 **Location:** Cross streets 400 W and 300 S. L D

J. WONG'S ASIAN BISTRO **Phone:** 801/350-0888 (22)

Asian
$9-$19

AAA Inspector Notes: Named for four brothers, the family bistro features a satay bar and a chic full-service bar featuring custom-made tabletops. The lunch menu features single-meal choices. At dinnertime, a variety of Chinese, Thai and select Asian specialty starters, soups, fried rice, noodles, beefsteak, pork, curry, vegetables and tofu dishes, as well as tangerine chicken, walnut shrimp and Chilean sea bass steak, are offered. Tender roast duck is available to those who phone ahead. **Bar:** full bar. **Address:** 163 W 200 S 84101 **Location:** Just e of 200 S and 200 W; across from Salt Palace Convention Center. **Parking:** valet and street only. L D

LA BELLA PIASTRA **Phone:** 801/961-8700 (29)

Italian
$9-$28

AAA Inspector Notes: Upscale contemporary Italian cuisine hits the mark with breaded and fried goat cheese croquettes with prosciutto and asparagus served with tomato and olive tapenade; grilled filet mignon duo; veal scaloppini; oven-baked cedar-plank salmon with sweet pea risotto; and delicious chicken piccata with lemon and capers. House-made desserts include an apple strudel pouch with caramel ice cream, chocolate crepes with raspberries and a cannoli duo plate. Windows overlook an ice skating rink. **Bar:** full bar. **Address:** 220 S State St 84111 **Location:** Cross streets State and 200 S; in Salt Lake City Marriott City Center. **Parking:** valet and street only.
B L D

LAMB'S GRILL CAFE **Phone:** 801/364-7166 (21)

American
$6-$25

AAA Inspector Notes: Located in the business district, this restaurant serves a wide variety of menu items, including seafood, chicken, lamb, steak, sandwiches, soups, salads and delicious desserts. Wearing white shirts and black aprons, the staff provides excellent service at booths and tables dressed in white linens or at a long black marble counter, which offers comfortable leather chairs. **Bar:** full bar. **Address:** 169 S Main St 84111 **Location:** 0.3 mi s of Temple Square; business district. **Parking:** on-site and street. **Classic Historic** B L D

LES MADELEINES CAFE & PATISSERIE
Phone: 801/355-2294 (51)

Breads/Pastries
$6-$11

AAA Inspector Notes: This delightful patisserie makes cakes, cookies, 17 types of cupcakes, candy, shortbread and tarts from scratch. Travel-inspired lunches feature tasty soups; macaroni with white cheddar and Gruyère cheeses; Chinese-style steamed buns filled with duck confit and served with edamame; a delicious sesame chicken salad, which is wrapped in butter lettuce then wrapped in rice paper and served with miso dressing; shrimp toast, a caprese sandwich; and chicken and goat cheese salad. **Address:** 216 E 500 S 84111 **Location:** Just e of 500 S and 200 E. **Parking:** street only. B L

THE LION HOUSE PANTRY
Phone: 801/363-5466 (10)

American
$6-$11

AAA Inspector Notes: Home-style food, fresh rolls and pastries are served in this cafeteria in the historic home of Brigham Young. Covered validated parking is available. **Address:** 63 E S Temple 84150 **Location:** At Temple Square; next to Joseph Smith Memorial Bldg. L D

LITTLE AMERICA DINING ROOM
Phone: 801/596-5704 (50)

Steak
$14-$49

AAA Inspector Notes: Evocative of an Old English-style club, the restaurant is decorated in leather and dark woods. **Bar:** full bar. **Reservations:** suggested. **Address:** 500 S Main 84101 **Location:** 1 mi s of Temple Square; just s of Main St and 500 S; in Little America Hotel. **Parking:** on-site and valet. B L D

MARKET STREET GRILL DOWNTOWN
Phone: 801/322-4668 (40)

Seafood
$11-$39

AAA Inspector Notes: Listed on the National Register of Historic Places, this local favorite serves breakfast, lunch and dinner and prepares steak, chicken, prime rib, pasta, salads and spectacular fresh seafood from around the world. **Bar:** full bar. **Address:** 48 W Market St 84101 **Location:** From Temple Square, 0.5 mi s on Main St, then just w. **Parking:** valet and street only. **Historic**
B L D

MARKET STREET GRILL UNIVERSITY
Phone: 801/583-8808 (49)

Seafood
$10-$28

AAA Inspector Notes: Close to the University of Utah, the restaurant presents a menu of fresh seafood flown in daily from around the world, including Atlantic and wild salmon, king crab legs, Hawaiian ahi tuna and Idaho trout. Other menu favorites include hickory-smoked barbecue baby back ribs, mesquite-broiled fish, tender steaks, pasta dishes and their famous clam chowder. Seafood lovers can pick up the fresh catch of the day in the eatery's fish market. **Bar:** full bar. **Address:** 260 S 1300 E 84102 **Location:** Cross streets 200 S and 1300 E; 2 mi e of Temple Square. **Historic** L D

MARTINE CAFE & TAPAS **Phone:** 801/363-9328 (15)

Provincial Mediterranean
$18-$28

AAA Inspector Notes: The flavors of North Africa, Spain and Provence come together in varied tapas dishes, including bay scallops and semolina-crusted calamari with pimiento aioli, and full entrées such as espresso-seared duck breast, grilled red trout and sable fish with lavender-leek cream and crimson lentils. Grilled gingerbread with caramel and house gelato ends the meal on a memorable note. **Bar:** full bar. **Reservations:** suggested. **Address:** 22 E 100 S 84111 **Location:** Just e of 100 S and Main St. **Parking:** valet and street only.
L D

MAZZA CAFE AT 9TH **Phone:** 801/521-4572 (59)

Middle Eastern
$7-$21

AAA Inspector Notes: The cozy neighborhood eatery offers specialty appetizer and entrée sampler platters with a choice of more than 20 mouthwatering items. Traditional dishes include grape leaves, falafel, mujaddara, muhamara made with pomegranate molasses, kafta, vegetarian kabesh, baba ghanoush, spinach fatayer and chicken, beef or lamb kebabs. The seafood platter features seasoned and broiled mahi mahi, shrimp and scallops. Most of the delicate baked desserts are served with a scrumptious orange blossom syrup. **Bar:** full bar. **Address:** 912 E 900 S 84105 **Location:** Just e of Temple Square to State St, 1.3 mi s, then 1.3 mi e. **Parking:** street only.
L D

(See map & index p. 422.)

NAKED FISH JAPANESE BISTRO

Phone: 801/595-8888 (13)

Sushi

$9-$24

AAA Inspector Notes: Lunch and dinner are served in several dining areas. **Bar:** full bar. **Address:** 67 W 100 S 84101 **Location:** Just e of SW Temple and 100 S. **Parking:** on-site (fee) and street.

[L] [D]

NAUVOO CAFE Phone: 801/539-3346 (9)

American

$6-$8

AAA Inspector Notes: Patrons enjoy hand-carved sandwiches and the famous potpies. Covered validated parking is available. **Address:** 15 E S Temple 84150 **Location:** In Joseph Smith Memorial Bldg, 1st Floor.

[B] [L] [D]

THE NEW YORKER Phone: 801/363-0166 (39)

American

$10-$48

AAA Inspector Notes: The restaurant offers classy contemporary dining with an emphasis on premium steaks, hand-made local pasta, game and lamb, not to mention shellfish and poultry. The specials are very imaginative, and the desserts are elegant. **Bar:** full bar. **Address:** 60 W Market St 84101 **Location:** Between Main St and W Temple. **Parking:** valet and street only.

[L] [D]

OASIS CAFE Phone: 801/322-0404 (28)

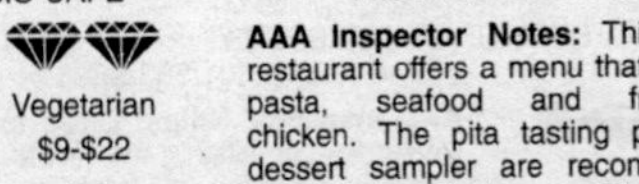

Vegetarian

$9-$22

AAA Inspector Notes: This casual restaurant offers a menu that includes pasta, seafood and free-range chicken. The pita tasting plate and dessert sampler are recommended. **Bar:** full bar. **Address:** 151 S 500 E 84102 **Location:** Cross street 100 S. **Parking:** on-site and street. [B] [L] [D]

PAGO Phone: 801/532-0777 (58)

Natural/Organic

$8-$37

AAA Inspector Notes: The neighborhood restaurant with an urban flare has a menu featuring delicious lamb burgers, a poached tuna salad sandwich, Wagyu steak salad, shallow poached Alaskan halibut, roasted quail and pork tenderloin roulade. For dessert, the mousse tasting is a favorite. The weekend brunch is very popular. **Bar:** full bar. **Address:** 878 S 900 E 84102 **Location:** Corner of 900 S and 900 E, just n. **Parking:** street only. [L] [D]

P.F. CHANG'S CHINA BISTRO

Phone: 801/539-0500 (32)

Chinese

$10-$21

AAA Inspector Notes: Trendy, upscale decor provides a pleasant backdrop for New Age Chinese dining. Appetizers, soups and salads are a meal by themselves. Vegetarian plates and sides, noodles, meins, chicken and meat dishes are created from exotic, fresh ingredients. **Bar:** full bar. **Address:** 174 W 300 S 84101 **Location:** Corner of 200 W and 300 S. **Parking:** valet and street only.

[L] [D] [LATE]

RED IGUANA Phone: 801/322-1489 (2)

Mexican

$9-$18

AAA Inspector Notes: Strong outdoor heat warmers keep diners toasty on the outdoor patio no matter what the weather. The authentic moles shouldn't be missed, but the cozy cucina also serves burritos, chimichangas, enchiladas, salads, seafood, soups, steaks, tacos and tostadas. The desserts are well worth consideration. **Bar:** full bar. **Address:** 736 W N Temple 84116 **Location:** 1 mi w of Temple Square. [L] [D]

RED IGUANA 2 Phone: 801/214-6050 (3)

Mexican

$9-$18

AAA Inspector Notes: Patrons can experience the true taste of authentic mole at this cozy and friendly spot. Burritos, chimichangas, enchiladas, salads, seafood, soups, steaks, tacos, tostadas and desserts also are available. **Bar:** full bar. **Address:** 866 W South Temple 84101 **Location:** 0.4 mi w of Temple Square via W South Temple, just n on 300 W, 0.7 mi w on W North Temple, just s on 800 W, just w on W South Temple. [L] [D]

RIO GRANDE CAFE Phone: 801/364-3302 (23)

Mexican

$8-$13

AAA Inspector Notes: Located in the historical Rio Grande train depot, the restaurant offers festive dining on consistently great Mexican fare, including carnitas, margaritas and more. Don't miss the model train running overhead. **Bar:** full bar. **Address:** 270 S Rio Grande St (455 W) 84101 **Location:** I-15 exit 306 (600 S), just e to 300 W, then 0.3 mi n; in Rio Grande Train Station Bldg. **Historic** [L] [D]

RODIZIO GRILL Phone: 801/220-0500 (55)

Brazilian

$17-$25

AAA Inspector Notes: This authentic Brazilian restaurant, offering unlimited appetizers and salad bar, has more than a dozen selections of delicious meats, which are served table side and hand carved by Brazilian gauchos. The live drums provide a night-in-Brazil feeling. **Bar:** full bar. **Address:** 459 Trolley Square 84102 **Location:** Main building, 2nd Level; in Trolley Square. [L] [D]

THE ROOF RESTAURANT Phone: 801/539-1911 (7)

American

$38

AAA Inspector Notes: Breathtaking views of downtown, Temple Square and the surrounding mountains can be seen from this restaurant's 10th-floor location. A gorgeous gourmet buffet of American and international dishes is prepared daily and includes a wide selection of salads, chilled shrimp, poached salmon, prime rib, baked ham, pasta, chef's choice of potatoes, seasonal fruit and vegetables. The mouthwatering desserts are colorfully displayed. **Reservations:** suggested. **Address:** 15 E S Temple St 84150 **Location:** Just w of State St and S Temple; in Joseph Smith Memorial Bldg, 10th Floor. [D] CALL [&M]

SAGE'S CAFE Phone: 801/322-3790 (43)

Natural/Organic

$7-$14

AAA Inspector Notes: The vegetarian cafe entices patrons with varied options, including pizza night on Tuesday and a four-course meal of gourmet raw cuisine on the last Friday of every month. **Bar:** beer & wine. **Address:** 473 E 300 S 84102 **Location:** Cross streets 300 S and 400 E. **Parking:** street only. [L] [D]

SAWADEE THAI RESTAURANT

Phone: 801/328-8424 (16)

Thai

$7-$15

AAA Inspector Notes: Featuring a popular lunch menu, soups, salads and curry dishes, diners enjoy gracious service at this charming downtown cafe. **Bar:** beer & wine. **Address:** 754 E S Temple 84102 **Location:** Cross street 700 E. [L] [D]

SETTEBELLO PIZZERIA NAPOLETANA

Phone: 801/322-3556 (27)

Pizza

$7-$13

AAA Inspector Notes: Diners can go healthy with caprese or arugula salads or instead opt for a traditional Napoli pizza, which can be served sliced or unsliced. The gelato choices are many. **Bar:** beer & wine. **Address:** 260 S 200 W 84101 **Location:** Just n of 200 S and 200 W. **Parking:** on-site and valet. [L] [D]

(See map & index p. 422.)

SPENCER'S FOR STEAKS AND CHOPS
Phone: 801/238-4748 (30)

Steak
$11-$49

AAA Inspector Notes: The classic steak house offers a sophisticated alternative, with an a la carte menu of classic favorites and world-class wines. Decadent desserts such as double-layer strawberry shortcake and the chocolate naughty are to be shared. **Bar:** full bar. **Address:** 255 S West Temple 84101 **Location:** Just s of cross streets 200 S and S W Temple; in Hilton Salt Lake City Center. **Parking:** valet and street only. L D

SQUATTER'S PUB BREWERY
Phone: 801/363-2739 (34)

American
$9-$15

AAA Inspector Notes: Patrons can enjoy the brewpub atmosphere from seats by the fireplace or on the patio. A variety of award-winning beers taste great paired with the selection of appetizers, soups, salads, sandwiches and pub favorites. The restaurant is open for breakfast, lunch and dinner. Vegetarian and low-carb items are offered. **Bar:** full bar. **Address:** 147 W Broadway (300 S) 84101 **Location:** Cross streets 300 S and 200 W. B L D

SU CASA MEXICAN RESTAURANT
Phone: 801/363-7771 (45)

Mexican
$6-$10

AAA Inspector Notes: Fast, friendly, upbeat service is provided at this downtown eatery offering all your favorite Mexican dishes. **Address:** 516 E 300 S 84102 **Location:** Corner of 500 E and 300 S. **Parking:** on-site and street. L D

TAKASHI
Phone: 801/519-9595 (42)

Sushi
$9-$24

AAA Inspector Notes: Hot small plates include braised Asian barbecue pork ribs brushed with ginger-soy glaze, wok-tossed asparagus in a garlic and shiitake mushroom sauce over glass noodles, assorted seafood in a lemon grass and cilantro broth, and shiitake lamb shank braised in a Japanese yellow curry. Also offered are sashimi and sushi combination plates, vegetarian items and creative and exciting specialty rolls. An excellent selection of sake, beer, wine and spirits is available. **Bar:** full bar. **Address:** 18 W Market St 84101 **Location:** From Temple Square, 0.5 mi s on Main St, then just w. **Parking:** valet and street only. L D

THAIFOON, TASTE OF ASIA
Phone: 801/456-8424 (5)

Asian
$9-$19

AAA Inspector Notes: A fun dining experience rooted in the exotic and fascinating cuisines of Asia, this family-friendly restaurant offers fresh, flavorful and familiar food that is meant to be shared. **Bar:** full bar. **Address:** 7 N 400 W 84101 **Location:** North end of The Gateway, 2nd Level. **Parking:** on-site and street. L D

TIN ANGEL BISTRO
Phone: 801/328-4155 (41)

Regional Natural/ Organic
$7-$21

AAA Inspector Notes: Local and organic produce are paramount at this downtown bistro where the menu changes often. Tapas may include prosciutto-wrapped shrimp drizzled with apricot Champagne vinaigrette or espresso-crusted beef tenderloin, while entrées trend toward bresaola carpaccio, chicken saltimbocca, wild mushroom risotto and lamb and chorizo stew. Whimsical seasonal desserts may include chardonnay-poached pear nestled in pastry cream on a caramel-glazed tart shell or elegant Italian panna cotta. **Bar:** full bar. **Reservations:** suggested. **Address:** 365 W 400 S 84101 **Location:** I-15 exit 307 (400 S), 0.3 mi e; across from Pioneer Park. L D

TONY CAPUTO'S MARKET & DELI
Phone: 801/531-8669 (31)

Regional Deli
$6-$8

AAA Inspector Notes: The menu features a good mix of Italian and Southern European dishes. **Address:** 314 W 300 S 84101 **Location:** Cross streets 300 S and 300 W. **Parking:** street only.

B L D

TUCCI'S CUCINA ITALIANA
Phone: 801/533-9111 (54)

Italian
$7-$18

AAA Inspector Notes: Guests see a colorful display of the chef's interesting entrées and desserts as they enter this restaurant, which boasts one of the city's largest covered patios. An attentive staff caters to diners as they enjoy such signature items as pasta mista, shrimp puttanesca, butternut squash ravioli and lamb a la Napoli. A kicky espresso goes great with dessert. **Bar:** full bar. **Address:** 515 S 700 E 84102 **Location:** Cross streets 500 S and 700 E; in Trolley Square. L D

VINTO
Phone: 801/539-9999 (33)

Pizza
$7-$11

AAA Inspector Notes: This casual Italian spot has chic and bright décor. Menu offerings include house-made meatballs the size of golf balls, delicious wood-fired pizzas, attractively presented salads, homemade breadsticks and flatbread and a thoughtful selection of wine, bottled water, tea and coffee. Children can select from their own menu. Flights of colorful house-made gelato and sorbetto hit the spot, while the molten cake and apple crostata should be shared. **Bar:** full bar. **Address:** 418 E 200 S 84111 **Location:** Corner of 200 S and 400 E.

L D

WILD GRAPE BISTRO
Phone: 801/746-5565 (12)

New American
$10-$32

AAA Inspector Notes: Creative dishes such as grilled lobster tail with saffron risotto and braised fennel, and spicy butternut squash soup with pear and cranberry chutney combine locally grown organic products whenever possible. Favorite sandwiches include a Colorado bison burger and a lamb burger with glazed onions. The wood-burning grill turns out choices such as cider-brined pork loin with caramelized pear and walnut chutney. Seasonal meal enders might include blue cheese cheesecake with mountain berry jam and fresh berries. **Bar:** full bar. **Address:** 481 E S Temple 84111 **Location:** 0.7 mi e of Temple Square on corner of S Temple and E St. B L D

SALT LAKE CITY

• **Restaurants p. 444**
• **Hotels & Restaurants map & index p. 426**

CANDLEWOOD SUITES AIRPORT
Phone: (801)359-7500 (13)

Extended Stay Hotel
$109-$159

Address: 2170 W N Temple 84116 **Location:** 3 mi w of Temple Square. **Facility:** 122 efficiencies. 3 stories, interior corridors. **Terms:** cancellation fee imposed. **Amenities:** high-speed Internet. **Activities:** exercise room. **Guest Services:** complimentary and valet laundry.

/ SOME UNITS FEE

COMFORT INN AIRPORT **Phone:** (801)746-5200 (4)

Hotel
$79-$179

Address: 200 N Admiral Byrd Rd 84116 **Location:** I-80 exit 113 (5600 W), 0.6 mi n, just e, then just s. Next to interstate. **Facility:** 155 units. 4 stories, interior corridors. **Terms:** cancellation fee imposed. **Amenities:** high-speed Internet. **Pool(s):** heated outdoor. **Activities:** sauna, whirlpool, exercise room. **Guest Services:** valet and coin laundry. **Free Special Amenities: full breakfast and high-speed Internet.**

SAVE BIZ FEE

/ SOME UNITS FEE

(See map & index p. 426.)

COMFORT SUITES Phone: (801)715-8688 12

Hotel
$79-$199

Address: 171 N 2100 W 84116 **Location:** 3 mi w of Temple Square. **Facility:** 104 units. 4 stories, interior corridors. **Terms:** cancellation fee imposed. **Amenities:** high-speed Internet. **Pool(s):** heated indoor. **Activities:** whirlpool, exercise room. **Guest Services:** valet and coin laundry.

BIZ

COURTYARD BY MARRIOTT AIRPORT
Phone: (801)532-4085 9

Hotel
$69-$160

AAA Benefit:
AAA hotel discounts of 5% or more.

Address: 4843 W Douglas Corrigan Way 84116 **Location:** I-80 exit 114 (Wright Brothers Dr), just n off ramp. **Facility:** 154 units. 3 stories, interior corridors. **Amenities:** video games (fee), high-speed Internet. **Pool(s):** heated indoor. **Activities:** whirlpool, exercise room. **Guest Services:** valet and coin laundry.

BIZ FEE

/ SOME UNITS

FAIRFIELD INN & SUITES AIRPORT
Phone: (801)355-3331 3

Hotel
$67-$123

AAA Benefit:
AAA hotel discounts of 5% or more.

Address: 230 N Admiral Byrd Rd 84116 **Location:** I-80 exit 113 (5600 W), 0.5 mi n, just e, then just s. **Facility:** 104 units. 3 stories, interior corridors. **Amenities:** high-speed Internet. **Pool(s):** heated indoor. **Activities:** whirlpool, exercise room. **Guest Services:** valet and coin laundry.

BIZ

HAMPTON INN & SUITES AIRPORT
Phone: (801)530-0088 2

Hotel
$99-$169

Hampton

AAA Benefit: Members save up to 10% everyday!

Address: 307 N Admiral Byrd Rd 84116 **Location:** I-80 exit 113 (5600 W), 0.6 mi n, just e, then just s. **Facility:** 100 units. 3 stories, interior corridors. **Terms:** 1-7 night minimum stay, cancellation fee imposed. **Amenities:** high-speed Internet. **Pool(s):** heated outdoor. **Activities:** whirlpool, exercise room. **Guest Services:** valet laundry. **Free Special Amenities: expanded continental breakfast and high-speed Internet.**

SAVE BIZ

/ SOME UNITS

HAMPTON INN CENTRAL **Phone:** 801/886-0703 17

Hotel
Rates not provided

AAA Benefit:
Members save up to 10% everyday!

Address: 2055 S Redwood Rd 84104 **Location:** I-15 exit 305C (2100 S), 1.5 mi w. **Facility:** 73 units. 3 stories, interior corridors. **Pool(s):** heated indoor. **Activities:** whirlpool, exercise room. **Guest Services:** valet and coin laundry.

BIZ / SOME UNITS

HILTON SALT LAKE CITY AIRPORT
Phone: (801)539-1515 5

Hotel
$79-$232

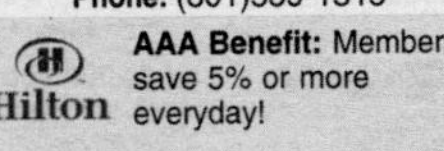

AAA Benefit: Members save 5% or more everyday!

Address: 5151 Wiley Post Way 84116 **Location:** I-80 exit 114 westbound, just n off ramp, then 0.4 mi w; exit 113 eastbound (5600 W), 0.5 mi n, 0.3 mi e on Amelia Earhart Dr, just s on Jimmy Doolittle Rd, then 0.3 mi e. **Facility:** 288 units. 3-5 stories, interior corridors. **Terms:** 1-7 night minimum stay, cancellation fee imposed. **Amenities:** video games (fee). **Dining:** Grill 114, see separate listing. **Pool(s):** outdoor, heated indoor. **Activities:** whirlpools, putting green, sports court, exercise room. **Guest Services:** valet and coin laundry. **Free Special Amenities: high-speed Internet and airport transportation.**

SAVE BIZ FEE

/ SOME UNITS FEE FEE

HOLIDAY INN & SUITES AIRPORT WEST
Phone: (801)741-1800 7

Hotel
$75-$219

Address: 5001 W Wiley Post Way 84116 **Location:** I-80 exit 114 (Wright Brothers Dr), just n off ramp, then 0.4 mi w; exit 113 (5600 W) eastbound, 0.5 mi n on 5600 W, 0.3 mi e on Amelia Earhart Dr, just s on Jimmy Doolittle Rd, then 0.5 mi e. **Facility:** 111 units. 4 stories, interior corridors. **Amenities:** high-speed Internet. **Dining:** Wing Tips, see separate listing. **Pool(s):** heated indoor. **Activities:** whirlpool, exercise room. **Guest Services:** valet and coin laundry.

FEE

/ SOME UNITS FEE

HOLIDAY INN EXPRESS AIRPORT EAST
Phone: (801)741-1500 11

Hotel
$159-$209 5/1-9/5
$129-$189 9/6-4/30

Address: 200 N 2100 W 84116 **Location:** I-80 exit 118 (Redwood Rd) westbound; exit 115 (N Temple) eastbound, 3.1 mi w of Temple Square. **Facility:** 92 units. 3 stories, interior corridors. **Terms:** 3 day cancellation notice-fee imposed. **Amenities:** video games (fee), high-speed Internet. **Pool(s):** heated indoor. **Activities:** whirlpool, exercise room. **Guest Services:** valet and coin laundry, area transportation-within 10 mi.

BIZ

/ SOME UNITS FEE

HYATT PLACE SALT LAKE CITY AIRPORT
Phone: (801)363-1400 10

Hotel
$79-$189

HYATT PLACE

AAA Benefit: Members save 10% or more everyday.

Address: 52 N Tommy Thompson Rd 84116 **Location:** I-80 exit 114 (Wright Brothers Dr), just n off ramp, just e, then just se. **Facility:** 123 units. 5 stories, interior corridors. **Terms:** cancellation fee imposed. **Amenities:** high-speed Internet. **Pool(s):** heated indoor. **Activities:** exercise room. **Guest Services:** valet and coin laundry. **Free Special Amenities: expanded continental breakfast and high-speed Internet.**

SAVE BIZ FEE

(See map & index p. 426.)

THE INN AT SOLITUDE **Phone:** (801)517-7717 19

Hotel

$209-$449

Address: 12000 Big Cottonwood Canyon 84121 **Location:** I-215 exit 6 (6200 S), 14 mi up Big Cottonwood Canyon, 2nd entrance. **Facility:** 46 units, some efficiencies. 4 stories, interior corridors. **Terms:** check-in 4 pm, 2 night minimum stay, 3 day cancellation notice. **Dining:** 2 restaurants, also, St. Bernard's at Solitude, see separate listing. **Pool(s):** heated outdoor. **Activities:** sauna, whirlpool, hiking trails, jogging, sports court, game room, horseshoes, volleyball, spa. *Fee:* downhill & cross country skiing, snowmobiling, ice skating, bicycles. **Guest Services:** coin laundry, area transportation-within resort & Nordic Center.

BIZ

/ SOME UNITS

QUALITY INN & SUITES AIRPORT **Phone:** 801/539-5005 1

Hotel

Rates not provided

Address: 315 N Admiral Byrd Rd 84116 **Location:** I-80 exit 113 (5600 W), 0.6 mi n, then just e. Adjacent to convenience store. **Facility:** 59 units. 2 stories, interior corridors. **Amenities:** high-speed Internet. **Pool(s):** heated outdoor. **Activities:** exercise room. **Guest Services:** coin laundry.

/ SOME UNITS FEE

RADISSON HOTEL SALT LAKE CITY AIRPORT **Phone:** 801/364-5800 14

Hotel

Rates not provided

Address: 2177 W North Temple 84116 **Location:** 3 mi w of Temple Square. **Facility:** 124 units. 3 stories, interior corridors. **Pool(s):** outdoor. **Activities:** whirlpool, exercise room. **Guest Services:** valet and coin laundry.

RESIDENCE INN BY MARRIOTT AIRPORT **Phone:** (801)532-4101 8

Extended Stay Hotel

$79-$149

AAA Benefit:
AAA hotel discounts of 5% or more.

Address: 4883 W Douglas Corrigan Way 84116 **Location:** I-80 exit 114 (Wright Brothers Dr), just n off ramp. **Facility:** 104 units, some two bedrooms, efficiencies and kitchens. 4 stories, interior corridors. **Amenities:** video games (fee). **Pool(s):** heated indoor. **Activities:** whirlpool, sports court, exercise room. **Guest Services:** valet and coin laundry.

CALL FEE

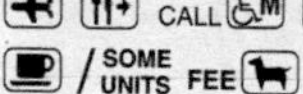
/ SOME UNITS FEE

(See map & index p. 426.)

SKY HARBOR SUITES **Phone:** (801)539-8420 15

Condominium
$79-$164

Address: 1876 W N Temple 84116 **Location:** 2.5 mi w of Temple Square. **Facility:** The property has fully furnished suites and a great location between downtown and the airport. 96 condominiums. 2 stories (no elevator), exterior corridors. **Terms:** office hours 7 am-11 pm, cancellation fee imposed. **Amenities:** high-speed Internet (fee). **Pool(s):** heated outdoor. **Activities:** sauna, whirlpools, racquetball court, jogging, playground, basketball, horseshoes, volleyball, exercise room. **Guest Services:** valet and coin laundry.

(See ad this page.)

 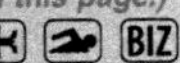  

SPRINGHILL SUITES BY MARRIOTT AIRPORT
Phone: (801)532-6633 6

Hotel
$69-$139

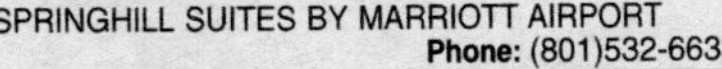

AAA Benefit:
AAA hotel discounts of 5% or more.

Address: 4955 Wiley Post Way 84116 **Location:** I-80 exit 114 (Wright Brothers Dr), just n off ramp, then just w. **Facility:** 143 kitchen units. 5 stories, interior corridors. **Amenities:** high-speed Internet. **Pool(s):** heated indoor. **Activities:** exercise room. **Guest Services:** valet and coin laundry.

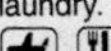 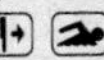    

UNIVERSITY GUEST HOUSE & CONFERENCE CENTER
Phone: 801/587-1000 16

Hotel
$89-$120

Address: 110 S Fort Douglas Blvd 84113 **Location:** I-80 exit 129 (Foothill Dr), 3 mi n, then just e of Foothill Dr. Located on University of Utah campus. **Facility:** 134 units. 4 stories, interior corridors. **Amenities:** high-speed Internet. **Activities:** exercise room. **Guest Services:** coin laundry.

WILDFLOWERS BED & BREAKFAST
Phone: (801)466-0600 18

Bed & Breakfast
$90-$145

Address: 936 E 1700 S 84105 **Location:** Cross streets 900 E and 1700 S, just e. **Facility:** 5 units. 3 stories (no elevator), interior/exterior corridors. **Terms:** 3 day cancellation notice-fee imposed. **Amenities:** high-speed Internet.

SOME UNITS

WHERE TO EAT

BOMBAY HOUSE CUISINE OF INDIA
Phone: 801/581-0222 18

Indian
$9-$17

AAA Inspector Notes: This great little restaurant has an authentic atmosphere and serves up delicate ethnic dishes; the flavor of curry abounds and is quite delightful. **Bar:** beer & wine. **Address:** 2731 E Parley's Way 84109 **Location:** I-80 exit 129, e off Foothill Dr; in Lamplighter Square. D

CITRIS GRILL AT 33RD **Phone:** 801/466-1202 20

American
$5-$19

AAA Inspector Notes: The soups, tidbits, salads, wood-fired pizza, sandwiches and entrées served in this friendly neighborhood eatery can be ordered in petite or hearty sizes. Sweet potato corn chowder is served daily, as are the delicious pepper-crusted risotto cakes, ham and cheese sandwich with cranberry aioli and apricot mustard on ciabatta, sesame seared salmon and made-in-house desserts such as the bread pudding smothered with candied pecans. **Bar:** full bar. **Address:** 2991 E 3300 S 84109 **Location:** I-215 exit 3 (3300 S/Wasatch Blvd), 0.7 mi w. B L D

DIAMOND LIL'S STEAK HOUSE
Phone: 801/533-0547 6

Steak
$6-$25

AAA Inspector Notes: The old-fashioned steak house serves up Calamity Jane, Jesse James, Butch Cassidy, Billy the Kid and other amusingly named entrées of mostly seafood and steak. Homemade pies are a specialty. **Bar:** full bar. **Address:** 1528 W North Temple 84116 **Location:** 2.5 mi w of Temple Square. L D

(See map & index p. 426.)

DODO RESTAURANT **Phone:** 801/486-2473 (16)

American
$10-$27

AAA Inspector Notes: It's hard to miss the modern purple building or the dodo birds socializing over drinks at this bistro. Delicious lunch, dinner and brunch items include the DoDo omelet, lemon-pepper seared ahi medallions, roasted tomato polenta cake, artichoke pie and spinach, mushroom and feta quiche. This place is known for its exquisite homemade desserts, including Butterfinger cheesecake and the signature Toll House pie. **Bar:** full bar. **Address:** 1355 E 2100 S 84105 **Location:** I-80 exit 126 (Sugar House), 0.5 mi n, just e. (L) (D) CALL (&M)

EGGS IN THE CITY **Phone:** 801/581-0809 (9)

Breakfast
$6-$11

AAA Inspector Notes: Formerly a gas station, this East Bench restaurant is appointed in clever and unusual décor. The cozy covered patio occupies what once was the garage. Quality ingredients keep the crowds coming. **Address:** 1675 E 1300 S 84105 **Location:** I-15 exit 305C (1300 S), 3.3 mi e, corner of 1300 S and 1700 S. **Parking:** on-site and street. (B) (L)

ENCORE GRILL **Phone:** 801/534-1996 (5)

American
$6-$16

AAA Inspector Notes: Located close to the airport, the restaurant serves a great breakfast. At lunch and dinner, pasta, seafood, steak, burgers, sandwiches and a daily special are offered, as are baklava and rice pudding desserts. Service is efficient but friendly. **Address:** 2080 W N Temple 84116 **Location:** 3 mi w of Temple Square. (B) (L) (D)

FRESCO ITALIAN CAFE **Phone:** 801/486-1300 (12)

Italian
$19-$29

AAA Inspector Notes: This charming cafe with its lovely landscaped patio is a hidden treasure. Creative and architecturally presented seasonal menu items may include the chef's soup of the evening, steamed mussels and clams, fresco-seared polenta with sauteed wild mushrooms, pan-seared shrimp with made-in-house black linguine, potato-crusted sea bass and pan-seared chicken served with artichokes, roasted tomatoes and pearl pasta. Mouthwatering desserts include panna cotta, gelato and robiola cheesecake. **Bar:** full bar. **Reservations:** suggested. **Address:** 1513 S 1500 E 84105 **Location:** Cross streets 1500 S and 1500 E. (D)

GRILL 114 **Phone:** 801/539-1515 (1)

American
$10-$25

AAA Inspector Notes: This casual spot is noteworthy for its wonderful views. **Bar:** full bar. **Address:** 5151 W Wiley Post Way 84116 **Location:** I-80 exit 114 westbound; exit 113 eastbound; in Hilton Salt Lake City Airport. (B) (L) (D)

KIMI'S MOUNTAINSIDE BISTRO AT SOLITUDE
Phone: 801/536-5787 (24)

European
$8-$29

AAA Inspector Notes: Whether guests are in the mood for a casual family meal, an apres-ski snack, fine dining in the evening or weekend brunch, the eclectic European fare is sure to please. Menu items include cheese and fruit fondue, duck confit tacos, chanterelle mushroom soup, roasted chicken and poblano chili, in addition to a wonderful selection of salads and wood-fired pizza. The dessert selections include Belgian chocolate fondue, Swedish lingonberry mousse and a mouthwatering tiramisu. **Bar:** full bar. **Reservations:** suggested. **Address:** 12000 Big Cottonwood Canyon 84121 **Location:** I-215 exit 6 (6200 S), 14 mi up Big Cottonwood Canyon, 2nd entrance. (D) (AC)

LOFTE'S PIZZERIA & RESTAURANT
Phone: 801/363-0808 (4)

Italian
$8-$13

AAA Inspector Notes: The casual restaurant with a bright atmosphere puts forth a creative menu for lunch and dinner. It features steaks, delicious wood-fired pizzas and freshly baked calzones. Locals favor the bruschetta smothered with balsamic-marinated tomatoes, capers and onions; the turkey, bacon and provolone sandwich on house-made bread; and build-your-own 8- and 12-inch pizzas. **Bar:** beer & wine. **Address:** 2110 W N Temple 84116 **Location:** 3 mi w of Temple Square. (L) (D)

LOG HAVEN
Menu on AAA.com **Phone:** 801/272-8255

New American
$15-$38

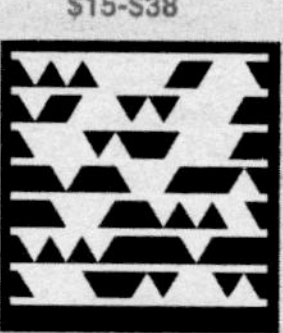

AAA Inspector Notes: Tucked away on a 40-acre site, the restaurant occupies a picture-postcard setting. Featured seasonal selections may include hazelnut pomegranate-glazed chicken, blackened wild shrimp, bison tenderloin, Kurabota pork scaloppini and Cornish game hen "under a brick." Tempting seasonal desserts include pineapple upside-down cake served with rhubarb ice cream and s'mores. Servers will gladly provide a validated canyon exit pass. **Bar:** full bar. **Reservations:** suggested. **Address:** 3800 Wasatch Blvd 84109 **Location:** I-215 exit 4 (3900 S), just e to Wasatch Blvd, just n to 3800 S/Millcreek Canyon, then 4 mi e up 3800 S/Millcreek Canyon; north side; in Wasatch National Forest. (D)

Historic Wilderness Mansion - Live Entertainment

LUGANO RESTAURANT **Phone:** 801/412-9994 (19)

Northern Italian
$11-$27

AAA Inspector Notes: Warm and personable staff enhance the dining experience at this east-side evening establishment. The Northern Italy-influenced dishes include roasted tomato and onion soup, wood-burning oven pasta and risotto, clay pot mussels, braised Angus beef short ribs, spaghetti with Napa cabbage and cauliflower, braised lamb shanks and mouthwatering desserts. **Bar:** full bar. **Address:** 3364 S 2300 E 84109 **Location:** I-80 exit 127 (2300 E), 1 mi s. **Parking:** on-site and street. (D)

MAZZA CAFE' AT 15TH **Phone:** 801/484-9259 (13)

Middle Eastern
$7-$17

AAA Inspector Notes: The cozy neighborhood eatery offers specialty appetizer and entrée sampler platters that include a choice of nearly two dozen mouthwatering dishes ranging from grape leaves, falafel, mujaddara and kafta to kabesh, baba ghanoush, muhamara made with pomegranate molasses, and chicken, beef and lamb kebabs. The seafood platter includes seasoned and broiled mahi-mahi, shrimp and scallops. Most desserts are served with orange blossom syrup. Gluten-free, vegetarian and vegan options are available. **Bar:** beer & wine. **Address:** 1515 S 1500 E 84105 **Location:** I-80 exit 126 (1300 E), 1.1 mi n, then 0.4 mi e. **Parking:** street only. (L) (D)

MEDITRINA SMALL PLATES & WINE BAR
Phone: 801/485-2055 (8)

Small Plates
$7-$12

AAA Inspector Notes: The carefully selected wines at this cozy spot are meant to complement seasonal small-plate choices such as steamed mussels in tomato-basil wine broth and lamb sirloin with roasted Roma tomatoes in feta butter and mint gastrique. The house-made desserts are decadent. **Bar:** beer & wine. **Address:** 1394 S W Temple St 84115 **Location:** 2 mi s of Temple Square. (L) (D)

(See map & index p. 426.)

THE PARIS BISTRO **Phone:** 801/486-5585 11

New American
$15-$30

AAA Inspector Notes: Inspired by Italian, French and Mediterranean food cultures, meals are a celebration at this elegant neighborhood bistro, where the gracious and attentive staff await your arrival. Wine selections complement seasonal hand-crafted salads, charcuterie, escargot, cheese courses, steamed clams, wild shrimp risotto, rotisserie chicken with lavender honey glaze, and roasted root vegetables. The grand dessert selection is tempting. **Bar:** full bar. **Address:** 1500 E 1500 S 84105 **Location:** I-80 exit 126 (1300 E), 1.2 mi n, then 0.3 mi e. **Parking:** street only. D

RINO'S ITALIAN RISTORANTE
Phone: 801/466-4614 17

Italian
$13-$30

AAA Inspector Notes: Experience the restaurant's cozy, romantic ambience in the Old World dining room or on the lovely grapevine-covered patio. Entrées, prepared with fresh ingredients, showcase cuisine from various regions of Italy. **Bar:** full bar. **Address:** 2302 E Parley's Way 84109 **Location:** I-80 exit 129 (Foothill Dr/Parley's Way), 2 mi nw; corner of Parley's Way (2100 S) and S 2300 E. D

ROBERTS RESTAURANT **Phone:** 801/364-3663 3

American
$6-$18

AAA Inspector Notes: The country-style eatery is a great spot for breakfast, lunch or dinner. Selections include daily homemade soup or chowder, great sandwiches and cheddar cheese-topped apple pie. **Bar:** full bar. **Address:** 145 N Wright Brothers Dr 84116 **Location:** I-80 exit 114 (Wright Brothers Dr), just n.
B L D

ROCKY MOUNTAIN PIZZA CO
Phone: 801/272-9888 22

Pizza
$6-$19

AAA Inspector Notes: This neighborhood eatery offers a nice salad bar; appetizers; calzones; a wide variety of specialty pizzas with delicious red or a white garlic sauce; sandwiches, spinach, chipotle and wheat wraps; and economical family specials. The dessert pizza combines light strudel crumbles with thick cinnamon-glaze topping. **Bar:** beer only. **Address:** 3977 S Wasatch Blvd 84124 **Location:** I-215 exit 4, 0.3 mi e, then 0.3 mi s; in Olympus Hills Shopping Center. L D

RUTH'S DINER **Phone:** 801/582-5807 7

American
$7-$20

AAA Inspector Notes: When the weather is nice, guests can sit under the trees on the creekside patio to enjoy salads, sandwiches and deluxe plates from the varied menu. **Bar:** full bar. **Address:** 4160 Emigration Canyon Rd 84108 **Location:** I-80 exit 129, 2.6 mi n on Foothill Dr, then 2.8 mi e via Sunnyside Ave and Emigration Canyon Rd. B L D

ST. BERNARD'S AT SOLITUDE
Phone: 801/517-7717 23

French
$26-$32

AAA Inspector Notes: Professional and knowledgeable servers help guests pair fine wines with seasonal country French dishes such as five-onion soup with Gruyère cheese; country pork and rabbit paté filled with cranberries; duck confit with butternut squash risotto, sage-brown butter sauce and caramelized apples with lavender-cheddar tuile; free-range organic chicken braised with red wine and crimini mushrooms; or the chef's daily fresh fish. A shared serving of luscious mousse ends the meal on the right note. **Bar:** full bar. **Reservations:** suggested. **Address:** 12000 Big Cottonwood Canyon 84121 **Location:** I-215 exit 6 (6200 S), 14 mi up Big Cottonwood Canyon, 2nd entrance; in The Inn at Solitude. **Parking:** on-site and valet.
B D

SALT LAKE PIZZA & PASTA
Phone: 801/484-1804 15

Italian
$7-$17

AAA Inspector Notes: The eatery features a variety of salads and sandwiches as well as house specialties of pizza and pasta. **Bar:** full bar. **Address:** 1063 E 2100 S 84106 **Location:** Cross streets 1100 E and 2100 S; in Sugar House. L D

SAMPAN **Phone:** 801/467-3663 14

Chinese
$8-$12

AAA Inspector Notes: Every dish arrives at the table fresh from the wok at this simple contemporary restaurant. The lettuce wraps make a great appetizer. **Bar:** beer & wine. **Address:** 675 E 2100 S, Suite C 84106 **Location:** I-80 exit 125 (700 E), 0.6 mi n; in 7-21 Plaza; northwest corner. L D

SEA SALT **Phone:** 801/349-1480 10

Southern Italian
$8-$19

AAA Inspector Notes: The spacious restaurant offers a wonderful variety of to-be-shared appetizers; minestrone and pasta e faioli soups; salads; wood-fired, Neopolitan-style, hand-tossed pizza; pasta with creative twists; grilled salmon; and chicken with cream polenta and braised greens. The rhubarb, strawberry, pistachio and buttermilk panna cotta is nice and light, but the budino chocolate cake sprinkled with sea salt and drizzled with olive oil is worth coming back for. **Bar:** full bar. **Reservations:** suggested. **Address:** 1709 E 1300 S 84108 **Location:** I-15 exit 305C (1300 S), 3 mi e; corner of 1700 E and 1300 S. **Parking:** street only. L D

STELLA GRILL **Phone:** 801/288-0051 21

American
$8-$20

AAA Inspector Notes: Soups, daily pasta salads, sandwiches and entrées, including oven-roasted game hen, rib-eye steak and Mexican dishes served with Southwest corn succotash and black beans, make up the menu. The desserts are scrumptious. **Bar:** full bar. **Address:** 4291 S 900 E 84107 **Location:** I-15 exit 301 (4500 S), 2 mi e to 900 E, then just n. L D

WING TIPS **Phone:** 801/741-1800 2

American
$9-$19

AAA Inspector Notes: Energizing and upscale décor paves the way for an enjoyable dinner with selections such as carpaccio, soups, salads, lasagna and New York strip grilled with olive oil and rosemary. The dessert menu is varied. **Bar:** full bar. **Address:** 5001 W Wiley Post Way 84116 **Location:** I-80 exit 114 westbound; exit 113 eastbound; in Holiday Inn Hotel & Suites Airport West.
B L D

MARKET STREET OYSTER BAR DOWNTOWN
Phone: 801/531-6044

fyi Not evaluated. Feast on spectacular fresh seafood from around the world. **Address:** 54 W Market St (350 S) 84101 **Location:** Just e on S Temple, 0.5 mi w on S Main St, then just w.

SANDY (B-3) pop. 87,461, elev. 4,465'

• Hotels & Restaurants map & index p. 426
• Part of Salt Lake City area — see map p. 412

THE LIVING PLANET AQUARIUM is .5 mi. e. on East 8800 South, 2.2 mi. s. on South 700 East/SR 71, then .1 mi. e. to 725 East 10600 South. The aquarium showcases more than 1,200 creatures in three main exhibit areas: Journey to South America, Ocean Explorer and Discover Utah. Visitors view such species as sharks, seahorses, jellyfish, octopus, piranha and caiman, while touch pools offer hands-on interaction with Southern stingrays. The facility also is home to a rescued green sea turtle and a colony of Gentoo penguins.

Time: Allow 1 hour minimum. **Hours:** Daily 10-6. Closed Thanksgiving and Christmas. **Cost:** $9; $8 (ages 65+ and students and military with ID); $7 (ages 3-17). **Phone:** (801) 355-3474.

BEST WESTERN PLUS COTTONTREE INN
Phone: (801)523-8484 66

Hotel
$99-$124

AAA Benefit: Members save up to 20%, plus 10% bonus points with Best Western Rewards®.

Address: 10695 S Auto Mall Dr 84070 **Location:** I-15 exit 293 (10600 S), 0.3 mi e, then just s. **Facility:** 111 units. 4 stories, interior corridors. **Amenities:** video games (fee). **Pool(s):** heated indoor. **Activities:** whirlpool, exercise room. **Guest Services:** valet and coin laundry, area transportation-within 5 mi. **Free Special Amenities: local telephone calls and high-speed Internet.**

 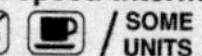  
SAVE / SOME UNITS FEE

COURTYARD BY MARRIOTT SANDY
Phone: (801)571-3600 64

Hotel
$161-$197

AAA Benefit:
AAA hotel discounts of 5% or more.

Address: 10701 S Holiday Park Dr 84070 **Location:** I-15 exit 293 (10600 S), just e, then just s. **Facility:** 124 units. 4 stories, interior corridors. **Amenities:** high-speed Internet. **Pool(s):** heated indoor. **Activities:** whirlpool, exercise room. **Guest Services:** valet and coin laundry, area transportation-within 3 mi.

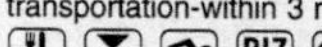

BIZ FEE

HAMPTON INN SANDY **Phone:** (801)571-0800 63

Hotel
$79-$149

AAA Benefit:
Members save up to 10% everyday!

Address: 10690 S Holiday Park Dr 84070 **Location:** I-15 exit 293 (10600 S), just e. **Facility:** 130 units. 4 stories, interior corridors. **Terms:** 1-7 night minimum stay, cancellation fee imposed. **Amenities:** video games (fee). **Pool(s):** heated indoor. **Activities:** whirlpool, exercise room. **Guest Services:** valet and coin laundry, area transportation-within 2 mi. BIZ

HILTON GARDEN INN SANDY
Phone: (801)352-9400 62

Hotel
$99-$209

AAA Benefit:
Unparalleled hospitality at a special Member rate.

Address: 277 W Sego Lilly Dr 84070 **Location:** I-15 exit 293 (10600 S), 0.4 mi e to State St, 0.7 mi n to 10000 S, then 0.3 mi w. **Facility:** 150 units. 5 stories, interior corridors. **Terms:** 1-7 night minimum stay, cancellation fee imposed. **Amenities:** high-speed Internet. **Pool(s):** heated indoor. **Activities:** whirlpool, exercise room. **Guest Services:** valet and coin laundry, area transportation-within 5 mi.

FEE BIZ

HOLIDAY INN EXPRESS & SUITES SANDY
Phone: 801/495-1317 65

Hotel
Rates not provided

Address: 10680 S Auto Mall Dr 84070 **Location:** I-15 exit 293 (10600 S), 0.3 mi e, then just s. **Facility:** 88 units. 3 stories, interior corridors. **Pool(s):** heated indoor. **Activities:** whirlpool, exercise room. **Guest Services:** valet and coin laundry.

BIZ / SOME UNITS FEE

HYATT SUMMERFIELD SUITES SALT LAKE CITY SANDY
Phone: (801)304-5700 60

Extended Stay Hotel
$89-$329

HYATT SUMMERFIELD SUITES

AAA Benefit: Members save 10% or more everyday.

Address: 9685 S Monroe St 84070 **Location:** I-15 exit 295 (9000 S), 0.3 mi e to Frontage Rd, then 1 mi s. **Facility:** 137 units, some two bedrooms, efficiencies and kitchens. 4 stories, interior corridors. *Bath:* shower only. **Terms:** cancellation fee imposed. **Pool(s):** heated outdoor. **Activities:** whirlpool, exercise room. **Guest Services:** valet and coin laundry, area transportation-within 5 mi. **Free Special Amenities: full breakfast and high-speed Internet.**

SAVE FEE BIZ

RESIDENCE INN BY MARRIOTT SANDY
Phone: (801)561-5005 61

Extended Stay Hotel
$99-$279

AAA Benefit:
AAA hotel discounts of 5% or more.

Address: 270 W 10000 S 84070 **Location:** I-15 exit 293 (10600 S), 0.4 mi e to State St, 0.7 mi n to 10000 S, then 0.3 mi w. **Facility:** 153 units, some two bedrooms and kitchens. 3 stories, interior corridors. **Amenities:** high-speed Internet. **Pool(s):** heated indoor. **Activities:** whirlpool, sports court, exercise room. **Guest Services:** valet and coin laundry, area transportation-within 3 mi.

BIZ / SOME UNITS FEE

WHERE TO EAT

CARVERS STEAKS & SEAFOOD
Phone: 801/572-5177 63

Steak
$19-$34

AAA Inspector Notes: This restaurant features relaxed dining in one of several unique dining rooms. Steaks, chops, seafood and choice prime rib offerings are available for your dining pleasure. **Bar:** full bar. **Reservations:** suggested. **Address:** 10720 S Holiday Park Dr 84070 **Location:** I-15 exit 293 (10600 S), 0.3 mi e, then just s. D

(See map & index p. 426.)

FRATELLI RISTORANTE **Phone:** 801/495-4550 (60)

Italian
$7-$26

AAA Inspector Notes: Owned and managed by two brothers, the upscale eatery offers traditional Italian dishes. Ingredients from Italy are used in some of grandmother's secret recipes. Menu items include a lovely caprese salad, a Sicilian citrus arugula salad, Margherita pizza and classic pasta dishes such as bucatini carbonara. Among entrées are yellowfin tuna with citrus pesto and certified Angus Tuscan steak in rosemary marinade. Pistachio cake layered with lemon mousse and raspberries is addictive. **Bar:** full bar. **Address:** 9236 S Village Shop Dr 84094 **Location:** I-15 exit 295 (9000 S), 3 mi e; in Quarry Bend Shopping Center. L D

IGGY'S SPORTS GRILL **Phone:** 801/495-1885

American
$8-$19

AAA Inspector Notes: Every seat offers a view of the sports action on multiple TVs. Among the many menu choices are salads, soups, steaks, pasta, ribs, chicken and seafood. A kids' menu is available. **Bar:** full bar. **Address:** 10631 S Holiday Park Dr 84070 **Location:** I-15 exit 293 (10600 S), 0.3 mi e, then just s. L D

JOE'S CRAB SHACK **Phone:** 801/255-9571

Seafood
$6-$25

AAA Inspector Notes: The popular seafood restaurant specializes in a year-round variety of crab: Alaskan king, Dungeness, snow and blue. Among other offerings are fresh shrimp, hearty gumbo, clam chowder and classic steaks and chicken. **Bar:** full bar. **Address:** 65 E 9400 S 84070 **Location:** I-15 exit 295 (9000 S); jct State St and 9400 S; in Jordan Commons. L D LATE

LA CAILLE **Phone:** 801/942-1751 (62)

Continental
$36-$68

AAA Inspector Notes: Cross the château gates and look for the swans, then step into a storybook in this restaurant, where the charming French atmosphere envelops an 18th-century estate surrounded by spacious, well-landscaped grounds. **Bar:** full bar. **Reservations:** suggested. **Address:** 9565 Wasatch Blvd 84092 **Location:** I-215 exit 6 (6200 S), e toward ski areas, 4 mi s to jct Little Cottonwood Rd, then continue 0.8 mi s on Wasatch Blvd. **Parking:** valet only. D

MI RANCHITO GRILL **Phone:** 801/233-0571 (61)

Mexican
$8-$17

AAA Inspector Notes: Fresh, quality ingredients are the first priority at this family restaurant. The menu includes delicious appetizers; cheese, chicken or beef nachos; chili verde burritos; grilled chicken breast chimichangas; enchiladas smothered in mole sauce; seasoned steak strips wrapped in flour tortillas; halibut tacos; tortillas stuffed with sautéed shrimp; and pan-fried, sizzling jumbo shrimp wrapped in bacon and served with grilled onions, peppers and tomatoes. Popular platters also are available. **Bar:** full bar. **Address:** 9550 S State St 84070 **Location:** I-15 exit 295 (9000 S), 0.5 mi e to State St, then 0.7 mi s. L D

TIBURON FINE DINING **Phone:** 801/255-1200 (59)

New American
$27-$38

AAA Inspector Notes: The restaurant's friendly greetings and great ambience signal warmth and class. Recommendations include grilled New Zealand elk tenderloin with green peppercorn demi glacé or dry-packed scallops in light chipotle cream sauce. Tastefully created desserts are not to be missed. **Bar:** full bar. **Reservations:** suggested. **Address:** 8256 S 700 E 84070 **Location:** I-15 exit 295 (9000 S), 1 mi e, then 1 mi n. D

SANTA CLARA (G-1) pop. 6,003, elev. 2,759'

JACOB HAMBLIN HOME is at Santa Clara Blvd. and Hamblin Dr. The house was the 1863 residence of a Mormon missionary noted for his peacemaking achievements with the Native Americans. The furnishings and implements are from the 1880s. **Time:** Allow 30 minutes minimum. **Hours:** Daily 10-7, May-Sept.; 10-5, rest of year. Last tour begins 30 minutes before closing. **Cost:** Free. **Phone:** (435) 673-2161, or (435) 673-5181 for the Temple Visitor Center Annex to schedule tours.

SANTAQUIN pop. 9,128

LESLIE'S FAMILY TREE RESTAURANT **Phone:** 801/754-3499

American
$5-$16

AAA Inspector Notes: This downtown cafe serves hot lunches, sandwiches, burgers on homemade buns, salads, shrimp and chicken baskets and a few south-of-the-border items. In addition, nice selections of steaks are featured for dinner. Beware, a 15-inch scone with honey butter is presented with entrées. **Address:** 77 W Main St 84655 **Location:** I-15 exit 244, 0.7 mi w. **Parking:** street only. B L D

SEVIER (E-3) elev. 5,542'

FREMONT INDIAN STATE PARK is 5 mi. s.w. off I-70 exit 17. The 1,784-acre park was established to protect the area's heritage of rock art and archeological sites. A museum interprets the evolution of the Fremont Anasazi Indian culture A.D. 500-1300 and displays artifacts and pictographs taken from nearby Five Fingers Hill. *See Recreation Chart.*

Time: Allow 30 minutes minimum. **Hours:** Daily 9-6, mid-May to mid-Sept.; 9-5, rest of year. Closed Jan. 1, Thanksgiving and Christmas. **Cost:** $6 (per private vehicle, maximum eight people) or $3 (per person arriving by other means); free (ages 0-5). Camping $13. **Phone:** (435) 527-4631.

SNOWBIRD B-3 elev. 8,163'

• **Hotels & Restaurants map & index p. 426**
• **Part of Salt Lake City area — see map p. 412**

RECREATIONAL ACTIVITIES

Skiing

- **Snowbird Ski and Summer Resort** is off I-215 exit 6; take 6200 South s.e., then SR 210 e. up Little Cottonwood Canyon. Other activities are offered. **Hours:** Winter activities daily 9-4:45, late Nov.-late May. Schedule varies rest of year; phone ahead. **Phone:** (801) 933-2222 or (800) 232-9542.

(See map & index p. 426.)

THE CLIFF LODGE, SPA & CONFERENCE CENTER **Phone:** 801/933-2222 (69)

Resort Hotel

Rates not provided

Address: Little Cottonwood Canyon Rd 84092 **Location:** 8 mi e on Little Cottonwood Canyon Rd, Level 4. **Facility:** Catering to skiers, this resort offers a luxurious spa, ski-in/ski-out accessibility and spacious indoor lockers and boot dryers. 457 units, some kitchens. 9 stories, interior corridors. **Parking:** on-site and valet. **Terms:** check-in 4 pm. **Amenities:** safes. **Dining:** 2 restaurants, also, Aerie Restaurant at Snowbird, see separate listing. **Pool(s):** heated outdoor. **Activities:** whirlpools, 2 tennis courts, recreation programs, bicycle trails, hiking trails, jogging, playground, sports court, basketball, horseshoes, volleyball, spa. *Fee:* downhill & cross country skiing, snowmobiling, horseback riding, game room, exercise room. **Guest Services:** complimentary laundry, area transportation-within 1 mi.

FEE BIZ

WHERE TO EAT

AERIE RESTAURANT AT SNOWBIRD **Phone:** 801/933-2160 (66)

New American

$21-$48

AAA Inspector Notes: The chef prepares innovative seafood creations in the sushi bar, which has breathtaking mountain views as its backdrop. Dining room specialties include pan-seared scallops, filet mignon and an assortment of seasonal desserts, including a signature fondue. **Bar:** full bar. **Reservations:** suggested. **Address:** Little Cottonwood Canyon Rd 84092 **Location:** 8 mi e on Little Cottonwood Canyon Rd, Level 4; in The Cliff Lodge, Spa & Conference Center. **Parking:** on-site and valet. D

SOUTH JORDAN pop. 50,418

- **Hotels & Restaurants map & index p. 426**
- **Part of Salt Lake City area — see map p. 412**

COUNTRY INN & SUITES BY CARLSON, SOUTH SALT LAKE CITY SOUTH TOWNE **Phone:** (801)553-1151 (57)

Hotel

$109-$149 11/1-4/30

$99-$139 5/1-10/31

Address: 10499 S Jordan Gateway 84095 **Location:** I-15 exit 293 (10600 S), just w, then just n. **Facility:** 128 units. 6 stories, interior corridors. **Terms:** cancellation fee imposed. **Amenities:** video games (fee), high-speed Internet. **Pool(s):** heated indoor. **Activities:** whirlpool, exercise room. **Guest Services:** valet and coin laundry, area transportation-within 5 mi. **Free Special Amenities: expanded continental breakfast and manager's reception.**

SAVE ECO FEE BIZ FEE

/SOME UNITS

WHERE TO EAT

GECKO'S MEXICAN GRILL **Phone:** 801/253-8668 (55)

Mexican

$8-$15

AAA Inspector Notes: The restaurant offers an authentic atmosphere and a friendly staff; guests shouldn't be surprised to see the owner preparing the food and delivering it to the tables. **Address:** 781 W 10600 S 84095 **Location:** I-15 exit 293 (10600 S), 0.5 mi w. L D

MADELINES STEAKHOUSE & GRILL **Phone:** 801/446-6639 (54)

Steak

$7-$28

AAA Inspector Notes: This family-owned restaurant serves made-from-scratch fare for lunch and dinner. Choices include large mushrooms stuffed with Italian sausage and cream cheese, salads with gluten-free dressings, certified Angus beef cuts such as the Grande Dame porterhouse and filet mignon, and seafood specialties of raspberry halibut and teriyaki salmon. Among luscious desserts are Alicia's cheesecake, cookies-and-cream mud pie and peanut butter cup. **Bar:** full bar. **Address:** 1133 W 10600 S 84095 **Location:** I-15 exit 293, 1 mi w. L D

MARKET STREET GRILL SOUTH JORDAN **Phone:** 801/302-2262 (56)

Seafood

$14-$38

AAA Inspector Notes: After warm bread, delicious soup and a fresh salad, guests then choose from a variety of blackened or broiled fresh fish and other seafood dishes centered on oysters, clams, mussels, shrimp, ahi tuna, Atlantic salmon and lobster. Although it's nowhere near, this place has an ocean-close atmosphere. A delightful selection of mouthwatering desserts rounds out the meal. **Bar:** full bar. **Address:** 10702 S River Front Pkwy 84095 **Location:** I-15 exit 293 (10600 S), 0.4 mi w, then just s; located in RiverPark. L D

MARKET STREET OYSTER BAR SOUTH JORDAN **Phone:** 801/302-2264

fyi Not evaluated. Feast on spectacular fresh seafood from around the world. **Address:** 10702 S River Front Pkwy 84095 **Location:** I-15 exit 293 (10600 S), 0.4 mi w, then just s; in RiverPark.

SOUTH SALT LAKE pop. 23,617

- **Hotels & Restaurants map & index p. 426**
- **Part of Salt Lake City area — see map p. 412**

LEFT FORK GRILL **Phone:** 801/266-4322 (33)

Comfort Food

$7-$14

AAA Inspector Notes: The diner serves great classic selections, including soups made fresh daily, meatloaf sandwiches, chicken schnitzel and open-faced hot turkey and steak sandwiches. Fresh seasonal pies, such as the exquisite banana, blueberry or peach cream, are the signature here. **Bar:** beer & wine. **Address:** 68 W 3900 S 84107 **Location:** I-15 exit 303, just e to 300 W, 1 mi s to 3900 S, then just e. L D

PAT'S BARBECUE **Phone:** 801/487-7287 (31)

Barbecue

$9-$15

AAA Inspector Notes: This barbecue-and-blues joint features award-winning hand rubbed-and-smoked pulled pork and beef brisket, pork ribs, chicken and Southern comfort food. Daily weekday specials are not to be missed and include burnt ends each Friday. Homemade desserts vary daily, but the sweet potato pie is a hit. Patrons can enjoy live music during lunch and dinner. **Bar:** beer only. **Address:** 155 W Commonwealth Ave 84115 **Location:** 2.8 mi s from Temple Square via S West Temple St, then just s of 2100 S; located in industrial neighborhood. **Parking:** on-site and street. L D

VERTICAL DINER **Phone:** 801/484-8378 (32)

Vegan

$6-$11

AAA Inspector Notes: This interesting diner serves vegetarian comfort food. **Bar:** beer & wine. **Address:** 2280 S W Temple 84115 **Location:** 3.3 mi s of Temple Square. L D

SPANISH FORK pop. 34,691

WESTERN INN **Phone:** 801/798-9400

Motel

$50-$80

Address: 632 Kirby Ln 84660 **Location:** I-15 exit 257 northbound (US 6/Price), exit 258 southbound (US 6/Price), 1 mi se. **Facility:** 47 units, some efficiencies. 2 stories, interior corridors. **Terms:** cancellation fee imposed. **Guest Services:** coin laundry. **Free Special Amenities: continental breakfast and high-speed Internet.**

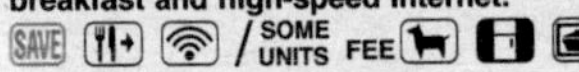

SPRINGDALE (G-2) pop. 529, elev. 3,912'

Springdale was founded by Mormon pioneers in the 1850s. Because of its location at the south entrance to Zion National Park *(see place listing p. 461)*, the town supports a number of accommodations and shops for park visitors.

The O.C. Tanner Amphitheater, just outside the entrance to Zion National Park, is a 2,000-seat site of outdoor concerts presented on Saturdays, Memorial Day through Labor Day. The amphitheater's mountain backdrop provides natural acoustics; phone (435) 652-7994 for ticket information.

ZION CANYON GIANT SCREEN THEATRE is at 145 Zion Park Blvd. Using a six-story-high, 82-foot-wide screen and digital surround sound, "Zion Canyon Treasure of the Gods" showcases Zion National Park and the canyonlands. Other large-format nature films and Hollywood blockbusters also are screened. **Hours:** Presentations are given daily on the hour 11-7. Phone ahead for film schedule. **Cost:** $8; $6 (ages 0-11 and 60+). **Phone:** (435) 772-2400 or (888) 256-3456.

ZION OUTBACK SAFARIS departs from local hotels. Visitors experience the backcountry of Zion National Park in comfortable, open-air safari vehicles. Guides discuss the park's ecosystem, geology, history and wildlife as well as local folklore. A sunset safari tour also is offered. **Time:** Allow 3 hours minimum. **Hours:** Outback safari tours depart Mon.-Sat. at noon, Sun. at 1. Sunset tours depart daily 2 hours before dusk. Phone ahead to confirm schedule. **Cost:** Outback safari tour $59; $41 (ages 1-11). Sunset tour $64; $46 (ages 1-11). **Phone:** (866) 946-6494.

BEST WESTERN ZION PARK INN **Phone:** (435)772-3200

Hotel

$89-$150

AAA Benefit: Members save up to 20%, plus 10% bonus points with Best Western Rewards®.

Address: 1215 Zion Park Blvd 84767 **Location:** 2 mi s of park entrance. **Facility:** 120 units, some efficiencies. 2 stories, interior corridors. **Amenities:** video games (fee). **Dining:** Switchback Grille, see separate listing. **Pool(s):** heated outdoor. **Activities:** whirlpool, putting green, hiking trails, basketball, horseshoes, volleyball. **Guest Services:** coin laundry. **Free Special Amenities: local telephone calls and high-speed Internet.** *(See ad p. 467.)*

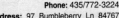

BUMBLEBERRY INN **Phone:** 435/772-3224

Motel

$58-$128

Address: 97 Bumbleberry Ln 84767 **Location:** SR 9, 1 mi s of south gate to Zion National Park. **Facility:** 48 units. 2 stories (no elevator), interior corridors. **Terms:** 3 day cancellation notice. **Pool(s):** heated outdoor. **Activities:** whirlpool, racquetball court, limited exercise equipment. **Guest Services:** coin laundry. **Free Special Amenities: local telephone calls and high-speed Internet.** *(See ad p. 467.)*

CANYON RANCH MOTEL **Phone:** 435/772-3357

Motel

Rates not provided

Address: 668 Zion Park Blvd 84767 **Location:** SR 9, just s of south gate to Zion National Park. **Facility:** 22 units, some efficiencies. 1 story, exterior corridors. **Pool(s):** outdoor. **Activities:** whirlpool. ***(See ad p. 466.)***

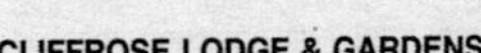

CLIFFROSE LODGE & GARDENS **Phone:** (435)772-3234

Motel

$129-$429 5/1-10/31
$79-$429 11/1-4/30

Address: 281 Zion Park Blvd 84767 **Location:** Just s of south gate to Zion National Park. **Facility:** 50 units, some two bedrooms and efficiencies. 2 stories (no elevator), exterior corridors. **Terms:** 3 day cancellation notice-fee imposed. **Pool(s):** heated outdoor. **Activities:** whirlpool, playground. *Fee:* massage. **Guest Services:** coin laundry. *(See ad p. 466.)*

/ SOME UNITS

DESERT PEARL INN **Phone:** 435/772-8888

Motel

Rates not provided

Address: 707 Zion Park Blvd 84767 **Location:** SR 9, just s of south gate to Zion National Park. **Facility:** 73 units, some efficiencies and kitchens. 2 stories (no elevator), exterior corridors. **Terms:** seasonal. **Amenities:** safes. **Pool(s):** heated outdoor. **Activities:** whirlpool. *Fee:* massage. **Guest Services:** coin laundry.

FLANIGAN'S INN & DEEP CANYON ADVENTURE SPA **Phone:** 435/772-3244

Motel
Rates not provided

Address: 450 Zion Park Blvd 84767 **Location:** Just s of south gate to Zion National Park. Located in a quiet area. **Facility:** 34 units, some two bedrooms. 1-2 stories (no elevator), exterior corridors. **Dining:** Spotted Dog Cafe at Flanigan's Inn, see separate listing. **Pool(s):** heated outdoor. **Activities:** whirlpool, hiking trails, spa. **Guest Services:** coin laundry. **Free Special Amenities: local telephone calls and high-speed Internet.** *(See ad p. 466.)*

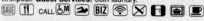

MAJESTIC VIEW LODGE **Phone:** (435)772-0665

Hotel
$89-$269

Address: 2400 Zion Park Blvd 84767 **Location:** 3.5 mi s of park entrance. **Facility:** 69 units. 2 stories (no elevator), exterior corridors. **Dining:** Arkansas Al's Pub & Eatery, see separate listing. **Pool(s):** heated outdoor. **Activities:** whirlpool, hiking trails. **Guest Services:** coin laundry, area transportation-Zion National Park. **Free Special Amenities: newspaper and high-speed Internet.** *(See ad p. 467.)*

/ SOME UNITS

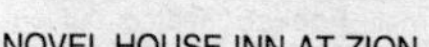

NOVEL HOUSE INN AT ZION **Phone:** (435)772-3650

Bed & Breakfast
$139-$159

Address: 73 Paradise Rd 84767 **Location:** Just off SR 9, 1 mi s of Zion National Park. **Facility:** This romantic getaway with spacious rooms inspired by famous authors offers a library with board games and books, a covered porch and a secluded patio. 10 units. 2 stories (no elevator), interior corridors. **Terms:** 2 night minimum stay - seasonal and/or weekends, age restrictions may apply, 7 day cancellation notice-fee imposed. ***(See ad p. 466.)***

PIONEER LODGE **Phone:** (435)772-3233

Motel
$109-$299 5/1-10/31
$69-$169 11/1-4/30

Address: 838 Zion Park Blvd 84767 **Location:** Center. **Facility:** 43 units, some three bedrooms and kitchens. 2 stories (no elevator), exterior corridors. **Terms:** 3 day cancellation notice-fee imposed. **Dining:** restaurant, see separate listing. **Pool(s):** heated outdoor. **Activities:** whirlpool. **Guest Services:** coin laundry.

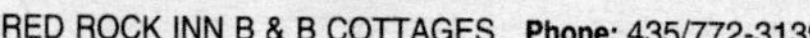

RED ROCK INN B & B COTTAGES **Phone:** 435/772-3139

Cottage
$89-$219

Address: 998 Zion Park Blvd 84767 **Location:** SR 9, just w of center. **Facility:** Shaded lawn. Flower and cactus garden. 5 cottages. 1 story, exterior corridors. **Terms:** check-in 4 pm, 7 day cancellation notice. **Amenities:** safes.

UNDER THE EAVES INN **Phone:** 435/772-3457

Bed & Breakfast
Rates not provided

Address: 980 Zion Park Blvd 84767 **Location:** SR 9, just w of center. **Facility:** 6 units. 2 stories (no elevator), interior/exterior corridors. **Terms:** age restrictions may apply.

WHERE TO EAT

ARKANSAS AL'S PUB & EATERY **Phone:** 435/772-0665

American
$13-$30

AAA Inspector Notes: Perched atop a large hill, the restaurant affords amazing views of the surrounding Zion Mountains through the floor-to-ceiling windows in its rustic dining room. High ceilings and a stone waterfall lend visual impact to the setting. Representative of its casual American cuisine are burgers, New York steak and trout. **Bar:** beer & wine. **Address:** 2400 Zion Park Blvd 84767 **Location:** 3.5 mi s of park entrance; in Majestic View Lodge.

L D

BIT AND SPUR SALOON & RESTAURANT **Phone:** 435/772-3498

Mexican
$9-$25

AAA Inspector Notes: Near Zion National Park, this upbeat restaurant offers Southwestern cuisine, baby back ribs and Mexican favorites. **Bar:** full bar. **Reservations:** suggested. **Address:** 1212 Zion Park Blvd 84767 **Location:** 2 mi s of park entrance. D

BLONDIE'S DINER **Phone:** 435/772-0595

American
$3-$9

AAA Inspector Notes: Next to an antelope and buffalo farm, the small country-style spot has a diner feel in its small dining room, where many signs display joking phrases. Examples of the simple home-style cooking include burgers, chicken breast and homemade pies. Guests can munch on buffalo burgers while watching the buffalo roam right outside. **Address:** 736 Zion Park Blvd 84767 **Location:** SR 9, 0.9 mi s of south gate to Zion National Park. B L D

CAFE SOLEIL **Phone:** 435/772-0505

American
$4-$9

AAA Inspector Notes: Just outside the entrance to the park, the small cafe employs friendly staff members who serve guests behind the counter. This place is known for great breakfasts, which might include a fresh bagel, oatmeal or fruit. Fresh coffee gets patrons going in the morning. Packed lunches are available to purchase and take on a hike. **Bar:** beer only. **Address:** 205 Zion Park Blvd 84767 **Location:** Just s of south gate to Zion National Park. B L D

PIONEER LODGE INTERNET CAFE **Phone:** 435/772-3233

American
$3-$5

AAA Inspector Notes: Internet access is hard to find in this rural location, but luckily this small Internet cafe helps travelers stay connected. In addition to specialty coffee drinks and smoothies, patrons can order food selections from the limited breakfast and lunch menu. **Address:** 838 Zion Park Blvd 84767 **Location:** Center; in Pioneer Lodge. B L

PIONEER RESTAURANT **Phone:** 435/772-3009

American
$6-$25

AAA Inspector Notes: Springdale's historic restaurant features a rustic, pioneer atmosphere along with country cooking, prime rib and, on weekends, Navajo tacos. Diners enjoy delicious daily specials and a vegetarian menu, all within the shadows of Zion National Park. **Bar:** full bar. **Address:** 838 Zion Park Blvd 84767 **Location:** Center; in Pioneer Lodge. B L D

SPOTTED DOG CAFE AT FLANIGAN'S INN **Phone:** 435/772-0700

Continental
$14-$27

AAA Inspector Notes: A pearl in the desert just outside Zion National Park, the cafe offers a seasonal menu with rabbit, Utah lamb and fresh local vegetables. **Bar:** full bar. **Address:** 428 Zion Park Blvd 84767 **Location:** Just s of south gate to Zion National Park; in Flanigan's Inn & Deep Canyon Adventure Spa. B D

SWITCHBACK GRILLE **Phone:** 435/772-3700

Steak
$7-$34

AAA Inspector Notes: Patrons relax in the attractive dining room while savoring delicious preparations of beef, seafood and poultry. Service is attentive. **Bar:** full bar. **Address:** 1149 Zion Park Blvd 84767 **Location:** 2 mi s of park entrance; adjacent to Best Western Zion Park Inn.

B D

WILDCAT WILLIE'S RESTAURANT **Phone:** 435/772-0115

American

$10-$30

AAA Inspector Notes: The central and easy-to-find restaurant is an easy walk from most parts of town. Bare wood walls, cast-iron chandeliers and wooden booths and tables scream the West. The menu features many Western favorites, including rib-eye steak, sea bass, Idaho trout and the unforgettable bumbleberry pie for dessert. Friendly servers gladly make suggestions. **Bar:** full bar. **Address:** 897 Zion Park Blvd 84767 **Location:** SR 9, 1 mi s of south gate to Zion National Park; adjacent to Bumbleberry Inn. B L D

ZION PIZZA & NOODLE CO. **Phone:** 435/772-3815

Italian

$10-$15

AAA Inspector Notes: The popular restaurant in the center of town has guests line up at the counter to order and pay for their pizza and pasta favorites. Because seating in the main dining room is limited, many head to the front or back patio. The freshly brewed wheat beer is recommended. **Bar:** beer & wine. **Address:** 868 Zion Park Blvd 84767 **Location:** Center. D

SPRINGVILLE (C-3) pop. 29,466, elev. 4,571'

Springville, overshadowed by the Wasatch Mountains on the east and bordered by Utah Lake on the west, is an important agricultural center. The town, settled by eight pioneer families in 1850, was originally called Hobble Creek because the pioneers' horses were often hobbled and left along the stream to graze; if they wandered into the creek their hobbles came off.

The Daughters of Utah Pioneers Museum, 151 S. Main St., houses relics of area pioneers; phone the chamber of commerce at (801) 489-4681. Jeep tours, fishing, hunting and snowmobiling are available nearby.

Springville Area Chamber of Commerce: 224 S. Main St., #440, Springville, UT 84663. **Phone:** (801) 489-4681.

SPRINGVILLE MUSEUM OF ART is at 126 E. 400 South. The museum has six galleries containing works by Utah painters, sculptors and printmakers from 1850 to the present, and seven galleries housing changing exhibitions. The museum, said to be Utah's oldest art museum, contains a collection of Soviet socialist realist paintings and the Utah Photographic Art Reference Archive, which documents the history of Utah art.

The museum grounds contain sculptures. Museum tours and a research library are available. **Hours:** Tues.-Sat. 10-5 (also Wed. 5-9), Sun. 3-6. Closed major holidays. **Cost:** Free. **Phone:** (801) 489-2727.

BEST WESTERN MOUNTAIN VIEW INN **Phone:** (801)489-3641

Hotel

$70-$160

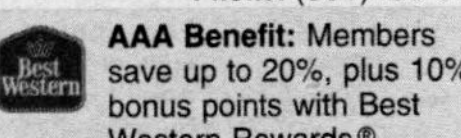

AAA Benefit: Members save up to 20%, plus 10% bonus points with Best Western Rewards®.

Address: 1455 N 1750 W 84663 **Location:** I-15 exit 261, just e. **Facility:** 55 units. 2 stories (no elevator), interior corridors. **Terms:** check-in 4 pm. **Pool(s):** heated outdoor. **Activities:** whirlpool. **Guest Services:** coin laundry. **Free Special Amenities: full breakfast and high-speed Internet.**

/ SOME UNITS FEE

CABLE MOUNTAIN LODGE **Phone:** (435)772-3366

Hotel

$149-$249 5/1-10/31
$89-$159 11/1-4/30

Address: 147 Zion Park Blvd 84767 **Location:** Just s of Zion National Park entrance; in Toaquim's Village. **Facility:** 50 units, some kitchens. 2 stories, exterior corridors. **Terms:** 3 day cancellation notice-fee imposed. **Amenities:** high-speed Internet. **Pool(s):** heated outdoor. **Activities:** whirlpool. **Guest Services:** coin laundry. *(See ad p. 467.)*

DAYS INN **Phone:** (801)491-0300

Motel

$44-$95

Address: 520 S 2000 W 84663 **Location:** I-15 exit 260, just w. **Facility:** 64 units. 3 stories, interior corridors. **Pool(s):** outdoor. **Activities:** whirlpool.

TEASDALE pop. 191

MULEY TWIST INN BED & BREAKFAST **Phone:** (435)425-3640

Bed & Breakfast

$99-$150

Address: 249 W 125 S 84773 **Location:** 4.5 mi w of jct SR 12 and 24 to Teasdale Rd (CR 3262), 1.5 mi s to 125 S, then 0.5 mi w. **Facility:** Specialty omelets, South-rim eggs, homemade bagels and gourmet coffee set the tone for breakfast at this B&B. Rocking chairs are on the covered wraparound porch. 5 units. 2 stories (no elevator), interior corridors. **Terms:** open 5/1-10/15 & 4/15-4/30, check-in 4 pm, 10 day cancellation notice-fee imposed. **Activities:** bicycles, hiking trails, jogging. CALL

TIMPANOGOS CAVE NATIONAL MONUMENT (C-2)

Seven miles east of American Fork on SR 92, Timpanogos Cave National Monument covers 250 acres in the American Fork Canyon on the north slope of 11,750-foot Mount Timpanogos. The visitor center is 10 miles east off I-15 exit 287 between Salt Lake City and Provo; a 20-minute introductory film is shown upon request.

Three large limestone caverns are connected by man-made tunnels. About 1,800 feet in length, the limestone caves maintain an average temperature of 45 F with nearly 100 percent humidity. Dripstone is still forming, and spectacular helictites, aragonite crystals, stalagmites and stalactites are found throughout the lighted caverns. The cave entrance, about 1,065 feet above the canyon floor, is reached from the visitor center by a strenuous, 1.5-mile paved foot trail. Wheelchairs and strollers are not permitted on the trail. The round-trip takes about 3 hours, including the cave tour. A self-guiding trail booklet is available at the visitor center.

Visitors must purchase tickets for cave tours at the visitor center before hiking up the 1.5-mile paved trail. Tours are limited to 20 people. Arrive as early as possible or phone ahead, since tours are often filled by mid-morning. Expect to wait several hours on Saturdays and holidays. A caving instructional tour also is available Memorial Day through Labor Day for ages 14 and older. Tickets can be purchased up to 30 days in advance; phone (801) 756-5238.

Picnicking is permitted. Food is available. The visitor center and the cave are open daily 7-5:30, Memorial Day weekend-Labor Day weekend; 8-5, Mother's Day weekend-day before Memorial Day weekend and day after Labor Day-Columbus Day. Cave tours begin every 10-20 minutes 8-3:30. Last tour begins 1 hour before closing, Memorial Day weekend-Labor Day; 90 minutes before closing, Mother's Day weekend-day before Memorial Day weekend and day after Labor Day-Columbus Day. The cave tour is $7; $5 (ages 6-15); $3.50 (ages 62+ with America the Beautiful–National Parks and Federal Recreational Lands Pass–Senior Pass); $3 (ages 3-5). The Introduction to Caving tour is $15; under 15 are not permitted. There is a fee of $6 (or $12 for 7 days) to drive the Canyon Road (also known as SR 92 and American Fork Canyon-Alpine Loop Scenic Backway).

For further information contact the Superintendent, Timpanogos Cave National Monument, R.R. 3, Box 200, American Fork, UT 84003; phone (801) 756-5239.

TOOELE (C-3) pop. 31,605, elev. 4,885'

BENSON GRIST MILL is on SR 138 adjacent to Stansbury Park. The grist mill was built in 1854 under the direction of Ezra Taft Benson, an apostle of The Church of Jesus Christ of Latter-day Saints, to serve the early Mormon settlers in Tooele County. The site also includes a blacksmith shop, cabins, a miller's home and a museum. **Time:** Allow 1 hour minimum. **Hours:** Mon.-Sat. 10-4, May-Oct. **Cost:** Free. **Phone:** (435) 882-7678.

TOOELE VALLEY RAILROAD MUSEUM is at 35 N. Broadway. The area's history is depicted through artifacts pertaining to railroading, smelting and mining. The museum's centerpiece is a 1910 steam locomotive that has been restored and converted into an interpretive display. A miniature train offers rides to visitors on some Saturdays. **Time:** Allow 30 minutes minimum. **Hours:** Tues.-Sat. 1-4, Memorial Day weekend-Labor Day. **Cost:** Donations. **Phone:** (435) 882-2836.

AMERICAN INN & SUITES **Phone:** 435/882-6100

Hotel

Rates not provided

Address: 491 S Main St 84074 **Location:** I-80 exit 99, 12 mi s. **Facility:** 50 units. 2 stories (no elevator), exterior corridors. **Pool(s):** heated outdoor. **Activities:** whirlpool, exercise room. **Guest Services:** coin laundry.

BEST WESTERN INN TOOELE **Phone:** (435)882-5010

Hotel

$90-$139

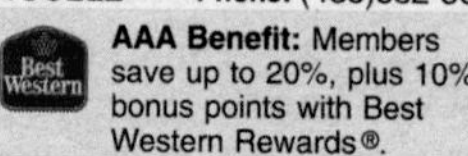

AAA Benefit: Members save up to 20%, plus 10% bonus points with Best Western Rewards®.

Address: 365 N Main St 84074 **Location:** I-80 exit 99, 11 mi s. **Facility:** 31 units, some houses. 2 stories (no elevator), interior/exterior corridors. **Amenities:** *Some:* high-speed Internet. **Pool(s):** heated indoor. **Activities:** whirlpool, exercise room. **Guest Services:** coin laundry. **Free Special Amenities: full breakfast and high-speed Internet.**

HAMPTON INN TOOELE **Phone:** (435)843-7700

Hotel

$129-$149

AAA Benefit:
Members save up to 10% everyday!

Address: 461 S Main St 84074 **Location:** I-80 exit 99, 12 mi s. **Facility:** 51 units. 4 stories, interior corridors. **Terms:** 1-7 night minimum stay, cancellation fee imposed. **Pool(s):** heated indoor. **Activities:** whirlpool, exercise room. **Guest Services:** coin laundry.

HOLIDAY INN EXPRESS & SUITES TOOELE
Phone: (435)833-0500

Hotel

$199-$205 5/1-10/1
$129-$139 10/2-4/30

Address: 1531 N Main St 84074 **Location:** I-80 exit 99, 11 mi s. **Facility:** 64 units. 3 stories, interior corridors. **Terms:** 3 day cancellation notice-fee imposed. **Amenities:** high-speed Internet. **Pool(s):** heated indoor. **Activities:** whirlpool, exercise room. **Guest Services:** coin laundry.

FEE

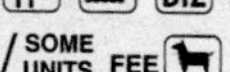

/ SOME UNITS FEE

WHERE TO EAT

SOSTANZA ON MAIN **Phone:** 435/882-4922

American

$9-$29

AAA Inspector Notes: This new restaurant offers American fusion food in an upscale atmosphere. The menu includes a wide selection of salads, filet mignon served with chipotle potato gratin and sautéed shiitake mushrooms, pan-seared half chicken, broasted halibut, baked Dover sole, chicken penne, red-pesto gnocchi with prawns and caramelized pulled pork. The ample and eye-pleasing dessert selection is presented on a tray. **Bar:** full bar. **Address:** 29 N Main St 84074 **Location:** Just n of center.

L D

THAI HOUSE **Phone:** 435/882-7579

Thai

$8-$13

AAA Inspector Notes: Among the many Thai specialties are cashew-nut stir-fry, vegetarian dishes and house-made coconut ice cream. The warm ambience and friendly service keep guests coming back. **Address:** 297 N Main St 84074 **Location:** I-80 exit 99, 11 mi s.

L D

TORREY pop. 182

AUSTINS CHUCK WAGON LODGE

Phone: (435)425-3335

Motel
$79

Address: 12 W Main St 84775 **Location:** On SR 24, 1.2 mi w of SR 12. **Facility:** 18 units, some cabins. 1-2 stories (no elevator), exterior corridors. **Terms:** open 5/1-11/1 & 3/15-4/30. **Pool(s):** heated outdoor. **Activities:** whirlpool, bicycles, hiking trails, jogging. **Guest Services:** coin laundry. **Free Special Amenities: local telephone calls and high-speed Internet.**

(See ad this page.)

/ SOME UNITS

BEST WESTERN CAPITOL REEF RESORT

Phone: (435)425-3761

Motel
$100-$120

AAA Benefit: Members save up to 20%, plus 10% bonus points with Best Western Rewards®.

Address: 2600 E Hwy 24 84775 **Location:** 2 mi e of jct SR 12 and 24. **Facility:** 100 units. 1-2 stories (no elevator), exterior corridors. **Terms:** check-in 4 pm, cancellation fee imposed. **Amenities:** *Some:* high-speed Internet. **Dining:** Red Cliff Restaurant, see separate listing. **Pool(s):** heated outdoor. **Activities:** whirlpool, lighted tennis court, basketball. **Guest Services:** coin laundry. **Free Special Amenities: local telephone calls and high-speed Internet.**

/ SOME UNITS FEE

COWBOY HOMESTEAD CABINS

Phone: 435/425-3414

Cabin
$79-$89 5/1-10/31
$69-$79 11/1-4/30

Address: 2323 S Hwy 12 84775 **Location:** 3.3 mi s of jct SR 12 and 24. **Facility:** 4 cabins. 1 story, exterior corridors. **Terms:** check-in 4 pm, 7 day cancellation notice-fee imposed. **Activities:** hiking trails, jogging. *Fee:* fishing.

DAYS INN TORREY

Phone: (435)425-3111

Hotel
$41-$108

Address: 675 E Hwy 24 84775 **Location:** Jct SR 12 and 24. **Facility:** 39 units. 2 stories (no elevator), interior corridors. **Pool(s):** heated indoor. **Activities:** whirlpool. **Guest Services:** coin laundry.

/ SOME UNITS

HOWARD JOHNSON

Phone: (435)425-3866

Hotel
$62-$98

Address: 877 N SR 24 84775 **Location:** 1.5 mi ne of jct SR 12 and 24. **Facility:** 40 units. 2 stories (no elevator), exterior corridors. **Activities:** exercise room. **Guest Services:** coin laundry.

/ SOME UNITS FEE

RED SANDS HOTEL

Phone: 435/425-3688

Hotel
Rates not provided

Address: 670 E Hwy 24 84775 **Location:** 0.3 mi w of jct SR 12 and 24. **Facility:** 35 units. 2 stories (no elevator), interior corridors. **Terms:** seasonal. **Pool(s):** heated indoor. **Activities:** whirlpool. **Guest Services:** coin laundry. **Free Special Amenities: continental breakfast and preferred room (subject to availability with advance reservations).**

/ SOME UNITS FEE

RIM ROCK INN **Phone:** (435)425-3398

Motel
$59-$79

Address: 2523 E Hwy 24 84775 **Location:** 2.5 mi ne of jct SR 12 and 24. **Facility:** 19 units. 1 story, exterior corridors. **Terms:** open 5/1-11/1, cancellation fee imposed. **Dining:** restaurant, see separate listing. **Activities:** hiking trails, horseshoes. **Free Special Amenities: continental breakfast and high-speed Internet.**

SKYRIDGE INN BED & BREAKFAST **Phone:** 435/425-3222

Bed & Breakfast
$119-$164

Address: 1090 E Hwy 24 84775 **Location:** Just e of jct SR 12 and 24. **Facility:** Southwest sophistication and magnificent views are part of the package at this Territorial-style house, set on 75 acres overlooking red rock cliffs. 6 units. 3 stories (no elevator), interior/exterior corridors. **Terms:** open 5/1-12/20 & 3/1-4/30, check-in 4 pm, 11 day cancellation notice-fee imposed. **Activities:** whirlpool, hiking trails. **Free Special Amenities: full breakfast and high-speed Internet.**

TORREY SCHOOLHOUSE BED & BREAKFAST **Phone:** 435/633-4643

Bed & Breakfast
$110-$160

Address: 150 N Center St 84775 **Location:** 1 mi w of jct SR 12 and 24, then just n. **Facility:** At this beautiful inn, the spectacular views are the star attraction. The spacious, school-themed rooms have names like Music, Arithmetic, Reading and Writing. There's a Teacher's Lounge, too. 10 units. 3 stories (no elevator), interior corridors. **Terms:** open 5/1-11/1, age restrictions may apply, 7 day cancellation notice-fee imposed. SOME UNITS

WHERE TO EAT

CAFE DIABLO **Phone:** 435/425-3070

Southwestern
$22-$29

AAA Inspector Notes: Friendly, attentive service are hallmarks of this casually upscale cafe. Among the menu favorites are painted salmon, pecan chicken, empanadas, duck mariachi, rattlesnake cakes and pumpkin seed trout, all innovatively presented. Wonderful homemade ice cream and pastries also are offered. Seating is seasonally available on a patio beside the herb and tulip garden. **Bar:** full bar. **Address:** 599 W Main St 84775 **Location:** 1 mi w of jct SR 12 and 24. L D

CAPITOL REEF CAFE **Phone:** 435/425-3271

Southwestern
$6-$19

AAA Inspector Notes: The cafe serves a variety of fresh local items, including a standout 10-vegetable salad. A mural of the Red Mountains graces the entrance, where guests also may notice the soothing sounds of calming music. Large windows afford panoramic views of the mountains themselves. Among the healthful choices are chicken, salmon and trout. **Bar:** beer & wine. **Address:** 360 W Main St 84775 **Location:** 1 mi w of jct SR 12 and 24.

B L D

CASTLE ROCK COFFEE & CANDY **Phone:** 435/425-2100

Coffee/Tea
$5-$8

AAA Inspector Notes: Fresh-from-the-oven breakfast sandwiches, cinnamon rolls, croissants, English scones, Japanese banana bread, muffins and incredibly delicious all-grain trail bars are served at this popular eatery. Homemade power bagels are served with peanut butter, banana, cranberries and walnuts, and the smoked flaked salmon with cream cheese is a delicious treat. Soups and freshly squeezed juices and smoothies are great thirst-quenchers after a day in the dessert. Wireless Internet is available. **Address:** 685 Hwy 24 84775 **Location:** Jct SR 12 and 24. B L

RED CLIFF RESTAURANT **Phone:** 435/425-3797

American
$8-$23

AAA Inspector Notes: Patrons can choose from a good selection of comfort food for both breakfast and dinner. The salad bar complements beef, pork, seafood and pasta dishes. **Bar:** full bar. **Address:** 2600 E Hwy 24 84775 **Location:** 2 mi e of jct SR 12 and 24; in Best Western Capitol Reef Resort. B D

RIM ROCK PATIO **Phone:** 435/425-3389

Italian
$6-$13

AAA Inspector Notes: The eatery has mostly patio seating with a small bar area inside. Guests can play darts, disc golf and horseshoes while they wait for their food or after their meal. The menu consists of pizza, sandwiches, beer and prepackaged desserts. **Bar:** beer only. **Address:** 2523 E Hwy 24 84775 **Location:** 2 mi e of jct SR 12 and 24. L D

RIM ROCK RESTAURANT **Phone:** 435/425-3388

American
$11-$29

AAA Inspector Notes: Perched atop a red rock cliff, this restaurant features 10 large windows with stunning views of the rim rocks. House-made pepper fettuccine, brown and wild rice, baked potato and baked beans are just a few of the eight side-dish selections available with each entrée. The popular nightly seasonal mixed grill may include elk bratwurst, Utah trout and quail. Vegetarian items also are available, including a tasty mole enchilada. **Bar:** full bar. **Reservations:** suggested. **Address:** 2523 E Hwy 24 84775 **Location:** 2.5 mi ne of jct SR 12 and 24; in Rim Rock Inn.

D

TREMONTON pop. 7,647

HAMPTON INN **Phone:** (435)257-6000

Hotel
$89-$109

AAA Benefit:
Members save up to 10% everyday!

Address: 2145 W Main St 84337 **Location:** I-84 exit 40, 0.4 mi e. **Facility:** 67 units. 3 stories, interior corridors. **Terms:** 1-7 night minimum stay, cancellation fee imposed. **Amenities:** high-speed Internet. **Pool(s):** heated indoor. **Activities:** whirlpool, exercise room. **Guest Services:** valet and coin laundry.

SOME UNITS FEE

WESTERN INN **Phone:** 435/257-3399

Motel
$56-$83

Address: 2301 W Main St 84337 **Location:** I-84 exit 40, just e. **Facility:** 46 units. 2 stories (no elevator), interior corridors. **Free Special Amenities: continental breakfast and local telephone calls.**

TROPIC pop. 530

• **Restaurants p. 456**

BRYCE COUNTRY CABINS **Phone:** 435/679-8643

Cabin
$95-$165 5/1-11/1
$75-$145 4/1-4/30

Address: 320 N Hwy 12 84776 **Location:** On SR 12, 0.3 mi n. **Facility:** 10 cabins. 1 story, exterior corridors. **Terms:** open 5/1-11/1 & 4/1-4/30, 7 day cancellation notice-fee imposed.

BRYCE POINT BED & BREAKFAST

Phone: 435/679-8629

Bed & Breakfast

$70-$160

Address: 61 N 400 West 84776 **Location:** From SR 12, 0.4 mi w via Bryce Way. Located in a quiet area. **Facility:** 6 units, some cottages. 2 stories (no elevator), interior/exterior corridors. **Terms:** open 5/1-10/31 & 3/1-4/30, 7 day cancellation notice. **Activities:** whirlpool.

/ SOME UNITS

BRYCE TRAILS BED & BREAKFAST

Phone: (435)679-8700

Bed & Breakfast

$105-$175

Address: 1001 W Bryce Way 84776 **Location:** Jct SR 12, 1 mi w. **Facility:** This modern B&B has spacious rooms and wonderful views from its location "under the rim" of Bryce Canyon National Park. 7 units. 2 stories (no elevator), interior corridors. **Terms:** 2 night minimum stay - seasonal, 14 day cancellation notice-fee imposed. **Activities:** basketball.

BULLBERRY INN BED & BREAKFAST

Phone: 435/679-8820

Bed & Breakfast

Rates not provided

Address: 412 S Hwy 12 84776 **Location:** 1 mi s of town. **Facility:** 5 units. 2 stories (no elevator), interior/exterior corridors. **Terms:** check-in 4 pm. **Guest Services:** complimentary laundry.

BYBEE'S STEPPING STONE MOTEL

Phone: 435/679-8998

fyi Not evaluated. **Address:** 21 S Main St 84776 **Location:** 0.3 mi s of center. Facilities, services, and decor characterize an economy property.

WHERE TO EAT

CLARKE'S RESTAURANT **Phone:** 435/679-8383

American

$6-$30

AAA Inspector Notes: In the center of town, the rustic restaurant is hard to miss. An old-fashioned candy store at the entrance lends to the inviting ambience. Among the casual American dishes on the varied menu are salmon steak, New York strip and chicken tenders. **Bar:** beer & wine. **Address:** 141 N Main St 84776 **Location:** On SR 12, 10 mi e of Bryce Canyon National Park; in Americas Best Value Inn & Suites Bryce Valley Inn.

B L D

THE PIZZA PLACE **Phone:** 435/679-8888

Pizza

$6-$18

AAA Inspector Notes: The hard-to-miss downtown restaurant has bright wooden booths, floors and walls, making it an inviting place in which to enjoy house-made pizza and yummy specialty breadsticks. **Address:** 21 N Main St 84776 **Location:** On SR 12. L D

UINTA NATIONAL FOREST (C-4)

Elevations in the forest range from 4,828 ft. at the mouth of the Provo River to 11,877 ft. at Mount Nebo. Refer to AAA maps for additional elevation information.

Extending in a rough semicircle around Provo, Uinta National Forest encompasses 949,848 acres of mountainous timber and rangeland. In 2007, the forest merged with Wasatch-Cache National Forest *(see place listing p. 458)* to form a ecologically diverse expanse comprising more than 2 million acres.

One of Uinta's highest points is 11,750-foot Mount Timpanogos; northwest is Timpanogos Cave National Monument *(see place listing p. 452)*. The forest offers scenic drives and has three wilderness areas: Lone Peak and Timpanogos on the north and Nebo on the south.

Mount Nebo Recreation Area lies 10 miles from Nephi in the left fork of Salt Creek Canyon. Nebo Scenic Byway is a 32-mile paved drive through the mountains, passing overlooks of surrounding valleys. The loop begins at Payson and ends near Nephi. Mount Nebo, which can be seen from the highway, is the highest peak in the Wasatch mountain range. In autumn the drive provides a view of brilliant colors.

Twelve miles southeast of Payson on FR 15 are Payson Lakes and Blackhawk recreation areas, where swimming and fishing are permitted. Payson Canyon Road is open when there is no snow. At the other end of the loop is Devil's Kitchen, resembling Bryce Canyon on a smaller scale.

Strawberry Reservoir Recreation Area, 23 miles south of Heber City, is known for its trout fishing and sailing opportunities. The area has boat ramps, a marina and camping facilities. Heber Mountain, 13 miles east of Heber City, provides many miles of groomed snowmobile trails. A visitor center provides exhibits and interpretive trails explaining the natural resources of Strawberry Reservoir. The center is open all year but closes for several weeks in winter for maintenance; phone (435) 548-2321.

For further information contact the Forest Supervisor's Office, Uinta-Wasatch-Cache National Forest, 88 West 100 North, Provo, UT 84601; phone (801) 342-5100. *See Recreation Chart.*

VERNAL (C-6) pop. 9,089, elev. 5,050'

• **Restaurants p. 458**

The Bank of Vernal building on Main Street was constructed of bricks sent parcel post from Salt Lake City in 1919, when railroad freight charges were $1.70 per pound and parcel post charges were only $1.05. Because the postal code forbade mailing more than 50 pounds in one package and mailing more than 500 pounds in a shipment to the same address, the bricks had to be sent in packages of seven, to a dozen Vernal addresses.

With mineral deposits and Native American petroglyphs nearby, Vernal is in an area of ancient and renewed geologic interest. The Flaming Gorge-Uintas National Scenic Byway, north from Vernal on US 191 and US 44 to Manila, passes geological formations where many different strata are exposed. Wildlife is abundant along the corridor. Signs along the scenic byway explain the sights. Local tour operators offer float trips on the Green and Yampa rivers.

Uintah County Travel & Tourism: 152 East 100 North, Vernal, UT 84078. **Phone:** (435) 781-6765 or (800) 477-5558.

Self-guiding tours: Self-guiding tour brochures are available at most local restaurants, motels and service stations as well as at the travel board. Areas covered by the tours include Dry Fork Canyon, Red Fleet Reservoir, Dinosaur National Monument *(see place listing p. 342)* and other area attractions. The travel board also has information about a walking tour of Vernal's historic sites.

JONES HOLE NATIONAL FISH HATCHERY, 40 mi. n.e. via SR 44 and Jones Hole Rd., raises trout for Utah, Wyoming and Colorado streams, lakes and reservoirs. Indoor hatching pools and outdoor ponds contain trout in various stages of growth. Rainbow trout account for the majority of the stocked fish, but cutthroat, brook and brown trout also are raised.

A trout stream emerges from a hole in the canyon wall nearby, joining the Green River 3.5 miles downstream. A hiking trail connects the hatchery and the river. **Time:** Allow 30 minutes minimum. **Hours:** Daily 7-3:30. Closed major holidays. **Cost:** Free. **Phone:** (435) 789-4481.

McCONKIE RANCH is 10 mi. n.w. in Dry Fork Canyon to 6228 McConkie Rd. On the property are Fremont Indian petroglyphs thought to have been created A.D. 1000-1200. Self-guiding tour brochures are available at the travel board and at local restaurants, hotels and service stations. **Time:** Allow 1 hour minimum. **Hours:** Daily dawn-dusk. **Cost:** Donations. **Phone:** (435) 789-6733.

UTAH FIELD HOUSE OF NATURAL HISTORY STATE PARK MUSEUM, 1 mi. e. at 496 E. Main St., has hands-on exhibits that depict the prehistoric background of the Uinta Basin. Visitors are greeted by a 90-foot skeleton of a diplodocus, a plant-eating dinosaur, before entering a theater to view a brief film. Several other dinosaur skeletons, a simulated dig site, sights and sounds from millions of years ago, a wall of leaf fossils, and a fenced dinosaur garden with life-size replicas also can be seen.

Time: Allow 1 hour minimum. **Hours:** Mon.-Sat. 9-5. Closed Jan. 1, Martin Luther King Jr. Day, Thanksgiving and Christmas. **Cost:** $6; $3 (ages 6-12 and 62+). **Phone:** (435) 789-3799.

WESTERN HERITAGE MUSEUM, 328 East 200 South, has memorabilia from Uintah County, Old West exhibits and mounted wildlife. Displays depict the lives of the pioneers, particularly early settlers, miners and soldiers. The museum also features one of the largest collections of Fremont and Ute Indian artifacts. An outdoor display of horse-drawn equipment is on-site, along with an amphitheater, arena, art gallery, equestrian complex, convention center and playground.

Time: Allow 1 hour minimum. **Hours:** Mon.-Fri. 9-6, Sat. 10-4, Memorial Day-Labor Day; Mon.-Fri. 9-5, Sat. 10-2, rest of year. Closed major holidays. **Cost:** Donations. **Phone:** (435) 789-7399.

RECREATIONAL ACTIVITIES

White-water Rafting

- **Don Hatch River Expeditions** departs from 221 North 400 East. **Hours:** Trips are offered daily, mid-May to mid-Sept. Departures times vary. **Phone:** (435) 789-4316 or (800) 342-8243.

BEST WESTERN ANTLERS Phone: (435)789-1202

Motel
$120-$130

AAA Benefit: Members save up to 20%, plus 10% bonus points with Best Western Rewards®.

Address: 423 W Main St 84078 **Location:** 0.4 mi w on US 40. **Facility:** 44 units. 2 stories (no elevator), exterior corridors. **Pool(s):** heated outdoor. **Activities:** whirlpool, playground, exercise room. **Guest Services:** valet and coin laundry. **Free Special Amenities: local telephone calls and high-speed Internet.**

BEST WESTERN DINOSAUR INN
Phone: (435)789-2660

Hotel
$120-$145

AAA Benefit:
Members save up to 20%, plus 10% bonus points with Best Western Rewards®.

Address: 251 E Main St 84078 **Location:** 0.3 mi e on US 40. **Facility:** 60 units. 2 stories (no elevator), exterior corridors. **Pool(s):** heated outdoor. **Activities:** whirlpool, playground, horseshoes, volleyball, exercise room. **Guest Services:** valet and coin laundry, area transportation-within 5 mi. **Free Special Amenities: expanded continental breakfast and use of on-premises laundry facilities.**

Dinosaur Inn offers 60 spaciously appointed rooms, complimentary continental bkft., pool & spa.

LANDMARK INN Phone: (435)781-1800

Motel
$79-$159

Address: 288 E 100 S 84078 **Location:** Corner of 300 E and 100 S. Located in a residential and small business area. **Facility:** 12 units, some kitchens. 3 stories (no elevator), interior corridors. **Terms:** off-site registration, cancellation fee imposed. / SOME UNITS

LANDMARK INN & SUITES Phone: (435)781-1800

Hotel
$79-$159

Address: 301 E 100 S 84078 **Location:** Corner of 300 E and 100 S. Located in a residential and small business area. **Facility:** 36 units, some kitchens. 3 stories, interior corridors. **Terms:** cancellation fee imposed. **Activities:** exercise room. **Guest Services:** valet and coin laundry.

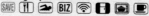

SPRINGHILL SUITES BY MARRIOTT

Phone: (435)781-9000

Historic Retro Resort Hotel

$109-$189

AAA Benefit:
AAA hotel discounts of 5% or more.

Address: 1205 W Hwy 40 84078 **Location:** 1.3 mi w. **Facility:** The stylish, smartly designed rooms have well-lit desks, large closets and a convenient pantry area. 97 units. 4 stories, interior corridors. **Amenities:** high-speed Internet. **Pool(s):** heated indoor. **Activities:** whirlpool, exercise room. **Guest Services:** valet and coin laundry.

SUPER 8

Phone: (435)789-4326

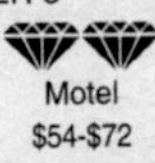

Motel

$54-$72

Address: 1624 W Hwy 40 84078 **Location:** 2 mi w on US 40. **Facility:** 42 units. 2 stories (no elevator), interior corridors. **Pool(s):** heated indoor. **Activities:** whirlpool.

WHERE TO EAT

7-11 RANCH CAFE

Phone: 435/789-1170

American

$6-$19

AAA Inspector Notes: Wagon-wheel chandeliers hang from the ceilings of this Western-theme restaurant, where the menu focuses on homemade country comfort food, including fruit and potato salads, fresh soups, blackened steak, fried chicken, prime rib and seasonal fruit and cream pies. Fresh scones accompany every meal. **Address:** 77 E Main St 84078 **Location:** On SR 40, just e of Vernal Ave; downtown. **Parking:** street only.

B L D

DON PEDRO'S

Phone: 435/789-3402

Mexican

$7-$14

AAA Inspector Notes: This eatery features traditional Mexican dishes such as tortilla soup, taco salad, huevos rancheros, chicken taquitos and sizzling fajitas. Also available are vegetarian choices and a menu for little amigos. **Bar:** full bar. **Address:** 3340 N Vernal Ave 84078 **Location:** 3.3 mi n of jct US 40 and US 191 (Vernal Ave). L D

WASATCH-CACHE NATIONAL FOREST (A-3)

Elevations in the forest range from 5,000 ft. at the West Desert Salt Lake Valley to 13,512 ft. at Gilbert Peak in the High Uintas Wilderness. Refer to AAA maps for additional elevation information.

Wasatch-Cache National Forest lies along the Wasatch, Uinta and Stansbury ranges of northeastern and north-central Utah. A small portion of the 1,259,160-acre forest, which merged with 949,848-acre Uinta National Forest *(see place listing p. 456)* in 2007, extends into Wyoming, and its northern sector reaches the Idaho border.

Some of the tallest mountains in Utah are found in the Uinta and Wasatch mountain ranges. (Wasatch is a Native American word meaning "high mountain pass.") Among the first white explorers to visit this area of Utah were trapper Jim Bridger, guide Kit Carson, trader and explorer Jedediah Smith, and the Rocky Mountain Fur Co. trappers. They found Paiute and Ute Indians living in the semidesert valleys.

Access throughout Wasatch-Cache is provided by 1,391 miles of road and 1,500 miles of trails. The forest has seven wilderness areas, more than 70 campgrounds and more than 30 picnic areas.

The forest terrain is very diverse, from the dry Great Basin Desert to the lush green meadows and high peaks of the Uinta Mountains. In the forest's easternmost section lies part of the High Uintas Wilderness Area *(see Ashley National Forest p. 322)*, with peaks 12,000 to 13,512 feet high. The wilderness area contains hundreds of glacial lakes, many of which are stocked with trout. More than half the people in Utah depend on water produced from the forest's municipal watersheds.

Wasatch-Cache National Forest is an important wildlife and fishery forest, providing a habitat for an estimated 300 species, predominantly birds and mammals. Two endangered species, the peregrine falcon and bald eagle, are seasonal residents. Much of the forest is suitable for livestock grazing.

There are snowmobile trails at Mirror Lake North, Mirror Lake South, Wolf Creek Pass, the Bridger Lake area and between Monte Cristo and Woodruff; because of the high altitudes, snowmobiling is best after the snow has settled. Snowshoeing as well as downhill and cross-country skiing trails also are available.

Other recreational opportunities include deer and elk hunting. A winter feeding ground for elk at Hardware Ranch is managed by the Division of Wildlife Resources. Elk and deer can be observed by telescope from a visitor center November through April. Phone (435) 753-6168.

A scenic drive from Provo Canyon via US 189 and SR 150 (Mirror Lake Highway) at Kamas winds through the forest and ends in Evanston, Wyo. Another scenic drive is SR 39 between the Monte Cristo Range and Woodruff. Pineview Lake, about 9 miles up Ogden Canyon, can be reached via SR 39. Logan Canyon is a recreation area east of the college town of Logan. Logan Canyon Scenic Byway, a 45-mile-long winding route, part of US 89, runs between Logan eastward to Bear Lake.

Snowbasin, on the east slope of Mount Ogden, offers year-round recreation. Notable ski areas include Alta and Snowbird, both within the forest.

For further information contact the Forest Supervisor, Uinta-Wasatch-Cache National Forest, 88 West 100 North, Provo, UT 84601; phone (801) 342-5100, (877) 444-6777, or TTY (877) 833-6777 for camping reservations. *See Recreation Chart.*

MIRROR LAKE is 33 mi. from Kamas via Bald Mountain Pass. The 10,687-foot Bald Mountain rises from the lake's western shore, providing views of the Uinta Range. The summit can be reached by trail.

WASHINGTON pop. 18,761

HOLIDAY INN EXPRESS & SUITES
Phone: (435)986-1313

Hotel
$89-$149

Address: 2450 N Town Center Dr 84780 **Location:** I-15 exit 16, just e. **Facility:** 100 units, some two bedrooms and kitchens. 3 stories, interior corridors. **Terms:** check-in 4 pm. **Amenities:** high-speed Internet. **Pool(s):** heated outdoor. **Activities:** whirlpool, exercise room. **Guest Services:** coin laundry.

BIZ / SOME UNITS FEE

WELLSVILLE (A-3) pop. 3,432, elev. 4,547'

AMERICAN WEST HERITAGE CENTER is at 4025 S. US 89/91. This 160-acre living-history site's Pioneer Settlement, Mountain Man Camp and Native American Encampment revive the Old West. Displays highlight pioneer music, folk life, values and other aspects of 1820-1920 American life. Jensen Historical Farm comprises 126 acres of orchards, meadows, fields, gardens and buildings, all of which combine to resemble a 1917 Mormon farm. Activities such as sheep shearing, gardening, woodworking and threshing are demonstrated. Special events are held throughout the year.

Time: Allow 1 hour minimum. **Hours:** Tues.-Sat. and holidays 9-4 (historic sites open at 11), June-Aug.; Mon.-Thurs. 10-10, Fri.-Sat. 10 a.m.-11 p.m., Sept. 1-late Oct. Phone for schedule rest of year. Closed Jan. 1, Thanksgiving and Christmas. **Cost:** $8; $6 (ages 3-11 and 55+). Prices vary for special events. **Phone:** (435) 245-6050 or (800) 225-3378.

SHERWOOD HILLS RESORT CONFERENCE CENTER & SPA
Phone: 435/245-5054

Hotel
Rates not provided

Address: 7877 S Hwy 89 & 91 84339 **Location:** I-15 exit 362 (Logan), 17 mi e on north side of US 89/91. **Facility:** 60 units, some two bedrooms. 3 stories, interior corridors. **Pool(s):** heated indoor. **Activities:** whirlpool, 2 tennis courts, cross country skiing, hiking trails, horseshoes, volleyball, exercise room, spa. *Fee:* golf-9 holes.

/ SOME UNITS

WENDOVER (B-1) pop. 1,400, elev. 4,291'

Located on the Utah-Nevada border at the western edge of the Great Salt Lake Desert, Wendover was established in 1907 as a Western Pacific Railroad stop. In 1940 the Army established an air base just south of town. During World War II it became a major training center for bomber pilots, including the crews that dropped the atomic bombs on Hiroshima and Nagasaki.

From vicinity hillsides it is possible to see the curvature of the earth. Looking east across the vast, level expanse of the Great Salt Lake Desert, the straight lines of the interstate and parallel railroad tracks and utility lines appear to curve away to the horizon.

WENDOVER AIRFIELD MUSEUM is at 345 S. Airport Apron. Operational 1942-69, Wendover is one of the country's most intact World War II-era training airfields. A museum housed in the operations building just south of the control tower has exhibits about the onetime Army airfield and Air Force base. Models of aircraft, vintage flight instruments, and flight gear and military uniforms are displayed. An 8-minute video is shown in the former pilot's lounge on the second floor. One-hour guided tours of the base, which includes an atomic bomb loading pit, are available.

Hours: Guided tours require a minimum of four people, and reservations are recommended. Museum daily 8-6:30. Last admission 1 hour before closing. Closed Thanksgiving and Christmas. **Cost:** Museum admission by donation. Guided tour $10. **Phone:** (435) 665-2308.

BEST WESTERN SALT FLAT INN **Phone:** (435)665-7811

Motel
$69-$99

AAA Benefit: Members save up to 20%, plus 10% bonus points with Best Western Rewards®.

Address: 935 E Wendover Blvd 84083 **Location:** I-80 exit 2, 2 mi w. **Facility:** 24 units. 2 stories (no elevator), exterior corridors. **Amenities:** *Some:* high-speed Internet. **Pool(s):** heated outdoor. **Activities:** sauna, whirlpool, steamroom. **Free Special Amenities: local telephone calls and high-speed Internet.**

SAVE BIZ / SOME UNITS

Nearby Nevada

WEST WENDOVER pop. 4,410

PEPPERMILL HOTEL & CASINO **Phone:** 775/664-2255

Hotel
$45-$299

Address: 680 Wendover Blvd 89883 **Location:** I-80 exit 410, just sw. **Facility:** Pamper yourself in unexpected comfort; watch the sun set over the high desert at this exciting hotel and casino. 382 units. 4 stories, interior corridors. **Amenities:** video games (fee). **Dining:** 3 restaurants, entertainment. **Guest Services:** area transportation-within 3 mi.

CALL FEE / SOME UNITS

RAINBOW HOTEL & CASINO **Phone:** 775/664-4000

fyi Not evaluated. **Address:** 1045 Wendover Blvd 89883 **Location:** I-80 exit 410, 0.3 mi w. Facilities, services, and decor characterize a mid-scale property.

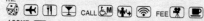

WHERE TO EAT

ROMANZA RISTORANTE ITALIANO
Phone: 775/664-9100

Italian
$15-$36

AAA Inspector Notes: Surrounded by an aquatic theme, guests can dine on fresh seafood and steaks. Crescent booths are finished in green and blue textures with plasma screens mounted overhead playing videos of graceful sea life creating an oceanic experience. **Bar:** full bar. **Reservations:** suggested. **Address:** 100 Wendover Blvd 89883 **Location:** I-80 exit 410, just s, then 0.8 mi e; in Montego Bay Casino & Resort. D

THE STEAK HOUSE **Phone:** 775/664-4000

Steak
$20-$48

AAA Inspector Notes: Diners enjoy fresh fish and seafood appetizers and entrées, steak, prime rib or pasta in this eatery's relaxed atmosphere. A glass of wine from an extensive wine list as well as professional, courteous staff members enhance the dining experience. **Bar:** full bar. **Address:** 1045 Wendover Blvd 89883 **Location:** I-80 exit 410, 0.3 mi w; in Rainbow Hotel & Casino. D

This ends the Wendover section and resumes the alphabetical city listings for Utah.

WEST JORDAN pop. 103,712

- **Hotels & Restaurants map & index p. 426**
- **Part of Salt Lake City area — see map p. 412**

ARCHIBALD'S RESTAURANT AT GARDNER VILLAGE **Phone:** 801/566-6940 (69)

American
$7-$19

AAA Inspector Notes: The Gardner Mill, which is part of historic Gardner Village, was built in 1877 and is on the National Register of Historic Places. The restaurant menu includes fried green tomatoes, batter-dipped halibut with chips, and homemade carrot cake. **Bar:** beer & wine. **Address:** 1100 W 7800 S 84084 **Location:** I-15 exit 297 (7200 S), 0.4 mi w, 0.7 mi s on 700th W, then just w. **Historic** L D

SALSA LEEDOS MEXICAN GRILL **Phone:** 801/565-8818 (70)

Mexican
$8-$15

AAA Inspector Notes: This eatery combines a very bright and festive atmosphere with flavorful dishes; the chile verde and beef or chicken fajitas are recommended. **Bar:** full bar. **Address:** 9155 S Redwood Rd 84088 **Location:** I-15 exit 295 (9000 S), 2 mi w, then just s.

L D

WEST VALLEY CITY pop. 129,480

- **Hotels & Restaurants map & index p. 426**
- **Part of Salt Lake City area — see map p. 412**

BAYMONT INN & SUITES WEST VALLEY **Phone:** (801)886-1300 (35)

Hotel
$44-$89

Address: 2229 W City Center Ct 84119 **Location:** I-215 exit 18 (3500 S), just e, then just w. **Facility:** 101 units. 4 stories, interior corridors. **Amenities:** video games (fee). **Pool(s):** heated indoor. **Activities:** whirlpool, exercise room. **Guest Services:** valet and coin laundry.

FEE / SOME UNITS

COUNTRY INN & SUITES BY CARLSON WEST VALLEY **Phone:** (801)908-0311 (36)

Hotel
$89-$129

Address: 3422 S Decker Lake Dr 84119 **Location:** I-215 exit 18 (3500 S), just e, then just n. **Facility:** 81 units. 3 stories, interior corridors. **Pool(s):** heated indoor. **Activities:** whirlpool. **Guest Services:** valet and coin laundry.

/ SOME UNITS FEE

CRYSTAL INN WEST VALLEY **Phone:** (801)736-2000 (34)

Hotel
$79-$139

Address: 2254 W City Center Ct 84119 **Location:** I-215 exit 18 (3500 S), just e, then 0.3 mi n. **Facility:** 122 units. 3 stories, interior corridors. **Amenities:** *Some:* high-speed Internet. **Pool(s):** heated indoor. **Activities:** whirlpool, exercise room. **Guest Services:** valet and coin laundry. ***(See ad p. 432.)***

HOLIDAY INN EXPRESS WATERPARK WEST VALLEY **Phone:** (801)517-4000 (33)

Contemporary Hotel
$90-$150

Address: 3036 S Decker Lake Dr 84119 **Location:** I-215 exit 18A (3500 S), just e, 0.6 mi n, then just w. Across from E Center. **Facility:** 94 units. 3 stories, interior corridors. **Amenities:** high-speed Internet. **Pool(s):** heated indoor. **Activities:** whirlpool, waterslide, sports court, exercise room. *Fee:* game room. **Guest Services:** valet and coin laundry, area transportation-within 5 mi.

BIZ / SOME UNITS FEE

HOME2 SUITES BY HILTON SALT LAKE CITY/WEST VALLEY CITY **Phone:** (801)679-8222

fyi
Hotel
$129-$169

AAA Benefit: AAA members can save up to 10% everyday.

Too new to rate, opening scheduled for November 2011. **Address:** 4028 Parkway Blvd 84120 **Location:** I-15 exit 305A (West Valley/2100 S), 4.2 mi w on CR 201 exit 13 (Bangerter Hwy), 1.2 mi s to Parkway Blvd, then 0.3 mi w. **Amenities:** 79 units, pets, coffeemakers, microwaves, refrigerators, pool, exercise facility. **Terms:** 1-7 night minimum stay, cancellation fee imposed.

LA QUINTA INN SALT LAKE CITY WEST **Phone:** (801)954-9292 (38)

Hotel
$84-$144

Address: 3540 S 2200 W 84119 **Location:** I-215 exit 18 (3500 S), just e, then just s. **Facility:** 59 units. 3 stories, interior corridors. **Pool(s):** heated indoor. **Activities:** whirlpool, limited exercise equipment. **Guest Services:** valet and coin laundry.

BIZ / SOME UNITS FEE

SLEEP INN WEST VALLEY **Phone:** (801)975-1888 (37)

Motel
$69-$139

Address: 3440 S 2200 W 84119 **Location:** I-215 exit 18 (3500 S), just e, then just n. **Facility:** 73 units. 2 stories (no elevator), interior corridors. *Bath:* shower only. **Terms:** cancellation fee imposed. **Activities:** whirlpool. **Guest Services:** valet and coin laundry.

/ SOME UNITS

STAYBRIDGE SUITES WEST VALLEY **Phone:** (801)746-8400 (32)

Extended Stay Contemporary Hotel
$99-$169

Address: 3038 S Decker Lake Dr 84119 **Location:** I-215 exit 18A (3500 S), just e, 0.6 mi n, then just w. **Facility:** 97 efficiencies, some two bedrooms. 3 stories, interior corridors. **Pool(s):** heated indoor. **Activities:** whirlpool, waterslide, sports court, exercise room. *Fee:* game room. **Guest Services:** complimentary and valet laundry, area transportation-within 5 mi.

CALL BIZ

/ SOME UNITS FEE

WHITEROCKS (C-5) pop. 289, elev. 6,033'

WHITEROCKS STATE FISH HATCHERY is 2 mi. n. on Whiterocks Rd. The hatchery supplies brook, brown, cutthroat and rainbow trout as well as kokanee salmon to Utah waters, including the Green River, Strawberry Reservoir and the lakes in the Uinta Basin and Flaming Gorge National Recreation Area *(see place listing p. 346)*. Nearly 1.5 million trout are raised on the 14-acre site annually. **Time:** Allow 30 minutes minimum. **Hours:** Daily 8-4. **Cost:** Free. **Phone:** (435) 353-4855.

WOODS CROSS pop. 9,761

- **Hotels & Restaurants map & index p. 426**
- **Part of Salt Lake City area — see map p. 412**

COMFORT INN & SUITES SALT LAKE CITY NORTH - WOODS CROSS **Phone:** 801/298-3900 29

Hotel
Rates not provided

Address: 2437 S Wildcat Way 84010 **Location:** I-15 exit 315, just e, then 0.8 mi n on frontage road. **Facility:** 78 units. 3 stories, interior corridors. **Pool(s):** heated indoor. **Activities:** whirlpool. **Guest Services:** valet and coin laundry.

SAVE FEE

HAMPTON INN SALT LAKE CITY NORTH - WOODS CROSS **Phone:** (801)296-1211 28

Hotel
$79-$99

AAA Benefit:
Members save up to 10% everyday!

Address: 2393 S 800 W 84087 **Location:** I-15 exit 315, just w, then just n. **Facility:** 60 units. 3 stories, interior corridors. **Terms:** 1-7 night minimum stay, cancellation fee imposed. **Amenities:** video games (fee). **Pool(s):** heated indoor. **Activities:** whirlpool. **Guest Services:** valet and coin laundry, area transportation-within 10 mi.

BIZ FEE

/ SOME UNITS

ZION NATIONAL PARK (F-2)

• Hotels p. 463 • Restaurants p. 463

Elevations in the park range from 3,666 ft. at Coalpits Wash to 8,726 ft. at Horse Ranch Mountain. Refer to AAA maps for additional elevation information.

Zion National Park's entrances on the southwestern and eastern edges are connected by SR 9 (Zion-Mount Carmel Highway), which joins I-15 on the west and US 89 on the east. The park's northwestern entrance is accessible from I-15, but no other road connects this part of the park with the Zion Canyon section.

Desert terrain and huge, sculpted rock formations coexist with hanging gardens. The gigantic stone masses of the West Temple and the Watchman guard the southern entrance to the park. From a multicolored stairway, the red-brown Watchman looms 2,555 feet above the canyon floor. The 7,810-foot West Temple is one of the most prominent formations in the southern section.

Just north of the southern entrance is the beginning of Zion Canyon, a spectacular gorge being carved through strangely colored sandstones and shale by the Virgin River. About a half-mile deep and a half-mile wide at its mouth, the canyon narrows to about 300 feet at the Temple of Sinawava, the narrowest portion of the canyon accessible by car and about 8 miles from the park entrance.

From the west the main park road, a continuation of SR 9 known as Zion-Mount Carmel Highway *(see attraction listing)*, climbs the talus slope of Pine Creek Canyon in six switchbacks, enters 5,607-foot Zion-Mount Carmel Tunnel (completed in 1930) and continues to ascend on a 5-percent grade. This road's construction is considered a remarkable engineering feat.

The Kolob Canyons section in the northwest corner of the park contains fingerlike red sandstone canyons at the edge of Kolob Terrace. Within this area is the Hurricane Fault, where layers of ancient rock are clearly exposed. Kolob Arch is accessible via a 14-mile round-trip trail. At 310 feet across, it is one of the largest freestanding arches in the world.

General Information and Activities

The park and its main roads are open all year. Scenic drives include a 13-mile round-trip through Zion Canyon from the southern entrance and a 22-mile round-trip from the eastern entrance to Zion Canyon. A paved road from SR 9 at Virgin joins an unpaved road leading north to Lava Point and Kolob Reservoir; the unpaved road is closed in the winter. A 5-mile drive from the Kolob Canyons Visitor Center at I-15 exit 40 affords spectacular views. Zion Canyon Scenic Drive stretches from Zion Canyon Visitor Center to the Temple of Sinawava. **Note:** Use caution and good judgment when driving along SR 9 to Bryce Canyon City. The road is not lit at night and contains hairpin turns that are difficult to maneuver; there are no guardrails.

From early April through October, the Zion Canyon Scenic Drive is only accessible by park shuttle bus. Parking at the Zion Canyon Visitor Center fills up quickly during peak summer months; free parking is available throughout the town of Springdale, near the south entrance of the park. A free shuttle provides regular transportation to and from the park from several sites throughout the town daily 6 a.m.-11 p.m., Memorial Day weekend-Labor Day; 6:30 a.m.-10 p.m., early Apr.-day before Memorial Day weekend and day after Labor Day-late Nov. Schedule may vary; phone ahead.

The town shuttle drops off its passengers just outside the park entrance. There, visitors enter the park on foot and walk a short distance to the Zion Canyon Visitor Center, where they may board another shuttle for Zion Canyon Scenic Drive. Shuttles run on a continuous loop, making stops at the park's points of interest; visitors may disembark and board another shuttle as many times as they wish between 5:35 a.m. and 11 p.m. in summer and between 6:45 a.m. and 10 p.m. in spring and in fall. Schedule may vary; phone ahead. Shuttles run between 7 and 30 minutes apart and are equipped with storage areas for bicycles. Pets are not permitted on shuttles; a kennel service is available in Springdale.

When private transportation is used, vehicles wider than 7 feet 10 inches (including mirrors) and/or higher than 11 feet 4 inches must be escorted through the Zion-Mount Carmel Tunnel, which is on the park road between the east entrance and Zion Canyon. The fee for this service is $15, which includes two trips for the same vehicle within 7 days from date of purchase. Escorts are stationed at tunnel entrances daily 8-8, mid-Apr. to mid-Sept.; schedule varies rest of year. Phone ahead to check tunnel escort availability, or, upon arrival, confirm hours at the main park entrance stations. Phone (435) 772-3256. Single vehicles more than 40 feet long or combined vehicles longer than 50 feet are prohibited. Vehicles exceeding 19 feet in length may not park in the Weeping Rock Parking Area or at the Temple of Sinawava.

About 65 miles of trails are open all year; some in the canyon may close due to potential danger of ice falling from above. Permits are required for all backcountry camping and day trips going down the Narrows and its tributaries, the Subway and all canyons that require mechanical aid; a fee is charged for the permits. Phone (435) 772-0170 for backcountry information.

Ranger-naturalists offer talks and guided walks April through the summer each year and, most years, through October (weather permitting). The Junior Ranger Program, an outdoor learning experience for ages 6 through 12, is held at the park nature center Memorial Day through Labor Day. *See Recreation Chart.*

ADMISSION is $25 (per private vehicle); $12 (per person arriving by other means). The above fees permit entrance to the park for 7 calendar days from date of purchase. **Note:** Visitors who do not plan to take the Zion Canyon Scenic Drive are still required to pay the $25 park entrance fee to use SR 9 between Springdale and the east Zion entrance station. The Zion-Mount Carmel Tunnel is within the park boundaries.

PETS must be physically restrained at all times and are not permitted in public buildings, on trails or aboard shuttles.

ADDRESS inquiries to the Superintendent, Zion National Park, Springdale, UT 84767-1099; phone (435) 772-3256.

ANGELS LANDING TRAIL is accessible from the Grotto Picnic Area in Zion National Park. The steep 2.5-mile climb to the top of Angels Landing offers spectacular views of the canyon. **Note:** While portions of the route are paved, the trail is not recommended for those afraid of heights or for young children. The last half-mile of the trail to the summit is strenuous and involves traveling along a narrow ridge flanked by dizzying drop-offs. Support chains are anchored intermittently along the route. Footing can be slippery even when the rock is dry.

BRIDGE MOUNTAIN is in Zion National Park on the eastern flank of the canyon. Named for the natural arch high on its face, the mountain is visible from Zion Canyon Visitor Center. East Temple, Twin Brothers and Mountain of the Sun also are visible. On the opposite side of the canyon are the Altar of Sacrifice, the Beehives and the Sentinel. Farther up is the Court of the Patriarchs, and rising above that are the Three Patriarchs. Lady Mountain, Castle Dome, The Spearhead and Mount Majestic also are visible on the same side of the canyon.

CANYON OVERLOOK TRAIL is in Zion National Park and begins at the parking area at the east end

▼ *See AAA listing p. 463* ▼

of Zion-Mount Carmel Tunnel. A moderately difficult half-mile nature trail, it offers excellent views of the western side of the canyon.

GREAT WHITE THRONE is beyond Zion Lodge against the east wall. Seen through a saddle in a low red rock wall, this towering monolith gradually changes shade from white at its top to red near the bottom. The iron minerals that produce the red color in the rock have been leached from the upper part of the formation. Opposite the Great White Throne is a smaller monolith, Angels Landing.

KOLOB CANYONS VISITOR CENTER is off I-15 exit 40 at the entrance to the Kolob Canyons area. The center provides Zion National Park information. **Hours:** Daily 8-6, in summer; 8-5, in spring; 8-4:30, rest of year. Closed Christmas. Phone ahead to confirm schedule. **Cost:** Free. **Phone:** (435) 586-9548.

TEMPLE OF SINAWAVA is in Zion National Park at the north end of Zion Canyon Dr. In the center of the Temple of Sinawava, which is a huge natural amphitheater, are two large stone pillars known as The Altar and The Pulpit. Many springs trickle from the walls of the canyon, and cascades tumble everywhere in early spring and after summer rains.

Riverside Walk is in Zion National Park and runs along the Virgin River from the Temple of Sinawava to the beginning of the Narrows. This spectacular section of the canyon at one point is more than 1,000 feet deep and less than 20 feet wide at its bottom. The 1-mile paved trail is Zion's most popular footpath. **Note:** Inquire about potential flood danger before starting out. **Time:** Allow 1 hour, 30 minutes minimum. **Hours:** Daily dawn-dusk (weather permitting).

ZION CANYON VISITOR CENTER is on SR 9 inside Zion National Park's south entrance. The center offers park information and orientation, literature, maps, permits and educational activities. **Hours:** Daily 8-7:30, in summer; 8-6, in fall and spring; 8-5, rest of year. Closed Christmas. Phone ahead to confirm schedule. **Cost:** Free. **Phone:** (435) 772-3256. ***(See ad p. 462.)***

ZION HUMAN HISTORY MUSEUM is on SR 9, .5 mi. n. of the south entrance to Zion National Park. This small museum was the park's main visitor center before the larger one was completed at the park's southern boundary in 2000. Inside are panels describing the canyon's human history; a few historic items are on display.

A 22-minute orientation film shown every half-hour introduces visitors to the park, explaining its geological origins and human history. Exhibits focus on early pioneers and Native Americans. **Time:** Allow 30 minutes minimum. **Hours:** Daily 9-7, in summer; 10-5, in spring; 9-6, in fall. Closed in winter. **Cost:** Free. **Phone:** (435) 772-3256.

ZION-MOUNT CARMEL HIGHWAY connects Zion National Park's east entrance with its south entrance and Zion Canyon Scenic Drive. The 10-mile road ascends from the floor of Zion Canyon through the mile-long Zion-Mount Carmel Tunnel and out into a broad area of slickrock, ancient sand dunes that have been turned to stone and eroded into unusual shapes.

One highlight is Checkerboard Mesa, a weathered sandstone hill crosshatched with fissures in a checkerboard pattern; a turnout allows drivers to take a closer look at the formation. The Canyon Overlook Trail *(see attraction listing)* begins at the tunnel's eastern end.

Note: Vehicles wider than 7 feet 10 inches (including mirrors) and/or higher than 11 feet 4 inches must be escorted through the narrow tunnel for a round-trip fee of $15. **Phone:** (435) 772-3256.

RECREATIONAL ACTIVITIES

Horseback Riding

- **Canyon Trail Rides** departs from the corral near Zion Lodge. **Hours:** One-hour Virgin River and half-day Sand Bench Trail trips are offered daily, Mar.-Oct. Departure times vary. **Phone:** (435) 679-8665 for reservations or (435) 834-5500.

ZION LODGE **Phone:** 435/772-7700

fyi Not evaluated. **Address:** Zion Lodge 84767 **Location:** SR 9, 4 mi n of south gate; in Zion Canyon. Facilities, services, and decor characterize an upscale property.

WHERE TO EAT

CASTLE DOME CAFE **Phone:** 435/772-7700

American

$2-$8

AAA Inspector Notes: Those on the go can grab a quick bite to eat here. Continental breakfast is served in the morning. Burgers, hot dogs and soft-serve ice cream are on the menu for the rest of the day and at night. On a hot day, it's hard to beat a yummy cone. **Bar:** beer only. **Address:** Zion Lodge 84767 **Location:** SR 9, 4 mi n of south gate; in Zion Canyon; in Zion Lodge. B L D

RED ROCK GRILL **Phone:** 435/772-7760

American

$6-$22

AAA Inspector Notes: Inside Zion National Park, the restaurant treats diners to great views. The uniformed full-service staff willingly helps guests with whatever they need. Items on the American menu include prime rib, flat-iron steak, stuffed chicken breast and even a vegan dish. **Bar:** full bar. **Address:** Zion Lodge 84767 **Location:** SR 9, 4 mi n of south gate; in Zion Canyon; in Zion Lodge.

B L D

▼ See AAA listing p. 379 ▼

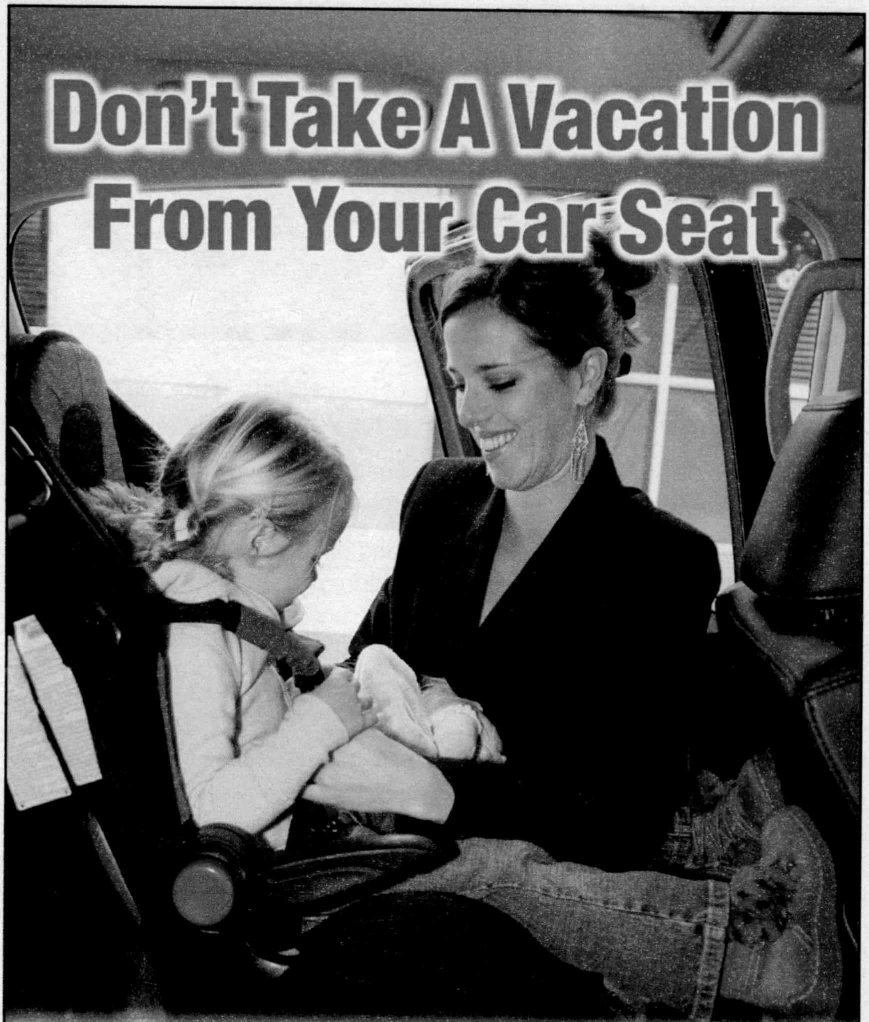

ENJOY A MAGICAL DISNEY VACATION WITH

What's the best way to experience all the enchantment of a vacation to the *Walt Disney World*® Resort in Florida or the *Disneyland*® Resort in California? How do you squeeze the most magic out of the Theme Parks and the whimsically themed *Disney Resort* hotels? And how can you enjoy great savings and exclusive benefits not available anywhere else? By booking a *AAA Vacations*® package from AAA Travel, of course!

DISNEYLAND® RESORT, CALIFORNIA

- Stay just steps away from the magic at a *Disneyland*® Resort Hotel.
- Catch World of Color, a nighttime spectacular at *Disney California Adventure*™ Park.

Disneyland® Resort Hotels

World of Color

LET AAA BE YOUR GUIDE...

With a *AAA Vacations*® package, you can create the Disney vacation that fits your family, your taste and your budget. And not only will your AAA/CAA Travel professional help put everything (like accommodations, flights and tickets) together, you'll also get to enjoy great Disney benefits on top of the exclusive AAA benefits and savings once you get there! Then all you need to do is relax and have fun.

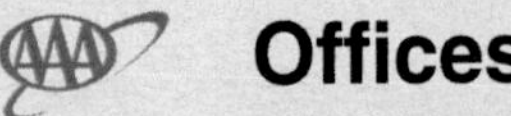

Offices

Cities with main offices are listed in **BOLD TYPE** and toll-free member service numbers in *ITALIC TYPE.*
All are closed Saturdays, Sundays and holidays unless otherwise indicated.
The addresses, phone numbers and hours for any AAA/CAA office are subject to change.
The type of service provided is designated below the name of the city where the office is located:

- ✚ Auto travel services, including books and maps, and on-demand TripTik® routings.
- ● Auto travel services, including selected books and maps, and on-demand TripTik® routings.
- ■ Books/maps only, no marked maps or on-demand TripTik® routings.
- ▲ Travel Agency Services, cruise, tour, air, car and rail reservations; domestic and international hotel reservations; passport photo services; international and domestic travel guides and maps; travel money products; and International Driving Permits. In addition, assistance with travel related insurance products including trip cancellation, travel accident, lost luggage, trip delay and assistance products.
- ✪ Insurance services provided. If only this icon appears, only insurance services are provided at that office.
- ✖ Car Care Plus Facility provides car care services.

AAA NATIONAL OFFICE: 1000 AAA DRIVE, HEATHROW, FLORIDA 32746-5063, (407) 444-7000

COLORADO

AURORA—AAA COLORADO, 1096 S SABLE BLVD, 80012. WEEKDAYS (M-F) 8:30-5:30, SAT 9:00-1:00. (303) 753-8800 EXT 8300, *(877) 244-9790.* ● ▲ ✪

BOULDER—AAA COLORADO, 1933 28TH ST # 200, 80301. WEEKDAYS (M-F) 8:30-5:30, SAT 9:00-1:00. (303) 753-8800 EXT 8600, *(877) 244-9790.* ● ▲ ✪

CENTENNIAL—AAA COLORADO, 7400 S UNIVERSITY BLVD, 80122. WEEKDAYS (M-F) 8:30-5:30, SAT 9:00-1:00. (303) 753-8800 EXT 8500, *(877) 244-9790.* ● ▲ ✪

COLORADO SPRINGS—AAA COLORADO, 3525 N CAREFREE CIR, 80917. WEEKDAYS (M-F) 8:30-5:30, SAT 9:00-1:00. (719) 591-2222 EXT 5400, *(877) 244-9790.* ● ▲ ✪

DENVER—**AAA COLORADO**, 4100 E ARKANSAS AVE, 80222. WEEKDAYS (M-F) 8:30-5:30, SAT 9:00-1:00. (303) 753-8800 EXT 8000, *(877) 244-9790.* ✚ ▲ ✪

DURANGO—AAA COLORADO, 16 TOWN PLAZA, 81301. WEEKDAYS (M-F) 8:30-5:30. (970) 247-2273 EXT 3900, *(877) 244-9790.* ● ▲

FORT COLLINS—AAA COLORADO, 3636 S COLLEGE AVE UNIT 2, 80525. WEEKDAYS (M-F) 8:30-5:30, SAT 9:00-1:00. (970) 223-1111 EXT 2200, *(877) 244-9790.* ● ▲ ✪

GRAND JUNCTION—AAA COLORADO, 2454 US HWY 6 & 50 #109, 81505. WEEKDAYS (M-F) 8:30-5:30. (970) 245-2236 EXT 3800, *(877) 244-9790.* ● ▲ ✪

LITTLETON—AAA COLORADO, 8601 W CROSS DR STE B1, 80123. WEEKDAYS (M-F) 8:30-5:30, SAT 9:00-1:00. (303) 753-8800 EXT 8800, *(877) 244-9790.* ● ▲ ✪

WESTMINSTER—AAA COLORADO, 5140 W 120TH AVE UNIT 300, 80020. WEEKDAYS (M-F) 8:30-5:30, SAT 9:00-1:00. (303) 753-8800 EXT 8900, *(877) 244-9790.* ● ▲ ✪

WHEAT RIDGE—AAA COLORADO, 7770 W 44TH AVE, 80033. WEEKDAYS (M-F) 8:30-5:30, SAT 9:00-1:00. (303) 753-8800 EXT 8400, *(877) 244-9790.* ● ▲ ✪

UTAH

DRAPER—AAA NORTHERN CALIFORNIA NEVADA & UTAH, 185 E 12300 S #100, 84020. WEEKDAYS (M-F) 9:00-6:00 (SAT BY APPOINTMENT ONLY.). (801) 878-8500 ✚ ✪

MURRAY—AAA NORTHERN CALIFORNIA NEVADA & UTAH, 5207 S STATE ST STE 2, 84107. WEEKDAYS (M-F) 9:00-6:00 (SAT BY APPOINTMENT ONLY.). (801) 266-8472 ✚ ▲ ✪

OGDEN—AAA NORTHERN CALIFORNIA NEVADA & UTAH, 5705 S HARRISON BLVD, 84403. WEEKDAYS (M-F) 9:00-6:00 (SAT BY APPOINTMENT ONLY.). (801) 605-0098 ✚ ✪

OREM—AAA NORTHERN CALIFORNIA NEVADA & UTAH, 160 E UNIVERSITY PKY ST F, 84058. WEEKDAYS (M-F) 9:00-6:00 (SAT BY APPOINTMENT ONLY.). (801) 788-3300 ✚ ✪

SALT LAKE CITY—AAA NORTHERN CALIFORNIA NEVADA & UTAH, 1400 S FOOTHILL DR ST 154, 84108. WEEKDAYS (M-F) 9:00-6:00 (SAT BY APPOINTMENT ONLY.). (801) 238-1250 ✚ ✪

WASHINGTON—AAA NORTHERN CALIFORNIA NEVADA & UTAH, 844 W TELEGRAPH RD STE 4, 84780. WEEKDAYS (M-F) 9:00-6:00 (SAT BY APPOINTMENT ONLY.). (435) 652-6920 ● ✪

Metric Equivalents Chart

TEMPERATURE

To convert Fahrenheit to Celsius, subtract 32 from the Fahrenheit temperature, multiply by 5 and divide by 9. To convert Celsius to Fahrenheit, multiply by 9, divide by 5 and add 32.

Celsius °		Fahrenheit °
100	**BOILING**	**212**
37		100
35		95
32		90
29		85
27		80
24		75
21		70
18		65
16		60
13		55
10		50
7		45
4		40
2		35
0	**FREEZING**	**32**
-4		25
-7		20
-9		15
-12		10
-15		5
-18		0
-21		-5
-24		-10
-27		-15

ACRES

1 acre = 0.4 hectare (ha) 1 hectare = 2.47 acres

MILES AND KILOMETERS

Note: A kilometer is approximately 5/8 or 0.6 of a mile. To convert kilometers to miles multiply by 0.6.

Miles/Kilometers		Kilometers/Miles	
15	24.1	30	18.6
20	32.2	35	21.7
25	40.2	40	24.8
30	48.3	45	27.9
35	56.3	50	31.0
40	64.4	55	34.1
45	72.4	60	37.2
50	80.5	65	40.3
55	88.5	70	43.4
60	96.6	75	46.6
65	104.6	80	49.7
70	112.7	85	52.8
75	120.7	90	55.9
80	128.7	95	59.0
85	136.8	100	62.1
90	144.8	105	65.2
95	152.9	110	68.3
100	160.9	115	71.4

LINEAR MEASURE

Customary	Metric
1 inch = 2.54 centimeters	1 centimeter = 0.4 inches
1 foot = 30 centimeters	1 meter = 3.3 feet
1 yard = 0.91 meters	1 meter = 1.09 yards
1 mile = 1.6 kilometers	1 kilometer = .62 miles

LIQUID MEASURE

Customary	Metric
1 fluid ounce = 30 milliliters	1 milliliter = .03 fluid ounces
1 cup = .24 liters	1 liter = 2.1 pints
1 pint = .47 liters	1 liter = 1.06 quarts
1 quart = .95 liters	1 liter = .26 gallons
1 gallon = 3.8 liters	

WEIGHT

If You Know:	Multiply By:	To Find:
Ounces	28	Grams
Pounds	0.45	Kilograms
Grams	0.035	Ounces
Kilograms	2.2	Pounds

PRESSURE

Air pressure in automobile tires is expressed in kilopascals. Multiply pound-force per square inch (psi) by 6.89 to find kilopascals (kPa).

24 psi = 165 kPa 28 psi = 193 kPa
26 psi = 179 kPa 30 psi = 207 kPa

GALLONS AND LITERS

Gallons/Liters				Liters/Gallons			
5	19.0	12	45.6	10	2.6	40	10.4
6	22.8	14	53.2	15	3.9	50	13.0
7	26.6	16	60.8	20	5.2	60	15.6
8	30.4	18	68.4	25	6.5	70	18.2
9	34.2	20	76.0	30	7.8	80	20.8
10	38.0	25	95.0	35	9.1	90	23.4

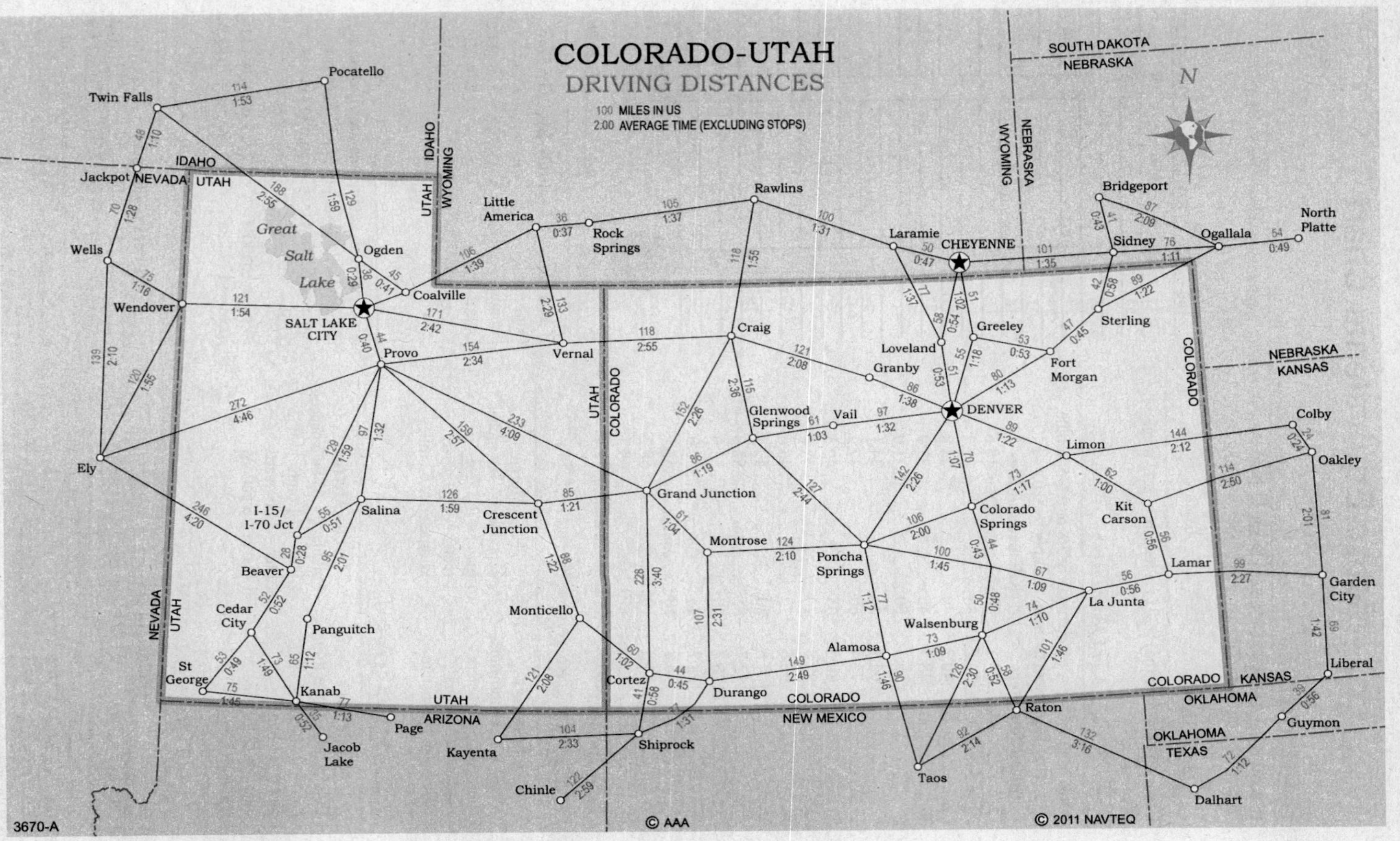
COLORADO-UTAH
DRIVING DISTANCES
100 MILES IN US
2:00 AVERAGE TIME (EXCLUDING STOPS)
N
SOUTH DAKOTA
NEBRASKA
WYOMING
IDAHO
UTAH
NEVADA
COLORADO
KANSAS
OKLAHOMA
TEXAS
NEW MEXICO
ARIZONA
Twin Falls
Pocatello
Jackpot
Wells
Wendover
Ely
Great Salt Lake
Ogden
Coalville
SALT LAKE CITY
Provo
Little America
Rock Springs
Rawlins
Vernal
Laramie
CHEYENNE
Bridgeport
Sidney
Ogallala
North Platte
Sterling
Greeley
Loveland
Fort Morgan
Craig
Granby
DENVER
Glenwood Springs
Vail
Limon
Colby
Oakley
Kit Carson
Colorado Springs
Grand Junction
Salina
I-15/ I-70 Jct
Crescent Junction
Montrose
Poncha Springs
Lamar
Garden City
La Junta
Beaver
Cedar City
Panguitch
Monticello
Walsenburg
Alamosa
St George
Kanab
Cortez
Durango
Liberal
Page
Jacob Lake
Kayenta
Shiprock
Raton
Guymon
Taos
Dalhart
Chinle
3670-A
© AAA
© 2011 NAVTEQ

Points of Interest Index

Attractions appear at the top of each category and offer a Great Experience for Members®.

ART & CULTURE

Index Legend

- NB. . . . . national battlefield
- NBP. . . . . national battlefield park
- NC. . . . . national cemetery
- NF. . . . . national forest
- NHM. . . . . national historic(al) monument
- NHP. . . . . national historic(al) park
- NHS. . . . . national historic(al) site
- NL. . . . . national lakeshore
- NME. . . . . national memorial
- NMO. . . . . national monument
- NMP. . . . . national military park
- NP. . . . . national park
- NRA. . . . . national recreation area
- NR. . . . . national river
- NS. . . . . national seashore
- NWR. . . . . national wildlife refuge
- PHP. . . . . provincial historic(al) park
- PHS. . . . . provincial historic(al) site
- PP. . . . . provincial park
- SF. . . . . state forest
- SHM. . . . . state historic(al) monument
- SHP. . . . . state historic(al) park
- SHS. . . . . state historic(al) site
- SME. . . . . state memorial
- SP. . . . . state park
- SRA. . . . . state recreation area

CHILDREN'S ACTIVITIES

EVENTS & FESTIVALS

HISTORIC SITES & EXHIBITS

OUTDOORS & SCIENCE

TOURS & SIGHTSEEING

Photo Credits

Page numbers are in bold type. Picture credit abbreviations are as follows:
■ (i) numeric sequence from top to bottom, left to right ■ (AAA) AAA Travel library.

- (Cover) Native American Powwow in Mesa Verde, CO / © Aurora Photos / awl-images
- **2** (i) © David R. Frazier Photolibrary, Inc. / Alamy
- **2** (ii) © Dave G. Houser / Alamy
- **7** © Monashee Frantz / age fotostock
- **13** © Adivin / iStockphoto
- **18** (i) © Richard Cummins / Lonely Planet Images
- **18** (ii) © Richard Cummins / Lonely Planet Images
- **19** © Richard Cummins / Lonely Planet Images
- **20** (i) Courtesy of Wikimedia Commons
- **20** (ii) © Bill Bachmann / Alamy
- **23** (i) © John Elk III / Lonely Planet Images
- **23** (ii) © Danita Delimont / Alamy
- **23** (iii) © Lee Foster / Lonely Planet Images
- **23** (iv) © Richard Cummins / Lonely Planet Images
- **23** (v) © H. Mark Weidman Photography / Alamy
- **24** (i) © David R. Frazier Photolibrary, Inc. / Alamy
- **24** (ii) © Danita Delimont / Alamy
- **24** (iii) © Jim Havey / Alamy
- **24** (iv) © SuperStock / Alamy
- **84** © Richard Cummins / Lonely Planet Images
- **87** © ClassicStock / Alamy
- **88** © Waldrons Photography / Colorado Springs Philharmonic
- **122** © Steve Vidler / eStock Photo
- **125** © Christian Aslund / Lonely Planet Images
- **126** © David R. Frazier Photolibrary, Inc. / Alamy
- **127** © Richard Cummins / Lonely Planet Images
- **128** Courtesy of the Brown Palace Hotel
- **129** © Ed Endicott / WYSIWYG Foto, LLC / Alamy
- **130** © Richard Cummins / Lonely Planet Images
- **306** (i) © Mark Newman / Lonely Planet Images
- **306** (ii) © Richard Cummins / Lonely Planet Images
- **307** © SCPhotos / Alamy
- **308** (i) Courtesy of Wikimedia Commons
- **308** (ii) Courtesy of Wikimedia Commons
- **311** (i) © Richard Cummins / Lonely Planet Images
- **311** (ii) © Richard Cummins / Lonely Planet Images
- **311** (iii) © Peter Ptschelinzew / Lonely Planet Images
- **311** (iv) © Felix Rioux / Lonely Planet Images

(cont'd)

- **311** (v) © Holger Leue / Lonely Planet Images
- **312** (i) © Blaine Harrington III / Alamy
- **312** (ii) © Dave G. Houser / Alamy
- **312** (iii) © JTB Photo Communications, Inc. / Alamy
- **312** (iv) © SuperStock / age fotostock
- **411** © Richard Cummins / Lonely Planet Images
- **414** © Andre Jenny / Alamy
- **415** © Richard Cummins / Lonely Planet Images
- **416** © Richard Cummins / Lonely Planet Images

KEEP YOUR CHILDREN
SAFE IN THE CAR

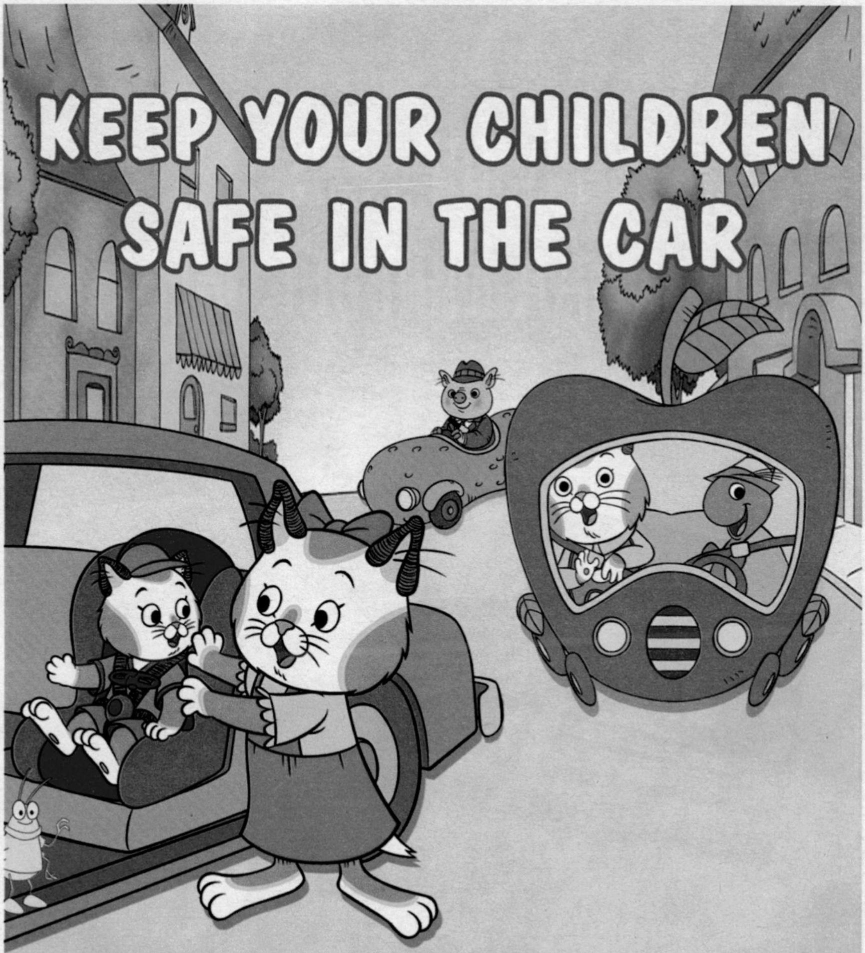

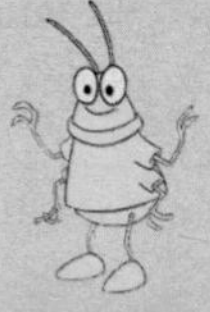

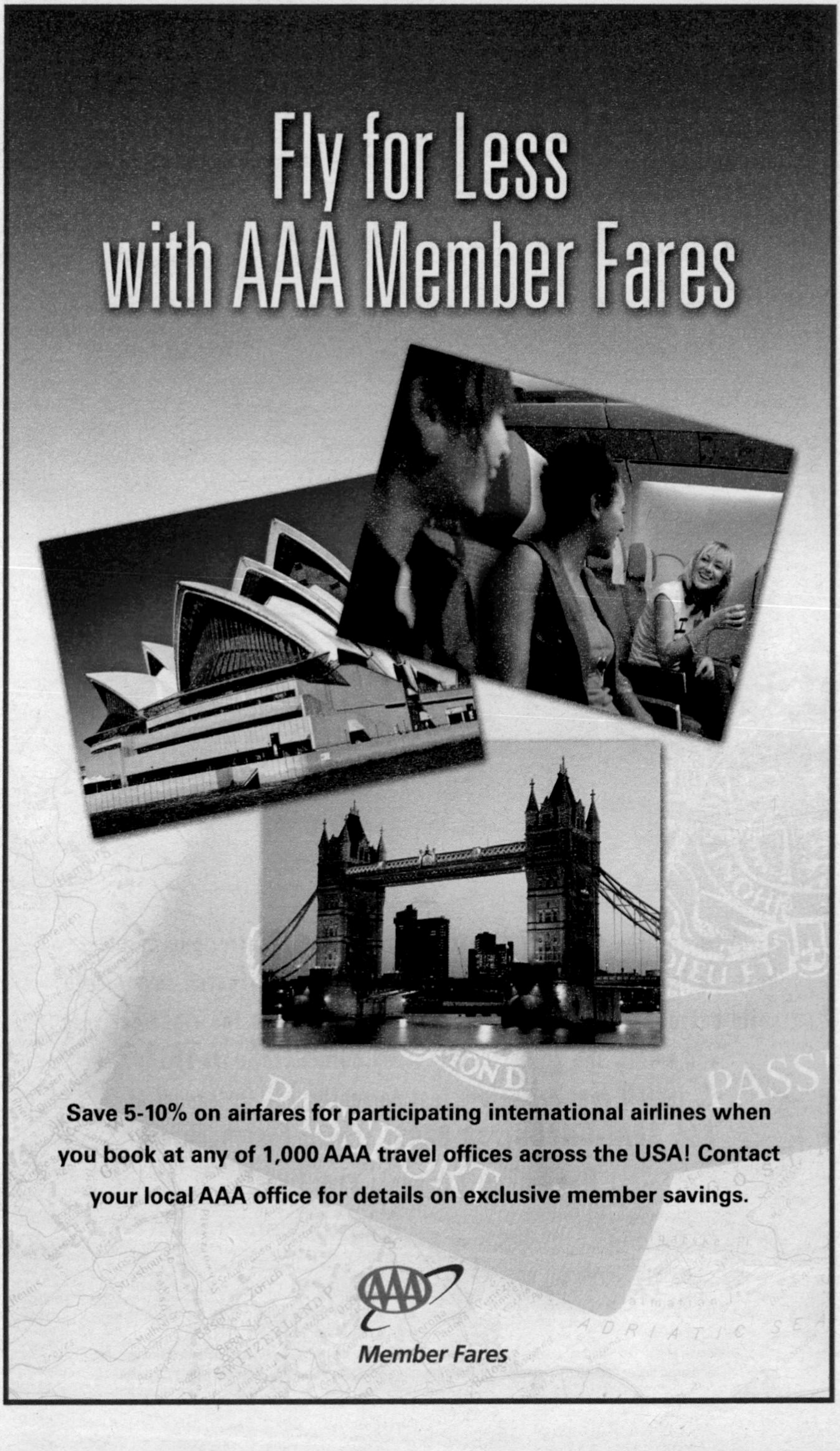
Fly for Less
with AAA Member Fares
Save 5-10% on airfares for participating international airlines when you book at any of 1,000 AAA travel offices across the USA! Contact your local AAA office for details on exclusive member savings.
AAA
Member Fares

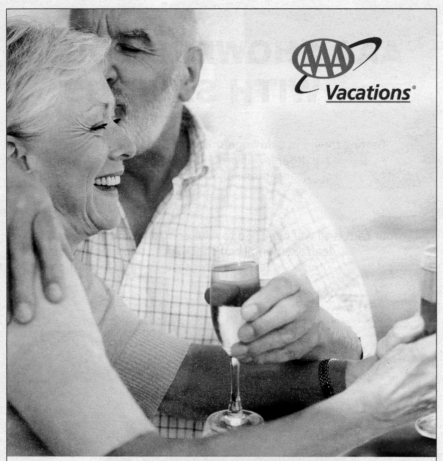